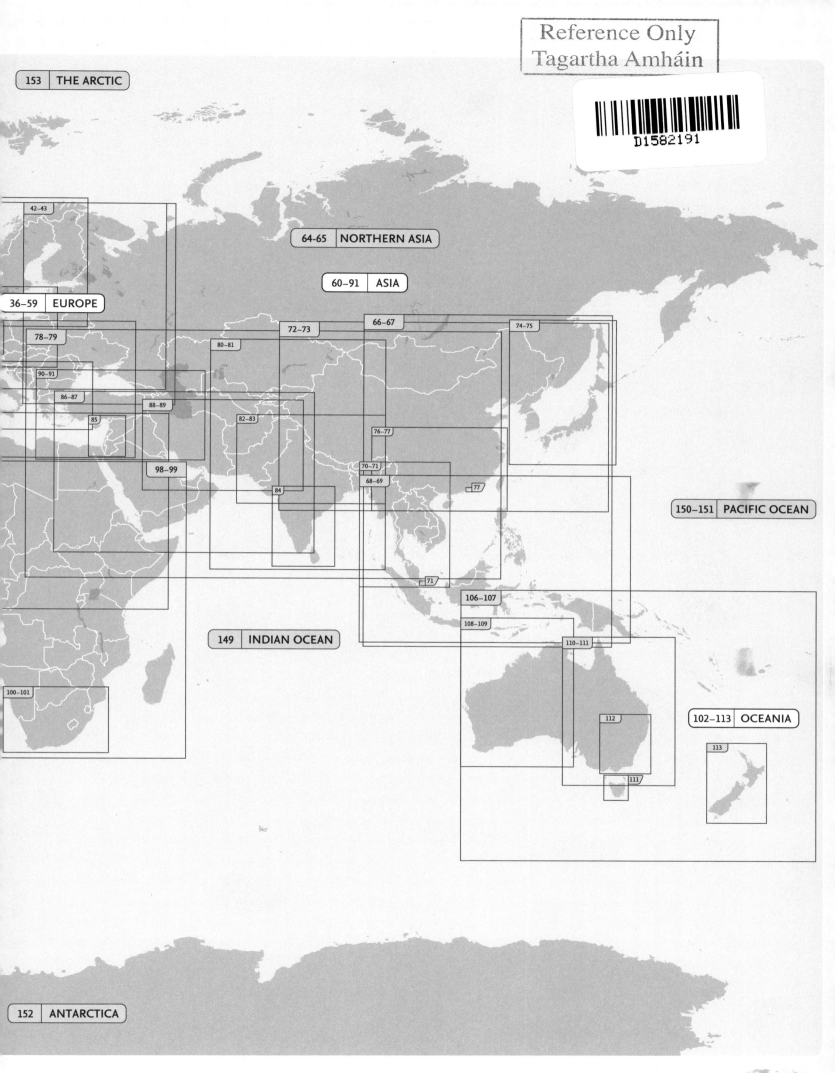

153 | THE ARCTIC

42–43

64-65 | NORTHERN ASIA

60–91 | ASIA

36–59 | EUROPE

78–79

72–73

80–81

66–67

74–75

90–91

86–87

88–89

85

82–83

76–77

98–99

70–71

84

68–69

77

150–151 | PACIFIC OCEAN

71

106–107

149 | INDIAN OCEAN

108–109

110–111

112

102–113 | OCEANIA

113

111

100–101

152 | ANTARCTICA

Find your map

Collins

WC
AT

REFEREN

Contents

Contents

Map Symbols
and Time Zones

Southern Europe

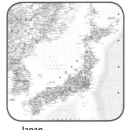

Japan

Antarctica

Settlements

Population	National capital	Administrative capital	Other city or town
over 10 million	BEIJING ⊛	Karachi ◉	New York ◉
5 million to 10 million	LONDON ✡	Tianjin ◎	Santos ◎
1 million to 5 million	KĀBUL ✶	Sydney ◎	Kaohsiung ◎
500 000 to 1 million	BANGUI ✶	Trujillo ◉	Amritsar ◎
100 000 to 500 000	WELLINGTON ✦	Mansa ◉	Apucarana ⊙
50 000 to 100 000	PORT OF SPAIN ✿	Potenza ◉	Arecibo ◦
10 000 to 50 000	MALABO ✿	Chinhoyi ◉	Ceres ◦
under 10 000	VALLETTA ✿	Ati ◦	Venta ◦

⬤ Built-up area

Boundaries

—————— International boundary

·—·—·—· Disputed international boundary
or alignment unconfirmed

- - - - Disputed territory boundary

—————— Administrative boundary

········· Ceasefire line

//////// UN Buffer zone

Miscellaneous

---------- National park

---------- Reserve or
Regional park

✿ Site of specific interest

⌷⌷⌷⌷⌷ Wall

Land and sea features

Desert

⌄ Oasis

Lava field

Marsh

1234
△ Volcano
height in metres

Ice cap or Glacier

⌐⌐⌐ Escarpment

········ Coral reef

ᵢᵢ *1234* Pass
height in metres

Lakes and rivers

Lake

Impermanent lake

Salt lake or lagoon

Impermanent salt lake

Dry salt lake or salt pan

123 Lake height
surface height above
sea level, in metres

—————— River

Impermanent river
or watercourse

‖ Waterfall

| Dam

ı Barrage

Relief

Contour intervals and layer colours

Height
metres		feet
5000		16404
3000		9843
2000		6562
1000		3281
500		1640
200		656
0		0
below sea level		
0		0
200		656
2000		6562
4000		13124
6000		19686

Depth

1234
▲ Summit
height in metres

-123 Spot height
height in metres

123 Ocean deep
depth in metres

Transport

→ ····· Motorway (tunnel; under construction)

→ ····· Main road (tunnel; under construction)

→ ····· Secondary road (tunnel; under construction)

········· Track

·—·—·—◇ ····· Main railway (tunnel; under construction)

·—·—◇ ····· Secondary railway (tunnel; under construction)

·—·—◇ ····· Other railway (tunnel; under construction)

—————— Canal

✈ Main airport

✈ Regional airport

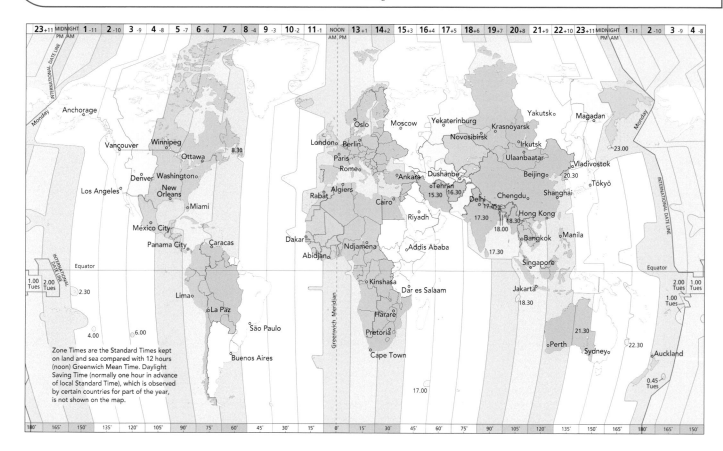

Zone Times are the Standard Times kept
on land and sea compared with 12 hours
(noon) Greenwich Mean Time. Daylight
Saving Time (normally one hour in advance
of local Standard Time), which is observed
by certain countries for part of the year,
is not shown on the map.

The Alps

Paris, France

Europe		Area sq km	Area sq miles	Population	Capital	Languages ('de facto' speakers over one per cent of population)	Religions ('de facto' adherents over one per cent of population)	Currency
ALBANIA		28 748	11 100	2 897 000	Tirana	Albanian, Greek	Sunni Muslim, Albanian Orthodox, Roman Catholic	Lek
ANDORRA		465	180	70 000	Andorra la Vella	Spanish, Catalan, French	Roman Catholic	Euro
AUSTRIA		83 855	32 377	8 545 000	Vienna	German, Croatian, Turkish	Roman Catholic, Protestant	Euro
BELARUS		207 600	80 155	9 496 000	Minsk	Belarusian, Russian	Belarusian Orthodox, Roman Catholic	Belarusian rouble
BELGIUM		30 520	11 784	11 299 000	Brussels	Dutch (Flemish), French (Walloon), German	Roman Catholic, Protestant	Euro
BOSNIA AND HERZEGOVINA		51 130	19 741	3 810 000	Sarajevo	Bosnian, Serbian, Croatian	Sunni Muslim, Serbian Orthodox, Roman Catholic, Protestant	Convertible mark
BULGARIA		110 994	42 855	7 150 000	Sofia	Bulgarian, Turkish, Romany, Macedonian	Bulgarian Orthodox, Sunni Muslim	Lev
CROATIA		56 538	21 829	4 240 000	Zagreb	Croatian, Serbian	Roman Catholic, Serbian Orthodox, Sunni Muslim	Kuna
CZECHIA (CZECH REPUBLIC)		78 864	30 450	10 543 000	Prague	Czech, Moravian, Slovak	Roman Catholic, Protestant	Koruna
DENMARK		43 075	16 631	5 669 000	Copenhagen	Danish	Protestant	Danish krone
ESTONIA		45 200	17 452	1 313 000	Tallinn	Estonian, Russian	Protestant, Estonian and Russian Orthodox	Euro
FINLAND		338 145	130 559	5 503 000	Helsinki	Finnish, Swedish, Sami languages	Protestant, Greek Orthodox	Euro
FRANCE		543 965	210 026	64 395 000	Paris	French, German dialects, Italian, Arabic, Breton	Roman Catholic, Protestant, Sunni Muslim	Euro
GERMANY		357 022	137 849	80 689 000	Berlin	German, Turkish	Protestant, Roman Catholic	Euro
GREECE		131 957	50 949	10 955 000	Athens	Greek	Greek Orthodox, Sunni Muslim	Euro
HUNGARY		93 030	35 919	9 855 000	Budapest	Hungarian	Roman Catholic, Protestant	Forint
ICELAND		102 820	39 699	329 000	Reykjavík	Icelandic	Protestant	Icelandic króna
IRELAND		70 282	27 136	4 688 000	Dublin	English, Irish	Roman Catholic, Protestant	Euro
ITALY		301 245	116 311	59 798 000	Rome	Italian	Roman Catholic	Euro
KOSOVO		10 908	4 212	1 805 000	Prishtinë (Priština)	Albanian, Serbian	Sunni Muslim, Serbian Orthodox	Euro
LATVIA		64 589	24 938	1 971 000	Rīga	Latvian, Russian	Protestant, Roman Catholic, Russian Orthodox	Euro
LIECHTENSTEIN		160	62	38 000	Vaduz	German	Roman Catholic, Protestant	Swiss franc
LITHUANIA		65 200	25 174	2 878 000	Vilnius	Lithuanian, Russian, Polish	Roman Catholic, Protestant, Russian Orthodox	Euro
LUXEMBOURG		2 586	998	567 000	Luxembourg	Letzeburgish, German, French	Roman Catholic	Euro
MACEDONIA (F.Y.R.O.M.)		25 713	9 928	2 078 000	Skopje	Macedonian, Albanian, Turkish	Macedonian Orthodox, Sunni Muslim	Macedonian denar
MALTA		316	122	419 000	Valletta	Maltese, English	Roman Catholic	Euro
MOLDOVA		33 700	13 012	4 069 000	Chișinău	Romanian, Ukrainian, Gagauz, Russian	Romanian Orthodox, Russian Orthodox	Moldovan leu
MONACO		2	1	38 000	Monaco-Ville	French, Monegasque, Italian	Roman Catholic	Euro
MONTENEGRO		13 812	5 333	626 000	Podgorica	Serbian (Montenegrin), Albanian	Montenegrin Orthodox, Sunni Muslim	Euro
NETHERLANDS		41 526	16 033	16 925 000	Amsterdam/The Hague	Dutch, Frisian	Roman Catholic, Protestant, Sunni Muslim	Euro
NORWAY		323 878	125 050	5 211 000	Oslo	Norwegian, Sami languages	Protestant, Roman Catholic	Norwegian krone
POLAND		312 683	120 728	38 612 000	Warsaw	Polish, German	Roman Catholic, Polish Orthodox	Złoty
PORTUGAL		88 940	34 340	10 350 000	Lisbon	Portuguese	Roman Catholic, Protestant	Euro
ROMANIA		237 500	91 699	19 511 000	Bucharest	Romanian, Hungarian	Romanian Orthodox, Protestant, Roman Catholic	Romanian leu
RUSSIA		17 075 400	6 592 849	143 457 000	Moscow	Russian, Tatar, Ukrainian, other local languages	Russian Orthodox, Sunni Muslim, Protestant	Russian rouble
SAN MARINO		61	24	32 000	San Marino	Italian	Roman Catholic	Euro
SERBIA		77 453	29 904	7 046 000	Belgrade	Serbian, Hungarian	Serbian Orthodox, Roman Catholic, Sunni Muslim	Serbian dinar
SLOVAKIA		49 035	18 933	5 426 000	Bratislava	Slovak, Hungarian, Czech	Roman Catholic, Protestant, Orthodox	Euro
SLOVENIA		20 251	7 819	2 068 000	Ljubljana	Slovene, Croatian, Serbian	Roman Catholic, Protestant	Euro
SPAIN		504 782	194 897	46 122 000	Madrid	Spanish, Castilian, Catalan, Galician, Basque	Roman Catholic	Euro
SWEDEN		449 964	173 732	9 779 000	Stockholm	Swedish, Sami languages	Protestant, Roman Catholic	Swedish krona
SWITZERLAND		41 293	15 943	8 299 000	Bern	German, French, Italian, Romansch	Roman Catholic, Protestant	Swiss franc
UKRAINE		603 700	233 090	44 824 000	Kiev	Ukrainian, Russian	Ukrainian Orthodox, Ukrainian Catholic, Roman Catholic	Hryvnia
UNITED KINGDOM		243 609	94 058	64 716 000	London	English, Welsh, Gaelic	Protestant, Roman Catholic, Muslim	Pound sterling
VATICAN CITY		0.5	0.2	800	Vatican City	Italian	Roman Catholic	Euro

Dependent and disputed territories		Territorial status	Area sq km	Area sq miles	Population	Capital	Languages	Religions	Currency
Azores		Autonomous Region of Portugal	2 300	888	247 413	Ponta Delgada	Portuguese	Roman Catholic, Protestant	Euro
Crimea		Disputed Territory	27 000	10 400	2 348 600	Simferopol'	Ukrainian, Russian	Russian Orthodox, Sunni Muslim	Russian rouble
Faroe Islands		Self-governing Danish Territory	1 399	540	48 000	Tórshavn	Faroese, Danish	Protestant	Danish krone
Gibraltar		United Kingdom Overseas Territory	7	3	32 000	Gibraltar	Engllish, Spanish	Roman Catholic, Protestant, Sunni Muslim	Gibraltar pound
Guernsey		British Crown Dependency	78	30	65 000	St Peter Port	English, French	Protestant, Roman Catholic	Pound sterling
Isle of Man		British Crown Dependency	572	221	88 000	Douglas	English	Protestant, Roman Catholic	Pound sterling
Jersey		British Crown Dependency	116	45	101 000	St Helier	English, French	Protestant, Roman Catholic	Pound sterling
Transnistria		Disputed Territory	4 200	1 622	...	Tiraspol	Russian, Ukrainian, Moldovan	Eastern Orthodox, Roman Catholic	Transnistrian rouble, Moldovan leu

World
States and Territories

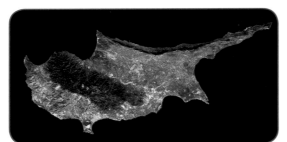

Cyprus, eastern Mediterranean

Angkor, Cambodia

Asia		Area sq km	Area sq miles	Population	Capital	Languages ('de facto' speakers over one per cent of population)	Religions ('de facto' adherents over one per cent of population)	Currency
AFGHANISTAN		652 225	251 825	32 527 000	Kābul	Dari, Pashto (Pashtu), Uzbek, Turkmen	Sunni Muslim, Shi'a Muslim	Afghani
ARMENIA		29 800	11 506	3 018 000	Yerevan	Armenian, Kurdish	Armenian Orthodox	Dram
AZERBAIJAN		86 600	33 436	9 754 000	Baku	Azeri, Armenian, Russian, Lezgian	Shi'a Muslim, Sunni Muslim, Russian and Armenian Orthodox	Azerbaijani manat
BAHRAIN		691	267	1 377 000	Manama	Arabic, English	Shi'a Muslim, Sunni Muslim, Christian	Bahraini dinar
BANGLADESH		143 998	55 598	160 996 000	Dhaka	Bengali, English	Sunni Muslim, Hindu	Taka
BHUTAN		46 620	18 000	775 000	Thimphu	Dzongkha, Nepali, Assamese	Buddhist, Hindu	Ngultrum, Indian rupee
BRUNEI		5 765	2 226	423 000	Bandar Seri Begawan	Malay, English, Chinese	Sunni Muslim, Buddhist, Christian	Bruneian dollar
CAMBODIA		181 035	69 884	15 578 000	Phnom Penh	Khmer	Buddhist, Roman Catholic, Sunni Muslim	Riel
CHINA		9 606 802	3 709 186	1 383 925 000	Beijing	Mandarin (Putonghua), Wu, Cantonese, Hsiang, regional languages	Confucian, Taoist, Buddhist, Christian, Sunni Muslim	Yuan, HK dollar**, Macau pataca
CYPRUS		9 251	3 572	1 165 000	Nicosia	Greek, Turkish, English	Greek Orthodox, Sunni Muslim	Euro
EAST TIMOR (TIMOR-LESTE)		14 874	5 743	1 185 000	Dili	Portuguese, Tetun, English	Roman Catholic	United States dollar
GEORGIA		69 700	26 911	4 000 000	Tbilisi	Georgian, Russian, Armenian, Azeri, Ossetian, Abkhaz	Georgian Orthodox, Russian Orthodox, Sunni Muslim	Lari
INDIA		3 166 620	1 222 632	1 311 051 000	New Delhi	Hindi, English, many regional languages	Hindu, Sunni Muslim, Shi'a Muslim, Sikh, Christian	Indian rupee
INDONESIA		1 919 445	741 102	257 564 000	Jakarta	Indonesian, other local languages	Sunni Muslim, Protestant, Roman Catholic, Hindu, Buddhist	Rupiah
IRAN		1 648 000	636 296	79 109 000	Tehrān	Farsi, Azeri, Kurdish, regional languages	Shi'a Muslim, Sunni Muslim	Iranian rial
IRAQ		438 317	169 235	36 423 000	Baghdād	Arabic, Kurdish, Turkmen	Shi'a Muslim, Sunni Muslim, Christian	Iraqi dinar
ISRAEL		20 770	8 019	8 064 000	Jerusalem (Yerushalayim) (El Quds)*	Hebrew, Arabic	Jewish, Sunni Muslim, Christian, Druze	Shekel
JAPAN		377 727	145 841	126 573 000	Tōkyō	Japanese	Shintoist, Buddhist, Christian	Yen
JORDAN		89 206	34 443	7 595 000	'Ammān	Arabic	Sunni Muslim, Christian	Jordanian dinar
KAZAKHSTAN		2 717 300	1 049 155	17 625 000	Astana	Kazakh, Russian, Ukrainian, German, Uzbek, Tatar	Sunni Muslim, Russian Orthodox, Protestant	Tenge
KUWAIT		17 818	6 880	3 892 000	Kuwait	Arabic	Sunni Muslim, Shi'a Muslim, Christian, Hindu	Kuwaiti dinar
KYRGYZSTAN		198 500	76 641	5 940 000	Bishkek	Kyrgyz, Russian, Uzbek	Sunni Muslim, Russian Orthodox	Kyrgyz som
LAOS		236 800	91 429	6 802 000	Vientiane	Lao, other local languages	Buddhist, traditional beliefs	Kip
LEBANON		10 452	4 036	5 851 000	Beirut	Arabic, Armenian, French	Shi'a Muslim, Sunni Muslim, Christian	Lebanese pound
MALAYSIA		332 965	128 559	30 331 000	Kuala Lumpur/Putrajaya	Malay, English, Chinese, Tamil, other local languages	Sunni Muslim, Buddhist, Hindu, Christian, traditional beliefs	Ringgit
MALDIVES		298	115	364 000	Male	Divehi (Maldivian)	Sunni Muslim	Rufiyaa
MONGOLIA		1 565 000	604 250	2 959 000	Ulan Bator	Khalka (Mongolian), Kazakh, other local languages	Buddhist, Sunni Muslim	Tugrik (tögrög)
MYANMAR (BURMA)		676 577	261 228	53 897 000	Nay Pyi Taw	Burmese, Shan, Karen, other local languages	Buddhist, Christian, Sunni Muslim	Kyat
NEPAL		147 181	56 827	28 514 000	Kathmandu	Nepali, Maithili, Bhojpuri, English, other local languages	Hindu, Buddhist, Sunni Muslim	Nepalese rupee
NORTH KOREA		120 538	46 540	25 155 000	P'yŏngyang	Korean	Traditional beliefs, Chondoist, Buddhist	North Korean won
OMAN		309 500	119 499	4 491 000	Muscat	Arabic, Baluchi, Indian languages	Ibadhi Muslim, Sunni Muslim	Omani rial
PAKISTAN		881 888	340 497	188 925 000	Islamabad	Urdu, Punjabi, Sindhi, Pashto (Pashtu), English, Balochi	Sunni Muslim, Shi'a Muslim, Christian, Hindu	Pakistani rupee
PALAU		497	192	21 000	Melekeok (Ngerulmud)	Palauan, English	Roman Catholic, Protestant, traditional beliefs	United States dollar
PHILIPPINES		300 000	115 831	100 699 000	Manila	English, Filipino, Tagalog, Cebuano, other local languages	Roman Catholic, Protestant, Sunni Muslim, Aglipayan	Philippine peso
QATAR		11 437	4 416	2 235 000	Doha	Arabic	Sunni Muslim	Qatari riyal
RUSSIA		17 075 400	6 592 849	143 457 000	Moscow	Russian, Tatar, Ukrainian, other local languages	Russian Orthodox, Sunni Muslim, Protestant	Russian rouble
SAUDI ARABIA		2 200 000	849 425	31 540 000	Riyadh	Arabic	Sunni Muslim, Shi'a Muslim	Saudi Arabian rial
SINGAPORE		639	247	5 604 000	Singapore	Chinese, English, Malay, Tamil	Buddhist, Taoist, Sunni Muslim, Christian, Hindu	Singapore dollar
SOUTH KOREA		99 274	38 330	50 293 000	Seoul	Korean	Buddhist, Protestant, Roman Catholic	South Korean won
SRI LANKA		65 610	25 332	20 715 000	Sri Jayewardenepura Kotte	Sinhalese, Tamil, English	Buddhist, Hindu, Sunni Muslim, Roman Catholic	Sri Lankan rupee
SYRIA		185 180	71 498	18 502 000	Damascus	Arabic, Kurdish, Armenian	Sunni Muslim, Shi'a Muslim, Christian	Syrian pound
TAIWAN+		36 179	13 969	23 462 000	Taipei (Taibei)	Mandarin (Putonghua), Min, Hakka, other local languages	Buddhist, Taoist, Confucian, Christian	New Taiwan dollar
TAJIKISTAN		143 100	55 251	8 482 000	Dushanbe	Tajik, Uzbek, Russian	Sunni Muslim	Somoni
THAILAND		513 115	198 115	67 959 000	Bangkok	Thai, Lao, Chinese, Malay, Mon-Khmer languages	Buddhist, Sunni Muslim	Baht
TURKEY		779 452	300 948	78 666 000	Ankara	Turkish, Kurdish	Sunni Muslim, Shi'a Muslim	Lira
TURKMENISTAN		488 100	188 456	5 374 000	Aşgabat (Ashgabad)	Turkmen, Uzbek, Russian	Sunni Muslim, Russian Orthodox	Turkmen manat
UNITED ARAB EMIRATES		77 700	30 000	9 157 000	Abu Dhabi (Abū ẓaby)	Arabic, English	Sunni Muslim, Shi'a Muslim	United Arab Emirates dirham
UZBEKISTAN		447 400	172 742	29 893 000	Toshkent (Tashkent)	Uzbek, Russian, Tajik, Kazakh	Sunni Muslim, Russian Orthodox	Uzbek som
VIETNAM		329 565	127 246	93 448 000	Ha Nôi (Hanoi)	Vietnamese, Thai, Khmer, Chinese, other local languages	Buddhist, Taoist, Roman Catholic, Cao Dai, Hoa Hao	Dong
YEMEN		527 968	203 850	26 832 000	Şan'ā'	Arabic	Sunni Muslim, Shi'a Muslim	Yemeni rial

Dependent and disputed territories	Territorial status		Area sq km	Area sq miles	Population	Capital	Languages	Religions	Currency
Abkhazia	Disputed territory		8 700	3 359	...	Sokhumi (Aq"a)	Abkhaz, Russian, Georgian	Abkhaz Orthodox, Sunni Muslim	Russian rouble, Abkhaz apsar
Christmas Island	Australian External Territory		135	52	2 240	The Settlement	English	Buddhist, Sunni Muslim, Protestant, Roman Catholic	Australian dollar
Cocos (Keeling) Islands	Australian External Territory		14	5	590	West Island	English	Sunni Muslim, Christian	Australian dollar
Gaza	Disputed territory		363	140	1 820 000	Gaza	Arabic	Sunni Muslim, Shi'a Muslim	Israeli shekel
Nagorno-Karabakh	Disputed territory		6 000	2 317	149 000	Xankändi (Stepanakert)	Armenian	Armenian Orthodox	Armenian dram
South Ossetia	Disputed territory		4 000	1 544	...	Tskhinvali	Ossetian, Russian, Georgian	Eastern Orthodox	Russian rouble
West Bank	Disputed territory		5 860	2 263	2 862 000		Arabic, Hebrew	Sunni Muslim, Jewish, Shi'a Muslim, Christian	Jordanian dinar, Israeli shekel

+China claims Taiwan as its 23rd province   *De facto capital. Disputed   **Hong Kong dollar

Victoria Falls, Zambia/Zimbabwe

Africa		Area sq km	Area sq miles	Population	Capital	Languages ('de facto' speakers over one per cent of population)	Religions ('de facto' adherents over one per cent of population)	Currency
ALGERIA		2 381 741	919 595	39 667 000	Algiers (Alger)	Arabic, French, Berber	Sunni Muslim	Algerian dinar
ANGOLA		1 246 700	481 354	25 022 000	Luanda	Portuguese, Bantu, other local languages	Roman Catholic, Protestant, traditional beliefs	Kwanza
BENIN		112 620	43 483	10 880 000	Porto-Novo	French, Fon, Yoruba, Adja, other local languages	Traditional beliefs, Roman Catholic, Sunni Muslim	CFA franc*
BOTSWANA		581 370	224 468	2 262 000	Gaborone	English, Setswana, Shona, other local languages	Traditional beliefs, Protestant, Roman Catholic	Pula
BURKINA FASO		274 200	105 869	18 106 000	Ouagadougou	French, Moore (Mossi), Fulani, other local languages	Sunni Muslim, traditional beliefs, Roman Catholic	CFA franc*
BURUNDI		27 835	10 747	11 179 000	Bujumbura	Kirundi (Hutu, Tutsi), French	Roman Catholic, traditional beliefs, Protestant	Burundian franc
CAMEROON		475 442	183 569	23 344 000	Yaoundé	French, English, Fang, Bamileke, other local languages	Roman Catholic, traditional beliefs, Sunni Muslim, Protestant	CFA franc*
CAPE VERDE		4 033	1 557	521 000	Praia	Portuguese, creole	Roman Catholic, Protestant	Cape Verdean escudo
CENTRAL AFRICAN REPUBLIC		622 436	240 324	4 900 000	Bangui	French, Sango, Banda, Baya, other local languages	Protestant, Roman Catholic, traditional beliefs, Sunni Muslim	CFA franc*
CHAD		1 284 000	495 755	14 037 000	Ndjamena	Arabic, French, Sara, other local languages	Sunni Muslim, Roman Catholic, Protestant, traditional beliefs	CFA franc*
COMOROS		1 862	719	788 000	Moroni	Shikomor (Comorian), French, Arabic	Sunni Muslim, Roman Catholic	Comorian franc
CONGO		342 000	132 047	4 620 000	Brazzaville	French, Kongo, Monokutuba, other local languages	Roman Catholic, Protestant, traditional beliefs, Sunni Muslim	CFA franc*
CONGO, DEM. REP. OF THE		2 345 410	905 568	77 267 000	Kinshasa	French, Lingala, Swahili, Kongo, other local languages	Christian, Sunni Muslim	Congolese franc
CÔTE D'IVOIRE (IVORY COAST)		322 463	124 504	22 702 000	Yamoussoukro	French, creole, Akan, other local languages	Sunni Muslim, Roman Catholic, traditional beliefs, Protestant	CFA franc*
DJIBOUTI		23 200	8 958	888 000	Djibouti	Somali, Afar, French, Arabic	Sunni Muslim, Christian	Djiboutian franc
EGYPT		1 001 450	386 660	91 508 000	Cairo (Al Qāhirah)	Arabic	Sunni Muslim, Coptic Christian	Egyptian pound
EQUATORIAL GUINEA		28 051	10 831	845 000	Malabo	Spanish, French, Fang	Roman Catholic, traditional beliefs	CFA franc*
ERITREA		117 400	45 328	5 228 000	Asmara	Tigrinya, Tigre	Sunni Muslim, Coptic Christian	Nakfa
ETHIOPIA		1 133 880	437 794	99 391 000	Addis Ababa	Oromo, Amharic, Tigrinya, other local languages	Ethiopian Orthodox, Sunni Muslim, traditional beliefs	Birr
GABON		267 667	103 347	1 725 000	Libreville	French, Fang, other local languages	Roman Catholic, Protestant, traditional beliefs	CFA franc*
THE GAMBIA		11 295	4 361	1 991 000	Banjul	English, Malinke, Fulani, Wolof	Sunni Muslim, Protestant	Dalasi
GHANA		238 537	92 100	27 410 000	Accra	English, Hausa, Akan, other local languages	Christian, Sunni Muslim, traditional beliefs	Cedi
GUINEA		245 857	94 926	12 609 000	Conakry	French, Fulani, Malinke, other local languages	Sunni Muslim, traditional beliefs, Christian	Guinean franc
GUINEA-BISSAU		36 125	13 948	1 844 000	Bissau	Portuguese, crioulo, other local languages	Traditional beliefs, Sunni Muslim, Christian	CFA franc*
KENYA		582 646	224 961	46 050 000	Nairobi	Swahili, English, other local languages	Christian, traditional beliefs	Kenyan shilling
LESOTHO		30 355	11 720	2 135 000	Maseru	Sesotho, English, Zulu	Christian, traditional beliefs	Loti, S. African rand
LIBERIA		111 369	43 000	4 503 000	Monrovia	English, creole, other local languages	Traditional beliefs, Christian, Sunni Muslim	Liberian dollar
LIBYA		1 759 540	679 362	6 278 000	Tripoli	Arabic, Berber	Sunni Muslim	Libyan dinar
MADAGASCAR		587 041	226 658	24 235 000	Antananarivo	Malagasy, French	Traditional beliefs, Christian, Sunni Muslim	Ariary
MALAWI		118 484	45 747	17 215 000	Lilongwe	Chichewa, English, other local languages	Christian, traditional beliefs, Sunni Muslim	Malawian kwacha
MALI		1 240 140	478 821	17 600 000	Bamako	French, Bambara, other local languages	Sunni Muslim, traditional beliefs, Christian	CFA franc*
MAURITANIA		1 030 700	397 955	4 068 000	Nouakchott	Arabic, French, other local languages	Sunni Muslim	Ouguiya
MAURITIUS		2 040	788	1 273 000	Port Louis	English, creole, Hindi, Bhojpurī, French	Hindu, Roman Catholic, Sunni Muslim	Mauritian rupee
MOROCCO		446 550	172 414	34 378 000	Rabat	Arabic, Berber, French	Sunni Muslim	Moroccan dirham
MOZAMBIQUE		799 380	308 642	27 978 000	Maputo	Portuguese, Makua, Tsonga, other local languages	Traditional beliefs, Roman Catholic, Sunni Muslim	Metical
NAMIBIA		824 292	318 261	2 459 000	Windhoek	English, Afrikaans, German, Ovambo, other local languages	Protestant, Roman Catholic	Namibian dollar
NIGER		1 267 000	489 191	19 899 000	Niamey	French, Hausa, Fulani, other local languages	Sunni Muslim, traditional beliefs	CFA franc*
NIGERIA		923 768	356 669	182 202 000	Abuja	English, Hausa, Yoruba, Ibo, Fulani, other local languages	Sunni Muslim, Christian, traditional beliefs	Naira
RWANDA		26 338	10 169	11 610 000	Kigali	Kinyarwanda, French, English	Roman Catholic, traditional beliefs, Protestant	Rwandan franc
SÃO TOMÉ AND PRÍNCIPE		964	372	190 000	São Tomé	Portuguese, creole	Roman Catholic, Protestant	Dobra
SENEGAL		196 720	75 954	15 129 000	Dakar	French, Wolof, Fulani, other local languages	Sunni Muslim, Roman Catholic, traditional beliefs	CFA franc*
SEYCHELLES		455	176	96 000	Victoria	English, French, creole	Roman Catholic, Protestant	Seychelles rupee
SIERRA LEONE		71 740	27 699	6 453 000	Freetown	English, creole, Mende, Temne, other local languages	Sunni Muslim, traditional beliefs	Leone
SOMALIA		637 657	246 201	10 787 000	Mogadishu	Somali, Arabic	Sunni Muslim	Somali shilling
SOUTH AFRICA		1 219 090	470 693	54 490 000	Bloemfontein/ Cape Town/Pretoria	Afrikaans, English, nine official other local languages	Protestant, Roman Catholic, Sunni Muslim, Hindu	Rand
SOUTH SUDAN		644 329	248 775	12 340 000	Juba	English, Arabic, Dinka, Nuer, other local languages	Traditional beliefs, Christian	South Sudanese pound
SUDAN		1 861 484	718 725	40 235 000	Khartoum	Arabic, Dinka, Nubian, Beja, Nuer, other local languages	Sunni Muslim, traditional beliefs, Christian	Sudanese pound (Sudani)
SWAZILAND		17 364	6 704	1 287 000	Mbabane	Swazi, English	Christian, traditional beliefs	Lilangeni, South African rand
TANZANIA		945 087	364 900	53 470 000	Dodoma	Swahili, English, Nyamwezi, other local languages	Shi'a Muslim, Sunni Muslim, traditional beliefs, Christian	Tanzanian shilling
TOGO		56 785	21 925	7 305 000	Lomé	French, Ewe, Kabre, other local languages	Traditional beliefs, Christian, Sunni Muslim	CFA franc*
TUNISIA		164 150	63 379	11 254 000	Tunis	Arabic, French	Sunni Muslim	Tunisian dinar
UGANDA		241 038	93 065	39 032 000	Kampala	English, Swahili, Luganda, other local languages	Roman Catholic, Protestant, Sunni Muslim, traditional beliefs	Ugandan shilling
ZAMBIA		752 614	290 586	16 212 000	Lusaka	English, Bemba, Nyanja, Tonga, other local languages	Christian, traditional beliefs	Zambian kwacha
ZIMBABWE		390 759	150 873	15 603 000	Harare	16 official languages including English, Shona and Ndebele	Christian, traditional beliefs	US dollar and other currencies

Dependent and disputed territories		Territorial status		Area sq km	Area sq miles	Population	Capital	Languages	Religions	Currency
Canary Islands		Autonomous Community of Spain		7 447	2 875	...	Santa Cruz de Tenerife/Las Palmas	Spanish	Roman Catholic	Euro
Madeira		Autonomous Region of Portugal		779	301	259 000	Funchal	Portuguese	Roman Catholic, Protestant	Euro
Mayotte		French Overseas Department		373	144	240 000	Dzaoudzi	French, Mahorian	Sunni Muslim, Christian	Euro
Réunion		French Overseas Department		2 551	985	861 000	St-Denis	French, creole	Roman Catholic	Euro
St Helena, Ascension and Tristan da Cunha		United Kingdom Overseas Territory		410	158	5 793	Jamestown	English	Protestant, Roman Catholic	St Helena pound
Somaliland		Disputed territory		140 000	54 054	3 850 000	Hargeysa	Somali, Arabic, English	Sunni Muslim	Somaliland shilling
Western Sahara		Disputed territory (Morocco)		266 000	102 703	573 000	Laâyoune	Arabic	Sunni Muslim	Moroccan dirham

*Communauté Financière Africaine franc

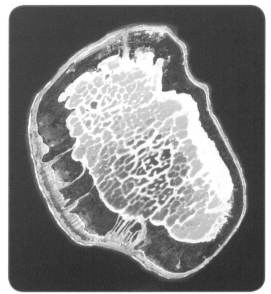

Mataiva Atoll, Tuamotu Archipelago, French Polynesia

Uluṟu (Ayers Rock), Australia

Oceania		Area sq km	Area sq miles	Population	Capital	Languages ('de facto' speakers over one per cent of population)	Religions ('de facto' adherents over one per cent of population)	Currency
AUSTRALIA		7 692 024	2 969 907	23 969 000	Canberra	English, Italian, Greek	Protestant, Roman Catholic, Orthodox	Australian dollar
FIJI		18 330	7 077	892 000	Suva	English, Fijian, Hindi	Christian, Hindu, Sunni Muslim	Fijian dollar
KIRIBATI		717	277	112 000	Bairiki	Gilbertese, English	Roman Catholic, Protestant	Australian dollar
MARSHALL ISLANDS		181	70	53 000	Delap-Uliga-Djarrit	English, Marshallese	Protestant, Roman Catholic	United States dollar
MICRONESIA, FEDERATED STATES OF		701	271	526 000	Palikir	English, Chuukese, Pohnpeian, other local languages	Roman Catholic, Protestant	United States dollar
NAURU		21	8	10 000	Yaren (de facto capital)	Nauruan, English	Protestant, Roman Catholic	Australian dollar
NEW ZEALAND		270 534	104 454	4 529 000	Wellington	English, Maori	Protestant, Roman Catholic	New Zealand dollar
PAPUA NEW GUINEA		462 840	178 704	7 619 000	Port Moresby	English, Tok Pisin (creole), other local languages	Protestant, Roman Catholic, traditional beliefs	Kina
SAMOA		2 831	1 093	193 000	Apia	Samoan, English	Protestant, Roman Catholic	Tala
SOLOMON ISLANDS		28 370	10 954	584 000	Honiara	English, creole, local languages	Protestant, Roman Catholic	Solomon Islands dollar
TONGA		748	289	106 000	Nuku'alofa	Tongan, English	Protestant, Roman Catholic	Pa'anga
TUVALU		25	10	9 916	Vaiaku	Tuvaluan, English	Protestant	Australian dollar
VANUATU		12 190	4 707	265 000	Port Vila	English, Bislama (creole), French	Protestant, Roman Catholic, traditional beliefs	Vatu

Dependent territories		Territorial status	Area sq km	Area sq miles	Population	Capital	Languages	Religions	Currency
American Samoa		United States Unincorporated Territory	197	76	56 000	Fagatogo	Samoan, English	Protestant, Roman Catholic	United States dollar
Cook Islands		Self-governing New Zealand Territory	293	113	21 000	Avarua	English, Maori	Protestant, Roman Catholic	New Zealand dollar
French Polynesia		French Overseas Country	3 265	1 261	283 000	Papeete	French, Tahitian, other Polynesian languages	Protestant, Roman Catholic	CFP franc*
Guam		United States Unincorporated Territory	541	209	170 000	Hagåtña (Agana)	Chamorro, English, Tapalog	Roman Catholic	United States dollar
New Caledonia		French Overseas Collectivity	19 058	7 358	263 000	Nouméa	French, other local languages	Roman Catholic, Protestant, Sunni Muslim	CFP franc*
Niue		Self-governing New Zealand Overseas Territory	258	100	1 610	Alofi	English, Niuean	Christian	New Zealand dollar
Norfolk Island		Australian External Territory	35	14	2 302	Kingston	English	Protestant, Roman Catholic	Australian Dollar
Northern Mariana Islands		United States Commonwealth	477	184	55 000	Capitol Hill	English, Chamorro, other local languages	Roman Catholic	United States dollar
Pitcairn Islands		United Kingdom Overseas Territory	45	17	49	Adamstown	English	Protestant	New Zealand dollar
Tokelau		New Zealand Overseas Territory	10	4	1 250		English, Tokelauan	Christian	New Zealand dollar
Wallis and Futuna		French Overseas Collectivity	274	106	13 000	Matā'utu	French, Wallisian, Futunian	Roman Catholic	CFP franc*

*Franc des Comptoirs Français du Pacifique

Queenstown and Lake Wakatipu, New Zealand

Liberty Island, New York, USA

Cuba, Caribbean Sea

North America		Area sq km	Area sq miles	Population	Capital	Languages ('de facto' speakers over one per cent of population)	Religions ('de facto' adherents over one per cent of population)	Currency
ANTIGUA AND BARBUDA		442	171	92 000	St John's	English, creole	Protestant, Roman Catholic	East Caribbean dollar
THE BAHAMAS		13 939	5 382	388 000	Nassau	English, creole	Protestant, Roman Catholic	Bahamian dollar
BARBADOS		430	166	284 000	Bridgetown	English, creole	Protestant, Roman Catholic	Barbadian dollar
BELIZE		22 965	8 867	359 000	Belmopan	English, Spanish, Mayan, creole	Roman Catholic, Protestant	Belizean dollar
CANADA		9 984 670	3 855 103	35 940 000	Ottawa	English, French, other local languages	Roman Catholic, Protestant, Eastern Orthodox, Jewish	Canadian dollar
COSTA RICA		51 100	19 730	4 808 000	San José	Spanish	Roman Catholic, Protestant	Costa Rican colón
CUBA		110 860	42 803	11 390 000	Havana	Spanish	Roman Catholic, Protestant	Cuban peso
DOMINICA		750	290	73 000	Roseau	English, creole	Roman Catholic, Protestant	East Caribbean dollar
DOMINICAN REPUBLIC		48 442	18 704	10 528 000	Santo Domingo	Spanish, creole	Roman Catholic, Protestant	Dominican peso
EL SALVADOR		21 041	8 124	6 127 000	San Salvador	Spanish	Roman Catholic, Protestant	United States dollar
GRENADA		378	146	107 000	St George's	English, creole	Roman Catholic, Protestant	East Caribbean dollar
GUATEMALA		108 890	42 043	16 343 000	Guatemala City	Spanish, Mayan languages	Roman Catholic, Protestant	Quetzal
HAITI		27 750	10 714	10 711 000	Port-au-Prince	French, creole	Roman Catholic, Protestant, Voodoo	Gourde
HONDURAS		112 088	43 277	8 075 000	Tegucigalpa	Spanish, Amerindian languages	Roman Catholic, Protestant	Lempira
JAMAICA		10 991	4 244	2 793 000	Kingston	English, creole	Protestant, Roman Catholic	Jamaican dollar
MEXICO		1 972 545	761 604	127 017 000	Mexico City	Spanish, Amerindian languages	Roman Catholic, Protestant	Mexican peso
NICARAGUA		130 000	50 193	6 082 000	Managua	Spanish, Amerindian languages	Roman Catholic, Protestant	Córdoba
PANAMA		77 082	29 762	3 929 000	Panama City	Spanish, English, Amerindian languages	Roman Catholic, Protestant, Sunni Muslim	Balboa
ST KITTS AND NEVIS		261	101	56 000	Basseterre	English, creole	Protestant, Roman Catholic	East Caribbean dollar
ST LUCIA		616	238	185 000	Castries	English, creole	Roman Catholic, Protestant	East Caribbean dollar
ST VINCENT AND THE GRENADINES		389	150	109 000	Kingstown	English, creole	Protestant, Roman Catholic	East Caribbean dollar
TRINIDAD AND TOBAGO		5 130	1 981	1 360 000	Port of Spain	English, creole, Hindi	Roman Catholic, Hindu, Protestant, Sunni Muslim	Trinidad and Tobago dollar
UNITED STATES OF AMERICA		9 826 635	3 794 085	321 774 000	Washington DC	English, Spanish	Protestant, Roman Catholic, Sunni Muslim, Jewish	United States dollar

Dependent territories		Territorial status	Area sq km	Area sq miles	Population	Capital	Languages	Religions	Currency
Anguilla		United Kingdom Overseas Territory	155	60	15 000	The Valley	English	Protestant, Roman Catholic	East Caribbean dollar
Aruba		Self-governing Netherlands Territory	193	75	104 000	Oranjestad	Papiamento, Dutch, English	Roman Catholic, Protestant	Arubian florin
Bermuda		United Kingdom Overseas Territory	54	21	62 000	Hamilton	English	Protestant, Roman Catholic	Bermuda dollar
Cayman Islands		United Kingdom Overseas Territory	259	100	60 000	George Town	English	Protestant, Roman Catholic	Cayman Islands dollar
Curaçao		Self-governing Netherlands territory	444	171	157 000	Willemstad	Dutch, Papiamento	Roman Catholic, Protestant	Netherlands Antillean guilder
Greenland		Self-governing Danish Territory	2 175 600	840 004	56 000	Nuuk	Greenlandic, Danish	Protestant	Danish krone
Guadeloupe		French Overseas Department	1 780	687	468 000	Basse-Terre	French, creole	Roman Catholic	Euro
Martinique		French Overseas Department	1 079	417	396 000	Fort-de-France	French, creole	Roman Catholic, traditional beliefs	Euro
Montserrat		United Kingdom Overseas Territory	100	39	5 125	Brades (Temporary capital)	English	Protestant, Roman Catholic	East Caribbean dollar
Puerto Rico		United States Commonwealth	9 104	3 515	3 683 000	San Juan	Spanish, English	Roman Catholic, Protestant	United States dollar
St Pierre and Miquelon		French Territorial Collectivity	242	93	6 288	St-Pierre	French	Roman Catholic	Euro
Turks and Caicos Islands		United Kingdom Overseas Territory	430	166	34 000	Grand Turk	English	Protestant	United States dollar
Virgin Islands (U.K.)		United Kingdom Overseas Territory	153	59	30 000	Road Town	English	Protestant, Roman Catholic	United States dollar
Virgin Islands (U.S.A.)		United States Unincorporated Territory	352	136	106 000	Charlotte Amalie	English, Spanish	Protestant, Roman Catholic	United States dollar

South America		Area sq km	Area sq miles	Population	Capital	Languages ('de facto' speakers over one per cent of population)	Religions ('de facto' adherents over one per cent of population)	Currency
ARGENTINA		2 766 889	1 068 302	43 417 000	Buenos Aires	Spanish, Italian, Amerindian languages	Roman Catholic, Protestant	Argentinian peso
BOLIVIA		1 098 581	424 164	10 725 000	La Paz/Sucre	Spanish, Quechua, Aymara	Roman Catholic, Protestant, Baha'i	Boliviano
BRAZIL		8 514 879	3 287 613	207 848 000	Brasília	Portuguese	Roman Catholic, Protestant	Real
CHILE		756 945	292 258	17 948 000	Santiago	Spanish, Amerindian languages	Roman Catholic, Protestant	Chilean peso
COLOMBIA		1 141 748	440 831	48 229 000	Bogotá	Spanish, Amerindian languages	Roman Catholic, Protestant	Colombian peso
ECUADOR		272 045	105 037	16 144 000	Quito	Spanish, Quechua, and other Amerindian languages	Roman Catholic	US dollar
GUYANA		214 969	83 000	767 000	Georgetown	English, creole, Amerindian languages	Protestant, Hindu, Roman Catholic, Sunni Muslim	Guyanese dollar
PARAGUAY		406 752	157 048	6 639 000	Asunción	Spanish, Guaraní	Roman Catholic, Protestant	Guaraní
PERU		1 285 216	496 225	31 377 000	Lima	Spanish, Quechua, Aymara	Roman Catholic, Protestant	Nuevo sol
SURINAME		163 820	63 251	543 000	Paramaribo	Dutch, Surinamese, English, Hindi	Hindu, Roman Catholic, Protestant, Sunni Muslim	Surinamese dollar
URUGUAY		176 215	68 037	3 432 000	Montevideo	Spanish	Roman Catholic, Protestant, Jewish	Uruguayan peso
VENEZUELA		912 050	352 144	31 108 000	Caracas	Spanish, Amerindian languages	Roman Catholic, Protestant	Bolívar

Dependent territories		Territorial status	Area sq km	Area sq miles	Population	Capital	Languages	Religions	Currency
Falkland Islands		United Kingdom Overseas Territory	12 170	4 699	2 903	Stanley	English	Protestant, Roman Catholic	Falkland Islands pound
French Guiana		French Overseas Department	90 000	34 749	269 000	Cayenne	French, creole	Roman Catholic	Euro

The current pattern of the world's countries and territories is a result of a long history of exploration, colonialism, conflict and politics. The fact that there are currently 196 independent countries in the world – the most recent, South Sudan, only being created in July 2011 – illustrates the significant political changes which have occurred since 1950 when there were only eighty-two. There has been a steady progression away from colonial influences over the last fifty years, although many dependent overseas territories remain.

The shapes of countries and the pattern of international boundaries reflect both physical and political processes. Some borders follow natural features – rivers, mountain ranges, etc. – others are defined according to political agreement or as a result of war. Some are still subject to dispute between two or more countries, and many remain undefined on the ground.

Facts

- The longest single continuous land border stretches for 6 416 kilometres between Canada and the USA
- Both China and Russia have land borders with 14 different countries
- Vatican City, the smallest independent country, was created in 1929 as an enclave within Rome, the capital of Italy
- All countries of the world are members of the United Nations except Kosovo, Taiwan and Vatican City

Internet Links

United Nations	www.un.org
Foreign and Commonwealth Office	www.fco.gov.uk
International Boundaries Research Unit	www.dur.ac.uk/ibru
Permanent Committee on Geographical Names	www.pcgn.org.uk
U.S. Board on Geographic Names	geonames.usgs.gov

Abbreviation Key

A.	ANDORRA	HUN.	HUNGARY	ROM.	ROMANIA
AL.	ALBANIA	ISR.	ISRAEL	RU.	RUSSIA
ARM.	ARMENIA	JOR.	JORDAN	S.	SERBIA
AUST.	AUSTRIA	K.	KOSOVO	SL.	SLOVENIA
AZER.	AZERBAIJAN	L.	LUXEMBOURG	SLA.	SLOVAKIA
B.	BURUNDI	LAT.	LATVIA	SUR.	SURINAME
BE.	BENIN	LEB.	LEBANON	SW.	SWITZERLAND
BEL.	BELGIUM	LITH.	LITHUANIA	T.	TOGO
B.H.	BOSNIA AND HERZEGOVINA	M.	MONTENEGRO	TAJIK.	TAJIKISTAN
BULG.	BULGARIA	MA.	MACEDONIA	TURKM.	TURKMENISTAN
CR.	CROATIA	MOL.	MOLDOVA	U.A.E.	UNITED ARAB EMIRATES
CZ.	CZECHIA (CZECH REPUBLIC)	NETH.	NETHERLANDS	U.K.	UNITED KINGDOM
EST.	ESTONIA	N.Z.	NEW ZEALAND	U.S.A.	UNITED STATES OF AMERICA
GEOR.	GEORGIA	R.	RWANDA	UZBEK.	UZBEKISTAN

Aerial view of the **Vatican City**, the world's smallest country by both population and area.

International boundaries in the sea shown on this map indicate ownership of islands and island groups only. They do not infer the alignments of legal maritime boundaries.

World extremes

Countries			
Largest country (area)	**Russia**	17 075 400 sq km	6 592 849 sq miles
Smallest country (area)	**Vatican City**	0.5 sq km	0.2 sq miles
Largest country (population)	**China**	1 383 925 000	
Smallest country (population)	**Vatican City**	800	
Most densely populated country	**Monaco**	19 000 per sq km	38 000 per sq mile
Least densely populated country	**Mongolia**	1.8 per sq km	4.7 per sq mile
Capitals			
Largest national capital (population)	**Tōkyō, Japan**	38 197 000	
Smallest national capital (population)	**Melekeok, (Ngerulmud) Palau**	391	
Most northerly national capital	**Reykjavík, Iceland**	64° 08'N	
Most southerly national capital	**Wellington, New Zealand**	41° 18'S	
Highest national capital	**La Paz, Bolivia**	3 636 m	11 910 ft

World
Landscapes

The Earth's physical features, both on land and on the sea bed, closely reflect its geological structure. The current shapes of the continents and oceans have evolved over millions of years. Movements of the tectonic plates which make up the Earth's crust have created some of the best-known and most spectacular features. The processes which have shaped the Earth continue today with earthquakes, volcanoes, erosion, climatic variations and man's activities all affecting the Earth's landscapes.

The total topographic range of the Earth's surface is nearly 20 000 metres, from the highest point Mount Everest, to the lowest point in the Mariana Trench. Major mountain ranges include the Himalaya, the Andes and the Rocky Mountains, each of which give rise to some of the world's greatest rivers. In contrast, the deserts of the Sahara, Australia, the Arabian Peninsula and the Gobi cover vast areas and each provide unique landscapes.

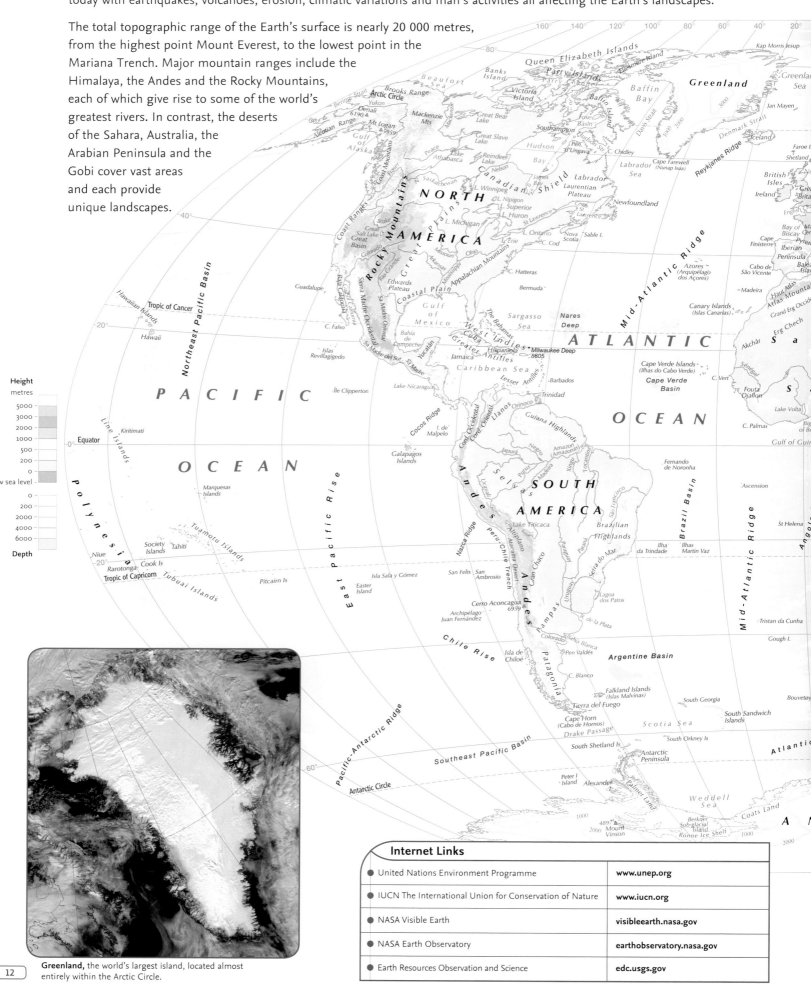

Greenland, the world's largest island, located almost entirely within the Arctic Circle.

Internet Links

● United Nations Environment Programme	**www.unep.org**
● IUCN The International Union for Conservation of Nature	**www.iucn.org**
● NASA Visible Earth	**visibleearth.nasa.gov**
● NASA Earth Observatory	**earthobservatory.nasa.gov**
● Earth Resources Observation and Science	**edc.usgs.gov**

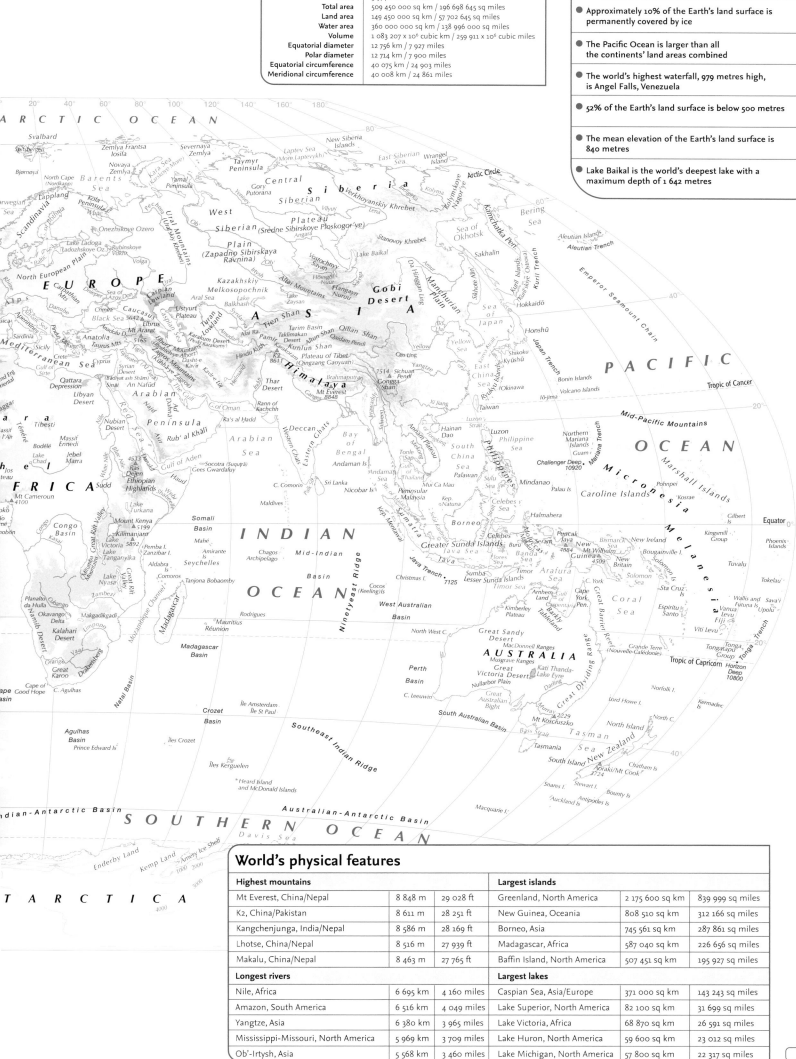

Earth's dimensions

Mass	5.974 x 10²¹ tonnes
Total area	509 450 000 sq km / 196 698 645 sq miles
Land area	149 450 000 sq km / 57 702 645 sq miles
Water area	360 000 000 sq km / 138 996 000 sq miles
Volume	1 083 207 x 10⁶ cubic km / 259 911 x 10⁶ cubic miles
Equatorial diameter	12 756 km / 7 927 miles
Polar diameter	12 714 km / 7 900 miles
Equatorial circumference	40 075 km / 24 903 miles
Meridional circumference	40 008 km / 24 861 miles

Facts

- Approximately 10% of the Earth's land surface is permanently covered by ice
- The Pacific Ocean is larger than all the continents' land areas combined
- The world's highest waterfall, 979 metres high, is Angel Falls, Venezuela
- 52% of the Earth's land surface is below 500 metres
- The mean elevation of the Earth's land surface is 840 metres
- Lake Baikal is the world's deepest lake with a maximum depth of 1 642 metres

World's physical features

Highest mountains			Largest islands		
Mt Everest, China/Nepal	8 848 m	29 028 ft	Greenland, North America	2 175 600 sq km	839 999 sq miles
K2, China/Pakistan	8 611 m	28 251 ft	New Guinea, Oceania	808 510 sq km	312 166 sq miles
Kangchenjunga, India/Nepal	8 586 m	28 169 ft	Borneo, Asia	745 561 sq km	287 861 sq miles
Lhotse, China/Nepal	8 516 m	27 939 ft	Madagascar, Africa	587 040 sq km	226 656 sq miles
Makalu, China/Nepal	8 463 m	27 765 ft	Baffin Island, North America	507 451 sq km	195 927 sq miles
Longest rivers			**Largest lakes**		
Nile, Africa	6 695 km	4 160 miles	Caspian Sea, Asia/Europe	371 000 sq km	143 243 sq miles
Amazon, South America	6 516 km	4 049 miles	Lake Superior, North America	82 100 sq km	31 699 sq miles
Yangtze, Asia	6 380 km	3 965 miles	Lake Victoria, Africa	68 870 sq km	26 591 sq miles
Mississippi-Missouri, North America	5 969 km	3 709 miles	Lake Huron, North America	59 600 sq km	23 012 sq miles
Ob'-Irtysh, Asia	5 568 km	3 460 miles	Lake Michigan, North America	57 800 sq km	22 317 sq miles

Earthquakes and volcanoes hold a constant fascination because of their power, their beauty, and the fact that they cannot be controlled or accurately predicted. Our understanding of these phenomena relies mainly on the theory of plate tectonics. This defines the Earth's surface as a series of 'plates' which are constantly moving relative to each other, at rates of a few centimetres per year. As plates move against each other enormous pressure builds up and when the rocks can no longer bear this pressure they fracture, and energy is released as an earthquake. The pressures involved can also melt the rock to form magma which then rises to the Earth's surface to form a volcano. The distribution of earthquakes and volcanoes therefore relates closely to plate boundaries. In particular, most active volcanoes and much of the Earth's seismic activity are centred on the 'Ring of Fire' around the Pacific Ocean.

Facts

- Over 900 earthquakes of magnitude 5.0 or greater occur every year
- An earthquake of magnitude 8.0 releases energy equivalent to 1 billion tons of TNT explosive
- Ground shaking during an earthquake in Alaska in 1964 lasted for 3 minutes
- Indonesia has more than 120 volcanoes and over 30% of the world's active volcanoes
- Volcanoes can produce very fertile soil and important industrial materials and chemicals

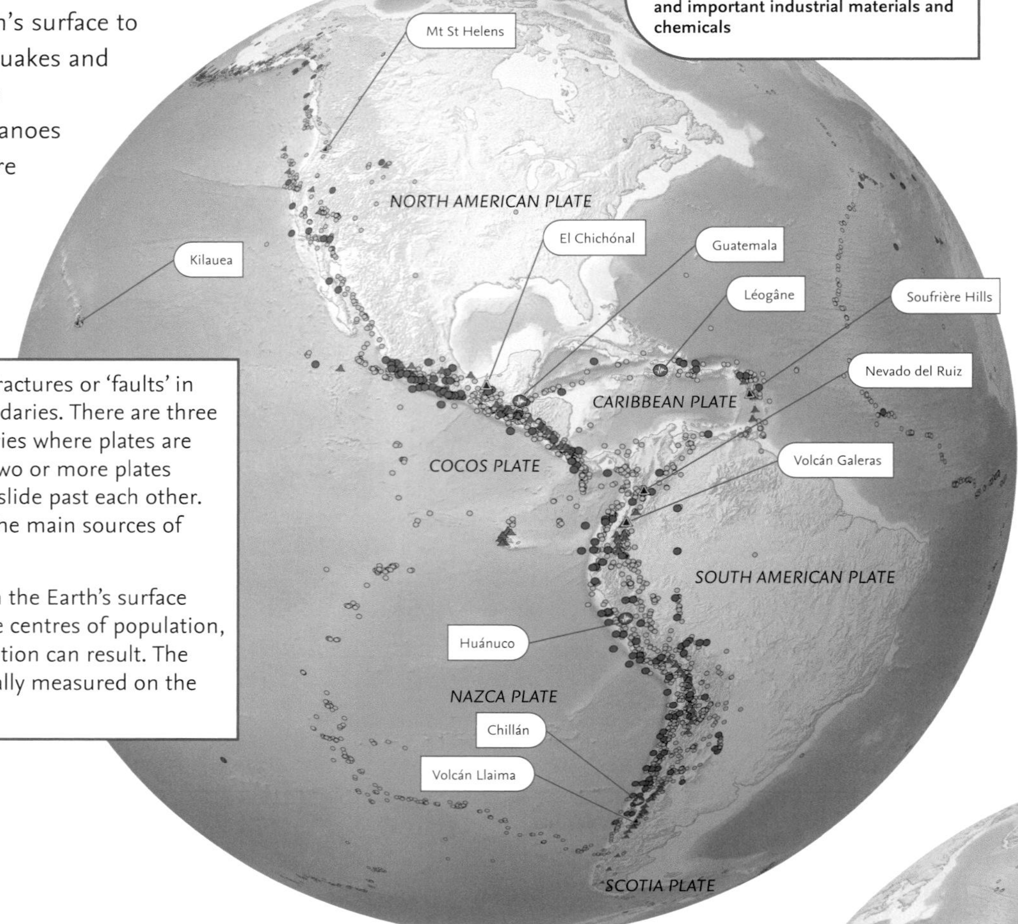

Earthquakes

Earthquakes are caused by movement along fractures or 'faults' in the Earth's crust, particularly along plate boundaries. There are three types of plate boundary: constructive boundaries where plates are moving apart; destructive boundaries where two or more plates collide; conservative boundaries where plates slide past each other. Destructive and conservative boundaries are the main sources of earthquake activity.

The epicentre of an earthquake is the point on the Earth's surface directly above its source. If this is near to large centres of population, and the earthquake is powerful, major devastation can result. The size, or magnitude, of an earthquake is generally measured on the Richter Scale.

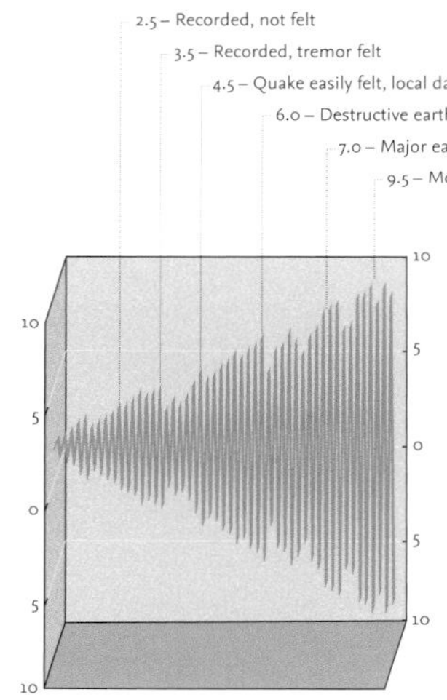

2.5 – Recorded, not felt
3.5 – Recorded, tremor felt
4.5 – Quake easily felt, local damage caused
6.0 – Destructive earthquake
7.0 – Major earthquake
9.5 – Most powerful earthquake recorded

Earthquake magnitude – the Richter Scale

The scale measures the energy released by an earthquake. It is a logarithmic scale: an earthquake measuring 4 is thirty times more powerful than one measuring 3, and a quake measuring 6 is 27 000 times more powerful than one measuring 3.

Mt St Helens

Kilauea

NORTH AMERICAN PLATE

El Chichónal

Guatemala

Léogâne

Soufrière Hills

Nevado del Ruiz

CARIBBEAN PLATE

COCOS PLATE

Volcán Galeras

SOUTH AMERICAN PLATE

Huánuco

NAZCA PLATE

Chillán

Volcán Llaima

SCOTIA PLATE

Chlef

SOUTH AMERICAN PLATE

Plate boundaries

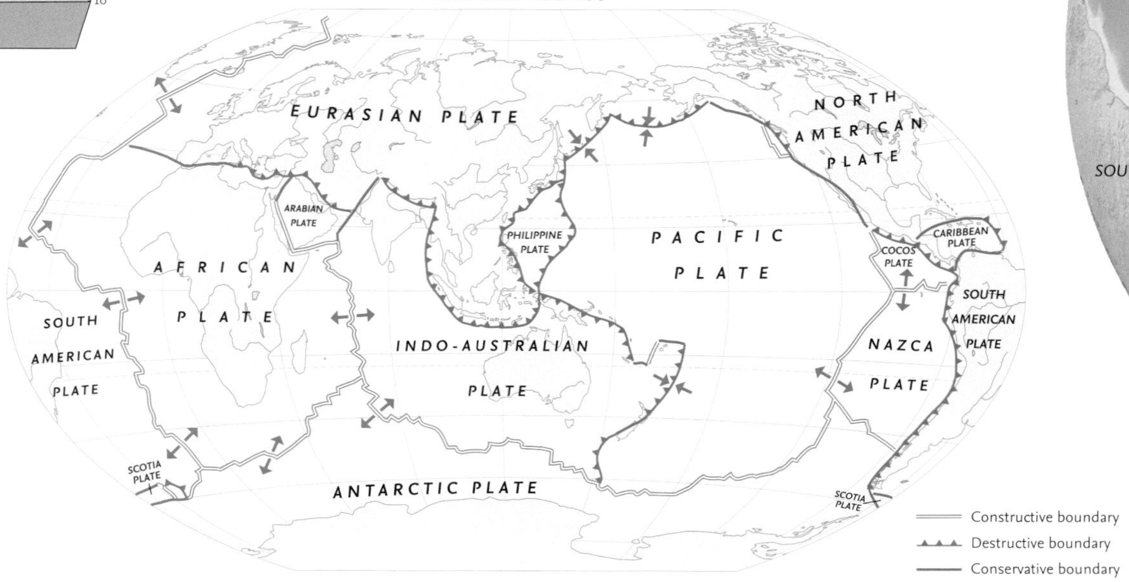

EURASIAN PLATE

NORTH AMERICAN PLATE

ARABIAN PLATE

PHILIPPINE PLATE

PACIFIC PLATE

COCOS PLATE

CARIBBEAN PLATE

AFRICAN PLATE

SOUTH AMERICAN PLATE

INDO-AUSTRALIAN PLATE

NAZCA PLATE

SOUTH AMERICAN PLATE

SCOTIA PLATE

ANTARCTIC PLATE

SCOTIA PLATE

‾‾‾ Constructive boundary
▲▲▲ Destructive boundary
‾‾‾ Conservative boundary

Volcanoes

The majority of volcanoes occur along destructive plate boundaries in the 'subduction zone' where one plate passes under another. The friction and pressure causes the rock to melt and to form magma which is forced upwards to the Earth's surface where it erupts as molten rock (lava) or as particles of ash or cinder. This process created the numerous volcanoes in the Andes, where the Nazca Plate is passing under the South American Plate. Volcanoes can be defined by the nature of the material they emit. 'Shield' volcanoes have extensive, gentle slopes formed from free-flowing lava, while steep-sided 'continental' volcanoes are created from thicker, slow-flowing lava and ash.

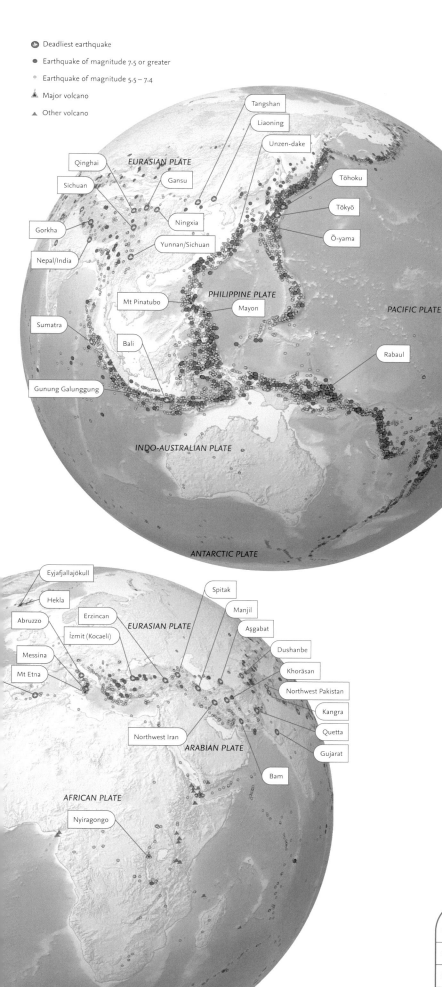

Legend

- Deadliest earthquake
- Earthquake of magnitude 7.5 or greater
- Earthquake of magnitude 5.5 – 7.4
- Major volcano
- Other volcano

Major volcanic eruptions 1980–2014

Volcano	Country	Date
Mt St Helens	USA	1980
El Chichónal	Mexico	1982
Gunung Galunggung	Indonesia	1982
Kilauea	Hawaii, USA	1983
Ō-yama	Japan	1983
Nevado del Ruiz	Colombia	1985
Mt Pinatubo	Philippines	1991
Unzen-dake	Japan	1991
Mayon	Philippines	1993
Volcán Galeras	Colombia	1993
Volcán Llaima	Chile	1994
Rabaul	Papua New Guinea	1994
Soufrière Hills	Montserrat	1997
Hekla	Iceland	2000
Mt Etna	Italy	2001
Nyiragongo	Dem. Rep. of the Congo	2002
Eyjafjallajökull	Iceland	2010

Deadliest earthquakes since 1900

Year	Location	Deaths
1905	Kangra, India	19 000
1907	west of Dushanbe, Tajikistan	12 000
1908	Messina, Italy	110 000
1915	Abruzzo, Italy	35 000
1917	Bali, Indonesia	15 000
1920	Ningxia Province, China	200 000
1923	Tōkyō, Japan	142 807
1927	Qinghai Province, China	200 000
1932	Gansu Province, China	70 000
1933	Sichuan Province, China	10 000
1934	Nepal/India	10 700
1935	Quetta, Pakistan	30 000
1939	Chillán, Chile	28 000
1939	Erzincan, Turkey	32 700
1948	Aşgabat, Turkmenistan	19 800
1962	northwest Iran	12 225
1970	Huánuco Province, Peru	66 794
1974	Yunnan and Sichuan Provinces, China	20 000
1975	Liaoning Province, China	10 000
1976	central Guatemala	22 778
1976	Tangshan, Hebei Province, China	255 000
1978	Khorāsan Province, Iran	20 000
1980	Chlef, Algeria	11 000
1988	Spitak, Armenia	25 000
1990	Manjil, Iran	50 000
1999	İzmit (Kocaeli), Turkey	17 000
2001	Gujarat, India	20 000
2003	Bam, Iran	26 271
2004	off Sumatra, Indian Ocean	> 225 000
2005	northwest Pakistan	74 648
2008	Sichuan Province, China	> 60 000
2009	Abruzzo region, Italy	308
2009	Sumatra, Indonesia	> 1 100
2010	Léogâne, Haiti	222 570
2011	Tōhoku, Japan	15 891
2015	Gorkha, Nepal	8 831

Internet Links

USGS Earthquake Hazards Program	**earthquake.usgs.gov**
USGS Volcano Hazards Program	**volcanoes.usgs.gov**
British Geological Survey	**www.bgs.ac.uk**
NASA Natural Hazards	**earthobservatory.nasa.gov/NaturalHazards**
Volcano World	**volcano.oregonstate.edu**

World
Climate and Weather

The climate of a region is defined by its long-term prevailing weather conditions. Classification of Climate Types is based on the relationship between temperature and humidity and how these factors are affected by latitude, altitude, ocean currents and winds. Weather is the specific short term condition which occurs locally and consists of events such as thunderstorms, hurricanes, blizzards and heat waves. Temperature and rainfall data recorded at weather stations can be plotted graphically and the graphs shown here, typical of each climate region, illustrate the various combinations of temperature and rainfall which exist worldwide for each month of the year. Data used for climate graphs are based on average monthly figures recorded over a minimum period of thirty years.

World Statistics: see pages 154–160

Major climate regions, ocean currents and sea surface temperatures

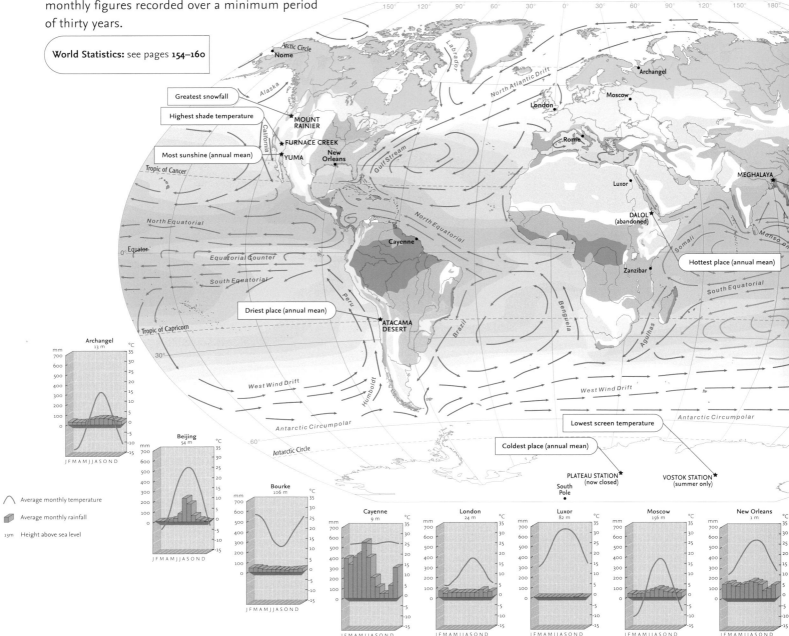

Climate change

The temperatures in 2015 were the warmest on record with a global average 0.9 °C above the 20th century average. Globally fifteen of the sixteen hottest years have been recorded this century. Most of this warming is caused by human activities which result in a build-up of greenhouse gases, mainly carbon dioxide, allowing heat to be trapped within the atmosphere. Carbon dioxide emissions have increased since the beginning of the industrial revolution due to burning of fossil fuels, increased urbanization, population growth, deforestation and industrial pollution.

Annual climate indicators such as number of frost-free days, length of growing season, heat wave frequency, number of wet days, length of dry spells and frequency of weather extremes are used to monitor climate change. The map opposite shows how future changes in temperature will not be spread evenly around the world. Some regions will warm faster than the global average, while others will warm more slowly. The Arctic is warming twice as fast as other areas mainly due to ice melting and there being less to reflect sunlight to keep the surface cool.

Projection of global temperatures 2090–2099

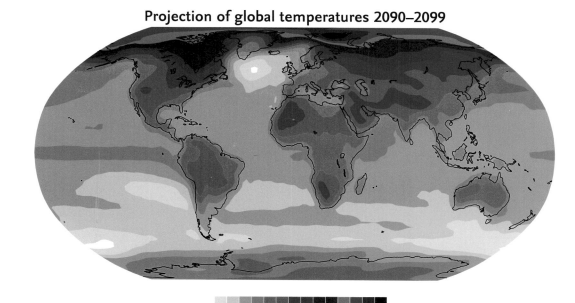

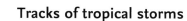

0.5 1 1.5 2 2.5 3 3.5 4 4.5 5 5.5 6 6.5 7 7.5

Change in average surface temperature (°C)

Tracks of tropical storms

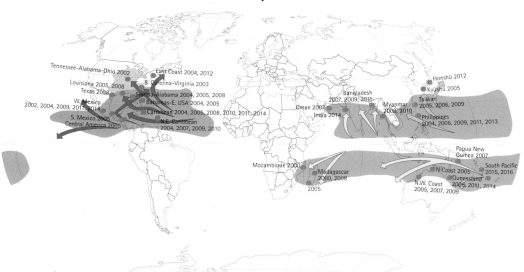

Tennessee-Alabama-Ohio 2002
East Coast 2004, 2012
Louisiana 2005, 2008
S. Carolina-Virginia 2003
Texas 2008
W. Mexico 2002, 2004, 2009, 2011, 2014
Florida-Alabama 2004, 2005, 2008
Bahamas-E. USA 2004, 2005
Caribbean 2004, 2005, 2008, 2010, 2011, 2014
S. Mexico 2005
Central America 2005
N.E. Caribbean 2004, 2007, 2009, 2010
Honshū 2012
Kyūshū 2005
Bangladesh 2007, 2009, 2011
Myanmar 2008, 2010
Taiwan 2005, 2006, 2009
Oman 2007
India 2014
Philippines 2004, 2006, 2009, 2011, 2013
Papua New Guinea 2007
Mozambique 2000
Madagascar 2000, 2008
N Coast 2005
South Pacific 2015, 2016
Queensland 2006, 2011, 2014
N.W. Coast 2005, 2007, 2009
2005

Cyclone track
Hurricane track
Typhoon track
Major tropical storm (2000–2016)
Source area of tropical storms
Tornado high risk areas

Tropical storms

Tropical storms are among the most powerful and destructive weather systems on Earth. Of the eighty to one hundred which develop annually over the tropical oceans, many make landfall and cause considerable damage to property and loss of life as a result of high winds and heavy rain. Although the number of tropical storms is projected to decrease, their intensity, and therefore their destructive power, is likely to increase.

Hurricane Sandy off the east coast of the USA, October 2012.

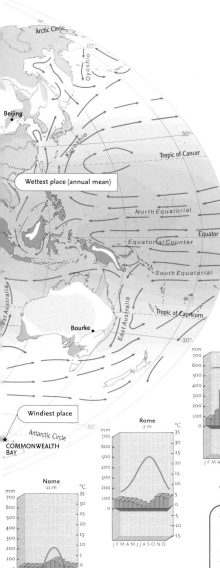

Arctic Circle
Oyashio
Beijing
Kuroshio
Tropic of Cancer
Wettest place (annual mean)
North Equatorial
Equatorial Counter
Equator
South Equatorial
West Australia
East Australia
Bourke
Tropic of Capricorn
Windiest place
Antarctic Circle
COMMONWEALTH BAY

Zanzibar 15 m

Rome 2 m

Nome 11 m

World
Land Cover

The oxygen- and water-rich environment of the Earth has helped create a wide range of habitats. Forest and woodland ecosystems form the predominant natural land cover over most of the Earth's surface. Tropical rainforests are part of an intricate land-atmosphere relationship that is disturbed by land cover changes. Forests in the tropics are believed to hold most of the world's bird, animal, and plant species. Grassland, shrubland and deserts collectively cover most of the unwooded land surface, with tundra on frozen subsoil

at high northern latitudes. These areas tend to have lower species diversity than most forests, with the notable exception of Mediterranean shrublands, which support some of the most diverse floras on the Earth. Humans have extensively altered most grassland and shrubland areas, usually through conversion to agriculture, burning and introduction of domestic livestock. They have had less immediate impact on tundra and true desert regions, although these remain vulnerable to global climate change.

World land cover

Evergreen needleleaf forest	Grasslands
Evergreen broadleaf forest	Permanent wetlands
Deciduous needleleaf forest	Croplands
Deciduous broadleaf forest	Urban and built-up
Mixed forest	Cropland/Natural vegetation mosaic
Closed shrublands	Snow and Ice
Open shrublands	Barren or sparsely vegetated
Woody savannas	Water bodies
Savannas	

Land cover

The land cover map shown here was developed at Boston University in Boston, MA, U.S.A. using data from the Moderate-resolution Imaging-Spectroradiometer (MODIS) instrument aboard NASA's Terra satellite. The high resolution (ground resolution of 1km) of the imagery used to compile the data set and map allows detailed interpretation of land cover patterns across the world. Important uses include managing forest resources, improving estimates of the Earth's water and energy cycles, and modelling climate change.

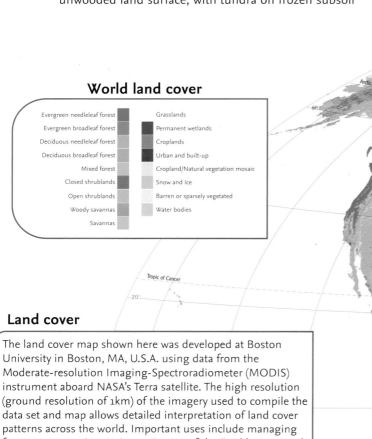

Urban, Tōkyō, capital of Japan and the largest city in the world.

Internet Links

World Resources Institute	**www.wri.org**
World Conservation Monitoring Centre	**www.unep-wcmc.org**
United Nations Environment Programme (UNEP)	**www.unep.org**
IUCN, International Union for Conservation of Nature	**www.iucn.org**
MODIS Land Cover Group at Boston University	**www.bu.edu/lcsc**

Cropland, near Consuegra, Spain.

Barren/Shrubland, Mojave Desert, California, United States of America.

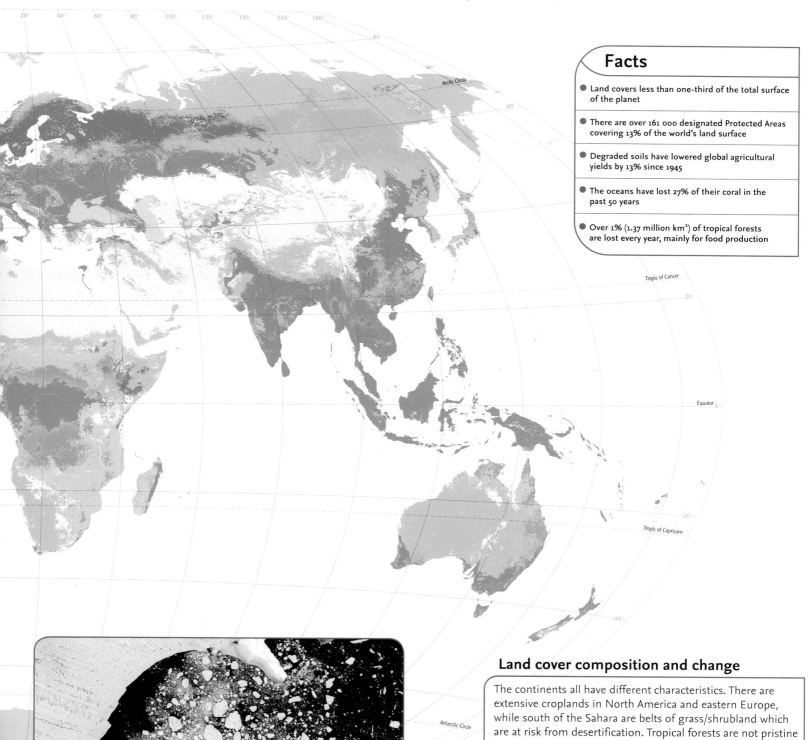

Snow and ice, Larsen Ice Shelf, Antarctica.

Land cover composition and change

The continents all have different characteristics. There are extensive croplands in North America and eastern Europe, while south of the Sahara are belts of grass/shrubland which are at risk from desertification. Tropical forests are not pristine areas either as they show signs of human activity in deforestation of land for crops or grazing.

World
Population

After increasing very slowly for most of human history, world population more than doubled in the last half century. Whereas world population did not pass the one billion mark until 1804 and took another 123 years to reach two billion in 1927, it then added the third billion in 33 years, the fourth in 14 years and the fifth in 13 years. Just twelve years later on October 12, 1999 the United Nations announced that the global population had reached the six billion mark, with seven billion being reached only eleven years later, on October 31, 2011. It is expected that another two billion people will have been added to the world's population by 2043.

World Statistics: see pages **154–160**

World population distribution
Population density (2005), continental populations (2013) and continental population change (2010–2015)

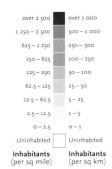

Inhabitants (per sq mile)	Inhabitants (per sq km)
over 2 500	over 1 000
1 250 – 2 500	500 – 1 000
625 – 1 250	250 – 500
250 – 625	100 – 250
125 – 250	50 – 100
62.5 – 125	25 – 50
12.5 – 62.5	5 – 25
2.5 – 12.5	1 – 5
0 – 2.5	0 – 1
Uninhabited	Uninhabited

World population change

Population growth since 1950 has been spread very unevenly between the continents. While overall numbers have been growing rapidly since 1950, a massive 89 per cent increase has taken place in the less developed regions, especially southern and eastern Asia. In contrast, Europe's population level has been almost stationary and is expected to decrease in the future. India and China alone are responsible for over one-third of current growth. Most of the highest rates of growth are to be found in Sub-Saharan Africa and, until population growth is brought under tighter control, the developing world in particular will continue to face enormous problems of supporting a rising population.

North America
Total population 358 000 000
Population change 0.8%

Europe
Total population 738 000 000
Population change 0.1%

Latin America and the Caribbean
Total population 634 000 000
Population change 1.1%

World
Total population 7 349 000 000
Population change 1.2%

World population growth, 1750–2050

Population (millions)

Year

Legend: World, Asia, Africa, Latin America and the Caribbean, Europe, North America, Oceania

Top 10 countries by population, 2015

Rank	Country	Population
1	China	1 383 925 000
2	India	1 311 051 000
3	United States of America	321 774 000
4	Indonesia	257 564 000
5	Brazil	207 848 000
6	Pakistan	188 925 000
7	Nigeria	182 202 000
8	Bangladesh	160 996 000
9	Russia	143 457 000
10	Mexico	127 017 000

The island nation of **Singapore,** the world's second most densely populated country.

Kuna Indians inhabit this congested island off the north coast of Panama.

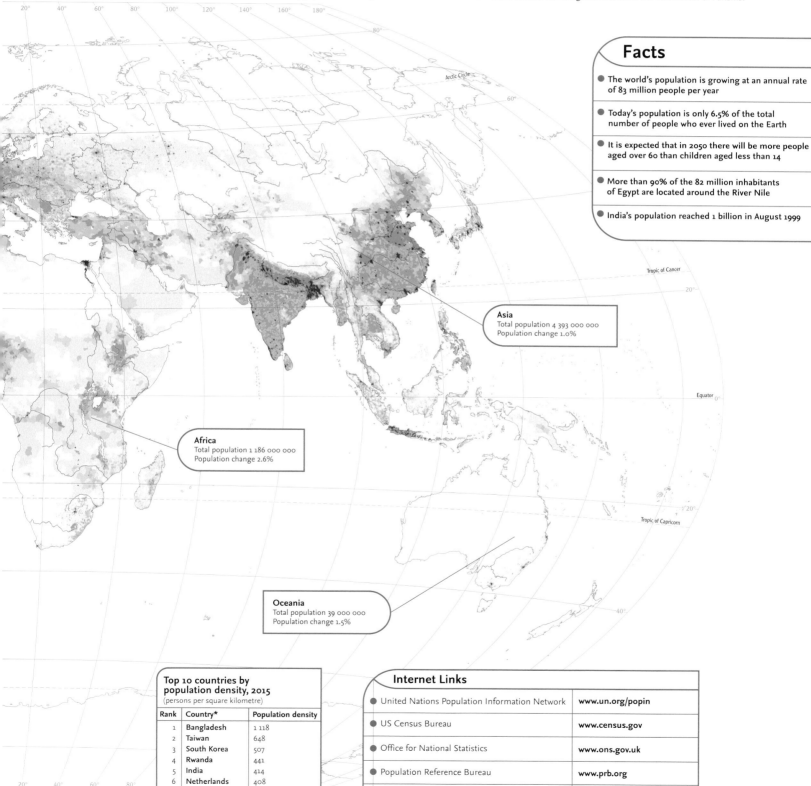

Asia
Total population 4 393 000 000
Population change 1.0%

Africa
Total population 1 186 000 000
Population change 2.6%

Oceania
Total population 39 000 000
Population change 1.5%

Facts

- The world's population is growing at an annual rate of 83 million people per year

- Today's population is only 6.5% of the total number of people who ever lived on the Earth

- It is expected that in 2050 there will be more people aged over 60 than children aged less than 14

- More than 90% of the 82 million inhabitants of Egypt are located around the River Nile

- India's population reached 1 billion in August 1999

Top 10 countries by population density, 2015
(persons per square kilometre)

Rank	Country*	Population density
1	Bangladesh	1 118
2	Taiwan	648
3	South Korea	507
4	Rwanda	441
5	India	414
6	Netherlands	408
7	Burundi	402
8	Haiti	386
9	Belgium	370
10	Philippines	336

*Only countries with a population of over 10 million are considered

Internet Links

United Nations Population Information Network	**www.un.org/popin**
US Census Bureau	**www.census.gov**
Office for National Statistics	**www.ons.gov.uk**
Population Reference Bureau	**www.prb.org**
Socioeconomic Data and Applications Center	**sedac.ciesin.columbia.edu**

World
Urbanization and Cities

The world is becoming increasingly urban but the level of urbanization varies greatly between and within continents. At the beginning of the twentieth century only fourteen per cent of the world's population was urban and by 1950 this had increased to thirty per cent. In the more developed regions and in Latin America and the Caribbean over seventy per cent of the population is urban while in Africa and Asia the figure is forty per cent. In recent decades urban growth has increased rapidly to over fifty per cent and in 2015 there are more than 500 cities with over 1 000 000 inhabitants. It is in the developing regions that the most rapid increases are taking place and it is expected that by 2030 over half of urban dwellers worldwide will live in Asia. Migration from the countryside to the city in the search for better job opportunities is the main factor in urban growth.

World Statistics: see pages **154–160**

Characteristic high-rise urban development **Hong Kong,** China.

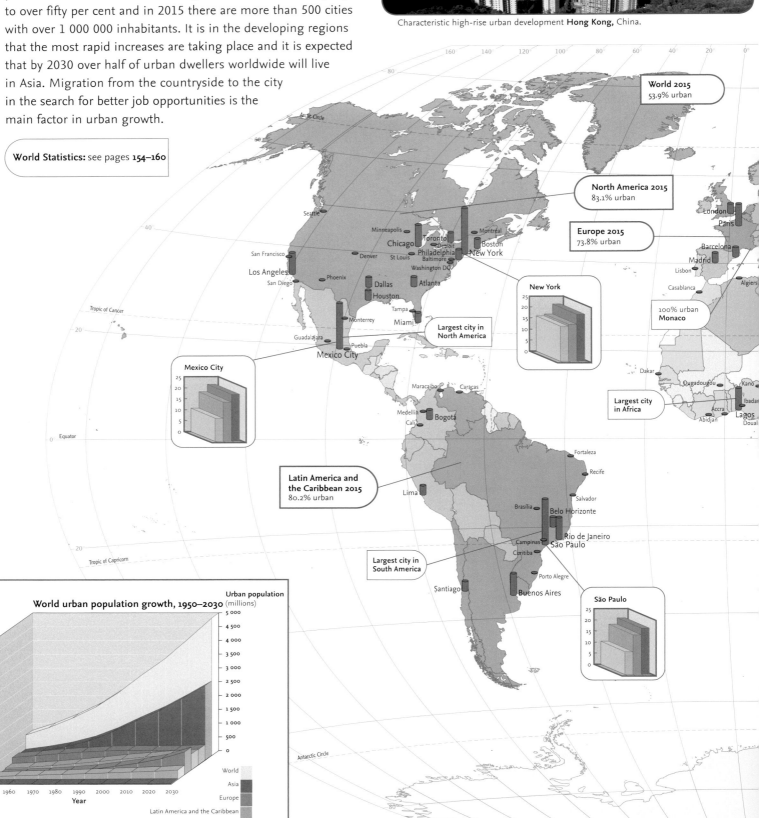

World 2015
53.9% urban

North America 2015
83.1% urban

Europe 2015
73.8% urban

100% urban
Monaco

Largest city in North America
New York

Largest city in Africa

Mexico City

Latin America and the Caribbean 2015
80.2% urban

Largest city in South America

São Paulo

World urban population growth, 1950–2030

Urban population (millions)

Year

- World
- Asia
- Europe
- Latin America and the Caribbean
- Africa
- North America
- Oceania

Level of urbanization and the world's largest cities

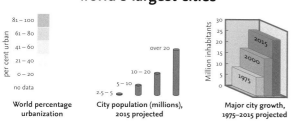

per cent urban
- 81 – 100
- 61 – 80
- 41 – 60
- 21 – 40
- 0 – 20
- no data

World percentage urbanization

City population (millions), 2015 projected
- 2.5 – 5
- 5 – 10
- 10 – 20
- over 20

Million inhabitants

Major city growth, 1975–2015 projected
- 1975
- 2000
- 2015

Megacities

There are currently sixty-nine cities in the world with over 5 000 000 inhabitants. Twenty-nine of these, often referred to as megacities, have over 10 000 000 inhabitants and one has over 30 000 000. Tōkyō, with 38 197 000 inhabitants, has remained the world's largest city since 1970 and is likely to remain so for the next decade. Other cities over 20 000 000 inhabitants in 2015 are Mumbai, São Paulo, Delhi, Shanghai, New York and Mexico City. Sixteen of the world's megacities are in Asia.

Facts

- From mid-2009, cities occupying less than 2% of the Earth's land surface housed over 50% of the human population

- Urban growth rates in Africa are the highest in the world

- Antarctica is uninhabited and most settlements in the Arctic regions have less than 5 000 inhabitants

- In 2015 India will have 56 cities with over one million inhabitants

- London was the first city to reach a population of over 5 million

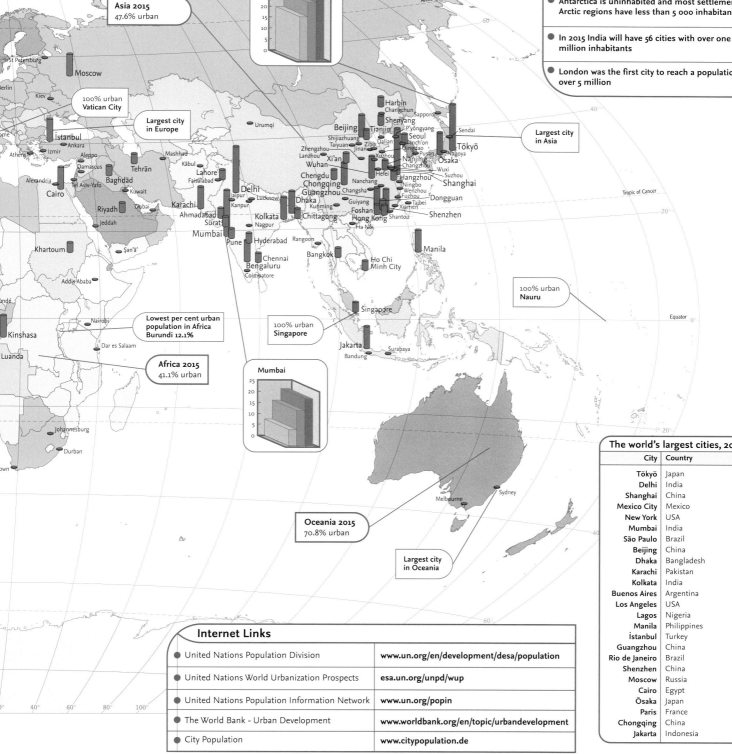

Asia 2015
47.6% urban

100% urban
Vatican City

Largest city in Europe

Largest city in Asia

Tōkyō

Lowest per cent urban population in Africa
Burundi 12.1%

100% urban
Singapore

100% urban
Nauru

Africa 2015
41.1% urban

Mumbai

Oceania 2015
70.8% urban

Largest city in Oceania

Internet Links

United Nations Population Division	www.un.org/en/development/desa/population
United Nations World Urbanization Prospects	esa.un.org/unpd/wup
United Nations Population Information Network	www.un.org/popin
The World Bank - Urban Development	www.worldbank.org/en/topic/urbandevelopment
City Population	www.citypopulation.de

The world's largest cities, 2015

City	Country	Population
Tōkyō	Japan	38 197 000
Delhi	India	25 629 000
Shanghai	China	22 963 000
Mexico City	Mexico	21 706 000
New York	USA	21 326 000
Mumbai	India	21 214 000
São Paulo	Brazil	21 028 000
Beijing	China	18 079 000
Dhaka	Bangladesh	17 382 000
Karachi	Pakistan	15 500 000
Kolkata	India	15 076 000
Buenos Aires	Argentina	14 151 000
Los Angeles	USA	14 081 000
Lagos	Nigeria	13 121 000
Manila	Philippines	12 856 000
İstanbul	Turkey	12 459 000
Guangzhou	China	12 385 000
Rio de Janeiro	Brazil	12 380 000
Shenzhen	China	12 337 000
Moscow	Russia	12 144 000
Cairo	Egypt	11 944 000
Ōsaka	Japan	11 783 000
Paris	France	11 097 000
Chongqing	China	11 054 000
Jakarta	Indonesia	10 470 000

Increased availability and ownership of telecommunications equipment over the last thirty years has aided the globalization of the world economy. Over half of the world's fixed telephone lines have been installed since 1987, and the majority of the world's Internet hosts have come on line since 1997. Cellular subscribers, particularly using digital technologies, are increasing much more rapidly than fixed telephone lines as in many countries they are a more practical option. Mobile broadband subscribers have now overtaken fixed broadband subscribers in all regions.

Internet users have been increasing rapidly since 1991 when there were only 4.4 million, with many large jumps especially in the last ten years, to 2 497 million in 2012, a figure that is more than double that of 2005. However, access levels vary, with approximately twenty countries still with less than 3 per cent Internet penetration.

Facts

- The first transatlantic telegraph cable came into operation in 1858
- In 2014, forty percent of the world's population were using the Internet
- The Falkland Islands have the world's highest density of Internet subscribers
- In 2011, 45 percent of Internet users were below the age of twenty-five

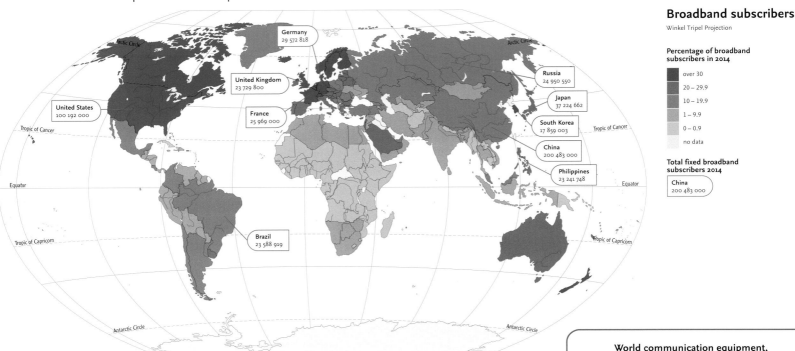

United States
100 192 000

Germany
29 572 818

United Kingdom
23 729 800

France
25 969 000

Russia
24 950 550

Japan
37 224 662

South Korea
17 859 003

China
200 483 000

Philippines
23 241 748

Brazil
23 588 919

Broadband subscribers
Winkel Tripel Projection

Percentage of broadband subscribers in 2014

- over 30
- 20 – 29.9
- 10 – 19.9
- 1 – 9.9
- 0 – 0.9
- no data

Total fixed broadband subscribers 2014

China
200 483 000

The Internet

Broadband connections for access to the Internet are relatively recent, but in that short time huge developments have been made in the technology and access speeds have shown a steady rise which is still continuing. Broadband access has had an impact on the delivery of electronic services in many areas such as health, education and finance. Mobile broadband (or mobile Internet) is wireless high-speed Internet access available through a portable modem device on a laptop computer and increasingly widely on hand-held tablets and mobile cellular telephones. In 2005 all regions with broadband access showed at least 64 per cent of all subscriptions were for fixed broadband. By 2008 almost all regions showed mobile broadband subscriptions had overtaken fixed as the technology improved and users were offered more options.

Top Broadband Economies 2014
Countries with the highest broadband penetration rate – subscribers per 100 inhabitants

	Top Economies – Fixed Broadband	Rate
1	Monaco	46.8
2	Switzerland	46.0
3	Denmark	41.4
4	Netherlands	41.0
5	Liechtenstein	40.3
6	France	40.2
7	South Korea	38.8
8	Norway	38.1
9	United Kingdom	37.4
10	San Marino	37.0

	Top Economies – Mobile Broadband	Rate
1	Singapore	156.1
2	Kuwait	139.8
3	Finland	138.5
4	Bahrain	126.2
5	Japan	121.4
6	Estonia	117.0
7	Sweden	116.3
8	Denmark	115.8
9	United Arab Emirates	114.0
10	Australia	112.2

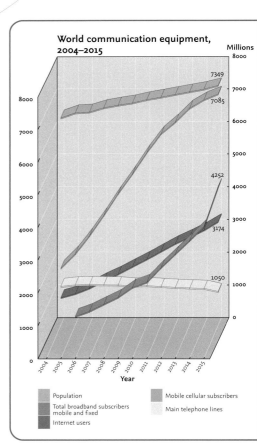

World communication equipment, 2004–2015

Millions

7349
7085
4252
3174
1050

Year

- Population
- Total broadband subscribers mobile and fixed
- Internet users
- Mobile cellular subscribers
- Main telephone lines

Mobile phone subscribers

Winkel Tripel Projection

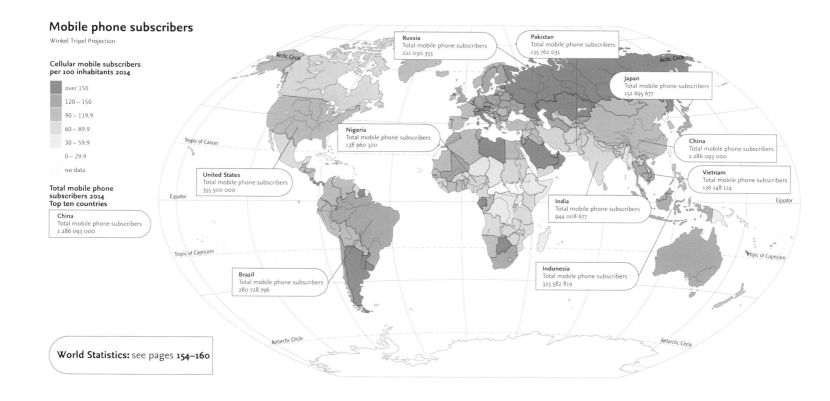

Cellular mobile subscribers per 100 inhabitants 2014

- over 150
- 120 – 150
- 90 – 119.9
- 60 – 89.9
- 30 – 59.9
- 0 – 29.9
- no data

Total mobile phone subscribers 2014 Top ten countries

China
Total mobile phone subscribers
1 286 093 000

Russia
Total mobile phone subscribers
221 030 353

Pakistan
Total mobile phone subscribers
135 762 031

Japan
Total mobile phone subscribers
152 695 677

Nigeria
Total mobile phone subscribers
138 960 320

China
Total mobile phone subscribers
1 286 093 000

Vietnam
Total mobile phone subscribers
136 148 124

United States
Total mobile phone subscribers
355 500 000

India
Total mobile phone subscribers
944 008 677

Brazil
Total mobile phone subscribers
280 728 796

Indonesia
Total mobile phone subscribers
325 582 819

World Statistics: see pages **154–160**

Mobile phone subscribers

In 2014, there were almost seven billion mobile cellular subscribers and it was estimated that out of every one hundred people, ninety-six of them owned a mobile. One area showing a recent change with the development of new mobile cellular technology, is mobile broadband where subscribers are now more than triple the number of fixed broadband subscribers in all regions. The total number of Short Message Service (SMS) or text messages sent globally tripled between 2007 and 2010 to over 6 trillion messages, around 200 000 every second. Many phone packages now include "unlimited" free text messages encouraging many shorter messages to be sent.

Internet Links

● OECD Organisation for Economic Co-operation and Development	**www.oecd.org**
● TeleGeography	**www.telegeography.com**
● International Telecommunication Union	**www.itu.int**

Fixed telephone lines

Winkel Tripel Projection

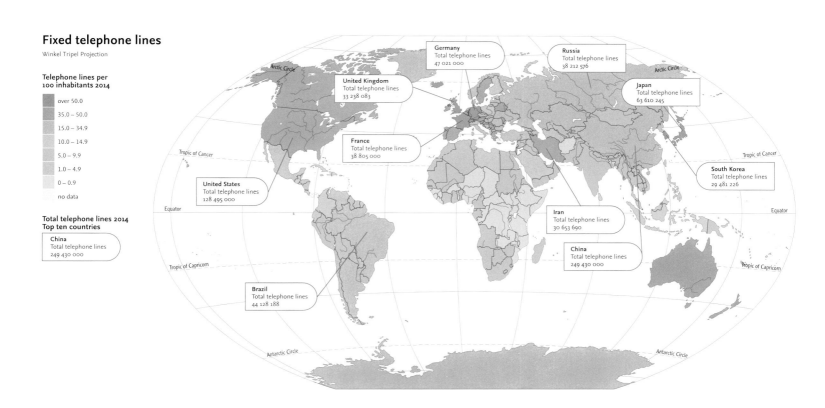

Telephone lines per 100 inhabitants 2014

- over 50.0
- 35.0 – 50.0
- 15.0 – 34.9
- 10.0 – 14.9
- 5.0 – 9.9
- 1.0 – 4.9
- 0 – 0.9
- no data

Total telephone lines 2014 Top ten countries

China
Total telephone lines
249 430 000

Germany
Total telephone lines
47 021 000

Russia
Total telephone lines
38 212 576

United Kingdom
Total telephone lines
33 238 083

Japan
Total telephone lines
63 610 245

France
Total telephone lines
38 805 000

South Korea
Total telephone lines
29 481 226

United States
Total telephone lines
128 495 000

Iran
Total telephone lines
30 653 690

China
Total telephone lines
249 430 000

Brazil
Total telephone lines
44 128 188

World
Social Indicators

Countries are often judged on their level of economic development, but national and personal wealth are not the only measures of a country's status. Numerous other indicators can give a better picture of the overall level of development and standard of living achieved by a country. The availability and standard of health services, levels of educational provision and attainment, levels of nutrition, water supply, life expectancy and mortality rates are just some of the factors which can be measured to assess and compare countries.

While nations strive to improve their economies, and hopefully also to improve the standard of living of their citizens, the measurement of such indicators often exposes great discrepancies between the countries of the 'developed' world and those of the 'less developed' world. They also show great variations within continents and regions and at the same time can hide great inequalities within countries.

World Statistics: see pages 154–160

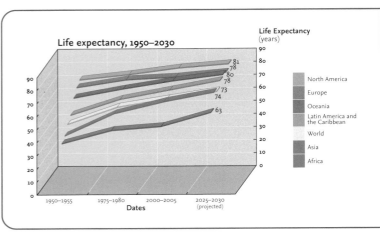

Life expectancy, 1950–2030

Life Expectancy (years)

North America	
Europe	
Oceania	
Latin America and the Caribbean	
World	
Asia	
Africa	

Internet Links

● United Nations Development Programme	**www.undp.org**
● World Health Organization	**www.who.int**
● United Nations Statistics Division	**unstats.un.org**
● United Nations Millennium Development Goals Indicators	**www.un.org/millenniumgoals**

Under-five mortality rate, 2015 and life expectancy by continent, 2015–2020

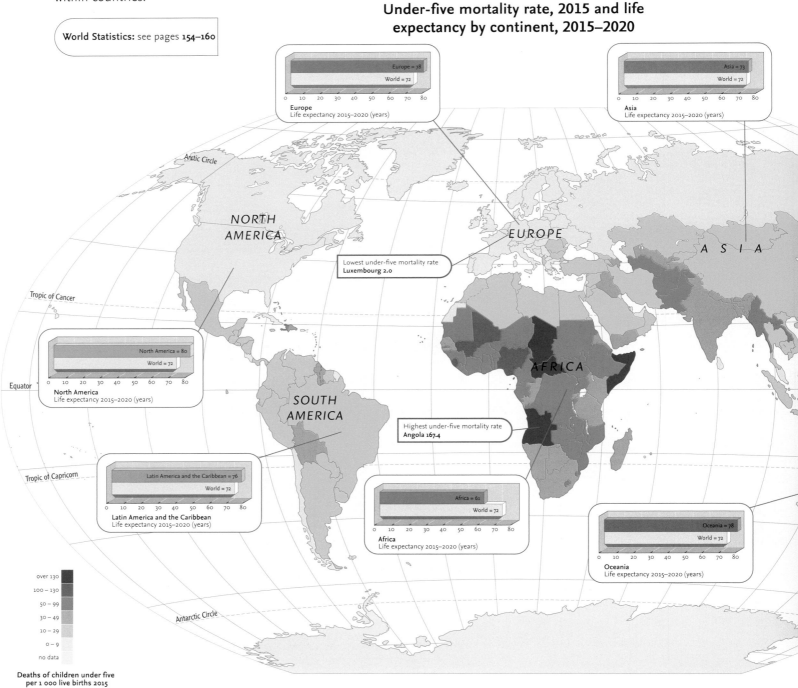

Europe = 78
World = 72
Europe
Life expectancy 2015–2020 (years)

Asia = 73
World = 72
Asia
Life expectancy 2015–2020 (years)

North America = 80
World = 72
North America
Life expectancy 2015–2020 (years)

Latin America and the Caribbean = 76
World = 72
Latin America and the Caribbean
Life expectancy 2015–2020 (years)

Africa = 61
World = 72
Africa
Life expectancy 2015–2020 (years)

Oceania = 78
World = 72
Oceania
Life expectancy 2015–2020 (years)

Lowest under-five mortality rate
Luxembourg 2.0

Highest under-five mortality rate
Angola 167.4

NORTH AMERICA

EUROPE

ASIA

AFRICA

SOUTH AMERICA

Arctic Circle
Tropic of Cancer
Equator
Tropic of Capricorn
Antarctic Circle

over 130
100 – 130
50 – 99
30 – 49
10 – 29
0 – 9
no data

Deaths of children under five per 1 000 live births 2015

- All of the 7 countries with under-5 mortality rates of more than 100 per 1000 live births, are in Africa

- Many western countries believe they have achieved satisfactory levels of education and no longer closely monitor levels of literacy

- Children born in Nepal have only a 12% chance of their birth being attended by trained health personnel; for most European countries the figure is 100%

- The illiteracy rate among young women in the Middle East and north Africa is almost twice the rate for young men

Health and education

Perhaps the most important indicators used for measuring the level of national development are those relating to health and education. Both of these key areas are vital to the future development of a country, and if there are concerns in standards attained in either (or worse, in both) of these, then they may indicate fundamental problems within the country concerned. The ability to read and write (literacy) is seen as vital in educating people and encouraging development, while easy access to appropriate health services and specialists is an important requirement in maintaining satisfactory levels of basic health.

Adult Literacy rate

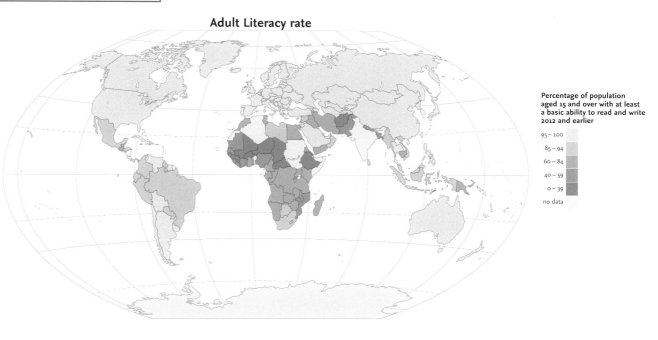

Percentage of population aged 15 and over with at least a basic ability to read and write 2012 and earlier

- 95 – 100
- 85 – 94
- 60 – 84
- 40 – 59
- 0 – 39
- no data

Doctors per 100 000 people

- over 350
- 250 – 350
- 150 – 249
- 50 – 149
- 0 – 49
- no data

Number of trained doctors per 100 000 people 2012 and earlier

UN Sustainable Development Goals Target for these to be reached is 2030		
Goal 1	End poverty in all its forms everywhere	
Goal 2	End hunger, achieve food security and improved nutrition and promote sustainable agriculture	
Goal 3	Ensure healthy lives and promote well-being for all at all ages	
Goal 4	Ensure inclusive and equitable quality education and promote lifelong learning opportunities for all	
Goal 5	Achieve gender equality and empower all women and girls	
Goal 6	Ensure availability and sustainable management of water and sanitation for all	
Goal 7	Ensure access to affordable, reliable, sustainable and modern energy for all	
Goal 8	Promote sustained, inclusive and sustainable economic growth, full and productive employment and decent work for all	
Goal 9	Build resilient infrastructure, promote inclusive and sustainable industrialization and foster innovation	
Goal 10	Reduce inequality within and among countries
Goal 11	Make cities and human settlements inclusive, safe, resilient and sustainable
Goal 12	Ensure sustainable consumption and production patterns
Goal 13	Take urgent action to combat climate change and its impacts
Goal 14	Conserve and sustainably use the oceans, seas and marine resources for sustainable development
Goal 15	Protect, restore and promote sustainable use of terrestrial ecosystems, sustainably manage forests, combat desertification, and halt and reverse land degradation and halt biodiversity loss
Goal 16	Promote peaceful and inclusive societies for sustainable development, provide access to justice for all and build effective, accountable and inclusive institutions at all levels
Goal 17	Strengthen the means of implementation and revitalize the global partnership for sustainable development

World
Economy and Wealth

The globalization of the economy is making the world appear a smaller place. However, this shrinkage is an uneven process. Countries are being included in and excluded from the global economy to differing degrees. The wealthy countries of the developed world, with their market-led economies, access to productive new technologies and international markets, dominate the world economic system. Great inequalities exist between and within countries. There may also be discrepancies between social groups within countries due to gender and ethnic divisions. Differences between countries are evident by looking at overall wealth on a national and individual level.

Many of the world's largest financial institutions are to be found in the City of London.

World Statistics: see pages 154–160

Poverty and inequality

In 2005, 25 per cent of the population of low- and middle-income economies lived in extreme poverty. With continued growth of average incomes, that number was expected to fall to less than 900 million by 2015. Even then there will be more than 2 billion people living on less than $2.00 a day or $730 a year. The greatest number of the extreme poor live in the large, lower-middle income economies of Asia – India and China – which together account for almost half of the people living in extreme poverty. But these are fast growing economies, where poverty rates have been falling rapidly. The highest rates of poverty are found in Sub-Saharan Africa, where economic growth was slowest in the 1990s and the regional poverty rate has only recently fallen below 50 per cent and was expected to reach 36 per cent by 2015. Since the mid-1990s, income inequality, as measured by the Gini index, has increased in slightly more than half of developing countries with available data.

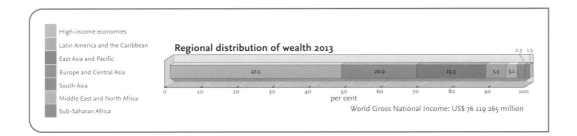

High-income economies
Latin America and the Caribbean
East Asia and Pacific
Europe and Central Asia
South Asia
Middle East and North Africa
Sub-Saharan Africa

Regional distribution of wealth 2013

| 47.5 | 20.9 | 19.3 | 5.5 | 3.1 | 2.3 | 1.5 |

per cent

World Gross National Income: US$ 76 119 265 million

Income inequality

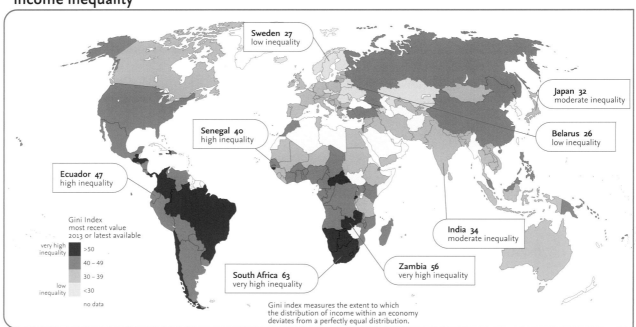

Sweden 27
low inequality

Japan 32
moderate inequality

Senegal 40
high inequality

Belarus 26
low inequality

Ecuador 47
high inequality

India 34
moderate inequality

South Africa 63
very high inequality

Zambia 56
very high inequality

Gini Index
most recent value
2013 or latest available

very high inequality	>50
	40 – 49
	30 – 39
low inequality	<30
no data	

Gini index measures the extent to which the distribution of income within an economy deviates from a perfectly equal distribution.

Rural village, **Malawi** – most of the world's poorest countries are in Africa.

Gross National Income per capita

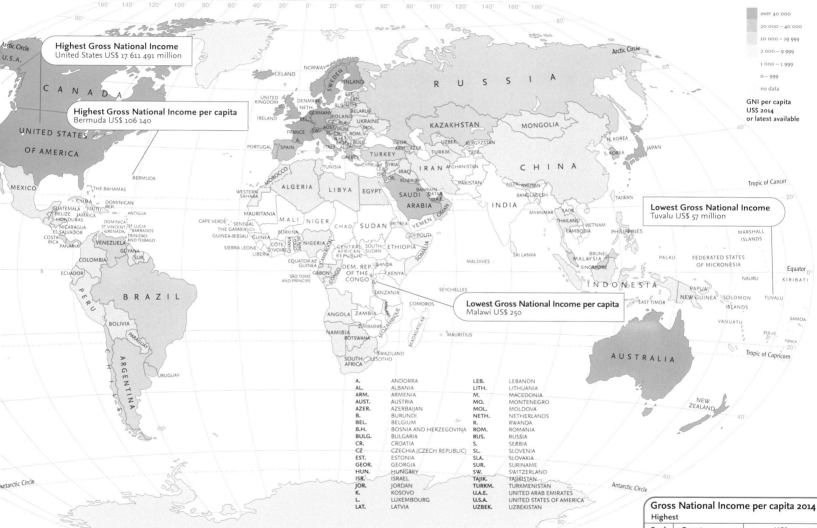

Highest Gross National Income
United States US$ 17 611 491 million

Highest Gross National Income per capita
Bermuda US$ 106 140

Lowest Gross National Income
Tuvalu US$ 57 million

Lowest Gross National Income per capita
Malawi US$ 250

	GNI per capita US$ 2014 or latest available
	over 40 000
	20 000 – 40 000
	10 000 – 19 999
	2 000 – 9 999
	1 000 – 1 999
	0 – 999
	no data

A.	ANDORRA	LEB.	LEBANON
AL.	ALBANIA	LITH.	LITHUANIA
ARM.	ARMENIA	M.	MACEDONIA
AUST.	AUSTRIA	MO.	MONTENEGRO
AZER.	AZERBAIJAN	MOL.	MOLDOVA
B.	BURUNDI	NETH.	NETHERLANDS
BEL.	BELGIUM	R.	RWANDA
B.H.	BOSNIA AND HERZEGOVINA	ROM.	ROMANIA
BULG.	BULGARIA	RUS.	RUSSIA
CR.	CROATIA	S.	SERBIA
CZ	CZECHIA (CZECH REPUBLIC)	SL.	SLOVENIA
EST.	ESTONIA	SLA.	SLOVAKIA
GEOR.	GEORGIA	SUR.	SURINAME
HUN.	HUNGARY	SW.	SWITZERLAND
ISR.	ISRAEL	TAJIK.	TAJIKISTAN
JOR.	JORDAN	TURKM.	TURKMENISTAN
K.	KOSOVO	U.A.E.	UNITED ARAB EMIRATES
L.	LUXEMBOURG	U.S.A.	UNITED STATES OF AMERICA
LAT.	LATVIA	UZBEK.	UZBEKISTAN

Measuring wealth

One of the indicators used to determine a country's wealth is its Gross National Income (GNI). This gives a broad measure of an economy's performance. This is the value of the final output of goods and services produced by a country plus net income from non-resident sources. The total GNI is divided by the country's population to give an average figure of the GNI per capita. From this it is evident that the developed countries dominate the world economy with the United States having the highest GNI. China is a rapidly growing world economic player with the second highest GNI figure and a relatively high GNI per capita (US$7 400) in proportion to its huge population.

Internet Links

United Nations Statistics Division	unstats.un.org
The World Bank	www.worldbank.org
International Monetary Fund	www.imf.org
OECD Organisation for Economic Co-operation and Development	www.oecd.org

Gross National Income per capita 2014

Highest

Rank	Country	US$
1	Bermuda	106 140
2	Norway	103 620
3	Qatar	92 200
4	Switzerland	84 720
5	Luxembourg	75 960
6	Australia	64 600
7	Sweden	61 570
8	Denmark	61 330
9	USA	55 230
10	Singapore	55 150

Lowest

Rank	Country	US$
178	Eritrea	480
179	Guinea	470
180	The Gambia	460
181	Madagascar	440
182	Niger	410
183	Dem. Rep. of the Congo	380
184	Liberia	370
185	Central African Republic	320
186	Burundi	270
187	Malawi	250

Geo-political issues shape the countries of the world and the current political situation in many parts of the world reflects a long history of armed conflict. Since the Second World War conflicts have been fairly localized, but there are numerous 'flash points' where factors such as territorial claims, ideology, religion, ethnicity and access to resources can cause friction between two or more countries. Such factors also lie behind the recent growth in global terrorism.

Military expenditure can take up a disproportionate amount of a country's wealth – South Sudan, with a Gross Domestic Product (GDP) per capita of US$1 115 spends nearly ten per cent of its total GDP on military activity. There is an encouraging trend towards wider international cooperation, mainly through the United Nations (UN) and the North Atlantic Treaty Organization (NATO), to prevent escalation of conflicts and on peacekeeping missions.

Military spending 2014, and conflicts since 1946

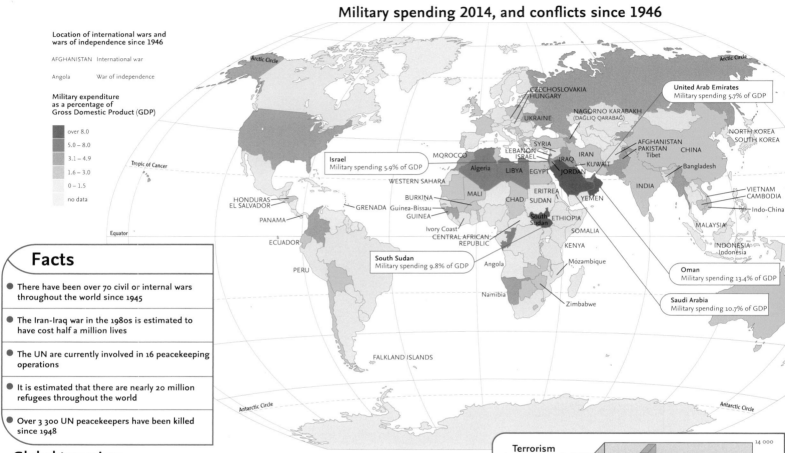

Location of international wars and wars of independence since 1946

AFGHANISTAN International war

Angola War of independence

Military expenditure as a percentage of Gross Domestic Product (GDP)

- over 8.0
- 5.0 – 8.0
- 3.1 – 4.9
- 1.6 – 3.0
- 0 – 1.5
- no data

Israel
Military spending 5.9% of GDP

United Arab Emirates
Military spending 5.7% of GDP

South Sudan
Military spending 9.8% of GDP

Oman
Military spending 13.4% of GDP

Saudi Arabia
Military spending 10.7% of GDP

Facts

- There have been over 70 civil or internal wars throughout the world since 1945

- The Iran-Iraq war in the 1980s is estimated to have cost half a million lives

- The UN are currently involved in 16 peacekeeping operations

- It is estimated that there are nearly 20 million refugees throughout the world

- Over 3 300 UN peacekeepers have been killed since 1948

Global terrorism

Terrorism is defined by the United Nations as "All criminal acts directed against a State and intended or calculated to create a state of terror in the minds of particular persons or a group of persons or the general public". The world has become increasingly concerned about terrorism and the possibility that terrorists could acquire and use nuclear, chemical and biological weapons. One common form of terrorist attack is suicide bombing. Pioneered by Tamil secessionists in Sri Lanka, it has been widely used by Palestinian groups fighting against Israeli occupation of the West Bank and Gaza. In recent years it has also been used by the Al Qaida network in its attacks on the western world. Suicide bombings have also been used in Iraq and Afghanistan. The most recent terrorist organisation to be designated as such by the United Nations and many countries around the world is the Islamic State, also known as ISIS or ISIL. It is renowned for internet and social media propaganda, for the beheadings of civilians, journalists, soldiers and aid workers, and for the deliberate destruction of cultural heritage sites.

Internet Links

United Nations Peacekeeping	www.un.org/en/peacekeeping
United Nations Refugee Agency	www.unhcr.org
NATO	www.nato.int
BBC News	www.bbc.co.uk/news
International Boundaries Research Unit	www.dur.ac.uk/ibru
Peace Research Institute Oslo	www.prio.org

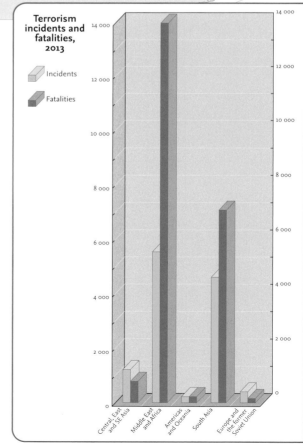

Terrorism incidents and fatalities, 2013

- Incidents
- Fatalities

United Nations peacekeeping

United Nations peacekeeping was developed by the Organization as a way to help countries torn by conflict create the conditions for lasting peace. The first UN peacekeeping mission was established in 1948, when the Security Council authorized the deployment of UN military observers to the Middle East to monitor the Armistice Agreement between Israel and its Arab neighbours. Since then, there have been a total of 69 UN peacekeeping operations around the world.

UN peacekeeping goals were primarily limited to maintaining ceasefires and stabilizing situations on the ground, so that efforts could be made at the political level to resolve the conflict by peaceful means. Today's peacekeepers undertake a wide variety of complex tasks, from helping to build sustainable institutions of governance, to human rights monitoring, to security sector reform, to the disarmament, demobilization and reintegration of former combatants.

United Nations peacekeeping operations 1948–2016
Current peacekeeping operations are named on the map

Many refugees from **Myanmar** (Burma) live in villages in Thailand.

Major terrorist incidents

Date	Location	Summary	Killed	Injured
December 1988	Lockerbie, Scotland	Airline bombing	270	5
March 1995	Tōkyō, Japan	Sarin gas attack on subway	12	5 510
April 1995	Oklahoma City, USA	Bomb in the Federal building	168	over 800
August 1998	Nairobi, Kenya and Dar es Salaam, Tanzania	US Embassy bombings	225	over 4 000
August 1998	Omagh, Northern Ireland	Town centre bombing	29	220
September 2001	New York and Washington D.C., USA	Airline hijacking and crashing	3 018	over 6 200
October 2002	Bali, Indonesia	Car bomb outside nightclub	202	over 200
October 2002	Moscow, Russia	Theatre siege	170	over 600
March 2004	Bāghdad and Karbalā', Iraq	Suicide bombing of pilgrims	181	over 400
March 2004	Madrid, Spain	Train bombings	191	1 800
September 2004	Beslan, Russia	School siege	385	over 700
July 2005	London, UK	Underground and bus bombings	56	700
July 2005	Sharm ash Shaykh, Egypt	Bombs at tourist sites	88	200
July 2006	Mumbai, India	Train bombings	209	700
August 2007	Qahtaniya, Iraq	Suicide bombing in town centres	796	over 1 500
November 2008	Mumbai, India	Coordinated shootings at eight sites	183	over 300
October 2011	Mogadishu, Somalia	Suicide truck bomb	139	over 90
March 2012	Zinjibar, Yemen	Army base attack	210	n/a
September 2013	Nairobi, Kenya	Shopping centre attack	72	201
May 2014	Gamboru and Ngala, Nigeria	Attack on market	310	n/a
April 2015	Garissa, Kenya	College shooting	147	79
November 2015	Paris, France	Attacks at six sites	130	368
March 2016	Brussels, Belgium	Bombings at three sites	32	340

Terrorist incidents

Number of terrorist incidents 2008-2013

- over 2000
- 1000 – 2000
- 100 – 999
- 10 – 99
- 1 – 9
- no incidents recorded

☆ Major terrorist incident location

With the process of globalization has come an increased awareness of, and direct interest in, issues which have global implications. Social issues can now affect large parts of the world and can impact on large sections of society. Perhaps the current issues of greatest concern are those of national security, including the problem of international terrorism, health, crime and natural resources. The three social issues highlighted here reflect this and are of immediate concern.

The international drugs trade, and the crimes commonly associated with it, can impact on society and individuals in devastating ways; scarcity of water resources and lack of access to safe drinking water can have major economic implications and cause severe health problems; and the AIDS epidemic is having disastrous consequences in large parts of the world, particularly in sub-Saharan Africa.

The drugs trade

The international trade in illegal drugs is estimated to be worth over US$400 billion. While it may be a lucrative business for the criminals involved, the effects of the drugs on individual users and on society in general can be devastating. Patterns of drug production and abuse vary, but there are clear centres for the production of the most harmful drugs – the opiates (opium, morphine and heroin) and cocaine. The 'Golden Triangle' of Laos, Myanmar and Thailand, and western South America respectively are the main producing areas for these drugs. Significant efforts are expended to counter the drugs trade, and there have been signs recently of downward trends in the production of heroin and cocaine.

The **opium poppy** is the plant from which opium is extracted.

The international drugs trade

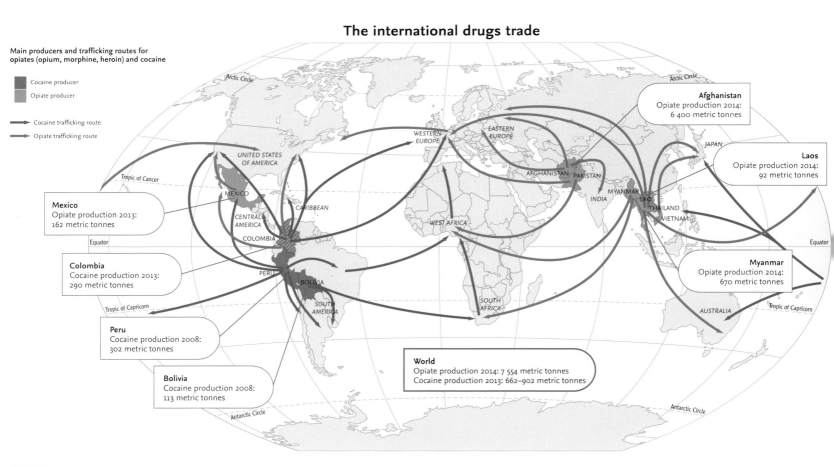

Main producers and trafficking routes for opiates (opium, morphine, heroin) and cocaine

- Cocaine producer
- Opiate producer

→ Cocaine trafficking route
→ Opiate trafficking route

Afghanistan
Opiate production 2014:
6 400 metric tonnes

Laos
Opiate production 2014:
92 metric tonnes

Mexico
Opiate production 2013:
162 metric tonnes

Colombia
Cocaine production 2013:
290 metric tonnes

Myanmar
Opiate production 2014:
670 metric tonnes

Peru
Cocaine production 2008:
302 metric tonnes

World
Opiate production 2014: 7 554 metric tonnes
Cocaine production 2013: 662–902 metric tonnes

Bolivia
Cocaine production 2008:
113 metric tonnes

AIDS epidemic

With 35 million people living with HIV/AIDS (Human Immunodeficiency Virus/Acquired Immune Deficiency Syndrome) and more than 20 million deaths from the disease, the AIDS epidemic poses one of the biggest threats to public health. The UNAIDS project estimated that 2.1 million people were newly infected in 2013 and that 1.5 million AIDS sufferers died. This is nearly one half the number of infections than the peak of 3.2 million in 1997. As well as the death count itself, there are millions of living African children, between the ages of 10 and 17, that have been orphaned as a result of the disease. Treatment to prevent HIV transmission to babies has resulted in 33 per cent drop in infections.

Population living with HIV/AIDS, 2013

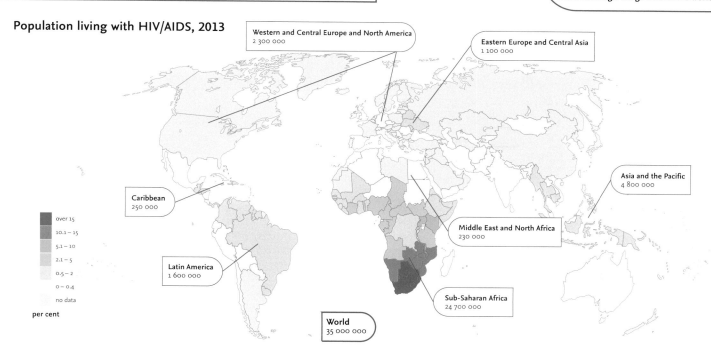

Western and Central Europe and North America
2 300 000

Eastern Europe and Central Asia
1 100 000

Caribbean
250 000

Asia and the Pacific
4 800 000

Middle East and North Africa
230 000

Latin America
1 600 000

Sub-Saharan Africa
24 700 000

World
35 000 000

over 15
10.1 – 15
5.1 – 10
2.1 – 5
0.5 – 2
0 – 0.4
no data

per cent

Water resources

Water is one of the fundamental requirements of life, and yet in some countries it is becoming more scarce due to increasing population and climate change. Safe drinking water, basic hygiene, health education and sanitation facilities are often virtually nonexistent for impoverished people in developing countries throughout the world. WHO/UNICEF estimate that the combination of these conditions results in over 4 000 deaths every day, most of these being children. Currently, 1.8 billion people drink untreated water and expose themselves to serious health risks, while political struggles over diminishing water resources are increasingly likely to be the cause of international conflict.

Domestic use of **untreated water** in Varanasi, India

Access to safe water, 2015
Percentage of population with access to improved drinking water

91 – 100
81 – 90
71 – 80
51 – 70
40 – 50
no data

per cent

World
Environmental Threats

The Earth has a rich and diverse environment which is under threat from both natural and man-induced forces. Forests and woodland form the predominant natural land cover with tropical rain forests – currently disappearing at alarming rates – believed to be home to the majority of animal and plant species. Grassland and scrub tend to have a lower natural species diversity but have suffered the most impact from man's intervention through conversion to agriculture, burning and the introduction of livestock. Wherever man interferes with existing biological and environmental processes degradation of that environment occurs to varying degrees. This interference also affects inland water and oceans where pollution, over-exploitation of marine resources and the need for fresh water has had major consequences on land and sea environments.

Facts

- The Sundarbans stretching across the Ganges delta is the largest area of mangrove forest in the world, covering 10 000 square kilometres (3 861 square miles) and forming an important ecological area, home to 260 species of birds, the Bengal tiger and other threatened species

- Over 90 000 square kilometres of precious tropical forest and wetland habitats are lost each year

- The surface level of the Dead Sea has fallen by more than 35 metres over the last 50 years

- Climate change and mismanagement of land areas can lead to soils becoming degraded and semi-arid grasslands becoming deserts – a process known as desertification

Environmental change

Whenever natural resources are exploited by man, the environment is changed. Approximately half the area of post-glacial forest has been cleared or degraded, and the amount of old-growth forest continues to decline. Desertification caused by climate change and the impact of man can turn semi-arid grasslands into arid desert. Regions bordering tropical deserts, such as the Sahel region south of the Sahara and regions around the Thar Desert in India, are most vulnerable to this process. Coral reefs are equally fragile environments, and many are under threat from coastal development, pollution and over-exploitation of marine resources.

Water resources in certain parts of the world are becoming increasingly scarce and competition for water is likely to become a common cause of conflict. The Aral Sea in central Asia was once the world's fourth largest lake but it now ranks only sixteenth after shrinking by more than 51 000 square kilometres since the 1960s. This shrinkage has been due to climatic change and to the diversion, for farming purposes, of the major rivers which feed the lake. The change has had a devastating effect on the local fishing industry and the exposure of chemicals on the lake bed has caused health problems for the local population.

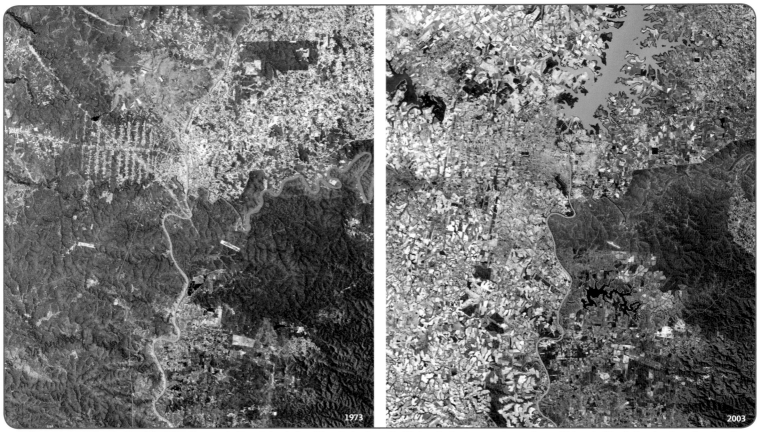

1973

2003

Deforestation and the creation of the **Itaipu Dam** on the Paraná river in Brazil have had a dramatic effect on the landscape and ecosystems of this part of South America. Some forest on the right of the images lies within Iguaçu National Park and has been protected from destruction.

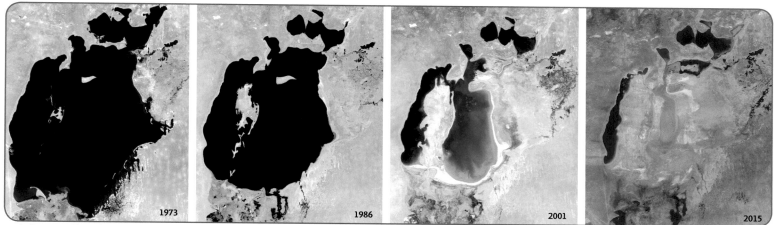

Aral Sea, Kazakhstan/Uzbekistan 1973-2015 Climate change and the diversion of rivers have caused its dramatic shrinkage.

Environmental Impacts

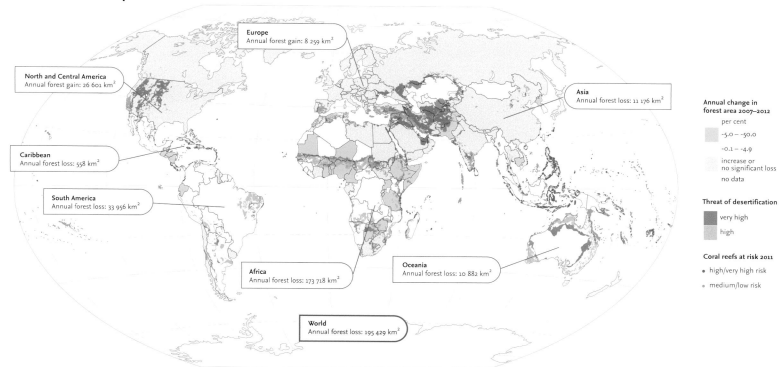

North and Central America
Annual forest gain: 26 601 km²

Europe
Annual forest gain: 8 259 km²

Asia
Annual forest loss: 11 176 km²

Caribbean
Annual forest loss: 558 km²

South America
Annual forest loss: 33 956 km²

Africa
Annual forest loss: 173 718 km²

Oceania
Annual forest loss: 10 882 km²

World
Annual forest loss: 195 429 km²

Annual change in
forest area 2007–2012
per cent

-5.0 – -50.0

-0.1 – -4.9

increase or
no significant loss

no data

Threat of desertification

very high

high

Coral reefs at risk 2011

• high/very high risk

• medium/low risk

Internet links	
United Nations Environment Programme (UNEP)	www.unep.org
IUCN International Union for Conservation of Nature	www.iucn.org
UNESCO World Heritage	whc.unesco.org

Environmental protection

Top 10 protected areas by size

Rank	Protected area	Country	Size (sq km)	Designation
1	Natural Park of the Coral Sea	New Caledonia, France	1 292 967	Marine Protected Area
2	South Georgia and South Sandwich Islands Marine Protected Area	South Georgia and South Sandwich Islands, United Kingdom	1 070 000	Marine Protected Area
3	Coral Sea Reserve	Australia	989 842	Marine Protected Area
4	Northeast Greenland	Greenland	972 000	National Park
5	Rub' al-Khālī	Saudi Arabia	640 000	Wildlife Management Area
6	Chagos Marine Protected Area	BIOT, United Kingdom	640 000	Marine Protected Area
7	Kermadec Islands Marine Reserve	New Zealand	469 276	Marine Protected Area
8	Phoenix Islands Protected Area	Kiribati	410 500	Marine Protected Area
9	Papahānaumokuākea Marine National Monument	United States	362 075	Marine Protected Area
10	Great Barrier Reef Marine Park	Australia	348 700	Marine Protected Area

Great Barrier Reef, Australia, the world's seventh largest protected area.

Europe
Landscapes

Europe, the westward extension of the Asian continent and the second smallest of the world's continents, has a remarkable variety of physical features and landscapes. The continent is bounded by mountain ranges of varying character – the highlands of Scandinavia and northwest Britain, the Pyrenees, the Alps, the Carpathian Mountains, the Caucasus and the Ural Mountains. Two of these, the Caucasus and Ural Mountains, define the eastern limits of Europe, with the Black Sea and the Bosporus defining its southeastern boundary with Asia.

Across the centre of the continent stretches the North European Plain, broken by some of Europe's greatest rivers, including the Volga and the Dnieper and containing some of its largest lakes. To the south, the Mediterranean Sea divides Europe from Africa. The Mediterranean region itself has a very distinct climate and landscape.

Facts

- The Danube flows through 7 countries and has 7 different name forms
- Lakes cover almost 10% of the total land area of Finland
- The Strait of Gibraltar, separating the Atlantic Ocean from the Mediterranean Sea and Europe from Africa, is only 13 kilometres wide at its narrowest point
- The highest mountain in the Alps is Mont Blanc, 4 810 metres, on the France/Italy border

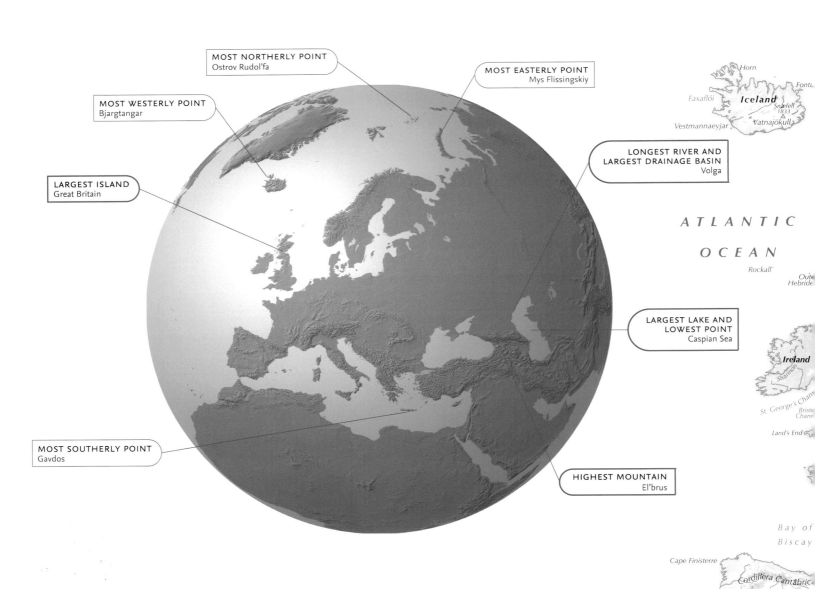

Europe's greatest physical features

Highest mountain	El'brus, Russia	5 642 metres	18 510 feet
Longest river	Volga, Russia	3 688 km	2 292 miles
Largest lake	Caspian Sea	371 000 sq km	143 243 sq miles
Largest island	Great Britain, United Kingdom	218 476 sq km	84 354 sq miles
Largest drainage basin	Volga, Russia	1 380 000 sq km	532 818 sq miles

Europe's extent

TOTAL LAND AREA	9 908 599 sq km / 3 825 710 sq miles
Most northerly point	Ostrov Rudol'fa, Russia
Most southerly point	Gavdos, Crete, Greece
Most westerly point	Bjargtangar, Iceland
Most easterly point	Mys Flissingskiy, Russia

Iceland in winter, one of Europe's largest islands.

Jan Mayen

Barents Sea

Ostrov Kolguyev

North Cape

Varanger Halvøya

Poluostrov Rybachiy

Poluostrov Kanin

Usa

Ostrov Severnyy

Novaya Zemlya

Ostrov Yuzhnyy

Chesskaya Guba

Pechora

Mezen

Vesterålen

Inarijärvi

Kola Peninsula

Lofoten

Vestfjorden

Ozero Ekostrovskaya Imandra

White Sea

Dvinskaya Guba

L a p p l a n d

Iule

Kem

N o r w e g i a n S e a

Ozero Topozero

Severnaya Dvina

Vychegda

Kama

U r a l M o u n t a i n s

Umeå

Lake Onega

Ozero Beloye

Kamskoye Vodokhranilishche

Galdhøpiggen 2470

S c a n d i n a v i a

Indals

Lake Ladoga

Rybinskoye Vodokhranilishche

Faroe Islands

Shetland Islands

Åland Islands

Ozero Il'men'

Kuybyshevskoye Vodokhranilishche

Cape Wrath

Orkney Islands

Boknafjorden

Vänern

Mälaren

Hiiumaa

Gulf of Finland

Lake Peipus

Volga

Moray Firth

Ben Nevis 1343

Grampian Mountains

Skagerrak

Vättern

Saaremaa

Valdayskaya Vozvyshennost'

British Isles

ish Sea

N o r t h S e a

Jutland

Gotland

Öland

Gulf of Riga

B a l t i c S e a

Zealand

Fyn

Bornholm

Gulf of Gdańsk

Central Russian Upland

Pennines

Cambrian Mountains

Great Britain

Lolland

Frisian Islands

IJsselmeer

Weser

N o r t h E u r o p e a n P l a i n

Wisła

Warta

Bug

Pripet Marshes

Kyyivs'ke Vodoskhovyshche

Don

English Channel

Strait of Dover

Channel Islands

Maas

Elbe

Oder

Wisła

Dniester

Tsimlyanskoye Vodokhranilishche

Volga

Seine

Marne

Rhine

Moselle

Ardennes

Erzgebirge

Sudety

Kremenchuts'ka Vodoskhovyshche

Kakhovs'ke Vodoskhovyshche

Loire

Vosges

Danube

Böhmer Wald

Inn

Danube

Carpathian Mountains

Dnieper

Dnieper

Ozero Manych-Gudilo

A S I A

Vienne

Jura

Lake Constance

Tisza

Gulf of Taganrog

Stavropol'skaya Vozvyshennost'

Dordogne

Lake Geneva

Mont Blanc 4810

A l p s

Lake Garda

Dolomites

Lake Balaton

Mureșul

Transylvanian Alps

Sava

Sea of Azov

Crimea

Karkinits'ka Zatoka

El'brus 5642

C a u c a s u s

C a s p i a n S e a

Massif Central

Rhône

Po

Dinaric Alps

Danube

B l a c k S e a

Garonne

Pyrenees

Aneto 3404

Golfe du Lion

A d r i a t i c S e a

Moravo

Balkan Mountains

L i g u r i a n S e a

A p e n n i n e s

Rhodope Mountains

Bosporus

Cap Corse

Isola d'Elba

Pindus Mts

Sea of Marmara

Balearic Islands

Corsica

Sardinia

T y r r h e n i a n S e a

Golfo di Taranto

Strait of Otranto

Thasos

Aegean Sea

Golfo de Valencia

Capo Carbonara

Ionian Islands

Limnos

Lesbos

Evvoia

Chios

Ibiza

Majorca

Minorca

Isole Lipari

Mount Etna 3323

Sicily

Ionian Sea

Peloponnese

Andros

Dodecanese

Rhodes

Formentera

Capo Carbonara

Sicilian Channel

Krytiko Pelagos

M e d i t e r r a n e a n

ICA

Malta

Kythira

Crete

Karpathos

S e a

Europe
Countries

The predominantly temperate climate of Europe has led to it becoming the most densely populated of the continents. It is highly industrialized, and has exploited its great wealth of natural resources and agricultural land to become one of the most powerful economic regions in the world.

The current pattern of countries within Europe is a result of numerous and complicated changes throughout its history. Ethnic, religious and linguistic differences have often been the cause of conflict, particularly in the Balkan region which has a very complex ethnic pattern. Current boundaries reflect, to some extent, these divisions which continue to be a source of tension. The historic distinction between 'Eastern' and 'Western' Europe is no longer made, following the collapse of Communism and the break up of the Soviet Union in 1991.

Facts

- The European Union was founded by six countries: Belgium, France, Germany, Italy, Luxembourg, and the Netherlands. It now has 28 members

- The newest member of the European Union, Croatia, joined in 2013

- Europe has the two smallest independent countries in the world – Vatican City and Monaco

- Vatican City is an independent country entirely within the city of Rome, and is the centre of the Roman Catholic Church

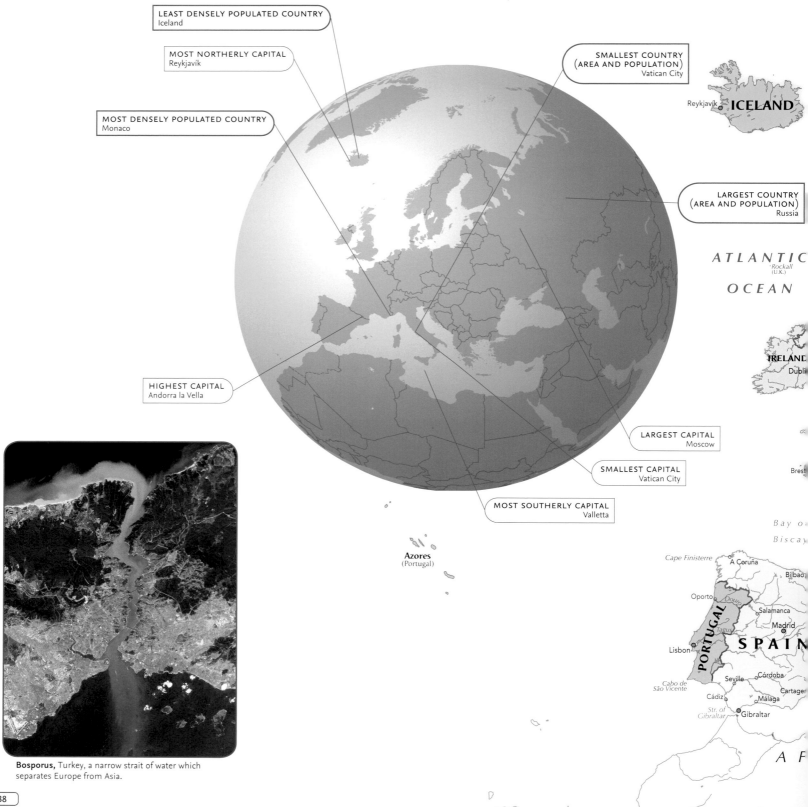

LEAST DENSELY POPULATED COUNTRY
Iceland

MOST NORTHERLY CAPITAL
Reykjavík

MOST DENSELY POPULATED COUNTRY
Monaco

SMALLEST COUNTRY
(AREA AND POPULATION)
Vatican City

Reykjavík · ICELAND

LARGEST COUNTRY
(AREA AND POPULATION)
Russia

ATLANTIC
·Rockall
(U.K.)

OCEAN

HIGHEST CAPITAL
Andorra la Vella

IRELAND
Dubli

LARGEST CAPITAL
Moscow

SMALLEST CAPITAL
Vatican City

Brest

MOST SOUTHERLY CAPITAL
Valletta

Bay o
Biscay

Azores
(Portugal)

Cape Finisterre · A Coruña
Bilbao
Oporto
Douro
Salamanca
PORTUGAL
Tagus
Madrid
Lisbon
SPAIN
Cabo de
São Vicente
Seville · Córdoba
Cádiz
Málaga · Cartager
Str. of
Gibraltar · Gibraltar

A F

Bosporus, Turkey, a narrow strait of water which separates Europe from Asia.

Europe's capitals

Largest capital (population)	Moscow, Russia	12 144 000	
Smallest capital (population)	Vatican City	800	
Most northerly capital	Reykjavík, Iceland	64° 39'N	
Most southerly capital	Valletta, Malta	35° 54'N	
Highest capital	Andorra la Vella, Andorra	1 029 metres	3 376 feet

Europe's countries

Largest country (area)	Russia	17 075 400 sq km	6 592 849 sq miles
Smallest country (area)	Vatican City	0.5 sq km	0.2 sq miles
Largest country (population)	Russia	143 457 000	
Smallest country (population)	Vatican City	800	
Most densely populated country	Monaco	19 000 per sq km	38 000 per sq mile
Least densely populated country	Iceland	3 per sq km	8 per sq mile

Internet Links

European Union	europa.eu/
UK Foreign and Commonwealth Office	www.fco.gov.uk
CIA World Factbook	www.cia.gov/library/publications/ the-world-factbook/index.html

Conic Equidistant Projection

1:10 000 000

0   100   200   300   400 miles

0   100   200   300   400   500   600 km

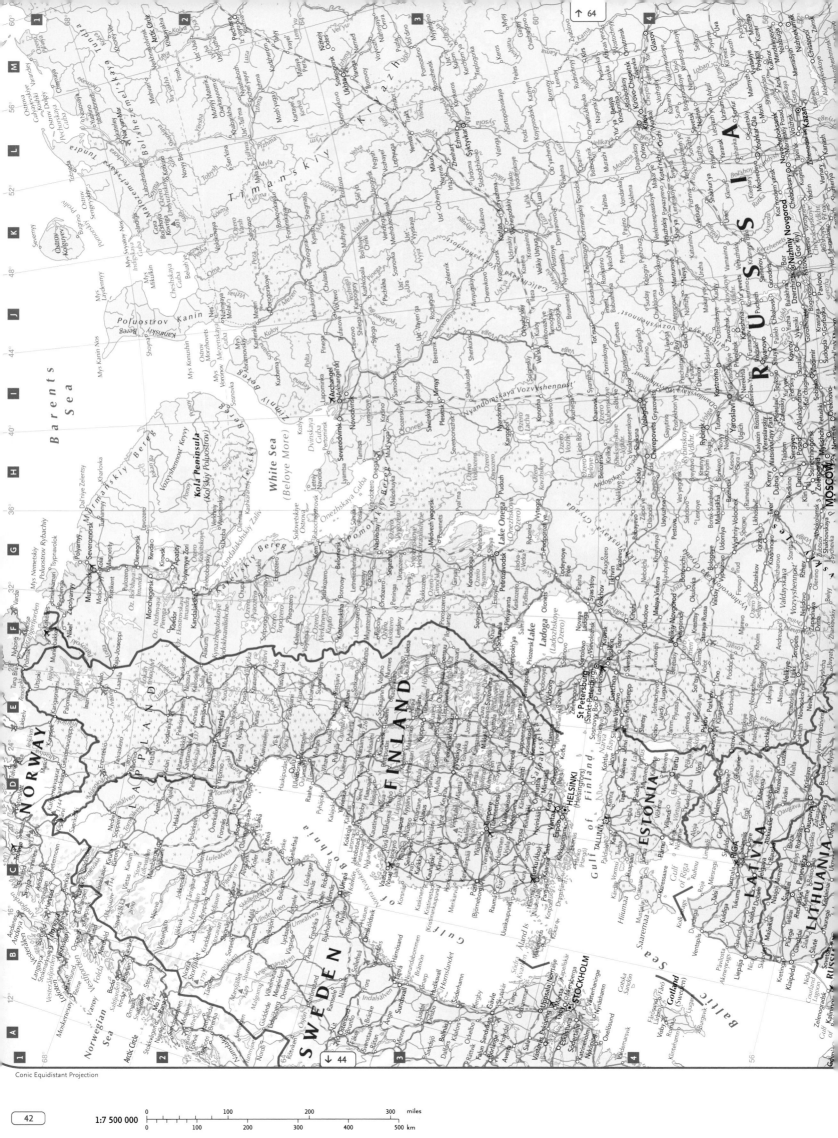

Conic Equidistant Projection

↓ 44

1:7 500 000

| 0 | 100 | 200 | 300 | miles |

| 0 | 100 | 200 | 300 | 400 | 500 km |

Europe
Western Russia

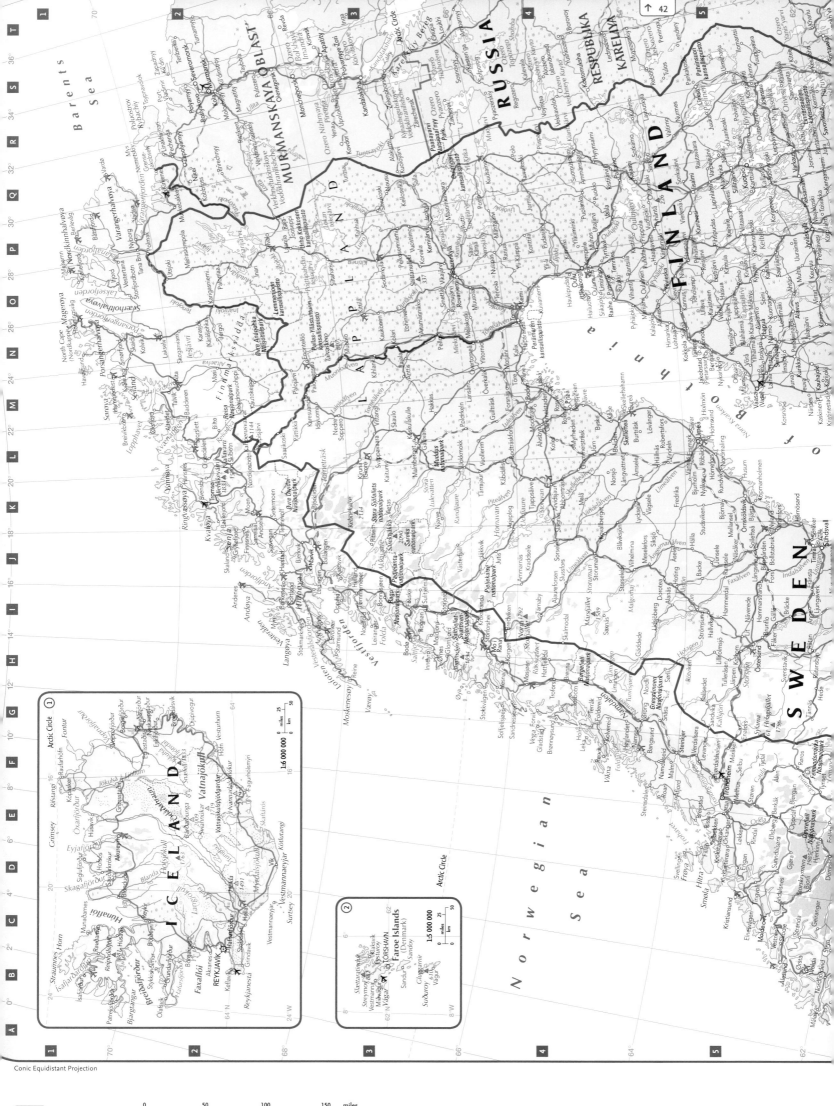

Conic Equidistant Projection

1:5 000 000

| | 0 | 50 | 100 | 150 | miles |
| 0 | 50 | 100 | 150 | 200 | 250 km |

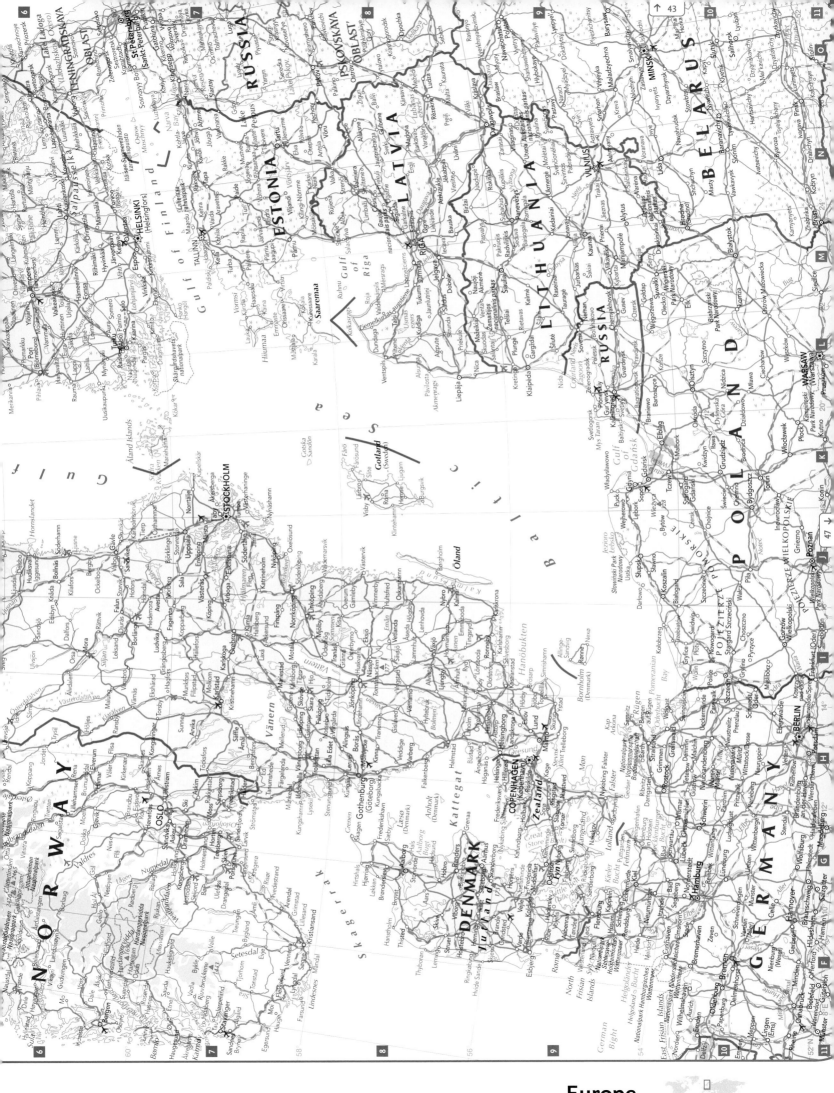

Europe

Scandinavia and the Baltic States

Europe
Northwest Europe

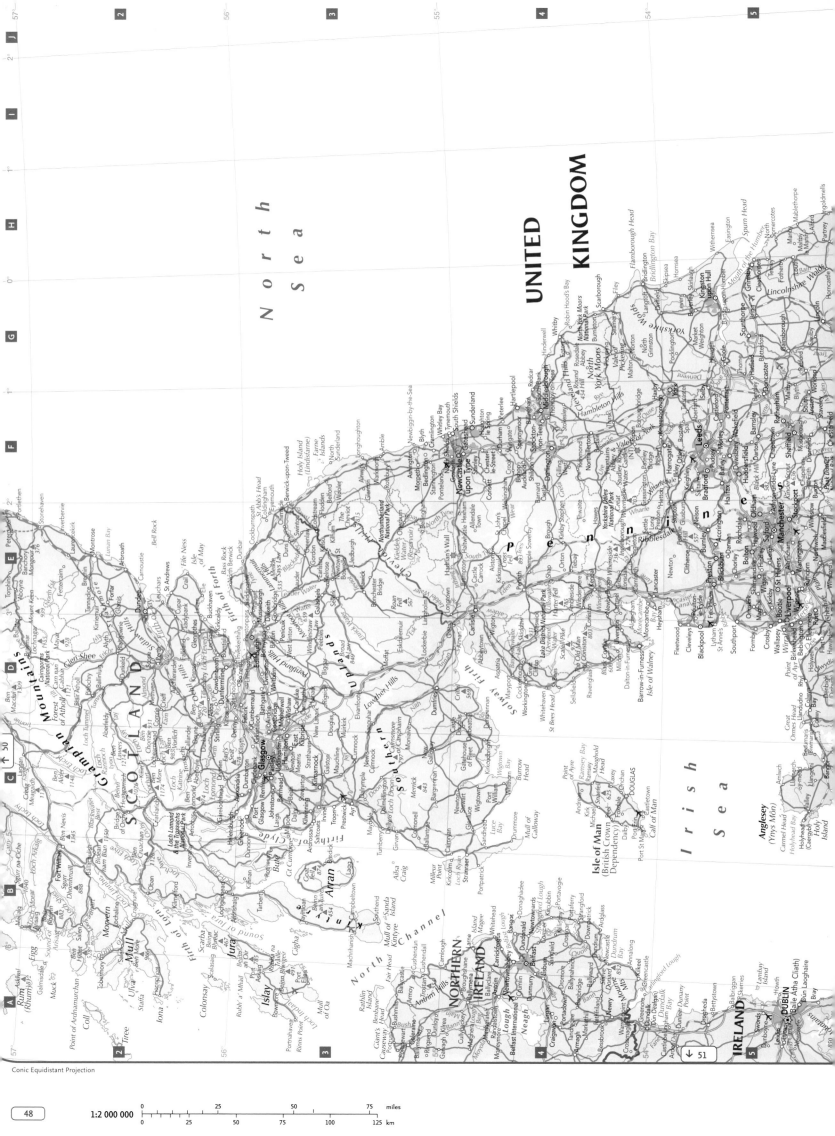

North Sea

UNITED

KINGDOM

Irish Sea

North Channel

NORTHERN
IRELAND

IRELAND

SCOTLAND

Grampian Mountains

Cairngorms National Park

Forest of Atholl

Loch Lomond & the Trossachs National Park

Southern Uplands

Cheviot Hills

Pennines

Lake District National Park

Yorkshire Dales National Park

North York Moors National Park

Yorkshire Wolds

Lincolnshire Wolds

Northumberland National Park

Anglesey (Ynys Môn)

Isle of Man (British Crown Dependency)

DOUGLAS

DUBLIN · Baile Átha Cliath

Glasgow

Edinburgh

Dundee

Newcastle upon Tyne

Middlesbrough

Leeds

Bradford

Manchester

Liverpool

Sheffield

Kingston upon Hull

Belfast

Conic Equidistant Projection

1:2 000 000

0   25   50   75   miles

0   25   50   75   100   125 km

↓ 51

← 50

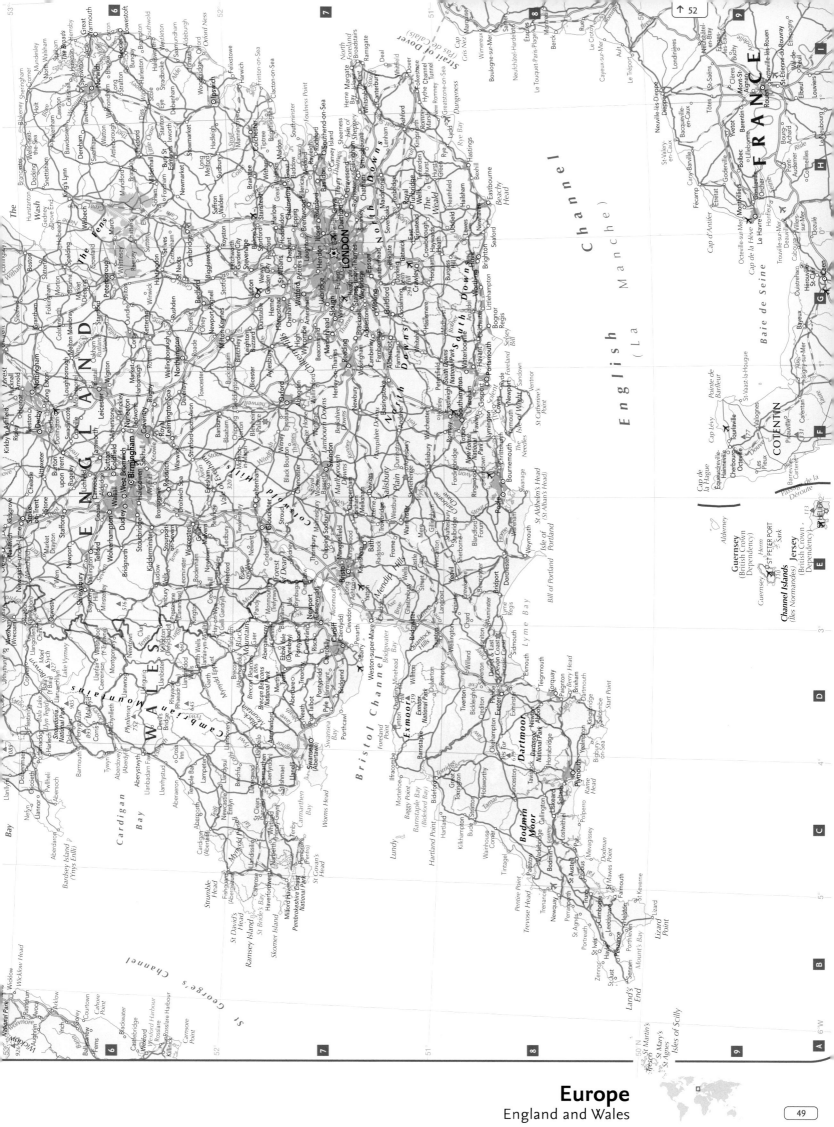

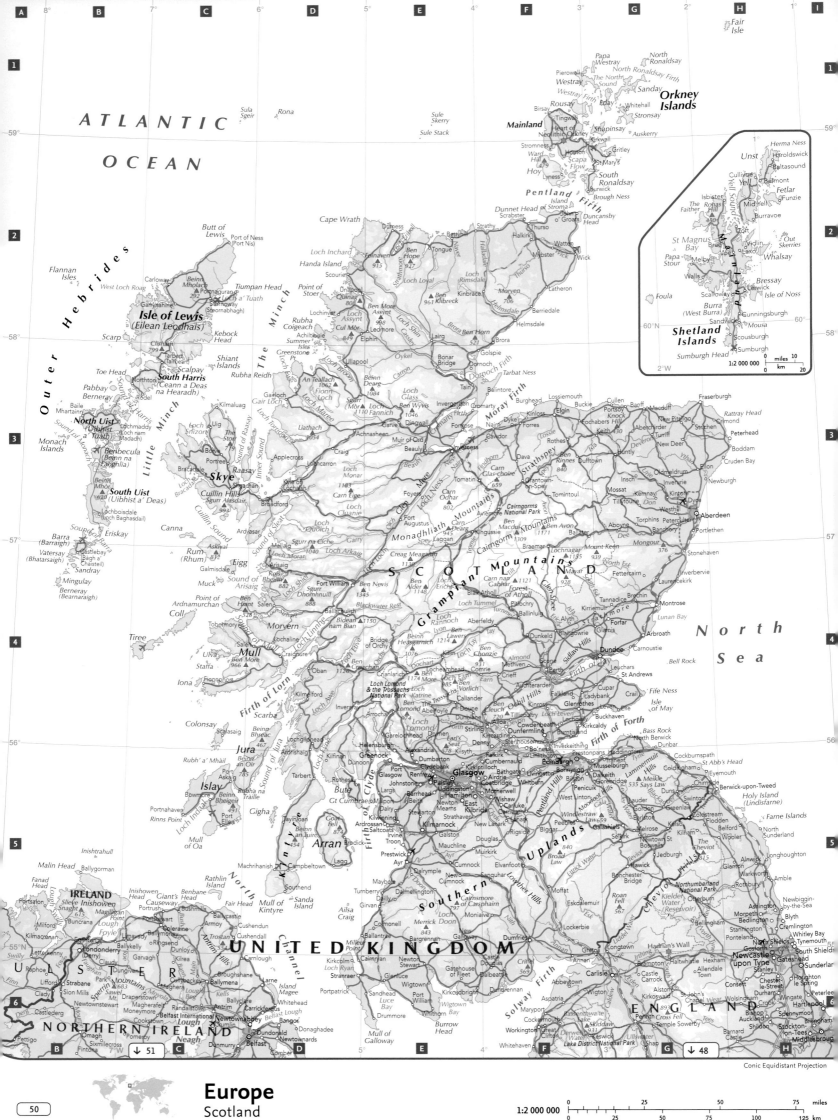

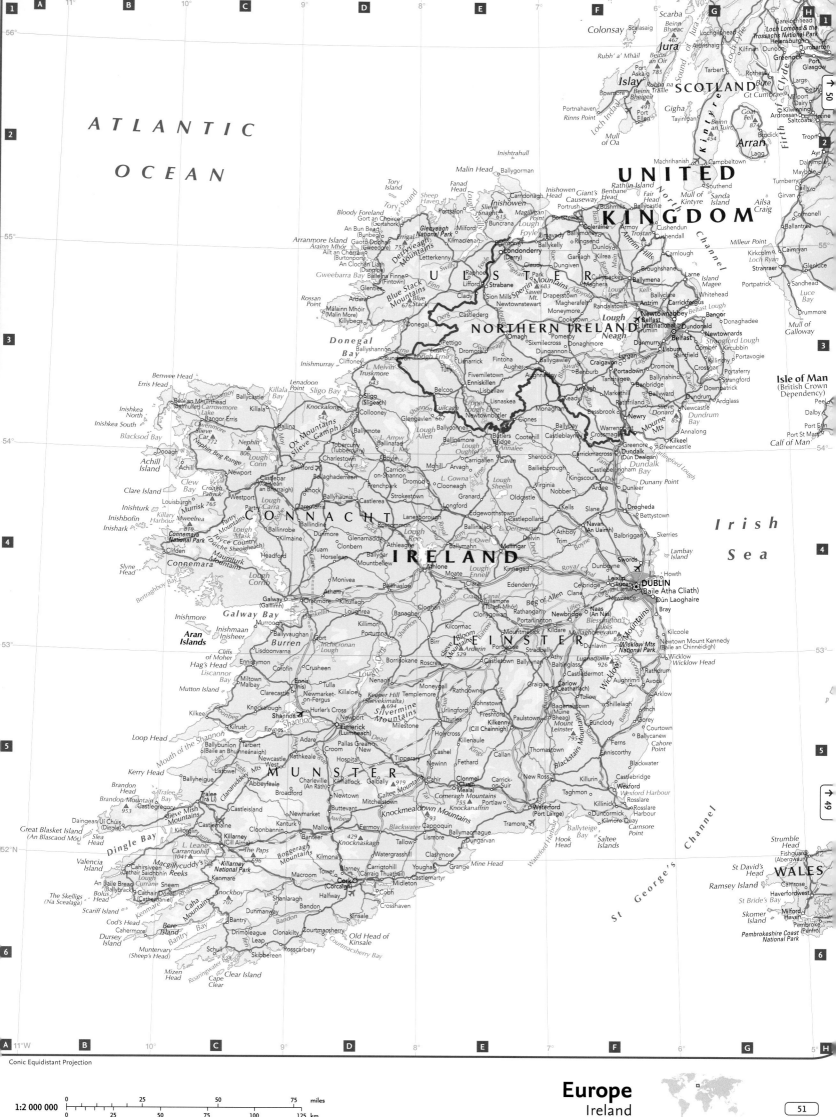

1:2 000 000

0 25 50 75 miles
0 25 50 75 100 125 km

Europe
Southern Europe and the Mediterranean

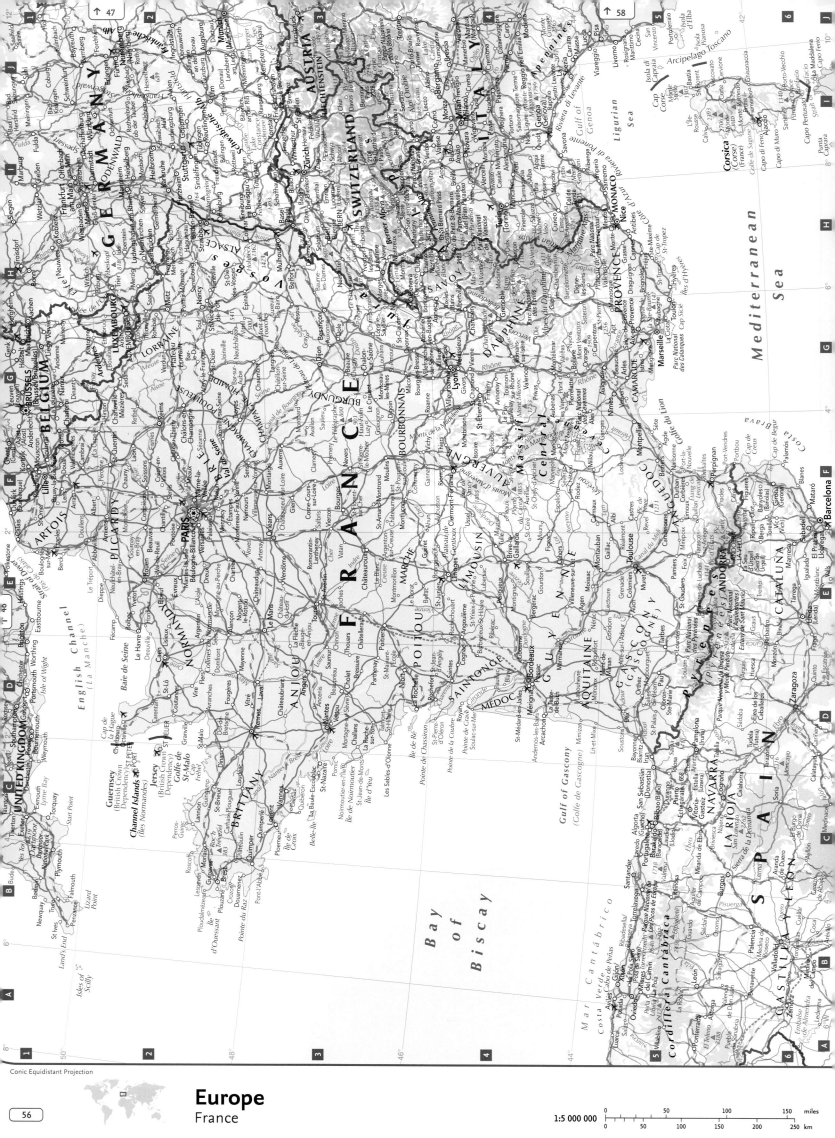

Conic Equidistant Projection

Europe
France

1:5 000 000

miles
0   50   100   150

km
0   50   100   150   200   250

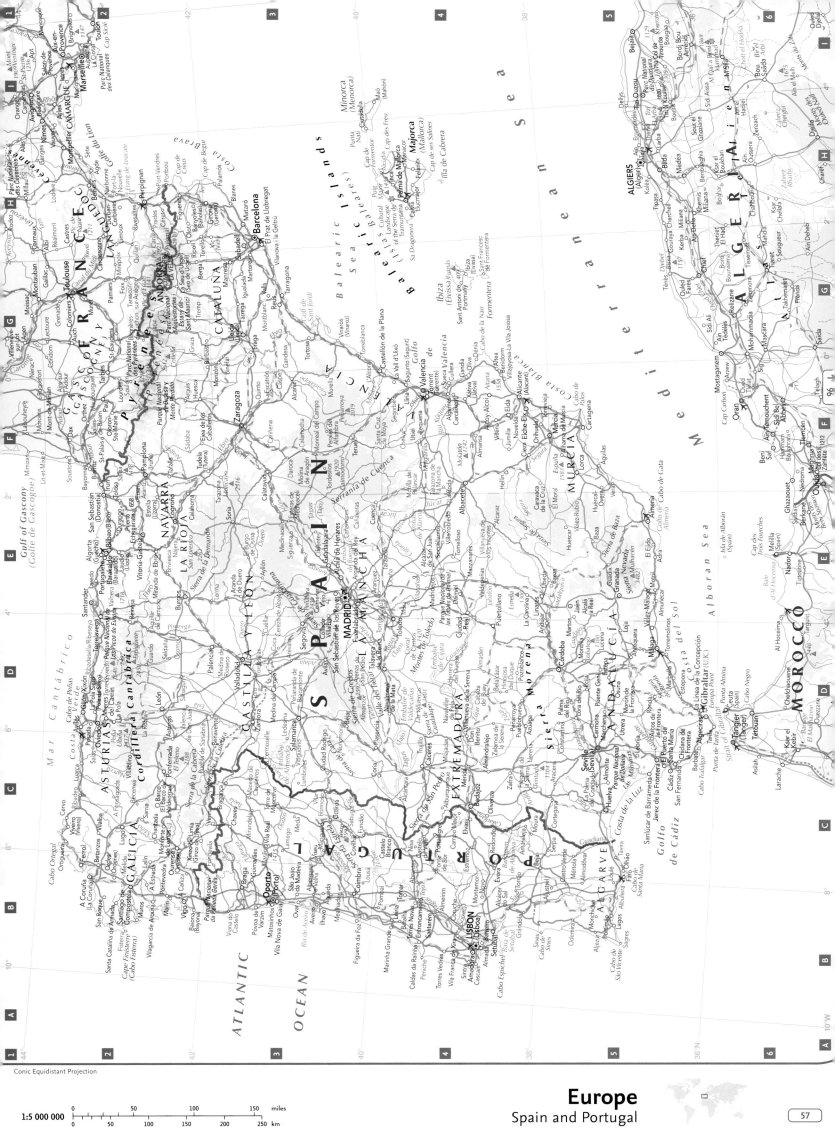

Chalon-
sur-Saône
St-Amour
Bourg-en-
Bresse
Lyon
Vienne

SWITZERLAND
BERN
Alpen
A L P S

LIECHTENSTEIN

AUSTRIA

Innsbruck

SLOVENIA
LJUBLJANA
ZAGREB

CROATIA

Turin
Torino
Milan
Milano

Genoa
Genova

FRANCE

PROVENCE

MONACO
Nice
Cannes

Marseille
Toulon

BOSNIA
AND
HERZEGOVINA
SARAJEVO

Ligurian Sea

Livorno

Corsica
(Corse)
(France)

Ajaccio

Florence
Firenze

SAN MARINO

Adriatic
Sea

ROME
(Roma)
VATICAN CITY

Sardinia
(Sardegna)
(Italy)

Naples
(Napoli)

Cagliari

Tyrrhenian

Sea

Sicily
(Sicilia)
Palermo

Mediterranean

Ionian

Sea

ALGERIA

TUNISIA
TUNIS

Catania

MALTA
VALLETTA

Conic Equidistant Projection

1:5 000 000

| 0 | 50 | 100 | 150 miles |
| 0 | 50 | 100 | 150 | 200 | 250 km |

Asia
Landscapes

Asia is the world's largest continent and occupies almost one-third of the world's total land area. Stretching across approximately 165° of longitude from the Mediterranean Sea to the easternmost point of the Russian Federation on the Bering Strait, it contains the world's highest and lowest points and some of the world's greatest physical features. Its mountain ranges include the Himalaya, Hindu Kush, Karakoram and the Ural Mountains and its major rivers – including the Yangtze, Tigris-Euphrates, Indus, Ganges and Mekong – are equally well-known and evocative.

Asia's deserts include the Gobi, the Taklimakan, and those on the Arabian Peninsula, and significant areas of volcanic and tectonic activity are present on the Kamchatka Peninsula, in Japan, and on Indonesia's numerous islands. The continent's landscapes are greatly influenced by climatic variations, with great contrasts between the islands of the Arctic Ocean and the vast Siberian plains in the north, and the tropical islands of Indonesia.

The **Yangtze**, China, Asia's longest river, flowing into the East China Sea near Shanghai.

Asia's physical features

Highest mountain	Mt Everest, China/Nepal	8 848 metres	29 028 feet
Longest river	Yangtze, China	6 380 km	3 965 miles
Largest lake	Caspian Sea	371 000 sq km	143 243 sq miles
Largest island	Borneo	745 561 sq km	287 861 sq miles
Largest drainage basin	Ob'-Irtysh, Kazakhstan/Russia	2 990 000 sq km	1 154 439 sq miles
Lowest point	Dead Sea, Israel/Jordan	-428 metres	-1 404 feet

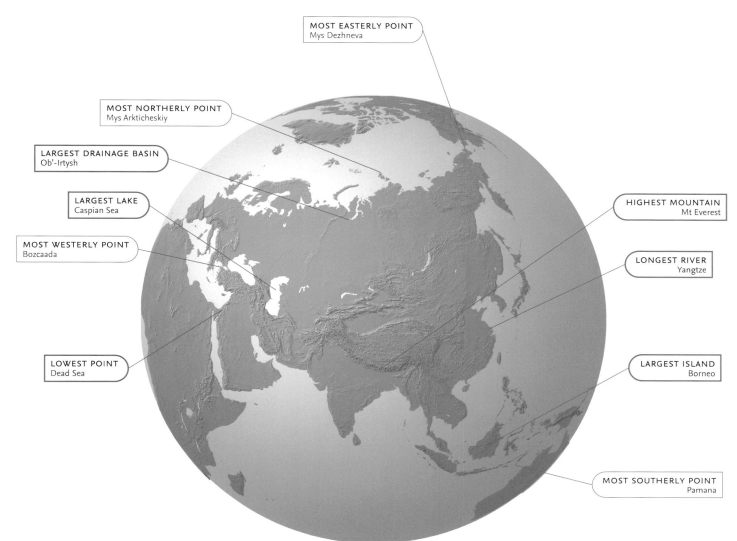

MOST EASTERLY POINT
Mys Dezhneva

MOST NORTHERLY POINT
Mys Arkticheskiy

LARGEST DRAINAGE BASIN
Ob'-Irtysh

LARGEST LAKE
Caspian Sea

MOST WESTERLY POINT
Bozcaada

LOWEST POINT
Dead Sea

HIGHEST MOUNTAIN
Mt Everest

LONGEST RIVER
Yangtze

LARGEST ISLAND
Borneo

MOST SOUTHERLY POINT
Pamana

Hahajima-rettō
Bonin Islands
Volcano Islands

Palau Islands

PACIFIC OCEAN

Jazirah Doberai
Puncak Jaya
4884
New Guinea

Kepulauan Aru
Kepulauan Tanimbar
Arafura Sea

Asia's extent

TOTAL LAND AREA	45 036 492 sq km / 17 388 686 sq miles
Most northerly point	Mys Arkticheskiy, Russia
Most southerly point	Pamana, Indonesia
Most westerly point	Bozcaada, Turkey
Most easterly point	Mys Dezhneva, Russia

Facts

- 90 of the world's 100 highest mountains are in Asia

- The Indonesian archipelago is made up of over 13 500 islands

- The height of the land in Nepal ranges from 60 metres to 8 848 metres

- The deepest lake in the world is Lake Baikal, Russia, with a maximum depth of 1 642 metres

Caspian Sea, Europe/Asia, the world's largest expanse of inland water.

61

Asia
Countries

With approximately sixty per cent of the world's population, Asia is home to numerous cultures, people groups and lifestyles. Several of the world's earliest civilizations were established in Asia, including those of Sumeria, Babylonia and Assyria. Cultural and historical differences have led to a complex political pattern, and the continent has been, and continues to be, subject to numerous territorial and political conflicts – including the current disputes in the Middle East and in Jammu and Kashmir.

Separate regions within Asia can be defined by the cultural, economic and political systems they support. The major regions are: the arid, oil-rich, mainly Islamic southwest; southern Asia with its distinct cultures, isolated from the rest of Asia by major mountain ranges; the Indian- and Chinese-influenced monsoon region of southeast Asia; the mainly Chinese-influenced industrialized areas of eastern Asia; and Soviet Asia, made up of most of the former Soviet Union.

Timor island in southeast Asia, on which East Timor, Asia's newest independent state, is located.

Internet Links

●	UK Foreign and Commonwealth Office	www.fco.gov.uk
●	CIA World Factbook	www.cia.gov/library/publicaions/the-world-factbook/index.html
●	Asian Development Bank	www.adb.org
●	Association of Southeast Asian Nations (ASEAN)	www.asean.org
●	Asia-Pacific Economic Cooperation	www.apec.org

Asia's countries

Largest country (area)	Russia	17 075 400 sq km	6 592 849 sq miles
Smallest country (area)	Maldives	298 sq km	115 sq miles
Largest country (population)	China	1 383 925 000	
Smallest country (population)	Palau	21 000	
Most densely populated country	Singapore	8 469 per sq km	21 911 per sq mile
Least densely populated country	Mongolia	2 per sq km	5 per sq mile

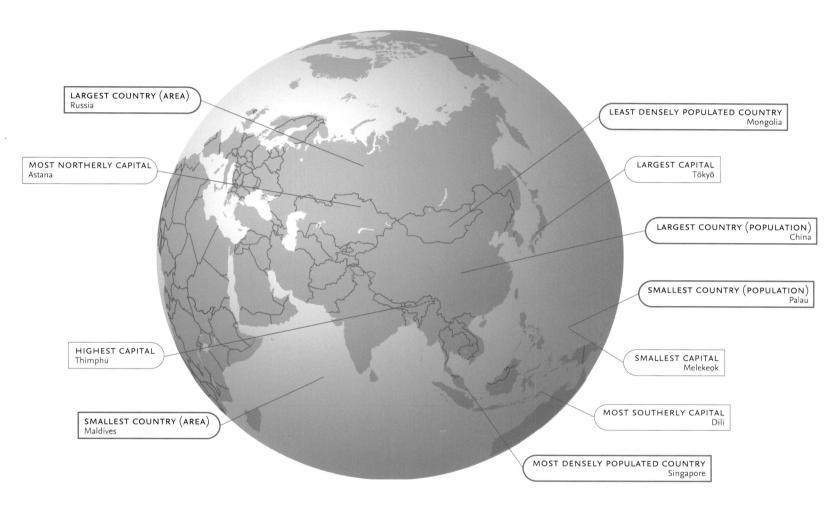

LARGEST COUNTRY (AREA)
Russia

MOST NORTHERLY CAPITAL
Astana

HIGHEST CAPITAL
Thimphu

SMALLEST COUNTRY (AREA)
Maldives

LEAST DENSELY POPULATED COUNTRY
Mongolia

LARGEST CAPITAL
Tōkyō

LARGEST COUNTRY (POPULATION)
China

SMALLEST COUNTRY (POPULATION)
Palau

SMALLEST CAPITAL
Melekeok

MOST SOUTHERLY CAPITAL
Dili

MOST DENSELY POPULATED COUNTRY
Singapore

Asia's capitals

Largest capital (population)	Tōkyō, Japan	38 197 000
Smallest capital (population)	Melekeok, Palau	391
Most northerly capital	Astana, Kazakhstan	51° 10'N
Most southerly capital	Dili, East Timor	8° 35'S
Highest capital	Thimphu, Bhutan	2 423 metres 7 949 feet

Facts

- Over 60% of the world's population live in Asia

- Asia has 11 of the world's 20 largest cities

- The Korean peninsula was divided into North Korea and South Korea in 1948 approximately along the 38th parallel

Beijing, capital of China, the most populous country in the world.

Conic Equidistant Projection

1:20 000 000

| 0 | 200 | 400 | 600 | miles |
| 0 | 200 | 400 | 600 | 800 | 1000 km |

Asia
Northern Asia

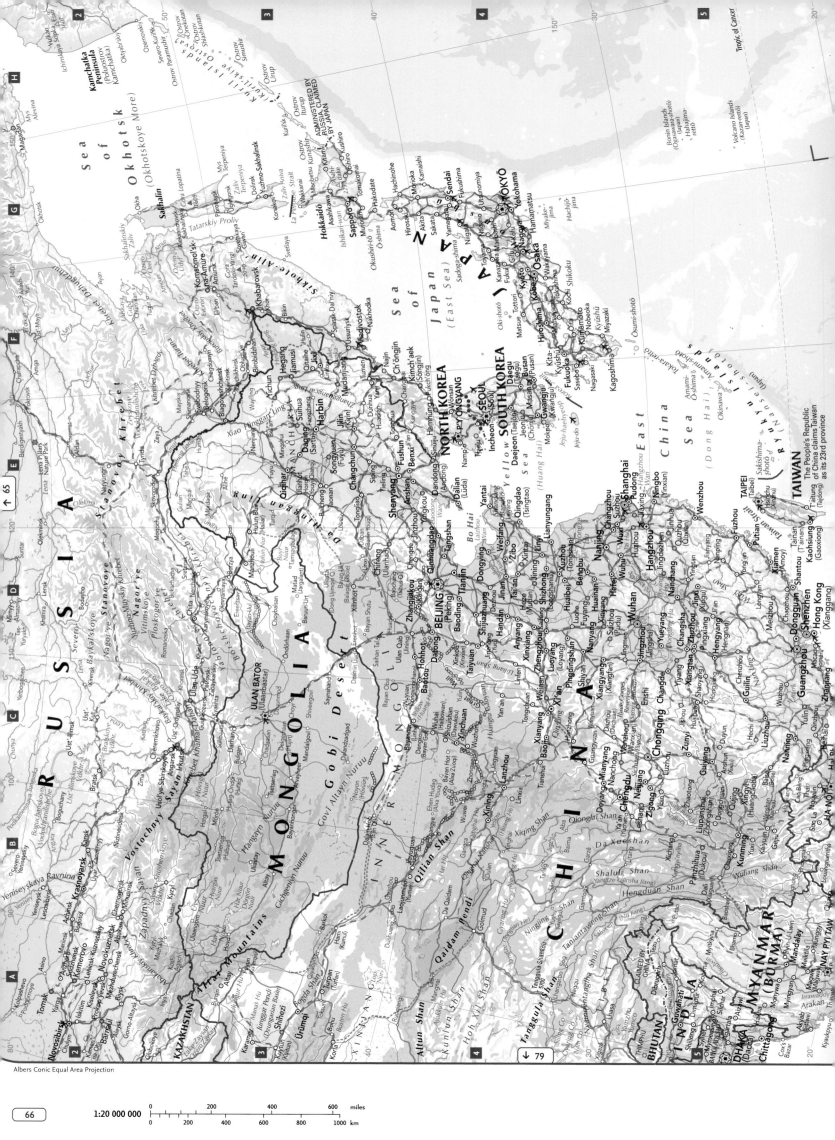

Albers Conic Equal Area Projection

1:20 000 000

| 0 | 200 | 400 | 600 | miles |

| 0 | 200 | 400 | 600 | 800 | 1000 | km |

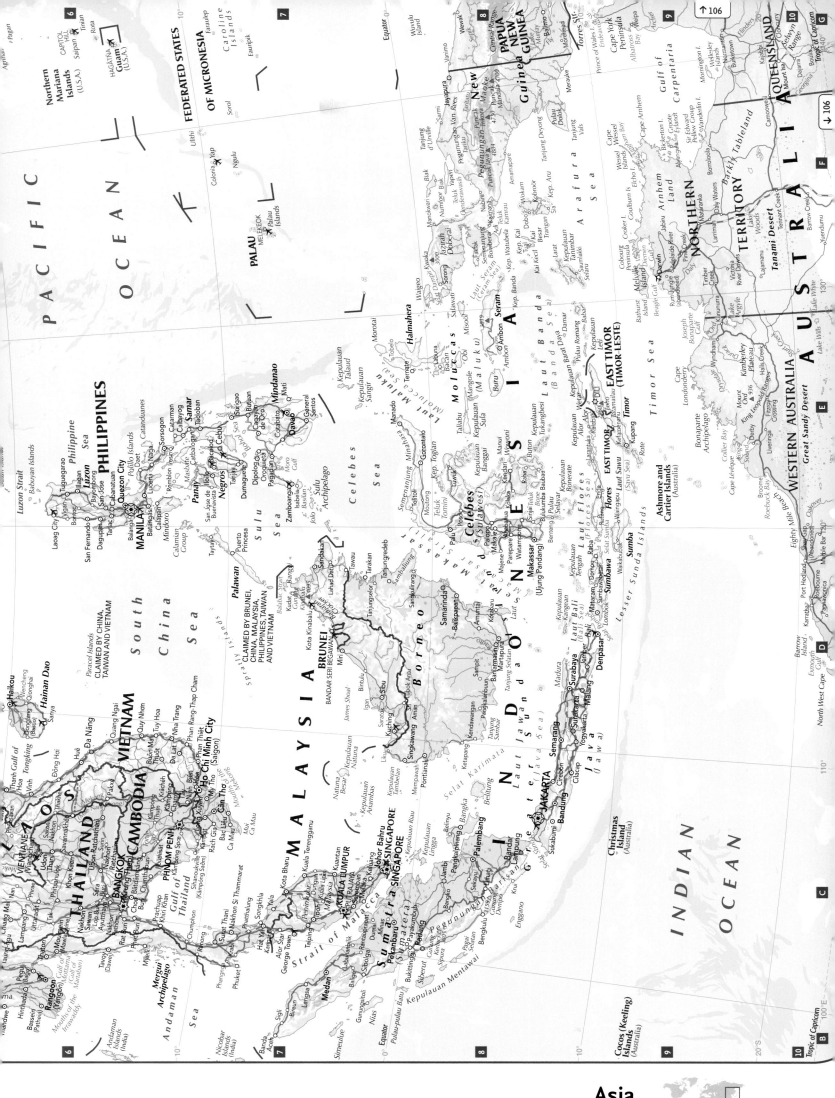

Asia
Eastern and Southeast Asia

Asia

Southeast Asia

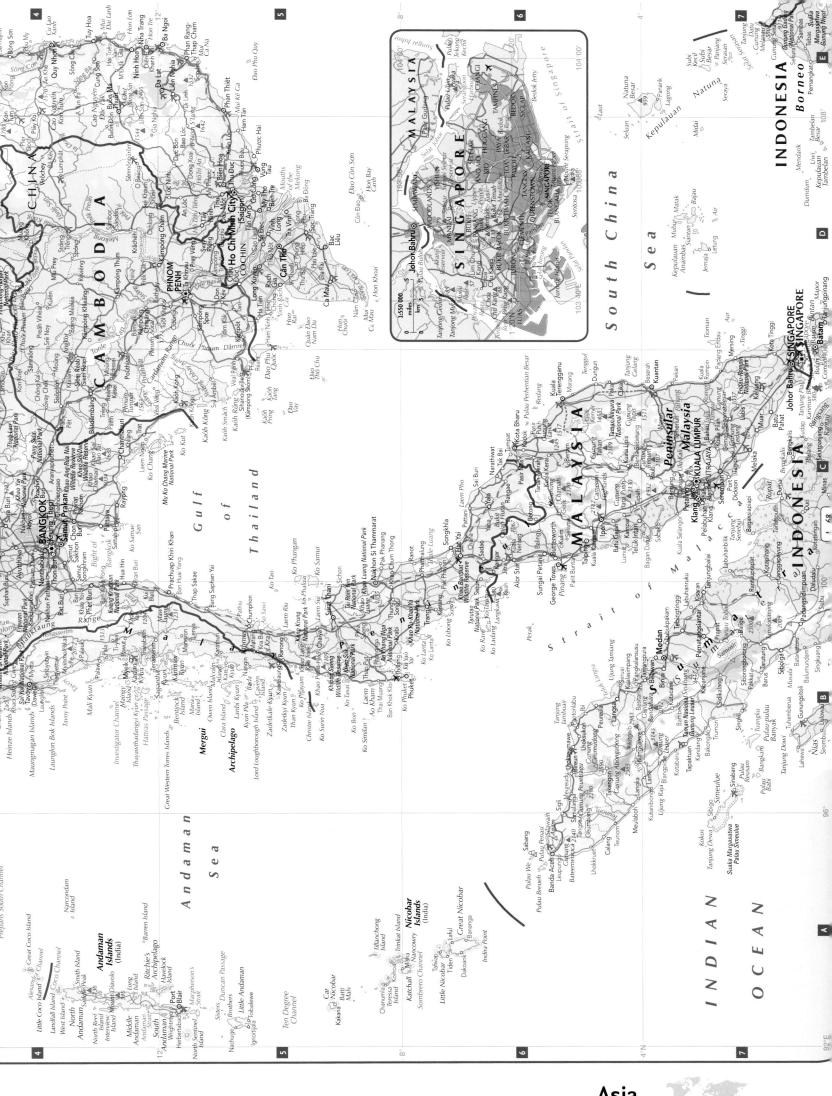

Asia
Myanmar, Thailand, Peninsular Malaysia and Indo-China

Asia
Eastern Asia

H

148°

G

144°

Sea
of
Okhotsk
(Okhotskoye More)

Sakhalin

SAKHALINSKAYA
OBLAST

ADMINISTERED BY
RUSSIA, CLAIMED
BY JAPAN

Kuril Islands
(Kuril'skiye Ostrova)

Ostrov
Iturup

Ostrov
Shikotan
(Shikotan-tō)

F

140°

Tatarskiy Proliv

La Pérouse Strait

Sōya-misaki

Hokkaidō

Sapporo

Hakodate

E

Mys
Vrangelya

136°

RUSSIA

KHABAROVSKIY KRAY

Khabarovsk
Komsomol'sk-na-Amure

SIKHOTE-ALIN'

PRIMORSKIY
KRAY

D

132°

AMURSKAYA OBLAST

YEVREYSKAYA
AVTONOMNAYA
OBLAST

Birobidzhan

Lake
Khanka

Vladivostok

C

↑ 65

128°

Blagoveshchensk

MANCHURIA

Harbin

HEILONGJIANG

Mudanjiang

Ussuriysk

B

124°

NEI MONGOL
ZIZHIQU

Qiqihar

Daqing (Saertu)

Changchun

JILIN
(Kirin)

Ch'ŏngjin

A

CHITINSKAYA
OBLAST

Shenyang
LIAONING

Fushun

Anshan

Conic Equidistant Projection

1:7 000 000

0   100   200   miles

0   100   200   300   400 km

73 ↓

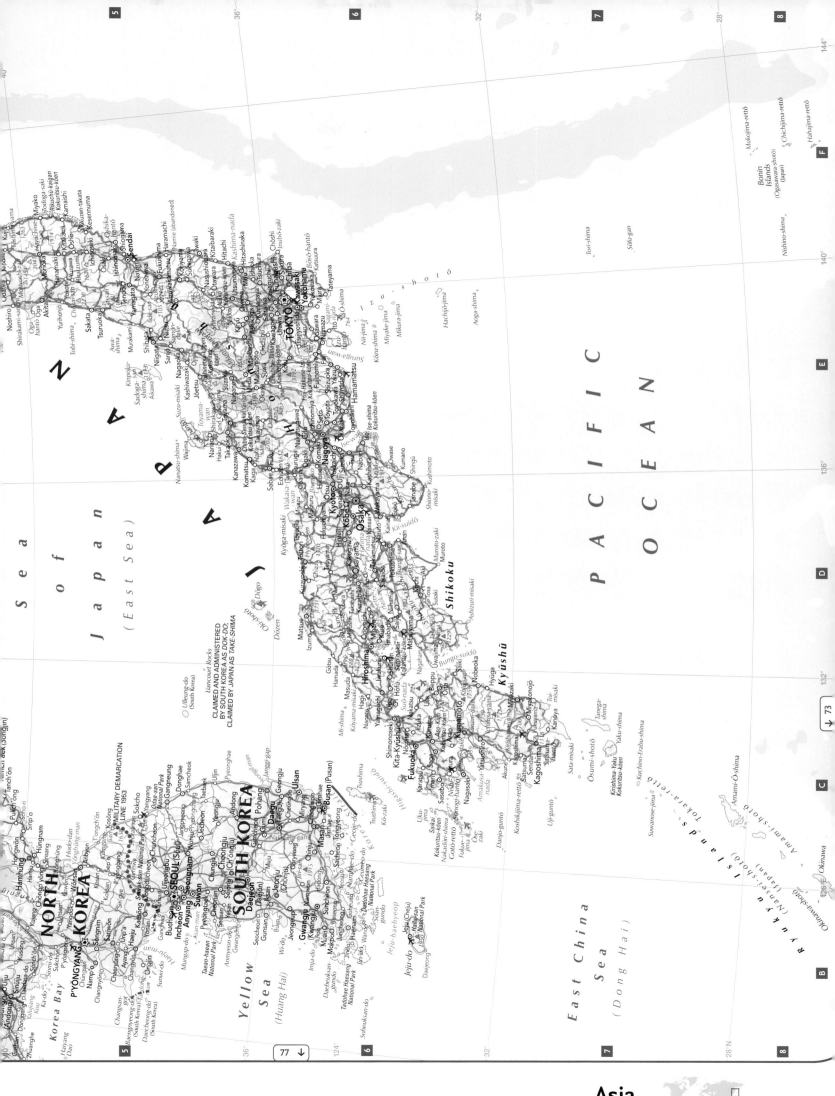

Asia
Japan, North Korea and South Korea

Conic Equidistant Projection

1:7 000 000

	100	200	miles
0			
0	100	200	300	400 km

Asia
Southeast China

Albers Conic Equal Area Projection

1:20 000 000

| | 200 | 400 | 600 | miles |
| 0 | 200 | 400 | 600 | 800 | 1000 | km |

Asia

Central and Southern Asia

Asia

Southern Asia

Conic Equidistant Projection

Administrative divisions in India
numbered on the map:

1. DADRA AND NAGAR HAVELI (C5)
2. DAMAN AND DIU (B5, C5)

1:7 000 000

| 0 | 100 | 200 | miles |

| 0 | 100 | 200 | 300 | 400 | km |

Asia

Northern India, Nepal, Bhutan and Bangladesh

Asia
Southern India and Sri Lanka

1:7 000 000

Administrative divisions in India numbered on the map:

1. DADRA AND NAGAR HAVELI (B1)
2. DAMAN AND DIU (A1, B1)
3. PUDUCHERRY (C4)

Conic Equidistant Projection

Albers Conic Equal Area Projection

1:13 000 000

| 0 | 100 | 200 | 300 | 400 | 500 miles |
| 0 | 100 | 200 | 300 | 400 | 500 | 600 | 700 | 800 km |

Conic Equidistant Projection

1:7 000 000

0   100   200   miles
0   100   200   300   400   km

Asia

The Gulf, Iran, Afghanistan and Pakistan

Asia

Eastern Mediterranean, the Caucasus and Iraq

Africa
Landscapes

Some of the world's greatest physical features are in Africa, the world's second largest continent. Variations in climate and elevation give rise to the continent's great variety of landscapes. The Sahara, the world's largest desert, extends across the whole continent from west to east, and covers an area of over nine million square kilometres. Other significant African deserts are the Kalahari and the Namib. In contrast, some of the world's greatest rivers flow in Africa, including the Nile, the world's longest, and the Congo.

The Great Rift Valley is perhaps Africa's most notable geological feature. It stretches for nearly 3 000 kilometres from Jordan, through the Red Sea and south to Mozambique, and contains many of Africa's largest lakes. Significant mountain ranges on the continent are the Atlas Mountains and the Ethiopian Highlands in the north, the Ruwenzori in east central Africa, and the Drakensberg in the far southeast.

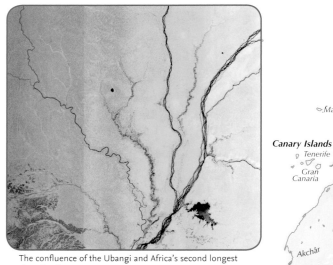

The confluence of the Ubangi and Africa's second longest river, the **Congo**.

Africa's extent

TOTAL LAND AREA	30 343 578 sq km / 11 715 655 sq miles
Most northerly point	La Galite, Tunisia
Most southerly point	Cape Agulhas, South Africa
Most westerly point	Santo Antão, Cape Verde
Most easterly point	Raas Xaafuun, Somalia

Internet Links

● NASA Visible Earth	**visibleearth.nasa.gov**
● NASA Astronaut Photography	**eol.jsc.nasa.gov**
● Peace Parks Foundation	**www.peaceparks.org**

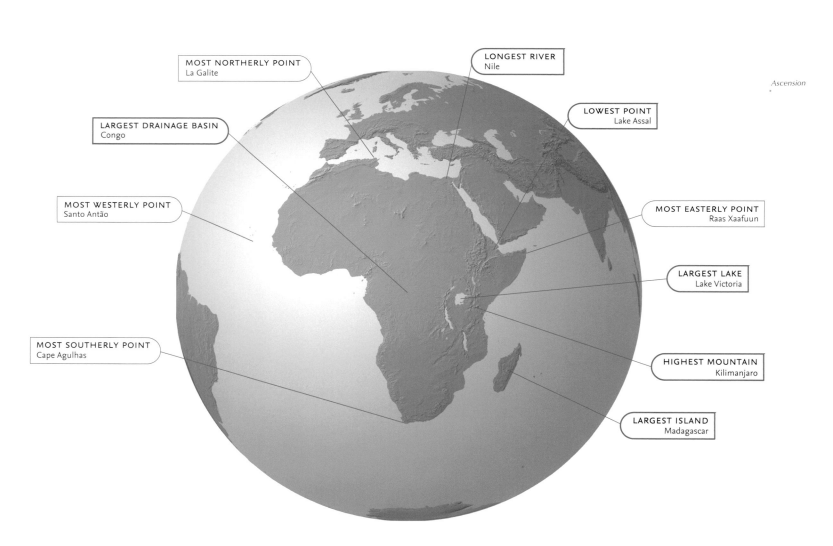

MOST NORTHERLY POINT
La Galite

LONGEST RIVER
Nile

LARGEST DRAINAGE BASIN
Congo

LOWEST POINT
Lake Assal

MOST WESTERLY POINT
Santo Antão

MOST EASTERLY POINT
Raas Xaafuun

LARGEST LAKE
Lake Victoria

MOST SOUTHERLY POINT
Cape Agulhas

HIGHEST MOUNTAIN
Kilimanjaro

LARGEST ISLAND
Madagascar

Lake Victoria, Africa's largest lake, and Lake Albert lie within Africa's Great Rift Valley.

Africa's physical features

Highest mountain	Kilimanjaro, Tanzania	5 892 metres	19 330 feet
Longest river	Nile	6 695 km	4 160 miles
Largest lake	Lake Victoria	68 870 sq km	26 591 sq miles
Largest island	Madagascar	587 040 sq km	226 656 sq miles
Largest drainage basin	Congo, Congo/Dem. Rep. Congo	3 700 000 sq km	1 428 570 sq miles
Lowest point	Lake Assal, Djibouti	-156 metres	-512 feet

Facts

- The Atlas Mountains are part of the same geological system as the Alps
- Lake Chad has shrunk by almost 95% over the last 40 years
- The Suez Canal, linking the Mediterranean Sea to the Red Sea, is 163 kilometres long and opened in 1869
- The Sahara desert covers 9 million square kilometres, approximately 30% of Africa's total land area
- Lake Assal in Djibouti is one of the saltiest lakes in the world

Africa
Countries

Africa is a complex continent, with over fifty independent countries and a long history of political change. It supports a great variety of ethnic groups, with the Sahara creating the major divide between Arab and Berber groups in the north and a diverse range of groups, including the Yoruba and Masai, in the south.

The current pattern of countries in Africa is a product of a long and complex history, including the colonial period, which saw European control of the vast majority of the continent from the fifteenth century until widespread moves to independence began in the 1950s. Despite its great wealth of natural resources, Africa is by far the world's poorest continent. Many of its countries are heavily dependent upon foreign aid and many are also subject to serious political instability.

Facts

- Africa has over 1 000 linguistic and cultural groups

- Only Liberia and Ethiopia have remained free from colonial rule throughout their history

- Over 30% of the world's minerals, and over 46% of the world's diamonds, come from Africa

- 9 of the 10 poorest countries in the world are in Africa

Madeira
(Portugal)

Canary Islands
(Spain)

Laâyoune

WESTERN
SAHARA

Nouâdhibou

MAURITANI
Nouakchott

CAPE VERDE
(Cabo Verde)
Praia

St-Louis

Dakar
Banjul
THE GAMBIA
Bissau

Kayes
SENEGAL
Kaolack

GUINEA-
BISSAU

GUINEA

Conakry
Freetown

Kank

SIERRA
LEONE
Monrovia

LIBER

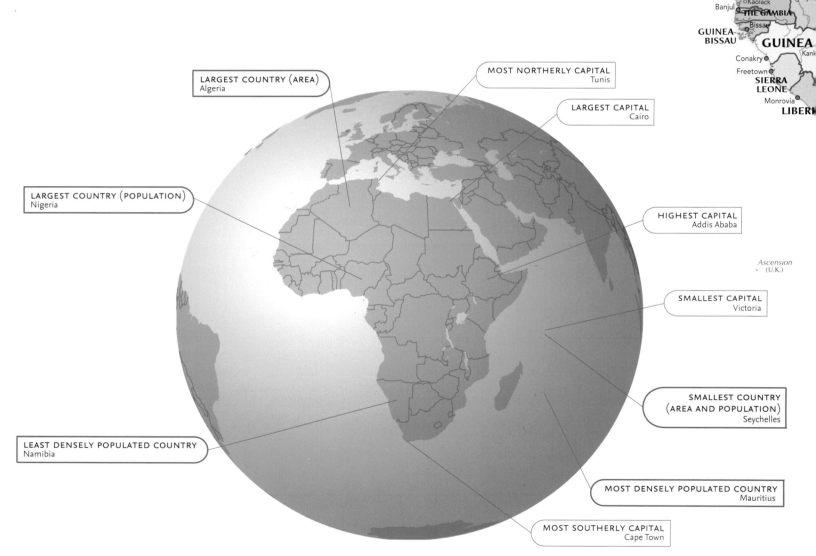

LARGEST COUNTRY (AREA)
Algeria

MOST NORTHERLY CAPITAL
Tunis

LARGEST CAPITAL
Cairo

LARGEST COUNTRY (POPULATION)
Nigeria

HIGHEST CAPITAL
Addis Ababa

Ascension
(U.K.)

SMALLEST CAPITAL
Victoria

SMALLEST COUNTRY
(AREA AND POPULATION)
Seychelles

LEAST DENSELY POPULATED COUNTRY
Namibia

MOST DENSELY POPULATED COUNTRY
Mauritius

MOST SOUTHERLY CAPITAL
Cape Town

Internet Links	
UK Foreign and Commonwealth Office	www.fco.gov.uk
CIA World Factbook	www.cia.gov/library/publications/ the-world-factbook/index.html
Southern African Development Community	www.sadc.int
African Union (AU)	www.au.int

EUROPE

Strait of Gibraltar
Rabat
Casablanca
Beni Mellal
Marrakech
Tangier
Fès
MOROCCO
Atlas Mountains
Oran
Sidi Bel
Abbès
Ech Chélif
Béchar
Algiers
Bejaïa
Skikda
Annaba
Constantine
Tunis
TUNISIA
Sfax
Gabès
Tripoli
Al Baydā'
Laghouat
Mişrātah
Gulf of Sirte
Benghazi

Mediterranean Sea

ALGERIA

Sahara

LIBYA

Libyan Desert

Alexandria
Port Said
Tantā
Giza
Cairo
Suez
Al Minyā
EGYPT
Asyūţ
Qinā
Luxor
Aswān
Lake Nasser

Red Sea

ASIA

MALI
Gao
Niger
Mopti
Ségou
Bamako
Ouagadougou
BURKINA FASO
Bobo-Dioulasso
CÔTE D'IVOIRE (IVORY COAST)
Yamoussoukro
Bouaké
Kumasi
Abidjan
GHANA
TOGO
BENIN
Accra
Cape Coast
Lomé
Porto-Novo

NIGER
Niamey
Agadez
Zinder

CHAD
Lake Chad
Abéché
Ndjamena
Sokoto
Kano
Maiduguri
Zaria
Maroua
Kumo
NIGERIA
Abuja
Ibadan
Ogbomosho
Lagos
Onitsha
Warri
Uyo
Port Harcourt
Parakou

SUDAN
Omdurman
Khartoum
Wad Medani
El Obeid
Blue Nile
Gedaref
Port Sudan

ERITREA
Asmara
Mek'elē
Bahir Dar
DJIBOUTI
Djibouti
Berbera
SOMALILAND
Hargeysa
Gulf of Aden

Addis Ababa
Dirē Dawa
ETHIOPIA

CENTRAL AFRICAN REPUBLIC
Bangui
Bossangoa
Bouar
Moundou
Sarh
Ngaoundéré
CAMEROON
Yaoundé
Nkongsamba
Douala
Malabo
EQUATORIAL GUINEA

SOUTH SUDAN
Wau
Juba

KENYA
Nairobi
Nakuru
Kisumu
UGANDA
Kampala
Lake Victoria
Mount Kenya 5199
SOMALIA
Mogadishu
Kismaayo

SÃO TOMÉ AND PRÍNCIPE
São Tomé
Gulf of Guinea
Libreville
Port-Gentil
GABON
Franceville
CONGO
Brazzaville
Pointe-Noire
CABINDA (Angola)
Matadi
Kinshasa

DEMOCRATIC REPUBLIC OF THE CONGO
Kisangani
Mbandaka
Congo
Bandundu
Kikwit
Kananga
Mbuji-Mayi
Kasai
Kamina
Kalemie
Kigoma
RWANDA
Bukavu
Kigali
BURUNDI
Bujumbura
Mwanza
Arusha
Kilimanjaro 5895
Lake Tanganyika
Tabora
Dodoma
TANZANIA
Tanga
Mombasa
Zanzibar
Zanzibar Island
Dar es Salaam
Iringa
Mbeya

INDIAN OCEAN

Victoria
SEYCHELLES

Aldabra Islands

ATLANTIC OCEAN

Luanda
Cuanza
ANGOLA
Lobito
Benguela
Huambo
Namibe
Lubango
Mongu
Livingstone
Cubango
ZAMBIA
Lusaka
Solwezi
Lubumbashi
Likasi
Ndola
Kabwe
Kasama
Mansa
Chingola
Chipata
Lake Nyasa
MALAWI
Lilongwe
Blantyre
Nampula
Nacala
Pemba

Moroni
COMOROS
Antsiranana
Mayotte (France)
Mahajanga
Toamasina

* St Helena (U.K.)
St Helena, Ascension and Tristan da Cunha (U.K.)

Etosha Pan
Okavango Delta
Francistown
Windhoek
NAMIBIA
Namib Desert
Zambezi
Harare
Chitungwiza
ZIMBABWE
Gweru
Bulawayo
Mutare
Tete
Quelimane
MOZAMBIQUE
Beira
Mozambique Channel
MADAGASCAR
Antananarivo
Fianarantsoa
Toliara

Port Louis **MAURITIUS**
Réunion (France)

BOTSWANA
Gaborone
Xai-Xai
Inhambane
Maputo
Pretoria (Tshwane)
Johannesburg
Carletonville
Soweto
Mbabane
SWAZILAND
Kimberley
Bloemfontein
LESOTHO
Maseru
Durban

SOUTH AFRICA
Cape Town
Khayelitsha
Cape of Good Hope
Cape Agulhas
East London
Port Elizabeth

Tristan da Cunha (U.K.)

Orange

Cape Town, legislative capital of the Republic of South Africa and the most southerly African capital city.

Africa's capitals

Largest capital (population)	Cairo, Egypt	11 944 000
Smallest capital (population)	Victoria, Seychelles	26 000
Most northerly capital	Tunis, Tunisia	36° 46'N
Most southerly capital	Cape Town, South Africa	33° 57'S
Highest capital	Addis Ababa, Ethiopia	2 408 metres 7 900 feet

Africa's countries

Largest country (area)	Algeria	2 381 741 sq km	919 595 sq miles
Smallest country (area)	Seychelles	455 sq km	176 sq miles
Largest country (population)	Nigeria	182 202 000	
Smallest country (population)	Seychelles	96 000	
Most densely populated country	Mauritius	610 per sq km	1 579 per sq mile
Least densely populated country	Namibia	3 per sq km	7 per sq mile

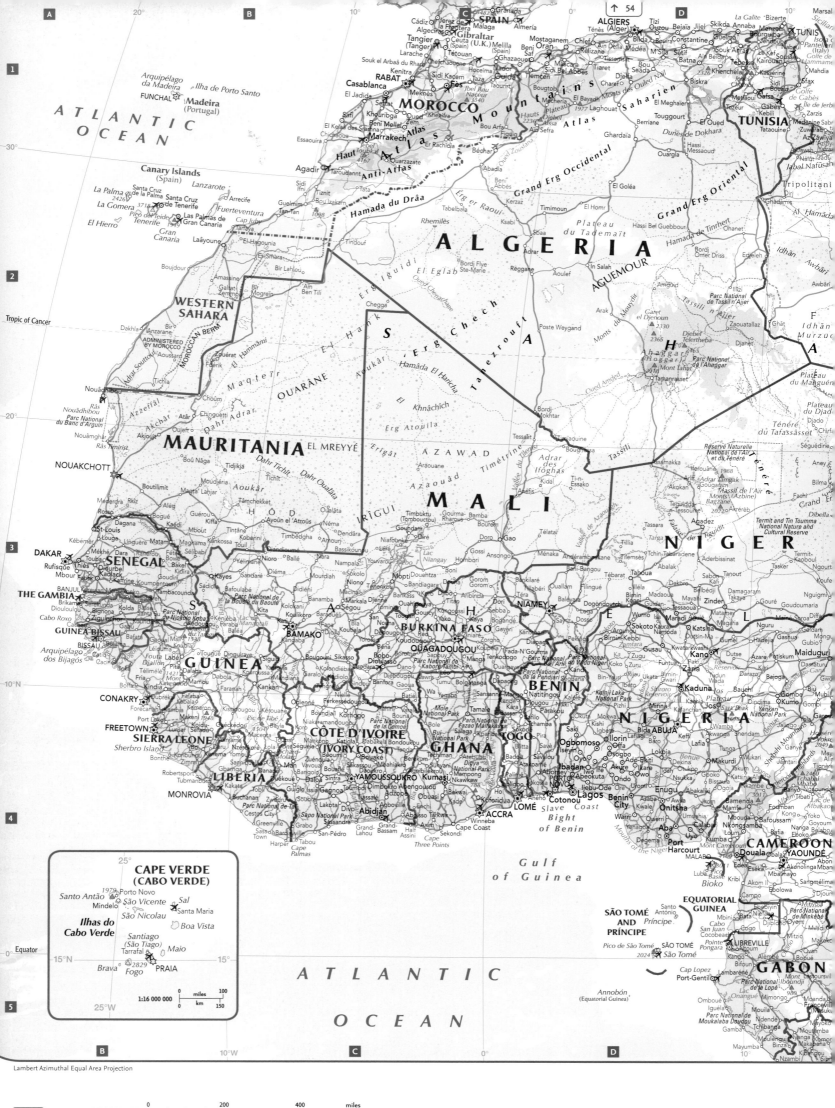

Africa
Northern Africa

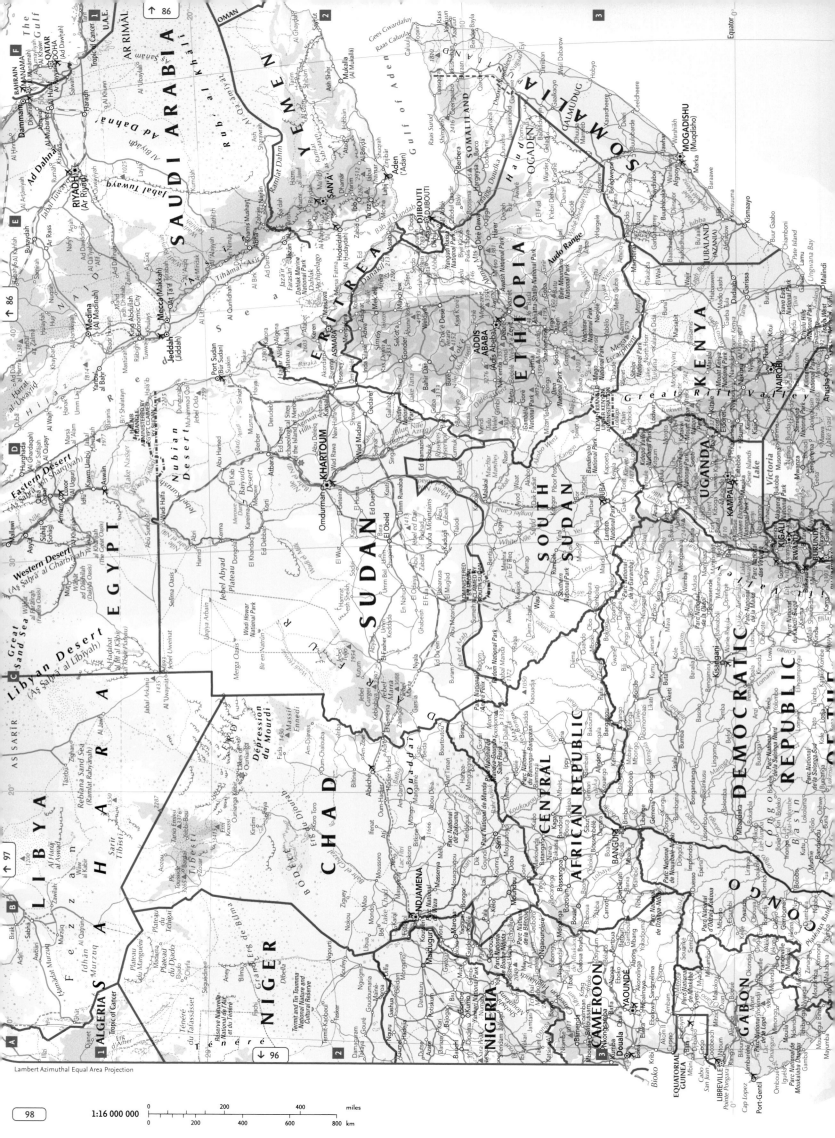

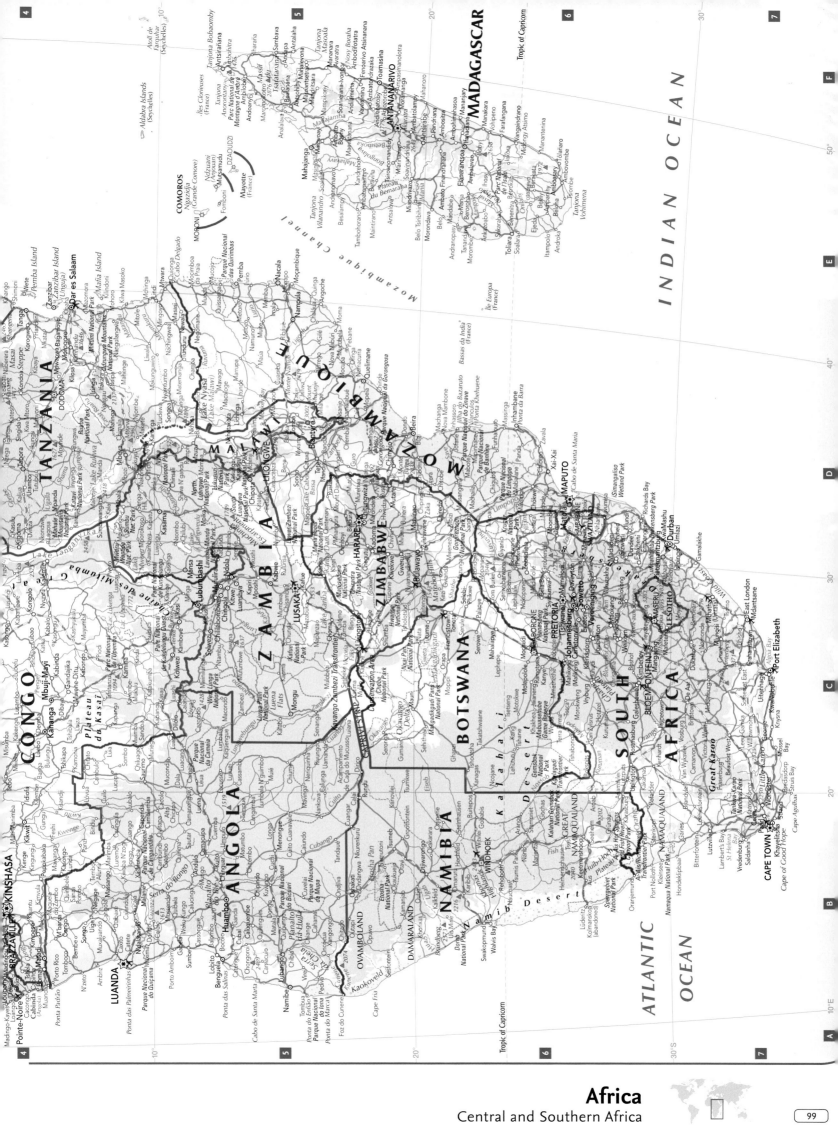

Africa

Central and Southern Africa

ATLANTIC

OCEAN

GHANZI

BOTSWANA

Central Kalahari Game Reserve

KWENENG

SOUTHERN

Kalahari

Kgalagadi Transfrontier Park

NAMIBIA

ERONGO

KHOMAS

WINDHOEK

HARDAP

GREAT NAMAQUALAND

!KARAS

NAMAQUALAND

NORTHERN

CAPE

AFRIC

WESTERN CAPE

CAPE TOWN

Lambert Azimuthal Equal Area Projection

1:5 000 000

miles

km

Africa
South Africa

Oceania
Landscapes

Oceania comprises Australia, New Zealand, New Guinea and the islands of the Pacific Ocean. It is the smallest of the world's continents by land area. Its dominating feature is Australia, which is mainly flat and very dry. Australia's western half consists of a low plateau, broken in places by higher mountain ranges, which has very few permanent rivers or lakes. The narrow, fertile coastal plain of the east coast is separated from the interior by the Great Dividing Range, which includes the highest mountain in Australia.

The numerous Pacific islands of Oceania are generally either volcanic in origin or consist of coral. They can be divided into three main regions - Micronesia, north of the equator between Palau and the Gilbert islands; Melanesia, stretching from mountainous New Guinea to Fiji; and Polynesia, covering a vast area of the eastern and central Pacific Ocean.

Princess Chatlotte Bay, on the east coast of Cape York Peninsula and the Claremont Isles National Park.

Facts

- Australia's Great Barrier Reef is the world's largest coral reef and stretches for over 2 000 kilometres

- The highest point of Tuvalu is less than 5 metres above sea level

- New Zealand lies directly on the boundary between the Pacific and Indo-Australian tectonic plates

- The Mariana Trench in the Pacific Ocean contains the earth's deepest point – Challenger Deep, 10 920 metres below sea level

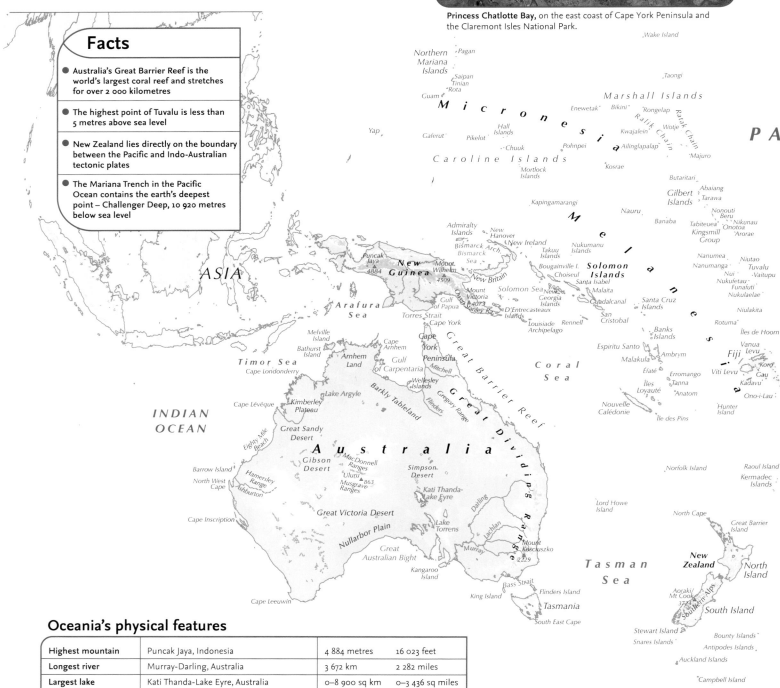

Oceania's physical features

Highest mountain	Puncak Jaya, Indonesia	4 884 metres	16 023 feet
Longest river	Murray-Darling, Australia	3 672 km	2 282 miles
Largest lake	Kati Thanda-Lake Eyre, Australia	0–8 900 sq km	0–3 436 sq miles
Largest island	New Guinea, Indonesia/Papua New Guinea	808 510 sq km	312 166 sq miles
Largest drainage basin	Murray-Darling, Australia	1 058 000 sq km	408 494 sq miles
Lowest point	Kati Thanda-Lake Eyre, Australia	-16 metres	-52 feet

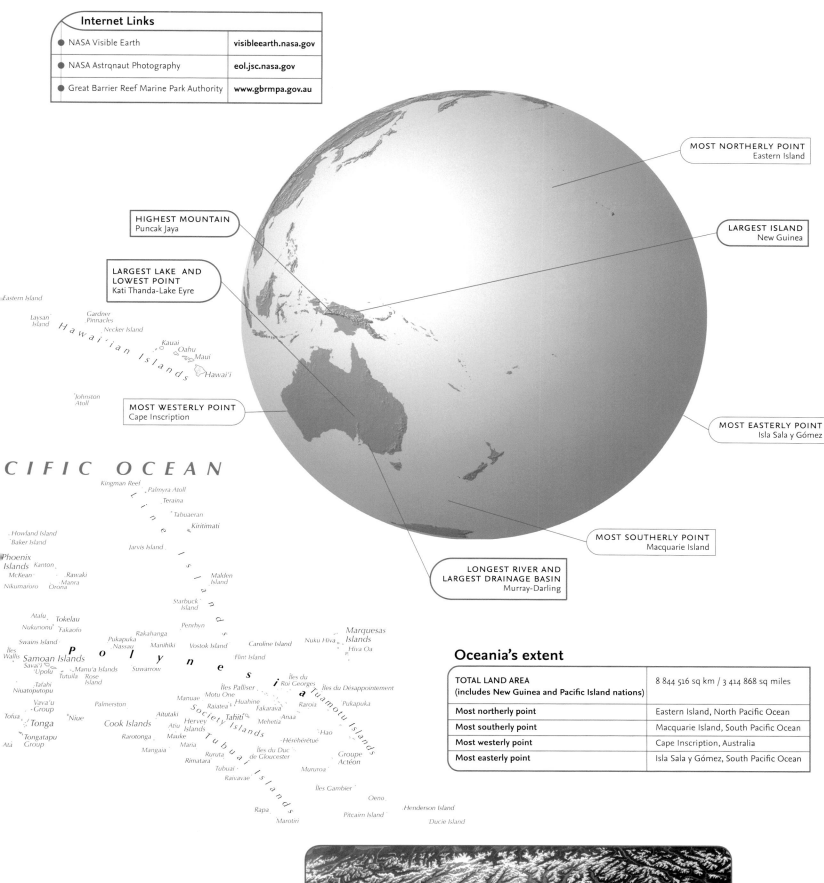

Internet Links

NASA Visible Earth	visibleearth.nasa.gov
NASA Astronaut Photography	eol.jsc.nasa.gov
Great Barrier Reef Marine Park Authority	www.gbrmpa.gov.au

MOST NORTHERLY POINT
Eastern Island

LARGEST ISLAND
New Guinea

HIGHEST MOUNTAIN
Puncak Jaya

LARGEST LAKE AND LOWEST POINT
Kati Thanda-Lake Eyre

Eastern Island

Laysan Island

Gardner Pinnacles

Necker Island

H a w a i ʻ i a n   I s l a n d s

Kauai
Oahu
Maui
Hawaiʻi

Johnston Atoll

MOST WESTERLY POINT
Cape Inscription

MOST EASTERLY POINT
Isla Sala y Gómez

C I F I C   O C E A N

Kingman Reef

Palmyra Atoll

Teraina

Tabuaeran

Kiritimati

L i n e   I s l a n d s

Howland Island
Baker Island

Jarvis Island

Malden Island

Phoenix Islands
Kanton
McKean
Rawaki
Nikumaroro
Orona
Manra

Starbuck Island

MOST SOUTHERLY POINT
Macquarie Island

LONGEST RIVER AND LARGEST DRAINAGE BASIN
Murray-Darling

Atafu
Tokelau
Nukunonu
Fakaofo

Rakahanga
Penrhyn

Marquesas Islands
Nuku Hiva
Hiva Oa

Swains Island
Pukapuka
Nassau
Manihiki
Vostok Island
Caroline Island

Îles Wallis

P o l y n e s i a

Samoan Islands
Savaiʻi
Upolu
Manuʻa Islands
Rose Island
Tutuila

Flint Island

Îles du Roi Georges
Îles du Désappointement

Tafahi
Niuatoputopu

Manuae
Motu One
Raiatea
Huahine
Fakarava
Raroia
Pukapuka

Vavaʻu Group
Palmerston

Aitutaki
Atiu
Hervey Islands
Tahiti
Mehetia
Anaa

Tofua
Tonga
Niue

Cook Islands
Rarotonga
Mauke
Maria

Society Islands

Hao

Tuamotu Islands

S o c i e t y   I s l a n d s

Tongatapu Group
Atā
Mangaia

Ruruta
Rimatara
Tubuai
Raivavae
Rapa
Marotiri

Îles du Duc de Gloucester

Héréhérétué

Groupe Actéon

Mururoa

T u b u a i   I s l a n d s

Îles Gambier

Oeno
Henderson Island
Pitcairn Island
Ducie Island

Oceania's extent

TOTAL LAND AREA (includes New Guinea and Pacific Island nations)	8 844 516 sq km / 3 414 868 sq miles
Most northerly point	Eastern Island, North Pacific Ocean
Most southerly point	Macquarie Island, South Pacific Ocean
Most westerly point	Cape Inscription, Australia
Most easterly point	Isla Sala y Gómez, South Pacific Ocean

Chatham Islands
Pitt Island

H E R N   O C E A N

Banks Peninsula, Canterbury Plains and the **Southern Alps,** South Island, New Zealand.

Oceania
Countries

Stretching across almost the whole width of the Pacific Ocean, Oceania has a great variety of cultures and an enormously diverse range of countries and territories. Australia, by far the largest and most industrialized country in the continent, contrasts with the numerous tiny Pacific island nations which have smaller, and more fragile economies based largely on agriculture, fishing and the exploitation of natural resources.

The division of the Pacific island groups into the main regions of Micronesia, Melanesia and Polynesia – often referred to as the South Sea islands – broadly reflects the ethnological differences across the continent. There is a long history of colonial influence in the region, which still contains dependent territories belonging to Australia, France, New Zealand, the UK and the USA.

Nouméa, capital of the French dependency of New Caledonia in the southern Pacific Ocean.

Facts

- Over 91% of Australia's population live in urban areas
- The Maori name for New Zealand is Aotearoa, meaning 'land of the long white cloud'
- Auckland, New Zealand, has the largest Polynesian population of any city in Oceania
- Over 800 different languages are spoken in Papua New Guinea

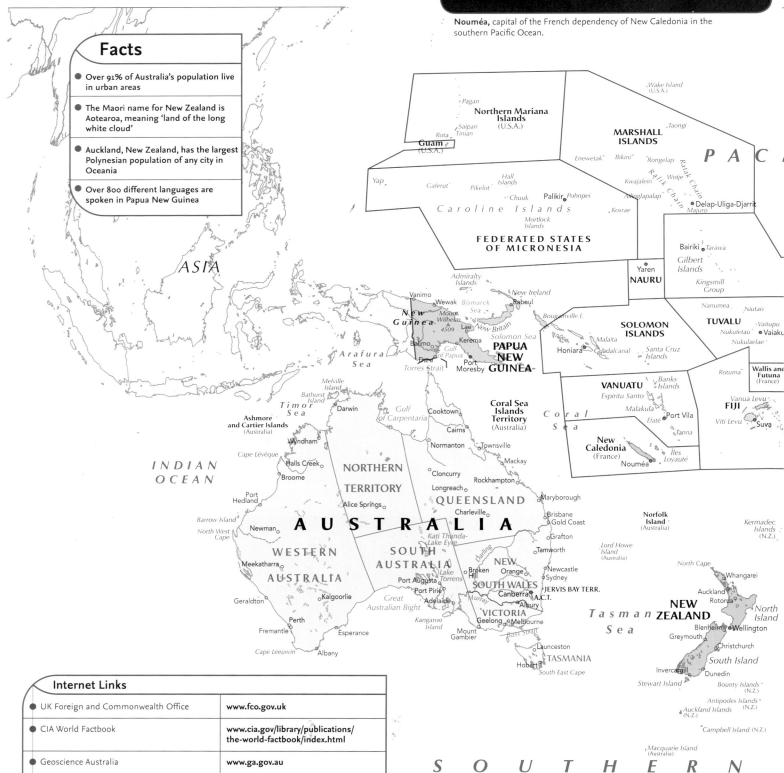

Internet Links

UK Foreign and Commonwealth Office	www.fco.gov.uk
CIA World Factbook	www.cia.gov/library/publications/the-world-factbook/index.html
Geoscience Australia	www.ga.gov.au

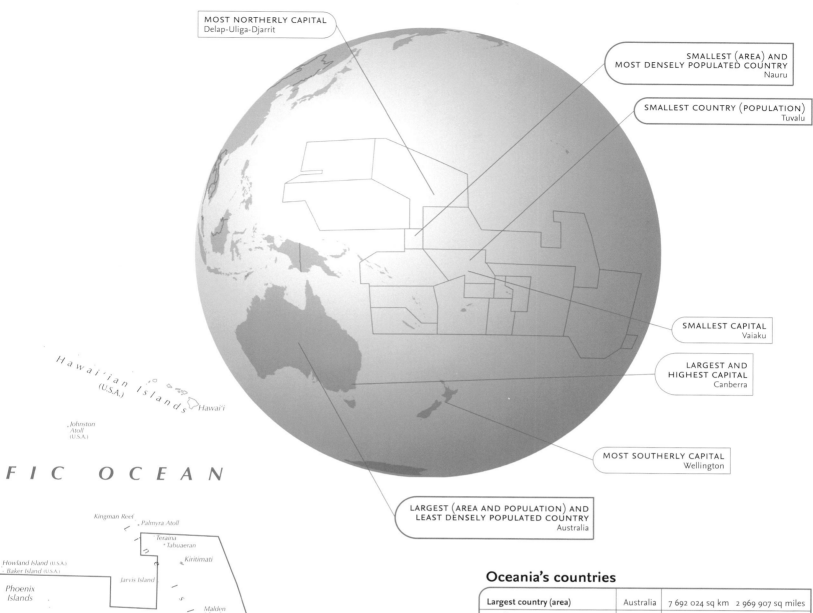

MOST NORTHERLY CAPITAL
Delap-Uliga-Djarrit

SMALLEST (AREA) AND
MOST DENSELY POPULATED COUNTRY
Nauru

SMALLEST COUNTRY (POPULATION)
Tuvalu

SMALLEST CAPITAL
Vaiaku

LARGEST AND
HIGHEST CAPITAL
Canberra

MOST SOUTHERLY CAPITAL
Wellington

LARGEST (AREA AND POPULATION) AND
LEAST DENSELY POPULATED COUNTRY
Australia

Hawai'ian Islands
(U.S.A.)

Hawai'i

Johnston Atoll
(U.S.A.)

FIC OCEAN

Kingman Reef

Palmyra Atoll

Teraina
Tabuaeran

Kiritimati

Howland Island (U.S.A.)
Baker Island (U.S.A.)

Jarvis Island

Phoenix Islands

Malden Island

K I R I B A T I

Starbuck Island

Tokelau
(N.Z.)

Penrhyn

Samoan Islands

Nuku Hiva • *Marquesas Islands*

SAMOA
Savai'i • *Upolu* — *Apia* • *Manu'a Islands*

Hiva Oa

American Samoa
(U.S.A.)

Îles du Roi Georges

Vava'u Group

Îles Palliser

TONGA
Nuku'alofa

Alofi
Niue
(N.Z.)

Cook Islands
(N.Z.)

Aitutaki
Hervey Islands

Society Islands • *Tahiti* • *Moorea*

Tuamotu Islands

F r e n c h

Tongatapu Group

Rarotonga

Tubuai Islands

Îles du Duc de Gloucester

Groupe Actéon

Tubuai

Mururoa

P o l y n e s i a

Îles Gambier

Pitcairn Is
(U.K.) *Henderson Island*

Rapa

Pitcairn Island

Oceania's countries

Largest country (area)	Australia	7 692 024 sq km	2 969 907 sq miles
Smallest country (area)	Nauru	21 sq km	8 sq miles
Largest country (population)	Australia	23 969 000	
Smallest country (population)	Tuvalu	9 916	
Most densely populated country	Nauru	476 per sq km	1 250 per sq mile
Least densely populated country	Australia	3 per sq km	8 per sq mile

Chatham Islands
(N.Z.)

Oceania's capitals

Largest capital (population)	Canberra, Australia	415 000
Smallest capital (population)	Vaiaku, Tuvalu	516
Most northerly capital	Delap-Uliga-Djarrit, Marshall Islands	7° 7'N
Most southerly capital	Wellington, New Zealand	41° 18'S
Highest capital	Canberra, Australia	581 metres 1 906 feet

Wellington, capital of New Zealand.

O C E A N

Oceania
Australia, New Zealand and Southwest Pacific

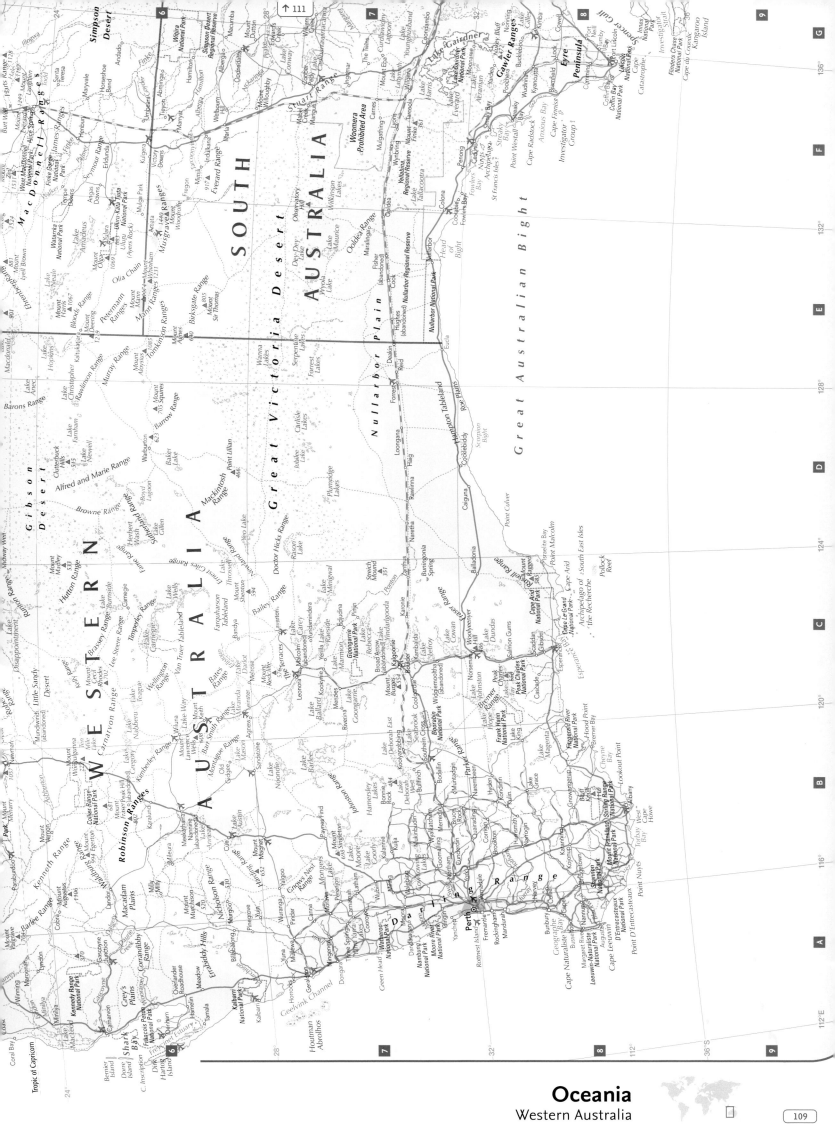

Oceania
Western Australia

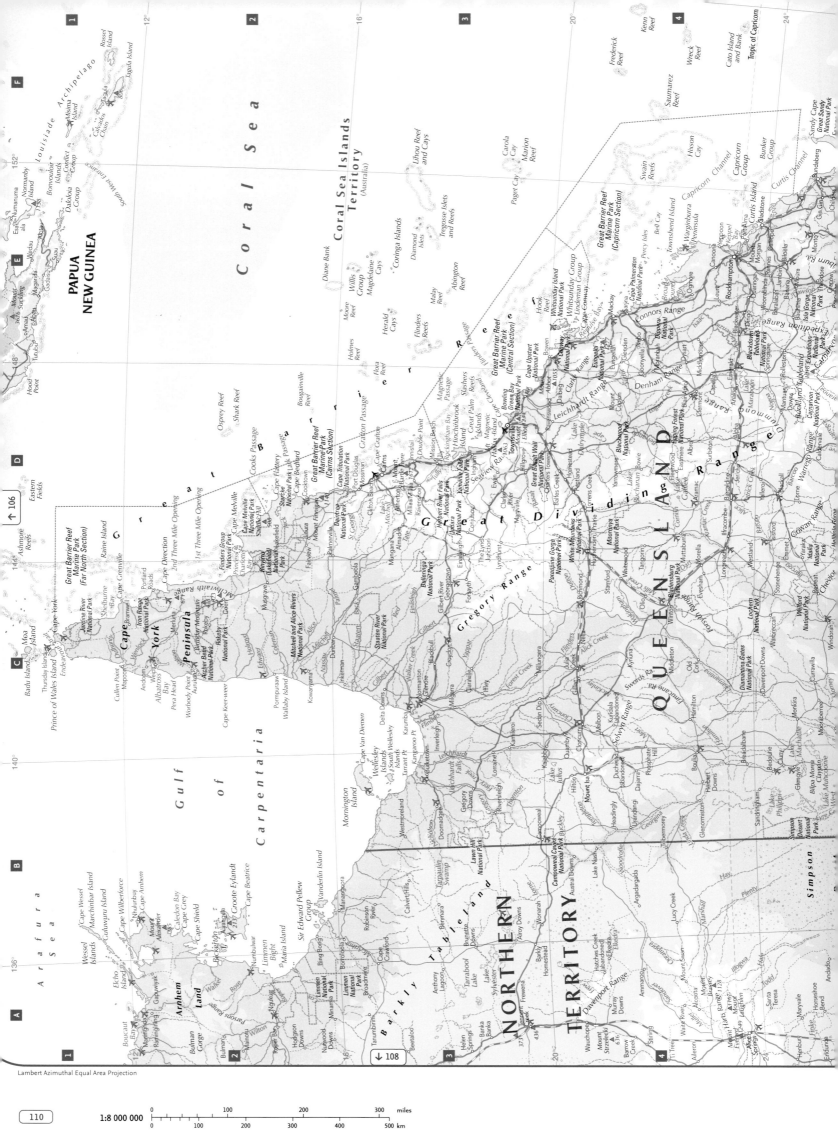

Lambert Azimuthal Equal Area Projection

1:8 000 000

| 0 | 100 | 200 | 300 | miles |

| 0 | 100 | 200 | 300 | 400 | 500 | km |

Oceania
Eastern Australia

Oceania
Southeast Australia

Lambert Azimuthal Equal Area Projection

1:5 000 000

QUEENSLAND

AUSTRALIA

NEW
SOUTH WALES

VICTORIA

AUSTRALIAN
CAPITAL
TERRITORY

JERVIS BAY TERRITORY

Darling
Downs

Tasman

Sea

Bass Strait

Conic Equidistant Projection

1:5 250 000

Oceania
New Zealand

North America
Landscapes

North America, the world's third largest continent, supports a wide range of landscapes from the Arctic north to sub-tropical Central America. The main physiographic regions of the continent are the mountains of the west coast, stretching from Alaska in the north to Mexico and Central America in the south; the vast, relatively flat Canadian Shield; the Great Plains which make up the majority of the interior; the Appalachian Mountains in the east; and the Atlantic coastal plain.

These regions contain some significant physical features, including the Rocky Mountains, the Great Lakes – three of which are amongst the five largest lakes in the world – and the Mississippi-Missouri river system which is the world's fourth longest river. The Caribbean Sea contains a complex pattern of islands, many volcanic in origin, and the continent is joined to South America by the narrow Isthmus of Panama.

Internet Links

● NASA Visible Earth	**visibleearth.nasa.gov**
● U.S. Geological Survey	**www.usgs.gov**
● Natural Resources Canada	**www.nrcan.gc.ca/home**
● Satellite imagery	**www.geo-airbusds.com**

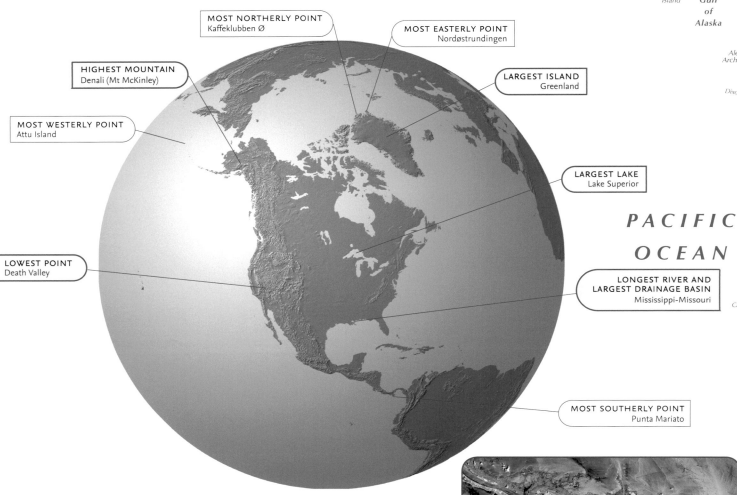

MOST NORTHERLY POINT
Kaffeklubben Ø

MOST EASTERLY POINT
Nordøstrundingen

HIGHEST MOUNTAIN
Denali (Mt McKinley)

LARGEST ISLAND
Greenland

MOST WESTERLY POINT
Attu Island

LARGEST LAKE
Lake Superior

LOWEST POINT
Death Valley

**LONGEST RIVER AND
LARGEST DRAINAGE BASIN**
Mississippi-Missouri

MOST SOUTHERLY POINT
Punta Mariato

PACIFIC OCEAN

North America's physical features

Highest mountain	Denali (Mt McKinley), USA	6 190 metres	20 310 feet
Longest river	Mississippi-Missouri, USA	5 969 km	3 709 miles
Largest lake	Lake Superior, Canada/USA	82 100 sq km	31 699 sq miles
Largest island	Greenland	2 175 600 sq km	839 999 sq miles
Largest drainage basin	Mississippi-Missouri, USA	3 250 000 sq km	1 254 825 sq miles
Lowest point	Death Valley, USA	-86 metres	-282 feet

North America's longest river system, the **Mississippi-Missouri**, flows into the Gulf of Mexico through the Mississippi Delta.

North America's extent

TOTAL LAND AREA (including Hawai'ian Islands)	24 680 331 sq km / 9 529 076 sq miles
Most northerly point	Kaffeklubben Ø, Greenland
Most southerly point	Punta Mariato, Panama
Most westerly point	Attu Island, USA
Most easterly point	Nordøstrundingen, Greenland

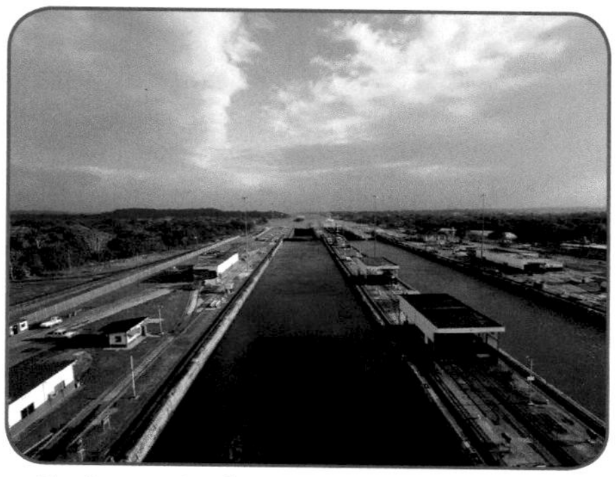

The **Panama Canal,** Panama, linking the Pacific Ocean to the Atlantic Ocean.

Facts

- Devon Island, Canada, is the world's largest uninhabited island
- Canada has the longest coastline of any country in the world
- Lake Superior is the world's largest freshwater lake
- Over 320 000 square kilometres of the USA is protected for conservation purposes

ARCTIC OCEAN
Kaffeklubben Ø
Greenland Sea
Shannon Ø
Kong Frederik VIII Land
Kong Oscars Fjord
Kangertittivaq
Kong Christian X Land
Denmark Strait
Kong Christian IX Land
Greenland
3000
2000
1000
Qimusseriarsuaq
Qeqertarsuaq
Davis Strait
Kong Frederik VI Kyst
Cape Farewell
Ellesmere Island
Axel Heiberg Island
Ellef Ringnes Island
Borden Island
Queen Elizabeth Islands
Nares Strait
Point Barrow
Prince Patrick Island
Parry Islands
Melville Island
Devon Island
Beaufort Sea
Banks Island
Parry Channel
Bylot Island
Baffin Bay
Prince of Wales Island
Somerset Island
Brodeur Peninsula
Gulf of Boothia
Boothia Peninsula
Victoria Island
King William Island
Queen Maud Gulf
Baffin Island
Home Bay
Cumberland Peninsula
Cumberland Sound
Prince Charles Island
Nettilling Lake
Melville Peninsula
Foxe Basin
Foxe Pen.
Amadjuak Lake
Frobisher Bay
Southampton Island
Hudson Strait
C. Chidley
Labrador Sea
Coats Island
Mansel Island
Péninsule d'Ungava
Ungava Bay
Hudson Bay
Labrador
Lac Caniapiscau
Smallwood Reservoir
Laurentian Plateau
Belcher Islands
Lac Bienville
James Bay
Réservoir La Grande
Newfoundland
Cape Race
Île d'Anticosti
Gulf of St Lawrence
Cabot Strait
Cape Breton Island
ATLANTIC OCEAN
Sable Island
Nova Scotia
Bay of Fundy
Cape Sable
Massachusetts Bay
Cape Cod
Long Island
Chesapeake Bay
Cape Hatteras
Cape Fear
Porcupine
Yukon
Mackenzie
Mackenzie Mountains
Selwyn Mountains
Cassiar Mountains
Great Bear Lake
Liard
Dubawnt Lake
Great Slave Lake
Caribou Mountains
Lake Athabasca
Athabasca
Wollaston Lake
Reindeer Lake
Churchill
Southern Indian Lake
Nelson
Peace
Fraser
Mount Robson 3954
North Saskatchewan
Saskatchewan
South Saskatchewan
Severn
Albany
Lake Winnipeg
Lake Winnipegosis
Canadian Shield
Lake Nipigon
Great Lakes
Lake Superior
Lake Michigan
Lake Huron
Lake Erie
Lake Ontario
Ottawa
St Lawrence
Hudson
Lake of the Woods
Coast Mountains
Vancouver Island
Rocky Mountains
Mount Rainier 4392
Cascade Range
F. D. Roosevelt Lake
Columbia
Coast Ranges
Bitterroot Range
Fort Peck Reservoir
Missouri
Yellowstone
Lake Sakakawea
Great Plains
Lake Oahe
Snake
Great Salt Lake
Great Basin
Sierra Nevada
San Joaquin
Death Valley
Sangre de Cristo Range
Mount Elbert 4398
Colorado
Grand Canyon
Colorado Plateau
Platte
Arkansas
Mississippi
Illinois
Ohio
Lake of the Ozarks
Ozark Plateau
Allegheny Mts
Appalachian Mountains
Mount Mitchell 2037
Tennessee
Alabama
Canadian
Rio Grande
Gila
Llano Estacado
Pecos
Edwards Plateau
Brazos
Red
Coastal Plain
Guadalupe
Baja California
Gulf of California
Yaqui
Conchos
Sierra Madre Occidental
Sierra Madre Oriental
Cape Canaveral
Grand Bahama
The Bahamas
Great Abaco
Mississippi Delta
Padre Island
Gulf of Mexico
Straits of Florida
Andros
West Indies
Acklins Island
Turks and Caicos Islands
Great Inagua
Virgin Islands
Anguilla
Puerto Rico
Guadaloupe
Dominica
Martinique
St Lucia
Barbados
Cuba
Hispaniola
Cayman Islands
Greater Antilles
Lesser Antilles
Jamaica
Yucatan Channel
Cabo Falso
Cabo Corrientes
Yucatán
Bahía de Campeche
Islas Revillagigedo
Volcán Popocatépetl 5452
Sierra Madre del Sur
Islas de la Bahía
Caribbean Sea
Tobago
Trinidad
Aruba
Curaçao
Sierra Madre
Gulf of Tehuantepec
Golfo de Fonseca
Lake Nicaragua
Peninsula de Nicoya
Cordillera Central
Panama Canal
Golfo del Darién
Isthmus of Panama
Gulf of Panamá
SOUTH AMERICA
Île Clipperton

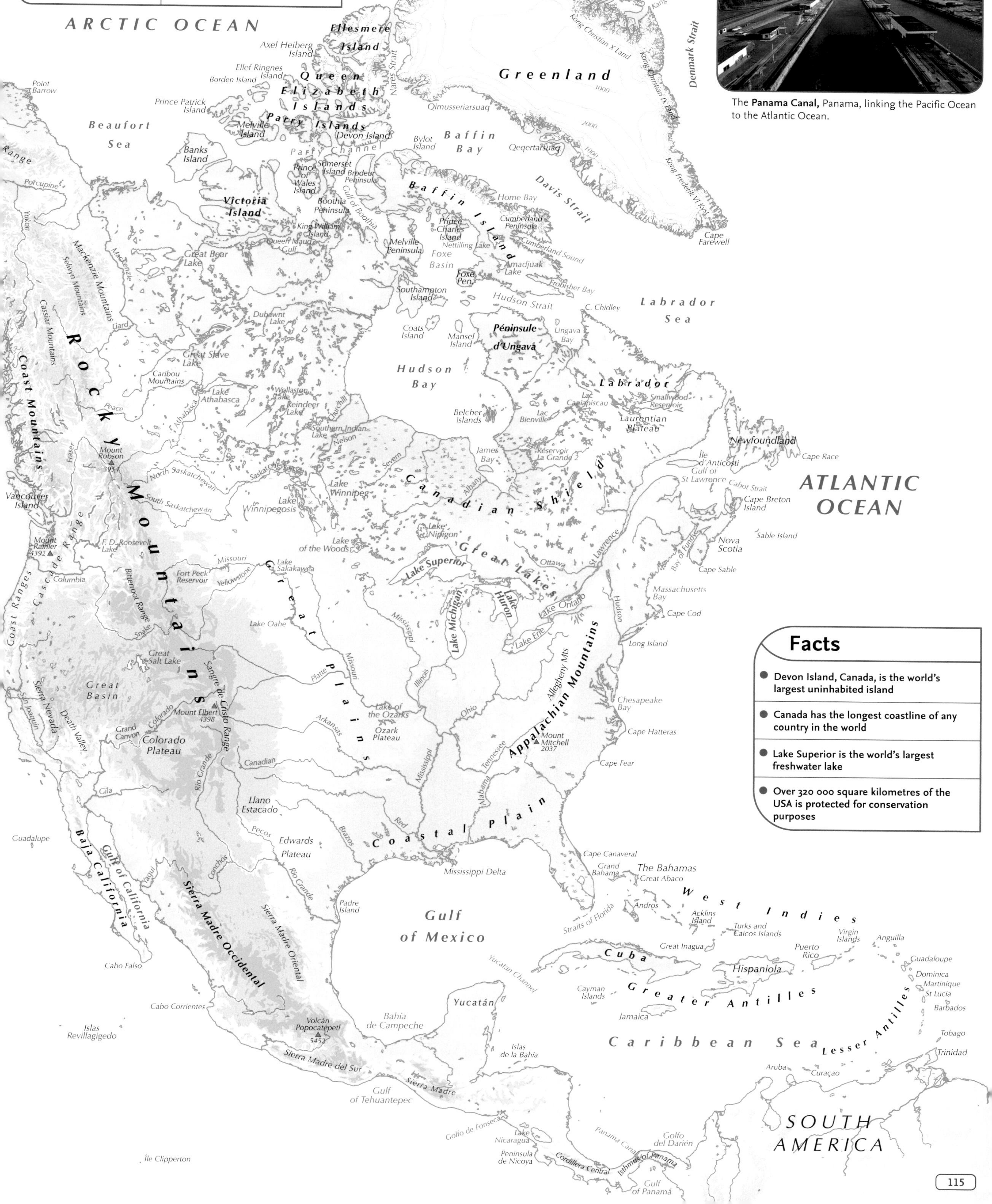

North America
Countries

North America has been dominated economically and politically by the USA since the nineteenth century. Before that, the continent was subject to colonial influences, particularly of Spain in the south and of Britain and France in the east. The nineteenth century saw the steady development of the western half of the continent. The wealth of natural resources and the generally temperate climate were an excellent basis for settlement, agriculture and industrial development which has led to the USA being the richest nation in the world today.

Although there are twenty-three independent countries and fourteen dependent territories in North America, Canada, Mexico and the USA have approximately eighty-five per cent of the continent's population and eighty-eight per cent of its land area. Large parts of the north remain sparsely populated, while the most densely populated areas are in the northeast USA, and the Caribbean.

North America's capitals

Largest capital (population)	Mexico City, Mexico	21 706 000
Smallest capital (population)	Roseau, Dominica	15 000
Most northerly capital	Ottawa, Canada	45° 25'N
Most southerly capital	Panama City, Panama	8° 56'N
Highest capital	Mexico City, Mexico	2 300 metres 7 546 feet

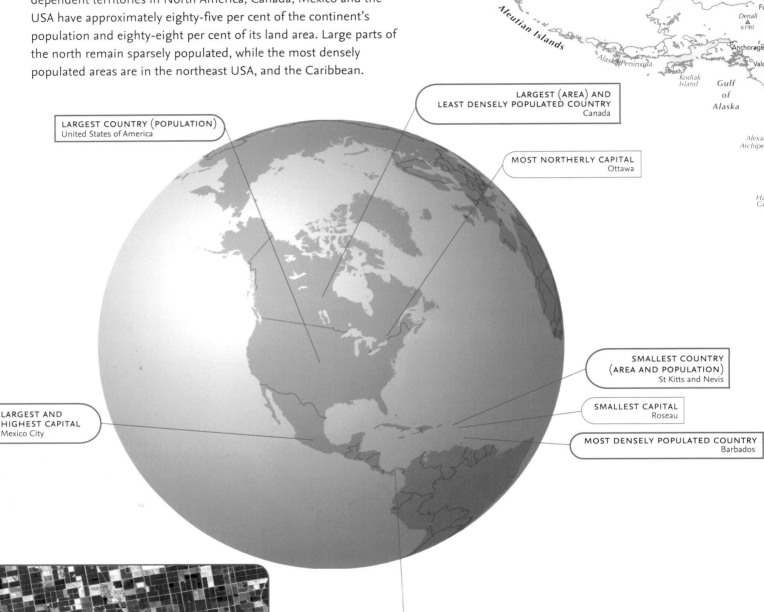

LARGEST COUNTRY (POPULATION)
United States of America

LARGEST (AREA) AND LEAST DENSELY POPULATED COUNTRY
Canada

MOST NORTHERLY CAPITAL
Ottawa

SMALLEST COUNTRY (AREA AND POPULATION)
St Kitts and Nevis

SMALLEST CAPITAL
Roseau

MOST DENSELY POPULATED COUNTRY
Barbados

LARGEST AND HIGHEST CAPITAL
Mexico City

MOST SOUTHERLY CAPITAL
Panama City

False-colour satellite image of the **Mexico-USA** boundary at Mexicali.

North America's countries

Largest country (area)	Canada	9 984 670 sq km	3 855 103 sq miles
Smallest country (area)	St Kitts and Nevis	261 sq km	101 sq miles
Largest country (population)	United States of America	321 774 000	
Smallest country (population)	St Kitts and Nevis	56 000	
Most densely populated country	Barbados	663 per sq km	1 717 per sq mile
Least densely populated country	Canada	4 per sq km	9 per sq mile

The Bahamas, a chain of islands in the North Atlantic Ocean, lying southeast of Florida, USA.

Facts

- ● The Panama Canal, opened in 1914, cut the journey between the Atlantic and the Pacific by over 14 000 km

- ● Mexico City is the highest city in North America and houses approximately 18% of Mexico's population

- ● The state of Alaska was bought by the USA from Russia in 1867

- ● The territory of Nunavut is Canada's newest administrative division, created in 1999 from the eastern part of Northwest Territories

Station Nord

Greenland Sea

Daneborg

Greenland
(Denmark)

Ellesmere Island

Queen Elizabeth Islands

Parry Islands

Barrow

Beaufort Sea

A.

Dundas

Nuussuaq

Ammassalik

Ilulissat

Melville Island

Devon Island

Banks Island

Sachs Harbour

Inuvik

Dawson

Potcupine

Prince of Wales Island

Somerset Island

Parry Channel

Pond Inlet

Clyde River

Davis Strait

Nuuk

Nanortalik

Juneau

YUKON

Whitehorse

Déline

Fort Simpson

Yellowknife

Great Bear Lake

Victoria Island

Hall Beach

Prince Charles Island

Baffin Island

Baffin Bay

Cumberland Sound

Cape Dorset

Iqaluit

NORTHWEST TERRITORIES

NUNAVUT

Foxe Basin

Repulse Bay

Fort Nelson

Liard

Fort Simpson

Great Slave Lake

Uranium City

Lake Athabasca

Southampton Island

Chesterfield Inlet

Arviat

Hudson Bay

Ivujivik

Kangirsuk

Ungava Bay

Nain

NEWFOUNDLAND AND LABRADOR

Strait of Belle Isle

Prince Rupert

BRITISH COLUMBIA

ALBERTA

Grande Prairie

Jasper

Fort McMurray

La Ronge

SASKATCHEWAN

The Pas

Churchill

Churchill

Nelson

Lake Winnipeg

Severn

MANITOBA

James Bay

Moosonee

Chisasibi

Reservoir La Grande 2

Schefferville

Smallwood Reservoir

QUÉBEC

Gander

Newfoundland

Corner Brook

St John's

C A N A D A

Peace

Kamloops

Vancouver Island

Vancouver

Victoria

Calgary

Lethbridge

Medicine Hat

Edmonton

Lloydminster

Saskatoon

Regina

Winnipeg

Thunder Bay

International Falls

Sault Sainte Marie

ONTARIO

Lake Nipigon

Rouyn-Noranda

Chicoutimi

Québec

Montréal

Ottawa

St Lawrence

Gulf of St Lawrence

Île d'Anticosti

Sept-Îles

Cabot Strait

St Pierre and Miquelon
(France)

P.E.I.

Charlottetown

NEW BRUNSWICK

Fredericton

NOVA SCOTIA

Halifax

Sable Island

Cape Sable

MAINE

Augusta

Olympia

WASHINGTON

Seattle

Spokane

Portland

Salem

Olympia

Columbia

OREGON

Boise

IDAHO

Helena

MONTANA

Missouri

Yellowstone

Billings

NORTH DAKOTA

Bismarck

Grand Forks

MINNESOTA

Duluth

Pierre

SOUTH DAKOTA

Sioux Falls

Minneapolis

St Paul

WISCONSIN

Madison

Milwaukee

Lake Superior

Lake Michigan

Lake Huron

MICHIGAN

Lansing

Detroit

Lake Erie

Lake Ontario

Toronto

Buffalo

Erie

NEW YORK

Albany

VT.

N.H.

Montpelier

Concord

Boston

MASS.

Providence

RHODE I.

Hartford

CONNECTICUT

New York

N.J.

Trenton

Philadelphia

PENNSYLVANIA

Pittsburgh

Dover

DELAWARE

WYOMING

Casper

Cheyenne

Snake

Great Salt Lake

Salt Lake City

Reno

Carson City

Sacramento

San Francisco

San Jose

NEVADA

Las Vegas

UTAH

Denver

Colorado Springs

COLORADO

Colorado

NEBRASKA

North Platte

Omaha

Platte

Des Moines

IOWA

Missouri

Chicago

ILLINOIS

Indianapolis

INDIANA

Columbus

OHIO

Cleveland

Columbus

Cincinnati

Frankfort

KENTUCKY

Charleston

W.V.

Richmond

VIRGINIA

Washington D.C.

MD.

Annapolis

Baltimore

Raleigh

N. CAROLINA

Charlotte

Cape Hatteras

U N I T E D   S T A T E S
O F   A M E R I C A

CALIFORNIA

Los Angeles

San Diego

KANSAS

Topeka

Wichita

Arkansas

MISSOURI

Jefferson City

Kansas City

St Louis

Nashville

Knoxville

TENNESSEE

Memphis

Ohio

Columbia

S. CAROLINA

ARIZONA

Phoenix

Tucson

Mexicali

Ensenada

Guadalupe (Mex.)

Baja California

Gulf of California

NEW MEXICO

Albuquerque

Rio Grande

OKLAHOMA

Oklahoma City

Little Rock

ARKANSAS

MISS.

Jackson

ALABAMA

Montgomery

GEORGIA

Atlanta

Columbus

Alabama

Nashville

El Paso

Ciudad Juárez

Hermosillo

Chihuahua

Conchos

Los Mochis

La Paz

Durango

Mazatlán

MEXICO

Islas Revillagigedo (Mex.)

Tepic

Guadalajara

León

San Luis Potosí

Mexico City

5452

Volcán Popocatépetl

TEXAS

Fort Worth

Dallas

Pecos

Rio Grande

Brazos

Austin

San Antonio

Houston

Corpus Christi

Nuevo Laredo

Monterrey

Matamoros

Tampico

Veracruz

LOUISIANA

Baton Rouge

New Orleans

Mississippi

Jacksonville

Tallahassee

Orlando

Tampa

FLORIDA

Miami

Gulf of Mexico

Straits of Florida

THE BAHAMAS

Nassau

Turks & Caicos Islands (U.K.)

Havana

Santa Clara

Holguin

CUBA

Cayman Islands (U.K.)

Montego Bay

Kingston

JAMAICA

Greater Antilles

HAITI

Port-au-Prince

DOMINICAN REP.

Santo Domingo

San Juan

Puerto Rico (U.S.A.)

Virgin Islands (U.K.)

Virgin Islands (U.S.A.)

Anguilla (U.K.)

ANTIGUA & BARBUDA

Montserrat (U.K.)

ST KITTS & NEVIS

Guadeloupe (France)

DOMINICA

Martinique (Fr.)

ST LUCIA

BARBADOS

ST VINCENT & THE GRENADINES

GRENADA

TRINIDAD & TOBAGO

Port of Spain

Lesser Antilles

Caribbean Sea

Aruba (Neth.)

Curaçao (Neth.)

BELIZE

Belmopan

San Pedro Sula

GUATEMALA

HONDURAS

Tegucigalpa

San Salvador

EL SALVADOR

NICARAGUA

Managua

Lake Nicaragua

COSTA RICA

San José

Colón

PANAMA

Panama City

Golfo de los Mosquitos

Golfo del Darién

Gulf of Panama

Mérida

Yucatán

Campeche

Bahía de Campeche

Villahermosa

Oaxaca

Acapulco

Gulf of Tehuantepec

Yucatán Channel

Ciudad Victoria

P A C I F I C

O C E A N

Île Clipperton (France)

S O U T H

A M E R I C A

A T L A N T I C
O C E A N

PACIFIC

OCEAN

ARCTIC

OCEAN

Beaufort Sea

Bering

Sea

Gulf

of

Alaska

U.S.A.

ALASKA

RUSSIA

INUVIALUIT

NORTHWEST TERRITORIES

YUKON

BRITISH

COLUMBIA

ALBERTA

SASKATCHEWAN

CANADA

Victoria

Vancouver

Island

WASHINGTON

OREGON

IDAHO

MONTANA

NORTH

DAKOTA

WYOMING

SOUTH

DAKOTA

NEBRASKA

NEVADA

UTAH

CALIFORNIA

UNITED STATES OF

Edmonton

Calgary

Vancouver

Seattle

Portland

San Francisco

San Jose

Sacramento

Aleutian Islands

↓ 124

Lambert Conformal Conic Projection

1:16 000 000

0   200   400   miles

0   200   400   600   800   km

North America
Canada

Conic Equidistant Projection

1:7 000 000

North America
Western Canada

North America
Eastern Canada

Lambert Conformal Conic Projection

1:12 000 000

| 0 | 100 | 200 | 300 | 400 | miles |

| 0 | 100 | 200 | 300 | 400 | 500 | 600 | 700 | km |

North America
United States of America

Lambert Conformal Conic Projection

1:7 000 000

miles
100   200

0   100   200   300   400 km

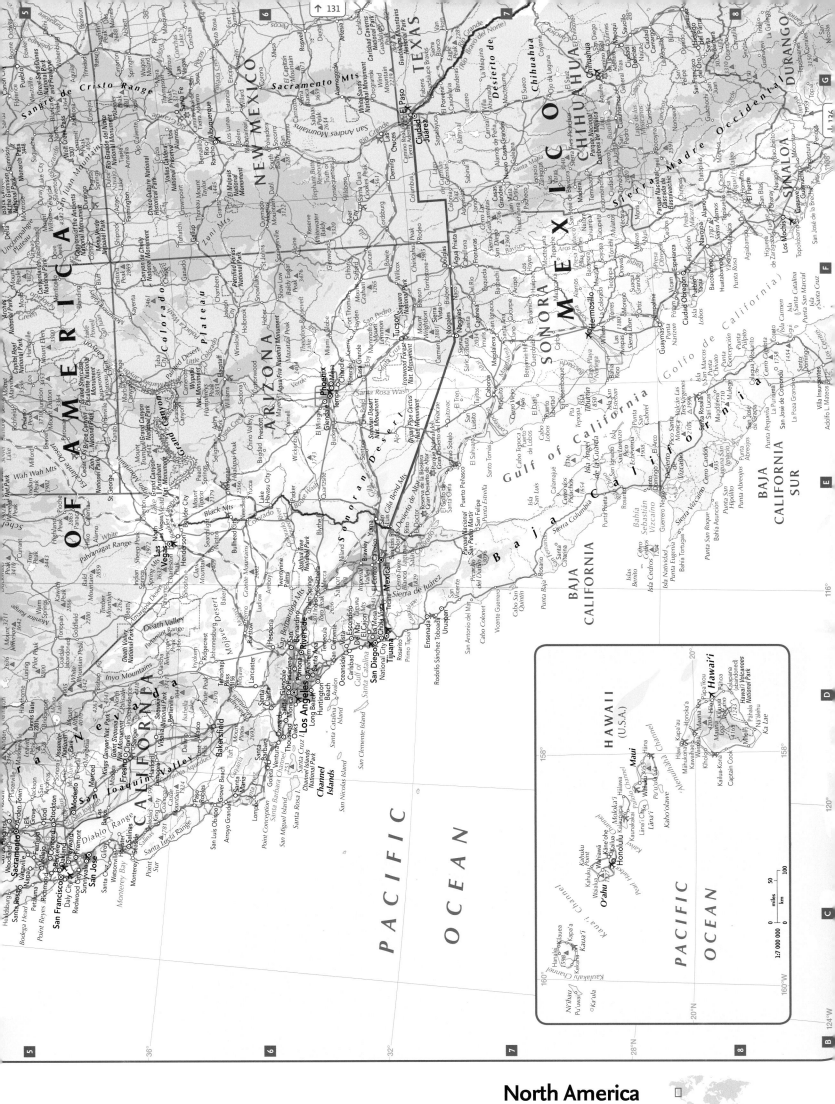

North America

Western United States

Lambert Conformal Conic Projection

1:3 500 000

↑ 133

↓ 127

→ 136

North America
Central United States

States in the U.S.A.
numbered on the map:

1. CONNECTICUT (F3)
2. DELAWARE (F4)
3. MASSACHUSETTS (F3)
4. RHODE ISLAND (G3)

Lambert Conformal Conic Projection

132

1:7 000 000

0   100   200   miles

0   100   200   300   400   km

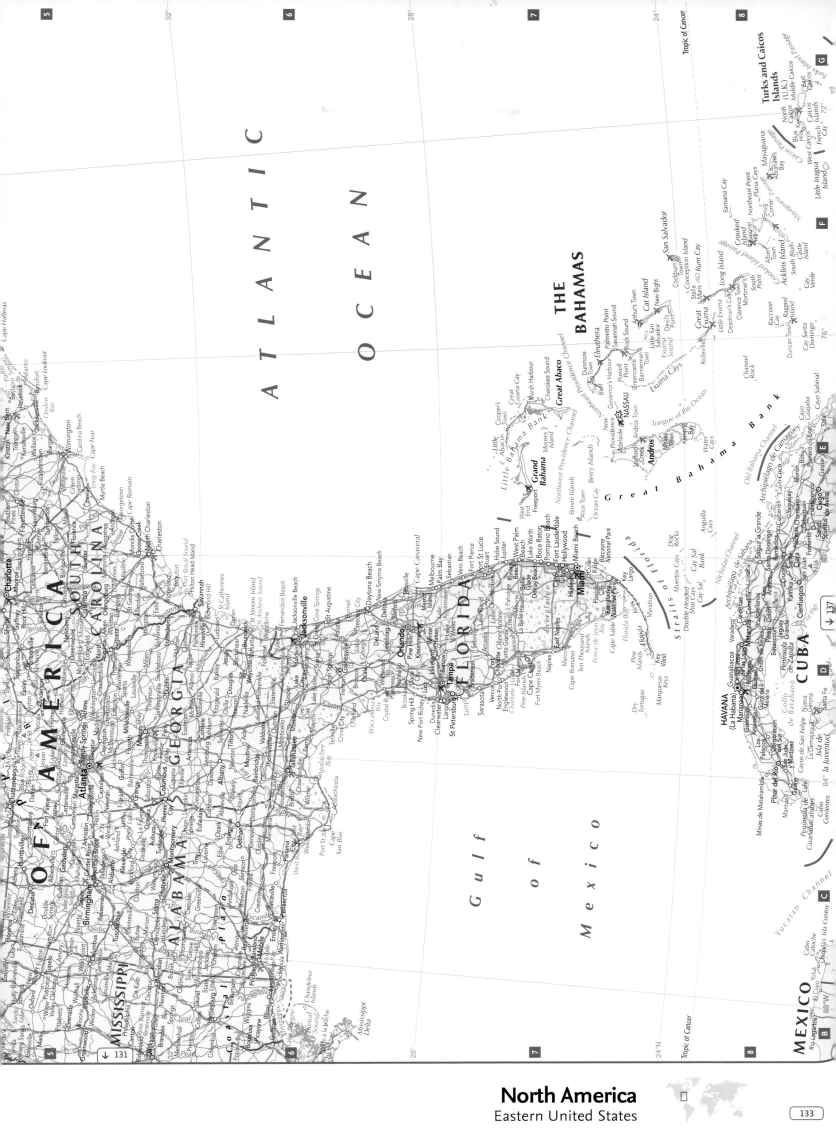

North America
Eastern United States

Lambert Conformal Conic Projection

1:3 500 000

0   50   100   miles

0   50   100   150   200   km

North America
Northeast United States

PACIFIC

OCEAN

Gulf

of

Mexico

Bahía
de Campeche

Gulf of
Tehuantepec

MEXICO

Baja California

Gulf of California

UNITED STATES OF AMERICA

CALIFORNIA

ARIZONA

NEW MEXICO

TEXAS

OKLAHOMA

KANSAS

MISSOURI

ARKANSAS

LOUISIANA

MISSISSIPPI

TENN

ILLINOIS

AL

COLORADO

Tropic of Cancer

GUATEMALA

BELIZE

EL SALVADOR

HO

Yucatán

Islas
Revillagigedo
(Mexico)

Guadalupe
(Mexico)

Isla
Socorro

Isla
San Benedicto

Isla
Clarión

Île Clipperton
(France)

Lambert Conformal Conic Projection

1:14 000 000

| 0 | 200 | 400 | miles |

| 0 | 200 | 400 | 600 | 800 km |

ATLANTIC

OCEAN

HAMILTON ✈ **Bermuda**
(U.K.)

Tropic of Cancer

THE BAHAMAS

Little
Abaco
Marsh Harbour
Great Abaco
Grand
Bahama Eleuthera
Freeport Governor's
Harbour
Berry
Islands Bimini
Islands ✈ NASSAU
Andros Town Cat Island
Andros San Salvador
Exuma Sound
Great Exuma Rum Cay
Long
Island
W
e
s
Crooked Island t
Turks and
Mayaguana Caicos Islands I
Caicos (U.K.) n
Acklins Islands d
Island GRAND TURK i
Great (Cockburn Town) e
Inagua Turks s
Matthew Islands
Town Silver Bank

HAVANA
(La Habana)
Cárdenas
Matanzas Sagua
Santa Clara la Grande
Guane Pinar del Río Guines Cienfuegos Sancti
Spiritus
Trinidad Ciego
de Ávila Nuevitas
Las
Tunas Cabo
Lucrecia
Banes
Puerto
CUBA Camagüey
Santa Cruz Holguín Baracoa
del Sur
1994 Bayamo Hispaniola
Manzanillo Santiago Guantánamo Monte Puerto
de Cuba Port-de-Paix Cristi Plata
Cap-Haïtien Santiago
HAITI St-Marc Pico La Vega
Île de Duarte
la Gonâve Elías San Pedro Higüey
PORT-AU- Piña de Macorís La Romana
PRINCE SANTO
Jérémie DOMINGO Puerto Rico
Les Jacmel Barahona (U.S.A.)
Cayes DOMINICAN
Cabo REPUBLIC
Beata

Virgin
Islands
(U.K.)
ROAD
TOWN
SAN
JUAN ✈
CHARLOTTE St Maarten
AMALIE (Neth.)
Mayagüez Virgin
Ponce Islands
(U.S.A.)

Anguilla
(U.K.)
THE VALLEY
St-Martin (France)
St-Barthélemy
(France) Barbuda
St Eustatius (Neth.) ANTIGUA
BASSETERRE AND BARBUDA
ST KITTS ST JOHN'S
AND NEVIS Antigua
Montserrat
(U.K.)
BASSE- Guadeloupe
TERRE (France)
Pointe-à-Pitre
Marie-Galante
DOMINICA
ROSEAU
FORT-DE-FRANCE ✈
Martinique
(France)
CASTRIES ST LUCIA
Kingstown BARBADOS
St Vincent Passage BRIDGETOWN
ST VINCENT
AND
THE GRENADINES
The Grenadines
GRENADA
ST GEORGE'S

BRAZIL

South America
Landscapes

South America is a continent of great contrasts, with landscapes varying from the tropical rainforests of the Amazon Basin, to the Atacama Desert, the driest place on earth, and the sub-Antarctic regions of southern Chile and Argentina. The dominant physical features are the Andes, stretching along the entire west coast of the continent and containing numerous mountains over 6 000 metres high, and the Amazon, which is the second longest river in the world and has the world's largest drainage basin.

The Altiplano is a high plateau lying between two of the Andes ranges. It contains Lake Titicaca, the world's highest navigable lake. By contrast, large lowland areas dominate the centre of the continent, lying between the Andes and the Guiana and Brazilian Highlands. These vast grasslands stretch from the Llanos of the north through the Selvas and the Gran Chaco to the Pampas of Argentina.

Confluence of the **Amazon** and **Negro** rivers at Manaus, northern Brazil.

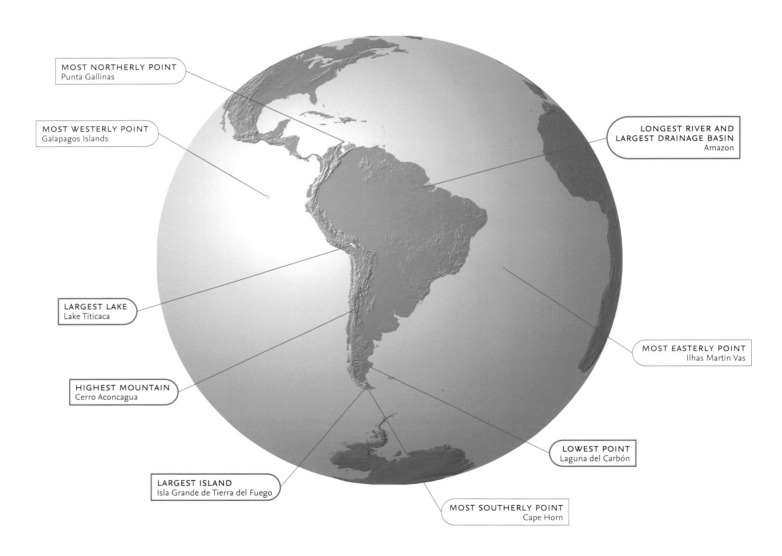

MOST NORTHERLY POINT
Punta Gallinas

MOST WESTERLY POINT
Galapagos Islands

LONGEST RIVER AND
LARGEST DRAINAGE BASIN
Amazon

LARGEST LAKE
Lake Titicaca

HIGHEST MOUNTAIN
Cerro Aconcagua

MOST EASTERLY POINT
Ilhas Martin Vas

LOWEST POINT
Laguna del Carbón

LARGEST ISLAND
Isla Grande de Tierra del Fuego

MOST SOUTHERLY POINT
Cape Horn

South America's physical features

Highest mountain	Cerro Aconcagua, Argentina	6 959 metres	22 831 feet
Longest river	Amazon	6 516 km	4 049 miles
Largest lake	Lake Titicaca, Bolivia/Peru	8 340 sq km	3 220 sq miles
Largest island	Isla Grande de Tierra del Fuego, Argentina/Chile	47 000 sq km	18 147 sq miles
Largest drainage basin	Amazon	7 050 000 sq km	2 722 005 sq miles
Lowest point	Laguna del Carbón, Argentina	-105 metres	-345 feet

Caribbean Sea

NORTH AMERICA

Punta Gallinas

Isla
de Margarita

Golfo de Venezuela

Orinoco
Delta   Waini Point

Golfo
del Darién

Lake
Maracaibo

Orinoco

Cabo Corrientes

Cerro Yavi
2285 ▲

Guiana Highlands

La Gran
Sabana

Pakaraima Mountains

Cabo Orange

Gulf
of Panama

Cordillera Occidental

Cordillera Central

Magdalena

Cordillera Oriental

Llanos

Meta

Ilha de Maracá

Isla de Malpelo

Guaviare

Orinoco

Branco

Mouths of
the Amazon

Caquetá

Amazon   Basin

Amazon

Ilha
de Marajó

Volcán Cotopaxi
5896 ▲

Putumayo

Japurá

Represa
de Balbina

Negro

Point Isère

Maroni

6310 ▲
Chimborazo

Amazon

Yavari

Juruá

Purus

Madeira

Tapajós

Xingu

Tocantins

Represa
Tucuruí

Baía de São Marcos

Parnaíba

Cabo
de São
Roque

Punta Santa Elena

Golfo de Guayaquil

Marañón

Ucayali

S e l v a s

Madeira

Teles Pires

Iriri

Galapagos Islands

Punta Negra

Nevado
de Huascarán
6768 ▲

A n d e s

Cordillera Central

Cordillera Oriental

Beni

Mamoré

Guaporé

Juruena

Arinos

Araguaia

Tocantins

Barragem
de Sobradinho

São Francisco

Chapada Diamantina

PACIFIC
OCEAN

Cordillera Oriental

Cordillera Occidental

Altiplano

Yungas

Lake
Titicaca

Lago
de San Luis

San Miguel

Paraguai

Represa
Serra da Mesa

São Francisco

Cabo Santo Antonio

Ponta da Baleia

South America's extent

TOTAL LAND AREA	17 815 420 sq km / 6 878 534 sq miles
Most northerly point	Punta Gallinas, Colombia
Most southerly point	Cape Horn, Chile
Most westerly point	Galapagos Islands, Ecuador
Most easterly point	Ilhas Martin Vas, Atlantic Ocean

Punta de Coles

Bañados
del Izozog

Pantanal

Brazilian
Highlands

Cabo de São Tomé

Lago de Poopó

Salar
de
Uyuni

Gran Chaco

Pilcomayo

Paraguay

Paraná

Paranapanema

Punta Tetas

Atacama Desert

Teuco

Salado

Punta Ballena

Nevado Ojos
del Salado
6908 ▲
Cerro Bonete
6872 ▲

Ilha de São Sebastião

Iguaçu
Falls

Iguaçu

Paraná

Islas
Desventuradas

Salinas Grandes

Salado

Uruguay

ATLANTIC
OCEAN

Archipiélago
Juan Fernández

A n d e s

Cerro
Aconcagua
6959 ▲

Sierras de Córdoba

Desaguadero

Pampas

Paraná

Negro

Lagoa
dos Patos

Serra do Mar

Salado

Lagoa Mirim

Punta Lavapié

Colorado

Río de la Plata
Punta Norte
Punta Sur

Facts

● Water flow along the Amazon is over 1 500 times that of the River Thames

● Cerro Aconcagua, 6 959 metres, is the highest point in the western hemisphere

● The Amazon rainforest supports approximately half of all the world's living species

● The Pantanal in Brazil is the largest area of wetland in the world

● The world's driest desert is the Atacama, where only 1mm of rain may fall as infrequently as once every 5–20 years

Punta Galera

Negro

Bahía Blanca

Golfo San Matías

Isla de Chiloé

Chubut

Península
Valdés

P a t a g o n i a

Golfo de
San Jorge

Cabo Tres Puntas

Archipiélago
de los Chonos

Golfo de Penas

Lago San Martín

Lago Argentino

Bahía Grande

West
Falkland   East
Falkland

Falkland Islands

Strait of Magellan

Isla Grande
de Tierra del Fuego

Isla de los Estados

South Georgia

Cape Horn

Drake Passage

Scotia Sea

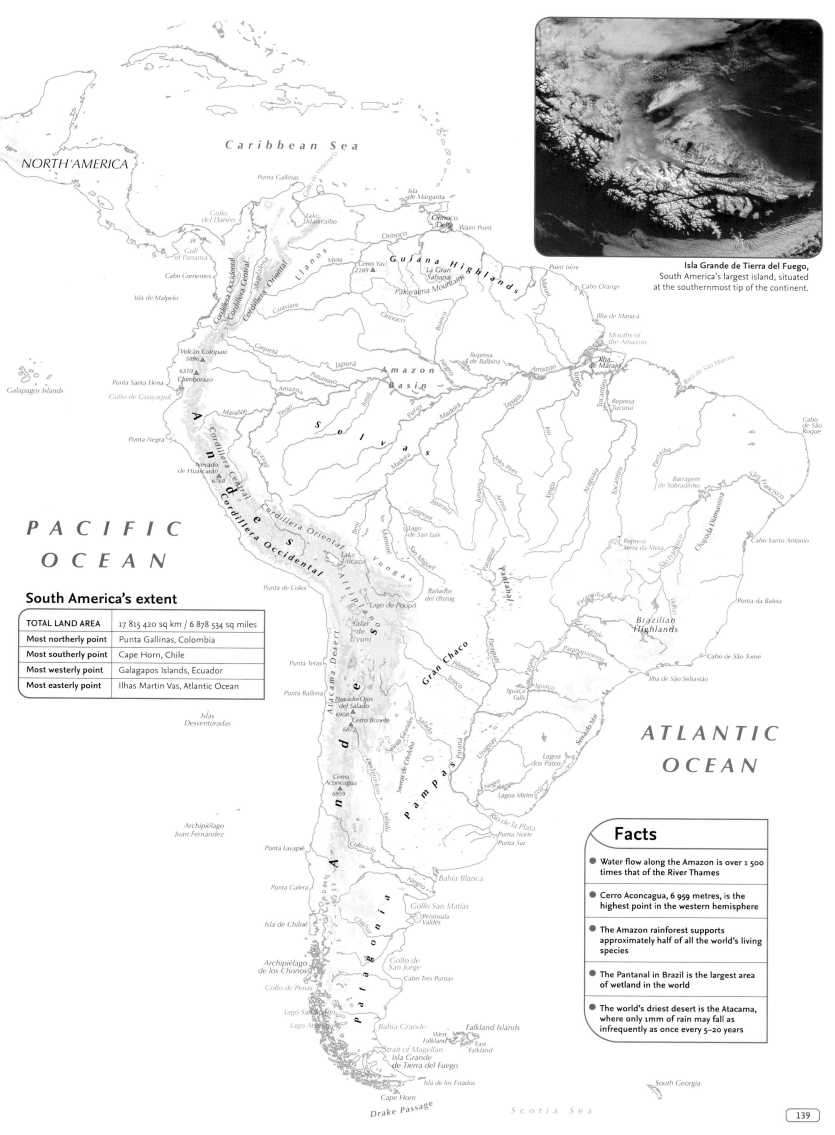

Isla Grande de Tierra del Fuego,
South America's largest island, situated
at the southernmost tip of the continent.

South America
Countries

French Guiana, a French Department, is the only remaining territory under overseas control on a continent which has seen a long colonial history. Much of South America was colonized by Spain in the sixteenth century, with Britain, Portugal and the Netherlands each claiming territory in the northeast of the continent. This colonization led to the conquering of ancient civilizations, including the Incas in Peru. Most countries became independent from Spain and Portugal in the early nineteenth century.

The population of the continent reflects its history, being composed primarily of indigenous Indian peoples and mestizos – reflecting the long Hispanic influence. There has been a steady process of urbanization within the continent, with major movements of the population from rural to urban areas. The majority of the population now lives in the major cities and within 300 kilometres of the coast.

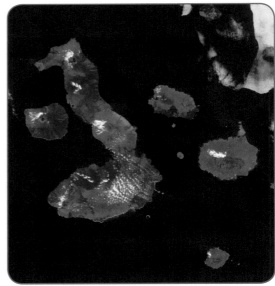

Galapagos Islands, an island territory of Ecuador which lies on the equator in the eastern Pacific Ocean over 900 kilometres west of the coast of Ecuador.

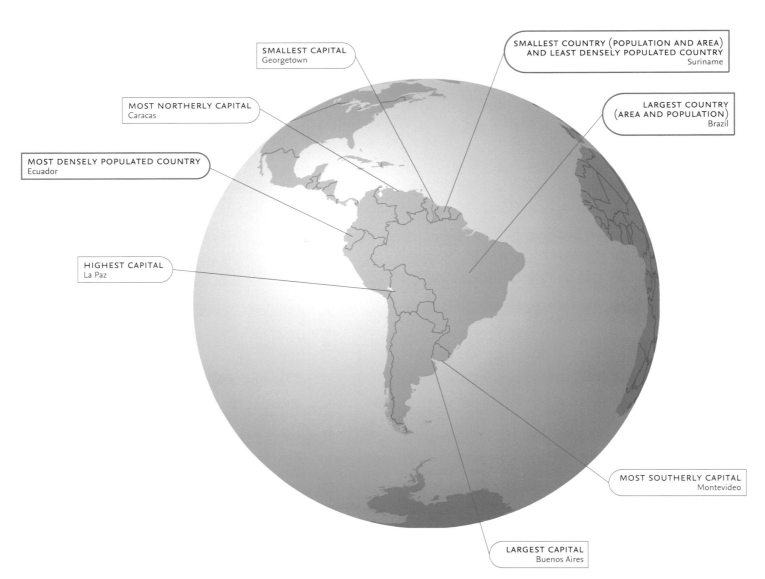

SMALLEST CAPITAL
Georgetown

SMALLEST COUNTRY (POPULATION AND AREA) AND LEAST DENSELY POPULATED COUNTRY
Suriname

MOST NORTHERLY CAPITAL
Caracas

LARGEST COUNTRY (AREA AND POPULATION)
Brazil

MOST DENSELY POPULATED COUNTRY
Ecuador

HIGHEST CAPITAL
La Paz

MOST SOUTHERLY CAPITAL
Montevideo

LARGEST CAPITAL
Buenos Aires

South America's countries

Largest country (area)	Brazil	8 514 879 sq km	3 287 613 sq miles
Smallest country (area)	Suriname	163 820 sq km	63 251 sq miles
Largest country (population)	Brazil	207 848 000	
Smallest country (population)	Suriname	543 000	
Most densely populated country	Ecuador	58 per sq km	150 per sq mile
Least densely populated country	Suriname	3 per sq km	9 per sq mile

Internet Links

UK Foreign and Commonwealth Office	www.fco.gov.uk
CIA World Factbook	www.cia.gov/library/publications/the-world-factbook/index.html
Caribbean Community (Caricom)	www.caricom.org
Latin American Network Information Center	lanic.utexas.edu

South America's capitals

Largest capital (population)	Buenos Aires, Argentina	14 151 000
Smallest capital (population)	Georgetown, Guyana	124 000
Most northerly capital	Caracas, Venezuela	10° 28'N
Most southerly capital	Montevideo, Uruguay	34° 52'S
Highest capital	La Paz, Bolivia	3 630 metres 11 909 feet

NORTH AMERICA

Caribbean Sea

Punta Gallinas
Barranquilla
Cartagena
Maracaibo
Cabimas Maracay Caracas
Barquisimeto Valencia Cumaná
Monteria San Cristóbal Ciudad Bolívar
VENEZUELA
Medellín Tunja Orinoco Georgetown
Puerto Paramaribo
Bogotá Ayacucho **GUYANA** Cayenne
Ibagué **COLOMBIA** **SURINAME** French
Cali Guaviare Guiana
Neiva Orinoco Boa Vista
Isla de Malpelo
(Colombia)
Pasto
Esmeraldas Caquetá Mouths of
Quito Japurá Represa the Amazon
Manta **ECUADOR** Putumayo de Balbina Amazon Belém
Guayaquil Tonantins Manaus Santarém São
Cuenca Iquitos Amazon Luís Parnaíba
Marañón Yavari Represa Fortaleza
Sullana Tucuruí Teresina
Chiclayo Juruá Carauari Maraba Natal
Trujillo Tarapoto **B R A Z I L** João Pessoa
Pucallpa Cruzeiro do Sul Madeira Teles Pires São Floresta Recife
P E R U Rio Branco Porto Juàzeiro
Callao Huancayo Velho Aracaju
Lima Puerto Iparaná Salvador
Ica Maldonado Guaporé Ilhéus
PACIFIC Cusco Beni Trinidad Cuiabá Brasília
Juliaca Mamoré Goiânia Teófilo
OCEAN Lake Santa Cruz Otoni
Titicaca La Paz **BOLIVIA** Pantanal Patos de Minas Uberaba
Arequipa Cochabamba Campo Aracatuba Ribeirão Belo
Arica Sucre Grande Preto Horizonte
Potosí Maringá Campinas Vitória
Iquique Tarija **PARAGUAY** Pedro Juan São Nova Iguaçu
Caballero Paulo Rio de Janeiro
Antofagasta San Salvador Asunción Foz do Iguaçu Curitiba
de Jujuy Formosa Encarnación Joinville
San Miguel Resistencia Posadas Florianópolis
Copiapó de Tucumán Corrientes
Catamarca Santa **ATLANTIC**
La Rioja Maria Porto Alegre **OCEAN**
Islas San Lagoa
Desventuradas Juan Santa Fe Paraná Concordia dos Patos
(Chile) Córdoba Uruguay Paysandú Rio Grande
Cerro San Luis Rosario **URUGUAY**
Aconcagua Montevideo
Valparaíso 6959 Mendoza Buenos Aires
Archipiélago Santiago San Rafael La Plata
Juan Fernández Talca **ARGENTINA** Río de la Plata
(Chile) Chillán Santa
Concepción Colorado Rosa
Bahía
Valdivia Blanca Mar del Plata
Puerto Montt Negro Neuquén
Isla de Chiloé Viedma

Facts

- South America is often referred to as 'Latin America', reflecting the historic influences of Spain and Portugal

- The largest city in each South American country is the capital, except in Brazil and Ecuador

- South America has only two landlocked countries – Bolivia and Paraguay

- Chile is over 4 000 kilometres long but has an average width of only 177 kilometres

Trelew
Comodoro Rivadavia
Archipiélago Golfo de
de los Chonos San Jorge
Punta Medanosa
Falkland Islands (U.K.)
Bahía Grande
Río Gallegos Stanley
Puerto Natales
Punta Arenas Isla Grande
de Tierra del Fuego
Cape Horn Ushuaia

Falkland Islands, an overseas UK territory in the South Atlantic Ocean.

South Georgia (U.K.)

141

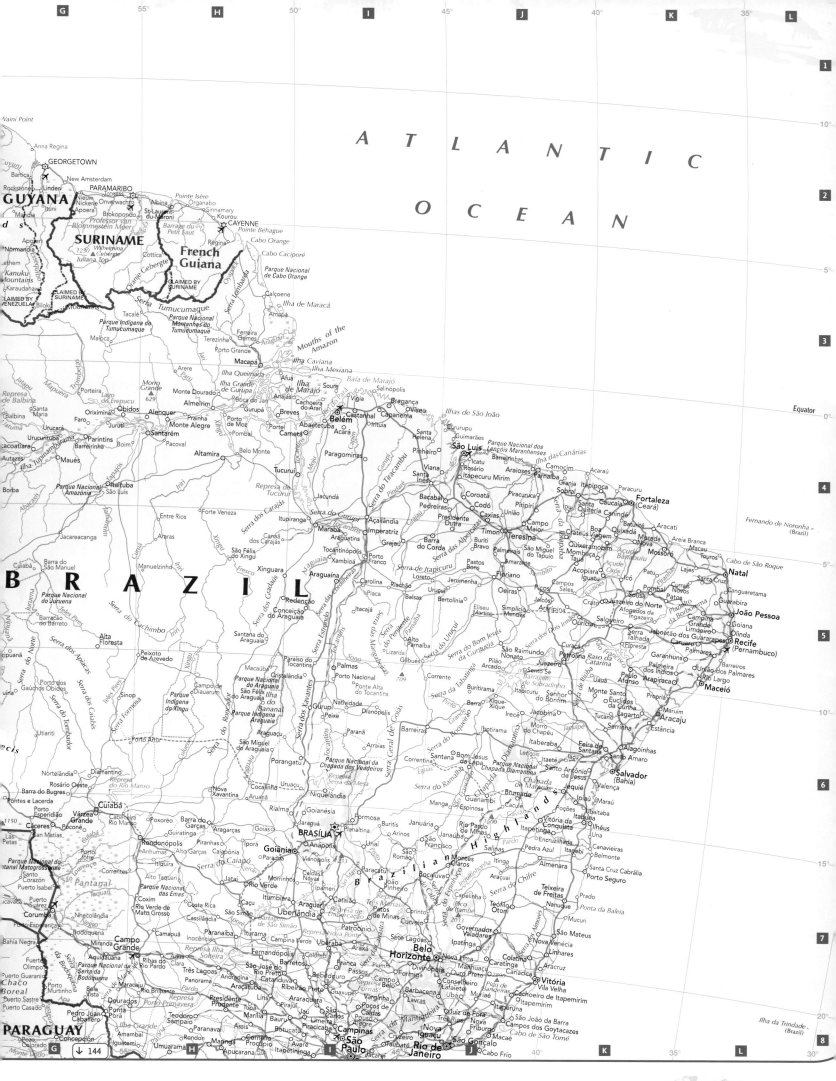

South America
Northern South America

↓ 144

South America
Southern South America

1:14 000 000

Lambert Azimuthal Equal Area Projection

Between them, the world's oceans and polar regions cover approximately seventy per cent of the Earth's surface. The oceans contain ninety-six per cent of the Earth's water and a vast range of flora and fauna. They are a major influence on the world's climate, particularly through ocean currents. The Arctic and Antarctica are the coldest and most inhospitable places on the Earth. They both have vast amounts of ice which, if global warming continues, could have a major influence on sea level across the globe.

Our understanding of the oceans and polar regions has increased enormously over the last twenty years through the development of new technologies, particularly that of satellite remote sensing, which can generate vast amounts of data relating to, for example, topography (both on land and the seafloor), land cover and sea surface temperature.

The oceans

The world's major oceans are the Pacific, the Atlantic and the Indian Oceans. The Arctic Ocean is generally considered as part of the Atlantic, and the Southern Ocean, which stretches around the whole of Antarctica is usually treated as an extension of each of the three major oceans.

One of the most important factors affecting the earth's climate is the circulation of water within and between the oceans. Differences in temperature and surface winds create ocean currents which move enormous quantities of water around the globe. These currents re-distribute heat which the oceans have absorbed from the sun, and so have a major effect on the world's climate system. El Niño is one climatic phenomenon directly influenced by these ocean processes.

Pacific Ocean
World's largest ocean: 166 241 000 sq km
Average depth: 4 200m

Challenger Deep: 10 920 metres
Mariana Trench
Deepest point

South Pacific Ocean
Average depth: 3 935 metres

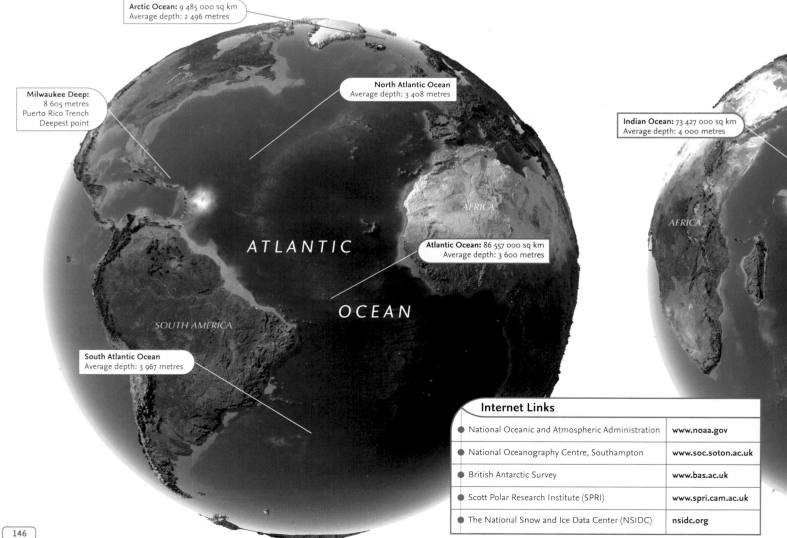

Arctic Ocean: 9 485 000 sq km
Average depth: 2 496 metres

Milwaukee Deep:
8 605 metres
Puerto Rico Trench
Deepest point

North Atlantic Ocean
Average depth: 3 408 metres

Indian Ocean: 73 427 000 sq km
Average depth: 4 000 metres

Atlantic Ocean: 86 557 000 sq km
Average depth: 3 600 metres

South Atlantic Ocean
Average depth: 3 967 metres

Internet Links	
National Oceanic and Atmospheric Administration	**www.noaa.gov**
National Oceanography Centre, Southampton	**www.soc.soton.ac.uk**
British Antarctic Survey	**www.bas.ac.uk**
Scott Polar Research Institute (SPRI)	**www.spri.cam.ac.uk**
The National Snow and Ice Data Center (NSIDC)	**nsidc.org**

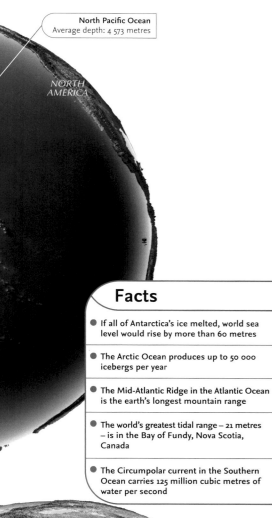

North Pacific Ocean
Average depth: 4 573 metres

NORTH
AMERICA

ASIA

Java Trench: 7 125 metres
Deepest point

INDIAN

OCEAN

Southern Ocean
Average depth: 3 239 metres

AUSTRALIA

ANTARCTICA

Facts

- If all of Antarctica's ice melted, world sea level would rise by more than 60 metres

- The Arctic Ocean produces up to 50 000 icebergs per year

- The Mid-Atlantic Ridge in the Atlantic Ocean is the earth's longest mountain range

- The world's greatest tidal range – 21 metres – is in the Bay of Fundy, Nova Scotia, Canada

- The Circumpolar current in the Southern Ocean carries 125 million cubic metres of water per second

Polar regions

Although a harsh climate is common to the two polar regions, there are major differences between the Arctic and Antarctica. The North Pole is surrounded by the Arctic Ocean, much of which is permanently covered by sea ice, while the South Pole lies on the huge land mass of Antarctica. This is covered by a permanent ice cap which reaches a maximum thickness of over four kilometres. Antarctica has no permanent population, but Europe, Asia and North America all stretch into the Arctic region which is populated by numerous ethnic groups. Antarctica is subject to the Antarctic Treaty of 1959 which does not recognize individual land claims and protects the continent in the interests of international scientific cooperation.

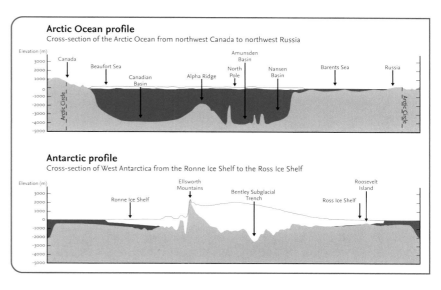

Arctic Ocean profile
Cross-section of the Arctic Ocean from northwest Canada to northwest Russia

Antarctic profile
Cross-section of West Antarctica from the Ronne Ice Shelf to the Ross Ice Shelf

Antarctica's physical features

Highest mountain: Mt Vinson	4 897 m	16 066 ft
Total land area (excluding ice shelves)	12 093 000 sq km	4 669 107 sq miles
Ice shelves	1 559 000 sq km	601 930 sq miles
Exposed rock	49 000 sq km	18 919 sq miles
Lowest bedrock elevation (Bentley Subglacial Trench)	2 496 m below sea level	8 189 ft below sea level
Maximum ice thickness (Astrolabe Subglacial Basin)	4 776 m	15 669 ft
Mean ice thickness (including ice shelves)	1 859 m	6 099 ft
Volume of ice sheet (including ice shelves)	25 400 000 cubic km	6 094 628 cubic miles

The **Antarctic Peninsula** and the **Larsen Ice Shelf** in western Antarctica.

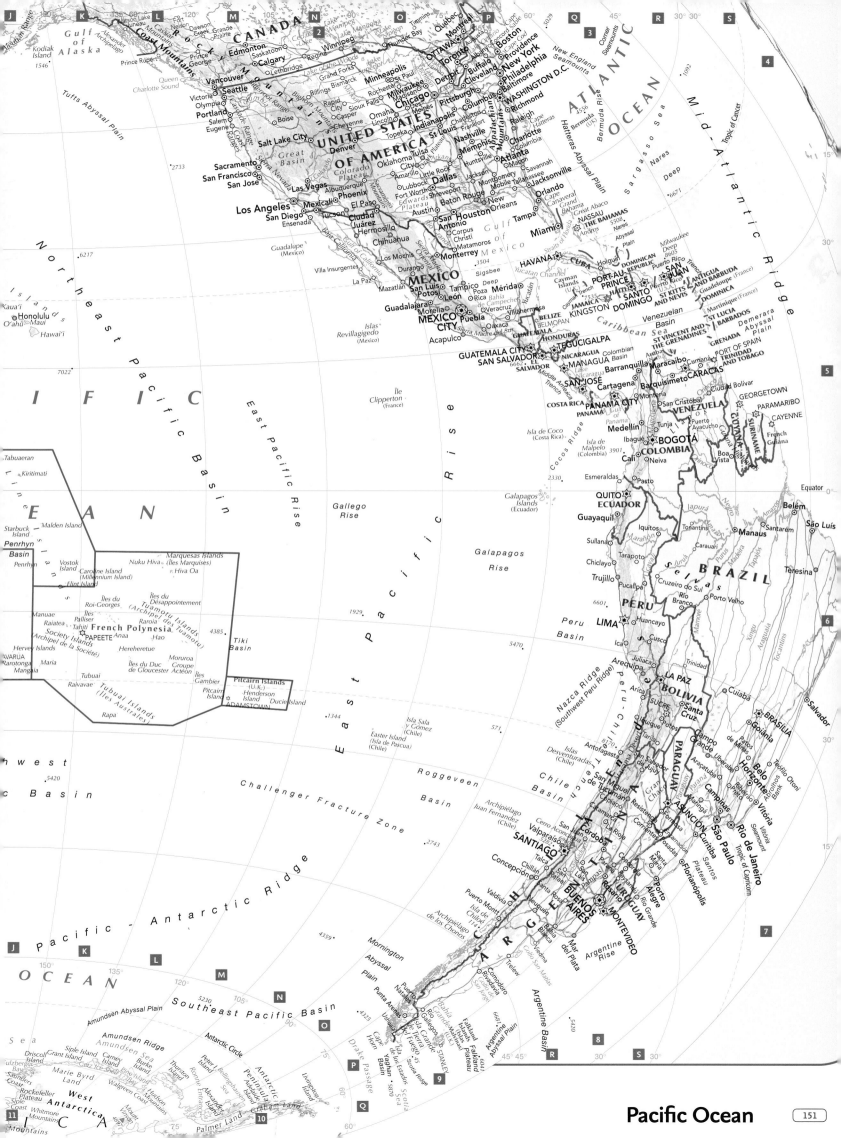

Pacific Ocean

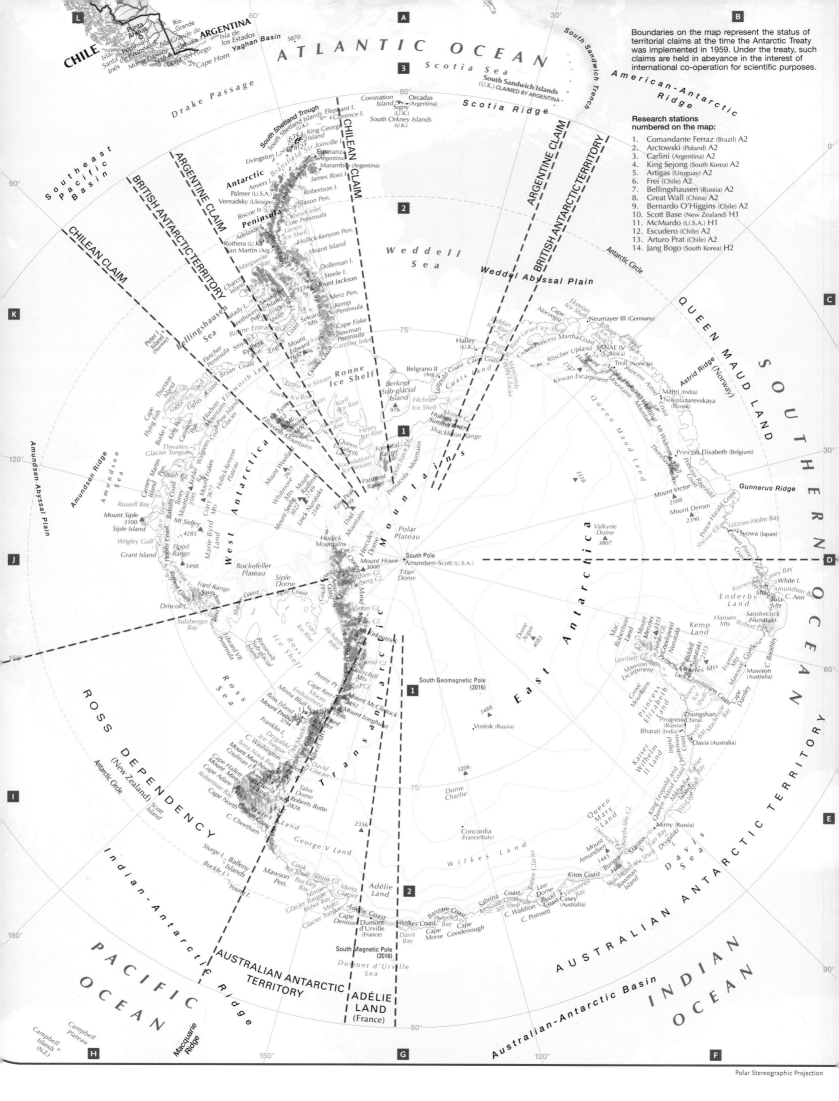

CHILE ARGENTINA

Punta
Arenas
Rio Grande
Isla Grande de Tierra del Fuego
Ushuaia
Isla de los Estados
Isla Santa Inés
Monte Darwin
3248
Peninsula
Cape Horn
Tierra del Fuego

A

3
Scotia Sea

B

Boundaries on the map represent the status of
territorial claims at the time the Antarctic Treaty
was implemented in 1959. Under the treaty, such
claims are held in abeyance in the interest of
international co-operation for scientific purposes.

ATLANTIC OCEAN

South Sandwich Trench

American-Antarctic

Ridge

**Research stations
numbered on the map:**

1. Comandante Ferraz (Brazil) A2
2. Arctowski (Poland) A2
3. Carlini (Argentina) A2
4. King Sejong (South Korea) A2
5. Artigas (Uruguay) A2
6. Frei (Chile) A2
7. Bellingshausen (Russia) A2
8. Great Wall (China) A2
9. Bernardo O'Higgins (Chile) A2
10. Scott Base (New Zealand) H1
11. McMurdo (U.S.A.) H1
12. Escudero (Chile) A2
13. Arturo Prat (Chile) A2
14. Jang Bogo (South Korea) H2

South Sandwich Islands
(U.K.) CLAIMED BY ARGENTINA

Scotia Ridge

Yaghan Basin 5870

Drake Passage

South Shetland Trough

Coronation
Island
Signy
(U.K.)
Orcadas
(Argentina)
South Orkney Islands
(U.K.)

Antarctic Circle

C

ARGENTINE CLAIM

CHILEAN CLAIM

BRITISH ANTARCTIC TERRITORY

ARGENTINE CLAIM

BRITISH ANTARCTIC TERRITORY

Weddell
Sea

QUEEN MAUD LAND

SOUTHERN OCEAN

K

CHILEAN CLAIM

Peter I
Island
(Norway)

Bellingshausen Sea

Weddell Abyssal Plain

Neumayer III (Germany)

SANAE IV
(South Africa)

Troll (Norway)

Maitri (India)
Novolazarevskaya
(Russia)

Astrid Ridge (Norway)

Southeast
Pacific
Basin

Halley
(U.K.)

Belgrano II
(Arg.)

Princess Elisabeth (Belgium)

Gunnerus Ridge

Amundsen Ridge

Amundsen Abyssal Plain

J

Ronne
Ice Shelf

Berkner
Sub-glacial
Island
976

Filchner
Ice Shelf

Polar
Plateau

South Pole
Amundsen-Scott (U.S.A.)

Valkyrie
Dome
3807

Syowa (Japan)

Enderby
Land

Ross
Sea

Ross Ice Shelf

West Antarctica

Transantarctic Mountains

East Antarctica

Dome
Argus
4093

3488

Vostok (Russia)

3206

Zhongshan
(China)
Progress (China)
Bharati (India)

Davis (Australia)

I

ROSS
DEPENDENCY
(New Zealand)

Antarctic Circle

South Geomagnetic
Pole (2016)

Dome
Charlie

Concordia
(France/Italy)

Mawson
(Australia)

Mirny (Russia)

E

Indian-Antarctic Ridge

Macquarie Ridge

Campbell
Islands
(N.Z.)
Campbell
Plateau

H

AUSTRALIAN ANTARCTIC
TERRITORY

ADÉLIE
LAND
(France)

Adélie
Land

South Magnetic Pole
(2016)

Dumont d'Urville
Sea

Wilkes Land

Casey (Australia)

AUSTRALIAN ANTARCTIC TERRITORY

Australian-Antarctic Basin

G

INDIAN
OCEAN

F

PACIFIC
OCEAN

Antarctica

Polar Stereographic Projection

1:26 000 000

| 0 | 200 | 400 | 600 | 800 | 1000 miles |

| 0 | 200 | 400 | 600 | 800 | 1000 | 1200 | 1400 | 1600 km |

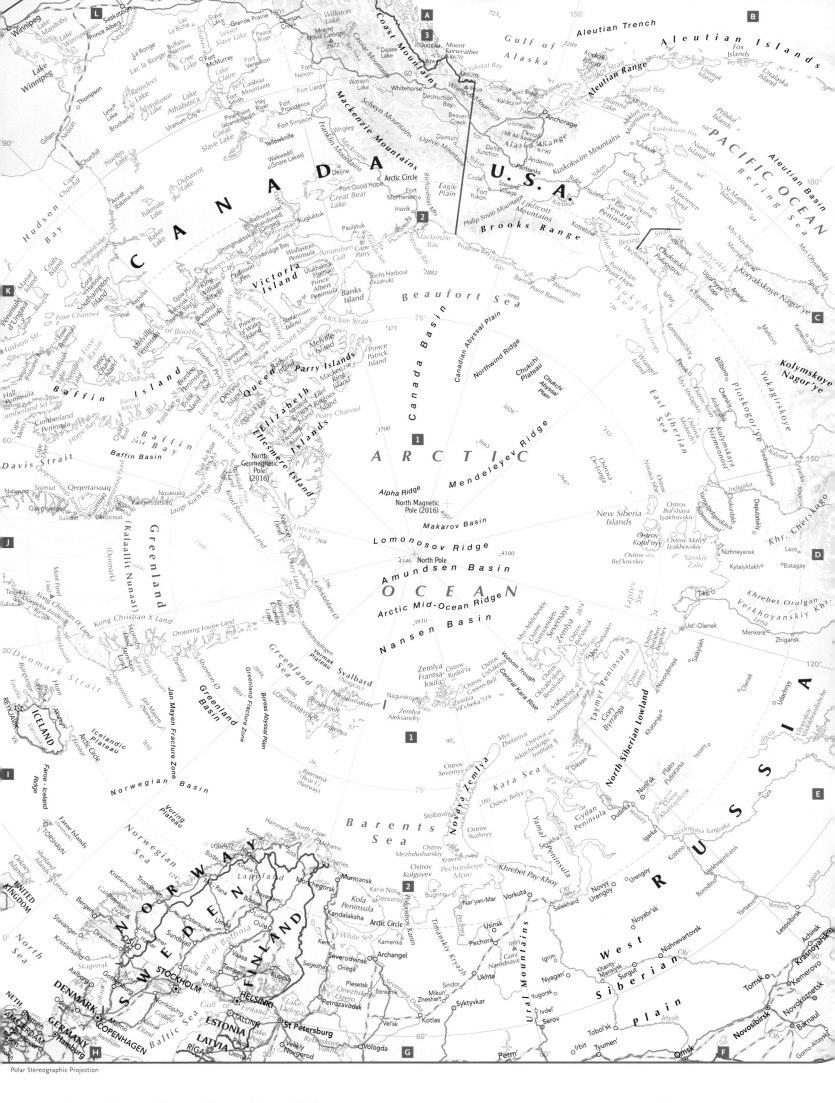

Polar Stereographic Projection

1:26 000 000

0   200   400   600   800   1000 miles
0 200 400 600 800 1000 1200 1400 1600 km

The Arctic

153

World
Statistics

See page 160 for explanatory table and sources

	Population							Economy					
	Total population	Population change (%)	% urban	Total fertility	Population by age (%)		2050 projected population	Total Gross National Income (GNI) (US$M)	GNI per capita (US$)	Debt service ratio (% GNI)	Total debt service (US$)	Aid receipts (% GNI)	Military spending (% GDP)
					0–14	65 or over							
WORLD	7 349 472 000	1.2	53.4	2.5	26.2	8.1	9 725 148 000	78 399 394	10 799	...	...	0.6	2.3
AFGHANISTAN	32 527 000	2.4	26.3	4.8	44.9	2.4	55 955 000	21 395	680	0.2	38 035 000	23.0	1.3
ALBANIA	2 897 000	-0.1	56.4	1.8	18.9	12.1	2 710 000	12 875	4 450	2.6	334 434 000	2.1	1.3
ALGERIA	39 667 000	1.8	70.1	2.9	28.2	5.8	56 461 000	213 784	5 490	0.1	298 308 000	0.1	5.6
ANDORRA	70 000	1.2	85.6	...	...	...	72 000	3 284	43 270	...	...	...	...
ANGOLA	25 022 000	3.1	43.3	6.1	47.9	2.3	65 473 000	...	...	...	7 303 904 000	0.2	...
ANTIGUA AND BARBUDA	92 000	1.0	24.2	2.1	24.6	7.1	114 000	1 209	13 300	...	...	0.2	...
ARGENTINA	43 417 000	0.9	91.6	2.3	25.3	10.8	55 445 000	579 220	13 480	...	...	0.0	0.9
ARMENIA	3 018 000	0.2	62.8	1.5	18.7	10.6	2 729 000	12 083	4 020	11.8	1 436 204 000	2.3	3.9
AUSTRALIA	23 969 000	1.6	89.3	1.9	18.7	14.7	33 496 000	1 516 201	64 600	...	...	...	1.8
AUSTRIA	8 545 000	0.6	65.9	1.4	14.3	18.6	8 846 000	423 906	49 600	...	...	...	0.8
AZERBAIJAN	9 754 000	1.3	54.4	2.0	22.0	5.6	10 963 000	72 425	7 600	2.5	1 791 147 000	0.3	4.6
THE BAHAMAS	388 000	1.4	82.8	1.9	21.1	8.0	489 000	8 037	20 980	...	...	...	...
BAHRAIN	1 377 000	0.9	88.7	2.1	21.2	2.4	1 822 000	28 424	21 060	...	...	...	4.4
BANGLADESH	160 996 000	1.2	33.5	2.2	30.0	5.0	202 209 000	171 250	1 080	0.9	1 740 720 000	1.3	0.0
BARBADOS	284 000	0.5	31.6	1.8	19.4	13.8	282 000	4 311	15 310	...	...	..	..
BELARUS	9 496 000	0.0	76.3	1.6	15.8	14.0	8 125 000	69 533	7 340	7.2	5 342 376 000	0.2	1.3
BELGIUM	11 299 000	0.4	97.8	1.8	16.9	18.0	12 527 000	530 558	47 240	...	...	...	1.0
BELIZE	359 000	2.3	44.1	2.6	33.1	3.8	588 000	1 496	4 350	...	91 973 000	..	1.0
BENIN	10 880 000	2.6	43.5	4.8	42.5	2.9	22 549 000	9 472	890	1.1	105 024 000	6.9	1.0
BHUTAN	775 000	1.5	37.9	2.0	27.4	5.0	950 000	1 811	2 370	4.5	82 792 000	7.4	...
BOLIVIA	10 725 000	1.6	68.1	3.0	32.9	6.3	15 963 000	30 344	2 870	3.2	995 658 000	2.1	1.9
BOSNIA AND HERZEGOVINA	3 810 000	-0.1	39.6	1.3	13.6	15.0	3 069 000	18 482	4 840	4.3	813 280 000	3.4	1.0
BOTSWANA	2 262 000	0.9	57.2	2.8	32.2	3.5	3 389 000	16 067	7 240	0.4	55 828 000	0.6	2.4
BRAZIL	207 848 000	0.8	85.4	1.8	23.5	7.6	238 270 000	2 429 720	11 790	2.5	59 895 313 000	0.0	1.4
BRUNEI	423 000	1.3	76.9	1.9	23.5	4.2	546 000	15 133	37 320	...	...	...	3.1
BULGARIA	7 150 000	-0.5	73.6	1.5	14.0	19.7	5 154 000	55 042	7 620	10.4	5 772 714 000	...	1.5
BURKINA FASO	18 106 000	2.8	29.0	5.5	45.8	2.4	42 789 000	12 278	700	0.7	91 488 000	9.0	1.6
BURUNDI	11 179 000	3.1	11.8	5.9	44.6	2.5	28 668 000	2 880	270	0.9	29 180 000	16.2	2.0
CAMBODIA	15 578 000	1.8	20.5	2.6	31.8	4.0	22 545 000	15 595	1 020	1	165 062 000	5.0	1.7
CAMEROON	23 344 000	2.5	53.8	4.7	42.8	3.2	48 362 000	30 763	1 350	1.4	444 977 000	2.6	1.3
CANADA	35 940 000	1.1	81.7	1.6	16.0	15.7	44 136 000	1 835 099	51 630	...	...	...	1.0
CAPE VERDE (CABO VERDE)	521 000	0.9	64.8	2.3	30.0	4.7	707 000	1 772	3 450	2.5	43 645 000	12.9	0.5
CENTRAL AFRICAN REPUBLIC	4 900 000	2.0	39.8	4.3	39.4	3.9	8 782 000	1 559	320	0.9	15 525 000	34.1	...
CHAD	14 037 000	3.0	22.3	6.2	48.0	2.5	35 131 000	13 292	980	0.9	125 660 000	2.9	2.8
CHILE	17 948 000	0.9	89.4	1.8	20.5	10.7	21 601 000	264 761	14 910	...	...	0.1	2.0
CHINA	1 383 925 000	0.5	54.4	1.6	17.2	9.2	1 357 042 000	10 096 966	7 400	0.5	51 736 841 000	0.0	1.9
COLOMBIA	48 229 000	1.3	76.2	1.9	24.7	6.8	54 927 000	380 998	7 970	3.6	13 233 040 000	0.3	3.1
COMOROS	788 000	2.4	28.2	4.5	40.5	2.8	1 502 000	605	790	0.1	592 000	11.4	...
CONGO	4 620 000	2.5	65.0	4.9	42.6	3.6	10 732 000	12 256	2 720	2.6	303 851 000	0.9	5.0
CONGO, DEM. REPUBLIC OF THE	77 267 000	2.7	42.0	6.0	46.2	3.0	195 277 000	28 730	380	1.4	410 141 000	8.3	1.0
COSTA RICA	4 808 000	1.3	75.9	1.8	22.7	8.6	5 759 000	48 140	10 120	7.2	3 464 431 000	0.1	0.0
CÔTE D'IVOIRE (IVORY COAST)	22 702 000	2.4	53.5	5.0	42.7	3.0	48 797 000	32 196	1 450	5.1	1 672 574 000	2.8	1.5
CROATIA	4 240 000	-0.5	58.7	1.5	15.0	18.6	3 554 000	55 017	12 980	...	...	..	1.6
CUBA	11 390 000	-0.1	77.0	1.6	16.6	13.6	10 339 000	66 620	5 880	...	...	..	...
CYPRUS	1 165 000	1.0	67.0	1.4	16.7	12.6	1 402 000	22 519	26 370	...	...	...	1.5
CZECHIA (CZECH REPUBLIC)	10 543 000	0.0	73.0	1.5	14.8	17.5	9 965 000	193 121	18 350	...	...	...	1.0
DENMARK	5 669 000	0.4	87.5	1.7	17.1	18.5	6 299 000	345 784	61 330	...	...	...	1.2
DJIBOUTI	888 000	1.5	77.3	3.2	33.0	4.1	1 186 000	...	...	...	41 480 000	..	...
DOMINICA	73 000	0.5	69.3	...	...	...	74 000	501	6 930	3.8	19 292 000	3.0	...
DOMINICAN REPUBLIC	10 528 000	1.2	78.1	2.5	30.3	6.5	13 238 000	62 862	6 040	5.3	3 239 166 000	0.3	0.7
EAST TIMOR (TIMOR-LESTE)	1 185 000	2.7	32.1	5.1	42.3	5.5	2 162 000	3 244	2 680	...	...	6.4	2.1
ECUADOR	16 144 000	1.5	63.5	2.5	29.3	6.5	23 013 000	96 845	6 090	4	4 001 602 000	0.2	2.9
EGYPT	91 508 000	1.6	43.1	3.3	33.0	5.2	151 111 000	287 683	3 210	2	5 994 632 000	1.3	1.7
EL SALVADOR	6 127 000	0.7	66.3	1.9	27.6	8.0	6 390 000	23 935	3 920	5.2	1 246 732 000	0.4	0.9
EQUATORIAL GUINEA	845 000	2.7	39.8	4.8	39.4	2.9	1 816 000	8 379	10 210	...	...	0.0	1.1
ERITREA	5 228 000	3.2	22.2	4.3	42.8	2.6	10 421 000	2 313	480	...	46 287 000	2.2	...
ESTONIA	1 313 000	-0.3	67.6	1.5	15.8	18.5	1 129 000	24 994	19 010	...	...	...	1.9
ETHIOPIA	99 391 000	2.5	19.0	4.4	42.1	3.5	188 455 000	53 621	550	1.4	767 725 000	6.6	0.7
FIJI	892 000	0.7	53.4	2.6	28.8	5.6	924 000	4 314	4 870	1.2	51 551 000	2.3	1.0
FINLAND	5 503 000	0.5	84.1	1.8	16.3	19.8	5 752 000	264 554	48 440	...	...	...	1.3
FRANCE	64 395 000	0.4	79.3	2.0	18.5	18.7	71 137 000	2 844 284	42 950	...	...	...	2.2
GABON	1 725 000	2.3	86.9	3.9	37.3	5.2	3 164 000	16 401	9 720	2.6	421 033 000	0.7	1.1
THE GAMBIA	1 991 000	3.2	59.0	5.7	46.3	2.3	4 981 000	878	460	5.3	43 385 000	12.7	1.7
GEORGIA	4 000 000	0.4	53.5	1.8	17.2	14.1	3 483 000	16 742	4 490	11.4	1 871 172 000	3.4	2.5

	Social Indicators					Environment				Communications			
Child mortality rate	Life expectancy	Literacy rate (%)	Access to safe water (%)	Doctors per 100 000 people	Forest area (%)	Annual change in forest area (%)	Protected land area (%)	CO_2 emissions (metric tonnes per capita)	Main telephone lines per 100 people	Cellular phone subscribers per 100 people	Fixed broadband subscribers per 100 people	International dialling code	Time zone
42.5	**71.5**	**85.2**	**91.0**	**154**	**31.0**	**-0.1**	**14**	**4.9**	**15.1**	**96.9**	**10.6**	**...**	**...**
91.1	60.4	31.7	55.3	27	2.1	0.0	0	0.4	0.3	74.9	0	93	+4.5
14.0	77.8	97.2	95.1	115	28.2	-0.2	11	1.6	7.4	105.5	6.6	355	+1
25.5	74.8	...	83.6	121	0.6	-0.6	7	3.3	7.8	92.9	4	213	+1
2.8	...	...	100.0	400	34.0	0.0	10	6.0	47.7	82.6	35.9	376	+1
156.9	52.3	70.8	49.0	17	46.7	-0.2	12	1.4	1.3	63.5	0.4	244	+1
8.1	75.9	98.9	97.9	...	22.3	0.0	10	5.8	21.9	132.1	11.8	1 268	-4
12.5	76.2	98.0	99.1	386	10.6	-0.8	7	4.6	23	158.8	15.6	54	-3
14.1	74.7	99.7	100.0	270	8.9	-1.5	8	1.7	19.2	115.9	9.1	374	+4
3.8	82.3	...	100.0	327	19.2	-0.6	13	16.5	38.9	131.2	27.7	61	+8 to +10.5
3.5	81.3	...	100.0	483	47.3	0.1	24	7.8	38.2	151.9	27.7	43	+1
31.7	70.8	99.8	87.0	340	11.3	0.0	7	3.6	18.9	110.9	19.9	994	+4
12.1	75.2	...	98.4	282	51.4	0.0	14	5.2	32.8	82.3	20.2	1 242	-5
6.2	76.7	94.6	100.0	92	0.7	3.3	3	17.9	21.2	173.3	21.4	973	+3
37.6	71.6	59.7	86.9	36	11.0	-0.2	5	0.4	0.6	80	2	880	+6
13.0	75.5	...	99.7	181	19.4	0.0	0	5.6	52.9	128.7	27.2	1 246	-4
4.6	73	99.6	99.7	393	42.9	0.5	8	6.7	48.5	122.5	28.8	375	+2
4.1	80.6	...	100.0	489	22.5	0.2	23	8.8	40.7	114.3	36	32	+1
16.5	70.1	...	99.5	83	60.2	-0.7	37	1.7	6.7	50.7	2.9	501	-6
99.5	59.5	...	77.9	6	39.6	-1.1	26	0.5	1.8	99.7	0.4	229	+1
32.9	69.5	...	100.0	26	85.8	0.3	28	0.8	3.1	82.1	3.3	975	+6
38.4	68.3	94.5	90.0	47	52.2	-0.5	21	1.6	8.1	96.3	1.6	591	-4
5.4	76.4	98.3	99.9	193	42.8	0.0	1	6.2	22.2	91.3	14.2	387	+1
43.6	64.4	87.3	96.2	34	19.6	-1.0	37	2.3	8.3	167.3	1.6	267	+2
16.4	74.4	91.5	98.1	189	61.6	-0.4	26	2.2	21.8	139	11.7	55	-2 to -5
10.2	78.8	96.1	...	144	71.4	-0.5	44	24.4	11.4	110.1	7.1	673	+8
10.4	75.4	98.4	99.4	387	37.2	1.5	37	6.7	25.3	137.7	20.7	359	+2
88.6	58.6	...	82.3	5	20.2	-1.0	15	0.1	0.7	71.7	0	226	UTC
81.7	56.7	86.9	75.9	...	6.6	-1.0	5	0.0	0.2	30.5	0	257	+2
28.7	68.2	73.9	75.5	17	55.7	-1.2	26	0.3	2.3	132.7	0.4	855	+7
87.9	55.5	71.3	75.6	8	41.2	-1.1	11	0.3	4.6	75.7	0.1	237	+1
4.9	82	...	99.8	207	34.1	0.0	9	14.1	46.2	81	35.4	1	-3.5 to -8
24.5	73.1	85.3	91.7	31	21.3	0.4	2	0.9	11.6	121.8	3.4	238	-1
130.1	50.7	36.8	68.5	5	36.2	-0.1	18	0.1	0	24.5	..	236	+1
138.7	51.6	38.2	50.8	...	9.0	-0.7	17	0.0	0.2	39.8	0.1	235	+1
8.1	81.5	96.7	99.0	103	21.9	0.2	19	4.6	19.2	133.3	14.1	56	-4
10.7	75.8	95.1	95.5	194	22.6	1.4	17	6.7	17.9	92.3	14.4	86	+8
15.9	74	93.6	91.4	147	54.3	-0.2	21	1.6	14.7	113.1	10.3	57	-5
73.5	63.3	76.6	90.1	...	1.2	-9.7	10	0.2	3.1	50.9	0.2	269	+3
45.0	62.3	79.3	76.5	10	65.6	-0.1	30	0.5	0.4	108.1	0	242	+1
98.3	58.7	75.0	52.4	...	67.7	-0.2	12	0.1	0	53.5	0	243	+1 & +2
9.7	79.4	97.4	97.8	111	51.9	0.9	27	1.7	17.8	143.8	10.5	506	-6
92.6	51.6	41.0	81.9	14	32.7	0.0	23	0.3	1.2	106.2	0.6	225	UTC
4.3	77.3	99.1	99.6	300	34.4	0.2	14	4.8	36.7	104.4	23	385	+1
5.5	79.4	99.8	94.9	672	27.6	1.3	12	3.2	11.2	22.5	0.1	53	-5
2.7	80.1	98.7	100.0	233	18.8	0.0	41	6.7	28.4	96.3	21.1	357	+2
3.4	78.3	...	100.0	362	34.5	0.1	22	10.4	18.6	129.5	27.9	420	+1
3.5	80.5	...	100.0	349	12.9	0.4	18	7.2	33.2	125.9	41.3	45	+1
65.3	62	...	90.0	23	0.2	0.0	0	0.6	2.5	32.4	2.3	253	+3
21.2	...	...	...	...	58.8	-0.6	22	1.7	24.3	127.5	15.8	1 767	-4
30.9	73.5	90.9	84.7	149	40.8	0.0	19	2.2	11.6	78.9	5.7	1 809	-4
52.6	68.3	58.3	71.9	7	48.4	-1.4	9	0.2	0.3	119.4	0.1	670	+9
21.6	75.9	93.3	86.9	172	38.1	-1.9	24	2.4	15.3	103.9	8.3	593	-5
24.0	71.1	75.1	99.4	283	0.1	0.9	11	2.6	7.6	114.3	3.7	20	+2
16.8	72.8	86.8	93.8	160	13.4	-1.5	8	1.1	14.9	144	5	503	-6
94.1	57.6	94.8	47.9	...	57.1	-0.7	21	8.9	1.9	66.4	0.5	240	+1
46.5	63.7	71.6	57.8	...	15.1	-0.3	5	0.1	1	6.4	0	291	+3
2.9	77.2	99.9	99.6	324	51.8	-0.3	21	14.0	31.7	160.7	28.9	372	+2
59.2	64	...	57.3	2	12.0	-1.1	18	0.1	0.8	31.6	0.5	251	+3
22.4	70.1	...	95.7	43	55.9	0.3	4	1.4	8.5	98.8	1.4	679	+12
2.3	81.1	...	100.0	291	72.9	0.0	15	10.2	11.7	139.7	32.3	358	+2
4.3	82.4	...	100.0	319	29.3	0.3	25	5.2	60	101.2	40.2	33	+1
50.8	64.4	82.3	93.2	...	85.4	0.0	20	1.4	1.1	171.4	0.6	241	+1
68.9	60.2	53.2	90.2	4	47.8	0.4	5	0.2	2.9	119.6	0.1	220	UTC
11.9	74.7	99.7	100.0	427	39.4	-0.1	4	1.8	25.4	124.9	12.2	995	+4

World
Statistics

See page 160 for explanatory table and sources

	Population				Population by age (%)		2050 projected population	Economy					
	Total population	Population change (%)	% urban	Total fertility	0–14	65 or over		Total Gross National Income (GNI) (US$M)	GNI per capita (US$)	Debt service ratio (% GNI)	Total debt service (US$)	Aid receipts (% GNI)	Military spending (% GDP)
GERMANY	80 689 000	0.3	75.1	1.4	13.0	21.1	74 513 000	3 853 623	47 590	...	...	...	1.2
GHANA	27 410 000	2.1	53.4	4.2	38.9	3.4	50 071 000	42 653	1 590	2.1	778 640 000	3.0	0.5
GREECE	10 955 000	-0.6	77.7	1.3	14.6	20.9	9 705 000	250 095	22 810	...	...	...	2.3
GRENADA	107 000	0.4	35.6	2.1	26.6	7.1	110 000	841	7 910	3	25 493 000	4.6	...
GUATEMALA	16 343 000	2.5	51.1	3.2	37.1	4.8	27 754 000	55 005	3 430	3.6	2 058 290 000	0.5	0.4
GUINEA	12 609 000	2.5	36.7	5.0	42.7	3.1	27 486 000	5 773	470	1.2	76 381 000	9.1	3.8
GUINEA-BISSAU	1 844 000	2.4	48.6	4.8	41.0	3.1	3 564 000	995	550	0.2	1 989 000	10.6	2.1
GUYANA	767 000	0.5	28.5	2.6	29.8	4.9	806 000	3 000	3 940	2.1	65 655 000	4.9	1.3
HAITI	10 711 000	1.4	57.4	3.0	34.2	4.6	14 189 000	8 651	820	0.3	24 382 000	12.4	0.0
HONDURAS	8 075 000	2.0	54.1	2.4	32.5	4.7	11 217 000	18 085	2 270	3.9	701 959 000	3.3	1.6
HUNGARY	9 855 000	-0.3	70.8	1.4	14.5	17.5	8 318 000	131 595	13 340	...	...	...	0.9
ICELAND	329 000	1.2	94.0	1.9	20.4	13.3	389 000	15 005	46 350	...	...	...	...
INDIA	1 311 051 000	1.2	32.4	2.4	29.2	5.5	1 705 333 000	2 027 964	1 570	4.6	92 518 516 777	0.1	2.5
INDONESIA	257 564 000	1.2	53.0	2.5	28.0	5.1	322 237 000	923 738	3 630	5.4	46 356 059 000	0.0	0.8
IRAN	79 109 000	1.3	72.9	1.7	23.5	5.0	92 219 000	548 968	7 120	...	506 167 000	..	2.3
IRAQ	36 423 000	2.5	69.4	4.6	41.1	3.1	83 652 000	227 343	6 530	...	...	0.6	4.3
IRELAND	4 688 000	0.3	63.0	2.0	21.6	12.7	5 789 000	214 711	46 520	...	...	...	0.5
ISRAEL	8 064 000	1.9	92.1	3.1	27.8	11.0	12 610 000	290 180	35 320	...	...	...	5.9
ITALY	59 798 000	1.8	68.8	1.4	13.8	22.0	56 513 000	2 102 247	34 580	...	...	...	1.5
JAMAICA	2 793 000	0.2	54.6	2.0	24.2	9.0	2 710 000	14 014	5 150	11.4	1 542 786 000	..	0.9
JAPAN	126 573 000	-0.2	93.0	1.4	12.9	25.7	107 411 000	5 339 076	42 000	...	...	...	1.0
JORDAN	7 595 000	2.3	83.4	3.4	35.8	3.8	11 717 000	34 070	5 160	3.9	1 395 649 000	7.6	4.3
KAZAKHSTAN	17 625 000	1.5	53.3	2.7	26.1	6.7	22 447 000	204 800	11 850	16	31 170 530 000	0.0	1.1
KENYA	46 050 000	2.7	25.2	4.3	42.1	2.8	95 505 000	58 086	1 290	2	1 237 038 000	4.4	1.3
KIRIBATI	112 000	1.5	44.2	3.7	35.0	3.7	178 000	326	2 950	...	...	35.1	...
KOSOVO	1 805 000	0.3	...	2.1	...	...	...	7 275	3 990	2	152 659 000	7.8	0.7
KUWAIT	3 892 000	3.2	98.3	2.1	22.5	1.9	5 924 000	185 026	49 300	...	...	...	3.6
KYRGYZSTAN	5 940 000	2.0	35.6	3.2	31.0	4.2	8 248 000	7 318	1 250	5.6	401 960 000	8.7	3.4
LAOS	6 802 000	1.8	37.6	3.0	35.1	3.8	10 172 000	11 078	1 660	3.1	357 268 000	4.2	...
LATVIA	1 971 000	-1.1	67.4	1.5	14.6	19.3	1 593 000	30 413	15 250	...	...	...	1.0
LEBANON	5 851 000	1.0	87.7	1.7	24.1	8.1	5 610 000	45 600	10 030	7.2	3 306 124 000	1.8	5.0
LESOTHO	2 135 000	1.1	26.8	3.2	36.3	4.2	2 987 000	2 804	1 330	1.6	40 922 000	4.0	2.2
LIBERIA	4 503 000	2.4	49.3	4.7	42.6	3.0	9 436 000	1 637	370	1	17 378 000	43.9	0.7
LIBYA	6 278 000	0.8	78.4	2.5	29.7	4.5	8 375 000	48 974	7 820	...	...	0.5	8.0
LIECHTENSTEIN	38 000	0.7	14.3	1.5	...	...	43 000	...	...	...	...	...	...
LITHUANIA	2 878 000	-1.0	66.5	1.6	14.5	18.6	2 375 000	45 185	15 410	...	...	...	0.9
LUXEMBOURG	567 000	2.3	89.9	1.6	16.7	14.0	803 000	42 256	75 960	...	...	...	0.4
MACEDONIA (F.Y.R.O.M.)	2 078 000	0.1	57.0	1.5	17.1	12.0	1 938 000	10 686	5 150	8.9	977 515 000	1.9	1.1
MADAGASCAR	24 235 000	2.8	34.5	4.4	42.0	2.8	55 294 000	10 403	440	0.9	95 919 000	5.7	0.7
MALAWI	17 215 000	2.8	16.1	5.1	45.4	3.4	43 155 000	4 180	250	1.6	65 301 000	22.8	1.3
MALAYSIA	30 331 000	1.6	74.0	1.9	25.0	5.6	40 725 000	332 507	11 120	4	12 947 893 000	0.0	1.5
MALDIVES	364 000	1.9	44.5	2.1	27.6	4.7	494 000	2 570	6 410	2.9	76 984 000	0.9	...
MALI	17 600 000	3.0	39.1	6.2	47.5	2.6	45 404 000	11 038	650	0.8	87 371 000	10.6	1.8
MALTA	419 000	0.9	95.3	1.4	14.8	18.7	411 000	8 889	21 000	...	...	...	0.4
MARSHALL ISLANDS	53 000	0.3	72.4	...	...	...	67 000	232	4 390	...	...	...	...
MAURITANIA	4 068 000	2.4	59.3	4.6	40.3	3.2	8 049 000	5 033	1 270	4.6	220 978 000	5.4	2.9
MAURITIUS	1 273 000	0.2	39.8	1.4	19.8	9.1	1 249 000	12 149	9 630	28.5	3 512 427 000	0.4	0.3
MEXICO	127 017 000	1.2	79.0	2.2	28.1	6.3	163 754 000	1 237 533	9 870	4.1	52 242 252 000	0.1	0.7
MICRONESIA, FED. STATES OF	526 000	0.3	22.4	3.2	34.6	4.2	690 000	333	3 200	...	...	..	...
MOLDOVA	4 069 000	-0.1	44.9	1.3	15.8	9.9	3 243 000	9 090	2 560	6.7	591 208 000	5.9	0.3
MONACO	38 000	0.6	100.0	...	...	...	44 000	...	...	...	...	...	...
MONGOLIA	2 959 000	1.5	71.2	2.7	27.9	4.0	4 028 000	12 458	4 280	12.2	1 361 263 000	2.8	0.9
MONTENEGRO	626 000	0.1	63.8	1.7	18.9	13.3	574 000	4 549	7 320	5.8	270 878 000	2.2	1.5
MOROCCO	34 378 000	1.5	59.7	2.5	27.3	6.1	43 696 000	105 831	3 070	4.5	4 799 518 000	2.2	3.7
MOZAMBIQUE	27 978 000	2.4	31.9	5.4	45.5	3.3	65 544 000	16 421	600	1.1	176 837 000	12.8	1.0
MYANMAR (BURMA)	53 897 000	0.9	33.6	2.2	28.1	5.2	63 575 000	68 129	1 270	0.1	62 035 000	2.2	3.7
NAMIBIA	2 459 000	1.9	45.7	3.5	36.9	3.5	4 322 000	13 531	5 630	...	...	1.7	4.2
NAURU	10 000	...	...	...	...	...	11 000	...	...	...	...	..	...
NEPAL	28 514 000	1.2	18.2	2.2	33.5	5.4	36 159 000	20 643	730	1.1	226 524 000	4.4	1.6
NETHERLANDS	16 925 000	0.3	89.9	1.7	16.7	17.7	17 602 000	874 591	51 860	...	...	...	1.2
NEW ZEALAND	4 529 000	1.5	86.3	1.9	20.3	14.4	5 607 000	185 214	41 070	...	...	...	1.1
NICARAGUA	6 082 000	1.4	58.5	2.3	30.5	5.0	7 863 000	11 264	1 870	6.5	744 028 636	3.7	0.7
NIGER	19 899 000	3.9	18.5	7.6	50.4	2.6	72 238 000	7 838	410	0.7	59 054 000	11.4	...
NIGERIA	182 202 000	2.8	46.9	5.7	44.1	2.7	398 508 000	526 467	2 970	0.1	702 825 000	0.5	0.4
NORTH KOREA	25 155 000	0.5	60.7	2.0	21.4	9.6	26 907 000	...	...	...	...	..	...
NORWAY	5 211 000	1.1	80.2	1.8	18.1	16.0	6 658 000	532 277	103 620	...	...	...	1.5

	Social Indicators					Environment				Communications				
Child mortality rate	Life expectancy	Literacy rate (%)	Access to safe water (%)	Doctors per 100 000 people	Forest area (%)	Annual change in forest area (%)	Protected land area (%)	CO$_2$ emissions (metric tonnes per capita)	Main telephone lines per 100 people	Cellular phone subscribers per 100 people	Fixed broadband subscribers per 100 people	International dialling code	Time zone
3.7	80.8	...	100.0	389	31.8	0.0	48	8.9	56.9	120.4	35.8	49	+1
61.6	61.3	71.5	88.7	10	20.7	-2.2	15	0.4	1	114.8	0.3	233	UTC
4.6	81.3	97.5	100.0	617	30.7	0.8	35	7.6	46.9	110.3	28.4	30	+2
11.8	73.4	...	96.6	...	50.0	0.0	2	2.4	25.7	110.2	18.3	1 473	-4
29.1	71.7	77.0	92.8	93	33.1	-1.5	31	0.7	10.8	106.6	2.7	502	-6
93.7	58.7	25.3	76.8	10	26.3	-0.5	28	0.2	0	72.1	0	224	UTC
92.5	55.2	57.8	79.3	5	71.2	-0.5	16	0.1	0.3	63.5	0.1	245	UTC
39.4	66.4	85.0	98.3	21	77.2	0.0	5	2.4	19.9	70.5	5.6	592	-4
69.0	62.7	...	57.7	...	3.6	-0.8	0	0.2	0.4	64.7	0	509	-5
20.4	73.1	85.5	91.2	...	44.3	-2.2	21	1.1	6.4	93.5	1.4	504	-6
5.9	75.9	99.0	100.0	308	22.6	0.5	23	4.9	30.3	118.1	27.3	36	+1
2.0	82.1	...	100.0	348	0.3	3.3	20	5.9	51.5	111.1	35.9	354	UTC
47.7	68	69.3	94.1	70	23.1	0.2	5	1.7	2.1	74.5	1.2	91	+5.5
27.2	68.9	92.8	87.4	20	51.4	-0.7	15	2.3	10.4	128.8	1.2	62	+7 to +9
15.5	75.4	83.6	96.2	89	6.8	0.0	7	7.8	39.1	87.8	9.5	98	+3.5
32.0	69.4	79.3	86.6	61	1.9	0.0	0	4.2	5.6	94.9	..	964	+3
3.6	81.2	...	97.9	267	11.0	1.2	14	7.9	43.2	105.1	26.9	353	UTC
4.0	82.2	...	100.0	334	7.1	-0.1	17	9.0	37.1	121.5	27.2	972	+2
3.5	82.7	99.1	100.0	376	31.6	0.9	22	6.7	33.7	154.3	23.5	39	+1
15.7	75.7	87.9	93.8	41	31.0	-0.1	16	2.9	9.1	107.4	5.4	1 876	-5
2.7	83.6	...	100.0	230	68.6	0.0	17	9.3	50.1	120.2	29.3	81	+9
17.9	74.1	97.9	96.9	256	1.1	0.0	...	3.6	5	147.8	4.7	962	+2
14.1	71.6	99.7	92.9	362	1.2	-0.2	3	15.8	26.2	172.2	12.9	7	+5 & +6
49.4	61.6	...	63.2	20	6.1	-0.3	12	0.3	0.4	73.8	0.2	254	+3
55.9	66	...	66.9	38	15.0	0.0	22	0.6	8.9	17.4	1.2	686	+12 to +14
...	71.1	...	...	...	...	...	...	...	..	..	..	381	+1
8.6	74.6	95.6	99.0	270	0.4	2.4	18	28.1	14.2	218.4	1.4	965	+3
21.3	70.4	99.2	90.0	197	5.1	1.9	6	1.2	7.9	134.5	4.2	996	+6
66.7	66.1	...	75.7	18	67.6	-0.5	17	0.2	13.4	67	0.2	856	+7
7.9	74.2	99.9	99.3	358	54.3	0.3	19	3.8	19.6	116.8	24.7	371	+2
8.3	79.4	...	99.0	320	13.4	0.1	1	4.7	19.4	88.3	22.8	961	+2
90.2	49.7	75.8	81.8	...	1.5	0.5	1	1.1	2	85	0.1	266	+2
69.9	60.8	...	75.6	1	44.3	-0.7	3	0.2	0.2	73.4	0.1	231	UTC
13.4	71.7	90.3	...	190	0.1	0.0	0	6.2	11.3	161.1	1	218	+1
...	82.3	...	...	...	43.1	0.0	43	1.4	48.5	109.3	42	423	+1
5.2	74	99.8	96.6	412	34.7	0.4	17	4.5	19.5	147	26.7	370	+2
1.9	82.2	...	100.0	290	33.5	0.0	40	20.9	50.5	149.5	34.8	352	+1
5.5	75.3	97.6	99.4	263	39.9	0.5	7	4.5	18.2	105.5	16.8	389	+1
49.6	65.1	64.5	51.5	16	21.4	-0.5	5	0.1	1.1	41.2	0.1	261	+3
64.0	62.7	61.3	90.2	2	33.6	-1.0	18	0.1	0.4	33.5	0.1	265	+2
7.0	74.7	93.1	98.2	120	61.7	-0.4	18	7.9	14.6	148.8	10.1	60	+8
8.6	76.8	...	98.6	142	3.0	0.0	...	3.3	6.1	189.4	5.6	960	+5
114.7	58	33.6	77.0	8	10.1	-0.6	6	0.1	1	149.1	0	223	UTC
6.4	81.7	93.3	100.0	349	0.9	0.0	22	6.0	53.6	127	35.2	356	+1
36.0	...	...	94.6	44	70.2	0.0	3	2.0	4.5	29.4	2.6	692	+12
84.7	63	...	57.9	13	0.2	-2.0	1	0.6	1.3	94.2	0.2	222	UTC
13.5	74.2	89.2	99.9	...	17.3	0.1	4	3.1	29.8	132.2	14.6	230	+4
13.2	76.7	94.0	96.1	210	33.2	-0.2	13	3.9	17.8	82.2	10.5	52	-5 to -8
34.7	69.1	...	89.0	18	91.7	0.0	4	1.2	6.8	..	3	691	+10 & +11
15.8	71.5	99.2	88.4	298	12.0	1.2	4	1.4	35.2	108	14.7	373	+2
3.5	...	...	100.0	717	...	...	36	...	133	88.5	46.8	377	+1
22.4	69.5	98.3	64.4	284	6.9	-0.7	14	6.9	7.9	105.1	6.8	976	+7 & +8
4.7	76.2	98.4	99.7	211	40.4	0.0	15	4.1	26.5	163	16.7	382	+1
27.6	74	67.1	85.4	62	11.5	0.2	22	1.7	7.4	131.7	3	212	UTC
78.5	55	50.6	51.1	4	49.1	-0.5	18	0.1	0.3	69.8	0.1	258	+2
50.0	65.9	92.8	80.6	61	47.7	-1.0	7	0.2	1	54	0.3	95	+6.5
45.4	64.7	...	91.0	37	8.7	-1.0	43	1.2	7.8	113.8	1.8	264	+1
...	...	...	...	...	...	...	...	...	...	...	...	674	+12
35.8	69.6	59.6	91.6	...	25.4	0.0	16	0.2	3	81.9	0.9	977	+5.75
3.8	81.3	...	100.0	286	10.8	0.0	20	10.1	41.3	116.4	40.8	31	+1
5.7	81.4	...	100.0	274	31.3	-0.1	27	7.1	40.6	112.1	31	64	+12 & +12.75
22.1	74.8	...	87.0	...	24.7	-2.1	31	0.8	5.5	114.6	2.5	505	-6
95.5	61.5	15.5	58.2	2	0.9	-1.0	17	0.1	0.6	44.4	0	227	+1
108.8	52.8	51.1	68.5	40	9.0	-4.0	14	0.5	0.1	77.8	0	234	+1
24.9	70.1	100.0.	99.7	...	45.0	-2.1	2	3.0	4.7	11.2	..	850	+8.5
2.6	81.8	...	100.0	428	28.0	0.8	16	9.2	21.2	116.1	38.8	47	+1

	Population							Economy					
	Total population	Population change (%)	% urban	Total fertility	Population by age (%) 0–14	Population by age (%) 65 or over	2050 projected population	Total Gross National Income (GNI) (US$M)	GNI per capita (US$)	Debt service ratio (% GNI)	Total debt service (US$)	Aid receipts (% GNI)	Military spending (% GDP)
OMAN	4 491 000	7.8	77.2	2.8	21.1	2.5	5 844 000	65 921	16 870	...	...	..	13.4
PAKISTAN	188 925 000	1.6	38.3	3.6	35.2	4.5	309 640 000	258 311	1 400	2.3	5 947 830 000	1.4	3.5
PALAU	21 000	0.9	86.5	...	...	...	28 000	234	11 110	...		9.7	...
PANAMA	3 929 000	1.6	66.3	2.4	27.5	7.4	5 599 000	43 064	11 130	3.2	1 401 124 000	-0.4	0.0
PAPUA NEW GUINEA	7 619 000	2.1	13.0	3.8	37.5	3.0	13 240 000	16 724	2 240	7.1	1 165 245 000	..	0.7
PARAGUAY	6 639 000	1.7	59.4	2.5	30.6	5.9	8 895 000	28 803	4 400	9.3	2 714 653 000	0.2	1.4
PERU	31 377 000	1.3	78.3	2.5	28.2	6.7	41 899 000	196 931	6 360	2.6	5 065 622 000	0.2	1.4
PHILIPPINES	100 699 000	1.7	44.5	3.0	32.2	4.5	148 260 000	347 458	3 500	1.8	6 096 397 000	0.2	1.1
POLAND	38 612 000	-0.1	60.6	1.3	14.9	15.0	33 136 000	520 138	13 680	...		...	1.9
PORTUGAL	10 350 000	-0.6	62.9	1.2	14.2	20.4	9 216 000	222 126	21 360	...		...	1.8
QATAR	2 235 000	4.5	99.2	2.0	15.3	1.2	3 205 000	200 262	92 200	...		...	...
ROMANIA	19 511 000	-0.4	54.4	1.4	15.6	16.9	15 207 000	189 513	9 520	12.6	24 622 485 000	...	1.4
RUSSIA	143 457 000	0.2	73.9	1.7	16.4	13.2	128 599 000	1 930 634	13 220	...		...	4.6
RWANDA	11 610 000	2.7	27.8	3.9	41.4	2.7	21 187 000	7 885	700	0.7	56 702 000	13.3	1.2
ST KITTS AND NEVIS	56 000	1.1	32.0	...	...	...	68 000	820	14 920	...		..	...
ST LUCIA	185 000	0.7	18.5	1.9	23.5	8.9	207 000	1 333	7 260	2.7	37 064 000	1.3	...
ST VINCENT AND THE GRENADINES	109 000	0.0	50.2	2.0	24.8	7.2	109 000	723	6 610	4.3	31 247 000	1.3	...
SAMOA	193 000	0.8	19.3	4.1	37.5	5.2	241 000	778	4 060	2.5	19 063 000	12.0	...
SAN MARINO	32 000	0.6	94.2	...	...	...	33 000	...	...	...		..	...
SÃO TOMÉ AND PRÍNCIPE	190 000	2.5	64.5	4.6	42.9	3.2	353 000	312	1 670	4.1	13 655 000	11.6	...
SAUDI ARABIA	31 540 000	1.9	82.9	2.8	28.8	2.8	46 059 000	759 271	25 140	...		...	10.7
SENEGAL	15 129 000	2.9	43.4	5.1	43.8	3.0	36 223 000	15 361	1 050	2.3	359 629 000	7.2	1.5
SERBIA	7 046 000	-0.5	55.5	1.4	16.5	16.6	7 331 000	41 505	5 820	19.7	8 296 307 000	0.9	2.1
SEYCHELLES	96 000	1.8	53.6	2.3	23.2	6.8	100 000	1 291	14 120	...		0.7	2.4
SIERRA LEONE	6 453 000	1.8	39.6	4.6	42.7	2.7	11 392 000	4 410	700	0.8	34 801 000	20.9	1.0
SINGAPORE	5 604 000	1.3	100.0	1.3	15.9	11.1	6 681 000	301 633	55 150	...		...	3.1
SLOVAKIA	5 426 000	0.1	53.8	1.3	15.1	13.5	4 892 000	96 200	17 750	...		...	1.0
SLOVENIA	2 068 000	0.1	49.7	1.6	14.6	17.6	1 942 000	48 625	23 580	...		...	1.0
SOLOMON ISLANDS	584 000	2.1	21.9	4.0	39.8	3.4	992 000	1 048	1 830	1.6	17 372 000	18.1	...
SOMALIA	10 787 000	2.9	39.1	6.5	46.9	2.8	27 030 000	...	...	0	35 000	..	0.0
SOUTH AFRICA	54 490 000	1.6	64.3	2.4	29.5	5.0	65 540 000	367 201	6 800	2.9	10 035 454 000	0.3	1.1
SOUTH KOREA	50 293 000	0.4	82.4	1.2	14.3	12.7	50 593 000	1 365 797	27 090	...		...	2.6
SOUTH SUDAN	12 340 000	3.8	18.6	5.0	42.4	3.5	25 855 000	11 609	970	...		20.0	9.8
SPAIN	46 122 000	-0.5	79.4	1.3	14.9	18.4	44 840 000	1 366 027	29 390	...		...	1.2
SRI LANKA	20 715 000	0.8	18.3	2.1	24.8	8.9	20 836 000	71 360	3 440	3.4	2 490 324 000	0.7	2.6
SUDAN	40 235 000	2.1	33.6	4.4	40.9	3.3	80 284 000	67 285	1 710	0.4	260 725 000	1.2	...
SURINAME	543 000	0.9	66.1	2.4	27.1	6.8	624 000	5 358	9 950	...		..	...
SWAZILAND	1 287 000	1.4	21.3	3.3	37.6	3.5	1 792 000	4 512	3 550	0.7	30 235 000	2.7	1.8
SWEDEN	9 779 000	0.9	85.7	1.9	17.1	19.6	11 881 000	596 941	61 570	...		...	1.1
SWITZERLAND	8 299 000	1.2	73.8	1.5	14.8	17.8	10 019 000	693 726	84 720	...		...	0.7
SYRIA	18 502 000	2.0	57.3	3.0	36.8	3.9	34 902 000	...	...	...	213 000	..	...
TAIWAN	23 462 000	...	...	...	...	...	...	...	...	...		...	...
TAJIKISTAN	8 482 000	2.4	26.7	3.5	34.9	3.1	14 288 000	8 948	1 080	4.6	419 012 000	3.9	1.1
TANZANIA	53 470 000	3.0	30.9	5.1	45.2	3.2	137 136 000	46 375	920	0.5	251 780 000	5.5	1.0
THAILAND	67 959 000	0.3	49.2	1.5	18.0	10.1	62 452 000	391 696	5 780	3.9	14 974 717 000	0.1	1.4
TOGO	7 305 000	2.6	39.5	4.6	42.4	2.8	15 681 000	4 047	570	1.5	59 679 000	5.1	1.8
TONGA	106 000	0.4	23.6	3.7	37.0	5.9	140 000	449	4 260	1.5	6 640 000	18.0	...
TRINIDAD AND TOBAGO	1 360 000	0.2	8.6	1.8	20.8	9.2	1 291 000	27 185	20 070	...		..	0.7
TUNISIA	11 254 000	1.0	66.6	2.2	23.3	7.5	13 476 000	46 537	4 230	4.1	1 928 073 000	..	1.9
TURKEY	78 666 000	1.2	72.9	2.1	25.9	7.4	95 819 000	822 450	10 830	7.1	55 900 086 000	0.4	2.2
TURKMENISTAN	5 374 000	1.3	49.7	2.3	28.4	4.1	6 555 000	42 544	8 020	0.1	55 705 000	0.1	...
TUVALU	9 916	0.2	58.8	...	...	...	11 000	57	5 720	...		..	...
UGANDA	39 032 000	3.3	15.8	5.8	48.3	2.5	101 873 000	25 303	670	0.4	98 519 000	6.3	1.2
UKRAINE	44 824 000	-0.3	69.5	1.5	14.6	15.3	35 117 000	152 065	3 560	13.7	17 878 190 000	1.1	3.1
UNITED ARAB EMIRATES	9 157 000	1.1	85.3	1.8	13.8	1.0	12 789 000	405 225	44 600	...		...	5.7
UNITED KINGDOM	64 716 000	0.6	82.3	1.8	17.7	17.5	75 361 000	2 801 499	43 390	...		...	2.0
UNITED STATES OF AMERICA	321 774 000	0.7	81.4	1.9	19.1	14.4	388 865 000	17 611 491	55 230	...		...	3.5
URUGUAY	3 432 000	0.3	95.2	2.0	21.6	14.3	3 667 000	55 915	16 350	...		0.2	1.5
UZBEKISTAN	29 893 000	1.6	36.3	2.2	28.5	4.6	37 126 000	64 266	2 090	1.4	887 704 000	0.5	...
VANUATU	265 000	2.2	25.8	3.3	36.8	4.1	476 000	819	3 160	1	7 852 000	..	...
VATICAN CITY	800	...	...	...	...	...	824	...	...	...		..	...
VENEZUELA	31 108 000	1.5	88.9	2.4	28.4	6.1	41 562 000	373 257	12 500	...		0.0	...
VIETNAM	93 448 000	1.1	33.0	2.0	23.1	6.6	112 783 000	171 905	1 890	3.8	6 716 374 000	2.4	2.3
YEMEN	26 832 000	2.3	34.0	4.2	40.7	2.7	47 170 000	33 319	1 300	...	305 611 000	..	...
ZAMBIA	16 212 000	3.3	40.5	5.4	46.1	2.9	42 975 000	26 396	1 680	1.6	410 375 000	3.9	1.6
ZIMBABWE	15 603 000	3.1	32.5	3.9	41.6	3.0	29 615 000	12 821	840	25.3	3 308 351 000	6.0	2.6

	Social Indicators					Environment				Communications			
Child mortality rate	Life expectancy	Literacy rate (%)	Access to safe water (%)	Doctors per 100 000 people	Forest area (%)	Annual change in forest area (%)	Protected land area (%)	CO$_2$ emissions (metric tonnes per capita)	Main telephone lines per 100 people	Cellular phone subscribers per 100 people	Fixed broadband subscribers per 100 people	International dialling code	Time zone
11.6	77.1	86.9	93.4	243	0.0	0.0	11	20.2	9.6	157.8	4.5	968	+4
81.1	66.2	56.8	91.4	83	2.1	-2.4	11	0.9	2.6	73.3	1.1	92	+5
16.4	...	99.5	...	138	87.6	0.0	16	10.9	33.8	90.6	9.4	680	+9
17.0	77.6	94.1	94.7	165	43.4	-0.4	21	2.6	15	158.1	7.9	507	-5
57.3	62.6	63.3	40.0	6	62.8	-0.5	3	0.7	1.9	44.9	0.2	675	+10 & +11
20.5	72.9	93.9	98.0	123	43.4	-1.0	6	0.8	5.4	105.6	2.4	595	-4
16.9	74.5	93.8	86.7	113	52.9	-0.2	19	1.8	9.9	103.6	5.7	51	-5
28.0	68.3	95.4	91.8	...	26.1	0.7	11	0.9	3.1	111.2	23.2	63	+8
5.2	77.3	99.8	98.3	222	30.7	0.3	34	8.3	12.6	148.9	18.9	48	+1
3.6	80.7	94.5	100.0	410	37.8	0.1	22	4.7	43.2	112.1	25.7	351	UTC
8.0	78.6	97.5	100.0	774	0.0	...	3	44.0	18.4	145.8	9.9	974	+3
11.1	75.1	98.6	100.0	245	28.9	0.6	19	4.2	21.1	105.9	18.5	40	+2
9.6	70.4	99.7	96.9	431	49.4	0.0	11	12.6	26.8	155.1	17.5	7	+2 to +12
41.7	64	68.3	76.1	6	18.4	2.5	11	0.1	0.4	64	0	250	+2
10.5	...	...	98.3	...	42.3	0.0	4	5.1	35.4	118.6	25.6	1 869	-4
14.3	75	...	96.3	11	77.0	0.0	17	2.3	17.9	102.6	15.4	1 758	-4
18.3	72.9	...	95.1	...	68.9	0.3	11	2.2	21.9	105.2	14.9	1 784	-4
17.5	73.5	99.0	99.0	48	60.4	0.0	7	1.3	6.1	55.5	1.1	685	+13
2.9	...	...	...	510	0.0	...	...	...	58.8	118.8	37	378	+1
47.3	66.4	69.5	97.1	...	28.1	0.0	...	0.6	3.4	64.9	0.6	239	UTC
14.5	74.3	94.4	97.0	249	0.5	0.0	31	18.1	12.3	179.6	23.4	966	+3
47.2	66.4	42.8	78.5	6	43.6	-0.5	25	0.6	2.1	98.8	0.7	221	UTC
6.7	75.5	98.0	99.2	211	32.1	1.9	6	6.8	37.3	122.1	15.6	381	+1
13.6	73.2	94.0	95.7	107	88.5	0.0	42	6.8	22.7	162.2	12.7	248	+4
120.4	50.9	45.7	62.6	2	37.2	-0.7	10	0.2	0.3	76.7	..	232	UTC
2.7	82.6	96.5	100.0	195	3.3	0.0	5	4.3	36.2	146.9	26.7	65	+8
7.3	76.7	...	100.0	332	40.2	0.0	36	6.4	16.8	116.9	21.8	421	+1
2.6	80.5	99.7	99.5	252	62.4	0.2	55	7.5	37.1	112.1	26.6	386	+1
28.1	67.9	...	80.8	22	78.7	-0.3	2	0.4	1.3	65.8	0.2	677	+11
136.8	55.4	...	...	4	10.5	-1.1	1	0.1	0.5	50.9	0.6	252	+3
40.5	57.2	93.7	93.2	78	7.6	0.0	6	9.3	6.9	149.2	3.2	27	+2
3.4	82.2	...	...	214	63.8	-0.1	6	11.8	59.5	115.7	38.8	82	+9
92.6	55.7	26.8	58.7	...	...	...	...	...	0	24.5	0	211	+3
4.1	83.1	98.1	100.0	495	37.1	1.0	29	5.8	40.6	107.8	27.3	34	+1
9.8	74.8	91.2	95.6	68	29.2	-0.8	22	0.7	12.5	103.2	2.6	94	+5.5
70.1	63.5	74.3	...	28	...	-0.1	...	0.3	1.1	72.2	0.1	249	+3
21.3	71.2	94.7	94.8	...	94.6	0.0	15	3.6	15.6	170.6	8.5	597	-3
60.7	48.9	83.1	74.1	17	33.2	0.8	3	0.9	3.5	72.3	0.4	268	+2
3.0	82	...	100.0	393	69.2	0.0	15	5.5	39.2	127.8	34.1	46	+1
3.9	82.8	...	100.0	405	31.6	0.4	26	4.6	53.6	136.7	42.5	41	+1
12.9	70.1	85.5	90.1	146	2.7	1.3	1	2.7	16.5	63.9	2.3	963	+2
...	...	...	...	...	...	...	...	...	...	...	...	886	+8
44.8	69.6	99.8	73.8	192	2.9	0.0	5	0.4	5.2	95.1	0.1	992	+5
48.7	64.9	79.0	55.6	3	36.8	-1.2	32	0.2	0.3	62.8	0.2	255	+3
12.3	74.4	96.4	97.8	39	37.2	0.1	19	4.5	8.5	144.4	8.5	66	+7
78.4	59.7	60.4	63.1	5	4.9	-5.8	25	0.3	0.8	64.6	0.2	228	UTC
16.7	72.8	99.4	99.6	56	12.5	0.0	16	1.0	11.3	64.3	1.7	676	+13
20.4	70.4	98.9	95.1	118	43.9	-0.3	33	37.1	21.5	147.3	17.6	1 868	-4
14.0	74.1	79.7	97.7	122	6.7	1.7	5	2.4	8.5	128.5	4.5	216	+1
13.5	75.2	95.3	100.0	171	15.0	1.1	2	4.4	16.5	94.8	11.7	90	+2
51.4	65.6	99.7	...	239	8.8	0.0	3	12.2	11.8	135.8	0	993	+5
27.1	...	...	97.7	109	33.3	0.0	2	...	15.2	38.4	9.1	688	+12
54.6	58.5	70.2	79.0	12	14.1	-2.7	11	0.1	0.8	52.4	0.3	256	+3
9.0	71.2	99.7	96.2	354	16.8	0.3	4	6.3	24.6	144.1	9.3	380	+2 & +4 (Crimea)
6.8	77.4	...	99.6	253	3.8	0.3	18	20.4	22.3	178.1	11.6	971	+4
4.2	81.1	...	100.0	281	12.0	0.3	28	7.1	52.4	123.6	37.4	44	UTC
6.5	78.9	...	99.2	245	33.3	0.1	14	17.0	39.8	110.2	31.1	1	-5 to -10
10.1	77	98.4	99.7	374	10.5	2.8	3	2.3	31.7	160.8	24.6	598	-3
39.1	68.3	99.5	...	253	7.7	-0.1	3	3.9	8.6	78.4	1.9	998	+5
27.5	71.9	84.0	94.5	12	36.1	0.0	4	0.6	2.2	60.4	1.8	678	+11
...	...	...	...	...	...	0.0	...	...	...	...	...	39	+1
14.9	74.2	94.8	93.1	...	51.8	-0.6	53	6.4	25.3	99	7.8	58	-4
21.7	75.6	93.5	97.6	119	45.4	1.1	6	2.0	6	147.1	6.5	84	+7
41.9	63.8	67.6	...	20	1.0	0.0	1	0.9	4.7	68.5	1.4	967	+3
64.0	60	...	65.4	17	66.1	-0.3	38	0.2	0.8	67.3	0.1	260	+2
70.7	57.5	83.6	76.9	8	38.7	-2.0	27	0.7	2.3	80.8	1	263	+2

Definitions

Indicator	Definition
Population	
Total population	Interpolated mid-year population, 2015.
Population change	Population growth (annual %), 2014.
% urban	Urban population as a percentage of the total population, 2014.
Total fertility	Average number of children a woman will have during her child-bearing years, 2014.
Population by age	Percentage of population in age groups 0–14 and 65 or over, 2014.
2050 projected population	Projected total population for the year 2050.
Economy	
Total Gross National Income (GNI)	The sum of value added to the economy by all resident producers plus taxes, less subsidies, plus net receipts of primary income from abroad. Data are in U.S. dollars (millions), 2014 or latest available. Formerly known as Gross National Product (GNP).
GNI per capita	Gross National Income per person in U.S. dollars using the World Bank Atlas method, 2014 or latest available.
Debt service ratio	Debt service as a percentage of GNI, 2014.
Total debt service	Sum of principal repayments and interest paid on long-term debt, interest paid on short-term debt and repayments to the International Monetary Fund (IMF), 2014.
Aid receipts	Aid received as a percentage of GNI from the Development Assistance Committee (DAC) countries of the Organization for Economic Co-operation and Development (OECD), 2014.
Military spending	Military-related spending, including recruiting, training, construction and the purchase of military supplies and equipment, as a percentage of Gross Domestic Product (GDP), 2014.
Social Indicators	
Child mortality rate	Number of deaths of children aged under 5 per 1 000 live births, 2015.
Life expectancy	Average life expectancy, at birth in years, male and female, 2014.
Adult literacy rate	Percentage of population aged 15 or over with at least a basic ability to read and write, 2013 and earlier.
Access to safe water	Percentage of population using improved drinking water, 2015.
Doctors	Number of trained doctors per 100 000 people, 2013 and earlier.
Environment	
Forest area	Percentage of total land area covered by forest, 2012.
Change in forest area	Average annual percentage change in forest area, 2005-2010.
Protected land area	Percentage of total land area designated as protected land, 2012.
CO_2 emissions	Emissions of carbon dioxide from the burning of fossil fuels and the manufacture of cement, divided by the population, expressed in metric tons per capita, 2011.
Communications	
Telephone lines	Main (fixed) telephone lines per 100 inhabitants, 2014.
Cellular phone subscribers	Cellular mobile subscribers per 100 inhabitants, 2014.
Fixed broadband subscribers	Fixed broadband subscribers per 100 inhabitants, 2014.
International dialling code	The country code prefix to be used when dialling from another country.
Time zone	Time difference in hours between local standard time and Coordinated Universal Time.

Main Statistical Sources	Internet Links
● United Nations Department of Economic and Social Affairs (UDESA) World Population Prospects: The 2010 Revision. World Urbanization Prospects: The 2009 Revision.	www.un.org/esa/population/unpop
● UNESCO Education Data Centre	stats.uis.unesco.org
● UN Human Development Report 2011	hdr.undp.org
● World Bank World Development Indicators online	www.worldbank.org/data
● OECD: Development Co-operation Report 2011	www.oecd.org
● UNICEF: The State of the World's Children 2011	www.unicef.org
● Food and Agriculture Organization (FAO) of the UN: Global Forest Resources Assessment 2010	www.fao.org
● World Resources Institute Biodiversity and Protected Areas Database	www.wri.org
● International Telecommunications Union (ITU)	www.itu.int

Introduction to the index

The index includes all names shown on the reference maps in the atlas. Each entry includes the country or geographical area in which the feature is located, a page number and an alphanumeric reference. Additional entry details and aspects of the index are explained below.

Name forms

The names policy in this atlas is generally to use local name forms which are officially recognized by the governments of the countries concerned. Rules established by the Permanent Committee on Geographical Names for British Official Use (PCGN) are applied to the conversion of non-roman alphabet names, for example in the Russian Federation, into the roman alphabet used in English.

However, English conventional name forms are used for the most well-known places for which such a form is in common use. In these cases, the local form is included in brackets on the map and appears as a cross-reference in the index. Other alternative names, such as well-known historical names or those in other languages, may also be included in brackets on the map and as cross-references in the index. All country names and those for international physical features appear in their English forms. Names appear in full in the index, although they may appear in abbreviated form on the maps.

Referencing

Names are referenced by page number and by grid reference. The grid reference relates to the alphanumeric values which appear on the edges of each map. These reflect the graticule on the map – the letter relates to longitude divisions, the number to latitude divisions. Names are generally referenced to the largest scale map page on which they appear. For large geographical features, including countries, the reference is to the largest scale map on which the feature appears in its entirety, or on which the majority of it appears.

Rivers are referenced to their lowest downstream point – either their mouth or their confluence with another river. The river name will generally be positioned as close to this point as possible.

Alternative names

Alternative names appear as cross-references and refer the user to the index entry for the form of the name used on the map.

For rivers with multiple names - for example those which flow through several countries - all alternative name forms are included within the main index entries, with details of the countries in which each form applies.

Administrative qualifiers

Administrative divisions are included in entries to differentiate duplicate names - entries of exactly the same name and feature type within the one country - where these division names are shown on the maps. In such cases, duplicate names are alphabetized in the order of the administrative division names.

Additional qualifiers are included for names within selected geographical areas, to indicate more clearly their location.

Descriptors

Entries, other than those for towns and cities, include a descriptor indicating the type of geographical feature. Descriptors are not included where the type of feature is implicit in the name itself, unless there is a town or city of exactly the same name.

Insets

Where relevant, the index clearly indicates [inset] if a feature appears on an inset map.

Alphabetical order

The Icelandic characters Ð and þ are transliterated and alphabetized as 'Th' and 'th'. The German character ß is alphabetized as 'ss'. Names beginning with Mac or Mc are alphabetized exactly as they appear. The terms Saint, Sainte, etc, are abbreviated to St, Ste, etc, but alphabetized as if in the full form.

Numerical entries

Entries beginning with numerals appear at the beginning of the index, in numerical order. Elsewhere, numerals are alphabetized before 'a'.

Permuted terms

Names beginning with generic geographical terms are permuted - the descriptive term is placed after, and the index alphabetized by, the main part of the name. For example, Mount Everest is indexed as Everest, Mount; Lake Superior as Superior, Lake. This policy is applied to all languages. Permuting has not been applied to names of towns, cities or administrative divisions beginning with such geographical terms. These remain in their full form, for example, Lake Isabella, USA.

Gazetteer entries

Selected entries have been extended to include gazetteer-style information. Important geographical facts which relate specifically to the entry are included within the entry.

Abbreviations

admin. dist.	administrative district	IA	Iowa	Pak.	Pakistan
admin. div.	administrative division	ID	Idaho	Para.	Paraguay
admin. reg.	administrative region	IL	Illinois	P.E.I.	Prince Edward Island
Afgh.	Afghanistan	imp. l.	impermanent lake	pen.	peninsula
AK	Alaska	IN	Indiana	Phil.	Philippines
AL	Alabama	Indon.	Indonesia	plat.	plateau
Alg.	Algeria	is	islands	P.N.G.	Papua New Guinea
AR	Arkansas	Kazakh.	Kazakhstan	Port.	Portugal
Arg.	Argentina	KS	Kansas	pref.	prefecture
aut. comm.	autonomous community	KY	Kentucky	prov.	province
aut. reg.	autonomous region	Kyrg.	Kyrgyzstan	pt	point
aut. rep.	autonomous republic	l.	lake	Qld	Queensland
AZ	Arizona	LA	Louisiana	Que.	Québec
Azer.	Azerbaijan	lag.	lagoon	r.	river
b.	bay	Lith.	Lithuania	reg.	region
Bangl.	Bangladesh	Lux.	Luxembourg	res.	reserve
B.C.	British Columbia	MA	Massachusetts	resr	reservoir
B.I.O.T.	British Indian Ocean Territory	Madag.	Madagascar	RI	Rhode Island
Bol.	Bolivia	Madh. Prad.	Madhya Pradesh	S.	South, Southern
Bos. & Herz.	Bosnia and Herzegovina	Mahar.	Maharashtra	S.A.	South Australia
Bulg.	Bulgaria	Man.	Manitoba	Sask.	Saskatchewan
c.	cape	MD	Maryland	SC	South Carolina
CA	California	ME	Maine	SD	South Dakota
Cent. Afr. Rep.	Central African Republic	Mex.	Mexico	Sing.	Singapore
chan.	channel	MI	Michigan	Switz.	Switzerland
CO	Colorado	MN	Minnesota	Tajik.	Tajikistan
Col.	Colombia	MO	Missouri	Tanz.	Tanzania
CT	Connecticut	Moz.	Mozambique	Tas.	Tasmania
DC	District of Columbia	MS	Mississippi	terr.	territory
DE	Delaware	MT	Montana	Thai.	Thailand
Dem. Rep. Congo	Democratic Republic of the Congo	mt.	mountain	TN	Tennessee
depr.	depression	mts	mountains	Trin. and Tob.	Trinidad and Tobago
des.	desert	mun.	municipality	Turkm.	Turkmenistan
disp. terr.	disputed territory	N.	North, Northern	TX	Texas
Dom. Rep.	Dominican Republic	nat. park	national park	U.A.E.	United Arab Emirates
E.	East, Eastern	N.B.	New Brunswick	U.K.	United Kingdom
Equat. Guinea	Equatorial Guinea	NC	North Carolina	Ukr.	Ukraine
esc.	escarpment	ND	North Dakota	U.S.A.	United States of America
est.	estuary	NE	Nebraska	UT	Utah
Eth.	Ethiopia	Neth.	Netherlands	Uttar Prad.	Uttar Pradesh
Fin.	Finland	Nfld and Lab.	Newfoundland and Labrador	Uzbek.	Uzbekistan
FL	Florida	NH	New Hampshire	VA	Virginia
for.	forest	NJ	New Jersey	Venez.	Venezuela
Fr. Guiana	French Guiana	NM	New Mexico	Vic.	Victoria
Fr. Polynesia	French Polynesia	N.S.	Nova Scotia	vol.	volcano
F.Y.R.O.M.	Former Yugoslav Republic of Macedonia	N.S.W.	New South Wales	vol. crater	volcanic crater
g.	gulf	N.T.	Northern Territory	VT	Vermont
GA	Georgia	NV	Nevada	W.	West, Western
Guat.	Guatemala	N.W.T.	Northwest Territories	WA	Washington
hd	headland	NY	New York	W.A.	Western Australia
HI	Hawaii	N.Z.	New Zealand	WI	Wisconsin
Hima. Prad.	Himachal Pradesh	OH	Ohio	WV	West Virginia
hist. area	historical area	OK	Oklahoma	WY	Wyoming
H.K.	Hong Kong	Ont.	Ontario	Y.T.	Yukon
Hond.	Honduras	OR	Oregon		
i.	island	PA	Pennsylvania		

1

1st Three Mile Opening sea chan. Australia 110 D2
2nd Three Mile Opening sea chan. Australia 110 C2
5 de Outubro Angola see Xá-Muteba
9 de Julio Arg. 144 D5
25 de Mayo Buenos Aires Arg. 144 D5
25 de Mayo La Pampa Arg. 144 C5
70 Mile House Canada 120 F5
100 Mile House Canada 120 F5
150 Mile House Canada 120 F4

A

Aabenraa Denmark 45 F9
Aachen Germany 52 G4
Aalborg Denmark 45 F8
Aalborg Bugt b. Denmark 45 G8
Aalen Germany 53 K6
Aalesund Norway see Ålesund
Aaley Lebanon see Aley
Aalo India 83 H3
Aalst Belgium 52 E4
Aanaar Fin. see Inari
Aarhus Denmark 45 G8
Aarlen Belgium see Arlon
Aars Denmark 45 F8
Aarschot Belgium 52 E4
Aasiaat Greenland 119 M3
Aath Belgium see Ath
Aba China 76 D1
Aba Dem. Rep. Congo 98 D3
Aba Nigeria 96 D4
Abacaxis r. Brazil 143 G4
Ābādān Iran 88 C4
Abadan Turkm. 88 E2
Ābādeh Iran 88 D4
Ābādeh Ţashk Iran 88 D4
Abadla Alg. 54 D5
Abaeté Brazil 145 B2
Abaetetuba Brazil 143 I4
Abagnar Qi China see Xilinhot
Abaiang atoll Kiribati 150 H5
Abajo Peak U.S.A. 129 I3
Abakaliki Nigeria 96 D4
Abakan Russia 72 G2
Abakanskiy Khrebet mts Russia 72 F2
Abalak Niger 96 D3
Abana Turkey 90 D2
Abancay Peru 142 D6
Abariringa atoll Kiribati see Kanton
Abarkūh Iran 88 D4
Abarkūh, Kavīr-e des. Iran 88 D4
Abarshahr Iran see Neyshābūr
Abashiri Japan 74 G3
Abashiri-wan b. Japan 74 G3
Abasolo Mex. 131 D7
Abau P.N.G. 110 E1
Abaya, Lake Eth. 98 D3
Ābaya Hāyk' l. Eth. see Abaya, Lake
Ābay Wenz r. Eth./Sudan see Blue Nile
Abaza Russia 72 G2
Abba Cent. Afr. Rep. 98 B3
'Abbāsābād Eşfahān Iran 88 D3
'Abbāsābād Semnān Iran 88 E2
Abbasanta Sardinia Italy 58 C4
Abbatis Villa France see Abbeville
Abbe, Lake Djibouti/Eth. 86 F7
Abbeville France 52 B4
Abbeville AL U.S.A. 133 C6
Abbeville GA U.S.A. 133 D6
Abbeville LA U.S.A. 131 E6
Abbeville SC U.S.A. 133 D5
Abbey Canada 121 I5
Abbeyfeale Ireland 51 C5
Abbeytown U.K. 48 D4
Abborrträsk Sweden 44 K4
Abbot, Mount Australia 110 D4
Abbot Ice Shelf Antarctica 152 K2
Abbotsford Canada 120 F5
Abbott NM U.S.A. 127 G5
Abbott VA U.S.A. 134 E5
Abbottabad Pak. 89 I3
'Abd al 'Azīz hill Syria 91 F3
'Abd al Kūrī i. Yemen 86 H7
'Abd Allah, Khawr sea chan. Iraq/Kuwait 88 C4
Abd al Ma'asīr well Saudi Arabia 85 D4
Ābdānān Iran 88 B3
'Abdollāhābād Iran 88 D3
Abdulino Russia 41 Q5
Abéché Chad 97 F3
Ab-e Garm, Chashmeh-ye spring Iran 88 E3
Abellinum Italy see Avellino
Abel Tasman National Park N.Z. 113 D5
Abengourou Côte d'Ivoire 96 C4
Åbenrå Denmark see Aabenraa
Abensberg Germany 53 L6
Abeokuta Nigeria 96 D4
Aberaeron U.K. 49 C6
Aberchirder U.K. 50 G3
Abercorn Zambia see Mbala
Abercrombie r. Australia 112 D4
Aberdare U.K. 49 D7
Aberdaron U.K. 49 C6
Aberdaugleddau U.K. see Milford Haven
Aberdeen Australia 112 E4
Aberdeen H.K. China 77 [inset]
Aberdeen S. Africa 100 G7
Aberdeen U.K. 50 G3
Aberdeen U.S.A. 130 D2
Aberdeen Lake Canada 121 L1
Aberdovey U.K. 49 C6
Aberdyfi U.K. see Aberdovey
Aberfeldy U.K. 50 F4
Aberford U.K. 48 F5
Aberfoyle U.K. 50 E4
Abergavenny U.K. 49 D7
Abergwaun U.K. see Fishguard
Aberhonddu U.K. see Brecon
Abermaw U.K. see Barmouth
Abernathy U.S.A. 131 C5
Aberporth U.K. 49 C6
Abersoch U.K. 49 C6
Abertawe U.K. see Swansea
Aberteifi U.K. see Cardigan
Aberystwyth U.K. 49 C6
Abeshr Chad see Abéché
Abez' Russia 41 S2
Ābgāh Iran 89 E5
Abhā Saudi Arabia 86 F6
Abhar Iran 88 C2
Abiad, Bahr el r. Africa see White Nile

Abidjan Côte d'Ivoire 96 C4
Former capital of Côte d'Ivoire (Ivory Coast).

Abijatta-Shalla National Park Eth. 98 D3
Ab-i-Kavīr salt flat Iran 88 E3
Abilene KS U.S.A. 130 D4
Abilene TX U.S.A. 131 D5
Abingdon U.K. 49 F7
Abingdon U.S.A. 134 D5
Abington Reef Australia 110 E3
Abinsk Russia 90 E1
Abitau Lake Canada 121 J2
Abitibi, Lake Canada 122 E4
Abkhazia disp. terr. Georgia 91 F2
Āb Khūrak Iran 88 E3
Abminga Australia 109 F6
Abnūb Egypt 90 C6
Åbo Fin. see Turku
Abohar India 82 C3
Aboisso Côte d'Ivoire 96 C4
Aboite U.S.A. 134 C3
Abomey Benin 96 D4
Abongabong, Gunung mt. Indon. 71 B6
Abong Mbang Cameroon 96 E4
Abou Déia Chad 97 E3
Abovyan Armenia 91 G2
Aboyne U.K. 50 G3
Abqaiq Saudi Arabia 88 C5
Abraham's Bay Bahamas 133 F8
Abramovskiy, Mys pt Russia 42 I2
Abrantes Port. 57 B4
Abra Pampa Arg. 144 C2
Abreojos, Punta pt Mex. 127 E8
'Abri Sudan 86 D5
Abrolhos Bank sea feature S. Atlantic Ocean 148 F7
Abruzzo, Lazio e Molise, Parco Nazionale d' nat. park Italy 58 E4
Absaroka Range mts U.S.A. 126 F3
Abtar, Jabal al hills Syria 85 C2
Abtsgmünd Germany 53 J6
Abū aḑ Ḑuhūr Syria 85 C2
Abū al Abyaḑ i. U.A.E. 88 D5
Abū al Ḩusayn, Qā' imp. l. Jordan 85 D3
Abū 'Alī i. Saudi Arabia 88 C5
Abū 'Āmūd, Wādī watercourse Jordan 85 C4
Abū 'Arīsh Saudi Arabia 86 F6
Abu 'Aweigîla well Egypt see Abū 'Uwayqilah
Abu Deleiq Sudan 86 D6

Abu Dhabi U.A.E. 88 D5
Capital of the United Arab Emirates.

Abū Du'ān Syria 85 D1
Abu Gubeiha Sudan 86 D7
Abū Ḩafnah, Wādī watercourse Jordan 85 D3
Abu Haggag Egypt see Ra's al Ḩikmah
Abū Ḩallūfah, Jabal hill Jordan 85 C4
Abu Hamed Sudan 86 D6

Abuja Nigeria 96 D4
Capital of Nigeria.

Abū Jifān well Saudi Arabia 88 B5
Abū Jurdhān Jordan 85 B4
Abū Kamāl Syria 91 F4
Abu Matariq Sudan 97 F3
Abumombazi Dem. Rep. Congo 98 C3
Abu Musa i. The Gulf see Abū Mūsá, Jazīreh-ye
Abū Mūsá, Jazīreh-ye i. The Gulf 88 D5
Abunā r. Bol. 142 E5
Abunā Brazil 142 E5
Ābune Yosēf mt. Eth. 86 E7
Abū Nujaym Libya 97 E1
Abū Qa'ţūr Syria 85 C2
Abū Rawthah, Jabal mt. Egypt 85 B5
Aburo mt. Dem. Rep. Congo 98 D3
Abu Road India 79 G4
Abū Rujmayn, Jabal mts Syria 85 D2
Abu Rûtha, Gebel mt. Egypt see Abū Rawthah, Jabal
Abū Sawādah well Saudi Arabia 88 C5
Abu Simbil Egypt see Abū Sunbul
Abū Sunbul Egypt 86 D5
Abū Ţarfā', Wādī watercourse Egypt 85 A5
Abut Head hd N.Z. 113 C6
Abū 'Uwayqilah well Egypt 85 B4
Abu Zabad Sudan 86 C7
Abū Ẓaby U.A.E. see Abu Dhabi
Abūzam Iran 88 C4
Abū Zanīmah Egypt 90 D5
Abu Zenîma Egypt see Abū Zanīmah
Abyad Sudan 86 C7
Abyaḑ, Jabal al mts Syria 85 C2
Abyār al Ḩakīm well Libya 90 A5
Abydos Australia 108 B5
Abyei Sudan 86 C8
Abyssinia country Africa see Ethiopia
Academician Vernadskiy research station Antarctica see Vernadsky
Academy Bay Russia see Akademii, Zaliv
Acadia prov. Canada see Nova Scotia
Acadia National Park U.S.A. 132 G2
Açailândia Brazil 143 I5
Acamarachi mt. Chile see Pili, Cerro
Acampamento de Caça do Mucusso Angola 99 C5
Acandí Col. 142 C2
A Cañiza Spain 57 B2
Acaponeta Mex. 136 C4
Acapulco Mex. 136 E5
Acapulco de Juárez Mex. see Acapulco
Acará Brazil 143 I4
Acarai Mountains hills Brazil/Guyana 143 G3
Acaraú Brazil 143 J4
Acaray, Represa de resr Para. 144 E3
Acarigua Venez. 142 E2
Acatlán Mex. 136 E5
Accho Israel see 'Akko
Accomac U.S.A. 135 H5
Accomack U.S.A. see Accomac

Accra Ghana 96 C4
Capital of Ghana.

Accrington U.K. 48 E5
Ach r. Germany 53 L6
Achacachi Bol. 142 E7
Achaguas Venez. 142 E2
Achalpur India 82 D5
Achampet India 84 C2
Achan Russia see Bolon'
Achayvayam Russia 65 S3
Acheng China 74 B3
Achhota India 84 D1
Achicourt France 52 C4
Achill Ireland 51 C4
Achillbeg Island Ireland 51 C4
Achill Island Ireland 51 B4
Achiltibuie U.K. 50 D2
Achim Germany 53 J1
Achinsk Russia 64 K4
Achit Russia 41 R4
Achit Nuur l. Mongolia 80 H2
Achkhoy-Martan Russia 91 G2
Achna Cyprus 85 A2
Achnasheen U.K. 50 D3
Acıgöl l. Turkey 59 M6
Acıpayam Turkey 59 M6
Acireale Sicily Italy 58 F6
Ackerman U.S.A. 131 F5
Ackley U.S.A. 130 E3
Acklins Island Bahamas 133 F8
Acle U.K. 49 I6

Aconcagua, Cerro mt. Arg. 144 B4
Highest mountain in South America.

Acopiara Brazil 143 K5
Açores terr. N. Atlantic Ocean see Azores
Açores, Arquipélago dos terr. N. Atlantic Ocean see Azores
A Coruña Spain 57 B2
Acquaviva delle Fonti Italy 58 G4
Acqui Terme Italy 58 C2
Acra U.S.A. 135 H2
Acragas Sicily Italy see Agrigento
Acraman, Lake salt flat Australia 111 A7
Acre r. Brazil 142 E6
Acre Israel see 'Akko
Acre, Bay of Israel see Haifa, Bay of
Acri Italy 58 G5
Ács Hungary 47 Q7
Actaeon Group is Fr. Polynesia see Actéon, Groupe
Actéon, Groupe is Fr. Polynesia 151 K7
Acton Canada 134 E2
Acton U.S.A. 128 D4
Açungui Brazil 145 A4
Acunum Acusio France see Montélimar
Ada MN U.S.A. 130 D2
Ada OH U.S.A. 134 D3
Ada OK U.S.A. 131 D5
Ada WI U.S.A. 134 B2
Adabazar Turkey see Adapazarı
Adaja r. Spain 57 D3
Adalia Turkey see Antalya
Adam Oman 87 I5
Adam, Mount hill Falkland Is 144 E8
Adamantina Brazil 145 A3
Adams IN U.S.A. 134 C4
Adams KY U.S.A. 134 D4
Adams MA U.S.A. 135 I2
Adams NY U.S.A. 135 G2
Adams, Mount U.S.A. 126 C3
Adams Center U.S.A. 135 G2
Adams Lake Canada 120 G5
Adams Mountain U.S.A. 120 D4
Adam's Peak Sri Lanka 84 D5
Adams Peak U.S.A. 128 C2

Adamstown Pitcairn Is 151 L7
Capital of the Pitcairn Islands.

'Adan Yemen see Aden
Adana Turkey 85 B1
Adana prov. Turkey 85 B1
Adana Yemen see Aden
Adapazarı Turkey 59 N4
Adare Ireland 51 D5
Adare, Cape Antarctica 152 H2
Adavale Australia 111 D5
Ad Dabbah Sudan see Ed Debba
Ad Ḑabbīyah well Saudi Arabia 88 C5
Ad Dafinah Saudi Arabia 86 F5
Ad Dahnā' des. Saudi Arabia 86 G5
Ad Dakhla W. Sahara see Dakhla
Ad Damir Sudan see Ed Damer
Ad Dammām Saudi Arabia see Dammam
Addanki India 84 C3
Ad Dār al Ḩamrā' Saudi Arabia 86 E4
Ad Darb Saudi Arabia 86 F6
Ad Dawādimī Saudi Arabia 86 F5
Ad Dawḩah Qatar see Doha
Ad Dawr Iraq 91 F4
Ad Daww plain Syria 85 C2
Ad Dayr Iraq 91 G5
Ad Dibdibah plain Saudi Arabia 88 B5
Aḑ Ḑiffah plat. Egypt see Libyan Plateau
Ad Dir'īyah Saudi Arabia 88 B5

Addis Ababa Eth. 98 D3
Capital of Ethiopia.

Addison U.S.A. 135 G2
Ad Dīwānīyah Iraq 91 G5
Addlestone U.K. 49 G7
Addo Elephant National Park S. Africa 101 G7
Addoo Atoll Maldives see Addu Atholhu
Addu Atholhu Maldives 81 D12
Ad Duqm Oman 87 I6
Ad Duwayd well Saudi Arabia 91 F5
Ad Duwaym Sudan see Ed Dueim
Ad Duwayris well Saudi Arabia 88 C6
Adegaon India 82 D5
Adel GA U.S.A. 133 D6
Adel IA U.S.A. 130 E3

Adelaide Australia 111 B7
Capital of South Australia.

Adelaide r. Australia 108 E3
Adelaide Bahamas 133 E7
Adelaide Island Antarctica 152 L2
Adelaide River Australia 108 E3
Adele Island Australia 108 C3
Adélie Coast Antarctica 152 G2
Adélie Land reg. Antarctica 152 G2
Adelong Australia 112 D5
Aden Yemen 86 F7
Aden, Gulf of Somalia/Yemen 86 G7
Adena U.S.A. 134 E3
Adenau Germany 52 G4
Adendorf Germany 53 K1
Aderbissinat Niger 96 D3
Aderno Sicily Italy see Adrano
Adesar India 82 B5
Adhan, Jabal mt. U.A.E. 88 E5
Adh Dhāyūf well Saudi Arabia 91 G6
'Adhfā' well Saudi Arabia 91 F5
'Ādhirīyāt, Jibāl al mts Jordan 85 C4
Adi i. Indon. 69 I7
Ādī Ārk'ay Eth. 86 E7
Adige r. Italy 58 E2
Ādīgrat Eth. 98 D2
Adilabad India 84 C2
Adilcevaz Turkey 91 F3
Adin U.S.A. 126 C4
Adīrī Libya 97 E2
Adirondack Mountains U.S.A. 135 H1
Ādīs Ābeba Eth. see Addis Ababa
Adi Ugri Eritrea see Mendefera
Adıyaman Turkey 90 E3
Adjud Romania 59 L1
Adjuntas, Presa de las resr Mex. 131 D8
Adlavik Islands Canada 123 K3
Admiralty Island Canada 119 H3
Admiralty Island U.S.A. 120 C3
Admiralty Island National Monument-Kootznoowoo Wilderness nat. park U.S.A. 120 C3
Admiralty Islands P.N.G. 69 L7
Ado-Ekiti Nigeria 96 D4
Adok South Sudan 86 D8
Adolfo L. Mateos Mex. 127 E8
Adolphus U.S.A. 134 B5
Adonara i. Indon. 108 C2
Adoni India 84 C3
Adorf (Diemelsee) Germany 53 I3
Adorf/Vogtland Germany 53 M4
Ado-Tymovo Russia 74 F2
Adour r. France 56 D5
Adra Spain 57 E5
Adramyttium Turkey see Edremit
Adramyttium, Gulf of Turkey see Edremit Körfezi
Adrano Sicily Italy 58 F6
Adrar Alg. 96 C2
Adrar hills Mali see Ifôghas, Adrar des
Adrar, Ḑahr hills Mauritania 96 B3
Adré Chad 97 F3
Adrian MI U.S.A. 134 C3
Adrian TX U.S.A. 131 C5
Adrianople Turkey see Edirne
Adrianopolis Turkey see Edirne
Adriatic Sea Europe 58 E2
Adua Eth. see Ādwa
Adunara i. Indon. see Adonara
Adusa Dem. Rep. Congo 98 C3
Aduwa Eth. see Ādwa
Adverse Well Australia 108 C5
Ādwa Eth. 98 D2
Adycha r. Russia 65 O3
Adyk Russia 43 J7
Adzopé Côte d'Ivoire 96 C4
Aegean Sea Greece/Turkey 59 K5
Aegina i. Greece see Aigina
Aegyptus country Africa see Egypt
Aela Jordan see Al 'Aqabah
Aelana Jordan see Al 'Aqabah
Aelia Capitolina Israel/West Bank see Jerusalem
Aelōnlaplap atoll Marshall Is see Ailinglaplap
Aenus Turkey see Enez
Aerzen Germany 53 J2
Aesernia Italy see Isernia
A Estrada Spain 57 B2
Afabet Eritrea 86 E6
Afanas'yevo Russia 42 L4
Affreville Alg. see Khemis Miliana
Afghānestān country Asia see Afghanistan
Afghanistan country Asia 89 G3
Afgooye Somalia 98 E3
'Afīf Saudi Arabia 86 F5
Afiun Karahissar Turkey see Afyon
Åfjord Norway 44 G5
Aflou Alg. 54 E5
Afmadow Somalia 98 E3
Afogados da Ingazeira Brazil 143 K5
A Fonsagrada Spain 57 C2
Afonso Cláudio Brazil 145 C3
Āfrēra vol. Eth. 86 F7
Africa Nova country Africa see Tunisia
'Afrīn Syria 85 C1
'Afrīn, Nahr r. Syria/Turkey 85 C1
Afşin Turkey 90 E3
Afsluitdijk barrage Neth. 52 F2
Afton U.S.A. 126 F4
Afuá Brazil 143 H4
'Afula Israel 85 B3
Afyon Turkey 59 N5
Afyonkarahisar Turkey see Afyon
Aga Germany 53 M4
Agadès Niger see Agadez
Agadez Niger 96 D3
Agadir Morocco 96 C1
Agalega Islands Mauritius 149 L6
Agana Guam see Hagåtña
Agara Georgia 91 F2
Agartala India 83 G5
Agashi India 84 B2
Agate Canada 122 E4
Agathe France see Agde
Agathonisi i. Greece 59 L6
Agats Indon. 69 J8
Agatti i. India 84 B4
Agboville Côte d'Ivoire 96 C4
Ağcabādi Azer. 91 G2
Ağdam (abandoned) Azer. 91 G3
Ağdaş Azer. 91 G2
Agdash Azer. see Ağdaş
Agde France 56 F5
Agdzhabedi Azer. see Ağcabādi
Agedabia Libya see Ajdābiyā
Agen France 56 E4
Aggeneys S. Africa 100 D5
Aggteleki nat. park Hungary 47 R6
Aghil Dawan China 82 D1
Agiabampo Mex. 127 F8
Agiguan i. N. Mariana Is see Aguijan
Ağın Turkey 90 E3
Aginskoye Russia 72 G1
Aginum France see Agen
Agios Dimitrios Greece 59 J6
Agios Efstratios i. Greece 59 K5
Agios Georgios i. Greece 59 J6
Agios Nikolaos Greece 59 K7
Agios Theodoros Cyprus 85 B2
Agiou Orous, Kolpos b. Greece 59 J4
Agirwat Hills Sudan 86 E6
Agisanang S. Africa 101 G4
Agnes, Mount hill Australia 109 E6
Agnew Australia 109 C6
Agnibilékrou Côte d'Ivoire 96 C4
Agnita Romania 59 K2
Agniye-Afanas'yevsk Russia 74 E2
Agra India 82 D4
Agrakhanskiy Poluostrov pen. Russia 91 G2
Agram Croatia see Zagreb
Ağrı Turkey 91 F3
Agria Gramvousa i. Greece 59 J7
Ağrı Dağı mt. Turkey see Ararat, Mount
Agrigan i. N. Mariana Is see Agrihan
Agrigento Sicily Italy 58 E6
Agrigentum Sicily Italy see Agrigento
Agrihan i. N. Mariana Is 69 L3
Agrinio Greece 59 I5
Agropoli Italy 58 F4
Agryz Russia 41 Q4
Ağsu Azer. 91 H2
Agua, Volcán de vol. Guat. 136 F6
Água Clara Brazil 144 F2
Aguadilla Puerto Rico 137 K5
Agua Escondida Arg. 144 C5
Agua Fria r. U.S.A. 129 G5
Agua Fria National Monument nat. park U.S.A. 129 G4
Aguanaval r. Mex. 131 C7
Aguanga U.S.A. 128 E5
Aguanish r. Canada 123 J4
Aguapeí r. Brazil 145 A3
Agua Prieta Mex. 127 F7
Aguaro-Guariquito, Parque Nacional nat. park Venez. 142 E2
Aguascalientes Mex. 136 D4
Águas Lindas de Goiás Brazil 145 A1
Agudos Brazil 145 A3
Águeda Port. 57 B3
Aguemour reg. Alg. 96 D2
Aguié Niger 96 D3
Aguijan i. N. Mariana Is 69 L4
Aguilar U.S.A. 127 G5
Aguilar de Campoo Spain 57 D2
Águilas Spain 57 F5

Agulhas, Cape S. Africa 100 E8
Most southerly point of Africa.

Agulhas Basin sea feature Southern Ocean 149 J9
Agulhas Negras mt. Brazil 145 B3
Agulhas Plateau sea feature Southern Ocean 149 J8
Agulhas Ridge sea feature S. Atlantic Ocean 148 I8
Ağva Turkey 59 M4
Agvali Russia 91 G2
Ahaggar plat. Alg. 96 D2
Ahaggar, Tassili oua-n- plat. Alg. 96 D2
Āhangarān Iran 89 F3
Ahar Iran 88 B2
Ahaura N.Z. 113 C6
Ahaus Germany 52 H2
Ahipara Bay N.Z. 113 D2
Ahiri India 84 D2
Ahklun Mountains U.S.A. 118 B4
Ahlen Germany 53 H3
Ahmadabad India 82 C5
Aḩmadābād Iran 89 E3
Aḩmad al Bāqir, Jabal mt. Jordan 85 B5
Ahmadī Iran 88 E5
Ahmadnagar India 84 B2
Ahmadpur East Pak. 89 H4
Ahmar Mountains mts Eth. 98 E3
Ahmedabad India see Ahmadabad
Ahmednagar India see Ahmadnagar
Ahorn Germany 53 K4
Ahr r. Germany 52 H4
Ahram Iran 88 C4
Ahrensburg Germany 53 K1
Āhtäri Fin. 44 N5
Ahtme Estonia 45 O7
Ahu China 77 H1
Āhū Iran 88 C4
Ahun France 56 F3
Ahuzhen China see Ahu
Ahvāz Iran 88 C4
Ahwa India 84 B1
Ahwāz Iran see Ahvāz
Ai-Ais Namibia 100 C4
Ai-Ais Hot Springs and Fish River Canyon Park nature res. Namibia 100 C4
Ai-Ais/Richtersveld Transfrontier Park Namibia/S. Africa 100 C5
Aibak Afgh. 89 H2
Aichwara India 82 D4
Aid U.S.A. 134 D4
Aigialousa Cyprus 85 B2
Aigina i. Greece 59 J6
Aigio Greece 59 J5
Aigle de Chambeyron mt. France 56 H4
Aigüestortes i Estany de Sant Maurici, Parc Nacional d' nat. park Spain 57 G2
Ai He r. China 74 B4
Aihua China see Yunxian
Aihui China see Heihe
Aijal India see Aizawl
Aikawa Japan 75 E5
Aiken U.S.A. 133 D5
Ailao Shan mts China 76 D3
Aileron Australia 108 F5
Ailinglabelab atoll Marshall Is see Ailinglaplap
Ailinglaplap atoll Marshall Is 150 H5
Ailly-sur-Noye France 52 C5
Ailsa Craig Canada 134 E2
Ailsa Craig i. U.K. 50 D5
Ailt an Chorráin Ireland 51 D3
Aimorés, Serra dos hills Brazil 145 C2
Aïn Beïda Alg. 58 B7
'Aïn Ben Tili Mauritania 96 C2
'Aïn Dâlla spring Egypt see 'Ayn Dāllah
Aïn Defla Alg. 57 H5
Aïn Deheb Alg. 57 G6
Aïn el Hadjel Alg. 57 H6
'Aïn el Maqfi spring Egypt see 'Ayn al Maqfī
Aïn el Melh Alg. 57 I6
Aïn Mdila well Alg. 58 B7
Aïn-M'Lila Alg. 54 F4
Aïn Oussera Alg. 57 H6
Aïn Salah Alg. see In Salah
Aïn Sefra Alg. 54 D5
Ainsworth U.S.A. 130 D3
Aintab Turkey see Gaziantep
Aïn Taya Alg. 57 H5
Aïn Tédélès Alg. 57 G6
Aïn Temouchent Alg. 57 F6
'Aïn Tibaghbagh spring Egypt see 'Ayn Tabaghbugh
'Aïn Timeira spring Egypt see 'Ayn Tumayrah
'Aïn Zeitûn Egypt see 'Ayn az Zaytūn
Aiquile Bol. 142 E7
Air i. Indon. 71 D7
Aïr, Massif de l' mts Niger 96 D3
Airaines France 52 B5
Airdrie Canada 120 H5
Airdrie U.K. 50 F5
Aire r. France 52 E5
Aire, Canal d' France 52 C4
Aire-sur-l'Adour France 56 D5
Air Force Island Canada 119 K3
Airpanas Indon. 108 D1
Aisatung Mountain Myanmar 70 A2
Aisch r. Germany 53 L5
Aishihik Canada 120 B2
Aishihik Lake Canada 120 B2
Aisne r. France 52 C5
Aïssa, Djebel mt. Alg. 54 D5
Aitamännikkö Fin. 44 N3
Aitana mt. Spain 57 F4
Aït Benhaddou tourist site Morocco 54 C5
Aiterach r. Germany 53 M6
Aitkin U.S.A. 130 E2
Aiud Romania 59 J1
Aix France see Aix-en-Provence
Aix-en-Provence France 56 G5
Aix-la-Chapelle Germany see Aachen
Aix-les-Bains France 56 G4
Aíyina i. Greece see Aigina
Aíyion Greece see Aigio
Aizawl India 83 H5
Aizkraukle Latvia 45 N8
Aizpute Latvia 45 L8
Aizuwakamatsu Japan 75 E5
Ajaccio Corsica France 56 I6
Ajanta India 84 B1
Ajanta Range hills India see Sahyadriparvat Range
Ajaureforsen Sweden 44 I4
Ajax Canada 134 F2
Ajayameru India see Ajmer
Ajban U.A.E. 88 D5
Ajdābiyā Libya 97 F1
a-Jiddét des. Oman see Ḩarāsīs, Jiddat al
Ajjer, Tassili n' plat. Alg. 96 D2
'Ajlūn Jordan 85 B3
'Ajman U.A.E. 88 D5
Ajmer India 82 C4
Ajmer-Merwara India see Ajmer
Ajnala India 82 C3
Ajo U.S.A. 129 G5
Ajo, Mount U.S.A. 129 G5
Ajrestān Afgh. 89 G3
Ajyyap Turkm. 88 D2
Akademii, Zaliv b. Russia 74 E1
Akademii Nauk, Khrebet mt. Tajik. see Akademiyai Fanho, Qatorkŭhi
Akademiyai Fanho, Qatorkŭhi mt. Tajik. 89 H2
Akadyr Kazakh. 80 D2
Akagera National Park Rwanda 98 D4
Akalkot India 84 C2
Akama, Akra c. Cyprus see Arnauti, Cape
Akamagaseki Japan see Shimonoseki
Akan Kokuritsu-kōen nat. park Japan 74 G4
Akaroa N.Z. 113 D6
Akas reg. India 76 B3
'Akāshāt Iraq 91 E4
Akbarābād Iran 91 I5
Akbarpur Uttar Prad. India 82 E4
Akbarpur Uttar Prad. India 83 E4
Akbaytal, Pereval pass Tajik. 89 I2
Akbaytal Pass Tajik. see Akbaytal, Pereval
Akbez Turkey 85 C1
Akçadağ Turkey 90 E3
Akçakale Turkey 85 D1
Akçakoca Turkey 59 N4
Akçakoca Dağları mts Turkey 59 N4
Akçakoyunlu Turkey 85 C1
Akçalı Dağları mts Turkey 85 A1
Akchâr reg. Mauritania 96 B3
Akchi Kazakh. see Akshi
Akdağlar mts Turkey 59 M6
Akdağmadeni Turkey 90 D3
Akdere Turkey 85 A1
Akelamo Indon. 69 H6
Åkersberga Sweden 45 K7
Akersloot Neth. 52 E2
Aketi Dem. Rep. Congo 98 C3
Akgyr Erezi hills Turkm. 88 D1
Akhali-Afoni Georgia see Akhali Atoni
Akhali Atoni Georgia 91 F2
Akhḑar, Al Jabal al mts Libya 97 F1
Akhḑar, Jabal mts Oman 88 E6
Akhisar Turkey 59 L5
Akhnoor India 82 C2
Akhsu Azer. see Ağsu

Akhta Armenia see Hrazdan
Akhtarīn Syria 85 C1
Akhtubinsk Russia 43 J6
Akhty Russia 91 G2
Akhtyrka Ukr. see Okhtyrka
Aki Japan 75 D6
Akiéni Gabon 98 B4
Akimiski Island Canada 122 E3
Akishma r. Russia 74 D1
Akita Japan 75 F5
Akjoujt Mauritania 96 B3
Akkajaure l. Sweden 44 J3
Akkerman Ukr. see Bilhorod-Dnistrovs'kyy
Akkeshi Japan 74 G4
'Akko Israel 85 B3
Akkol' Akmolinskaya Oblast' Kazakh. 80 D1
Akkol' Atyrauskaya Oblast' Kazakh. 43 K7
Akku Kazakh. 80 E1
Akkul' Kazakh. see Akkol'
Akkuş Turkey 90 E2
Akkyr, Gory hills Turkm. see Akgyr Erezi
Aklavik Canada 118 E3
Aklera India 82 D4
Ak-Mechet Kazakh. see Kyzylorda
Akmeņrags pt Latvia 45 L8
Akmeqit China 82 D1
Akmola Kazakh. see Astana
Akmolinsk Kazakh. see Astana
Akobo South Sudan 97 G4
Akobo Wenz r. Eth./South Sudan 98 D3
Akokan Niger 96 D3
Akola India 84 C1
Akom II Cameroon 96 E4
Akonolinga Cameroon 96 E4
Akordat Eritrea 86 E6
Akören Turkey 90 D3
Akot India 82 D5
Akpatok Island Canada 123 I1
Akqi China 80 E3
Akra, Jabal mt. Syria/Turkey see Aqra', Jabal al
Akranes Iceland 44 [inset 1]
Åkrehamn Norway 45 D7
Akréréb Niger 96 D3
Akron CO U.S.A. 130 C3
Akron IN U.S.A. 134 B3
Akron OH U.S.A. 134 E3
Akrotiri Bay Cyprus 85 A2
Akrotirion Bay Cyprus see Akrotiri Bay
Akrotiriou, Kolpos b. Cyprus see Akrotiri Bay
Akrotiri Sovereign Base Area military base Cyprus 85 A2
Aksai Chin terr. Asia 82 D2
Aksaray Turkey 90 D3
Aksay China 80 H4
Aksay Kazakh. 41 Q5
Ak-Say r. Kyrg. 87 M1
Aksay Russia 43 H7
Akşehir Turkey 59 N5
Akşehir Gölü l. Turkey 59 N5
Akseki Turkey 90 C3
Aksha Russia 73 K2
Akshi Kazakh. 80 E3
Akshiganak Kazakh. 80 B2
Akshukyr Kazakh. 91 H2
Aksu China 80 F3
Aksu Kazakh. 80 E1
Aksu r. Tajik. see Oqsu
Aksu r. Turkey 59 N6
Aksuat Kazakh. 80 F2
Aksu-Ayuly Kazakh. 80 D2
Aksubayevo Russia 43 K5
Āksum Eth. 86 E7
Aktag mt. China 83 F1
Aktas Dağı mt. Turkey 91 G3
Aktau Kazakh. 78 E2
Akto China 89 J2
Aktobe Kazakh. 78 E1
Aktogay Karagandinskaya Oblast' Kazakh. 80 E2
Aktogay Vostochnyy Kazakhstan Kazakh. 80 E2
Aktsyabrski Belarus 43 F5
Aktyubinsk Kazakh. see Aktobe
Akulivik Canada 119 K3
Akune Japan 75 C6
Akure Nigeria 96 D4
Akuressa Sri Lanka 84 D5
Akureyri Iceland 44 [inset 1]
Akusha Russia 43 J8
Akwanga Nigeria 96 D4
Akxokesay China 83 G1
Akyab Myanmar 70 A2
Akyatan Gölü salt l. Turkey 85 B1
Akyazı Turkey 59 N4
Akzhaykyn, Ozero salt l. Kazakh. 80 C3
Ål Norway 45 F6
'Alā, Jabal al hills Syria 85 C2
Alabama r. U.S.A. 133 C6
Alabama state U.S.A. 133 C5
Alabaster AL U.S.A. 133 C5
Alabaster MI U.S.A. 134 D1
Al 'Abṭīyah well Iraq 91 G5
Alaca Turkey 90 D2
Alacahan Turkey 90 E3
Alaçam Turkey 90 D2
Alaçam Dağları mts Turkey 59 M5
Alacant Spain see Alicante
Alaçatı Turkey 59 L5
Aladağ Turkey 90 D3
Ala Dağlar mts Turkey 91 F3
Ala Dağları mts Turkey 90 D3
Al 'Adam Libya 90 A5
Al Aflāj reg. Saudi Arabia 88 B6
Alag Hu l. China 76 C1
Alagir Russia 91 G2
Alagoinhas Brazil 145 D1
Alahärmä Fin. 44 M5
Al Aḥmadī Kuwait 88 C4
Alai Range mts Asia 89 H2
Alaivān Iran 88 D3
Ālājah Syria 85 B2
Alajärvi Fin. 44 M5
Al 'Ajrūd well Egypt 85 B4
Alakanuk U.S.A. 118 B3
Al Akhḍar Saudi Arabia 90 E5
Alakol', Ozero salt l. Kazakh. 80 F2
Ala Kul salt l. Kazakh. see Alakol', Ozero
Alakurtti Russia 44 Q3
Al 'Alamayn Egypt 90 C5
Al 'Alayyah Saudi Arabia 86 F6
Alama Somalia 98 E3
Alamagan i. N. Mariana Is 69 L3
Alamaguan i. N. Mariana Is see Alamagan
Al 'Amārah Iraq 91 G5
'Alam ar Rūm, Ra's pt Egypt 90 B5
'Alāmarvdasht watercourse Iran 88 D4
Alameda U.S.A. 128 B3
'Alam el Rûm, Râs pt Egypt see 'Alam ar Rūm, Ra's
Al Amghar waterhole Iraq 91 G5
Al 'Āmirīyah Egypt 90 C5
Alamítos, Sierra de los mt. Mex. 131 C7
Alamo GA U.S.A. 133 D5
Alamo NV U.S.A. 129 F3
Alamo Dam U.S.A. 129 G4
Alamogordo U.S.A. 127 G6
Alamo Heights U.S.A. 131 D6
Alamos Sonora Mex. 127 F7
Alamos Sonora Mex. 127 F8
Alamos r. Mex. 131 C7
Alamos, Sierra mts Mex. 127 F8
Alamosa U.S.A. 127 G5
Alamos de Peña Mex. 127 G7
Alampur India 84 C3
Alan Myanmar see Aunglan
Alanäs Sweden 44 I4
Åland is Fin. see Åland Islands
Aland r. Germany 53 L1
Aland India 84 C2
Åland Islands Fin. 45 K6
Alando China 76 B2
Alandur India 84 D3
Alanson U.S.A. 134 C1
Alanya Turkey 90 D3
Alaplı Turkey 59 N4
Alappuzha India 84 C4
Alapuzha India see Alappuzha
Al 'Aqabah Jordan 85 B5
'Alāqahdārī Gēlān Afgh. 89 G3
'Alāqahdārī Gulistān Afgh. 89 F3
'Alāqahdārī Shāh Jōy Afgh. 89 G3
'Alāqahdārī Shumūlzaī Afgh. 89 G4
'Alāqahdārī-ye Kirān wa Munjān Afgh. 89 H2
Al 'Aqīq Saudi Arabia 86 F5
Al 'Arabīyah as Sa'ūdīyah country Asia see Saudi Arabia
Alarcón, Embalse de resr Spain 57 E4
Al 'Arīsh Egypt 85 A4
Al Arṭāwīyah Saudi Arabia 86 G4
Alas, Selat sea chan. Indon. 108 B2
Alaşehir Turkey 59 M5
Alashiya country Asia see Cyprus
Al Ashmūnayn Egypt 90 C6
Alaska state U.S.A. 118 D3
Alaska, Gulf of U.S.A. 118 D4
Alaska Highway Canada/U.S.A. 120 A2
Alaska Peninsula U.S.A. 118 B4
Alaska Range mts U.S.A. 118 D3
Älät Azer. 91 H3
Alat Uzbek. see Olot
Alataw Shankou pass China/Kazakh. see Dzungarian Gate
Al Atwā' well Saudi Arabia 91 F5
Alatyr' Russia 43 J5
Alatyr' r. Russia 43 J5
Alausí Ecuador 142 C4
Alaverdi Armenia 91 G2
Alavieska Fin. 44 N4
'Alavījeh Iran 88 C3
Alavus Fin. 44 M5
Alawbum Myanmar 70 B1
Alawoona Australia 111 C7
Alay Kyrka Toosu mts Asia see Alai Range
Al 'Ayn Oman 88 E6
Al 'Ayn U.A.E. 88 D5
Alayskiy Khrebet mts Asia see Alai Range
Al 'Azīzīyah Iraq 91 G4
Al 'Azīzīyah Libya 55 G5
Al Azraq al Janūbī Jordan 85 C4
Alba Italy 58 C2
Alba U.S.A. 134 C1
Al Bāb Syria 85 C1
Albacete Spain 57 F4
Al Badī' Saudi Arabia 88 B6
Al Bādiyah al Janūbīyah hill Iraq 91 G5
Al Bahrayn country Asia see Bahrain
Alba Iulia Romania 59 J1
Al Bajā' well U.A.E. 88 C5
Albājī Iran 88 C4
Al Bakhrā well Saudi Arabia 88 B5
Albanel, Lac l. Canada 123 G4
Albania country Europe 59 H4
Albany Australia 109 B8
Albany r. Canada 122 E3
Albany GA U.S.A. 133 C6
Albany IN U.S.A. 134 C3
Albany KY U.S.A. 134 C5
Albany MO U.S.A. 130 E3

▶Albany NY U.S.A. 135 I2
Capital of New York state.

Albany OH U.S.A. 134 D4
Albany OR U.S.A. 126 C3
Albany TX U.S.A. 131 D5
Albany Downs Australia 112 D1
Al Bāridah hills Saudi Arabia 85 D5
Al Başrah Iraq see Basra
Al Baṭḥa' marsh Iraq 91 G5
Al Bāṭinah reg. Oman 88 E5
Albatross Bay Australia 110 C2
Albatross Island Australia 111 [inset]
Al Bawīṭī Egypt 90 C5
Al Bayḍā' Libya 86 B3
Al Bayḍā' Yemen 86 G7
Albemarle U.S.A. 133 D5
Albemarle Sound sea chan. U.S.A. 132 E5
Albenga Italy 58 C2
Alberche r. Spain 57 D4
Alberga Australia 111 A5
Alberga watercourse Australia 111 A5
Albergaria-a-Velha Port. 57 B3
Albert Australia 112 C4
Albert France 52 C5
Albert, Lake Dem. Rep. Congo/Uganda 98 D3
Albert, Parc National nat. park Dem. Rep. Congo see Virunga, Parc National des
Alberta prov. Canada 120 H4
Alberta U.S.A. 135 G5
Albert Kanaal canal Belgium 52 F4
Albert Lea U.S.A. 130 E3
Albert Nile r. South Sudan/Uganda 97 G4
Alberto de Agostini, Parque Nacional nat. park Chile 144 B8
Alberton S. Africa 101 I4
Alberton U.S.A. 126 E3
Albert Town Bahamas 133 F8
Albertville Dem. Rep. Congo see Kalemie
Albertville France 56 H4
Albertville U.S.A. 133 C5
Albestroff France 52 G6
Albi France 56 F5
Albia U.S.A. 130 E3
Al Bīḍah des. Saudi Arabia 88 C5
Albina Suriname 143 H2
Albino Italy 58 C2
Albion CA U.S.A. 128 B2
Albion IL U.S.A. 130 F4
Albion IN U.S.A. 134 C3
Albion MI U.S.A. 134 C2
Albion NE U.S.A. 130 D3
Albion NY U.S.A. 135 F2
Albion PA U.S.A. 134 E3
Al Biqā' valley Lebanon see El Béqaa
Al Bi'r Saudi Arabia 90 E5
Al Birk Saudi Arabia 86 F6
Al Biyāḍh reg. Saudi Arabia 86 G5
Alborán, Isla de i. Spain 57 E6
Alboran Sea sea Europe 57 E5
Ålborg Denmark see Aalborg
Ålborg Bugt b. Denmark see Aalborg Bugt
Albro Australia 110 D4
Al Budayyi' Bahrain 88 C5
Albufeira Port. 57 B5
Al Buḥayrāt al Murrah lakes Egypt see Bitter Lakes
Albuquerque U.S.A. 127 G6
Al Burayj Syria 85 C2
Al Buraymī Oman 88 D5
Al Burdī Libya 90 B5
Al Burj Jordan 85 B5
Alburquerque Spain 57 C4
Albury Australia 112 C6
Al Buşayrah Syria 91 F4
Al Busayṭā' plain Saudi Arabia 85 D4
Al Bushūk well Saudi Arabia 88 B4
Alcácer do Sal Port. 57 B4
Alcalá de Henares Spain 57 E3
Alcalá la Real Spain 57 E5
Alcamo Sicily Italy 58 E6
Alcañiz Spain 57 F3
Alcántara Spain 57 C4
Alcantara Lake Canada 121 I2
Alcaraz Spain 57 E4
Alcázar de San Juan Spain 57 E4
Alcazarquivir Morocco see Ksar el Kebir
Alchevs'k Ukr. 43 H6
Alcobaça Brazil 145 D2
Alcoi Spain see Alcoy-Alcoi
Alcoota Australia 108 F5
Alcova U.S.A. 126 G4
Alcoy Spain see Alcoy-Alcoi
Alcoy-Alcoi Spain 57 F4
Alcúdia Spain 57 H4
Aldabra Islands Seychelles 99 E4
Aldan Russia 65 N4
Aldan r. Russia 65 N3
Al Dayyen Qatar 88 C5
Alde r. U.K. 49 I6
Aldeboarn Neth. 52 F1
Aldeburgh U.K. 49 I6
Alder Creek U.S.A. 135 H2
Alderney i. Channel Is 49 E9
Alder Peak U.S.A. 128 C4
Aldershot U.K. 49 G7
Al Dhafrah reg. U.A.E. 88 D6
Aldingham U.K. 48 D4
Aldridge U.K. 49 F6
Aleg Mauritania 96 B3
Alegre Espírito Santo Brazil 145 C3
Alegre Minas Gerais Brazil 145 B2
Alegrete Brazil 144 E3
Alegros Mountain U.S.A. 129 I4
Aleksandra, Mys hd Russia 74 E1
Aleksandriya Ukr. see Oleksandriya
Aleksandro-Nevskiy Russia 43 I5
Aleksandropol Armenia see Gyumri
Aleksandrov Russia 42 H4
Aleksandrov Gay Russia 43 K6
Aleksandrovsk Russia 41 R4
Aleksandrovsk Ukr. see Zaporizhzhya
Aleksandrovskiy Russia see Aleksandrovsk
Aleksandrovskoye Russia 91 F1
Aleksandrovsk-Sakhalinskiy Russia 74 F2
Aleksandry, Zemlya i. Russia 64 F1
Alekseyevka Akmolinskaya Oblast' Kazakh. see Akkol'
Alekseyevka Vostochnyy Kazakhstan Kazakh. see Terekty
Alekseyevka Amurskaya Oblast' Russia 74 B1
Alekseyevka Belgorodskaya Oblast' Russia 43 H6
Alekseyevka Belgorodskaya Oblast' Russia 43 H6
Alekseyevskaya Russia 43 I6
Alekseyevskoye Russia 42 K5
Aleksin Russia 43 H5
Aleksinac Serbia 59 I3
Alèmbé Gabon 98 B4
Ålen Norway 44 G5
Alençon France 56 E2
Alenquer Brazil 143 H4
'Alenuihāhā Channel U.S.A. 127 [inset]
Alep Syria see Aleppo
Aleppo Syria 85 C1
Alert Canada 119 L1
Alerta Peru 142 D6
Alès France 56 G4
Aleşd Romania 59 J1
Aleshki Ukr. see Tsyurupyns'k
Aleşkirt Turkey see Eleşkirt
Alessandria Italy 58 C2
Alessio Albania see Lezhë
Ålesund Norway 44 E5
Aleutian Basin sea feature Bering Sea 150 H2
Aleutian Islands U.S.A. 118 A4
Aleutian Range mts U.S.A. 118 C4
Aleutian Trench sea feature N. Pacific Ocean 150 I2
Alevina, Mys c. Russia 65 Q4
Alevişik Turkey see Samandağı
Alexander U.S.A. 130 C2
Alexander, Kap c. Greenland see Ullersuaq
Alexander, Mount hill Australia 110 B2
Alexander Archipelago is U.S.A. 120 B3
Alexander Bay b. Namibia/S. Africa 100 C5
Alexander Bay S. Africa 100 C5
Alexander City U.S.A. 133 C5
Alexander Island Antarctica 152 L2
Alexandra Australia 112 B6
Alexandra N.Z. 113 B7
Alexandra, Cape S. Georgia 144 I8
Alexandra Channel India 71 A4
Alexandra Land i. Russia see Aleksandry, Zemlya
Alexandreia Greece 59 J4
Alexandretta Turkey see İskenderun
Alexandria Afgh. see Ghaznī
Alexandria Canada 135 H1
Alexandria Egypt 90 C5
Alexandria Romania 59 K3
Alexandria S. Africa 101 H7
Alexandria Turkm. see Mary
Alexandria U.K. 50 E5
Alexandria IN U.S.A. 134 C3
Alexandria KY U.S.A. 134 C4
Alexandria LA U.S.A. 131 E6
Alexandria VA U.S.A. 135 G4
Alexandria Arachoton Afgh. see Kandahār
Alexandria Areion Afgh. see Herāt
Alexandria Bay U.S.A. 135 H1
Alexandria Prophthasia Afgh. see Farāh
Alexandrina, Lake Australia 111 B7
Alexandroupoli Greece 59 K4
Alexis r. Canada 123 K3
Alexis Creek Canada 120 F4
Aley Lebanon 85 B3
Aleyak Iran 88 E2
Aleysk Russia 72 E2
Alf Germany 52 H4
Al Farwānīyah Kuwait 88 B4
Al Fas Morocco see Fès
Al Fatḥah Iraq 91 F4
Al Fāw Iraq 91 H5
Al Fayyūm Egypt 90 C5
Alfeld (Leine) Germany 53 J3
Alfenas Brazil 145 B3
Alford U.K. 48 H5
Alfred ME U.S.A. 135 J2
Alfred NY U.S.A. 135 G2
Alfred and Marie Range hills Australia 109 D6
Al Fujayrah U.A.E. see Fujairah
Al Fuqahā' Libya 97 E2
Al Furāt r. Asia see Euphrates
Alga Kazakh. 80 A2
Ålgård Norway 45 D7
Algarrobo del Aguilla Arg. 144 C5
Algarve reg. Port. 57 B5
Algeciras Spain 57 D5
Algemesí Spain 57 F4
Algena Eritrea 86 E6
Alger Alg. see Algiers
Alger U.S.A. 134 C1

▶Algeria country Africa 96 C2
Largest country in Africa and 10th largest in the world.

Algérie country Africa see Algeria
Algermissen Germany 53 J2
Algha Kazakh. see Alga
Al Ghāfāt Oman 88 E6
Al Ghammās Iraq 91 G5
Al Ghardaqah Egypt see Hurghada
Al Ghawr plain Jordan/West Bank 85 B4
Al Ghayḍah Yemen 86 H6
Alghero Sardinia Italy 58 C4
Al Ghurdaqah Egypt see Hurghada
Al Ghuwayr well Qatar 88 C5

▶Algiers Alg. 57 H5
Capital of Algeria.

Algoa Bay S. Africa 101 G7
Algoma U.S.A. 134 B1
Algona U.S.A. 130 E3
Algonac U.S.A. 134 D2
Algonquin Park Canada 135 F1
Algonquin Provincial Park Canada 135 F1
Algorta Spain 57 E2
Algueirao Moz. see Hacufera
Al Habakah well Saudi Arabia 91 F5
Al Ḥabbānīyah Iraq 91 F4
Al Ḥadaqah well Saudi Arabia 88 B4
Al Ḥadd Bahrain 88 C5
Al Hadhālīl plat. Saudi Arabia 91 F5
Al Ḥadīthah Iraq 91 F4
Al Hadīthah Saudi Arabia 85 C4
Al Ḥaḍr Iraq see Hatra
Al Ḥafār well Saudi Arabia 91 F5
Al Ḥaffah Syria 85 C2
Al Ḥajar al Gharbī mts Oman 88 E5
Al Ḥajar ash Sharqī mts Oman 88 E6
Al Ḥamād plain Asia 90 E5
Alhama de Murcia Spain 57 F5
Al Ḥamar Saudi Arabia 88 B6
Al Ḥamdānīyah Syria 85 C2
Al Ḥamīdīyah Syria 85 B2
Al Ḥammām Egypt 90 C5
Al Ḥanākīyah Saudi Arabia 86 F5
Al Haniyah esc. Iraq 91 G5
Al Hariq Saudi Arabia 88 B6
Al Ḥarrah Egypt 90 C5
Al Harūj al Aswad hills Libya 97 E2
Al Hasa reg. Saudi Arabia 88 C5
Al Ḥasakah Syria 91 F3
Al Hawi salt pan Saudi Arabia 85 D5
Al Ḥawīyah Saudi Arabia 86 F5
Al Hawjā' Saudi Arabia 90 E5
Al Ḥawṭah reg. Saudi Arabia 88 B6
Al Ḥayy Iraq 91 G4
Al Hayz Egypt 90 C5
Al Hazīm Jordan 85 C4
Al Ḥazm Saudi Arabia 90 E5
Al Ḥibāk des. Saudi Arabia 87 H6
Al Ḥījānah Syria 85 C3
Al Ḥillah Iraq see Hillah
Al Ḥillah Saudi Arabia 86 G5
Al Ḥinnāh Saudi Arabia 98 E1
Al Ḥinw mt. Saudi Arabia 85 D4
Al Hirrah well Saudi Arabia 88 C6
Al Hīshah Syria 85 D1
Al Ḥismā plain Saudi Arabia 90 D5
Al Ḥiṣn Jordan 85 B3
Al Hoceima Morocco 57 E6
Al Hoceima, Baie d' b. Morocco 57 E6
Al Ḥudaydah Yemen see Hodeidah
Al Ḥufrah reg. Saudi Arabia 90 E5
Al Hufūf Saudi Arabia 86 G4
Al Hūj hills Saudi Arabia 90 E5
Al Husayfīn Oman 88 E5
Al Huwwah Saudi Arabia 88 B6
Ali China 82 D2
'Alīābād Afgh. 89 H2
'Alīābād Golestān Iran 88 D2
'Alīābād Hormozgān Iran 88 D4
'Alīābād Khorāsān-e Jonūbī Iran 89 F4
'Alīābād, Kūh-e mt. Iran 88 C3
'Alīābād-e Marān Iran 88 B2
'Ali'Addé Djibouti 86 F7
Aliağa Turkey 59 L5
Aliakmonas r. Greece 59 J4
Alibag India 84 B2
Alicante Spain 57 F4
Alice r. Australia 110 C2
Alice watercourse Australia 110 D5
Alice U.S.A. 131 D7
Alice, Punta pt Italy 58 G5
Alice Springs Australia 109 F5
Alice Town Bahamas 133 E7
Aliceville U.S.A. 131 F5
Alichur Tajik. 89 I2
Alichur r. Tajik. 89 I2
Alick Creek r. Australia 110 C4
Alifu Atoll Maldives see Ari Atholhu
Al Ifẓī'iyyah i. U.A.E. 88 C5
Aliganj India 82 D4
Aligarh Rajasthan India 82 D4
Aligarh Uttar Prad. India 82 D4
Alīgūdarz Iran 88 C3
Alihe China 74 A2
'Alījūq, Kūh-e mt. Iran 88 C4
'Alī Khēl Afgh. 89 H3
Al Imārāt al 'Arabīyah at Muttaḥidah country Asia see United Arab Emirates
Alimia i. Greece 59 L6
Alindao Cent. Afr. Rep. 98 C3
Alingsås Sweden 45 H8
Aliova r. Turkey 59 M5
Alipura India 82 D4
Alipur Duar India 83 G4
Alirajpur India 82 C5
Al 'Irāq country Asia see Iraq
Al 'Īsāwīyah Saudi Arabia 85 C4
Al Iskandarīyah Egypt see Alexandria
Al Iskandarīyah Iraq 91 G4
Al Ismā'īlīyah Egypt 90 D5
Al Ismā'īlīyah governorate Egypt 85 A4
Aliveri Greece 59 K5
Aliwal North S. Africa 101 H6
Alix Canada 120 H4
Al Jafr Jordan 85 C4
Al Jāfūrah des. Saudi Arabia 88 C5
Al Jaghbūb Libya 90 B5
Al Jahrah Kuwait 88 B4
Al Jarāwī well Saudi Arabia 85 D4
Al Jauf Saudi Arabia see Dawmat al Jandal
Al Jawb reg. Saudi Arabia 88 C6
Al Jawf Libya 97 F2
Al Jawsh Libya 96 E1
Al Jaza'ir country Africa see Algeria
Al Jaza'ir Alg. see Algiers
Aljezur Port. 57 B5
Al Jībān reg. Saudi Arabia 88 C5
Al Jil well Iraq 91 F5
Al Jilh esc. Saudi Arabia 88 B5
Al Jithāmīyah Saudi Arabia 91 F6
Al Jīzah Egypt see Giza
Al Jīzah Jordan 85 B4
Al Jubayl hills Saudi Arabia 88 B5
Al Jubaylah Saudi Arabia 88 B5
Al Jufrah Libya 97 E2
Al Julayqah well Saudi Arabia 88 C5
Al Jumaylīyah Qatar 88 C5
Aljustrel Port. 57 B5
Al Juwayf depr. Syria 85 C3
Al Kahfah Ash Sharqīyah Saudi Arabia 88 C5
Al Kahfah Ḥā'il Saudi Arabia 86 F4
Alkali Lake Canada 120 F5
Al Karak Jordan 85 B4
Al Kāẓimīyah Iraq 91 G4
Al Khābūrah Oman 88 E6
Al Khalīl West Bank see Hebron
Al Khāliṣ Iraq 91 G4
Al Khamāsīn Saudi Arabia 86 F5
Al Khārijah Egypt 86 D4
Al Kharj reg. Saudi Arabia 88 B6
Al Kharrārah Qatar 88 C5
Al Kharrūbah Egypt 85 A4
Al Khaṣab Oman 88 E5
Al Khatam reg. U.A.E. 88 D5
Al Khawkhah Yemen 86 F7
Al Khawr Qatar 88 C5
Al Khizāmī well Saudi Arabia 88 C5
Al Khums Libya 97 E1
Al Khunfah sand area Saudi Arabia 90 E5
Al Khunn Saudi Arabia 98 E1
Al Kifl Iraq 91 G4
Al Kir'ānah Qatar 88 C5
Al Kiswah Syria 85 C3
Alkmaar Neth. 52 E2
Al Kūbrī Egypt 85 A4
Al Kūfah Iraq 91 G4
Al Kumayt Iraq 91 G4
Al Kuntillah Egypt 85 B5
Al Kusūr hills Saudi Arabia 85 D4
Al Kūt Iraq 91 G4
Al Kuwayt country Asia see Kuwait
Al Kuwayt Kuwait see Kuwait
Al Labbah plain Saudi Arabia 91 F5
Al Lādhiqīyah Syria see Latakia
Allagadda India 84 C3
Allahabad India 83 E4
Al Lajā lava field Syria 85 C3
Allakaket U.S.A. 118 C3
Allakh-Yun' Russia 65 O3
Allanmyo Myanmar see Aunglan
Allanridge S. Africa 101 H4
Allapalli India 84 D2
'Allāqī, Wādī al watercourse Egypt 86 D5
'Allāqi, Wâdi el watercourse Egypt see 'Allāqī, Wādī al
Allardville Canada 123 I5
Alldays S. Africa 101 I2
Allegan U.S.A. 134 C2
Allegheny r. U.S.A. 134 F3
Allegheny Mountains U.S.A. 134 D5
Allegheny Reservoir U.S.A. 135 F3
Allen, Lough l. Ireland 51 D3
Allendale U.S.A. 133 D5
Allendale Town U.K. 48 E4
Allende Coahuila Mex. 131 C6
Allende Nuevo León Mex. 131 C7
Allendorf (Lumda) Germany 53 I4
Allenford Canada 134 E1
Allenstein Poland see Olsztyn
Allensville U.S.A. 134 B5
Allentown U.S.A. 135 H3
Alleppey India see Alappuzha
Aller r. Germany 53 J2
Alliance NE U.S.A. 130 C3
Alliance OH U.S.A. 134 E3
Al Lībīyah country Africa see Libya
Allier r. France 56 F3
Al Lihābah well Saudi Arabia 88 B5
Allinge-Sandvig Denmark 45 I9
Al Lişāfah well Saudi Arabia 88 B5
Al Lisān pen. Jordan 85 B4
Alliston Canada 134 F1
Al Līth Saudi Arabia 86 F5
Al Liwā' oasis U.A.E. 88 D6
Alloa U.K. 50 F4
Allons U.S.A. 134 C5
Allora Australia 112 F2
Allur India 84 D3
Alluru Kottapatnam India 84 D3
Al Lussuf well Iraq 91 F5
Alma Canada 123 H4
Alma MI U.S.A. 134 C2
Alma NE U.S.A. 130 D3
Alma WI U.S.A. 130 F2
Al Ma'ānīyah Iraq 91 F5
Alma-Ata Kazakh. see Almaty
Almada Port. 57 B4
Al Madāfi' plat. Saudi Arabia 90 E5
Al Ma'danīyāt well Iraq 91 G5
Almaden Australia 110 D3
Almadén Spain 57 D4
Al Madīnah Saudi Arabia see Medina
Al Mafraq Jordan 85 C3
Al Maghrib country Africa see Morocco
Al Maghrib reg. U.A.E. 88 D6
Al Maḥajjah depr. Saudi Arabia 90 E6
Al Mahākīk reg. Saudi Arabia 88 C6
Al Maḥwīt Yemen 86 F6
Al Malsūnīyah reg. Saudi Arabia 88 C5
Almalyk Uzbek. see Olmaliq
Al Manadir reg. Oman 88 D6
Al Manāmah Bahrain see Manama
Al Manjūr well Saudi Arabia 88 B6
Almanor, Lake U.S.A. 128 C1
Almansa Spain 57 F4
Al Manṣūrah Egypt 90 C5
Almanzor mt. Spain 57 D3
Al Mariyyah U.A.E. 88 D6
Al Marj Libya 97 F1
Almas, Rio das r. Brazil 145 A1
Al Maṭarīyah Egypt 90 D5

▶Almaty Kazakh. 80 E3
Former capital of Kazakhstan.

Al Mawşil Iraq see Mosul
Al Mayādīn Syria 91 F4
Al Mazār Egypt 85 A4
Almaznyy Russia 65 M3
Almeirim Brazil 143 H4
Almeirim Port. 57 B4
Almelo Neth. 52 G2
Almenara Brazil 145 C2
Almendra, Embalse de resr Spain 57 C3
Almendralejo Spain 57 C4
Almere Neth. 52 F2
Almería Spain 57 E5
Almería, Golfo de b. Spain 57 E5
Almetievsk Russia see Al'met'yevsk
Al'met'yevsk Russia 41 Q5
Älmhult Sweden 45 I8
Almina, Punta pt Spain 57 D6
Al Mindak Saudi Arabia 86 F5
Al Minyā Egypt 90 C5
Almirós Greece see Almyros
Al Mish'āb Saudi Arabia 88 C4
Almodôvar Port. 57 B5
Almond r. U.K. 50 F4
Almont U.S.A. 134 D2
Almonte Spain 57 C5
Almora India 82 D3
Al Mu'ayzīlah hill Saudi Arabia 85 D5
Al Mubarrez Saudi Arabia 86 G4
Al Muḍaibī Oman 87 I5
Al Muḍairib Oman 88 E6
Al Muḥarraq Bahrain 88 C5
Al Mukallā Yemen see Mukalla
Al Mukhā Yemen see Mocha
Al Mukhaylī Libya 86 B3
Al Munbaṭiḥ des. Saudi Arabia 88 C6
Almuñécar Spain 57 E5
Al Muqdādīyah Iraq 91 G4
Al Mūrītānīyah country Africa see Mauritania
Al Murūt well Saudi Arabia 91 E5
Almus Turkey 90 E2
Al Musannāh ridge Saudi Arabia 88 B4
Al Musayyib Iraq 88 B3
Al Muwaqqar Jordan 85 C4
Almyros Greece 59 J5
Almyrou, Ormos b. Greece 59 K7
Alnwick U.K. 48 F3

▶Alofi Niue 107 J3
Capital of Niue.

Aloja Latvia 45 N8
Alon Myanmar 70 A2

Anne Marie Lake Canada **123** J3
Annen Neth. **52** G1
Annette Island U.S.A. **120** D4
An Nimārah Syria **85** C3
An Nimāş Saudi Arabia **86** F6
Anning China **76** D3
Anniston U.S.A. **133** C5
Annobón *i.* Equat. Guinea **96** D5
Annonay France **56** G4
An Nu'mānīyah Iraq **91** G4
Anonima *atoll* Micronesia *see* **Namonuito**
Anorontany, Tanjona *hd* Madag. **99** E5
Ano Viannos Greece *see* **Viannos**
Anpu Gang *b.* China **77** F4
Anqing China **77** H2
Anren China **77** G3
Ans Belgium **52** F4
Ansbach Germany **53** K5
Anser Group *is* Australia **112** C7
Anshan China **74** A4
Anshun *Guizhou* China **76** E3
Anshun *Sichuan* China **76** D2
Ansley U.S.A. **130** D3
Anson U.S.A. **131** D5
Anson Bay Australia **108** E3
Ansongo Mali **96** D3
Ansonville Canada **122** E4
Ansted U.S.A. **134** E4
Ansudu Indon. **69** J7
Antabamba Peru **142** D6
Antakya Turkey **85** C1
Antalaha Madag. **99** F5
Antalya Turkey **59** N6
Antalya *prov.* Turkey **85** A1
Antalya Körfezi *g.* Turkey **59** N6

▶**Antananarivo** Madag. **99** E5
Capital of Madagascar.

An tAonach Ireland *see* **Nenagh**

▶**Antarctica 152**
Most southerly and coldest continent, and the continent with the highest average elevation.

Antarctic Peninsula Antarctica **152** L2
Antas *r.* Brazil **145** A5
An Teallach *mt.* U.K. **50** D3
Antelope Island U.S.A. **129** G1
Antelope Range *mts* U.S.A. **128** E2
Antequera Spain **57** D5
Anthony Lagoon Australia **110** A3
Anti-Atlas *mts* Morocco **54** C6
Antibes France **56** H5
Anticosti, Île d' *i.* Canada **123** J4
Anticosti Island Canada *see* **Anticosti, Île d'**
Antifer, Cap d' *c.* France **49** H9
Antigo U.S.A. **130** F2
Antigonish Canada **123** J5
Antigua *i.* Antigua and Barbuda **137** L5
Antigua *country* West Indies *see* **Antigua and Barbuda**
Antigua and Barbuda *country* West Indies **137** L5
Antikythira *i.* Greece **59** J7
Antikythiro, Steno *sea chan.* Greece **59** J7
Anti Lebanon *mts* Lebanon/Syria *see* **Sharqī, Jabal ash**
Antimilos *i.* Greece **59** K6
Antimony U.S.A. **129** H2
An tInbhear Mór Ireland *see* **Arklow**
Antioch Turkey *see* **Antakya**
Antioch U.S.A. **128** C2
Antiocheia ad Cragum *tourist site* Turkey **85** A1
Antiochia Turkey *see* **Antakya**
Antiparos *i.* Greece **59** K6
Antipodes Islands N.Z. **107** H6
Antipsara *i.* Greece **59** K5
Antium Italy *see* **Anzio**
Antlers U.S.A. **131** E5
Antofagasta Chile **144** B2
Antofagasta de la Sierra Arg. **144** C3
Antofalla, Volcán *vol.* Arg. **144** C3
Antoing Belgium **52** D4
Antonine Wall *tourist site* U.K. **50** E5
António Enes Moz. *see* **Angoche**
Antri India **82** D4
Antrim U.K. **51** F3
Antrim Hills U.K. **51** F2
Antrim Plateau Australia **108** E4
Antropovo Russia **42** I4
Antsalova Madag. **99** E5
Antseranana Madag. *see* **Antsiraṅana**
Antsirabe Madag. **99** E5
Antsiraṅana Madag. **99** E5
Antsla Estonia **45** O8
Antsohihy Madag. **99** E5
Anttis Sweden **44** M3
Anttola Fin. **45** O6
An Tuc Vietnam *see* **An Khê**
Antwerp Belgium **52** E3
Antwerp U.S.A. **135** H1
Antwerpen Belgium *see* **Antwerp**
An Uaimh Ireland *see* **Navan**
Anuc, Lac *l.* Canada **122** G2
Anuchino Russia **74** D4
Anugul India *see* **Angul**
Anupgarh India **82** C3
Anuradhapura Sri Lanka **84** D4
Anveh Iran **88** D5
Anvers Island Antarctica **152** L2
Anvik U.S.A. **118** B3
Anvil Range *mts* Canada **120** C2
Anxi China **77** H3
Anxiang China **77** G2
Anxious Bay Australia **109** F8
Anyang *Guangxi* China *see* **Du'an**
Anyang *Henan* China **73** K5
Anyang S. Korea **75** B5
A'nyêmaqên Shan *mts* China **76** C1
Anyuan *Jiangxi* China **77** G3
Anyuan *Jiangxi* China **77** G3
Anyue China **76** E2
Anyuy *r.* Russia **74** E2
Anyuysk Russia **65** R3
Anzac *Alta* Canada **121** I3
Anzac *B.C.* Canada **120** F4
Anzhero-Sudzhensk Russia **64** J4
Anzi Dem. Rep. Congo **98** C4
Anzio Italy **58** E4
Aoba *i.* Vanuatu **107** G3
Aoga-shima *i.* Japan **75** E6
Ao Kham, Laem *pt* Thai. **71** B5
Aomen China *see* **Macao**
Aomen *aut. reg.* China *see* **Macao**
Aomen Tebie Xingzhengqu *aut. reg.* China *see* **Macao**
Aomori Japan **74** F4
Ao Phang Nga National Park Thai. **71** B5

▶**Aoraki/Mount Cook** *mt.* N.Z. **113** C6
Highest mountain in New Zealand.

Aoraki/Mount Cook National Park N.Z. **113** C6
Aôral, Phnum *mt.* Cambodia **71** D4
Aorangi *mt.* N.Z. *see* **Aoraki/Mount Cook**
Aosta Italy **58** B2
Aotearoa *country* Oceania *see* **New Zealand**
Aouk, Bahr *r.* Cent. Afr. Rep./Chad **97** E4
Aoukâr *reg.* Mali/Mauritania **96** C2
Aoulef Alg. **96** D2
Aoussard W. Sahara **96** B2
Aozou Chad **97** E2
Apa *r.* Brazil **144** E2
Apache Creek U.S.A. **129** I5
Apache Junction U.S.A. **129** H5
Apaiang *atoll* Kiribati *see* **Abaiang**
Apalachee Bay U.S.A. **133** C6
Apalachicola U.S.A. **133** C6
Apalachicola *r.* U.S.A. **133** C6
Apalachin U.S.A. **135** G2
Apamea Turkey *see* **Dinar**
Apaporis *r.* Col. **142** E4
Aparecida do Tabuado Brazil **145** A3
Aparima N.Z. *see* **Riverton**
Aparri Phil. **150** E4
Apatity Russia **44** R3
Apatzingán Mex. **136** D5
Ape Latvia **45** O8
Apeldoorn Neth. **52** F2
Apelern Germany **53** J2
Apennines *mts* Italy **58** C2
Apensen Germany **53** J1
Apex Mountain Canada **120** B2
Api *mt.* Nepal **82** E3
Api *i.* Vanuatu *see* **Épi**
Apia *atoll* Kiribati *see* **Abaiang**

▶**Apia** Samoa **107** I3
Capital of Samoa.

Apiacas, Serra dos *hills* Brazil **143** G6
Apiaí Brazil **145** A4
Apishapa *r.* U.S.A. **130** C4
Apiti N.Z. **113** E4
Apizolaya Mex. **131** C7
Apkhazeti *disp. terr.* Georgia *see* **Abkhazia**
Aplao Peru **142** D7
Apo, Mount *vol.* Phil. **69** H5
Apoera Suriname **143** G2
Apolda Germany **53** L3
Apollo Bay Australia **112** A7
Apollonia Bulg. *see* **Sozopol**
Apolo Bol. **142** E6
Aporé Brazil **145** A2
Aporé *r.* Brazil **145** A2
Apostelens Tommelfinger *mt.* Greenland **119** N3
Apostle Islands U.S.A. **130** F2
Apostolos Andreas, Cape Cyprus **85** B2
Apoteri Guyana **143** G3
Apozai Pak. **89** H4
Appalachian Mountains U.S.A. **134** D5
Appalla *i.* Fiji *see* **Kabara**
Appennino *mts* Italy *see* **Apennines**
Appennino Abruzzese *mts* Italy **58** E3
Appennino Tosco-Emiliano *mts* Italy **58** D3
Appennino Umbro-Marchigiano *mts* Italy **58** E3
Appingedam Neth. **52** G1
Applecross U.K. **50** D3
Appleton *MN* U.S.A. **130** D2
Appleton *WI* U.S.A. **134** A1
Apple Valley U.S.A. **128** E4
Appomattox U.S.A. **135** F5
Aprilia Italy **58** E4
Aprunyi India **76** B2
Apsheronsk Russia **91** E1
Apsheronskaya Russia *see* **Apsheronsk**
Apsley Canada **135** F1
Apt France **56** G5
Apucarana Brazil **145** A3
Apucarana, Serra da *hills* Brazil **145** A3
Apuka Russia **65** R3
Apulum Romania *see* **Alba Iulia**
Aq"a Georgia *see* **Sokhumi**
'Aqaba Jordan *see* **Al 'Aqabah**
Aqaba, Gulf of Asia **90** D5
'Aqaba, Wâdi el *watercourse* Egypt *see* **'Aqabah, Wādī al**
'Aqabah, Birkat al *well* Iraq **88** A4
'Aqabah, Wādī al *watercourse* Egypt **85** A4
Aqadyr Kazakh. *see* **Akadyr**
Aqdoghmish *r.* Iran **88** B2
Aqköl *Akmolinskaya Oblast'* Kazakh. *see* **Akkol'**
Aqköl *Atyrauskaya Oblast'* Kazakh. *see* **Akkol'**
Aqmola Kazakh. *see* **Astana**
Aqqan China **83** F1
Aqqikkol Hu *salt l.* China **83** G1
Aqra', Jabal al *mt.* Syria/Turkey **85** B2
'Aqran *hill* Saudi Arabia **85** D4
Aqsay Kazakh. *see* **Aksay**
Aqsayqin *terr.* China *see* **Aksai Chin**
Aqshī Kazakh. *see* **Akshi**
Aqshuqyr Kazakh. *see* **Akshukyr**
Aqsū Kazakh. *see* **Aksu**
Aqsūat Kazakh. *see* **Aksuat**
Aqsū-Ayuly Kazakh. *see* **Aksu-Ayuly**
Aqtaū Kazakh. *see* **Aktau**
Aqtöbe Kazakh. *see* **Aktobe**
Aqtoghay Kazakh. *see* **Aktogay**
Aquae Grani Germany *see* **Aachen**
Aquae Gratianae France *see* **Aix-les-Bains**
Aquae Sextiae France *see* **Aix-en-Provence**
Aquae Statiellae Italy *see* **Acqui Terme**
Aquarius Mountains U.S.A. **129** G4
Aquarius Plateau U.S.A. **129** H3
Aquidauana Brazil **144** E2
Aquiles Mex. **127** G7
Aquincum Hungary *see* **Budapest**
Aquiry *r.* Brazil *see* **Acre**
Aquisgranum Germany *see* **Aachen**
Aquitaine *reg.* France **56** D5
Aquitania *reg.* France *see* **Aquitaine**
Aqzhayqyn Köli *salt l.* Kazakh. *see* **Akzhaykyn, Ozero**
Ara India *see* **Arrah**
Āra Ārba Eth. **98** E3
'Arab Afgh. **89** G4
Arab, Bahr el *watercourse* Sudan **97** F4
'Arab, Khalîg el *b.* Egypt *see* **'Arab, Khalīj al**
'Arab, Khalīj al *b.* Egypt **90** C5
'Arabah, Wādī al *watercourse* Israel/Jordan **85** B5
Arabian Basin *sea feature* Indian Ocean **149** M5
Arabian Gulf Asia *see* **The Gulf**
Arabian Peninsula Asia **86** G5
Arabian Sea Indian Ocean **87** K6
Araç Turkey **90** D2
Araça *r.* Brazil **142** F4
Aracaju Brazil **143** K6
Aracati Brazil **143** K4
Aracatu Brazil **145** C1
Araçatuba Brazil **145** A3
Aracena Spain **57** C5
Aracruz Brazil **145** C2
Araçuaí Brazil **145** C2
Araçuaí *r.* Brazil **145** C2
'Arad Israel **85** B4
Arad Romania **59** I1
'Arādah U.A.E. **88** D6
Arafura Sea Australia/Indon. **106** D2
Arafura Shelf *sea feature* Australia/Indon. **150** E6
Aragarças Brazil **143** H7
Aragón *r.* Spain **57** F2
Araguaçu Brazil **145** A1
Araguaia *r.* Brazil **145** A1
Araguaia, Parque Nacional do *nat. park* Brazil **143** H6
Araguaiana Brazil **145** A1
Araguaína Brazil **143** I5
Araguari Brazil **145** A2
Araguari *r.* Brazil **143** H3
Araguatins Brazil **143** I5
Araí Brazil **145** B1
'Arâif el Naga, Gebel *hill* Egypt *see* **'Urayf an Nāqah, Jabal**
Araioses Brazil **143** J4
Arak Alg. **96** D2
Ārāk Iran **88** C3
Arak Syria **85** D2
Arakan *reg.* Myanmar **70** A2
Arakan Yoma *mts* Myanmar **70** A2
Arakkonam India **84** C3
Araks *r.* Azer. *see* **Araz**
Araku India **84** D2
Aral China **80** F3
Aral Kazakh. *see* **Aral'sk**
Aral Tajik. *see* **Vose'**
Aralkum *des.* Kazakh./Uzbek. **80** A3

▶**Aral Sea** *salt l.* Kazakh./Uzbek. **80** A3
4th largest lake in Asia.

Aral'sk Kazakh. **80** B2
Aral'skoye More *salt l.* Kazakh./Uzbek. *see* **Aral Sea**
Aralsor, Ozero *l.* Kazakh. **43** K6
Aral Tengizi *salt l.* Kazakh./Uzbek. *see* **Aral Sea**
Aramac Australia **110** D4
Aramac Creek *watercourse* Australia **110** D4
Aramah *plat.* Saudi Arabia **88** B5
Aramberri Mex. **131** D7
Aramia *r.* P.N.G. **69** K8
Aran *r.* India **84** C2
Aranda de Duero Spain **57** E3
Arandai Indon. **69** I7
Aranđelovac Serbia **59** I2
Arandis Namibia **100** B2
Arang India **83** E5
Arani India **84** C3
Aran Islands Ireland **51** C4
Aranjuez Spain **57** E3
Aranos Namibia **100** D3
Aransas Pass U.S.A. **131** D7
Arantangi India **84** C4
Aranuka *atoll* Kiribati **107** H1
Aranyaprathet Thai. **71** C4
Arao Japan **75** C6
Araouane Mali **96** C3
Arapaho U.S.A. **131** D5
Arapgir Turkey **90** E3
Arapiraca Brazil **143** K5
Arapis, Akra *pt* Greece *see* **Arapis, Akrotirio**
Arapis, Akrotirio *pt* Greece **59** K4
Arapkir Turkey *see* **Arapgir**
Arapongas Brazil **145** A3
Araquari Brazil **145** A4
'Ar'ar Saudi Arabia **91** F5
Araranguá Brazil **145** A5
Araraquara Brazil **145** A3
Araras Brazil **143** H5
Ararat Armenia **91** G3
Ararat Australia **112** A6
Ararat, Mount **91** G3
Araria India **83** F4
Araripina Brazil **143** J5
Aras *r.* Azer. *see* **Araz**
Aras Turkey **91** F3
Arataca Brazil **145** D1
Arauca Col. **142** D2
Arauca *r.* Venez. **142** E2
Aravalli Range *mts* India **82** C4
Aravete Estonia **45** N7
Arawa P.N.G. **106** F2
Araxá Brazil **145** B2
Araxes *r.* Azer. *see* **Araz**
Arayıt Dağı *mt.* Turkey **59** N5
Araz *r.* Azer. **91** H2
also spelt Araks (Armenia), Aras (Turkey), formerly known as Araxes
Arbailu Iraq *see* **Arbīl/Hewlêr**
Arbela Iraq *see* **Arbīl/Hewlêr**
Arberth U.K. *see* **Narberth**
Arbīl/Hewlêr Iraq **91** G3
Arboga Sweden **45** I7
Arborfield Canada **121** K4
Arborg Canada **121** L5
Arbroath U.K. **50** G4
Arbuckle U.S.A. **128** B2
Arbū-ye Shamālī, Dasht-e *des.* Afgh. **89** F4
Arcachon France **56** D4
Arcade U.S.A. **135** F2
Arcadia *FL* U.S.A. **133** D7
Arcadia *LA* U.S.A. **131** E5
Arcadia *MI* U.S.A. **134** B1
Arcanum U.S.A. **134** C4
Arcata U.S.A. **126** B4
Arc Dome *mt.* U.S.A. **128** E2
Arcelia Mex. **136** D5
Archaeological Sites of the Island of Meroe *tourist site* Sudan **97** G3
Archangel Russia **42** I2
Archer *r.* Australia **67** G9
Archer Bend National Park Australia **110** C2
Archer City U.S.A. **131** D5
Arches National Park U.S.A. **129** I2
Archipel-de-Mingan, Réserve du Parc National de l' *nat. park* Canada **123** J4
Archipiélago Los Roques, Parque Nacional *nat. park* Venez. **142** E1
Ärçivan Azer. **91** H3
Arckaringa *watercourse* Australia **111** A6
Arco U.S.A. **126** E4
Arcos Brazil **145** B3
Arcos de la Frontera Spain **57** D5
Arctic Bay Canada **119** J2
Arctic Institute Islands Russia *see* **Arkticheskogo Instituta, Ostrova**
Arctic Mid-Ocean Ridge *sea feature* Arctic Ocean **153** H1
Arctic Ocean 153 B1
Arctic Red *r.* Canada **118** E3
Arctowski *research station* Antarctica **152** A2
Arda *r.* Bulg. **59** L4
also known as Ardas (Greece)
Ardabīl Iran **88** C2
Ardahan Turkey **91** F2
Ardakān Iran **88** D3
Årdalstangen Norway **45** E6
Ardara Ireland **51** D3
Ardas *r.* Bulg. *see* **Arda**
Arḍ aş Şawwān *plain* Jordan **85** C4
Ardatov *Nizhegorodskaya Oblast'* Russia **43** I5
Ardatov *Respublika Mordoviya* Russia **43** J5
Ardee Ireland **51** F4
Ardennes *plat.* Belgium **52** F5
Ardennes, Canal des France **52** E5
Arden Town U.S.A. **128** C2
Arderin *hill* Ireland **51** E4
Ardestān Iran **88** D3
Ardglass U.K. **51** G3
Ardila *r.* Port. **57** C4
Ardlethan Australia **112** C5
Ardmore U.S.A. **131** D5
Ardnamurchan, Point of U.K. **50** C4
Ardon Russia **91** G2
Ardrishaig U.K. **50** D4
Ardrossan U.K. **50** E5
Ardvasar U.K. **50** D3
Areia Branca Brazil **143** K4
Arel Belgium *see* **Arlon**
Arelas France *see* **Arles**
Arelate France *see* **Arles**
Aremberg *hill* Germany **52** G4
Arena, Point U.S.A. **128** B2
Arenas de San Pedro Spain **57** D3
Arendal Norway **45** F7
Arendsee (Altmark) Germany **53** L2
Areopoli Greece **59** J6
Arequipa Peru **142** D7
Arere Brazil **143** H4
Arévalo Spain **57** D3
Arezzo Italy **58** D3
'Arfajah *well* Saudi Arabia **85** D4
Argadargada Australia **110** B4
Arganda del Rey Spain **57** E3
Argel Alg. *see* **Algiers**
Argentan France **56** D2
Argentario, Monte *hill* Italy **58** D3
Argentera, Cima dell' *mt.* Italy **58** B2
Argenthal Germany **53** H5

▶**Argentina** *country* S. America **144** C5
2nd largest and 3rd most populous country in South America and 8th largest in the world.

Argentine Abyssal Plain *sea feature* S. Atlantic Ocean **148** E9
Argentine Basin *sea feature* S. Atlantic Ocean **148** F8
Argentine Republic *country* S. America *see* **Argentina**
Argentine Rise *sea feature* S. Atlantic Ocean **148** E8
Argentino, Lago *l.* Arg. **144** B8
Argenton-sur-Creuse France **56** E3
Argentoratum France *see* **Strasbourg**
Argeş *r.* Romania **59** L2
Arg-e Zārī Afgh. **89** G3
Arghandāb Rōd *r.* Afgh. **89** G4
Argi *r.* Russia **74** C1
Argolikos Kolpos *b.* Greece **59** J6
Argos Greece **59** J6
Argos U.S.A. **134** B3
Argostoli Greece **59** I5
Arguis Spain **57** F2
Argun' *r.* China/Russia **73** M2
Argun Russia **91** G2
Argungu Nigeria **96** D3
Argus, Dome *ice feature* Antarctica **152** E1
Argus Range *mts* U.S.A. **128** E4
Argyle Canada **123** I6
Argyle, Lake Australia **108** E4
Argyrokastron Albania *see* **Gjirokastër**
Ar Horqin Qi China *see* **Tianshan**
Århus Denmark *see* **Aarhus**
Ariah Park Australia **112** C5
Ariamsvlei Namibia **100** D5
Ariana Tunisia *see* **L'Ariana**
Ariano Irpino Italy **58** F4
Ari Atholhu Maldives **81** D11
Aribinda Burkina Faso **96** C3
Arica Chile **142** D7
Arid, Cape Australia **109** C8
Arigza China **76** C1
Arīḩā Syria **85** C2
Arīḩā West Bank *see* **Jericho**
Arikaree *r.* U.S.A. **130** C3
Arima Trin. and Tob. **137** L6
Ariminum Italy *see* **Rimini**
Arinos Brazil **145** B1
Aripuanã Brazil **143** G6
Aripuanã *r.* Brazil **142** F5
Ariquemes Brazil **142** F5
Aris Namibia **100** C2
Arisaig U.K. **50** D4
Arisaig, Sound of *sea chan.* U.K. **50** D4
'Arīsh, Wādī al *watercourse* Egypt **85** A4
Aristazabal Island Canada **120** D4
Arixang China *see* **Wenquan**
Ariyalur India **84** C4
Arizaro, Salar de *salt flat* Arg. **144** C2
Arizona Arg. **144** C5
Arizona *state* U.S.A. **127** F6
Arizpe Mex. **127** F7
'Arjah Saudi Arabia **86** F5
Arjasa Indon. **68** F8
Arjeplog Sweden **44** J3
Arjuni *Chhattisgarh* India **84** D1
Arjuni *Mahar.* India **82** E5
Arkadak Russia **43** I6
Arkadelphia U.S.A. **131** E5
Arkaig, Loch *l.* U.K. **50** D4
Arkalyk Kazakh. **80** C1
Arkansas *r.* U.S.A. **131** F5
Arkansas *state* U.S.A. **131** E5
Arkansas City *AR* U.S.A. **131** F5
Arkansas City *KS* U.S.A. **131** D4
Arkanū, Jabal *mt.* Libya **86** B5
Arka Tag *mts* China **83** G1
Arkell, Mount Canada **120** C2
Arkhangel'sk Russia *see* **Archangel**
Arkhara Russia **74** C2
Arkhipovka Russia **74** D4
Árki *i.* Greece *see* **Arkoi**
Arklow Ireland **51** F5
Arkoi *i.* Greece **59** L6
Arkona Canada **134** E2
Arkona, Kap *c.* Germany **47** N3
Arkonam India *see* **Arakkonam**
Arkport U.S.A. **135** G2

▶**Arkticheskiy, Mys** *c.* Russia **153** E1
Most northerly point of Asia.

Arkticheskogo Instituta, Ostrova *is* Russia **64** J2
Arkul' Russia **42** K4
Arlandag *mt.* Turkm. **88** D2
Arles France **56** G5
Arli, Parc National de l' *nat. park* Burkina Faso **96** D3
Arlington S. Africa **101** H5
Arlington *NY* U.S.A. **135** I3
Arlington *OH* U.S.A. **134** D3
Arlington *SD* U.S.A. **130** D2
Arlington *VA* U.S.A. **135** G4
Arlington Heights U.S.A. **134** A2
Arlit Niger **96** D3
Arlon Belgium **52** F5
Arm *r.* Canada **121** J5
Armadale Australia **109** A8
Armagh U.K. **51** F3
Arma Konda *mt.* India **84** D2
Armant Egypt **86** D4
Armavir Armenia **91** G2
Armavir Russia **91** F1
Armenia *country* Asia **91** G2
Armenia Col. **142** C3
Armenopolis Romania *see* **Gherla**
Armeria Mex. **136** D5
Armidale Australia **112** E3
Armington U.S.A. **126** F3
Armit Lake Canada **121** N1
Armori India **84** D1
Armour U.S.A. **130** D3
Armoy U.K. **51** F2
Armstrong *r.* Australia **108** E4
Armstrong Canada **122** C4
Armstrong, Mount Canada **120** C2
Armstrong Island Cook Is *see* **Rarotonga**
Armu *r.* Russia **74** E3
Armur India **84** C2
Armutçuk Dağı *mts* Turkey **59** L5
Armyanskaya S.S.R. *country* Asia *see* **Armenia**
Arnaoutis, Cape Cyprus *see* **Arnauti, Cape**
Arnaud *r.* Canada **123** H2
Arnauti, Cape Cyprus **85** A2
Årnes Norway **45** G6
Arnett U.S.A. **131** D4
Arnhem Neth. **52** F3
Arnhem, Cape Australia **110** B2
Arnhem Land *reg.* Australia **108** F3
Arniston S. Africa **100** E8
Arno *r.* Italy **58** D3
Arno Bay Australia **111** B7
Arnold U.K. **49** F5
Arnold's Cove Canada **123** L5
Arnon *r.* Jordan *see* **Mawjib, Wādī al**
Arnprior Canada **135** G1
Arnsberg Germany **53** I3
Arnstadt Germany **53** K4
Arnstein Germany **53** J5
Arnstorf Germany **53** M6
Aroab Namibia **100** D4
Aroland Canada **122** D4
Arolsen Germany **53** J3
Aroma Sudan **86** E6
Arona Italy **58** C2
Arorae *i.* Kiribati **107** H2
Arore *i.* Kiribati *see* **Arorae**
Aros *r.* Mex. **127** F7
Arossi *i.* Solomon Is *see* **Makira**
Arqalyq Kazakh. *see* **Arkalyk**
Arquipélago da Madeira *aut. reg.* Port. **96** B1
Arrabury Australia **111** C5
Arrah India **83** F4
Arraias Brazil **145** B1
Arraias, Serra de *hills* Brazil **145** B1
Ar Ramādī Iraq **91** F4
Ar Ramlah Jordan **85** B5
Ar Ramthā Jordan **85** C3
Arran *i.* U.K. **50** D5
Arranmore Island Ireland **51** D3
Ar Raqqah Syria **85** D2
Arras France **52** C4
Ar Rass Saudi Arabia **86** F4
Ar Rastan Syria **85** C2
Ar Rayyān Qatar **88** C5
Arrecife Canary Is **96** B2
Arretium Italy *see* **Arezzo**
Arriagá Mex. **136** F5
Ar Rifā'ī Iraq **91** G5
Ar Rihāb *salt flat* Iraq **91** G5
Ar Rimāl *reg.* Saudi Arabia **98** F1
Arrington U.S.A. **135** F5
Ar Riyāḑ Saudi Arabia *see* **Riyadh**
Arrochar U.K. **50** E4
Arrojado *r.* Brazil **145** B1
Arrow, Lough *l.* Ireland **51** D3
Arrowsmith, Mount N.Z. **113** C6
Arroyo Grande U.S.A. **128** C4
Ar Rubay'īyah Saudi Arabia **88** B5
Ar Rummān Jordan **85** B3
Ar Ruq'ī *well* Saudi Arabia **88** B4
Ar Ruşayfah Jordan **85** C3
Ar Rustāq Oman **88** E6
Ar Ruṭbah Iraq **91** F4
Ar Ruwaydah Saudi Arabia **88** B5
Ar Ruwayḑah Saudi Arabia **88** B6
Ar Ruwayḑah Syria **85** C2
Års Denmark *see* **Aars**
Ars Iran **88** B2
Arseno Lake Canada **120** H1
Arsen'yev Russia **74** D3
Arsk Russia **42** K4
Arta Greece **59** I5
Artem Russia **74** D4
Artemisa Cuba **133** D8
Artemivs'k Ukr *see* **Bakhmut**
Artemovsk Ukr. *see* **Artemivs'k**
Artenay France **56** E2
Artesia *AZ* U.S.A. **129** I5
Artesia *NM* U.S.A. **127** G6
Arthur Canada **134** E2
Arthur *NE* U.S.A. **130** C3
Arthur *TN* U.S.A. **134** D5
Arthur, Lake U.S.A. **134** E3
Arthur's Pass National Park N.Z. **113** C6
Arthur's Town Bahamas **133** F7
Arti Russia **41** R4
Artigas *research station* Antarctica **152** A2
Artigas Uruguay **144** E4
Art'ik Armenia **91** F2
Artillery Lake Canada **121** I2
Artisia Botswana **101** H3
Artois *reg.* France **52** B4
Artois, Collines d' *hills* France **52** B4
Artos Dağı *mt.* Turkey **91** F3
Artova Turkey **90** E2
Artsakh *disp. terr.* Azer. *see* **Nagorno-Karabakh**
Artsiz Ukr. *see* **Artsyz**
Artsyz Ukr. **59** M2
Artur de Paiva Angola *see* **Kuvango**
Arturo Prat *research station* Antarctica **152** A2
Artux China **80** E4
Artvin Turkey **91** F2
Artyk Turkm. **88** E2
Aru, Kepulauan *is* Indon. **108** F1
Arua Uganda **98** D3
Aruanã Brazil **145** A1

▶**Aruba** *terr.* West Indies **137** K6
Self-governing Netherlands territory.

Arumã Brazil **142** F4
Arunachal Pradesh *state* India **83** H4
Arundel U.K. **49** G8
Arun Gol *r.* China *see* **Arun He**
Arun He *r.* China **74** B3
Arun Qi China *see* **Naji**
Aruppukkottai India **84** C4
Arusha Tanz. **98** D4
Aruwimi *r.* Dem. Rep. Congo **98** C3
Arvada U.S.A. **126** G5
Arvagh Ireland **51** E4
Arvayheer Mongolia **80** J2
Arviat Canada **121** M2
Arvidsjaur Sweden **44** K4
Arvika Sweden **45** H7
Arvonia U.S.A. **135** F5
Arwā' Saudi Arabia **88** B6
Arwād, Jazīrat *i.* Syria **85** B2
Arwala Indon. **108** D1
Arxan China **73** L3
Aryanah Tunisia *see* **L'Ariana**
Āryanshahr Iran **88** E3
Arys Kazakh. **80** C3
Arzamas Russia **43** I5
Arzanah *i.* U.A.E. **88** D5
Arzberg Germany **53** M4
Arzew Alg. **57** F6
Arzgir Russia **91** G1
Arzila Morocco *see* **Asilah**
Aš Czechia **53** M4
Asaba Nigeria **96** D4
Asad, Buḩayrat al *resr* Syria **85** D1
Asadābād Afgh. **89** H3
Asadābād Iran **88** C3
Asahi-dake *vol.* Japan **74** F4
Asahikawa Japan **74** F4
'Asal Egypt **85** A5
Āsalē *l.* Eth. **98** E2
Asālem Iran **88** C2
'Asalūyeh Iran **88** D5
Asan-man *b.* S. Korea **75** B5
Asansol India **83** F5
Āsayita Eth. **98** E2
Asbach Germany **53** H4
Asbestos Mountains S. Africa **100** F5
Asbury Park U.S.A. **135** H3
Ascalon Israel *see* **Ashqelon**
Ascea Italy **58** F4
Ascensión Bol. **142** F7
Ascensión Mex. **127** G7
Ascension *atoll* Micronesia *see* **Pohnpei**

Az Zāhirīyah West Bank 85 B4
Az Zahrān Saudi Arabia see Dhahran
Az Zaqāzīq Egypt 90 C5
Az Zarbah Syria 85 C1
Az Zarqā' Jordan 85 C3
Az Za'tarī Jordan 85 C3
Az Za'yin Qatar see Al Dayyen
Azzeffâl hills Mauritania/W. Sahara 96 B
Az Zubayr Iraq 91 G5
Az Zuqur i. Yemen 86 F7

B

Ba, Sông r. Vietnam 71 E4
Baa Indon. 108 C2
Baabda Lebanon 85 B3
Ba'albek Lebanon 85 C2
Baan Baa Australia 112 D3
Baardheere Somalia 98 E3
Bab India 82 D4
Bābā, Kōh-e mts Afgh. 89 H3
Baba Burnu pt Turkey 59 L5
Babadağ mt. Azer. 91 H2
Babadag Romania 59 M2
Babadurmaz Turkm. 88 E2
Babaeski Turkey 59 L4
Babahoyo Ecuador 142 C4
Babai India 82 D5
Babai r. Nepal 83 E3
Bābā Kalān Iran 88 C4
Bāb al Mandab strait Africa/Asia 86 F7
Babanusa Sudan 86 C7
Babao Qinghai China see Qilian
Babao Yunnan China 76 E4
Babar i. Indon. 108 E1
Babar, Kepulauan is Indon. 108 E1
Babati Tanz. 99 D4
Babayevo Russia 42 G4
Babayurt Russia 91 G2
B'abdā Lebanon see Baabda
Bab el Mandeb, Straits of Africa/Asia see Bāb al Mandab
Babi, Pulau i. Indon. 71 B7
Babian Jiang r. China 76 D4
Babine r. Canada 120 E4
Babine Lake Canada 120 E4
Babine Range mts Canada 120 E4
Bābol Iran 88 D2
Bābolsar Iran 88 D2
Babongo Cameroon 97 E4
Baboon Point S. Africa 100 D7
Baboua Cent. Afr. Rep. 98 B3
Babruysk Belarus 43 F5
Babstovo Russia 74 D2
Babu China see Hezhou
Babuhri India 82 B4
Babusar Pass Pak. 89 I3
Babushkina, imeni Russia 42 I4
Babuyan i. Phil. 69 G3
Babuyan Channel Phil. 69 G3
Babuyan Islands Phil. 69 G3
Bacaadweyn Somalia 98 E3
Bacabal Brazil 143 J4
Bacan i. Indon. 69 H7
Bacanora Mex. 127 F7
Bacău Romania 59 L1
Baccaro Point Canada 123 I6
Bắc Giang Vietnam 70 D2
Bacha China 74 D2
Bach Ice Shelf Antarctica 152 L2
Bach Long Vi, Đao i. Vietnam 70 D2
Bachu China 80 E4
Bachuan China see Tongliang
Back r. Australia 110 C3
Back r. Canada 121 M1
Bačka Palanka Serbia 59 H2
Backbone Mountain U.S.A. 134 F4
Backbone Ranges mts Canada 120 D2
Backe Sweden 44 J5
Backstairs Passage Australia 111 B7
Bac Liêu Vietnam 71 D5
Bắc Ninh Vietnam 70 D2
Bacoachi Mex. 127 F7
Bacoachi watercourse Mex. 127 F7
Bacobampo Mex. 127 F8
Bacolod Phil. 69 G4
Bacqueville, Lac l. Canada 122 G2
Bacqueville-en-Caux France 49 H9
Bacubirito Mex. 127 G8
Bada China see Xilin
Bada mt. Eth. 98 D3
Bada i. Myanmar 71 B5
Badabayhan Turkm. 89 F2
Bad Abbach Germany 53 M6
Badain Jaran Shamo des. China 80 J3
Badajoz Spain 57 C4
Badami India 84 B3
Badampaharh India 83 F5
Badamsha Kazakh. 80 A1
Badanah Saudi Arabia 91 F5
Badanjilin Shamo des. China see Badain Jaran Shamo
Badaojiang China see Baishan
Badarpur India 83 H4
Badaun India see Budaun
Bad Axe U.S.A. 134 D2
Bad Bederkesa Germany 53 I1
Bad Belzig Germany 53 M2
Bad Bergzabern Germany 53 H5
Bad Berleburg Germany 53 I3
Bad Bevensen Germany 53 K1
Bad Blankenburg Germany 53 L4
Bad Camberg Germany 53 I4
Badderen Norway 44 M2
Bad Driburg Germany 53 J3
Bad Düben Germany 53 M3
Bad Dürkheim Germany 53 I5
Bad Dürrenberg Germany 53 M3
Bademli Turkey see Aladağ
Bademli Geçidi pass Turkey 90 C3
Bad Ems Germany 53 H4
Baden Austria 47 P6
Baden Switz. 56 I3
Baden-Baden Germany 53 I6
Baden-Württemberg land Germany 53 I6
Bad Essen Germany 53 I2
Bad Fallingbostel Germany 53 J2
Bad Grund (Harz) Germany 53 K3
Bad Harzburg Germany 53 K3
Bad Hersfeld Germany 53 J4
Bad Hofgastein Austria 47 N7
Bad Homburg vor der Höhe Germany 53 I4
Badia Polesine Italy 58 D2
Badin Pak. 89 H5
Bad Ischl Austria 47 N7
Bādiyat ash Shām des. Asia see Syrian Desert
Bad Kissingen Germany 53 K4
Bad Königsdorff Poland see Jastrzębie-Zdrój
Bad Kösen Germany 53 L3
Bad Kötzting Germany 53 M5
Bad Kreuznach Germany 53 H5
Bad Laasphe Germany 53 I4
Badlands reg. ND U.S.A. 130 C2
Badlands reg. SD U.S.A. 130 C3
Badlands National Park U.S.A. 130 C3
Bad Langensalza Germany 53 K3
Bad Lauterberg im Harz Germany 53 K3
Bad Liebenwerda Germany 53 N3
Bad Lippspringe Germany 53 I3
Bad Marienberg (Westerwald) Germany 53 H4
Bad Mergentheim Germany 53 J5
Bad Nauheim Germany 53 I4
Badnawar India 82 C5
Badnera India 84 C1
Bad Neuenahr-Ahrweiler Germany 52 H4
Bad Neustadt an der Saale Germany 53 K4
Badnor India 82 C4
Badong China 77 F2
Ba Đông Vietnam 71 D5
Badou Togo 96 D4
Bad Pyrmont Germany 53 J3
Badrah Iraq 91 G4
Badreh Iran 88 B3
Bad Reichenhall Germany 47 N7
Badr Hunayn Saudi Arabia 86 E5
Bādrūd Iran 88 D3
Bad Sachsa Germany 53 K3
Bad Salzdetfurth Germany 53 K2
Bad Salzuflen Germany 53 I2
Bad Salzungen Germany 53 K4
Bad Schwalbach Germany 53 I4
Bad Schwartau Germany 47 M4
Bad Segeberg Germany 47 M4
Bad Sobernheim Germany 53 H5
Bad Staffelstein Germany 53 K4
Badu Island Australia 110 C1
Badulla Sri Lanka 84 D5
Bad Vilbel Germany 53 I4
Bad Wilsnack Germany 53 L2
Bad Windsheim Germany 53 K5
Badzhal Russia 74 D2
Badzhal'skiy Khrebet mts Russia 74 D2
Bad Zwischenahn Germany 53 I1
Bae Colwyn U.K. see Colwyn Bay
Baengnyeong-do i. S. Korea 75 B5
Baesweiler Germany 52 G4
Baeza Spain 57 E5
Bafatá Guinea-Bissau 96 B3
Baffa Pak. 89 I3
Baffin Bay sea Canada/Greenland 119 L2

▶Baffin Island Canada 119 L3
2nd largest island in North America and 5th in the world.

Bafia Cameroon 96 E4
Bafilo Togo 96 D4
Bafing r. Africa 96 B3
Bafoulabé Mali 96 B3
Bafoussam Cameroon 96 E4
Bāfq Iran 88 D4
Bafra Turkey 90 D2
Bafra Burnu pt Turkey 90 D2
Bāft Iran 88 E4
Bafwaboli Dem. Rep. Congo 98 C3
Bafwasende Dem. Rep. Congo 98 C3
Bagaha India 83 F4
Bagalkot India 84 B2
Bagalkote India see Bagalkot
Bagamoyo Tanz. 99 D4
Bagan China 76 C1
Bagan Datoh Malaysia see Bagan Datuk
Bagan Datuk Malaysia 71 C7
Bagansiapiapi Indon. 71 C7
Bagata Dem. Rep. Congo 98 B4
Bagdad U.S.A. 129 G4
Bagdarin Russia 73 K2
Bagé Brazil 144 F4
Bagenalstown Ireland 51 F5
Bagerhat Bangl. 83 G5
Bageshwar India 82 D3
Baggs U.S.A. 126 G4
Baggy Point U.K. 49 C7
Bagh India 82 C5
Bāgh, Chāh-e well Iran 88 D4
Bàgh a'Chaisteil U.K. see Castlebay
Baghak Pak. 89 G4
Baghbaghū Iran 89 F2

▶Baghdād Iraq 91 G4
Capital of Iraq.

Bāgh-e Malek Iran 88 C4
Bagherhat Bangl. see Bagerhat
Bāghīn Iran 88 E4
Baghlān Afgh. 89 H2
Baghrān Afgh. 89 G3
Bağırsak r. Turkey 85 C1
Bağırsak Deresi r. Syria/Turkey see Sājūr, Nahr
Bagley U.S.A. 130 E2
Baglung Nepal 83 E3
Bagnères-de-Luchon France 56 E5
Bago Myanmar see Pegu
Bago Phil. 69 G4
Bagong China see Sansui
Bagor India 89 I5
Bagrationovsk Russia 45 L9
Bagrax China see Bohu
Bagrax Hu l. China see Bosten Hu
Baguio Phil. 69 G3
Bagur, Cabo c. Spain see Begur, Cap de
Bagzane, Monts mts Niger 96 D3
Bahādorābād Iran 88 E4
Bahalda India 83 F5
Bahamas, The country West Indies 133 E7
Bahara Pak. 89 G5
Baharampur India 83 G4
Bahardipur Pak. 89 H5
Bahariya Oasis oasis Egypt see Bahrīyah, Wāḩāt al
Bahau Malaysia 71 C7
Bahawalnagar Pak. 89 I4
Bahawalpur Pak. 89 H4
Bahçe Adana Turkey 85 B1
Bahçe Osmaniye Turkey 90 E3
Baher Dar Eth. see Bahir Dar
Baheri India 82 D3
Bahia Brazil see Salvador
Bahia state Brazil 145 C1
Bahía, Islas de la is Hond. 137 G5
Bahía Asunción Mex. 127 E8
Bahía Blanca Arg. 144 D5
Bahía Kino Mex. 127 F7
Bahía Laura Arg. 144 C7
Bahía Negra Para. 144 E2
Bahía Tortugas Mex. 127 E8
Bahir Dar Eth. 98 D2
Bahl India 82 C3
Bahlā Oman 88 E6
Bahomonte Indon. 69 G7
Bahraich India 83 E4
Bahrain country Asia 88 C5
Bahrain, Gulf of Asia 88 C5
Bahrāmābād Iran see Rafsanjān
Bahrām Beyg Iran 88 C2
Bahrāmjerd Iran 88 E4
Bahrīyah, Wāḩāt al oasis Egypt 90 C6
Bahuaja-Sonene, Parque Nacional nat. park Peru 142 E6
Baia Mare Romania 59 J1
Baicang China 83 G3
Baicheng Jilin China 74 A3
Baicheng Xinjiang China 80 F3
Baidoa Somalia see Baydhabo
Baidoi Co l. China 83 F2
Baidu China 77 H3
Baie-aux-Feuilles Canada see Tasiujaq
Baie-Comeau Canada 123 H4
Baie-du-Poste Canada see Mistissini
Baie-St-Paul Canada 123 H5
Baie-Trinité Canada 123 I4
Baie Verte Canada 123 K4
Baiguan China see Shangyu
Baiguo Hubei China 77 G2
Baiguo Hunan China 77 G3
Baihar India 82 E5
Baihe Jilin China 74 C4
Baihe Shaanxi China 77 F1
Baiji Iraq see Bayjī

▶Baikal, Lake Russia 72 J2
Deepest lake in Asia and the world, and 2nd largest lake in Asia and 8th in the world.

Baikalu Shan mt. China 74 A1
Baikunthpur India 83 E5
Baile Átha Cliath Ireland see Dublin
Baile Átha Luain Ireland see Athlone
Baile Mhartainn U.K. 50 B3
Baile na Finne Ireland 51 D3
Băilești Romania 59 J2
Bailey Range hills Australia 109 C7
Bailianhe Shuiku resr China 77 G2
Bailieborough Ireland 51 F4
Bailleul France 52 C4
Baillie r. Canada 121 J1
Bailong China see Hadapu
Bailong Jiang r. China 76 E1
Baima Qinghai China 76 D1
Baima Xizang China see Baxoi
Baima Jian mt. China 77 H2
Baimuru P.N.G. 69 K8
Bain r. U.K. 48 G5
Bainang China see Norkyung
Bainbridge GA U.S.A. 133 C6
Bainbridge IN U.S.A. 134 B4
Bainbridge NY U.S.A. 135 H2
Bainduru India 84 B3
Baingoin China see Porong
Baini China see Yuqing
Baiona Spain 57 B2
Baiqên China 76 D1
Baiquan China 74 B3
Bā'ir Jordan 85 C4
Bā'ir, Wādī watercourse Jordan/Saudi Arabia 85 C4
Bairab Co l. China 83 E2
Bairat India 82 D4
Baird U.S.A. 131 D5
Baird Mountains U.S.A. 118 C3

▶Bairiki Kiribati 150 H5
Capital of Kiribati, on Tarawa atoll.

Bairin Youqi China see Daban
Bairnsdale Australia 112 C6
Baise China 76 E4
Baisha Chongqing China 76 E2
Baisha Hainan China 77 F5
Baisha Sichuan China 77 F2
Baishan Guangxi China see Mashan
Baishan Jilin China 74 B4
Baishan Jilin China 74 B4
Baishanzhen China see Baishan
Baishui Shaanxi China 77 F1
Baishui Sichuan China 76 E1
Baishui Jiang r. China 76 E1
Baisogala Lith. 45 M9
Baitadi Nepal 82 E3
Baitang China 76 C1
Bai Thương Vietnam 70 D3
Baitou Shan mt. China/N. Korea 74 C4
Baixi China see Yibin
Baiyashi China see Dong'an
Baiyin China 72 I5
Baiyü China 76 C2
Baiyuda Desert Sudan 86 D6
Baja Hungary 58 H1
Baja, Punta pt Mex. 127 E7
Baja California pen. Mex. 127 E7
Baja California state Mex. 127 E7
Baja California Norte state Mex. see Baja California
Baja California Sur state Mex. 127 E8
Bajan Mex. 131 C7
Bajau i. Indon. 71 D7
Bajaur reg. Pak. 89 H3
Bajawa Indon. 108 C2
Baj Baj India 83 G5
Bājgīrān Iran 88 E2
Bajiang China 77 F3
Bājil Yemen 86 F7
Bajo Caracoles Arg. 144 B7
Bajoga Nigeria 96 E3
Bajoi China 76 D2
Bajrakot India 83 F5
Bakala Cent. Afr. Rep. 97 F4
Bakanas Kazakh. 80 E3
Bakar Pak. 89 H5
Bakel Senegal 96 B3
Baker CA U.S.A. 128 E4
Baker ID U.S.A. 126 E3
Baker LA U.S.A. 131 F6
Baker MT U.S.A. 126 G3
Baker NV U.S.A. 129 F2
Baker WV U.S.A. 135 F4
Baker, Mount vol. U.S.A. 126 C2
Baker Butte mt. U.S.A. 129 H4
Baker City U.S.A. 126 D3

▶Baker Island terr. N. Pacific Ocean 107 I1
United States Unincorporated Territory.

Baker Island U.S.A. 120 C4
Baker Lake salt flat Australia 109 D6
Baker Lake Canada 121 M1
Baker Lake l. Canada 121 M1
Baker's Dozen Islands Canada 122 F2
Bakersfield U.S.A. 128 D4
Bakersville U.S.A. 132 D4
Bâ Kêv Cambodia 71 D4
Bakhardok Turkm. see Bokurdak
Bākharz, Kūhhā-ye mts Iran 89 F3
Bakhasar India 82 B4
Bakhirevo Russia 74 C2
Bakhmach Ukr. 43 G6
Bakhma Dam Iraq see Békma, Sadd
Bakhmut Ukr. 43 H6
Bākhtarān Iran see Kermānshāh
Bakhtegan, Daryācheh-ye l. Iran 88 D4
Bakhtiari Country reg. Iran 88 C3
Bakı Azer. see Baku
Baki Somalia 98 E2
Bakırköy Turkey 59 M4
Bakkejord Norway 44 K2
Bakloh India 82 C2
Bako Eth. 98 D3
Bakongan Indon. 71 B7
Bakouma Cent. Afr. Rep. 98 C3
Baksan Russia 91 F2

▶Baku Azer. 91 H2
Capital of Azerbaijan.

Baku Dem. Rep. Congo 98 D3
Bakutis Coast Antarctica 152 J2
Baky Azer. see Baku
Balâ Turkey 90 D3
Bala U.K. 49 D6
Bala, Cerros de mts Bol. 142 E6
Balabac i. Phil. 68 F5
Balabac Strait Malaysia/Phil. 68 F5
Baladeh Māzandarān Iran 88 C2
Baladeh Māzandarān Iran 88 C2
Baladek Russia 74 D1
Balagar Gaole China see Bayan Ul
Balaghat India 82 E5
Balaghat Range hills India 84 B2
Bālā Ḩowz Iran 88 E4
Balaka Malawi 99 D5
Balakān Azer. 91 G2
Balakhna Russia 42 I4
Balakhta Russia 72 G1
Balaklava Australia 111 B7
Balaklava Crimea 90 D1
Balakleya Ukr. see Balakliya
Balakliya Ukr. 43 H6
Balakovo Russia 43 J5
Bala Lake l. U.K. 49 D6
Balaman India 82 E4
Balan India 82 B4
Balanda Russia see Kalininsk
Balanda r. Russia 43 J6
Balan Dağı hill Turkey 59 M6
Balanga Phil. 69 G4
Ba Lang An, Mui pt Vietnam 70 E4
Balangir India 84 D1
Balaözen r. Kazakh./Russia see Saryozen
Balarampur India see Balrampur
Bālā Shahr Iran 88 E5
Balashov Russia 43 I6
Balasore India see Baleshwar
Balaton, Lake Hungary 58 G1
Balatonboglár Hungary 58 G1
Balatonfüred Hungary 58 G1
Balbina Brazil 143 G4
Balbina, Represa de resr Brazil 143 G4
Balbriggan Ireland 51 F4
Balchik Bulg. 59 M3
Bal Chirāgh Afgh. 89 G3
Balclutha N.Z. 113 B8
Balcones Escarpment U.S.A. 131 C6
Bald Knob U.S.A. 134 E5
Bald Mountain U.S.A. 129 F3
Baldock Lake Canada 121 L3
Baldwin Canada 134 F1
Baldwin FL U.S.A. 133 D6
Baldwin MI U.S.A. 134 C2
Baldwin PA U.S.A. 134 F3
Baldy Mount Canada 126 D2
Baldy Mountain hill Canada 121 K5
Baldy Peak U.S.A. 129 I5
Bale Indon. 68 C7
Bâle Switz. see Basel
Baléa Mali 96 B3
Baleares is Spain see Balearic Islands
Baleares, Islas is Spain see Balearic Islands
Baleares Insulae is Spain see Balearic Islands
Balearic Islands is Spain 57 G4
Balearic Sea Spain 57 G3
Balears is Spain see Balearic Islands
Balears, Illes is Spain see Balearic Islands
Baleia, Ponta da pt Brazil 145 D2
Baleine, Grande Rivière de la r. Canada 122 F3
Baleine, Petite Rivière de la r. Canada 122 F3
Baleine, Rivière à la r. Canada 123 I2
Bale Mountains National Park Eth. 98 D3
Baler Phil. 69 G3
Baleshwar India 83 F5
Balestrand Norway 45 E6
Balestrieri, Punta mt. Italy 58 C4
Baléyara Niger 96 D3
Balezino Russia 41 Q4
Balfes Creek Australia 110 D4
Balfour Downs Australia 108 C5
Balgo Australia 108 D5
Balguntay China 80 G3
Bali India 82 C4
Bali i. Indon. 108 A2
Bali, Laut sea Indon. 108 A1
Balia India see Ballia
Baliapal India 83 F5
Balige Indon. 71 B7
Baliguda India 84 D1
Balıkesir Turkey 59 L5
Balīkh r. Syria/Turkey 85 D2
Balikpapan Indon. 68 F7
Balimila Reservoir India 84 D2
Balimo P.N.G. 69 K8
Balin China 74 A2
Baling Malaysia 71 C6
Balingen Germany 47 L6
Balintore U.K. 50 F3
Bali Sea Indon. see Bali, Laut
Balk Neth. 52 F2
Balkanabat Turkm. 88 D2
Balkan Mountains Bulg./Serbia 59 J3
Balkash Kazakh. 80 D2
Balkassar Pak. 89 I3
Balkh r. Afgh. 89 G2

▶Balkhash, Lake Kazakh. 80 D2
3rd largest lake in Asia.

Balkhash, Ozero l. Kazakh. see Balkhash, Lake
Balkuduk Kazakh. 43 J7
Ballachulish U.K. 50 D4
Balladonia Australia 109 C8
Balladoran Australia 112 D3
Ballaghaderreen Ireland 51 D4
Ballan Australia 112 B6
Ballangen Norway 44 J2
Ballantine U.S.A. 126 F3
Ballantrae U.K. 50 E5
Ballarat Australia 112 A6
Ballard, Lake salt flat Australia 109 C7
Ballari India 84 C3
Ballarpur India 84 C2
Ballater U.K. 50 F3
Ballé Mali 96 C3
Ballena, Punta pt Chile 144 B3
Balleny Islands Antarctica 152 H2
Ballia India 83 F4
Ballina Australia 112 F2
Ballina Ireland 51 C3
Ballinafad Ireland 51 D3
Ballinalack Ireland 51 E4
Ballinamore Ireland 51 E3
Ballinasloe Ireland 51 D4
Ballindine Ireland 51 D4
Ballinger U.S.A. 131 D6
Ballinluig U.K. 50 F4
Ballinrobe Ireland 51 C4
Ballston Spa U.S.A. 135 I2
Ballybay Ireland 51 F3
Ballybunion Ireland 51 C5
Ballycanew Ireland 51 F5
Ballycastle Ireland 51 C3
Ballycastle U.K. 51 F2
Ballyclare U.K. 51 G3
Ballyconnell Ireland 51 E3
Ballygar Ireland 51 D4
Ballygawley U.K. 51 E3
Ballygorman Ireland 51 E2
Ballyhaunis Ireland 51 D4
Ballyheigue Ireland 51 C5
Ballykelly U.K. 51 E2
Ballylynan Ireland 51 E5
Ballymacmague Ireland 51 E5
Ballymahon Ireland 51 E4
Ballymena U.K. 51 F3
Ballymoney U.K. 51 F2
Ballymote Ireland 51 D3
Ballynahinch U.K. 51 G3
Ballyshannon Ireland 51 D3
Ballyteige Bay Ireland 51 F5
Ballyvaughan Ireland 51 C4
Ballyward U.K. 51 F3
Balmartin U.K. see Baile Mhartainn
Balmer India see Barmer
Balmertown Canada 121 M5
Balmorhea U.S.A. 131 C6
Balochistan prov. Pak. 89 G4
Balombo Angola 99 B5
Balonne r. Australia 112 D2
Balotra India 82 C4
Balqash Kazakh. see Balkash
Balqash Köli l. Kazakh. see Balkhash, Lake
Balrampur India 83 E4
Balranald Australia 112 A5
Balș Romania 59 K2
Balsam Lake Canada 135 F1
Balsas Brazil 143 I5
Balta Ukr. 43 F7
Baltasound U.K. 50 [inset]
Baltay Russia 43 J5
Bălți Moldova 43 E7
Baltic U.S.A. 134 E3
Baltic Sea g. Europe 45 J9
Baltīm Egypt 90 C5
Baltîm Egypt see Baltīm
Baltimore S. Africa 101 I2
Baltimore MD U.S.A. 135 G4
Baltimore OH U.S.A. 134 D4
Baltinglass Ireland 51 F5
Baltistan reg. Pak. 82 C2
Baltiysk Russia 45 K9
Balu India 76 B3
Baluarte, Arroyo watercourse U.S.A. 131 D7
Baluch Ab well Iran 88 E4
Balumundam Indon. 71 B7
Balurghat India 83 G4
Balve Germany 53 H3
Balvi Latvia 45 O8
Balya Turkey 59 L5
Balykchy Kyrg. 80 E3
Balykshi Kazakh. 78 E2
Balyqshy Kazakh. see Balykshi
Bam Iran 88 E4
Bām Iran 88 E2
Bama China 76 E3

▶Bamako Mali 96 C3
Capital of Mali.

Bamba Mali 96 C3
Bambari Cent. Afr. Rep. 98 C3
Bambel Indon. 71 B7
Bamberg Germany 53 K5
Bamberg U.S.A. 133 D5
Bambili Dem. Rep. Congo 98 C3
Bambio Cent. Afr. Rep. 98 B3
Bamboesberg mts S. Africa 101 H6
Bamboo Creek Australia 108 C5
Bambouti Cent. Afr. Rep. 98 C3
Bambuí Brazil 145 B3
Bamda China 76 C2
Bamenda Cameroon 96 E4
Bamiantong China see Muling
Bamingui Cent. Afr. Rep. 98 C3
Bamingui-Bangoran, Parc National du nat. park Cent. Afr. Rep. 98 B3
Bâmnák Cambodia 71 D4
Bamnet Narong Thai. 70 C4
Bamor India 82 D4
Bamori India 84 C1
Bamposht reg. Iran 89 F5
Bampton U.K. 49 D8
Bampūr Iran 89 F5
Bampūr watercourse Iran 89 E5
Bamrūd Iran 89 F3
Bāmyān Afgh. 89 G3
Bamyili Australia 108 F3
Banaba i. Kiribati 107 G2
Banabuiu, Açude resr Brazil 143 K5
Banagher Ireland 51 E4
Banalia Dem. Rep. Congo 98 C3
Banamana, Lagoa l. Moz. 101 K2
Banamba Mali 96 C3
Banámichi Mex. 127 F7
Banana Australia 110 E5
Bananal, Ilha do i. Brazil 143 H6
Bananga India 71 A6
Banapur India 84 E2
Banas r. India 82 D4
Banaz Turkey 59 M5
Ban Ban Laos 70 C3
Banbān, 'Irq des. Saudi Arabia 88 B5
Banbar China see Domartang
Ban Bo Laos 70 C3
Banbridge U.K. 51 F3
Ban Bua Chum Thai. 70 C4
Ban Bua Yai Thai. 70 C4
Ban Bungxai Laos 70 D4
Banbury U.K. 49 F6
Ban Cang Vietnam 70 C2
Banc d'Arguin, Parc National du nat. park Mauritania 96 B2
Ban Channabot Thai. 70 C3
Banchory U.K. 50 G3
Bancroft Canada 135 G1
Bancroft Zambia see Chililabombwe
Banda Dem. Rep. Congo 98 C3
Banda India 82 E4
Banda, Kepulauan is Indon. 69 H7
Banda, Laut sea Indon. 69 H8
Banda Aceh Indon. 71 A6
Banda Banda, Mount Australia 112 F3
Banda Daud Shah Pak. 89 H3
Bandahara, Gunung mt. Indon. 71 B7
Bandama r. Côte d'Ivoire 96 C4
Bandān Kūh mts Iran 89 F4
Bandar India see Machilipatnam
Bandar Moz. 99 D5
Bandar Abbas Iran see Bandar-e 'Abbās
Bandarban Bangl. 83 H5
Bandar-e 'Abbās Iran 88 E5
Bandar-e Anzalī Iran 88 C2
Bandar-e Būshehr Iran 88 C4
Bandar-e Dayyer Iran 88 C5
Bandar-e Deylam Iran 88 C4
Bandar-e Emām Khomeynī Iran 88 C4
Bandar-e Ganāveh Iran 88 C4
Bandar-e Ḩeydarābād Iran 88 B2
Bandar-e Jāsk Iran 88 E5
Bandar-e Kangān Iran 88 D5
Bandar-e Lengeh Iran 88 D5
Bandar-e Māhshahr Iran 88 C4
Bandar-e Nakhīlū Iran 88 D5
Bandar-e Pahlavī Iran see Bandar-e Anzalī
Bandar-e Shāh Iran see Bandar-e Torkaman
Bandar-e Torkaman Iran 88 D2
Bandar Labuan Malaysia see Labuan
Bandar Lampung Indon. 68 D8
Bandarpunch mt. India 82 D3

▶Bandar Seri Begawan Brunei 68 E6
Capital of Brunei.

Banda Sea sea Indon. see Banda, Laut
Band-e Bābā, Silsilah-ye Kōh-e mts Afgh. 89 F3
Band-e Bamposht, Kūh-e mts Iran 89 F5
Bandeira Brazil 145 C1
Bandeirante Brazil 145 A1
Bandeiras, Pico de mt. Brazil 145 C3
Bandelierkop S. Africa 101 I2
Banderas Mex. 131 B6
Banderas, Bahía de b. Mex. 136 C4
Band-e Sar Qom Iran 88 D3
Bandhi Pak. 89 H5
Bandhogarh India 82 E5
Bandi r. India 82 C4
Bandiagara Mali 96 C3
Bandikui India 82 D4
Bandingilo National Park South Sudan 97 G4
Bandipur National Park India 84 C4
Bandırma Turkey 59 L4
Bandjarmasin Indon. see Banjarmasin
Bandon Ireland 51 D6
Bandon r. Ireland 51 D6
Ban Don Thai. see Surat Thani

Bandon U.S.A. 126 B4
Band Qīr Iran 88 C4
Bandra India 84 B2
Bandundu Dem. Rep. Congo 98 B4
Bandung Indon. 68 D8
Bandya Australia 109 C6
Bāneh Iran 88 B3
Banera India 82 C4
Banes Cuba 137 I4
Banff Canada 120 H5
Banff U.K. 50 G3
Banff National Park Canada 120 G5
Banfora Burkina Faso 96 C3
Banga Dem. Rep. Congo 99 C4
Bangalore India see Bengaluru
Bangalow Australia 112 F2
Bangaon India 83 G5
Bangar Brunei 68 F6
Bangassou Cent. Afr. Rep. 98 C3
Bangdag Co salt l. China 83 E2
Banggai Indon. 69 G7
Banggai, Kepulauan is Indon. 69 G7
Banggi i. Malaysia 68 F5
Banghāzī Libya see Benghazi
Banghiang, Xé r. Laos 70 D3
Bangka i. Indon. 68 D7
Bangka, Selat sea chan. Indon. 68 D7
Bangkalan Indon. 68 E8
Bangkaru i. Indon. 71 B7
Bangko Indon. 68 C7

▶Bangkok Thai. 71 C4
Capital of Thailand.

Bangkok, Bight of b. Thai. 71 C4
Bangkor China 83 F3
Bangla state India see West Bengal

▶Bangladesh country Asia 83 G4
5th most populous country in Asia and 8th in the world.

Bangma Shan mts China 76 C4
Bang Mun Nak Thai. 70 C3
Ba Ngoi Vietnam 71 E5
Bangolo Côte d'Ivoire 96 C4
Bangong Co salt l. China/India 82 D2
Bangor Northern Ireland U.K. 51 G3
Bangor Wales U.K. 48 C5
Bangor ME U.S.A. 132 G2
Bangor MI U.S.A. 134 B2
Bangor PA U.S.A. 135 H3
Bangor Erris Ireland 51 C3
Bangs, Mount U.S.A. 129 G3
Bang Saphan Yai Thai. 71 B5
Bangsund Norway 44 G4
Bangued Phil. 69 G3

▶Bangui Cent. Afr. Rep. 98 B3
Capital of the Central African Republic.

Bangweulu, Lake Zambia 99 C5
Banhā Egypt 90 C5
Banhine, Parque Nacional de nat. park Moz. 101 K2
Ban Hin Heup Laos 70 C3
Ban Houei Sai Laos see Houayxay
Ban Huai Khon Thai. 70 C3
Ban Huai Yang Thai. 71 B5
Bani, Jebel ridge Morocco 54 C6
Bania Cent. Afr. Rep. 98 B3
Bani-Bangou Niger 96 D3
Banifing r. Mali 96 C3
Banihal Pass and Tunnel India 82 C2
Banister r. U.S.A. 134 F5
Banī Suwayf Egypt 90 C5
Banī Walīd Libya 97 E1
Banī Wuṭayfān well Saudi Arabia 88 C5
Bāniyās Israel 85 B3
Bāniyās Syria 85 B2
Bani Yas reg. U.A.E. 88 D6
Banja Luka Bos. & Herz. 58 G2
Banjarmasin Indon. 68 E7
Banjës, Liqeni i resr Albania 59 I4

▶Banjul Gambia 96 B3
Capital of The Gambia.

Banka India 83 F4
Banka Banka Australia 108 F4
Bankapur India 84 B3
Bankass Mali 96 C3
Ban Kèngkabao Laos 70 D3
Ban Khao Yoi Thai. 71 B4
Ban Khok Kloi Thai. 71 B5
Bankilaré Niger 96 D3
Banks Island B.C. Canada 120 D4
Banks Island N.W.T. Canada 118 F2
Banks Islands Vanuatu 107 G3
Banks Lake Canada 121 M2
Banks Lake U.S.A. 126 D3
Banks Peninsula N.Z. 113 D6
Banks Strait Australia 111 [inset]
Bankura India 83 F5
Ban Lamduan Thai. 71 C4
Banlan China 77 F3
Ban Mae La Luang Thai. 70 B3
Banmaw Myanmar see Bhamo
Banmo Myanmar see Bhamo
Bann r. Ireland 51 F5
Bann r. U.K. 51 F2
Ban Nakham Laos 70 D3
Bannerman Town Bahamas 133 E7
Banning U.S.A. 128 E5
Banningville Dem. Rep. Congo see Bandundu
Ban Noi Myanmar 70 B3
Ban Nonghèt Laos 70 D3
Ban Nong Kung Thai. 70 D3
Bannu Pak. 89 H3
Bano India 83 F5
Bañolas Spain see Banyoles
Ban Phai Thai. 70 C3
Ban Phôn Laos see Xékong
Ban Phôn-Hông Laos 70 C3
Banqiao Yunnan China 76 C3
Banqiao Yunnan China 76 E3
Bansi Bihar India 83 F4
Bansi Rajasthan India 82 C4
Bansi Uttar Prad. India 82 D4
Bansi Uttar Prad. India 83 E4
Bansihari India 83 G4
Banská Bystrica Slovakia 47 Q6
Banspani India 83 F5
Bansur India 82 D4
Ban Sut Ta Thai. 70 B3
Ban Suwan Wari Thai. 70 D4
Banswara India 82 C5
Banteer Ireland 51 D5
Ban Tha Song Yang Thai. 70 B3
Banthat mts Cambodia/Thai. see Cardamom Range
Ban Tha Tum Thai. 70 C4
Ban Tôp Laos 70 D3
Bantry Ireland 51 C6
Bantry Bay Ireland 51 C6
Bantval India 84 B3
Ban Wang Chao Thai. 70 B3
Ban Woen Laos 70 C3
Ban Xepian Laos 70 D4
Banyak, Pulau-pulau is Indon. 71 B7
Ban Yang Yong Thai. 71 B4
Banyo Cameroon 96 E4
Banyoles Spain 57 H2
Banyuwangi Indon. 108 A2
Banzare Coast Antarctica 152 G2
Banzare Seamount sea feature Indian Ocean 149 N9
Banzart Tunisia see Bizerte
Banzkow Germany 53 L1
Banzyville Dem. Rep. Congo see Mobayi-Mbongo
Bao'an China see Shenzhen
Baochang China 73 L4
Baocheng China 76 E1
Baoding China 73 L5
Baofeng China 77 G1
Baohe China see Weixi
Baoji China 76 E1
Baokang Hubei China 77 F2
Baokang Nei Mongol China 74 A3
Bao Lac Vietnam 70 D2
Baolin China 74 C3
Bao Lôc Vietnam 71 D5
Baoqing China 74 D3
Baoro Cent. Afr. Rep. 98 B3
Baoshan China 76 C3
Baotou China 73 K4
Baoulé r. Mali 96 C3
Baoxing China 76 D2
Baoying China 77 H1
Baoyou China see Ledong
Bap India 82 C4
Bapatla India 84 D3
Bapaume France 52 C4
Baptiste Lake Canada 135 F1
Bapu China see Meigu
Baq'ā' oasis Saudi Arabia 91 F6
Baqbaq Egypt see Buqbuq
Baqên Xizang China 76 B1
Baqên Xizang China 76 B2
Baqiu China 77 G3
Ba'qūbah Iraq 91 G4
Bar Montenegro 59 H3
Bara Sudan 86 D7
Baraawe Somalia 98 E3
Bara Banki India see Barabanki
Barabanki India 82 E4
Baraboo U.S.A. 130 F3
Baracaju r. Brazil 145 A1
Baracaldo Spain see Barakaldo
Baracoa Cuba 137 J4
Baradá, Nahr r. Syria 85 C3
Baradine Australia 112 D3
Baradine r. Australia 112 D3
Baragarh India see Bargarh
Barahona Dom. Rep. 137 J5
Barail Range mts India 83 H4
Baraka watercourse Eritrea/Sudan 97 G3
Barakaldo Spain 57 E2
Barakī Barak Afgh. 89 H3
Baralaba Australia 110 E5
Bara Lacha La India 82 D2
Baralzon Lake Canada 121 L3
Baram India 83 F5
Baram r. Malaysia 68 E6
Baramati India 84 B2
Baramula India see Baramulla
Baramulla India 82 C2
Baran India 82 D4
Baran r. Pak. 89 H5
Bārān, Kūh-e mts Iran 89 F3
Barana Pak. 89 I4
Baranavichy Belarus 45 O10
Barang, Dasht-e des. Afgh. 89 F3
Baranikha Russia 65 R3
Baranīs Egypt 86 E5
Baranîs Egypt see Baranīs
Baranda India 82 E4
Baranof Island U.S.A. 120 C3
Baranovichi Belarus see Baranavichy
Baranowicze Belarus see Baranavichy
Baraouéli Mali 96 C3
Baraque de Fraiture hill Belgium 52 F4
Barasat India 83 G5
Barat Daya, Kepulauan is Indon. 108 D1
Baraut India 82 D3
Barbacena Brazil 145 C3
Barbados country West Indies 137 M6
Barbar, Gebel el mt. Egypt see Barbar, Jabal
Barbar, Jabal mt. Egypt 85 A5
Barbara Lake Canada 122 D4
Barbastro Spain 57 G2
Barbate Spain 57 D5
Barbaza Phil. 69 G4
Barberton S. Africa 101 J3
Barberton U.S.A. 134 E3
Barbezieux-St-Hilaire France 56 D4
Barbour Bay Canada 121 M2
Barbourville U.S.A. 134 D5
Barbuda i. Antigua and Barbuda 137 L5
Barby Germany 53 L3
Barcaldine Australia 110 D4
Barce Libya see Al Marj
Barcelona Spain 57 H3
Barcelona Venez. 142 F1
Barcelonnette France 56 H4
Barcelos Brazil 142 F4
Barchfeld Germany 53 K4
Barcino Spain see Barcelona
Barclay de Tolly atoll Fr. Polynesia see Raroia
Barclayville Liberia 96 C4
Barcoo watercourse Australia 110 C5
Barcoo Creek watercourse Australia see Cooper Creek
Barcoo National Park Australia see Welford National Park
Barcs Hungary 58 G2
Bārdā Azer. 91 G2
Bardaï Chad 97 E2
Bárðarbunga mt. Iceland 44 [inset 1]
Bardawīl, Khabrat al salt pan Saudi Arabia 85 D4
Bardawīl, Sabkhat al lag. Egypt 85 A4
Barddhaman India 83 F5
Bardejov Slovakia 43 D6
Bardera Somalia see Baardheere
Bardeskan Iran 88 E3
Bardhaman India see Barddhaman
Bardsey Island U.K. 49 C6
Bardsīr Iran 88 E4
Barðsneshorn pt Iceland 40 D2
Bardstown U.S.A. 134 C5
Barduli Italy see Barletta
Bardwell U.S.A. 131 F4
Bareilly India 82 D3
Barellan Australia 112 C5
Barentin France 49 H9
Barentsburg Svalbard 64 C2
Barents Sea Arctic Ocean 42 I1
Barentu Eritrea 86 E6
Barfleur, Pointe de pt France 49 F9
Bārgāh Iran 88 E5
Bargarh India 83 E5
Barghamad Iran 88 E2
Bargrennan U.K. 50 E5
Bargteheide Germany 53 K1
Barguna Bangl. 83 G5
Barhaj India 83 E4
Barham Australia 112 B5
Bari Italy 58 G4
Bariadi Tanz. 98 D4
Bari Doab lowland Pak. 89 I4
Barika Alg. 54 F4
Barinas Venez. 142 D2
Baripada India 83 F5
Bariri Brazil 145 A3
Bari Sadri India 82 C4
Barisal Bangl. 83 G5
Barisan, Pegunungan mts Indon. 68 C7
Barito r. Indon. 68 E7
Barium Italy see Bari
Barkal Bangl. 83 H5
Barkam China 76 D2
Barkan, Ra's-e pt Iran 88 C4
Barkava Latvia 45 O8
Bark Lake Canada 135 G1
Barkly East S. Africa 101 H6
Barkly Homestead Australia 110 A3
Barkly-Oos S. Africa see Barkly East
Barkly Tableland reg. Australia 110 A3
Barkly-Wes S. Africa see Barkly West
Barkly West S. Africa 100 G5
Barkol China 80 H3
Barla Turkey 59 N5
Bârlad Romania 59 L1
Bar-le-Duc France 52 F6
Barlee, Lake salt flat Australia 109 B7
Barlee Range hills Australia 109 A5
Barletta Italy 58 G4
Barlow Canada 120 B2
Barlow Lake Canada 121 K2
Barmah Forest Australia 112 B5
Barmedman Australia 112 C5
Barmen-Elberfeld Germany see Wuppertal
Barmer India 82 B4
Barm Fīrūz, Kūh-e mt. Iran 88 C4
Barmouth U.K. 49 C6
Barnala India 82 C3
Barnard Castle U.K. 48 F4
Barnato Australia 112 B3
Barnaul Russia 72 E2
Barnegat Bay U.S.A. 135 H4
Barnes Icecap Canada 119 K2
Barnesville GA U.S.A. 133 D5
Barnesville MN U.S.A. 130 D2
Barneveld Neth. 52 F2
Barneville-Carteret France 49 F9
Barneys Lake imp. l. Australia 112 B4
Barney Top mt. U.S.A. 129 H3
Barnsley U.K. 48 F5
Barnstable U.S.A. 135 J3
Barnstaple U.K. 49 C7
Barnstaple Bay U.K. 49 C7
Barnstorf Germany 53 I2
Baro Nigeria 96 D4
Baroda Gujarat India see Vadodara
Baroda Madh. Prad. India 82 D4
Barong China 76 C2
Barons Range hills Australia 109 D6
Barpathar India 76 B3
Barpeta India 83 G4
Bar Pla Soi Thai. see Chon Buri
Barques, Point Aux U.S.A. 134 D1
Barquisimeto Venez. 142 E1
Barra Brazil 143 J6
Barra i. U.K. 50 B4
Barra, Ponta da pt Moz. 101 L2
Barra, Sound of sea chan. U.K. 50 B3
Barraba Australia 112 E3
Barra Bonita Brazil 145 A3
Barracão do Barreto Brazil 143 G5
Barra do Bugres Brazil 143 G7
Barra do Corda Brazil 143 I5
Barra do Cuieté Brazil 145 C2
Barra do Garças Brazil 143 H7
Barra do Piraí Brazil 145 C3
Barra do São Manuel Brazil 143 G5
Barra do Turvo Brazil 145 A4
Barra Falsa, Ponta da pt Moz. 101 L2
Barraigh i. U.K. see Barra
Barra Mansa Brazil 145 B3
Barranca Peru 142 C4
Barranqueras Arg. 144 E3
Barranquilla Col. 142 D1
Barre MA U.S.A. 135 I2
Barre VT U.S.A. 135 I1
Barre des Écrins mt. France 56 H4
Barreiras Brazil 143 J6
Barreirinha Brazil 143 G4
Barreirinhas Brazil 143 J4
Barreiro Port. 57 B4
Barreiros Brazil 143 K5
Barren Island India 71 A4
Barren Island Kiribati see Starbuck Island
Barren River Lake U.S.A. 134 B5
Barretos Brazil 145 A3
Barrett, Mount hill Australia 108 D4
Barrhead Canada 120 H4
Barrhead U.K. 50 E5
Barrie Canada 134 F1
Barrier Bay Antarctica 152 E2
Barrière Canada 120 F5
Barrier Range hills Australia 111 C6
Barrington Canada 123 I6
Barrington, Mount Australia 112 E4
Barrington Tops National Park Australia 112 E4
Barringun Australia 112 B2
Barro Alto Brazil 145 A1
Barrocão Brazil 145 C2
Barron U.S.A. 130 F2
Barrow r. Ireland 51 F5
Barrow U.S.A. 118 C2
Barrow, Point pt U.S.A. 118 C2
Barrow Creek Australia 108 F5
Barrow-in-Furness U.K. 48 D4
Barrow Island Australia 108 A5
Barrow Range hills Australia 109 D6
Barrow Strait Canada 119 I2
Barr Smith Range hills Australia 109 C6
Barry U.K. 49 D7
Barrydale S. Africa 100 E7
Barry Mountains Australia 112 C6
Barrys Bay Canada 135 G1
Barryville U.S.A. 135 H3
Barsalpur India 82 C3
Barshatas Kazakh. 80 E2
Barshi India see Barsi
Barsi India 84 B2
Barsinghausen Germany 53 J2
Barstow U.S.A. 128 E4
Barsur India 84 D2
Bar-sur-Aube France 56 G2
Bartang Tajik. 89 H2
Barth Germany 47 N3
Bartica Guyana 143 G2
Bartın Turkey 90 D2
Bartle Frere, Mount Australia 110 D3
Bartlett U.S.A. 130 D3
Bartlett Reservoir U.S.A. 129 H5
Barton U.S.A. 135 I1
Barton-upon-Humber U.K. 48 G5
Bartoszyce Poland 47 R3
Bartow U.S.A. 133 D7
Barú, Volcán vol. Panama 137 H7
Barung i. Indon. 68 E8
Barunga Australia see Bamyili
Barun-Torey, Ozero l. Russia 73 L2
Barus Indon. 71 B7
Baruunturuun Mongolia 80 H2
Baruun-Urt Mongolia 73 K3
Baruva India 84 E2
Barwani India 82 C5
Barwéli Mali see Baraouéli
Barwon r. Australia 112 C3
Barygaza India see Bharuch
Barysaw Belarus 45 P9
Barysh Russia 43 J5
Basaga Turkm. 89 G2
Basăk, Tônlé r. Cambodia 71 D5
Basalt r. Australia 110 D3
Basalt Island H.K. China 77 [inset]
Basankusu Dem. Rep. Congo 98 B3
Basar India 84 C2
Basarabi Romania 59 M2
Basargechar Armenia see Vardenis
Basaseachic, Parque Nacional Cascada de nat. park Mex. 127 F7
Bascuñán, Cabo c. Chile 144 B3
Basel Switz. 56 H3
Bāsh Ābdān Afgh. 89 H2
Bashäkerd, Kūhhā-ye mts Iran 88 E5
Bashanta Russia see Gorodovikovsk
Bashaw Canada 120 H4
Bāshī Iran 88 C4
Bashi Channel Phil./Taiwan 69 G2
Bashmakovo Russia 43 I5
Bāsht Iran 88 C4
Bashtanka Ukr. 43 G7
Basi Punjab India 82 D3
Basi Rajasthan India 82 D4
Basia India 83 F5
Basilan i. Phil. 69 G5
Basildon U.K. 49 H7
Basile, Pico mt. Equat. Guinea 96 D4
Basin U.S.A. 126 F3
Basingstoke U.K. 49 F7
Basin Lake Canada 121 J4
Basirhat India 83 G5
Basīṭ, Ra's al pt Syria 85 B2
Başkale Turkey 91 G3
Baskatong, Réservoir resr Canada 122 G5
Baskerville, Cape Australia 108 C4
Başkomutan Tarıhı Milli Parkı nat. park Turkey 59 N5
Başköy Turkey 85 A1
Baskunchak, Ozero l. Russia 43 J6
Basle Switz. see Basel
Basmat India 84 C2
Basoko Dem. Rep. Congo 98 C3
Basol r. Pak. 89 G5
Basra Iraq 91 G5
Bassano Canada 121 H5
Bassano del Grappa Italy 58 D2
Bassar Togo 96 D4
Bassas da India reef Indian Ocean 99 D6
Bassas de Pedro Padua Bank sea feature India 84 B3
Bassein Myanmar 70 A3
Bassein r. Myanmar 70 A3
Bassenthwaite Lake U.K. 48 D4
Basse Santa Su Gambia 96 B3

▶Basse-Terre Guadeloupe 137 L5
Capital of Guadeloupe.

▶Basseterre St Kitts and Nevis 137 L5
Capital of St Kitts and Nevis.

Bassett NE U.S.A. 130 D3
Bassett VA U.S.A. 134 F5
Bassikounou Mauritania 96 C3
Bass Rock i. U.K. 50 G4
Bass Strait Australia 111 D8
Bassum Germany 53 I2
Basswood Lake Canada 122 C4
Båstad Sweden 45 H8
Bastheim Germany 53 K4
Basti India 83 E4
Bastia Corsica France 56 I5
Bastioes r. Brazil 143 K5
Bastogne Belgium 52 F4
Bastrop LA U.S.A. 131 F5
Bastrop TX U.S.A. 131 D6
Basuo China see Dongfang
Basutoland country Africa see Lesotho
Başyayla Turkey 85 A1
Bata Equat. Guinea 96 D4
Batabanó, Golfo de b. Cuba 137 H4
Batagay Russia 65 O3
Batala India 82 C3
Batalha Port. 57 B4
Batam Indon. 71 D7
Batam i. Indon. 71 D7
Batamay Russia 65 N3
Batamshy Kazakh. see Badamsha
Batan Jiangsu China 77 I1
Batan Qinghai China 76 D1
Batan i. Phil. 69 G2
Batang China 76 C2
Batangafo Cent. Afr. Rep. 98 B3
Batangas Phil. 69 G4
Batangtoru Indon. 71 B7
Batan Islands Phil. 69 G2
Batavia Indon. see Jakarta
Batavia NY U.S.A. 135 F2
Batavia OH U.S.A. 134 C4
Bataysk Russia 43 H7
Batchawana Mountain hill Canada 122 D5
Bătdâmbâng Cambodia 71 C4
Batéké, Plateaux Congo 98 B4
Batemans Bay Australia 112 E5
Bates Range hills Australia 109 C6
Batesville AR U.S.A. 131 F5
Batesville IN U.S.A. 134 C4
Batesville MS U.S.A. 131 F5
Batetskiy Russia 42 F4
Bath N.B. Canada 123 I5
Bath Ont. Canada 135 G1
Bath U.K. 49 E7
Bath ME U.S.A. 135 K2
Bath NY U.S.A. 135 G2
Bath PA U.S.A. 135 H3
Batha watercourse Chad 97 E3
Bathéay Cambodia 71 D5
Bathgate U.K. 50 F5
Bathinda India 82 C3
Bathurst Australia 112 D4
Bathurst Canada 123 I5
Bathurst Gambia see Banjul
Bathurst S. Africa 101 H7
Bathurst, Cape Canada 118 F2
Bathurst, Lake Australia 112 D5
Bathurst Inlet inlet Canada 118 H3
Bathurst Inlet (abandoned) Canada 118 H3
Bathurst Island Australia 108 E2
Bathurst Island Canada 119 I2
Bathyz Döwlet Gorugy nature res. Turkm. 89 F3
Batié Burkina Faso 96 C4
Batı Menteşe Dağları mts Turkey 59 L6
Batı Toroslar mts Turkey 59 N6
Batken Kyrg. 80 D4
Batkes Indon. 108 E1
Bāṭlāq-e Gavkhūnī marsh Iran 88 D3
Batley U.K. 48 F5
Batlow Australia 112 D5
Batman Turkey 91 F3
Batna Alg. 54 F4
Batok, Bukit hill Sing. 71 [inset]

▶Baton Rouge U.S.A. 131 F6
Capital of Louisiana.

Batopilas Mex. 127 G8
Batouri Cameroon 97 E4
Batrā' tourist site Jordan see Petra
Batrā', Jabal al mt. Jordan 85 B5
Batroûn Lebanon 85 B2
Båtsfjord Norway 44 P1
Battambang Cambodia see Bătdâmbâng
Batticaloa Sri Lanka 84 D5
Batti Malv i. India 71 A5
Battipaglia Italy 58 F4
Battle r. Canada 121 I4
Battle Creek U.S.A. 134 C2
Battleford Canada 121 I4
Battle Mountain U.S.A. 128 E1
Battle Mountain mt. U.S.A. 128 E1
Battura Glacier Pak. 82 C1
Batu mt. Eth. 98 D3
Batu, Pulau-pulau is Indon. 68 B7
Batudaka i. Indon. 69 G7
Batu Gajah Malaysia 71 C6
Batum Georgia see Bat'umi
Bat'umi Georgia 91 F2
Batu Pahat Malaysia 71 C7
Batu Putih, Gunung mt. Malaysia 71 C6
Baturaja Indon. 68 C7
Baturité Brazil 143 K4
Batyrevo Russia 43 J5
Batys Qazaqstan admin. div. Kazakh. see Zapadnyy Kazakhstan
Bau Sarawak Malaysia 68 E6
Baubau Indon. 69 G8
Baucau East Timor 108 D2
Bauchi Nigeria 96 D3
Bauda India 84 E1
Baudette U.S.A. 130 E1
Baudh India see Bauda
Baugé-en-Anjou France 56 D3
Bauhinia Australia 110 E5
Baukau East Timor see Baucau
Bauld, Cape Canada 123 L4
Baume-les-Dames France 56 H3
Baunach r. Germany 53 K5
Baura Bangl. 83 G4
Bauru Brazil 145 A3
Bausendorf Germany 52 G4
Bauska Latvia 45 N8
Bautino Kazakh. 91 H1
Bautzen Germany 47 O5
Bavānāt Iran 88 D4
Bavaria land Germany see Bayern
Bavaria reg. Germany 53 L6
Bavda India 84 B2
Baviaanskloofberge mts S. Africa 100 F7
Bavispe r. Mex. 127 F7
Bavla India 82 C5
Bavly Russia 41 Q5
Baw Myanmar 70 A2
Bawal India 82 D3
Baw Baw National Park Australia 112 C6
Bawdeswell U.K. 49 I6
Bawdwin Myanmar 70 B2
Bawean i. Indon. 68 E8
Bawinkel Germany 53 H2
Bawlake Myanmar 70 B3
Bawolung China 76 D2
Baxi China 76 D1
Baxley U.S.A. 133 D6
Baxoi China 76 C2
Baxter Mountain U.S.A. 129 J2
Bay China see Baicheng
Bayamo Cuba 137 I4
Bayan Heilong. China 74 B3
Bayan Qinghai China 76 C1
Bayana India 82 D4
Bayan-Adarga Mongolia 73 K3
Bayanauyl Kazakh. 80 E1
Bayanbulak China 80 F3
Bayanday Russia 72 J2
Bayan Gol China see Dengkou
Bayan Har Shan mts China 76 B1
Bayan Har Shankou pass China 76 C1
Bayanhongor Mongolia 80 J2
Bayan Hot China 72 J5
Bayānlū Iran 88 B3
Bayannur China 73 J4
Bayan Obo China 73 J4
Bayan Shutu China 73 K4
Bayantsagaan Mongolia 80 I2
Bayan Ul China 73 L4
Bayan-Uul Mongolia 73 K3
Bayard U.S.A. 129 I5
Bayat Turkey 59 N5
Bayāẓ Iran 88 E4
Bayāẓīyeh Iran 88 D3
Baybay Phil. 69 G4
Bayboro U.S.A. 133 E5
Bayburt Turkey 91 F2
Bay Canh, Hon i. Vietnam 71 D5
Bay City MI U.S.A. 134 D2
Bay City TX U.S.A. 131 D6
Baydaratskaya Guba Russia 64 H3
Baydhabo Somalia 98 E3
Bayerischer Wald mts Germany 47 N6
Bayerischer Wald, Nationalpark nat. park Germany 47 N6
Bayern land Germany 53 L6
Bayeux France 49 G9
Bayfield Canada 134 E2
Bayındır Turkey 59 L5
Bay Islands is Hond. see Bahía, Islas de la
Bayizhen China see Nyingchi
Bayjī Iraq 91 F4
Baykal, Ozero l. Russia see Baikal, Lake
Baykal-Amur Magistral Russia 74 C1
Baykal Range mts Russia see Baykal'skiy Khrebet
Baykal'skiy Khrebet mts Russia 73 J2
Baykan Turkey 91 F3
Bay-Khaak Russia 80 H1
Baykibashevo Russia 41 R4
Baykonur Kazakh. see Baykonyr
Baykonyr Kazakh. 80 B2
Baymak Russia 64 G4
Bay Minette U.S.A. 133 C6
Baynūna'h reg. U.A.E. 88 D6
Bayombong Phil. 69 G3
Bayona Spain see Baiona
Bayonne France 56 D5
Bayonne U.S.A. 135 H3
Bay Port U.S.A. 134 D2
Bayqongyr Kazakh. see Baykonyr
Bayram-Ali Turkm. see Baýramaly
Baýramaly Turkm. 89 F2
Bayramiç Turkey 59 L5
Bayreuth Germany 53 L5
Bayrūt Lebanon see Beirut
Bays, Lake of Canada 134 F1
Bay Shore MI U.S.A. 134 C1
Bay Shore NY U.S.A. 135 I3
Bay Springs U.S.A. 131 F6
Bayston Hill U.K. 49 E6
Baysun Uzbek. see Boysun
Bayt Jālā West Bank 85 B4
Bayt Lahm West Bank see Bethlehem
Baytown U.S.A. 131 E6
Bay View N.Z. 113 F4
Bayy al Kabīr, Wādī watercourse Libya 97 E1
Baza Spain 57 E5
Baza, Sierra de mts Spain 57 E5
Bāzārak Afgh. 89 G3
Bazardüzü Dağı mt. Azer./Russia see Bazardyuzyu, Gora
Bazardyuzyu, Gora mt. Azer./Russia 91 G2
Bāzār-e Māsāl Iran 88 C2
Bazarnyy Karabulak Russia 43 J5
Bazaruto, Ilha do i. Moz. 99 D6
Bazdar Pak. 89 G5
Bazhong China 76 E2
Bazhou China see Bazhong
Bazin r. Canada 122 G5
Bazmān Iran 89 F5
Bazmān, Kūh-e mt. Iran 89 F4
Bcharré Lebanon 85 C2
Be, Sông r. Vietnam 71 D5
Beach U.S.A. 130 C2
Beachy Head hd U.K. 49 H8
Beacon U.S.A. 135 I3
Beacon Bay S. Africa 101 H7
Beaconsfield U.K. 49 G7
Beagle, Canal sea chan. Arg. 144 C8
Beagle Bank reef Australia 108 C3
Beagle Bay Australia 108 C4
Beagle Gulf Australia 108 E3
Bealanana Madag. 99 E5
Béal an Átha Ireland see Ballina
Béal an Mhuirthead Ireland 51 C3
Béal Átha na Sluaighe Ireland see Ballinasloe

Beale, Lake India 84 B2
Beaminster U.K. 49 E8
Bear r. U.S.A. 126 E4
Bearalváhki Norway see Berlevåg
Bear Cove Point Canada 121 O2
Beardmore Canada 122 D4
Beardmore Glacier Antarctica 152 H1
Bear Island Arctic Ocean see Bjørnøya
Bear Island Canada 122 E3
Bear Lake l. Canada 122 A3
Bear Lake U.S.A. 134 B1
Bear Lake l. U.S.A. 126 F4
Bearma r. India 82 D4
Bear Mountain U.S.A. 130 C3
Bearnaraigh i. U.K. see Berneray
Bear Paw Mountain U.S.A. 126 F2
Bearpaw Mountains U.S.A. 126 F2
Bearskin Lake Canada 121 N4
Beas Dam India 82 C3
Beata, Cabo c. Dom. Rep. 137 J5
Beatrice U.S.A. 130 D3
Beatrice, Cape Australia 110 B2
Beatton r. Canada 120 F3
Beatton River Canada 120 F3
Beatty U.S.A. 128 E3
Beattyville Canada 122 F4
Beattyville U.S.A. 134 D5
Beaucaire France 56 G5
Beauchene Island Falkland Is 144 E8
Beaufort Australia 112 A6
Beaufort NC U.S.A. 133 E5
Beaufort SC U.S.A. 133 D5
Beaufort Island H.K. China 77 [inset]
Beaufort Sea Canada/U.S.A. 118 D2
Beaufort West S. Africa 100 F7
Beaulieu r. Canada 121 H2
Beauly U.K. 50 E3
Beauly r. U.K. 50 E3
Beaumaris U.K. 48 C5
Beaumont Belgium 52 E4
Beaumont N.Z. 113 B7
Beaumont MS U.S.A. 131 F6
Beaumont TX U.S.A. 131 E6
Beaune France 56 G3
Beaupréau France 56 D3
Beauquesne France 52 C4
Beauraing Belgium 52 E4
Beauséjour Canada 121 L5
Beauvais France 52 C5
Beauval France 52 C4
Beaver r. Alba/Sask. Canada 121 J4
Beaver r. Ont. Canada 122 D3
Beaver r. Y.T. Canada 120 E3
Beaver OK U.S.A. 131 C4
Beaver PA U.S.A. 134 E3
Beaver UT U.S.A. 129 G2
Beaver r. U.S.A. 129 G2
Beaver Creek Canada 153 A2
Beavercreek U.S.A. 134 C4
Beaver Creek r. MT U.S.A. 130 B1
Beaver Creek r. ND U.S.A. 130 C2
Beaver Dam KY U.S.A. 134 B5
Beaver Dam WI U.S.A. 130 F3
Beaver Falls U.S.A. 134 E3
Beaverhead Mountains U.S.A. 126 E3
Beaverhill Lake Alta Canada 121 H4
Beaver Hill Lake Canada 121 M4
Beaverhill Lake N.W.T. Canada 121 J2
Beaver Island U.S.A. 132 C2
Beaverlodge Canada 120 G4
Beaverton Canada 134 F1
Beaverton MI U.S.A. 134 C2
Beaverton OR U.S.A. 126 C3
Beawar India 82 C4
Beazley Arg. 144 C4
Bebedouro Brazil 145 A3
Bebington U.K. 48 D5
Bebra Germany 53 J4
Bêca China 76 C2
Bécard, Lac l. Canada 123 G1
Beccles U.K. 49 I6
Bečej Serbia 59 I2
Becerreá Spain 57 C2
Béchar Alg. 54 D5
Bechhofen Germany 53 K5
Bechuanaland country Africa see Botswana
Beckley U.S.A. 134 E5
Beckum Germany 53 I3
Becky Peak U.S.A. 129 F2
Bečov nad Teplou Czechia 53 M4
Bedale U.K. 48 F4
Bedburg Germany 52 G4
Bedelē Eth. 98 D3
Bedford N.S. Canada 123 J5
Bedford Que. Canada 135 I1
Bedford E. Cape S. Africa 101 H7
Bedford KwaZulu-Natal S. Africa 101 J5
Bedford U.K. 49 G6
Bedford IN U.S.A. 134 B4
Bedford KY U.S.A. 134 C4
Bedford PA U.S.A. 135 F3
Bedford VA U.S.A. 134 F5
Bedford, Cape Australia 110 D2
Bedford Downs Australia 108 D4
Bedgerebong Australia 112 C4
Bedi India 82 B5
Bedla India 82 C4
Bedlington U.K. 48 F3
Bedok Sing. 71 [inset]
Bedok Jetty Sing. 71 [inset]
Bedok Reservoir Sing. 71 [inset]
Bedourie Australia 110 B5
Bedum Neth. 52 G1
Bedworth U.K. 49 F6
Beechworth Australia 112 C6
Beechy Canada 121 J5
Beecroft Peninsula Australia 112 E5
Beed India see Bid
Beelitz Germany 53 M2
Beenleigh Australia 112 F1
Beernem Belgium 52 D3
Beersheba Israel 85 B4
Be'ér Sheva' Israel see Beersheba
Be'ér Sheva', Naḥal watercourse Israel 85 B4
Beervlei Dam S. Africa 100 F7
Beerwah Australia 112 F1
Beetaloo Australia 108 F4
Beethoven Peninsula Antarctica 152 L2
Beeville U.S.A. 131 D6
Befori Dem. Rep. Congo 98 C3
Beg, Lough l. U.K. 51 F3
Bega Australia 112 D6
Begari r. Pak. 89 H4
Begicheva, Ostrov i. Russia see Bol'shoy Begichev, Ostrov
Begur, Cap de c. Spain 57 H3
Begusarai India 83 F4
Behābād Iran 88 E3
Béhague, Pointe pt Fr. Guiana 143 H3
Behbahān Iran 88 C4
Behchokǫ̀ Canada 120 G2
Behrūsī Iran 88 D4
Behshahr Iran 88 D2
Bei'an China 74 B2
Bei'ao China see Dongtou
Beibei China 76 E2
Beichuan China see Qushan
Beida Libya see Al Bayḍā'
Beigang Taiwan 77 I4
Beiguan China see Anyang
Beihai China 77 F4
Bei Hulsan Hu salt l. China 83 H1
▶Beijing China 73 L5
Capital of China. 5th most populous city in Asia and 8th in the world.
Beijing mun. China 73 L4
Beik Myanmar see Myeik
Beilen Neth. 52 G2
Beiliu China 77 F4
Beilngries Germany 53 L5
Beiluheyan China 76 B1
Beinn an Oir hill U.K. 50 D5
Beinn an Tuirc hill U.K. 50 D5
Beinn Bheigeir hill U.K. 50 C5
Beinn Bhreac hill U.K. 50 D4
Beinn Dearg mt. U.K. 50 E3
Beinn Heasgarnich mt. U.K. 50 E4
Beinn Mholach hill U.K. 50 C2
Beinn Mhòr hill U.K. 50 B3
Beinn na Faoghlia i. U.K. see Benbecula
Beipan Jiang r. China 76 E3
Beipiao China 73 M4
Beira Moz. 99 D5
▶Beirut Lebanon 85 B3
Capital of Lebanon.
Bei Shan mts China 80 I3
Beitbridge Zimbabwe 99 C6
Beith U.K. 50 E5
Beja Port. 57 C4
Béja Tunisia 58 C6
Bejaïa Alg. 57 I5
Béjar Spain 57 D3
Beji r. Pak. 80 C6
Bekaa valley Lebanon see El Béqaa
Békés Hungary 59 I1
Békéscsaba Hungary 59 I1
Bekily Madag. 99 E6
Bēkma, Sadd dam Iraq 91 G3
Bekovo Russia 43 I5
Bekwai Ghana 96 C4
Bela India 83 E4
Bela Pak. 89 G5
Belab r. Pak. 89 H4
Bela-Bela S. Africa 101 I3
Bélabo Cameroon 96 E4
Bela Crkva Serbia 59 I2
Belagavi India 84 B3
Bel Air U.S.A. 135 G4
Belalcázar Spain 57 D4
Bělá nad Radbuzou Czechia 53 M5
Belapur India 84 B2
Belarus country Europe 43 E5
Belau country N. Pacific Ocean see Palau
Bela Vista Brazil 144 E2
Bela Vista Moz. 101 K4
Bela Vista de Goiás Brazil 145 A2
Belawan Indon. 71 B7
Belaya r. Russia 65 S3 also known as Bila
Belaya Glina Russia 43 I7
Belaya Kalitva Russia 43 I6
Belaya Kholunitsa Russia 42 K4
Belaya Tserkva Ukr. see Bila Tserkva
Belbédji Niger 96 D3
Bełchatów Poland 47 Q5
Belcher U.S.A. 134 D5
Belcher Islands Canada 122 F2
Belcoo U.K. 51 E3
Belden U.S.A. 128 C1
Belding U.S.A. 134 C2
Beleapani reef India see Cherbaniani Reef
Belebey Russia 41 Q5
Beledweyne Somalia 98 E3
Belém Brazil 143 I4
Belém Novo Brazil 145 A5
Belén Arg. 144 C3
Belen Antalya Turkey 85 A1
Belen Hatay Turkey 85 C1
Belen U.S.A. 127 G6
Belep, Îles is New Caledonia 107 G3
Belev Russia 43 H5
▶Belfast U.K. 51 G3
Capital of Northern Ireland.
Belfast U.S.A. 132 G2
Belfast Lough inlet U.K. 51 G3
Bēlfodiyo Eth. 98 D2
Belford U.K. 48 F3
Belfort France 56 H3
Belgaum India see Belagavi
Belgern Germany 53 N3
Belgian Congo country Africa see Congo, Democratic Republic of the
België country Europe see Belgium
Belgique country Europe see Belgium
Belgium country Europe 52 E4
Belgorod Russia 43 H6
Belgorod-Dnestrovskyy Ukr. see Bilhorod-Dnistrovs'kyy
▶Belgrade Serbia 59 I2
Capital of Serbia.
Belgrade ME U.S.A. 135 K1
Belgrade MT U.S.A. 126 F3
Belgrano II research station Antarctica 152 A1
Belice r. Sicily Italy 58 E6
Belinskiy Russia 43 I5
Belinyu Indon. 68 D7
Belitung i. Indon. 68 D7
Belize Angola 99 B4
▶Belize Belize 136 G5
Former capital of Belize.
Belize country Central America 136 G5
Beljak Austria see Villach
Belkina, Mys pt Russia 74 E3
Bel'kovskiy, Ostrov i. Russia 65 O2
Bell Australia 112 E1
Bell r. Australia 112 D4
Bell r. Canada 122 F4
Bella Bella Canada 120 D4
Bellac France 56 E3
Bella Coola Canada 120 E4
Bellaire U.S.A. 134 C1
Bellary India see Ballari
Bellata Australia 112 D2
Bella Unión Uruguay 144 E4
Bella Vista U.S.A. 128 B1
Bellbrook Australia 112 F3
Bell Cay reef Australia 110 E4
Belledonne mts France 56 G4
Bellefontaine U.S.A. 134 D3
Bellefonte U.S.A. 135 G3
Belle Fourche U.S.A. 130 C2
Belle Fourche r. U.S.A. 130 C2
Belle Glade U.S.A. 133 D7
Belle-Île i. France 56 C3
Belle Isle i. Canada 123 L4
Belle Isle, Strait of Canada 123 K4
Belleville Canada 135 G1
Belleville IL U.S.A. 130 F4
Belleville KS U.S.A. 130 D4
Bellevue IA U.S.A. 130 F3
Bellevue MI U.S.A. 134 C2
Bellevue OH U.S.A. 134 D3
Bellevue WA U.S.A. 126 C3
Bellin Canada see Kangirsuk
Bellingham U.K. 48 E3
Bellingham U.S.A. 126 C2
Bellingshausen research station Antarctica 152 A2
Bellingshausen Sea Antarctica 152 L2
Bellinzona Switz. 56 I3
Bellows Falls U.S.A. 135 I2
Bellpat Pak. 89 H4
Belluno Italy 58 E1
Bell Ville Arg. 144 D4
Bellville S. Africa 100 D7
Belm Germany 53 I2
Belmont Australia 112 E4
Belmont U.K. 50 [inset]
Belmont U.S.A. 135 F2
Belmonte Brazil 145 D1
▶Belmopan Belize 136 G5
Capital of Belize.
Belmore, Mount hill Australia 112 F2
Belo Madag. 99 E6
Belo Campo Brazil 145 C1
Belœil Belgium 52 D4
Belogorsk Crimea see Bilohirs'k
Belogorsk Russia 74 C2
Beloha Madag. 99 E6
Belo Horizonte Brazil 145 C2
Beloit KS U.S.A. 130 D4
Beloit WI U.S.A. 130 F3
Belokurikha Russia 80 F1
Belo Monte Brazil 143 H4
Belomorsk Russia 42 G2
Belonia India 83 G5
Belorechensk Russia 91 E1
Belorechenskaya Russia see Belorechensk
Belören Turkey 90 D3
Beloretsk Russia 64 G4
Belorussia country Europe see Belarus
Belorusskaya S.S.R. country Europe see Belarus
Belostok Poland see Białystok
Belot, Lac l. Canada 118 F3
Belo Tsiribihina Madag. 99 E5
Belovo Russia 72 F2
Beloyarskiy Russia 41 T3
Beloye, Ozero l. Russia 42 H3
Beloye More sea Russia see White Sea
Belozersk Russia 42 H3
Belpre U.S.A. 134 E4
Beltana Australia 111 B6
Belted Range mts U.S.A. 128 E3
Belton U.S.A. 131 D6
Bel'ts' Moldova see Bălţi
Bel'tsy Moldova see Bălţi
Belukha, Gora mt. Kazakh./Russia 80 G2
Belush'ye Russia 42 J2
Belvidere IL U.S.A. 130 F3
Belvidere NJ U.S.A. 135 H3
Belyando r. Australia 110 D4
Belyayevka Ukr. see Bilyayivka
Belyy Russia 42 G5
Belyy, Ostrov i. Russia 64 I2
Belzoni U.S.A. 131 F5
Bemaraha, Plateau du Madag. 99 E5
Bembe Angola 99 B4
Bemidji U.S.A. 130 E2
Béna Burkina Faso 96 C3
Bena Dibele Dem. Rep. Congo 98 C4
Ben Alder mt. U.K. 50 E4
Benalla Australia 112 B6
Benares India see Varanasi
Ben Arous Tunisia 58 D6
Benavente Spain 57 D2
Ben Avon mt. U.K. 50 F3
Benbane Head hd U.K. 51 F2
Benbecula i. U.K. 50 B3
Ben Boyd National Park Australia 112 E6
Benburb U.K. 51 F3
Bencha China 77 I1
Ben Chonzie hill U.K. 50 F4
Ben Cleuch hill U.K. 50 F4
Ben Cruachan mt. U.K. 50 D4
Bend U.S.A. 126 C3
Bendearg mt. S. Africa 101 H6
Bender Moldova 59 M1
Bender-Bayla Somalia 98 F3
Bendery Moldova see Bender
Bendigo Australia 112 B6
Bendoc Australia 112 D6
Bene Moz. 99 D5
Benedict, Mount hill Canada 123 K3
Benenitra Madag. 99 E6
Benešov Czechia 47 O6
Bénestroff France 52 G6
Benevento Italy 58 F4
Beneventum Italy see Benevento
Benezette U.S.A. 135 F3
Beng, Nâm r. Laos 70 C3
Bengal, Bay of sea Indian Ocean 81 G8
Bengaluru India 84 C3
Bengamisa Dem. Rep. Congo 98 C3
Bengbu China 77 H1
Benghazi Libya 97 F1
Bengkalis Indon. 71 C7
Bengkalis i. Indon. 71 C7
Bengkulu Indon. 68 C7
Bengtsfors Sweden 45 H7
Benguela Angola 99 B5
Benha Egypt see Banhā
Ben Hiant hill U.K. 50 C4
Ben Hope hill U.K. 50 E2
Ben Horn hill U.K. 50 E2
Beni r. Bol. 142 E6
Beni Dem. Rep. Congo 98 C3
Beni Nepal 83 E3
Beni Abbès Alg. 54 D5
Beniah Lake Canada 121 H2
Benidorm Spain 57 F4
Beni Hammad, Al Qal'a tourist site Alg. 57 I6
Beni Mellal Morocco 54 C5
Benin country Africa 96 D4
Benin, Bight of g. Africa 96 D4
Benin City Nigeria 96 D4
Beni Saf Alg. 57 F6
Beni Snassen, Monts des mts Morocco 57 E6
Beni Suef Egypt see Banī Suwayf
Benito, Islas is Mex. 127 E7
Benito Juárez Arg. 144 E5
Benito Juárez Mex. 129 F5
Benjamin U.S.A. 131 D5
Benjamin Constant Brazil 142 E4
Benjamín Hill Mex. 127 F7
Benjina Indon. 69 I8
Benkelman U.S.A. 130 C3
Ben Klibreck hill U.K. 50 E2
Ben Lavin Nature Reserve S. Africa 101 I2
Ben Lawers mt. U.K. 50 E4
Ben Lomond mt. Australia 112 E3
Ben Lomond hill U.K. 50 E4
Ben Lomond National Park Australia 111 [inset]
Ben Macdui mt. U.K. 50 F3
Benmara Australia 110 B3
Ben More hill U.K. 50 C4
Ben More mt. U.K. 50 E4
Benmore, Lake N.Z. 113 C7
Ben More Assynt hill U.K. 50 E2
Bennäs Fin. 44 M5
Bennetta, Ostrov i. Russia 65 P2
Bennett Island Russia see Bennetta, Ostrov
Bennett Lake Canada 120 C3
Bennettsville U.S.A. 133 E5
Ben Nevis mt. U.K. 50 D4
Bennington NH U.S.A. 135 J2
Bennington VT U.S.A. 135 I2
Benoni S. Africa 101 I4
Bénoué, Parc National de la nat. park Cameroon 97 E4
Ben Rinnes hill U.K. 50 F3
Bensheim Germany 53 I5
Benson AZ U.S.A. 129 H6
Benson MN U.S.A. 130 E2
Benta Seberang Malaysia 71 C6
Benteng Indon. 69 G8
Bentinck Island Myanmar 71 B5
Bentiu South Sudan 86 C8
Bent Jbaïl Lebanon 85 B3
Bentley U.K. 48 F5
Bento Gonçalves Brazil 145 A5
Benton AR U.S.A. 131 E5
Benton CA U.S.A. 128 D3
Benton IL U.S.A. 130 F4
Benton KY U.S.A. 131 F4
Benton LA U.S.A. 131 E5
Benton MO U.S.A. 131 F4
Benton PA U.S.A. 135 G3
Bentong Malaysia see Bentung
Benton Harbor U.S.A. 134 B2
Bentonville U.S.A. 131 E4
Bên Tre Vietnam 71 D5
Bentung Malaysia 71 C7
Benue r. Nigeria 96 D4
Benum, Gunung mt. Malaysia 71 C7
Ben Vorlich hill U.K. 50 E4
Benwee Head hd Ireland 51 C3
Benwood U.S.A. 134 E3
Ben Wyvis mt. U.K. 50 E3
Benxi Liaoning China 74 A4
Benxi Liaoning China 74 B4
Beograd Serbia see Belgrade
Béoumi Côte d'Ivoire 96 C4
Beppu Japan 75 C6
Béqaa valley Lebanon see El Béqaa
Berach r. India 82 C4
Beraketa Madag. 99 E6
Bérard, Lac l. Canada 123 H2
Berasia India 82 D5
Berat Albania 59 H4
Beravina Madag. 99 E5
Berbak, Taman Nasional nat. park Indon. 68 C7
Berber Sudan 86 D6
Berbera Somalia 98 E2
Berbérati Cent. Afr. Rep. 98 B3
Berchtesgaden, Nationalpark nat. park Germany 47 N7
Berck France 52 B4
Berdichev Ukr. see Berdychiv
Berdigestyakh Russia 65 N3
Berdyans'k Ukr. 43 H7
Berdychiv Ukr. 43 F6
Berea KY U.S.A. 134 C5
Berea OH U.S.A. 134 E3
Beregovo Ukr. see Berehove
Beregovoy Russia 74 B1
Berehove Ukr. 43 D6
Bereina P.N.G. 69 L8
Bere Island Ireland 51 C6
Bereket Turkm. 88 D2
Berekum Ghana 96 C4
Berenice Egypt see Baranīs
Berenice Libya see Benghazi
Berens r. Canada 121 L4
Berens Island Canada 121 L4
Berens River Canada 121 L4
Beresford U.S.A. 130 D3
Bereza Belarus see Byaroza
Berezino Belarus see Byerazino
Berezivka Ukr. 43 F7
Berezne Ukr. 43 E6
Bereznik Russia 42 I3
Berezniki Russia 41 R4
Berezov Russia see Berezovo
Berezovka Russia 74 B2
Berezovka Ukr. see Berezivka
Berezovo Russia 41 T3
Berezovyy Russia 74 D2
Berga Germany 53 L3
Berga Spain 57 G2
Bergama Turkey 59 L5
Bergamo Italy 58 C2
Bergby Sweden 45 J6
Bergen Germany 53 J2
Bergen Norway 45 D6
Bergen U.S.A. 135 G2
Bergen auf Rügen Germany 47 N3
Bergen op Zoom Neth. 52 E3
Bergerac France 56 E4
Bergères-lès-Vertus France 52 E6
Bergheim Germany 52 G4
Bergisches Land reg. Germany 53 H4
Bergisch Gladbach Germany 52 H4
Bergland Namibia 100 C2
Bergomum Italy see Bergamo
Bergoo U.S.A. 134 E4
Bergpark Wilhelmshöhe tourist site Germany 47 L5
Bergsjö Sweden 45 J6
Bergsviken Sweden 44 L4
Bergtheim Germany 53 K5
Bergues France 52 C4
Bergum Neth. see Burgum
Bergville S. Africa 101 I5
Berhampur India see Baharampur
Beringa, Ostrov i. Russia 65 R4
Beringen Belgium 52 F3
Beringovskiy Russia 65 S3
Bering Sea N. Pacific Ocean 65 S4
Bering Strait Russia/U.S.A. 65 U3
Berīs, Ra's pt Iran 89 F5
Berislav Ukr. see Beryslav
Berkåk Norway 44 G5
Berkane Morocco 57 E6
Berkel r. Neth. 52 G2
Berkeley U.S.A. 128 B3
Berkeley Springs U.S.A. 135 F4
Berkhout Neth. 52 F2
Berkner Sub-glacial Island Antarctica 152 A1
Berkovitsa Bulg. 59 J3
Berkshire Downs hills U.K. 49 F7
Berkshire Hills U.S.A. 135 I2
Berland r. Canada 120 G4
Berlare Belgium 52 E3
Berlevåg Norway 44 P1
▶Berlin Germany 53 N2
Capital of Germany.
Berlin land Germany 53 N2
Berlin MD U.S.A. 135 H4
Berlin NH U.S.A. 135 J1
Berlin PA U.S.A. 135 F4
Berlin Lake U.S.A. 134 E3
Bermagui Australia 112 E6
Bermejo r. Arg./Bol. 144 E3
Bermejo Bol. 142 F8
Bermen, Lac l. Canada 123 H3
▶Bermuda terr. N. Atlantic Ocean 137 L2
United Kingdom Overseas Territory.
Bermuda Rise sea feature N. Atlantic Ocean 148 D4
▶Bern Switz. 56 H3
Capital of Switzerland.
Bernalillo U.S.A. 127 G6
Bernardino de Campos Brazil 145 A3
Bernardo O'Higgins research station Antarctica 152 A2
Bernardo O'Higgins, Parque Nacional nat. park Chile 144 B7
Bernasconi Arg. 144 D5
Bernau bei Berlin Germany 53 N2
Bernburg (Saale) Germany 53 L3
Berne Germany 53 I1
Berne Switz. see Bern
Berne U.S.A. 134 C3
Berner Alpen mts Switz. 56 H3
Berneray i. Scotland U.K. 50 B3
Berneray i. Scotland U.K. 50 B4
Bernier Island Australia 109 A6
Bernina, Piz mt. Italy/Switz. 58 C1
Bernina Pass Switz. 56 J3
Bernkastel-Kues Germany 52 H5
Beroea Greece see Veroia
Beroea Syria see Aleppo
Beroroha Madag. 99 E6
Beroun Czechia 47 O6
Berounka r. Czechia 47 O6
Berovina Madag. see Beravina
Berri Australia 111 C7
Berriane Alg. 54 E5
Berridale Australia 112 D6
Berriedale U.K. 50 F2
Berrigan Australia 112 B5
Berrima Australia 112 E5
Berrouaghia Alg. 57 H5
Berry Australia 112 E5
Berry U.S.A. 134 C4
Berryessa, Lake U.S.A. 128 B2
Berry Head hd U.K. 49 D8
Berry Islands Bahamas 133 E7
Berryville U.S.A. 135 G4
Berseba Namibia 100 C4
Bersenbrück Germany 53 H2
Bertam Malaysia 71 C6
Berté, Lac l. Canada 123 H4
Berthoud Pass U.S.A. 126 G5
Bertolínia Brazil 143 J5
Bertoua Cameroon 96 E4
Bertraghboy Bay Ireland 51 C4
Beru atoll Kiribati 107 H2
Beruri Brazil 142 F4
Beruwala Sri Lanka 84 C5
Berwick Australia 112 B7
Berwick U.S.A. 135 G3
Berwick-upon-Tweed U.K. 48 E3
Berwyn hills U.K. 49 D6
Beryslav Ukr. 59 O1
Berytus Lebanon see Beirut
Besalampy Madag. 99 E5
Besançon France 56 H3
Besar, Gunung mt. Malaysia 71 C7
Besbay Kazakh. 80 A2
Beserah Malaysia 71 C7
Beshkent Uzbek. 89 G2
Beshneh Iran 88 D4
Besikama Indon. 108 D2
Besitang Indon. 71 B6
Beskra Alg. see Biskra
Beslan Russia 91 G2
Besnard Lake Canada 121 J4
Besni Turkey 90 E3
Besor, Naḥal watercourse Israel 85 B4
Beşparmak Dağları mts Cyprus see Pentadaktylos Range
Bessbrook U.K. 51 F3
Bessemer U.S.A. 133 C5
Besshoky, Gora hill Kazakh. 91 I1
Besskorbnaya Russia 43 I7
Bessonovka Russia 43 J5
Betalongchhip mt. India 83 H5
Betanzos Spain 57 B2
Bet Guvrin Israel 85 B4
Bethal S. Africa 101 I4
Bethanie Namibia 100 C4
Bethany U.S.A. 130 E3
Bethel U.S.A. 123 H5
Bethel Park U.S.A. 134 E3
Bethesda U.K. 48 C5
Bethesda MD U.S.A. 135 G4
Bethesda OH U.S.A. 134 E3
Bethlehem S. Africa 101 I5
Bethlehem U.S.A. 135 H3
Bethlehem West Bank 85 B4
Bethulie S. Africa 101 G6
Béthune France 52 C4
Beti Pak. 89 H4
Betim Brazil 145 B2
Bet Lehem West Bank see Bethlehem
Betma India 82 C5
Betong Thai. 71 C6
Betoota (abandoned) Australia 110 C5
Betpakdala plain Kazakh. 80 D2
Betroka Madag. 99 E6
Bet She'an Israel 85 B3
Betsiamites Canada 123 H4
Betsiamites r. Canada 123 H4
Betsukai Japan 74 G4
Bettiah India 83 F4
Bettyhill U.K. 50 E2
Bettystown Ireland 51 F4
Betul India 82 D5
Betung Kerihun, Taman Nasional nat. park Indon. 68 E6
Betwa r. India 82 D4
Betws-y-coed U.K. 49 D5
Betzdorf Germany 53 H4
Beulah Australia 111 C7
Beulah MI U.S.A. 134 B1
Beulah ND U.S.A. 130 C2
Beult r. U.K. 49 H7
Beuthen Poland see Bytom
Bever r. Germany 53 H2
Beverley U.K. 48 G5
Beverly MA U.S.A. 135 J2
Beverly OH U.S.A. 134 E4
Beverly Hills U.S.A. 128 D4
Beverly Lake Canada 121 K1
Beverstedt Germany 53 I1
Beverungen Germany 53 J3
Beverwijk Neth. 52 E2
Bewani P.N.G. 69 K7
Bexbach Germany 53 H5
Bexhill U.K. 49 H8
Bexley, Cape Canada 118 G3
Beyce Turkey see Orhaneli
Bey Dağları mts Turkey 59 N6
Beykoz Turkey 59 M4
Beyla Guinea 96 C4
Beylagan Azer. see Beyläqan
Beyläqan Azer. 91 G3
Beyneu Kazakh. 78 E2
Beypazarı Turkey 59 N4
Beypınarı Turkey 90 E3
Beypore India 84 B4
Beyrouth Lebanon see Beirut
Beyşehir Turkey 90 C3
Beyşehir Gölü l. Turkey 90 C3
Beytonovo Russia 74 B1
Beytüşşebap Turkey 91 F3
Bezameh Iran 88 E3
Bezbozhnik Russia 42 K4
Bezhanitsy Russia 42 F4
Bezhetsk Russia 42 H4
Béziers France 56 F5
Bezmein Turkm. see Abadan
Bezwada India see Vijayawada
Bhabha India see Bhabua
Bhabhar India 82 B4
Bhabhua India see Bhabua
Bhabua India 83 E4
Bhachau India 82 B5
Bhachbhar India 82 B4
Bhadgaon Nepal see Bhaktapur
Bhadohi India 83 E4
Bhadra India 82 C3
Bhadrachalam Road Station India see Kottagudem
Bhadrak India 83 F5
Bhadrakh India see Bhadrak
Bhadravati India 84 B3
Bhag Pak. 89 G4
Bhagalpur India 83 F4
Bhainsa India 84 C2

Bhainsdehi India 82 D5
Bhairab Bazar Bangl. 83 G4
Bhairi Hol mt. Pak. 89 G5
Bhaktapur Nepal 83 F4
Bhalki India 84 C2
Bhamo Myanmar 70 B1
Bhamragarh India 84 D2
Bhandal India 82 C2
Bhandara India 82 D5
Bhanjanagar India 84 E2
Bhanrer Range hills India 82 D5
Bhaptiahi India 83 F4
Bharat country Asia see India
Bharati research station Antarctica 152 E2
Bharatpur India 82 D4
Bhareli r. India 83 H4
Bharuch India 82 C5
Bhatapara India 83 E5
Bhatarsaigh i. U.K. see Vatersay
Bhatghar Lake India 84 B2
Bhatinda India see Bathinda
Bhatnair India see Hanumangarh
Bhatpara India 83 G5
Bhaunagar India see Bhavnagar
Bhavani r. India 84 C4
Bhavani Sagar l. India 84 C4
Bhavnagar India 82 C5
Bhawana Pak. 89 I4
Bhawanipatna India 84 D2
Bhearnaraigh, Eilean i. U.K. see Berneray
Bheemavaram India see Bhimavaram
Bhekuzulu S. Africa 101 J4
Bhera Pak. 89 I3
Bhigvan India 84 B2
Bhikhna Thori Nepal 83 F4
Bhilai India 82 E5
Bhildi India 82 C4
Bhilwara India 82 C4
Bhima r. India 84 C2
Bhimar India 82 B4
Bhimavaram India 84 D2
Bhimlath India 82 E5
Bhind India 82 D4
Bhinga India 83 E4
Bhisho S. Africa 101 H7
Bhiwandi India 84 B2
Bhiwani India 82 D3
Bhogaipur India 82 D4
Bhojpur Nepal 83 F4
Bhola Bangl. 83 G5
Bhongweni S. Africa 101 I6
Bhopal India 82 D5
Bhopalpatnam India 84 D2
Bhrigukaccha India see Bharuch
Bhuban India 84 E1
Bhubaneshwar India 84 E1
Bhubaneswar India see Bhubaneshwar
Bhuj India 82 B5
Bhusawal India 82 C5
Bhutan country Asia 83 G4
Bhuttewala India 82 B4
Bia r. Ghana 96 C4
Bīabān mts Iran 88 E5
Biafo Glacier Pak. 82 C2
Biak Indon. 69 J7
Biak i. Indon. 69 J7
Biała Podlaska Poland 43 D5
Białogard Poland 47 O4
Białystok Poland 43 D5
Bianco, Monte mt. France/Italy see Blanc, Mont
Biandan Gang r. mouth China 77 I1
Bianzhao China 74 A3
Bianzhuang China see Cangshan
Biaora India 82 D5
Biarritz France 56 D5
Bi'ār Tabrāk well Saudi Arabia 88 B5
Bibai Japan 74 F4
Bibbenluke Australia 112 D6
Bibbiena Italy 58 D3
Bibby Island Canada 121 M2
Biberach an der Riß Germany 47 L6
Bibile Sri Lanka 84 D5
Biblis Germany 53 I5
Biblos Lebanon see Jbail
Bicas Brazil 145 C3
Biçer Turkey 59 N5
Bicester U.K. 49 F7
Bichabhera India 82 C4
Bicheng China see Bishan
Bichevaya Russia 74 D3
Bichi r. Russia 74 E1
Bickerton Island Australia 110 B2
Bickleigh U.K. 49 D8
Bicknell U.S.A. 134 B4
Bicuari, Parque Nacional do nat. park Angola 99 B5
Bid India 84 B2
Bida Nigeria 96 D4
Bidar India 84 C2
Biddeford U.S.A. 135 J2
Biddinghuizen Neth. 52 F2
Bidean nam Bian mt. U.K. 50 D4
Bideford U.K. 49 C7
Bideford Bay U.K. see Barnstaple Bay
Bīdokht Iran 88 E3
Bidzhan Russia 74 C3
Bié Angola see Kuito
Bié, Planalto do Angola 99 B5
Biebrzański Park Narodowy nat. park Poland 45 M10
Biedenkopf Germany 53 I4
Bielawa Poland 47 P5
Biel/Bienne Switz. 56 H3
Bielefeld Germany 53 I2
Bielitz Poland see Bielsko-Biała
Biella Italy 58 C2
Bielsko-Biała Poland 47 Q6
Bielstein hill Germany 53 J3
Bienenbüttel Germany 53 K1
Biên Hoa Vietnam 71 D5
Bienne Switz. see Biel/Bienne
Bienville, Lac l. Canada 123 G3
Bierbank Australia 112 B1
Biesiesvlei S. Africa 101 G4
Bietigheim-Bissingen Germany 53 J6
Bièvre Belgium 52 F5
Bifoun Gabon 98 B4
Big r. Canada 123 K3
Biga Turkey 59 L4
Bigadiç Turkey 59 M5
Biga Yarımadası pen. Turkey 59 L5
Big Baldy Mountain U.S.A. 126 F3
Big Bar Creek Canada 120 F5
Big Bear Lake U.S.A. 128 E4
Big Belt Mountains U.S.A. 126 F3
Big Bend Swaziland 101 J4
Big Bend National Park U.S.A. 131 C6
Bigbury-on-Sea U.K. 49 D8
Big Canyon watercourse U.S.A. 131 C6
Biger Nuur salt l. Mongolia 80 I2
Big Falls U.S.A. 130 E1
Big Fork r. U.S.A. 130 E1
Biggar Canada 121 J4
Biggar U.K. 50 F5
Biggar, Lac l. Canada 122 G4
Bigge Island Australia 108 D3
Biggenden Australia 111 F5
Bigger, Mount Canada 120 B3
Biggesee l. Germany 53 H3
Biggleswade U.K. 49 G6
Biggs U.S.A. 128 C2
Biggs Junction U.S.A. 126 C3
Big Hole r. U.S.A. 126 E3
Bighorn r. U.S.A. 126 G3
Bighorn Mountains U.S.A. 126 G3
Big Island Nunavut Canada 119 K3
Big Island N.W.T. Canada 120 G2
Big Island Ont. Canada 121 M5
Big Kalzas Lake Canada 120 C2
Big Lake l. Canada 121 H1
Big Lake U.S.A. 131 C6
Big Pine U.S.A. 128 D3
Big Pine Peak U.S.A. 128 D4
Big Raccoon r. U.S.A. 134 B4
Big Rapids U.S.A. 134 C2
Big River Canada 121 J4
Big Sable Point U.S.A. 134 B1
Big Salmon r. Canada 120 C2
Big Sand Lake Canada 121 L3
Big Sandy r. U.S.A. 126 F4
Big Sandy Lake Canada 121 J4
Big Smokey Valley U.S.A. 128 E2
Big South Fork National River and Recreation Area park U.S.A. 134 C5
Big Spring U.S.A. 131 C5
Big Stone Canada 121 I5
Big Stone Gap U.S.A. 134 D5
Bigstone Lake Canada 121 M4
Big Timber U.S.A. 126 F3
Big Trout Lake Canada 121 N4
Big Trout Lake l. Canada 121 N4
Big Valley Canada 121 H4
Big Water U.S.A. 129 H3
Bihać Bos. & Herz. 58 F2
Bihar state India 83 F4
Bihariganj India 83 F4
Bihar Sharif India 83 F4
Bihor, Vârful mt. Romania 59 J1
Bihoro Japan 74 G4
Bijagós, Arquipélago dos is Guinea-Bissau 96 B3
Bijaipur India 82 D4
Bijapur India see Vijayapura
Bījār Iran 88 B3
Bijbehara India 82 C2
Bijeljina Bos. & Herz. 59 H2
Bijelo Polje Montenegro 59 H3
Bijiang China see Zhiziluo
Bijie China 76 E3
Bijji India 84 D2
Bijnor India 82 D3
Bijnore India see Bijnor
Bijnot Pak. 89 H4
Bijrān well Saudi Arabia 88 C5
Bijrān, Khashm hill Saudi Arabia 88 C5
Bikampur India 82 C4
Bikaner India 82 C3
Bīkhūyeh Iran 88 D5
Bikin Russia 74 D3
Bikin r. Russia 74 D3
Bikini atoll Marshall Is 150 H5
Bikori Sudan 86 D7
Bikoro Dem. Rep. Congo 98 B4
Bikou China 76 E1
Bikramganj India 83 F4
Bilād Banī Bū 'Alī Oman 87 I5
Bilaigarh India 84 D1
Bilara India 82 C4
Bilaspur Chhattisgarh India 83 E5
Bilaspur Hima. Prad. India 82 D3
Biläsuvar Azer. 91 H3
Bila Tserkva Ukr. 43 F6
Bilauktaung Range mts Myanmar/Thai. 71 B4
Bilbao Spain 57 E2
Bilbays Egypt 90 C5
Bilbeis Egypt see Bilbays
Bilbo Spain see Bilbao
Bilecik Turkey 59 M4
Biłgoraj Poland 43 D6
Bilharamulo Tanz. 98 D4
Bilhaur India 82 E4
Bilhorod-Dnistrovs'kyy Ukr. 59 N1
Bili Dem. Rep. Congo 98 C3
Bilibino Russia 65 R3
Bilin Myanmar 70 B3
Bill U.S.A. 126 G4
Billabalong Australia 109 A6
Billabong Creek r. Australia see Moulamein Creek
Billericay U.K. 49 H7
Billiluna Australia 108 D4
Billingham U.K. 48 F4
Billings U.S.A. 126 F3
Billiton i. Indon. see Belitung
Bill of Portland hd U.K. 49 E8
Bill Williams r. U.S.A. 129 F4
Bill Williams Mountain U.S.A. 129 G4
Bilma Niger 96 E3
Bilma, Grand Erg de des. Niger 96 E3
Bilo r. Russia see Belaya
Biloela Australia 110 E5
Bilohirs'k Crimea 90 D1
Bilohir"ya Ukr. 43 E6
Biloku Guyana 143 G3
Biloli India 84 C2
Bilovods'k Ukr. 43 H6
Biloxi U.S.A. 131 F6
Bilpa Morea Claypan salt flat Australia 110 B5
Bilston U.K. 50 F5
Biltine Chad 97 F3
Bilto Norway 44 L2
Bilugyun Island Myanmar 70 B3
Bilyayivka Ukr. 59 N1
Bilzen Belgium 52 F4
Bima Indon. 108 B2
Bimberi, Mount Australia 112 D5
Bimbo Cent. Afr. Rep. 97 E4
Bimini Islands Bahamas 133 E7
Bimlipatam India 84 D2
Bina-Etawa India 82 D4
Binaija, Gunung mt. Indon. 67 E8
Bīnālūd, Reshteh Kūh-e mts Iran 88 E2
Binboğa Daği mt. Turkey 90 E3
Bincheng China see Binzhou
Binchuan China 76 D3
Bindebango Australia 112 C1
Bindle Australia 112 D1
Bindu Dem. Rep. Congo 99 B4
Bindura Zimbabwe 99 D5
Binéfar Spain 57 G3
Binga Zimbabwe 99 C5
Binga, Monte mt. Moz. 99 D5
Bingara Australia 112 B2
Bingaram i. India 84 B4
Bing Bong Australia 110 B2
Bingen am Rhein Germany 53 H5
Bingham U.S.A. 135 K1
Binghamton U.S.A. 135 H2
Bingmei China see Congjiang
Bingöl Turkey 91 F3
Bingol Dağı mt. Turkey 91 F3
Bingxi China see Yushan
Bingzhongluo China 76 C2
Binh Gia Vietnam 70 D2
Binika India 83 E5
Binjai Indon. 71 B7
Bin Mürkhan well U.A.E. 88 D5
Binnaway Australia 112 D3
Binpur India 83 F5
Bintan i. Indon. 71 D7
Bint Jbeil Lebanon see Bent Jbaïl
Bintulu Sarawak Malaysia 68 E6
Binxian Heilong. China 74 B3
Binxian Shaanxi China 77 F1
Binya Australia 112 C5
Binyang China 77 F4
Bin-Yauri Nigeria 96 D3
Binzhou Guangxi China see Binyang
Binzhou Heilong. China see Binxian
Binzhou Shandong China 73 L5
Bioco i. Equat. Guinea see Bioko
Biograd na Moru Croatia 58 F3
Bioko i. Equat. Guinea 96 D4
Biokovo mts Croatia 58 G3
Biquinhas Brazil 145 B2
Bir India see Bid
Bira Russia 74 D2
Bi'r Abū Jady oasis Syria 85 D1
Birāk Libya 97 E2
Birakan Russia 74 C2
Bi'r al 'Abd Egypt 85 A4
Bi'r al Ḥalbā well Syria 85 D2
Bi'r al Jifjāfah well Egypt 85 A4
Bi'r al Khamsah well Egypt 90 B5
Bi'r al Māliḥah well Egypt 85 A5
Bi'r al Mulūsi Iraq 91 F4
Bi'r al Munbaṭiḥ well Syria 85 D2
Bi'r al Qaṭrānī well Egypt 90 B5
Bi'r al Ubbayiḍ well Egypt 90 B6
Bi'r an Nuṣf well Egypt see Bi'r an Nuṣṣ
Bi'r an Nuṣṣ well Egypt 90 B5
Bir Anzarane W. Sahara 96 B2
Birao Cent. Afr. Rep. 98 C2
Bi'r ar Rābiyah well Egypt 90 B5
Birata Turkm. 89 F1
Biratnagar Nepal 83 F4
Bi'r aṭ Ṭarfāwī well Libya 90 B5
Bi'r Başīrī well Syria 85 C2
Bi'r Bayḍā' well Egypt 85 B4
Bi'r Baylī well Egypt 90 B5
Bîr Beiḍa well Egypt see Bi'r Bayḍā'
Bi'r Buṭaymān Syria 91 E3
Birch r. Canada 121 H3
Birch Hills Canada 121 J4
Birch Island Canada 120 G5
Birch Lake N.W.T. Canada 120 G2
Birch Lake Ont. Canada 121 M5
Birch Lake Sask. Canada 121 I4
Birch Mountains Canada 120 H3
Birch River U.S.A. 134 E4
Birch Run U.S.A. 134 D2
Bircot Eth. 98 E3
Birdaard Neth. see Burdaard
Bîr Dignâsh well Egypt see Bi'r Diqnāsh
Bi'r Diqnāsh well Egypt 90 B5
Bird Island N. Mariana Is see Farallon de Medinilla
Birdseye U.S.A. 129 H2
Birdsville Australia 111 B5
Birecik Turkey 90 E3
Bîr el 'Abd Egypt see Bi'r al 'Abd
Bir el Arbi well Alg. 57 I6
Bîr el Istabl well Egypt see Bi'r Istabl
Bîr el Khamsa well Egypt see Bi'r al Khamsah
Bîr el Nuṣṣ well Egypt see Bi'r an Nuṣṣ
Bîr el Obeiyid well Egypt see Bi'r al Ubbayiḍ
Bîr el Qaṭrāni well Egypt see Bi'r al Qaṭrānī
Bîr el Râbia well Egypt see Bi'r ar Rābiyah
Birendranagar Nepal see Surkhet
Bir en Natrûn well Sudan 86 C6
Bireun Indon. 71 B6
Bi'r Fāḍil well Saudi Arabia 88 C6
Bi'r Fajr well Saudi Arabia 90 E5
Bi'r Fu'ād well Egypt 90 B5
Bīrg, Kūh-e mts Iran 89 F5
Bîr Gifgâfa well Egypt see Bi'r al Jifjāfah
Bi'r Ḥajal well Syria 85 D2
Bi'r Ḥasanah well Egypt 85 A4
Bi'r Ḥayzān well Saudi Arabia 90 E6
Bi'r Ibn Hirmās Saudi Arabia see Al Bi'r
Bir Ibn Juhayyim Saudi Arabia 88 C6
Birigui Brazil 145 A3
Bīrīn Syria 85 C2
Bi'r Istabl well Egypt 90 B5
Bīrjand Iran 88 E3
Bi'r Jubnī well Libya 90 B5
Birkát Hamad well Iraq 91 G5
Birkenfeld Germany 53 H5
Birkenhead U.K. 48 D5
Birkirkara Malta 58 F7
Birksgate Range hills Australia 109 E6
Bîrlad Romania see Bârlad
Bi'r Lahfān well Egypt 85 A4
Bir Lahlou W. Sahara 96 C2
Birlik Kazakh. 80 D3
Birmal reg. Afgh. 89 H3
Birmingham U.K. 49 F6
Birmingham U.S.A. 133 C5
Bîr Mogreïn Mauritania 96 B2
Bi'r Muḥaymid al Wazwaz well Syria 85 D2
Bi'r Nāḥid oasis Egypt 90 C5
Birnin-Gwari Nigeria 96 D3
Birnin-Kebbi Nigeria 96 D3
Birnin Konni Niger 96 D3
Birobidzhan Russia 74 D2
Bi'r Qaṣīr as Sirr well Egypt 90 B5
Birr Ireland 51 E4
Bi'r Rawḍ Sālim well Egypt 85 A4
Birrie r. Australia 112 C2
Birrindudu Australia 108 E4
Bîr Rôḍ Sâlim well Egypt see Bi'r Rawḍ Sālim
Birsay U.K. 50 F1
Bi'r Shalatayn Egypt 86 E5
Bîr Shalatein Egypt see Bi'r Shalatayn
Birsk Russia 41 R4
Birstall U.K. 49 F6
Birstein Germany 53 J4
Bir Ṭalḥah well Saudi Arabia 88 B6
Birthday Mountain hill Australia 110 C2
Birtle Canada 121 K5
Biru China 76 B2
Birur India 84 B3
Bi'r Usaylīlah well Saudi Arabia 88 B6
Biruxiong China see Biru
Biržai Lith. 45 N8
Bisa India 70 A1
Bisa i. Indon. 69 H7
Bisalpur India 82 D3
Bisau India 82 C3
Bisbee U.S.A. 127 F7
Biscay, Bay of sea France/Spain 56 B4
Biscay Abyssal Plain sea feature N. Atlantic Ocean 148 H3
Biscayne National Park U.S.A. 133 D7
Biscoe Islands Antarctica 152 L2
Biscotasi Lake Canada 122 E5
Biscotasing Canada 122 E5
Bisezhai China 76 D4
Bishan China 76 E2
Bishbek Kyrg. see Bishkek
Bishenpur India see Bishnupur

▶Bishkek Kyrg. 80 D3
Capital of Kyrgyzstan.

Bishnupur Manipur India 83 H4
Bishnupur W. Bengal India 83 F5
Bishop U.S.A. 128 D3
Bishop Auckland U.K. 48 F4
Bishop Lake Canada 120 G1
Bishop's Stortford U.K. 49 H7
Bishopville U.S.A. 133 D5
Bishrī, Jabal hills Syria 85 D2
Bishui Heilong. China 74 A1
Bishui Henan China see Biyang
Biskra Alg. 54 F5
Bislig Phil. 69 H5

▶Bismarck U.S.A. 130 C2
Capital of North Dakota.

Bismarck Archipelago is P.N.G. 69 L7
Bismarck Range mts P.N.G. 69 K7
Bismarck Sea P.N.G. 69 L7
Bismark (Altmark) Germany 53 L2
Bismil Turkey 91 F3
Bismo Norway 44 F6
Bison U.S.A. 130 C2
Bispgården Sweden 44 J5
Bispingen Germany 53 K1
Bissa, Djebel mt. Alg. 57 G5
Bissagos Islands Guinea-Bissau see Bijagós, Arquipélago dos
Bissamcuttak India 84 D2

▶Bissau Guinea-Bissau 96 B3
Capital of Guinea-Bissau.

Bissaula Nigeria 96 E4
Bissett Canada 121 M5
Bistcho Lake Canada 120 G3
Bistrița Romania 59 K1
Bistrița r. Romania 59 L1
Bitburg Germany 52 G5
Bitche France 53 H5
Bithur India 82 E4
Bithynia hist. area Turkey 59 M4
Bitkine Chad 97 E3
Bitlis Turkey 91 F3
Bitola Macedonia 59 I4
Bitolj Macedonia see Bitola
Bitonto Italy 58 G4
Bitrān, Jabal hill Saudi Arabia 88 B6
Bitra Par reef India 84 B4
Bitter Creek r. U.S.A. 129 I2
Bitterfeld Germany 53 M3
Bitterfontein S. Africa 100 D6
Bitter Lakes Egypt 90 D5
Bitterroot r. U.S.A. 126 E3
Bitterroot Range mts U.S.A. 126 E3
Bitterwater U.S.A. 128 C3
Bittkau Germany 53 L2
Bitung Indon. 69 H6
Biu Nigeria 96 E3
Biwa-ko l. Japan 75 D6
Biwmaris U.K. see Beaumaris
Biyang China 77 G1
Bīye K'obē Posīs T'abīya Eth. 98 E2
Biysk Russia 72 F2
Bizana S. Africa 101 I6
Bizerta Tunisia see Bizerte
Bizerte Tunisia 58 C6

▶Bjargtangar hd Iceland 44 [inset 1]
Most westerly point of Europe.

Bjästa Sweden 44 K5
Bjelovar Croatia 58 G2
Bjerkvik Norway 44 J2
Bjerringbro Denmark 45 F8
Bjørgan Norway 44 G5
Björkliden Sweden 44 K2
Björklinge Sweden 45 J6
Bjorli Norway 44 F5
Björna Sweden 44 K5
Björneborg Fin. see Pori

▶Bjørnøya i. Arctic Ocean 64 C2
Part of Norway.

Bjurholm Sweden 44 K5
Bla Mali 96 C3
Black r. Man. Canada 121 L5
Black r. Ont. Canada 122 E4
Black r. AR U.S.A. 131 F5
Black r. AZ U.S.A. 129 H5
Black r. Vietnam 70 D2
Blackadder Water r. U.K. 50 G5
Blackall Australia 110 D5
Blackbear r. Canada 121 N4
Black Birch Lake Canada 121 J3
Black Bourton U.K. 49 F7
Blackbull Australia 110 C3
Blackburn U.K. 48 E5
Blackbutt Australia 112 F1
Black Butte mt. U.S.A. 128 B2
Black Butte Lake U.S.A. 128 B2
Black Canyon gorge U.S.A. 129 F4
Black Canyon of the Gunnison National Park U.S.A. 129 J2
Black Combe hill U.K. 48 D4
Black Creek watercourse U.S.A. 129 I4
Black Donald Lake Canada 135 G1
Blackdown Tableland National Park Australia 110 E4
Blackduck U.S.A. 130 E2
Blackfalds Canada 120 H4
Blackfoot U.S.A. 126 E4
Black Foot r. U.S.A. 126 E3
Black Forest mts Germany 47 L7
Black Hill hill U.K. 48 F3
Black Hills SD U.S.A. 124 G3
Black Hills SD U.S.A. 126 G3
Black Island Canada 121 L5
Black Lake Canada 121 J3
Black Lake l. Canada 121 J3
Black Lake l. U.S.A. 134 C1
Black Mesa mt. U.S.A. 129 I5
Black Mesa ridge U.S.A. 129 H3
Black Mountain Pak. 89 I3
Black Mountain hill U.K. 49 D7
Black Mountain AK U.S.A. 118 B3
Black Mountain CA U.S.A. 128 E4
Black Mountain KY U.S.A. 134 D5
Black Mountain NM U.S.A. 129 I5
Black Mountains hills U.K. 49 D7
Black Mountains U.S.A. 129 F4
Black Nossob watercourse Namibia 100 D2
Black Pagoda India see Konarka
Blackpool U.K. 48 D5
Black Range mts U.S.A. 129 I5
Black River MI U.S.A. 134 D1
Black River NY U.S.A. 135 H1
Black River Falls U.S.A. 130 F2
Black Rock hill Jordan see 'Unāb, Jabal al
Black Rock Desert U.S.A. 126 D4
Blacksburg U.S.A. 134 E5
Black Sea Asia/Europe 43 H8
Blacks Fork r. U.S.A. 126 F4
Blackshear U.S.A. 133 D6
Blacksod Bay Ireland 51 B3
Black Springs U.S.A. 128 D2
Blackstairs Mountains hills Ireland 51 F5
Blackstone U.S.A. 135 F5
Black Sugarloaf mt. Australia 112 E3
Black Tickle Canada 123 L3
Blackville Australia 112 E3
Blackwater Australia 110 E4
Blackwater Ireland 51 F5
Blackwater r. Ireland 51 E5
Blackwater r. Ireland/U.K. 51 F3
Blackwater watercourse U.S.A. 131 C5
Blackwater Lake Canada 120 F2
Blackwater Reservoir U.K. 50 E4
Blackwood r. Australia 109 A8
Blackwood National Park Australia 110 D4
Bladensburg National Park Australia 110 C4
Blaenavon U.K. 49 D7
Blagodarnyy Russia 91 F1
Blagoevgrad Bulg. 59 J3
Blagoveshchensk Amurskaya Oblast' Russia 74 B2
Blagoveshchensk Respublika Bashkortostan Russia 41 R4
Blaikiston, Mount Canada 120 H5
Blaine Lake Canada 121 J4
Blair U.S.A. 130 D3
Blair Athol Australia 110 D4
Blair Atholl U.K. 50 F4
Blairgowrie U.K. 50 F4
Blairsden U.S.A. 128 C2
Blairsville U.S.A. 133 D5
Blakely U.S.A. 133 C6
Blakeney U.K. 49 I6

▶Blanc, Mont mt. France/Italy 56 H4
5th highest mountain in Europe.

Blanca, Bahía b. Arg. 144 D5
Blanca, Sierra mt. U.S.A. 127 G6
Blanca Peak U.S.A. 127 G5
Blanche, Lake salt flat S.A. Australia 111 B6
Blanche, Lake salt flat W.A. Australia 108 C5
Blanchester U.S.A. 134 D4
Blanc Nez, Cap c. France 52 B4
Blanco r. Bol. 142 F6
Blanco U.S.A. 129 J3
Blanco, Cape U.S.A. 126 B4
Blanc-Sablon Canada 123 K4
Bland r. Australia 112 C4
Bland U.S.A. 134 E5
Blanda r. Iceland 44 [inset 1]
Blandford Forum U.K. 49 E8
Blanding U.S.A. 129 I3
Blanes Spain 57 H3
Blangah, Telok Sing. 71 [inset]
Blangkejeren Indon. 71 B7
Blangpidie Indon. 71 B7
Blankenberge Belgium 52 D3
Blankenheim Germany 52 G4
Blanquilla, Isla i. Venez. 142 F1
Blansko Czechia 47 P6
Blantyre Malawi 99 D5
Blarney Ireland 51 D6
Blaufelden Germany 53 J5
Blåviksjön Sweden 44 K4
Blaye France 56 D4
Blayney Australia 112 D4
Blaze, Point Australia 108 E3
Bleckede Germany 53 K1
Bleilochtalsperre resr Germany 53 L4
Blenheim Canada 134 E2
Blenheim N.Z. 113 D5
Blenheim Palace tourist site U.K. 49 F7
Blerick Neth. 52 G3
Blessington Lakes Ireland 51 F4
Bletchley U.K. 49 G6
Blida Alg. 57 H5
Blies r. Germany 53 H5
Bligh Water b. Fiji 107 H3
Blind River Canada 122 E5
Bliss U.S.A. 126 E4
Blissfield U.S.A. 134 D3
Blitta Togo 96 D4
Blocher U.S.A. 134 C4
Block Island U.S.A. 135 J3
Block Island Sound sea chan. U.S.A. 135 J3
Bloemfontein S. Africa 101 H5
Bloemhof S. Africa 101 G4
Bloemhof Dam S. Africa 101 G4
Bloemhof Dam Nature Reserve S. Africa 101 G4
Blomberg Germany 53 J3
Blönduós Iceland 44 [inset 1]
Blongas Indon. 108 B2
Bloods Range mts Australia 109 E6
Bloodsworth Island U.S.A. 135 G4
Bloodvein r. Canada 121 L5
Bloody Foreland pt Ireland 51 D2
Bloomer U.S.A. 130 F2
Bloomfield Canada 135 G2
Bloomfield IA U.S.A. 130 E3
Bloomfield IN U.S.A. 134 B4
Bloomfield MO U.S.A. 131 F4
Bloomfield NM U.S.A. 129 J3
Blooming Prairie U.S.A. 130 E3
Bloomington IL U.S.A. 130 F3
Bloomington IN U.S.A. 134 B4
Bloomington MN U.S.A. 130 E2
Bloomsburg U.S.A. 135 G3
Blossburg U.S.A. 135 G3
Blosseville Kyst coastal area Greenland 119 P3
Blouberg S. Africa 101 I2
Blouberg Nature Reserve S. Africa 101 I2
Blountstown U.S.A. 133 C6
Blountville U.S.A. 134 D5
Bloxham U.K. 49 F6
Blue r. Canada 120 D3
Blue watercourse U.S.A. 129 I5
Blue Bell Knoll mt. U.S.A. 129 H2
Blueberry r. Canada 120 F3
Blue Diamond U.S.A. 129 F3
Blue Earth U.S.A. 130 E3
Bluefield VA U.S.A. 132 D4
Bluefield WV U.S.A. 134 E5
Bluefields Nicaragua 137 H6
Blue Hills Turks and Caicos Is 133 F8
Blue Knob hill U.S.A. 135 F3
Blue Mesa Reservoir U.S.A. 129 J2
Blue Mountain hill Canada 123 K4
Blue Mountain Lake U.S.A. 135 H2
Blue Mountain Pass Lesotho 101 H5
Blue Mountains Australia 112 D4
Blue Mountains U.S.A. 126 D3
Blue Mountains National Park Australia 112 E4
Blue Nile r. Eth./Sudan 86 D6
also known as Ābay Wenz (Ethiopia), Bahr el Azraq (Sudan)
Bluenose Lake Canada 118 G3
Blue Ridge GA U.S.A. 133 C5
Blue Ridge VA U.S.A. 134 F5
Blue Ridge mts U.S.A. 134 E5
Blue Stack hill Ireland 51 D3
Blue Stack Mountains hills Ireland 51 D3
Bluestone Lake U.S.A. 134 E5
Bluewater U.S.A. 129 J4
Bluff N.Z. 113 B8
Bluff U.S.A. 129 I3
Bluffdale U.S.A. 129 H1
Bluff Island H.K. China 77 [inset]
Bluff Knoll mt. Australia 109 B8
Bluffton IN U.S.A. 134 C3
Bluffton OH U.S.A. 134 D3
Blumenau Brazil 145 A4
Blustry Mountain Canada 126 C2
Blyde River Canyon Nature Reserve S. Africa 101 J3
Blyth Canada 134 E2
Blyth England U.K. 48 F3
Blyth England U.K. 48 F5
Blythe U.S.A. 129 F5
Blytheville U.S.A. 131 F5
Bø Norway 45 F7
Bo Sierra Leone 96 B4
Boa Esperança Brazil 145 B3
Bo'ai Henan China 77 G1
Bo'ai Yunnan China 76 E4
Boali Cent. Afr. Rep. 98 B3
Boalsert Neth. see Bolsward
Boane Moz. 101 K4
Boa Nova Brazil 145 C1
Boardman U.S.A. 134 E3
Boatlaname Botswana 101 G2
Boa Viagem Brazil 143 K5
Boa Vista Brazil 142 F3
Boa Vista i. Cape Verde 96 [inset]
Bobadah Australia 112 C4
Bobai China 77 F4
Bobaomby, Tanjona c. Madag. 99 E5
Bobbili India 84 D2
Bobcaygeon Canada 135 F1
Bobo-Dioulasso Burkina Faso 96 C3
Bobotov Kuk mt. Montenegro see Durmitor
Bobriki Russia see Novomoskovsk

Bratsk Russia 72 I1
Bratskoye Vodokhranilishche *resr* Russia 72 I1
Brattleboro U.S.A. 135 I2
Braunau am Inn Austria 47 N6
Braunfels Germany 53 I4
Braunlage Germany 53 K3
Braunsbedra Germany 53 L3
Braunschweig Germany 53 K2
Brava *i.* Cape Verde 96 [inset]
Brave U.S.A. 134 E4
Bråviken *inlet* Sweden 45 J7
Bravo, Cerro *mt.* Bol. 142 F7
Bravo del Norte, Río *r.* Mex. 124 H6
Bravo del Norte, Río *r.* Mex./U.S.A. *see* Rio Grande
Brawley U.S.A. 129 F5
Bray Ireland 51 F4
Bray, Pays de *reg.* France 52 B5
Bray Island Canada 119 K3
Brazeau *r.* Canada 120 H4
Brazeau, Mount Canada 120 G4

▶Brazil *country* S. America 143 G5
Largest and most populous country in South America and 5th largest and 5th most populous in the world.

Brazil U.S.A. 134 B4
Brazil Basin *sea feature* S. Atlantic Ocean 148 G7
Brazos *r.* U.S.A. 131 E6

▶Brazzaville Congo 99 B4
Capital of Congo.

Brčko Bos. & Herz. 58 H2
Bré Ireland *see* Bray
Breadalbane Australia 110 B4
Breaksea Sound *inlet* N.Z. 113 A7
Bream Bay N.Z. 113 E2
Brechfa U.K. 49 C7
Brechin U.K. 50 G4
Brecht Belgium 52 E3
Breckenridge *MI* U.S.A. 134 C2
Breckenridge *MN* U.S.A. 130 D2
Breckenridge *TX* U.S.A. 131 D5
Břeclav Czechia 47 P6
Brecon U.K. 49 D7
Brecon Beacons *reg.* U.K. 49 D7
Brecon Beacons National Park U.K. 49 D7
Breda Neth. 52 E3
Bredasdorp S. Africa 100 E8
Bredbo Australia 112 D5
Breddin Germany 53 M2
Bredevoort Neth. 52 G3
Bredviken Sweden 44 I3
Bree Belgium 52 F3
Breed U.S.A. 134 A1
Bregenz Austria 47 L7
Breiðafjörður *b.* Iceland 44 [inset 1]
Breiðdalsvík Iceland 44 [inset 1]
Breidenbach Germany 53 I4
Breien U.S.A. 130 C2
Breitenfelde Germany 53 K1
Breitengüßbach Germany 53 K5
Breiter Luzinsee *l.* Germany 53 N1
Breivikbotn Norway 44 M1
Breizh *reg.* France *see* Brittany
Brejo Velho Brazil 145 C1
Brekstad Norway 44 F5
Bremen Germany 53 I1
Bremen *land* Germany 53 I1
Bremen *IN* U.S.A. 134 B3
Bremen *OH* U.S.A. 134 D4
Bremer Bay Australia 109 B8
Bremerhaven Germany 53 I1
Bremer Range *hills* Australia 109 C8
Bremersdorp Swaziland *see* Manzini
Bremervörde Germany 53 J1
Bremm Germany 52 H4
Brenham U.S.A. 131 D6
Brenna Norway 44 H4
Brennero, Passo di *pass* Austria/Italy *see* Brenner Pass
Brennerpaß *pass* Austria/Italy *see* Brenner Pass
Brenner Pass Austria/Italy 58 D1
Brentwood U.K. 49 H7
Brescia Italy 58 D2
Breslau Poland *see* Wrocław
Bresle *r.* France 52 B4
Brésolles, Lac *l.* Canada 123 H3
Bressanone Italy 58 D1
Bressay *i.* U.K. 50 [inset]
Bressuire France 56 D3
Brest Belarus 45 M10
Brest France 56 B2
Brest-Litovsk Belarus *see* Brest
Bretagne *reg.* France *see* Brittany
Breteuil France 52 C5
Brétigny-sur-Orge France 52 C6
Breton Canada 120 H4
Breton Sound *b.* U.S.A. 131 F6
Brett, Cape N.Z. 113 E2
Bretten Germany 53 I5
Bretton U.K. 48 E5
Breueh, Pulau *i.* Indon. 71 A6
Brevard U.S.A. 133 D5
Breves Brazil 143 H4
Brewarrina Australia 112 C2
Brewer U.S.A. 132 G2
Brewster *NE* U.S.A. 130 D3
Brewster *OH* U.S.A. 134 E3
Brewster, Kap *c.* Greenland *see* Kangikajik
Brewster, Lake *imp. l.* Australia 112 B4
Brewton U.S.A. 133 C6
Breyten S. Africa 101 I4
Breytovo Russia 42 H4
Brezhnev Russia *see* Naberezhnyye Chelny
Brezno Slovakia 47 Q6
Brezovo Bulg. 59 K3
Brezovo Polje *hill* Croatia 58 G2
Bria Cent. Afr. Rep. 98 C3
Briançon France 56 H4
Brian Head *mt.* U.S.A. 129 G3
Bribbaree Australia 112 C5
Bribie Island Australia 112 F1
Briceni Moldova 43 E6
Brichany Moldova *see* Briceni
Brichen' Moldova *see* Briceni
Bridgend U.K. 49 D7
Bridge of Orchy U.K. 50 E4
Bridgeport *CA* U.S.A. 128 D2
Bridgeport *CT* U.S.A. 135 I3
Bridgeport *IL* U.S.A. 134 B4
Bridgeport *NE* U.S.A. 130 C3
Bridger Peak U.S.A. 126 G4
Bridgeton U.S.A. 135 H4
Bridgetown Australia 109 B8

▶Bridgetown Barbados 137 M6
Capital of Barbados.

Bridgetown Canada 123 I5
Bridgeville U.S.A. 135 H4
Bridgewater Canada 123 I5
Bridgewater U.S.A. 135 H2
Bridgnorth U.K. 49 E6
Bridgton U.S.A. 135 J1
Bridgwater U.K. 49 D7
Bridgwater Bay U.K. 49 D7
Bridlington U.K. 48 G4
Bridlington Bay U.K. 48 G4
Bridport Australia 111 [inset]
Bridport U.K. 49 E8
Brie *reg.* France 56 F2
Brie-Comte-Robert France 52 C6
Brieg Poland *see* Brzeg
Briery Knob *mt.* U.S.A. 134 E4
Brig Switz. 56 H3
Brigg U.K. 48 G5
Brigham City U.S.A. 126 E4
Brightlingsea U.K. 49 I7
Brighton Canada 135 G1
Brighton U.K. 49 G8
Brighton *CO* U.S.A. 126 G5
Brighton *MI* U.S.A. 134 D2
Brighton *NY* U.S.A. 135 G2
Brighton *WV* U.S.A. 134 D4
Brignoles France 56 H5
Brikama Gambia 96 B3
Brillion U.S.A. 134 A1
Brilon Germany 53 I3
Brindisi Italy 58 G4
Brinkley U.S.A. 131 F5
Brion, Île *i.* Canada 123 J5
Brioude France 56 F4
Brisay Canada 123 H3

▶Brisbane Australia 112 F1
Capital of Queensland. 3rd most populous city in Oceania.

Brisbane Ranges National Park Australia 112 B6
Bristol U.K. 49 E7
Bristol *CT* U.S.A. 135 I3
Bristol *FL* U.S.A. 133 C6
Bristol *NH* U.S.A. 135 J2
Bristol *RI* U.S.A. 135 J3
Bristol *TN* U.S.A. 134 D5
Bristol *VT* U.S.A. 135 I1
Bristol Bay U.S.A. 118 B4
Bristol Channel *est.* U.K. 49 C7
Bristol Lake U.S.A. 129 F4
Britannia Island New Caledonia *see* Maré
British Antarctic Territory *reg.* Antarctica 152 L2
British Columbia *prov.* Canada 120 F5
British Empire Range *mts* Canada 119 J1
British Guiana *country* S. America *see* Guyana
British Honduras *country* Central America *see* Belize

▶British Indian Ocean Territory *terr.* Indian Ocean 149 M6
United Kingdom Overseas Territory.

British Solomon Islands *country* S. Pacific Ocean *see* Solomon Islands
Brito Godins Angola *see* Kiwaba N'zogi
Brits S. Africa 101 H3
Britstown S. Africa 100 F6
Brittany *reg.* France 56 C2
Britton U.S.A. 130 D2
Brive-la-Gaillarde France 56 E4
Briviesca Spain 57 E2
Brixham U.K. 49 D8
Brixia Italy *see* Brescia
Brlik Kazakh. *see* Birlik
Brno Czechia 47 P6
Broach India *see* Bharuch
Broad *r.* U.S.A. 133 D5
Broadalbin U.S.A. 135 H2
Broad Arrow (abandoned) Australia 109 C7
Broadback *r.* Canada 122 F4
Broad Bay U.K. *see* Tuath, Loch a'
Broadford Australia 112 B6
Broadford Ireland 51 D5
Broadford U.K. 50 D3
Broad Law *hill* U.K. 50 F5
Broadmere Australia 110 A3
Broad Peak China/Pak. 89 J3
Broad Sound *sea chan.* Australia 110 E4
Broadstairs U.K. 49 I7
Broadus U.S.A. 126 G3
Broadview Canada 121 K5
Broadway U.S.A. 135 F4
Broadwood N.Z. 113 D2
Brochet Canada 121 K3
Brochet, Lac *l.* Canada 121 K3
Brochet, Lac au *l.* Canada 123 H4
Brocken *mt.* Germany 53 K3
Brockman, Mount Australia 108 B5
Brockport *NY* U.S.A. 135 G2
Brockport *PA* U.S.A. 135 F3
Brockton U.S.A. 135 J2
Brockville Canada 135 H1
Brockway U.S.A. 135 F3
Brodeur Peninsula Canada 119 J2
Brodhead U.S.A. 134 C5
Brodick U.K. 50 D5
Brodnica Poland 47 Q4
Brody Ukr. 43 E6
Broghil, Kōtal-e Afgh. 89 I2
Broken Arrow U.S.A. 131 E4
Broken Bay Australia 112 E4
Broken Bow *NE* U.S.A. 130 D3
Broken Bow *OK* U.S.A. 131 E5
Brokenhead *r.* Canada 121 L5
Broken Hill Australia 111 C6
Broken Hill Zambia *see* Kabwe
Broken Plateau *sea feature* Indian Ocean 149 O8
Brokopondo Suriname 143 G2
Brokopondo Stuwmeer *resr* Suriname *see* Professor van Blommestein Meer
Bromberg Poland *see* Bydgoszcz
Brome Germany 53 K2
Bromsgrove U.K. 49 E6
Brønderslev Denmark 45 F8
Brønnøysund Norway 44 H4
Bronson *FL* U.S.A. 133 D6
Bronson *MI* U.S.A. 134 C3
Brooke U.K. 49 I6
Brookfield U.S.A. 134 A2
Brookhaven U.S.A. 131 F6
Brookings *OR* U.S.A. 126 B4
Brookings *SD* U.S.A. 130 D2
Brookline U.S.A. 135 J2
Brooklyn U.S.A. 134 C2
Brooklyn Park U.S.A. 130 E2
Brookneal U.S.A. 135 F5
Brooks Canada 121 I5
Brooks Brook Canada 120 C2
Brooks Range *mts* U.S.A. 118 D3
Brookston U.S.A. 134 B3
Brooksville *FL* U.S.A. 133 D6
Brooksville *KY* U.S.A. 134 C4
Brookton Australia 109 B8
Brookville *IN* U.S.A. 134 C4
Brookville *PA* U.S.A. 134 F3
Brookville Lake U.S.A. 134 C4
Broom, Loch *inlet* U.K. 50 D3
Broome Australia 108 C4
Brora U.K. 50 F2
Brora *r.* U.K. 50 F2
Brösarp Sweden 45 I9
Brosna *r.* Ireland 51 E4
Brosville U.S.A. 134 F5
Brothers *is* India 71 A5
Brough U.K. 48 E4
Brough Ness *pt* U.K. 50 G2
Broughshane U.K. 51 F3
Broughton Island Canada *see* Qikiqtarjuaq
Broughton Islands Australia 112 F4
Brovary Ukr. 43 F6
Brovinia Australia 111 E5
Brovst Denmark 45 F8
Brown City U.S.A. 134 D2
Brown Deer U.S.A. 134 B2
Browne Range *hills* Australia 109 D6
Brownfield U.S.A. 131 C5
Browning U.S.A. 126 E2
Brown Mountain U.S.A. 128 E4
Brownstown U.S.A. 134 B4
Brownsville *KY* U.S.A. 134 B5
Brownsville *PA* U.S.A. 134 F3
Brownsville *TN* U.S.A. 131 F5
Brownsville *TX* U.S.A. 131 D7
Brownwood U.S.A. 131 D6
Browse Island Australia 108 C3
Bruay-la-Buissière France 52 C4
Bruce Peninsula Canada 134 E1
Bruce Peninsula National Park Canada 134 E1
Bruce Rock Australia 109 B7
Bruchsal Germany 53 I5
Brück Germany 53 M2
Bruck an der Mur Austria 47 O7
Brue *r.* U.K. 49 E7
Bruges Belgium *see* Brugge
Brugge Belgium 52 D3
Brühl *Baden-Württemberg* Germany 53 I5
Brühl *Nordrhein-Westfalen* Germany 52 G4
Bruin *KY* U.S.A. 134 D4
Bruin *PA* U.S.A. 134 F3
Bruini India 83 I3
Bruin Point *mt.* U.S.A. 129 H2
Brûk, Wâdi el *watercourse* Egypt *see* Burūk, Wādī al
Brukkaros Namibia 100 D3
Brûlé Canada 120 G4
Brûlé, Lac *l.* Canada 123 J3
Brûly Belgium 52 E5
Brumado Brazil 145 C1
Brumath France 53 H6
Brumunddal Norway 45 G6
Brunau Germany 53 L2
Brundisium Italy *see* Brindisi
Bruneau U.S.A. 126 E4
Brunei *country* Asia 68 E6
Brunei Brunei *see* Bandar Seri Begawan
Brunette Downs Australia 110 A3
Brunflo Sweden 44 I5
Brunico Italy 58 D1
Brünn Czechia *see* Brno
Brunner, Lake N.Z. 113 C6
Bruno Canada 121 J4
Brunswick Germany *see* Braunschweig
Brunswick *GA* U.S.A. 133 D6
Brunswick *MD* U.S.A. 135 G4
Brunswick *ME* U.S.A. 135 K2
Brunswick, Península de *pen.* Chile 144 B8
Brunswick Bay Australia 108 D3
Brunswick Lake Canada 122 E4
Bruntál Czechia 47 P6
Brunt Ice Shelf Antarctica 152 B2
Bruntville S. Africa 101 J5
Bruny Island Australia 111 [inset]
Brusa Turkey *see* Bursa
Brusenets Russia 42 I3
Brushton U.S.A. 135 H1
Brusque Brazil 145 A4
Brussel Belgium *see* Brussels

▶Brussels Belgium 52 E4
Capital of Belgium.

Bruthen Australia 112 C6
Bruxelles Belgium *see* Brussels
Bruzual Venez. 142 E2
Bryan *OH* U.S.A. 134 C3
Bryan *TX* U.S.A. 131 D6
Bryan, Mount *hill* Australia 111 B7
Bryan Coast Antarctica 152 L2
Bryansk *Bryanskaya Oblast'* Russia 43 G5
Bryansk *Respublika Dagestan* Russia 91 G1
Bryant Pond U.S.A. 135 J1
Bryantsburg U.S.A. 134 C4
Bryce Canyon National Park U.S.A. 129 G3
Bryce Mountain U.S.A. 129 I5
Brynbuga U.K. *see* Usk
Bryne Norway 45 D7
Bryukhovetskaya Russia 43 H7
Brzeg Poland 47 P5
Brześć nad Bugiem Belarus *see* Brest
Bua *r.* Malawi 99 D5
Bu'aale Somalia 98 E3
Buala Solomon Is 107 F2
Buan S. Korea 75 B6
Bu'ayj *well* Saudi Arabia 88 C5
Būbiyān, Jazīrat Kuwait 88 C4
Bucak Turkey 59 N6
Bucaramanga Col. 142 D2
Buccaneer Archipelago *is* Australia 108 C4
Buchanan Liberia 96 B4
Buchanan *MI* U.S.A. 134 B3
Buchanan *VA* U.S.A. 134 F5
Buchanan, Lake *salt flat* Australia 110 D4
Buchan Gulf Canada 119 K2

▶Bucharest Romania 59 L2
Capital of Romania.

Büchen Germany 53 K1
Buchen (Odenwald) Germany 53 J5
Bucheon S. Korea 75 B5
Buchholz Germany 53 M1
Buchholz in der Nordheide Germany 53 J1
Buchon, Point U.S.A. 128 C4
Buchy France 52 B5
Bucin, Pasul *pass* Romania 59 K1
Buckambool Mountain *hill* Australia 112 B3
Bückeburg Germany 53 J2
Bücken Germany 53 J2
Buckeye U.S.A. 129 G5
Buckhannon U.S.A. 134 E4
Buckhaven U.K. 50 F4
Buckhorn Lake Canada 135 F1
Buckie U.K. 50 G3
Buckingham U.K. 49 G6
Buckingham U.S.A. 135 F5
Buckingham Bay Australia 67 F9
Buckland Tableland *reg.* Australia 110 E5
Buckleboo Australia 109 G8
Buckle Island Antarctica 152 H2
Buckley *watercourse* Australia 110 B4
Buckley Bay Antarctica 152 G2
Bucklin U.S.A. 130 D4
Buckskin Mountains U.S.A. 129 G4
Bucks Mountain U.S.A. 128 C2
Bucksport U.S.A. 123 H5
Bückwitz Germany 53 M2
București Romania *see* Bucharest
Bucyrus U.S.A. 134 D3
Buda-Kashalyova Belarus 43 F5
Budalin Myanmar 70 A2

▶Budapest Hungary 59 H1
Capital of Hungary.

Budaun India 82 D3
Budawang National Park Australia 112 E5
Budda Australia 112 B3
Budd Coast Antarctica 152 F2
Buddusò *Sardinia* Italy 58 C4
Bude U.K. 49 C8
Bude U.S.A. 131 F6
Budennovsk Russia 91 G1
Buderim Australia 112 F1
Būding Iran 88 E5
Büdingen Germany 53 J4
Budīyah, Jabal *hills* Egypt 85 A5
Budongquan China 83 H2
Budoni *Sardinia* Italy 58 C4
Budū, Ḩadabat al *plain* Saudi Arabia 88 C6
Budū', Sabkhat al *salt pan* Saudi Arabia 88 C6
Budweis Czechia *see* České Budějovice
Buenaventura Col. 142 C3
Buena Vista *i.* N. Mariana Is *see* Tinian
Buena Vista *CO* U.S.A. 126 G5
Buena Vista *VA* U.S.A. 134 F5
Buendía, Embalse de *resr* Spain 57 E3

▶Buenos Aires Arg. 144 E4
Capital of Argentina. 2nd most populous city in South America.

Buenos Aires, Lago *l.* Arg./Chile 144 B7
Buerarema Brazil 145 D1
Buet *r.* Canada 123 H1
Búfalo Mex. 131 B7
Buffalo *r.* Canada 120 H2
Buffalo *KY* U.S.A. 134 C5
Buffalo *MO* U.S.A. 130 E4
Buffalo *NY* U.S.A. 135 F2
Buffalo *OK* U.S.A. 131 D4
Buffalo *SD* U.S.A. 130 C2
Buffalo *TX* U.S.A. 131 D6
Buffalo *WY* U.S.A. 126 G3
Buffalo Head Hills Canada 120 G3
Buffalo Head Prairie Canada 120 G3
Buffalo Hump *mt.* U.S.A. 126 E3
Buffalo Lake *Alta* Canada 121 H4
Buffalo Lake *N.W.T.* Canada 120 H2
Buffalo Narrows Canada 121 I4
Buffels *watercourse* S. Africa 100 C5
Buffels Drift S. Africa 101 H2
Buftea Romania 59 K2
Bug *r.* Poland 47 S5
Buga Col. 142 C3
Bugaldie Australia 112 D3
Bugdaýly Turkm. 88 D2
Buggenhout Belgium 52 E3
Bugojno Bos. & Herz. 58 G2
Bugrino Russia 42 K1
Bugsuk *i.* Phil. 68 F5
Bugt China 74 A2
Bugul'ma Russia 41 Q5
Būgür China *see* Luntai
Buguruslan Russia 41 Q5
Buhera Zimbabwe 99 D5
Bühl Germany 53 I6
Buhuşi Romania 59 L1
Buick Canada 120 F3
Builth Wells U.K. 49 D6
Buin, Piz *mt.* Austria/Switz. 47 M7
Bui National Park Ghana 96 C4
Buinsk Russia 43 K5
Bu'īn Zahrā Iran 88 C3
Buitepos Namibia 100 D2
Bujanovac Serbia 59 I3

▶Bujumbura Burundi 98 C4
Capital of Burundi.

Bukachacha Russia 73 L2
Bukadaban Feng *mt.* China 83 G1
Buka Island P.N.G. 106 F2
Būkān Iran 88 B2
Būkand Iran 88 D4
Bukavu Dem. Rep. Congo 98 C4
Bukhara Uzbek. *see* Buxoro
Bukhoro Uzbek. *see* Buxoro
Bukit Baka-Bukit Raya, Taman Nasional *nat. park* Indon. 68 E7
Bukittinggi Indon. 68 C7
Bukkapatnam India 84 C3
Bukoba Tanz. 98 D4
Bükreş Romania *see* Bucharest
Būl, Kūh-e *mt.* Iran 88 D4
Bula P.N.G. 69 K8
Bülach Switz. 56 I3
Bulan *i.* Indon. 71 C7
Bulancak Turkey 90 E2
Bulandshahr India 82 D3
Bulanık Turkey 91 F3
Bulava Russia 74 F2
Bulawayo Zimbabwe 99 C6
Buldan Turkey 59 M5
Buldana India 84 C1
Buldhana India *see* Buldana
Buleda *reg.* Pak. 89 F5
Bulembu Swaziland 101 J3
Bulgan *Bulgan* Mongolia 80 J2
Bulgan *Hovd* Mongolia 80 H2
Bulgar Russia *see* Bolgar
Bulgaria *country* Europe 59 K3
Bŭlgariya *country* Europe *see* Bulgaria
Bulkley Ranges *mts* Canada 120 D4
Bullawarra, Lake *salt flat* Australia 112 A1
Bullen *r.* Canada 121 K1
Buller *r.* N.Z. 113 C5
Buller, Mount Australia 112 C6
Bulleringa National Park Australia 110 C3
Bullfinch Australia 109 B7
Bullhead City U.S.A. 129 F4
Bulli Australia 112 E5
Bullion Mountains U.S.A. 128 E4
Bullo *r.* Australia 108 E3
Bulloo Downs Australia 111 C6
Bulloo Lake *salt flat* Australia 111 C6
Büllsport Namibia 100 C3
Bully Choop Mountain U.S.A. 128 B1
Bulman Australia 108 F3
Bulman Gorge Australia 108 F3
Bulmer Lake Canada 120 F2
Buloh, Pulau *i.* Sing. 71 [inset]
Buloke, Lake *dry lake* Australia 112 A6
Bulolo P.N.G. 69 L8
Bulsar India *see* Valsad
Bultfontein S. Africa 101 H5
Bulukumba Indon. 69 G8
Bulun Russia 65 N2
Bulungu Dem. Rep. Congo 99 C4
Bulung'ur Uzbek. 89 G2
Bumba Dem. Rep. Congo 98 C3
Būmbah Libya 90 A4
Bumbah, Khalīj al *b.* Libya 90 A4
Bumhkang Myanmar 70 B1
Bumhpa Bum *mt.* Myanmar 70 B1
Buna Dem. Rep. Congo 98 B4
Buna Kenya 98 D3
Bunayyān *well* Saudi Arabia 88 C6
Bunazi Tanz. 98 D4
Bunbury Australia 109 A8
Bunclody Ireland 51 F5
Buncrana Ireland 51 E2
Bunda Tanz. 98 D4
Bundaberg Australia 110 F5
Bundaleer Australia 112 C2
Bundarra Australia 112 E3
Bundi India 82 C4
Bundjalung National Park Australia 112 F2
Bundoran Ireland 51 D3
Bundukia South Sudan 97 G4
Buner *reg.* Pak. 89 I3
Bungalaut, Selat *sea chan.* Indon. 68 B7
Bungay U.K. 49 I6
Bungendore Australia 112 D5
Bunger Hills Antarctica 152 F2
Bungle Bungle National Park Australia *see* Purnululu National Park
Bungo-suidō *sea chan.* Japan 75 D6
Bunguran, Kepulauan *is* Indon. *see* Natuna, Kepulauan
Bunguran, Pulau *i.* Indon. *see* Natuna Besar
Bunia Dem. Rep. Congo 98 D3
Buniangra Dem. Rep. Congo 98 C4
Buningonia *well* Australia 109 C7
Bunji Pak. 82 C2
Bunker Group *atolls* Australia 110 F4
Bunkeya Dem. Rep. Congo 99 C5
Bunnell U.S.A. 133 D6
Bünsum China 83 E3
Bunya Mountains National Park Australia 112 E1
Bünyan Turkey 90 D3
Bunyu *i.* Indon. 68 F6
Buôn Đôn Vietnam 71 D4
Buôn Ma Thuột Vietnam 71 E4
Buor-Khaya, Guba *b.* Russia 65 O2
Bup *r.* China 83 F3
Buqayq Saudi Arabia *see* Abqaiq
Buqbuq Egypt 90 B5
Bura Kenya 98 D4
Buraan Somalia 98 E2
Buram Sudan 97 F3
Buran Kazakh. *see* Boran
Buranhaém *r.* Brazil 145 D2
Buranhém Brazil 145 C2
Burāq Syria 85 C3
Buray *r.* India 82 C5
Buraydah Saudi Arabia 86 F4
Burbach Germany 53 I4
Burbank U.S.A. 128 D4
Burcher Australia 112 C4
Burco Somalia 98 E3
Burdaard Neth. 52 F1
Burdalyk Turkm. 89 G2
Burdigala France *see* Bordeaux
Burdur Turkey 59 N6
Burdur Gölü *l.* Turkey 59 N6
Burdwan India *see* Barddhaman
Burē Eth. 98 D2
Bure *r.* U.K. 49 I6
Bureå Sweden 44 L4
Bureinskiy Khrebet *mts* Russia 74 D2
Bureinskiy Zapovednik *nature res.* Russia 74 D2
Burewala Pak. 89 I4
Bureya *r.* Russia 74 C2
Bureya Range *mts* Russia *see* Bureinskiy Khrebet
Burford Canada 134 E2
Burg Germany 53 L2
Burgas Bulg. 59 L3
Burgaw U.S.A. 133 E5
Burgbernheim Germany 53 K5
Burgdorf Germany 53 K2
Burgeo Canada 123 K5
Burgersdorp S. Africa 101 H6
Burgersfort S. Africa 101 J3
Burges, Mount *hill* Australia 109 C7
Burgess Hill U.K. 49 G8
Burghaun Germany 53 J4
Burghausen Germany 47 N6
Burghead U.K. 50 F3
Burgh-Haamstede Neth. 52 D3
Burgio, Serra di *hill* Sicily Italy 58 F6
Burglengenfeld Germany 53 M5
Burgos Mex. 131 D7
Burgos Spain 57 E2
Burgstädt Germany 53 M4
Burgsvik Sweden 45 K8
Burgum Neth. 52 G1
Burgundy *reg.* France 56 G3
Burhan Budai Shan *mts* China 80 H4
Burhaniye Turkey 59 L5
Burhanpur India 82 D5
Burhar-Dhanpuri India 83 E5
Buri Brazil 145 A3
Burias *i.* Phil. 69 G4
Burin Canada 123 L5
Burin Peninsula Canada 123 L5
Buriram Thai. 70 C4
Buritama Brazil 145 A3
Buriti Alegre Brazil 145 A2
Buriti Bravo Brazil 143 J5
Buritirama Brazil 143 J6
Buritis Brazil 145 B1
Burj Aziz Khan Pak. 89 G4
Burke U.S.A. 130 D3
Burke Island Antarctica 152 K2
Burke Pass N.Z. *see* Burkes Pass
Burkes Pass N.Z. 113 C7
Burkesville U.S.A. 134 C5
Burketown Australia 110 B3
Burkeville U.S.A. 135 F5
Burkina *country* Africa *see* Burkina Faso
Burkina Faso *country* Africa 96 C3
Burk's Falls Canada 122 F5
Burley U.S.A. 126 E4
Burlington Canada 134 F2
Burlington *CO* U.S.A. 130 C4
Burlington *IA* U.S.A. 130 F3
Burlington *KS* U.S.A. 130 E4
Burlington *KY* U.S.A. 134 C4
Burlington *VT* U.S.A. 135 I1
Burlington *WI* U.S.A. 134 A2
Burma *country* Asia *see* Myanmar
Burmantovo Russia 41 S3
Burnaby Canada 120 F5
Burnet U.S.A. 131 D6
Burney U.S.A. 128 C1
Burney, Monte *vol.* Chile 144 B8
Burnham U.S.A. 135 G3
Burnie Australia 111 [inset]
Burniston U.K. 48 G4
Burnley U.K. 48 E5
Burns U.S.A. 126 D4
Burnside *r.* Canada 118 H3
Burnside U.S.A. 134 C5
Burnside, Lake *salt flat* Australia 109 C6
Burns Junction U.S.A. 126 D4
Burns Lake Canada 120 E4
Burntisland U.K. 50 F4
Burnt Lake Canada *see* Brûlé, Lac
Burntwood *r.* Canada 121 L4
Burog Co *l.* China 83 F2
Buron *r.* Canada 123 H2
Burovoy Uzbek. 89 F1
Burqin China 80 G2
Burqu' Jordan 85 D3
Burqu', Qaşr *tourist site* Jordan 85 C3
Burra Australia 111 B7
Burra *i.* U.K. 50 [inset]
Burravoe U.K. 50 [inset]
Burrel Albania 59 I4
Burrel U.S.A. 128 D3
Burren *reg.* Ireland 51 C4
Burrendong, Lake Australia 112 D4
Burren Junction Australia 112 D3
Burrewarra Point Australia 112 E5
Burrinjuck Australia 112 D5
Burrinjuck Reservoir Australia 112 D5
Burro, Serranías del *mts* Mex. 131 C6
Burr Oak Reservoir U.S.A. 134 D4
Burro Creek *watercourse* U.S.A. 129 G4
Burro Peak U.S.A. 129 I5
Burrowa Pine Mountain National Park Australia 112 C6
Burrow Head *hd* U.K. 50 E6
Burrows U.S.A. 134 B3
Burrundie Australia 108 E3
Bursa Turkey 59 M4
Būr Safāga Egypt *see* Būr Safājah
Būr Safājah Egypt 86 D4
Būr Sa'īd Egypt *see* Port Said
Būr Sa'īd Egypt *see* Port Said
Būr Sa'īd *governorate* Egypt *see* Būr Sa'īd
Būr Sa'īd *governorate* Egypt 85 A4
Bürstadt Germany 53 I5
Būr Sudan Sudan *see* Port Sudan
Burt Lake U.S.A. 132 C2
Burton U.S.A. 134 D2

Burton, Lac l. Canada 122 F3
Burton upon Trent U.K. 49 F6
Burträsk Sweden 44 L4
Burt Well Australia 109 F5
Buru i. Indon. 69 H7
Burūk, Wādī al watercourse Egypt 85 A4
Burullus, Baḥra el lag. Egypt see Burullus, Lake
Burullus, Buḥayrat al lag. Egypt see Burullus, Lake
Burullus, Lake lag. Egypt 90 C5
Burultokay China see Fuhai
Burūn, Ra's pt Egypt 85 A4
Burundi country Africa 98 C4
Burunniy Russia see Tsagan Aman
Bururi Burundi 98 C4
Burwash Landing Canada 120 B2
Burwick U.K. 50 G2
Buryn' Ukr. 43 G6
Bury St Edmunds U.K. 49 H6
Burzil Pass Pak. 82 C2
Busambra, Rocca mt. Sicily Italy 58 E6
Busan S. Korea 75 C6
Busanga Dem. Rep. Congo 98 C4
Busby U.S.A. 126 G3
Buseire Syria see Al Buşayrah
Bush r. U.K. 51 F2
Bushêngcaka China 83 E2
Bushenyi Uganda 98 D4
Bushire Iran see Bandar-e Būshehr
Bushmills U.K. 51 F2
Bushnell U.S.A. 133 D6
Businga Dem. Rep. Congo 98 C3
Buşrá ash Shām Syria 85 C3
Busse Russia 74 B2
Busselton Australia 109 A8
Bussum Neth. 52 F2
Bustillos, Lago l. Mex. 127 G7
Busto Arsizio Italy 58 C2
Buta Dem. Rep. Congo 98 C3
Butare Rwanda 98 C4
Butaritari atoll Kiribati 150 H5
Bute Australia 111 B7
Bute i. U.K. 50 D5
Butedale (abandoned) Canada 120 D4
Butha-Buthe Lesotho 101 I5
Butha Qi China see Zalantun
Buthidaung Myanmar 70 A2
Butler AL U.S.A. 131 F5
Butler GA U.S.A. 133 C5
Butler IN U.S.A. 134 C3
Butler KY U.S.A. 134 C4
Butler MO U.S.A. 130 E4
Butler PA U.S.A. 134 F3
Butlers Bridge Ireland 51 E3
Buton i. Indon. 69 G7
Bütow Germany 53 M1
Butte MT U.S.A. 126 E3
Butte NE U.S.A. 130 D3
Buttelstedt Germany 53 L3
Butterworth Malaysia 71 C6
Butterworth S. Africa see Gcuwa
Buttes, Sierra mt. U.S.A. 128 C2
Buttevant Ireland 51 D5
Butt of Lewis hd U.K. 50 C2
Button Bay Canada 121 M3
Butuan Phil. 69 H5
Butuo China 76 D3
Buturlinovka Russia 43 I6
Butwal Nepal 83 E4
Butzbach Germany 53 I4
Buulobarde Somalia 98 E3
Buur Gaabo Somalia 98 E4
Buurhabaka Somalia 98 E3
Buutsagaan Mongolia 80 I2
Buxar India 83 F4
Buxoro Uzbek. 89 G2
Buxtehude Germany 53 J1
Buxton U.K. 48 F5
Buy Russia 42 I4
Buynaksk Russia 91 G2
Buyr Nuur l. Mongolia 73 L3
Büyükçekmece Turkey 90 C2
Büyük Egri Dağ mt. Turkey 85 A1
Büyükmenderes r. Turkey 59 L6
Buzancy France 52 E5
Buzău Romania 59 L2
Buzdyak Russia 41 Q5
Búzi Moz. 99 D5
Büzmeýin Turkm. see Abadan
Buzuluk Russia 41 Q5
Buzuluk r. Russia 43 I6
Buzzards Bay U.S.A. 135 J3
Byakar Bhutan see Jakar
Byala Bulg. 59 K3
Byala Slatina Bulg. 59 J3
Byalynichy Belarus 43 F5
Byarezina r. Belarus 43 F5
Byaroza Belarus 45 N10
Byblos tourist site Lebanon 85 B2
Bydgoszcz Poland 47 Q4
Byelorussia country Europe see Belarus
Byerazino Belarus 43 F5
Byers U.S.A. 126 G5
Byeshankovichy Belarus 43 F5
Byesville U.S.A. 134 E4
Bygland Norway 45 E7
Bykhaw Belarus 43 F5
Bykhov Belarus see Bykhaw
Bykle Norway 45 E7
Bykovo Russia 43 J6
Bylas U.S.A. 129 H5
Bylot Island Canada 119 K2
Byramgore Reef India 84 A4
Byrd Glacier Antarctica 152 H1
Byrdstown U.S.A. 134 C5
Byrkjelo Norway 45 E6
Byrock Australia 112 C3
Byron U.S.A. 135 J1
Byron, Cape Australia 112 F2
Byron Bay Australia 112 F2
Byron Island Kiribati see Nikunau
Byrranga, Gory mts Russia 65 K2
Byske Sweden 44 L4
Byssa Russia 74 C1
Byssa r. Russia 74 C1
Bytom Poland 47 Q5
Bytów Poland 47 P3
Byurgyutli Turkm. 88 D2
Byzantium Turkey see İstanbul

C

Ca, Sông r. Vietnam 70 D3
Caacupé Para. 144 E3
Caatinga Brazil 145 B2
Caazapá Para. 144 E3
Cabaiguán Cuba 133 E8
Caballas Peru 142 C6
Caballococha Peru 142 D4
Caballos Mesteños, Llano de los plain Mex. 131 B6
Cabanaconde Peru 142 D7
Cabanatuan Phil. 69 G3
Cabano Canada 123 H5
Cabdul Qaadir Somalia 98 E2
Cabeceira Rio Manso Brazil 143 G7
Cabeceiras Brazil 145 B1
Cabeza del Buey Spain 57 D4
Cabezas Bol. 142 F7
Cabimas Venez. 142 D1
Cabinda Angola 99 B4
Cabinda prov. Angola 99 B5
Cabinet Inlet Antarctica 152 L2
Cabinet Mountains U.S.A. 126 E2
Cabistra Turkey see Ereğli
Cabo Frio Brazil 145 C3
Cabo Frio, Ilha do i. Brazil 145 C3
Cabonga, Réservoir resr Canada 122 F5
Cabool U.S.A. 131 E4
Caboolture Australia 112 F1
Cabo Orange, Parque Nacional de nat. park Brazil 143 H3
Cabo Pantoja Peru 142 C4
Cabora Bassa, Lake resr Moz. 99 D5
Cabo Raso Arg. 144 C6
Caborca Mex. 127 E7
Cabo San Lucas Mex. 136 C4
Cabot Head hd Canada 134 E1
Cabot Strait Canada 123 J5
Cabourg France 49 G9
Cabo Verde country Africa see Cape Verde
Cabo Verde, Ilhas do is N. Atlantic Ocean 96 [inset]
Cabo Yubi Morocco see Tarfaya
Cabral, Serra do mts Brazil 145 B2
Cäbrayıl Azer. 91 G3
Cabrera, Illa de i. Spain 57 H4
Cabrera, Sierra de la mts Spain 57 C2
Cabri Canada 121 I5
Cabullona Mex. 127 F7
Caçador Brazil 145 A4
Cacagoin China see Qagca
Čačak Serbia 59 I3
Caccia, Capo c. Sardinia Italy 58 C4
Çäçe Turkm. 89 F2
Cacequi Brazil 144 F3
Cáceres Brazil 143 G7
Cáceres Spain 57 C4
Cache Creek Canada 120 F5
Cache Peak U.S.A. 126 E4
Cacheu Guinea-Bissau 96 B3
Cachi, Nevados de mts Arg. 144 C2
Cachimbo, Serra do hills Brazil 143 H5
Cachoeira Brazil 145 D1
Cachoeira Alta Brazil 145 A2
Cachoeira de Goiás Brazil 145 A2
Cachoeira do Arari Brazil 143 I4
Cachoeiro de Itapemirim Brazil 145 C3
Cacine Guinea-Bissau 96 B3
Caciporé, Cabo c. Brazil 143 H3
Cacolo Angola 99 B5
Cacongo Angola 99 B4
Cactus U.S.A. 131 C4
Caçu Brazil 145 A2
Caculé Brazil 145 C1
Čadca Slovakia 47 Q6
Cadereyta Mex. 131 C7
Cadibarrawirracanna, Lake salt flat Australia 111 A6
Cadillac Canada 121 J5
Cadillac U.S.A. 134 C1
Cadiz Phil. 69 G4
Cádiz Spain 57 C5
Cadiz IN U.S.A. 134 C4
Cadiz KY U.S.A. 132 C4
Cadiz OH U.S.A. 134 E3
Cádiz, Golfo de g. Spain 57 C5
Cadiz Lake U.S.A. 129 F4
Cadomin Canada 120 G4
Cadotte r. Canada 120 G3
Cadotte Lake Canada 120 G3
Caen France 56 D2
Caerdydd U.K. see Cardiff
Caerffili U.K. see Caerphilly
Caerfyrddin U.K. see Carmarthen
Caergybi U.K. see Holyhead
Caernarfon U.K. 49 C5
Caernarfon Bay U.K. 49 C5
Caernarvon U.K. see Caernarfon
Caerphilly U.K. 49 D7
Caesaraugusta Spain see Zaragoza
Caesarea Alg. see Cherchell
Caesarea Cappadociae Turkey see Kayseri
Caesarea Philippi Syria see Bāniyās
Caesarodunum France see Tours
Caesaromagus U.K. see Chelmsford
Caetité Brazil 145 C1
Cafayate Arg. 144 C3
Cafelândia Brazil 145 A3
Caffa Crimea see Feodosiya
Cagayan de Oro Phil. 69 G5
Cagayan de Tawi-Tawi i. Phil. 68 F5
Cagles Mill Lake U.S.A. 134 B4
Cagli Italy 58 E3
Cagliari Sardinia Italy 58 C5
Cagliari, Golfo di b. Sardinia Italy 58 C5
Çagyl Turkm. 91 I2
Cahama Angola 99 B5
Caha Mountains hills Ireland 51 C6
Cahermore Ireland 51 B6
Cahersiveen Ireland see Cahirsiveen
Cahir Ireland 51 E5
Cahirsiveen Ireland 51 B6
Cahora Bassa, Lago de resr Moz. see Cabora Bassa, Lake
Cahore Point Ireland 51 F5
Cahors France 56 E4
Cahuapanas Peru 142 C5
Cahul Moldova 59 M2
Caia Moz. 99 D5
Caiabis, Serra dos hills Brazil 143 G6
Caianda Angola 99 C5
Caiapó r. Brazil 145 A1
Caiapó, Serra do mts Brazil 145 A2
Caiapônia Brazil 145 A2
Caibarién Cuba 133 E8
Cai Bầu, Đao i. Vietnam 70 D2
Caicara Venez. 142 E2
Caicos Islands Turks and Caicos Is 137 J4
Caicos Passage Bahamas/Turks and Caicos Is 133 F8
Caidian China 77 G2
Caiguna Australia 109 D8
Caimodorro mt. Spain 57 F3
Cainnyigoin China 76 D1
Cains Store U.S.A. 134 C5
Caipe Arg. 144 C2
Caird Coast Antarctica 152 B1
Cairngorm Mountains U.K. 50 F3
Cairngorms National Park U.K. 50 F3
Cairnryan U.K. 50 D6
Cairns Australia 110 D3
Cairnsmore of Carsphairn hill U.K. 50 E5

▶Cairo Egypt 90 C5
Capital of Egypt. 2nd most populous city in Africa.

Cairo U.S.A. 133 C6
Caisleán an Bharraigh Ireland see Castlebar
Caiundo Angola 99 B5
Caiwarro (abandoned) Australia 112 B2
Caiyuanzhen China see Shengsi
Caizi Hu l. China 77 H2
Cajamarca Peru 142 C5
Cajati Brazil 145 A4
Cajuru Brazil 145 B3
Čakovec Croatia 58 G1
Çal Denizli Turkey 59 M5
Çal Hakkâri Turkey see Çukurca
Cala S. Africa 101 H6
Calabar Nigeria 96 D4
Calabogie Canada 135 G1
Calabria, Parco Nazionale della nat. park Italy 58 G5
Calafat Romania 59 J3
Calagua Mex. 127 F8
Calagurris Spain see Calahorra
Calahorra Spain 57 F2
Calai Angola 99 B5
Calais France 52 B4
Calais U.S.A. 123 I5
Calalasteo, Sierra de mts Arg. 144 C3
Calama Brazil 142 F5
Calama Chile 144 C2
Calamajué Mex. 127 E7
Calamar Col. 142 D1
Calamian Group is Phil. 68 F4
Calamocha Spain 57 F3
Calandula Angola 99 B4
Calang Indon. 71 A6
Calanques, Parc National des nat. park France 56 G5
Calapan Phil. 69 G4
Călărași Romania 59 L2
Calatayud Spain 57 F3
Calayan i. Phil. 69 G3
Calbayog Phil. 69 G4
Calbe (Saale) Germany 53 L3
Calçoene Brazil 143 H3
Calcutta India see Kolkata
Caldas da Rainha Port. 57 B4
Caldas Novas Brazil 143 I7
Calden Germany 53 J3
Calder r. Canada 120 G1
Caldera Chile 144 B3
Caldervale Australia 110 D5
Caldew r. U.K. 48 E4
Caldwell ID U.S.A. 126 D4
Caldwell KS U.S.A. 131 D4
Caldwell OH U.S.A. 134 E4
Caldwell TX U.S.A. 131 D6
Caledon r. Lesotho/S. Africa 101 H6
Caledon S. Africa 100 D8
Caledon Bay Australia 110 B2
Caledonia Canada 134 F2
Caledonia admin. div. U.K. see Scotland
Caledonia U.S.A. 135 G2
Caleta el Cobre Chile 144 B2
Calexico U.S.A. 129 F5
Calf of Man i. Isle of Man 48 C4
Calgary Canada 120 H5
Calhoun U.S.A. 134 B5
Cali Col. 142 C3
Calicut India see Kozhikode
Caliente U.S.A. 129 F3
California U.S.A. 134 F3
California state U.S.A. 127 C4
California, Gulf of g. Mex. 127 E7
California Aqueduct canal U.S.A. 128 C3
Cälilabad Azer. 91 H3
Calingasta Arg. 144 C4
Calipatria U.S.A. 129 F5
Calistoga U.S.A. 128 B2
Calkiní Mex. 136 F4
Callabonna, Lake salt flat Australia 111 C6
Callaghan, Mount U.S.A. 128 E2
Callan Ireland 51 E5
Callan r. U.K. 51 F3
Callander Canada 122 F5
Callander U.K. 50 E4
Callao Peru 142 C6
Callao U.S.A. 129 G2
Callicoon U.S.A. 135 H3
Calling Lake Canada 120 H4
Callington U.K. 49 C8
Calliope Australia 110 E5
Callipolis Turkey see Gallipoli
Calmar U.S.A. 130 F3
Caloosahatchee r. U.S.A. 133 D7
Caloundra Australia 112 F1
Caltagirone Sicily Italy 58 F6
Caltanissetta Sicily Italy 58 F6
Calucinga Angola 99 B5
Calulo Angola 99 B4
Calunga Angola 99 B5
Caluquembe Angola 99 B5
Caluula Somalia 98 F2
Caluula, Raas pt Somalia 98 F2
Calvados Chain is P.N.G. 110 F1
Calvert Hills Australia 110 B3
Calvert Island Canada 120 D5
Calvi Corsica France 56 I5
Calvià Spain 57 H4
Calvinia S. Africa 100 D6
Calvo, Monte mt. Italy 58 F4
Cam r. U.K. 49 H6
Camaçari Brazil 145 D1
Camache Reservoir U.S.A. 128 C2
Camachigama r. Canada 122 F5
Camacho Mex. 131 C7
Camacuio Angola 99 B5
Camacupa Angola 99 B5
Camagüey Cuba 137 I4
Camagüey, Archipiélago de is Cuba 137 I4
Camamu Brazil 145 D1
Camaná Peru 142 D7
Camanongue Angola 99 C5
Camapuã Brazil 143 H7
Camaquã Brazil 144 F4
Çamardı Turkey 90 D3
Camargo Bol. 142 E8
Camargue reg. France 56 G5
Camarillo U.S.A. 128 D4
Camarones Arg. 144 C6
Camarones, Bahía b. Arg. 144 C6
Camas r. U.S.A. 126 E4
Ca Mau Vietnam 71 D5
Ca Mau, Mui c. Vietnam 71 D5
Cambay India see Khambhat
Cambay, Gulf of India see Khambhat, Gulf of
Camberley U.K. 49 G7
Cambodia country Asia 71 D4
Camboriú Brazil 145 A4
Camborne U.K. 49 B8
Cambrai France 52 D4
Cambria admin. div. U.K. see Wales
Cambrian Mountains hills U.K. 49 D6
Cambridge Canada 134 E2
Cambridge N.Z. 113 E3
Cambridge U.K. 49 H6
Cambridge MA U.S.A. 135 J2
Cambridge MD U.S.A. 135 G4
Cambridge MN U.S.A. 130 E2
Cambridge NY U.S.A. 135 I2
Cambridge OH U.S.A. 134 E3
Cambridge Bay Canada 119 H3
Cambridge City U.S.A. 134 C4
Cambridge Springs U.S.A. 134 E3
Cambrien, Lac l. Canada 123 H2
Cambulo Angola 99 C4
Cambundi-Catembo Angola 99 B5
Cambuquira Brazil 145 B3
Cam Co l. China 83 E2
Camdeboo National Park S. Africa 100 G7
Camden AL U.S.A. 133 C5
Camden AR U.S.A. 131 E5
Camden NJ U.S.A. 135 H4
Camden NY U.S.A. 135 H2
Camden SC U.S.A. 133 D5
Camdenton U.S.A. 130 E4
Cameia Angola 99 C5
Cameia, Parque Nacional da nat. park Angola 99 C5
Cameron AZ U.S.A. 129 H4
Cameron LA U.S.A. 131 E6
Cameron MO U.S.A. 130 E4
Cameron TX U.S.A. 131 D6
Cameron Highlands mts Malaysia 71 C6
Cameron Hills Canada 120 G3
Cameron Island Canada 119 H2
Cameron Park U.S.A. 128 C2
Cameroon country Africa 96 E4
Cameroon, Mount vol. Cameroon see Cameroun, Mont
Cameroon Highlands slope Cameroon/Nigeria 96 E4
Caméroun country Africa see Cameroon
Cameroun, Mont vol. Cameroon 96 D4
Cametá Brazil 143 I4
Camiña Chile 142 E7
Camino Real de Tierra Adentro tourist site Mex. 131 B6
Camiri Bol. 142 F8
Camisea Peru 142 D6
Camocim Brazil 143 J4
Camooweal Australia 110 B3
Camooweal Caves National Park Australia 110 B4
Camorta i. India 81 H10
Campana Mex. 131 C7
Campana, Isla i. Chile 144 A7
Campania Island Canada 120 D4
Campbell S. Africa 100 F5
Campbell, Cape N.Z. 113 E5
Campbell, Mount hill Australia 108 E5
Campbellford Canada 135 G1
Campbell Hill hill U.S.A. 134 D3
Campbell Island N.Z. 150 H9
Campbell Lake Canada 121 J2
Campbell Plateau sea feature S. Pacific Ocean 150 H9
Campbell Range hills Australia 108 D3
Campbell River Canada 120 E5
Campbellsville U.S.A. 134 C5
Campbellton Canada 123 I5
Campbelltown Australia 112 E5
Campbeltown U.K. 50 D5
Campeche Mex. 136 F5
Campeche, Bahía de g. Mex. 136 F5
Camperdown Australia 112 A7
Câmpina Romania 59 K2
Campina Grande Brazil 143 K5
Campinas Brazil 145 B3
Campina Verde Brazil 145 A2
Campo Cameroon 96 D4
Campobasso Italy 58 F4
Campo Belo Brazil 145 B3
Campo Belo do Sul Brazil 145 A4
Campo de Diauarum Brazil 143 H6
Campo Florido Brazil 145 A2
Campo Gallo Arg. 144 D3
Campo Grande Brazil 144 F2
Campo Largo Brazil 145 A4
Campo Maior Brazil 143 J4
Campo Maior Port. 57 C4
Campo Mourão Brazil 144 F2
Campos Altos Brazil 145 B2
Campos dos Goytacazes Brazil 145 C3
Campos Novos Brazil 145 A4
Campos Sales Brazil 143 J5
Campton U.S.A. 134 D5
Câmpulung Romania 59 K2
Câmpulung Moldovenesc Romania 59 K1
Camp Verde U.S.A. 129 H4
Camrose Canada 121 H4
Camrose U.K. 49 B7
Camsell Lake Canada 121 I2
Camsell Portage Canada 121 I3
Camsell Range mts Canada 120 F2
Camulodunum U.K. see Colchester
Çan Turkey 59 L4
Ca Na, Mui hd Vietnam 71 E5
Canaã dos Carajás Brazil 143 H5
Canaan r. Canada 123 I5
Canaan U.S.A. 135 I2
Canaan Peak U.S.A. 129 H3
Canabrava Brazil 145 B2
Canacona India 84 B3

▶Canada country N. America 118 H4
Largest country in North America and 2nd in the world. 3rd most populous country in North America.

Canada Basin sea feature Arctic Ocean 153 A1
Canadian U.S.A. 131 C5
Canadian r. U.S.A. 131 E5
Canadian Abyssal Plain sea feature Antarctica 153 A1
Cañadón Grande, Sierra mts Arg. 144 C7
Canaima, Parque Nacional nat. park Venez. 142 F2
Çanakkale Turkey 59 L4
Çanakkale Boğazı strait Turkey see Dardanelles
Canalejas Arg. 144 C5
Canal-Supe, Sacred City of tourist site Peru 142 C6
Cañamares Spain 57 E3
Canandaigua U.S.A. 135 G2
Cananea Mex. 127 F7
Cananéia Brazil 145 B4
Canápolis Brazil 145 A2
Cañar Ecuador 142 C4
Canarias terr. N. Atlantic Ocean see Canary Islands
Canárias, Ilha das i. Brazil 143 J4
Canarias, Islas terr. N. Atlantic Ocean see Canary Islands
Canarreos, Archipiélago de los is Cuba 137 H4

▶Canary Islands terr. N. Atlantic Ocean 96 B2
Autonomous Community of Spain.

Canaseraga U.S.A. 135 G2
Canastota U.S.A. 135 H2
Canastra, Serra da mts Goiás Brazil 145 A1
Canastra, Serra da mts Minas Gerais Brazil 145 B2
Canatiba Brazil 145 C1
Canatlán Mex. 131 B7
Canaveral, Cape U.S.A. 133 D6
Cañaveras Spain 57 E3
Canavieiras Brazil 145 D1
Canbelego Australia 112 C3

▶Canberra Australia 112 D5
Capital of Australia and Australian Capital Territory.

Cancún Mex. 137 G4
Çandar Turkey see Kastamonu
Çandarlı Turkey 59 L5
Candela Mex. 131 C7
Candela r. Mex. 131 C7
Candelaria Mex. 127 G7
Candia Greece see Iraklion
Cândido de Abreu Brazil 145 A4
Çandır Turkey 90 D2
Candle Lake Canada 121 J4
Candlewood, Lake U.S.A. 135 I3
Cando U.S.A. 130 D1
Cane r. Australia 108 A5
Canea Greece see Chania
Canela Brazil 145 A5
Canelones Uruguay 144 E4
Cane Valley U.S.A. 134 C5
Cangallo Peru 142 D6
Cangamba Angola 99 B5
Cangandala, Parque Nacional de nat. park Angola 99 B4
Cango Caves S. Africa 100 F7
Cangola Angola 99 B4
Cangshan China 77 H1
Canguaretama Brazil 143 K5
Canguçu Brazil 144 F4
Canguçu, Serra do hills Brazil 144 F4
Cangwu China 77 F4
Cangzhou China 73 L5
Caniapiscau Canada 123 H3
Caniapiscau r. Canada 123 H2
Caniapiscau, Réservoir de l. Canada 123 H3
Caniçado Moz. see Guija
Canicatti Sicily Italy 58 E6
Canim Lake Canada 120 F5
Canindé Brazil 143 K4
Canisteo U.S.A. 135 G2
Canisteo r. U.S.A. 135 G2
Canisteo Peninsula Antarctica 152 K2
Cañitas de Felipe Pescador Mex. 131 C8
Çankırı Turkey 90 D2
Canna Australia 109 A7
Canna i. U.K. 50 C3
Cannanore India see Kannur
Cannanore Islands India 84 B4
Cannelton U.S.A. 134 B5
Cannes France 56 H5
Cannock U.K. 49 E6
Cannon Beach U.S.A. 126 C3
Cann River Australia 112 D6
Canoas Brazil 145 A5
Canōas, Rio das r. Brazil 145 A4
Canoeiros Brazil 145 B2
Canoe Lake Canada 121 I4
Canoe Lake l. Canada 121 I4
Canoinhas Brazil 145 A4
Canon City U.S.A. 127 G5
Cañon Largo watercourse U.S.A. 129 J3
Canoona Australia 110 E4
Canora Canada 121 K5
Canowindra Australia 112 D4
Canso Canada 123 J5
Canso, Cape Canada 123 J5
Cantabrian Mountains Spain see Cantábrica, Cordillera
Cantábrica, Cordillera mts Spain 57 D2
Cantábrico, Mar sea Spain 57 C2
Cantagalo Brazil 145 C3
Canterbury U.K. 49 I7
Canterbury Bight b. N.Z. 113 C7
Canterbury Plains N.Z. 113 C6
Cần Thơ Vietnam 71 D5
Cantil U.S.A. 128 E4
Canton GA U.S.A. 133 C5
Canton IL U.S.A. 130 F3
Canton MO U.S.A. 130 F3
Canton MS U.S.A. 131 F5
Canton NY U.S.A. 135 H1
Canton OH U.S.A. 134 E3
Canton PA U.S.A. 135 G3
Canton SD U.S.A. 130 D3
Canton TX U.S.A. 131 E5
Canton Island atoll Kiribati see Kanton
Cantuaria U.K. see Canterbury
Canunda National Park Australia 111 C8
Canutama Brazil 142 F5
Canutillo Mex. 131 B7
Canvey Island U.K. 49 H7
Canwood Canada 121 J4
Cany-Barville France 49 H9
Canyon U.S.A. 131 C5
Canyon City U.S.A. 126 D3
Canyon City (abandoned) Canada 120 B2
Canyondam U.S.A. 128 C1
Canyon de Chelly National Monument nat. park U.S.A. 129 I3
Canyon Ferry Lake U.S.A. 126 F3
Canyon Lake U.S.A. 129 H5
Canyonlands National Park U.S.A. 129 I2
Canyon Ranges mts Canada 120 E2
Canyons of the Ancients National Monument nat. park U.S.A. 129 I3
Canyonville U.S.A. 126 C4
Cao Bằng Vietnam 70 D2
Caocheng China see Caoxian
Caohai China see Weining
Caohe China see Qichun
Caohu China 80 F3
Caojiahe China see Qichun
Caojian China 76 C3
Caoshi China 74 B4
Caoxian China 77 G1
Caozhou China see Heze
Capac U.S.A. 134 D2
Çapakçur Turkey see Bingöl
Capanaparo r. Venez. 142 E2
Capanema Brazil 143 I4
Capão Bonito Brazil 145 A4
Caparaó, Serra do mts Brazil 145 C3
Cap-aux-Meules Canada 123 J5
Cap-de-la-Madeleine Canada 123 G5
Cape r. Australia 110 D4
Cape Arid National Park Australia 109 C8
Cape Barren Island Australia 111 [inset]
Cape Basin sea feature S. Atlantic Ocean 148 I8
Cape Breton Highlands National Park Canada 123 J5
Cape Breton Island Canada 123 J5
Cape Charles Canada 123 L3
Cape Charles U.S.A. 135 G5
Cape Coast Ghana 96 C4
Cape Coast Castle Ghana see Cape Coast
Cape Cod Bay U.S.A. 135 J3
Cape Cod National Seashore nature res. U.S.A. 135 K3
Cape Coral U.S.A. 133 D7
Cape Crawford Australia 110 A3
Cape Dorset Canada 119 K3
Cape Fanshaw U.S.A. 120 C3
Cape Fear r. U.S.A. 133 E5
Cape George Canada 123 J5
Cape Girardeau U.S.A. 131 F4
Cape Johnson Depth sea feature N. Pacific Ocean 150 E5
Cape Juby Morocco see Tarfaya
Cape Krusenstern National Monument nat. park U.S.A. 118 B3
Capel Australia 109 A8
Cape Le Grand National Park Australia 109 C8
Capelinha Brazil 145 C2
Capella Australia 110 E4
Capelle aan den IJssel Neth. 52 E3
Capelongo Angola see Kuvango
Cape May U.S.A. 135 H4
Cape May Court House U.S.A. 135 H4
Cape May Point U.S.A. 135 H4
Cape Melville National Park Australia 110 D2
Capenda-Camulemba Angola 99 B4
Cape Palmerston National Park Australia 110 E4
Cape Range National Park Australia 108 A5
Cape St George Canada 123 K4

▶Cape Town S. Africa 100 D7
Legislative capital of South Africa.

Cape Tribulation National Park Australia 110 D2
Cape Upstart National Park Australia 110 D3
Cape Verde country Africa 96 [inset]
Cape Verde Basin sea feature N. Atlantic Ocean 148 F5
Cape Verde Plateau sea feature N. Atlantic Ocean 148 F4
Cape Vincent U.S.A. 135 G1
Cape York Peninsula Australia 110 C2
Cap-Haïtien Haiti 137 J5
Capim r. Brazil 143 I4

Châlons-en-Champagne France 52 E6
Châlons-sur-Marne France see Châlons-en-Champagne
Chalon-sur-Saône France 56 G3
Chālūs Iran 88 C2
Cham Germany 53 M5
Cham, Cu Lao i. Vietnam 70 E4
Cham, Kūh-e hill Iran 88 C3
Chamah, Gunung mt. Malaysia 71 C6
Chamaico Arg. 144 D5
Chamais Bay Namibia 100 B4
Chaman Pak. 78 F3
Chaman Bīd Iran 88 E2
Chamao, Khao mt. Thai. 71 C4
Chamarajanagar India 84 C4
Chamba India 82 D2
Chamba Tanz. 99 D5
Chambal r. India 82 D4
Chambas Cuba 133 E8
Chambeaux, Lac l. Canada 123 H3
Chamberlain r. Australia 108 D4
Chamberlain Canada 121 J5
Chamberlain U.S.A. 130 D3
Chamberlain Lake U.S.A. 132 G2
Chambers U.S.A. 129 I4
Chambersburg U.S.A. 135 G4
Chambers Island U.S.A. 134 B1
Chambéry France 56 G4
Chambeshi r. Zambia 99 C5
Chambi, Jebel mt. Tunisia 58 C7
Chambūk Iran 88 E3
Chamdo China see Qamdo
Chamechaude mt. France 56 G4
Chamiss Bay Canada 120 E5
Chamoli India see Gopeshwar
Chamonix-Mont-Blanc France 56 H4
Champa India 83 E5
Champagne-Ardenne admin. reg. France see Alsace, Champagne-Ardenne et Lorraine
Champagne Castle mt. S. Africa 101 I5
Champagne Humide reg. France 56 G2
Champagne Pouilleuse reg. France 56 F2
Champagnole France 56 G3
Champagny Islands Australia 108 D3
Champaign U.S.A. 130 F3
Champasak Laos 70 D4
Champdoré, Lac l. Canada 123 I3
Champhai India 83 H5
Champion Canada 120 H5
Champlain U.S.A. 135 G4
Champlain, Lake Canada/U.S.A. 135 I1
Champotón Mex. 136 F5
Chamzinka Russia 43 J5
Chana Thai. 71 C6
Chanak Turkey see Çanakkale
Chañaral Chile 144 B3
Chanda India see Chandrapur
Chandalar r. U.S.A. 118 D3
Chandausi India 82 D3
Chandbali India 83 F5
Chandeleur Islands U.S.A. 131 F6
Chanderi India 82 D4
Chandigarh India 82 D3
Chandil India 83 F5
Chandir Uzbek. 89 G2
Chandler Canada 123 I4
Chandler AZ U.S.A. 129 H5
Chandler IN U.S.A. 134 B4
Chandler OK U.S.A. 131 D5
Chandod India 82 C5
Chandos Lake Canada 135 G1
Chandpur Bangl. 83 G5
Chandpur India 82 D3
Chandragiri India 84 C3
Chandrapur India 84 C2
Chandvad India 84 B1
Chang, Ko i. Thai. 71 C4
Chang'an China 77 F1
Changane r. Moz. 101 K3
Changbai China 74 C4
Changbai Shan mts China/N. Korea 74 B4
Chang Cheng research station Antarctica see Great Wall
Changcheng China 77 F5
Changchow Fujian China see Zhangzhou
Changchow Jiangsu China see Changzhou
Changchun China 74 B4
Changchunling China 74 B3
Changde China 77 F2
Changgang China 77 G3
Changge China 77 G1
Changgo China 83 F3
Chang Hu l. China 77 G2
Changhua Taiwan 77 I3
Changhwa Taiwan see Changhua
Changi Sing. 71 [inset]
Changji China 80 G3
Changjiang China 77 F5
Chang Jiang r. China see Yangtze
Changjiang Kou China see Mouth of the Yangtze
Changjin-ho resr N. Korea 75 B4
Changkiang China see Zhanjiang
Changlang India 83 H4
Changleng China see Xinjian
Changling China 74 A3
Changlung India 87 M3
Changma China 83 I4
Changna China 83 F3
Changning Jiangxi China see Xunwu
Changning Sichuan China 76 E2
Changnyŏn N. Korea 75 B5
Ch'ang-pai Shan mts China/N. Korea see Changbai Shan
Changpu China see Suining
Changsan-got pt N. Korea 75 B5
Changsha China 77 G2
Changshan China 77 H2
Changshi China 76 E3
Changshou China 77 G2
Changshoujie China see Changshou
Changshu China 77 I2
Changtai China 77 H3
Changteh China see Changde
Changting Fujian China 77 H3
Changting Heilong. China 74 C3
Changwon S. Korea 75 C6
Changxing China 77 H2
Changyang China 77 F2
Changyŏn N. Korea 75 B5
Changyuan China 77 G1
Changzhi China 73 K5
Changzhou China 77 H2
Chañi, Nevado de mt. Arg. 144 C2
Chania Greece 59 K7
Chanion, Kolpos b. Greece 59 J7
Chankou China 76 E1
Channahon U.S.A. 134 A3
Channapatna India 84 C3
Channel Islands English Chan. 49 E9
Channel Islands U.S.A. 128 D5
Channel Islands National Park U.S.A. 128 D4
Channel-Port-aux-Basques Canada 123 K5
Channel Rock i. Bahamas 133 E8
Channel Tunnel France/U.K. 49 I7
Channing U.S.A. 131 C5
Chantada Spain 57 C2
Chanthaburi Thai. 71 C4
Chantilly France 52 C5
Chanumla India 71 A5
Chanute U.S.A. 130 E4
Chanuwala Pak. 89 I3
Chany, Ozero salt l. Russia 64 I4
Chaohu China 77 H2
Chao Hu l. China 77 H2
Chaor He r. China 74 A3
Chaowula Shan mt. China 76 C1
Chaoyang Guangdong China 77 H4
Chaoyang Heilong. China see Jiayin
Chaoyang Liaoning China 73 M4
Chaoyang Nei Mongol China 74 B2
Chaoyang Hu l. China 83 F2
Chaozhong China 74 A2
Chaozhou China 77 H4
Chapada Diamantina, Parque Nacional nat. park Brazil 145 C1
Chapada dos Veadeiros, Parque Nacional da nat. park Brazil 145 B1
Chapais Canada 122 G4
Chapak Gozār Afgh. 89 G2
Chapala, Laguna de l. Mex. 136 D4
Chāpārī, Kōtal-e Afgh. 89 G3
Chapayeva, imeni Turkm. see S. A. Nyýazow Adyndaky
Chapayevo Kazakh. 78 E1
Chapayevsk Russia 43 K5
Chapecó Brazil 144 F3
Chapecó r. Brazil 144 F3
Chapel-en-le-Frith U.K. 48 F5
Chapelle-lez-Herlaimont Belgium 52 E4
Chapeltown U.K. 48 F5
Chapleau Canada 122 E5
Chaplin Canada 121 J5
Chaplin Lake Canada 121 J5
Chaplygin Russia 43 H5
Chapman, Mount Canada 120 G5
Chapmanville U.S.A. 134 D5
Chappell U.S.A. 130 C3
Chappell Islands Australia 111 [inset]
Chapra Bihar India 83 F4
Chapra Jharkhand India see Chatra
Chaqmaqtīn, Kōl-e Afgh. 89 I2
Charagua Bol. 142 F7
Charay Mex. 127 F8
Charcas Mex. 136 D4
Charcot Island Antarctica 152 L2
Chard Canada 121 I4
Chard U.K. 49 E8
Chardara Kazakh. see Shardara
Chardara, Step' plain Kazakh. see Shardara, Step'
Chardon U.S.A. 134 E3
Chardzhev Turkm. see Türkmenabat
Chardzhou Turkm. see Türkmenabat
Charef Alg. 57 H6
Charef, Oued watercourse Morocco 54 D5
Charente r. France 56 D4
Chari r. Cameroon/Chad 97 E3
Chārī Iran 88 E4
Chārīkār Afgh. 89 H3
Chariton U.S.A. 130 E3
Chärjew Turkm. see Türkmenabat
Charkayuvom Russia 42 L2
Charkhlik China see Ruoqiang
Charleroi Belgium 52 E4
Charles, Cape U.S.A. 135 H5
Charlesbourg Canada 123 H5
Charles City IA U.S.A. 130 E3
Charles City VA U.S.A. 135 G5
Charles Hill Botswana 100 E2
Charles Lake Canada 121 I3
Charles Point Australia 108 E3
Charleston N.Z. 113 C5
Charleston IL U.S.A. 130 F4
Charleston MO U.S.A. 131 F4
Charleston SC U.S.A. 133 E5
▶Charleston WV U.S.A. 134 E4
Capital of West Virginia.
Charleston Peak U.S.A. 129 F3
Charlestown Ireland 51 D4
Charlestown IN U.S.A. 134 C4
Charlestown NH U.S.A. 135 I2
Charlestown RI U.S.A. 135 J3
Charles Town U.S.A. 135 G4
Charleville Australia 111 D5
Charleville Ireland 51 D5
Charleville-Mézières France 52 E5
Charlevoix U.S.A. 134 C1
Charlie, Dome ice feature Antarctica 152 F2
Charlie Lake Canada 120 F3
Charlotte MI U.S.A. 134 C2
Charlotte NC U.S.A. 133 D5
Charlotte TN U.S.A. 134 B5
▶Charlotte Amalie Virgin Is (U.S.A.) 137 L5
Capital of the U.S. Virgin Islands.
Charlotte Harbor b. U.S.A. 133 D7
Charlotte Lake Canada 120 E4
Charlottesville U.S.A. 135 F4
▶Charlottetown Canada 123 J5
Capital of Prince Edward Island.
Charlton Australia 112 A6
Charlton Island Canada 122 F3
Charron Lake Canada 121 M4
Charsadda Pak. 89 H3
Charshanga Turkm. see Köýtendag
Charshangngy Turkm. see Köýtendag
Charters Towers Australia 110 D4
Chartres France 56 E2
Chas India 83 F5
Chase Canada 120 G5
Chase U.S.A. 134 C2
Chase City U.S.A. 135 F5
Chashmeh Nūrī Iran 88 E3
Chashmeh-ye Palasi Iran 88 D3
Chashniki Belarus 43 F5
Chaska U.S.A. 130 E2
Chaslands Mistake c. N.Z. 113 B8
Chasŏng N. Korea 74 B4
Chasseral mt. Switz. 47 K7
Chassiron, Pointe de pt France 56 D3
Chastab, Kūh-e mts Iran 88 D3
Chāt Iran 88 D2
Chatanika U.S.A. 118 D3
Châteaubriant France 56 D3
Château-du-Loir France 56 E3
Châteaudun France 56 E2
Chateaugay U.S.A. 135 H1
Châteauguay Canada 135 I1
Châteauguay r. Canada 123 H2
Châteauguay, Lac l. Canada 123 H2
Châteaulin France 56 B2
Châteaumeillant France 56 F3
Châteauneuf-en-Thymerais France 52 B6
Châteauneuf-sur-Loire France 56 F3
Chateau Pond l. Canada 123 K3
Châteauroux France 56 E3
Château-Salins France 52 G6
Château-Thierry France 52 D5
Chateh Canada 120 G3
Châtelet Belgium 52 E4
Châtellerault France 56 E3
Chatfield U.S.A. 122 B6
Chatham Canada 134 D2
Chatham U.K. 49 H7
Chatham MA U.S.A. 135 K3
Chatham NY U.S.A. 135 I2
Chatham PA U.S.A. 135 H4
Chatham VA U.S.A. 134 F5
Chatham, Isla i. Chile 144 B8
Chatham Island N.Z. 107 I6
Chatham Island Samoa see Savai'i
Chatham Islands N.Z. 107 I6
Chatham Rise sea feature S. Pacific Ocean 150 I8
Chatham Strait U.S.A. 120 C3
Châtillon-sur-Seine France 56 G3
Chatkal Range mts Kyrg./Uzbek. 80 D3
Chatom U.S.A. 131 F6
Chatra India 83 F4
Chatra Nepal 83 F4
Chatsworth Canada 134 E1
Chatsworth U.S.A. 135 H4
Chattagam Bangl. see Chittagong
Chattanooga U.S.A. 133 C5
Chattarpur India see Chhatarpur
Chatteris U.K. 49 H6
Chattisgarh state India see Chhattisgarh
Chatturat Thai. 70 C4
Chatyr-Tash Kyrg. 80 E3
Châu Đôc Vietnam 71 D5
Chauhtan India 82 B4
Chauk Myanmar 70 A2
Chaumont France 56 G2
Chauncey U.S.A. 134 D4
Chaungzon Myanmar 70 B3
Chaunskaya Guba b. Russia 65 R3
Chauny France 52 D5
Châu Phu Vietnam see Châu Đôc
Chausy Belarus see Chavusy
Chautauqua, Lake U.S.A. 134 F2
Chauter Pak. 89 G4
Chauvin Canada 121 I4
Chavakachcheri Sri Lanka 84 D4
Chavakkad India 84 B4
Chaves Port. 57 C3
Chavigny, Lac l. Canada 122 G2
Chavusy Belarus 43 F5
Chawal r. Pak. 89 G4
Chây, Sông r. Vietnam 70 D2
Chayatyn, Khrebet ridge Russia 74 E1
Chayevo Russia 42 H4
Chaykovskiy Russia 41 Q4
Chazhegovo Russia 42 L3
Chazy U.S.A. 135 I1
Cheadle U.K. 49 F6
Cheaha Mountain hill U.S.A. 133 C5
Cheat r. U.S.A. 134 F4
Cheatham Lake U.S.A. 134 B5
Cheb Czechia 53 M4
Chebba Tunisia 58 D7
Cheboksarskoye Vodokhranilishche resr Russia 42 J5
Cheboksary Russia 42 J4
Cheboygan U.S.A. 132 C2
Chechen', Ostrov i. Russia 91 G2
Chedabucto Bay Canada 123 J5
Cheddar U.K. 49 E7
Cheduba Myanmar see Man-aung
Cheduba Island i. Myanmar see Man-aung Kyun
Chée r. France 52 E6
Cheektowaga U.S.A. 135 F2
Cheepie Australia 112 B1
Cheetham, Cape Antarctica 152 H2
Chefchaouene Morocco 57 D6
Chefoo China see Yantai
Chefornak U.S.A. 118 B3
Chefu Moz. 101 K2
Chegdomyn Russia 74 D2
Chegga Mauritania 96 C2
Chegutu Zimbabwe 99 D5
Chehalis U.S.A. 126 C3
Chehardeh Iran 88 E3
Chehel Chashmeh, Kūh-e hill Iran 88 B3
Chehel Dokhtarān, Kūh-e mt. Iran 89 F4
Chehel Pāyeh Iran 88 E4
Cheju S. Korea see Jeju
Cheju-do i. S. Korea 75 B6
Chekhov Moskovskaya Oblast' Russia 43 H5
Chekhov Sakhalinskaya Oblast' Russia 74 F3
Chekiang prov. China see Zhejiang
Chekichler Turkm. see Çekiçler
Chek Lap Kok reg. H.K. China 77 [inset]
Chekunda Russia 74 D2
Chela, Serra da mts Angola 99 B5
Chelan, Lake U.S.A. 126 C2
Cheleken Turkm. see Hazar
Cheline Moz. 101 L2
Chelkar Kazakh. see Shalkar
Chełm Poland 43 D6
Chelmer r. U.K. 49 H7
Chełmno Poland 47 Q4
Chelmsford U.K. 49 H7
Chelsea MI U.S.A. 134 C2
Chelsea VT U.S.A. 135 I2
Cheltenham U.K. 49 E7
Chelva Spain 57 F4
Chelyabinsk Russia 64 H4
Chemba Moz. 99 D5
Chêm Co l. China 82 D2
Chemnitz Germany 53 M4
Chemulpo S. Korea see Incheon
Chenab r. India/Pak. 82 B3
Chenachane, Oued watercourse Alg. 96 C2
Chenārān Iran 88 E2
Chencang China 76 E1
Chendir r. Turkm. see Çendir
Cheney U.S.A. 126 D3
Cheney Reservoir U.S.A. 130 D4
Chengalpattu India 84 D3
Chengbu China 77 F3
Chengchow China see Zhengzhou
Chengde China 73 L4
Chengdu China 76 E2
Chengele India 76 C2
Chenggong China 76 D3
Chenghai China 77 H4
Cheng Hai l. China 76 D3
Chengjiang China see Taihe
Chengjiang Fossil Site tourist site China 76 D3
Chengmai China 77 F5
Chengtu China see Chengdu
Chengwu China 77 G1
Chengxian China 76 E1
Chengxiang Chongqing China see Wuxi
Chengxiang Jiangxi China see Quannan
Chengzhong China see Ningming
Cheniu Shan i. China 77 H1
Chenkaladi Sri Lanka 84 D5
Chennai India 84 D3
Chenqing China 74 B2
Chenqingqiao China see Chenqing
Chenstokhov Poland see Częstochowa
Chenxi China 77 F3
Chenyang China see Chenxi
Chenying China see Wannian
Chenzhou China 77 G3
Cheonan S. Korea 75 B5
Cheongdo S. Korea 75 C6
Cheongju S. Korea 75 B5
Chepén Peru 142 C5
Chepes Arg. 144 C4
Chepo Panama 137 I7
Chepstow U.K. 49 E7
Cheptsa r. Russia 42 K4
Chequamegon Bay U.S.A. 130 F2
Cher r. France 56 E3
Chera state India see Kerala
Cheraw U.S.A. 133 E5
Cherbaniani Reef India 84 A3
Cherbourg-Octeville France 56 D2
Cherchell Alg. 57 H5
Cherchen China see Qiemo
Cherdakly Russia 43 K5
Cherdyn' Russia 41 R3
Chereapani reef India see Byramgore Reef
Cheremkhovo Russia 72 I2
Cheremshany Russia 74 D3
Cheremukhovka Russia 42 K4
Cherepanovo Russia 72 E2
Cherepovets Russia 42 H4
Cherevkovo Russia 42 J3
Chergui, Chott ech imp. l. Alg. 54 D5
Chéria Alg. 58 B7
Cheriton U.S.A. 135 H5
Cheriyakara, Suheli India 84 B4
Cheriyam atoll India 84 B4
Cherkassy Ukr. see Cherkasy
Cherkasy Ukr. 43 G6
Cherkessk Russia 91 F1
Cherla India 84 D2
Chernaya Russia 42 M1
Chernaya r. Russia 42 M1
Chernigov Ukr. see Chernihiv
Chernigovka Russia 74 D3
Chernihiv Ukr. 43 F6
Cherninivka Ukr. 43 H7
Chernivtsi Ukr. 43 E6
Chernobyl' Ukr. see Chornobyl'
Chernogorsk Russia 72 G2
Chernovtsy Ukr. see Chernivtsi
Chernoye More sea Asia/Europe see Black Sea
Chernushka Russia 41 R4
Chernyakhiv Ukr. 43 F6
Chernyakhovsk Russia 45 L9
Chernyanka Russia 43 H6
Chernyayevo Russia 74 B1
Chernyshevsk Russia 73 L2
Chernyshevskiy Russia 65 M3
Chernyshkovskiy Russia 43 I6
Chernyye Zemli reg. Russia 43 J7
Chernyy Irtysh r. China/Kazakh. see Ertix He
Chernyy Porog Russia 42 G3
Chernyy Yar Russia 43 J6
Cherokee U.S.A. 130 E3
Cherokee Sound Bahamas 133 E7
▶Cherrapunji India 83 G4
Highest recorded annual rainfall in the world.
Cherry Creek r. U.S.A. 130 C2
Cherry Creek Mountains U.S.A. 129 F1
Cherry Hill U.S.A. 135 H4
Cherry Island Solomon Is 107 G3
Cherry Lake U.S.A. 128 D2
Cherskiy Russia 153 C2
Cherskogo, Khrebet mts Russia 65 P3
Chertkov Ukr. see Chortkiv
Chertkovo Russia 43 I6
Cherven Bryag Bulg. 59 K3
Chervonoarmeyskoye Ukr. see Vil'nyans'k
Chervonoarmiys'k Donets'ka Oblast' Ukr. see Krasnoarmiys'k
Chervonoarmiys'k Rivnens'ka Oblast' Ukr. see Radyvyliv
Chervonograd Ukr. see Chervonohrad
Chervonohrad Ukr. 43 E6
Chervyen' Belarus 43 F5
Cherwell r. U.K. 49 F7
Cherykaw Belarus 43 F5
Chesapeake U.S.A. 135 G5
Chesapeake Bay U.S.A. 135 G4
Chesham U.K. 49 G7
Cheshire Plain U.K. 48 E5
Cheshme Vtoroy Turkm. 89 F2
Cheshskaya Guba b. Russia 42 J2
Cheshtebe Tajik. 89 I2
Cheshunt U.K. 49 G7
Chesnokovka Russia see Novoaltaysk
Chester Canada 123 I5
Chester U.K. 48 E5
Chester CA U.S.A. 128 C1
Chester IL U.S.A. 130 F4
Chester MT U.S.A. 126 F2
Chester OH U.S.A. 134 E4
Chester SC U.S.A. 133 D5
Chester r. U.S.A. 135 G4
Chesterfield U.K. 48 F5
Chesterfield U.S.A. 135 G5
Chesterfield, Îles is New Caledonia 107 F3
Chesterfield Inlet Canada 121 N2
Chesterfield Inlet inlet Canada 121 M2
Chester-le-Street U.K. 48 F4
Chestertown MD U.S.A. 135 G4
Chestertown NY U.S.A. 135 I2
Chesterville Canada 135 H1
Chestnut Ridge U.S.A. 134 F3
Chesuncook Lake U.S.A. 132 G2
Chetaïbi Alg. 58 B6
Chéticamp Canada 123 J5
Chetlat i. India 84 B4
Chetumal Mex. 136 G5
Chetwynd Canada 120 F4
Cheung Chau H.K. China 77 [inset]
Chevelon Creek r. U.S.A. 129 H4
Cheviot N.Z. 113 D6
Cheviot Hills U.K. 48 E3
Cheviot Range hills Australia 110 C5
Chevreulx r. Canada 122 G3
Cheyenne OK U.S.A. 131 D5
▶Cheyenne WY U.S.A. 126 G4
Capital of Wyoming.
Cheyenne r. U.S.A. 130 C2
Cheyenne Wells U.S.A. 130 C4
Cheyne Bay Australia 109 B8
Cheyur India 84 D3
Chezacut Canada 120 E4
Chhapra India see Chapra
Chhata India 82 D4
Chhatak Bangl. 83 G4
Chhatarpur Jharkhand India 83 F4
Chhatarpur Madh. Prad. India 82 D4
Chhatr Pak. 89 H4
Chhatrapur India 84 E2
Chhattisgarh state India 83 E5
Chhay Arêng, Stœng r. Cambodia 71 C5
Chhindwara India 82 D5
Chhitkul India see Chitkul
Chhlong Cambodia 71 D4
Chhukha Bhutan 83 G4
Chi, Lam r. Thai. 71 C4
Chi, Mae Nam r. Thai. 70 D4
Chiai Taiwan see Jiayi
Chiamboni Somalia 98 E4
Chiange Angola 99 B5
Chiang Kham Thai. 70 C3
Chiang Khan Thai. 70 C3
Chiang Mai Thai. 70 B3
Chiang Rai Thai. 70 B3
Chiang Saen Thai. 70 C2
Chiari Italy 58 C2
Chiautla Mex. 136 E5
Chiavenna Italy 58 C1
Chiayi Taiwan see Jiayi
Chiba Japan 75 F6
Chibi China 77 G2
Chibia Angola 99 B5
Chibizovka Russia see Zherdevka
Chiboma Moz. 99 D6
Chibougamau Canada 122 G4
Chibougamau, Lac l. Canada 122 G4
Chibuto Moz. 101 K3
Chibuzhang Co l. China 83 G2
Chicacole India see Srikakulam
▶Chicago U.S.A. 134 B3
4th most populous city in North America.
Chic-Chocs, Monts mts Canada 123 I4
Chichagof U.S.A. 120 B3
Chichagof Island U.S.A. 120 C3
Chichak r. Pak. 89 G5
Chichaoua Morocco 54 C5
Chichatka Russia 74 A1
Chicheng China see Pengxi
Chichester U.K. 49 G8
Chichester Range mts Australia 108 B5
Chichgarh India 84 D1
Chichibu Japan 75 E6
Chichibu-Tama Kokuritsu-kōen nat. park Japan 75 E6
Chichijima-rettō is Japan 75 F8
Chickasha U.S.A. 131 D5
Chiclana de la Frontera Spain 57 C5
Chiclayo Peru 142 C5
Chico r. Arg. 144 C6
Chico U.S.A. 128 C2
Chicomo Moz. 101 L3
Chicopee U.S.A. 135 I2
Chicoutimi Canada 123 H4
Chicualacuala Moz. 101 J2
Chidambaram India 84 C4
Chidenguele Moz. 101 L3
Chidley, Cape Canada 119 L3
Chido China see Sêndo
Chiducuane Moz. 101 L3
Chiefland U.S.A. 133 D6
Chiemsee l. Germany 47 N7
Chiengmai Thai. see Chiang Mai
Chiers r. France 52 F5
Chieti Italy 58 F3
Chifeng China 73 L4
Chifre, Serra do mts Brazil 145 C2
Chiginagak Volcano, Mount U.S.A. 118 C4
Chigu China 83 G3
Chigubo Moz. 101 K2
Chigu Co l. China 83 G3
Chihil Abdālān, Kōh-e mts Afgh. 89 G3
Chihli, Gulf of China see Bo Hai
Chihuahua Mex. 127 G7
Chihuahua state Mex. 127 G7
Chikalda India 82 D5
Chikan China 77 F4
Chikaskia r. U.S.A. 131 D4
Chikhli India 84 C1
Chikishlyar Turkm. see Çekiçler
Chikkamagaluru India 84 B3
Chikodi India 84 B2
Chilanko r. Canada 120 F4
Chilas Pak. 82 C2
Chilaw Sri Lanka 84 C5
Chilcotin r. Canada 120 F5
Childers Australia 110 F5
Childress U.S.A. 131 C5
Chile country S. America 144 B4
Chile Basin sea feature S. Pacific Ocean 151 O8
Chile Chico Chile 144 B7
Chile Rise sea feature S. Pacific Ocean 151 O8
Chilgir Russia 43 J7
Chilhowie U.S.A. 134 E5
Chilia-Nouă Ukr. see Kiliya
Chilika Lake India 84 E2
Chililabombwe Zambia 99 C5
Chilko r. Canada 120 F4
Chilko Lake Canada 120 E5
Chilkoot Pass Canada/U.S.A. 120 C3
Chilkoot Trail National Historic Site nat. park Canada 120 C3
Chillán Chile 144 B5
Chillicothe MO U.S.A. 130 E4
Chillicothe OH U.S.A. 134 D4
Chilliwack Canada 120 F5
Chilo India 82 C4
Chiloé, Isla de i. Chile 144 B6
Chiloé, Isla Grande de i. Chile see Chiloé, Isla de
Chilpancingo Mex. 136 E5
Chilpancingo de los Bravos Mex. see Chilpancingo
Chilpi Pak. 82 C1
Chiltern Hills U.K. 49 G7
Chilton U.S.A. 134 A1
Chiluage Angola 99 C4
Chilubi Zambia 99 C5
Chilung Taiwan see Jilong
Chilwa, Lake Malawi 99 D5
Chimala Tanz. 99 D4
Chimaltenango Guat. 136 F6
Chi Ma Wan H.K. China 77 [inset]
Chimay Belgium 52 E4
Chimbas Arg. 144 C4
Chimbay Uzbek. see Chimboy
Chimborazo mt. Ecuador 142 C4
Chimbote Peru 142 C5
Chimboy Uzbek. 80 A3
Chimishliya Moldova see Cimişlia
Chimkent Kazakh. see Shymkent
Chimney Rock U.S.A. 129 J3
Chimoio Moz. 99 D5
Chimtargha, Qullai mt. Tajik. 89 H2
Chimtorga, Gora mt. Tajik. see Chimtargha, Qullai
▶China country Asia 72 H5
Most populous country in Asia and the world. 2nd largest country in Asia and 4th largest in the world.
China Mex. 131 D7
China, Republic of country Asia see Taiwan
China Bakir r. Myanmar see To
China Lake CA U.S.A. 128 E4
China Lake ME U.S.A. 135 K1
Chinandega Nicaragua 136 G6
China Point U.S.A. 128 D5
Chinati Peak U.S.A. 131 B6
Chincha Alta Peru 142 C6
Chinchaga r. Canada 120 G3
Chinchilla Australia 112 E1
Chincholi India 84 C2
Chinchorro, Banco sea feature Mex. 137 G5
Chincoteague Bay U.S.A. 135 H5
Chinde Moz. 99 D5
Chindwin r. Myanmar 70 A2
Chinese Turkestan aut. reg. China see Xinjiang Uygur Zizhiqu
Chinghai prov. China see Qinghai
Chingleput India see Chengalpattu
Chingola Zambia 99 C5
Chinguar Angola 99 B5
Chinguețți Mauritania 96 B2
Chinhoyi Zimbabwe 99 D5
Chini India see Kalpa
Chining China see Jining
Chiniot Pak. 89 I4
Chinipas Mex. 127 F8
Chinit, Stœng r. Cambodia 71 D4
Chinju S. Korea 75 C6
Chinle U.S.A. 129 I3
Chinmen Taiwan see Jinmen
Chinmen Tao i. Taiwan see Jinmen Dao
Chinnamp'o N. Korea see Namp'o
Chinnur India 84 C2
Chino Creek watercourse U.S.A. 129 G4
Chinon France 56 E3
Chinook U.S.A. 126 F2
Chinook Trough sea feature N. Pacific Ocean 150 I3
Chino Valley U.S.A. 129 G4
Chinsali Zambia 99 D5
Chin-shan China see Zhujing
Chintamani India 84 C3
Chioggia Italy 58 E2
Chios Greece 59 L5
Chios i. Greece 59 K5
Chipata Zambia 99 D5
Chipchihua, Sierra de mts Arg. 144 C6

Chiphu Cambodia 71 D5
Chipindo Angola 99 B5
Chipinga Zimbabwe see Chipinge
Chipinge Zimbabwe 99 D6
Chipley U.S.A. 133 C6
Chipman Canada 123 I5
Chippenham U.K. 49 E7
Chippewa, Lake U.S.A. 130 F2
Chippewa Falls U.S.A. 130 F2
Chipping Norton U.K. 49 F7
Chipping Sodbury U.K. 49 E7
Chipurupalle Andhra Prad. India 84 D2
Chipurupalle Andhra Prad. India 84 D2
Chiquilá Mex. 133 C8
Chiquinquirá Col. 142 D2
Chir r. Russia 43 I6
Chirada India 84 D3
Chirala India 84 D3
Chīras Afgh. 89 G3
Chirchiq Uzbek. 80 C3
Chiredzi Zimbabwe 99 D6
Chirfa Niger 96 E2
Chiricahua National Monument nat. park U.S.A. 129 I5
Chiricahua Peak U.S.A. 129 I6
Chirikof Island U.S.A. 118 C4
Chiriquí, Golfo de b. Panama 137 H7
Chiriquí, Volcán de vol. Panama see Barú, Volcán
Chirk U.K. 49 D6
Chirnside U.K. 50 G5
Chirripó mt. Costa Rica 137 H7
Chisamba Zambia 99 C5
Chisana r. U.S.A. 120 A2
Chisasibi Canada 122 F3
Chishima-retto is Russia see Kuril Islands
Chisholm Canada 120 H4
Chishtian Pak. 89 I4
Chishui Guizhou China 76 E2
Chishui Sichuan China 76 E3
Chisimaio Somalia see Kismaayo

▶Chişinău Moldova 59 M1
Capital of Moldova.

Chistopol' Russia 42 K5
Chita Russia 73 K2
Chitado Angola 99 B5
Chitaldrug India see Chitradurga
Chitalwana India 82 B4
Chitambo Zambia 99 D5
Chitato Angola 99 C4
Chitek Lake Canada 121 J4
Chitek Lake l. Canada 121 L4
Chitembo Angola 99 B5
Chitina U.S.A. 118 D3
Chitipa Malawi 99 D4
Chitkul India 82 D3
Chitobe Moz. 99 D6
Chitoor India see Chittoor
Chitor India see Chittaurgarh
Chitose Japan 74 F4
Chitradurga India 84 C3
Chitrakoot India 82 E4
Chitrakut India see Chitrakoot
Chitral Pak. 89 H3
Chitral r. Pak. 89 H3
Chitravati r. India 84 C3
Chitré Panama 137 H7
Chitrod India 82 B5
Chittagong Bangl. 83 G5
Chittaurgarh India 82 C4
Chittoor India 84 C3
Chittor India see Chittoor
Chittorgarh India see Chittaurgarh
Chittur India 84 C4
Chitungwiza Zimbabwe 99 D5
Chiume Angola 99 C5
Chivasso Italy 58 B2
Chívato, Punta pt Mex. 127 F8
Chivhu Zimbabwe 99 D5
Chixixu China 77 G4
Chizarira National Park Zimbabwe 99 C5
Chizhou China 77 H2
Chizu Japan 75 D6
Chkalov Russia see Orenburg
Chkalovsk Russia 42 I4
Chkalovskoye Russia 74 D3
Chlef Alg. 57 G5
Chlef, Oued r. Alg. 57 G5
Chloride U.S.A. 129 F4
Chlya, Ozero l. Russia 74 F1
Choa Chu Kang Sing. 71 [inset]
Choa Chu Kang hill Sing. 71 [inset]
Chobe National Park Botswana 99 C5
Chodov Czechia 53 M4
Choele Choel Arg. 144 C5
Chogar r. Russia 74 D1
Chogori Feng mt. China/Pak. see K2
Chograyskoye Vodokhranilishche resr Russia 43 J7
Choiseul i. Solomon Is 107 F2
Choix Mex. 127 F8
Chojnice Poland 47 P4
Chōkai-san vol. Japan 75 F5
Ch'ok'ē mts Eth. 98 D2
Ch'ok'ē Mountains Eth. see Ch'ok'ē
Ch'ok'ē Terara mt. Eth. 98 D2
Chokola mt. China 82 E3
Choksum China 83 F3
Chokue Moz. see Chókwè
Chokurdakh Russia 65 P2
Chókwè Moz. 101 K3
Cho La pass China 76 C2
Cholame U.S.A. 128 C4
Cholet France 56 D3
Cholpon-Ata Kyrg. 80 E3
Choluteca Hond. 137 G6
Choma Zambia 99 C5
Chomo Ganggar mt. China 83 G3
Chơ Moi Vietnam 70 D2
Chomo Lhari mt. Bhutan/China 83 G4
Chom Thong Thai. 70 B3
Chomutov Czechia 47 N5
Chon Buri Thai. 71 C4
Ch'ŏnch'ŏn N. Korea 74 B4
Chone Ecuador 142 B4
Ch'ŏngch'ŏn-gang r. N. Korea 75 B5
Chonggye China see Qonggyai
Ch'ŏngjin N. Korea 74 C4
Ch'ŏngju S. Korea see Cheongju
Chŏng Kal Cambodia 71 C4
Chongkü China 76 C2
Chonglong China see Zizhong
Chongming Dao i. China 77 I2
Chongoroi Angola 99 B5
Chŏngp'yŏng N. Korea 75 B5
Chongqing China 76 E2
Chongqing mun. China 76 E2
Chonguene Moz. 101 K3
Chongyang China 77 G2
Chongyi China 77 G3
Chongzuo China 76 E4
Chŏnju S. Korea see Jeonju
Chonos, Archipiélago de los is Chile 144 A6

▶Cho Oyu mt. China/Nepal 83 F3
6th highest mountain in Asia and the world.

Chopda India 82 C5
Chor Pak. 89 H5
Chora Sfakion Greece 59 K7
Chorley U.K. 48 E5
Chornobyl' Ukr. 43 F6
Chornomors'k Ukr. 43 F7
Chornomors'ke Crimea 59 O2
Chortkiv Ukr. 43 E6
Ch'osan N. Korea 74 B4
Chōshi Japan 75 F6
Chosŏn country Asia see South Korea
Chosŏn-minjujuŭi-inmin-konghwaguk country Asia see North Korea
Choszczno Poland 47 O4
Chota Peru 142 C5
Chota Sinchula hill India 83 G4
Choteau U.S.A. 126 E3
Choti Pak. 89 H4
Choûm Mauritania 96 B2
Chowchilla U.S.A. 128 C3
Chown, Mount Canada 120 G4
Choybalsan Mongolia 73 K3
Choyr Mongolia 73 J3
Chrétiens, Île aux i. Canada see Christian Island
Chřiby hills Czechia 47 P6
Chrisman U.S.A. 134 B4
Chrissiesmeer S. Africa 101 J4
Christchurch N.Z. 113 D6
Christchurch U.K. 49 F8
Christian, Cape Canada 119 L2
Christiana S. Africa 101 G4
Christiania Norway see Oslo
Christian Island Canada 134 E1
Christiansburg U.S.A. 134 E5
Christianshåb Greenland see Qasigiannguit
Christie Bay Canada 121 I2
Christie Island Myanmar 71 B5
Christina r. Canada 121 I3
Christina, Mount N.Z. 113 B7

▶Christmas Island terr. Indian Ocean 68 D9
Australian External Territory.

Christopher, Lake salt flat Australia 109 D6
Chrudim Czechia 47 O6
Chrysi i. Greece see Gaïdouronisi
Chrysochou Bay Cyprus 85 A2
Chrysochous, Kolpos b. Cyprus see Chrysochou Bay
Chu Kazakh. see Shu
Chuadanga Bangl. 83 G5
Chuali, Lago l. Moz. 101 K3
Chuanhui China see Zhoukou
Chuansha China 77 I2
Chubalung China 76 C2
Chubarovka Ukr. see Polohy
Chubartau Kazakh. see Barshatas
Chūbu-Sangaku Kokuritsu-kōen nat. park Japan 75 E5
Chu-ching China see Zhujing
Chuchkovo Russia 43 I5
Chuckwalla Mountains U.S.A. 129 F5
Chudniv Ukr. 43 F6
Chudovo Russia 42 F4
Chudskoye, Ozero l. Estonia/Russia see Peipus, Lake
Chugach Mountains U.S.A. 118 D3
Chūgoku-sanchi mts Japan 75 D6
Chugqênsumdo China see Jigzhi
Chuguchak China see Tacheng
Chuguyev Ukr. see Chuhuyiv
Chuguyevka Russia 74 D3
Chugwater U.S.A. 126 G4
Chuhai China see Zhuhai
Chuhuyiv Ukr. 43 H6
Chujiang China see Shimen
Chukai Malaysia see Cukai
Chukchagirskoye, Ozero l. Russia 74 E1
Chukchi Abyssal Plain sea feature Arctic Ocean 153 B1
Chukchi Peninsula Russia see Chukotskiy Poluostrov
Chukchi Plateau sea feature Arctic Ocean 153 B1
Chukchi Sea Russia/U.S.A. 65 T3
Chukhloma Russia 42 I4
Chukotskiy, Mys c. Russia 118 A3
Chukotskiy Poluostrov pen. Russia 65 T3
Chulakkurgan Kazakh. see Sholakkorgan
Chulaktau Kazakh. see Karatau
Chulasa Russia 42 J2
Chula Vista U.S.A. 128 E5
Chulucanas Peru 142 B5
Chulung Pass Pak. 82 D2
Chulym Russia 64 J4
Chumar India 82 D2
Chumbicha Arg. 144 C3
Chumda China 76 C1
Chumikan Russia 65 O4
Chum Phae Thai. 70 C3
Chumphon Thai. 71 B5
Chum Saeng Thai. 70 C4
Chunar India 83 E4
Chuncheon S. Korea 75 B5
Chunga Zambia 99 C5
Chung-hua Jen-min Kung-ho-kuo country Asia see China
Chung-hua Min-kuo country Asia see Taiwan
Chungju S. Korea 75 B5
Chungking China see Chongqing
Ch'ungmu S. Korea see Tongyeong
Chŭngsan N. Korea 75 B5
Chunian Pak. 89 I4
Chunskiy Russia 72 H1
Chunya r. Russia 65 K3
Chuôi, Hon i. Vietnam 71 D5
Chuosijia China see Guanyinqiao
Chupa Russia 44 R3
Chūplū Iran 88 B2
Chuquicamata Chile 144 C2
Chur Switz. 56 I3
Churachandpur India 83 H4
Chūrān Iran 88 D4
Churapcha Russia 65 O3
Churchill Canada 121 M3
Churchill r. Man. Canada 121 M3
Churchill r. Nfld. and Lab. Canada 123 J3
Churchill, Cape Canada 121 M3
Churchill Falls Canada 123 J3
Churchill Lake Canada 121 I4
Churchill Mountains Antarctica 152 H1
Churchill Sound sea chan. Canada 122 F2
Churchs Ferry U.S.A. 130 D1
Churchville U.S.A. 134 F4
Churia Ghati Hills Nepal 83 F4
Churu India 82 C3
Churubusco U.S.A. 134 C3
Churún-Merú waterfall Venez. see Angel Falls
Chushul India 82 D2
Chuska Mountains U.S.A. 129 I3
Chusovaya r. Russia 41 R4
Chusovoy Russia 41 R4
Chust Ukr. see Khust
Chute-des-Passes Canada 123 H4
Chutia Assam India 83 H4
Chutia Jharkhand India 83 F5
Chutung Taiwan see Zhudong
Chuuk is Micronesia 150 G5
Chuxiong China 76 D3
Chüy r. Kazakh./Kyrg. see Shu
Chuzhou Anhui China 77 H1
Chuzhou Jiangsu China 77 H1
Chymyshliya Moldova see Cimişlia
Chyulu Hills National Park Kenya 98 D4
Ciadâr-Lunga Moldova see Ciadîr-Lunga
Ciadîr-Lunga Moldova 59 M1
Ciamis Indon. 68 D8
Cianjur Indon. 68 D8
Cianorte Brazil 144 F2
Cibecue U.S.A. 129 H4
Cibolo Creek r. U.S.A. 131 D6
Cibuta, Sierra mt. Mex. 127 F7
Čičarija mts Croatia 58 E2
Cicero U.S.A. 134 B3
Cidade Velha Cape Verde 96 [inset]
Cide Turkey 90 D2
Ciechanów Poland 47 R4
Ciego de Ávila Cuba 137 I4
Ciénaga Col. 142 D1
Ciénega Mex. 131 C7
Ciénega de Flores Mex. 131 C7
Cienfuegos Cuba 137 H4
Cieza Spain 57 F4
Çiftlik Turkey see Kelkit
Cifuentes Spain 57 E3
Cigüela r. Spain 57 E4
Cihanbeyli Turkey 90 D3
Cíjara, Embalse de resr Spain 57 D4
Cilacap Indon. 68 D8
Çıldır Turkey 91 F2
Çıldır Gölü l. Turkey 91 F2
Çıldıroba Turkey 85 C1
Cilento, Vallo di Diano e Alburni, Parco Nazionale del nat. park Italy 58 F4
Cili China 77 F2
Cilician Gates pass Turkey see Gülek Boğazı
Cill Airne Ireland see Killarney
Cill Chainnigh Ireland see Kilkenny
Cill Mhantáin Ireland see Wicklow
Çilmämmetgum des. Turkm. 88 D1
Cilo Dağı mt. Turkey 91 G3
Çilov Adası i. Azer. 91 H2
Cimarron CO U.S.A. 129 J2
Cimarron KS U.S.A. 130 C4
Cimarron NM U.S.A. 127 G5
Cimarron r. U.S.A. 131 D4
Cimişlia Moldova 59 M1
Cimone, Monte mt. Italy 58 D2
Cîmpina Romania see Câmpina
Cîmpulung Romania see Câmpulung
Cîmpulung Moldovenesc Romania see Câmpulung Moldovenesc
Cina, Tanjung c. Indon. 68 C8
Çınar Turkey 91 F3
Cinca r. Spain 57 G3
Cincinnati U.S.A. 134 C4
Cinco de Outubro Angola see Xá-Muteba
Cinderford U.K. 49 E7
Çine Turkey 59 M6
Ciney Belgium 52 F4
Cintalapa Mex. 136 F5
Cinto, Monte mt. France 56 I5
Ciping China 77 G3
Circeo, Parco Nazionale del nat. park Italy 58 E4
Circle AK U.S.A. 118 D3
Circle MT U.S.A. 126 G3
Circleville OH U.S.A. 134 D4
Circleville UT U.S.A. 129 G2
Cirebon Indon. 68 D8
Cirencester U.K. 49 F7
Cirò Marina Italy 58 G5
Cirta Alg. see Constantine
Cisco (abandoned) U.S.A. 129 I2
Cisne, Islas del is Caribbean Sea 137 H5
Citlaltépetl vol. Mex. see Orizaba, Pico de
Čitluk Bos. & Herz. 58 G3
Citronelle U.S.A. 131 F6
Citrus Heights U.S.A. 128 C2
Città di Castello Italy 58 E3
Ciucaş, Vârful mt. Romania 59 K2
Ciudad Acuña Mex. 131 C6
Ciudad Altamirano Mex. 136 D5
Ciudad Bolívar Venez. 142 F2
Ciudad Camargo Mex. 131 B7
Ciudad Constitución Mex. 136 B3
Ciudad del Carmen Mex. 136 F5
Ciudad Delicias Mex. 131 B6
Ciudad de Panamá Panama see Panama City
Ciudad de Valles Mex. 136 E4
Ciudad Flores Guat. see Flores
Ciudad Guayana Venez. 142 F2
Ciudad Guerrero Mex. 127 G7
Ciudad Guzmán Mex. 136 D5
Ciudad Juárez Mex. 127 G7
Ciudad Lerdo Mex. 131 C7
Ciudad Mante Mex. 136 E4
Ciudad Obregón Mex. 127 F8
Ciudad Real Spain 57 E4
Ciudad Río Bravo Mex. 131 D7
Ciudad Rodrigo Spain 57 C3
Ciudad Trujillo Dom. Rep. see Santo Domingo
Ciudad Victoria Mex. 131 D8
Ciutadella Spain 57 H3
Cıva Burnu pt Turkey 90 E2
Cividale del Friuli Italy 58 E1
Civitanova Marche Italy 58 E3
Civitavecchia Italy 58 D3
Çivril Turkey 59 M5
Cixi China 77 I2
Cizre Turkey 91 F3
Clacton-on-Sea U.K. 49 I7
Clady U.K. 51 E3
Claire, Lake Canada 121 H3
Clairfontaine Alg. see El Aouinet
Clamecy France 56 F3
Clane Ireland 51 F4
Clanton U.S.A. 133 C5
Clanwilliam Dam S. Africa 100 D7
Clara Ireland 51 E4
Clara Island Myanmar 71 B5
Claraville Australia 110 C3
Clare N.S.W. Australia 112 A4
Clare S.A. Australia 111 B7
Clare r. Ireland 51 C4
Clare U.S.A. 134 C2
Clarecastle Ireland 51 D5
Clare Island Ireland 51 B4
Claremont U.S.A. 135 I2
Claremore U.S.A. 131 E4
Claremorris Ireland 51 D4
Clarence r. Australia 112 F2
Clarence N.Z. 113 D6
Clarence Island Antarctica 152 A2
Clarence Strait Iran see Khūran
Clarence Strait U.S.A. 120 C3
Clarence Town Bahamas 133 F8
Clarendon AR U.S.A. 131 F5
Clarendon PA U.S.A. 134 F3
Clarendon TX U.S.A. 131 C5
Clarenville Canada 123 L4
Claresholm Canada 120 H5
Clarie Coast Antarctica see Wilkes Coast
Clarinda U.S.A. 130 E3
Clarington U.S.A. 134 E4
Clarion IA U.S.A. 130 E3
Clarion PA U.S.A. 134 F3
Clarion r. U.S.A. 134 F3
Clarión, Isla i. Mex. 136 B5
Clark U.S.A. 130 D2
Clark, Mount Canada 120 F1
Clarkdale U.S.A. 129 G4
Clarkebury S. Africa 101 I6
Clarke Range mts Australia 110 D4
Clarke River Australia 110 D3
Clarke's Head Canada 123 L4
Clark Mountain U.S.A. 129 F4
Clark Point Canada 134 E1
Clarksburg U.S.A. 134 E4
Clarksdale U.S.A. 131 F5
Clarks Hill U.S.A. 134 B3
Clarksville AR U.S.A. 131 E5
Clarksville TN U.S.A. 134 B5
Clarksville TX U.S.A. 131 E5
Clarksville VA U.S.A. 135 F5
Claro r. Goiás Brazil 145 A2
Claro r. Mato Grosso Brazil 145 A1
Clashmore Ireland 51 E5
Claude U.S.A. 131 C5
Claudy U.K. 51 E3
Clavier Belgium 52 F4
Claxton U.S.A. 133 D5
Clay U.S.A. 134 E4
Clayburg U.S.A. 135 I1
Clay Center KS U.S.A. 130 D4
Clay Center NE U.S.A. 130 D3
Clay City IN U.S.A. 134 B4
Clay City KY U.S.A. 134 D5
Clayhole Wash watercourse U.S.A. 129 G3
Claypool U.S.A. 129 H5
Clay Springs U.S.A. 129 H4
Clayton DE U.S.A. 135 H4
Clayton GA U.S.A. 133 D5
Clayton MI U.S.A. 134 C3
Clayton MO U.S.A. 130 F4
Clayton NM U.S.A. 131 C4
Clayton NY U.S.A. 135 G1
Claytor Lake U.S.A. 134 E5
Clay Village U.S.A. 134 C4
Clear, Cape Ireland 51 C6
Clearco U.S.A. 134 E4
Clear Creek Canada 134 E2
Clear Creek r. U.S.A. 129 H4
Cleare, Cape U.S.A. 118 D4
Clearfield PA U.S.A. 135 F3
Clearfield UT U.S.A. 126 E4
Clear Fork Brazos r. U.S.A. 131 D5
Clear Hills Canada 120 G3
Clear Island Ireland 51 C6
Clear Lake IA U.S.A. 130 E3
Clear Lake SD U.S.A. 130 D2
Clear Lake l. CA U.S.A. 128 B2
Clear Lake l. UT U.S.A. 129 G2
Clearmont U.S.A. 126 G3
Clearwater Canada 120 G5
Clearwater r. Alta/Sask. Canada 121 I3
Clearwater r. Alta Canada 120 H4
Clearwater U.S.A. 133 D7
Clearwater Lake Canada 121 K4
Clearwater Mountains U.S.A. 126 E3
Cleaton U.S.A. 134 B5
Cleburne U.S.A. 131 D5
Cleethorpes U.K. 48 G5
Clementi Sing. 71 [inset]
Clendenin U.S.A. 134 E4
Clendening Lake U.S.A. 134 E3
Clères France 52 B5
Clerf Lux. see Clervaux
Clerke Reef Australia 108 B4
Clermont Australia 110 D4
Clermont France 52 C5
Clermont-en-Argonne France 52 F5
Clermont-Ferrand France 56 F4
Clervaux Lux. 52 G4
Cles Italy 58 D1
Clevedon U.K. 49 E7
Cleveland MS U.S.A. 131 F5
Cleveland OH U.S.A. 134 E3
Cleveland TN U.S.A. 133 C5
Cleveland UT U.S.A. 129 H2
Cleveland WI U.S.A. 134 B2
Cleveland, Cape Australia 110 D3
Cleveland, Mount U.S.A. 126 E2
Cleveland Heights U.S.A. 134 E3
Cleveland Hills U.K. 48 F4
Cleveleys U.K. 48 D5
Cleves Germany see Kleve
Clew Bay Ireland 51 C4
Clifden Ireland 51 B4
Cliff U.S.A. 129 I5
Cliffoney Ireland 51 D3
Clifton Australia 112 E1
Clifton U.S.A. 129 I5
Clifton Beach Australia 110 D3
Clifton Forge U.S.A. 134 F5
Clifton Park U.S.A. 135 I2
Climax Canada 121 I5
Climax U.S.A. 134 C2
Clinch Mountain mts U.S.A. 134 D5
Cline River Canada 120 G4
Clinton B.C. Canada 120 F5
Clinton Ont. Canada 134 E2
Clinton IA U.S.A. 130 F3
Clinton IL U.S.A. 130 F3
Clinton IN U.S.A. 134 B4
Clinton KY U.S.A. 131 F4
Clinton MI U.S.A. 134 D2
Clinton MO U.S.A. 130 E4
Clinton MS U.S.A. 131 F5
Clinton NC U.S.A. 133 E5
Clinton NJ U.S.A. 135 H3
Clinton OK U.S.A. 131 D5
Clinton-Colden Lake Canada 121 J1
Clintwood U.S.A. 134 D5

▶Clipperton, Île terr. N. Pacific Ocean 151 M5
Part of France. Most easterly point of Oceania.

Clisham hill U.K. 50 C3
Clitheroe U.K. 48 E5
Clive Lake Canada 120 G2
Cliza Bol. 142 E7
Clocolan S. Africa 101 H5
Cloghan Ireland 51 E4
Clonakilty Ireland 51 D6
Clonbern Ireland 51 D4
Cloncurry Australia 110 C4
Cloncurry r. Australia 110 C3
Clones Ireland 51 E3
Clonmel Ireland 51 E5
Clonygowan Ireland 51 E4
Cloonbannin Ireland 51 C5
Clooneagh Ireland 51 E4
Cloppenburg Germany 53 I2
Cloquet U.S.A. 130 E2
Cloquet r. U.S.A. 130 E2
Cloud Peak WY U.S.A. 124 F3
Cloud Peak WY U.S.A. 126 G3
Clova Canada 122 G4
Clover U.S.A. 129 G1
Cloverdale CA U.S.A. 128 B2
Cloverdale IN U.S.A. 134 B4
Cloverport U.S.A. 134 B5
Clovis CA U.S.A. 128 D3
Clovis NM U.S.A. 131 C5
Cloyne Canada 135 G1
Cluain Meala Ireland see Clonmel
Cluanie, Loch l. U.K. 50 D3
Cluff Lake Mine Canada 121 I3
Cluj-Napoca Romania 59 J1
Clun U.K. 49 D6
Clunes Australia 112 A6
Cluny Australia 110 B5
Cluses France 56 H3
Cluster Springs U.S.A. 135 F5
Clut Lake Canada 120 G1
Clutterbuck Head hd Canada 123 H1
Clutterbuck Hills hill Australia 109 D6
Clwydian Range hills U.K. 48 D5
Clyde Canada 120 H4
Clyde r. U.K. 50 E5
Clyde NY U.S.A. 135 G2
Clyde OH U.S.A. 134 D3
Clyde, Firth of est. U.K. 50 E5
Clydebank U.K. 50 E5
Clyde River Canada 119 L2
Côa r. Port. 57 C3
Coachella U.S.A. 128 E5
Coahuila state Mex. 131 C7
Coahuila de Zaragoza state Mex. see Coahuila
Coal r. Canada 120 E3
Coal City U.S.A. 134 A3
Coaldale (abandoned) U.S.A. 128 E2
Coalgate U.S.A. 131 D5
Coal Harbour Canada 120 E5
Coalinga U.S.A. 128 C3
Coalport U.S.A. 135 F3
Coal River Canada 120 E3
Coal Valley U.S.A. 129 F3
Coalville U.K. 49 F6
Coalville U.S.A. 129 H1
Coari Brazil 142 F4
Coari r. Brazil 142 F4
Coarsegold U.S.A. 128 D3
Coastal Plain U.S.A. 131 E6
Coast Mountains Canada 120 E4
Coast Range hills Australia 111 E5
Coast Ranges mts U.S.A. 128 B1
Coatbridge U.K. 50 E5
Coatesville U.S.A. 135 H4
Coaticook Canada 135 J1
Coats Island Canada 119 J3
Coats Land reg. Antarctica 152 A1
Coatzacoalcos Mex. 136 F5
Cobar Australia 112 B3
Cobargo Australia 112 D6
Cobden Australia 112 A7
Cobh Ireland 51 D6
Cobham r. Canada 121 M4
Cobija Bol. 142 E6
Coblenz Germany see Koblenz
Cobleskill U.S.A. 135 H2
Cobourg Peninsula Australia 108 F2
Cobra Australia 109 B6
Cobram Australia 112 B5
Coburg Germany 53 K4
Coburg Island Canada 119 K2
Coca Ecuador 142 C4
Coca Spain 57 D3
Cocalinho Brazil 145 A1
Cocanada India see Kakinada
Cochabamba Bol. 142 E7
Cochem Germany 53 H4
Cochin India see Kochi
Cochin reg. Vietnam 71 D5
Cochinos, Bahía de b. Cuba see Pigs, Bay of
Cochise U.S.A. 129 I5
Cochise Head mt. U.S.A. 129 I5
Cochrane Alta Canada 120 H5
Cochrane Ont. Canada 122 E4
Cochrane r. Canada 121 K3
Cockburn Australia 111 C7
Cockburnspath U.K. 50 G5
Cockburn Town Bahamas 133 F7
Cockburn Town Turks and Caicos Is see Grand Turk
Cockermouth U.K. 48 D4
Cocklebiddy Australia 109 D8
Cockscomb mt. S. Africa 100 G7
Coco r. Hond./Nicaragua 137 H6
Coco, Cayo i. Cuba 133 E8
Coco, Isla de i. N. Pacific Ocean 137 G7
Cocobeach Gabon 98 A3
Coco Channel India 71 A4
Cocomórachic Mex. 127 G7
Coconino Plateau U.S.A. 129 G4
Cocopara National Park Australia 112 C5
Cocos Brazil 145 B1

▶Cocos (Keeling) Islands terr. Indian Ocean 68 B9
Australian External Territory.

Cocos Basin sea feature Indian Ocean 149 O5
Cocos Ridge sea feature N. Pacific Ocean 151 O5
Cocuy, Sierra Nevada del mt. Col. 142 D2
Cod, Cape U.S.A. 135 J3
Codajás Brazil 142 F4
Coderre Canada 121 J5
Codfish Island N.Z. 113 A8
Codigoro Italy 58 E2
Cod Island Canada 123 J2
Codlea Romania 59 K2
Codó Brazil 143 J4
Codsall U.K. 49 E6
Cod's Head hd Ireland 51 B6
Cody U.S.A. 126 F3
Coeburn U.S.A. 134 D5
Coen Australia 110 C2
Coesfeld Germany 53 H3
Coeur d'Alene U.S.A. 126 D3
Coeur d'Alene Lake U.S.A. 126 D3
Coevorden Neth. 52 G2
Coffee Bay S. Africa 101 I6
Coffee Cultural Landscape of Colombia tourist site Col. 142 C2
Coffeyville U.S.A. 131 E4
Coffin Bay Australia 111 A7
Coffin Bay National Park Australia 111 A7
Coffs Harbour Australia 112 F3
Cofimvaba S. Africa 101 H7
Cognac France 56 D4
Cogo Equat. Guinea 96 D4
Coguno Moz. 101 L3
Cohoes U.S.A. 135 I2
Cohuna Australia 112 B5
Coiba, Isla de i. Panama 137 H7
Coigeach, Rubha pt U.K. 50 D2
Coihaique Chile 144 B7
Coimbatore India 84 C4
Coimbra Port. 57 B3
Coipasa, Salar de salt flat Bol. 142 E7
Coire Switz. see Chur
Colac Australia 112 A7
Colair Lake India see Kolleru Lake
Colatina Brazil 145 C2
Colbitz Germany 53 L2
Colborne Canada 135 G2
Colby U.S.A. 130 C4
Colchester U.K. 49 H7
Colchester U.S.A. 135 I3
Cold Bay U.S.A. 118 B4
Coldingham U.K. 50 G5
Colditz Germany 53 M3
Cold Lake Canada 121 I4
Cold Lake l. Canada 121 I4
Coldspring U.S.A. 131 E6
Coldstream Canada 120 G5
Coldstream U.K. 50 G5
Coldwater Canada 134 F1
Coldwater KS U.S.A. 131 D4
Coldwater MI U.S.A. 134 C3
Coldwater r. U.S.A. 131 F5
Coleambally Australia 112 B5
Colebrook U.S.A. 135 J1
Coleman r. Australia 110 C2
Coleman U.S.A. 131 D6
Çölemerik Turkey see Hakkâri
Colenso S. Africa 101 I5
Cole Peninsula Antarctica 152 L2
Coleraine Australia 111 C8
Coleraine U.K. 51 F2
Coles, Punta de pt Peru 142 D7
Coles Bay Australia 111 [inset]
Colesberg S. Africa 101 G6
Coleville Canada 121 I5
Colfax CA U.S.A. 128 C2
Colfax LA U.S.A. 131 E6
Colfax WA U.S.A. 126 D3
Colhué Huapí, Lago l. Arg. 144 C7
Coligny S. Africa 101 H4
Colima Mex. 136 D5
Colima, Nevado de vol. Mex. 136 D5

Coll *i.* U.K. 50 C4
Collado Villalba Spain 57 E3
Collarenebri Australia 112 D2
College Station U.S.A. 131 D6
Collerina Australia 112 C2
Collie *N.S.W.* Australia 112 D3
Collie *W.A.* Australia 109 B8
Collier Bay Australia 108 D4
Collier Range National Park Australia 109 B6
Collingwood Canada 134 E1
Collingwood N.Z. 113 D5
Collins U.S.A. 131 F6
Collins Glacier Antarctica 152 E2
Collinson Peninsula Canada 119 H2
Collipulli Chile 144 B5
Collmberg *hill* Germany 53 N3
Collooney Ireland 51 D3
Colmar France 56 H2
Colmenar Viejo Spain 57 E3
Colmonell U.K. 50 E5
Colne *r.* U.K. 49 H7
Cologne Germany 52 G4
Coloma U.S.A. 134 B2
Colomb-Béchar Alg. *see* Béchar
Colômbia Brazil 145 A3
Colombia Mex. 131 D7

► Colombia *country* S. America 142 D3
2nd most populous and 4th largest country in South America.

Colombian Basin *sea feature* S. Atlantic Ocean 148 C5

► Colombo Sri Lanka 84 C5
Former capital of Sri Lanka.

Colomiers France 56 E5
Colón *Buenos Aires* Arg. 144 D4
Colón *Entre Ríos* Arg. 144 E4
Colón Cuba 133 D8
Colón Panama 137 I7
Colón U.S.A. 134 C3
Colón, Archipiélago de *is* Ecuador *see* Galapagos Islands
Colona Australia 109 F7
Colonelganj India 83 E4
Colonel Hill Bahamas 133 F8
Colonet, Cabo *c.* Mex. 127 D7
Colônia *r.* Brazil 145 D1
Colonia Micronesia 69 J5
Colonia Agrippina Germany *see* Cologne
Colonia Díaz Mex. 127 F7
Colonia Julia Fenestris Italy *see* Fano
Colonial Heights U.S.A. 135 G5
Colonna, Capo *c.* Italy 58 G5
Colonsay *i.* U.K. 50 C4
Colorado *r.* Arg. 144 D5
Colorado *r.* Mex./U.S.A. 127 E7
Colorado *r.* U.S.A. 131 D6
Colorado *state* U.S.A. 126 G5
Colorado City *AZ* U.S.A. 129 G3
Colorado City *TX* U.S.A. 131 C5
Colorado Desert U.S.A. 128 C5
Colorado National Monument *nat. park* U.S.A. 129 I2
Colorado Plateau U.S.A. 129 I3
Colorado River Aqueduct *canal* U.S.A. 129 F4
Colorado Springs U.S.A. 126 G5
Colossae Turkey *see* Honaz
Colotlán Mex. 136 D4
Cölpin Germany 53 N1
Colquiri Bol. 142 E7
Colquitt U.S.A. 133 C6
Colson U.S.A. 134 D5
Colsterworth U.K. 49 G6
Colstrip U.S.A. 126 G3
Coltishall U.K. 49 I6
Colton *CA* U.S.A. 128 E4
Colton *NY* U.S.A. 135 H1
Colton (abandoned) U.S.A. 129 H2
Columbia *KY* U.S.A. 134 C5
Columbia *LA* U.S.A. 131 E5
Columbia *MD* U.S.A. 135 G4
Columbia *MO* U.S.A. 130 E4
Columbia *MS* U.S.A. 131 F6
Columbia *NC* U.S.A. 132 E5
Columbia *PA* U.S.A. 135 G3

► Columbia *SC* U.S.A. 133 D5
Capital of South Carolina.

Columbia *TN* U.S.A. 132 C5
Columbia *r.* U.S.A. 126 C3
Columbia, District of *admin. dist.* U.S.A. 135 G4
Columbia, Mount Canada 120 G4
Columbia, Sierra *mts* Mex. 127 E7
Columbia City U.S.A. 134 C3
Columbia Lake Canada 120 H5
Columbia Mountains Canada 120 F4
Columbia Plateau U.S.A. 126 D3
Columbine, Cape S. Africa 100 C7
Columbus *GA* U.S.A. 133 C5
Columbus *IN* U.S.A. 134 C4
Columbus *MS* U.S.A. 131 F5
Columbus *MT* U.S.A. 126 F3
Columbus *NC* U.S.A. 133 D5
Columbus *NM* U.S.A. 127 G7

► Columbus *OH* U.S.A. 134 D4
Capital of Ohio.

Columbus *TX* U.S.A. 131 D6
Columbus Grove U.S.A. 134 C3
Columbus Salt Marsh U.S.A. 128 D2
Colusa U.S.A. 128 B2
Colville N.Z. 113 E3
Colville U.S.A. 126 D2
Colville *r.* U.S.A. 118 C2
Colville Channel N.Z. 113 E3
Colville Lake Canada 118 F3
Colwyn Bay U.K. 48 D5
Comacchio Italy 58 E2
Comacchio, Valli di *lag.* Italy 58 E2
Comai China 83 G3
Comalcalco Mex. 136 F5
Comanche U.S.A. 131 D6

Comandante Ferraz *research station* Antarctica 152 A2
Comandante Salas Arg. 144 C4
Comăneşti Romania 59 L1
Combahee U.S.A. 133 D5
Combarbalá Chile 144 B4
Comber U.K. 51 G3
Combermere Bay Myanmar 70 A3
Combles France 52 C4
Combol *i.* Indon. 71 C7
Combomune Moz. 101 K2
Comboyne Australia 112 F3
Comencho, Lac *l.* Canada 122 G4
Comendador Dom. Rep. *see* Elías Piña
Comendador Gomes Brazil 145 A2
Comeragh Mountains *hills* Ireland 51 E5
Comercinho Brazil 145 C2
Cometela Moz. 101 L1
Comfort U.S.A. 131 D6
Comilla Bangl. 83 G5
Comines Belgium 52 C4
Comino, Capo *c.* Sardinia Italy 58 C4
Comitán de Domínguez Mex. 136 F5
Commack U.S.A. 135 I3
Commentry France 56 F3
Committee Bay Canada 119 J3
Commonwealth Territory *admin. div.* Australia *see* Jervis Bay Territory
Como Italy 58 C2
Como, Lago di Italy *see* Como, Lake
Como, Lake Italy 58 C2
Como Chamling *l.* China 83 G3
Comodoro Rivadavia Arg. 144 C7
Comoé, Parc National de la *nat. park* Côte d'Ivoire 96 C4
Comores *country* Africa *see* Comoros
Comorin, Cape India 84 C4
Comoro Islands *country* Africa *see* Comoros
Comoros *country* Africa 99 E5
Compiègne France 52 C5
Comprida, Ilha *i.* Brazil 145 B4
Comrat Moldova 59 M1
Comrie U.K. 50 F4
Comstock U.S.A. 131 C6
Côn, Sông *r.* Vietnam 71 E4
Cona China 83 G4

► Conakry Guinea 96 B4
Capital of Guinea.

Cona Niyeo Arg. 144 C6
Conceição *r.* Brazil 145 B2
Conceição da Barra Brazil 145 D2
Conceição do Araguaia Brazil 143 I5
Conceição do Mato Dentro Brazil 145 C2
Concepción Chile 144 B5
Concepción Mex. 131 B8
Concepción *Para.* 144 E2
Concepción, Punta *pt* Mex. 127 F8
Concepción de la Vega Dom. Rep. *see* La Vega
Conception, Point U.S.A. 128 C4
Conception Island Bahamas 133 F8
Conchas U.S.A. 127 G6
Conchas Lake U.S.A. 127 G6
Concho U.S.A. 129 I4
Conchos *r.* Chihuahua Mex. 131 B6
Conchos *r.* Nuevo León/Tamaulipas Mex. 131 D7
Concord *CA* U.S.A. 128 B3
Concord *NC* U.S.A. 133 D5

► Concord *NH* U.S.A. 135 J2
Capital of New Hampshire.

Concord *VT* U.S.A. 135 J1
Concordia *research station* Antarctica 152 G2
Concordia Arg. 144 E4
Concórdia Mex. 131 B8
Concordia Peru 142 D4
Concordia S. Africa 100 C5
Concordia *KS* U.S.A. 130 D4
Concordia *KY* U.S.A. 134 B4
Concord Peak Afgh. 89 I2
Con Cuông Vietnam 70 D3
Condamine Australia 112 E1
Condamine *r.* Australia 112 D1
Côn Đao Vietnam 71 D5
Condé-sur-Noireau France 49 F9
Condeúba Brazil 145 C1
Condobolin Australia 112 C4
Condom France 56 E5
Condon U.S.A. 126 C3
Cóndor, Cordillera del *mts* Ecuador/Peru 142 C4
Condroz *reg.* Belgium 52 E4
Conecuh *r.* U.S.A. 133 C6
Conegliano Italy 58 E2
Conejos Mex. 131 C7
Conejos U.S.A. 127 G5
Conemaugh *r.* U.S.A. 134 F3
Conestogo Lake Canada 134 E2
Conesus Lake U.S.A. 135 G2
Conflict Group *is* P.N.G. 110 E1
Confoederatio Helvetica *country* Europe *see* Switzerland
Confusion Range *mts* U.S.A. 129 G2
Congdü China 83 F3
Conghua China 77 G4
Congjiang China 77 F3
Congleton U.K. 48 E5
Congo *country* Africa 98 B4

► Congo *r.* Congo/Dem. Rep. Congo 98 B4
2nd longest river in Africa and 8th in the world.
Formerly known as Zaïre.

Congo (Brazzaville) *country* Africa *see* Congo
Congo (Kinshasa) *country* Africa *see* Congo, Democratic Republic of the

► Congo, Democratic Republic of the *country* Africa 98 C4
2nd largest and 4th most populous country in Africa.

Congo, Republic of *country* Africa *see* Congo
Congo Basin Dem. Rep. Congo 98 C4
Congo Cone *sea feature* S. Atlantic Ocean 148 I6
Congo Free State *country* Africa *see* Congo, Democratic Republic of the
Congonhas Brazil 145 C3
Congress U.S.A. 129 G4
Conimbla National Park Australia 112 D4
Coningsby U.K. 49 G5
Coniston Canada 122 E5
Coniston U.K. 48 D4
Conjuboy Australia 110 D3
Conklin Canada 121 I4
Conn *r.* Canada 122 F3
Conn, Lough *l.* Ireland 51 C3
Connacht *reg.* Ireland 51 C4
Connaught *reg.* Ireland *see* Connacht
Conneaut U.S.A. 134 E3
Connecticut *state* U.S.A. 135 I3
Connellsville U.S.A. 134 C4
Connemara *reg.* Ireland 51 C4
Connemara National Park Ireland 51 C4
Connersville U.S.A. 134 C4
Connolly, Mount Canada 120 C2
Connors Range *hills* Australia 110 E4
Conoble Australia 112 B4
Conquista Brazil 145 B2
Conrad U.S.A. 126 F2
Conrad Rise *sea feature* Southern Ocean 149 K9
Conroe U.S.A. 131 E6
Conselheiro Lafaiete Brazil 145 C3
Consett U.K. 48 F4
Consolación del Sur Cuba 133 D8
Côn Sơn, Đao *i.* Vietnam 71 D5
Consort Canada 121 I4
Constance Germany *see* Konstanz
Constance, Lake Germany/Switz. 47 L7
Constância dos Baetas Brazil 142 F5
Constância Germany *see* Konstanz
Constantia *tourist site* Cyprus *see* Salamis
Constantina Spain 57 D5
Constantine Alg. 54 F4
Constantine, Cape U.S.A. 118 C4
Constantinople Turkey *see* İstanbul
Constitución de 1857, Parque Nacional *nat. park* Mex. 129 F5
Consul Canada 121 I5
Contact U.S.A. 126 E4
Contamana Peru 142 C5
Contas *r.* Brazil 145 D1
Contay, Isla *i.* Mex. 133 C8
Contria Brazil 145 B2
Contwoyto Lake Canada 121 I1
Convención Col. 142 D2
Convent U.S.A. 131 F6
Conway *AR* U.S.A. 131 E5
Conway *ND* U.S.A. 130 D1
Conway *NH* U.S.A. 135 J2
Conway *SC* U.S.A. 133 E5
Conway, Cape Australia 110 E4
Conway, Lake *salt flat* Australia 111 A6
Conway National Park Australia 110 E4
Conway Reef Fiji *see* Ceva-i-Ra
Conwy U.K. 48 D5
Conwy *r.* U.K. 49 D5
Coober Pedy Australia 109 F7
Coochbehar India *see* Koch Bihar
Cooch Behar India *see* Koch Bihar
Cook Australia 109 E7
Cook, Cape Canada 120 E5
Cook, Grand Récif de *reef* New Caledonia 107 G3
Cook, Mount N.Z. *see* Aoraki/Mount Cook
Cookes Peak U.S.A. 127 G6
Cookeville U.S.A. 132 C4
Cookhouse S. Africa 101 G7
Cook Ice Shelf Antarctica 152 H2
Cook Inlet *sea chan.* U.S.A. 118 C3

► Cook Islands *terr.* S. Pacific Ocean 150 J7
Self-governing New Zealand overseas territory.

Cooksburg U.S.A. 135 H2
Cooks Passage Australia 110 D2
Cookstown U.K. 51 F3
Cooktown Australia 110 D2
Coolabah Australia 112 C3
Cooladdi Australia 112 B1
Coolah Australia 112 D3
Coolamon Australia 112 C5
Coolgardie Australia 109 C7
Coolibah Australia 108 E3
Coolidge U.S.A. 129 H5
Coolum Beach Australia 111 F5
Cooma Australia 112 D6
Coombah Australia 111 C7
Coonabarabran Australia 112 D3
Coonamble Australia 112 D3
Coondambo Australia 111 A6
Coondapoor India *see* Kundapura
Coongoola Australia 112 B1
Coonoor India 84 C4
Coopracambra National Park Australia 112 D6
Coorabie Australia 109 F7
Coorong National Park Australia 111 B8
Coorow Australia 109 B7
Coosa *r.* U.S.A. 133 C5
Coos Bay U.S.A. 126 B4
Coos Bay *b.* U.S.A. 126 B4
Cootamundra Australia 112 D5
Cootehill Ireland 51 E3
Cooyar Australia 112 E1
Copala Mex. 136 E5
Cope U.S.A. 130 C4
Copemish U.S.A. 134 C1

Çorovodë Albania 59 I4
Corowa Australia 112 C5
Corpus Christi U.S.A. 131 D7
Corque Bol. 142 E7

► Copenhagen Denmark 45 H9
Capital of Denmark.

Copenhagen U.S.A. 135 H2
Copertino Italy 58 H4
Cô Pi, Phou *mt.* Laos/Vietnam 70 D3
Copiapó Chile 144 B3
Copley Australia 111 B6
Copparo Italy 58 D2
Copper Cliff Canada 122 E5
Copper Harbor U.S.A. 132 C2
Coppermine Canada *see* Kugluktuk
Coppermine *r.* Canada 120 H1
Coppermine Point Canada 122 D5
Copperton S. Africa 100 F5
Copp Lake Canada 120 H2
Coquihatville Dem. Rep. Congo *see* Mbandaka
Coquille *i.* Micronesia *see* Pikelot
Coquille U.S.A. 126 B4
Coquimbo Chile 144 B3
Coquitlam Canada 120 F5
Corabia Romania 59 K3
Coração de Jesus Brazil 145 B2
Coracesium Turkey *see* Alanya
Coraki Australia 112 F2
Coral Bay Australia 109 A5
Coral Harbour Canada 119 J3
Coral Sea S. Pacific Ocean 106 F3
Coral Sea Basin S. Pacific Ocean 150 E4

► Coral Sea Islands Territory *terr.* Australia 106 F3
Australian External Territory.

Corangamite, Lake Australia 112 A7
Corat Azer. 91 H2
Corbeny France 52 D5
Corbett Inlet Canada 121 M2
Corbett National Park India 82 D3
Corbie France 52 C5
Corbin U.S.A. 134 C5
Corby U.K. 49 G6
Corcaigh Ireland *see* Cork
Corcoran U.S.A. 128 D3
Corcovado, Golfo de *sea chan.* Chile 144 B6
Corcyra *i.* Greece *see* Corfu
Cordele U.S.A. 133 D6
Cordelia U.S.A. 128 B2
Cordell U.S.A. 131 D5
Cordilheiras, Serra das *hills* Brazil 143 I5
Cordillera Azul, Parque Nacional *nat. park* Peru 142 C5
Cordillera de los Picachos, Parque Nacional *nat. park* Col. 142 D3
Cordillo Downs Australia 111 C5
Cordisburgo Brazil 145 B2
Córdoba *Durango* Mex. 131 C7
Córdoba *Veracruz* Mex. 136 E5
Córdoba Spain 57 D5
Córdoba, Sierras de *mts* Arg. 144 D4
Cordova Spain *see* Córdoba
Cordova U.S.A. 118 D3
Corduba Spain *see* Córdoba
Corfu *i.* Greece 59 H5
Coria Spain 57 C4
Coribe Brazil 145 B1
Coricudgy *mt.* Australia 112 E4
Corigliano Calabro Italy 58 G5
Coringa Islands Australia 110 E3
Corinium U.K. *see* Cirencester
Corinth Greece 59 J6
Corinth *KY* U.S.A. 134 C4
Corinth *MS* U.S.A. 131 F5
Corinth *NY* U.S.A. 135 I2
Corinth, Gulf of *sea chan.* Greece 59 J5
Corinthus Greece *see* Corinth
Corinto Brazil 145 B2
Cork Ireland 51 D6
Corleone Sicily Italy 58 E6
Çorlu Turkey 59 L4
Cormeilles France 49 H9
Cornelia S. Africa 101 I4
Cornélio Procópio Brazil 145 A3
Cornélios Brazil 145 A5
Cornell U.S.A. 130 F2
Corner Brook Canada 123 K4
Corner Inlet *b.* Australia 112 C7
Corner Seamounts *sea feature* N. Atlantic Ocean 148 E3
Corneto Italy *see* Tarquinia
Cornillet, Mont *hill* France 52 E5
Corning *AR* U.S.A. 131 F4
Corning *CA* U.S.A. 128 B1
Corning *NY* U.S.A. 135 G2
Cornish *watercourse* Australia 110 D4
Corn Islands *is* Nicaragua *see* Maíz, Islas del
Corno di Campo *mt.* Italy/Switz. 56 J3
Corno Grande *mt.* Italy 58 E3
Cornwall Canada 135 H1
Cornwallis Island Canada 119 I2
Cornwall Island Canada 119 I2
Coro Venez. 142 E1
Coroaci Brazil 145 C2
Coroatá Brazil 143 J4
Corofin Ireland 51 C5
Coromandel Brazil 145 B2
Coromandel Coast India 84 D4
Coromandel Peninsula N.Z. 113 E3
Coromandel Range *hills* N.Z. 113 E3
Corona U.S.A. 128 E5
Corona *NM* U.S.A. 127 G6
Coronado U.S.A. 128 E5
Coronado, Bahía de *b.* Costa Rica 137 H7
Coronation U.S.A. 118 D3
Coronation Gulf Canada 118 G3
Coronation Island S. Atlantic Ocean 152 A2
Coronda Arg. 144 D4
Coronel Chile 144 B5
Coronel Fabriciano Brazil 145 C2
Coronel Oviedo Para. 144 E3
Coronel Pringles Arg. 144 D5
Coronel Suárez Arg. 144 D5
Coropuna, Nudo *mt.* Peru 142 D7

Couture, Lac *l.* Canada 122 G2
Couvin Belgium 52 E4
Cove Fort U.S.A. 129 G2
Cove Island Canada 134 E1
Cove Mountains *hills* U.S.A. 135 F4
Coventry U.K. 49 F6
Covesville U.S.A. 135 F5
Covilhã Port. 57 C3
Covington *GA* U.S.A. 133 D5
Covington *IN* U.S.A. 134 B3
Covington *KY* U.S.A. 134 C4
Covington *LA* U.S.A. 131 F6
Covington *MI* U.S.A. 130 F2
Covington *TN* U.S.A. 131 F5
Covington *VA* U.S.A. 134 E5
Cowal, Lake *dry lake* Australia 112 C4
Cowan, Lake *salt flat* Australia 109 C7
Cowansville Canada 135 I1
Cowargarzê China 76 C1
Cowcowing Lakes *salt flat* Australia 109 B7
Cowdenbeath U.K. 50 F4
Cowell Australia 111 B7
Cowes U.K. 49 F8
Cowichan Lake Canada 120 E5
Cowley Australia 112 B1
Cowper Point Canada 119 G2
Cowra Australia 112 D4
Cox *r.* Australia 110 A2
Coxá *r.* Brazil 145 B1
Coxen Hole Hond. *see* Roatán
Coxilha de Santana *hills* Brazil/Uruguay 144 E4
Coxilha Grande *hills* Brazil 144 F3
Coxim Brazil 143 H7
Cox's Bazar Bangl. 83 G5
Coyame Mex. 131 B6
Coyhaique Chile *see* Coihaique
Coyote Lake U.S.A. 128 E4
Coyote Peak *hill* U.S.A. 129 F5
Cozhê *Xizang* China 83 F3
Cozhê *Xizang* China 83 F3
Cozie, Alpi *mts* France/Italy *see* Cottian Alps
Cozumel Mex. 137 G4
Cozumel, Isla de *i.* Mex. 137 G4
Craboon Australia 112 D4
Cracovia Poland *see* Kraków
Cracow Australia 110 E5
Cracow Poland *see* Kraków
Cradle Mountain Lake St Clair National Park Australia 111 [inset]
Cradock S. Africa 101 G7
Craig U.K. 50 D3
Craig *AK* U.S.A. 120 C4
Craig *CO* U.S.A. 129 J1
Craigavon U.K. 51 F3
Craigieburn Australia 112 B6
Craig Island Taiwan *see* Mianhua Yu
Craignure U.K. 50 D4
Craigsville U.S.A. 134 E4
Crail U.K. 50 G4
Crailsheim Germany 53 K5
Cranberry Lake U.S.A. 135 H1
Cranberry Portage Canada 121 K4
Cranborne Chase *for.* U.K. 49 E8
Cranbourne Australia 112 B7
Cranbrook Canada 120 H5
Crandon U.S.A. 130 F2
Crane Lake Canada 121 I5
Cranston *NC* U.S.A. 134 D4
Cranston *RI* U.S.A. 135 J3
Cranz Russia *see* Zelenogradsk
Crary Ice Rise Antarctica 152 I1
Crary Mountains Antarctica 152 J1
Crater Lake National Park U.S.A. 126 C4
Crater Peak U.S.A. 128 C1
Craters of the Moon National Monument *nat. park* U.S.A. 126 E4
Crateús Brazil 143 J5
Crato Brazil 143 K5
Crawford *CO* U.S.A. 129 J2
Crawford *NE* U.S.A. 130 C3
Crawfordsville U.S.A. 134 B3
Crawfordville *FL* U.S.A. 133 C6
Crawfordville *GA* U.S.A. 133 D5
Crawley U.K. 49 G7
Crazy Mountains U.S.A. 126 F3
Creag Meagaidh *mt.* U.K. 50 E4
Crécy-en-Ponthieu France 52 B4
Credenhill U.K. 49 E6
Crediton U.K. 49 D8
Cree *r.* Canada 121 J3
Creede U.S.A. 127 G5
Creel Mex. 127 G8
Cree Lake Canada 121 J3
Creemore Canada 134 E1
Creighton Canada 121 K4
Creil France 52 C5
Creil Neth. 52 F2
Crema Italy 58 C2
Cremlingen Germany 53 K2
Cremona Canada 120 H5
Cremona Italy 58 D2
Crépy-en-Valois France 52 C5
Cres *i.* Croatia 58 F2
Crescent U.S.A. 126 C4
Crescent City *CA* U.S.A. 126 B4
Crescent City *FL* U.S.A. 133 D6
Crescent Group *is* Paracel Is 68 E3
Crescent Head Australia 112 F3
Crescent Junction U.S.A. 129 I2
Crescent Valley U.S.A. 128 E1
Cressy Australia 112 A7
Crestline U.S.A. 134 D3
Creston Canada 120 G5
Creston *IA* U.S.A. 130 E3
Creston *WY* U.S.A. 126 G4
Crestview U.S.A. 133 C6
Creswick Australia 112 A6
Creta *i.* Greece *see* Crete
Crete *i.* Greece 59 K7
Crete U.S.A. 130 D3
Creus, Cap de *c.* Spain 57 H2
Creuse *r.* France 56 E3
Creußen Germany 53 L5
Creutzwald France 52 G5
Creuzburg Germany 53 K3
Crevasse Valley Glacier Antarctica 152 J1
Crewe U.K. 49 E5
Crewe U.S.A. 135 F5

Crewkerne U.K. 49 E8
Crianlarich U.K. 50 E4
Criccieth U.K. 49 C6
Criciúma Brazil 145 A5
Crieff U.K. 50 F4
Crifell hill U.K. see Criffel
Criffel hill U.K. 50 F6
Crikvenica Croatia 58 F2
Crillon, Mount U.S.A. 120 B3
Crimea disp. terr. Europe 55 K2
Crimmitschau Germany 53 M4
Crimond U.K. 50 H3
Crisfield U.S.A. 135 H5
Cristalândia Brazil 143 I6
Cristalina Brazil 145 B2
Cristalino r. Brazil see Mariembero
Cristóbal Colón, Pico mt. Col. 142 D1
Crixás Brazil 145 A1
Crixás Açu r. Brazil 145 A1
Crixás Mirim r. Brazil 145 A1
Crna Gora country Europe see Montenegro
Crni Vrh mt. Serbia 59 J2
Črnomelj Slovenia 58 F2
Croagh Patrick hill Ireland 51 C4
Croajingolong National Park Australia 112 D6
Croatia country Europe 58 G2
Crocker, Banjaran mts Malaysia 68 E6
Crockett U.S.A. 131 E6
Crofton KY U.S.A. 134 B5
Crofton NE U.S.A. 130 D3
Croghan U.S.A. 135 H2
Croisilles France 52 C4
Croker, Cape Canada 134 E1
Croker Island Australia 108 F2
Cromarty U.K. 50 E3
Cromarty Firth est. U.K. 50 E3
Cromer U.K. 49 I6
Crook U.K. 48 F4
Crooked Harbour b. H.K. China 77 [inset]
Crooked Island Bahamas 133 F8
Crooked Island H.K. China 77 [inset]
Crooked Island Passage Bahamas 133 F8
Crookston U.S.A. 130 D2
Crooksville U.S.A. 134 D4
Crookwell Australia 112 D5
Croom Ireland 51 D5
Croppa Creek Australia 112 E2
Crosby U.K. 48 D5
Crosby MN U.S.A. 130 E2
Crosby ND U.S.A. 130 C1
Crosbyton U.S.A. 131 C5
Cross Bay Canada 121 M2
Cross City U.S.A. 133 D6
Cross Fell hill U.K. 48 E4
Crossfield Canada 120 H5
Crossgar U.K. 51 G3
Crosshaven Ireland 51 D6
Cross Inn U.K. 49 C6
Cross Lake Canada 121 L4
Cross Lake l. Canada 121 L4
Cross Lake l. U.S.A. 135 G2
Crossmaglen U.K. 51 F3
Crossman Peak U.S.A. 129 F4
Crossville U.S.A. 132 C5
Crotch Lake Canada 135 G1
Croton Italy see Crotone
Crotone Italy 58 G5
Crouch r. U.K. 49 H7
Crow r. Canada 120 E3
Crow Agency U.S.A. 126 G3
Crowal watercourse Australia 112 C3
Crowborough U.K. 49 H7
Crowdy Bay National Park Australia 112 F3
Crowell U.S.A. 131 D5
Crowland U.K. 49 G6
Crowley U.S.A. 131 E6
Crowley, Lake U.S.A. 128 D3
Crown Point IN U.S.A. 134 B3
Crownpoint U.S.A. 129 I4
Crown Point NY U.S.A. 135 I2
Crown Prince Olav Coast Antarctica 152 D2
Crown Princess Martha Coast Antarctica 152 B1
Crows Nest Australia 112 F1
Crowsnest Pass Canada 120 H5
Crowsnest Pass pass Canada 120 H5
Crow Wing r. U.S.A. 130 E2
Croydon Australia 110 C3
Crozet U.S.A. 135 F4
Crozet, Îles is Indian Ocean 149 L9
Crozet Basin sea feature Indian Ocean 149 M8
Crozet Plateau sea feature Indian Ocean 149 K8
Crozon France 56 B2
Cruces Cuba 133 D8
Cruden Bay U.K. 50 H3
Cruillas Mex. 131 D7
Crum U.S.A. 134 D5
Crumlin U.K. 51 F3
Crusheen Ireland 51 D5
Cruz Alta Brazil 144 F3
Cruz del Eje Arg. 144 D4
Cruzeiro Brazil 145 B3
Cruzeiro do Sul Brazil 142 D5
Cry Lake Canada 120 D3
Crysdale, Mount Canada 120 F4
Crystal U.S.A. 129 I3
Crystal City Canada 121 L5
Crystal City U.S.A. 131 D6
Crystal Falls U.S.A. 130 F2
Crystal Lake U.S.A. 134 A2
Crystal River U.S.A. 133 D6
Csongrád Hungary 59 I1
Cưa Lớn, Sông r. Vietnam 71 D5
Cuamba Moz. 99 D5
Cuando r. Angola/Zambia 99 C5
Cuangar Angola 99 B5
Cuango Angola 99 B4
Cuanza r. Angola 99 B4
Cuatro Ciénegas Mex. 131 C7
Cuauhtémoc Mex. 127 G7
Cuba NM U.S.A. 127 G5
Cuba NY U.S.A. 135 F2

▶Cuba country West Indies 137 H4
5th largest island and 5th most populous country in North America.

Cubal Angola 99 B5
Cubango r. Angola/Namibia 99 C5
Cubatão Brazil 145 B3
Cub Hills Canada 121 J4
Çubuk Turkey 90 D2
Cucapa, Sierra mts Mex. 129 F5
Cuchi Angola 99 B5
Cuchilla Grande hills Uruguay 144 E4
Cucuí Brazil 142 E3
Cucurpe Mex. 127 F7
Cúcuta Col. 142 D2
Cudal Australia 112 D4
Cuddalore India 84 C4
Cuddapah India see Kadapa
Cuddeback Lake U.S.A. 128 E4
Cue Australia 109 B6
Cuéllar Spain 57 D3
Cuemba Angola 99 B5
Cuenca Ecuador 142 C4
Cuenca Spain 57 E3
Cuenca, Serranía de mts Spain 57 E3
Cuencamé Mex. 131 C7
Cuernavaca Mex. 136 E5
Cuero U.S.A. 131 D6
Cuervos Mex. 129 F5
Cugir Romania 59 J2
Cuiabá Amazonas Brazil 143 G5
Cuiabá Mato Grosso Brazil 143 G7
Cuiabá r. Brazil 143 G7
Cuihua China see Daguan
Cuijiang China see Ninghua
Cuijk Neth. 52 F3
Cuilcagh hill Ireland/U.K. 51 E3
Cuillin Hills U.K. 50 C3
Cuillin Sound sea chan. U.K. 50 C3
Cuilo Angola 99 B4
Cuiluan China 74 C3
Cuité r. Brazil 145 C2
Cuito r. Angola 99 C5
Cuito Cuanavale Angola 99 B5
Cukai Malaysia 71 C6
Çukurca Turkey 88 A2
Çukurova plat. Turkey 85 B1
Culcairn Australia 112 C5
Culebra, Sierra de la mts Spain 57 C3
Culfa Azer. 91 G3
Culgoa r. Australia 112 C2
Culiacán Mex. 136 C4
Culiacán Rosales Mex. see Culiacán
Culion Phil. 69 F4
Culion i. Phil. 68 F4
Cullen U.K. 50 G3
Cullen Point Australia 110 C1
Cullera Spain 57 F4
Cullivoe U.K. 50 [inset]
Cullman U.S.A. 133 C5
Cullybackey U.K. 51 F3
Cul Mòr hill U.K. 50 D2
Culpeper U.S.A. 135 G4
Cultural Landscape of the Serra de Tramuntana tourist site Spain 57 H4
Cultural Sites of Al Ain tourist site U.A.E. 87 I5
Culuene r. Brazil 143 H6
Culver, Point Australia 109 D8
Culverden N.Z. 113 D6
Cumaná Venez. 142 F1
Cumari Brazil 145 A2
Cumbal, Nevado de vol. Col. 142 C3
Cumberland KY U.S.A. 134 D5
Cumberland MD U.S.A. 135 F4
Cumberland VA U.S.A. 135 F5
Cumberland r. U.S.A. 132 C4
Cumberland, Lake U.S.A. 134 C5
Cumberland Lake Canada 121 K4
Cumberland Mountains U.S.A. 134 D5
Cumberland Peninsula Canada 119 L3
Cumberland Plateau U.S.A. 132 C5
Cumberland Point U.S.A. 130 F2
Cumberland Sound sea chan. Canada 119 L3
Cumbernauld U.K. 50 F5
Cumbres de Majalca, Parque Nacional nat. park Mex. 127 G7
Cumbres de Monterey, Parque Nacional nat. park Mex. 131 C7
Cumbum India 84 C3
Cumlosen Germany 53 L1
Cummings U.S.A. 128 B2
Cummins Australia 111 A7
Cummins Range hills Australia 108 D4
Cumnock Australia 112 D4
Cumnock U.K. 50 E5
Çumra Turkey 90 D3
Cumuruxatiba Brazil 145 D2
Cunagua Cuba see Bolivia
Cunderdin Australia 109 B7
Cunene r. Angola 99 B5
also known as Kunene
Cuneo Italy 58 B2
Cung Sơn Vietnam 71 E4
Cunnamulla Australia 112 B2
Cunningsburgh U.K. 50 [inset]
Cupar U.K. 50 F4
Cupica, Golfo de b. Col. 142 C2
Curaçá Brazil 143 K5
Curaçá r. Brazil 142 D4

▶Curaçao terr. West Indies 137 K6
Self-governing Netherlands territory.

Curaray r. Ecuador 142 D4
Curdlawidny Lagoon salt flat Australia 111 B6
Curia Switz. see Chur
Curicó Chile 144 B4
Curitiba Brazil 145 A4
Curitibanos Brazil 145 A4
Curlewis Australia 112 E3
Curnamona Australia 111 B6
Currabubula Australia 112 E3
Currais Novos Brazil 143 K5
Curran U.S.A. 134 D1
Currane, Lough l. Ireland 51 B6
Currant U.S.A. 129 F2
Curranyalpa Australia 112 B3
Currawilla Australia 110 C5
Currawinya National Park Australia 112 B2
Currie Australia 106 E5
Currie U.S.A. 129 F1
Currituck U.S.A. 135 G5
Currockbilly, Mount Australia 112 E5
Curtis Channel Australia 110 F5
Curtis Island Australia 110 E4
Curtis Island N.Z. 107 I5
Curuá r. Brazil 143 H5
Curup Indon. 68 C7
Curupira, Serra mts Brazil/Venez. 142 F3
Cururupu Brazil 143 J4
Curvelo Brazil 145 B2
Curwood, Mount hill U.S.A. 130 F2
Cusco Peru 142 D6
Cushendall U.K. 51 F2
Cushendun U.K. 51 F2
Cushing U.S.A. 131 D4
Cusseta U.S.A. 133 C5
Custer MT U.S.A. 126 G3
Custer SD U.S.A. 130 C3
Cut Bank U.S.A. 126 E2
Cuthbert U.S.A. 133 C6
Cuthbertson Falls Australia 108 F3
Cut Knife Canada 121 I4
Cutler Ridge U.S.A. 133 D7
Cuttaburra Creek r. Australia 112 B2
Cuttack India 84 E1
Cuvelai Angola 99 B5
Cuxhaven Germany 47 L4
Cuya Chile 142 D7
Cuyahoga Falls U.S.A. 134 E3
Cuyama U.S.A. 128 D4
Cuyama r. U.S.A. 128 C4
Cuyo Islands Phil. 69 G4
Cuyuni r. Guyana 143 G2
Cuzco Peru see Cusco
Cwmbrân U.K. 49 D7
Cyangugu Rwanda 98 C4
Cyclades is Greece 59 K6
Cydonia Greece see Chania
Cygnet U.S.A. 134 D3
Cymru admin. div. U.K. see Wales
Cynthiana U.S.A. 134 C4
Cypress Hills Canada 121 I5
Cyprus country Asia 85 A2
Cyrenaica hist. area Libya 97 F2
Cythera i. Greece see Kythira
Czar Canada 121 I4
Czechia country Europe 47 O6

▶Czechoslovakia
Divided in 1993 into the Czech Republic and Slovakia.

Czech Republic country see Czechia
Czernowitz Ukr. see Chernivtsi
Czersk Poland 47 P4
Częstochowa Poland 47 Q5

D

Đa, Sông r. Vietnam see Black
Da'an China 74 B3
Ḍabāb, Jabal aḍ mt. Jordan 85 B4
Dabakala Côte d'Ivoire 96 C4
Daban China 73 L4
Dabao China 76 D2
Daba Shan mts China 77 F1
Dabba China see Daocheng
Dabein Myanmar 70 B3
Dabhoi India 82 C5
Ḍab'ī, Wādī aḍ watercourse Jordan 85 C4
Dabie Shan mts China 77 G2
Dablana India 82 C4
Dabola Guinea 96 B3
Dabqig China 73 J5
Dąbrowa Górnicza Poland 47 Q5
Dabs Nur l. China 74 A3
Dabu Guangdong China 77 H3
Dabu Guangxi China see Liucheng
Dabusu Pao l. China see Dabs Nur
Dacca Bangl. see Dhaka
Dachau Germany 47 M6
Dachuan China see Dazhou
Dacre Canada 135 G1
Dadaab Kenya 98 E3
Daday Turkey 90 D2
Dade City U.S.A. 133 D6
Dadeville U.S.A. 133 C5
Dādkān Iran 89 F5
Dadohae Haesang National Park S. Korea 75 B6
Dadong China see Donggang
Dadra India see Achalpur
Dadu Pak. 89 G5
Daecheong-do i. S. Korea 75 B5
Daegu S. Korea 75 C6
Daeheuksan-gundo is S. Korea 75 B6
Daejeon S. Korea 75 B5
Daejeong S. Korea 75 B6
Daet Phil. 69 G4
Dafang China 76 E3
Dafeng China 77 I1
Dafla Hills India 83 H4
Dafoe Canada 121 J5
Dafoe r. Canada 121 M4
Dagana Senegal 96 B3
Dagcagoin China see Zoigê
Dagcanglhamo China see Langmusi
Daghmar Oman 88 E6
Dağlıq Qarabağ disp. terr. Azer. see Nagorno-Karabakh
Daglung China 83 G3
Dagö i. Estonia see Hiiumaa
Dagon Myanmar see Rangoon
Daguan China 76 D3
Daguokui Shan hill China 74 C3
Dagupan Phil. 69 G3
Dagxoi Sichuan China see Sowa
Dagxoi Sichuan China see Yidun
Dagzê China 83 G3
Dagzê Co salt l. China 83 F3
Dahadinni r. Canada 120 E2
Dahalach, Isole is Eritrea see Dahlak Archipelago
Dahana des. Saudi Arabia see Ad Dahnā'
Dahe Guangxi China see Ziyuan
Dahe Heilong. China 74 D3
Daheiding Shan mt. China 74 C3
Dahei Shan mts China 74 B4
Dahej India 82 C5
Da Hinggan Ling mts China 74 A2
Dahl, Nafūd ad des. Saudi Arabia 88 B6
Dahlak Archipelago is Eritrea 86 F6
Dahlak Marine National Park Eritrea 86 F6
Dahl al Furayy well Saudi Arabia 88 B5
Dahlem Germany 52 G4
Dahlenburg Germany 53 K1
Dahm, Ramlat des. Saudi Arabia/Yemen 86 G6
Dahmani Tunisia 58 C7
Dahme/Mark Germany 53 N3
Dahn Germany 53 H5
Dahnā' plain Saudi Arabia 88 B5
Dahod India 82 C5
Dahomey country Africa see Benin
Dahongliutan China 82 D2
Dahra Senegal see Dara
Dähre Germany 53 K2
Dahūk/Dihok Iraq 91 F3
Dai i. Indon. 108 E1
Daik Indon. 68 C7
Daik-U Myanmar 70 B3
Đai Lanh, Mui pt Vietnam 71 E4
Dailekh Nepal 83 E3
Dailly U.K. 50 E5
Daimiel Spain 57 E4
Daingean Uí Chúis Ireland 51 B5
Dainkognubma China 76 C1
Daintree National Park Australia 110 D3
Dair, Jebel ed mt. Sudan 86 D7
Dairen China see Dalian
Dai-sen vol. Japan 75 D6
Daisetsu-zan Kokuritsu-kōen nat. park Japan 74 F4
Daishan China 77 I2
Daiyun Shan mts China 77 H3
Dajarra Australia 110 B4
Dajin Chuan r. China 76 D2
Da Juh China 83 H1

▶Dakar Senegal 96 B3
Capital of Senegal.

Dākhilah, Wāḥāt ad oasis Egypt 86 C4
Dakhla W. Sahara 96 B2
Dakhla Oasis oasis Egypt see Dākhilah, Wāḥāt ad
Đắk Lắk, Cao Nguyên plat. Vietnam 71 E4
Dakoank India 71 A6
Dakol'ka r. Belarus 43 F5
Dakor India 82 C5
Dakoro Niger 96 D3
Dakota City IA U.S.A. 130 E3
Dakota City NE U.S.A. 130 D3
Đakovica Kosovo see Gjakovë
Đakovo Croatia 58 H2
Daktuy Russia 74 B1
Dala Angola 99 C5
Dalaba Guinea 96 B3
Dalai China see Da'an
Dalain Hob China 80 J3
Dalākī Iran 88 C4
Dalälven r. Sweden 45 J6
Dalaman Turkey 59 M6
Dalandzadgad Mongolia 72 I4
Dalap-Uliga-Darrit Marshall Is see Delap-Uliga-Djarrit
Đa Lat Vietnam 71 E5
Dalatando Angola see N'dalatando
Dalaud India 82 C5
Dalauda India 82 C5
Dalbandin Pak. 89 G4
Dalbeattie U.K. 50 F6
Dalbeg Australia 110 D4
Dalby Australia 112 E1
Dalby Isle of Man 48 C4
Dale Hordaland Norway 45 D6
Dale Sogn og Fjordane Norway 45 D6
Dale City U.S.A. 135 G4
Dale Hollow Lake U.S.A. 134 C5
Dalen Neth. 52 G2
Dalet Myanmar 70 A3
Daletme Myanmar 70 A2
Dalfors Sweden 45 I6
Dalgān Iran 88 E5
Dalgety Australia 112 D6
Dalgety r. Australia 109 A6
Dalhart U.S.A. 131 C4
Dalhousie Canada 123 I4
Dalhousie, Cape Canada 118 F2
Dali Shaanxi China 77 F1
Dali Yunnan China 76 D3
Dalian China 73 M5
Daliang China see Shunde
Daliang Shan mts China 76 D2
Dalin China 74 A4
Dalizi China 74 B4
Dalkeith U.K. 50 F5
Dallas OR U.S.A. 126 C3
Dallas TX U.S.A. 131 D5
Dalles City U.S.A. see The Dalles
Dall Island U.S.A. 120 C4
Dalmā i. U.A.E. 88 D5
Dalmacija reg. Bos. & Herz./Croatia see Dalmatia
Dalmas, Lac l. Canada 123 H3
Dalmatia reg. Bos. & Herz./Croatia 78 A2
Dalmau India 82 E4
Dalmellington U.K. 50 E5
Dalmeny Canada 121 J4
Dalmi India 83 F5
Dal'negorsk Russia 74 D3
Dal'nerechensk Russia 74 D3
Dal'niye Zelentsy Russia 42 H1
Dalny China see Dalian
Daloa Côte d'Ivoire 96 C4

▶Dalol (abandoned) Eth. 86 F7
Highest recorded annual mean temperature in the world.

Daloloia Group is P.N.G. 110 E1
Dalou Shan mts China 76 E3
Dalqān well Saudi Arabia 88 B5
Dalry U.K. 50 E5
Dalrymple U.K. 50 E5
Dalrymple, Lake Australia 110 D4
Daltenganj India see Daltonganj
Dalton Canada 122 D4
Dalton S. Africa 101 J5
Dalton GA U.S.A. 133 C5
Dalton MA U.S.A. 135 I2
Dalton PA U.S.A. 135 H3
Daltonganj India 83 F4
Dalton-in-Furness U.K. 48 D4
Daludalu Indon. 71 C7
Daluo China 76 D4
Daly r. Australia 108 E3
Daly City U.S.A. 128 B3
Daly River Australia 108 E3
Daly Waters Australia 108 F4
Damagaram Takaya Niger 96 D3
Daman India 84 B1
Daman and Diu union terr. India 84 A1
Damanhūr Egypt 90 C5
Damanhûr Egypt see Damanhūr
Damant Lake Canada 121 J2
Damão India see Daman
Damar i. Indon. 108 E1
Damara Cent. Afr. Rep. 98 B3
Damaraland reg. Namibia 99 B6
Damas Syria see Damascus

▶Damascus Syria 85 C3
Capital of Syria.

Damascus U.S.A. 134 E5
Damaturu Nigeria 96 E3
Damāvand Iran 88 D3
Damāvand, Qolleh-ye mt. Iran 88 D3
Dambulla Sri Lanka 84 D5
Damdy Kazakh. 80 B1
Dāmghān Iran 88 D2
Damianópolis Brazil 145 B1
Damietta Egypt see Dumyāṭ
Daming Shan mt. China 77 F4
Dāmiyā Jordan 85 B3
Damjong China 76 B1
Damlasu Turkey 85 D1
Dammam Saudi Arabia 86 H4
Damme Belgium 52 D3
Damme Germany 53 I2
Damoh India 82 D5
Damour Lebanon 85 B3
Dampar, Tasik l. Malaysia 71 C7
Dampier Archipelago is Australia 108 B5
Dampier Island P.N.G. see Karkar Island
Dampier Land reg. Australia 108 C4
Dampier Strait P.N.G. 69 L8
Dampir, Selat sea chan. Indon. 69 I7
Damqoq Zangbo r. China 83 F3
Dam Qu r. China 76 B1
Dâmrei, Chuŏr Phnum mts Cambodia 71 D5
Damroh India 76 B2
Damwâld Neth. 52 G1
Damwoude Neth. see Damwâld
Damxoi China see Comai
Damxung China see Gongtang
Ḍānā Jordan 85 B4
Dana Nepal 83 E3
Danakil reg. Africa 98 E2
Danané Côte d'Ivoire 96 C4
Đa Năng Vietnam 70 E3
Đa Năng, Vung b. Vietnam 70 E3
Danao Phil. 69 G4
Danata Turkm. 88 D2
Danba China 76 D2
Danbury CT U.S.A. 135 I3
Danbury NC U.S.A. 132 D4
Danby U.S.A. 135 I2
Danby Lake U.S.A. 129 F4
Dandaragan Australia 109 A7
Dande Eth. 98 D3
Dandeldhura Nepal 82 E3
Dandeli India 84 B3
Dandong China 75 B4
Dandot Pak. 89 I3
Dandridge U.S.A. 132 D4
Dane r. U.K. 48 E5
Daneborg Greenland 153 I2
Danese U.S.A. 134 E5
Danfeng China see Shizong
Dangan Liedao i. China 77 G4
Dangara Tajik. see Danghara
Dangbi China 74 C3
Dangchang China 76 E1
Dangchengwan China see Subei
Danger Islands atoll Cook Is see Pukapuka
Danger Point S. Africa 100 D8
Danghara Tajik. 89 H2
Danghe Nanshan mts China 80 H4
Dang La pass China see Tanggula Shankou
Dangla Shan mts China see Tanggula Shan
Dangqên China 83 G3
Dângrêk, Chuŏr Phnum mts Cambodia/Thai. see Phanom Dong Rak, Thiu Khao
Dangriga Belize 136 G5
Dangshan China 77 H1
Dangtu China 77 H2
Daniel's Harbour Canada 123 K4
Danielskuil S. Africa 100 F5
Danilov Russia 42 I4
Danilovka Russia 43 J6
Danilovskaya Vozvyshennost' hills Russia 42 H4
Danjiang China see Leishan
Danjiangkou China 77 F1
Danjiangkou Shuiku resr China 77 F1
Danjo-guntō is Japan 75 C6
Ḍank Oman 88 E6
Dankhar India 82 D2
Dankov Russia 43 H5
Danlí Hond. 137 G6
Danmark country Europe see Denmark
Dannebrog Ø i. Greenland see Qillak
Dannenberg (Elbe) Germany 53 L1
Dannenwalde Germany 53 N1
Dannevirke N.Z. 113 F5
Dannhauser S. Africa 101 J5
Dano Burkina Faso 96 C3
Danshui Taiwan 77 I3
Dansville U.S.A. 135 G2
Danta India 82 C4
Dantan India 83 F5
Dantevada India see Dantewada
Dantewada India 84 D2
Dantewara India see Dantewada
Dantu China see Zhenjiang

▶Danube r. Europe 47 P6
2nd longest river in Europe.
Also spelt Donau (Austria/Germany) or Duna (Hungary) or Dunaj (Slovakia) or Dunărea (Romania) or Dunav (Bulgaria/Croatia/Yugoslavia) or Dunay (Ukraine).

Danube Delta Romania/Ukr. 59 M2
Danubyu Myanmar 70 A3
Danville IL U.S.A. 134 B3
Danville IN U.S.A. 134 B4
Danville KY U.S.A. 134 C5
Danville OH U.S.A. 134 D3
Danville PA U.S.A. 135 G3
Danville VA U.S.A. 134 F5
Danville VT U.S.A. 135 I1
Danxian China see Danzhou
Danzhai China 76 E3
Danzhou Guangxi China 77 F3
Danzhou Hainan China 77 F5
Danzig Poland see Gdańsk
Danzig, Gulf of Poland/Russia see Gdańsk, Gulf of
Daocheng China 76 D2
Daokou China see Huaxian
Dao Tay Sa is S. China Sea see Paracel Islands
Daoud Alg. see Aïn Beïda
Daoukro Côte d'Ivoire 96 C4
Daozhen China 76 E2
Dapaong Togo 96 D3
Dapha Bum mt. India 83 I4
Dapitan Phil. 69 G5
Daporijo India 83 H4
Đập Sơn La resr Vietnam 70 C2
Dapu China see Liucheng
Da Qaidam China 80 I4
Daqiao China 76 D3
Daqing China 74 B3
Daqiu China 77 H3
Dāq Mashī Iran 88 E3
Daqu Shan i. China 77 I2
Dara Senegal 96 B3
Dar'ā Syria 85 C3
Dâra, Gebel mt. Egypt see Dārah, Jabal
Dārāb Iran 88 D4
Darāgāh Iran 88 D4
Dārah, Jabal mt. Egypt 90 D6
Dārākūyeh Iran 88 D4
Dārān Iran 88 C3
Daraut-Korgon Kyrg. 89 I2
Darazo Nigeria 96 E3
Darband Tajik. 89 H2
Darband, Kūh-e mt. Iran 88 E4
Darband-e Hajjī Boland Turkm. 89 F2
Darbhanga India 83 F4
Darcang China 76 C1
Dardanelle U.S.A. 131 E5
Dardanelles strait Turkey 59 L4
Dardania prov. Europe see Kosovo
Dardesheim Germany 53 K3
Dardo China see Kangding
Dar el Beida Morocco see Casablanca
Darende Turkey 90 E3

▶Dar es Salaam Tanz. 99 D4
Former capital of Tanzania.

Dāreyn, Kūh-e mt. Iran 88 E3
Darfo Boario Terme Italy 58 D2
Dargai Pak. 89 H3
Dargaville N.Z. 113 D2
Dargo Australia 112 C6
Dargo Zangbo r. China 83 F3
Darhan Mongolia 72 J3
Darien U.S.A. 133 D6
Darién, Golfo del g. Col. 142 C2
Darién, Parque Nacional de nat. park Panama 137 I7
Dariga Pak. 89 G5
Darīganga Mongolia 73 K3
Darjeeling India see Darjiling
Darjiling India 83 G4
Darkhazīneh Iran 88 C4

▶Darling r. Australia 112 B3
2nd longest river in Oceania, and a major part of the longest (Murray-Darling).

Darling Downs hills Australia 112 D1
Darling Range hills Australia 109 A8
Darlington U.K. 48 F4
Darlington U.S.A. 130 F3
Darlington Point Australia 112 C5
Darlot, Lake salt flat Australia 109 C6
Darłowo Poland 47 P3
Darma Pass China/India 82 E3
Darmstadt Germany 53 I5
Darnah Libya 90 A4
Darnall S. Africa 101 J5
Darnick Australia 112 A4
Darnley, Cape Antarctica 152 E2
Daroca Spain 57 F3
Darong China 77 H3
Daroot-Korgon Kyrg. see Daraut-Korgon
Darovskoy Russia 42 J4
Darr watercourse Australia 110 C4
Darreh Bīd Iran 88 E3
Darreh-ye Bāhābād Iran 88 D4
Darsi India 84 C3
Dart r. U.K. 49 D8
Dartford U.K. 49 H7
Dartmoor hills U.K. 49 C8
Dartmoor National Park U.K. 49 D8
Dartmouth Canada 123 J5
Dartmouth U.K. 49 D8
Dartmouth, Lake salt flat Australia 111 D5
Dartmouth Reservoir Australia 112 C6
Darton U.K. 48 F5
Daru P.N.G. 69 K8
Daru Sierra Leone 96 B4
Daruba Indon. 69 H6
Darvaza Turkm. see Içoguz
Darvoz, Qatorkŭhi mts Tajik. 89 H2
Darwāzagēy Afgh. 89 G4
Darwen U.K. 48 E5

Die France 56 G4
Dieblich Germany 53 H4
Diébougou Burkina Faso 96 C3
Dieburg Germany 53 I5
Diedenhofen France see Thionville
Diefenbaker, Lake Canada 121 I5
Diego de Almagro, Isla i. Chile 144 A8
Diégo Suarez Madag. see Antsirañana
Diekirch Lux. 52 G5
Diéma Mali 96 C3
Diemel r. Germany 53 J3
Điện Biên Vietnam see Điện Biên Phu
Điện Biên Phu Vietnam 70 C2
Diên Châu Vietnam 70 D3
Diên Khanh Vietnam 71 E4
Diepholz Germany 53 I2
Dieppe France 52 B5
Dierks U.S.A. 131 E5
Di'er Songhua Jiang r. China see Songhua Jiang
Diessen Neth. 52 F3
Diest Belgium 52 F4
Dietikon Switz. 56 I3
Diez Germany 53 I4
Diffa Niger 96 E3
Digby Canada 123 I5
Diggi India 82 C4
Diglur India 84 C2
Digne France see Digne-les-Bains
Digne-les-Bains France 56 H4
Digoin France 56 F3
Digos Phil. 69 H5
Digras India 84 C1
Digri Pak. 89 H5
Digul r. Indon. 69 K8
Digya National Park Ghana 96 C4
Dihang r. India see Brahmaputra
Dihok Iraq see Dahūk/Dihok
Dihourse, Lac l. Canada 123 I2
Diinsoor Somalia 98 E3
Dijon France 56 G3
Dik Chad 97 E4
Diken India 82 C4
Dikhil Djibouti 86 F7
Dikili Turkey 59 L5
Dik'losmta mt. Russia 43 J8
Diksmuide Belgium 52 C3
Dikson Russia 64 J2
Dīla Eth. 98 D3
Dilārām Afgh. 89 F3
Dilaram Iran 88 E4

▶Dili East Timor 108 D2
Capital of East Timor (Timor-Leste).

Di Linh Vietnam 71 E5
Dillenburg Germany 53 I4
Dilley U.S.A. 131 D6
Dillingen an der Donau Germany 47 M6
Dillingen/Saar Germany 52 G5
Dillingham U.S.A. 118 C4
Dillon r. Canada 121 I4
Dillon MT U.S.A. 126 E3
Dillon SC U.S.A. 133 E5
Dillwyn U.S.A. 135 F5
Dilolo Dem. Rep. Congo 99 C5
Dilsen Belgium 52 F3
Dimapur India 83 H4
Dimashq Syria see Damascus
Dimbokro Côte d'Ivoire 96 C4
Dimboola Australia 111 C8
Dimitrov Ukr. see Dymytrov
Dimitrovgrad Bulg. 59 K3
Dimitrovgrad Russia 43 K5
Dimitrovo Bulg. see Pernik
Dimmitt U.S.A. 131 C5
Dimona Israel 85 B4
Dimpho Pan salt pan Botswana 100 E3
Dinagat i. Phil. 69 H4
Dinajpur Bangl. 83 G4
Dinan France 56 C2
Dinant Belgium 52 E4
Dinapur India 83 F4
Dinar Turkey 59 N5
Dīnār, Kūh-e mt. Iran 88 C4
Dinara Planina mts Bos. & Herz./Croatia see Dinaric Alps
Dinaric Alps mts Bos. & Herz./Croatia 58 G2
Dinbych U.K. see Denbigh
Dinbych-y-pysgod U.K. see Tenby
Dinder National Park Sudan 97 G3
Dindi r. India 84 C2
Dindigul India 84 C4
Dindima Nigeria 96 E3
Dindiza Moz. 101 K2
Dindori India 82 E5
Dingcheng China see Dingyuan
Dingelstädt Germany 53 K3
Dinggyê China 83 F3
Dingla Nepal 83 F4
Dingle Ireland see Daingean Uí Chúis
Dingle Bay Ireland 51 B5
Dingnan China 77 G3
Dingo Australia 110 E4
Dingolfing Germany 53 M6
Dingping China see Linshui
Dingtao China 77 G1
Dinguiraye Guinea 96 B3
Dingwall U.K. 50 E3
Dingxi China 76 E1
Dingyuan China 77 H1
Dinh Lâp Vietnam 70 D2
Dinkelsbühl Germany 53 K5
Dinokwe Botswana 101 H2
Dinosaur U.S.A. 129 I1
Dinosaur National Monument nat. park U.S.A. 129 I1
Dinslaken Germany 52 G3
Dinwiddie U.S.A. 135 G5
Dioïla Mali 96 C3
Dionísio Cerqueira Brazil 144 F3
Diorama Brazil 145 A2
Dioscurias Georgia see Sokhumi
Diouloulou Senegal 96 B3
Diourbel Senegal 96 B3
Dipayal Nepal 82 E3
Diphu India 83 H4
Dipkarpaz Cyprus see Rizokarpason
Diplo Pak. 89 H5
Dipperu National Park Australia 110 E4
Dipu China see Anji
Dir reg. Pak. 89 I3
Dirang India 83 H4
Diré Mali 96 C3
Direction, Cape Australia 110 C2
Dirē Dawa Eth. 98 E3
Dirico Angola 99 C5
Dirj Libya 96 E1
Dirk Hartog Island Australia 109 A6
Dirranbandi Australia 112 D2
Ḍirs Saudi Arabia 98 E2
Dirschau Poland see Tczew
Dirty Devil r. U.S.A. 129 H3
Disa India 82 C4
Disang r. India 83 H4
Disappointment, Cape S. Georgia 144 I8
Disappointment, Cape U.S.A. 126 B3
Disappointment, Lake salt flat Australia 109 C5
Disappointment Islands Fr. Polynesia see Désappointement, Îles du
Disappointment Lake Canada 123 J3
Disaster Bay Australia 112 D6
Discovery Bay Australia 111 C8
Disko i. Greenland see Qeqertarsuaq
Disko Bugt b. Greenland see Qeqertarsuup Tunua
Dismal Swamp U.S.A. 132 E4
Dispur India 83 G4
Disputanta U.S.A. 135 G5
Disraeli Canada 123 H5
Diss U.K. 49 I6
Distrito Federal admin. dist. Brazil 145 B1
Disūq Egypt 90 C5
Ditloung S. Africa 100 F5
Dittaino r. Sicily Italy 58 F6
Diu India 84 A1
Dīvāndarreh Iran 88 B3
Divehi country Indian Ocean see Maldives
Divi, Point India 84 D3
Divichi Azer. see Şabran
Divide Mountain U.S.A. 120 A2
Divinópolis Brazil 145 B3
Divnoye Russia 43 I7
Divo Côte d'Ivoire 96 C4
Divriği Turkey 90 E3
Diwana Pak. 89 G5
Diwaniyah Iraq see Ad Dīwānīyah
Dixfield U.S.A. 135 J1
Dixon CA U.S.A. 128 C2
Dixon IL U.S.A. 130 F3
Dixon KY U.S.A. 134 B5
Dixon MT U.S.A. 126 E3
Dixon Entrance sea chan. Canada/U.S.A. 120 C4
Dixonville Canada 120 G3
Dixville Canada 135 J1
Diyadin Turkey 91 F3
Diyarbakır Turkey 91 F3
Diz Pak. 89 F5
Diz Chah Iran 88 D3
Dize Turkey see Yüksekova
Dizney U.S.A. 134 D5
Djado Niger 96 E2
Djado, Plateau du Niger 96 E2
Djaja, Puntjak mt. Indon. see Jaya, Puncak
Djakarta Indon. see Jakarta
Djakovica Kosovo see Gjakovë
Djakovo Croatia see Đakovo
Djambala Congo 98 B4
Djanet Alg. 96 D2
Djarrit-Uliga-Dalap Marshall Is see Delap-Uliga-Djarrit
Djelfa Alg. 57 H6
Djéma Cent. Afr. Rep. 98 C3
Djenné Mali 96 C3
Djenoun, Garet el mt. Alg. 96 D2
Djibloho Equat. Guinea 96 E4
Djibo Burkina Faso 96 C3
Djibouti country Africa 86 F7

▶Djibouti Djibouti 86 F7
Capital of Djibouti.

Djidjelli Alg. see Jijel
Djizak Uzbek. see Jizzax
Djougou Benin 96 D4
Djoum Cameroon 96 E4
Djourab, Erg du des. Chad 97 E3
Djúpivogur Iceland 44 [inset 1]
Djurås Sweden 45 I6
Djurdjura, Parc National du nat. park Alg. 57 I5
Dmitriya Lapteva, Proliv sea chan. Russia 65 P2
Dmitriyev-L'govskiy Russia 43 G5
Dmitriyevsk Ukr. see Makiyivka
Dmitrov Russia 42 H4
Dmytriyevs'k Ukr. see Makiyivka
Dnepr r. Europe see Dnieper
Dneprodzerzhinsk Ukr. see Dniprodzerzhyns'k
Dnepropetrovsk Ukr. see Dnipropetrovs'k

▶Dnieper r. Europe 43 G7
3rd longest river in Europe.
Also spelt Dnepr (Russia) or Dnipro (Ukraine) or Dnyapro (Belarus).

Dniester r. Ukr. 43 F6
also spelt Dnister (Ukraine) or Nistru (Moldova)
Dnipro r. Europe see Dnieper
Dniprodzerzhyns'k Ukr. 43 G6
Dnipropetrovs'k Ukr. 43 G6
Dnister r. Ukr. see Dniester
Dno Russia 42 F4
Dnyapro r. Europe see Dnieper
Doaba Pak. 89 H3
Đoan Hung Vietnam 70 D2
Doba Chad 97 E4
Doba China see Toiba
Dobele Latvia 45 M8
Döbeln Germany 53 N3
Doberai, Jazirah pen. Indon. 69 I7
Doberai Peninsula Indon. see Doberai, Jazirah
Dobo Indon. 69 I8
Doboj Bos. & Herz. 58 H2
Doborji Iran 88 D4
Döbraberg hill Germany 53 L4
Dobrich Bulg. 59 L3
Dobrinka Russia 43 I5
Dobroye Russia 43 H5
Dobrudja reg. Romania see Dobruja
Dobruja reg. Romania 59 L3
Dobrush Belarus 43 F5
Dobryanka Russia 41 R4
Dobzha China 83 G3
Đôc, Mui pt Vietnam 70 D3
Doce r. Brazil 145 D2
Dochart r. U.K. 50 E4
Docking U.K. 49 H6
Doctor Hicks Range hills Australia 109 D7
Doctor Pedro P. Peña Para. 144 D2
Doda India 82 C2
Doda Betta mt. India 84 C4
Dod Ballapur India 84 C3
Dodecanese is Greece 59 L7
Dodekanisa is Greece see Dodecanese
Dodekanisos is Greece see Dodecanese
Dodge City U.S.A. 130 C4
Dodgeville U.S.A. 130 F3
Dodman Point U.K. 49 C8

▶Dodoma Tanz. 99 D4
Capital of Tanzania.

Dodsonville U.S.A. 134 D4
Doetinchem Neth. 52 G3
Dog r. Canada 122 C4
Dogai Coring salt l. China 83 G2
Dogaicoring Qangco salt l. China 83 G2
Doğanşehir Turkey 90 E3
Dogên Co l. China 83 G3
Doghārūn Iran 89 F3
Dog Island Canada 123 J2
Dog Lake Man. Canada 121 L5
Dog Lake Ont. Canada 122 C4
Dog Lake Ont. Canada 122 D4
Dōgo i. Japan 75 D5
Dogondoutchi Niger 96 D3
Dog Rocks is Bahamas 133 E7
Doğubeyazıt Turkey 91 G3
Doğu Menteşe Dağları mts Turkey 59 M6
Dogxung Zangbo r. China 83 F3
Do'gyaling China 83 G3

▶Doha Qatar 88 C5
Capital of Qatar.

Dohad India see Dahod
Dohazari Bangl. 83 H5
Dohrighat India 83 E4
Doi i. Fiji 107 I4
Doi Inthanon National Park Thai. 70 B3
Doi Luang National Park Thai. 70 B3
Doire U.K. see Londonderry
Doi Saket Thai. 70 B3
Dois Irmãos, Serra dos hills Brazil 143 J5
Dokan, Sadd Iraq 91 G4
Dok-do i. N. Pacific Ocean see Liancourt Rocks
Dokhara, Dunes de des. Alg. 54 F5
Dokka Norway 45 G6
Dokkum Neth. 52 F1
Dokog He r. China 76 D2
Dokri Pak. 89 H5
Dokshukino Russia see Nartkala
Dokshytsy Belarus 45 O9
Dokuchayeva, Mys c. Russia 74 G3
Dokuchayevka Kazakh. see Karamendy
Dokuchayevs'k Ukr. 43 H7
Dolbenmaen U.K. 49 C6
Dol-de-Bretagne France 56 D2
Dole France 56 G3
Dolgellau U.K. 49 D6
Dolgen Germany 53 N1
Dolgiy, Ostrov i. Russia 42 L1
Dolgorukovo Russia 43 H5
Dolina Ukr. see Dolyna
Dolinsk Russia 74 F3
Dolisie Congo 99 B4
Dolleman Island Antarctica 152 L2
Dollnstein Germany 53 L6
Dolok, Pulau i. Indon. 69 J8
Dolomites mts Italy 58 D2
Dolomiti mts Italy see Dolomites
Dolomiti Bellunesi, Parco Nazionale delle nat. park Italy 58 D1
Dolomitiche, Alpi mts Italy see Dolomites
Dolonnur China see Duolun
Dolo Odo Eth. 98 E3
Dolores Arg. 144 E5
Dolores Uruguay 144 E4
Dolores U.S.A. 129 I3
Dolphin and Union Strait Canada 118 G3
Dolphin Head hd Namibia 100 B3
Đô Lương Vietnam 70 D3
Dolyna Ukr. 43 D6
Domaila India 82 D3
Domaniç Turkey 59 M5
Domar China 80 F5
Domartang China 76 B2
Domažlice Czechia 53 M5
Domba China 76 B1
Dom Bākh Iran 88 B3
Dombås Norway 44 F5
Dombóvár Hungary 58 H1
Dombrau Poland see Dąbrowa Górnicza
Dombrovitsa Ukr. see Dubrovytsya
Dombrowa Poland see Dąbrowa Górnicza
Domda China see Qingshuihe
Dome Creek Canada 120 F4
Dome Rock Mountains U.S.A. 129 F5
Domeyko Chile 144 B3
Domfront France 56 D2
Dominica country West Indies 137 L5
Dominicana, República country West Indies see Dominican Republic
Dominican Republic country West Indies 137 J5
Dominion, Cape Canada 119 K3
Dominique i. Fr. Polynesia see Hiva Oa
Dömitz Germany 53 L1
Dom Joaquim Brazil 145 C2
Dommel r. Neth. 52 F3
Domo Eth. 98 E3
Domokos Greece 59 J5
Dompu Indon. 108 B2
Domula China see Duomula
Domuyo, Volcán vol. Arg. 144 B5
Domville, Mount hill Australia 112 E2
Don Mex. 127 F8

▶Don r. Russia 43 H7
5th longest river in Europe.

Don r. U.K. 50 G3
Don, Xé r. Laos 70 D4
Donaghadee U.K. 51 G3
Donaghmore U.K. 51 F3
Donald Australia 112 A6
Donaldsonville U.S.A. 131 F6
Donalsonville U.S.A. 133 C6
Doñana, Parque Nacional de nat. park Spain 57 C5
Donau r. Europe see Danube
Donauwörth Germany 53 K6
Don Benito Spain 57 D4
Doncaster U.K. 48 F5
Dondo Angola 99 B4
Dondo Moz. 99 D5
Dondra Head hd Sri Lanka 84 D5
Donegal Ireland 51 D3
Donegal Bay Ireland 51 D3
Donets'k Ukr. 43 H7
Donetsko-Amrovsiyevka Ukr. see Amvrosiyivka
Donets'kyy Kryazh hills Russia/Ukr. 43 H6
Donga r. Cameroon/Nigeria 96 D4
Dong'an China 77 F3
Dongane, Lagoa lag. Moz. 101 L3
Dongara Australia 109 A7
Dongbo China see Mêdog
Dongchuan Yunnan China see Yao'an
Dongchuan Yunnan China see Tangdan
Dongchuan Yunnan China 76 D3
Dongco China 83 F2
Dong Co l. China 83 F2
Dong Dabsan Hu salt l. China 83 H1
Dongducheon S. Korea 75 B5
Dongfang China 77 F5
Dongfanghong China 74 D3
Donggang Liaoning China 75 B5
Donggang Shandong China 77 H1
Donggi Conag l. China 76 C1
Donggou China see Donggang
Donggu China 77 G3
Dongguan China 77 G4
Donghae S. Korea 75 C5
Dong Hai sea N. Pacific Ocean see East China Sea
Dong Haxat China 74 B3
Đông Hơi Vietnam 70 D3
Donghuang China see Xishui
Dongjiang Shuiku resr China 77 G3
Dongjug China 76 B2
Dongkou China 77 F3
Donglan China 76 E3
Dongliao He r. China 74 A4
Dongmen China see Luocheng
Dongminzhutun China 74 A3
Dongning China 74 C3
Dongo Angola 99 B5
Dongo Dem. Rep. Congo 98 B3
Dongola Sudan 86 D6
Dongou Congo 98 B3
Dong Phraya Yen esc. Thai. 70 C4
Dongping Guangdong China 77 G4
Dongping Hunan China see Anhua
Dongpo China see Meishan
Dongqiao China 83 G3
Dongshan Fujian China 77 H4
Dongshan Jiangsu China 77 I2
Dongshan Jiangxi China see Shangyou
Dongshao China 77 G3
Dongsheng Nei Mongol China 73 K5
Dongsheng Sichuan China see Shuangliu
Dongtai China 77 I1
Dongting Hu l. China 77 G2
Dongtou China 77 I3
Đông Triều Vietnam 70 D2
Dong Ujimqin Qi China see Uliastai
Đông Văn Vietnam 70 D2
Dongxiang China 77 H2
Dongxi Liandao i. China 77 H1
Dongxing Guangxi China 76 E4
Dongxing Heilong. China 74 B3
Dongyang China 77 I2
Dongying China 73 L5
Dongzhi China 77 H2
Donkerbroek Neth. 52 G1
Don Kêv Cambodia 71 D5
Donnacona Canada 123 H5
Donnellys Crossing N.Z. 113 D2
Donner Pass U.S.A. 128 C2
Donnersberg hill Germany 53 H5
Donostia Spain see San Sebastián
Donousa i. Greece 59 K6
Donoussa i. Greece see Donousa
Donskoye Russia 43 I7
Donyztau, Sor dry lake Kazakh. 80 A2
Dooagh Ireland 51 B4
Doomadgee Australia 110 B3
Doon r. U.K. 50 E5
Doon, Loch l. U.K. 50 E5
Doonbeg r. Ireland 51 C5
Doorn Neth. 52 F2
Door Peninsula U.S.A. 134 B1
Doorwerth Neth. 52 F3
Doqêmo China 76 B2
Doqên Co l. China 83 G3
Dor Israel 85 B3
Dora U.S.A. 131 C5
Dora, Lake salt flat Australia 108 C5
Dorado Mex. 131 B7
Dorah Pass Pak. 89 H2
Doran Lake Canada 121 I2
Dorbiljin China see Emin
Dorbod China 74 B3
Dorbod Qi China see Ulan Hua
Dorchester U.K. 49 E8
Dordabis Namibia 100 C2
Dordogne r. France 56 D4
Dordrecht Neth. 52 E3
Dordrecht S. Africa 101 H6
Doreenville Namibia 100 D2
Doré Lake Canada 121 J4
Doré Lake l. Canada 121 J4
Dores do Indaiá Brazil 145 B2
Dorgê Co l. China 83 I2
Dörgön Nuur salt l. Mongolia 80 H2
Dori Burkina Faso 96 C3
Doring r. S. Africa 100 D6
Dorisvale Australia 108 E3
Dorking U.K. 49 G7
Dormagen Germany 52 G3
Dormans France 52 D5
Dormidontovka Russia 74 D3
Dornoch U.K. 50 E3
Dornoch Firth est. U.K. 50 E3
Dornum Germany 53 H1
Doro Mali 96 C3
Dorob National Park Namibia 100 B2
Dorogobuzh Russia 43 G5
Dorogorskoye Russia 42 J2
Doroḩ Iran 89 F3
Dorohoi Romania 43 E7
Dorostol Bulg. see Silistra
Dorotea Sweden 44 J4
Dorpat Estonia see Tartu
Dorre Island Australia 109 A6
Dorrigo Australia 112 F3
Dorris U.S.A. 126 C4
Dorset Canada 135 F1
Dorsoidong Co l. China 83 G2
Dortmund Germany 53 H3
Dörtyol Turkey 85 C1
Dorūd Iran 88 C3
Dorum Germany 53 I1
Doruma Dem. Rep. Congo 98 C3
Dorūneh, Kūh-e mts Iran 88 E3
Dörverden Germany 53 J2
Dorylaeum Turkey see Eskişehir
Dos Bahías, Cabo c. Arg. 144 C6
Dos de Mayo Peru 142 C5
Doshakh, Koh-i- mt. Afgh. see Dū Shākh, Kōh-e
Đỗ Sơn Vietnam 70 D2
Dos Palos U.S.A. 128 C3
Dosse r. Germany 53 M2
Dosso Niger 96 D3
Dothan U.S.A. 133 C6
Dotsero U.S.A. 129 J2
Douai France 52 D4
Douala Cameroon 96 D4
Douarnenez France 56 B2
Double Headed Shot Cays is Bahamas 133 D8
Double Island H.K. China 77 [inset]
Double Island Point Australia 111 F5
Double Mountain Fork r. U.S.A. 131 C5
Double Peak U.S.A. 128 D4
Double Point Australia 110 D3
Double Springs U.S.A. 133 C5
Doubs r. France/Switz. 56 G3
Doubtful Sound inlet N.Z. 113 A7
Doubtless Bay N.Z. 113 D2
Douentza Mali 96 C3
Dougga tourist site Tunisia 58 C6

▶Douglas Isle of Man 48 C4
Capital of the Isle of Man.

Douglas S. Africa 100 F5
Douglas U.K. 50 F5
Douglas AZ U.S.A. 127 F7
Douglas GA U.S.A. 133 D6
Douglas WY U.S.A. 126 G4
Douglas Reef i. Japan see Okino-Tori-shima
Douglasville U.S.A. 133 C5
Douhudi China see Gong'an
Doulatpur Bangl. see Daulatpur
Douliu Taiwan 77 I4
Doullens France 52 C4
Douna Mali 96 C3
Doune U.K. 50 E4
Doupovské hory mts Czechia 53 N4
Dourada, Serra hills Brazil 145 A2
Dourada, Serra mts Brazil 145 A1
Dourados Brazil 144 F2
Douro r. Port. 57 B3
also known as Duero (Spain)
Doushi China see Gong'an
Doushui Shuiku resr China 77 G3
Douve r. France 49 F9
Douzy France 52 F5
Dove r. U.K. 49 F6
Dove Brook Canada 123 K3
Dove Creek U.S.A. 129 I3
Dover U.K. 49 I7

▶Dover DE U.S.A. 135 H4
Capital of Delaware.

Dover NH U.S.A. 135 J2
Dover NJ U.S.A. 135 H3
Dover OH U.S.A. 134 E3
Dover TN U.S.A. 132 C4
Dover, Strait of France/U.K. 56 E1
Dover-Foxcroft U.S.A. 135 K1
Dovey r. U.K. 49 D6
Dovrefjell Nasjonalpark nat. park Norway 44 F5
Dowagiac U.S.A. 134 B3
Dowi, Tanjung pt Indon. 71 B7
Dowlaiswaram India 84 D2
Dowlatābād Afgh. 89 F3
Dowlatābād Fārs Iran 88 C4
Dowlatābād Fārs Iran 88 D4
Dowlatābād Khorāsān-e Razavī Iran 88 E2
Dowlatābād Khorāsān-e Razavī Iran 89 F2
Dowlat Khān Afgh. 89 H3
Dowlatyār Afgh. 89 G3
Downieville U.S.A. 128 C2
Downpatrick U.K. 51 G3
Downsville U.S.A. 135 H2
Doyle U.S.A. 128 C1
Doylestown U.S.A. 135 H3
Dozdān r. Iran 88 E5
Dōzen is Japan 75 D5
Dozois, Réservoir resr Canada 122 F5
Dozulé France 49 G9
Drâa, Hamada du plat. Alg. 54 C6
Dracena Brazil 145 A3
Drachten Neth. 52 G1
Drăgăneşti-Olt Romania 59 K2
Drăgăşani Romania 59 K2
Dragonera, Isla i. Spain see Sa Dragonera
Dragoon U.S.A. 129 H5
Dragsfjärd Fin. 45 M6
Draguignan France 56 H5
Drahichyn Belarus 45 N10
Drake Australia 112 F2
Drake U.S.A. 130 C2
Drakensberg mts S. Africa 101 I3
Drake Passage S. Atlantic Ocean 148 D9
Drakes Bay U.S.A. 128 B3
Drama Greece 59 K4
Drammen Norway 45 G7
Drang, Ia r. Cambodia 71 D4
Drangedal Norway 45 F7
Dransfeld Germany 53 J3
Draper, Mount U.S.A. 120 B3
Draperstown U.K. 51 F3
Drapsaca Afgh. see Kunduz
Dras India 82 C2
Drasan Pak. 89 I2
Drau r. Europe see Drava
Dráva r. Europe see Drava
Drava r. Europe 58 H2
also known as Drau (Austria), Drave or Drava (Slovenia and Croatia), Dráva (Hungary)
Drave r. Europe see Drava
Drayton Valley Canada 120 H4
Drazinda Pak. 89 H4
Dréan Alg. 58 B6
Dreistelzberge hill Germany 53 J4
Drentse Hoofdvaart canal Neth. 52 G2
Drepano, Akra pt Greece see Laimos, Akrotirio
Dresden Canada 134 D2
Dresden Germany 47 N5
Dreux France 52 B6
Drevsjø Norway 45 H6
Drewryville U.S.A. 135 G5
Dri China 76 C2
Driffield U.K. 48 G4
Driftwood U.S.A. 135 F3
Driggs U.S.A. 126 F4
Drillham Australia 112 E1
Drimoleague Ireland 51 C6
Drina r. Bos. & Herz./Serbia 59 H2
Driscoll Island Antarctica 152 J1
Drissa Belarus see Vyerkhnyadzvinsk
Drniš Croatia 58 G3
Drobeta-Turnu Severin Romania 59 J2
Drochtersen Germany 53 J1
Drogheda Ireland 51 F4
Drogichin Belarus see Drahichyn
Drogobych Ukr. see Drohobych
Drohobych Ukr. 43 D6
Droichead Átha Ireland see Drogheda
Droichead Nua Ireland see Newbridge
Droitwich U.K. see Droitwich Spa
Droitwich Spa U.K. 49 E6
Dromedary, Cape Australia 112 E6
Dromod Ireland 51 E4
Dromore Northern Ireland U.K. 51 E3
Dromore Northern Ireland U.K. 51 F3
Dronfield U.K. 48 F5
Dronning Louise Land reg. Greenland 153 I1
Dronning Maud Land reg. Antarctica see Queen Maud Land
Dronten Neth. 52 F2
Druk-Yul country Asia see Bhutan
Drumheller Canada 121 H5
Drummond atoll Kiribati see Tabiteuea
Drummond U.S.A. 126 E3
Drummond, Lake U.S.A. 135 G5
Drummond Island Kiribati see McKean
Drummond Range hills Australia 110 D5
Drummondville Canada 123 G5
Drummore U.K. 50 E6
Drury Lake Canada 120 C2
Druskieniki Lith. see Druskininkai
Druskininkai Lith. 45 N10
Druzhina Russia 65 P3
Druzhnaya Gorka Russia 45 Q7
Dry r. Australia 108 F3
Dryanovo Bulg. 59 K3
Dryberry Lake Canada 121 M5
Dryden Canada 121 M5
Dryden U.S.A. 135 G2
Dry Fork r. U.S.A. 126 G4
Drygalski Ice Tongue Antarctica 152 H1
Drygalski Island Antarctica 152 F2
Dry Lake U.S.A. 129 F3
Dry Lake l. U.S.A. 130 D1
Drymen U.K. 50 E4
Dry Ridge U.S.A. 134 C4
Drysdale r. Australia 108 D3
Drysdale River National Park Australia 108 D3
Dry Tortugas is U.S.A. 133 D7
Du'an China 77 F4
Duaringa Australia 110 E4
Duarte, Pico mt. Dom. Rep. 137 J5
Duartina Brazil 145 A3
Ḍubā Saudi Arabia 86 E4
Dubai U.A.E. 88 D5
Dubakella Mountain U.S.A. 128 B1
Dubawnt r. Canada 121 L2
Dubawnt Lake Canada 121 K2
Dubayy U.A.E. see Dubai
Dubbo Australia 112 D4

▶Dublin Ireland 51 F4
Capital of Ireland.

Dublin U.S.A. 133 D5
Dubna Russia 42 H4
Dubno Ukr. 43 E6
Dubois ID U.S.A. 126 E3
Dubois IN U.S.A. 134 B4
Du Bois U.S.A. 135 F3
Dubovka Russia 43 J6
Dubovskoye Russia 43 I7
Dubréka Guinea 96 B4
Dubris U.K. see Dover
Dubrovnik Croatia 58 H3
Dubrovytsya Ukr. 43 E6
Dubuque U.S.A. 130 F3
Dubysa r. Lith. 45 M9
Đức Bôn Vietnam 71 D5
Duc de Gloucester, Îles du is Fr. Polynesia 151 K7
Duchang China 77 H2
Ducheng China see Yunan
Duchesne U.S.A. 129 H1
Duchesne r. U.S.A. 129 I1

El Arba, Tizi *hill* Alg. 57 H5
El Arco Mex. 127 E7
El Ariana Tunisia *see* L'Ariana
El Aricha Alg. 54 D5
El 'Arîsh Egypt *see* Al 'Arīsh
El Arrouch Alg. 58 B6
El Ashmûnein Egypt *see* Al Ashmūnayn
El Asnam Alg. *see* Chlef
Elassona Greece 59 J5
Elat Israel *see* Eilat
Elato *atoll* Micronesia 69 L5
Elazığ Turkey 91 E3
Elba U.S.A. 133 C6
Elba, Isola d' *i.* Italy 58 D3
El'ban Russia 74 E2
El Barco de Valdeorras Spain *see* O Barco
El Barreal *salt l.* Mex. 127 G7
Elbasan Albania 59 I4
El Batroun Lebanon *see* Batroûn
El Baúl Venez. 142 E2
El Bawîti Egypt *see* Al Bawītī
El Bayadh Alg. 54 E5
Elbe *r.* Germany 53 J1
also known as Labe (Czech Republic)
Elbe-Havel-Kanal *canal* Germany 53 L2
El Béqaa *valley* Lebanon 85 C2
Elbert, Mount U.S.A. 126 G5
Elberta U.S.A. 129 H2
Elberton U.S.A. 133 D5
Elbeuf France 56 E2
Elbeyli Turkey 85 C1
Elbing Poland *see* Elbląg
Elbistan Turkey 90 E3
Elbląg Poland 47 Q3
El Boulaïda Alg. *see* Blida
Elbow Canada 121 J5
Elbow Lake U.S.A. 130 D2
El Bozal Mex. 131 C8
El Brasil Mex. 131 C7

►El'brus *mt.* Russia 91 F2
Highest mountain in Europe.

Elburg Neth. 52 F2
El Burgo de Osma Spain 57 E3
Elburz Mountains Iran 88 C2
El Cajon U.S.A. 128 E5
El Callao Venez. 142 F2
El Campo U.S.A. 131 D6
El Capitan Mountain U.S.A. 127 G6
El Capulín *r.* Mex. 131 C7
El Casco Mex. 131 B7
El Centro U.S.A. 129 F5
El Cerro Bol. 142 F7
Elche Spain *see* Elche-Elx
Elche-Elx Spain 57 F4
El Chilicote Mex. 131 B6
Elcho Island Australia 110 A1
El Coca Ecuador *see* Coca
El Cocuy, Parque Nacional *nat. park* Col. 142 D2
El Cuyo Mex. 133 C8
Elda Spain 57 F4
El Dátil Mex. 127 E7
El Desemboque Mex. 127 E7
El Diamante Mex. 131 C6
El'dikan Russia 65 O3
El Djezair *country* Africa *see* Algeria
El Djezair Alg. *see* Algiers
El Doctor Mex. 129 F6
Eldon U.S.A. 130 E4
Eldorado Arg. 144 F3
Eldorado Brazil 145 A4
El Dorado Col. 142 D3
El Dorado Mex. 124 F7
El Dorado *AR* U.S.A. 131 E5
El Dorado *KS* U.S.A. 130 D4
Eldorado U.S.A. 131 C6
El Dorado Venez. 142 F2
Eldorado Mountains U.S.A. 129 F4
Eldoret Kenya 98 D3
Elea, Cape Cyprus *see* Elaia, Cape
Eleanor U.S.A. 134 E4
Electric Peak U.S.A. 126 F3
Elefantes *r.* Moz./S. Africa *see* Olifants
El Eglab *plat.* Alg. 96 C2
El Ejido Spain 57 E5
El Encanto Col. 142 D4
Elend Germany 53 K3
Elephanta Caves *tourist site* India 84 B2
Elephant Butte Reservoir U.S.A. 127 G6
Elephant Island Antarctica 152 A2
Elephant Pass Sri Lanka 84 D4
Elephant Point Bangl. 83 H5
Eleşkirt Turkey 91 F3
El Eulma Alg. 54 F4
Eleuthera *i.* Bahamas 133 E7
Eleven Point *r.* U.S.A. 131 F4
El Fahs Tunisia 58 C6
El Faiyûm Egypt *see* Al Fayyūm
El Fasher Sudan 97 F3
El Ferrol Spain *see* Ferrol
El Ferrol del Caudillo Spain *see* Ferrol
Elfershausen Germany 53 J4
El Fud Eth. 98 E3
El Fuerte Mex. 127 F8
El Fula Sudan 98 C2
El Gara Egypt *see* Qārah
El Geneina Sudan 97 F3
El Geteina Sudan 86 D7
El Ghardaqa Egypt *see* Hurghada
El Ghor *plain* Jordan/West Bank *see* Al Ghawr
Elgin U.K. 50 F3
Elgin *IL* U.S.A. 130 F3
Elgin *ND* U.S.A. 130 C2
Elgin *NV* U.S.A. 129 F3
Elgin *TX* U.S.A. 131 D6
El'ginskiy Russia 65 P3
El Gîza Egypt *see* Giza
El Goléa Alg. 54 E5
El Golfo de Santa Clara Mex. 127 E7
Elgon, Mount Kenya/Uganda 78 C6
El Hadjar Alg. 58 B6
El-Hagounia W. Sahara 96 B2
El Ḥammâm Egypt *see* Al Ḥammām
El Ḥammâmi *reg.* Mauritania 96 B2
El Ḥank *esc.* Mali/Mauritania 96 C2
El Ḥarra Egypt *see* Al Ḥarrah
El Hazim Jordan *see* Al Hazīm
El Ḥeiz Egypt *see* Al Ḥayz
El Hierro *i.* Canary Is 96 B2
El Homr Alg. 54 E6
El Homra Sudan 86 D7
Elhovo Bulg. 59 L3
Eliase Indon. 108 E2
Elías Piña Dom. Rep. 137 J5
Elichpur India *see* Achalpur
Elida U.S.A. 134 C3
Elie U.K. 50 G4
Elila *r.* Dem. Rep. Congo 98 C4
Elim U.S.A. 118 B3
Elimberrum France *see* Auch
Eling China *see* Yinjiang
Elingampangu Dem. Rep. Congo 98 C4
Eliot, Mount Canada 123 J2
Élisabethville Dem. Rep. Congo *see* Lubumbashi
Eliseu Martins Brazil 143 J5
El Iskandarîya Egypt *see* Alexandria
Elista Russia 43 J7
Elizabeth *NJ* U.S.A. 135 H3
Elizabeth *WV* U.S.A. 134 E4
Elizabeth, Mount *hill* Australia 108 D4
Elizabeth Bay Namibia 100 B4
Elizabeth City U.S.A. 132 E4
Elizabeth Island Pitcairn Is *see* Henderson Island
Elizabeth Point Namibia 100 B4
Elizabethton U.S.A. 132 D4
Elizabethtown *IL* U.S.A. 130 F4
Elizabethtown *KY* U.S.A. 134 C5
Elizabethtown *NC* U.S.A. 133 E5
Elizabethtown *NY* U.S.A. 135 I1
El Jadida Morocco 54 C5
El Jaralito Mex. 131 B7
El Jem Tunisia 58 D7
Elk *r.* Canada 120 H5
Ełk Poland 47 S4
Elk *r.* U.S.A. 135 H4
El Kaa Lebanon *see* Qaa
El Kab Sudan 86 D6
Elkader U.S.A. 130 F3
El Kala Alg. 58 C6
Elk City U.S.A. 131 D5
Elkedra Australia 110 A4
Elkedra *watercourse* Australia 110 B4
El Kef Tunisia *see* Le Kef
El Kelaâ des Srarhna Morocco 54 C5
Elkford Canada 120 H5
Elk Grove U.S.A. 128 C2
El Khalil West Bank *see* Hebron
El Khandaq Sudan 86 D6
El Khârga Egypt *see* Al Khārijah
El Kharrûba Egypt *see* Al Kharrūbah
Elkhart *IN* U.S.A. 134 C3
Elkhart *KS* U.S.A. 131 C4
El Khartûm Sudan *see* Khartoum
El Khenachich *esc.* Mali *see* El Khnâchîch
El Khnâchîch *esc.* Mali 96 C2
Elkhorn U.S.A. 130 F3
Elkhorn City U.S.A. 134 D5
Elki Turkey *see* Beytüşşebap
Elkin U.S.A. 132 D4
Elkins U.S.A. 134 F4
Elk Island National Park Canada 121 H4
Elk Lake Canada 122 E5
Elk Lake *l.* U.S.A. 134 C1
Elkland U.S.A. 135 G3
Elk Mountain U.S.A. 126 G4
Elk Mountains U.S.A. 129 J2
Elko Canada 120 H5
Elko U.S.A. 129 F1
Elk Point Canada 121 I4
Elk Point U.S.A. 130 D3
Elk Springs U.S.A. 129 I1
Elkton *MD* U.S.A. 135 H4
Elkton *VA* U.S.A. 135 F4
El Kûbri Egypt *see* Al Kubrī
El Kuntilla Egypt *see* Al Kuntillah
Elkview U.S.A. 134 E4
Ellas *country* Europe *see* Greece
Ellaville U.S.A. 133 C5
Ell Bay Canada 121 O1
Ellef Ringnes Island Canada 119 H2
Ellen, Mount U.S.A. 129 H2
Ellenburg Depot U.S.A. 135 I1
Ellendale U.S.A. 130 D2
Ellensburg U.S.A. 126 C3
Ellenville U.S.A. 135 H3
El León, Cerro *mt.* Mex. 131 B7
Ellesmere, Lake N.Z. 113 D6

►Ellesmere Island Canada 119 J2
4th largest island in North America and 10th in the world.

Ellesmere Island National Park Reserve Canada *see* Quttinirpaaq National Park
Ellesmere Port U.K. 48 E5
Ellettsville U.S.A. 134 B4
Ellice *r.* Canada 121 K1
Ellice Island *atoll* Tuvalu *see* Funafuti
Ellice Islands *country* S. Pacific Ocean *see* Tuvalu
Ellicott City U.S.A. 135 G4
Ellijay U.S.A. 133 C5
Ellingen Germany 53 K5
Elliot S. Africa 101 H6
Elliot, Mount Australia 110 D3
Elliotdale S. Africa 101 I6
Elliot Knob *mt.* U.S.A. 134 F4
Elliot Lake Canada 122 E5
Elliott Australia 108 F4
Elliston U.S.A. 134 E5
Ellon U.K. 50 G3
Ellora Caves *tourist site* India 84 B1
Ellsworth *KS* U.S.A. 130 D4
Ellsworth *ME* U.S.A. 132 G2
Ellsworth *NE* U.S.A. 130 C3
Ellsworth *WI* U.S.A. 130 E2
Ellsworth Land *reg.* Antarctica 152 K1
Ellsworth Mountains Antarctica 152 L1
Ellwangen (Jagst) Germany 53 K6
El Maghreb *country* Africa *see* Morocco
Elmakuz Dağı *mt.* Turkey 85 A1
Elmalı Turkey 59 M6
El Malpais National Monument *nat. park* U.S.A. 129 J4
El Manṣûra Egypt *see* Al Manṣūrah
El Maṭarîya Egypt *see* Al Maṭarīyah
El Mazâr Egypt *see* Al Mazār
El Meghaïer Alg. 54 F5
El Milia Alg. 54 F4
El Minya Egypt *see* Al Minyā
Elmira *Ont.* Canada 134 E2
Elmira *P.E.I.* Canada 123 J5
Elmira *MI* U.S.A. 134 C1
Elmira *NY* U.S.A. 135 G2
El Mirage U.S.A. 129 G5
El Moral Spain 57 E5
Elmore Australia 112 B6
El Mreyyé *reg.* Mauritania 96 C3
Elmshorn Germany 53 J1
El Muglad Sudan 86 C7
Elmvale Canada 134 F1
Elnesvågen Norway 44 E5
El Nevado, Cerro *mt.* Col. 142 D3
El Oasis Mex. 129 F5
El Obeid Sudan 86 D7
El Odaiya Sudan 86 C7
El Oro Mex. 131 C7
Elorza Venez. 142 E2
El Oued Alg. 54 F5
Eloy U.S.A. 129 H5
El Palmito Mex. 131 B7
El Paso *IL* U.S.A. 130 F3
El Paso *KS* U.S.A. *see* Derby
El Paso *TX* U.S.A. 127 G7
Elphin U.K. 50 D2
Elphinstone Island *i.* Myanmar *see* Thayawthadangyi Kyun
El Portal U.S.A. 128 D3
El Porvenir Mex. 131 B6
El Porvenir Panama 137 I7
El Prat de Llobregat Spain 57 H3
El Progreso Hond. 136 G5
El Puerto de Santa María Spain 57 C5
El Qâhira Egypt *see* Cairo
El Qasimiye *r.* Lebanon 85 B3
El Quds Israel/West Bank *see* Jerusalem
El Quṣeima Egypt *see* Al Quṣaymah
El Quṣeir Egypt *see* Al Quṣayr
El Qûṣîya Egypt *see* Al Qūṣīyah
El Regocijo Mex. 131 B8
El Reno U.S.A. 131 D5
Elrose Canada 121 I5
Elsa Canada 120 C2
El Ṣâff Egypt *see* Aṣ Ṣaff
El Sahuaro Mex. 127 E7
El Salado Mex. 131 C7
El Salto Mex. 131 B8
El Salvador *country* Central America 136 G6
El Salvador Chile 144 C3
El Salvador Mex. 131 C7
Elsass *reg.* France *see* Alsace
El Sauz Mex. 127 G7
Else *r.* Germany 53 I2
El Sellûm Egypt *see* As Sallūm
Elsey Australia 108 F3
El Shallûfa Egypt *see* Ash Shallūfah
El Sharana Australia 108 F3
El Shaṭṭ Egypt *see* Ash Shaṭṭ
Elsie U.S.A. 134 C2
Elsinore Denmark *see* Helsingør
Elsinore U.S.A. 129 G2
Elsinore Lake U.S.A. 128 E5
El Sueco Mex. 127 G7
El Suweis Egypt *see* Suez
El Suweis *governorate* Egypt *see* As Suways
El Tama, Parque Nacional *nat. park* Venez. 142 D2
El Tarf Alg. 58 C6
El Teleno *mt.* Spain 57 C2
El Temascal Mex. 131 D7
El Thamad Egypt *see* Ath Thamad
El Tigre Venez. 142 F2
Eltmann Germany 53 K5
El'ton Russia 43 J6
El'ton, Ozero *l.* Russia 43 J6
El Tren Mex. 127 E7
El Tuparro, Parque Nacional *nat. park* Col. 142 E2
El Ṭûr Egypt *see* Aṭ Ṭūr
El Turbio Arg. 144 B8
El Uqṣur Egypt *see* Luxor
Eluru India 84 D2
Elva Estonia 45 O7
Elvanfoot U.K. 50 F5
Elvas Port. 57 C4
Elverum Norway 45 G6
Elvira Brazil 142 D5
El Wak Kenya 98 E3
El Wâṭya *well* Egypt *see* Al Wāṭiyah
Elwood *IN* U.S.A. 134 C3
Elwood *NE* U.S.A. 130 D3
El Wuz Sudan 86 D7
Elx Spain *see* Elche-Elx
Elxleben Germany 53 K3
Ely U.K. 49 H6
Ely *MN* U.S.A. 130 F2
Ely *NV* U.S.A. 129 F2
Elyria U.S.A. 134 D3
Elz Germany 53 I4
El Zagâzîg Egypt *see* Az Zaqāzīq
Elze Germany 53 J2
Émaé *i.* Vanuatu 107 G3
eMakhazeni S. Africa 101 J3
eMalahleni S. Africa 101 I3
Emām Taqī Iran 88 E2
Emån *r.* Sweden 45 J8
eManzimtoti S. Africa 101 J6
Emas, Parque Nacional das *nat. park* Brazil 143 H7
Emba Kazakh. 80 A2
Embalenhle S. Africa 101 I4
Embarcación Arg. 144 D2
Embarras Portage Canada 121 I3
Embi Kazakh. *see* Emba
Embira *r.* Brazil *see* Envira
Emborcação, Represa de *resr* Brazil 145 B2
Embrun Canada 135 H1
Embu Kenya 98 D4
Emden Germany 53 H1
Emden Deep *sea feature* N. Pacific Ocean *see* Cape Johnson Depth
Emei China *see* Emeishan
Emeishan China 76 D2
Emei Shan *mt.* China 76 D2
Emerald Australia 110 E4
Emeril Canada 123 I3
Emerita Augusta Spain *see* Mérida
Emerson Canada 121 L5
Emerson U.S.A. 134 D4
Emery U.S.A. 129 H2
Emesa Syria *see* Homs
Emet Turkey 59 M5
Emgwenya S. Africa 101 J3
eMgwenya S. Africa 101 J3
Emigrant Pass U.S.A. 128 E1
Emigrant Valley U.S.A. 129 F3
Emi Koussi *mt.* Chad 97 E3
Emile *r.* Canada 120 G2
Emiliano Zapata Mex. 136 F5
Emin China 80 F2
Emine, Nos *pt* Bulg. 59 L3
Eminence U.S.A. 134 C4
Eminska Planina *hills* Bulg. 59 L3
Emirdağ Turkey 59 N5
Emir Dağı *mt.* Turkey 59 N5
Emir Dağları *mts* Turkey 59 N5
Emissi, Tarso *mt.* Chad 97 E2
eMjindini S. Africa 101 J3
eMkhondo S. Africa 101 J4
Emmaboda Sweden 45 I8
Emmaste Estonia 45 M7
Emmaville Australia 112 E2
Emmeloord Neth. 52 F2
Emmelshausen Germany 53 H4
Emmen Neth. 52 G2
Emmen Switz. 56 I3
Emmerich am Rhein Germany 52 G3
Emmet Australia 110 D5
Emmetsburg U.S.A. 130 E3
Emmett U.S.A. 126 D4
Emmiganuru India 84 C3
Emo Canada 121 M5
Emona Slovenia *see* Ljubljana
eMondlo S. Africa 101 J4
Emory Peak U.S.A. 131 C6
Empalme Mex. 127 F8
Empangeni S. Africa 101 J5
Emperor Seamount Chain *sea feature* N. Pacific Ocean 150 H2
Emperor Trough *sea feature* N. Pacific Ocean 150 H2
Empingham Reservoir U.K. *see* Rutland Water
Emplawas Indon. 108 E2
Empoli Italy 58 D3
Emporia *KS* U.S.A. 130 D4
Emporia *VA* U.S.A. 135 G5
Emporium U.S.A. 135 F3
Empress Canada 121 I5
Empty Quarter *des.* Saudi Arabia *see* Rub' al Khālī
Ems *r.* Germany 53 H1
Emsdale Canada 134 F1
Emsdetten Germany 53 H2
Ems-Jade-Kanal *canal* Germany 53 H1
eMzinoni S. Africa 101 I4
Enafors Sweden 44 H5
Encantadas, Serra das *hills* Brazil 144 F4
Encarnación Para. 144 E3
Enchi Ghana 96 C4
Encinal U.S.A. 131 D6
Encinitas U.S.A. 128 E5
Encino U.S.A. 127 G6
Encruzilhada Brazil 145 C1
Endako Canada 120 E4
Endau-Rompin National Park *nat. park* Malaysia 71 C7
Ende Indon. 108 C2
Endeavour Strait Australia 110 C1
Endeh Indon. *see* Ende
Enderby Canada 120 G5
Enderby *atoll* Micronesia *see* Puluwat
Enderby Land *reg.* Antarctica 152 D2
Endicott U.S.A. 135 G2
Endicott Mountains U.S.A. 118 C3
EnenKio *terr.* N. Pacific Ocean *see* Wake Island
Energodar Ukr. *see* Enerhodar
Enerhodar Ukr. 43 G7
Enewetak *atoll* Marshall Is 150 G5
Enez Turkey 59 L4
Enfe Lebanon 85 B2
Enfião, Ponta do *pt* Angola 99 B5
Enfidaville Tunisia 58 D6
Enfield U.S.A. 132 E4
Engan Norway 44 F5
Engaru Japan 74 F3
En Gedi Israel 85 B4
Engelhard U.S.A. 132 F5
Engel's Russia 43 J6
Engelschmangat *sea chan.* Neth. 52 E1
Enggano *i.* Indon. 68 C8
Enghien Belgium 52 E4
England *admin. div.* U.K. 49 E6
Englee Canada 123 L4
Englehart Canada 122 F5
Englewood *FL* U.S.A. 133 D7
Englewood *OH* U.S.A. 134 C4
English *r.* Canada 121 M5
English U.S.A. 134 B4
English Bazar India *see* Ingraj Bazar
English Channel France/U.K. 49 F9
English Coast Antarctica 152 L2
Engozero Russia 42 G2
Enhlalakahle S. Africa 101 J5
Enid U.S.A. 131 D4
Eniwa Japan 74 F4
Eniwetok *atoll* Marshall Is *see* Enewetak
Enjiang China *see* Yongfeng
Enkeldoorn Zimbabwe *see* Chivhu
Enkhuizen Neth. 52 F2
Enköping Sweden 45 J7
Enna *Sicily* Italy 58 F6
Ennadai Lake Canada 121 K2
En Nahud Sudan 86 C7
Ennedi, Massif *mts* Chad 97 F3
Ennell, Lough *l.* Ireland 51 E4
Enngonia Australia 112 B2
Enning U.S.A. 130 C2
Ennis Ireland 51 D5
Ennis *MT* U.S.A. 126 F3
Ennis *TX* U.S.A. 131 D5
Enniscorthy Ireland 51 F5
Enniskillen U.K. 51 E3
Ennistymon Ireland 51 C5
Enn Nâqoûra Lebanon 85 B3
Enns *r.* Austria 47 O6
Eno Fin. 44 Q5
Enoch U.S.A. 129 G3
Enontekiö Fin. 44 M2
Enosburg Falls U.S.A. 135 I1
Enos Corner U.S.A. 134 B4
Enping China 77 G4
Ens Neth. 52 F2
Ensay Australia 112 C6
Enschede Neth. 52 G2
Ense Germany 53 I3
Ensenada Mex. 127 D7
Enshi China 77 F2
Ensley U.S.A. 133 C6
Entebbe Uganda 98 D3
Enterprise Canada 120 G2
Enterprise *AL* U.S.A. 133 C6
Enterprise *OR* U.S.A. 126 D3
Enterprise *UT* U.S.A. 129 G3
Entre Ríos Bol. 142 F8
Entre Rios Brazil 143 H5
Entre Rios de Minas Brazil 145 B3
Entroncamento Port. 57 B4
Enugu Nigeria 96 D4
Enurmino Russia 65 T3
Envira Brazil 142 D5
Envira *r.* Brazil 142 D5
'En Yahav Israel 85 B4
Enyamba Dem. Rep. Congo 98 C4
Eochaill Ireland *see* Youghal
Epe Neth. 52 F2
Epéna Congo 98 B3
Épernay France 52 D5
Ephraim U.S.A. 129 H2
Ephrata U.S.A. 135 G3
Épi *i.* Vanuatu 107 G3
Epidamnus Albania *see* Durrës
Épinal France 56 H2
Episkopi Bay Cyprus 85 A2
Episkopis, Kolpos *b.* Cyprus *see* Episkopi Bay
ePitoli S. Africa *see* Pretoria
Epomeo, Monte *hill* Italy 58 E4
Epping U.K. 49 H7
Epping Forest National Park Australia 110 D4
Eppstein Germany 53 I4
Eppynt, Mynydd *hills* U.K. 49 D6
Epsom U.K. 49 G7
Epte *r.* France 52 B5
Eqlīd Iran 88 D4
Equatorial Guinea *country* Africa 96 D4
Équeurdreville-Hainneville France 49 F9
Erac Creek *watercourse* Australia 112 B1
Erandol India 84 B1
Erawadi *r.* Myanmar *see* Irrawaddy
Erawan National Park Thai. 71 B4
Erbaa Turkey 90 E2
Erbendorf Germany 53 M5
Erbeskopf *hill* Germany 52 H5
Erbet Iraq 91 G4
Ercan *airport* Cyprus 85 A2
Erciş Turkey 91 F3
Erciyes Dağı *mt.* Turkey 90 D3
Érd Hungary 58 H1
Erdaobaihe China *see* Baihe
Erdaogou Bingzhan China 76 B1
Erdao Jiang *r.* China 74 B4
Erdek Turkey 59 L4
Erdemli Turkey 85 B1
Erdenedalay Mongolia 72 I3
Erdenet Mongolia 80 J2
Erdenetsagaan Mongolia 73 L3
Erdi *reg.* Chad 97 F3
Erdniyevskiy Russia 43 J7

►Erebus, Mount *vol.* Antarctica 152 H1
Highest active volcano in Antarctica.

Erechim Brazil 144 F3
Ereentsav Mongolia 73 L3
Ereğli *Konya* Turkey 90 D3
Ereğli *Zonguldak* Turkey 59 N4
Erego Moz. *see* Errego
Erei, Monti *mts Sicily* Italy 58 F6
Erementaū Kazakh. *see* Yereymentau
Erenhot China 73 K4
Erepucu, Lago de *l.* Brazil 143 G4
Erevan Armenia *see* Yerevan
Erfurt Germany 53 L4
Erfurt *airport* Germany 53 K4
Ergani Turkey 91 E3
'Erg Chech *des.* Alg./Mali 96 C2
Ergene *r.* Turkey 59 L4
Ērgli Latvia 45 N8
Ergu China 74 C3
Ergun China 73 M2
Ergun He *r.* China/Russia *see* Argun'
Ergun Youqi China *see* Ergun
Ergun Zuoqi China *see* Gegen Gol
Er Hai *l.* China 76 D3
Erhulai China 74 B4
Eriboll, Loch *inlet* U.K. 50 E2
Ericht *r.* U.K. 50 F4
Ericht, Loch *l.* U.K. 50 E4
Erickson Canada 121 L5
Erie *KS* U.S.A. 131 E4
Erie *PA* U.S.A. 134 E2
Erie, Lake Canada/U.S.A. 134 E2
'Erîgât *des.* Mali 96 C3
Erik Eriksenstretet *sea chan.* Svalbard 64 D2
Eriksdale Canada 121 L5
Erimo-misaki *c.* Japan 74 F4
Erin Canada 134 E2
Erinpura Road India 82 C4
Eriskay *i.* U.K. 50 B3
Eritrea *country* Africa 86 E6
Erlangen Germany 53 L5
Erlangping China 77 F1
Erldunda Australia 109 F6
Erlistoun *watercourse* Australia 109 C6
Erlong Shan *mt.* China 74 C4
Erlongshan Shuiku *resr* China 74 B4
Ermak Kazakh. *see* Aksu
Ermelo Neth. 52 F2
Ermelo S. Africa 101 I4
Ermenek Turkey 85 A1
Ermenek *r.* Turkey 85 A1
Ermont Egypt *see* Armant
Ermoupoli Greece 59 K6
Ernakulam India 84 C4
Erne *r.* Ireland/U.K. 51 D3
Ernest Giles Range *hills* Australia 109 C6
Erode India 84 C4
Eromanga Australia 111 C5
Erongo *admin. reg.* Namibia 100 B1
Erp Neth. 52 F3
Erqu China *see* Zhouzhi
Errabiddy Hills Australia 109 A6
Er Rachidia Morocco 54 D5
Errego Moz. 99 D5
Er Remla Tunisia 58 D7
Er Renk South Sudan 86 D7
Errigal *hill* Ireland 51 D2
Errinundra National Park Australia 112 D6
Erris Head *hd* Ireland 51 B3
Errol U.S.A. 135 J1
Erromango *i.* Vanuatu 107 G3
Erronan *i.* Vanuatu *see* Futuna
Erseka Albania *see* Ersekë
Ersekë Albania 59 I4
Erskine U.S.A. 130 D2
Ersmark Sweden 44 L5
Ertai China 80 H2
Ertil' Russia 43 I6
Ertis *r.* Kazakh./Russia *see* Irtysh
Ertix He *r.* China/Kazakh. 80 G2
Ērtra *country* Africa *see* Eritrea
Eruh Turkey 91 F3
Erwin U.S.A. 132 D4
Erwitte Germany 53 I3
Erxleben *Sachsen-Anhalt* Germany 53 L2
Erxleben *Sachsen-Anhalt* Germany 53 L2
Eryuan China 76 C3
Erzerum Turkey *see* Erzurum
Erzgebirge *mts* Czechia/Germany 53 N4
Erzhan China 74 B2
Erzin Turkey 85 C1
Erzincan Turkey 91 E3
Erzurum Turkey 91 F3
Esa-ala P.N.G. 110 E1
Esan-misaki *pt* Japan 74 F4
Esashi Japan 74 F3
Esbjerg Denmark 45 F9
Esbo Fin. *see* Espoo
Escalante U.S.A. 129 H3
Escalante *r.* U.S.A. 129 H3
Escalante Desert U.S.A. 129 G3
Escalón Mex. 131 B7
Escambia *r.* U.S.A. 133 C6
Escanaba U.S.A. 132 C2
Escárcega Mex. 136 F5
Escatrón Spain 57 F3
Escaut *r.* Belgium 52 D4
Esch Neth. 52 F3
Eschede Germany 53 K2
Eschscholtz *atoll* Marshall Is *see* Bikini
Esch-sur-Alzette Lux. 52 F5
Eschwege Germany 53 K3
Eschweiler Germany 52 G4
Escondido *r.* Mex. 131 C6
Escondido U.S.A. 128 E5
Escudilla *mt.* U.S.A. 129 I5
Escuinapa Mex. 136 C4
Escuintla Guat. 136 F6
Eséka Cameroon 96 E4
Eşen Turkey 59 M6
Esenguly Turkm. 88 D2
Esenguly Döwlet Gorugy *nature res.* Turkm. 88 D2
Esens Germany 53 H1
Eşfahān Iran 88 C3
Esfarayen, Reshteh-ye *mts* Iran 88 E2
Esfedān Iran 89 E3
Eshan China 76 D3
Eshkanān Iran 88 D5
Eshowe S. Africa 101 J5
'Eshqābād Iran 88 E3
eSikhaleni S. Africa 101 J5
Esil Kazakh. *see* Yesil'
Esil *r.* Kazakh./Russia *see* Yesil'
Esk Australia 112 F1
Esk *r.* Australia 111 [inset]
Esk *r.* U.K. 48 D4
Eskdalemuir U.K. 50 F5
Esker Canada 123 I3
Eskifjörður Iceland 44 [inset 1]
Eski Gediz Turkey 59 M5
Eskilstuna Sweden 45 J7
Eskimo Lakes Canada 118 E3
Eskimo Point Canada *see* Arviat
Eskipazar Turkey 90 D2
Eskişehir Turkey 59 N5
Eski-Yakkabog' Uzbek. 89 G2
Esla *r.* Spain 57 C3
Eslāmābād-e Gharb Iran 88 B3
Esler Dağı *mt.* Turkey 59 M6
Eslohe (Sauerland) Germany 53 I3
Eslöv Sweden 45 H9
Esmā'īlī-ye Pā'īn Iran 88 E4
Eşme Turkey 59 M5
Esmeraldas Ecuador 142 C3
Esmont U.S.A. 135 F5
Esnagami Lake Canada 122 D4
Esnes France 52 D4
Espakeh Iran 89 F5
Espalion France 56 F4
España *country* Europe *see* Spain
Espanola Canada 122 E5
Espanola U.S.A. 131 B4
Espelkamp Germany 53 I2
Esperance Australia 109 C8
Esperance Bay Australia 109 C8
Esperanza *research station* Antarctica 152 A2
Esperanza Arg. 144 B8
Esperanza Mex. 127 F8
Espichel, Cabo *c.* Port. 57 B4
Espigão, Serra do *mts* Brazil 145 A4
Espigüete *mt.* Spain 57 D2
Espinazo Mex. 131 C7
Espinhaço, Serra do *mts* Brazil 145 C2
Espinosa Brazil 145 C1
Espírito Santo Brazil *see* Vila Velha
Espírito Santo *state* Brazil 145 C2
Espírito Santo do Pinhal Brazil 145 B3
Espiritu Santo *i.* Vanuatu 107 G3
Espíritu Santo, Isla *i.* Mex. 124 E7
Espoo Fin. 45 N6
Espuña *mt.* Spain 57 F5
Esqueda Mex. 127 F7
Esquel Arg. 144 B6

Esquimalt Canada 120 F5
Essaouira Morocco 96 C1
Essen Belgium 52 E3
Essen Germany 52 H3
Essen (Oldenburg) Germany 53 H2
Essequibo *r.* Guyana 143 G2
Essex Canada 134 D2
Essex *CA* U.S.A. 129 F4
Essex *MD* U.S.A. 135 G4
Essex *NY* U.S.A. 135 I1
Essexville U.S.A. 134 D2
Esslingen am Neckar Germany 53 J6
Es-Smara W. Sahara 96 B2
Esso Russia 65 Q4
Essoyla Russia 42 G3
Est, Canal de l' France 52 G6
Est, Île de l' *i.* Canada 123 J5
Est, Pointe de l' *pt* Canada 123 J4
Estación Marítima Antárctica *research station* Chile 152 A2
Estados, Isla de los *i.* Arg. 144 D8
Eşṭahbān Iran 88 D4
Estância Brazil 143 K6
Estancia U.S.A. 127 G6
Estand, Kūh-e *mt.* Iran 89 F4
Estats, Pic d' *mt.* France/Spain 56 E5
Estcourt S. Africa 101 I5
Este *r.* Germany 53 J1
Estelí Nicaragua 137 G6
Estella Spain 57 E2
Estepa Spain 57 D5
Estepona Spain 57 D5
Esteras de Medinaceli Spain 57 E3
Esterhazy Canada 121 K5
Estero Bay U.S.A. 128 C4
Esteros Para. 144 D2
Estevan Canada 121 K5
Estevan Group *is* Canada 120 D4
Estherville U.S.A. 130 E3
Estill U.S.A. 133 D5
Eston Canada 121 I5
Estonia *country* Europe 45 N7
Estonskaya S.S.R. *country* Europe *see* **Estonia**
Estrées-St-Denis France 52 C5
Estrela Brazil 145 A5
Estrela, Serra da *mts* Port. 57 C3
Estrela do Sul Brazil 145 B2
Estrella *mt.* Spain 57 E4
Estrella, Punta *pt* Mex. 127 E7
Estremoz Port. 57 C4
Estrondo, Serra *hills* Brazil 143 I5
Etadunna Australia 111 B6
Etah India 82 D4
Étain France 52 F5
Étamamiou Canada 123 K4
Étampes France 56 F2
Étaples France 52 B4
Etawah *Rajasthan* India 82 D4
Etawah *Uttar Prad.* India 82 D4
Ethandakukhanya S. Africa 101 J4
Ethelbert Canada 121 K5
Ethel Creek Australia 109 C5
E'Thembini S. Africa 100 F5

▶**Ethiopia** *country* Africa 98 D3
2nd most populous country in Africa.

Etimesgut Turkey 90 D3
Etive, Loch *inlet* U.K. 50 D4

▶**Etna, Mount** *vol. Sicily* Italy 58 F6
Highest active volcano in Europe.

Etne Norway 45 D7
Etobicoke Canada 134 F2
Etolin Strait U.S.A. 118 B3
Etorofu-tō *i.* Russia *see* **Iturup, Ostrov**
Etosha National Park Namibia 99 B5
Etosha Pan *salt pan* Namibia 99 B5
Etoumbi Congo 98 B3
Etrek *r.* Iran/Turkm. *see* **Atrek**
Etrek Turkm. 88 D2
Étrépagny France 52 B5
Étretat France 49 H9
Ettelbruck Lux. 52 G5
Etten-Leur Neth. 52 E3
Ettlingen Germany 53 I6
Ettrick Water *r.* U.K. 50 F5
Euabalong Australia 112 C4
Euboea *i.* Greece *see* **Evvoia**
Eucla Australia 109 E7
Euclid U.S.A. 134 E3
Euclides da Cunha Brazil 143 K6
Eucumbene, Lake Australia 112 D6
Eudistes, Lac des *l.* Canada 123 I4
Eudora U.S.A. 131 F5
Eudunda Australia 111 B7
Eufaula *AL* U.S.A. 133 C6
Eufaula *OK* U.S.A. 131 E5
Eufaula Lake *resr* U.S.A. 131 E5
Eugene U.S.A. 126 C3
Eugenia, Punta *pt* Mex. 127 E8
Eugowra Australia 112 D4
Eulo Australia 112 B2
Eumungerie Australia 112 D3
Eungella Australia 110 E4
Eungella National Park Australia 110 E4
Eunice *LA* U.S.A. 131 E6
Eunice *NM* U.S.A. 131 C5
Eupen Belgium 52 G4

▶**Euphrates** *r.* Asia 91 G5
Longest river in western Asia. Also known as Al Furāt (Iraq/Syria) or Fırat (Turkey).

Eura Fin. 45 M6
Eure *r.* France 52 B5
Eureka *CA* U.S.A. 126 B4
Eureka *KS* U.S.A. 130 D4
Eureka *MT* U.S.A. 126 E2
Eureka *NV* U.S.A. 129 F2
Eureka *OH* U.S.A. 134 D4
Eureka *SD* U.S.A. 130 D2
Eureka *UT* U.S.A. 129 G2
Eureka Sound *sea chan.* Canada 119 J2
Eureka Springs U.S.A. 131 E4
Eureka Valley U.S.A. 128 E3
Euriowie Australia 111 C6
Euroa Australia 112 B6
Eurombah Australia 111 E5
Eurombah Creek *r.* Australia 111 E5
Europa, Île *i.* Indian Ocean 99 E6
Europa, Punta de *pt* Gibraltar *see* **Europa Point**
Europa Point Gibraltar 57 D5
Euskirchen Germany 52 G4
Eutaw U.S.A. 133 C5
Eutsuk Lake Canada 120 E4
Eutzsch Germany 53 M3
Eva Downs Australia 108 F4
Evans, Lac *l.* Canada 122 F4
Evans, Mount U.S.A. 126 G5
Evansburg Canada 120 H4
Evans City U.S.A. 134 E3
Evans Head Australia 112 F2
Evans Head *hd* Australia 112 F2
Evans Ice Stream Antarctica 152 L1
Evans Strait Canada 121 P2
Evanston *IL* U.S.A. 134 B2
Evanston *WY* U.S.A. 126 F4
Evansville Canada 122 E5
Evansville *IN* U.S.A. 134 B5
Evansville *WY* U.S.A. 126 G4
Evant U.S.A. 131 D6
Eva Perón Arg. *see* **La Plata**
Evart U.S.A. 134 C2
Evaton S. Africa 101 H4
Evaz Iran 88 D5
Evening Shade U.S.A. 131 F4
Evensk Russia 65 Q3
Everard, Lake *salt flat* Australia 111 A6
Everard, Mount Australia 109 F5
Everard Range *hills* Australia 109 F6
Everdingen Neth. 52 F3
Everek Turkey *see* **Develi**

▶**Everest, Mount** China/Nepal 83 F4
Highest mountain in Asia and the world.

Everett *PA* U.S.A. 135 F3
Everett *WA* U.S.A. 126 C3
Evergem Belgium 52 D3
Everglades *swamp* U.S.A. 133 D7
Everglades National Park U.S.A. 133 D7
Evergreen U.S.A. 133 C6
Evesham Australia 110 C4
Evesham U.K. 49 F6
Evesham, Vale of *valley* U.K. 49 F6
Evijärvi Fin. 44 M5
Evje Norway 45 E7
Évora Port. 57 C4
Evoron, Ozero *l.* Russia 74 E2
Évreux France 52 B5
Evros *r.* Bulg. *see* **Maritsa**
Evros *r.* Turkey *see* **Meriç**
Evrotas *r.* Greece 59 J6
Évry France 52 C6
Evrychou Cyprus 85 A2
Evrykhou Cyprus *see* **Evrychou**
Evvoia *i.* Greece 59 K5
Ewan Australia 110 D3
Ewaso Ngiro *r.* Kenya 98 E3
Ewe, Loch *b.* U.K. 50 D3
Ewing U.S.A. 134 D5
Ewo Congo 98 B4
Exaltación Bol. 142 E6
Excelsior S. Africa 101 H5
Excelsior Mountain U.S.A. 128 D2
Excelsior Mountains U.S.A. 128 D2
Exe *r.* U.K. 49 D8
Exeter Australia 112 E5
Exeter Canada 134 E2
Exeter U.K. 49 D8
Exeter *CA* U.S.A. 128 D3
Exeter *NH* U.S.A. 135 J2
Exeter Lake Canada 121 I1
Exloo Neth. 52 G2
Exminster U.K. 49 D8
Exmoor *hills* U.K. 49 D7
Exmoor National Park U.K. 49 D7
Exmore U.S.A. 135 H5
Exmouth Australia 108 A5
Exmouth U.K. 49 D8
Exmouth, Mount Australia 112 D3
Exmouth Gulf Australia 108 A5
Exmouth Lake Canada 120 H1
Exmouth Plateau *sea feature* Indian Ocean 149 P7
Expedition National Park Australia 110 E5
Expedition Range *mts* Australia 110 E5
Exploits *r.* Canada 123 L4
Exton U.S.A. 135 H3
Extremadura *aut. comm.* Spain 57 D4
Exuma Cays *is* Bahamas 133 E7
Exuma Sound *sea chan.* Bahamas 133 F7
Eyasi, Lake *salt l.* Tanz. 98 D4
Eyawadi *r.* Myanmar *see* **Irrawaddy**
Eye U.K. 49 I6
Eyeberry Lake Canada 121 J2
Eyelenoborsk Russia 41 S3
Eyemouth U.K. 50 G5
Eyjafjörður *inlet* Iceland 44 [inset 1]
Eyl Somalia 98 E3
Eylau Russia *see* **Bagrationovsk**
Eynsham U.K. 49 F7
Eyre Creek *watercourse* Australia 110 B5
Eyre Mountains N.Z. 113 B7
Eyre Peninsula Australia 111 A7
Eystrup Germany 53 J2
Eysturoy *i.* Faroe Is 44 [inset 2]
Ezakheni S. Africa 101 J5
Ezel U.S.A. 134 D5
Ezenzeleni S. Africa 101 I4
Ezequiel Ramos Mexía, Embalse *resr* Arg. 144 C5
Ezhou China 77 G2
Ezhva Russia 42 K3
Ezine Turkey 59 L5
Ezo *i.* Japan *see* **Hokkaidō**
Ezousa *r.* Cyprus 85 A2

F

Faaborg Denmark 45 G9
Faadhippolhu Maldives 84 B5
Faafxadhuun Somalia 98 E3
Fabens U.S.A. 127 G7
Faber, Mount *hill* Sing. 71 [inset]
Faber Lake Canada 120 G2
Fåborg Denmark *see* **Faaborg**
Fabriano Italy 58 E3
Faches-Thumesnil France 52 D4
Fachi Niger 96 E3
Fada Chad 97 F3
Fada-N'Gourma Burkina Faso 96 D3
Fadghāmī Syria 91 F4
Fadiffolu Atoll Maldives *see* **Faadhippolhu**
Fadippolu Atoll Maldives *see* **Faadhippolhu**
Faenza Italy 58 D2
Færoerne *terr.* N. Atlantic Ocean *see* **Faroe Islands**
Faeroes *terr.* N. Atlantic Ocean *see* **Faroe Islands**
Făgăraş Romania 59 K2

▶**Fagatogo** American Samoa 107 I3
Capital of American Samoa.

Fagersta Sweden 45 I7
Fagne *reg.* Belgium 52 E4
Fagurhólsmýri Iceland 44 [inset 1]
Fagwir South Sudan 86 D8
Fahraj Iran 88 D4
Fā'id Egypt 90 D5
Fairbanks U.S.A. 118 D3
Fairborn U.S.A. 134 C4
Fairbury U.S.A. 130 D3
Fairchance U.S.A. 134 F4
Fairfax U.S.A. 135 G4
Fairfield *CA* U.S.A. 128 B2
Fairfield *IA* U.S.A. 130 F3
Fairfield *ID* U.S.A. 126 E4
Fairfield *IL* U.S.A. 130 F4
Fairfield *OH* U.S.A. 134 C4
Fairfield *TX* U.S.A. 131 D6
Fair Haven U.S.A. 135 I2
Fair Head *hd* U.K. 51 F2
Fair Isle *i.* U.K. 50 H1
Fairlee U.S.A. 135 I2
Fairlie N.Z. 113 C7
Fairmont *MN* U.S.A. 130 E3
Fairmont *WV* U.S.A. 134 E4
Fair Oaks U.S.A. 134 B3
Fairview Australia 110 D2
Fairview Canada 120 G3
Fairview *MI* U.S.A. 134 C1
Fairview *OK* U.S.A. 131 D4
Fairview *PA* U.S.A. 134 E2
Fairview *UT* U.S.A. 129 H2
Fairview Park *H.K.* China 77 [inset]
Fairweather, Cape U.S.A. 120 B3
Fairweather, Mount Canada/U.S.A. 120 B3
Fais *i.* Micronesia 69 K5
Faisalabad Pak. 89 I4
Faissault France 52 E5
Faith U.S.A. 130 C2
Faīẕābād Afgh. 89 H2
Faizabad Afgh. *see* **Faīẕābād**
Faizabad India 83 E4
Fakaofo *atoll* Tokelau 107 I2
Fakaofu *atoll* Tokelau *see* **Fakaofo**
Fakenham U.K. 49 H6
Fåker Sweden 44 I5
Fakfak Indon. 69 I7
Fakhrābād Iran 88 D4
Fakiragram India 83 G4
Fako *vol.* Cameroon *see* **Cameroun, Mont**
Fal *r.* U.K. 49 C8
Falaba Sierra Leone 96 B4
Falaise Lake Canada 120 G2
Falam Myanmar 70 A2
Falāvarjān Iran 88 C3
Falcon Lake Canada 121 M5
Falcon Lake *l.* Mex./U.S.A. 131 D7
Falenki Russia 42 K4
Falfurrias U.S.A. 131 D7
Falher Canada 120 G4
Falkenberg Sweden 45 H8
Falkenberg/Elster Germany 53 N3
Falkenhagen Germany 53 M1
Falkenhain Germany 53 M3
Falkensee Germany 53 N2
Falkenstein Germany 53 M5
Falkirk U.K. 50 F5
Falkland U.K. 50 F4
Falkland Escarpment *sea feature* S. Atlantic Ocean 148 E9

▶**Falkland Islands** *terr.* S. Atlantic Ocean 144 E8
United Kingdom Overseas Territory.

Falkland Plateau *sea feature* S. Atlantic Ocean 148 E9
Falkland Sound *sea chan.* Falkland Is 144 D8
Falköping Sweden 45 H7
Fallbrook U.S.A. 128 E5
Fallieres Coast Antarctica 152 L2
Falling Spring U.S.A. 134 E5
Fallon U.S.A. 128 D2
Fall River U.S.A. 135 J3
Fall River Pass U.S.A. 126 G4
Falls City U.S.A. 130 E3
Falmouth U.K. 49 B8
Falmouth *KY* U.S.A. 134 C4
Falmouth *VA* U.S.A. 135 G4
False *r.* Canada 123 H2
False Bay S. Africa 100 D8
False Point India 83 F5
Falster *i.* Denmark 45 G9
Fălticeni Romania 43 E7
Falun Sweden 45 I6
Famagusta Cyprus 85 A2
Famagusta Bay Cyprus *see* **Ammochostos Bay**
Fameck France 52 G5
Fāmenīn Iran 88 C3
Fame Range *hills* Australia 109 C6
Family Lake Canada 121 M5
Family Well Australia 108 D5
Fāmūr, Daryācheh-ye *l.* Iran 88 C4
Fana Mali 96 C3
Fanad Head *hd* Ireland 51 E2
Fandriana Madag. 99 E6
Fane *r.* Ireland 51 F4
Fang Thai. 70 B3
Fangcheng *Guangxi* China 77 F4
Fangcheng *Henan* China 77 G1
Fangchenggang China *see* **Fangcheng**
Fangdou Shan *mts* China 77 F2
Fangliao Taiwan 77 I4
Fangshan Taiwan 77 I4
Fangxian China 77 F1
Fangzheng China 74 C3
Fankuai China 77 F2
Fankuaidian China *see* **Fankuai**
Fanling *H.K.* China 77 [inset]
Fannich, Loch *l.* U.K. 50 D3
Fannūj Iran 89 E5
Fano Italy 58 E3
Fanshan *Anhui* China 77 H2
Fanshan *Zhejiang* China 77 I3
Fanum Fortunae Italy *see* **Fano**
Faqīh Aḥmadān Iran 88 C4
Farab Turkm. *see* **Farap**
Faraba Mali 96 B3
Faradofay Madag. *see* **Tôlañaro**
Farafangana Madag. 99 E6
Farāfirah, Wāḥāt al *oasis* Egypt 86 C4
Farafra Oasis *oasis* Egypt *see* **Farāfirah, Wāḥāt al**
Farāh Afgh. 89 F3
Faraḥābād Iran *see* **Khezerābād**
Farallon de Medinilla *i.* N. Mariana Is 69 L3
Farallon de Pajaros *vol.* N. Mariana Is 69 K2
Farallones de Cali, Parque Nacional *nat. park* Col. 142 C3
Faranah Guinea 96 B3
Farap Turkm. 89 F2
Fararah Oman 87 I6
Farasān, Jazā'ir *is* Saudi Arabia 86 F6
Faraulep *atoll* Micronesia 69 K5
Fareham U.K. 49 F8
Farewell, Cape Greenland 119 N3
Farewell, Cape N.Z. 113 D5
Farewell Spit N.Z. 113 D5
Färgelanda Sweden 45 H7
Farghona Uzbek. *see* **Farg'ona**
Fargo U.S.A. 130 D2
Farg'ona Uzbek. 87 L1
Faribault U.S.A. 130 E2
Faribault, Lac *l.* Canada 123 H2
Faridabad India 82 D3
Faridkot India 82 C3
Faridpur Bangl. 83 G5
Farīmān Iran 89 E3
Farkhār Afgh. 89 H2
Farkhor Tajik. 89 H2
Farmahīn Iran 88 C3
Farmer Island Canada 122 E2
Farmerville U.S.A. 131 E5
Farmington Canada 120 F4
Farmington *ME* U.S.A. 135 J1
Farmington *MO* U.S.A. 130 F4
Farmington *NH* U.S.A. 135 J2
Farmington *NM* U.S.A. 129 I3
Farmington Hills U.S.A. 134 D2
Far Mountain Canada 120 E4
Farmville U.S.A. 135 F5
Farnborough U.K. 49 G7
Farne Islands U.K. 48 F3
Farnham U.K. 49 G7
Farnham, Lake *salt flat* Australia 109 D6
Farnham, Mount Canada 120 G5
Faro Brazil 143 G4
Faro Canada 120 C2
Faro Port. 57 C5
Fårö *i.* Sweden 45 K8
Faroe-Iceland Ridge *sea feature* Arctic Ocean 153 I2

▶**Faroe Islands** *terr.* N. Atlantic Ocean 44 [inset 2]
Self-governing Danish territory.

Fårösund Sweden 45 K8
Farquhar, Atoll de *is* Seychelles 99 F5
Farquharson Tableland *hills* Australia 109 C6
Farrāshband Iran 88 D4
Farr Bay Antarctica 152 F2
Farristown U.S.A. 134 C5
Farsund Norway 45 E7
Fārūj Iran 88 E2
Farwell *MI* U.S.A. 134 C2
Farwell *TX* U.S.A. 131 C5
Fasā Iran 88 D4
Fasano Italy 58 G4
Faşikan Geçidi *pass* Turkey 85 A1
Faßberg Germany 53 K2
Fastiv Ukr. 43 F6
Fastov Ukr. *see* **Fastiv**
Fatehabad India 82 C3
Fatehgarh India 82 D4
Fatehpur *Rajasthan* India 82 C4
Fatehpur *Uttar Prad.* India 82 E4
Fatick Senegal 96 B3
Fattoilep *atoll* Micronesia *see* **Faraulep**
Faughan *r.* U.K. 51 E2
Faulkton U.S.A. 130 D2
Faulquemont France 52 G5
Fauresmith S. Africa 101 G5
Fauske Norway 44 I3
Faust Canada 120 H4
Fawcett Canada 120 H4
Fawley U.K. 49 F8
Fawn *r.* Canada 121 N4
Faxaflói *b.* Iceland 44 [inset 1]
Faxälven *r.* Sweden 44 J5
Faya Chad 97 E3
Fayette *AL* U.S.A. 133 C5
Fayette *MO* U.S.A. 130 E4
Fayette *MS* U.S.A. 131 F6
Fayette *OH* U.S.A. 134 C3
Fayetteville *AR* U.S.A. 131 E4
Fayetteville *NC* U.S.A. 133 E5
Fayetteville *TN* U.S.A. 133 C5
Fayetteville *WV* U.S.A. 134 E4
Fâyid Egypt *see* **Fā'id**
Faylakah *i.* Kuwait 88 C4
Fazao Malfakassa, Parc National de *nat. park* Togo 96 D4
Fazilka India 82 C3
Fazrān, Jabal *hill* Saudi Arabia 88 C5
Fdérik Mauritania 96 B2
Fead Group *is* P.N.G. *see* **Nuguria Islands**
Feale *r.* Ireland 51 C5
Fear, Cape U.S.A. 133 E5
Featherston N.Z. 113 E5
Feathertop, Mount Australia 112 C6
Fécamp France 56 E2
Federal District *admin. dist.* Brazil *see* **Distrito Federal**
Federalsburg U.S.A. 135 H4
Federated Malay States *country* Asia *see* **Malaysia**
Fedusar India 82 C4
Fehet Lake Canada 121 M1
Fehmarn *i.* Germany 47 M3
Fehrbellin Germany 53 M2
Feia, Lagoa *lag.* Brazil 145 C3
Feicheng China *see* **Feixian**
Feijó Brazil 142 D5
Feilding N.Z. 113 E5
Feio *r.* Brazil *see* **Aguapeí**
Feira de Santana Brazil 145 D1
Feixi China 77 H2
Feixian China 77 H1
Fejd el Abiod *pass* Alg. 58 B6
Feke Turkey 90 D3
Felanitx Spain 57 H4
Feldberg Germany 53 N1
Feldberg *mt.* Germany 47 L7
Feldkirch Austria 47 L7
Feldkirchen in Kärnten Austria 47 O7
Felidhe Atholhu Maldives 81 D11
Felidu Atoll Maldives *see* **Felidhe Atholhu**
Felipe C. Puerto Mex. 136 G5
Felixlândia Brazil 145 B2
Felixstowe U.K. 49 I7
Felixton S. Africa 101 J5
Fellowsville U.S.A. 134 F4
Felsina Italy *see* **Bologna**
Felton U.S.A. 135 H4
Feltre Italy 58 D1
Femunden *l.* Norway 44 G5
Femundsmarka Nasjonalpark *nat. park* Norway 44 H5
Fenaio, Punta del *pt* Italy 58 D3
Fence Lake U.S.A. 129 I4
Fener Burnu *hd* Turkey 85 B1
Fénérive Madag. *see* **Fenoarivo Atsinanana**
Fengari *mt.* Greece 59 K4
Fengcheng *Fujian* China *see* **Yongding**
Fengcheng *Fujian* China *see* **Anxi**
Fengcheng *Fujian* China *see* **Lianjiang**
Fengcheng *Guangdong* China *see* **Xinfeng**
Fengcheng *Guangxi* China *see* **Fengshan**
Fengcheng *Guizhou* China *see* **Tianzhu**
Fengcheng *Jiangxi* China 77 G2
Fenggang *Fujian* China *see* **Shaxian**
Fenggang *Guizhou* China 76 E3
Fenggang *Jiangxi* China *see* **Yihuang**
Fengguang China 74 B3
Fenghuang China 77 F3
Fengjiaba China *see* **Wangcang**
Fengjie China 77 F2
Fengkai China 77 F4
Fenglin Taiwan 77 I4
Fengman China 74 B4
Fengming *Shaanxi* China *see* **Qishan**
Fengming *Sichuan* China *see* **Pengshan**
Fengqing China 76 C3
Fengshan *Fujian* China *see* **Luoyuan**
Fengshan *Guangxi* China 76 E3
Fengshan *Hubei* China *see* **Luotian**
Fengshan *Yunnan* China *see* **Fengqing**
Fengshuba Shuiku *resr* China 77 G3
Fengtongzhai Nature Reserve *nature res.* China 76 D2
Fengxian China 76 E1
Fengxiang *Heilong.* China *see* **Luobei**
Fengxiang *Yunnan* China *see* **Lincang**
Fengyang China 77 H1
Fengyuan Taiwan 77 I3
Fengzhen China 73 K4
Feni Bangl. 83 G5
Feni Islands P.N.G. 106 F2
Fennville U.S.A. 134 B2
Feno, Capo di *c. Corsica* France 56 I6
Fenoarivo Atsinanana Madag. 99 E5
Fenshui Guan *pass* China 77 H3
Fenton U.S.A. 134 D2
Fenua Ura *atoll* Fr. Polynesia *see* **Manuae**
Fenyi China 77 G3
Feodosiya Crimea 90 D1
Fer, Cap de *c.* Alg. 58 B6
Férai Greece *see* **Feres**
Ferdows Iran 88 E3
Fère-Champenoise France 52 D6
Feres Greece 59 L4
Fergus Canada 134 E2
Fergus Falls U.S.A. 130 D2
Ferguson Lake Canada 121 L2
Fergusson Island P.N.G. 106 F2
Fériana Tunisia 58 C7
Ferizaj Kosovo 59 I3
Ferkessédougou Côte d'Ivoire 96 C4
Fermo Italy 58 E3
Fermont Canada 123 I3
Fermoselle Spain 57 C3
Fermoy Ireland 51 D5
Fernandina, Isla *i. Galápagos* Ecuador 142 [inset]
Fernandina Beach U.S.A. 133 D6
Fernando de Magallanes, Parque Nacional *nat. park* Chile 144 B8
Fernando de Noronha *i.* Brazil 148 F6
Fernandópolis Brazil 145 A3
Fernando Poó *i.* Equat. Guinea *see* **Bioko**
Fernão Dias Brazil 145 B2
Ferndale U.S.A. 128 A1
Ferndown U.K. 49 F8
Fernlee Australia 112 C2
Fernley U.S.A. 128 D2
Ferns Ireland 51 F5
Ferozepore India *see* **Firozpur**
Ferrara Italy 58 D2
Ferreira Gomes Brazil 143 H3
Ferro, Capo *c. Sardinia* Italy 58 C4
Ferrol Spain 57 B2
Ferron U.S.A. 129 H2
Ferros Brazil 145 C2
Ferryland Canada 123 L5
Ferryville Tunisia *see* **Menzel Bourguiba**
Fertő-tavi *nat. park* Hungary 58 G1
Ferwerd Neth. 52 F1
Ferwert Neth. *see* **Ferwerd**
Fès Morocco 54 D5
Feshi Dem. Rep. Congo 99 B4
Fessenden U.S.A. 130 D2
Festus U.S.A. 130 F4
Fété Bowé Senegal 96 B3
Fethard Ireland 51 E5
Fethiye *Malatya* Turkey *see* **Yazıhan**
Fethiye *Muğla* Turkey 59 M6
Fethiye Körfezi *b.* Turkey 59 M6
Fetisovo Kazakh. 91 I2
Fetlar *i.* U.K. 50 [inset]
Fettercairn U.K. 50 G4
Feucht Germany 53 L5
Feuchtwangen Germany 53 K5
Feuilles, Rivière aux *r.* Canada 123 H2
Fevral'sk Russia 74 C1
Fevzipaşa Turkey 90 E3
Feyẕābād *Kermān* Iran 88 D4
Feyẕābād *Khorāsān-e Raẓavī* Iran 88 E3
Fez Morocco *see* **Fès**
Fezzan *hist. area* Libya 96 E2
Ffestiniog U.K. 49 D6
Fianarantsoa Madag. 99 E6
Fichē Eth. 98 D3
Fichtelgebirge *hills* Germany 53 M4
Field U.S.A. 134 D5
Fier Albania 59 H4
Fiery Creek *r.* Australia 110 B3
Fiery Cross Reef S. China Sea 68 E5
Fife Lake U.S.A. 134 C1
Fife Ness *pt* U.K. 50 G4
Fifield Australia 112 C4
Fifth Meridian Canada 120 H3
Figeac France 56 F4
Figueira da Foz Port. 57 B3
Figueras Spain *see* **Figueres**
Figueres Spain 57 H2
Figuig Morocco 54 D5
Figuil Cameroon 97 E4

▶**Fiji** *country* S. Pacific Ocean 107 H3
4th most populous and 5th largest country in Oceania.

Fīk' Eth. 98 E3
Filadelfia Para. 144 D2
Filchner Ice Shelf Antarctica 152 A1
Filey U.K. 48 G4
Filibe Bulg. *see* **Plovdiv**
Filingué Niger 96 D3
Filipinas *country* Asia *see* **Philippines**
Filippiada Greece 59 I5
Filipstad Sweden 45 I7
Fillan Norway 44 F5
Fillmore *CA* U.S.A. 128 D4
Fillmore *UT* U.S.A. 129 G2
Fils *r.* Germany 53 J6
Fīltu Eth. 98 E3
Fimbul Ice Shelf Antarctica 152 C2
Finch Canada 135 H1
Findhorn *r.* U.K. 50 F3
Fındık Turkey 88 A2
Findlay U.S.A. 134 D3
Fine U.S.A. 135 H1
Fīn-e 'Olyā Iran 88 C3
Finger Lake Canada 121 M4
Finger Lakes U.S.A. 135 G2
Finike Turkey 59 N6
Finike Körfezi *b.* Turkey 59 N6
Finisterre Spain *see* **Fisterra**
Finisterre, Cabo *c.* Spain *see* **Finisterre, Cape**
Finisterre, Cape Spain 57 B2
Finke *watercourse* Australia 110 A5
Finke, Mount *hill* Australia 109 F7
Finke Bay Australia 108 E3
Finke Gorge National Park Australia 109 F6
Finland *country* Europe 44 O5
Finland, Gulf of Europe 45 M7

▶**Finlay** *r.* Canada 120 E3
Part of the Mackenzie-Peace-Finlay, the 2nd longest river in North America.

Finlay, Mount Canada 120 E3
Finlay Forks Canada 120 F4
Finley U.S.A. 130 D2
Finn *r.* Ireland 51 E3
Finne *ridge* Germany 53 L3
Finnigan, Mount Australia 110 D2
Finniss, Cape Australia 109 F8
Finnmarksvidda *reg.* Norway 44 H2
Finnsnes Norway 44 J2
Fins Oman 88 E6
Finschhafen P.N.G. 69 L8
Finspång Sweden 45 I7
Fintona U.K. 51 E3
Finucane Range *hills* Australia 110 C4
Fionn Loch *l.* U.K. 50 D3
Fionnphort U.K. 50 C4
Fiordland National Park N.Z. 113 A7
Fir *reg.* Saudi Arabia 88 B4
Fırat *r.* Asia *see* **Euphrates**
Firebaugh U.S.A. 128 C3
Firedrake Lake Canada 121 J2
Firenze Italy *see* **Florence**
Fireside Canada 120 E3
Firk, Sha'īb *watercourse* Iraq 91 G5
Firmat Arg. 144 D4
Firminy France 56 G4
Firmum Italy *see* **Fermo**
Firmum Picenum Italy *see* **Fermo**
Firovo Russia 42 G4
Firozabad India 82 D4
Firozkoh *reg.* Afgh. 89 G3
Firozpur India 82 C3
First State National Historical Site *nat. park* U.S.A. 135 H4
Fīrūzābād Iran 88 D4
Fīrūzkūh Iran 88 D3
Firyuza Turkm. *see* **Pöwrize**
Fischbach Germany 53 H5
Fischersbrunn Namibia 100 B3
Fish *watercourse* Namibia 100 C5
Fisher (abandoned) Australia 109 E7
Fisher Bay Antarctica 152 G2
Fisher Glacier Antarctica 152 E2
Fisher River Canada 121 L5
Fishers U.S.A. 134 B4
Fishers Island U.S.A. 135 J3

German South-West Africa country Africa see Namibia
Germantown OH U.S.A. 134 C4
Germantown WI U.S.A. 134 A2

▶Germany country Europe 47 L5
2nd most populous country in Europe.

Germersheim Germany 53 I5
Germī Iran 88 C2
Gernsheim Germany 53 I5
Gerolstein Germany 52 G4
Gerolzhofen Germany 53 K5
Gerona Spain see Girona
Gerrit Denys is P.N.G. see Lihir Group
Gers r. France 56 E4
Gersfeld (Rhön) Germany 53 J4
Gersoppa India 84 B3
Gerstungen Germany 53 K4
Gerwisch Germany 53 L2
Géryville Alg. see El Bayadh
Gêrzê China 83 F2
Gerze Turkey 90 D2
Gescher Germany 52 H3
Gesoriacum France see Boulogne-sur-Mer
Gessie U.S.A. 134 B3
Gestro Wenz, Wabē r. Eth. 78 D6
Gete r. Belgium 52 F4
Gettysburg PA U.S.A. 135 G4
Gettysburg SD U.S.A. 130 D2
Gettysburg National Military Park nat. park U.S.A. 135 G4
Getz Ice Shelf Antarctica 152 J2
Geumeo-do i. S. Korea 75 B6
Geumpang Indon. 71 B6
Geureudong, Gunung vol. Indon. 71 B6
Geurie Australia 112 D4
Gevaş Turkey 91 F3
Gevgelija Macedonia 59 J4
Gēwārām Band Afgh. 89 G4
Gexto Spain see Algorta
Gey Iran see Nīkshahr
Geyikli Turkey 59 L5
Geylegphug Bhutan 83 G4
Geysdorp S. Africa 101 G4
Geyserville U.S.A. 128 B2
Geyve Turkey 59 N4
Gezīr Iran 88 D5
Ghaap Plateau S. Africa 100 F4
Ghāb, Wādī al r. Syria 85 C2
Ghabāghib Syria 85 C3
Ghabeish Sudan 86 C7
Ghadaf, Wādī al watercourse Jordan 85 C4
Ghadamés Libya see Ghadāmis
Ghadāmis Libya 96 D1
Ghaghara r. India 83 F4
Ghaibi Dero Pak. 89 G5
Ghalend Iran 89 F4
Ghallaorol Uzbek. see G'allaorol
Ghana country Africa 96 C4
Ghanādah, Rās pt U.A.E. 88 D5
Ghantila India 82 B5
Ghanwā Saudi Arabia 86 G4
Ghanzi Botswana 99 C6
Ghanzi admin. dist. Botswana 100 F2
Ghap'an Armenia see Kapan
Ghār, Ras al pt Saudi Arabia 88 C5
Ghardaïa Alg. 54 E5
Gharghoda India 84 D1
Ghârib, Gebel mt. Egypt see Ghārib, Jabal
Ghārib, Jabal mt. Egypt 90 D5
Gharm Tajik. 89 H2
Gharqābād Iran 88 C3
Gharwa India see Garhwa
Gharyān Libya 97 E1
Ghāt Libya 96 E2
Ghatgaon India 83 F5
Ghatol India 82 C5
Ghawdex i. Malta see Gozo
Ghazal, Bahr el watercourse Chad 97 E3
Ghazaouet Alg. 57 F6
Ghaziabad India 82 D3
Ghazi Ghat Pak. 89 H4
Ghazipur India 83 E4
Ghazna Afgh. see Ghaznī
Ghaznī Afgh. 89 H3
Ghaznī Rōd r. Afgh. 89 G3
Ghazzah Gaza see Gaza
Ghebar Gumbad Iran 88 E3
Ghent Belgium 52 D3
Gheorghe Gheorghiu-Dej Romania see Onești
Gheorgheni Romania 59 K1
Gherla Romania 59 J1
Ghijduwon Uzbek. see G'ijduvon
Ghilzai reg. Afgh. 89 G4
Ghīnah, Wādī al watercourse Saudi Arabia 85 D4
Ghisonaccia Corsica France 56 I5
Ghōrak Afgh. 89 G3
Ghōriyān Afgh. 89 F3
Ghost Lake Canada 120 H2
Ghotaru India 82 B4
Ghotki Pak. 89 H5
Ghudamis Libya see Ghadāmis
Ghugri r. India 83 F4
Ghurayfah hill Saudi Arabia 85 C4
Ghūrī Iran 88 D4
Ghurrab, Jabal hill Saudi Arabia 88 B5
Ghuwayṭah, Nafūd al des. Saudi Arabia 85 D5
Ghuzor Uzbek. see G'uzor
Ghyvelde France 52 C3
Giaginskaya Russia 91 F1
Gialias r. Cyprus 85 A2
Gia Nghia Vietnam 71 D4
Gianisada i. Greece 59 L7
Giannitsa Greece 59 J4
Giant's Castle mt. S. Africa 101 I5
Giant's Causeway lava field U.K. 51 F2
Gianysada i. Greece see Gianisada
Gia Rai Vietnam 71 D5
Giarre Sicily Italy 58 F6
Gibb r. Australia 108 D3
Gibbonsville U.S.A. 126 E3
Gibeon Namibia 100 C3
Gibraltar terr. Europe 57 D5

▶Gibraltar Gibraltar 148 H3
United Kingdom Overseas Territory.

Gibraltar, Strait of Morocco/Spain 57 C6
Gibraltar Range National Park Australia 112 F2
Gibson Australia 109 C8
Gibson City U.S.A. 134 A3
Gibson Desert Australia 109 C6
Gichgeniyn Nuruu mts Mongolia 80 H2
Gidar Pak. 89 G4
Giddalur India 84 C3
Gīddi, Gebel el hill Egypt see Jiddī, Jabal al
Giddings U.S.A. 131 D6
Gīdolē Eth. 97 G4
Gien France 56 F3
Gießen Germany 53 I4
Gīfān-e 'Olyā Iran 88 E2
Gifford r. Canada 119 J2
Gifhorn Germany 53 K2
Gift Lake Canada 120 H4
Gifu Japan 75 E6
Giganta, Cerro mt. Mex. 127 F8
Gigha i. U.K. 50 D5
Gīgīga Eth. see Jijiga
G'ijduvon Uzbek. 89 G1
Gijón Spain see Gijón/Xixón
Gijón/Xixón Spain 57 D2
Gila r. U.S.A. 129 F5
Gila Bend U.S.A. 129 G5
Gila Bend Mountains U.S.A. 129 G5
Gīlān-e Gharb Iran 88 B3
Gilbert r. Australia 110 C3
Gilbert AZ U.S.A. 129 H5
Gilbert WV U.S.A. 134 E5
Gilbert Islands Kiribati 150 H5
Gilbert Islands country Pacific Ocean see Kiribati
Gilbert Peak U.S.A. 129 H1
Gilbert Ridge sea feature Pacific Ocean 150 H6
Gilbert River Australia 110 C3
Gilbués Brazil 143 I5
Gil Chashmeh Iran 88 E3
Gilé Moz. 99 D5
Gilead hist. area Jordan 85 B3
Giles Creek r. Australia 108 E4
Gilford Island Canada 120 E5
Gilgai Australia 112 E2
Gilgandra Australia 112 D3
Gil Gil Creek r. Australia 112 D2
Gilgit Pak. 82 C2
Gilgit r. Pak. 87 L2
Gilgit-Baltistan admin. div. Pak. 89 I2
Gilgunnia Australia 112 C4
Gılındire Turkey see Aydıncık
Gillam Canada 121 M3
Gillen, Lake salt flat Australia 109 D6
Gilles, Lake salt flat Australia 111 B7
Gillett U.S.A. 135 G3
Gillette U.S.A. 126 G3
Gilliat Australia 110 C4
Gillingham England U.K. 49 E7
Gillingham England U.K. 49 H7
Gilling West U.K. 48 F4
Gilman U.S.A. 134 B3
Gilmer U.S.A. 131 E5
Gilmour Island Canada 122 F2
Gilroy U.S.A. 128 C3
Gīmbī Eth. 98 D3
Gimcheon S. Korea 75 C5
Gimhae S. Korea 75 C6
Gimhwa S. Korea 75 B5
Gimli Canada 121 L5
Gimol'skoye, Ozero l. Russia 42 G3
Ginebra, Laguna l. Bol. 142 E6
Gineifa Egypt see Junayfah
Gin Gin Australia 110 E5
Gingin Australia 109 A7
Gingolx Canada 120 D4
Gīnīr Eth. 98 E3
Ginosa Italy 58 G4
Ginzo de Limia Spain see Xinzo de Limia
Gioia del Colle Italy 58 G4
Gipouloux r. Canada 122 G3
Gippsland reg. Australia 112 B7
Girā, Wâdi watercourse Egypt see Jirā', Wādī
Gīrān Rīg mt. Iran 88 E4
Girard U.S.A. 134 E2
Girardin, Lac l. Canada 123 I2
Girdab Iran 88 E3
Giresun Turkey 90 E2
Girgenti Sicily Italy see Agrigento
Giridh India see Giridih
Giridih India 83 F4
Girilambone Australia 112 C3
Girishk Afgh. 89 G4
Girna r. India 82 C5
Gir National Park India 82 B5
Girne Cyprus see Kyrenia
Girón Ecuador 142 C4
Giron Sweden see Kiruna
Girona Spain 57 H3
Gironde est. France 56 D4
Girot Pak. 89 I3
Girral Australia 112 C4
Girraween National Park Australia 112 E2
Girvan U.K. 50 E5
Girvas Russia 42 G3
Gisborne N.Z. 113 G4
Giscome Canada 120 F4
Gislaved Sweden 45 H8
Gisors France 52 B5
Gissar Tajik. see Hisor
Gissar Range mts Tajik./Uzbek. 89 G2
Gissarskiy Khrebet mts Tajik./Uzbek. see Gissar Range
Gitarama Rwanda 98 C4
Gitega Burundi 98 C4
Giuba r. Somalia see Jubba
Giulianova Italy 58 E3
Giurgiu Romania 59 K3
Giuvala, Pasul pass Romania 59 K2
Gīvar Iran 88 E2
Givet France 52 E4
Givors France 56 G4
Givry-en-Argonne France 52 E6
Giyani S. Africa 101 J2
Giza Egypt 90 C5
Gizhiga Russia 65 R3
Gjakovë Kosovo 59 I3
Gjilan Kosovo 59 I3
Gjirokastër Albania 59 I4
Gjirokastra Albania see Gjirokastër
Gjoa Haven Canada 119 I3
Gjøra Norway 44 F5
Gjøvik Norway 45 G6
Gkinas, Akrotirio pt Greece 59 M6
Glace Bay Canada 123 K5
Glacier Bay National Park and Preserve U.S.A. 120 B3
Glacier National Park Canada 120 G5
Glacier National Park U.S.A. 126 E2
Glacier Peak vol. U.S.A. 126 C2
Gladstad Norway 44 G4
Gladstone Australia 110 E4
Gladstone Canada 121 L5
Gladwin U.S.A. 134 C2
Gladys U.S.A. 134 F5
Gladys Lake Canada 120 C3
Glamis U.K. 50 F4
Glamis U.S.A. 129 F5
Glamoč Bos. & Herz. 58 G2
Glan r. Germany 53 H5
Glandorf Germany 53 I2
Glanton U.K. 48 F3
Glasgow U.K. 50 E5
Glasgow KY U.S.A. 134 C5
Glasgow MT U.S.A. 126 G2
Glasgow VA U.S.A. 134 F5
Glaslyn Canada 121 I4
Glass, Loch l. U.K. 50 E3
Glass Mountain U.S.A. 128 D3
Glastonbury U.K. 49 E7
Glauchau Germany 53 M4
Glazov Russia 42 L4
Gleiwitz Poland see Gliwice
Glen U.S.A. 135 J1
Glen Allen U.S.A. 135 G5
Glen Alpine Dam S. Africa 101 I2
Glenamaddy Ireland 51 D4
Glenamoy r. Ireland 51 C3
Glen Arbor U.S.A. 134 C1
Glenbawn, Lake Australia 112 E4
Glenboro Canada 121 L5
Glen Canyon gorge U.S.A. 129 H3
Glen Canyon Dam U.S.A. 129 H3
Glencoe Canada 134 E2
Glencoe S. Africa 101 J5
Glencoe U.S.A. 130 E2
Glendale AZ U.S.A. 129 G5
Glendale CA U.S.A. 128 D4
Glendale UT U.S.A. 129 G3
Glendale Lake U.S.A. 135 F3
Glen Davis Australia 112 E4
Glenden Australia 110 E4
Glendive U.S.A. 126 G3
Glendon Canada 121 I4
Glendo Reservoir U.S.A. 126 G4
Glenfield U.S.A. 135 H2
Glengavlen Ireland 51 E3
Glengyle Australia 110 B5
Glen Innes Australia 112 E2
Glenluce U.K. 50 E6
Glen Lyon U.S.A. 135 G3
Glenlyon Peak Canada 120 C2
Glen More valley U.K. 50 E3
Glenmorgan Australia 112 D1
Glenn U.S.A. 128 B2
Glennallen U.S.A. 118 D3
Glennie U.S.A. 134 D1
Glenns Ferry U.S.A. 126 E4
Glenora Canada 120 D3
Glenore Australia 110 C3
Glenormiston Australia 110 B4
Glenreagh Australia 112 F3
Glen Rose U.S.A. 131 D5
Glenrothes U.K. 50 F4
Glens Falls U.S.A. 135 I2
Glen Shee valley U.K. 50 F4
Glenties Ireland 51 D3
Glenveagh National Park Ireland 51 E2
Glenville U.S.A. 134 E4
Glenwood AR U.S.A. 131 E5
Glenwood IA U.S.A. 130 E3
Glenwood MN U.S.A. 130 E2
Glenwood NM U.S.A. 129 I5
Glenwood Springs U.S.A. 129 J2
Glevum U.K. see Gloucester
Glinde Germany 53 K1
Glittertinden mt. Norway 45 F6
Gliwice Poland 47 Q5
Globe U.S.A. 129 H5
Glogau Poland see Głogów
Głogów Poland 47 P5
Glomfjord Norway 44 H3
Glomma r. Norway 44 G7
Glommersträsk Sweden 44 K4
Glorieuses, Îles is Indian Ocean 99 E5
Glorioso Islands Indian Ocean see Glorieuses, Îles
Gloster U.S.A. 131 F6
Gloucester Australia 112 E3
Gloucester U.K. 49 E7
Gloucester MA U.S.A. 135 J2
Gloucester VA U.S.A. 135 G5
Gloversville U.S.A. 135 H2
Glovertown Canada 123 L4
Glöwen Germany 53 M2
Glubinnoye Russia 74 D3
Glubokiy Krasnoyarskiy Kray Russia 72 H2
Glubokiy Rostovskaya Oblast' Russia 43 I6
Glubokoye Belarus see Hlybokaye
Glubokoye Kazakh. 80 F1
Gluggarnir hill Faroe Is 44 [inset 2]
Glukhov Ukr. see Hlukhiv
Glusburn U.K. 48 F5
Glynebwy U.K. see Ebbw Vale
Gmelinka Russia 43 J6
Gmünd Austria 47 O6
Gmunden Austria 47 N7
Gnarp Sweden 45 J5
Gnarrenburg Germany 53 J1
Gnesen Poland see Gniezno
Gniezno Poland 47 P4
Gnjilane Kosovo see Gjilan
Gnowangerup Australia 109 B8
Gnows Nest Range hills Australia 109 B7
Goa India 84 B3
Goa state India 84 B3
Goageb Namibia 100 C4
Goalen Head hd Australia 112 E6
Goalpara India 83 G4
Goat Fell hill U.K. 50 D5
Goba Eth. 98 E3
Gobabis Namibia 100 D2
Gobannium U.K. see Abergavenny
Gobas Namibia 100 D4
Gobernador (abandoned) U.S.A. 129 J3
Gobi Desert des. China/Mongolia 72 J4
Gobindpur India 83 F5
Gobles U.S.A. 134 C2
Gobō Japan 75 D6
Goch Germany 52 G3
Gochas Namibia 100 D3
Go Công Vietnam 71 D5
Godalming U.K. 49 G7
Godavari r. India 84 D2
Godavari, Cape India 84 D2
Godda India 83 F4
Godē Eth. 98 E3
Godere Eth. 98 E3
Goderich Canada 134 E2
Goderville France 49 H9
Godhavn Greenland see Qeqertarsuaq
Godhra India 82 C5
Godia Creek b. India 89 H6
Gods r. Canada 121 M3
Gods Lake Canada 121 M4
God's Mercy, Bay of Canada 121 O2
Godthåb Greenland see Nuuk
Godwin-Austen, Mount China/Pak. see K2
Goedereede Neth. 52 D3
Goedgegun Swaziland see Nhlangano
Goegap Nature Reserve S. Africa 100 D5
Goélands, Lac aux l. Canada 123 J3
Goes Neth. 52 D3
Gogama Canada 122 E5
Gogebic Range hills U.S.A. 130 F2
Gogra r. India see Ghaghara
Goheung S. Korea 75 B6
Goiana Brazil 143 L5
Goiandira Brazil 145 A2
Goianésia Brazil 145 A1
Goiânia Brazil 145 A2
Goiás Brazil 145 A1
Goiás state Brazil 145 A2
Goidhoo Maldives 84 B5
Goifulha Fehendhu Atoll Maldives see Goidhoo
Goinsargoin China 76 C2
Goioerê Brazil 144 F2
Gojra Pak. 89 I4
Gokak India 84 B2
Gokarn India 84 B3
Gök Çay r. Turkey 85 A1
Gökçeada i. Turkey 59 K4
Gökdepe Turkm. see Gëkdepe
Gökdere r. Turkey 85 A1
Goklenkuy, Solonchak salt l. Turkm. 88 E1
Gökova Körfezi b. Turkey 59 L6
Gokprosh Hills Pak. 89 F5
Göksun Turkey 90 E3
Göksu Parkı Turkey 85 A1
Gokteik Myanmar 70 B2
Gokwe Zimbabwe 99 C5
Gol Norway 45 F6
Golaghat India 83 H4
Golbāf Iran 88 E4
Gölbaşı Turkey 90 E3
Golconda U.S.A. 128 E1
Gölcük Turkey 59 M4
Gold U.S.A. 135 G3
Gołdap Poland 47 S3
Gold Beach U.S.A. 126 B4
Goldberg Germany 53 M1
Gold Coast country Africa see Ghana
Gold Coast Australia 112 F2
Golden U.S.A. 126 G5
Golden Bay N.Z. 113 D5
Goldendale U.S.A. 126 C3
Goldene Aue reg. Germany 53 K3
Golden Gate Highlands National Park S. Africa 101 I5
Golden Hinde mt. Canada 120 E5
Golden Lake Canada 135 G1
Golden Prairie Canada 121 I5
Goldenstedt Germany 53 I2
Goldfield U.S.A. 128 E3
Goldsand Lake Canada 121 K3
Goldsboro U.S.A. 133 E5
Goldstone Lake U.S.A. 128 E4
Goldsworthy (abandoned) Australia 108 B5
Goldthwaite U.S.A. 131 D6
Goldvein U.S.A. 135 G4
Göle Turkey 91 F2
Goleta U.S.A. 128 D4
Golets-Davydov, Gora mt. Russia 73 J2
Gölgeli Dağları mts Turkey 59 M6
Goliad U.S.A. 131 D6
Golingka China see Gongbo'gyamda
Gölköy Turkey 90 E2
Gollel Swaziland see Lavumisa
Golm Germany 53 M2
Golmberg hill Germany 53 N2
Golmud China 80 H4
Golovnino Russia 74 G4
Golpāyegān Iran 88 C3
Gölpazarı Turkey 59 N4
Golspie U.K. 50 F3
Gol Vardeh Iran 89 F3
Golyama Syutkya mt. Bulg. 59 K4
Golyam Persenk mt. Bulg. 59 K4
Golyshi Russia see Vetluzhskiy
Golzow Germany 53 M2
Goma Dem. Rep. Congo 98 C4
Gōmal Kêlay Afgh. 89 H3
Gomang Co salt l. China 83 G3
Gomati r. India 87 N4
Gombak, Bukit hill Sing. 71 [inset]
Gombe Nigeria 96 E3
Gombe r. Tanz. 99 D4
Gombi Nigeria 96 E3
Gombroon Iran see Bandar-e 'Abbās
Gomel' Belarus see Homyel'
Gómez Palacio Mex. 131 C7
Gomīsh Tappeh Iran 88 D2
Gommern Germany 53 L2
Gomo Co salt l. China 83 F2
Gonābād Iran 88 E2
Gonaïves Haiti 137 J5
Gonarezhou National Park Zimbabwe 99 D6
Gonâve, Île de la i. Haiti 137 J5
Gonbad, Chāh-e well Iran 88 D3
Gonbad-e Kāvūs Iran 88 D2
Gonda India 83 E4
Gondal India 82 B5
Gondar Eth. see Gonder
Gonder Eth. 98 D2
Gondia India see Gondiya
Gondiya India 82 E5
Gönen Turkey 59 L4
Gonfreville-l'Orcher France 49 H9
Gong'an China 77 G2
Gongbalou China see Gamba
Gongbo'gyamda China 76 B2
Gongchang China see Longxi
Gongcheng China 77 F3
Gongga Shan mt. China 76 D2
Gonghe Qinghai China 80 J4
Gonghe Yunnan China see Mouding
Gongjiang China see Yudu
Gongogi r. Brazil 145 D1
Gongolgon Australia 112 C3
Gongquan China 76 E2
Gongtang China 83 G3
Gongwang Shan mts China 76 D3
Gongxian China see Gongquan
Gonjo China see Kasha
Gonjog China see Coqên
Gonzales CA U.S.A. 128 C3
Gonzales TX U.S.A. 131 D6
Gonzha Russia 74 B1
Goochland U.S.A. 135 G5
Goodenough, Cape Antarctica 152 G2
Goodenough Island P.N.G. 106 F2
Gooderham Canada 135 F1
Good Hope, Cape of S. Africa 100 D8
Good Hope Mountain Canada 126 B2
Gooding U.S.A. 126 E4
Goodland IN U.S.A. 134 B3
Goodland KS U.S.A. 130 C4
Goodlettsville U.S.A. 134 B5
Goodooga Australia 112 C2
Goodspeed Nunataks Antarctica 152 E2
Goole U.K. 48 G5
Goolgowi Australia 112 B5
Goolma Australia 112 D4
Gooloogong Australia 112 D4
Goomalling Australia 109 B7
Goombalie Australia 112 B2
Goondiwindi Australia 112 E2
Goongarrie, Lake salt flat Australia 109 C7
Goongarrie National Park Australia 109 C7
Goonyella Australia 110 D4
Goorly, Lake salt flat Australia 109 B7
Goose Bay Canada see Happy Valley-Goose Bay
Goose Creek U.S.A. 133 D5
Goose Lake U.S.A. 126 C4
Gooty India 84 C3
Gopalganj Bangl. 83 G5
Gopalganj India 83 F4
Gopeshwar India 82 D3
Göppingen Germany 53 J6
Gorakhnath mt. India 82 B5
Gorakhpur India 83 E4
Goražde Bos. & Herz. 58 H3
Gorczański Park Narodowy nat. park Poland 47 R6
Gorda, Punta pt U.S.A. 128 A1
Gördes Turkey 59 M5
Gordil Cent. Afr. Rep. 98 C3
Gordon r. Canada 121 O1
Gordon U.K. 50 G5
Gordon U.S.A. 130 C3
Gordon, Lake Australia 111 [inset]
Gordon Downs Australia 108 E4
Gordon Lake Canada 121 I3
Gordon Lake U.S.A. 135 F4
Gordonsville U.S.A. 135 F4
Goré Chad 97 E4
Gorē Eth. 98 D3
Gore N.Z. 113 B8
Gore U.S.A. 135 F4
Gorebridge U.K. 50 F5
Gore Point pt U.S.A. 118 C4
Gorey Ireland 51 F5
Gorg Iran 89 E4
Gorgān Iran 88 D2
Gorgān, Khalīj-e Iran 88 D2
Gorge Range hills Australia 108 B5
Gorgona, Isla i. Col. 142 C3
Gorham U.S.A. 135 J1
Gori Georgia 86 F1
Gorinchem Neth. 52 E3
Goris Armenia 91 G3
Gorizia Italy 58 E2
Gorki Belarus see Horki
Gor'kiy Russia see Nizhniy Novgorod
Gor'kovskoye Vodokhranilishche resr Russia 42 I4
Gorlice Poland 43 D6
Görlitz Germany 47 O5
Gorlovka Ukr. see Horlivka
Gorna Dzhumaya Bulg. see Blagoevgrad
Gorna Oryahovitsa Bulg. 59 K3
Gornji Milanovac Serbia 59 I2
Gornji Vakuf Bos. & Herz. 58 G3
Gorno-Altaysk Russia 80 G1
Gornotrakiyska Nizina lowland Bulg. 59 K3
Gornozavodsk Permskiy Kray Russia 41 R4
Gornozavodsk Sakhalinskaya Oblast' Russia 74 F3
Gornyak Russia 80 F1
Gornyy Russia 43 K6
Gornyye Klyuchi Russia 74 D3
Goro i. Fiji see Koro
Gorodenka Ukr. see Horodenka
Gorodets Russia 42 I4
Gorodishche Penzenskaya Oblast' Russia 43 J5
Gorodishche Volgogradskaya Oblast' Russia 43 J6
Gorodok Belarus see Haradok
Gorodok Russia see Zakamensk
Gorodok Khmel'nyts'ka Oblast' Ukr. see Horodok
Gorodok L'vivs'ka Oblast' Ukr. see Horodok
Gorodovikovsk Russia 43 I7
Goroka P.N.G. 69 L8
Gorokhovets Russia 42 I4
Gorom Gorom Burkina Faso 96 C3
Gorong, Kepulauan is Indon. 69 I7
Gorongosa mt. Moz. 99 D5
Gorongosa, Parque Nacional da nat. park Moz. 99 D5
Gorontalo Indon. 69 G6
Gorshechnoye Russia 43 H6
Gort Ireland 51 D4
Gort an Choirce Ireland 51 D2
Gorūh Iran 88 E4
Gorutuba r. Brazil 145 C1
Goryachiy Klyuch Russia 91 E1
Goryeong S. Korea 75 C6
Görzke Germany 53 M2
Gorzów Wielkopolski Poland 47 O4
Gosainthan mt. China see Xixabangma Feng
Gosforth U.K. 48 F3
Goshen CA U.S.A. 128 D3
Goshen IN U.S.A. 134 C3
Goshen NH U.S.A. 135 I2
Goshen NY U.S.A. 135 H3
Goshen VA U.S.A. 134 F5
Goshoba Turkm. see Goşoba
Goslar Germany 53 K3
Goşoba Turkm. 91 I2
Gospić Croatia 58 F2
Gosport U.K. 49 F8
Gossi Mali 96 C3
Gostivar Macedonia 59 I4
Gosu China 76 C1
Göteborg Sweden see Gothenburg
Götene Sweden 45 H7
Gotenhafen Poland see Gdynia
Gotha Germany 53 K4
Gothenburg Sweden 45 G8
Gothenburg U.S.A. 130 C3
Gotland i. Sweden 45 K8
Gotō-rettō is Japan 75 C6
Gotse Delchev Bulg. 59 J4
Gotska Sandön i. Sweden 45 K7
Gōtsu Japan 75 D6
Göttingen Germany 53 J3
Gott Peak Canada 120 F5
Gottwaldow Czechia see Zlín
Gouda Neth. 52 E2
Goudiri Senegal 96 B3
Goudoumaria Niger 96 E3
Goûgaram Niger 96 D3

▶Gough Island S. Atlantic Ocean 148 H8
Dependency of Tristan da Cunha.

Gouin, Réservoir resr Canada 122 G4
Goulburn Australia 112 D5
Goulburn r. N.S.W. Australia 112 E4
Goulburn r. Vic. Australia 112 B6
Goulburn Islands Australia 108 F2
Goulburn River National Park Australia 112 E4
Gould Coast Antarctica 152 J1
Goulou atoll Micronesia see Ngulu
Goundam Mali 96 C3
Goundi Chad 97 E4
Goupil, Lac l. Canada 123 H3
Gouraya Alg. 57 G5
Gourcy Burkina Faso 96 C3
Gourdon France 56 E4
Gouré Niger 96 E3
Gouripur Bangl. 83 G4
Gourits r. S. Africa 100 E8
Gourma-Rharous Mali 96 C3
Gournay-en-Bray France 52 B5
Goussainville France 52 C5
Gouverneur U.S.A. 135 H1
Governador Valadares Brazil 145 C2
Governor's Harbour Bahamas 133 E7
Govĭ Altayn Nuruu mts Mongolia 80 I3
Govind Ballash Pant Sagar resr India 83 E4
Gowanda U.S.A. 135 F2
Gowan Range hills Australia 110 D5
Gowna, Lough l. Ireland 51 E4
Goya Arg. 144 E3
Göyçay Azer. 91 G2
Goyder watercourse Australia 109 F6
Göygöl Azer. 91 G2
Goymatdag hills Turkm. 88 D1
Göynük Turkey 59 N4
Goyoum Cameroon 96 E4
Goz-Beïda Chad 97 F3
Gozha Co salt l. China 82 E2
Gözkaya Turkey 85 C1
Gozo i. Malta 58 F6
Graaff-Reinet S. Africa 100 G7
Grabfeld plain Germany 53 K4
Grabo Côte d'Ivoire 96 C4
Grabouw S. Africa 100 D8
Grabow Germany 53 L1
Gračac Croatia 58 F2
Gracefield Canada 122 F5
Gracey U.S.A. 134 B5
Gradaús, Serra dos hills Brazil 143 H5
Gradiška Bos. & Herz. see Bosanska Gradiška
Grady U.S.A. 131 C5
Gräfenhainichen Germany 53 M3
Grafenwöhr Germany 53 L5
Grafton Australia 112 F2
Grafton ND U.S.A. 130 D1
Grafton WI U.S.A. 134 B2
Grafton WV U.S.A. 134 E4
Grafton, Cape Australia 110 D3
Grafton, Mount U.S.A. 129 F2
Grafton Passage Australia 110 D3
Graham NC U.S.A. 132 E4
Graham TX U.S.A. 131 D5
Graham, Mount U.S.A. 129 I5
Graham Bell Island Russia see Greem-Bell, Ostrov
Graham Island B.C. Canada 120 C4
Graham Island Nunavut Canada 119 I2
Graham Land reg. Antarctica 152 L2
Grahamstown S. Africa 101 H7
Grahovo Bos. & Herz. see Bosansko Grahovo
Graigue Ireland 51 F5
Grajaú Brazil 143 I5
Grajaú r. Brazil 143 J4
Grammont Belgium see Geraardsbergen
Grammos mt. Greece 59 I4
Grampian Mountains U.K. 50 E4
Grampians National Park Australia 111 C8
Granada Nicaragua 137 G6
Granada Spain 57 E5

Granada U.S.A. 130 C4
Granard Ireland 51 E4
Granbury U.S.A. 131 D5
Granby Canada 123 G5
Gran Canaria i. Canary Is 96 B2
Gran Chaco reg. Arg./Para. 144 D3
Grand r. MO U.S.A. 134 B2
Grand r. SD U.S.A. 130 C2
Grand Atlas mts Morocco see Haut Atlas
Grand Bahama i. Bahamas 133 E7
Grand Ballon mt. France 47 K7
Grand Bank Canada 123 L5
Grand Banks of Newfoundland sea feature N. Atlantic Ocean 148 E3
Grand-Bassam Côte d'Ivoire 96 C4
Grand Bay-Westfield Canada 123 I5
Grand Bend Canada 134 E2
Grand Blanc U.S.A. 134 D2
Grand Canal Ireland 51 E4
Grand Canary i. Canary Is see Gran Canaria
Grand Canyon U.S.A. 129 G3
Grand Canyon gorge U.S.A. 129 G3
Grand Canyon National Park U.S.A. 129 G3
Grand Canyon-Parashant National Monument nat. park U.S.A. 129 G3
Grand Cayman i. Cayman Is 137 H5
Grand Drumont mt. France 47 K7
Grande r. Bahia Brazil 145 B1
Grande r. São Paulo Brazil 145 A3
Grande, Bahía b. Arg. 144 C8
Grande, Ilha i. Brazil 145 B3
Grande Cache Canada 120 G4
Grande Comore i. Comoros see Ngazidja
Grande de Matagalpa r. Nicaragua 137 H6
Grande Prairie Canada 120 G4
Grand Erg Occidental des. Alg. 54 D5
Grand Erg Oriental des. Alg. 54 F6
Grande-Rivière Canada 123 I4
Gran Desierto de Altar, Reserva de la Biosfera tourist site Mex. 127 E7
Gran Desierto del Pinacate, Parque Natural del tourist site Mex. 127 E7
Grandes, Salinas salt marsh Arg. 144 C4
Grande-Vallée Canada 123 I4
Grand Falls Canada 123 I5
Grand Falls-Windsor Canada 123 L4
Grand Forks Canada 120 G5
Grand Forks U.S.A. 130 D2
Grand Gorge U.S.A. 135 H2
Grand Haven U.S.A. 134 B2
Grandin, Lac l. Canada 120 G1
Grandioznyy, Pik mt. Russia 72 H2
Grand Island U.S.A. 130 D3
Grand Isle U.S.A. 131 F6
Grand Junction U.S.A. 129 I2
Grand-Lahou Côte d'Ivoire 96 C4
Grand Lake N.B. Canada 123 I5
Grand Lake Nfld. and Lab. Canada 123 J3
Grand Lake Nfld. and Lab. Canada 123 K4
Grand Lake LA U.S.A. 131 E6
Grand Lake MI U.S.A. 134 D1
Grand Lake St Marys U.S.A. 134 C3
Grand Ledge U.S.A. 134 C2
Grand Manan Island Canada 123 I5
Grand Marais MI U.S.A. 132 C2
Grand Marais MN U.S.A. 130 F2
Grand-Mère Canada 123 G5
Grand Mesa U.S.A. 129 J2
Grândola Port. 57 B4
Grand Passage New Caledonia 107 G3
Grand Pré, Landscape of tourist site Canada 123 I5
Grand Rapids Canada 121 L4
Grand Rapids MI U.S.A. 134 C2
Grand Rapids MN U.S.A. 130 E2
Grand-Sault Canada see Grand Falls
Grand St-Bernard, Col du pass Italy/Switz. see Great St Bernard Pass
Grand Teton mt. U.S.A. 126 F4
Grand Teton National Park U.S.A. 126 F4
Grand Traverse Bay U.S.A. 134 C1
▶Grand Turk Turks and Caicos Is 137 J4
Capital of the Turks and Caicos Islands.
Grandville U.S.A. 134 C2
Grandvilliers France 52 B5
Grand Wash Cliffs mts U.S.A. 129 F4
Grange Ireland 51 E6
Grängesberg Sweden 45 I6
Grangeville U.S.A. 126 D3
Granisle Canada 120 E4
Granite Falls U.S.A. 130 E2
Granite Mountain U.S.A. 128 E1
Granite Mountains CA U.S.A. 129 F4
Granite Mountains CA U.S.A. 129 F5
Granite Peak MT U.S.A. 126 F3
Granite Peak UT U.S.A. 129 G1
Granite Range mts AK U.S.A. 120 A3
Granite Range mts NV U.S.A. 128 D1
Granitola, Capo c. Sicily Italy 58 E6
Granja Brazil 143 J4
Gran Laguna Salada l. Arg. 144 C6
Gränna Sweden 45 I7
Gran Paradiso mt. Italy 58 B2
Gran Paradiso, Parco Nazionale del nat. park Italy 58 B2
Gran Pilastro mt. Austria/Italy 47 M7
Gran San Bernardo, Colle del pass Italy/Switz. see Great St Bernard Pass
Gran Sasso e Monti della Laga, Parco Nazionale del nat. park Italy 58 E3
Granschütz Germany 53 M3
Gransee Germany 53 N1
Grant U.S.A. 130 C3
Grant, Mount U.S.A. 128 E2
Grantham U.K. 49 G6
Grant Island Antarctica 152 J2
Grant Lake Canada 120 G1
Grantown-on-Spey U.K. 50 F3
Grant Range mts U.S.A. 129 F2
Grants U.S.A. 129 J4
Grants Pass U.S.A. 126 C4
Grantsville UT U.S.A. 129 G1
Grantsville WV U.S.A. 134 E4
Granville France 56 D2
Granville AZ U.S.A. 129 I5
Granville NY U.S.A. 135 I2
Granville TN U.S.A. 134 C5
Granville (abandoned) Canada 120 B2
Granville Lake Canada 121 K3
Grão Mogol Brazil 145 C2
Grapevine Mountains U.S.A. 128 E3
Gras, Lac de l. Canada 121 I1
Graskop S. Africa 101 J3
Grasplatz Namibia 100 B4
Grass r. Canada 121 L3
Grass r. U.S.A. 135 H1
Grasse France 56 H5
Grassflat U.S.A. 135 F3
Grassington U.K. 48 F4
Grasslands National Park Canada 121 J5
Grass Range U.S.A. 126 F3
Grass Valley U.S.A. 128 C2
Grassy Butte U.S.A. 130 C2
Grästorp Sweden 45 H7
Gratz U.S.A. 134 C4
Graudenz Poland see Grudziądz
Graus Spain 57 G2
Gravataí Brazil 145 A5
Grave, Pointe de pt France 56 D4
Gravelbourg Canada 121 J5
Gravel Hill Lake Canada 121 K2
Gravelines France 52 C4
Gravelotte S. Africa 101 J2
Gravenhurst Canada 134 F1
Grave Peak U.S.A. 126 E3
Gravesend Australia 112 E2
Gravesend U.K. 49 H7
Gravina in Puglia Italy 58 G4
Grawn U.S.A. 134 C1
Gray France 56 G3
Gray GA U.S.A. 133 D5
Gray KY U.S.A. 134 C5
Gray ME U.S.A. 135 J2
Grayback Mountain U.S.A. 126 C4
Gray Lake Canada 121 I2
Grayling r. Canada 120 E3
Grayling U.S.A. 134 C1
Grays U.K. 49 H7
Grays Harbor inlet U.S.A. 126 B3
Grays Lake U.S.A. 126 F4
Grayson U.S.A. 134 D4
Graz Austria 47 O7
Greasy Lake Canada 120 F2
Great Abaco i. Bahamas 133 E7
Great Australian Bight g. Australia 109 E8
Great Baddow U.K. 49 H7
Great Bahama Bank sea feature Bahamas 133 E7
Great Barrier Island N.Z. 113 E3
Great Barrier Reef Australia 110 D1
Great Barrier Reef Marine Park (Cairns Section) Australia 110 D3
Great Barrier Reef Marine Park (Capricorn Section) Australia 110 E4
Great Barrier Reef Marine Park (Central Section) Australia 110 E3
Great Barrier Reef Marine Park (Far North Section) Australia 110 D2
Great Barrington U.S.A. 135 I2
Great Basalt Wall National Park Australia 110 D3
Great Basin U.S.A. 128 E2
Great Basin National Park U.S.A. 129 F2
Great Bear r. Canada 120 E1
▶Great Bear Lake Canada 120 G1
4th largest lake in North America and 7th in the world.
Great Belt sea chan. Denmark 45 G9
Great Bend U.S.A. 130 D4
Great Bitter Lake Egypt 85 A4
Great Blasket Island Ireland 51 B5
▶Great Britain i. U.K. 46 G4
Largest island in Europe and 8th in the world.
Great Clifton U.K. 48 D4
Great Coco Island Cocos Is 68 A4
Great Cumbrae i. U.K. 50 E5
Great Dismal Swamp National Wildlife Refuge nature res. U.S.A. 135 G5
Great Dividing Range mts Australia 112 B6
Great Eastern Erg des. Alg. see Grand Erg Oriental
Greater Antarctica reg. Antarctica see East Antarctica
Greater Antilles is Caribbean Sea 137 H4
Greater Khingan Mountains China see Da Hinggan Ling
Greater Tunb i. The Gulf see Tonb-e Bozorg, Jazīreh-ye
Great Exuma i. Bahamas 133 F8
Great Falls U.S.A. 126 F3
Great Fish r. S. Africa 101 H7
Great Fish Point S. Africa 101 H7
Great Fish River Reserve Complex nature res. S. Africa 101 H7
Great Gandak r. India 83 F4
Great Ganges atoll Cook Is see Manihiki
Great Guana Cay i. Bahamas 133 E7
Great Himalayan National Park India 82 D3
Great Inagua i. Bahamas 137 J4
Great Karoo plat. S. Africa 100 F7
Great Kei r. S. Africa 101 I7
Great Lake Australia 111 [inset]
Great Limpopo Transfrontier Park Africa 101 J2
Great Malvern U.K. 49 E6
Great Meteor Tablemount sea feature N. Atlantic Ocean 148 G4
Great Namaqualand reg. Namibia 100 C4
Great Nicobar i. India 71 A6
Great Ormes Head hd U.K. 48 D5
Great Ouse r. U.K. 49 H6
Great Oyster Bay Australia 111 [inset]
Great Palm Islands Australia 110 D3
Great Plains U.S.A. 130 C3
Great Point U.S.A. 135 J3
Great Rift Valley Africa 98 D4
Great Ruaha r. Tanz. 99 D4
Great Sacandaga Lake U.S.A. 135 H2
Great St Bernard Pass Italy/Switz. 58 B2
Great Salt Lake U.S.A. 129 G1
Great Salt Lake Desert U.S.A. 129 G1
Great Sand Hills Canada 121 I5
Great Sand Sea des. Egypt/Libya 90 B5
Great Sandy Desert Australia 108 C5
Great Sandy Island Australia see Fraser Island
Great Sandy National Park Austr. 111 F5
Great Sea Reef Fiji 107 H3
▶Great Slave Lake Canada 120 H2
Deepest and 5th largest lake in North America and 10th largest in the world.
Great Smoky Mountains U.S.A. 133 C5
Great Smoky Mountains National Park U.S.A. 132 D5
Great Snow Mountain Canada 120 E3
Greatstone-on-Sea U.K. 49 H8
Great Stour r. U.K. 49 I7
Great Torrington U.K. 49 C8
Great Victoria Desert Australia 109 E7
Great Wall research station Antarctica 152 A2
Great Wall tourist site China 73 L4
Great Waltham U.K. 49 H7
Great Western Erg des. Alg. see Grand Erg Occidental
Great Western Torres Islands Myanmar 71 B5
Great Whernside hill U.K. 48 F4
Great Yarmouth U.K. 49 I6
Grebenkovskiy Ukr. see Hrebinka
Grebyonka Ukr. see Hrebinka
Greco, Cape Cyprus see Greko, Cape
Gredos, Sierra de mts Spain 57 D3
Greece country Europe 59 I5
Greece U.S.A. 135 G2
Greeley CO U.S.A. 126 G4
Greeley NE U.S.A. 130 D3
Greem-Bell, Ostrov i. Russia 64 H1
Green r. KY U.S.A. 134 B5
Green r. WY U.S.A. 129 I2
Green Bay U.S.A. 134 A1
Green Bay b. U.S.A. 134 B1
Greenbrier U.S.A. 134 B5
Greenbrier r. U.S.A. 134 E5
Green Cape Australia 112 E6
Greencastle Bahamas 133 E7
Greencastle U.K. 51 F3
Greencastle U.S.A. 134 B4
Green Cove Springs U.S.A. 133 D6
Greene ME U.S.A. 135 J1
Greene NY U.S.A. 135 H2
Greeneville U.S.A. 132 D4
Greenfield CA U.S.A. 128 C3
Greenfield IN U.S.A. 134 C4
Greenfield MA U.S.A. 135 I2
Greenfield OH U.S.A. 134 D4
Green Head hd Australia 109 A7
Greenhill Island Australia 108 F2
Green Island Taiwan see Lü Dao
Green Lake Canada 121 J4
▶Greenland terr. N. America 119 N3
Self-governing Danish territory. Largest island in North America and the world, and 3rd largest political entity in North America.
Greenland Basin sea feature Arctic Ocean 153 I2
Greenland Fracture Zone sea feature Arctic Ocean 153 I1
Greenland Sea Greenland/Svalbard 64 A2
Greenlaw U.K. 50 G5
Green Mountains U.S.A. 135 I1
Greenock U.K. 50 E5
Greenore Ireland 51 F3
Greenport U.S.A. 135 I3
Green River P.N.G. 69 K7
Green River UT U.S.A. 129 H2
Green River WY U.S.A. 126 F4
Green River Lake U.S.A. 134 C5
Greensboro U.S.A. 133 D5
Greensburg IN U.S.A. 134 C4
Greensburg KS U.S.A. 130 D4
Greensburg KY U.S.A. 134 C5
Greensburg LA U.S.A. 131 F6
Greensburg PA U.S.A. 134 F3
Greens Peak U.S.A. 129 I4
Greenstone Point U.K. 50 D3
Green Swamp U.S.A. 133 E5
Greentown U.S.A. 134 C3
Greenup IL U.S.A. 130 F4
Greenup KY U.S.A. 134 D4
Green Valley Canada 135 H1
Greenville Liberia 96 C4
Greenville AL U.S.A. 133 C6
Greenville IL U.S.A. 130 F4
Greenville KY U.S.A. 134 B5
Greenville ME U.S.A. 132 G2
Greenville MI U.S.A. 134 C2
Greenville MS U.S.A. 131 F5
Greenville NC U.S.A. 132 E5
Greenville NH U.S.A. 135 J2
Greenville OH U.S.A. 134 C3
Greenville PA U.S.A. 134 E3
Greenville SC U.S.A. 133 D5
Greenville TX U.S.A. 131 D5
Greenwich atoll Micronesia see Kapingamarangi
Greenwich CT U.S.A. 135 I3
Greenwich OH U.S.A. 134 D3
Greenwood AR U.S.A. 131 E5
Greenwood IN U.S.A. 134 B4
Greenwood MS U.S.A. 131 F5
Greenwood SC U.S.A. 133 D5
Gregory r. Australia 110 B3
Gregory, Lake salt flat S.A. Australia 111 B6
Gregory, Lake salt flat W.A. Australia 108 D5
Gregory, Lake salt flat W.A. Australia 109 B6
Gregory Downs Australia 110 B3
Gregory National Park Australia 108 E4
Gregory Range hills Qld Australia 110 C3
Gregory Range hills W.A. Australia 108 C5
Greifswald Germany 47 N3
Greiz Germany 53 M4
Greko, Cape Cyprus 85 B2
Gremyachinsk Russia 41 R4
Grenå Denmark see Grenaa
Grenaa Denmark 45 G8
Grenada U.S.A. 131 F5
Grenada country West Indies 137 L6
Grenade France 56 E5
Grenen spit Denmark 45 G8
Grenfell Australia 112 D4
Grenfell Canada 121 K5
Grenoble France 56 G4
Grense-Jakobselv Norway 44 Q2
Grenville, Cape Australia 110 C1
Grenville Island Fiji see Rotuma
Greshak Pak. 89 G5
Gresham U.S.A. 126 C3
Gressåmoen Nasjonalpark nat. park Norway 44 H4
Greta r. U.K. 48 E4
Gretna U.K. 50 F6
Gretna LA U.S.A. 131 F6
Gretna VA U.S.A. 134 F5
Greußen Germany 53 K3
Grevelingen sea chan. Neth. 52 D3
Greven Germany 53 H2
Grevena Greece 59 I4
Grevenbicht Neth. 52 F3
Grevenbroich Germany 52 G3
Grevenmacher Lux. 52 G5
Grevesmühlen Germany 47 M4
Grey, Cape Australia 110 B2
Greybull U.S.A. 126 F3
Greybull r. U.S.A. 126 F3
Grey Hunter Peak Canada 120 C2
Grey Islands Canada 123 L4
Greylock, Mount U.S.A. 135 I2
Greymouth N.Z. 113 C6
Grey Range hills Australia 112 A2
Grey's Plains Australia 109 A6
Greytown S. Africa 101 J5
Grez-Doiceau Belgium 52 E4
Gribanovskiy Russia 43 I6
Gridley U.S.A. 128 C2
Griffin U.S.A. 133 C5
Griffith Australia 112 C5
Grigan i. N. Mariana Is see Agrihan
Grik Malaysia see Gerik
Grim, Cape Australia 111 [inset]
Grimari Cent. Afr. Rep. 98 C3
Grimma Germany 53 M3
Grimmen Germany 47 N3
Grimnitzsee l. Germany 53 N2
Grimsby U.K. 48 G5
Grímsey i. Iceland 44 [inset 1]
Grimshaw Canada 120 G3
Grímsstaðir Iceland 44 [inset 1]
Grimstad Norway 45 F7
Grindavík Iceland 44 [inset 1]
Grindsted Denmark 45 F9
Grind Stone City U.S.A. 134 D1
Grindul Chituc spit Romania 59 M2
Grinnell Peninsula Canada 119 I2
Griqualand East reg. S. Africa 101 I6
Griqualand West reg. S. Africa 100 F5
Griquatown S. Africa 100 F5
Grise Fiord Canada 119 J2
Grishino Ukr. see Krasnoarmiys'k
Gris Nez, Cap c. France 52 B4
Gritley U.K. 50 G2
Grizzly Bear Mountain hill Canada 120 F1
Grmeč mts Bos. & Herz. 58 G2
Grobbendonk Belgium 52 E3
Groblersdal S. Africa 101 I3
Groblershoop S. Africa 100 F5
Grodno Belarus see Hrodna
Groen watercourse N. Cape S. Africa 100 F6
Groen watercourse Northern Cape/Western Cape S. Africa 100 C6
Groix, Île de i. France 56 C3
Grombalia Tunisia 58 D6
Gronau (Westfalen) Germany 52 H2
Grong Norway 44 H4
Groningen Neth. 52 G1
Groninger Wad tidal flat Neth. 52 G1
Grønland terr. N. America see Greenland
Groom Lake U.S.A. 129 F3
Groot-Aar Pan salt pan S. Africa 100 E4
Groot Berg r. S. Africa 100 D7
Groot Brakrivier S. Africa 100 F8
Grootdraaidam dam S. Africa 101 I4
Grootdrink S. Africa 100 E5
Groote Eylandt i. Australia 110 B2
Grootfontein Namibia 99 B5
Groot Karas Berg plat. Namibia 100 D4
Groot Letaba r. S. Africa 101 J2
Groot Marico S. Africa 101 H3
Groot Swartberge mts S. Africa 100 E7
Grootvloer salt pan S. Africa 100 E5
Groot Winterberg mt. S. Africa 101 H7
Gros Morne National Park Canada 123 K4
Gross Barmen Namibia 100 C2
Große Aue r. Germany 53 J2
Große Laaber r. Germany 53 M6
Großengottern Germany 53 K3
Großenkneten Germany 53 I2
Großenlüder Germany 53 J4
Großer Arber mt. Germany 53 N5
Großer Beerberg hill Germany 53 K4
Großer Eyberg hill Germany 53 H5
Großer Gleichberg hill Germany 53 K4
Großer Kornberg hill Germany 53 M4
Großer Osser mt. Czechia/Germany 53 N5
Großer Rachel mt. Germany 47 N6
Grosser Speikkogel mt. Austria 47 O7
Grosseto Italy 58 D3
Grossevichi Russia 74 E3
Groß-Gerau Germany 53 I5
Großglockner mt. Austria 47 N7
Groß Oesingen Germany 53 K2
Großrudestedt Germany 53 L3
Groß Schönebeck Germany 53 N2
Gross Ums Namibia 100 D2
Großvenediger mt. Austria 47 N7
Gros Ventre Range mts U.S.A. 126 F4
Groswater Bay Canada 123 K3
Groton U.S.A. 130 D2
Grottoes U.S.A. 135 F4
Grou Neth. 52 F1
Groundhog r. Canada 122 E4
Grouw Neth. see Grou
Grove U.S.A. 131 E4
Grove City U.S.A. 134 D4
Grove Hill U.S.A. 133 C6
Grove Mountains Antarctica 152 E2
Grover Beach U.S.A. 128 C4
Grovertown U.S.A. 134 B3
Groveton NH U.S.A. 135 J1
Groveton TX U.S.A. 131 E6
Growler Mountains U.S.A. 129 G5
Groznyy Russia 91 G2
Grubišno Polje Croatia 58 G2
Grudovo Bulg. see Sredets
Grudziądz Poland 47 Q4
Grünau Namibia 100 D4
Grünberg Poland see Zielona Góra
Grundarfjörður Iceland 44 [inset 1]
Grundy U.S.A. 134 D5
Gruñidora Mex. 131 C7
Grünstadt Germany 53 I5
Gruver U.S.A. 131 C4
Gruzinskaya S.S.R. country Asia see Georgia
Gryazi Russia 43 H5
Gryazovets Russia 42 I4
Gryfice Poland 47 O4
Gryfino Poland 47 O4
Gryfów Śląski Poland 47 O5
Gryllefjord Norway 44 J2
Grytviken S. Georgia 144 I8
Gua India 83 F5
Guacanayabo, Golfo de b. Cuba 137 I4
Guachochi Mex. 127 G8
Guadajoz r. Spain 57 D5
Guadalajara Mex. 136 D4
Guadalajara Spain 57 E3
Guadalcanal i. Solomon Is 107 G2
Guadalete r. Spain 57 C5
Guadalope r. Spain 57 F3
Guadalquivir r. Spain 57 C5
Guadalupe Mex. 131 C7
Guadalupe i. Mex. 127 D7
Guadalupe watercourse Mex. 128 E5
Guadalupe U.S.A. 128 C4
Guadalupe, Sierra de mts Spain 57 D4
Guadalupe Aguilera Mex. 131 B7
Guadalupe Bravos Mex. 127 G7
Guadalupe Mountains National Park U.S.A. 127 G7
Guadalupe Peak U.S.A. 127 G7
Guadalupe Victoria Baja California Mex. 129 F5
Guadalupe Victoria Durango Mex. 131 B7
Guadarrama, Sierra de mts Spain 57 D3
▶Guadeloupe terr. West Indies 137 L5
French Overseas Department.
Guadeloupe Passage Caribbean Sea 137 L5
Guadiana r. Port./Spain 57 C5
Guadix Spain 57 E5
Guafo, Isla i. Chile 144 B6
Guaíba Brazil 145 A5
Guaiçuí Brazil 145 B2
Guaíra Brazil 144 F2
Guajaba, Cayo i. Cuba 133 E8
Guaje, Llano de plain Mex. 131 C7
Guajira, Península de la pen. Col. 142 D1
Gualala U.S.A. 128 B2
Gualeguay Arg. 144 E4
Gualeguaychu Arg. 144 E4
Gualicho, Salina salt flat Arg. 144 C6
▶Guam terr. N. Pacific Ocean 69 K4
United States Unincorporated Territory.
Guamblin, Isla i. Chile 144 A6
Guampí, Sierra de mts Venez. 142 E2
Guamúchil Mex. 127 F8
Guanabacoa Cuba 133 D8
Guanacevi Mex. 131 B7
Guanahacabibes, Península de pen. Cuba 133 C8
Guanajay Cuba 133 D8
Guanajuato Mex. 136 D4
Guanambi Brazil 145 C1
Guanare Venez. 142 E2
Guandu China 77 G3
Guane Cuba 137 H4
Guang'an China 76 E2
Guangchang China 77 H3
Guangdong prov. China 77 [inset]
Guanghai China 77 G4
Guanghan China 76 E2
Guanghua China see Laohekou
Guangming China see Xide
Guangming Ding mt. China 77 H2
Guangnan China 76 E3
Guangshan China 77 G2
Guangxi aut. reg. China see Guangxi Zhuangzu Zizhiqu
Guangxi Zhuangzu Zizhiqu aut. reg. China 76 F4
Guangyuan China 76 E1
Guangze China 77 H3
Guangzhou China 77 G4
Guanhães Brazil 145 C2
Guanhe Kou r. mouth China 77 H1
Guanipa r. Venez. 142 F2
Guanling China 76 E3
Guanmian Shan mts China 77 F2
Guannan China 77 H1
Guanpo China 77 F1
Guanshui China 74 B4
Guansuo China see Guanling
Guantánamo Cuba 137 I4
Guanxian China see Dujiangyan
Guanyang China 77 F3
Guanyinqiao China 76 D2
Guanyun China 77 H1
Guapé Brazil 145 B3
Guapí Col. 142 C3
Guaporé r. Bol./Brazil 142 E6
Guaporé Brazil 145 A5
Guaqui Bol. 142 E7
Guará r. Brazil 145 B1
Guarabira Brazil 143 K5
Guaranda Ecuador 142 C4
Guarapari Brazil 145 C3
Guarapuava Brazil 145 A4
Guararapes Brazil 145 A3
Guaratinguetá Brazil 145 B3
Guaratuba Brazil 145 A4
Guaratuba, Baía de b. Brazil 145 A4
Guarda Port. 57 C3
Guardafui, Cape Somalia see Gwardafuy, Gees
Guardiagrele Italy 58 F3
Guardo Spain 57 D2
Guárico, del Embalse resr Venez. 142 E2
Guarujá Brazil 145 B3
Guasave Mex. 127 F8
Guasdualito Venez. 142 D2
▶Guatemala country Central America 136 F5
4th most populous country in North America.
▶Guatemala City Guat. 136 F6
Capital of Guatemala.
Guaviare r. Col. 142 E3
Guaxupé Brazil 145 B3
Guayaquil Ecuador 142 C4
Guayaquil, Golfo de g. Ecuador 142 B4
Guaymas Mex. 127 F8
Guazhou China 80 I3
Guba Eth. 98 D2
Gubakha Russia 41 R4
Gubbi India 84 C3
Gubio Nigeria 96 E3
Gubkin Russia 43 H6
Gucheng Hubei China 77 F1
Gucheng Yunnan China 76 D3
Gudari India 84 D2
Gudbrandsdalen valley Norway 45 F6
Gudermes Russia 91 G2
Gudivada India 84 D2
Gudiyattam India 84 C3
Gudur Andhra Prad. India 84 C3
Gudur Andhra Prad. India 84 C3
Gudvangen Norway 45 E6
Gudzhal r. Russia 74 D2
Gué, Rivière du r. Canada 123 H2
Guecho Spain see Algorta
Guéckédou Guinea 96 B4
Guelma Alg. 58 B6
Guelmim Morocco 96 B2
Guelph Canada 134 E2
Guémez Mex. 131 D8
Guénange France 52 G5
Guerara Alg. 54 E5
Guérard, Lac l. Canada 123 I2
Guercif Morocco 54 D5
Guéret France 56 E3
▶Guernsey terr. Channel Is 49 E9
British Crown Dependency.
Guernsey U.S.A. 126 G4
Guérou Mauritania 96 B3
Guerrah Et-Tarf salt pan Alg. 58 B7
Guerrero Negro Mex. 127 E8
Guers, Lac l. Canada 123 I2
Gueugnon France 56 G3
Gufeng China see Pingnan
Gufu China see Xingshan
Gugē mt. Eth. 98 D3
Gügerd, Kūh-e mts Iran 88 D3
Guguan i. N. Mariana Is 69 L3
Guhakolak, Tanjung pt Indon. 68 D8
Guhe China 77 H2
Gūh Kūh mt. Iran 88 E5
Guhrān Iran 88 E5
Guhuai China see Pingyu
Guiana Basin sea feature N. Atlantic Ocean 148 E5
Guiana Highlands mts S. America 142 E2
Guichi China see Chizhou
Guidan-Roumji Niger 96 D3
Guider Cameroon 97 E4
Guiding China 76 E3
Guidong China 77 G3
Guidonia Montecelio Italy 58 E4
Guigang China 77 F4
Guiglo Côte d'Ivoire 96 C4
Guignicourt France 52 D5
Guija Moz. 101 K3
Guiji Shan mts China 77 I2
Guildford U.K. 49 G7
Guilford U.S.A. 132 G2
Guilherme Capelo Angola see Cacongo
Guilin China 77 F3
Guillaume-Delisle, Lac l. Canada 122 F2
Guimarães Brazil 143 J4
Guimarães Port. 57 B3
Guinan China see Mangra
Guinea country Africa 96 B3
Guinea, Gulf of Africa 96 D4
Guinea Basin sea feature N. Atlantic Ocean 148 H5
Guinea-Bissau country Africa 96 B3
Guinea-Conakry country Africa see Guinea
Guinea Ecuatorial country Africa see Equatorial Guinea
Guiné-Bissau country Africa see Guinea-Bissau
Guinée country Africa see Guinea
Güines Cuba 137 H4
Guînes France 52 B4
Guines, Lac l. Canada 123 J3
Guingamp France 56 C2
Guipavas France 56 B2
Guiping China 77 F4
Güira de Melena Cuba 133 D8
Guiratinga Brazil 143 H7
Guiscard France 52 D5
Guise France 52 D5
Guishan China see Xinping
Guishan Dao i. Taiwan 77 I3
Guishun China 76 E3
Guixi Chongqing China see Dianjiang
Guixi Jiangxi China 77 H2
Guiyang Guizhou China 76 E3
Guiyang Hunan China 77 G3
Guizhou prov. China 76 E3
Guizi China 77 F4
Gujarat state India 82 C5
Gujar Khan Pak. 89 I3
Gujerat state India see Gujarat
Gujranwala Pak. 89 I3
Gujrat Pak. 89 I3
Gukovo Russia 43 H6
Gulabgarh India 82 D2
Gulbarga India see Kalaburagi
Gulbene Latvia 45 O8
Gul'cha Kyrg. see Gülchö
Gülchö Kyrg. 80 D3
Gülcihan Turkey 85 B1

Harlow U.K. 49 H7
Harlowton U.S.A. 126 F3
Harly France 52 D5
Harman U.S.A. 134 F4
Harmancık Turkey 59 M5
Harmanli Bulg. 59 K4
Harmony U.S.A. 135 K1
Harmsdorf Germany 53 K1
Harnai India 84 B2
Harnai Pak. 89 G4
Harnes France 52 C4
Harney Basin U.S.A. 126 D4
Harney Lake U.S.A. 126 D4
Härnösand Sweden 44 J5
Harns Neth. see Harlingen
Har Nuur l. Mongolia 80 H2
Haroldswick U.K. 50 [inset]
Harper Liberia 96 C4
Harper U.S.A. 131 D4
Harper, Mount U.S.A. 118 D3
Harper Creek r. Canada 120 H3
Harper Lake U.S.A. 128 E4
Harp Lake Canada 123 J3
Harpstedt Germany 53 I2
Harquahala Mountains U.S.A. 127 E6
Harrai India 82 D5
Harran Turkey 85 D1
Harrand Pak. 89 H4
Harricana, Rivière d' r. Canada 122 F4
Harriet Tubman Underground Railroad National Monument nat. park U.S.A. 135 H4
Harrington Australia 112 F3
Harrington U.S.A. 135 H4
Harris, Lake salt flat Australia 111 A6
Harris, Mount Australia 109 E6
Harris, Sound of sea chan. U.K. 50 B3
Harrisburg AR U.S.A. 131 F5
Harrisburg IL U.S.A. 130 F4
Harrisburg NE U.S.A. 130 C3

▶Harrisburg PA U.S.A. 135 G3
Capital of Pennsylvania.

Harrismith Australia 109 B8
Harrison AR U.S.A. 131 E4
Harrison MI U.S.A. 134 C1
Harrison NE U.S.A. 130 C3
Harrison OH U.S.A. 134 C4
Harrison, Cape Canada 123 K3
Harrison Bay U.S.A. 118 C2
Harrisonburg LA U.S.A. 131 F6
Harrisonburg VA U.S.A. 135 F4
Harrisonville U.S.A. 130 E4
Harriston Canada 134 E2
Harrisville MI U.S.A. 134 D1
Harrisville NY U.S.A. 135 H1
Harrisville PA U.S.A. 134 E3
Harrisville WV U.S.A. 134 E4
Harrodsburg IN U.S.A. 134 B4
Harrodsburg KY U.S.A. 134 C5
Harrodsville N.Z. see Otorohanga
Harrogate U.K. 48 F5
Harrowsmith Canada 135 G1
Harry S. Truman Reservoir U.S.A. 130 E4
Har Sai Shan mt. China 76 C1
Harsefeld Germany 53 J1
Harsīn Iran 88 B3
Harşit r. Turkey 90 E2
Hârşova Romania 59 L2
Harstad Norway 44 J2
Harsud India 82 D5
Harsum Germany 53 J2
Hart r. Canada 118 E3
Hart U.S.A. 134 B2
Hartbees watercourse S. Africa 100 E5
Hartberg Austria 47 O7
Harteigan mt. Norway 45 E6
Harter Fell hill U.K. 48 E4

▶Hartford CT U.S.A. 135 I3
Capital of Connecticut.

Hartford KY U.S.A. 134 B5
Hartford MI U.S.A. 134 B2
Hartford City U.S.A. 134 C3
Hartland U.K. 49 C8
Hartland U.S.A. 135 K1
Hartland Point U.K. 49 C7
Hartlepool U.K. 48 F4
Hartley U.S.A. 131 C5
Hartley Zimbabwe see Chegutu
Hartley Bay Canada 120 D4
Hartola Fin. 45 O6
Harts r. S. Africa 101 G5
Härtsfeld hills Germany 53 K6
Harts Range mts Australia 109 F5
Hartsville U.S.A. 134 B5
Hartswater S. Africa 100 G4
Hartville U.S.A. 131 E4
Hartwell U.S.A. 133 D5
Ḩarūrī, 'Irq al des. Saudi Arabia 88 B5
Har Us Nuur l. Mongolia 80 H2
Hārūt r. Afgh. 89 F3
Harūz Iran 88 E4
Harvard, Mount U.S.A. 126 G5
Harvey Australia 109 A8
Harvey U.S.A. 130 C2
Harvey Mountain U.S.A. 128 C1
Harwich U.K. 49 I7
Haryana state India 82 D3
Harz hills Germany 47 M5
Har Zin Israel 85 B4
Ḩaşāh, Wādī al watercourse Jordan 85 B4
Ḩaşāh, Wādī al watercourse Jordan/Saudi Arabia 85 C4
Hasalbag China 89 J2
Häsänabad Azer. 91 H3
Ḩasanah, Wādī watercourse Egypt 85 A4
Hasan Dağı mts Turkey 90 D3
Hasan Guli Turkm. see Esenguly
Hasankeyf Turkey 91 F3
Ḩasan Kūlah Afgh. 89 F3
Hasanur India 84 C4
Hasardag mt. Turkm. 88 E2
Hasbaïya Lebanon 85 B3
Hasbaya Lebanon see Hasbaïya
Hase r. Germany 53 H2
Haselünne Germany 53 H2
HaSharon plain Israel 85 B3
Hashtgerd Iran 88 C3
Hashtpar Iran see Tālesh
Hashtrūd Iran 88 B2
Haskell U.S.A. 131 D5
Haskovo Bulg. 59 K4
Haslemere U.K. 49 G7
Hăşmaşul Mare mt. Romania 59 K1
Ḩaşş, Jabal al hills Syria 85 C1
Hassan India 84 C3
Hassayampa watercourse U.S.A. 129 G5
Haßberge hills Germany 53 K4
Hasselt Belgium 52 F4
Hasselt Neth. 52 G2
Hassi Bel Guebbour Alg. 96 D2
Hassi Messaoud Alg. 54 F5
Hässleholm Sweden 45 H8
Hastings Australia 112 B7
Hastings r. Australia 112 F3
Hastings Canada 135 G1
Hastings N.Z. 113 F4
Hastings U.K. 49 H8
Hastings MI U.S.A. 134 C2
Hastings MN U.S.A. 130 E2
Hastings NE U.S.A. 130 D3
Hata India 83 E4
Hatanbulag Mongolia 73 J4
Hatay Turkey see Antakya
Hatay prov. Turkey 85 C1
Hatch U.S.A. 129 G3
Hatches Creek (abandoned) Australia 110 A4
Hatchet Lake Canada 121 K3
Hatfield Australia 112 A4
Hatfield U.K. 48 G5
Hatgal Mongolia 80 J1
Hath India 84 D1
Hat Head National Park Australia 112 F3
Hathras India 82 D4
Ha Tiên Vietnam 71 D5
Ha Tinh Vietnam 70 D3
Hatisar Bhutan see Geylegphug
Hatod India 82 C5
Hato Hud East Timor see Hatudo
Hatra Iraq 91 F4
Hattah Australia 111 C7
Hattah Kulkyne National Park Australia 111 C7
Hatteras, Cape U.S.A. 133 F5
Hatteras Abyssal Plain sea feature S. Atlantic Ocean 148 D4
Hattfjelldal Norway 44 H4
Hattiesburg U.S.A. 131 F6
Hattingen Germany 53 H3
Hattras Passage Myanmar 71 B4
Hatudo East Timor 108 D2
Hat Yai Thai. 71 C6
Hau Bon Vietnam see A Yun Pa
Haubstadt U.S.A. 134 B4
Haud reg. Eth. 98 E3
Hauge Norway 45 E7
Haugesund Norway 45 D7
Haukeligrend Norway 45 E7
Haukipudas Fin. 44 N4
Haukivesi l. Fin. 44 P5
Haultain r. Canada 121 J4
Hauraki Gulf N.Z. 113 E3
Haut Atlas mts Morocco 54 C5
Haute-Normandie admin. reg. France see Normandie
Haute-Volta country Africa see Burkina Faso
Haut-Folin hill France 56 G3
Hauts Plateaux Alg. 54 D5

▶Havana Cuba 137 H4
Capital of Cuba.

Havana U.S.A. 130 F3
Havant U.K. 49 G8
Havasu, Lake U.S.A. 129 F4
Havel r. Germany 53 L2
Havelange Belgium 52 F4
Havelberg Germany 53 M2
Havelock Canada 135 G1
Havelock N.Z. 113 D5
Havelock Swaziland see Bulembu
Havelock U.S.A. 133 E5
Havelock Falls Australia 108 F3
Havelock Island India 71 A5
Havelock North N.Z. 113 F4
Haverfordwest U.K. 49 C7
Haverhill U.S.A. 135 J2
Haveri India 84 B3
Haversin Belgium 52 F4
Havixbeck Germany 53 H3
Havlíčkův Brod Czechia 47 O6
Havøysund Norway 44 N1
Havran Turkey 59 L5
Havre U.S.A. 126 F2
Havre Aubert, Île du i. Canada 123 J5
Havre Rock i. Kermadec Is 107 I5
Havre-St-Pierre Canada 123 J4
Havza Turkey 90 D2
Hawai'i i. U.S.A. 127 [inset]
Hawai'ian Islands N. Pacific Ocean 150 I4
Hawaiian Ridge sea feature N. Pacific Ocean 150 I4
Hawai'i Volcanoes National Park U.S.A. 127 [inset]
Ḩawallī Kuwait 88 C4
Hawar i. Bahrain see Ḩuwār
Hawarden U.K. 48 D5
Hawea, Lake N.Z. 113 B7
Hawera N.Z. 113 E4
Hawes U.K. 48 E4
Hawesville U.S.A. 134 B5
Hāwī U.S.A. 127 [inset]
Hawick U.K. 50 G5
Ḩawīzah, Hawr al imp. l. Iraq 91 G5
Hawkdun Range mts N.Z. 113 B7
Hawke Bay N.Z. 113 F4
Hawkes Bay Canada 123 K4
Hawkins Peak U.S.A. 129 G3
Hawlêr Iraq see Arbīl/Hewlêr
Hawley U.S.A. 135 H3
Hawng Luk Myanmar 70 B2
Ḩawrān, Wādī watercourse Iraq 91 F4
Ḩawshah, Jibāl al mts Saudi Arabia 88 B6
Hawston S. Africa 100 D8
Hawthorne U.S.A. 128 D2
Haxby U.K. 48 F4
Hay Australia 112 B5
Hay watercourse Australia 110 B5
Hay r. Canada 120 H2
Hayachine-san mt. Japan 75 F5
Hayastan country Asia see Armenia
Haydān, Wādī al r. Jordan 85 B4
Hayden AZ U.S.A. 129 H5
Hayden CO U.S.A. 129 J1
Hayden IN U.S.A. 134 C4
Hayes r. Man. Canada 121 M3
Hayes r. Nunavut Canada 119 I3
Hayes Halvø pen. Greenland 119 L2
Hayfield Reservoir U.S.A. 129 F5
Hayfork U.S.A. 128 B1
Hayl, Wādī watercourse Syria 85 C3
Hayl, Wādī al watercourse Syria 85 D2
Hayle U.K. 49 B8
Haymā' Oman 87 I6
Haymana Turkey 90 D3
Haymarket U.S.A. 135 G4
Hay-on-Wye U.K. 49 D6
Hayrabolu Turkey 59 L4
Hay River Canada 118 G3
Hay River Reserve Canada 120 H2
Hays KS U.S.A. 130 D4
Hays MT U.S.A. 126 F2
Ḩays Yemen 86 F7
Haysville U.S.A. 131 D4
Haysyn Ukr. 43 F6
Ḩayṭān, Jabal hill Egypt 85 A4
Hayward CA U.S.A. 128 B3
Hayward WI U.S.A. 130 F2
Haywards Heath U.K. 49 G8
Hazar Turkm. 88 D2
Hazārah Jāt reg. Afgh. 89 G3
Hazard U.S.A. 134 D5
Hazaribag India see Hazaribagh
Hazaribagh India 83 F5
Hazaribagh Range mts India 83 E5
Hazār Masjed, Kūh-e mts Iran 88 E2
Hazebrouck France 52 C4
Hazelton Canada 120 E4
Hazen Strait Canada 119 G2
Hazerswoude-Rijndijk Neth. 52 E2
Hazhdanahr reg. Afgh. 89 G2
Hazira India 82 C5
Hazleton IN U.S.A. 134 B4
Hazleton PA U.S.A. 135 H3
Hazlett, Lake salt flat Australia 108 E5
Ḩazm al Jawf Yemen 86 F6
Ḩazrat-e Sulṭān Afgh. 89 G2
H. Bouchard Arg. 144 D4
Headford Ireland 51 C4
Headingly Australia 110 B4
Head of Bight b. Australia 109 E7
Healdsburg U.S.A. 128 B2
Healesville Australia 112 B6
Healy U.S.A. 118 D3
Heanor U.K. 49 F5
Hearadh, Ceann a Deas na pen. U.K. see South Harris
Heard Island Indian Ocean 149 M9

▶Heard Island and McDonald Islands terr. Indian Ocean 149 M9
Australian External Territory.

Hearne U.S.A. 131 D6
Hearne Lake Canada 121 H2
Hearrenfean Neth. see Heerenveen
Hearst Canada 122 E4
Hearst Island Antarctica 152 L2
Heart r. U.S.A. 130 C2
Heart of Neolithic Orkney tourist site U.K. 50 F1
Heathcote Australia 112 B6
Heathfield U.K. 49 H8
Heathsville U.S.A. 135 G5
Hebbardsville U.S.A. 134 B5
Hebbronville U.S.A. 131 D7
Hebei prov. China 73 L5
Hebel Australia 112 C2
Heber U.S.A. 129 H4
Heber City U.S.A. 129 H1
Heber Springs U.S.A. 131 E5
Hebi China see Shancheng
Hebron Canada 123 J2
Hebron U.S.A. 130 D3
Hebron West Bank 85 B4
Hecate Strait Canada 120 D4
Hecheng Jiangxi China see Zixi
Hecheng Zhejiang China see Qingtian
Hechi China 77 F3
Hechuan Chongqing China 76 E2
Hechuan Jiangxi China see Yongxin
Hecla Island Canada 121 L5
Hede China see Sheyang
Hede Sweden 44 H5
Hedemora Sweden 45 I6
He Devil Mountain U.S.A. 126 D3
Hedi Shuiku resr China 77 F4
Heech Neth. see Heeg
Heeg Neth. 52 F2
Heek Germany 52 H2
Heer Belgium 52 E4
Heerde Neth. 52 G2
Heerenveen Neth. 52 F2
Heerhugowaard Neth. 52 E2
Heerlen Neth. 52 F4
Hefa Israel see Haifa
Hefa, Mifraz Israel see Haifa, Bay of
Hefei China 77 H2
Hefeng China 77 F2
Heflin U.S.A. 133 C5
Hegang China 74 C3
Heho Myanmar 70 B2
Heidan r. Jordan see Haydān, Wādī al
Heidberg hill Germany 53 L3
Heide Germany 47 L3
Heide Namibia 100 C2
Heidelberg Germany 53 I5
Heidelberg S. Africa 101 I4
Heidenheim an der Brenz Germany 53 K6
Heihe China 74 B2
Heilbron S. Africa 101 H4
Heilbronn Germany 53 J5
Heiligenhafen Germany 47 M3
Hei Ling Chau i. H.K. China 77 [inset]
Heilongjiang prov. China 74 C3
Heilong Jiang r. China/Russia 74 D2
also known as Amur (Russia)
Heilsbronn Germany 53 K5
Heilungkiang prov. China see Heilongjiang
Heinola Fin. 45 O6
Heinze Islands Myanmar 71 B4
Heirnkut Myanmar 70 A1
Heishi Beihu l. China 83 E2
Heishui China 76 D1
Heisker Islands U.K. see Monach Islands
Heist-op-den-Berg Belgium 52 E3
Ḩeiṭân, Gebel hill Egypt see Ḩayṭān, Jabal
Hejaz reg. Saudi Arabia see Hijaz
Hejiang China 76 E2
He Jiang r. China 77 F4
Hejing China 80 G3
Hekimhan Turkey 90 E3
Hekla vol. Iceland 44 [inset 1]
Hekou Gansu China 72 I5
Hekou Hubei China 77 G2
Hekou Jiangxi China see Yanshan
Hekou Sichuan China see Yajiang
Hekou Yunnan China 76 D4
Helagsfjället mt. Sweden 44 H5
Helam India 76 B3
Helan Shan mts China 72 J5
Helbra Germany 53 L3
Helen atoll Palau 69 I6
Helena AR U.S.A. 131 F5

▶Helena MT U.S.A. 126 E3
Capital of Montana.

Helen Reef Palau 69 I6
Helensburgh U.K. 50 E4
Helen Springs Australia 108 F4
Ḩelez Israel 85 B4
Helgoland i. Germany 47 K3
Helgoländer Bucht g. Germany 47 L3
Heligoland i. Germany see Helgoland
Heligoland Bight g. Germany see Helgoländer Bucht
Heliopolis Lebanon see Ba'albek
Helixi China see Ningguo
Hella Iceland 44 [inset 1]
Helland Norway 44 J2
Hellas country Europe see Greece
Helleh r. Iran 88 C4
Hellespont strait Turkey see Dardanelles
Hellevoetsluis Neth. 52 E3
Hellhole Gorge National Park Australia 110 D5
Hellín Spain 57 F4
Hellinikon tourist site Greece 90 A3
Hells Canyon gorge U.S.A. 126 D3
Hell-Ville Madag. see Andoany
Helmand r. Afgh. 89 F4
Helmand, Hāmūn salt flat Afgh./Iran 89 F4
Helmantica Spain see Salamanca
Helmbrechts Germany 53 L4
Helme r. Germany 53 L3
Helmeringhausen Namibia 100 C3
Helmond Neth. 52 F3
Helmsdale U.K. 50 F2
Helmsdale r. U.K. 50 F2
Helmstedt Germany 53 L2
Helong China 74 C4
Helper U.S.A. 129 H2
Helpter Berge hills Germany 53 N1
Helsingborg Sweden 45 H8
Helsingfors Fin. see Helsinki
Helsingør Denmark 45 H8

▶Helsinki Fin. 45 N6
Capital of Finland.

Helston U.K. 49 B8
Helvécia Brazil 145 D2
Helvetic Republic country Europe see Switzerland
Ḩelwân Egypt see Ḩulwān
Hemel Hempstead U.K. 49 G7
Hemet U.S.A. 128 E5
Hemingford U.S.A. 130 C3
Hemlock Lake U.S.A. 135 G2
Hemmingen Germany 53 J2
Hemmingford Canada 135 I1
Hemmoor Germany 53 J1
Hempstead U.S.A. 131 D6
Hemsby U.K. 49 I6
Hemse Sweden 45 K8
Henan China 76 D1
Henan prov. China 77 G1
Henares r. Spain 57 E3
Henashi-zaki pt Japan 75 E4
Henbury Australia 109 F6
Hendek Turkey 59 N4
Henderson KY U.S.A. 134 B5
Henderson NC U.S.A. 132 E4
Henderson NV U.S.A. 129 F3
Henderson NY U.S.A. 135 G2
Henderson TN U.S.A. 131 F5
Henderson TX U.S.A. 131 E5
Henderson Island Pitcairn Is 151 L7
Hendersonville NC U.S.A. 133 D5
Hendersonville TN U.S.A. 134 B5
Henderville atoll Kiribati see Aranuka
Hendon U.K. 49 G7
Hendorābī, Jazīreh-ye i. Iran 88 D5
Hendy-Gwyn U.K. see Whitland
Hengām Iran 89 E5
Hengduan Shan mts China 76 C2
Hengelo Neth. 52 G2
Hengfeng China 77 H2
Hengnan China see Hengyang
Hengshan China 74 C3
Heng Shan mt. China 77 G3
Hengshui Hebei China 73 L5
Hengshui Jiangxi China see Chongyi
Hengxian China 77 F4
Hengyang Hunan China 77 G3
Hengyang Hunan China 77 G3
Hengzhou China see Hengxian
Heniches'k Ukr. 43 G7
Henley N.Z. 113 C7
Henley-on-Thames U.K. 49 G7
Henlopen, Cape U.S.A. 135 H4
Hennef (Sieg) Germany 53 H4
Hennenman S. Africa 101 H4
Hennepin U.S.A. 130 F3
Hennessey U.S.A. 131 D4
Hennigsdorf Germany 53 N2
Henniker U.S.A. 135 J2
Henning U.S.A. 134 B3
Henrietta U.S.A. 131 D5
Henrietta Maria, Cape Canada 122 E3
Henrieville U.S.A. 129 H3
Henrique de Carvalho Angola see Saurimo
Henry, Cape U.S.A. 135 G5
Henry Ice Rise Antarctica 152 A1
Henryk Arctowski research station Antarctica see Arctowski
Henry Kater, Cape Canada 119 L3
Henry Mountains U.S.A. 129 H2
Hensall Canada 134 E2
Henshaw, Lake U.S.A. 128 E5
Henteyn Nuruu mts Mongolia 73 J3
Hentiesbaai Namibia 100 B2
Henty Australia 112 C5
Henzada Myanmar see Hinthada
Heping Guangdong China 77 G3
Heping Guizhou China see Huishui
Heping Guizhou China see Yanhe
Hepo China see Jiexi
Heppner U.S.A. 126 D3
Heptanesus is Greece see Ionian Islands
Hepu China 77 F4
Heqing China 76 D3
Heraclea Turkey see Ereğli
Heraclea Pontica Turkey see Ereğli
Heraklion Greece see Iraklion
Herald Cays atolls Australia 110 E3
Herāt Afgh. 89 F3
Hérault r. France 56 F5
Herbertabad India 71 A5
Herbert Downs Australia 110 B4
Herbert River Falls National Park Australia 110 D3
Herbert Wash salt flat Australia 109 D6
Herborn Germany 53 I4
Herbstein Germany 53 J4
Hercules Dome ice feature Antarctica 152 K1
Herdecke Germany 53 H3
Herdorf Germany 53 H4
Hereford U.K. 49 E6
Hereford U.S.A. 131 C5
Hereheretue atoll Fr. Polynesia 151 K7
Herent Belgium 52 E4
Herford Germany 53 I2
Heringen (Werra) Germany 53 K4
Herington U.S.A. 130 D4
Herīs Iran 88 B2
Herisau Switz. 56 I3
Herkimer U.S.A. 135 H2
Herlen Gol r. China/Mongolia 73 L3
Herlen He r. China/Mongolia see Herlen Gol
Herleshausen Germany 53 K3
Herlong U.S.A. 128 C1
Herm i. Channel Is 49 E9
Hermanas Mex. 131 C7
Herma Ness hd U.K. 50 [inset]
Hermann U.S.A. 130 F4
Hermannsburg Germany 53 K2
Hermanus S. Africa 100 D8
Hermel Lebanon 85 C2
Hermes, Cape S. Africa 101 I6
Hermidale Australia 112 C3
Hermiston U.S.A. 126 D3
Hermitage MO U.S.A. 130 E4
Hermitage PA U.S.A. 134 E3
Hermitage Bay Canada 123 K5
Hermite, Islas is Chile 144 C9
Hermit Islands P.N.G. 69 L7
Hermon, Mount Lebanon/Syria 85 B3
Hermonthis Egypt see Armant
Hermopolis Magna Egypt see Al Ashmūnayn
Hermosa U.S.A. 129 J3
Hermosillo Mex. 127 F7
Hernandarias Para. 144 F3
Hernando U.S.A. 131 F5
Herndon CA U.S.A. 128 D3
Herndon PA U.S.A. 135 G3
Herndon WV U.S.A. 134 E5
Herne Germany 53 H3
Herne Bay U.K. 49 I7
Herning Denmark 45 F8
Heroica Nogales Mex. see Nogales
Heroica Puebla de Zaragoza Mex. see Puebla
Hérouville-St-Clair France 49 G9
Herowābād Iran see Khalkhāl
Herrera del Duque Spain 57 D4
Herrieden Germany 53 K5
Hershey U.S.A. 135 G3
Hertford U.K. 49 G7
Hertzogville S. Africa 101 G5
Herve Belgium 52 F4
Hervé, Lac l. Canada 123 H3
Hervey Islands Cook Is 151 J7
Herzberg Germany 53 M2
Herzberg (Elster) Germany 53 N3
Herzlake Germany 53 H2
Herzliyya Israel 85 B3
Herzogenaurach Germany 53 K5
Herzsprung Germany 53 M1
Ḩeşār Būshehr Iran 88 C4
Ḩeşār Hormozgān Iran 88 E5
Ḩeşār Zanjān Iran 88 C2
Hesdin France 52 C4
Hesel Germany 53 H1
Heshan China 77 F4
Heshengqiao China 77 G2
Hesperia U.S.A. 128 E4
Hesperus U.S.A. 129 I3
Hesperus Peak U.S.A. 129 I3
Hesquiat Canada 120 E5
Hess r. Canada 120 C2
Heßdorf Germany 53 K5
Hesse land Germany see Hessen
Hesselberg hill Germany 53 K5
Hessen land Germany 53 J4
Hessisch Lichtenau Germany 53 J3
Hess Mountains Canada 120 C2
Het r. Laos 70 D2
Hetauda Nepal 83 F4
Heteren Neth. 52 F3
Hetou China 77 F4
Hettinger U.S.A. 130 C2
Hetton U.K. 48 E4
Hettstedt Germany 53 L3
Hève, Cap de la c. France 49 H9
Ḩevron West Bank see Hebron
Hexham U.K. 48 E4
Hexian Anhui China 77 H2
Hexian Guangxi China see Hezhou
Heyang China 77 F1
Ḩeydarābād Iran 89 F4
Heydebreck Poland see Kędzierzyn-Koźle
Heysham U.K. 48 E4
Heyshope Dam S. Africa 101 J4
Heyuan China 77 G4
Heywood U.K. 48 E5
Heze China 77 G1
Hezhang China 76 E3
Hezheng China 76 D1
Hezhou China 77 F3
Hezuo China 76 D1
Hezuozhen China see Hezuo
Hialeah U.S.A. 133 D7
Hiawassee U.S.A. 133 D5
Hiawatha U.S.A. 130 E4
Hibbing U.S.A. 130 E2
Hibbs, Point Australia 111 [inset]
Hibernia Reef Australia 108 C3
Hīchān Iran 89 F5
Hicks, Point Australia 112 D6
Hicks Bay N.Z. 113 G3
Hicks Lake Canada 121 K2
Hicksville U.S.A. 134 C3
Hico U.S.A. 131 D5
Hidaka Japan 74 F4
Hidaka-sanmyaku mts Japan 74 F4
Hidalgo Mex. 131 D7
Hidalgo del Parral Mex. 131 B7
Hidrolândia Brazil 145 A2
Hierosolyma Israel/West Bank see Jerusalem
Higashi-suidō sea chan. Japan 75 C6
Higgins U.S.A. 131 C4
Higgins Bay U.S.A. 135 H2
Higgins Lake U.S.A. 134 C1
High Atlas mts Morocco see Haut Atlas
High Desert U.S.A. 126 C4
High Island i. H.K. China 77 [inset]
High Island U.S.A. 131 E6
High Island Reservoir H.K. China 77 [inset]
Highland Peak CA U.S.A. 128 D2
Highland Peak NV U.S.A. 129 F3
Highlands U.S.A. 135 I3
Highland Springs U.S.A. 135 G5
High Level Canada 120 G3
Highmore U.S.A. 130 D2
High Point U.S.A. 132 E5
High Point hill U.S.A. 135 H3
High Prairie Canada 120 G4
High River Canada 120 H5
Highrock Lake Man. Canada 121 K4
Highrock Lake Sask. Canada 121 J3
High Springs U.S.A. 133 D6
High Tatras mts Poland/Slovakia see Tatra Mountains
High Wycombe U.K. 49 G7
Higuera de Zaragoza Mex. 127 F8
Higüey Dom. Rep. 137 K5
Hiiumaa i. Estonia 45 M7
Hījānah, Buḩayrat al imp. l. Syria 85 C3
Hijaz reg. Saudi Arabia 86 E4
Ḩikmah, Ra's al pt Egypt 90 B5
Hiko U.S.A. 129 F3
Hikone Japan 75 E6
Hikurangi mt. N.Z. 113 G3
Hila Indon. 108 D1
Hilāl, Jabal hill Egypt 85 A4
Hilāl, Ra's al pt Libya 86 B3
Hilary Coast Antarctica 152 H1
Hildale U.S.A. 129 G3
Hildburghausen Germany 53 K4
Hilders Germany 53 K4
Hildesheim Germany 53 J2
Hillah Iraq 91 G4
Hill City U.S.A. 130 D4
Hillegom Neth. 52 E2
Hill End Australia 112 D4
Hillerød Denmark 45 H9
Hillgrove Australia 110 D3
Hill Island Lake Canada 121 I2
Hillman U.S.A. 134 D1
Hillsboro ND U.S.A. 130 D2
Hillsboro NM U.S.A. 127 G6
Hillsboro OH U.S.A. 134 D4
Hillsboro OR U.S.A. 126 C3
Hillsboro TX U.S.A. 131 D5
Hillsdale IN U.S.A. 134 B4
Hillsdale MI U.S.A. 134 C3
Hillside Australia 108 B5
Hillston Australia 112 B4
Hillsville U.S.A. 134 E5
Hilo U.S.A. 127 [inset]
Hilton Australia 110 B4
Hilton S. Africa 101 J5
Hilton U.S.A. 135 G2
Hilton Head Island U.S.A. 133 D5
Hilvan Turkey 90 E3
Hilversum Neth. 52 F2
Himachal Pradesh state India 82 D3
Himalaya mts Asia 82 D2
Himalchul mt. Nepal 83 F3
Himanka Fin. 44 M4
Ḩimār, Wādī al watercourse Syria/Turkey 85 D1
Himarë Albania 59 H4
Himatnagar India 82 C5
Himeji Japan 75 D6
Ḩimş Syria see Homs
Ḩimş, Baḩrat resr Syria see Qaṭṭinah, Buḩayrat
Hinchinbrook Island Australia 110 D3
Hinckley U.K. 49 F6
Hinckley MN U.S.A. 130 E2
Hinckley UT U.S.A. 129 G2
Hinckley Reservoir U.S.A. 135 H2
Hindaun India 82 D4
Hinderwell U.K. 48 G4
Hindley U.K. 48 E5
Hindman U.S.A. 134 D5
Hindmarsh, Lake dry lake Australia 111 C8
Hindu Kush mts Afgh./Pak. 89 G3
Hindupur India 84 C3

Hines Creek Canada 120 G3
Hinesville U.S.A. 133 D6
Hinganghat India 84 C1
Hingoli India 84 C2
Hınıs Turkey 91 F3
Hinnøya i. Norway 44 I2
Hinojosa del Duque Spain 57 D4
Hinsdale U.S.A. 135 I2
Hinte Germany 53 H1
Hinthada Myanmar 70 A3
Hinton Canada 120 G4
Hinton U.S.A. 134 E5
Hiort i. U.K. see St Kilda
Hippolytushoef Neth. 52 E2
Hipponium Italy see Vibo Valentia
Hippo Regius Alg. see Annaba
Hippo Zarytus Tunisia see Bizerte
Hirabit Dağ mt. Turkey 91 G3
Hiraizumi tourist site Japan 75 F5
Hirakud Dam India 83 E5
Hirakud Reservoir India 83 E5
Hirapur India 82 D4
Hiriyur India 84 C3
Hirosaki Japan 74 F4
Hiroshima Japan 75 D6
Hirschaid Germany 53 L5
Hirschberg Germany 53 L4
Hirschberg mt. Germany 47 M7
Hirschberg Poland see Jelenia Góra
Hirschenstein mt. Germany 53 M6
Hirson France 52 E5
Hîrşova Romania see Hârşova
Hirtshals Denmark 45 F8
Hisar India 82 C3
Hisarköy Turkey see Domaniç
Hisarönü Turkey 59 O4
Ḩisb, Sha'īb watercourse Iraq 91 G5
Ḩisbān Jordan 85 B4
Hisiu P.N.G. 69 L8
Hisor Tajik. 89 H2
Hisor tizmasi mts Tajik./Uzbek. see Gissar Range
Hispalis Spain see Seville
Hispania country Europe see Spain

▶Hispaniola i. Caribbean Sea 137 J4
Consists of the Dominican Republic and Haiti.

Hispur Glacier Pak. 82 C1
Hissar India see Hisar
Hisua India 83 F4
Ḩisyah Syria 85 C2
Hīt Iraq 91 F4
Hitachi Japan 75 F5
Hitachinaka Japan 75 F5
Hitra i. Norway 44 F5
Hitzacker (Elbe) Germany 53 L1
Hiva Oa i. Fr. Polynesia 151 K6
Hixon Canada 120 F4
Hixson Cay reef Australia 110 F4
Hiyyon, Naḥal watercourse Israel 85 B4
Hizan Turkey 91 F3
Hjälmaren l. Sweden 45 I7
Hjerkinn Norway 44 F5
Hjo Sweden 45 I7
Hjørring Denmark 45 G8
Hkakabo Razi mt. China/Myanmar 76 C2
Hlaingdet Myanmar 70 B2
Hlane Royal National Park Swaziland 101 J4
Hlatikulu Swaziland 101 J4
Hlegu Myanmar 70 B3
Hlohlowane S. Africa 101 H5
Hlotse Lesotho 101 I5
Hluhluwe-Umfolozi Park nature res. S. Africa 101 J5
Hlukhiv Ukr. 43 G6
Hlung-Tan Myanmar 70 B2
Hlusha Belarus 43 F5
Hlybokaye Belarus 45 O9
Ho Ghana 96 D4
Hoa Binh Hoa Binh Vietnam 70 D2
Hoa Binh Nghê An Vietnam 70 D3
Hoachanas Namibia 100 D2
Hoagland U.S.A. 134 C3
Hoang Liên Sơn mts Vietnam 70 C2
Hoang Sa is S. China Sea see Paracel Islands

▶Hobart Australia 111 [inset]
Capital of Tasmania.

Hobart U.S.A. 131 D5
Hobbs U.S.A. 131 C5
Hobbs Coast Antarctica 152 J1
Hobe Sound U.S.A. 133 D7
Hobiganj Bangl. see Habiganj
Hobro Denmark 45 F8
Hobyo Somalia 98 E3
Hochharz nat. park Germany 53 J5
Hochfeiler mt. Austria/Italy see Gran Pilastro
Hochfeld Namibia 99 B6
Hochharz, Nationalpark nat. park Germany 53 K3
Hô Chi Minh Vietnam see Ho Chi Minh City
Ho Chi Minh City Vietnam 71 D5
Hochschwab mt. Austria 47 O7
Hochschwab mts Austria 47 O7
Hockenheim Germany 53 I5
Ḥôḍ reg. Mauritania 96 C3
Hoddesdon U.K. 49 G7
Hodeidah Yemen 86 F7
Hodgenville U.S.A. 134 C5
Hodgson Downs Australia 108 F3
Hódmezővásárhely Hungary 59 I1
Hodna, Chott el salt l. Alg. 57 I6
Hodo-dan pt N. Korea 75 B5
Ho Dynasty Citadel tourist site Vietnam 76 E4
Ho Dynasty Citadel tourist site Vietnam 70 D2
Hoek van Holland Neth. see Hook of Holland
Hoensbroek Neth. 52 F4
Hoeryŏng N. Korea 74 C4
Hof Germany 53 L4
Hoffman Mountain U.S.A. 135 I2
Hofheim in Unterfranken Germany 53 K4
Hofmeyr S. Africa 101 G6
Höfn Iceland 44 [inset 1]
Hofors Sweden 45 J6
Hofsjökull ice cap Iceland 44 [inset 1]
Hofsós Iceland 44 [inset 1]
Hōfu Japan 75 C6
Höganäs Sweden 45 H8
Hogan Group is Australia 112 C7
Hogansburg U.S.A. 135 H1
Hogback Mountain U.S.A. 130 C3
Hoge Vaart canal Neth. 52 F2
Hogg, Mount Canada 120 C2
Hoggar plat. Alg. see Ahaggar
Hog Island U.S.A. 135 H5
Högsby Sweden 45 J8
Hohenloher Ebene plain Germany 53 J5
Hohenmölsen Germany 53 M3
Hohennauen Germany 53 M2
Hohensalza Poland see Inowrocław
Hohenwald U.S.A. 132 C5
Hohenwartetalsperre resr Germany 53 L4
Hoher Dachstein mt. Austria 47 N7
Hohe Rhön mts Germany 53 J4
Hohe Tauern mts Austria 47 N7
Hohhot China 73 K4
Höhmorït Mongolia 80 H2
Hohneck mt. France 56 H2
Hoh Sai Hu l. China 83 H2
Hoh Xil Hu salt l. China 83 G2
Hoh Xil Shan mts China 83 G2
Hôi An Vietnam 70 E4
Hoima Uganda 98 D3
Hojagala Turkm. 88 E2
Hojai India 83 H4
Hojambaz Turkm. 89 G2
Højryggen mts Greenland 119 M2
Hokitika N.Z. 113 C6
Hokkaidō i. Japan 74 F4
Hokksund Norway 45 F7
Hol Norway 45 F6
Holbæk Denmark 45 G9
Holbeach U.K. 49 H6
Holbrook Australia 112 C5
Holbrook U.S.A. 129 H4
Holden U.S.A. 129 G2
Holdenville U.S.A. 131 D5
Holdrege U.S.A. 130 D3
Holgate U.S.A. 134 C3
Holguín Cuba 137 I4
Holin He r. China 74 B3
Höljes Sweden 45 H6
Holland country Europe see Netherlands
Holland MI U.S.A. 134 B2
Holland NY U.S.A. 135 F2
Hollandia Indon. see Jayapura
Hollick-Kenyon Peninsula Antarctica 152 L2
Hollick-Kenyon Plateau Antarctica 152 K1
Hollidaysburg U.S.A. 135 F3
Hollis AK U.S.A. 120 C4
Hollis OK U.S.A. 131 D5
Hollister U.S.A. 128 C3
Holly U.S.A. 134 D2
Hollyhill U.S.A. 134 C5
Holly Springs U.S.A. 131 F5
Hollywood CA U.S.A. 129 D4
Hollywood FL U.S.A. 133 D7
Holm Norway 44 H4
Holmes Reef Australia 110 D3
Holmes Summit Antarctica 152 B1
Holmestrand Norway 45 G7
Holmgard Russia see Velikiy Novgorod
Holm Ø i. Greenland see Kiatassuaq
Holmön i. Sweden 44 L5
Holmsund Sweden 44 L5
Ḥolon Israel 85 B3
Holoog Namibia 100 C4
Holothuria Banks reef Australia 108 D3
Holroyd r. Australia 110 C2
Holstebro Denmark 45 F8
Holstein U.S.A. 130 E3
Holsteinsborg Greenland see Sisimiut
Holston r. U.S.A. 132 D4
Holsworthy U.K. 49 C8
Holt U.K. 49 I6
Holt U.S.A. 134 C2
Holton U.S.A. 134 B2
Holwerd Neth. 52 F1
Holwert Neth. see Holwerd
Holycross Ireland 51 E5
Holy Cross U.S.A. 118 C3
Holy Cross, Mount of the U.S.A. 126 G5
Holyhead U.K. 48 C5
Holyhead Bay U.K. 48 C5
Holy Island England U.K. 48 F3
Holy Island Wales U.K. 48 C5
Holyoke U.S.A. 130 C3
Holy See Europe see Vatican City
Holywell U.K. 48 D5
Holzhausen Germany 53 M3
Holzkirchen Germany 47 M7
Holzminden Germany 53 J3
Homand Iran 89 E3
Homāyūnshahr Iran see Khomeynīshahr
Homberg (Efze) Germany 53 J3
Hombori Mali 96 C3
Homburg Germany 53 H5
Home Bay Canada 119 L3
Homécourt France 52 F5
Homer GA U.S.A. 133 D5
Homer LA U.S.A. 131 E5
Homer MI U.S.A. 134 C2
Homer NY U.S.A. 135 G2
Homerville U.S.A. 133 D6
Homestead Australia 110 D4
Homnabad India 84 C2
Homoine Moz. 101 L2
Homs Libya see Al Khums
Homs Syria 85 C2
Homyel' Belarus 43 F5
Honan prov. China see Henan
Honavar India 84 B3
Honawad India 84 B2
Honaz Turkey 59 M6
Hon Chông Vietnam 71 D5
Hondeklipbaai S. Africa 100 C6
Hondo U.S.A. 131 D6
Hondsrug reg. Neth. 52 G1

▶Honduras country Central America 137 G6
5th largest country in North America.

Hønefoss Norway 45 G6
Honesdale U.S.A. 135 H3
Honey Lake salt l. U.S.A. 128 C1
Honeyoye Lake U.S.A. 135 G2
Honfleur France 56 E2
Hong, Mouths of the Vietnam see Red River, Mouths of the
Hông, Sông r. Vietnam see Red
Hongchuan China see Hongya
Hongguo China see Panxian
Honghai Wan b. China 77 G4
Honghe China 76 D4
Hong He r. China 77 G1
Honghe Hani Rice Terraces tourist site China 76 D4
Honghu China 77 G2
Hongjiang Hunan China 77 F3
Hongjiang Sichuan China see Wangcang
Hong Kong H.K. China 77 [inset]
Hong Kong aut. reg. China 77 [inset]
Hong Kong Harbour sea chan. H.K. China 77 [inset]
Hong Kong Island H.K. China 77 [inset]
Hongliuwan China see Aksay
Hongliuyuan China 80 I3
Hongqiao China see Qidong
Hongqizhen China see Wuzhishan
Hongshan China 77 G2
Hongshilazi China 74 B4
Hongshui He r. China 76 F4
Honguedo, Détroit d' sea chan. Canada 123 I4
Hongwŏn N. Korea 75 B4
Hongxing China 74 A3
Hongya China 76 D2
Hongyuan China 76 D1
Hongze China 77 H1
Hongze Hu l. China 77 H1

▶Honiara Solomon Is 107 F2
Capital of the Solomon Islands.

Honiton U.K. 49 D8
Honkajoki Fin. 45 M6
Honningsvåg Norway 44 N1
Honoka'a U.S.A. 127 [inset]

▶Honolulu U.S.A. 127 [inset]
Capital of Hawaii.

▶Honshū i. Japan 75 D6
Largest island in Japan, 3rd largest in Asia and 7th in the world.

Hood, Mount vol. U.S.A. 126 C3
Hood Point Australia 109 B8
Hood Point P.N.G. 110 D1
Hood River U.S.A. 126 C3
Hoogeveen Neth. 52 G2
Hoogezand-Sappemeer Neth. 52 G1
Hooghly r. mouth India see Hugli
Hooker U.S.A. 131 C4
Hook Head hd Ireland 51 F5
Hook of Holland Neth. 52 E3
Hook Reef Australia 110 E3
Hoonah U.S.A. 120 C3
Hooper Bay U.S.A. 153 B2
Hooper Island U.S.A. 135 G4
Hoopeston U.S.A. 134 B3
Hoopstad S. Africa 101 G4
Höör Sweden 45 H9
Hoorn Neth. 52 F2
Hoosick U.S.A. 135 I2
Hoover Dam U.S.A. 129 F3
Hoover Memorial Reservoir U.S.A. 134 D3
Hopa Turkey 91 F2
Hope Canada 120 F5
Hope r. N.Z. 113 D6
Hope AR U.S.A. 131 E5
Hope IN U.S.A. 134 C4
Hope, Lake salt flat Australia 109 C8
Hope, Point pt U.S.A. 118 B3
Hopedale Canada 123 J3
Hopefield S. Africa 100 D7
Hopei prov. China see Hebei
Hope Mountains Canada 123 J3
Hope Saddle pass N.Z. 113 D5
Hopes Advance, Baie b. Canada 123 H2
Hopes Advance, Cap c. Canada 119 L3
Hopes Advance Bay Canada see Aupaluk
Hopetoun Australia 111 C7
Hopetown S. Africa 100 G5
Hopewell U.S.A. 135 G5
Hopewell Islands Canada 122 F2
Hopin Myanmar 70 B1
Hopkins r. Australia 111 C8
Hopkins, Lake salt flat Australia 109 E6
Hopkinsville U.S.A. 134 B5
Hopland U.S.A. 128 B2
Hoquiam U.S.A. 126 C3
Hor China 76 D1
Horasan Turkey 91 F2
Hörby Sweden 45 H9

▶Horizon Deep sea feature S. Pacific Ocean 150 I7
Deepest point in the Tonga Trench, and 2nd in the world.

Horki Belarus 43 F5
Horlick Mountains Antarctica 152 K1
Horlivka Ukr. 43 H6
Hormoz, Jazīreh-ye i. Iran 88 E5
Hormoz, Kūh-e mt. Iran 88 D5
Hormuz, Strait of Iran/Oman 88 E5
Horn Austria 47 O6
Horn r. Canada 120 G2
Horn c. Iceland 44 [inset 1]

▶Horn, Cape Chile 144 C9
Most southerly point of South America.

Horn, Îles de is Wallis and Futuna 107 I3
Hornavan l. Sweden 44 J3
Hornbrook U.S.A. 126 C4
Hornburg Germany 53 K2
Horncastle U.K. 48 G5
Horndal Sweden 45 J6
Horne, Îles de is Wallis and Futuna Is see Horn, Îles de
Horneburg Germany 53 J1
Hörnefors Sweden 44 K5
Hornell U.S.A. 135 G2
Hornepayne Canada 122 D4
Hornillos Mex. 127 F8
Hornisgrinde mt. Germany 47 L6
Hornkranz Namibia 100 C2
Horn Mountains Canada 120 F2
Hornos, Cabo de Chile see Horn, Cape
Hornoy-le-Bourg France 52 B5
Horn Peak Canada 120 D2
Hornsby Australia 112 E4
Hornsea U.K. 48 G5
Hornslandet pen. Sweden 45 J6
Horodenka Ukr. 43 E6
Horodnya Ukr. 43 F6
Horodok Khmel'nyts'ka Oblast' Ukr. 43 E6
Horodok L'vivs'ka Oblast' Ukr. 43 D6
Horokanai Japan 74 F3
Horoshiri-dake mt. Japan 74 F4
Horqin Youyi Qianqi China see Ulanhot
Horqin Zuoyi Houqi China see Ganjig
Horqin Zuoyi Zhongqi China see Baokang
Horrabridge U.K. 49 C8
Horrocks Australia 109 A7
Horru China 83 G3
Horse Cave U.S.A. 134 C5
Horsefly Canada 120 F4
Horseheads U.S.A. 135 G2
Horse Islands Canada 123 L4
Horseleap Ireland 51 D4
Horsens Denmark 45 F9
Horseshoe Bend Australia 109 F6
Horseshoe Reservoir U.S.A. 129 H4
Horseshoe Seamounts sea feature N. Atlantic Ocean 148 G3
Horsham Australia 111 C8
Horsham U.K. 49 G7
Horšovský Týn Czechia 53 M5
Horst hill Germany 53 J4
Hörstel Germany 53 H2
Horten Norway 45 G7
Hortobágyi nat. park Hungary 59 I1
Horton r. Canada 118 F3
Horwood Lake Canada 122 E4
Hosapete India 84 C3
Hösbach Germany 53 J4
Hose, Pegunungan mts Malaysia 68 E6
Ḩoseynābād Iran 88 B3
Ḩoseynīyeh Iran 88 C4
Hoshab Pak. 89 F5
Hoshangabad India 82 D5
Hoshiarpur India 82 C3
Hospital Ireland 51 D5
Hosta Butte mt. U.S.A. 129 I4
Hotagen r. Sweden 44 I5
Hotahudo East Timor see Hatudo
Hotan China 82 E1
Hotazel S. Africa 100 F4
Hot Creek Range mts U.S.A. 128 E2
Hotgi India 84 C2
Hotham r. Australia 109 B8
Hoting Sweden 44 J4
Hot Springs AR U.S.A. 131 E5
Hot Springs NM U.S.A. see Truth or Consequences
Hot Springs SD U.S.A. 130 C3
Hot Sulphur Springs U.S.A. 126 G4
Hottah Lake Canada 120 G1
Hottentots Bay Namibia 100 B4
Hottentots Point Namibia 100 B4
Houayxay Laos 70 C2
Houdan France 52 B6
Houffalize Belgium 52 F4
Hougang Sing. 71 [inset]
Houghton MI U.S.A. 130 F2
Houghton NY U.S.A. 135 F2
Houghton Lake U.S.A. 134 C1
Houghton Lake l. U.S.A. 134 C1
Houghton le Spring U.K. 48 F4
Houie Moc, Phou mt. Laos 70 C2
Houlton U.S.A. 132 H2
Houma China 77 F1
Houma U.S.A. 131 F6
Houmen China 77 G4
House Range mts U.S.A. 129 G2
Houston Canada 120 E4
Houston MO U.S.A. 131 F4
Houston MS U.S.A. 131 F5
Houston TX U.S.A. 131 E6
Houtman Abrolhos is Australia 109 A7
Houton U.K. 50 F2
Houwater S. Africa 100 F6
Hovd Mongolia 80 H2
Hove U.K. 49 G8
Hoveton U.K. 49 I6
Hovmantorp Sweden 45 I8
Hövsgöl Nuur l. Mongolia 80 J1
Howar, Wadi watercourse Sudan 86 C6
Howard Australia 110 F5
Howard PA U.S.A. 135 G3
Howard SD U.S.A. 130 D2
Howard WI U.S.A. 134 A1
Howard City U.S.A. 134 C2
Howard Lake Canada 121 J2
Howden U.K. 48 G5
Howe, Cape Australia 112 D6
Howe, Mount Antarctica 152 J1
Howell U.S.A. 134 D2
Howick Canada 135 I1
Howick S. Africa 101 J5
Howland U.S.A. 132 G2

▶Howland Island terr. N. Pacific Ocean 107 I1
United States Unincorporated Territory.

Howlong Australia 112 C5
Howrah India see Haora
Howth Ireland 51 F4
Ḩowz well Iran 88 E3
Ḩowz-e Khān well Iran 88 E3
Ḩowz-e Panj Iran 88 E4
Ḩowz-e Panj waterhole Iran 88 D3
Howz i-Mian i-Tak Iran 88 D3
Hô Xa Vietnam 70 D3
Höxter Germany 53 J3
Hoy i. U.K. 50 F2
Hoya Germany 53 J2
Høyanger Norway 45 E6
Hoyerswerda Germany 47 O5
Høylandet Norway 44 H4
Hoym Germany 53 L3
Höytiäinen l. Fin. 44 P5
Hoyt Peak U.S.A. 129 H1
Hpa-an Myanmar 70 B3
Hpapun Myanmar 70 B3
Hpungan Pass India/Myanmar 70 B1
Hradec Králové Czechia 47 O5
Hradiště hill Czechia 53 N4
Hrasnica Bos. & Herz. 58 H3
Hrazdan Armenia 91 G2
Hrebinka Ukr. 43 G6
Hrodna Belarus 45 M10
Hrvatska country Europe see Croatia
Hrvatsko Grahovo Bos. & Herz. see Bosansko Grahovo
Hsenwi Myanmar 70 B2
Hsiang Kang H.K. China see Hong Kong
Hsi-hseng Myanmar 70 B2
Hsin-chia-p'o country Asia see Singapore
Hsin-chia-p'o Sing. see Singapore
Hsinchu Taiwan 77 I3
Hsinking China see Changchun
Hsinying Taiwan see Xinying
Hsipaw Myanmar 70 B2
Hsi-sha Ch'ün-tao is S. China Sea see Paracel Islands
Hsü-chou China see Xuzhou
Hua watercourse Namibia 99 B6
Huachinera Mex. 127 F7
Huacho Peru 142 C6
Huachuan China 74 C3
Huade China 73 K4
Huadian China 74 B4
Huadu China 77 G4
Hua Hin Thai. 71 B4
Huai'an Jiangsu China see Chuzhou
Huai'an Jiangsu China 77 H1
Huaibei China 77 H1
Huaibin China 77 G1
Huaicheng Guangdong China see Huaiji
Huaicheng Jiangsu China see Chuzhou
Huaide China 74 B4
Huaidian China see Shenqiu
Huai Had National Park Thai. 70 D3
Huaihua China 77 F3
Huaiji China 77 G4
Huai Kha Khaeng Wildlife Reserve nature res. Thai. 70 B4
Huailillas mt. Peru 142 C5
Huainan China 77 H1
Huaining Anhui China 77 H2
Huaining Anhui China see Shipai
Huaiyang China 77 G1
Huaiyin Jiangsu China see Huai'an
Huaiyin Jiangsu China 77 H1
Huaiyuan China 77 H1
Huajialing China 76 E1
Huajuápan de León Mex. 136 E5
Hualapai Peak U.S.A. 129 G4
Hualian Taiwan see Hualien
Hualien Taiwan 77 I3
Huallaga r. Peru 142 C5
Huambo Angola 99 B5
Huanan China 74 C3
Huancane Peru 142 E7
Huancavelica Peru 142 C6
Huancayo Peru 142 C6
Huangbei China 77 G3
Huangcaoba China see Xingyi
Huang-chou China see Huanggang
Huangchuan China 77 G1
Huanggang China 77 G2
Huang Hai sea N. Pacific Ocean see Yellow Sea
Huang He r. China see Yellow River
Huangjian China 77 I1
Huang-kang China see Huanggang
Huangling China 77 F1
Huangliu China 77 F5
Huanglongsi China see Kaifeng
Huangmao Jian mt. China 77 H3
Huangmei China 77 G2
Huangpu China 77 G4
Huangqi China 77 H3
Huangshan China 77 H2
Huangshi China 77 G2
Huangtu Gaoyuan plat. China 73 J5
Huangyan China 77 I2
Huangzhou China see Huanggang
Huaning China 76 D3
Huanjiang China 77 F3
Huanren China 74 B4
Huanshan China see Yuhuan
Huánuco Peru 142 C5
Huaping China 76 D3
Huaping Yu i. Taiwan 77 I3
Huaqiao China 76 E2
Huaqiaozhen China see Huaqiao
Huaraz Peru 142 C5
Huarmey Peru 142 C6
Huarong China 77 G2
Huascarán, Nevado de mt. Peru 142 C5
Huasco Chile 144 B3
Hua Shan mt. China 77 F1
Huashixia China 76 C1
Huashulinzi China 74 B4
Huatabampo Mex. 127 F8
Huaxian Guangdong China see Huadu
Huaxian Henan China 77 G1
Huayang China see Jixi
Huayin China 77 F1
Huayuan China 77 F2
Huazangsi China see Tianzhu
Hubballi India 84 B3
Hubbard, Mount Canada/U.S.A. 120 B2
Hubbard, Pointe pt Canada 123 I2
Hubbard Lake U.S.A. 134 D1
Hubbart Point Canada 121 M3
Hubei prov. China 77 G2
Hubli India see Hubballi
Hückelhoven Germany 52 G3
Hucknall U.K. 49 F5
Huddersfield U.K. 48 F5
Huder China 74 A2
Hudiksvall Sweden 45 J6
Hudson MA U.S.A. 135 J2
Hudson MD U.S.A. 135 G4
Hudson MI U.S.A. 134 C3
Hudson NH U.S.A. 135 J2
Hudson NY U.S.A. 135 I2
Hudson r. U.S.A. 135 I3
Hudson, Baie d' sea Canada see Hudson Bay
Hudson, Détroit d' strait Canada see Hudson Strait
Hudson Bay Canada 121 K4
Hudson Bay sea Canada 119 J4
Hudson Falls U.S.A. 135 I2
Hudson Island Tuvalu see Nanumanga
Hudson Mountains Antarctica 152 K2
Hudson's Hope Canada 120 F3
Hudson Strait Canada 119 K3
Huê Vietnam 70 D3
Huehuetenango Guat. 136 F5
Huehueto, Cerro mt. Mex. 131 B7
Huelva Spain 57 C5
Huentelauquén Chile 144 B4
Huépac Mex. 127 F7
Huércal-Overa Spain 57 F5
Huertecillas Mex. 131 C7
Huesca Spain 57 F2
Huéscar Spain 57 E5
Hughenden Australia 110 D4
Hughes r. Canada 121 K3
Hughes (abandoned) Australia 109 E7
Hughson U.S.A. 128 C3
Hugli r. mouth India 83 F5
Hugli-Chinsurah India 83 G5
Hugo CO U.S.A. 130 C4
Hugo OK U.S.A. 131 E5
Hugo Lake U.S.A. 131 E5
Hugoton U.S.A. 131 C4
Huhehot China see Hohhot
Huhhot China see Hohhot
Huhudi S. Africa 100 G4
Hui'an China 77 H3
Hui'anpu China 72 J5
Huiarau Range mts N.Z. 113 F4
Huib-Hoch Plateau Namibia 100 C4
Huichang China 77 G3
Huicheng Anhui China see Shexian
Huicheng Guangdong China see Huilai
Huidong China 76 D3
Huijbergen Neth. 52 E3
Huila, Nevado de vol. Col. 142 C3
Huíla, Planalto da Angola 99 B5
Huilai China 77 H4
Huili China 76 D3
Huimanguillo Mex. 136 F5
Huinan China see Nanhui
Huining China 76 E1
Huishi China see Huining
Huishui China 76 E3
Huiten Nur l. China 83 G2
Huitong China 77 F3
Huittinen Fin. 45 M6
Huixian Gansu China 76 E1
Huixian Henan China 77 G1
Huiyang China see Huizhou
Huize China 76 D3
Huizhou China 77 G4
Hujr Saudi Arabia 86 F4
Hukawng Valley Myanmar 70 B1
Hukuntsi Botswana 100 E2
Hulan China 74 B3
Hulan Ergi China 74 A3
Ḩulayfah Saudi Arabia 86 F4
Ḩulayḩilah well Syria 85 D2
Huliao China see Dabu
Hulilan Iran 88 B3
Hulin China 74 D3
Hull Canada 135 H1
Hull U.K. see Kingston upon Hull
Hull Island atoll Kiribati see Orona
Hultsfred Sweden 45 I8
Hulun China see Hulun Buir
Hulun Buir China 73 L3
Hulun Nur l. China 73 L3
Ḩulwān Egypt 90 C5
Huma China 74 B2
Humahuaca Arg. 144 C2
Humaitá Brazil 142 F5
Humaya r. Mex. 127 G8
Humaym well U.A.E. 88 D6
Humayyān, Jabal hill Saudi Arabia 88 B5
Humber, Mouth of the U.K. 48 H5
Humboldt Canada 121 J4
Humboldt AZ U.S.A. 129 G4
Humboldt NE U.S.A. 130 E3
Humboldt NV U.S.A. 128 D1
Humboldt r. U.S.A. 128 D1
Humboldt Bay U.S.A. 126 B4
Humboldt Range mts U.S.A. 128 D1
Humbolt Salt Marsh U.S.A. 128 E2
Hume r. Canada 120 D1
Humeburn Australia 112 B1
Hu Men sea chan. China 77 G4
Hume Reservoir Australia 112 C5
Humphrey Island atoll Cook Is see Manihiki
Humphreys, Mount U.S.A. 128 D3
Humphreys Peak U.S.A. 129 H4
Hūn Libya 97 E2
Húnaflói b. Iceland 44 [inset 1]
Hunan prov. China 77 F3
Hundeluft Germany 53 M3
Hunedoara Romania 59 J2
Hünfeld Germany 53 J4
Hungary country Europe 55 H2
Hungerford Australia 112 B2
Hŭngnam N. Korea 75 B5
Hung Shui Kiu H.K. China 77 [inset]
Hưng Yên Vietnam 70 D2
Hunjiang China see Baishan
Huns Mountains Namibia 100 C4
Hunstanton U.K. 49 H6
Hunte r. Germany 53 I1
Hunter r. Australia 112 E4
Hunter Island Australia 111 [inset]
Hunter Island Canada 120 D5
Hunter Island S. Pacific Ocean 107 H4
Hunter Islands Australia 111 [inset]
Huntingburg U.S.A. 134 B4
Huntingdon Canada 135 H1
Huntingdon U.K. 49 G6

Huntingdon PA U.S.A. 135 G3
Huntingdon TN U.S.A. 131 F4
Huntington IN U.S.A. 134 C3
Huntington OR U.S.A. 126 D3
Huntington WV U.S.A. 134 D4
Huntington Beach U.S.A. 128 D5
Huntington Creek r. U.S.A. 129 F1
Huntly N.Z. 113 E3
Huntly U.K. 50 G3
Hunt Mountain U.S.A. 126 G3
Huntsville Canada 134 F1
Huntsville AL U.S.A. 133 C5
Huntsville AR U.S.A. 131 E4
Huntsville TN U.S.A. 134 C5
Huntsville TX U.S.A. 131 E6
Hunza reg. Pak. 82 C1
Huolin He r. China see Holin He
Huolongmen China 74 B2
Hương Khê Vietnam 70 D3
Huonville Australia 111 [inset]
Huoqiu China 77 H1
Huoshan China 77 H2
Huoshao Tao i. Taiwan see Lü Dao
Hupeh prov. China see Hubei
Hupnik r. Turkey 85 C1
Hupu India 76 B2
Ḩūr Iran 88 E4
Hurault, Lac l. Canada 123 H3
Ḩuraydin, Wādī watercourse Egypt 85 A4
Huraysān reg. Saudi Arabia 88 B6
Hurd, Cape Canada 134 E1
Hurd Island Kiribati see Arorae
Hüren Tovon Uul mt. Mongolia 80 I3
Hurghada Egypt 86 D4
Hurler's Cross Ireland 51 D5
Hurley NM U.S.A. 129 I5
Hurley WI U.S.A. 130 F2
Hurmagai Pak. 89 G4
Huron CA U.S.A. 128 C3
Huron SD U.S.A. 130 D2

▶Huron, Lake Canada/U.S.A. 134 D1
2nd largest lake in North America and 4th in the world.

Hurricane U.S.A. 129 G3
Hursley U.K. 49 F7
Hurst Green U.K. 49 H7
Husain Nika Pak. 89 H4
Húsavík Norðurland eystra Iceland 44 [inset 1]
Húsavík Vestfirðir Iceland 44 [inset 1]
Huseyinabat Turkey see Alaca
Huseyinli Turkey see Kızılırmak
Hūshak Iran 89 F5
Hushan Zhejiang China see Wuyi
Hushan Zhejiang China 77 H2
Hushan Zhejiang China see Cixi
Huşi Romania 59 M1
Huskvarna Sweden 45 I8
Husn Jordan see Al Ḩişn
Ḩuṣn Āl 'Abr Yemen 86 G6
Husnes Norway 45 D7
Husum Germany 47 L3
Husum Sweden 44 K5
Hutag-Öndör Mongolia 80 J2
Hutchinson KS U.S.A. 130 D4
Hutchinson MN U.S.A. 130 E2
Hutch Mountain U.S.A. 129 H4
Hutou China 74 D3
Hutsonville U.S.A. 134 B4
Hutton, Mount hill Australia 111 E5
Hutton Range hills Australia 109 C6
Huvadhu Atholhu Maldives 81 D11
Hüvek Turkey see Bozova
Hüvīān, Kūh-e mts Iran 89 E5
Ḩuwār i. Bahrain 88 C5
Huwaytat reg. Saudi Arabia 85 C5
Huxi China 77 G3
Huzhong China 74 A2
Huzhou China 77 I2
Hvannadalshnúkur vol. Iceland 44 [inset 1]
Hvar i. Croatia 58 G3
Hvide Sande Denmark 45 F8
Hvíta r. Iceland 44 [inset 1]
Hwange Zimbabwe 99 C5
Hwange National Park Zimbabwe 99 C5
Hwang Ho r. China see Yellow River
Hwedza Zimbabwe 99 D5
Hwlffordd U.K. see Haverfordwest
Hyannis MA U.S.A. 135 J3
Hyannis NE U.S.A. 130 C3
Hyargas Nuur salt l. Mongolia 80 H2
Hyco Lake U.S.A. 134 F5
Hyde N.Z. 113 C7
Hyden Australia 109 B8
Hyden U.S.A. 134 D5
Hyde Park U.S.A. 135 I1
Hyderabad India 84 C2
Hyderabad Pak. 89 H5
Hydra i. Greece see Ydra
Hyères France 56 H5
Hyères, Îles d' is France 56 H5
Hyesan N. Korea 74 C4
Hyland, Mount Australia 112 F3
Hyland Post Canada 120 D3
Hyllestad Norway 45 D6
Hyltebruk Sweden 45 H8
Hyndman Peak U.S.A. 126 E4
Hyōno-sen mt. Japan 75 D6
Hyrynsalmi Fin. 44 P4
Hysham U.S.A. 126 G3
Hythe Canada 120 G4
Hythe U.K. 49 I7
Hyūga Japan 75 C6
Hyvinkää Fin. 45 N6

I

Iaciara Brazil 145 B1
Iaco r. Brazil 142 E5
Iaçu Brazil 145 C1
Iadera Croatia see Zadar
Iaeger U.S.A. 134 E5
Iakora Madag. 99 E6
Ialomiţa r. Romania 59 L2
Ianca Romania 59 L2
Iaşi Romania 59 L1
Iba Phil. 69 F3
Ibadan Nigeria 96 D4
Ibagué Col. 142 C3
Ibaiti Brazil 145 A3
Ibapah U.S.A. 129 G1
Ibarra Ecuador 142 C3
Ibb Yemen 86 F7
Ibbenbüren Germany 53 H2
Iberá, Esteros del marsh Arg. 144 E3
Iberia Peru 142 E6

▶Iberian Peninsula Europe 57
Consists of Portugal, Spain and Gibraltar.

Iberville, Lac d' l. Canada 123 G3
Ibeto Nigeria 96 D3
iBhayi S. Africa see Port Elizabeth
Ibi Indon. 71 B6
Ibi Nigeria 96 D4
Ibiá Brazil 145 B2
Ibiaí Brazil 145 B2
Ibiapaba, Serra da hills Brazil 143 J4
Ibiassucê Brazil 145 C1
Ibicaraí Brazil 145 D1
Ibiquera Brazil 145 C1
Ibirama Brazil 145 A4
Ibiranhém Brazil 145 C2
Ibitinga Brazil 145 A3
Ibiza Spain 57 G4
Ibiza i. Spain 57 G4
Iblei, Monti mts Sicily Italy 58 F6
Ibn Buşayyiş well Saudi Arabia 88 B5
Ibotirama Brazil 143 J6
Iboundji, Mont hill Gabon 98 B4
Ibrā' Oman 88 E6
İbradı Turkey 90 C3
Ibrī Oman 88 E6
Ica r. Col. see Putumayo
Ica Peru 142 C6
Içana Brazil 142 E3
Içana r. Brazil 142 E3
Icaria i. Greece see Ikaria
Icatu Brazil 143 J4
Iceberg Canyon gorge U.S.A. 129 F3
İçel Turkey see Mersin

▶Iceland country Europe 44 [inset 1]
2nd largest island in Europe.

Iceland Basin sea feature N. Atlantic Ocean 148 G2
Icelandic Plateau sea feature N. Atlantic Ocean 153 I2
Ichalkaranji India 84 B2
Ichifusa-yama mt. Japan 75 C6
Ichinomiya Japan 75 E6
Ichinoseki Japan 75 F5
Ichinskaya Sopka, Vulkan vol. Russia 65 Q4
Ichkeul, Parc National de l' nat. park Tunisia 58 C6
Ichnya Ukr. 43 G6
Ichtegem Belgium 52 D3
Ichtershausen Germany 53 K4
Icó Brazil 143 K5
İçoguz Turkm. 88 E1
Iconha Brazil 145 C3
Iconium Turkey see Konya
Icosium Alg. see Algiers
Iculisma France see Angoulême
Icy Cape U.S.A. 118 B2
Id Turkey see Narman
Idabel U.S.A. 131 E5
Ida Grove U.S.A. 130 E3
Idah Nigeria 96 D4
Idaho state U.S.A. 126 E3
Idaho City U.S.A. 126 E4
Idaho Falls U.S.A. 126 E4
Idalia National Park Australia 110 D5
Idar India 82 C5
Idar-Oberstein Germany 53 H5
Ideriyn Gol r. Mongolia 80 J2
Idfū Egypt 86 D5
Idhra i. Greece see Ydra
Idi Amin Dada, Lake Dem. Rep. Congo/Uganda see Edward, Lake
Idiofa Dem. Rep. Congo 99 B4
Idivuoma Sweden 44 M2
Idkū Egypt 90 C5
Idle r. U.K. 48 G5
Idlewild airport U.S.A. see John F. Kennedy
Idlib Syria 85 C2
Idra i. Greece see Ydra
Idre Sweden 45 H6
Idrija Slovenia 58 E1
Idstein Germany 53 I4
Idutywa S. Africa see Dutywa
Idzhevan Armenia see Ijevan
Iecava Latvia 45 N8
Iepê Brazil 145 A3
Ieper Belgium 52 C4
Ierapetra Greece 59 K7
Ierissou, Kolpos b. Greece 59 J4
Iešjávri l. Norway 44 N2
Ifakara Tanz. 99 D4
Ifalik atoll Micronesia 69 K5
Ifaluk atoll Micronesia see Ifalik
Ifanadiana Madag. 99 E6
Ife Nigeria 96 D4
Ifenat Chad 97 E3
Iferouâne Niger 96 D3
Iffley Australia 110 C3
Ifjord Norway 44 O1
Ifôghas, Adrar des hills Mali 96 D3
Iforas, Adrar des hills Mali see Ifôghas, Adrar des
Igan Sarawak Malaysia 68 E6
Iganga Uganda 97 G4
Igarapava Brazil 145 B3
Igarka Russia 64 J3
Igatpuri India 84 B2
Igbeti Nigeria see Igbetti
Igbetti Nigeria 96 D4
Igdir Iran 88 B2
Iğdır Turkey 91 G3
Iggesund Sweden 45 J6
Igikpak, Mount U.S.A. 118 C3
Igizyar China 89 J2
Iglesias Sardinia Italy 58 C5
Iglesiente reg. Sardinia Italy 58 C5
Igloolik Canada 119 J3
Igluligaarjuk Canada see Chesterfield Inlet
Ignace Canada 121 N5
Ignacio Zaragoza Chihuahua Mex. 127 G7
Ignacio Zaragoza Zacatecas Mex. 131 C8
Ignalina Lith. 45 O9
İğneada Turkey 59 L4
İğneada Burnu pt Turkey 59 M4
Ignoitijala India 71 A5
iGoli S. Africa see Johannesburg
Igoumenitsa Greece 59 I5
Igra Russia 41 Q4
Igrim Russia 41 S3
Iguaçu r. Brazil 145 A4
Iguaçu, Saltos do waterfall Arg./Brazil see Iguaçu Falls
Iguaçu Falls Arg./Brazil 144 F3
Iguaí Brazil 145 C1
Iguala Mex. 136 E5
Igualada Spain 57 G3
Iguape Brazil 145 B4
Iguaraçu Brazil 145 A3
Iguatama Brazil 145 B3
Iguatemi Brazil 144 F2
Iguatu Brazil 143 K5
Iguazú, Cataratas do waterfall Arg./Brazil see Iguaçu Falls
Iguéla Gabon 98 A4
Iguidi, Erg des. Alg./Mauritania 96 C2
Igunga Tanz. 99 D4
Iharaña Madag. 99 E5
Ihavandhippolhu Maldives 84 B5
Ihavandiffulu Atoll Maldives see Ihavandhippolhu
Ihosy Madag. 99 E6
Ihtiman Bulg. 59 J3
Ih Tol Gol China 74 A2
Iide-san mt. Japan 75 E5
Iijärvi l. Fin. 44 O2
Iijoki r. Fin. 44 N4
Iisalmi Fin. 44 O5
Iizuka Japan 75 C6
Ijebu-Ode Nigeria 96 D4
Ijevan Armenia 91 G2
IJmuiden Neth. 52 E2
IJssel r. Neth. 52 F2
IJsselmeer l. Neth. 52 F2
Ijzer r. France see Yser
Ikaahuk Canada see Sachs Harbour
Ikaalinen Fin. 45 M6
Ikageleng S. Africa 101 H3
Ikageng S. Africa 101 H4
iKapa S. Africa see Cape Town
Ikare Nigeria 96 D4
Ikaria i. Greece 59 L6
Ikast Denmark 45 F8
Ikeda Japan 74 F4
Ikela Dem. Rep. Congo 98 C4
Ikhutseng S. Africa 100 G5
Iki-Burul Russia 43 J7
Ikom Nigeria 96 D4
Iksan S. Korea 75 B6
Ikungu Tanz. 99 D4
Ilagan Phil. 69 G3
Ilaisamis Kenya 98 D3
Īlām Iran 88 B3
Ilam Nepal 83 F4
Ilan Taiwan see Yilan
Ilave Peru 142 E7
Iława Poland 47 Q4
Ilazārān, Kūh-e mt. Iran 88 E4
Île-à-la-Crosse Canada 121 J4
Île-à-la-Crosse, Lac l. Canada 121 J4
Ilebo Dem. Rep. Congo 99 C4
Île-de-France admin. reg. France 52 C6
Île Europa i. Indian Ocean see Europa, Île
Ilek Kazakh. 41 Q5
Ilemi Triangle terr. Africa 98 D3
Ilen r. Ireland 51 C6
Ileret Kenya 98 D3
Ileza Russia 42 I3
Ilfeld Germany 53 K3
Ilford Canada 121 M3
Ilford U.K. 49 H7
Ilfracombe Australia 110 D4
Ilfracombe U.K. 49 C7
Ilgaz Turkey 90 D2
Ilgın Turkey 90 C3
Ilha Grande resr Brazil 144 F2
Ilha Solteíra, Represa resr Brazil 145 A3
Ílhavo Port. 57 B3
Ilhéus Brazil 145 D1
Ili Kazakh. see Kapshagay
Iliamna Lake U.S.A. 118 C4
İliç Turkey 90 E3
Il'ichevsk Azer. see Şärur
Il'ichevsk Ukr. see Chornomors'k
Ilici Spain see Elche-Elx
Iligan Phil. 69 G5
Ilimananngip Nunaa i. Greenland 119 P2
Il'inka Russia 43 J7
Il'inskiy Permskiy Kray Russia 41 R4
Il'inskiy Sakhalinskaya Oblast' Russia 74 F3
Il'insko-Podomskoye Russia 42 J3
Ilion U.S.A. 135 H2
Ilium tourist site Turkey see Troy
Iliysk Kazakh. see Kapshagay
Ilkal India 84 C3
Ilkeston U.K. 49 F6
Ilkley U.K. 48 F5
Illapel Chile 144 B4
Illéla Niger 96 D3
Iller r. Germany 47 L6
Illichivs'k Ukr. see Chornomors'k
Illimani, Nevado de mt. Bol. 142 E7
Illinois r. U.S.A. 130 F4
Illinois state U.S.A. 134 A3
Illizi Alg. 96 D2
Illogwa watercourse Australia 110 A5
Ilm r. Germany 53 L3
Ilmajoki Fin. 44 M5
Il'men', Ozero l. Russia 42 F4
Ilmenau Germany 53 K4
Ilmenau r. Germany 53 K1
Ilminster U.K. 49 E8
Ilo Peru 142 D7
Iloilo Phil. 69 G4
Ilomantsi Fin. 44 Q5
Ilong India 76 B3
Ilorin Nigeria 96 D4
Ilovlya Russia 43 I6
Ilsede Germany 53 K2
Iluka Australia 112 F2
Ilulissat Greenland 119 M3
Iluppur India 84 C4
Ilva i. Italy see Elba, Isola d'
Imabari Japan 75 D6
Imaichi Japan see Nikkō
Imala Moz. 99 D5
Imam-baba Turkm. 89 F2
İmamoğlu Turkey 90 D3
Imām Şāḩib Afgh. 89 H2
Iman Russia see Dal'nerechensk
Iman r. Russia 74 D3
Imari Japan 75 C6
Imaruí Brazil 145 A5
Imataca, Serranía de mts Venez. 142 F2
Imatra Fin. 45 P6
Imbituva Brazil 145 A4
imeni 26 Bakinskikh Komissarov Azer. see Häsänabad
imeni Petra Stuchki Latvia see Aizkraukle
Īmī Eth. 98 E3
Imishli Azer. see İmişli
İmişli Azer. 91 H3
Imit Pak. 82 C1
Imja-do i. S. Korea 75 B6
Imlay U.S.A. 128 D1
Imlay City U.S.A. 134 D2
Imola Italy 58 D2
iMonti S. Africa see East London
Impendle S. Africa 101 I5
Imperatriz Brazil 143 I5
Imperia Italy 58 C3
Imperial CA U.S.A. 129 F5
Imperial NE U.S.A. 130 C3
Imperial Beach U.S.A. 128 E5
Imperial Dam U.S.A. 129 F5
Imperial Valley plain U.S.A. 129 F5
Imperieuse Reef Australia 108 B4
Impfondo Congo 98 B3
Imphal India 83 H4
İmralı Adası i. Turkey 59 M4
İmroz Turkey 59 K4
İmroz i. Turkey see Gökçeada
Imtān Syria 85 C3
Imuris Mex. 127 F7
In r. Russia 74 D2
Ina Japan 75 E6
Inambari r. Peru 142 E6
Inari Fin. 44 O2
Inarijärvi l. Fin. 44 O2
Inarijoki r. Fin./Norway 44 N2
Inca Spain 57 H4
İnce Burnu pt Turkey 59 L4
İnce Burun pt Turkey 90 D2
Inch Ireland 51 F5
Inchard, Loch b. U.K. 50 D2
Incheon S. Korea 75 B5
Inchicronan Lough l. Ireland 51 D5
Inch'ŏn S. Korea see Incheon
Incirli Turkey see Karasu
Indaal, Loch b. U.K. 50 C5
Indalsälven r. Sweden 44 J5
Indalstø Norway 45 D6
Inda Silasē Eth. 98 D2
Indaw Myanmar 70 A2
Indawgyi Lake Myanmar 76 C3
Indé Mex. 131 B7
Independence CA U.S.A. 128 D3
Independence IA U.S.A. 130 F3
Independence KS U.S.A. 131 E4
Independence KY U.S.A. 134 C4
Independence MO U.S.A. 130 E4
Independence VA U.S.A. 134 E5
Independence Mountains U.S.A. 126 D4
Inder China 74 A3
Inderbor Kazakh. 78 E2
Indi India 84 C2

▶India country Asia 81 E7
2nd most populous country in Asia and the world. 3rd largest country in Asia and 7th in the world.

Indian r. Canada 120 B2
Indiana U.S.A. 134 F3
Indiana state U.S.A. 134 B3
Indian-Antarctic Ridge sea feature Southern Ocean 150 D9

▶Indianapolis U.S.A. 134 B4
Capital of Indiana.

Indian Cabins Canada 120 G3
Indian Desert India/Pak. see Thar Desert
Indian Harbour Canada 123 K3
Indian Head Canada 121 K5
Indian Lake U.S.A. 135 H2
Indian Lake l. NY U.S.A. 135 H2
Indian Lake l. OH U.S.A. 134 D3
Indian Lake l. PA U.S.A. 135 F3

▶Indian Ocean 149
3rd largest ocean in the world.

Indianola IA U.S.A. 130 E3
Indianola MS U.S.A. 131 F5
Indian Peak U.S.A. 129 G2
Indian Springs IN U.S.A. 134 B4
Indian Springs NV U.S.A. 129 F3
Indian Wells U.S.A. 129 H4
Indiga Russia 42 K2
Indigirka r. Russia 65 P2
Indigskaya Guba b. Russia 42 K2
Inđija Serbia 59 I2
Indin Lake Canada 120 H1
Indio U.S.A. 128 E5
Indira Point India 71 A6
Indira Priyadarshini Pench National Park India 82 D5
Indispensable Reefs Solomon Is 107 G3
Indjija Serbia see Inđija
Indo-China reg. Asia 70 D3

▶Indonesia country Asia 68 E7
3rd most populous country in Asia and 4th in the world.

Indore India 82 C5
Indrapura, Gunung vol. Indon. see Kerinci, Gunung
Indravati r. India 84 D2
Indre r. France 56 E3
Indulkana Australia 109 F6
Indur India see Nizamabad
Indus r. China/Pak. 89 G6
also known as Sênggê Zangbo or Shiquan He
Indus, Mouths of the Pak. 89 G5
Indus Cone sea feature Indian Ocean 149 M4
Indwe S. Africa 101 H6
İnebolu Turkey 90 D2
İnegöl Turkey 59 M4
Inevi Turkey see Cihanbeyli
Inez U.S.A. 134 D5
Infantes Spain see Villanueva de los Infantes
Infiernillo, Presa resr Mex. 136 D5
Ing, Nam Mae r. Thai. 70 C2
Inga Russia 44 S3
Ingalls, Mount U.S.A. 128 C2
Ingelmunster Belgium 52 D4
Ingenika r. Canada 120 E3
Ingersoll Canada 134 E2
Ingham Australia 110 D3
Ingichka Uzbek. 89 G2
Ingleborough hill U.K. 48 E4
Inglefield Land reg. Greenland 119 K2
Ingleton U.K. 48 E4
Inglewood Qld Australia 112 E2
Inglewood Vic. Australia 112 A6
Inglewood U.S.A. 128 D5
Ingoka Pum mt. Myanmar 70 B1
Ingoldmells U.K. 48 H5
Ingolstadt Germany 53 L6
Ingomar Australia 109 F7
Ingomar U.S.A. 126 G3
Ingonish Canada 123 J5
Ingraj Bazar India 83 G4
Ingram U.S.A. 134 F5
Ingray Lake Canada 120 G1
Ingrid Christensen Coast Antarctica 152 E2
Ingwavuma S. Africa 101 K4
Ingwavuma r. S. Africa/Swaziland see Ngwavuma
Ingwiller France 53 H6
Inhaca Moz. 101 K3
Inhaca, Península pen. Moz. 101 K4
Inhambane Moz. 101 L2
Inhambane prov. Moz. 101 L2
Inhaminga Moz. 99 D5
Inharrime Moz. 101 L3
Inhassoro Moz. 99 D6
Inhaúmas Brazil 145 B1
Inhobim Brazil 145 C1
Inhumas Brazil 145 A2
Inírida Col. 142 E3
Inis Ireland see Ennis
Inis Córthaidh Ireland see Enniscorthy
Inishark i. Ireland 51 B4
Inishbofin i. Ireland 51 B4
Inisheer i. Ireland 51 C4
Inishkea North i. Ireland 51 B3
Inishkea South i. Ireland 51 B3
Inishmaan i. Ireland 51 C4
Inishmore i. Ireland 51 C4
Inishmurray i. Ireland 51 D3
Inishowen pen. Ireland 51 E2
Inishowen Head hd Ireland 51 F2
Inishtrahull i. Ireland 51 E2
Inishturk i. Ireland 51 B4
Injune Australia 111 E5
Inkerman Australia 110 C3
Inkeroinen Fin. 45 O6
Inklin Canada 120 C3
Inklin r. Canada 120 C3
Inkylap Turkm. 89 F2
Inland Kaikoura Range mts N.Z. 113 D6
Inland Sea Japan see Seto-naikai
Inlet U.S.A. 135 H2
Inn r. Europe 47 M7
Innaanganeq c. Greenland 119 L2
Innamincka Australia 111 C5
Innamincka Regional Reserve nature res. Australia 111 C5
Inndyr Norway 44 I3
Inner Sound sea chan. U.K. 50 D3
Innes National Park Australia 111 B7
Innisfail Australia 110 D3
Innisfail Canada 120 H4
Innokent'yevka Russia 74 C2
Innoko r. U.S.A. 118 C3
Innsbruck Austria 47 M7
Innuksuak r. Canada 122 F2
Inny r. Ireland 51 E4
Inocência Brazil 145 A2
Inongo Dem. Rep. Congo 98 B4
İnönü Turkey 59 N5
Inoucdjouac Canada see Inukjuak
Inowrocław Poland 47 Q4
In Salah Alg. 96 D2
Insch U.K. 50 G3

▶Inscription, Cape Australia 110 B3
Most westerly point of Oceania.

Insein Myanmar 70 B3
Insterburg Russia see Chernyakhovsk
Inta Russia 41 S2
Interamna Italy see Teramo
Interlaken Switz. 56 H3
International Falls U.S.A. 130 E1
Interview Island India 71 A4
Intracoastal Waterway canal U.S.A. 131 E6
Intutu Peru 142 D4
Inubō-zaki pt Japan 75 F6
Inukjuak Canada 122 F2
Inuvialuit area Canada 118 E3
Inuvik Canada 118 E3
Inveraray U.K. 50 D4
Inverbervie U.K. 50 G4
Invercargill N.Z. 113 B8
Inverell Australia 112 E2
Invergordon U.K. 50 E3
Inverkeithing U.K. 50 F4
Inverleigh Australia 110 C3
Invermay Canada 121 K5
Inverness Canada 123 J5
Inverness U.K. 50 E3
Inverness CA U.S.A. 128 B2
Inverness FL U.S.A. 133 D6
Inverurie U.K. 50 G3
Investigator Channel Myanmar 71 B4
Investigator Group is Australia 109 F8
Investigator Ridge sea feature Indian Ocean 149 O6
Investigator Strait Australia 111 B7
Inwood U.S.A. 135 F4
Inya Russia 80 G1
Inyanga Zimbabwe see Nyanga
Inyokern U.S.A. 128 E4
Inyo Mountains U.S.A. 128 D3
Inyonga Tanz. 99 D4
Inza Russia 43 J5
Inzhavino Russia 43 I5
Ioannina Greece 59 I5
Iokan'ga r. Russia 42 H2
Iola U.S.A. 130 E4
Iolgo, Khrebet mts Russia 80 G1
Iolotan' Turkm. see Ýolöten
Iona Canada 123 J5
Iona i. U.K. 50 C4
Iona, Parque Nacional do nat. park Angola 99 B5
Ione U.S.A. 128 E2
Iongo Angola 99 B4
Ionia U.S.A. 134 C2
Ionian Islands Greece 59 H5
Ionian Sea Greece/Italy 58 H5
Ionioi Nisoi is Greece see Ionian Islands
Ios i. Greece 59 K6
Iowa state U.S.A. 130 E3
Iowa City U.S.A. 130 F3
Iowa Falls U.S.A. 130 E3
Ipameri Brazil 145 A2
Ipanema Brazil 145 C2
Iparía Peru 142 D5
Ipatinga Brazil 145 C2
Ipatovo Russia 43 I7
Ipelegeng S. Africa 101 G4
Ipiales Col. 142 C3
Ipiaú Brazil 145 D1
Ipirá Brazil 145 D1
Ipiranga Brazil 145 A4
iPitoli S. Africa see Pretoria
Ipixuna r. Brazil 142 F5
Ipoh Malaysia 71 C6
Iporá Brazil 145 A2
Ippy Cent. Afr. Rep. 98 C3
Ipsala Turkey 59 L4
Ipswich Australia 112 F1
Ipswich U.K. 49 I6
Ipswich U.S.A. 130 D2
Ipu Brazil 143 J4

▶Iqaluit Canada 119 L3
Capital of Nunavut.

Iquique Chile 144 B2
Iquiri r. Brazil see Ituxi
Iquitos Peru 142 D4
Īrafshān reg. Iran 89 F5
Iraí Brazil 144 F3
Irakleio Greece see Iraklion
Iraklion Greece 59 K7
Iramaia Brazil 145 C1
Iran country Asia 88 D3
Iran, Pegunungan mts Indon. 68 E6
Īrānshahr Iran 89 F5
Irapuato Mex. 136 D4
Iraq country Asia 91 F4
Irará Brazil 145 D1
Irati Brazil 145 A4
Irayel' Russia 42 L2
Irazú, Volcán vol. Costa Rica 137 H7
Irbid Jordan 85 B3
Irbil Iraq see Arbīl/Hewlêr
Irbit Russia 64 H4
Irecê Brazil 143 J6
Ireland country Europe 51 E4

▶Ireland i. Ireland/U.K. 51
3rd largest island in Europe.

Irema Dem. Rep. Congo 98 C4
Iri S. Korea see Iksan
Irian, Teluk b. Indon. see Cenderawasih, Teluk
Iriba Chad 97 F3
Īrī Dāgh mt. Iran 88 B2
Iriga Phil. 69 G4
Irîgui reg. Mali/Mauritania 96 C3
Iringa Tanz. 99 D4
Iriri r. Brazil 143 H4
Irish Free State country Europe see Ireland
Irish Sea Ireland/U.K. 51 G4
Irituia Brazil 143 I4
'Irj well Saudi Arabia 88 C5
Irkutsk Russia 72 I2
Irma Canada 121 I4
Irmak Turkey 90 D3
Irminger Basin sea feature N. Atlantic Ocean 148 F2
Iron Baron Australia 111 B7
Irondequoit U.S.A. 135 G2
Iron Mountain U.S.A. 130 F2
Iron Mountain mt. U.S.A. 129 G3
Iron Range National Park Australia 110 C2
Iron River U.S.A. 130 F2
Ironton MO U.S.A. 130 F4
Ironton OH U.S.A. 134 D4
Ironwood Forest National Monument nat. park U.S.A. 129 H5
Iroquois r. U.S.A. 134 B3
Iroquois Falls Canada 122 E4
Irosin Phil. 69 G4
Irpen' Ukr. see Irpin'
Irpin' Ukr. 43 F6
Irrawaddy r. Myanmar 70 A4
Irrawaddy, Mouths of the Myanmar 70 A4
Irshad Pass Afgh./Pak. 89 I2
Irta Russia 42 K3
Irthing r. U.K. 48 E4

▶Irtysh r. Kazakh./Russia 80 E1
5th longest river in Asia and 10th in the world, and a major part of the 2nd longest in Asia (Ob'-Irtysh).

Irun Spain 57 F2
Iruña Spain see Pamplona
Iruñea Spain see Pamplona
Irvine U.K. 50 E5

Jervis Bay Australia 112 E5
Jervis Bay b. Australia 112 E5
Jervis Bay Territory admin. div. Australia 112 E5
Jesenice Slovenia 58 F1
Jesenice, Vodní nádrž resr Czechia 53 M4
Jesi Italy 58 E3
Jesselton Sabah Malaysia see Kota Kinabalu
Jessen (Elster) Germany 53 M3
Jessheim Norway 45 G6
Jessore Bangl. 83 G5
Jesteburg Germany 53 J1
Jesu Maria Island P.N.G. see Rambutyo Island
Jesup U.S.A. 133 D6
Jesús María, Barra spit Mex. 131 D7
Jetmore U.S.A. 130 D4
Jetpur India 82 B5
Jever Germany 53 H1
Jewell Ridge U.S.A. 134 E5
Jewish Autonomous Oblast admin. div. Russia see Yevreyskaya Avtonomnaya Oblast'
Jeypur India see Jaypur
Jezercë, Maja mt. Albania 59 H3
Jezzine Lebanon 85 B3
Jhabua India 82 C5
Jhajhar India see Jhajjar
Jhajjar India 82 D3
Jhal Pak. 89 G4
Jhalawar India 82 D4
Jhal Jhao Pak. 89 G5
Jhang Pak. 89 I4
Jhansi India 82 D4
Jhanzi r. India 70 A1
Jhapa Nepal 83 F4
Jharia India 83 F5
Jharkhand state India 83 F5
Jharsuguda India 83 F5
Jhawani Nepal 83 F4
Jhelum r. India/Pak. 89 I4
Jhelum Pak. 89 I3
Jhenaidah Bangl. 83 G5
Jhenaidaha Bangl. see Jhenaidah
Jhenida Bangl. see Jhenaidah
Jhimpir Pak. 89 H5
Jhingtubum mt. India 76 B3
Jhudo Pak. 89 H5
Jhumritilaiya India 83 F4
Jhund India 82 B5
Jhunjhunun India 82 C3
Jiachuan China 76 E1
Jiachuanzhen China see Jiachuan
Jiading Jiangxi China see Xinfeng
Jiading Shanghai China 77 I2
Jiahe China 77 G3
Jiajiang China 76 D2
Jiamusi China 74 C3
Ji'an Jiangxi China 77 G3
Ji'an Jilin China 74 B4
Jianchuan China 76 C3
Jiande China 77 H2
Jiangbei China see Yubei
Jiangbiancun China 77 G3
Jiangcheng China 76 D4
Jiangcun China 77 F3
Jiangdu China 77 H1
Jiange China see Pu'an
Jianghong China 77 F4
Jiangjin China 76 E2
Jiangjunmiao China 80 G3
Jiangkou Guangdong China see Fengkai
Jiangkou Guizhou China 77 F3
Jiangkou Shaanxi China 76 E1
Jiangling China see Jingzhou
Jiangluo China 76 E1
Jiangmen China 77 G4
Jiangna China see Yanshan
Jiangshan China 77 H2
Jiangsi China see Dejiang
Jiangsu prov. China 77 H1
Jiangxi prov. China 77 G3
Jiangxia China 77 G2
Jiangyan China 77 I1
Jiangyin China 77 I2
Jiangyou China 76 E2
Jiangzhesongrong China 83 F3
Jianjun China see Yongshou
Jiankang China 76 D3
Jianli China 77 G2
Jian'ou China 77 H3
Jianping China see Langxi
Jianshe China see Baiyü
Jianshi China 77 F2
Jianshui China 76 D4
Jianshui Hu l. China 83 E2
Jianxing China 76 E2
Jianyang Fujian China 77 H3
Jianyang Sichuan China 76 E2
Jiaochang China 76 D1
Jiaochangba China see Jiaochang
Jiaocheng China see Jiaoling
Jiaohe China 74 B4
Jiaojiang China see Taizhou
Jiaokui China see Yiliang
Jiaoling China 77 H3
Jiaopingdu China 76 D3
Jiaowei China 77 H3
Jiaozuo China 77 G1
Jiasa China 76 D3
Jiashan China see Mingguang
Jia Tsuo La pass China 83 F3
Jiawang China 77 H1
Jiaxian China 77 G1
Jiaxing China 77 I2
Jiayi Taiwan 77 I4
Jiayin China 74 C2
Jiayuguan China 80 I4
Jiazi China 77 H4
Jībūtī country Africa see Djibouti
Jibuti Djibouti see Djibouti
Jiddah Saudi Arabia see Jeddah
Jiddī, Jabal al hill Egypt 85 A4
Jido S. Korea 75 B6
Jidong China 74 C3
Jiehkkevárri mt. Norway 44 K2
Jieshi China 77 G4
Jieshipu China 76 E1
Jieshi Wan b. China 77 G4
Jiexi China 77 G4
Jiexiu China 73 K5
Jieyang China 77 H4
Jieznas Lith. 45 N9
Jigzhi China 76 D1
Jiḥār, Wādī al watercourse Syria 85 C2
Jihlava Czechia 47 O6
Jījah Afgh. 89 F3
Jijel Alg. 54 F4
Jijiga Eth. 98 E3
Jījīrud Iran 88 C3
Jijü China 76 D2
Jil'ād reg. Jordan see Gilead
Jilf al Kabīr, Haḍabat al plat. Egypt 86 C5
Jilh al 'Ishār plain Saudi Arabia 88 B5
Jilib Somalia 98 E3
Jilin China 74 B4
Jilin prov. China 74 B4
Jilin Hada Ling mts China 74 B4
Jiliu He r. China 74 A2
Jilo India 82 C4
Jilong Taiwan see Keelung
Jīma Eth. 98 D3
Jiménez Chihuahua Mex. 131 B7
Jiménez Coahuila Mex. 131 C6
Jiménez Tamaulipas Mex. 131 D7
Jimía, Cerro mt. Hond. 136 G5
Jimsar China 80 G3
Jim Thorpe U.S.A. 135 H3
Jinan China 73 L5
Jin'an China see Songpan
Jinbi China see Dayao
Jinchang China 72 I5
Jincheng Shanxi China 77 G1
Jincheng Sichuan China 76 E2
Jincheng Yunnan China see Wuding
Jinchengjiang China see Hechi
Jinchuan Gansu China see Jinchang
Jinchuan Jiangxi China see Xingan
Jind India 82 D3
Jinding China see Lanping
Jindo S. Korea 75 B6
Jin-do i. S. Korea 75 B6
Jindřichův Hradec Czechia 47 O6
Jin'e China see Longchang
Jingbian China 73 J5
Jingchuan China 76 E1
Jingde China 77 H2
Jingdezhen China 77 H2
Jingellic Australia 112 C5
Jinggangshan China see Ciping
Jinggang Shan hill China 77 G3
Jinggongqiao China 77 H2
Jinggu China 76 D4
Jing He r. China 77 F1
Jinghong China 76 D4
Jingle China 73 K5
Jingmen China 77 G2
Jingpo China 74 C4
Jingpo Hu resr China 74 C4
Jingsha China see Jingzhou
Jingtai China 72 I5
Jingxi China 76 E4
Jingxian Anhui China 77 H2
Jingxian Hunan China see Jingzhou
Jingyang China see Jingde
Jingyu China 74 B4
Jingyuan China 72 I5
Jingzhou Hubei China 77 G2
Jingzhou Hubei China 77 G2
Jingzhou Hunan China 77 F3
Jinhae S. Korea 75 C6
Jinhe Nei Mongol China 74 A2
Jinhe Yunnan China see Jinping
Jinhu China 77 H1
Jinhua Yunnan China see Jianchuan
Jinhua Zhejiang China 77 H2
Jining Nei Mongol China see Ulan Qab
Jining Shandong China 77 H1
Jinja Uganda 98 D3
Jinjiang Hainan China see Chengmai
Jinjiang Yunnan China 76 D3
Jin Jiang r. China 77 G2
Jinka Eth. 98 D3
Jinmen Taiwan 77 H3
Jinmen Dao i. Taiwan 77 H3
Jinmu Jiao pt China 77 F5
Jinning China 76 D3
Jinotepe Nicaragua 137 G6
Jinping Guizhou China 77 F3
Jinping Yunnan China 76 D4
Jinping Yunnan China see Qiubei
Jinping Shan mts China 76 D3
Jinsen S. Korea see Incheon
Jinsha China 76 E3
Jinsha Jiang r. China see Yangtze
Jinshan Nei Mongol China see Guyang
Jinshan Shanghai China see Zhujing
Jinshan Yunnan China see Lufeng
Jinshi Hunan China 77 F2
Jinshi Hunan China see Xinning
Jintur India 84 C2
Jinxi Anhui China see Taihu
Jinxi Jiangxi China 77 H3
Jinxi Liaoning China see Lianshan
Jin Xi r. China 77 H3
Jinxian China 77 H2
Jinxiang China 77 H1
Jinyun China 77 I2
Jinz, Qā' al salt flat Jordan 85 C4
Jinzhai China 77 G2
Jinzhong China 73 K5
Jinzhou China 73 M4
Jinzhu China see Daocheng
Ji-Paraná Brazil 142 F6
Jipijapa Ecuador 142 B4
Ji Qu r. China 76 C2
Jiquiriçá Brazil 145 D1
Jiquitaia Brazil 145 D2
Jirā', Wādī watercourse Egypt 85 A5
Jirānīyāt, Shi'bān al watercourse Saudi Arabia 85 D4
Jirghatol Tajik. 89 H2
Jiri r. India 70 A1
Jiri-san mt. S. Korea 75 B6
Jīroft Iran 88 E4
Jirriiban Somalia 98 E3
Jirwān Saudi Arabia 88 C6
Jirwan well Saudi Arabia 88 C6
Jishou China 77 F2
Jisr ash Shughūr Syria 85 C2
Jitian China see Lianshan
Jitra Malaysia 71 C6
Jiu r. Romania 59 J3
Jiuding Shan mt. China 76 D2
Jiuhe China 76 C3
Jiujiang Jiangxi China 77 G2
Jiujiang Jiangxi China 77 H2
Jiulian China see Mojiang
Jiuling Shan mts China 77 G2
Jiulong China 76 D2
Jiuqian China 77 F3
Jiuquan China 80 I4
Jiuxu China 76 E3
Jiuzhou Jiang r. China 77 F4
Jiwani Pak. 89 F5
Jiwen China 74 A2
Jixi Anhui China 77 H2
Jixi Heilong. China 74 C3
Jixian China 74 C3
Jiyuan China 77 G1
Jīzah, Ahrāmāt al tourist site Egypt see Pyramids of Giza
Jizzakh Uzbek. see Jizzax
Jizzax Uzbek. 89 G1
Joaçaba Brazil 145 A4
Joaíma Brazil 145 C2
João Belo Moz. see Xai-Xai
João de Almeida Angola see Chibia
João Maria, Albardão do coastal area Brazil 144 F4
João Pessoa Brazil 143 L5
João Pinheiro Brazil 145 B2
Joaquín V. González Arg. 144 D3
Job Peak U.S.A. 128 D2
Jocketa Germany 53 M4
Joda India 83 F5
Jodhpur India 82 C4
Jodiya India 82 B5
Joensuu Fin. 44 P5
Jōetsu Japan 75 E5
Jofane Moz. 99 D6
Joffre, Mount Canada 120 H5
Jogbura Nepal 82 E3
Jõgeva Estonia 45 O7
Jogjakarta Indon. see Yogyakarta
Johannesburg S. Africa 101 H4
Johannesburg U.S.A. 128 E4
Johan Peninsula Canada 119 K2
Johi Pak. 89 G5
John Day U.S.A. 126 D3
John Day r. U.S.A. 126 C3
John D'Or Prairie Canada 120 H3
John F. Kennedy airport U.S.A. 135 I3
John H. Kerr Reservoir U.S.A. 135 F5
John Jay, Mount Canada/U.S.A. 120 D3
John o' Groats U.K. 50 F2
Johnson U.S.A. 130 C4
Johnsonburg U.S.A. 135 F3
Johnson City NY U.S.A. 135 H2
Johnson City TN U.S.A. 132 D4
Johnson City TX U.S.A. 131 D6
Johnsondale U.S.A. 128 D4
Johnson Draw watercourse U.S.A. 131 C6
Johnson's Crossing Canada 120 C2
Johnston, Lake salt flat Australia 109 C8
Johnston and Sand Islands terr. N. Pacific Ocean see Johnston Atoll

▶Johnston Atoll terr. N. Pacific Ocean 150 I4
United States Unincorporated Territory.

Johnstone U.K. 50 E5
Johnstone Lake Canada see Old Wives Lake
Johnston Range hills Australia 109 B7
Johnstown Ireland 51 E5
Johnstown NY U.S.A. 135 H2
Johnstown PA U.S.A. 135 F3
Johor, Selat strait Malaysia/Sing. 71 [inset]
Johor, Sungai r. Malaysia 71 [inset]
Johor Bahru Malaysia 71 [inset]
Johore Bahru Malaysia see Johor Bahru
Jõhvi Estonia 45 O7
Joinville Brazil 145 A4
Joinville France 56 G2
Joinville Island Antarctica 152 A2
Jokkmokk Sweden 44 K3
Jökulsá r. Iceland 44 [inset 1]
Jökulsá á Fjöllum r. Iceland 44 [inset 1]
Jökulsá í Fljótsdal r. Iceland 44 [inset 1]
Jolfā Iran 88 B2
Joliet U.S.A. 134 A3
Joliet, Lac l. Canada 122 F4
Joliette Canada 123 G5
Jolly Lake Canada 121 H1
Jolo Phil. 69 G5
Jolo i. Phil. 69 G5
Jomda China 76 C2
Jonancy U.S.A. 134 D5
Jonava Lith. 45 N9
Jonê China 76 D1
Jonesboro AR U.S.A. 131 F5
Jonesboro LA U.S.A. 131 E5
Jones Sound sea chan. Canada 119 J2
Jonesville MI U.S.A. 134 C3
Jonesville VA U.S.A. 134 D5
Jonglei Canal South Sudan 86 D8
Jönköping Sweden 45 I8
Jonquière Canada 123 H4
Joplin U.S.A. 131 E4
Joppa Israel see Tel Aviv-Yafo
Jora India 82 D4
Jordan country Asia 85 C4
Jordan r. Asia 85 B4
Jordan U.S.A. 126 G3
Jordan r. U.S.A. 126 D4
Jordânia Brazil 145 C1
Jordet Norway 45 H6
Jorhat India 83 H4
Jork Germany 53 J1
Jörn Sweden 44 L4
Joroinen Fin. 44 O5
Jørpeland Norway 45 E7
Jos Nigeria 96 D4
José de San Martín Arg. 144 B6
Joseph, Lac l. Canada 123 I3
Joseph Bonaparte Gulf Australia 108 E3
Joseph City U.S.A. 129 H4
Joshimath India 82 D3
Joshipur India 84 E1
Joshua Tree National Park U.S.A. 129 F5
Jos Plateau Nigeria 96 D4
Jostedalsbreen Nasjonalpark nat. park Norway 45 E6
Jotunheimen Nasjonalpark nat. park Norway 45 F6
Jouaiya Lebanon 85 B3
Joubertina S. Africa 100 F7
Jouberton S. Africa 101 H4
Jõuga Estonia 45 O7
Joûnié Lebanon 85 B3
Joure Neth. 52 F2
Joutsa Fin. 45 O6
Joutseno Fin. 45 P6
Jouy-aux-Arches France 52 G5
Jovellanos Cuba 133 D8
Jowai India 83 H4
Jowand Afgh. 89 G3
Jowr Deh Iran 88 C2
Joy, Mount Canada 120 C2
Joyce Country reg. Ireland 51 C4
Joypurhat Bangl. 83 G4
Juan Aldama Mex. 131 C7
Juancheng China 77 G1
Juan de Fuca Strait Canada/U.S.A. 124 C2
Juan Fernández, Archipiélago is S. Pacific Ocean 151 O8
Juan Fernández Islands S. Pacific Ocean see Juan Fernández, Archipiélago
Juanjuí Peru 142 C5
Juankoski Fin. 44 P5
Juan Mata Ortíz Mex. 127 F7
Juárez Mex. 131 C7
Juárez, Sierra de mts Mex. 127 D6
Juazeiro Brazil 143 J5
Juazeiro do Norte Brazil 143 K5
Juba r. Somalia see Jubba

▶Juba South Sudan 97 G4
Capital of South Sudan.

Jubba r. Somalia 98 E4
Jubbah Saudi Arabia 91 F5
Jubbulpore India see Jabalpur
Jubilee Lake salt flat Australia 109 D7
Juby, Cap c. Morocco 96 B2
Juchitán Mex. 136 E5
Jucuruçu Brazil 145 D2
Jucuruçu r. Brazil 145 D2
Judaberg Norway 45 D7
Judaidat al Hamir Iraq 91 F5
Judayyidat 'Ar'ar well Iraq 91 F5
Judenburg Austria 47 O7
Judian China 76 C3
Judith Gap U.S.A. 126 F3
Juegang China see Rudong
Juelsminde Denmark 45 G9
Juerana Brazil 145 D2
Jugar China see Sêrxü
Juigalpa Nicaragua 137 G6
Juillet, Lac l. Canada 123 J3
Juína Brazil 143 G6
Juist i. Germany 52 H1
Juiz de Fora Brazil 145 C3
Ju Ju Klu Turkm. 89 F2
Julaca Bol. 142 E8
Julesburg U.S.A. 130 C3
Julia Brazil 142 E4
Juliaca Peru 142 D7
Julia Creek Australia 110 C4
Julian U.S.A. 128 E5
Julian, Lac l. Canada 122 F3
Julianadorp Neth. 52 E2
Julian Alps mts Slovenia see Julijske Alpe
Julianatop mt. Indon. see Mandala, Puncak
Juliana Top mt. Suriname 143 G3
Julianehåb Greenland see Qaqortoq
Jülich Germany 52 G4
Julijske Alpe mts Slovenia 58 E1
Julimes Mex. 131 B6
Juliomagus France see Angers
Julius, Lake Australia 110 B4
Jullundur India see Jalandhar
Juma Uzbek. 89 G2
Jumbilla Peru 142 C5
Jumilla Spain 57 F4
Jumla Nepal 83 E3
Jümme r. Germany 53 H1
Jumna r. India see Yamuna
Jump r. U.S.A. 130 F2
Junagadh India 82 B5
Junagarh India 84 D2
Junan China 77 H1
Junayfah Egypt 85 A4
Junction TX U.S.A. 131 D6
Junction UT U.S.A. 129 G2
Junction City KS U.S.A. 130 D4
Junction City KY U.S.A. 134 C5
Junction City OR U.S.A. 126 C3
Jundiaí Brazil 145 B3
Jundian China 77 F1

▶Juneau AK U.S.A. 120 C3
Capital of Alaska.

Juneau WI U.S.A. 130 F3
Juneau Icefield Canada 120 C3
Junee Australia 112 C5
Jûn el Khudr b. Lebanon 85 B3
Jungar Qi China see Shagedu
Jungfrau mt. Switz. 56 H3
Junggar Pendi basin China 80 G2
Juniata r. U.S.A. 135 G3
Junín Arg. 144 D4
Junín Peru 142 C6
Junior U.S.A. 134 F4
Juniper Mountain U.S.A. 129 I1
Juniper Mountains U.S.A. 129 G4
Junipero Serro Peak U.S.A. 128 C3
Junlian China 76 E2
Junmenling China 77 G3
Juno U.S.A. 131 C6
Junsele Sweden 44 J5
Junshan Hu l. China 77 H2
Junxi China see Datian
Junxian China see Danjiangkou
Ju'nyung China 76 C1
Ju'nyunggoin China see Ju'nyung
Juodupė Lith. 45 N8
Jupiá Brazil 145 A3
Jupía, Represa resr Brazil 145 A3
Jupiter U.S.A. 133 D7
Juquiá r. Brazil 145 B4
Jur r. South Sudan 86 C8
Jura mts France/Switz. 56 G4
Jura i. U.K. 50 D4
Jur'ā, Nafūd al des. Saudi Arabia 88 B5
Jura, Sound of sea chan. U.K. 50 D5
Juracĭ Brazil 145 C1
Jurbarkas Lith. 45 M9
Jurf ad Darāwīsh Jordan 85 B4
Jürgenstorf Germany 53 M1
Jurhen Ul mts China 83 G2
Jurm Afgh. 89 H2
Jūrmala Latvia 45 M8
Jurmu Fin. 44 O4
Jurong Sing. 71 [inset]
Jurong, Sungai r. Sing. 71 [inset]
Jurong Island reg. Sing. 71 [inset]
Juruá r. Brazil 142 E4
Juruena r. Brazil 143 G5
Juruti Brazil 143 G4
Jurva Fin. 44 L5
Jūshqān Iran 88 E2
Jūsīyah Syria 85 C2
Jussara Brazil 145 A1
Justice U.S.A. 134 E5
Jutaí Brazil 142 E5
Jutaí r. Brazil 142 E4
Jüterbog Germany 53 N3
Jutiapa Guat. 136 G6
Juticalpa Hond. 137 G6
Jutis Sweden 44 J3
Jutland pen. Denmark 45 F8
Juuka Fin. 44 P5
Juva Fin. 44 O6
Juventud, Isla de la i. Cuba 137 H4
Juye China 77 H1
Jūyom Iran 88 D4
Jūzak Iran 89 F4
Južnoukrajinsk Ukr. see Yuzhnoukrayins'k
Jwaneng Botswana 100 G3
Jylland pen. Denmark see Jutland
Jyväskylä Fin. 44 N5

K

▶K2 mt. China/Pak. 82 D2
2nd highest mountain in Asia and the world.

Ka r. Nigeria 96 D3
Kaa-Iya del Gran Chaco, Parque Nacional nat. park Bol. 142 F7
Kaakhka Turkm. see Kaka
Ka'ala mt. U.S.A. 127 [inset]
Kaapstad S. Africa see Cape Town
Kaarina Fin. 45 M6
Kaarßen Germany 53 L1
Kaarst Germany 52 G3
Kaavi Fin. 44 P5
Kaba China see Habahe
Kabakly Turkm. see Gabakly
Kabala Sierra Leone 96 B4
Kabale Uganda 98 C4
Kabalega Falls National Park Uganda see Murchison Falls National Park
Kabalo Dem. Rep. Congo 99 C4
Kabambare Dem. Rep. Congo 99 C4
Kabanbay Kazakh. 80 F2
Kabangu Dem. Rep. Congo 99 C5
Kabanjahe Indon. 71 B7
Kabara i. Fiji 107 I3
Kabarega National Park Uganda see Murchison Falls National Park
Kabaw Valley Myanmar 70 A2
Kabbani r. India 84 C3
Kåbdalis Sweden 44 L3
Kabīd, Mushāsh al well Jordan 85 C5
Kabinakagami r. Canada 122 D4
Kabinakagami Lake Canada 122 D4
Kabinda Dem. Rep. Congo 99 C4
Kabīr, Nahr al r. Syria 85 B2
Kabīrkūh mts Iran 88 B3
Kabo Cent. Afr. Rep. 98 B3
Kābol Afgh. see Kābul
Kabompo r. Zambia 99 C5
Kabongo Dem. Rep. Congo 99 C4
Kaboré Tambi, Parc National de nat. park Burkina Faso 96 C3
Kabūdar Āhang Iran 88 C3
Kabūd Gonbad Iran see Kalāt

▶Kābul Afgh. 89 H3
Capital of Afghanistan.

Kābul r. Afgh. 89 I3
Kabuli P.N.G. 69 L7
Kabunda Dem. Rep. Congo 99 C5
Kabunduk Indon. 108 B2
Kaburuang i. Indon. 69 H6
Kabūtar Khān Iran 88 E4
Kabwe Zambia 99 C5
Kāchā Kūh mts Iran/Pak. 89 F4
Kachalinskaya Russia 43 J6
Kachchh, Great Rann of marsh India see Kachchh, Rann of
Kachchh, Gulf of India 82 B5
Kachchh, Little Rann of marsh India 82 B5
Kachchh, Rann of marsh India 82 B4
Kachia Nigeria 96 D4
Kachkanar Russia 41 R4
K'ach'reti Georgia 91 G2
Kachug Russia 72 J2
Kaçkar Dağı mt. Turkey 91 F2
Kadaingti Myanmar 70 B3
Kadaiyanallur India 84 C4
Kadanai r. Afgh./Pak. 89 G4
Kadan Kyun i. Myanmar 71 B4
Kadapa India 84 C3
Kadavu i. Fiji 107 H3
Kadavu Passage Fiji 107 H3
Kaddam l. India 84 C2
Kade Ghana 96 C4
Kadi India 82 C5
Kadıköy Turkey 59 M4
Kadınhanı Turkey 90 D3
Kadiolo Mali 96 C3
Kadiri India 84 C3
Kadirli Turkey 90 E3
Kadiyevka Ukr. see Stakhanov
Kadmat atoll India 84 B4
Ka-do i. N. Korea 75 B5
Kadok Malaysia 71 C6
Kadoka U.S.A. 130 C3
Kadoma Zimbabwe 99 C5
Kadonkani Myanmar 70 A4
Kadu Myanmar 70 B1
Kadugli Sudan 86 C7
Kaduna Nigeria 96 D3
Kaduna r. Nigeria 96 D4
Kadusam mt. China/India 83 I3
Kaduy Russia 42 H4
Kadyy Russia 42 I4
Kadzherom Russia 42 L2
Kaédi Mauritania 96 B3
Kaélé Cameroon 97 E3
Kaeng Krachan National Park Thai. 71 B4
Kaesŏng N. Korea 75 B5
Kāf Saudi Arabia 85 C4
Kafa Crimea see Feodosiya
Kafakumba Dem. Rep. Congo 99 C4
Kafan Armenia see Kapan
Kafanchan Nigeria 96 D4

▶Kaffeklubben Ø i. Greenland 153 I1
Most northerly point of North America.

Kaffrine Senegal 96 B3
Kafireas, Akra pt Greece see Ntoro, Kavo
Kafiristan reg. Pak. 89 H3
Kafr ash Shaykh Egypt 90 C5
Kafr el Sheikh Egypt see Kafr ash Shaykh
Kafue Zambia 99 C5
Kafue r. Zambia 99 C5
Kafue National Park Zambia 99 C5
Kaga Japan 75 E5
Kaga Bandoro Cent. Afr. Rep. 98 B3
Kagan Pak. 89 I3
Kagan Uzbek. see Kogon
Kagang China 76 D1
Kaganovichabad Tajik. see Kolkhozobod
Kaganovichi Pervyye Ukr. see Polis'ke (abandoned)
Kagarlyk Ukr. see Kaharlyk
Kåge Sweden 44 L4
Kağızman Turkey 91 F2
Kagmar Sudan 86 D7
Kagoshima Japan 75 C7
Kagoshima pref. Japan 75 C7
Kagul Moldova see Cahul
Kahama Tanz. 98 D4
Kaharlyk Ukr. 43 F6
Kaherekoau Mountains N.Z. 113 A7
Kahīrī Iran 89 F5
Kahla Germany 53 L4
Kahmard reg. Afgh. 89 G3
Kahnūj-e Pā'īn Iran 88 E4
Kahoka U.S.A. 130 F3
Kaho'olawe i. U.S.A. 127 [inset]
Kahperusvaarat mts Fin. 44 L2
Kahramanmaraş Turkey 90 E3
Kahror Pakka Pak. 89 H4
Kahta Turkey 90 E3
Kahuku U.S.A. 127 [inset]
Kahuku Point U.S.A. 127 [inset]
Kahurangi National Park N.Z. 113 D5
Kahurangi Point N.Z. 113 D5
Kahuta Pak. 89 I3
Kahuzi-Biega, Parc National du nat. park Dem. Rep. Congo 98 C4
Kai, Kepulauan is Indon. 69 I8
Kaiapoi N.Z. 113 D6
Kaibab U.S.A. 129 G3
Kaibab Plateau U.S.A. 129 G3
Kai Besar i. Indon. 69 I8
Kaibito Plateau U.S.A. 129 H3
Kaifeng Henan China 77 G1
Kaifeng Henan China 77 G1
Kaihua Yunnan China see Wenshan
Kaihua Zhejiang China 77 H2
Kaiingveld reg. S. Africa 100 E5
Kaijiang China 76 E2
Kai Kecil i. Indon. 69 I8
Kai Keung Leng H.K. China 77 [inset]
Kaikoura N.Z. 113 D6
Kailas mt. China see Kangrinboqê Feng
Kailasahar India see Kailashahar
Kailashahar India 83 H4
Kailas Range mts China see Gangdisê Shan
Kaili China 76 E3
Kailu China 73 M4
Kailua U.S.A. 127 [inset]
Kailua-Kona U.S.A. 127 [inset]
Kaimana Indon. 69 I7
Kaimanawa Mountains N.Z. 113 E4
Kaimar China 76 B1
Kaimur Range hills India 82 E4
Käina Estonia 45 M7
Kainan Japan 75 D6
Kainda Kyrg. see Kayyngdy
Kaindy Kyrg. see Kayyngdy
Kainji Lake National Park Nigeria 96 D4
Kaipara Harbour N.Z. 113 E3
Kaiparowits Plateau U.S.A. 129 H3
Kaiping China 77 G4
Kaipokok Bay Canada 123 K3
Kairana India 82 D3
Kairiru Island P.N.G. 69 K7
Kaironi Indon. 69 I7
Kairouan Tunisia 58 D7
Kaiserslautern Germany 53 H5
Kaiser Wilhelm II Land reg. Antarctica 152 E2
Kaitaia N.Z. 113 D2
Kaitangata N.Z. 113 B8
Kaitawa N.Z. 113 F4
Kaithal India 82 D3
Kaitum Sweden 44 L3
Kaiwatu Indon. 108 D2
Kaiwi Channel U.S.A. 127 [inset]
Kaixian China 77 F2
Kaiyang China 76 E3
Kaiyuan Liaoning China 74 B4
Kaiyuan Yunnan China 76 D4
Kajaani Fin. 44 O4
Kajabbi Australia 110 C4
Kajakī Suflá Afgh. 89 G3
Kajarabie, Lake Australia 112 D1
Kajrān Afgh. 89 G3
Kaka Turkm. 89 E2
Kakabeka Falls Canada 122 C4

Kāsah Murgh mts Afgh. 89 F3
Kasaï r. Dem. Rep. Congo 98 B4
also known as Kwa
Kasaï, Plateau du Dem. Rep. Congo 99 C4
Kasaji Dem. Rep. Congo 99 C5
Kasama Zambia 99 D5
Kasan Uzbek. see Koson
Kasane Botswana 99 C5
Kasaragod India 84 B3
Kasargod India see Kasaragod
Kasargode India see Kasaragod
Kasatkino Russia 74 C2
Kasba Lake Canada 121 K2
Kasba Tadla Morocco 54 C5
Kasenga Dem. Rep. Congo 99 C5
Kasengu Dem. Rep. Congo 99 C4
Kasese Dem. Rep. Congo 98 C4
Kasese Uganda 98 D3
Kasevo Russia see Neftekamsk
Kasganj India 82 D4
Kasha China 76 C2
Kashabowie Canada 122 C4
Kāshān Iran 88 C3
Kashary Russia 43 I6
Kashechewan Canada 122 E3
Kashgar China see Kashi
Kashi China 80 E4
Kashihara Japan 75 D6
Kashima-nada b. Japan 75 F5
Kashin Russia 42 H4
Kashipur India 82 D3
Kashira Russia 43 H5
Kashiwazaki Japan 75 E5
Kashkarantsy Russia 42 H2
Kashkū'īyeh Iran 88 D4
Kāshmar Iran 88 E3
Kashmir hist. area Asia 82 D2
Kashmir, Vale of reg. India 82 C2
Kashyr Kazakh. 72 D2
Kashyukulu Dem. Rep. Congo 99 C4
Kasi India see Varanasi
Kāsīgar Afgh. 89 H3
Kasimov Russia 43 I5
Kaskattama r. Canada 121 N3
Kaskinen Fin. 44 L5
Kas Klong i. Cambodia see Kŏng, Kaôh
Kaskö Fin. see Kaskinen
Kaslo Canada 120 G5
Kasmere Lake Canada 121 K3
Kasongo Dem. Rep. Congo 99 C4
Kasongo-Lunda Dem. Rep. Congo 99 B4
Kasos i. Greece 59 L7
Kaspiy Mangy Oypaty lowland Kazakh./Russia see Caspian Lowland
Kaspiysk Russia 91 G2
Kaspiyskiy Russia see Lagan'
Kaspiyskoye More l. Asia/Europe see Caspian Sea
Kassa Slovakia see Košice
Kassala Sudan 86 E6
Kassandras, Akra pt Greece see Kassandras, Akrotirio
Kassandras, Akrotirio pt Greece 59 J5
Kassandras, Kolpos b. Greece 59 J4
Kassel Germany 53 J3
Kasserine Tunisia 58 C7
Kastag Pak. 89 F5
Kastamonu Turkey 90 D2
Kastellaun Germany 53 H4
Kastelli Greece see Kissamos
Kastéllion Greece see Kissamos
Kastellorizon i. Greece see Megisti
Kasterlee Belgium 52 E3
Kastoria Greece 59 I4
Kastornoye Russia 43 H6
Kastsyukovichy Belarus 43 G5
Kasulu Tanz. 99 D4
Kasumkent Russia 91 H2
Kasungu Malawi 99 D5
Kasungu National Park Malawi 99 D5
Kasur Pak. 89 I4
Katâdtlit Nunât terr. N. America see Greenland
Katahdin, Mount U.S.A. 132 G2
Katah Sang Srah Afgh. 89 G3
Kataklik India 82 D2
Katako-Kombe Dem. Rep. Congo 98 C4
Katakwi Uganda 98 D3
Katana India 82 C5
Katangi India 82 D5
Katanning Australia 109 B8
Katavi National Park Tanz. 99 D4
Katāwāz reg. Afgh. 89 G3
Katchall i. India 71 A6
Katea Dem. Rep. Congo 99 C4
Katerini Greece 59 J4
Katesh Tanz. 99 D4
Kate's Needle mt. Canada/U.S.A. 120 C3
Katete Zambia 99 D5
Katherîna, Gebel mt. Egypt see Kātrīnā, Jabal
Katherine Australia 108 F3
Katherine Gorge National Park Australia see Nitmiluk National Park
Kathi India 89 I6
Kathiawar pen. India 82 B5
Kathihar India see Katihar
Kathiraveli Sri Lanka 84 D4
Kathiwara India 82 C5
Kathleen Falls Australia 108 E3

▶Kathmandu Nepal 83 F4
Capital of Nepal.

Kathu S. Africa 100 F4
Kathua India 82 C2
Kati Mali 96 C3
Katihar India 83 F4
Katikati S. Africa 101 H7
Katima Mulilo Namibia 99 C5
Katimik Lake Canada 121 L4
Katiola Côte d'Ivoire 96 C4
Kā Tiritiri o te Moana mts N.Z. see Southern Alps

▶Kati Thanda-Lake Eyre Australia 111 B6
Largest lake in Oceania and lowest point.

Kati Thanda-Lake Eyre (North) Australia 111 B6
Kati Thanda-Lake Eyre (South) Australia 111 B6
Kati Thanda-Lake Eyre National Park Australia 111 B6
Katkop Hills S. Africa 100 E6
Katlehong S. Africa 101 I4
Katmai National Park and Preserve U.S.A. 118 C4
Katmandu Nepal see Kathmandu
Katni India 82 E5
Kato Achaïa Greece 59 I5
Katoomba Australia 112 E4
Katowice Poland 47 Q5
Katoya India 83 G5
Katrancık Dağı mts Turkey 59 M6
Kātrīnā, Jabal mt. Egypt 90 D5
Katrine, Loch l. U.K. 50 E4
Katrineholm Sweden 45 J7
Katse Dam Lesotho 101 I5
Katsina Nigeria 96 D3
Katsina-Ala Nigeria 96 D4
Katsuura Japan 75 F6
Kattaktoc, Cap c. Canada 123 I2
Kattamudda Well Australia 108 D5
Kattaqo'rg'on Uzbek. 89 G2
Kattaqŭrghon Uzbek. see Kattaqo'rg'on
Kattegat strait Denmark/Sweden 45 G8
Kattowitz Poland see Katowice
Katumbar India 82 D4
Katunino Russia 42 J4
Katuri Pak. 89 H4
Katwa India see Katoya
Katwijk aan Zee Neth. 52 E2
Katzenbuckel hill Germany 53 J5
Kaua'i i. U.S.A. 127 [inset]
Kaua'i Channel U.S.A. 127 [inset]
Kaub Germany 53 H4
Kaufungen Germany 53 J3
Kauhajoki Fin. 44 M5
Kauhava Fin. 44 M5
Kaukauna U.S.A. 134 A1
Kaukkwè Hills Myanmar 70 B1
Kaukonen Fin. 44 N3
Ka'ula i. U.S.A. 127 [inset]
Kaulakahi Channel U.S.A. 127 [inset]
Kaumajet Mountains Canada 123 J2
Kaunakakai U.S.A. 127 [inset]
Kaunas Lith. 45 M9
Kaunata Latvia 45 O8
Kaundy, Vpadina depr. Kazakh. 91 I2
Kaunia Bangl. 83 G4
Kaura-Namoda Nigeria 96 D3
Kau Sai Chau i. H.K. China 77 [inset]
Kaustinen Fin. 44 M5
Kautokeino Norway 44 M2
Kau-ye Kyun i. Myanmar 71 B5
Kavadarci Macedonia 59 J4
Kavak Turkey 90 E2
Kavaklıdere Turkey 59 M6
Kavala Greece 59 K4
Kavalas, Kolpos b. Greece 59 K4
Kavalerovo Russia 74 D3
Kavali India 84 D3
Kavango Zambezi Transfrontier Conservation Area res. Africa 99 C5
Kavār Iran 88 D4
Kavaratti India 84 B4
Kavaratti atoll India 84 B4
Kavarna Bulg. 59 M3
Kavendou, Mont mt. Guinea 96 B3
Kaveri r. India 84 C4
Kavīr Iran 88 C3
Kavīr, Chāh-e well Iran 88 E3
Kavīr, Dasht-e des. Iran 88 D3
Kavīr Kūshk well Iran 88 E3
Kavkasioni mts Asia/Europe see Caucasus
Kawa Myanmar 70 B3
Kawagama Lake Canada 135 F1
Kawagoe Japan 75 E6
Kawaguchi Japan 75 E6
Kawaihae U.S.A. 127 [inset]
Kawaikini U.S.A. 127 [inset]
Kawakawa N.Z. 113 E2
Kawambwa Zambia 99 C4
Kawana Zambia 99 C5
Kawardha India 82 E5
Kawartha Highlands Signature Site park Canada 135 F1
Kawartha Lakes Canada 135 F1
Kawasaki Japan 75 E6
Kawau Island N.Z. 113 E3
Kawawachikamach Canada 123 I3
Kawdut Myanmar 70 B4
Kawerau N.Z. 113 F4
Kawhia N.Z. 113 E4
Kawhia Harbour N.Z. 113 E4
Kawich Peak U.S.A. 128 E3
Kawich Range mts U.S.A. 128 E3
Kawinaw Lake Canada 121 L4
Kaw Lake U.S.A. 131 D4
Kawlin Myanmar 70 A2
Kawm Umbū Egypt 86 D5
Kawngmeum Myanmar 70 B2
Kawthaung Myanmar 71 B5
Kaxgar China see Kashi
Kaxgar He r. China 80 E4
Kax He r. China 80 F3
Kaxtexi Shan mts China 83 E1
Kaya Burkina Faso 96 C3
Kayadibi Turkey 90 E3
Kayan r. Indon. 68 F6
Kayankulam India 84 C4
Kayar India 84 C2
Kaycee U.S.A. 126 G4
Kaydak, Sor dry lake Kazakh. 91 I1
Kaydanovo Belarus see Dzyarzhynsk
Kayembe-Mukulu Dem. Rep. Congo 99 C4
Kayenta U.S.A. 129 H3
Kayes Mali 96 B3
Kaylahgay (abandoned) Afgh. 89 H3
Kaymaz Turkey 59 N5
Kaynar Kazakh. 80 E2
Kaynar Turkey 90 E3
Kayseri Turkey 90 D3
Kayuyu Dem. Rep. Congo 98 C4
Kayyngdy Kyrg. 80 D3
Kazach'ye Russia 65 O2
Kazakh Azer. see Qazax
Kazakhskaya S.S.R. country Asia see Kazakhstan
Kazakhskiy Zaliv b. Kazakh. 91 I2

▶Kazakhstan country Asia 78 F2
4th largest country in Asia and 9th in the world.

Kazakhstan Kazakh. see Aksay
Kazakh Steppe plain Kazakh. see Saryarka
Kazakstan country Asia see Kazakhstan
Kazan r. Canada 121 M2
Kazan' Russia 42 K5
Kazandzhik Turkm. see Bereket
Kazanka r. Russia 42 K5
Kazanlak Bulg. 59 K3
Kazanlı Turkey 85 B1
Kazan-rettō is Japan see Volcano Islands
Kazatin Ukr. see Kozyatyn

▶Kazbek mt. Georgia/Russia 43 J8
4th highest mountain in Europe.

Kaz Dağı mts Turkey 59 L5
Kāzerūn Iran 88 C4
Kazhym Russia 42 K3
Kazidi Tajik. see Qozide
Kazi Magomed Azer. see Hacıqabul
Kazincbarcika Hungary 43 D6
Kaziranga National Park India 83 H4
K'azreti Georgia 91 G2
Kaztalovka Kazakh. 41 P6
Kazy Turkm. 88 E2
Kazym r. Russia 41 T3
Kazym-Mys Russia 41 T3
Kea i. Greece see Tzia
Keady U.K. 51 F3
Keams Canyon U.S.A. 129 H4
Kéamu i. Vanuatu see Anatom
Kearney U.S.A. 130 D3
Kearny U.S.A. 129 H5
Keban Turkey 90 E3
Keban Barajı resr Turkey 90 E3
Kébémèr Senegal 96 B3
Kebili Tunisia 54 F5
Kebīr, Nahr al r. Lebanon/Syria 85 B2
Kebkabiya Sudan 97 F3
Kebnekaise mt. Sweden 44 K3
Kebock Head hd U.K. 50 C2
K'ebrī Dehar Eth. 98 E3
Kech reg. Pak. 89 F5
Kechika r. Canada 120 E3
Keçiborlu Turkey 59 N6
Kecskemét Hungary 59 H1
Keda Georgia 91 F2
Kėdainiai Lith. 45 M9
Kedairu Passage Fiji see Kadavu Passage
Kedgwick Canada 123 I5
Kedian China 77 G2
Kedong China 74 B3
Kédougou Senegal 96 B3
Kedva r. Russia 42 L2
Kędzierzyn-Koźle Poland 47 Q5
Keele r. Canada 120 E1
Keele Peak Canada 120 D2
Keeler U.S.A. 128 E3
Keeley Lake Canada 121 I4
Keeling Islands terr. Indian Ocean see Cocos (Keeling) Islands
Keelung Taiwan 77 I3
Keen, Mount hill U.K. 50 G4
Keene CA U.S.A. 128 D4
Keene KY U.S.A. 134 C5
Keene NH U.S.A. 135 I2
Keene OH U.S.A. 134 E3
Keeper Hill hill Ireland 51 D5
Keepit, Lake resr Australia 112 E3
Keep River National Park Australia 108 E3
Keerbergen Belgium 52 E3
Keer-weer, Cape Australia 110 C2
Keetmanshoop Namibia 100 D4
Keewatin Canada 121 M5
Kefallinía i. Greece see Cephalonia
Kefallonia i. Greece see Cephalonia
Kefamenanu Indon. 108 D2
Kefe Crimea see Feodosiya
Keffi Nigeria 96 D4
Keflavík Iceland 44 [inset 1]
Kê Ga, Mui pt Vietnam 71 E5
Kegalla Sri Lanka 84 D5
Kegen Kazakh. 80 E3
Keglo, Baie de b. Canada 123 I2
Keg River Canada 120 G3
Kegul'ta Russia 43 J7
Kehra Estonia 45 N7
Kehsi Mansam Myanmar 70 B2
Keighley U.K. 48 F5
Keila Estonia 45 N7
Keimoes S. Africa 100 E5
Keitele Fin. 44 O5
Keitele l. Fin. 44 O5
Keith Australia 111 C8
Keith U.K. 50 G3
Keith Arm b. Canada 120 F1
Kejimkujik National Park Canada 123 I5
Kekaha U.S.A. 127 [inset]
Kékes mt. Hungary 47 R7
Kekri India 82 C4
Kelaa i. Maldives 84 B5
K'elafo Eth. 98 E3
Kelberg Germany 52 G4
Kelheim Germany 53 L6
Kelibia Tunisia 58 D6
Kelif Uzboýy marsh Turkm. 89 F2
Kelīrī Iran 88 E5
Kelkheim (Taunus) Germany 53 I4
Kelkit Turkey 91 E2
Kelkit r. Turkey 90 E2
Kéllé Congo 98 B4
Keller Lake Canada 120 F2
Kellett, Cape Canada 118 F2
Kelleys Island U.S.A. 134 D3
Kelliher Canada 121 K5
Kelloselkä Fin. 44 P3
Kells Ireland 51 F4
Kells r. U.K. 51 F3
Kelly U.S.A. 134 B5
Kelly Lake Canada 120 E1
Kelly Range hills Australia 109 C6
Kelmė Lith. 45 M9
Kelmis Belgium 52 G4
Kélo Chad 97 E4
Kelowna Canada 120 G5
Kelp Head hd Canada 120 E5
Kelseyville U.S.A. 128 B2
Kelso U.K. 50 G5
Kelso U.S.A. 126 C3
Kelso (abandoned) U.S.A. 129 F4
Keluang Malaysia 71 C7
Kelvington Canada 121 K4
Kem' Russia 42 G2
Kem' r. Russia 42 G2
Ke Macina Mali see Macina
Kemah Turkey 90 E3
Kemaliye Turkey 90 E3
Kemalpaşa Turkey 59 L5
Kemano (abandoned) Canada 120 E4
Kembé Cent. Afr. Rep. 98 C3
Kemeneshát hills Hungary 58 G1
Kemer Antalya Turkey 59 N6
Kemer Muğla Turkey 59 M6
Kemer Barajı resr Turkey 59 M6
Kemerovo Russia 64 J4
Kemi Fin. 44 N4
Kemijärvi Fin. 44 O3
Kemijärvi l. Fin. 44 O3
Kemijoki r. Fin. 44 N4
Kemiö Fin. see Kimito
Kemir Turkm. see Keymir
Kemmerer U.S.A. 126 F4
Kemnath Germany 53 L5
Kemnay U.K. 50 G3
Kemp Coast reg. Antarctica see Kemp Land
Kempele Fin. 44 N4
Kempen Germany 52 G3
Kempisch Kanaal canal Belgium 52 F3
Kemp Land reg. Antarctica 152 D2
Kemp Peninsula Antarctica 152 A2
Kemp's Bay Bahamas 133 E7
Kempsey Australia 112 F3
Kempt, Lac l. Canada 122 G5
Kempten (Allgäu) Germany 47 M7
Kempton U.S.A. 134 B3
Kempton Park S. Africa 101 I4
Kemptville Canada 135 H1
Kemujan i. Indon. 68 E8
Ken r. India 82 E4
Kenai U.S.A. 118 C3
Kenai Fiords National Park U.S.A. 118 C4
Kenai Mountains U.S.A. 118 C4
Kenamu r. Canada 123 K3
Kenansville U.S.A. 133 E5
Kenâyis, Râs el pt Egypt see Ḥikmah, Ra's al
Kenbridge U.S.A. 135 F5
Kendal U.K. 48 E4
Kendall Australia 112 F3
Kendall, Cape Canada 119 J3
Kendallville U.S.A. 134 C3
Kendari Indon. 69 G7
Kendawangan Indon. 68 E7
Kendégué Chad 97 E3
Kendirli-Kiyasan, Plato plat. Kazakh. 91 I2
Kendrapara India 83 F5
Kendraparha India see Kendrapara
Kendrick Peak U.S.A. 129 H4
Kendujhar India see Kendujhargarh
Kendujhargarh India 83 F5
Kendyrlisor, Solonchak salt l. Kazakh. 91 I2
Kenebri Australia 112 D3
Kenedy U.S.A. 131 D6
Kenema Sierra Leone 96 B4
Kenge Dem. Rep. Congo 99 B4
Keng Lap Myanmar 70 C2
Kengtung Myanmar 70 B2
Kenhardt S. Africa 100 E5
Kéniéba Mali 96 B3
Kenitra Morocco 54 C5
Kenmare Ireland 51 C6
Kenmare U.S.A. 130 C1
Kenmare River inlet Ireland 51 B6
Kenmore U.S.A. 135 F2
Kenn Germany 52 G5
Kenna U.S.A. 131 C5
Kennebec U.S.A. 130 D3
Kennebec r. U.S.A. 132 G2
Kennebunkport U.S.A. 135 J2
Kennedy, Cape U.S.A. see Canaveral, Cape
Kennedy Range National Park Australia 109 A6
Kennedy Town H.K. China 77 [inset]
Kenner U.S.A. 131 F6
Kennet r. U.K. 49 G7
Kenneth Range hills Australia 109 B5
Kennett U.S.A. 131 F4
Kennewick U.S.A. 126 D3
Kenn Reef Australia 110 F4
Kenogami r. Canada 122 D4
Keno Hill Canada 120 C2
Kenora Canada 121 M5
Kenosha U.S.A. 134 B2
Kenozero, Ozero l. Russia 42 H3
Kent r. U.K. 48 E4
Kent OH U.S.A. 134 E3
Kent TX U.S.A. 131 B6
Kent VA U.S.A. 134 E5
Kent WA U.S.A. 126 C3
Kentani S. Africa see Centane
Kent Group is Australia 111 [inset]
Kentland U.S.A. 134 B3
Kenton U.S.A. 134 D3
Kent Peninsula Canada 118 H3
Kentucky state U.S.A. 134 C5
Kentucky Lake U.S.A. 131 F4
Kenya country Africa 98 D3

▶Kenya, Mount Kenya 98 D4
2nd highest mountain in Africa.

Kenyir, Tasik resr Malaysia 71 C6
Keokuk U.S.A. 130 F3
Keoladeo National Park India 82 D4
Keonjhar India see Kendujhargarh
Keonjhargarh India see Kendujhargarh
Keosauqua U.S.A. 130 F3
Keowee, Lake resr U.S.A. 133 D5
Kepina r. Russia 42 I2
Keppel Bay Australia 110 E4
Kepsut Turkey 59 M5
Kera India 83 F5
Kerāh Iran 88 E4
Kerala state India 84 B4
Kerang Australia 112 A5
Kerava Fin. 45 N6
Kerba Alg. 57 G5
Kerbela Iraq see Karbalā'
Kerben Kyrg. 80 D3
Kerbi r. Russia 74 E1
Kerbodot, Lac l. Canada 123 I3
Kerch Crimea 90 E1
Kerchom"ya Russia 42 L3
Kerema P.N.G. 69 L8
Keremeos Canada 120 G5
Kerempe Burun pt Turkey 90 D2
Keren Eritrea 86 E6
Kerepakupai Merú waterfall Venez. see Angel Falls
Kerewan Gambia 96 B3
Kergeli Turkm. 88 E2
Kerguélen, Îles is Indian Ocean 149 M9
Kerguelen Islands Indian Ocean see Kerguélen, Îles
Kerguelen Plateau sea feature Indian Ocean 149 M9
Kericho Kenya 98 D4
Kerikeri N.Z. 113 D2
Kerimäki Fin. 44 P6
Kerinci, Gunung vol. Indon. 68 C7
Kerinci Seblat, Taman Nasional nat. park Indon. 68 C7
Kerintji vol. Indon. see Kerinci, Gunung
Keriya He watercourse China 72 E5
Keriya Shankou pass China 83 E2
Kerken Germany 52 G3
Kerkennah, Îles is Tunisia 58 D7
Kerkiçi Turkm. 89 G2
Kerkini, Limni l. Greece 59 J4
Kerkinitis, Limni l. Greece see Kerkini, Limni
Kérkira i. Greece see Corfu
Kerkouane tourist site Tunisia 58 D6
Kerkyra Greece 59 H5
Kerkyra i. Greece see Corfu
Kerma Sudan 86 D6
Kermadec Islands S. Pacific Ocean 107 I5

▶Kermadec Trench sea feature S. Pacific Ocean 150 I8
4th deepest trench in the world.

Kermān Iran 88 E4
Kerman U.S.A. 128 C3
Kermān, Bīābān-e Iran 88 E4
Kermānshāh Kermānshāh Iran 88 B3
Kermānshāh Yazd Iran 88 D4
Kermine Uzbek. see Navoiy
Kermit U.S.A. 131 C6
Kern r. U.S.A. 128 D4
Kernertut, Cap c. Canada 123 I2
Keros Russia 42 L3
Keross i. Greece 59 K6
Kérouané Guinea 96 C4
Kerpen Germany 52 G4
Kerr, Cape Antarctica 152 H1
Kerrobert Canada 121 I5
Kerrville U.S.A. 131 D6
Kerry Head hd Ireland 51 C5
Kerteminde Denmark 45 G9
Kerulen r. China/Mongolia see Herlen Gol
Kerur India 84 B2
Keryneia Cyprus see Kyrenia
Kerzaz Alg. 96 C2
Kerzhenets r. Russia 42 J4
Kesagami Lake Canada 122 E4
Kesälahti Fin. 44 P6
Keşan Turkey 59 L4
Keşap Turkey 43 H8
Kesariya India 83 F4
Kesennuma Japan 75 F5
Keshan China 74 B2
Keshena U.S.A. 134 A1
Keshod India 82 B5
Keshvar Iran 88 C3
Keskin Turkey 90 D3
Keskozero Russia 42 G3
Kesova Gora Russia 42 H4
Kessel Neth. 52 G3
Kestell S. Africa 101 I5
Kesten'ga Russia 44 Q4
Kestilä Fin. 44 O4
Keswick Canada 134 F1
Keswick U.K. 48 D4
Keszthely Hungary 58 G1
Ketapang Indon. 68 E7
Ketchikan U.S.A. 120 D4
Keti Bandar Pak. 89 G5
Ketmen', Khrebet mts China/Kazakh. 80 F3
Kettering U.K. 49 G6
Kettering U.S.A. 134 C4
Kettle r. Canada 120 G5
Kettle Creek r. U.S.A. 135 G3
Kettle Falls U.S.A. 126 D2
Kettleman City U.S.A. 128 D3
Kettle River Range mts U.S.A. 126 D2
Keuka U.S.A. 135 G2
Keuka Lake U.S.A. 135 G2
Keumgang, Mount N. Korea see Kumgang-san
Keumsang, Mount N. Korea see Kumgang-san
Keuruu Fin. 44 N5
Kew Turks and Caicos Is 133 F8
Kewanee U.S.A. 130 F3
Kewaunee U.S.A. 134 B1
Keweenaw Bay U.S.A. 130 F2
Keweenaw Peninsula U.S.A. 130 F2
Keweenaw Point U.S.A. 132 C2
Key, Lough l. Ireland 51 D3
Keyala South Sudan 97 G4
Keyano Canada 123 G3
Keya Paha r. U.S.A. 130 D3
Key Harbour Canada 122 E5
Keyihe China 74 A2
Key Largo U.S.A. 133 D7
Keymir Turkm. 88 D2
Keynsham U.K. 49 E7
Keyser U.S.A. 135 F4
Keystone Lake U.S.A. 131 D4
Keystone Peak U.S.A. 129 H6
Keysville U.S.A. 135 F5
Keytesville U.S.A. 130 E4
Keyvy, Vozvyshennost' hills Russia 42 H2
Key West U.S.A. 133 D7
Kez Russia 41 Q4
Kezi Zimbabwe 99 C6
Kgalagadi admin. dist. Botswana 100 E3
Kgalagadi Transfrontier Park Botswana/S. Africa 101 D2
Kgalazadi admin. dist. Botswana see Kgalagadi
Kgatlen admin. dist. Botswana see Kgatleng
Kgatleng admin. dist. Botswana 101 H3
Kgomofatshe Pan salt pan Botswana 100 E2
Kgoro Pan salt pan Botswana 100 G3
Kgotsong S. Africa 101 H4
Khabab Syria 85 C3
Khabar Iran 88 D4
Khabarikha Russia 42 L2
Khabarovsk Russia 74 D2
Khabarovskiy Kray admin. div. Russia 74 D2
Khabarovsk Kray admin. div. Russia see Khabarovskiy Kray
Khabary Russia 72 D2
Khabis Iran see Shahdād
Khachmas Azer. see Xaçmaz
Khadar, Jabal mt. Oman 88 E6
Khadīr Afgh. 89 G3
Khadro Pak. 89 H5
Khadzhiolen Turkm. 88 E2
Khafs Banbān well Saudi Arabia 88 B5
Khagaria India 83 F4
Khagrachari Bangl. 83 G5
Khagrachhari Bangl. see Khagrachari
Khairgarh Pak. 89 H4
Khairpur Punjab Pak. 89 I4
Khairpur Sindh Pak. 89 H5
Khāīz, Kūh-e mt. Iran 88 C4
Khajuha India 82 E4
Khāk-e Jabār-e Bālā Afgh. 89 H3
Khakhea Botswana 100 F3
Khākrēz Afgh. 89 G4
Khākrēz reg. Afgh. 89 G4
Khalajestan reg. Iran 88 C3
Khalatse India 82 D2
Khalifat mt. Pak. 89 G4
Khalīj Surt g. Libya see Sirte, Gulf of
Khalilabad India 83 E4
Khalīlī Iran 88 D5
Khalkabad Turkm. 89 F1
Khalkhāl Iran 88 C2
Khálki i. Greece see Chalki
Khalkís Greece see Chalkida
Khallikot India 84 E2
Khalturin Russia see Orlov
Khamar-Daban, Khrebet mts Russia 72 I2
Khamaria India 84 D1
Khambhat India 82 C5
Khambhat, Gulf of India 84 A2
Khamgaon India 84 C1
Khamis Mushayṭ Saudi Arabia 86 F6
Khamkeut Laos 70 D3
Khamma well Saudi Arabia 88 B5
Khammam India 84 D2
Khammouan Laos see Thakhèk
Khamr Yemen 86 F6
Khamra Russia 65 M3
Khamseh reg. Iran 88 C3
Khan, Nâm r. Laos 70 C3
Khānābād Afgh. 89 H2
Khān al Baghdādī Iraq 91 F4
Khān al Mashāhidah Iraq 91 G4
Khān al Muṣallá Iraq 91 G4
Khanapur India 84 B2
Khān ar Raḥbah Iraq 91 G5
Khanasur Pass Iran/Turkey 91 G3
Khanbalik China see Beijing
Khānch Iran 88 B2
Khandu India 89 I6
Khandwa India 82 D5
Khandyga Russia 65 O3
Khanewal Pak. 89 H4
Khanh Hung Vietnam see Soc Trăng
Khaniá Greece see Chania
Khānī Yek Iran 88 D4
Khanka, Lake China/Russia 74 D3
Khanka, Ozero l. China/Russia see Khanka, Lake
Khankendi Azer. see Xankändi
Khanna India 82 D3
Khannā, Qā' salt pan Jordan 85 C3
Khanpur Balochistan Pak. 89 H4
Khanpur Punjab Pak. 89 H4
Khān Ruḥābah Iraq see Khān ar Raḥbah
Khansar Pak. 89 H4
Khān Shaykhūn Syria 85 C2
Khantayskoye, Ozero l. Russia 64 K3
Khanthabouli Laos see Savannakhét
Khanty-Mansiysk Russia 64 H3
Khān Yūnus Gaza 85 B4
Khanzi admin. dist. Botswana see Ghanzi
Khao Ang Rua Nai Wildlife Reserve nature res. Thai. 71 C4
Khao Banthat Wildlife Reserve nature res. Thai. 71 B6
Khao Chum Thong Thai. 71 B5
Khaoen Si Nakarin National Park Thai. 71 B4
Khao Laem, Ang Kep Nam Thai. 70 B4
Khao Laem National Park Thai. 70 B4
Khao Luang National Park Thai. 71 B5
Khao Pu-Khao Ya National Park Thai. 71 B6
Khao Soi Dao Wildlife Reserve nature res. Thai. 71 C4
Khao Sok National Park Thai. 71 B5
Khao Yai National Park Thai. 71 C4
Khaplu Pak. 80 E4
Khaptad National Park Nepal 82 E3
Kharabali Russia 43 J7
Kharagpur Bihar India 83 F4
Kharagpur W. Bengal India 83 F5
Kharāmeh Iran 88 D4
Khārān r. Iran 87 I4
Kharānaq, Kūh-e mt. Iran 88 D3
Kharari India see Abu Road
Kharda India 84 B2
Khardi India 82 C6
Khardong La pass India see Khardung La
Khardung La pass India 82 D2
Kharfiyah Iraq 91 G5
Kharga Egypt see Al Khārijah
Kharga r. Russia 74 D1
Khârga, El Wâḥât el oasis Egypt see Khārijah, Wāḥāt al

Kharga Oasis Egypt see Khārijah, Wāḩāt al
Kharg Islands Iran 88 C4
Khargone India 82 C5
Khari r. Rajasthan India 82 C4
Khari r. Rajasthan India 82 C4
Kharian Pak. 89 I3
Khariar India 84 D1
Khārijah, Wāḩāt al oasis Egypt 86 D5
Kharîm, Gebel hill Egypt see Kharīm, Jabal
Kharīm, Jabal hill Egypt 85 A4
Kharkhara r. India 82 E5
Kharkiv Ukr. 43 H6
Khar'kov Ukr. see Kharkiv
Kharlovka Russia 42 H1
Kharlu Russia 44 Q6
Kharōṭī reg. Afgh. 89 H3
Kharovsk Russia 42 I4
Kharsia India 83 E5

▶Khartoum Sudan 86 D6
Capital of Sudan. 5th most populous city in Africa.

Kharwār reg. Afgh. 89 H3
Khasavyurt Russia 91 G2
Khāsh Iran 89 F4
Khāsh, Dasht-e Afgh. 89 F4
Khashm el Girba Sudan 86 E7
Khashm Şana' Saudi Arabia 90 E6
Khāsh Rōd Afgh. 89 F4
Khāsh Rōd r. Afgh. 89 F4
Khashuri Georgia 91 F2
Khasi Hills India 83 G4
Khatanga Russia 65 L2
Khatanga, Gulf of Russia see Khatangskiy Zaliv
Khatangskiy Zaliv b. Russia 65 L2
Khatayakha Russia 42 M2
Khatinza Pass Pak. 89 H2
Khatmat al Malāha Oman 88 E5
Khatyrka Russia 65 S3
Khaur Pak. 89 I3
Khavda India 82 B5
Khāwāk, Kōtal-e Afgh. 89 H3
Khayamnandi S. Africa 101 G6
Khayang mt. India 83 H4
Khaybar Saudi Arabia 86 E4
Khayelitsha S. Africa 100 D8
Khayrān, Ra's al pt Oman 88 E6
Khefa Israel see Haifa
Khehuene, Ponta pt Moz. 101 L2
Khemis Miliana Alg. 57 H5
Khemmarat Thai. 70 D3
Khenchela Alg. 58 B7
Khenifra Morocco 54 C5
Kherrata Alg. 57 I5
Kherreh Iran 88 D5
Khersan r. Iran 88 C4
Kherson Ukr. 59 O1
Kheta r. Russia 65 L2
Kheyrābād Iran 88 D4
Khezerābād Iran 88 D2
Khezrī Dasht-e Bayāz Iran 88 E3
Khiching India 83 F5
Khilok Russia 73 K2
Khilok r. Russia 73 J2
Khinganskiy Zapovednik nature res. Russia 74 C2
Khinsar Pak. 89 H5
Khíos i. Greece see Chios
Khipro Pak. 89 H5
Khisrow Afgh. 89 G3
Khitai Dawan pass China 82 D2
Khīyāv Iran 88 B2
Khiytola Russia 45 P6
Khlevnoye Russia 43 H5
Khlong, Mae r. Thai. 71 C4
Khlong Saeng Wildlife Reserve nature res. Thai. 71 B5
Khlong Wang Chao National Park Thai. 70 B3
Khlung Thai. 71 C4
Khmel'nik Ukr. see Khmil'nyk
Khmel'nitskiy Ukr. see Khmel'nyts'kyy
Khmel'nyts'kyy Ukr. 43 E6
Khmer Republic country Asia see Cambodia
Khmil'nyk Ukr. 43 E6
Khoai, Hon i. Vietnam 71 D5
Khobi Georgia 91 F2
Khodā Āfarīd spring Iran 88 E3
Khodzha-Kala Turkm. see Hojagala
Khodzhambaz Turkm. see Hojambaz
Khodzhent Tajik. see Khŭjand
Khodzheyli Uzbek. see Xo'jayli
Khojand Tajik. see Khŭjand
Khokhowe Pan salt pan Botswana 100 E3
Khokhropar Pak. 89 H5
Khoksar India 82 D2
Kholm Poland see Chełm
Kholm Russia 42 F4
Kholmsk Russia 74 F3
Kholon Israel see Ḥolon
Khomas admin. reg. Namibia 100 C2
Khomas Highland hills Namibia 100 B2
Khomeyn Iran 88 C3
Khomeynīshahr Iran 88 C3
Khong, Mae Nam r. Asia see Mekong
Khonj Iran 88 D5
Khonj, Kūh-e mts Iran 88 D5
Khon Kaen Thai. 70 C3
Khon Kriel Cambodia see Kon Kriel
Khonsa India 83 H4
Khonuu Russia 65 P3
Khoper r. Russia 43 I6
Khor Russia 74 D3
Khor r. Russia 74 D3
Khorāsān, Chāh-e well Iran 88 D3
Khorat Plateau Thai. 70 C3
Khorda India see Khordha
Khordha India 84 E1
Khorey-Ver Russia 42 M2
Khorinsk Russia 73 J2
Khorixas Namibia 99 B6
Khormūj, Kūh-e mt. Iran 88 C4
Khorog Tajik. see Khorugh
Khorol Russia 74 D3
Khorol Ukr. 43 G6
Khoroslū Dāgh hills Iran 88 B2
Khorramābād Iran 88 C3
Khorramshahr Iran 88 C4
Khorugh Tajik. 89 H2
Khosheutovo Russia 43 J7
Khoshgort Russia 41 T2
Khōst Afgh. 89 H3
Khōst reg. Afgh./Pak. 89 H3
Khosūyeh Iran 88 D4
Khotan China see Hotan
Khouribga Morocco 54 C5
Khovaling Tajik. 89 H2
Khowrjān Iran 88 D4
Khreum Myanmar 70 A2
Khroma r. Russia 65 P2
Khromtau Kazakh. 80 A1
Khrushchev Ukr. see Svitlovods'k
Khrysokhou Bay Cyprus see Chrysochou Bay
Khrystynivka Ukr. 43 F6
Khudumelapye Botswana 100 G2
Khudzhand Tajik. see Khŭjand
Khufaysah, Khashm al hill Saudi Arabia 88 B6
Khugiana Afgh. see Pīr Zādah
Khuis Botswana 100 E4
Khŭjand Tajik. 80 C3
Khŭjayli Uzbek. see Xo'jayli
Khu Khan Thai. 71 D4
Khulays Saudi Arabia 86 E5
Khulkhuta Russia 43 J7
Khulm Afgh. 89 G2
Khulm, Daryā-ye r. Afgh. 89 G2
Khulna Bangl. 83 G5
Khulo Georgia 91 F2
Khuma S. Africa 101 H4
Khunayzīr, Jabal al mts Syria 85 C2
Khūnīk Iran 88 E3
Khūnīnshahr Iran see Khorramshahr
Khunjerab Pass China/Pak. 82 C1
Khun Yuam Thai. 70 B3
Khūr Iran 88 E3
Khūran sea chan. Iran 88 D5
Khurays Saudi Arabia 86 G4
Khurda India see Khordha
Khurdha India see Khordha
Khurja India 82 D3
Khurmāliq Afgh. 89 F3
Khurmuli Russia 74 E2
Khushab Pak. 89 I3
Khushalgarh Pak. 89 H3
Khushshah, Wādī al watercourse Jordan/Saudi Arabia 85 C5
Khust Ukr. 43 D6
Khutse Game Reserve nature res. Botswana 100 G2
Khutsong S. Africa 101 H4
Khutu r. Russia 74 E2
Khuzdar Pak. 89 G5
Khvāf Iran 89 F3
Khvāf reg. Iran 89 F3
Khvājeh Iran 88 B2
Khvalynsk Russia 43 K5
Khvānsār Iran 88 C3
Khvodrān Iran 88 D4
Khvormūj Iran 88 C4
Khvors Iran 88 D3
Khvoy Iran 88 B2
Khvoynaya Russia 42 G4
Khwaja Amran mt. Pak. 89 G4
Khwājah Dū Kōh hill Afgh. 89 G2
Khwājah Muḩammad, Kōh-e mts Afgh. 89 H2
Khyber Pakhtunkhwa prov. Pak. 89 H3
Khyber Pass Afgh./Pak. 89 H3
Kiama Australia 112 E5
Kiamichi r. U.S.A. 131 E5
Kiangsi prov. China see Jiangxi
Kiangsu prov. China see Jiangsu
Kiantajärvi l. Fin. 44 P4
Kīāsar Iran 88 D2
Kiatassuaq i. Greenland 119 M2
Kibaha Tanz. 99 D4
Kibali r. Dem. Rep. Congo 98 C3
Kibangou Congo 98 B4
Kibaya Tanz. 99 D4
Kiboga Uganda 98 D3
Kibombo Dem. Rep. Congo 98 C4
Kibondo Tanz. 98 D4
Kibre Mengist Eth. 97 G4
Kibris country Asia see Cyprus
Kibungo Rwanda 98 D4
Kičevo Macedonia 59 I4
Kichmengskiy Gorodok Russia 42 J4
Kiçik Qafqaz mts Asia see Lesser Caucasus
Kicking Horse Pass Canada 120 G5
Kidal Mali 96 D3
Kidderminster U.K. 49 E6
Kidepo Valley National Park Uganda 98 D3
Kidira Senegal 96 B3
Kidmang India 82 D2
Kidnappers, Cape N.Z. 113 F4
Kidsgrove U.K. 49 E5
Kiel Germany 47 M3
Kiel U.S.A. 134 A2
Kiel Canal Germany 47 L3
Kielce Poland 47 R5
Kielder Water resr U.K. 48 E3
Kieler Bucht b. Germany 47 M3
Kienge Dem. Rep. Congo 99 C5
Kierspe Germany 53 H3

▶Kiev Ukr. 43 F6
Capital of Ukraine.

Kiffa Mauritania 96 B3
Kifisia Greece 59 J5
Kifrī Iraq 91 G4

▶Kigali Rwanda 98 D4
Capital of Rwanda.

Kiğı Turkey 91 F3
Kiglapait Mountains Canada 123 J2
Kigoma Tanz. 99 C4
Kihlanki Fin. 44 M3
Kihniö Fin. 44 M5
Kīholo U.S.A. 127 [inset]
Kiiminki Fin. 44 N4
Kii-sanchi mts Japan 75 D6
Kii-suidō sea chan. Japan 75 D6
Kikerino Russia 45 P7
Kikinda Serbia 59 I2
Kikki Pak. 89 F5
Kikládhes is Greece see Cyclades
Kiknur Russia 42 J4
Kikonai Japan 74 F4
Kikori P.N.G. 69 K8
Kikori r. P.N.G. 69 K8
Kikwit Dem. Rep. Congo 99 B4
Kilafors Sweden 45 J6
Kilar India 82 D2
Kīlauea U.S.A. 127 [inset]
Kīlauea Volcano U.S.A. 127 [inset]
Kilchu N. Korea 74 C4
Kilcoole Ireland 51 F4
Kilcormac Ireland 51 E4
Kilcoy Australia 112 F1
Kildare Ireland 51 F4
Kil'dinstroy Russia 44 R2
Kilemary Russia 42 J4
Kilembe Dem. Rep. Congo 99 B4
Kilfinan U.K. 50 D5
Kilgore U.S.A. 131 E5
Kilham U.K. 48 E3
Kilia Ukr. see Kiliya
Kılıç Dağı mt. Syria/Turkey see Aqra', Jabal al
Kilifi Kenya 98 D4
Kilik Pass China 82 C1

▶Kilimanjaro vol. Tanz. 98 D4
Highest mountain in Africa.

Kilimanjaro National Park Tanz. 98 D4
Kilinailau Islands P.N.G. 106 F2
Kilindoni Tanz. 99 D4
Kilingi-Nõmme Estonia 45 N7
Kilis Turkey 85 C1
Kilis prov. Turkey 85 C1
Kiliya Ukr. 59 M2
Kilkee Ireland 51 C5
Kilkeel U.K. 51 G3
Kilkenny Ireland 51 E5
Kilkhampton U.K. 49 C8
Kilkis Greece 59 J4
Killala Ireland 51 C3
Killala Bay Ireland 51 C3
Killaloe Ireland 51 D5
Killam Canada 121 I4
Killarney N.T. Australia 108 E4
Killarney Qld Australia 112 F2
Killarney Canada 122 E5
Killarney Ireland 51 C5
Killarney National Park Ireland 51 C6
Killary Harbour b. Ireland 51 C4
Killbuck U.S.A. 134 E3
Killeen U.S.A. 131 D6
Killenaule Ireland 51 E5
Killimor Ireland 51 D4
Killin U.K. 50 E4
Killinchy U.K. 51 G3
Killíni mt. Greece see Kyllini
Killinick Ireland 51 F5
Killorglin Ireland 51 C5
Killurin Ireland 51 F5
Killybegs Ireland 51 D3
Kilmacrenan Ireland 51 E2
Kilmaine Ireland 51 C4
Kilmallock Ireland 51 D5
Kilmaluag U.K. 50 C3
Kilmarnock U.K. 50 E5
Kilmelford U.K. 50 D4
Kil'mez' Russia 42 K4
Kil'mez' r. Russia 42 K4
Kilmona Ireland 51 D6
Kilmore Australia 112 B6
Kilmore Quay Ireland 51 F5
Kilosa Tanz. 99 D4
Kilpisjärvi Fin. 44 L2
Kilrea U.K. 51 F3
Kilrush Ireland 51 C5
Kilsyth U.K. 50 E5
Kiltan atoll India 84 B4
Kiltullagh Ireland 51 D4
Kilwa Masoko Tanz. 99 D4
Kilwinning U.K. 50 E5
Kim U.S.A. 131 C4
Kimba Australia 109 G8
Kimba Congo 98 B4
Kimball U.S.A. 130 C3
Kimball, Mount U.S.A. 118 D3
Kimbe P.N.G. 106 F2
Kimberley S. Africa 100 G5
Kimberley Plateau Australia 108 D4
Kimberley Range hills Australia 109 B6
Kimch'aek N. Korea 75 C4
Kimhae S. Korea see Gimhae
Kimhandu mt. Tanz. 99 D4
Kimi Greece see Kymi
Kimito Fin. 45 M6
Kimjŏngsuk N. Korea 74 B4
Kimmirut Canada 119 L3
Kimolos i. Greece 59 K6
Kimovsk Russia 43 H5
Kimpese Dem. Rep. Congo 99 B4
Kimpoku-san mt. Japan see Kinpoku-san
Kimry Russia 42 H4
Kimsquit Canada 120 E4
Kimvula Dem. Rep. Congo 99 B4
Kinabalu, Gunung mt. Sabah Malaysia 68 F5
Kinango Kenya 99 D4
Kinaskan Lake Canada 120 D3
Kinbasket Lake Canada 120 G4
Kinbrace U.K. 50 F2
Kincaid Canada 121 J5
Kincardine Canada 134 E1
Kincardine U.K. 50 F4
Kinchega National Park Australia 111 C7
Kincolith Canada see Gingolx
Kinda Dem. Rep. Congo 99 C4
Kindat Myanmar 70 A2
Kinde U.S.A. 134 D2
Kinder Scout hill U.K. 48 F5
Kindersley Canada 121 I5
Kindia Guinea 96 B3
Kindu Dem. Rep. Congo 98 C4
Kinel' Russia 43 K5
Kineshma Russia 42 I4
King Abdullah Economic City Saudi Arabia 78 C4
Kingaroy Australia 112 E1
King Christian Island Canada 119 H2
King City U.S.A. 128 C3
King Edward VII Land pen. Antarctica see Edward VII Peninsula
Kingfield U.S.A. 135 J1
Kingfisher U.S.A. 131 D5
King George U.S.A. 135 G4
King George, Mount Canada 126 E2
King George Island Antarctica 152 A2
King George Islands Canada 122 F2
King George Islands Fr. Polynesia see Roi Georges, Îles du
King Hill hill Australia 108 C5
Kingisepp Russia 45 P7
King Island Australia 111 [inset]
King Island Canada 120 E4
King Island Myanmar see Kadan Kyun
Kingisseppa Estonia see Kuressaare
Kinglake National Park Australia 112 B6
King Leopold and Queen Astrid Coast Antarctica 152 E2
King Leopold Range National Park Australia 108 D4
King Leopold Ranges hills Australia 108 D4
Kingman U.S.A. 129 F4

▶Kingman Reef terr. N. Pacific Ocean 150 J5
United States Unincorporated Territory.

King Mountain Canada 120 D3
King Mountain hill U.S.A. 131 C6
Kingoonya Australia 111 A6
King Peak Antarctica 152 L1
King Peninsula Antarctica 152 K2
Kingri Pak. 89 H4
Kings r. Ireland 51 E5
Kings r. CA U.S.A. 128 C3
Kings r. NV U.S.A. 126 D4
King Salmon U.S.A. 118 C4
Kingsbridge U.K. 49 D8
Kingsburg U.S.A. 128 D3
Kings Canyon National Park U.S.A. 128 D3
Kingscliff Australia 112 F2
Kingscote Australia 111 B7
Kingscourt Ireland 51 F4
King Sejong research station Antarctica 152 A2
King's Lynn U.K. 49 H6
Kingsmill Group is Kiribati 107 H2
Kingsnorth U.K. 49 H7
King Sound b. Australia 108 C4
Kings Peak U.S.A. 129 H1
Kingsport U.S.A. 132 D4
Kingston Australia 111 [inset]
Kingston Canada 135 G1

▶Kingston Jamaica 137 I5
Capital of Jamaica.

▶Kingston Norfolk I. 107 G4
Capital of Norfolk Island.

Kingston MO U.S.A. 130 E4
Kingston NY U.S.A. 135 H3
Kingston OH U.S.A. 134 D4
Kingston PA U.S.A. 135 H3
Kingston Peak U.S.A. 129 F4
Kingston South East Australia 111 B8
Kingston upon Hull U.K. 48 G5

▶Kingstown St Vincent 137 L6
Capital of St Vincent.

Kingstree U.S.A. 133 E5
Kingsville U.S.A. 131 D7
Kingswood U.K. 49 E7
Kington U.K. 49 D6
Kingungi Dem. Rep. Congo 99 B4
Kingurutik r. Canada 123 J2
Kingussie U.K. 50 E3
King William U.S.A. 135 G5
King William Island Canada 119 I3
King William's Town S. Africa 101 H7
Kingwood TX U.S.A. 131 E6
Kingwood WV U.S.A. 134 F4
Kinloch N.Z. 113 B7
Kinloss U.K. 50 F3
Kinmen Taiwan see Jinmen
Kinmen i. Taiwan see Jinmen Dao
Kinmount Canada 135 F1
Kinna Sweden 45 H8
Kinnegad Ireland 51 E4
Kinneret, Yam l. Israel see Galilee, Sea of
Kinniyai Sri Lanka 84 D4
Kinnula Fin. 44 N5
Kinoje r. Canada 122 E3
Kinoosao Canada 121 K3
Kinpoku-san mt. Japan 75 E5
Kinross U.K. 50 F4
Kinsale Ireland 51 D6
Kinsale U.S.A. 135 G4

▶Kinshasa Dem. Rep. Congo 99 B4
Capital of the Democratic Republic of the Congo. 3rd most populous city in Africa.

Kinsley U.S.A. 130 D4
Kinsman U.S.A. 134 E3
Kinston U.S.A. 133 E5
Kintore U.K. 50 G3
Kintyre pen. U.K. 50 D5
Kin-U Myanmar 70 A2
Kinushseo r. Canada 122 E3
Kinyeti mt. South Sudan 97 G4
Kinzig r. Germany 53 I4
Kiowa CO U.S.A. 126 G5
Kiowa KS U.S.A. 131 D4
Kipahigan Lake Canada 121 K4
Kiparissia Greece see Kyparissia
Kipawa, Lac l. Canada 122 F5
Kipling Canada 121 K5
Kipling Station Canada see Kipling
Kipnuk U.S.A. 118 B4
Kiptopeke U.S.A. 135 H5
Kipungo Angola see Quipungo
Kipushi Dem. Rep. Congo 99 C5
Kirakira Solomon Is 107 G3
Kirandul India 84 D2
Kirchdorf Germany 53 I2
Kirchheimbolanden Germany 53 I5
Kirchheim unter Teck Germany 53 J6
Kircubbin U.K. 51 G3
Kirdimi Chad 97 E3
Kirenga r. Russia 73 J1
Kirensk Russia 65 L4
Kireyevsk Russia 43 H5
Kirghizia country Asia see Kyrgyzstan
Kirghiz Range mts Kazakh./Kyrg. 80 D3
Kirgizskaya S.S.R. country Asia see Kyrgyzstan
Kirgizskiy Khrebet mts Kazakh./Kyrg. see Kirghiz Range
Kirgizstan country Asia see Kyrgyzstan
Kiri Dem. Rep. Congo 98 B4
Kiribati country Pacific Ocean 150 I6
Kırıkhan Turkey 85 C1
Kırıkkale Turkey 90 D3
Kirillov Russia 42 H4
Kirillovo (abandoned) Russia 74 F3
Kirin China see Jilin
Kirin prov. China see Jilin
Kirinda Sri Lanka 84 D5
Kirinyaga mt. Kenya see Kenya, Mount
Kirishi Russia 42 G4
Kirishima-Yaku Kokuritsu-kōen nat. park Japan 75 C7
Kirishima-yama vol. Japan 75 C7
Kiritimati atoll Kiribati 151 J5
Kiriwina Islands P.N.G. see Trobriand Islands
Kırkağaç Turkey 59 L5
Kirk Bulāg Dāgi mt. Iran 88 B2
Kirkby U.K. 48 E5
Kirkby in Ashfield U.K. 49 F5
Kirkby Lonsdale U.K. 48 E4
Kirkby Stephen U.K. 48 E4
Kirkcaldy U.K. 50 F4
Kirkcolm U.K. 50 D6
Kirkcudbright U.K. 50 E6
Kirkenær Norway 45 H6
Kirkenes Norway 44 Q2
Kirkfield Canada 135 F1
Kirkintilloch U.K. 50 E5
Kirkkonummi Fin. 45 N6
Kirkland U.S.A. 129 G4
Kirkland Lake Canada 122 E4
Kırklareli Turkey 59 L4
Kirklin U.S.A. 134 B3
Kirk Michael Isle of Man 48 C4
Kirkoswald U.K. 48 E4
Kirkpatrick, Mount Antarctica 152 H1
Kirksville U.S.A. 130 E3
Kirkūk Iraq 91 G4
Kirkwall U.K. 50 G2
Kirkwood S. Africa 101 G7
Kirman Iran see Kermān
Kirn Germany 53 H5
Kirov Kaluzhskaya Oblast' Russia 43 G5
Kirov Kirovskaya Oblast' Russia 42 K4
Kirova, imeni Kazakh. see Kopbirlik
Kirova, Zaliv b. Azer. see Qızılağac Körfäzi
Kirovabad Azer. see Gäncä
Kirovabad Tajik. see Panj
Kirovakan Armenia see Vanadzor
Kirovo Ukr. see Kirovohrad
Kirovo-Chepetsk Russia 42 K4
Kirovo-Chepetskiy Russia see Kirovo-Chepetsk
Kirovograd Ukr. see Kirovohrad
Kirovohrad Ukr. 43 G6
Kirovsk Leningradskaya Oblast' Russia 42 F4
Kirovsk Murmanskaya Oblast' Russia 44 R3
Kirovsk Turkm. see Badabaýhan
Kirovs'ke Crimea 90 D1
Kirovskiy Amurskaya Oblast' Russia 74 B1
Kirovskiy Primorskiy Kray Russia 74 D3
Kirovskoye Crimea see Kirovs'ke
Kırpaşa pen. Cyprus see Karpasia
Kirpili Turkm. 88 E2
Kirriemuir U.K. 50 F4
Kirs Russia 42 L4
Kirsanov Russia 43 I5
Kırşehir Turkey 90 D3
Kirthar National Park Pak. 89 G5
Kirthar Range mts Pak. 89 G5
Kirtland U.S.A. 129 I3
Kirtorf Germany 53 J4
Kiruna Sweden 44 L3
Kirundu Dem. Rep. Congo 98 C4
Kirwan Escarpment Antarctica 152 B2
Kiryū Japan 75 E5
Kisa Sweden 45 I8
Kisama, Parque Nacional de nat. park Angola see Quiçama, Parque Nacional do
Kisandji Dem. Rep. Congo 99 B4
Kisangani Dem. Rep. Congo 98 C3
Kisantu Dem. Rep. Congo 99 B4
Kisar i. Indon. 108 D2
Kisaran Indon. 71 B7
Kiselevka Russia 74 E2
Kiselevsk Russia 72 F2
Kīsh, Jazīreh-ye i. Iran 88 D5
Kishanganj India 83 F4
Kishangarh Madh. Prad. India 82 D4
Kishangarh Rajasthan India 82 B4
Kishangarh Rajasthan India 82 C4
Kishangarh Rajasthan India 82 D4
Kishi Nigeria 96 D4
Kishim Afgh. 89 H2
Kishindih-ye Bālā Afgh. 89 G2
Kishinev Moldova see Chişinău
Kishkenekol' Kazakh. 79 G1
Kishoreganj Bangl. 83 G4
Kishorganj Bangl. see Kishoreganj
Kisi Nigeria see Kishi
Kisii Kenya 98 D4
Kiska Island U.S.A. 65 S4
Kiskittogisu Lake Canada 121 L4
Kiskitto Lake Canada 121 L4
Kiskunfélegyháza Hungary 59 H1
Kiskunhalas Hungary 59 H1
Kiskunsági nat. park Hungary 59 H1
Kislovodsk Russia 91 F2
Kismaayo Somalia 98 E4
Kismayu Somalia see Kismaayo
Kisoro Uganda 97 F5
Kispiox Canada 120 E4
Kispiox r. Canada 120 E4
Kissamos Greece 59 J7
Kisseraing Island Myanmar see Kanmaw Kyun
Kissidougou Guinea 96 B4
Kissimmee U.S.A. 133 D6
Kissimmee, Lake U.S.A. 133 D7
Kississing Lake Canada 121 K4
Kistendey Russia 43 I5
Kistigan Lake Canada 121 M4
Kistna r. India see Krishna
Kisumu Kenya 98 D4
Kisykkamys Kazakh. see Zhanakala
Kita Mali 96 C3
Kitab Uzbek. see Kitob
Kita-Daitō-jima i. Japan 73 O7
Kitaibaraki Japan 75 F5
Kita-Iō-jima vol. Japan 69 K1
Kitakami Japan 75 F5
Kita-Kyūshū Japan 75 C6
Kitale Kenya 98 D3
Kitami Japan 74 F4
Kit Carson U.S.A. 130 C4
Kitchener Canada 134 E2
Kitchigama r. Canada 122 F4
Kitee Fin. 44 Q5
Kitgum Uganda 98 D3
Kíthira i. Greece see Kythira
Kíthnos i. Greece see Kythnos
Kiti, Cape Cyprus see Kitiou, Cape
Kitimat Canada 120 D4
Kitinen r. Fin. 44 O3
Kition, Cape Cyprus 85 A2
Kitiou, Akra c. Cyprus see Kition, Cape
Kitkatla Canada 120 D4
Kitob Uzbek. 89 G2
Kitsault Canada 120 D4
Kittanning U.S.A. 134 F3
Kittatinny Mountains hills U.S.A. 135 H3
Kittery U.S.A. 135 J2
Kittilä Fin. 44 N3
Kittur India 84 B3
Kitty Hawk U.S.A. 132 F4
Kitui Kenya 98 D4
Kitwanga Canada 120 D4
Kitwe Zambia 99 C5
Kitzbüheler Alpen mts Austria 47 N7
Kitzingen Germany 53 K5
Kitzscher Germany 53 M3
Kiu Lom, Ang Kep Nam Thai. 70 B3
Kiunga P.N.G. 69 K8
Kiuruvesi Fin. 44 O5
Kivalina U.S.A. 118 B3
Kivijärvi Fin. 44 N5
Kiviõli Estonia 45 O7
Kivu, Lac Dem. Rep. Congo/Rwanda 98 C4
Kiwaba N'zogi Angola 99 B4
Kiwai Island P.N.G. 69 K8
Kiyev Ukr. see Kiev
Kiyevskoye Vodokhranilishche resr Ukr. see Kyivs'ke Vodoskhovyshche
Kıyıköy Turkey 59 M4
Kizel Russia 41 R4
Kizema Russia 42 J3
Kızılcadağ Turkey 59 M6
Kızılca Dağ mt. Turkey 90 C3
Kızılcahamam Turkey 90 D2
Kızıldağ mt. Turkey 85 A1
Kızıldağ mt. Turkey 85 B1
Kızıl Dağı mt. Turkey 90 E3
Kızılırmak Turkey 90 D2
Kızılırmak r. Turkey 90 D2
Kızıltepe Turkey 91 F3
Kizilyurt Russia 91 G2
Kızkalesi Turkey 85 B1
Kizlyar Russia 91 G2
Kizlyarskiy Zaliv b. Russia 91 G1
Kizner Russia 42 K4
Kizyl-Arbat Turkm. see Serdar
Kizyl-Atrek Turkm. see Etrek
Kjøllefjord Norway 44 O1
Kjøpsvik Norway 44 J2
Kladno Czechia 47 O5
Klagenfurt am Wörthersee Austria 47 O7
Klagetoh U.S.A. 129 I4
Klaipėda Lith. 45 L9
Klaksvík Faroe Is 44 [inset 2]
Klamath U.S.A. 126 B4
Klamath r. U.S.A. 118 F5
Klamath Falls U.S.A. 126 C4
Klamath Mountains U.S.A. 126 C4
Klang Malaysia 71 C7
Klarälven r. Sweden 45 H7
Klatovy Czechia 47 N6
Klawer S. Africa 100 D6
Klazienaveen Neth. 52 G2
Kleides Islands Cyprus 85 B2
Kleinbegin S. Africa 100 E5
Klein Karas Namibia 100 D4
Klein Nama Land reg. S. Africa see Namaqualand
Klein Roggeveldberge mts S. Africa 100 E7
Kleinsee S. Africa 100 C5
Klemtu Canada 120 D4
Klerksdorp S. Africa 101 H4
Kletnya Russia 43 G5
Kletsk Belarus see Klyetsk
Kletskaya Russia 43 I6
Kletskiy Russia see Kletskaya
Kleve Germany 52 G3
Klidhes Islands Cyprus see Kleides Islands
Klimkovka Russia 42 K4
Klimovo Russia 43 G5
Klin Russia 42 H4
Klingenberg am Main Germany 53 J5
Klingenthal Germany 53 M4
Klingkang, Banjaran mts Indon./Malaysia 68 E6
Klink Germany 53 M1
Klínovec mt. Czechia 53 N4
Klintehamn Sweden 45 K8
Klintsy Russia 43 G5
Ključ Bos. & Herz. 58 G2
Kłodzko Poland 47 P5
Klondike r. Canada 120 B1
Klondike Gold Rush National Historical Park nat. park U.S.A. 120 C3
Kloosterhaar Neth. 52 G2
Klosterneuburg Austria 47 P6
Klötze (Altmark) Germany 53 L2
Kluane Lake Canada 120 B2
Kluane National Park Canada 120 B2
Kluang Malaysia see Keluang

Kluczbork Poland 47 Q5
Klukhori Russia see Karachayevsk
Klukhorskiy, Pereval Georgia/Russia 91 F2
Klukwan U.S.A. 120 C3
Klyetsk Belarus 45 O10
Klyuchevskaya Sopka, Vulkan vol. Russia 65 R4
Klyuchi Russia 74 B2
Knåda Sweden 45 I6
Knaresborough U.K. 48 F4
Knee Lake Man. Canada 121 M4
Knee Lake Sask. Canada 121 J4
Knetzgau Germany 53 K5
Knife r. U.S.A. 130 C2
Knight Inlet Canada 120 E5
Knighton U.K. 49 D6
Knights Landing U.S.A. 128 C2
Knightstown U.S.A. 134 C4
Knin Croatia 58 G2
Knittelfeld Austria 47 O7
Knjaževac Serbia 59 J3
Knob Lake Canada see Schefferville
Knob Lick U.S.A. 134 C5
Knob Peak hill Australia 108 E3
Knock Ireland 51 D4
Knockalongy hill Ireland 51 D3
Knockalough Ireland 51 C5
Knockanaffrin hill Ireland 51 E5
Knockboy hill Ireland 51 C6
Knock Hill hill U.K. 50 G3
Knockmealdown Mountains hills Ireland 51 D5
Knocknaskagh hill Ireland 51 D5
Knokke-Heist Belgium 52 D3
Knorrendorf Germany 53 N1
Knowle U.K. 49 F6
Knowlton Canada 135 I1
Knox IN U.S.A. 134 B3
Knox PA U.S.A. 134 F3
Knox, Cape Canada 120 C4
Knox Coast Antarctica 152 F2
Knoxville GA U.S.A. 133 D5
Knoxville TN U.S.A. 132 D5
Knud Rasmussen Land reg. Greenland 119 L2
Knysna S. Africa 100 F8
Ko, Gora mt. Russia 74 E3
Koartac Canada see Quaqtaq
Koba Indon. 68 D7
Kobanê Syria see 'Ayn al 'Arab
Kobbfoss Norway 44 P2
Kobda Kazakh. 80 A1
Kōbe Japan 75 D6
København Denmark see Copenhagen
Kobenni Mauritania 96 C3
Koblenz Germany 53 H4
Koboldo Russia 74 D1
Kobrin Belarus see Kobryn
Kobroör i. Indon. 69 I8
Kobryn Belarus 45 N10
Kobuk Valley National Park U.S.A. 118 C3
Kobuleti Georgia 91 F2
Kocaeli Turkey see İzmit
Kocaeli Yarımadası pen. Turkey 59 M4
Kočani Macedonia 59 J4
Kocasu r. Turkey 59 M4
Kočevje Slovenia 58 F2
Koch Bihar India 83 G4
Kocher r. Germany 53 J5
Kochevo Russia 41 Q4
Kochi India 84 C4
Kōchi Japan 75 D6
Koçhisar Turkey see Kızıltepe
Koch Island Canada 119 K3
Kochkor Kyrg. 80 E3
Kochkorka Kyrg. see Kochkor
Kochkurovo Russia 43 J5
Kochubeyevskoye Russia 91 F1
Kod India 84 B3
Kodala India 84 E2
Kodarma India 83 F4
Koderma India see Kodarma
Kodiak U.S.A. 118 C4
Kodiak Island U.S.A. 118 C4
Kodibeleng Botswana 101 H2
Kodino Russia 42 H3
Kodiyakkarai India 84 C4
Kodok South Sudan 86 D8
Kodyma Ukr. 43 F6
Kodzhaele mt. Bulg./Greece 59 K4
Koedoesberg mts S. Africa 100 E7
Koegrabie S. Africa 100 E5
Koekenaap S. Africa 100 D6
Koersel Belgium 52 F3
Koës Namibia 100 D3
Kofa Mountains U.S.A. 129 G5
Koffiefontein S. Africa 100 G5
Koforidua Ghana 96 C4
Kōfu Japan 75 E6
Kogaluc r. Canada 122 F2
Kogaluc, Baie de b. Canada 122 F2
Kogaluk r. Canada 123 J2
Kogan Australia 112 E1
Køge Denmark 45 H9
Kogon r. Guinea 96 B3
Kogon Uzbek. 89 G2
Kohan Pak. 89 G5
Kohat Pak. 89 H3
Koh-e Şayyād Afgh. 89 G2
Kōhestān reg. Afgh. 89 H3
Kohila Estonia 45 N7
Kohima India 83 H4
Kohistan reg. Pak. 89 I3
Kōhistānāt Afgh. 89 G3
Kohler Range mts Antarctica 152 K2
Kohlu Pak. 89 H4
Kohtla-Järve Estonia 45 O7
Koidern Mountain Canada 120 A2
Koidu Sierra Leone see Koidu-Sefadu
Koidu-Sefadu Sierra Leone 96 B4
Koihoa India 71 A5
Koilkonda India 84 C2
Koin N. Korea 75 B4
Koin r. Russia 42 K3
Kojonup Australia 109 B8
Kokand Uzbek. see Qo'qon
Kōkar Fin. 45 L7
Kokchetav Kazakh. see Kokshetau
Kokemäenjoki r. Fin. 45 L6
Kokerboom Namibia 100 D5
Ko Kha Thai. 70 B3
Kokkilai Sri Lanka 84 D4
Kokkola Fin. 44 M5
Koko Nigeria 96 D3
Kokomo U.S.A. 134 B3
Kokong Botswana 100 F3
Kokos i. Indon. 71 A7
Kokosi S. Africa 101 H4
Kokpekty Kazakh. 80 F2
Koksan N. Korea 75 B5
Kokshaal-Tau, Khrebet mts China/Kyrg. see Kakshaal-Too
Koksharka Russia 42 J4
Kokshetau Kazakh. 79 F1
Koksoak r. Canada 123 H2
Kokstad S. Africa 101 I6
Koktal Kazakh. 80 E3
Kokterek Kazakh. 43 K6
Kola i. Indon. 69 I8
Kola Russia 44 R2
Kolachi r. Pak. 89 G5
Kolahoi mt. India 82 C2
Kolaka Indon. 69 G7
Ko Lanta Thai. 71 B6
Kola Peninsula Russia 42 H2
Kolar Chhattisgarh India 84 D2
Kolar Karnataka India 84 C3
Kolār, Kūh-e hill Iran 88 C4
Kolaras India 82 D4
Kolar Gold Fields India 84 C3
Kolari Fin. 44 M3
Kolarovgrad Bulg. see Shumen
Kolasib India 83 H4
Kolayat India 82 C4
Kolberg Poland see Kołobrzeg
Kol'chugino Russia 42 H4
Kolda Senegal 96 B3
Kolding Denmark 45 F9
Kole Kasaï-Oriental Dem. Rep. Congo 98 C4
Kole Orientale Dem. Rep. Congo 98 C3
Koléa Alg. 57 H5
Koler Sweden 44 L4
Kolguyev, Ostrov i. Russia 42 K1
Kolhan reg. India 83 F5
Kolhapur India 84 B2
Kolhumadulu Maldives 81 D11
Kolikata India see Kolkata
Kõljala Estonia 45 M7
Kolkasrags pt Latvia 45 M8
Kolkata India 83 G5
Kolkhozabad Khatlon Tajik. see Vose'
Kolkhozabad Khatlon Tajik. see Kolkhozobod
Kolkhozobod Tajik. 89 H2
Kollam India 84 C4
Kolleru Lake India 84 D2
Kollum Neth. 52 G1
Kolmanskop (abandoned) Namibia 100 B4
Köln Germany see Cologne
Köln-Bonn airport Germany 53 H4
Kołobrzeg Poland 47 O3
Kologriv Russia 42 J4
Kolokani Mali 96 C3
Kolombangara i. Solomon Is 107 F2
Kolomea Ukr. see Kolomyya
Kolomna Russia 43 H5
Kołomyja Ukr. see Kolomyya
Kolomyya Ukr. 43 E6
Kolondiéba Mali 96 C3
Kolonedale Indon. 69 G7
Koloni Cyprus 85 A2
Kolonkwaneng Botswana 100 E4
Kolozsvár Romania see Cluj-Napoca
Kolpashevo Russia 64 J4
Kol'skiy Poluostrov pen. Russia see Kola Peninsula
Kölük Turkey see Kahta
Koluli Eritrea 86 F7
Kolumadulu Atoll Maldives see Kolhumadulu
Kolva r. Russia 42 M2
Kolvan India 84 B2
Kolvereid Norway 44 G4
Kolvik Norway 44 N1
Kolvitskoye, Ozero l. Russia 44 R3
Kolwa reg. Pak. 89 G5
Kolwezi Dem. Rep. Congo 99 C5
Kolyma r. Russia 65 R3
Kolyma Lowland Russia see Kolymskaya Nizmennost'
Kolyma Range mts Russia see Kolymskoye Nagor'ye
Kolymskaya Nizmennost' lowland Russia 65 Q3
Kolymskoye Nagor'ye mts Russia 65 R3
Kolyshley Russia 43 J5
Kom mt. Bulg. 59 J3
Komadugu-Gana watercourse Nigeria 96 E3
Komaggas S. Africa 100 C5
Komaio P.N.G. 69 K8
Komaki Japan 75 E6
Komandnaya, Gora mt. Russia 74 E2
Komandorskiye Ostrova is Russia 65 R4
Komárno Slovakia 47 Q7
Komati r. Swaziland 101 J3
Komatipoort S. Africa 101 J3
Komatsu Japan 75 E5
Komba i. Indon. 108 C1
Komga S. Africa 101 H7
Komintern Ukr. see Marhanets'
Kominternivs'ke Ukr. 59 N1
Komiža Croatia 58 G3
Komló Hungary 58 H1
Kommunarsk Ukr. see Alchevs'k
Komodo, Taman Nasional nat. park Indon. 108 B2
Kôm Ombo Egypt see Kawm Umbū
Komono Congo 98 B4
Komoran i. Indon. 69 J8
Komotini Greece 59 K4
Kompong Cham Cambodia see Kâmpóng Cham
Kompong Chhnang Cambodia see Kâmpóng Chhnăng
Kompong Kleang Cambodia see Kâmpóng Khleăng
Kompong Som Cambodia see Sihanoukville
Kompong Speu Cambodia see Kâmpóng Spœ
Kompong Thom Cambodia see Kâmpóng Thum
Komrat Moldova see Comrat
Komsberg mts S. Africa 100 E7
Komsomol Kazakh. see Karabalyk
Komsomolabad Tajik. see Darband
Komsomolets Kazakh. see Karabalyk
Komsomolets, Ostrov i. Russia 64 K1
Komsomol's'k Ukr. 43 G6
Komsomol'skiy Chukotskiy Avtonomnyy Okrug Russia 153 C2
Komsomol'skiy Khanty-Mansiyskiy Avtonomnyy Okrug-Yugra Russia see Yugorsk
Komsomol'skiy Respublika Kalmykiya-Khalm'g-Tangch Russia 43 J7
Komsomol'sk-na-Amure Russia 74 E2
Komsomol'skoye Kazakh. 80 B1
Komsomol'skoye Russia 43 J6
Kömürlü Turkey 91 F2
Kon India 83 E4
Konacık Turkey 85 B1
Konada India 84 D2
Konarak India see Konarka
Konarka India 83 F6
Konch India 82 D4
Kondagaon India 84 D2
Kondinin Australia 109 B8
Kondinskoye Russia see Oktyabr'skoye
Kondoa Tanz. 99 D4
Kondol' Russia 43 J5
Kondopoga Russia 42 G3
Kondoz Afgh. see Kunduz
Kondrovo Russia 43 G5
Köneürgenç Turkm. 87 I1
Kong Cameroon 96 E4
Kông, Kaôh i. Cambodia 71 C5
Kông, Tônlé r. Cambodia 71 D4
Kong, Xé r. Laos 70 D4
Kong Christian IX Land reg. Greenland 119 O3
Kong Christian X Land reg. Greenland 119 P2
Kongelab atoll Marshall Is see Rongelap
Kong Frederik IX Land reg. Greenland 119 M3
Kong Frederik VI Kyst coastal area Greenland 119 N3
Kongolo Dem. Rep. Congo 99 C4
Kongor South Sudan 97 G4
Kong Oscars Fjord inlet Greenland 119 P2
Kongoussi Burkina Faso 96 C3
Kongsberg Norway 45 F7
Kongsvinger Norway 45 H6
Kongur Shan mt. China 80 E4
Königsberg Russia see Kaliningrad
Königsee Germany 53 L4
Königswinter Germany 53 H4
Königs Wusterhausen Germany 53 N2
Konimekh Uzbek. see Konimex
Konimex Uzbek. 89 G1
Konin Poland 47 Q4
Konjic Bos. & Herz. 58 G3
Konkiep watercourse Namibia 100 C5
Kon Kriel Cambodia 71 C4
Könnern Germany 53 L3
Konnevesi Fin. 44 O5
Konosha Russia 42 I3
Konotop Ukr. 43 G6
Konpara India 83 E5
Kon Plông Vietnam 71 E4
Konqi He r. China 80 G3
Konso Eth. 98 D3
Konso Cultural Landscape tourist site Eth. 97 G4
Konstantinograd Ukr. see Krasnohrad
Konstantinovka Russia 74 B2
Konstantinovka Ukr. see Kostyantynivka
Konstantinovy Lázně Czechia 53 M5
Konstanz Germany 47 L7
Kontha Myanmar 70 B2
Kontiolahti Fin. 44 P5
Konttila Fin. 44 O4
Kon Tum Vietnam 71 D4
Kon Tum, Cao Nguyên Vietnam 71 E4
Könugard Ukr. see Kiev
Konushin, Mys pt Russia 42 I2
Konya Turkey 90 D3
Konz Germany 52 G5
Konzhakovskiy Kamen', Gora mt. Russia 41 R4
Koocanusa, Lake resr Canada/U.S.A. 120 H5
Kooch Bihar India see Koch Bihar
Kookynie Australia 109 C7
Koolyanobbing Australia 109 B7
Koondrook Australia 112 B5
Koorawatha Australia 112 D5
Koordarrie Australia 108 A5
Kootenay r. Canada 120 G5
Kootenay Lake Canada 120 G5
Kootenay National Park Canada 120 G5
Kootjieskolk S. Africa 100 E6
Kópasker Iceland 44 [inset 1]
Kopbirlik Kazakh. 80 E2
Koper Slovenia 58 E2
Kopet Dag mts Iran/Turkm. 88 E2
Kopet-Dag, Khrebet mts Iran/Turkm. see Kopet Dag
Köpetdag Gershi mts Iran/Turkm. see Kopet Dag
Kopili r. India 83 G4
Köping Sweden 45 J7
Köpmanholmen Sweden 44 K5
Kopong Botswana 101 G3
Koppal India 84 C3
Koppang Norway 45 G6
Kopparberg Sweden 45 I7
Koppeh Dāgh mts Iran/Turkm. see Kopet Dag
Köppel hill Germany 53 H4
Koppi r. Russia 74 F2
Koppies S. Africa 101 H4
Koppieskraal Pan salt pan S. Africa 100 E4
Koprivnica Croatia 58 G1
Köprülü Turkey 85 A1
Köprülü Kanyon Milli Parkı nat. park Turkey 59 N6
Kopyl' Belarus see Kapyl'
Kora India 82 E4
Korablino Russia 43 I5
K'orahē Eth. 98 E3
Korak Pak. 89 G5
Koramlik China 83 F1
Korangal India 84 C2
Korangi Pak. 89 G5
Koraput India 84 D2
Korat Thai. see Nakhon Ratchasima
Koratla India 84 C2
Korba India 83 E5
Korbach Germany 53 I3
Korçë Albania 59 I4
Korčula Croatia 58 G3
Korčula i. Croatia 58 G3
Korčulanski Kanal sea chan. Croatia 58 G3
Korday Kazakh. 80 D3
Kord Kūy Iran 88 D2
Kords reg. Iran 89 F5
Korea, North country Asia 75 B5
Korea, South country Asia 75 B5
Korea Bay g. China/N. Korea 75 B5
Korea Strait Japan/S. Korea 75 C6
Koregaon India 84 B2
Korenovsk Russia 91 E1
Korenovskaya Russia see Korenovsk
Korepino Russia 41 R3
Korets' Ukr. 43 E6
Körfez Turkey 59 M4
Korff Ice Rise Antarctica 152 L1
Korfovskiy Russia 74 D2
Korgalzhyn Kazakh. 80 D1
Korgen Norway 44 H3
Korhogo Côte d'Ivoire 96 C4
Koribundu Sierra Leone 96 B4
Kori Creek inlet India 82 B5
Korinthiakos Kolpos sea chan. Greece see Corinth, Gulf of
Korinthos Greece see Corinth
Kőris-hegy hill Hungary 58 G1
Koritnik mt. Albania 59 I3
Koritsa Albania see Korçë
Kōriyama Japan 75 F5
Korkuteli Turkey 59 N6
Korla China 80 G3
Kormakitis, Cape Cyprus 85 A2
Körmend Hungary 58 G1
Kornati, Nacionalni Park nat. park Croatia 58 F3
Korneyevka Russia 43 K6
Koro Côte d'Ivoire 96 C4
Koro i. Fiji 107 H3
Koro Mali 96 C3
Koroc r. Canada 123 I2
Köroğlu Dağları mts Turkey 59 O4
Köroğlu Tepesi mt. Turkey 90 D2
Korogwe Tanz. 99 D4
Koroneia, Limni l. Greece 59 J4
Korong Vale Australia 112 A6
Koronia, Limni l. Greece see Koroneia, Limni

▶Koror Palau 69 I5
Former capital of Palau.

Koro Sea b. Fiji 107 H3
Korosten' Ukr. 43 F6
Korostyshiv Ukr. 43 F6
Koro Toro Chad 97 E3
Korpilahti Fin. 44 N5
Korpo Fin. 45 L6
Korppoo Fin. see Korpo
Korsakov Russia 74 F3
Korsnäs Fin. 44 L5
Korsør Denmark 45 G9
Korsun'-Shevchenkivs'kyy Ukr. 43 F6
Korsun'-Shevchenkovskiy Ukr. see Korsun'-Shevchenkivs'kyy
Korsze Poland 47 R3
Kortesjärvi Fin. 44 M5
Korti Sudan 86 D6
Kortkeros Russia 42 K3
Kortrijk Belgium 52 D4
Korvala Fin. 44 O3
Koryakskaya Sopka, Vulkan vol. Russia 65 Q4
Koryakskoye Nagor'ye mts Russia 65 S3
Koryazhma Russia 42 J3
Kos i. Greece 59 L6
Kosa Russia 41 Q4
Kosam India 82 E4
Kosan N. Korea 75 B5
Kościan Poland 47 P4
Kosciusko, Mount Australia see Kosciuszko, Mount
Kosciuszko, Mount Australia 112 D6
Kosciuszko National Park Australia 112 D6
Köse Turkey 91 E2
Köseçobanlı Turkey 85 A1
Kosgi India 84 C2
Kosh-Agach Russia 80 G2
Koshikijima-rettō is Japan 75 C7
Koshk Afgh. 89 F3
Koshki Russia 43 K5
Kosi Bay S. Africa 101 K4
Košice Slovakia 43 D6
Kosigi India 84 C3
Koskullskulle Sweden 44 L3
Köslin Poland see Koszalin
Kosma r. Russia 42 K2
Koson Uzbek. 89 G2
Kosŏng N. Korea 75 C5
Kosova prov. Europe see Kosovo

▶Kosovo country Europe 59 I3
Gained independence from Serbia in February 2008.

Kosovo-Metohija prov. Europe see Kosovo
Kosovska Mitrovica Kosovo see Mitrovicë
Kosrae atoll Micronesia 150 G5
Kösseine hill Germany 53 L5
Kosta-Khetagurovo Russia see Nazran'
Kostanay Kazakh. 78 F1
Kostenets Bulg. 59 J3
Kosti Sudan 86 D7
Kostinbrod Bulg. 59 J3
Kostino Russia 64 J3
Kostomuksha Russia 44 Q4
Kostopil' Ukr. 43 E6
Kostopol' Ukr. see Kostopil'
Kostroma Russia 42 I4
Kostrzyn nad Odrą Poland 47 O4
Kostyantynivka Ukr. 43 H6
Kostyukovichi Belarus see Kastsyukovichy
Kos'yu Russia 41 R2
Koszalin Poland 47 P3
Kőszeg Hungary 58 G1
Kota Andhra Prad. India 84 D3
Kota Chhattisgarh India 83 E5
Kota Rajasthan India 82 C4
Kota Baharu Malaysia see Kota Bharu
Kotabaru Kalimantan Indon. 68 F7
Kotabaru Sumatra Indon. 71 B7
Kota Bharu Malaysia 71 C6
Kotabumi Indon. 68 C7
Kot Addu Pak. 89 H4
Kota Kinabalu Sabah Malaysia 68 F5
Kotamobagu Indon. 69 G6
Kotaneelee Range mts Canada 120 E2
Kotaparh India 84 D2
Kotapinang Indon. 71 C7
Kotatengah Indon. 71 C7
Kota Tinggi Malaysia 71 C7
Kotcho r. Canada 120 F3
Kotcho Lake Canada 120 F3
Kot Diji Pak. 89 H5
Kotel'nich Russia 42 K4
Kotel'nikovo Russia 43 I7
Kotel'nyy, Ostrov i. Russia 65 O2
Kotgar India 84 D2
Kotgarh India 82 D3
Kothagudem India see Kottagudem
Köthen (Anhalt) Germany 53 L3
Kotido Uganda 97 G4
Kotikovo Russia 74 D3
Kot Imamgarh Pak. 89 H5
Kotka Fin. 45 O6
Kot Kapura India 82 C3
Kotkino Russia 42 K2
Kotlas Russia 42 J3
Kotli Pak. 89 I3
Kotlik U.S.A. 118 B3
Kötlutangi pt Iceland 44 [inset 1]
Kotly Russia 45 P7
Kotovo Russia 43 J6
Kotovsk Russia 43 I5
Kotra India 82 C4
Kotra Pak. 89 G4
Kotri r. India 84 D2
Kot Sarae Pak. 89 G6
Kottagudem India 84 D2
Kottarakara India 84 C4
Kottayam India 84 C4
Kotte Sri Lanka see Sri Jayewardenepura Kotte
Kotto r. Cent. Afr. Rep. 98 C3
Kotturu India 84 C3
Kotuy r. Russia 65 L2
Kotzebue U.S.A. 118 B3
Kotzebue Sound sea chan. U.S.A. 118 B3
Kouango Cent. Afr. Rep. 98 C3
Koubia Guinea 96 B3
Kouchibouguac National Park Canada 123 I5
Koudougou Burkina Faso 96 C3
Kouebokkeveld mts S. Africa 100 D7
Koufey Niger 96 E3
Koufonisi i. Greece 59 L7
Kougaberge mts S. Africa 100 F7
Koukdjuak, Great Plain of the Canada 119 K3
Koukourou r. Cent. Afr. Rep. 98 B3
Koulen Cambodia see Kulên
Koulikoro Mali 96 C3
Koumac New Caledonia 107 G4
Koumpentoum Senegal 96 B3
Koumra Chad 97 E4
Koundâra Guinea 96 B3
Kountze U.S.A. 131 E6
Koupéla Burkina Faso 96 C3
Kourou Fr. Guiana 143 H2
Kouroussa Guinea 96 C3
Kousséri Cameroon 97 E3
Koutiala Mali 96 C3
Kouvola Fin. 45 O6
Kovallberget Sweden 44 J4
Kovdor Russia 44 Q3
Kovel' Ukr. 43 E6
Kovernino Russia 42 I4
Kovilpatti India 84 C4
Kovno Lith. see Kaunas
Kovrov Russia 42 I4
Kovylkino Russia 43 I5
Kovzhskoye, Ozero l. Russia 42 H3
Kowanyama Australia 110 C2
Kowloon H.K. China 77 [inset]
Kowloon Peak hill H.K. China 77 [inset]
Kowloon Peninsula H.K. China 77 [inset]
Kowŏn N. Korea 75 B5
Koxrap China 89 J2
Kōyama-misaki pt Japan 75 C6
Koyamutthoor India see Coimbatore
Köyceğiz Turkey 59 M6
Koygorodok Russia 42 K3
Koyna Reservoir India 84 B2
Köytendag Turkm. 89 G2
Koyuk U.S.A. 118 B3
Koyukuk r. U.S.A. 118 C3
Koyulhisar Turkey 90 E2
Kozağacı Turkey see Günyüzü
Kō-zaki pt Japan 75 C6
Kozan Turkey 90 D3
Kozani Greece 59 I4
Kozara mts Bos. & Herz. 58 G2
Kozara, Nacionalni Park nat. park Bos. & Herz. 58 G2
Kozarska Dubica Bos. & Herz. see Bosanska Dubica
Kozelets' Ukr. 43 F6
Kozel'sk Russia 43 G5
Kozhikode India 84 B4
Kozhva Russia 42 M2
Kozlu Turkey 59 N4
Kozly Russia 42 H2
Koz'modem'yansk Russia 42 J4
Kožuf mts Greece/Macedonia 59 J4
Kōzu-shima i. Japan 75 E6
Kozyatyn Ukr. 43 F6
Kpandae Ghana 96 C4
Kra, Isthmus of Thai. 71 B5
Krabi Thai. 71 B5
Kra Buri Thai. 71 B5
Krâchéh Cambodia 71 D4
Kraddsele Sweden 44 J4
Kragerø Norway 45 F7
Kraggenburg Neth. 52 F2
Kragujevac Serbia 59 I2

▶Krakatau vol. Indon. 68 D8
2nd deadliest recorded volcanic eruption (1883).

Krakau Poland see Kraków
Kraków Poland 47 Q5
Krakower See l. Germany 53 M1
Krâlănh Cambodia 71 C4
Kralendijk Bonaire 137 K6
Kramators'k Ukr. 43 H6
Kramfors Sweden 44 J5
Krammer est. Neth. 52 E3
Kranidi Greece 59 J6
Kranj Slovenia 58 F1
Kranji Reservoir Sing. 71 [inset]
Kranskop S. Africa 101 J5
Krasavino Russia 42 J3
Krasilov Ukr. see Krasyliv
Krasino Russia 64 G2
Kraskino Russia 74 C4
Krāslava Latvia 45 O9
Kraslice Czechia 53 M4
Krasnaya Gorbatka Russia 42 I5
Krasnoarmeysk Russia 43 J6
Krasnoarmeysk Ukr. see Krasnoarmiys'k
Krasnoarmiys'k Ukr. 43 H6
Krasnoborsk Russia 42 J3
Krasnodar Russia 90 E1
Krasnodar Kray admin. div. Russia see Krasnodarskiy Kray
Krasnodarskiy Kray admin. div. Russia 90 E1
Krasnodon Ukr. 43 H6
Krasnogorodsk Russia 45 P8
Krasnogorsk Russia 74 F2
Krasnogorskoye Russia 42 L4
Krasnograd Ukr. see Krasnohrad
Krasnogvardeysk Uzbek. see Bulung'ur
Krasnogvardeyskoye Russia 43 I7
Krasnohrad Ukr. 43 G6
Krasnohvardiys'ke Crimea 43 G7
Krasnokamsk Russia 41 R4
Krasnoperekops'k Crimea 43 G7
Krasnopol'ye Russia 74 F2
Krasnorechenskiy Russia 74 D3
Krasnoslobodsk Russia 43 I5
Krasnotur'insk Russia 41 S4
Krasnoufimsk Russia 41 R4
Krasnovishersk Russia 41 R3
Krasnovodsk Turkm. see Türkmenbaşy
Krasnovodsk, Mys pt Turkm. 88 D2
Krasnovodskoye Plato plat. Turkm. 91 I2
Krasnovodsk Aylagy b. Turkm. see Türkmenbaşy Aýlagy
Krasnoyarovo Russia 74 C2
Krasnoyarsk Russia 64 K4
Krasnoyarskoye Vodokhranilishche resr Russia 72 G2
Krasnoye Lipetskaya Oblast' Russia 43 H5
Krasnoye Respublika Kalmykiya-Khalm'g-Tangch Russia see Ulan Erge
Krasnoznamenskiy Kazakh. see Yegindykol'
Krasnoznamenskoye Kazakh. see Yegindykol'
Krasnyy Russia 43 F5
Krasnyy Chikoy Russia 73 J2
Krasnyye Baki Russia 42 J4
Krasnyy Kamyshanik Russia see Komsomol'skiy
Krasnyy Kholm Russia 42 H4
Krasnyy Kut Russia 43 J6
Krasnyy Luch Ukr. 43 H6
Krasnyy Lyman Ukr. see Lyman
Krasnyy Yar Russia 43 K7
Krasyliv Ukr. 43 E6
Kratie Cambodia see Krâchéh
Kratke Range mts P.N.G. 69 L8
Kraulshavn Greenland see Nuussuaq
Krâvanh, Chuŏr Phnum mts Cambodia/Thai. see Cardamom Range
Kraynovka Russia 91 G2
Krefeld Germany 52 G3
Kremenchug Ukr. see Kremenchuk
Kremenchugskoye Vodokhranilishche resr Ukr. see Kremenchuts'ke Vodoskhovyshche
Kremenchuk Ukr. 43 G6
Kremenchuts'ke Vodoskhovyshche resr Ukr. 43 G6
Křemešník hill Czechia 47 O6
Kremges Ukr. see Svitlovods'k
Kremmidi, Akra pt Greece see Kremmydi, Akrotirio
Kremmydi, Akrotirio pt Greece 59 J6
Krems Austria see Krems an der Donau
Krems an der Donau Austria 47 O6
Kresta, Zaliv g. Russia 65 T3
Kresttsy Russia 42 G4
Kretinga Lith. 45 L9
Kreuzau Germany 52 G4
Kreuztal Germany 53 H4
Kreva Belarus 45 O9
Kribi Cameroon 96 D4
Krichev Belarus see Krychaw
Kriel S. Africa see Ga-Nala
Krikellos Greece 59 I5
Kril'on, Mys c. Russia 74 F3
Krishna India 84 C2
Krishna r. India 84 D2
Krishnanagar India 83 G5
Krishnarajanagara India 84 C3
Krishnaraja Sagara l. India 84 C3
Kristiania Norway see Oslo
Kristiansand Norway 45 E7
Kristianstad Sweden 45 I8
Kristiansund Norway 44 E5
Kristiinankaupunki Fin. see Kristinestad
Kristinehamn Sweden 45 I7
Kristinestad Fin. 44 L5
Kristinopol' Ukr. see Chervonohrad
Kriti i. Greece see Crete
Kritiko Pelagos sea Greece 59 K6
Krivoy Rog Ukr. see Kryvyy Rih
Križevci Croatia 58 G1
Krk i. Croatia 58 F2

La Grita Venez. 142 D2
Laguna Brazil 145 A5
Laguna, Picacho de la mt. Mex. 136 B4
Laguna Dam U.S.A. 129 F5
Laguna Mountains U.S.A. 128 E5
Lagunas Chile 144 C2
Laguna San Rafael, Parque Nacional nat. park Chile 144 B7
Laha China 74 B2
La Habana Cuba see Havana
La Habra U.S.A. 128 E5
Lahad Datu Sabah Malaysia 68 F5
Laharpur India 82 E4
Lahat Indon. 68 C7
Lahe Myanmar 70 A1
Lahemaa rahvuspark nat. park Estonia 45 N7
Lahewa Indon. 71 B7
Laḥij Yemen 86 F7
Lāhījān Iran 88 C2
Lahn r. Germany 53 H4
Lahnstein Germany 53 H4
Laholm Sweden 45 H8
Lahontan Reservoir U.S.A. 128 D2
Lahore Pak. 89 I4
Lahri Pak. 89 H4
Lāhrūd Iran 88 B2
Lahti Fin. 45 N6
Laï Chad 97 E4
Lai'an China 77 H1
Laibach Slovenia see Ljubljana
Laibin China 77 F4
Laidley Australia 112 F1
Laifeng China 77 F2
L'Aigle France 56 E2
Laihia Fin. 44 M5
Lai-hka Myanmar 70 B2
Lai-Hsak Myanmar 70 B2
Laimakuri India 83 H4
Laimos, Akrotirio pt Greece 59 J5
Laingsburg S. Africa 100 E7
Laingsburg U.S.A. 134 C2
Lainioälven r. Sweden 44 M3
Lair U.S.A. 134 C4
Lairg U.K. 50 E2
La Isabela Cuba 133 D8
Laishevo Russia 42 K5
Laitila Fin. 45 L6
Laives Italy 58 D1
Laiwu China 73 L5
Laiwui Indon. 69 H7
Laiyang China 73 M5
Laizhou China 73 L5
Laizhou Wan b. China 73 L5
Lajamanu Australia 108 E4
Lajanurp'ekhi Georgia 91 F2
Lajeado Brazil 145 A5
Lajes Brazil 143 K5
La Junta Mex. 127 G7
La Junta U.S.A. 130 C4
Lakadiya India 82 B5
L'Akagera, Parc National de nat. park Rwanda see Akagera National Park
La Kagera, Parc National de nat. park Rwanda see Akagera National Park
Lake U.S.A. 134 D5
Lake Andes U.S.A. 130 D3
Lakeba i. Fiji 107 I3
Lake Bardawil Reserve nature res. Egypt 85 A4
Lake Bolac Australia 112 A6
Lake Butler U.S.A. 133 D6
Lake Cargelligo Australia 112 C4
Lake Cathie Australia 112 F3
Lake Charles U.S.A. 131 E6
Lake City CO U.S.A. 129 J3
Lake City FL U.S.A. 133 D6
Lake City MI U.S.A. 134 C1
Lake Clark National Park and Preserve U.S.A. 118 C3
Lake Clear U.S.A. 135 H1
Lake District National Park U.K. 48 D4
Lake Eildon National Park Australia 112 B6
Lake Elsinore U.S.A. 128 E5
Lakefield Australia 110 D2
Lakefield Canada 135 F1
Lake Forest U.S.A. 134 B2
Lake Gairdner National Park Australia 111 B7
Lake Geneva U.S.A. 130 F3
Lake George MI U.S.A. 134 C2
Lake George NY U.S.A. 135 I2
Lake Grace Australia 109 B8
Lake Harbour Canada see Kimmirut
Lake Havasu City U.S.A. 129 F4
Lakehurst U.S.A. 135 H3
Lake Isabella U.S.A. 128 D4
Lake Jackson U.S.A. 131 E6
Lake King Australia 109 B8
Lake Kopiago P.N.G. 69 K8
Lakeland FL U.S.A. 133 D7
Lakeland GA U.S.A. 133 D6
Lake Louise Canada 120 G5
Lakemba i. Fiji see Lakeba
Lake Mills U.S.A. 130 E3
Lake Nash Australia 110 B4
Lake Odessa U.S.A. 134 C2
Lake Paringa N.Z. 113 B6
Lake Placid FL U.S.A. 133 D7
Lake Placid NY U.S.A. 135 I1
Lake Pleasant U.S.A. 135 H2
Lakeport CA U.S.A. 128 B2
Lakeport MI U.S.A. 134 D2
Lake Providence U.S.A. 131 F5
Lake Range mts U.S.A. 128 D1
Lake River Canada 122 E3
Lakes Entrance Australia 112 D6
Lakeside AZ U.S.A. 129 I4
Lakeside VA U.S.A. 135 G5
Lakes of Ounianga tourist site Chad 97 F3
Lake Superior National Marine Conservation Area park Canada 122 D4
Lake Tabourie Australia 112 E5
Lake Tekapo N.Z. 113 C7
Lake Torrens National Park Australia 111 B6
Lakeview MI U.S.A. 134 C2
Lakeview OH U.S.A. 134 D3
Lakeview OR U.S.A. 126 C4
Lake Village U.S.A. 131 F5
Lake Wales U.S.A. 133 D7
Lakewood CO U.S.A. 126 G5
Lakewood NJ U.S.A. 135 H3
Lakewood NY U.S.A. 134 F2
Lakewood OH U.S.A. 134 E3
Lake Worth U.S.A. 133 D7
Lakha India 82 B4
Lakhdenpokh'ya Russia 44 Q6
Lakhimpur Assam India see North Lakhimpur
Lakhimpur Uttar Prad. India 82 E4
Lakhisarai India 83 F4
Lakhish, Naḥal r. Israel 85 B4
Lakhnadon India 82 D5
Lakhpat India 82 B5
Lakhtar India 82 B5
Lakin U.S.A. 130 C4
Lakitusaki r. Canada 122 E3
Lakki Marwat Pak. 89 H3
Lakonikos Kolpos b. Greece 59 J6
Lakor i. Indon. 108 E2
Lakota Côte d'Ivoire 96 C4
Lakota U.S.A. 130 D1
Laksefjorden sea chan. Norway 44 O1
Lakselv Norway 44 N1
Lakshadweep India 84 B4
Lakshadweep union terr. India 84 B4
Lakshettipet India 84 C2
Lakshmipur Bangl. 83 G5
Laksmipur Bangl. see Lakshmipur
Lalaghat India 83 H4
Lalara India 84 D1
L'Alcora Spain 57 F3
Lāleh Zār, Kūh-e mt. Iran 88 E4
Lalganj India 83 F4
Lālī Iran 88 C3
La Ligua Chile 144 B4
Laliki Indon. 108 D1
Lalin China 74 B3
Lalín Spain 57 B2
La Línea de la Concepción Spain 57 D5
Lalin He r. China 74 B3
Lalitpur India 82 D4
Lalitpur Nepal see Patan
Lalmanirhat Bangl. see Lalmonirhat
Lalmonirhat Bangl. 83 G4
La Loche Canada 121 I3
La Loche, Lac l. Canada 121 I3
La Louvière Belgium 52 E4
Lal'sk Russia 42 J3
Lalung La pass China 83 F3
Lama Bangl. 83 H5
La Macarena, Parque Nacional nat. park Col. 142 D3
La Maddalena Sardinia Italy 58 C4
Lamadian China 74 B3
Lamadianzi China see Lamadian
La Malbaie Canada 123 H5
La Mancha Mex. 131 C7
La Mancha reg. Spain 57 E4
La Manche strait France/U.K. see English Channel
La Máquina Mex. 131 B6
Lamar CO U.S.A. 130 C4
Lamar MO U.S.A. 131 E4
La Marmora, Punta mt. Sardinia Italy 58 C5
La Marque U.S.A. 131 E6
La Martre, Lac l. Canada 120 G2
Lamas r. Turkey 85 B1
La Mauricie, Parc National de nat. park Canada 123 G5
Lambaréné Gabon 98 B4
Lambasa Fiji see Labasa
Lambayeque Peru 142 C5
Lambay Island Ireland 51 G4
Lambert atoll Marshall Is see Ailinglaplap

▶Lambert Glacier Antarctica 152 E2
Largest glacier in the world.

Lambert's Bay S. Africa 100 D7
Lambeth Canada 134 E2
Lambi India 82 C3
Lambourn Downs hills U.K. 49 F7
Lame Indon. 71 B7
Lamego Port. 57 C3
Lamèque, Île i. Canada 123 I5
La Merced Arg. 144 C3
La Merced Peru 142 C6
Lāmerd Iran 88 D5
Lameroo Australia 111 C7
La Mesa U.S.A. 128 E5
Lamesa U.S.A. 131 C5
Lamia Greece 59 J5
Lamington National Park Australia 112 F2
La Misión Mex. 128 E5
Lamma Island H.K. China 77 [inset]
Lammerlaw Range mts N.Z. 113 B7
Lammermuir Hills U.K. 50 G5
Lammhult Sweden 45 I8
Lammi Fin. 45 N6
Lamont CA U.S.A. 128 D4
Lamont WY U.S.A. 126 G4
La Montaña de Covadonga, Parque Nacional de nat. park Spain see Picos de Europa, Parque Nacional de los
La Mora Mex. 131 C7
La Morita Chihuahua Mex. 131 B6
La Morita Coahuila Mex. 131 C6
Lamotrek atoll Micronesia 69 L5
LaMoure U.S.A. 130 D2
Lampang Thai. 70 B3
Lam Pao, Ang Kep Nam Thai. 70 C3
Lampasas U.S.A. 131 D6
Lampazos Mex. 131 C7
Lampedusa, Isola di i. Sicily Italy 58 E7
Lampeter U.K. 49 C6
Lamphun Thai. 70 B3
Lampsacus Turkey see Lâpseki
Lam Tin H.K. China 77 [inset]
Lamu Kenya 98 E4
Lamu Myanmar 70 A3
Lan, Loi mt. Myanmar/Thai. 70 B3
Lāna'i i. U.S.A. 127 [inset]
Lāna'i City U.S.A. 127 [inset]
Lanao, Lake Phil. 69 G5
Lanark Canada 135 G1
Lanark U.K. 50 F5
Lanbi Kyun i. Myanmar 71 B5
Lancang China 76 C4
Lancang Jiang r. Asia see Mekong
Lancaster Canada 135 H1
Lancaster U.K. 48 E4
Lancaster CA U.S.A. 128 D4
Lancaster KY U.S.A. 134 C5
Lancaster MO U.S.A. 130 E3
Lancaster NH U.S.A. 135 J1
Lancaster OH U.S.A. 134 D4
Lancaster PA U.S.A. 135 G3
Lancaster SC U.S.A. 133 D5
Lancaster VA U.S.A. 135 G5
Lancaster WI U.S.A. 130 F3
Lancaster Canal U.K. 48 E5
Lancaster Sound strait Canada 119 J2
Lanchow China see Lanzhou
Landana Angola see Cacongo
Landau an der Isar Germany 53 M6
Landau in der Pfalz Germany 53 I5
Landeck Austria 47 M7
Landeh Iran 88 C4
Lander watercourse Australia 108 E5
Lander U.S.A. 126 F4
Landesbergen Germany 53 J2
Landfall Island India 71 A4
Landhi Pak. 89 G5
Landis Canada 121 I4
Landor Australia 109 B6
Landsberg Poland see Gorzów Wielkopolski
Landsberg am Lech Germany 47 M6
Land's End pt U.K. 49 B8
Landshut Germany 53 M6
Landskrona Sweden 45 H9
Landstuhl Germany 53 H5
Land Wursten reg. Germany 53 I1
Lanesborough Ireland 51 E4
Lang, Nam r. Myanmar 70 B2
La'nga Co l. China 82 E3
Langao China 77 F1
Langar Afgh. 89 H3
Langberg mts S. Africa 100 F5
Langdon U.S.A. 130 D1
Langeac France 56 F4
Langeberg mts S. Africa 100 D7
Langeland i. Denmark 45 G9
Längelmäki Fin. 45 N6
Langelsheim Germany 53 K3
Langen Germany 53 I1
Langenburg Canada 121 K5
Langenhagen Germany 53 J2
Langenhahn Germany 53 H4
Langenlonsheim Germany 53 H5
Langenthal Switz. 56 H3
Langenweddingen Germany 53 L2
Langeoog Germany 53 H1
Langesund Norway 45 F7
Langfang China 73 L5
Langgapayung Indon. 71 B7
Langgar China 76 B2
Langgöns Germany 53 I4
Langholm U.K. 48 E3
Langjan Nature Reserve S. Africa 101 I2
Langjökull ice cap Iceland 44 [inset 1]
Langka Indon. 71 B6
Langkawi i. Malaysia 71 B6
Lang Kha Toek, Khao mt. Thai. 71 B5
Langklip S. Africa 100 E5
Langley Canada 120 F5
Langley U.S.A. 134 D5
Langlo Crossing Australia 111 D5
Langmusi China 76 D1
Langong, Xé r. Laos 70 D3
Langøya i. Norway 44 I2
Langphu mt. China 83 F3
Langport U.K. 49 E7
Langqên Zangbo r. China 82 D3
Langqi China 77 H3
Langres France 56 G3
Langres, Plateau de France 56 G3
Langru China 82 D1
Langsa Indon. 71 B6
Langsa, Teluk b. Indon. 71 B6
Långsele Sweden 44 J5
Lang Sơn Vietnam 70 D2
Langtang National Park Nepal 83 F3
Langtao Myanmar 70 B1
Langting India 83 H4
Langtoft U.K. 48 G4
Langtry U.S.A. 131 C6
Languan China see Lantian
Languedoc reg. France 56 E5
Långvattnet Sweden 44 L4
Langwedel Germany 53 J2
Langxi China 77 H2
Langzhong China 76 E2
Lanigan Canada 121 J5
Lanín, Parque Nacional nat. park Arg. 144 B5
Lanín, Volcán vol. Arg./Chile 144 B5
Lanji India 82 E5
Lanka country Asia see Sri Lanka
Länkäran Azer. 91 H3
Lannion France 56 C2
Lanping China 76 C3
Lansån Sweden 44 M3
L'Anse U.S.A. 130 F2
Lanshan China 77 G3

▶Lansing U.S.A. 134 C2
Capital of Michigan.

Lanta, Ko i. Thai. 71 B6
Lantau Island H.K. China 77 [inset]
Lantau Peak hill H.K. China 77 [inset]
Lantian China 77 F1
Lantoto National Park South Sudan 98 D3
Lanxi Heilong. China 74 B3
Lanxi Zhejiang China 77 H2
Lan Yu i. Taiwan 77 I4
Lanzarote i. Canary Is 96 B2
Lanzhou China 72 I5
Lanzi China 74 A3
Laoag City Phil. 69 G3
Laoang Phil. 69 H4
Laobie Shan mts China 76 C4
Laobu China 77 F3
Lao Cai Vietnam 70 C2
Laodicea Syria see Latakia
Laodicea Turkey see Denizli
Laodicea ad Lycum Turkey see Denizli
Laodicea ad Mare Syria see Latakia
Laohekou China 77 F1
Laohupo China see Logpung
Laojie China see Yongping
Laojunmiao China 80 I4
Lao Ling mts China 74 B4
Lao Mangnai China 80 H4
Laon France 52 D5
La Oroya Peru 142 C6
Laos country Asia 70 C3
Laotougou China 74 C4
Laotu Dingzi hill China 74 B4
Laowohi pass India see Khardung La
Laoye Ling mts Heilongjiang/Jilin China 74 C4
Laoye Ling mts Jilin China 74 B3
Lapa Brazil 145 A4
La Palma i. Canary Is 96 B2
La Palma Panama 137 I7
La Palma U.S.A. 129 H5
La Palma del Condado Spain 57 C5
La Panza Range mts U.S.A. 128 C4
La Paragua Venez. 142 F2
La Parilla Mex. 131 B8
La Paya, Parque Nacional nat. park Col. 142 D3
La Paz Arg. 144 E4

▶La Paz Bol. 142 E7
Joint capital (with Sucre) of Bolivia.

La Paz Hond. 136 G6
La Paz Mex. 136 B4
La Pedrera Col. 142 E4
Lapeer U.S.A. 134 D2
La Perla Mex. 131 B6
La Pérouse Strait Japan/Russia 74 F3
La Pesca Mex. 131 D8
Lapinlahti Fin. 44 O5
Lapithos Cyprus 85 A2
Lap Lae Thai. 70 C3
La Plant U.S.A. 130 C2
La Plata Arg. 144 E4
La Plata MD U.S.A. 135 G4
La Plata MO U.S.A. 130 E3
La Plata, Isla i. Ecuador 142 B4

▶La Plata, Río de sea chan. Arg./Uruguay 144 E4
Part of the Río de la Plata - Paraná, 2nd longest river in South America and 9th in the world.

La Plonge, Lac l. Canada 121 J4
Lapmežciems Latvia 45 M8
La Pola Spain 57 D2
La Pola Siero Spain 57 D2
Lapominka Russia 42 I2
La Porte U.S.A. 134 B3
Laporte U.S.A. 135 G3
Laporte, Mount Canada 120 E2
La Potherie, Lac l. Canada 123 G2
La Poza Grande Mex. 127 E8
Lappajärvi Fin. 44 M5
Lappajärvi l. Fin. 44 M5
Lappeenranta Fin. 45 P6
Lappersdorf Germany 53 M5
Lappi Fin. 45 L6
Lappland reg. Europe 44 K3
La Pryor U.S.A. 131 D6
Lâpseki Turkey 59 L4
Laptevo Russia see Yasnogorsk
Laptev Sea Russia 65 N2
Lapua Fin. 44 M5
Lapurdum France see Bayonne
La Purísima Mex. 127 E8
Laqiya Arbain well Sudan 86 C5
La Quiaca Arg. 144 C2
L'Aquila Italy 58 E3
La Quinta U.S.A. 128 E5
Lār Iran 88 D5
Larache Morocco 57 C6
Lārak, Jazīreh-ye i. Iran 88 E5
Laramie U.S.A. 126 G4
Laramie r. U.S.A. 126 G4
Laramie Mountains U.S.A. 126 G4
Laranda Turkey see Karaman
Laranjal Paulista Brazil 145 B3
Laranjeiras do Sul Brazil 144 F3
Laranjinha r. Brazil 145 A3
Larantuka Indon. 108 C2
Larat Indon. 108 E1
Larat i. Indon. 108 E1
Larba Alg. 57 H5
Lärbro Sweden 45 K8
L'Ardenne, Plateau de plat. Belgium see Ardennes
Laredo Spain 57 E2
Laredo U.S.A. 131 D7
La Reina Adelaida, Archipiélago de is Chile 144 B8
Largeau Chad see Faya
Largo U.S.A. 133 D7
Largs U.K. 50 E5
L'Ariana Tunisia 58 D6
Larimore U.S.A. 130 D2
La Rioja Arg. 144 C3
La Rioja aut. comm. Spain 57 E2
Larisa Greece 59 J5
Larissa Greece see Larisa
Laristan reg. Iran 88 E5
Larkana Pak. 89 H5
Lark Harbour Canada 123 K4
Lark Passage Australia 110 D2
Larnaca Cyprus 85 A2
Larnaka Cyprus see Larnaca
Larnaka Bay Cyprus 85 A2
Larnakos, Kolpos b. Cyprus see Larnaka Bay
Larne U.K. 51 G3
Larned U.S.A. 130 D4
La Robla Spain 57 D2
La Roche-en-Ardenne Belgium 52 F4
La Rochelle France 56 D3
La Roche-sur-Yon France 56 D3
La Roda Spain 57 E4
La Romana Dom. Rep. 137 K5
La Ronge Canada 121 J4
La Ronge, Lac l. Canada 121 J4
La Rosa Mex. 131 C7
La Rosita Mex. 131 C6
Larrey Point Australia 108 B4
Larrimah Australia 108 F3
Lars Christensen Coast Antarctica 152 E2
Larsen Ice Shelf Antarctica 152 L2
Larsmo Fin. 44 M5
Larvik Norway 45 G7
La Sal U.S.A. 129 I2
LaSalle Canada 135 I1
La Salle U.S.A. 122 C6
Las Animas U.S.A. 130 C4
Las Anod Somalia see Laascaanood
La Sarre Canada 122 F4
Las Avispas Mex. 127 F7
La Savonnière, Lac l. Canada 123 G3
Lascano Uruguay 144 F4
La Scie Canada 123 L4
Las Cruces CA U.S.A. 128 C4
Las Cruces NM U.S.A. 127 G6
La Selle, Pic mt. Haiti 137 J5
La Serena Chile 144 B3
Las Esperanças Mex. 131 C7
La Seu d'Urgell Spain 57 G2
Las Flores Arg. 144 E5
Las Guacamatas, Cerro mt. Mex. 127 F7
Lāshār, Rūd-e r. Iran 89 F5
Lashburn Canada 121 I4
Lāsh-e Juwayn Afgh. 89 F4
Las Heras Mendoza Arg. 144 C4
Las Heras Santa Cruz Arg. 144 C7
Lashio Myanmar 70 B2
Lashkar India 82 D4
Lashkar Gāh Afgh. 89 G4
Las Juntas Chile 144 C3
Las Lomitas Arg. 144 D2
Las Marismas marsh Spain 57 C5
Las Martinetas Arg. 144 C7
Las Mesteñas Mex. 131 B6
Las Minas, Cerro de mt. Hond. 136 G6
Las Nopaleras, Cerro mt. Mex. 131 C7
La Société, Archipel de is Fr. Polynesia see Society Islands
Las Palmas watercourse Mex. 128 E5

▶Las Palmas de Gran Canaria Canary Is 96 B2
Joint capital (with Santa Cruz de Tenerife) of the Canary Islands.

Las Petas Bol. 143 G7
La Spezia Italy 58 C2
Las Plumas Arg. 144 C6
Laspur Pak. 89 I2
Lassance Brazil 145 B2
Lassen Peak vol. U.S.A. 128 C1
Lassen Volcanic National Park U.S.A. 128 C1
Las Tablas Panama 137 H7
Last Chance U.S.A. 130 C4
Last Mountain Lake Canada 121 J5
Las Tórtolas, Cerro mt. Chile 144 C3
Lastoursville Gabon 98 B4
Lastovo i. Croatia 58 G3
Las Tres Vírgenes, Volcán vol. Mex. 127 E8
Lastrup Germany 53 H2
Las Tunas Cuba 137 I4
Las Varas Chihuahua Mex. 127 G7
Las Varas Nayarit Mex. 136 C4
Las Varillas Arg. 144 D4
Las Vegas NM U.S.A. 127 G6
Las Vegas NV U.S.A. 129 F3
Las Villuercas mt. Spain 57 D4
La Tabatière Canada 123 K4
Latacunga Ecuador 142 C4
Latady Island Antarctica 152 L2
Latakia Syria 85 B2
La Teste-de-Buch France 56 D4
Latham Australia 109 B7
Lathen Germany 53 H2
Latheron U.K. 50 F2
Lathi India 82 B4
Latho India 82 D2
Lathrop U.S.A. 128 C3
Latina Italy 58 E4
La Tortuga, Isla i. Venez. 142 E1
Latrobe U.S.A. 134 F3
Laṭrūn West Bank 85 B4
Lattaquié Syria see Latakia
Lattrop Neth. 52 G2
La Tuque Canada 123 G5
Latur India 84 C2
Latvia country Europe 45 N8
Latvija country Europe see Latvia
Latviyskaya S.S.R. country Europe see Latvia
Lauca, Parque Nacional nat. park Chile 142 E7
Lauchhammer Germany 47 N5
Lauder U.K. 50 G5
Laudio Spain 57 E2
Lauenbrück Germany 53 J1
Lauenburg (Elbe) Germany 53 K1
Lauf an der Pegnitz Germany 53 L5
Laufen Switz. 56 H3
Lauge Koch Kyst reg. Greenland 119 L2
Laughlen, Mount Australia 109 F5
Laughlin Peak U.S.A. 127 G5
Lauka Estonia 45 M7
Launceston Australia 111 [inset]
Launceston U.K. 49 C8
Laune r. Ireland 51 C5
Launggyaung Myanmar 70 B1
Launglon Myanmar 71 B4
Launglon Bok Islands Myanmar 71 B4
La Unión Bol. 142 F7
Laura Australia 110 D2
Laurel DE U.S.A. 135 H4
Laurel MS U.S.A. 131 F6
Laurel MT U.S.A. 126 F3
Laureldale U.S.A. 135 H3
Laurel Hill hills U.S.A. 134 F4
Laurencekirk U.K. 50 G4
Laurieton Australia 112 F3
Laurinburg U.S.A. 133 E5
Lauru i. Solomon Is see Choiseul
Lausanne Switz. 56 H3
Laut i. Indon. 68 E6
Laut i. Indon. 71 E6
Lautem East Timor 108 D2
Lauterbach (Hessen) Germany 53 J4
Laut Kecil, Kepulauan is Indon. 68 F8
Lautoka Fiji 107 H3
Lauvuskylä Fin. 44 P5
Lauwersmeer l. Neth. 52 G1
Lava Beds National Monument nat. park U.S.A. 126 C4
Laval Canada 122 G5
Laval France 56 D2
La Vall d'Uixó Spain 57 F4
Lāvān, Jazīreh-ye i. Iran 88 D5
Lavapié, Punta pt Chile 144 B5
Lāvar Iran 88 C4
Laveaga Peak U.S.A. 128 C3
La Vega Dom. Rep. 137 J5
Laverne U.S.A. 131 D4
Laverton Australia 109 C7
La Víbora Mex. 131 C7
La Vila Joíosa Spain see Villajoyosa-La Vila Joíosa
La Viña Peru 142 C5
Lavongal i. P.N.G. see New Hanover
Lavras Brazil 145 B3
Lavumisa Swaziland 101 J4
Lavushi-Manda National Park Zambia 99 D5
Lawa India 82 C4
Lawa Myanmar 70 B1
Lawa Pak. 89 H3
Lawashi r. Canada 122 E3
Law Dome ice feature Antarctica 152 F2
Lawit, Gunung mt. Malaysia 71 C6
Lawksawk Myanmar 70 B2
Lawn Hill National Park Australia 110 B3
Lawra Ghana 96 C3
Lawrence IN U.S.A. 134 B4
Lawrence KS U.S.A. 130 E4
Lawrence MA U.S.A. 135 J2
Lawrenceburg IN U.S.A. 134 C4
Lawrenceburg KY U.S.A. 134 C4
Lawrenceburg TN U.S.A. 132 C5
Lawrenceville GA U.S.A. 133 D5
Lawrenceville IL U.S.A. 134 B4
Lawrenceville VA U.S.A. 135 G5
Lawrence Wells, Mount hill Australia 109 C6
Lawton U.S.A. 131 D5
Lawz, Jabal al mt. Saudi Arabia 90 D5
Laxå Sweden 45 I7
Laxey Isle of Man 48 C4
Laxgalts'ap Canada 120 D4
Lax Kw'alaams Canada 120 D4
Laxo U.K. 50 [inset]
Laya r. Russia 42 M2
Laydennyy, Mys c. Russia 42 J1
Laylá Saudi Arabia 86 G5
Laylá salt pan Saudi Arabia 85 D4
Laysan Island U.S.A. 150 I4
Laytonville U.S.A. 128 B2
Layyah Pak. 89 H4
Laza Myanmar 70 B1
Lazarev Russia 74 F1
Lazarevac Serbia 59 I2
Lázaro Cárdenas Mex. 136 D5
Lazdijai Lith. 45 M9
Lazikou China 76 D1
Lazo Primorskiy Kray Russia 74 D4
Lazo Respublika Sakha (Yakutiya) Russia 65 O3
Lead U.S.A. 130 C2
Leader Water r. U.K. 50 G5
Leadville Australia 112 D4
Leaf r. U.S.A. 131 F6
Leaf Bay Canada see Tasiujaq
Leaf Rapids Canada 121 K3
Leakey U.S.A. 131 D6
Leaksville U.S.A. see Eden
Leamington Canada 134 D2
Leane, Lough l. Ireland 51 C5
Leap Ireland 51 C6
Leatherhead U.K. 49 G7
L'Eau d'Heure l. Belgium 52 E4
Leavenworth IN U.S.A. 134 B4
Leavenworth KS U.S.A. 130 E4
Leavenworth WA U.S.A. 126 C3
Leavitt Peak U.S.A. 128 D2
Lebach Germany 52 G5
Lebanon country Asia 85 B2
Lebanon IN U.S.A. 134 B3
Lebanon KY U.S.A. 134 C5
Lebanon MO U.S.A. 130 E4
Lebanon NH U.S.A. 135 I2
Lebanon OH U.S.A. 134 C4
Lebanon OR U.S.A. 126 C3
Lebanon PA U.S.A. 135 G3
Lebanon TN U.S.A. 132 C4
Lebanon VA U.S.A. 134 D5
Lebanon Junction U.S.A. 134 C5
Lebanon Mountains Lebanon see Liban, Jebel
Lebbeke Belgium 52 E3
Lebec U.S.A. 128 D4
Lebedyan' Russia 43 H5
Lebel-sur-Quévillon Canada 122 F4
Le Blanc France 56 E3
Lębork Poland 47 P3
Lebowakgomo S. Africa 101 I3
Lebrija Spain 57 C5
Łebsko, Jezioro lag. Poland 47 P3
Lebu Chile 144 B5
Lebyazh'ye Kazakh. see Akku
Lebyazh'ye Russia 42 K4
Le Caire Egypt see Cairo
Le Cateau-Cambrésis France 52 D4
Le Catelet France 52 D4
Lecce Italy 58 H4
Lecco Italy 58 C2
Lech r. Austria/Germany 47 M7
Lechaina Greece 59 I6
Lechang China 77 G3
Le Chasseron mt. Switz. 56 H3
Le Chesne France 52 E5
Lechtaler Alpen mts Austria 47 M7
Leck Germany 47 L3
Lecompte U.S.A. 131 E6
Le Creusot France 56 G3
Le Crotoy France 52 B4
Lectoure France 56 E5
Ledang, Gunung mt. Malaysia 71 C7
Ledbury U.K. 49 E6
Ledesma Spain 57 D3
Ledmore U.K. 50 E2
Ledmozero Russia 44 R4
Ledong Hainan China 70 E3
Ledong Hainan China 77 F5
Le Dorat France 56 E3
Leduc Canada 120 H4
Lee r. Ireland 51 D6
Lee IN U.S.A. 134 B3

Lee *MA* U.S.A. **135** I2
Leech Lake U.S.A. **130** E2
Leedstown U.K. **49** B8
Leek Neth. **52** G1
Leek U.K. **49** E5
Leende Neth. **52** F3
Leer (Ostfriesland) Germany **53** H1
Leesburg *FL* U.S.A. **133** D6
Leesburg *GA* U.S.A. **133** C6
Leesburg *OH* U.S.A. **134** D4
Leesburg *VA* U.S.A. **135** G4
Leese Germany **53** J2
Leesville U.S.A. **131** E6
Leesville Lake *OH* U.S.A. **134** E3
Leesville Lake *VA* U.S.A. **134** F5
Leeton Australia **112** C5
Leeu-Gamka S. Africa **100** E7
Leeuwarden Neth. **52** F1
Leeuwin, Cape Australia **109** A8
Leeuwin-Naturaliste National Park
   Australia **109** A8
Lee Vining U.S.A. **128** C3
Leeward Islands Caribbean Sea **137** L5
Lefka Cyprus **85** A2
Lefkada Greece **59** I5
Lefkada *i.* Greece **59** I5
Lefkás Greece *see* Lefkada
Lefke Cyprus *see* Lefka
Lefkimmi Greece **59** I5
Lefkoniko Cyprus *see* Lefkonikon
Lefkonikon Cyprus **85** A2
Lefkosa Cyprus *see* Nicosia
Lefkosia Cyprus *see* Nicosia
Lefroy *r.* Canada **122** D4
Lefroy, Lake *salt flat* Australia **109** C7
Legarde *r.* Canada **122** D4
Legazpi Phil. **69** G4
Legden Germany **53** H2
Legges Tor *mt.* Australia **111** [inset]
Leghorn Italy *see* Livorno
Legnago Italy **58** D2
Legnica Poland **47** P5
Le Grand U.S.A. **128** C3
Legune Australia **108** E3
Leh India **82** D2
Le Havre France **56** E2
Lehi U.S.A. **129** H1
Leighton U.S.A. **135** H3
Lehmo Fin. **44** P5
Lehre Germany **53** K2
Lehrte Germany **53** J2
Lehtimäki Fin. **44** M5
Lehututu Botswana **100** E2
Leibnitz Austria **47** O7
Leicester U.K. **49** F6
Leichhardt *r.* Australia **106** B3
Leichhardt Falls Australia **110** B3
Leichhardt Range *mts* Australia **110** D4
Leiden Neth. **52** E2
Leie *r.* Belgium **52** D3
Leigh N.Z. **113** E3
Leigh U.K. **48** E5
Leighton Buzzard U.K. **49** G7
Leiktho Myanmar **70** B3
Leimen Germany **53** I5
Leine *r.* Germany **53** J2
Leinefelde Germany **53** K3
Leinster Australia **109** C6
Leinster *reg.* Ireland **51** F4
Leinster, Mount *hill* Ireland **51** F5
Leipsic U.S.A. **134** D3
Leipsoi *i.* Greece **59** L6
Leipzig Germany **53** N3
Leipzig-Halle *airport* Germany **53** M3
Leiranger Norway **44** I3
Leiria Port. **57** B4
Leirvik Norway **45** D7
Leishan China **77** F3
Leisler, Mount *hill* Australia **109** E5
Leisnig Germany **53** M3
Leitchfield U.S.A. **134** B5
Leith Hill *hill* U.K. **49** G7
Leiva, Cerro *mt.* Col. **142** D3
Leixlip Ireland **51** F4
Leiyang China **77** G3
Leizhou China **77** F4
Leizhou Bandao *pen.* China **77** F4
Leizhou Wan *b.* China **77** F4
Lek *r.* Neth. **52** E3
Leka Norway **44** G4
Lékana Congo **98** B4
Le Kef Tunisia **58** C6
Lekhainá Greece *see* Lechaina
Lekitobi Indon. **69** G7
Lekkersing S. Africa **100** C5
Lékoni Gabon **98** B4
Leksand Sweden **45** I6
Leksozero, Ozero *l.* Russia **44** Q5
Lelai, Tanjung *pt* Indon. **69** H6
Leland U.S.A. **134** C1
Leli China *see* Tianlin
Lélouma Guinea **96** B3
Lelystad Neth. **52** F2
Le Maire, Estrecho de *sea chan.* Arg.
   144 C9
Léman, Lac *l.* France/Switz. *see*
   Geneva, Lake
Le Mans France **56** E2
Le Mars U.S.A. **130** D3
Lemberg France **53** H5
Lemberg Ukr. *see* L'viv
Lembruch Germany **53** I2
Lemdiyya Alg. *see* Médéa
Leme Brazil **145** B3
Lemele Neth. **52** G2
Lemesos Cyprus *see* Limassol
Lemgo Germany **53** I2
Lemhi Range *mts* U.S.A. **126** E3
Lemi Fin. **45** O6
Lemmenjoen kansallispuisto *nat. park*
   Fin. **44** N2
Lemmer Neth. **52** F2
Lemmon U.S.A. **130** C2
Lemmon, Mount U.S.A. **129** H5
Lemnos *i.* Greece *see* Limnos
Lemoncove U.S.A. **128** D3
Lemoore U.S.A. **128** D3
Le Moyne, Lac *l.* Canada **123** H2

Lemro *r.* Myanmar **70** A2
Lemtybozh Russia **41** R3
Le Murge *hills* Italy **58** G4
Lemvig Denmark **45** F8
Lem"yu *r.* Russia **42** M3
Lena *r.* Russia **72** J1
Lena U.S.A. **134** A1
Lena, Mount U.S.A. **129** I1
Lenadoon Point Ireland **51** C3
Lena Pillars Nature Park *tourist site* Russia
   65 N3
Lenchung Tso *salt l.* China **83** E2
Lençóis Brazil **145** C1
Lençóis Maranhenses, Parque Nacional
   dos *nat. park* Brazil **143** J4
Lendery Russia **44** Q5
Le Neubourg France **49** H9
Lengerich Germany **53** H2
Lenglong Ling *mts* China **72** I5
Lengshuijiang China **77** F3
Lenham U.K. **49** H7
Lenhovda Sweden **45** I8
Lenin, Qullai *mt.* Kyrg./Tajik. *see*
   Lenin Peak
Lenina, Pik *mt.* Kyrg./Tajik. *see* Lenin Peak
Leninabad Tajik. *see* Khŭjand
Leninakan Armenia *see* Gyumri
Lenin Atyndagy Choku *mt.* Kyrg./Tajik. *see*
   Lenin Peak
Lenine Crimea **90** D1
Leningrad Russia *see* St Petersburg
Leningrad. **89** I1
Leningrad Oblast *admin. div.* Russia *see*
   Leningradskaya
Leningradskaya Russia **43** H7
Leningradskaya Oblast' *admin. div.* Russia
   45 R7
Leningradskiy Russia **65** S3
Leningradskiy Tajik. *see* Leningrad
Lenino Crimea *see* Lenine
Leninobod Tajik. *see* Khŭjand
Lenin Peak Kyrg./Tajik. **89** I2
Leninsk Kazakh. *see* Baykonyr
Leninsk Russia **43** J6
Leninskiy Russia **43** H5
Leninsk-Kuznetskiy Russia **64** J4
Leninskoye *Kirovskaya Oblast'* Russia **42** L4
Leninskoye *Yevreyskaya Avtonomnaya
   Oblast'* Russia **74** D2
Lenkoran' Azer. *see* Länkäran
Lenne *r.* Germany **53** H3
Lennox Canada **135** J1
Lennoxville Canada **135** J1
Lenoir U.S.A. **132** D5
Lenore U.S.A. **134** D5
Lenore Lake Canada **121** J4
Lenox U.S.A. **135** I2
Lens France **52** C4
Lensk Russia **65** M3
Lenti Hungary **58** G1
Lentini *Sicily* Italy **58** F6
Lenya Myanmar **71** B5
Lenzen (Elbe) Germany **53** L1
Léo Burkina Faso **96** C3
Leoben Austria **47** O7
Leodhais, Eilean *i.* U.K. *see* Lewis, Isle of
Leominster U.K. **49** E6
Leominster U.S.A. **135** J2
León Mex. **136** D4
León Nicaragua **137** G6
León Spain **57** D2
Leon *r.* U.S.A. **131** D6
Leonardtown U.S.A. **135** G4
Leonardville Namibia **100** D2
Leongatha Australia **112** B7
Leonidi Greece *see* Leonidio
Leonidio Greece **59** J6
Leonidovo Russia **74** F2
Leonora Australia **109** C7
Leopold U.S.A. **134** E4
Leopold and Astrid Coast Antarctica *see*
   King Leopold and Queen Astrid Coast
Léopold II, Lac *l.* Dem. Rep. Congo *see*
   Mai-Ndombe, Lac
Leopoldina Brazil **145** C3
Leopoldo de Bulhões Brazil **145** A2
Léopoldville Dem. Rep. Congo *see*
   Kinshasa
Leoti U.S.A. **130** C4
Leoville Canada **121** J4
Lépa, Lac *l.* Russia **43** I5
Lepalale S. Africa **101** I2
Lepaya Latvia *see* Liepāja
Lepel' Belarus *see* Lyepyel'
Lepellé *r.* France **123** H1
Lephalala *r.* S. Africa **101** H2
Lephalale S. Africa **101** H2
Lephepe Botswana **101** G2
Lephoi S. Africa **101** G6
Leping China **77** H2
Lepontine Alps *mts* Italy/Switz. **58** C1
Leppävirta Fin. **44** O5
Lepreau, Point Canada **123** I5
Lepsa Kazakh. *see* Lepsi
Lepsi Kazakh. **80** E2
Le Puy France *see* Le Puy-en-Velay
Le Puy-en-Velay France **56** F4
Le Quesnoy France **52** D4
Lerala Botswana **101** H2
Leratswana S. Africa **101** H5
Léré Mali **96** C3
Lereh Indon. **69** J7
Leribe Lesotho *see* Hlotse
Lérida Col. **142** D4
Lérida Spain *see* Lleida
Lerik Azer. **91** H3
Lerma Spain **57** E2
Lermontov Russia **91** F1
Lermontovka Russia **74** D3
Lermontovskiy Russia *see* Lermontov
Leros *i.* Greece **59** L6
Le Roy U.S.A. **135** G2
Le Roy, Cap *c.* France **122** D2
Lerum Sweden **45** H8
Lerwick U.K. **50** [inset]
Les Amirantes *is* Seychelles *see*
   Amirante Islands
Lesbos *i.* Greece **59** K5
Les Cayes Haiti **137** J5
Leye *i.* Phil. **69** G4
Leshan China **76** D2
Leshukonskoye Russia **42** J2
Lesi *watercourse* South Sudan **97** F4
Leskhimstroy Ukr. *see* Syeverodonets'k

Leskovac Serbia **59** I3
Leslie U.S.A. **134** C2
Lesneven France **56** B2
Lesnoy *Kirovskaya Oblast'* Russia **42** L4
Lesnoy *Murmanskaya Oblast'* Russia *see*
   Umba
Lesnoye Russia **42** G4
Lesogorskoye Russia **74** F2
Lesopil'noye Russia **74** D3
Lesosibirsk Russia **64** K3
Lesotho *country* Africa **101** I5
Lesozavodsk Russia **74** D3
L'Espérance Rock *i.* Kermadec Is **107** I5
Les Pieux France **49** F9
Les Sables-d'Olonne France **56** D3
Lesse *r.* Belgium **52** E4
Lesser Antarctica *reg.* Antarctica *see*
   West Antarctica
Lesser Antilles *is* Caribbean Sea **137** K6
Lesser Caucasus *mts* Asia **91** F2
Lesser Himalaya *mts* India/Nepal **82** D3
Lesser Khingan Mountains China *see*
   Xiao Hinggan Ling
Lesser Slave Lake Canada **120** H4
Lesser Tunb *i.* The Gulf *see*
   Tonb-e Kūchek, Jazīreh-ye
Lessines Belgium **52** D4
Lester U.S.A. **134** E5
Lestijärvi Fin. **44** N5
Les Vans France **56** G4
Lesvos *i.* Greece *see* Lesbos
Leszno Poland **47** P5
Letaba S. Africa **101** J2
Letchworth Garden City U.K. **49** G7
Le Télégraphe *hill* France **56** G3
Leteri India **82** D4
Letha Range *mts* Myanmar **70** A2
Lethbridge *Alta* Canada **121** H5
Lethbridge *Nfld. and Lab.* Canada **123** L4
Leti *i.* Indon. **108** D2
Leti, Kepulauan *is* Indon. **108** D2
Leticia Col. **142** E4
Letlhakane Botswana **101** G3
Letlhakeng Botswana **101** G3
Letnerechenskiy Russia **42** G2
Letniy Navolok Russia **42** H2
Le Touquet-Paris-Plage France **52** B4
Letpadan Myanmar **70** A3
Le Tréport France **52** B4
Letsitele S. Africa **101** J2
Letsok-aw Kyun *i.* Myanmar **71** B5
Letsopa S. Africa **101** G4
Letterkenny Ireland **51** E3
Letung Indon. **71** D7
Lětzebuerg *country* Europe *see*
   Luxembourg
Letzlingen Germany **53** L2
Léua Angola **99** C5
Leucas Greece *see* Lefkada
Leucate, Étang de *l.* France **56** F5
Leuchars U.K. **50** G4
Leukas Greece *see* Lefkada
Leunovo Russia **42** I2
Leupp U.S.A. **129** H4
Leupung Indon. **71** A6
Leura Australia **110** E4
Leusden Neth. **52** F2
Leuser, Gunung *mt.* Indon. **71** B7
Leutershausen Germany **53** K5
Leuven Belgium **52** E4
Levadeia Greece *see* Livadeia
Levan U.S.A. **131** C4
Levanger Norway **44** G5
Levante, Riviera di *coastal area* Italy **58** C2
Levanto Italy **58** C2
Levashi Russia **91** G2
Levelland U.S.A. **131** C5
Leven *England* U.K. **48** F4
Leven *Scotland* U.K. **50** G4
Leven, Loch *l.* U.K. **50** F4
Lévêque, Cape Australia **108** C4
Leverkusen Germany **52** G3
Lévézou *mts* France **56** F4
Levice Slovakia **47** Q6
Levin N.Z. **113** E5
Lévis Canada **123** H5
Levitha *i.* Greece **59** L6
Levittown *NY* U.S.A. **135** I3
Levittown *PA* U.S.A. **135** H3
Levkás *i.* Greece *see* Lefkada
Levkímmi Greece *see* Lefkimmi
Levkosia Bulg. *see* Karlovo
Levski Bulg. *see* Karlovo
Lev Tolstoy Russia **43** H5
Levuka Fiji **107** H3
Lévy, Cap *c.* France **49** F9
Lewe Myanmar **70** B3
Lewerberg *mt.* S. Africa **100** C5
Lewes U.K. **49** H8
Lewes U.S.A. **135** H4
Lewis *CO* U.S.A. **129** I3
Lewis *IN* U.S.A. **134** B4
Lewis *KS* U.S.A. **130** D4
Lewis, Isle of *i.* U.K. **50** C2
Lewis, Lake *salt flat* Australia **108** F5
Lewisburg *KY* U.S.A. **134** B5
Lewisburg *PA* U.S.A. **135** G3
Lewisburg *WV* U.S.A. **134** E5
Lewis Cass, Mount Canada/U.S.A. **120** D3
Lewis Hills hill Canada **123** K4
Lewis Pass N.Z. **113** D6
Lewis Range *hills* Australia **108** E5
Lewis Range *mts* U.S.A. **126** E2
Lewis Smith, Lake U.S.A. **133** C5
Lewiston *ID* U.S.A. **126** D3
Lewiston *ME* U.S.A. **135** J1
Lewistown *IL* U.S.A. **130** F3
Lewistown *MT* U.S.A. **126** F3
Lewistown *PA* U.S.A. **135** G3
Lewisville U.S.A. **131** E5
Lexington *IL* U.S.A. **134** C4
Lexington *MI* U.S.A. **134** D2
Lexington *NC* U.S.A. **132** D5
Lexington *NE* U.S.A. **130** D3
Lexington *TN* U.S.A. **131** F5
Lexington *VA* U.S.A. **134** F5
Lexington Park U.S.A. **135** G4
Leyden Neth. *see* Leiden
Leye China **76** E3
Leyla Dāgh *mt.* Iran **88** B2
Leyte *i.* Phil. **69** G4
Lezha Albania *see* Lezhë
Lezhë Albania **59** H4
Lezhi China **76** E2

Leshu China **77** G4
L'gov Russia **43** G6
Lharigarbo China **83** G2
Lhasa China **83** G3
Lhasoi China **76** B2
Lhatog China **76** B2
Lhaviyani Atoll Maldives *see* Faadhippolhu
Lhazê *Xizang* China **76** B2
Lhazê *Xizang* China **83** F3
Lhazhong China **83** F3
Lhokkruet Indon. **71** A6
Lhokseumawe Indon. **71** B6
Lhoksukon Indon. **71** B6
Lhoma China **83** G3
Lhorong China **76** B2

▶ **Lhotse** *mt.* China/Nepal **83** F4
4th highest mountain in Asia and the world.

Lhozhag China **83** G3
Lhuentse Bhutan **83** G4
Lhünzê China **76** B2
Lhünzhub China *see* Poindo
Liakoura *mt.* Greece **59** J5
Liancheng China *see* Guangnan
Liancourt France **52** C5
Liancourt Rocks *i.* N. Pacific Ocean **75** C5
Liandu China *see* Lishui
Liangdang China **76** E1
Liangdaohe China *see* Zaring
Lianghe *Chongqing* China **77** F2
Lianghe *Sichuan* China **76** D2
Lianghe *Yunnan* China **76** C3
Lianghekou *Chongqing* China *see* Lianghe
Lianghekou *Gansu* China **76** E1
Liangping China **76** E2
Liangpran, Gunung *mt.* Indon. **68** F6
Liangshan China *see* Liangping
Liang Shan *mt.* Myanmar **70** B1
Liangshi China *see* Shaodong
Liangtian China **77** F4
Liangyuan China *see* Shangqiu
Liangzhou China *see* Wuwei
Liangzi Hu *l.* China **77** G2
Lianhe China *see* Qianjiang
Lianhua China **77** G3
Lianhua Shan *mts* China **77** G4
Lianjiang *Fujian* China **77** H3
Lianjiang *Jiangxi* China *see* Xingguo
Liannan China **77** G3
Lianping China **77** G3
Lianran China *see* Anning
Lianshan *Guangdong* China **77** G3
Lianshan *Liaoning* China **73** M4
Lianshui China **77** H1
Liant, Cape *i.* Thai. *see* Samae San, Ko
Liantang China *see* Nanchang
Lianxian China *see* Lianzhou
Lianyin China **74** A1
Lianyungang China **77** H1
Lianzhou *Guangdong* China **77** G3
Lianzhou *Guangxi* China *see* Hepu
Liaocheng China **73** L5
Liaodong Bandao *pen.* China **73** M5
Liaodong Wan *b.* China **73** M4
Liaogao China *see* Songtao
Liao He *r.* China **73** M4
Liaoning *prov.* China **74** A4
Liaoyang China **74** A4
Liaoyuan China **74** B4
Liaozhong China **74** A4
Liapades Greece **59** H5
Liard *r.* Canada **120** F2
Liard Highway Canada **120** F2
Liard Plateau Canada **120** E2
Liard River Canada **120** E3
Liari Pak. **89** G5
Liathach *mt.* U.K. **50** D3
Liban *country* Asia *see* Lebanon
Liban, Jebel *mts* Lebanon **85** C2
Libau Latvia *see* Liepāja
Libby U.S.A. **126** E2
Libenge Dem. Rep. Congo **98** B3
Liberal U.S.A. **131** C4
Liberdade Brazil **145** B3
Liberec Czechia **47** O5
Liberia *country* Africa **96** C4
Liberia Costa Rica **137** G6
Liberty *IN* U.S.A. **134** C4
Liberty *KY* U.S.A. **134** C5
Liberty *ME* U.S.A. **135** K1
Liberty *MO* U.S.A. **130** E4
Liberty *MS* U.S.A. **131** F6
Liberty *NY* U.S.A. **135** H3
Liberty *TX* U.S.A. **131** E6
Liberty Lake U.S.A. **135** G4
Libin Belgium **52** F5

▶ **Lilongwe** Malawi **99** D5
Capital of Malawi.

Lilydale Australia **111** B7

▶ **Lima** Peru **142** C6
*Capital of Peru. 4th most populous city in
South America.*

Lima *MT* U.S.A. **126** E3
Lima *NY* U.S.A. **135** G2
Lima *OH* U.S.A. **134** C3
Lima Duarte Brazil **145** C3
Liman Russia **43** J7
Limar Indon. **108** D1
Limassol Cyprus **85** A2
Limavady U.K. **51** F2
Limay *r.* Arg. **144** C5
Limbaži Latvia **45** N8
Limbunya Australia **108** E4
Limburg an der Lahn Germany **53** I4
Lim Chu Kang *hill* Sing. **71** [inset]
Lime Acres S. Africa **100** F5
Limeira Brazil **145** B3
Limerick Ireland **51** D5
Limestone Point Canada **121** L4
Limfjorden *sea chan.* Denmark *see* Little Belt
Limingen Norway **44** H4
Limingen *l.* Norway **44** H4
Limington U.S.A. **135** J2
Liminka Fin. **44** N4
Limmen Bight *b.* Australia **110** B2
Limmen National Park Australia **108** F3
Limnos *i.* Greece **59** K5
Limoeiro Brazil **143** K5
Limoges Canada **135** H1
Limoges France **56** E4
Limón Costa Rica *see* Puerto Limón
Limon U.S.A. **130** C4
Limonlu Turkey **85** B1
Limonum France *see* Poitiers
Limousin *reg.* France **56** E4
Limoux France **56** F5
Limpopo, Parque Nacional do *nat. park*
   S. Africa **101** J2

Limpopo *prov.* S. Africa **101** I2
Limpopo *r.* S. Africa **101** K3
Limu China **77** F3
Linah *well* Saudi Arabia **91** F5
Lin'an China *see* Jianshui
Linares Chile **144** B5
Linares Mex. **131** D7
Linares Spain **57** E4
Lincang China **76** D4
Lincheng *Hainan* China *see* Lingao
Lincheng *Hunan* China *see* Huitong
Linchuan China *see* Fuzhou
Linck Nunataks *nunataks* Antarctica **152** K1
Lincoln Arg. **144** D4
Lincoln U.K. **48** G5
Lincoln *CA* U.S.A. **128** C2
Lincoln *IL* U.S.A. **130** F3
Lincoln *MI* U.S.A. **134** D1

▶ **Lincoln** *NE* U.S.A. **130** D3
Capital of Nebraska.

Lincoln City *IN* U.S.A. **134** B4
Lincoln City *OR* U.S.A. **126** B3
Lincoln Island Paracel Is **68** E3
Lincoln National Park Australia **111** A7
Lincoln Sea Canada/Greenland **153** J1
Lincolnshire Wolds *hills* U.K. **48** G5
Lincolnton U.S.A. **133** D5
Linda, Serra *hills* Brazil **145** C1
Linda Creek *watercourse* Australia **110** B4
Lindau Germany **53** M2
Lindau (Bodensee) Germany **47** L7
Lindeman Group *is* Australia **110** E4
Linden Canada **120** H5
Linden Germany **53** I4
Linden Guyana **143** G2
Linden *AL* U.S.A. **133** C5
Linden *MI* U.S.A. **134** D2
Linden *TN* U.S.A. **132** C5
Linden *TX* U.S.A. **131** E5
Linden Grove U.S.A. **130** E2
Lindern (Oldenburg) Germany **53** H2
Lindesnes *c.* Norway **45** E7
Líndhos Greece *see* Lindos
Lindi *r.* Dem. Rep. Congo **98** C3
Lindi Tanz. **99** D4
Lindian China **74** B3
Lindisfarne *i.* U.K. *see* Holy Island
Lindley S. Africa **101** H4
Lindos Greece **59** S4
Lindos, Akra *pt* Greece *see*
   Gkinas, Akrotirio
Lindsay Canada **135** F1
Lindsay *CA* U.S.A. **128** D3
Lindsay *MT* U.S.A. **126** G3
Lindsborg U.S.A. **130** D4
Lindside U.S.A. **134** E5
Lindum U.K. *see* Lincoln
Line Islands Kiribati **151** J5
Linesville U.S.A. **134** E3
Linfen China **73** K5
Lingampet India **84** C2
Lingao China **77** F5
Lingayen Phil. **69** G3
Lingbi China **77** H1
Lingcheng *Anhui* China *see* Lingbi
Lingcheng *Guangxi* China *see* Lingshan
Lingcheng *Hainan* China *see* Lingshui
Lingchuan *Guangxi* China **77** F3
Lingchuan *Shanxi* China **77** G1
Lingelethu S. Africa **101** H7
Lingen (Ems) Germany **53** H2
Lingga, Kepulauan *is* Indon. **68** D7
Lingle U.S.A. **126** G4
Lingling China **77** F3
Lingomo Dem. Rep. Congo **98** C3
Lingshan China **77** F4
Lingshi China **77** F5
Lingshui China **77** F5
Lingshui Wan *b.* China **77** F5
Lingsugur India **84** C2
Lingtai China **76** E1
Linguère Senegal **96** B3
Lingui China **77** F3
Lingxi China *see* Yongshun
Lingxia China **74** A3
Lingxian China *see* Yanling
Lingxiang China **77** G2
Lingyang China *see* Cili
Lingyun China **76** E3
Lingzi Tang *reg.* China **82** D2
Linh, Ngok *mt.* Vietnam **70** D4
Linhai China **77** I2
Linhares Brazil **145** C2
Linhe China *see* Bayannur
Linhpa Myanmar **70** A1
Linjiang China **74** B4
Linjin China **77** F1
Linköping Sweden **45** I7
Linkou China **74** C3
Linli China **77** F2
Linlithgow U.K. **50** F5
Linn *MO* U.S.A. **130** F4
Linn *TX* U.S.A. **131** D7
Linn, Mount U.S.A. **128** B1
Linnansaaren kansallispuisto *nat. park*
   Fin. **44** P5
Linnhe, Loch *inlet* U.K. **50** D4
Linnich Germany **52** G4
Linosa, Isola di *i. Sicily* Italy **58** E7
Linquan China **77** G1
Linru *Henan* China *see* Ruzhou
Linru *Henan* China **77** G1
Lins Brazil **145** A3
Linshu China **77** H1
Linshui China **76** E2
Lintan China **76** D1
Lintao China **76** D1
Linton *IN* U.S.A. **134** B4
Linton *ND* U.S.A. **130** C2
Linwu China **77** G3
Linxi China **73** L4
Linxia China **76** D1
Linxiang China **77** G2
Linyi *Shandong* China **73** L5
Linyi *Shandong* China **77** H1
Linying China **77** G1
Linz Austria **47** O6
Lion, Golfe du *g.* France **56** F5

Lions, Gulf of France see Lion, Golfe du
Lions Bay Canada 120 F5
Lioua Chad 97 E3
Lipari Sicily Italy 58 F5
Lipari, Isole is Italy 58 F5
Lipetsk Russia 43 H5
Lipin Bor Russia 42 H3
Liping China 77 F3
Lipova Romania 59 I1
Lipovtsy Russia 74 C3
Lippe r. Germany 53 G3
Lippstadt Germany 53 I3
Lipsoi i. Greece see Leipsoi
Lipti Lekh pass Nepal 82 E3
Liptrap, Cape Australia 112 B7
Lipu China 77 F3
Lira Uganda 98 D3
Liranga Congo 98 B4
Lircay Peru 142 D6
Lisala Dem. Rep. Congo 98 C3
Lisbellaw U.K. 51 E3
Lisboa Port. see Lisbon

▶Lisbon Port. 57 B4
Capital of Portugal.

Lisbon ME U.S.A. 135 J1
Lisbon NH U.S.A. 135 J1
Lisbon OH U.S.A. 134 E3
Lisburn U.K. 51 F3
Liscannor Bay Ireland 51 C5
Lisdoonvarna Ireland 51 C4
Lishan Taiwan 77 I3
Lishe Jiang r. China 76 D3
Lishi China see Dingnan
Lishu China 74 B4
Lishui China 77 H2
Li Shui r. China 77 F2
Lisichansk Ukr. see Lysychans'k
Lisieux France 56 E2
Liskeard U.K. 49 C8
Liski Russia 43 H6
L'Isle-Adam France 52 C5
Lismore Australia 112 F2
Lismore Ireland 51 E5
Lisnarrick U.K. 51 E3
Lisnaskea U.K. 51 E3
Liss mt. Saudi Arabia 85 D4
Lissa Poland see Leszno
Lister, Mount Antarctica 152 H1
Listowel Canada 134 E2
Listowel Ireland 51 C5
Lit Sweden 44 I5
Litang Guangxi China 77 F4
Litang Sichuan China 76 D2
Līţānī, Nahr el r. Lebanon 85 B3
Litchfield CA U.S.A. 128 C1
Litchfield CT U.S.A. 135 I3
Litchfield IL U.S.A. 130 F4
Litchfield MI U.S.A. 134 C2
Litchfield MN U.S.A. 130 E2
Lit-et-Mixe France 56 D4
Lithgow Australia 112 E4
Lithino, Akra pt Greece see
Lithino, Akrotirio
Lithino, Akrotirio pt Greece 59 K7
Lithuania country Europe 45 M9
Lititz U.S.A. 135 G3
Litoměřice Czechia 47 O5
Litovko Russia 74 D2
Litovskaya S.S.R. country Europe see
Lithuania
Little r. U.S.A. 131 E6
Little Abaco i. Bahamas 133 E7
Little Abitibi r. Canada 122 E4
Little Abitibi Lake Canada 122 E4
Little Andaman i. India 71 A5
Little Bahama Bank sea feature Bahamas
133 E7
Little Barrier Island i. N.Z. 113 E3
Little Belt sea chan. Denmark 45 F9
Little Belt Mountains U.S.A. 126 F3
Little Bitter Lake Egypt 85 A4
Little Cayman i. Cayman Is 137 H5
Little Churchill r. Canada 121 M3
Little Chute U.S.A. 134 A1
Little Coco Island Cocos Is 71 A4
Little Colorado r. U.S.A. 129 H3
Little Creek Peak U.S.A. 129 G3
Little Current Canada 122 E5
Little Current r. Canada 122 D4
Little Desert National Park Australia
111 C8
Little Egg Harbor inlet U.S.A. 135 H4
Little Exuma i. Bahamas 133 F8
Little Falls U.S.A. 130 E2
Littlefield AZ U.S.A. 129 G3
Littlefield TX U.S.A. 131 C5
Little Fork r. U.S.A. 130 E1
Little Grand Rapids Canada 121 M4
Littlehampton U.K. 49 G8
Little Inagua Island Bahamas 133 F8
Little Karas Berg plat. Namibia 100 D4
Little Karoo plat. S. Africa 100 E7
Little Lake U.S.A. 128 E4
Little Mecatina r. Canada see
Petit Mécatina
Little Mecatina Island Canada see
Petit Mécatina, Île du
Little Minch sea chan. U.K. 50 B3
Little Missouri r. U.S.A. 130 C2
Little Namaqualand reg. S. Africa see
Namaqualand
Little Nicobar i. India 71 A6
Little Ouse r. U.K. 49 H6
Little Pamir mts Asia 89 I2
Little Rancheria r. Canada 120 D2
Little Red River Canada 120 H3

▶Little Rock U.S.A. 131 E5
Capital of Arkansas.

Littlerock U.S.A. 128 E4
Little Sable Point U.S.A. 134 B2
Little Salmon Lake Canada 120 C2
Little Salt Lake U.S.A. 129 G3
Little Sandy Desert Australia 109 B5
Little San Salvador i. Bahamas 133 F7
Little Smoky Canada 120 G4
Little Tibet reg. India/Pak. see Ladakh
Littleton U.S.A. 126 G5
Little Valley U.S.A. 135 F2
Little Wind r. U.S.A. 126 F4
Litunde Moz. 99 D5
Liu'an China see Lu'an
Liuba China 76 E1
Liucheng China 77 F3
Liuchong He r. China 76 E3
Liuchow China see Liuzhou
Liuhe China 74 B4
Liuheng Dao i. China 77 I2
Liujiachang China 77 F2
Liujiaxia Shuiku resr China 76 D1
Liukesong China 74 B3
Liulin China see Jonê
Liupan Shan mts China 76 E1
Liupanshui China 76 E3
Liuqiu Yu i. Taiwan 77 I4
Liuquan China 77 H1
Liuwa Plain National Park Zambia 99 C5
Liuyang China 77 G2
Liuzhan China 74 B2
Liuzhi China 76 E3
Liuzhou China 77 F3
Livadeia Greece 59 J5
Līvāni Latvia 45 O8
Live Oak U.S.A. 133 D6
Liveringa Australia 106 C3
Livermore CA U.S.A. 128 C3
Livermore KY U.S.A. 134 B5
Livermore, Mount U.S.A. 131 B6
Livermore Falls U.S.A. 135 J1
Liverpool Australia 112 E4
Liverpool Canada 123 I5
Liverpool U.K. 48 E5
Liverpool Bay Canada 118 E3
Liverpool Plains Australia 112 E3
Liverpool Range mts Australia 112 D3
Livia U.S.A. 134 B5
Livingston U.K. 50 F5
Livingston AL U.S.A. 131 F5
Livingston KY U.S.A. 134 C5
Livingston MT U.S.A. 126 F3
Livingston TN U.S.A. 134 C5
Livingston TX U.S.A. 131 E6
Livingston, Lake U.S.A. 131 E6
Livingstone Zambia 99 C5
Livingston Island Antarctica 152 L2
Livingston Manor U.S.A. 135 H3
Livno Bos. & Herz. 58 G3
Livny Russia 43 H5
Livojoki r. Fin. 44 O4
Livonia MI U.S.A. 134 D2
Livonia NY U.S.A. 135 G2
Livorno Italy 58 D3
Livramento de Nossa Senhora Brazil
145 C1
Liwā Oman 88 E5
Liwā', Wādī al watercourse Syria 85 C3
Liwale Tanz. 99 D4
Lixian Gansu China 76 E1
Lixian Sichuan China 76 D2
Lixiang Jiang r. China 76 D4
Lixus Morocco see Larache
Liyang China see Hexian
Liyuan China see Sangzhi
Lizard U.K. 49 B9
Lizarda Brazil 143 I5
Lizard Point U.K. 49 B9
Lizarra Spain see Estella
Lizemores U.S.A. 134 E4
Liziping China 76 D2
Lizy-sur-Ourcq France 52 D5
Ljouwert Neth. see Leeuwarden

▶Ljubljana Slovenia 58 F1
Capital of Slovenia.

Ljugarn Sweden 45 K8
Ljungan r. Sweden 44 J5
Ljungaverk Sweden 44 J5
Ljungby Sweden 45 H8
Ljusdal Sweden 45 J6
Ljusnan r. Sweden 45 J6
Ljusne Sweden 45 J6
Llaima, Volcán vol. Chile 144 B5
Llanandras U.K. see Presteigne
Llanbadarn Fawr U.K. 49 C6
Llanbedr Pont Steffan U.K. see Lampeter
Llanbister U.K. 49 D6
Llandeilo U.K. 49 D7
Llandissilio U.K. 49 C7
Llandovery U.K. 49 D7
Llandrindod Wells U.K. 49 D6
Llandudno U.K. 48 D5
Llandysul U.K. 49 C6
Llanegwad U.K. 49 C7
Llanelli U.K. 49 C7
Llanfair Caereinion U.K. 49 D6
Llanfair-ym-Muallt U.K. see Builth Wells
Llangefni U.K. 48 C5
Llangollen U.K. 49 D6
Llangurig U.K. 49 D6
Llanllyfni U.K. 49 C5
Llannerch-y-medd U.K. 48 C5
Llannor U.K. 49 C6
Llano Mex. 127 F7
Llano U.S.A. 131 D6
Llano r. U.S.A. 131 D6
Llano Estacado plain U.S.A. 131 C5
Llanos plain Col./Venez. 142 E2
Llanquihue, Lago l. Chile 144 B6
Llanrhystud U.K. 49 C6
Llantrisant U.K. 49 D7
Llanuwchllyn U.K. 49 D6
Llanwnog U.K. 49 D6
Llanymddyfri U.K. see Llandovery
Llay U.K. 49 D5
Lleida Spain 57 G3
Llerena Spain 57 C4
Llíria Spain 57 F4
Llodio Spain see Laudio
Lloyd George, Mount Canada 120 E3
Lloyd Lake Canada 121 I3
Lloydminster Canada 121 I4
Lluchmayor Spain see Llucmajor
Llucmajor Spain 57 H4

▶Llullaillaco, Volcán vol. Chile 144 C2
Highest active volcano in South America
and the world.

Lô, Sông r. China/Vietnam 70 D2
Loa r. Chile 144 B2
Loa U.S.A. 129 H2
Loango Congo 99 B4
Loban' r. Russia 42 K4
Lobatejo mt. Spain 57 D5
Lobatse Botswana 101 G3
Lobaye r. Cent. Afr. Rep. 98 B3
Löbejün Germany 53 L3
Lobéké, Parc National de nat. park
Cameroon 97 E4
Löbenberg hill Germany 53 M3
Loberia Arg. 144 E5
Lobito Angola 99 B5
Lobos Arg. 144 E5
Lobos, Cabo c. Mex. 127 E7
Lobos, Isla i. Mex. 127 F8
Lobos de Tierra, Isla i. Peru 142 B5
Loburg Germany 53 M2
Lôc Binh Vietnam 70 D2
Lochaline U.K. 50 D4
Loch Baghasdail U.K. see Lochboisdale
Lochboisdale U.K. 50 B3
Lochcarron U.K. 50 D3
Lochearnhead U.K. 50 E4
Lochem Neth. 52 G2
Lochern National Park Australia 110 C5
Loches France 56 E3
Loch Garman Ireland see Wexford
Lochgelly U.K. 50 F4
Lochgilphead U.K. 50 D4
Lochinver U.K. 50 D2
Loch Lomond and the Trossachs National
Park U.K. 50 E4
Lochmaddy U.K. 50 B3
Lochnagar mt. U.K. 50 F4
Loch na Madadh U.K. see Lochmaddy
Loch Raven Reservoir U.S.A. 135 G4
Lochy, Loch l. U.K. 50 E4
Lock Australia 111 A7
Lockerbie U.K. 50 F5
Lockhart Australia 112 C5
Lockhart U.S.A. 131 D6
Lock Haven U.S.A. 135 G3
Löcknitz r. Germany 53 L1
Lockport U.S.A. 135 F2
Lôc Ninh Vietnam 71 D5
Lod Israel 85 B4
Loddon r. Australia 112 A5
Lodève France 56 F5
Lodeynoye Pole Russia 42 G3
Lodge, Mount Canada/U.S.A. 120 B3
Lodhikheda India 82 D5
Lodhran Pak. 89 H4
Lodi Italy 58 C2
Lodi CA U.S.A. 128 C2
Lodi OH U.S.A. 134 D3
Lødingen Norway 44 I2
Lodja Dem. Rep. Congo 98 C4
Lodomeria Russia see Vladimir
Lodrani India 82 B5
Lodwar Kenya 98 D3
Łódź Poland 47 Q5
Loei Thai. 70 C3
Loeriesfontein S. Africa 100 D6
Lofoten is Norway 44 H2
Lofusa South Sudan 97 G4
Log Russia 43 I6
Loga Niger 96 D3
Logan IA U.S.A. 130 E3
Logan OH U.S.A. 134 D4
Logan UT U.S.A. 126 F4
Logan WV U.S.A. 134 E5

▶Logan, Mount Canada 120 A2
2nd highest mountain in North America.

Logan, Mount U.S.A. 126 C2
Logan Creek r. Australia 110 D4
Logan Lake Canada 120 F5
Logan Mountains Canada 120 D2
Logansport IN U.S.A. 134 B3
Logansport LA U.S.A. 131 E6
Logatec Slovenia 58 F2
Logpung China 76 D1
Logroño Spain 57 E2
Lohardaga India 83 F5
Loharu India 82 C3
Lohatlha S. Africa 100 F5
Lohawat India 82 C4
Lohfelden Germany 53 J3
Lohil r. China/India see Zayü Qu
Lohiniva Fin. 44 N3
Lohit r. India 83 H4
Lohjanjärvi l. Fin. 45 M6
Löhne Germany 53 I2
Lohne (Oldenburg) Germany 53 I2
Lohtaja Fin. 44 M4
Loi, Nam r. Myanmar 70 C2
Loikaw Myanmar 70 B3
Loi-lem Myanmar 70 B2
Loi Lun Myanmar 70 B2
Loimaa Fin. 45 M6
Loipyet Hills Myanmar 70 B1
Loire r. France 56 C3
Loja Ecuador 142 C4
Loja Spain 57 D5
Lokan tekojärvi l. Fin. 44 O3
Lokchim r. Russia 42 K3
Lokeren Belgium 52 E3
Lokgwabe Botswana 100 E3
Lokichar Kenya 78 C6
Lokichokio Kenya 98 D3
Lokilalaki, Gunung mt. Indon. 69 G7
Løkken Denmark 45 F8
Løkken Norway 44 F5
Loknya Russia 42 F4
Lokoja Nigeria 96 D4
Lokolama Dem. Rep. Congo 98 B4
Lokossa Benin 96 D4
Lokot' Russia 43 G5
Loktak Lake India 83 H4
Lol South Sudan 97 F4
Lola Guinea 96 C4
Lola, Mount U.S.A. 128 C2
Loleta U.S.A. 128 A1
Loliondo Tanz. 98 D4
Lolland i. Denmark 45 G9
Lolo U.S.A. 126 E3
Loloda Indon. 69 H6
Lolo Pass U.S.A. 126 E3
Lolowau Indon. 71 B7
Lolwane S. Africa 100 F4
Lom Bulg. 59 J3
Lom Norway 45 F6
Loma U.S.A. 129 I2
Lomami r. Dem. Rep. Congo 98 C3
Lomar Pass Afgh. 89 G3
Lomas, Bahía de b. Chile 144 C8
Lomas de Zamora Arg. 144 E4
Lombarda, Serra hills Brazil 143 H3
Lomblen i. Indon. 108 C2
Lombok Indon. 108 B2
Lombok i. Indon. 108 B2
Lombok, Selat sea chan. Indon.
108 A2

▶Lomé Togo 96 D4
Capital of Togo.

Lomela Dem. Rep. Congo 98 C4
Lomela r. Dem. Rep. Congo 97 F5
Lomira U.S.A. 134 A2
Lomme France 52 C4
Lommel Belgium 52 F3
Lomond Canada 123 K4
Lomond, Loch l. U.K. 50 E4
Lomonosov Russia 45 P7
Lomonosov Ridge sea feature Arctic Ocean
153 B1
Lomovoye Russia 42 I2
Lomphat Cambodia see Lumphăt
Lompoc U.S.A. 128 C4
Lom Sak Thai. 70 C3
Łomża Poland 47 S4
Lơn, Hon i. Vietnam 71 E4
Lonar India 84 C2
Londa Bangl. 83 G5
Londa India 84 B3
Londinières France 52 B5
Londinium U.K. see London
Londoko Russia 74 D2
London Canada 134 E2

▶London U.K. 49 G7
Capital of the United Kingdom and of
England. 4th most populous city in Europe.

London KY U.S.A. 134 C5
London OH U.S.A. 134 D4
Londonderry U.K. 51 E3
Londonderry OH U.S.A. 134 D4
Londonderry VT U.S.A. 135 I2
Londonderry, Cape Australia 108 D3
Londrina Brazil 145 A3
Lone Pine U.S.A. 128 D3
Long Thai. 70 B3
Longa Angola 99 B5
Longa, Proliv sea chan. Russia 65 S2
Long'an China 76 E4
Long Ashton U.K. 49 E7
Longbao China 76 C1
Long Bay U.S.A. 133 E5
Longbeach N.Z. 113 C7
Long Beach U.S.A. 128 D5
Longbo China see Shuangpai
Long Branch U.S.A. 135 I3
Longchang China 76 E2
Longcheng Anhui China see Xiaoxian
Longcheng Guangdong China see Longmen
Longcheng Yunnan China see Chenggong
Longchuan China see Nanhua
Longchuan Jiang r. China 76 C4
Long Creek r. Canada 121 K5
Long Creek U.S.A. 126 D3
Long Eaton U.K. 49 F6
Longford Ireland 51 E4
Longgang Chongqing China see Dazu
Longgang Guangdong China 77 G4
Longhoughton U.K. 48 F3
Longhui China 77 F3
Longhurst, Mount Antarctica 152 H1
Long Island Bahamas 133 F8
Long Island N.S. Canada 123 I5
Long Island Nunavut Canada 122 F3
Long Island India 71 A4
Long Island P.N.G. 69 L8
Long Island U.S.A. 135 I3
Long Island Sound sea chan. U.S.A. 135 I3
Longjiang China 74 A3
Longjin China see Qingliu
Longju China 76 B2
Longlac Canada 122 D4
Long Lake l. Canada 122 D4
Long Lake U.S.A. 135 H2
Long Lake l. ME U.S.A. 132 G2
Long Lake l. MI U.S.A. 134 D1
Long Lake l. ND U.S.A. 130 C2
Long Lake l. NY U.S.A. 135 H1
Longli China 76 E3
Longlin China 76 E3
Longling China 76 C3
Longmeadow U.S.A. 135 I2
Long Melford U.K. 49 H6
Longmen Guangdong China 77 G4
Longmen Heilong. China 74 B2
Longmen Shan hill China 77 F1
Longmen Shan mts China 76 E1
Longming China 76 E4
Longmont U.S.A. 126 G4
Longnan Gansu China 76 E1
Longnan Jiangxi China 77 G3
Long Phu Vietnam 71 D5
Longping China see Luodian
Long Point Canada 134 E2
Long Point Man. Canada 121 L4
Long Point Ont. Canada 134 E2
Long Point N.Z. 113 B8
Long Point Bay Canada 134 E2
Long Prairie U.S.A. 130 E2
Long Preston U.K. 48 E4
Longquan Guizhou China see Danzhai
Longquan Guizhou China see Fenggang
Longquan Hunan China see Xintian
Longquan Xi r. China 77 I2
Long Range Mountains Nfld. and Lab.
Canada 123 K4
Long Range Mountains Nfld. and Lab.
Canada 123 K5
Longreach Australia 110 D4
Longriba China 76 D1
Longshan Guizhou China see Longli
Longshan Hunan China 77 F2
Longshan Yunnan China see Longling
Long Shan mts China 76 E1
Longshanlu China see Shizhong
Longsheng China 77 F3
Longs Peak U.S.A. 126 G4
Long Stratton U.K. 49 I6
Longtom Lake Canada 120 G1
Longtown U.K. 48 E3
Longue-Pointe-de-Mingan Canada 123 I4
Longueuil Canada 122 G5
Longuyon France 52 F5
Longvale U.S.A. 128 B2
Longview TX U.S.A. 131 E5
Longview WA U.S.A. 126 C3
Longwangmiao China 74 D3
Longwei Co l. China 83 G2
Longxi China 76 E1
Longxian Guangdong China see Wengyuan
Longxian Shaanxi China 76 E1
Longxingchang China see Wuyuan
Longxi Shan mt. China 77 H3
Longxu China see Cangwu
Long Xuyên Vietnam 71 D5
Longyan China 77 H3

▶Longyearbyen Svalbard 64 C2
Capital of Svalbard.

Longzhen China 74 B2
Longzhou China 76 E4
Longzhouping China see Changyang
Löningen Germany 53 H2
Lonoke U.S.A. 131 F5
Lonpo Myanmar 70 B2
Lönsboda Sweden 45 I8
Lons-le-Saunier France 56 G3
Lonton Myanmar 70 B1
Looc Phil. 69 G4
Loochoo Islands Japan see Ryukyu Islands
Loogootee U.S.A. 134 B4
Lookout, Cape Canada 122 E3
Lookout, Cape U.S.A. 133 E5
Lookout, Point Australia 112 F1
Lookout, Point U.S.A. 134 D1
Lookout Mountain U.S.A. 129 I4
Lookout Point Australia 109 B8
Loolmalasin vol. crater Tanz. 98 D4
Loon Canada 122 C4
Loon r. Canada 120 H3
Loongana Australia 109 D7
Loon Lake Canada 121 I4
Loop Head hd Ireland 51 C5
Lop China 82 E1
Lopasnya Russia see Chekhov
Lopatina, Gora mt. Russia 74 F2
Lop Buri Thai. 70 C4
Lopez Phil. 69 G4
Lopez, Cap c. Gabon 98 A4
Lop Nur salt flat China 80 H3
Lopphavet b. Norway 44 L1
Loptyuga Russia 42 K3
Loqung China 76 C1
Lora Pak. 89 G5
Lora r. Venez. 142 D2
Lora, Hāmūn-i- dry lake Afgh./Pak. 89 G4
Lora del Río Spain 57 D5
Lorain U.S.A. 134 D3
Loralai Pak. 89 H4
Loralai r. Pak. 89 H4
Loramie, Lake U.S.A. 134 C3
Lorca Spain 57 F5
Lorch Germany 53 H4
Lordegān Iran 88 C4
Lord Howe Atoll Solomon Is see
Ontong Java Atoll
Lord Howe Island Australia 107 F5
Lord Howe Rise sea feature
S. Pacific Ocean 150 G7
Lord Loughborough Island Myanmar
71 B5
Lordsburg U.S.A. 129 I5
Lore East Timor 108 D2
Lore Lindu, Taman Nasional nat. park
Indon. 68 G7
Lorena Brazil 145 B3
Lorengau P.N.G. 69 L7
Lorentz, Taman Nasional nat. park Indon.
69 J7
Loreto Arg. 144 D3
Loreto Brazil 143 I5
Loreto Mex. 127 F8
Lorient France 56 C3
Lorillard r. Canada 121 N1
Loring U.S.A. 126 G2
Lorn, Firth of est. U.K. 50 D4
Lorne Australia 110 D5
Lorne watercourse Australia 110 B3
Loropéni Burkina Faso 96 C3
Lorrain, Plateau France 53 G6
Lorraine Australia 110 B3
Lorraine admin. reg. France see Alsace,
Champagne-Ardenne et Lorraine
Lorraine reg. France 52 F5
Lorsch Germany 53 I5
Lorup Germany 53 H2
Losal India 82 C4
Los Alamos CA U.S.A. 128 C4
Los Alamos NM U.S.A. 127 G6
Los Alerces, Parque Nacional nat. park
Arg. 144 B6
Los Ángeles Chile 144 B5

▶Los Angeles U.S.A. 128 D4
3rd most populous city in North America.

Los Angeles Aqueduct canal U.S.A. 128 D4
Los Arabos Cuba 133 D8
Los Banos U.S.A. 128 C3
Los Blancos Arg. 144 D2
Los Cerritos watercourse Mex. 127 F8
Los Coronados, Islas is Mex. 128 E5
Los Gigantes, Llanos de plain Mex. 131 B6
Los Glaciares, Parque Nacional nat. park
Arg. 144 B8
Losheim am See Germany 52 G5
Los Hoyos Mex. 127 F7
Lošinj i. Croatia 58 F2
Los Juríes Arg. 144 D3
Los Katios, Parque Nacional nat. park
Col. 137 I7
Loskop Dam S. Africa 101 I3
Los Lunas U.S.A. 127 G6
Los Menucos Arg. 144 C6
Los Mochis Mex. 127 F8
Los Molinos U.S.A. 128 B1
Losombo Dem. Rep. Congo 98 B3
Los Palacios Cuba 133 D8
Los Remedios r. Mex. 131 B7
Los Roques, Islas is Venez. 142 E1
Losser Neth. 52 G2
Lossie r. U.K. 50 F3
Lossiemouth U.K. 50 F3
Lößnitz Germany 53 M4
Lost Creek KY U.S.A. 134 D5
Lost Creek WV U.S.A. 134 E4
Los Teques Venez. 142 E1
Los Testigos is Venez. 142 F1
Lost Hills U.S.A. 128 D4
Lost Trail Pass U.S.A. 126 E3
Lostwithiel U.K. 49 C8
Los Vidrios Mex. 129 G6
Los Vilos Chile 144 B4
Lot r. France 56 E4
Lota Chile 144 B5
Loţfābād Turkm. 88 E2
Lothringen reg. France see Lorraine
Lotikipi Plain Kenya/South Sudan 98 D3
Loto Dem. Rep. Congo 98 C4
Lotsane r. Botswana 101 I2
Lot's Wife i. Japan see Sōfu-gan
Lotta r. Fin./Russia 44 Q2
also known as Lutto
Lotte Germany 53 H2
Louangnamtha Laos 70 C2
Louangphabang Laos 70 C3
Loubomo Congo see Dolisie
Loudéac France 56 C2
Loudi China 77 F3
Louga Senegal 96 B3
Loughborough U.K. 49 F6
Lougheed Island Canada 119 H2
Loughor r. U.K. 49 C7
Loughrea Ireland 51 D4
Loughton U.K. 49 H7
Louhans France 56 G3
Louisa KY U.S.A. 134 D4
Louisa VA U.S.A. 135 G4
Louisbourg Canada 123 K5
Louisburg Canada see Louisbourg
Louisburgh Ireland 51 C4
Louise Falls Canada 120 G2
Louis-Gentil Morocco see Youssoufia
Louisiade Archipelago is P.N.G. 110 F1
Louisiana U.S.A. 130 F4
Louisiana state U.S.A. 131 F6
Louis Trichardt S. Africa see Makhado
Louisville GA U.S.A. 133 D5
Louisville IL U.S.A. 130 F4
Louisville KY U.S.A. 134 C4
Louisville MS U.S.A. 131 F5
Louisville Ridge sea feature S. Pacific Ocean
150 I8
Louis-XIV, Pointe pt Canada 122 F3
Loukhi Russia 44 R3
Loukoléla Congo 98 B4
Loukouo Congo 97 E5
Loulé Port. 57 B5
Loum Cameroon 96 D4
Louny Czechia 47 N5
Loup r. U.S.A. 130 D3
Loups Marins, Lacs des lakes Canada
122 G2
Loups Marins, Petit lac des l. Canada
123 G2
Lourdes Canada 123 K4
Lourdes France 56 D5
Lourenço Marques Moz. see Maputo
Lousã Port. 57 B3
Loushan China 74 C3
Loushanguan China see Tongzi
Louth Australia 112 B3
Louth U.K. 48 G5
Loutra Aidipsou Greece 59 J5
Louvain Belgium see Leuven
Louviers France 52 B5
Louwater-Suid Namibia 100 C2
Louwsburg S. Africa 101 J4
Lövånger Sweden 44 L4
Lovat' r. Russia 42 F4
Lovech Bulg. 59 K3
Lovell U.S.A. 135 J1
Lovelock U.S.A. 128 D1
Lovendegem Belgium 52 D3
Lovers Leap mt. U.S.A. 134 E5
Loviisa Fin. 45 O6
Lovington U.S.A. 131 C5
Lovozero Russia 42 G1
Lóvua Lunda Norte Angola 99 C4
Lóvua Moxico Angola 99 C5
Low, Cape Canada 119 J3
Lowa Dem. Rep. Congo 98 C4
Lowa r. Dem. Rep. Congo 98 C4
Lowarai Pass Pak. 89 H3
Lowell IN U.S.A. 134 B3
Lowell MA U.S.A. 135 J2
Lower Arrow Lake Canada 120 G5
Lower California pen. Mex. see
Baja California
Lower Glenelg National Park Australia
111 C8
Lower Granite Gorge U.S.A. 129 G4
Lower Hutt N.Z. 113 E5
Lower Laberge Canada 120 C2
Lower Lake U.S.A. 128 B2
Lower Lough Erne l. U.K. 51 E3
Lower Post Canada 120 D3
Lower Red Lake U.S.A. 130 E2
Lower Saxony land Germany see
Niedersachsen
Lower Tunguska r. Russia see
Nizhnyaya Tunguska
Lower Zambezi National Park Zambia
99 C5
Lowestoft U.K. 49 I6
Łowicz Poland 47 Q4
Low Island Kiribati see Starbuck Island
Lowrah, Hāmūn-e dry lake Afgh./Pak. see
Lora, Hāmūn-i-
Lowther Hills U.K. 50 F5
Lowville U.S.A. 135 H2
Loxstedt Germany 53 I1

Maghâgha Egypt see Maghāghah
Maghāghah Egypt 90 C5
Maghama Mauritania 96 B3
Maghâra, Gebel hill Egypt see Magharah, Jabal
Magharah, Jabal hill Egypt 85 A4
Maghera U.K. 51 F3
Magherafelt U.K. 51 F3
Maghnia Alg. 57 F6
Maghull U.K. 48 E5
Magilligan Point U.K. 51 F2
Magma U.S.A. 129 H5
Magna Grande mt. Sicily Italy 58 F6
Magnetic Island Australia 110 D3
Magnetic Passage Australia 110 D3
Magnetity Russia 44 R2
Magnitogorsk Russia 64 G4
Magnolia AR U.S.A. 131 E5
Magnolia MS U.S.A. 131 F6
Magny-en-Vexin France 52 B5
Mago Russia 74 F1
Màgoé Moz. 99 D5
Magog Canada 135 I1
Mago National Park Eth. 98 D3
Magosa Cyprus see Famagusta
Magpie r. Canada 123 I4
Magpie, Lac l. Canada 123 I4
Magta' Lahjar Mauritania 96 B3
Magu, Chashmeh-ye well Iran 88 E3
Magu, Khrebet mts Russia 74 E1
Maguan China 76 E4
Magude Moz. 101 K3
Magueyal Mex. 131 C7
Magura Bangl. 83 G5
Maguse Lake Canada 121 M2
Magway Myanmar see Magwe
Magwe Myanmar 70 A2
Magyar Köztársaság country Europe see Hungary
Magyichaung Myanmar 70 A2
Mahābād Iran 88 B2
Mahabharat Range mts Nepal 83 F4
Mahaboobnagar India see Mahbubnagar
Mahad India 84 B2
Mahadeo Hills India 82 D5
Mahaffey U.S.A. 135 F3
Mahajan India 82 C3
Mahajanga Madag. 99 E5
Mahakam r. Indon. 68 F7
Mahalapye Botswana 101 H2
Mahale Mountains National Park Tanz. 99 C4
Mahalevona Madag. 99 E5
Maḥallāt Iran 88 C3
Māhān Iran 88 E4
Mahanadi r. India 84 E1
Mahanoro Madag. 99 E5
Maharashtra state India 84 B2
Maha Oya Sri Lanka 84 D5
Maha Sarakham Thai. 70 C3
Mahasham, Wâdi el watercourse Egypt see Muhashsham, Wādī al
Mahaxai Laos 70 D3
Mahbubabad India 84 D2
Mahbubnagar India 84 C2
Mahd adh Dhahab Saudi Arabia 86 F5
Mahdia Alg. 57 G6
Mahdia Guyana 143 G2
Mahdia Tunisia 58 D7
Mahdūm Syria 85 C1
Mahe China 76 E1
Mahé i. Seychelles 149 L6
Mahendragiri mt. India 84 E2
Mahendranagar Nepal 82 E3
Mahenge Tanz. 99 D4
Mahesana India 82 C5
Mahi r. India 82 C5
Mahia Peninsula N.Z. 113 F4
Mahikeng S. Africa 101 G3
Mahilyow Belarus 43 F5
Mahim India 84 B2
Māhīrūd Iran 89 F3
Mahjān Iran 88 D4
Mahlabatini S. Africa 101 J5
Mahlsdorf Germany 53 L2
Maḥmūdābād Iran 88 D2
Maḥmūd-e 'Erāqī Afgh. see Maḥmūd-e Rāqī
Maḥmūd-e Rāqī Afgh. 89 H3
Mahnomen U.S.A. 130 D2
Maho Sri Lanka 84 D5
Mahoba India 82 D4
Maholi India 82 E4
Mahón Spain see Maó
Mahony Lake Canada 120 E1
Mahrauni India 82 D4
Mahrès Tunisia 58 D7
Mahsana India see Mahesana
Mahudaung mts Myanmar 70 A2
Māhukona U.S.A. 127 [inset]
Mahur India 84 C2
Mahuva India 82 B5
Mahwa India 82 D4
Mahya Dağı mt. Turkey 59 L4
Mai i. Vanuatu see Émaé
Maiaia Moz. see Nacala
Maibong India 70 A1
Maicao Col. 142 D1
Maicasagi r. Canada 122 F4
Maicasagi, Lac l. Canada 122 F4
Maichen China 77 F4
Maīdān Shahr Afgh. 89 H3
Maidenhead U.K. 49 G7
Maidstone Canada 121 I4
Maidstone U.K. 49 H7
Maiduguri Nigeria 97 E3
Mai Gudo mt. Eth. 98 D3
Maigue r. Ireland 51 D5
Maihar India 82 E4
Maiji Shan mt. China 76 E1
Maikala Range hills India 82 E5
Maiko r. Dem. Rep. Congo 98 C3
Maiko, Parc National de la nat. park Dem. Rep. Congo 98 C4
Mailan Hill mt. India 83 E5
Mailly-le-Camp France 52 E6
Mailsi Pak. 89 I4
Maïmanah Afgh. 89 G3
Main r. Germany 53 I4
Main r. U.K. 51 F3
Main Brook Canada 123 L4
Mainburg Germany 53 L6
Main Channel lake channel Canada 134 E1
Maindargi India 84 C2
Mai-Ndombe, Lac l. Dem. Rep. Congo 98 B4
Main-Donau-Kanal canal Germany 53 K5
Maindong China see Coqên
Main Duck Island Canada 135 G2
Maine state U.S.A. 135 K1
Maine, Gulf of Canada/U.S.A. 135 K2
Maine Hanarí, Cerro hill Col. 142 D4
Maïné-Soroa Niger 96 E3
Maingkaing Myanmar 70 A1
Maingkwan Myanmar 70 B1
Maingy Island Myanmar 71 B4
Mainhardt Germany 53 J5
Mainkung China 76 C2
Mainland i. Scotland U.K. 50 F1
Mainland i. Scotland U.K. 50 [inset]
Mainleus Germany 53 L4
Mainoru Australia 108 F3
Mainpat reg. India 83 E5
Mainpuri India 82 D4
Main Range National Park Australia 112 F2
Maintenon France 52 B6
Maintirano Madag. 99 E5
Mainz Germany 53 I4
Maio i. Cape Verde 96 [inset]
Maipú Arg. 144 E5
Maish Vaya U.S.A. 129 G5
Maiskhal Island Bangl. 83 G5
Maisons-Laffitte France 52 C6
Maitengwe Botswana 99 C6
Maitland N.S.W. Australia 112 E4
Maitland S.A. Australia 111 B7
Maitland r. Australia 108 B5
Maitri research station Antarctica 152 C2
Maiwo i. Vanuatu see Maéwo
Maiyu, Mount hill Australia 108 E4
Maíz, Islas del is Nicaragua 137 H6
Maizar Pak. 89 H3
Maizuru Japan 75 D6
Majdel Aanjar tourist site Lebanon 85 B3
Majella, Parco Nazionale della nat. park Italy 58 F3
Majene Indon. 68 F7
Majestic U.S.A. 134 D5
Majḥūd well Saudi Arabia 88 C6
Majī Eth. 98 D3
Majiang Guangxi China 77 F4
Majiang Guizhou China 76 E3
Majiazi China 74 B2
Majnābād Iran 89 F3
Majōl country N. Pacific Ocean see Marshall Islands
Major, Puig mt. Spain 57 H4
Majorca i. Spain 57 H4
Mājro atoll Marshall Is see Majuro
Majunga Madag. see Mahajanga
Majuro atoll Marshall Is 150 H5
Majwemasweu S. Africa 101 H5
Makabana Congo 98 B4
Makale Indon. 69 F7

Makalu mt. China/Nepal 83 F4
5th highest mountain in Asia and the world.

Makalu Barun National Park Nepal 83 F4
Makanpur India 82 E4
Makanshy Kazakh. 80 F2
Makari Mountain National Park Tanz. see Mahale Mountains National Park
Makarov Russia 74 F2
Makarov Basin sea feature Arctic Ocean 153 B1
Makarska Croatia 58 G3
Makarwal Pak. 89 H3
Makar'ye Russia 42 K4
Makar'yev Russia 42 I4
Makasar, Selat strait Indon. see Makassar, Selat
Makassar Indon. 68 F8
Makassar, Selat str. Indon. 68 F7
Makassar Strait Indon. see Makassar, Selat
Makat Kazakh. 78 E2
Makatini Flats lowland S. Africa 101 K4
Makedonija country Europe see Macedonia
Makeni Sierra Leone 96 B4
Makete Tanz. 99 D4
Makeyevka Ukr. see Makiyivka
Makgadikgadi depr. Botswana 99 C6
Makgadikgadi Pans National Park Botswana 99 C6
Makhachkala Russia 91 G2
Makhad Pak. 89 H3
Makhado S. Africa 101 I2
Makhāzin, Kathīb al des. Egypt 85 A4
Makhâzin, Kathîb el des. Egypt see Makhāzin, Kathīb al
Makhazine, Barrage El dam Morocco 57 D6
Makhmūr/Mexmûr Iraq 91 F4
Makhtal India 84 C2
Makin atoll Kiribati see Butaritari
Makindu Kenya 98 D4
Makinsk Kazakh. 79 G1
Makira i. Solomon Is 107 G3
Makiyivka Ukr. 43 H6
Makkah Saudi Arabia see Mecca
Makkovik Canada 123 K3
Makkovik, Cape Canada 123 K3
Makkum Neth. 52 F1
Makó Hungary 59 I1
Makokou Gabon 98 B3
Makopong Botswana 100 F3
Makotipoko Congo 97 E5
Makran reg. Iran/Pak. 89 F5
Makrana India 82 C4
Makran Coast Range mts Pak. 89 F5
Makri India 84 D2
Maksatikha Russia 42 G4
Maksi India 82 D5
Maksimovka Russia 74 E3
Maksotag Iran 89 F4
Maksudangarh India 82 D5
Mākū Iran 88 B2
Makunguwiro Tanz. 99 D5
Makurdi Nigeria 96 D4
Makwassie S. Africa 101 G4
Mal India 83 G4
Mala Ireland see Mallow
Mala i. Solomon Is see Malaita
Malå Sweden 44 K4
Mala, Punta pt Panama 137 H7
Malabar Coast India 84 B3

Malabo Equat. Guinea 96 D4
Capital of Equatorial Guinea.

Malaca Spain see Málaga
Malacca Malaysia see Melaka
Malacca, Strait of Indon./Malaysia 71 B6
Malad City U.S.A. 126 E4
Maladzyechna Belarus 45 O9
Malá Fatra, Národný park nat. park Slovakia 47 Q6
Málaga Spain 57 D5
Malaga U.S.A. 131 B5
Malagasy Republic country Africa see Madagascar
Málainn Mhóir Ireland 51 D3
Malaita i. Solomon Is 107 G2
Malakal South Sudan 86 D8
Malakanagiri India see Malkangiri
Malakheti Nepal 82 E3
Malakula i. Vanuatu 107 G3
Malan, Ras pt Pak. 89 G5
Malang Indon. 68 E8
Malangana Nepal see Malangwa
Malange Angola see Malanje
Malangwa Nepal 83 F4
Malanje Angola 99 B4
Malappuram India 84 C4
Mälaren l. Sweden 45 J7
Malargüe Arg. 144 C5
Malartic Canada 122 F4
Malaspina Glacier U.S.A. 120 A3
Malatya Turkey 90 E3
Malavalli India 84 C3
Malawi country Africa 99 D5
Malawi, Lake Africa see Nyasa, Lake
Malawi National Park Zambia see Nyika National Park
Malaya pen. Malaysia see Peninsular Malaysia
Malaya Pera Russia 42 L2
Malaya Vishera Russia 42 G4
Malaybalay Phil. 69 H5
Malāyer Iran 88 C3
Malay Peninsula Asia 71 B4
Malay Reef Australia 110 E3
Malaysia country Asia 68 D5
Malaysia, Semenanjung pen. Malaysia see Peninsular Malaysia
Malazgirt Turkey 91 F3
Malbon Australia 110 C4
Malbork Poland 47 Q3
Malborn Germany 52 G5
Malchin Germany 47 N4
Malcolm (abandoned) Australia 109 C7
Malcolm, Point Australia 109 C8
Malcolm Island Myanmar 71 B5
Maldegem Belgium 52 D3
Malden U.S.A. 131 F4
Malden Island Kiribati 151 J6
Maldives country Indian Ocean 81 D10
Maldon Australia 112 B6
Maldon U.K. 49 H7
Maldonado Uruguay 144 F4

Male Maldives 81 D11
Capital of the Maldives.

Maleas, Akra pt Greece see Maleas, Akrotirio
Maleas, Akrotirio pt Greece 59 J6
Male Atholhu Maldives 81 D11
Male Atoll Maldives see Male Atholhu
Malebogo S. Africa 101 G5
Malegaon Mahar. India 84 B1
Malegaon Mahar. India 84 C2
Malek, Chāh-e well Iran 88 D3
Malé Karpaty hills Slovakia 47 P6
Malek Mīrzā, Chāh-e well Iran 88 D4
Malek Siāh Kōh mt. Afgh. 89 F4
Malele Dem. Rep. Congo 99 B4
Maler Kotla India 82 C3
Maleševski Planini mts Bulg./Macedonia 59 J4
Malgobek Russia 91 G2
Malgomaj l. Sweden 44 J4
Malḥa, Naqb mt. Egypt see Māliḥah, Naqb
Malhada Brazil 145 C1
Malheur r. U.S.A. 126 D3
Malheur Lake U.S.A. 126 D4
Mali country Africa 96 C3
Mali Dem. Rep. Congo 98 C4
Mali Guinea 96 B3
Maliana East Timor 108 D2
Malianjing China 80 I3
Māliḥah, Naqb mt. Egypt 85 A5
Malik Naro mt. Pak. 89 F4
Mali Kyun i. Myanmar 71 B4
Malili Indon. 69 G7
Malin Ukr. see Malyn
Malindi Kenya 98 E4
Malines Belgium see Mechelen
Malin Head hd Ireland 51 E2
Malipo China 76 E4
Mali Raginac mt. Croatia 58 F2
Malita Phil. 69 H5
Malka r. Russia 91 G2
Malkangiri India 84 D2
Malkapur India 84 B2
Malkara Turkey 59 L4
Mal'kavichy Belarus 45 O10
Malko Tarnovo Bulg. 59 L4
Mallacoota Australia 112 D6
Mallacoota Inlet b. Australia 112 D6
Mallaig U.K. 50 D4
Mallani reg. India 89 H5
Mallawī Egypt 90 C6
Mallee Cliffs National Park Australia 111 C7
Mallery Lake Canada 121 L1
Mallet Brazil 145 A4
Mallorca i. Spain see Majorca
Mallow Ireland 51 D5
Mallowa Well Australia 108 D5
Mallwyd U.K. 49 D6
Malm Norway 44 G4
Malmberget Sweden 44 L3
Malmedy Belgium 52 G4
Malmesbury S. Africa 100 D7
Malmesbury U.K. 49 E7
Malmö Sweden 45 H9
Malmyzh Russia 42 K4
Maloca Brazil 143 G3
Malone U.S.A. 135 H1
Malonje mt. Tanz. 99 D4
Maloshuyka Russia 42 H3
Måløy Norway 44 D6
Maloyaroslavets Russia 43 H5
Malozemel'skaya Tundra lowland Russia 42 K2
Malpelo, Isla de i. N. Pacific Ocean 137 H8
Malprabha r. India 84 C2
Malta country Europe 58 F7
Malta Latvia 45 O8
Malta ID U.S.A. 126 E4
Malta MT U.S.A. 126 G2
Malta Channel Italy/Malta 58 F6
Maltahöhe Namibia 100 C3
Maltby U.K. 48 F5
Maltby le Marsh U.K. 48 H5
Malton U.K. 48 G4
Maluku is Indon. see Moluccas
Maluku, Laut sea Indon. 69 H6
Ma'lūlā, Jabal mts Syria 85 C3
Malung Sweden 45 H6
Maluti Mountains Lesotho 101 I5
Malu'u Solomon Is 107 G2
Malvan India 84 B2
Malvasia Greece see Monemvasia
Malvern U.K. see Great Malvern
Malvern U.S.A. 131 E5
Malvérnia Moz. see Chicualacuala
Malvinas, Islas terr. S. Atlantic Ocean see Falkland Islands
Malyn Ukr. 43 F6
Malyy Anyuy r. Russia 65 R3
Malyye Derbety Russia 43 J7
Malyy Kavkaz mts Asia see Lesser Caucasus
Malyy Lyakhovskiy, Ostrov i. Russia 65 P2
Mamadysh Russia 42 K5
Mamafubedu S. Africa 101 I4
Mamatān Nāwēr l. Afgh. 89 G4
Mamba China 76 B2
Mambaí Brazil 145 B1
Mambasa Dem. Rep. Congo 98 C3
Mamburao Phil. 69 G4
Mamelodi S. Africa 101 I3
Mamfe Cameroon 96 D4
Mamit India 83 H5
Mammoth U.S.A. 129 H5
Mammoth Cave National Park U.S.A. 134 B5
Mammoth Reservoir U.S.A. 128 D3
Mamonas Brazil 145 C1
Mamoré r. Bol./Brazil 142 E6
Mamou Guinea 96 B3
Mampikony Madag. 99 E5
Mampong Ghana 96 C4
Mamuju Indon. 68 F7
Mamuno Botswana 100 E2
Man Côte d'Ivoire 96 C4
Man India 84 B2
Man r. India 84 B2
Man U.S.A. 134 E5

Man, Isle of terr. Irish Sea 48 C4
United Kingdom Crown Dependency.

Manacapuru Brazil 142 F4
Manacor Spain 57 H4
Manado Indon. 69 G6

Managua Nicaragua 137 G6
Capital of Nicaragua.

Manakara Madag. 99 E6
Manakau mt. N.Z. 113 D6
Manākhah Yemen 86 F6

Manama Bahrain 88 C5
Capital of Bahrain.

Manamadurai India 84 C4
Mana Maroka National Park S. Africa 101 H5
Manamelkudi India 84 C4
Manam Island P.N.G. 69 L7
Mananara Avaratra Madag. 99 E5
Manangoora Australia 110 B3
Mananjary Madag. 99 E6
Manantali, Lac de l. Mali 96 B3
Manantenina Madag. 99 E6
Mana Pass China/India 82 D3
Mana Pools National Park Zimbabwe 99 C5

Manapouri, Lake N.Z. 113 A7
Deepest lake in Oceania.

Manasa India 82 C4
Manas He r. China 80 G2
Manas Hu l. China 80 G2
Manāṣīr reg. U.A.E. 88 D6

Manaslu mt. Nepal 83 F3
8th highest mountain in Asia and the world.

Manas National Park nature res. Bhutan 83 G4
Manassas U.S.A. 135 G4
Manastir Macedonia see Bitola
Man-aung Myanmar 70 A3
Man-aung Kyun Myanmar 70 A3
Manaus Brazil 142 F4
Manavgat Turkey 90 C3
Manbazar India 83 F5
Manbij Syria 85 C1
Manby U.K. 48 H5
Mancelona U.S.A. 134 C1
Manchar India 84 B2
Manchester U.K. 48 E5
Manchester CT U.S.A. 135 I3
Manchester IA U.S.A. 130 F3
Manchester KY U.S.A. 134 D5
Manchester MD U.S.A. 135 G4
Manchester MI U.S.A. 134 C2
Manchester NH U.S.A. 135 J2
Manchester OH U.S.A. 134 D4
Manchester TN U.S.A. 132 C5
Manchester VT U.S.A. 135 I2
Mancılık Turkey 90 E3
Mand Pak. 89 F5
Mand, Rūd-e r. Iran 88 C4
Manda Tanz. 99 D4
Manda, Jabal mt. South Sudan 97 F4
Manda, Parc National de nat. park Chad 97 E4
Mandabe Madag. 99 E6
Mandai Sing. 71 [inset]
Mandal Norway 45 E7

Mandala, Puncak mt. Indon. 69 K7
3rd highest mountain in Oceania.

Mandalay Myanmar 70 B2
Mandale Myanmar see Mandalay
Mandalgovĭ Mongolia 72 J3
Mandalī Iraq 91 G4
Mandal-Ovoo Mongolia 72 I4
Mandalt China 73 K4
Mandan U.S.A. 130 C2
Mandas Sardinia Italy 58 C5
Mandasa India 84 E2
Mandasor India see Mandsaur
Mandav Hills India 82 B5
Mandera Kenya 98 E3
Manderfield U.S.A. 129 G2
Manderscheid Germany 52 G4
Mandeville Jamaica 137 I5
Mandeville N.Z. 113 B7
Mandha India 82 B4
Mandhoúdhion Greece see Mantoudi
Mandi India 82 D3
Mandiana Guinea 96 C3
Mandié Moz. 99 D5
Mandini S. Africa 101 J5
Mandira Dam India 83 F5
Mandla India 82 E5
Mandleshwar India 82 C5
Mandrael India 82 D4
Mandritsara Madag. 99 E5
Mandsaur India 82 C4
Mandurah Australia 109 A8
Manduria Italy 58 G4
Mandvi India 82 B5
Mandya India 84 C3
Manerbio Italy 58 D2
Manevychi Ukr. 43 E6
Manfalūṭ Egypt 90 C6
Manfredonia Italy 58 F4
Manfredonia, Golfo di g. Italy 58 G4
Manga Brazil 145 C1
Manga Burkina Faso 96 C3
Mangabeiras, Serra das hills Brazil 143 I6
Mangai Dem. Rep. Congo 98 B4
Mangaia i. Cook Is 151 J7
Mangakino N.Z. 113 E4
Mangalagiri India 84 D2
Mangaldai India see Mangaldoi
Mangaldoi India 70 A1
Mangalia Romania 59 M3
Mangalmé Chad 97 E3
Mangalore India see Mangaluru
Mangaluru India 84 B3
Mangaon India 84 B2
Mangareva Islands Fr. Polynesia see Gambier, Îles
Mangaung Free State S. Africa 101 H5
Mangaung Free State S. Africa see Bloemfontein
Mangawan India 83 E4
Ma'ngê China see Luqu
Mangea i. Cook Is see Mangaia
Mangghyshlaq Kazakh. see Mangistau
Mangghystaū Kazakh. see Mangistau
Mangghystaū admin. div. Kazakh. see Mangystauskaya Oblast'
Mangghyt Uzbek. see Mang'it
Manghāl Afgh. 89 F3
Manghit Uzbek. see Mang'it
Mangin Range mts Myanmar see Mingin Range
Mangistau Kazakh. 91 H2
Mang'it Uzbek. 80 B3
Mangla Bangl. see Mongla
Mangla China see Mangra
Mangla Pak. 89 I3
Mangnai China 80 H4
Mangochi Malawi 99 D5
Mangoky r. Madag. 99 E6
Mangole i. Indon. 69 H7
Mangoli India 84 B2
Mangotsfield U.K. 49 E7
Mangqystaū Shyghanaghy b. Kazakh. see Mangystau, Zaliv
Mangra China 76 D1
Mangrol India 82 B5
Mangrul India 84 C1
Mangshi China 76 C3
Mangualde Port. 57 C3
Manguéni, Plateau du Niger 96 E2
Mangui China 74 A2
Mangula Zimbabwe see Mhangura
Mangum U.S.A. 131 D5
Manguri Australia 109 F7
Mangyshlak Kazakh. see Mangistau
Mangyshlak Oblast admin. div. Kazakh. see Mangystauskaya Oblast'
Mangyshlakskaya Oblast' admin. div. Kazakh. see Mangystauskaya Oblast'
Mangystau Kazakh. see Mangistau
Mangystau, Poluostrov pen. Kazakh. 91 H1
Mangystau, Zaliv b. Kazakh. 91 H1
Mangystauskaya Oblast' admin. div. Kazakh. 91 I2
Manhā Brazil 145 B1
Manhattan U.S.A. 130 D4
Manhica Moz. 101 K3
Manhoca Moz. 101 K4
Manhuaçu Brazil 145 C3
Manhuaçu r. Brazil 145 C2
Mani China 83 F2
Mania r. Madag. 99 E5
Maniago Italy 58 E1
Manicouagan Canada 123 H4
Manicouagan r. Canada 123 H4
Manicouagan, Petit Lac l. Canada 123 I3
Manicouagan, Réservoir resr Canada 123 H4
Manic Trois, Réservoir resr Canada 123 H4
Manīfah Saudi Arabia 88 C5
Maniganggo China 76 C2
Manigotagan Canada 121 L5
Manihiki atoll Cook Is 150 J6
Maniitsoq Greenland 119 M3
Manikchhari Bangl. 83 H5
Manikgarh India see Rajura

Manila Phil. 69 G4
Capital of the Philippines.

Manila U.S.A. 126 F4
Manildra Australia 112 D4
Manilla Australia 112 E3
Maningrida Australia 108 F3
Manipur India see Imphal
Manipur state India 83 H4
Manisa Turkey 59 L5
Manistee U.S.A. 134 B1
Manistee r. U.S.A. 134 B1
Manistique U.S.A. 132 C2
Manitoba prov. Canada 121 L4
Manitoba, Lake Canada 121 L5
Manito Lake Canada 121 I4
Manitou Canada 121 L5
Manitou, Lake U.S.A. 134 B3
Manitou Beach U.S.A. 135 G2
Manitou Falls Canada 121 M5
Manitou Islands U.S.A. 134 B1
Manitoulin Island Canada 122 E5
Manitouwadge Canada 122 D4
Manitowoc U.S.A. 134 B1
Maniwaki Canada 122 G5
Manizales Col. 142 C2
Manja Madag. 99 E6
Manjarabad India 84 B3
Manjeri India 84 C4
Manjhand Pak. 89 H5
Manjhi India 83 F4
Manjra r. India 84 C2
Man Kabat Myanmar 70 B1
Mankaiana Swaziland see Mankayane
Mankato KS U.S.A. 130 D4
Mankato MN U.S.A. 130 E2
Mankayane Swaziland 101 J4
Mankera Pak. 89 H4
Mankono Côte d'Ivoire 96 C4
Mankota Canada 121 J5
Manlay Mongolia 72 J4
Manley Hot Springs U.S.A. 118 C3
Manmad India 84 B1
Mann r. Australia 108 F3
Mann, Mount Australia 109 E6
Manna Indon. 68 C7
Man Na Myanmar 70 B2
Mannahill Australia 111 B7
Mannar Sri Lanka 84 C4
Mannar, Gulf of India/Sri Lanka 84 C4
Manneru r. India 84 D3
Mannessier, Lac l. Canada 123 H3
Mannheim Germany 53 I5
Mannicolo Islands Solomon Is see Vanikoro Islands
Manning r. Australia 112 F3
Manning Canada 120 G3
Manning U.S.A. 133 D5
Mannington U.S.A. 134 E4
Manningtree U.K. 49 I7
Mann Ranges mts Australia 109 E6
Mannsville KY U.S.A. 134 C5
Mannsville NY U.S.A. 135 G2
Mannu, Capo c. Sardinia Italy 58 C4
Mannville Canada 121 I4
Manoel Ribas Brazil 145 A4
Manoel Vitorino Brazil 145 C1
Man-of-War Rocks is U.S.A. see Gardner Pinnacles
Manoharpur India 82 D4
Manohar Thana India 82 D4
Manokotak U.S.A. 118 C4
Manokwari Indon. 69 I7
Manoron Myanmar 71 B5
Manosque France 56 G5
Manouane r. Canada 123 H4
Manouane, Lac l. Canada 123 H4
Manouba Tunisia 58 D6
Manovo-Gounda Saint Floris, Parc National du nat. park Cent. Afr. Rep. 98 C3
Man Pan Myanmar 70 B2
Manp'o N. Korea 74 B4
Manra i. Kiribati 107 I2
Manresa Spain 57 G3
Mansa Gujarat India 82 C5
Mansa Punjab India 82 C3
Mansa Zambia 99 C5
Mansakonko Gambia 96 B3
Man Sam Myanmar 70 B2
Mansehra Pak. 87 L3
Mansel Island Canada 119 K3
Mansfield Australia 112 C6
Mansfield U.K. 49 F5
Mansfield LA U.S.A. 131 E5
Mansfield OH U.S.A. 134 D3
Mansfield PA U.S.A. 135 G3
Mansfield, Mount U.S.A. 135 I1
Man Si Myanmar 70 B1
Mansi Myanmar 70 A1
Manso r. Brazil see Mortes, Rio das
Manta Ecuador 142 B4
Mantaro r. Peru 142 D6
Manteca U.S.A. 128 C3
Mantena Brazil 145 C2
Manteo U.S.A. 132 F5
Mantes-la-Jolie France 52 B6
Mantiqueira, Serra da mts Brazil 145 B3
Manton U.S.A. 134 C1
Mantoudi Greece 59 J5
Mantova Italy see Mantua
Mäntsälä Fin. 45 N6
Mänttä Fin. 44 N5
Mantua Cuba 133 C8
Mantua Italy 58 D2
Mantuan Downs Australia 110 D5
Manturovo Russia 42 J4
Mäntyharju Fin. 45 O6
Mäntyjärvi Fin. 44 O3
Manú Peru 142 D6
Manu, Parque Nacional del nat. park Peru 142 D6

Manuae atoll Fr. Polynesia 151 J7
Manu'a Islands American Samoa 107 I3
Manuelzinho Brazil 143 H5
Manui i. Indon. 69 G7
Manukau N.Z. 113 E3
Manukau Harbour N.Z. 113 E3
Manunda watercourse Australia 111 B7
Manusela, Taman Nasional nat. park Indon. 69 H7
Manus Island P.N.G. 69 L7
Manvi India 84 C3
Many U.S.A. 131 E6
Manyakatana S. Africa 101 J3
Manyana Botswana 101 G3
Manyas Turkey 59 L4
Manyas Gölü l. Turkey see Kuş Gölü
Many Island Lake Canada 121 I5
Manyoni Tanz. 99 D4
Manzai Pak. 89 H3
Manzanares Spain 57 E4
Manzanillo Cuba 137 I4
Manzanillo Mex. 136 D5
Manzhouli China 73 L3
Manzini Swaziland 101 J4
Mao Chad 97 E3
Maó Spain 57 I4
Maoba Guizhou China 76 E3
Maoba Hubei China 77 F2
Maobi Tou c. Taiwan 77 I4
Mao'ergai China 76 D1
Maoke, Pegunungan mts Indon. 69 J7
Maokeng S. Africa 101 H4
Maokui Shan mt. China 74 A4
Maolin China 74 A4
Maoming China 77 F4
Ma On Shan hill H.K. China 77 [inset]
Maopi T'ou c. Taiwan see Maobi Tou
Maopora i. Indon. 108 D1
Maotou Shan mt. China 76 D3
Mapai Moz. 101 J2
Mapam Yumco l. China 83 E3
Mapanza Zambia 99 C5
Maphodi S. Africa 101 G6
Mapimí Mex. 131 C7
Mapimí, Bolsón de des. Mex. 131 B7
Mapinhane Moz. 101 L2
Mapiri Bol. 142 E7
Maple r. MI U.S.A. 134 C2
Maple r. ND U.S.A. 130 D2
Maple Creek Canada 121 I5
Maple Heights U.S.A. 134 E3
Maple Peak U.S.A. 129 I5
Mapmaker Seamounts sea feature N. Pacific Ocean 150 H4
Mapoon Australia 110 C1
Mapor i. Indon. 71 D7
Mapoteng Lesotho 101 H5
Maprik P.N.G. 69 K7
Mapuera r. Brazil 143 G4
Mapulanguene Moz. 101 K3
Mapungubwe National Park S. Africa 101 I2

▶Maputo Moz. 101 K3
Capital of Mozambique.

Maputo prov. Moz. 101 K3
Maputo r. Moz./S. Africa 101 K4
Maputo, Baía de b. Moz. 101 K4
Maputsoe Lesotho 101 H5
Maqanshy Kazakh. see Makanshy
Maqar an Na'am well Iraq 91 F5
Maqat Kazakh. see Makat
Maqên China 76 D1
Maqên Kangri mt. China 76 C1
Maqnā Saudi Arabia 90 D5
Maqṭeïr reg. Mauritania 96 B2
Maqu China 76 D1
Ma Qu r. China see Yellow River
Maquan He r. China see Damqoq Zangbo
Maquela do Zombo Angola 99 B4
Maquinchao Arg. 144 C6
Mar r. Pak. 89 G5
Mar, Serra do mts Rio de Janeiro/São Paulo Brazil 145 B3
Mar, Serra do mts Rio Grande do Sul/Santa Catarina Brazil 145 A5
Mara r. Canada 121 I1
Mara India 83 E5
Mara S. Africa 101 I2
Maraã Brazil 142 E4
Marabá Brazil 143 I5
Maraboon, Lake resr Australia 110 E4
Maracá, Ilha de i. Brazil 143 H3
Maracaibo Venez. 142 D1
Maracaibo, Lago de Venez. see Maracaibo, Lake
Maracaibo, Lake Venez. 142 D2
Maracaju Brazil 144 E2
Maracaju, Serra de hills Brazil 144 E2
Maracanda Uzbek. see Samarqand
Maracás Brazil 145 C1
Maracás, Chapada de hills Brazil 145 C1
Maracay Venez. 142 E1
Marādah Libya 97 E2
Maradi Niger 96 D3
Marāgheh Iran 88 B2
Marahuaca, Cerro mt. Venez. 142 E3
Marajó, Baía de est. Brazil 143 I4
Marajó, Ilha de i. Brazil 143 H4
Marakele National Park S. Africa 101 H3
Maralal Kenya 98 D3
Maralbashi China see Bachu
Maralinga Australia 109 E7
Maralwexi China see Bachu
Maramasike i. Solomon Is 107 G2
Maramba Zambia see Livingstone
Marambio research station Antarctica 152 A2
Maran Malaysia 71 C7
Marana U.S.A. 129 H5
Marand Iran 88 B2
Marandellas Zimbabwe see Marondera
Marang Malaysia 71 C6
Marang Myanmar 71 B5
Maranhão r. Brazil 145 A1
Maranoa r. Australia 112 D1
Marañón r. Peru 142 D4
Marão Moz. 101 L3
Marão mt. Port. 57 C3
Mara Rosa Brazil 145 A1
Maraş Turkey see Kahramanmaraş
Marathon Canada 122 D4
Marathon FL U.S.A. 133 D7
Marathon NY U.S.A. 135 G2
Marathon TX U.S.A. 131 C6
Maratua i. Indon. 68 F6
Maraú Brazil 145 D1
Maravillas Creek watercourse U.S.A. 131 C6
Marbella Spain 57 D5
Marble Bar Australia 108 B5
Marble Canyon U.S.A. 129 H3
Marble Canyon gorge U.S.A. 129 H3
Marble Hall S. Africa 101 I3
Marble Hill U.S.A. 131 F4
Marble Island Canada 121 N2
Marbul Pass India 82 C2
Marburg Germany 53 I4
Marburg S. Africa 101 J6
Marburg Slovenia see Maribor
Marca, Ponta do pt Angola 99 B5
Marcali Hungary 58 G1
Marcelino Ramos Brazil 145 A4
March U.K. 49 H6
Marche reg. France 56 E3
Marche-en-Famenne Belgium 52 F4
Marchena Spain 57 D5
Marchinbar Island Australia 110 B1
Mar Chiquita, Laguna l. Arg. 144 D4
Marchtrenk Austria 47 O6
Marco U.S.A. 133 D7
Marcoing France 52 D4
Marcona Peru 142 C7
Marcopeet Islands Canada 122 F2
Marcus Baker, Mount U.S.A. 118 D3
Marcy, Mount U.S.A. 135 I1
Mardan Pak. 89 I3
Mar del Plata Arg. 144 E5
Mardīān Afgh. 89 G2
Mardin Turkey 91 F3
Maré i. New Caledonia 107 G4
Maree, Loch l. U.K. 50 D3
Mareh Ḥoseynābād Iran 89 E5
Marengo IA U.S.A. 130 E3
Marengo IN U.S.A. 134 B4
Marengo OH U.S.A. 134 D3
Marevo Russia 42 G4
Marfa U.S.A. 131 B6
Marganets Ukr. see Marhanets'
Margao India 84 B3
Margaret r. Australia 108 D4
Margaret watercourse Australia 111 B6
Margaret, Mount hill Australia 108 B5
Margaret Lake Alta Canada 120 H3
Margaret Lake N.W.T. Canada 120 G1
Margaret River Australia 109 A8
Margaretville U.S.A. 135 H2
Margarita, Isla de i. Venez. 142 F1
Margaritovo Russia 74 D4
Margate U.K. 49 I7
Margeride, Monts de la mts France 56 F4
Margherita, Lake Eth. see Abaya, Lake

▶Margherita Peak Dem. Rep. Congo/Uganda 98 C3
3rd highest mountain in Africa.

Marghilon Uzbek. see Marg'ilon
Marg'ilon Uzbek. 80 D3
Mārgō, Dasht-e des. Afgh. 89 F4
Mārgō, Dasht-i- des. Afgh. see Mārgō, Dasht-e
Margog Caka l. China 83 F2
Margraten Neth. 52 F4
Marguerite Canada 120 F4
Marguerite, Pic mt. Dem. Rep. Congo/Uganda see Margherita Peak
Marguerite Bay Antarctica 152 L2
Margyang China 83 G3
Marhaj Khalīl Iraq 91 G4
Marhanets' Ukr. 43 G7
Marhoum Alg. 54 D5
Mari Myanmar 70 B1
Maria atoll Fr. Polynesia 151 J7
María Elena Chile 144 C2
Maria Island Australia 110 A2
Maria Island Myanmar 71 B5
Maria Island National Park Australia 111 [inset]
Mariala National Park Australia 111 D5
Mariana Brazil 145 C3
Marianao Cuba 133 D8
Mariana Ridge sea feature N. Pacific Ocean 150 F4

▶Mariana Trench sea feature N. Pacific Ocean 150 F5
Deepest trench in the world.

Mariani India 83 H4
Mariánica, Cordillera mts Spain see Morena, Sierra
Marian Lake Canada 120 G2
Marianna AR U.S.A. 131 F5
Marianna FL U.S.A. 133 C6
Mariano Machado Angola see Ganda
Mariánské Lázně Czechia 53 M5
Marias r. U.S.A. 126 F2
Marías, Islas is Mex. 136 C4

▶Mariato, Punta pt Panama 137 H7
Most southerly point of North America.

Maria van Diemen, Cape N.Z. 113 D2
Ma'rib Yemen 86 G6
Maribor Slovenia 58 F1
Marica r. Bulg. see Maritsa
Maricopa AZ U.S.A. 129 G5
Maricopa CA U.S.A. 128 D4
Maricopa Mountains U.S.A. 129 G5
Maridi South Sudan 97 F4
Marie Byrd Land reg. Antarctica 152 J1
Marie-Galante i. Guadeloupe 137 L5
Mariehamn Fin. 45 K6
Mariembero r. Brazil 145 A1
Marienbad Czechia see Mariánské Lázně
Marienberg Germany 53 N4
Marienburg Poland see Malbork
Marienhafe Germany 53 H1
Mariental Namibia 100 C3
Marienwerder Poland see Kwidzyn
Mariestad Sweden 45 H7
Mariet r. Canada 122 F2
Marietta GA U.S.A. 133 C5
Marietta OH U.S.A. 134 E4
Marietta OK U.S.A. 131 D5
Marignane France 56 G5
Marii, Mys pt Russia 66 G2
Mariinsk Russia 64 J4
Mariinskiy Posad Russia 42 J4
Marijampolė Lith. 45 M9
Marília Brazil 145 A3
Marillana Australia 108 B5
Marimba Angola 99 B4
Marín mt. Pak. 89 G4
Marín Spain 57 B2
Marina U.S.A. 128 C3
Marina di Gioiosa Ionica Italy 58 G5
Mar'ina Gorka Belarus see Mar"ina Horka
Mar"ina Horka Belarus 45 P10
Marinduque i. Phil. 69 G4
Marinette U.S.A. 134 B1
Maringá Brazil 145 A3
Maringa r. Dem. Rep. Congo 98 B3
Marinha Grande Port. 57 B4
Marion AL U.S.A. 133 C5
Marion AR U.S.A. 131 F5
Marion IL U.S.A. 130 F4
Marion IN U.S.A. 134 C3
Marion KS U.S.A. 130 D4
Marion MI U.S.A. 134 C1
Marion NY U.S.A. 135 G2
Marion OH U.S.A. 134 D3
Marion SC U.S.A. 133 E5
Marion VA U.S.A. 134 E5
Marion, Lake U.S.A. 133 D5
Marion Reef Australia 110 F3
Maripa Venez. 142 E2
Mariposa U.S.A. 128 D3
Marisa Indon. 69 G6
Mariscal José Félix Estigarribia Para. 144 D2
Maritime Alps mts France/Italy 56 H4
Maritime Kray admin. div. Russia see Primorskiy Kray
Maritimes, Alpes mts France/Italy see Maritime Alps
Maritsa r. Bulg. 59 L4
also known as Evros (Greece), Marica (Bulgaria), Meriç (Turkey)
Marittime, Alpi mts France/Italy see Maritime Alps
Mariupol' Ukr. 43 H7
Mariusa, Parque Nacional nat. park Venez. 142 F2
Marīvān Iran 88 B3
Marjan Afgh. see Mashōrēy
Marjayoûn Lebanon 85 B3
Marka Somalia 98 E3
Markakala Mali 96 C3
Markam China 76 C2
Markaryd Sweden 45 H8
Markaz-e Sayyidābād Afgh. 89 H3
Markdale Canada 134 E1
Marken S. Africa 101 I2
Markermeer l. Neth. 52 F2
Market Deeping U.K. 49 G6
Market Drayton U.K. 49 E6
Market Harborough U.K. 49 G6
Markethill U.K. 51 F3
Market Weighton U.K. 48 G5
Markha r. Russia 65 M3
Markham Canada 134 F2
Markit China 80 E4
Markkleeberg Germany 53 M3
Markleeville U.S.A. 128 D2
Marklohe Germany 53 J2
Markog Qu r. China 76 D1
Markounda Cent. Afr. Rep. 98 B3
Markovo Russia 65 S3
Markranstädt Germany 53 M3
Marks Russia 43 J6
Marks U.S.A. 131 F5
Marksville U.S.A. 131 E6
Marktheidenfeld Germany 53 J5
Marktredwitz Germany 53 M4
Marl Germany 52 H3
Marla Australia 109 F6
Marlborough Downs hills U.K. 49 F7
Marle France 52 D5
Marlette U.S.A. 134 D2
Marlin U.S.A. 131 D6
Marlinton U.S.A. 134 E4
Marlo Australia 112 D6
Marmagao India 84 B3
Marmande France 56 E4
Marmara, Sea of g. Turkey 59 M4
Marmara Denizi g. Turkey see Marmara, Sea of
Marmara Gölü l. Turkey 59 M5
Marmarica reg. Libya 90 B5
Marmaris Turkey 59 M6
Marmarth U.S.A. 130 C2
Marmet U.S.A. 134 E4
Marmion, Lake salt l. Australia 109 C7
Marmion Lake Canada 121 N5
Marmolada mt. Italy 58 D1
Marne r. France 52 C6
Marne au Rhin, Canal de la France 52 G6
Marne-la-Vallée France 52 C6
Marnitz Germany 53 L1
Maroantsetra Madag. 99 E5
Maroc country Africa see Morocco
Marol Pak. 82 D2
Maroldsweisach Germany 53 K4
Maromokotro mt. Madag. 99 E5
Marondera Zimbabwe 99 D5
Maroochydore Australia 112 F1
Maroonah Australia 109 A5
Maroon Peak U.S.A. 126 G5
Marosvásárhely Romania see Târgu Mureş
Marot Pak. 89 I4
Maroua Cameroon 97 E3
Marovoay Madag. 99 E5
Marqadah Syria 91 F4
Mar Qu r. China see Markog Qu
Marquard S. Africa 101 H5
Marquesas Islands Fr. Polynesia 151 K6
Marquesas Keys is U.S.A. 133 D7
Marquette U.S.A. 132 C2
Marquez U.S.A. 131 D6
Marquion France 52 D4
Marquise France 52 B4
Marquises, Îles is Fr. Polynesia see Marquesas Islands
Marra Australia 112 A3
Marra r. Australia 112 C3
Marra, Jebel mt. Sudan 97 F3
Marra, Jebel plat. Sudan 97 F3
Marracuene Moz. 101 K3
Marrakech Morocco 54 C5
Marrakesh Morocco see Marrakech
Marrangua, Lagoa l. Moz. 101 L3
Marrar Australia 112 C5
Marrawah Australia 111 [inset]
Marree Australia 111 B6
Marrowbone U.S.A. 134 C5
Marruecos country Africa see Morocco
Marrupa Moz. 99 D5
Marryat Australia 109 F6
Marsá al 'Alam Egypt 86 D4
Marsa 'Alam Egypt see Marsá al 'Alam
Marsá al Burayqah Libya 97 E1
Marsabit Kenya 98 D3
Marsala Sicily Italy 58 E6
Marsá Maṭrūḥ Egypt 90 B5
Marsberg Germany 53 I3
Marsciano Italy 58 E3
Marsden Australia 112 C4
Marsden Canada 121 I4
Marsdiep sea chan. Neth. 52 E2
Marseille France 56 G5
Marseilles France see Marseille
Marsfjället mt. Sweden 44 I4
Marshall watercourse Australia 110 B4
Marshall AR U.S.A. 131 E5
Marshall IL U.S.A. 134 B4
Marshall MI U.S.A. 134 C2
Marshall MN U.S.A. 130 E2
Marshall MO U.S.A. 130 E4
Marshall TX U.S.A. 131 E5
Marshall Islands country N. Pacific Ocean 150 H5
Marshalltown U.S.A. 130 E3
Marshfield MO U.S.A. 131 E4
Marshfield WI U.S.A. 130 F2
Marsh Harbour Bahamas 133 E7
Mars Hill U.S.A. 132 H2
Marsh Island U.S.A. 131 F6
Marsh Peak U.S.A. 129 I1
Marsh Point Canada 121 M3
Marsing U.S.A. 126 D4
Märsta Sweden 45 J7
Marsyaty Russia 41 S3
Martaban, Gulf of Myanmar see Mottama, Gulf of
Martapura Indon. 68 E7
Marten River Canada 122 F5
Marte R. Gómez, Presa resr Mex. 131 D7
Martha's Vineyard i. U.S.A. 135 J3
Martigny Switz. 56 H3
Martim Vaz, Ilhas is S. Atlantic Ocean see Martin Vas, Ilhas
Martin r. Canada 120 F2
Martin Slovakia 47 Q6
Martin MI U.S.A. 134 C2
Martin SD U.S.A. 130 C3
Martinez Lake U.S.A. 129 F5
Martinho Campos Brazil 145 B2

▶Martinique terr. West Indies 137 L6
French Overseas Department.

Martinique Passage Dominica/Martinique 137 L5
Martin Peninsula Antarctica 152 K2
Martinsburg U.S.A. 135 G4
Martins Ferry U.S.A. 134 E3
Martinsville IL U.S.A. 134 B4
Martinsville IN U.S.A. 134 B4
Martinsville VA U.S.A. 134 F5

▶Martin Vas, Ilhas is S. Atlantic Ocean 148 G7
Most easterly point of South America.

Martin Vaz Islands S. Atlantic Ocean see Martin Vas, Ilhas
Martök Kazakh. see Martok
Martok Kazakh. 78 E1
Marton N.Z. 113 E5
Martorell Spain 57 G3
Martos Spain 57 E5
Martuni Armenia 91 G2
Ma'rūf Afgh. 89 G4
Maruim Brazil 143 K6
Marukhis Ughelt'ekhili pass Georgia/Russia 91 F2
Marulan Australia 112 D5
Marusthali reg. India 89 H5
Marvast Iran 88 D4
Marvdasht Iran 88 D4
Marvejols France 56 F4
Marvine, Mount U.S.A. 129 H2
Marwayne Canada 121 I4
Mary r. Australia 108 E3
Mary Turkm. 89 F2
Maryborough Qld Australia 111 F5
Maryborough Vic. Australia 112 A6
Marydale S. Africa 100 F5
Mary Frances Lake Canada 121 J2
Mary Lake Canada 121 K2
Maryland state U.S.A. 135 G4
Maryport U.K. 48 D4
Mary's Harbour Canada 123 L3
Marysvale U.S.A. 129 G2
Marysville CA U.S.A. 128 C2
Marysville KS U.S.A. 130 D4
Marysville OH U.S.A. 134 D3
Maryvale N.T. Australia 109 F6
Maryvale Qld Australia 110 D3
Maryville MO U.S.A. 130 E3
Maryville TN U.S.A. 132 D5
Marzagão Brazil 145 A2
Marzahna Germany 53 M2
Masada tourist site Israel 85 B4
Masāhūn, Kūh-e mt. Iran 88 D4
Masai Steppe plain Tanz. 99 D4
Masaka Uganda 98 D4
Masakhane S. Africa 101 H6
Masalembu Besar i. Indon. 68 E8
Masallı Azer. 91 H3
Masan S. Korea 75 C6
Masasi Tanz. 99 D5
Masavi Bol. 142 F7
Masbate Phil. 69 G4
Masbate i. Phil. 69 G4
Mascara Alg. 57 G6
Mascarene Basin sea feature Indian Ocean 149 L7
Mascarene Plain sea feature Indian Ocean 149 L7
Mascarene Ridge sea feature Indian Ocean 149 L6
Mascote Brazil 145 D1
Masein Myanmar 70 A2
Masela Indon. 108 E2
Masela i. Indon. 108 E2

▶Maseru Lesotho 101 H5
Capital of Lesotho.

Mashai Lesotho 101 I5
Mashan China 77 F4
Masherbrum mt. Pak. 82 D2
Mashhad Iran 89 E2
Mashishing S. Africa 101 J3
Mashkel, Hamun-i- salt flat Pak. 89 F4
Mashkel, Rudi-i r. Pak. 89 F5
Mashki Chah Pak. 89 F4
Mashōrēy Afgh. 89 H3
Masi Norway 44 M2
Masiáca Mex. 127 F8
Masibambane S. Africa 101 H6
Masīlah, Wādī al watercourse Yemen 86 H6
Masilo S. Africa 101 H5
Masi-Manimba Dem. Rep. Congo 99 B4
Masindi Uganda 98 D3
Masinyusane S. Africa 100 F6
Masira, Gulf of Oman see Maşīrah, Khalīj
Maşīrah, Jazīrat i. Oman 87 I5
Maşīrah, Khalīj b. Oman 87 I6
Masira Island Oman see Maşīrah, Jazīrat
Masjed Soleymān Iran 88 C4
Mask, Lough l. Ireland 51 C4
Maskūtān Iran 89 E5
Maslovo Russia 41 S3
Masoala, Tanjona c. Madag. 99 F5
Mason MI U.S.A. 134 C2
Mason OH U.S.A. 134 C4
Mason TX U.S.A. 131 D6
Mason, Lake salt flat Australia 109 B6
Mason Bay N.Z. 113 A8
Mason City U.S.A. 130 E3
Masontown U.S.A. 134 F4
Masqaṭ Oman see Muscat
Masqaṭ reg. Oman see Muscat
'Masrūg well Oman 88 D6
Massa Italy 58 D2
Massachusetts state U.S.A. 135 I2
Massachusetts Bay U.S.A. 135 J2
Massadona U.S.A. 129 I1
Massafra Italy 58 G4
Massakory Chad 97 E3
Massa Marittima Italy 58 D3
Massangena Moz. 99 D6
Massango Angola 99 B4
Massawa Eritrea 86 E6
Massawippi, Lac l. Canada 135 I1
Massena U.S.A. 135 H1
Massenya Chad 97 E3
Masset Canada 120 C4
Massieville U.S.A. 134 D4
Massif Central mts France 56 F4
Massilia France see Marseille
Massillon U.S.A. 134 E3
Massinga Moz. 101 L2
Massingir Moz. 101 K2
Massingir, Barragem de resr Moz. 101 K2
Masson Island Antarctica 152 F2
Mastchoh Tajik. 89 H2
Masteksay Kazakh. 43 K6
Masterton N.Z. 113 E5
Masticho, Akra pt Greece see Oura, Akrotirio
Mastung Pak. 78 F4
Mastūrah Saudi Arabia 86 E5
Masty Belarus 45 N10
Masuda Japan 75 C6
Masuku Gabon see Franceville
Masulipatam India see Machilipatnam
Masulipatnam India see Machilipatnam
Masuna i. American Samoa see Tutuila
Masvingo Zimbabwe 99 D6
Masvingo prov. Zimbabwe 101 J1
Maswa Tanz. 98 D4
Maswaar i. Indon. 69 I7
Maşyāf Syria 85 C2
Mat, Nam r. Laos 70 D3
Mata Myanmar 70 B1
Matabeleland South prov. Zimbabwe 101 I1
Matachewan Canada 122 E5
Matad Mongolia 73 L3
Matadi Dem. Rep. Congo 99 B4
Matador U.S.A. 131 C5
Matagalpa Nicaragua 137 G6
Matagami Canada 122 F4
Matagami, Lac l. Canada 122 F4
Matagorda Island U.S.A. 131 D6
Matak i. Indon. 71 D7
Matakana Island N.Z. 113 F3
Matala Angola 99 B5
Maṭāli', Jabal hill Saudi Arabia 91 F6
Matam Senegal 96 B3
Matamey Niger 96 D3
Matamoras U.S.A. 135 H3
Matamoros Coahuila Mex. 131 C7
Matamoros Tamaulipas Mex. 131 D7
Matandu r. Tanz. 99 D4
Matane Canada 123 I4
Matanzas Cuba 137 H4
Matapan, Cape pt Greece see Tainaro, Akrotirio
Matapédia, Lac l. Canada 123 I4
Maṭār well Saudi Arabia 88 B5
Matara Sri Lanka 84 D5
Mataram Indon. 108 B2
Matarani Peru 142 D7
Mataranka Australia 108 F3
Matarípe Brazil 145 D1
Mataró Spain 57 H3
Matasiri i. Indon. 68 F7
Matatiele S. Africa 101 I6
Matatila Reservoir India 82 D4
Mataura N.Z. 113 B8
Mata-Utu Wallis and Futuna see Matā'utu

▶Matā'utu Wallis and Futuna 107 I3
Capital of Wallis and Futuna.

Matawai N.Z. 113 F4
Matay Kazakh. 80 E2
Matcha Tajik. see Mastchoh
Mat Con, Hon i. Vietnam 70 D3
Mategua Bol. 142 F6
Matehuala Mex. 131 C8
Matemanga Tanz. 99 D5
Matera Italy 58 G4
Mateur Tunisia 58 C6
Mathaji India 82 B4
Matheson Canada 122 E4
Mathews U.S.A. 135 G5
Mathis U.S.A. 131 D6
Mathoura Australia 112 B5
Mathura India 82 D4
Mati Phil. 69 H5
Matiali India 83 G4
Matias Cardoso Brazil 145 C1
Matías Romero Mex. 136 E5
Matimekosh Canada 123 I3
Matin India 83 E5
Matinenda Lake Canada 122 E5
Matizi China 76 D1
Matla r. India 83 G5
Matlabas r. S. Africa 101 H2
Matli Pak. 89 H5
Matlock U.K. 49 F5
Mato, Cerro mt. Venez. 142 E2
Matobo Hills Zimbabwe 99 C6
Mato Grosso state Brazil 145 A1
Mato Grosso, Planalto do plat. Brazil 143 H7
Matola Moz. 101 K3
Matopo Hills Zimbabwe see Matobo Hills
Matos Costa Brazil 145 A4
Matosinhos Port. 57 B3
Mato Verde Brazil 145 C1
Maṭraḥ Oman 88 E6
Matroosberg mt. S. Africa 100 D7
Matsue Japan 75 D6
Matsumoto Japan 75 E5
Matsu Tao i. Taiwan see Mazu Dao
Matsuyama Japan 75 D6
Mattagami r. Canada 122 E4
Mattamuskeet, Lake U.S.A. 132 E5
Mattawa Canada 122 F5
Matterhorn mt. Italy/Switz. 58 B2
Matterhorn mt. U.S.A. 126 E4
Matthew Town Bahamas 137 J4
Maţţī, Sabkhat salt pan Saudi Arabia 88 D6
Mattoon U.S.A. 130 F4
Matturai Sri Lanka see Matara
Matuku i. Fiji 107 H3
Matumbo Angola 99 B5
Maturín Venez. 142 F2
Matusadona National Park Zimbabwe 99 C5
Matwabeng S. Africa 101 H5
Maty Island P.N.G. see Wuvulu Island
Mau India see Maunath Bhanjan
Maúa Moz. 99 D5
Maubeuge France 52 D4
Maubin Myanmar 70 A3
Ma-ubin Myanmar 70 B1
Maubourguet France 56 E5
Mauchline U.K. 50 E5
Maudaha India 82 E4
Maude Australia 111 D7
Maud Seamount sea feature S. Atlantic Ocean 148 I10
Mau-é-ele Moz. see Marão
Maués Brazil 143 G4
Maughold Head hd Isle of Man 48 C4
Maug Islands N. Mariana Is 69 L2
Maui i. U.S.A. 127 [inset]
Maukkadaw Myanmar 70 A2
Maulbronn Germany 53 I6
Maule r. Chile 144 B5
Maulvi Bazar Bangl. see Moulvibazar
Maumee U.S.A. 134 D3
Maumee Bay U.S.A. 134 D3
Maumere Indon. 108 C2
Maumturk Mountains hills Ireland 51 C4
Maun Botswana 99 C5
Mauna Kea vol. U.S.A. 127 [inset]
Mauna Loa vol. U.S.A. 127 [inset]
Maunath Bhanjan India 83 E4
Maunatlala Botswana 101 H2
Maungaturoto N.Z. 113 E3
Maungdaw Myanmar 70 A2
Maungmagan Islands Myanmar 71 B4
Maurepas, Lake U.S.A. 131 F6
Mauriac France 56 F4
Maurice country Indian Ocean see Mauritius
Maurice, Lake salt flat Australia 109 E7
Maurik Neth. 52 F3
Mauritania country Africa 96 B3
Mauritanie country Africa see Mauritania
Mauritius country Indian Ocean 149 L7
Maurs France 56 F4
Mauston U.S.A. 130 F3
Mava Dem. Rep. Congo 98 C3
Mavago Moz. 99 D5
Mavan, Kūh-e hill Iran 88 E3
Mavanza Moz. 101 L2
Mavinga Angola 99 C5
Mavrovo nat. park Macedonia 59 I4
Mavume Moz. 101 L2
Mavuya S. Africa 101 H6
Ma Wan i. H.K. China 77 [inset]
Māwān, Khashm hill Saudi Arabia 88 B6
Mawana India 82 D3
Mawanga Dem. Rep. Congo 99 B4
Ma Wang Dui tourist site China 77 G2
Mawei China 77 H3
Mawjib, Wādī al r. Jordan 85 B4
Mawkmai Myanmar 70 B2
Mawlaik Myanmar 70 A2
Mawlamyaing Myanmar see Moulmein
Mawlamyine Myanmar see Moulmein
Mawqaq Saudi Arabia 91 F6

Mawson research station Antarctica 152 E2
Mawson Coast Antarctica 152 E2
Mawson Escarpment Antarctica 152 E2
Mawson Peninsula Antarctica 152 H2
Maw Taung mt. Myanmar 71 B5
Mawza' Yemen 86 F7
Maxán Arg. 144 C3
Maxhamish Lake Canada 120 F3
Maxia, Punta mt. Sardinia Italy 58 C5
Maxixe Moz. 101 L2
Maxmo Fin. 44 M5
May, Isle of i. U.K. 50 G4
Maya r. Russia 65 O3
Mayaguana i. Bahamas 133 F8
Mayaguana Passage Bahamas 133 F8
Mayagüez Puerto Rico 137 K5
Mayahi Niger 96 D3
Mayak Russia 74 E2
Mayakovskiy, Qullai mt. Tajik. 89 H2
Mayakovskogo, Pik mt. Tajik. see Mayakovskiy, Qullai
Mayama Congo 98 B4
Maya Mountains Belize/Guat. 136 G5
Mayan China see Mayanhe
Mayang China 77 F3
Mayanhe China 76 E1
Mayar hill U.K. 50 F4
Maybeury U.S.A. 134 E5
Maybole U.K. 50 E5
Maych'ew Eth. 98 D2
Maydān Shahr Afgh. see Maīdān Shahr
Maydh Somalia 86 G7
Maydos Turkey see Eceabat
Mayen Germany 53 H4
Mayenne France 56 D2
Mayenne r. France 56 D3
Mayer U.S.A. 129 G4
Mayêr Kangri mt. China 83 F2
Mayersville U.S.A. 131 F5
Mayerthorpe Canada 120 H4
Mayfield N.Z. 113 C6
Mayi He r. China 74 C3
Maykop Russia 91 F1
Mayna Respublika Khakasiya Russia 64 K4
Mayna Ul'yanovskaya Oblast' Russia 43 J5
Mayni India 84 B2
Maynooth Canada 135 G1
Mayo Canada 120 C2
Mayo U.S.A. 133 D6
Mayo Alim Cameroon 96 E4
Mayoko Congo 98 B4
Mayo Lake Canada 120 C2
Mayo Landing Canada see Mayo
Mayor, Puig mt. Spain see Major, Puig
Mayor Island N.Z. 113 F3
Mayor Pablo Lagerenza Para. 144 D1

▶Mayotte terr. Africa 99 E5
French Overseas Department.

Mayskiy Amurskaya Oblast' Russia 74 C1
Mayskiy Kabardino-Balkarskaya Respublika Russia 91 G2
Mays Landing U.S.A. 135 H4
Mayson Lake Canada 121 J3
Maysville U.S.A. 134 D4
Mayumba Gabon 98 B4
Mayum La pass China 83 E3
Mayuram India 84 C4
Mayville MI U.S.A. 134 D2
Mayville ND U.S.A. 130 D2
Mayville NY U.S.A. 134 F2
Mayville WI U.S.A. 134 A2
Mazabuka Zambia 99 C5
Mazaca Turkey see Kayseri
Mazagan Morocco see El Jadida
Mazar China 82 D1
Mazār, Kōh-e mt. Afgh. 89 G3
Mazara, Val di valley Sicily Italy 58 E6
Mazara del Vallo Sicily Italy 58 E6
Mazār-e Sharīf Afgh. 89 G2
Mazārī' reg. U.A.E. 88 D6
Mazatán Mex. 127 F7
Mazatlán Mex. 136 C4
Mazatzal Peak U.S.A. 129 H4
Mazdaj Iran 91 H4
Mazdāvand Iran 89 F2
Mažeikiai Lith. 45 M8
Maẓhūr, 'Irq al des. Saudi Arabia 88 A5
Mazīm Oman 88 E6
Mazocahui Mex. 127 F7
Mazocruz Peru 142 E7
Mazomora Tanz. 99 D4
Mazongshan China 80 I3
Mazowiecka, Nizina reg. Poland 47 R4
Mazu Dao i. Taiwan 77 I3
Mazunga Zimbabwe 99 C6
Mazyr Belarus 43 F5
Mazzouna Tunisia 58 C7

▶Mbabane Swaziland 101 J4
Capital of Swaziland.

Mbabo, Tchabal mt. Cameroon 96 E4
Mbahiakro Côte d'Ivoire 96 C4
Mbaïki Cent. Afr. Rep. 98 B3
Mbakaou, Lac de l. Cameroon 96 E4
Mbala Zambia 99 D4
Mbale Uganda 98 D3
Mbalmayo Cameroon 96 E4
Mbam r. Cameroon 96 E4
Mbandaka Dem. Rep. Congo 98 B4
M'banza Congo Angola 99 B4
Mbarara Uganda 97 G5
Mbari r. Cent. Afr. Rep. 98 C3
Mbaswana S. Africa 101 K4
Mbemkuru r. Tanz. 99 D4
Mbeya Tanz. 99 D4
Mbhashe r. S. Africa 101 I7
Mbinga Tanz. 99 D5
Mbini Equat. Guinea 96 D4
Mbizi Zimbabwe 99 D6
Mboki Cent. Afr. Rep. 98 C3
Mbombela S. Africa 101 J3
Mbomo Congo 98 B3
Mbouda Cameroon 96 E4
Mbour Senegal 96 B3
Mbout Mauritania 96 B3
Mbozi Tanz. 99 D4
Mbrès Cent. Afr. Rep. 98 B3
Mbuji-Mayi Dem. Rep. Congo 99 C4
Mbulu Tanz. 98 D4
Mburucuyá Arg. 144 E3
McAdam Canada 123 I5
McAlester U.S.A. 131 E5
McAlister mt. Australia 112 D5
McAllen U.S.A. 131 D7
McArthur r. Australia 110 B2
McArthur U.S.A. 134 D4
McArthur Mills Canada 135 G1
McBain U.S.A. 134 C1
McBride Canada 120 F4
McCall U.S.A. 126 D3
McCamey U.S.A. 131 C6
McCammon U.S.A. 126 E4
McCauley Island Canada 120 D4
McClintock, Mount Antarctica 152 H1
McClintock Channel Canada 119 H2
McClintock Range hills Australia 108 D4
McClure, Lake U.S.A. 128 C3
McClure Strait Canada 118 G2
McClusky U.S.A. 130 C2
McComb U.S.A. 131 F6
McConaughy, Lake U.S.A. 130 C3
McConnellsburg U.S.A. 135 G4
McConnelsville U.S.A. 134 E4
McCook U.S.A. 130 C3
McCormick U.S.A. 133 D5
McCrea r. Canada 120 H2
McCreary Canada 121 L5
McDame (abandoned) Canada 120 D3
McDermitt U.S.A. 126 D4
McDonald Islands Indian Ocean 149 M9
McDonald Peak U.S.A. 126 E3
McDonough U.S.A. 133 C5
McDougall's Bay S. Africa 100 C5
McDowell Peak U.S.A. 129 H5
McFarland U.S.A. 128 D4
McGill U.S.A. 129 F2
McGivney Canada 123 I5
McGrath AK U.S.A. 118 C3
McGrath MN U.S.A. 130 E2
McGraw U.S.A. 135 G2
McGregor r. Canada 120 F4
McGregor S. Africa 100 D7
McGregor, Lake Canada 120 H5
McGregor Range hills Australia 111 C5
McGuire, Mount U.S.A. 126 E3
Mchinga Tanz. 99 D4
Mchinji Malawi 99 D5
McIlwraith Range hills Australia 110 C2
McInnes Lake Canada 121 M4
McIntosh U.S.A. 130 C2
McKay Range hills Australia 108 C5
McKean i. Kiribati 107 I2
McKee U.S.A. 134 C5
McKenzie r. U.S.A. 126 C3
McKinlay r. Australia 110 C4
McKinley, Mount mt. U.S.A. see Denali
McKinney U.S.A. 131 D5
McKittrick U.S.A. 128 D4
McLaughlin U.S.A. 130 C2
McLeansboro U.S.A. 130 F4
McLennan Canada 120 G4
McLeod r. Canada 120 H4
McLeod Bay Canada 121 I2
McLeod Lake Canada 120 F4
McLoughlin, Mount U.S.A. 126 C4
McMillan, Lake U.S.A. 131 B5
McMinnville OR U.S.A. 126 C3
McMinnville TN U.S.A. 132 C5
McMurdo research station Antarctica 152 H1
McMurdo Sound b. Antarctica 152 H1
McNary U.S.A. 129 I4
McNaughton Lake Canada see Kinbasket Lake
McPherson U.S.A. 130 D4
McQuesten r. Canada 120 B2
McRae U.S.A. 133 D5
McTavish Arm b. Canada 120 G1
McVeytown U.S.A. 135 G3
McVicar Arm b. Canada 120 F1
Mdantsane S. Africa 101 H7
M'Daourouch Alg. 58 B6
M'Đrăk Vietnam 71 E4
Mê, Hon i. Vietnam 70 D3
Mead, Lake resr U.S.A. 129 F3
Meade U.S.A. 131 C4
Meade r. U.S.A. 118 C2
Meadow Australia 109 A6
Meadow SD U.S.A. 130 C2
Meadow UT U.S.A. 129 G2
Meadow Lake Canada 121 I4
Meadville MS U.S.A. 131 F6
Meadville PA U.S.A. 134 E3
Meaford Canada 134 E1
Meaken-dake vol. Japan 74 G4
Mealhada Port. 57 B3
Mealy Mountains Canada 123 K3
Meandarra Australia 112 D1
Meander River Canada 120 G3
Meaux France 52 C6
Mecca Saudi Arabia 86 E5
Mecca CA U.S.A. 128 E5
Mecca OH U.S.A. 134 E3
Mechanic Falls U.S.A. 135 J1
Mechanicsville U.S.A. 135 G5
Mechelen Belgium 52 E3
Mechelen Neth. 52 F4
Mecherchar i. Palau see Eil Malk
Mecheria Alg. 54 D5
Mechernich Germany 52 G4
Mecitözü Turkey 90 D2
Meckenheim Germany 52 H4
Mecklenburger Bucht b. Germany 47 M3
Mecklenburg-Vorpommern land Germany 53 M1
Mecklenburg-West Pomerania land Germany see Mecklenburg-Vorpommern
Meda r. Australia 108 C4
Meda Port. 57 C3
Medak India 84 C2
Medan Indon. 71 B7
Medanosa, Punta pt Arg. 144 C7
Médanos de Coro, Parque Nacional nat. park Venez. 142 E1
Medawachchiya Sri Lanka 84 D4
Médéa Alg. 57 H5
Medebach Germany 53 I3
Medellín Col. 142 C2
Meden r. U.K. 48 G5
Medenine Tunisia 54 G5
Mederdra Mauritania 96 B3
Medford NY U.S.A. 135 I3
Medford OK U.S.A. 131 D4
Medford OR U.S.A. 126 C4
Medford WI U.S.A. 130 F2
Medgidia Romania 59 M2
Media U.S.A. 135 H4
Mediaş Romania 59 K1
Medicine Bow r. U.S.A. 126 G4
Medicine Bow Mountains U.S.A. 126 G4
Medicine Bow Peak U.S.A. 126 G4
Medicine Hat Canada 121 I5
Medicine Lake U.S.A. 126 G2
Medicine Lodge U.S.A. 131 D4
Medina Brazil 145 C2
Medina Saudi Arabia 86 E5
Medina ND U.S.A. 130 D2
Medina NY U.S.A. 135 F2
Medina OH U.S.A. 134 E3
Medinaceli Spain 57 E3
Medina del Campo Spain 57 D3
Medina de Rioseco Spain 57 D3
Medina Lake U.S.A. 131 D6
Medinipur India 83 F5
Mediolanum Italy see Milan
Mediterranean Sea 54 K5
Medjerda, Monts de la mts Alg. 58 B6
Mednyy, Ostrov i. Russia 150 H2
Médoc reg. France 56 D4
Mêdog China 76 B2
Medora U.S.A. 130 C2
Medstead Canada 121 I4
Meduro atoll Marshall Is see Majuro
Medvedevo Russia 42 J4
Medveditsa r. Russia 43 I6
Medvednica mts Croatia 58 F2
Medvezh'i, Ostrova is Russia 65 R2
Medvezh'ya, Gora mt. Russia 74 E3
Medvezh'ya. Gora vol. Russia 74 H3
Medvezh'yegorsk Russia 42 G3
Medway r. U.K. 49 H7
Meekatharra Australia 109 B6
Meeker CO U.S.A. 129 J1
Meeker OH U.S.A. 134 D3
Meelpaeg Reservoir Canada 123 K4
Meemu Atoll Maldives see Mulakatholhu
Meerane Germany 53 M4
Meerlo Neth. 52 G3
Meerut India 82 D3
Mega Escarpment Eth./Kenya 98 D3
Megalopoli Greece 59 J6
Megamo Indon. 69 I7
Mégantic, Lac l. Canada 123 H5
Megara Greece 59 J5
Megezez mt. Eth. 98 D3

▶Meghalaya state India 83 G4
Highest mean annual rainfall in the world.

Meghasani mt. India 83 F5
Meghri Armenia 91 G3
Megin Turkm. 88 E2
Megisti i. Greece 59 M6
Megri Armenia see Meghri
Mehamn Norway 44 O1
Mehar Pak. 89 G5
Meharry, Mount Australia 109 B5
Mehbubnagar India see Mahbubnagar
Mehdia Tunisia see Mahdia
Meherpur Bangl. 83 G5
Meherrin U.S.A. 135 F5
Meherrin r. U.S.A. 135 G5
Mehlville U.S.A. 130 F4
Mehrakān salt marsh Iran 88 D5
Mehrān Hormozgān Iran 88 D5
Mehrān Īlām Iran 88 B3
Mehren Germany 52 G4
Mehrestān Iran 89 F4
Mehrīz Iran 88 D4
Mehsana India see Mahesana
Mehtar Lām Afgh. 89 H3
Meia Ponte r. Brazil 145 A2
Meicheng China see Minqing
Meiganga Cameroon 97 E4
Meighen Island Canada 119 I2
Meigu China 76 D2
Meihekou China 74 B4
Meikeng China 77 G3
Meikle r. Canada 120 G3
Meikle Says Law hill U.K. 50 G5
Meiktila Myanmar 70 A2
Meilin China see Ganxian
Meilleur r. Canada 120 E2
Meilü China see Wuchuan
Meine Germany 53 K2
Meinersen Germany 53 K2
Meiningen Germany 53 K4
Meishan Anhui China see Jinzhai
Meishan Sichuan China 76 D2
Meishan Shuiku resr China 77 G2
Meißen Germany 47 N5
Meister r. Canada 120 D2
Meitan China 76 E3
Meixi China 74 C3
Meixian China see Meizhou
Meixing China see Xiaojin
Meizhou China 77 H3
Mej r. India 82 D4
Mejicana mt. Arg. 144 C3
Mejillones Chile 144 B2
Mékambo Gabon 98 B3
Mek'elē Eth. 98 D2
Mekelle Eth. see Mek'elē
Mékhé Senegal 96 B3
Mekhtar Pak. 89 H4
Meknassy Tunisia 58 C7
Meknès Morocco 54 C5
Mekong r. Asia 70 D4
also known as Mae Nam Khong (Laos/Thailand)
Mekong, Mouths of the Vietnam 71 D5
Mekoryuk U.S.A. 118 B3
Melaka Malaysia 71 C7
Melanau, Gunung hill Indon. 71 E7
Melanesia is Pacific Ocean 150 G6
Melanesian Basin sea feature Pacific Ocean 150 G5

▶Melbourne Australia 112 B6
Capital of Victoria. 2nd most populous city in Oceania.

Melbourne U.S.A. 133 D6
Melby U.K. 50 [inset]
Meldorf Germany 47 L3

▶Melekeok Palau 69 I5
Capital of Palau.

Melekess Russia see Dimitrovgrad
Melenki Russia 43 I5
Melet Turkey see Mesudiye
Mélèzes, Rivière aux r. Canada 123 H2
Melfa U.S.A. 135 H5
Melfi Chad 97 E3
Melfi Italy 58 F4
Melfort Canada 121 J4
Melhus Norway 44 G5
Meliadine Lake Canada 121 M2
Melide Spain 57 C2

▶Melilla N. Africa 57 E6
Autonomous Community of Spain.

Melimoyu, Monte mt. Chile 144 B6
Meliskerke Neth. 52 D3
Melita Canada 121 K5
Melitene Turkey see Malatya
Melitopol' Ukr. 43 G7
Melk Austria 47 O6
Melka Guba Eth. 98 D3
Melksham U.K. 49 E7
Mellakoski Fin. 44 N3
Mellansel Sweden 44 K5
Melle Germany 53 I2
Mellerud Sweden 45 H7
Mellette U.S.A. 130 D2
Mellid Spain see Melide
Mellilia N. Africa see Melilla
Mellrichstadt Germany 53 K4
Mellum i. Germany 53 I1
Melmoth S. Africa 101 J5
Mel'nichoye Russia 74 D3
Melo Uruguay 144 F4
Meloco Moz. 99 D5
Melolo Indon. 108 C2
Melozitna r. U.S.A. 118 C3
Melrhir, Chott salt l. Alg. 54 F5
Melrose Australia 109 C6
Melrose U.K. 50 G5
Melrose U.S.A. 130 E2
Melsungen Germany 53 J3
Melton Australia 112 B6
Melton Mowbray U.K. 49 G6
Melun France 56 F2
Melville Canada 121 K5
Melville, Cape Australia 110 D2
Melville, Lake Canada 123 K3
Melville Bugt b. Greenland see Qimusseriarsuaq
Melville Island Australia 108 E2
Melville Island Canada 119 H2
Melville Peninsula Canada 119 J3
Melvin U.S.A. 134 A3
Melvin, Lough l. Ireland/U.K. 51 D3
Mêmar Co salt l. China 83 E2
Memba Moz. 99 E5
Memberamo r. Indon. 69 J7
Memel Lith. see Klaipėda
Memel S. Africa 101 I4
Memmelsdorf Germany 53 K5
Memmingen Germany 47 M7
Mempawah Indon. 68 D6
Memphis tourist site Egypt 90 C5
Memphis MI U.S.A. 134 D2
Memphis TN U.S.A. 131 F5
Memphis TX U.S.A. 131 C5
Memphrémagog, Lac l. Canada 135 I1
Mena Ukr. 43 G6
Mena U.S.A. 131 E5
Menado Indon. see Manado
Ménaka Mali 96 D3
Menard U.S.A. 131 D6
Menasha U.S.A. 134 A1
Mendanha Brazil 145 C2
Mendarik i. Indon. 71 D7
Mende France 56 F4
Mendefera Eritrea 86 E7
Mendeleyev Ridge sea feature Arctic Ocean 153 B1
Mendeleyevsk Russia 42 L5
Mendenhall U.S.A. 131 F6
Mendenhall, Cape U.S.A. 118 B4
Mendenhall Glacier U.S.A. 120 C3
Méndez Mex. 131 D7
Mendī Eth. 98 D3
Mendi P.N.G. 69 K8
Mendip Hills U.K. 49 E7
Mendocino U.S.A. 128 B2
Mendocino, Cape U.S.A. 128 A1
Mendocino, Lake U.S.A. 128 B2
Mendooran Australia 112 D3
Mendota CA U.S.A. 128 C3
Mendota IL U.S.A. 130 F3
Mendoza Arg. 144 C4
Menemen Turkey 59 L5
Ménerville Alg. see Thenia
Mengban China 76 D4
Mengcheng China 77 H1
Menghai China 76 D4
Mengjin China 77 G1
Mengla China 76 D4
Menglang China see Lancang
Menglie China see Jiangcheng
Mengyang China see Mingshan
Mengzi China 76 D4
Menihek Canada 123 I3
Menihek Lakes Canada 123 I3
Menindee Australia 111 C7
Menindee, Lake Australia 111 C7
Ménistouc, Lac l. Canada 123 I3
Menkere Russia 65 N3
Mennecy France 52 C6
Menominee U.S.A. 134 B1
Menomonee Falls U.S.A. 134 A2
Menomonie U.S.A. 130 F2
Menongue Angola 99 B5
Menorca i. Spain see Minorca
Mentawai, Kepulauan is Indon. 68 B7
Mentawai, Selat sea chan. Indon. 68 C7
Menteroda Germany 53 K3
Mentmore U.S.A. 129 I4
Menton France 56 H5
Mentone U.S.A. 131 C6
Menuf Egypt see Minūf
Menzel Bourguiba Tunisia 58 C6
Menzelet Barajı resr Turkey 90 E3
Menzelinsk Russia 41 Q4
Menzel Temime Tunisia 58 D6
Menzies Australia 109 C7
Menzies, Mount Antarctica 152 E2
Meobbaai b. Namibia 100 B3
Meoqui Mex. 131 B6
Meppel Neth. 52 G2
Meppen Germany 53 H2
Mepuze Moz. 101 K2
Meqheleng S. Africa 101 H5
Mequon U.S.A. 134 B2
Merak Indon. 68 D8
Meråker Norway 44 G5
Merano Italy 58 D1
Meratswe r. Botswana 100 G2
Merauke Indon. 69 K8
Merca Somalia see Marka
Mercantour, Parc National du nat. park France 56 H4
Merced U.S.A. 128 C3
Merced r. U.S.A. 128 C3
Mercedes Arg. 144 E3
Mercedes Uruguay 144 E4
Mercer ME U.S.A. 135 K1
Mercer PA U.S.A. 134 E3
Mercer WI U.S.A. 130 F2
Mercês Brazil 145 C3
Mercury Islands N.Z. 113 E3
Mercy, Cape Canada 119 L3
Merdenik Turkey see Göle
Mere Belgium 52 D4
Mere U.K. 49 E7
Meredith U.S.A. 135 J2
Meredith, Lake U.S.A. 131 C5
Merefa Ukr. 43 H6
Merga Oasis Sudan 86 C6
Mergui Myanmar see Myeik
Mergui Archipelago is Myanmar 71 B5
Meriç r. Turkey 59 L4
also known as Euros (Greece), Marica, Maritsa (Bulgaria)
Mérida Mex. 136 G4
Mérida Spain 57 C4
Mérida Venez. 142 D2
Mérida, Cordillera de mts Venez. 142 D2
Meriden U.S.A. 135 I3
Meridian MS U.S.A. 131 F5
Meridian TX U.S.A. 131 D6
Mérignac France 56 D4
Merijärvi Fin. 44 N4
Merikarvia Fin. 45 L6
Merimbula Australia 112 D6
Merín, Laguna l. Brazil/Uruguay see Mirim, Lagoa
Meringur Australia 111 C7
Merir i. Palau 69 I6
Merjayoun Lebanon see Marjayoûn
Merkel U.S.A. 131 C5
Merluna Australia 110 C2
Mermaid Reef Australia 108 B4
Meron, Har mt. Israel 85 B3
Merowe Sudan 86 D6
Merowe Dam Sudan 86 D6
Mêrqung Co l. China 83 F3
Merredin Australia 109 B7
Merrick hill U.K. 50 E5
Merrickville Canada 135 H1
Merrill MI U.S.A. 134 C2
Merrill WI U.S.A. 130 F2
Merrill, Mount Canada 120 E2
Merrillville U.S.A. 134 B3
Merriman U.S.A. 130 C3
Merritt Canada 120 F5
Merritt Island U.S.A. 133 D6
Merriwa Australia 112 E4
Merrygoen Australia 112 D3
Mersa Fatma Eritrea 86 F7
Mersa Maṭrûḥ Egypt see Marsá Maṭrūḥ
Mersch Lux. 52 G5
Merseburg Germany 53 L3
Mersey est. U.K. 48 E5
Mersin Turkey 85 B1
Mersin prov. Turkey 85 A1
Mersing Malaysia 71 C7
Mērsrags Latvia 45 M8
Merta India 82 C4
Merthyr Tydfil U.K. 49 D7
Mértola Port. 57 C5
Mertz Glacier Antarctica 152 G2
Mertz Glacier Tongue Antarctica 152 G2
Mertzon U.S.A. 131 C6
Méru France 52 C5

▶Meru vol. Tanz. 98 D4
4th highest mountain, and highest active volcano in Africa.

Merui Pak. 89 F4
Merv Turkm. see Mary
Merweville S. Africa 100 E7
Merzifon Turkey 90 D2
Merzig Germany 52 G5
Merz Peninsula Antarctica 152 L2
Mesa AZ U.S.A. 129 H5
Mesa NM U.S.A. 127 G6
Mesabi Range hills U.S.A. 130 E2
Mesagne Italy 58 G4
Mesa Negra mt. U.S.A. 129 J4
Mesara, Ormos b. Greece see Messaras, Kolpos
Mesa Verde National Park U.S.A. 129 I3
Meschede Germany 53 I3
Mese Myanmar 70 B3
Meselefors Sweden 44 J4
Mesgouez, Lac Canada 122 G4
Meshed Iran see Mashhad
Meshkān Iran 88 E2
Meshra' Er Req South Sudan 86 C8
Mesick U.S.A. 134 C1
Mesimeri Greece 59 J4
Mesolongi Greece 59 I5
Mesolóngion Greece see Mesolongi
Mesopotamia hist. area Iraq 91 F4
Mesopotamia Marshlands National Park Iraq 91 G5
Mesquita Brazil 145 C2
Mesquite NV U.S.A. 129 F3
Mesquite TX U.S.A. 131 D5
Mesquite Lake U.S.A. 129 F4
Messaad Alg. 54 E5
Messana Sicily Italy see Messina
Messaras, Kolpos b. Greece 59 K7
Messina Sicily Italy 58 F5
Messina, Strait of Italy 58 F5
Messina, Stretta di Italy see Messina, Strait of
Messini Greece 59 J6
Messiniakos Kolpos b. Greece 59 J6
Mesta r. Bulg. 59 K4
Mesta r. Greece see Nestos
Mesta, Akrotirio pt Greece 59 K5
Mestghanem Alg. see Mostaganem
Mestlin Germany 53 L1
Meston, Akra pt Greece see Mesta, Akrotirio
Mestre Italy 58 E2
Mesudiye Turkey 90 E2
Meta r. Col./Venez. 142 E2
Métabetchouan Canada 123 H4
Meta Incognita Peninsula Canada 119 L3
Metairie U.S.A. 131 F6
Metallifere, Colline mts Italy 58 D3
Metán Arg. 144 C3
Meteghan Canada 123 I5
Meteor Depth sea feature S. Atlantic Ocean 148 G9
Methoni Greece 59 I6
Methuen U.S.A. 135 J2
Methven U.K. 50 F4
Metionga Lake Canada 122 C4
Metković Croatia 58 G3
Metlaoui Tunisia 54 F5
Metoro Moz. 99 D5
Metro Indon. 68 D8
Metropolis U.S.A. 131 F4
Metsada tourist site Israel see Masada
Metter U.S.A. 133 D5
Mettet Belgium 52 E4
Mettingen Germany 53 H2
Mettler U.S.A. 128 D4
Mettur India 84 C4
Metu Eth. 98 D3
Metz France 52 G5
Metz U.S.A. 134 C3
Meulaboh Indon. 71 B6
Meureudu Indon. 71 B6
Meuse r. Belgium/France 52 F3
also known as Maas (Netherlands)
Meuse, Côtes de ridge France 52 E5
Meuselwitz Germany 53 M3
Mevagissey U.K. 49 C8
Mêwa China 76 D1
Mexia U.S.A. 131 D6
Mexiana, Ilha i. Brazil 143 I3
Mexicali Mex. 129 F5
Mexican Hat U.S.A. 129 I3
Mexicanos, Lago de los l. Mex. 127 G7
Mexican Water U.S.A. 129 I3

▶Mexico country Central America 136 D4
2nd most populous and 3rd largest country in North America, and 10th most populous country in the world.

México Mex. see Mexico City
Mexico ME U.S.A. 135 J1
Mexico MO U.S.A. 130 F4
Mexico NY U.S.A. 135 G2
Mexico, Gulf of Mex./U.S.A. 125 H6

▶Mexico City Mex. 136 E5
Capital of Mexico. Most populous city in North America and 4th in the world.

Meybod Iran 88 D3
Meydanī, Ra's-e pt Iran 88 E5
Meyenburg Germany 53 M1
Meyersdale U.S.A. 134 F4
Meymeh Iran 88 C3
Meynypil'gyno Russia 153 C2
Mezada tourist site Israel see Masada
Mezdra Bulg. 59 J3
Mezen' Russia 42 J2
Mezen' r. Russia 42 J2
Mézenc, Mont mt. France 56 G4
Mezenskaya Guba b. Russia 42 I2
Mezhdurechensk Kemerovskaya Oblast' Russia 72 F2
Mezhdurechensk Respublika Komi Russia 42 K3
Mezhdurech'ye Russia see Shali
Mezhdusharskiy, Ostrov i. Russia 64 G2
Mezitli Turkey 85 B1
Mezőtúr Hungary 59 I1
Mežvidi Latvia 45 O8
Mfolozi r. S. Africa 101 K5
Mhàil, Rubh' a' pt U.K. 50 C5
Mhangura Zimbabwe 99 D5
Mhlume Swaziland 101 J4
Mhow India 82 C5
Mi r. Myanmar 83 H5
Miahuatlán Mex. 136 E5
Miajadas Spain 57 D4
Miaméré Cent. Afr. Rep. 98 B3
Miami AZ U.S.A. 129 H5

▶Miami FL U.S.A. 133 D7
5th most populous city in North America.

Miami OK U.S.A. 131 E4
Miami Beach U.S.A. 133 D7
Miancaowan China 76 C1
Mīāndehī Iran 88 E3
Mīāndoāb Iran 88 B2
Miandrivazo Madag. 99 E5
Mīāneh Iran 88 B2
Miang, Phu mt. Thai. 70 C3
Mianhua Yu i. Taiwan 77 I3
Miani India 89 I4
Miani Hor b. Pak. 89 G5
Mīān Jōy Afgh. 89 G3
Mianning China 76 D2
Mianwali Pak. 89 H3

Mianxian China 76 E1
Mianyang *Hubei* China *see* Xiantao
Mianyang *Shaanxi* China *see* Mianxian
Mianyang *Sichuan* China 76 E2
Mianzhu China 76 E2
Miaoli Taiwan 77 I3
Miarinarivo Madag. 99 E5
Miarritze France *see* Biarritz
Miass Russia 64 H4
Mica Creek Canada 120 G4
Mica Mountain U.S.A. 129 H5
Micang Shan *mts* China 76 E1
Michalovce Slovakia 43 D6
Michel Canada 121 I4
Michelau in Oberfranken Germany 53 L4
Michelson, Mount U.S.A. 118 D3
Michelstadt Germany 53 J5
Michendorf Germany 53 N2
Micheng China *see* Midu
Michigan *state* U.S.A. 134 C2

▶Michigan, Lake U.S.A. 134 B2
3rd largest lake in North America and 5th in the world.

Michigan City U.S.A. 134 B3
Michinberi India 84 D2
Michipicoten Bay Canada 122 D5
Michipicoten Island Canada 122 D5
Michipicoten River Canada 122 D5
Michurin Bulg. *see* Tsarevo
Michurinsk Russia 43 I5
Micronesia *country* N. Pacific Ocean *see* Micronesia, Federated States of
Micronesia *is* Pacific Ocean 150 F5
Micronesia, Federated States of *country* N. Pacific Ocean 150 G5
Midai *i.* Indon. 71 D7
Mid-Atlantic Ridge *sea feature* Atlantic Ocean 148 E4
Mid-Atlantic Ridge *sea feature* Atlantic Ocean 148 G7
Middelburg Neth. 52 D3
Middelburg *E. Cape* S. Africa 101 G6
Middelburg *Mpumalanga* S. Africa 101 I3
Middelfart Denmark 45 F9
Middelharnis Neth. 52 E3
Middelwit S. Africa 101 H3
Middle Alkali Lake U.S.A. 126 C4
Middle America Trench *sea feature* N. Pacific Ocean 151 N5
Middle Andaman *i.* India 71 A4
Middle Atlas *mts* Morocco *see* Moyen Atlas
Middle Bay Canada 123 K4
Middlebourne U.S.A. 134 E4
Middleburg U.S.A. 135 G3
Middleburgh U.S.A. 135 H2
Middlebury *IN* U.S.A. 134 C3
Middlebury *VT* U.S.A. 135 I1
Middle Caicos *i.* Turks and Caicos Is 133 G8
Middle Concho *r.* U.S.A. 131 C6
Middle Congo *country* Africa *see* Congo
Middle Island Thai. *see* Tasai, Ko
Middle Loup *r.* U.S.A. 130 D3
Middlemarch N.Z. 113 C7
Middlemount Australia 110 E4
Middle River U.S.A. 135 G4
Middlesbrough U.K. 48 F4
Middle Strait India *see* Andaman Strait
Middleton Australia 110 C4
Middleton Canada 123 I5
Middleton Island *atoll* American Samoa *see* Rose Island
Middletown *CA* U.S.A. 128 B2
Middletown *CT* U.S.A. 135 I3
Middletown *NY* U.S.A. 135 H3
Middletown *VA* U.S.A. 135 F4
Midelt Morocco 54 D5
Midhurst U.K. 49 G8
Midi, Canal du France 56 F5
Mid-Indian Basin *sea feature* Indian Ocean 149 N6
Mid-Indian Ridge *sea feature* Indian Ocean 149 M7
Midland Canada 135 F1
Midland *IN* U.S.A. 134 B4
Midland *MI* U.S.A. 134 C2
Midland *SD* U.S.A. 130 C2
Midland *TX* U.S.A. 131 C5
Midland (abandoned) U.S.A. 129 F5
Midleton Ireland 51 D6
Midnapore India *see* Medinipur
Midnapur India *see* Medinipur
Midongy Atsimo Madag. 99 E6
Mid-Pacific Mountains *sea feature* N. Pacific Ocean 150 G4
Midu China 76 D3
Miðvágur Faroe Is 44 [inset 2]
Midway Oman *see* Thamarīt

▶Midway Islands *terr.* N. Pacific Ocean 150 I4
United States Unincorporated Territory.

Midway Well Australia 109 C5
Midwest U.S.A. 126 G4
Midwest City U.S.A. 131 D5
Midwoud Neth. 52 F2
Midyat Turkey 91 F3
Midye Turkey *see* Kıyıköy
Mid Yell U.K. 50 [inset]
Midzhur *mt.* Bulg./Serbia 90 A2
Miehikkälä Fin. 45 O6
Miekojärvi *l.* Fin. 44 N3
Mielec Poland 43 D6
Mieraslompola Fin. 44 O2
Mierašluoppal Fin. *see* Mieraslompola
Miercurea Ciuc Romania 59 K1
Mieres Spain *see* Mieres del Camín
Mieres del Camín Spain 57 D2
Mī'ēso Eth. 98 E3
Mieste Germany 53 L2
Mifflinburg U.S.A. 135 G3
Mifflintown U.S.A. 135 G3
Migang Shan *mt.* China 76 E1
Migdol S. Africa 101 G4
Miging India 76 B2
Miguel Auza Mex. 131 C7
Miguel Hidalgo, Presa *resr* Mex. 127 F8
Mihalıççık Turkey 59 N5
Mihara Japan 75 D6
Mihintale Sri Lanka 84 D4
Mihmandar Turkey 85 B1
Mijares *r.* Spain *see* Millárs
Mijdrecht Neth. 52 E2
Mikhaylov Russia 43 H5
Mikhaylovgrad Bulg. *see* Montana
Mikhaylov Island Antarctica 152 E2
Mikhaylovka *Amurskaya Oblast'* Russia 74 C2
Mikhaylovka *Primorskiy Kray* Russia 74 D4
Mikhaylovka *Tul'skaya Oblast'* Russia *see* Kimovsk
Mikhaylovka *Volgogradskaya Oblast'* Russia 43 I6
Mikhaylovsk Russia 91 F1
Mikhaylovskiy *Altayskiy Kray* Russia 80 E1
Mikhaylovskoye *Stavropol'skiy Kray* Russia *see* Mikhaylovsk
Mikhrot Timna Israel 85 B5
Mikir Hills India 83 H4
Mikkeli Fin. 45 O6
Mikkelin mlk Fin. 45 O6
Mikkwa *r.* Canada 120 H3
Mikonos *i.* Greece *see* Mykonos
Mikoyan Armenia *see* Yeghegnadzor
Mikulkin, Mys *c.* Russia 42 J2
Mikumi National Park Tanz. 99 D4
Mikun' Russia 42 K3
Mikuni-sanmyaku *mts* Japan 75 E5
Mikura-jima *i.* Japan 75 E6
Milaca U.S.A. 130 E2
Miladhunmadulu Maldives 84 B5
Miladummadulu Atoll Maldives *see* Miladhunmadulu
Milan Italy 58 C2
Milan *MI* U.S.A. 134 D2
Milan *MO* U.S.A. 130 E3
Milan *OH* U.S.A. 134 D3
Milange Moz. 99 D5
Milano Italy *see* Milan
Milas Turkey 59 L6
Milazzo *Sicily* Italy 58 F5
Milazzo, Capo di *c. Sicily* Italy 58 F5
Milbank U.S.A. 130 D2
Milbridge U.S.A. 132 H2
Milde *r.* Germany 53 L2
Mildenhall U.K. 49 H6
Mildura Australia 111 C7
Mile China 76 D3
Mileiz, Wâdi el *watercourse* Egypt *see* Mulayz, Wādī al
Miles Australia 112 E1
Miles City U.S.A. 126 G3
Milestone Ireland 51 D5
Miletto, Monte *mt.* Italy 58 F4
Mileura Australia 109 B6
Milford Ireland 51 E2
Milford *DE* U.S.A. 135 H4
Milford *IL* U.S.A. 134 B3
Milford *MA* U.S.A. 135 J2
Milford *MI* U.S.A. 134 D2
Milford *NE* U.S.A. 130 D3
Milford *NH* U.S.A. 135 J2
Milford *PA* U.S.A. 135 H3
Milford *UT* U.S.A. 129 G2
Milford *VA* U.S.A. 135 G4
Milford Haven U.K. 49 B7
Milford Sound N.Z. 113 A7
Milford Sound *inlet* N.Z. 113 A7
Milgarra Australia 110 C3
Milḥ, Baḥr al *l.* Iraq *see* Razāzah, Buḥayrat ar
Milḥ, Qurayyāt al *l.* Jordan 85 C4
Miliana Alg. 57 H5
Milid Turkey *see* Malatya
Milikapiti Australia 108 E2
Miling Australia 109 B7
Milk *r.* U.S.A. 126 G2
Milk, Wadi el *watercourse* Sudan 86 D6
Mil'kovo Russia 65 Q4
Millaa Millaa Australia 110 D3
Millárs *r.* Spain 57 F4
Millau France 56 F4
Millbrook Canada 135 F1
Mill Creek *r.* U.S.A. 128 B1
Milledgeville U.S.A. 133 D5
Mille Lacs *lakes* U.S.A. 130 E2
Mille Lacs, Lac des *l.* Canada 119 I5
Millen U.S.A. 133 D5
Millennium Island *atoll* Kiribati *see* Caroline Island
Miller U.S.A. 130 D2
Miller Lake Canada 134 E1
Millerovo Russia 43 I6
Millersburg *OH* U.S.A. 134 E3
Millersburg *PA* U.S.A. 135 G3
Millers Creek U.S.A. 134 D5
Millersville U.S.A. 135 G4
Millerton Lake U.S.A. 128 D3
Millet Canada 120 H4
Milleur Point U.K. 50 D5
Mill Hall U.S.A. 135 G3
Millicent Australia 111 C8
Millington *MI* U.S.A. 134 D2
Millington *TN* U.S.A. 131 F5
Millinocket U.S.A. 132 G2
Mill Island Canada 119 K3
Millmerran Australia 112 E1
Millom U.K. 48 D4
Millport U.K. 50 E5
Millsboro U.S.A. 135 H4
Mills Creek *watercourse* Australia 110 C4
Mills Lake Canada 120 G2
Millstone *KY* U.S.A. 134 D5
Millstone *WV* U.S.A. 134 E4
Millstream-Chichester National Park Australia 108 B5
Millthorpe Australia 112 D4
Milltown Canada 123 I5
Milltown U.S.A. 126 E3
Millungera Australia 110 C3
Millville U.S.A. 135 H4
Millwood U.S.A. 134 B5
Millwood Lake U.S.A. 131 E5
Milly Milly Australia 109 B6
Milne Land *i.* Greenland *see* Ilimananngip Nunaa
Milner U.S.A. 129 J1
Milo *r.* Guinea 96 C3
Milogradovo Russia 74 D4
Miloli'i U.S.A. 127 [inset]
Milos *i.* Greece 59 K6
Milparinka Australia 111 C6
Milpitas U.S.A. 128 C3
Milroy U.S.A. 135 G3
Milton N.Z. 113 B8
Milton *DE* U.S.A. 135 H4
Milton *NH* U.S.A. 135 J2
Milton *WV* U.S.A. 134 D4
Milton Keynes U.K. 49 G6
Miltown Malbay Ireland 51 C5
Miluo China 77 G2
Milverton Canada 134 E2
Milwaukee U.S.A. 134 B2

▶Milwaukee Deep *sea feature* Caribbean Sea 148 D4
Deepest point in the Puerto Rico Trench (deepest in the Atlantic).

Mimbres *watercourse* U.S.A. 129 J5
Mimili Australia 109 F6
Mimisal India 84 C4
Mimizan France 56 D4
Mimongo Gabon 98 B4
Mimosa Rocks National Park Australia 112 E6
Mina Mex. 131 C7
Mina U.S.A. 128 D2
Mīnāb Iran 88 E5
Minaçu Brazil 145 A1
Minahasa, Semenanjung *pen.* Indon. 69 G6
Minahassa Peninsula Indon. *see* Minahasa, Semenanjung
Minaker Canada *see* Prophet River
Minakh Syria 85 C1
Minaki Canada 121 M5
Minamia Australia 108 F3
Minami-Daitō-jima *i.* Japan 73 O7
Minami-Iō-jima *vol.* Japan 69 K2
Min'an China *see* Longshan
Minas Indon. 71 C7
Minas Uruguay 144 E4
Minas de Matahambre Cuba 133 D8
Minas Gerais *state* Brazil 145 B2
Minas Novas Brazil 145 C2
Minatitlán Mex. 136 F5
Minbu Myanmar 70 A2
Minbya Myanmar 70 A2
Minchinmávida *vol.* Chile 144 B6
Mindanao *i.* Phil. 69 H5
Mindanao Trench *sea feature* N. Pacific Ocean *see* Philippine Trench
Mindelo Cape Verde 96 [inset]
Minden Canada 135 F1
Minden Germany 53 I2
Minden *LA* U.S.A. 131 E5
Minden *NE* U.S.A. 124 H3
Minden *NV* U.S.A. 128 D2
Mindon Myanmar 70 A3
Mindoro *i.* Phil. 69 G4
Mindoro Strait Phil. 69 F4
Mindouli Congo 98 B4
Mine Head *hd* Ireland 51 E6
Minehead U.K. 49 D7
Mineola U.S.A. 135 I3
Mineral U.S.A. 135 G4
Mineral'nyye Vody Russia 91 F1
Mineral Wells *TX* U.S.A. 131 D5
Mineral Wells *WV* U.S.A. 134 E4
Minersville *PA* U.S.A. 135 G3
Minersville *UT* U.S.A. 129 G2
Minerva U.S.A. 134 E3
Minerva Reefs Fiji 107 I4
Minfeng China 83 E1
Minga Dem. Rep. Congo 99 C5
Mingäçevir Azer. 91 G2
Mingäçevir Su Anbarı *resr* Azer. 91 G2
Mingala Cent. Afr. Rep. 98 C3
Mingan, Îles de *is* Canada 123 J4
Mingan Archipelago National Park Reserve Canada *see* Archipel-de-Mingan, Réserve du Parc National de l'
Mingbuloq Uzbek. 80 B3
Mingechaur Azer. *see* Mingäçevir
Mingechaurskoye Vodokhranilishche *resr* Azer. *see* Mingäçevir Su Anbarı
Mingenew Australia 109 A7
Mingfeng China *see* Yuan'an
Minggang China 77 G1
Mingguang China 77 H1
Mingin Range *mts* Myanmar 70 A2
Minglanilla Spain 57 F4
Mingoyo Tanz. 99 D5
Mingshan China 76 D2
Mingshui *Gansu* China 80 I3
Mingshui *Heilong.* China 74 B3
Mingulay *i.* U.K. 50 B4
Mingxi China 77 H3
Mingzhou China *see* Suide
Minhe China *see* Jinxian
Minhla *Bago* Myanmar 70 A3
Minhla *Magway* Myanmar 70 A3
Minho *r.* Port./Spain *see* Miño
Minicoy *atoll* India 84 B4
Minigwal, Lake *salt flat* Australia 109 C7
Minilya Australia 109 A5
Minilya *r.* Australia 109 A5
Minipi Lake Canada 123 J3
Miniss Lake Canada 121 N5
Minitonas Canada 121 K4
Minjian China *see* Mabian
Min Jiang *r. Fujian* China 77 H3
Min Jiang *r. Sichuan* China 76 E2
Minna Nigeria 96 D4
Minna Bluff *pt* Antarctica 152 H1
Minne Sweden 44 I5
Minneapolis *KS* U.S.A. 130 D4
Minneapolis *MN* U.S.A. 130 E2
Minnedosa Canada 121 L5
Minnehaha Springs U.S.A. 134 F4
Minneola U.S.A. 131 C4
Minnesota *r.* U.S.A. 130 E2
Minnesota *state* U.S.A. 130 E2
Minnewaukan U.S.A. 130 D1
Minnitaki Lake Canada 121 N5
Miño *r.* Port./Spain 57 B3
also known as Minho
Minorca *i.* Spain 57 H3
Minot U.S.A. 130 C1
Minqing China 77 H3
Minquan China 77 G1
Min Shan *mts* China 76 D1
Minsin Myanmar 70 A1

▶Minsk Belarus 45 O10
Capital of Belarus.

Mińsk Mazowiecki Poland 47 R4
Minsterley U.K. 49 E6
Mintaka Pass China/Pak. 82 C1
Minto, Lac *l.* Canada 122 G2
Minto, Mount Antarctica 152 H2
Minto Inlet Canada 118 G2
Minton Canada 121 J5
Mīnūdasht Iran 88 D2
Minūf Egypt 90 C5
Minusinsk Russia 72 G2
Minvoul Gabon 98 B3
Minxian China 76 E1
Minya Konka *mt.* China *see* Gongga Shan
Minywa Myanmar 70 A2
Minzong India 83 I4
Mio U.S.A. 134 C1
Miquelon Canada 122 F4
Miquelon *i.* St Pierre and Miquelon 123 K5
Mīrābād Afgh. 89 F4
Mirabela Brazil 145 B2
Mirador, Parque Nacional de *nat. park* Brazil 143 I5
Mīrah, Wādī al *watercourse* Iraq/Saudi Arabia 91 F4
Miraí Brazil 145 C3
Miraj India 84 B2
Miramar Arg. 144 E5
Miramichi Canada 123 I5
Miramichi Bay Canada 123 I5
Mirampelou, Kolpos *b.* Greece 59 K7
Mirampelou, Kolpos *b.* Greece *see* Mirampelou, Kolpos
Miranda Brazil 144 E2
Miranda Moz. *see* Macaloge
Miranda U.S.A. 128 B1
Miranda, Lake *salt flat* Australia 109 C6
Miranda de Ebro Spain 57 E2
Mirandela Port. 57 C3
Mirandola Italy 58 D2
Mirante Brazil 145 C1
Mirante, Serra do *hills* Brazil 145 A3
Mirassol Brazil 145 A3
Mir-Bashir Azer. *see* Tärtär
Mirbāṭ Oman 87 H6
Mirboo North Australia 112 C7
Mirepoix France 56 E5
Mirgarh Pak. 89 I4
Mirgorod Ukr. *see* Myrhorod
Miri *Sarawak* Malaysia 68 E6
Miri *mt.* Pak. 89 F4
Mirialguda India 84 C2
Miri Hills India 83 H4
Mirim, Lagoa *l.* Brazil/Uruguay 144 F4
Mirim, Lagoa do *l.* Brazil 145 A5
Mirintu *watercourse* Australia 112 A2
Mirjan India 84 B3
Mirny *research station* Antarctica 152 F2
Mirnyy *Arkhangel'skaya Oblast'* Russia 42 I3
Mirnyy *Respublika Sakha (Yakutiya)* Russia 65 M3
Mirond Lake Canada 121 K4
Mironovka Ukr. *see* Myronivka
Mirow Germany 53 M1
Mirpur Khas Pak. 89 H5
Mirpur Sakro Pak. 89 G5
Mirs Bay *H.K.* China 77 [inset]
Mirtoan Sea Greece *see* Myrtoo Pelagos
Miryalaguda India *see* Mirialguda
Miryang S. Korea 75 C6
Mirzachirla Turkm. *see* Murzechirla
Mirzachul Uzbek. *see* Guliston
Mirzapur India 83 E4
Mirzawal India 82 C3
Misaw Lake Canada 121 K3
Miscou Island Canada 123 I5
Misehkow *r.* Canada 122 C4
Mīsh, Kūh-e *hill* Iran 88 E3
Misha India 71 A6
Mishawaka U.S.A. 134 B3
Mishicot U.S.A. 134 B1
Mi-shima *i.* Japan 75 C6
Mishmi Hills India 83 H3
Mishvan' Russia 42 L2
Misima Island P.N.G. 110 F1
Misis Dağ *hills* Turkey 85 B1
Miskin Oman 88 E6
Miskitos, Cayos *is* Nicaragua 137 H6
Miskolc Hungary 43 D6
Mismā, Tall al *hill* Jordan 85 C3
Misoöl *i.* Indon. 69 I7
Misquah Hills U.S.A. 130 F2
Misr *country* Africa *see* Egypt
Misraç Turkey *see* Kurtalan
Miṣrātah Libya 97 E1
Missinaibi *r.* Canada 122 E4
Mission Beach Australia 110 D3
Mission Viejo U.S.A. 128 E5
Missisa *r.* Canada 122 D3
Missisa Lake Canada 122 D3
Missisicabi *r.* Canada 122 F4
Mississagua Canada 134 F2
Mississinewa Lake U.S.A. 134 C3

▶Mississippi *r.* U.S.A. 131 F6
4th longest river in North America, and a major part of the longest (Mississippi-Missouri).

Mississippi *state* U.S.A. 131 F5
Mississippi Delta U.S.A. 131 F6
Mississippi Lake Canada 135 G1

▶Mississippi-Missouri *r.* U.S.A. 125 I4
Longest river in North America and 4th in the world.

Mississippi Sound *sea chan.* U.S.A. 131 F6
Missolonghi Greece *see* Mesolongi
Missoula U.S.A. 126 E3

▶Missouri *r.* U.S.A. 130 F4
3rd longest river in North America, and a major part of the longest (Mississippi-Missouri).

Missouri *state* U.S.A. 130 E4
Mistanipisipou *r.* Canada 123 J4
Mistassibi *r.* Canada 119 K5
Mistassini Canada 123 G4
Mistassini *r.* Canada 123 G4
Mistassini, Lac *l.* Canada 122 G4
Mistastin Lake Canada 123 J3
Mistelbach Austria 47 P6
Mistinibi, Lac *l.* Canada 123 J2
Mistissini Canada 122 G4
Misty Fiords National Monument Wilderness *nat. park* U.S.A. 120 D4
Misumba Dem. Rep. Congo 99 C4
Misuratah Libya *see* Miṣrātah
Mitchell Australia 111 D5
Mitchell *r. N.S.W.* Australia 112 F2
Mitchell *r. Qld* Australia 110 C2
Mitchell *r. Vic.* Australia 112 C6
Mitchell Canada 134 E2
Mitchell *IN* U.S.A. 134 B4
Mitchell *OR* U.S.A. 126 C3
Mitchell *SD* U.S.A. 130 D3
Mitchell, Lake Australia 110 D3
Mitchell, Mount U.S.A. 132 D5
Mitchell and Alice Rivers National Park Australia 110 C2
Mitchell Island Cook Is *see* Nassau
Mitchell Island *atoll* Tuvalu *see* Nukulaelae
Mitchell Point Australia 108 E2
Mitchelstown Ireland 51 D5
Mīt Ghamr Egypt 90 C5
Mît Ghamr Egypt *see* Mīt Ghamr
Mithi Pak. 89 H5
Mithrau Pak. 89 H5
Mithri Pak. 89 G4
Mitilíni Greece *see* Mytilini
Mitkof Island U.S.A. 120 C3
Mito Japan 75 F5
Mitole Tanz. 99 D4
Mitre *mt.* N.Z. 113 E5
Mitre Island Solomon Is 107 H3
Mitrofanovka Russia 43 H6
Mitrovica Kosovo *see* Mitrovicë
Mitrovicë Kosovo 59 I3
Mitsinjo Madag. 99 E5
Mits'iwa Eritrea *see* Massawa
Mitta Mitta Australia 112 C6
Mittellandkanal *canal* Germany 53 I2
Mitterteich Germany 53 M5
Mittimatalik Canada *see* Pond Inlet
Mittweida Germany 53 M4
Mitú Col. 142 D3
Mitumba, Chaîne des *mts* Dem. Rep. Congo 99 C5
Mitzic Gabon 98 B3
Miughalaigh *i.* U.K. *see* Mingulay
Miura Japan 75 E6
Mixian China *see* Xinmi
Miyake-jima *i.* Japan 75 E6
Miyako Japan 75 F5
Miyakonojō Japan 75 C7
Miyang China *see* Mile
Miyani India 82 B5
Miyazaki Japan 75 C7
Miyazu Japan 75 D6
Miyi China 76 D3
Miyoshi Japan 75 D6
Mīzān 'Alāqahdārī Afgh. 89 G3
Mīzan Teferī Eth. 98 D3
Mizdah Libya 97 E1
Mizen Head *hd* Ireland 51 C6
Mizhhir"ya Ukr. 43 D6
Mizo Hills *state* India *see* Mizoram
Mizoram *state* India 83 H5
Mizpé Ramon Israel 85 B4
Mjölby Sweden 45 I7
Mkata Tanz. 99 D4
Mkushi Zambia 99 C5
Mladá Boleslav Czechia 47 O5
Mladenovac Serbia 59 I2
Mława Poland 47 R4
Mlilwane Nature Reserve Swaziland 101 J4
Mljet *i.* Croatia 58 G3
Mlungisi S. Africa 101 H6
Mlu Prey Cambodia 71 D4
Mmabatho S. Africa 101 G3
Mmamabula Botswana 101 H2
Mmathethe Botswana 101 G3
Mo Norway 45 D6
Moa *i.* Indon. 108 E2
Moab *hist. area* Jordan 85 B4
Moab U.S.A. 129 I2
Moa Island Australia 110 C1
Moala *i.* Fiji 107 H3
Mo'allā Iran 88 D3
Moamba Moz. 101 K3
Moanda Gabon 98 B4
Moapa U.S.A. 129 F3
Moate Ireland 51 E4
Mobārakeh Iran 88 C3
Mobayembongo Dem. Rep. Congo *see* Mobayi-Mbongo
Mobayi-Mbongo Dem. Rep. Congo 98 C3
Moberly U.S.A. 130 E4
Moberly Lake Canada 120 F4
Mobha India 82 C5
Mobile *AL* U.S.A. 131 F6
Mobile *AZ* U.S.A. 129 G5
Mobile Bay U.S.A. 131 F6
Moble *watercourse* Australia 112 B1
Mobridge U.S.A. 130 C2
Mobutu, Lake Dem. Rep. Congo/Uganda *see* Albert, Lake
Mobutu Sese Seko, Lake Dem. Rep. Congo/Uganda *see* Albert, Lake
Moca Geçidi *pass* Turkey 85 A1
Moçambique *country* Africa *see* Mozambique
Moçambique Moz. 99 E5
Moçâmedes Angola *see* Namibe
Môc Châu Vietnam 70 D2
Mocha Yemen 86 F7
Mocha, Isla *i.* Chile 144 B5
Mochirma, Parque Nacional *nat. park* Venez. 142 F1
Mochudi Botswana 101 H3
Mochudi *admin. dist.* Botswana *see* Kgatleng
Mocimboa da Praia Moz. 99 E5
Möckern Germany 53 L2
Möckmühl Germany 53 J5
Mockträsk Sweden 44 L4
Mocoa Col. 142 C3
Mococa Brazil 145 B3
Mocoduene Moz. 101 L2
Mocorito Mex. 127 G8
Moctezuma *Chihuahua* Mex. 127 G7
Moctezuma *San Luis Potosí* Mex. 136 D4
Moctezuma *Sonora* Mex. 127 F7
Mocuba Moz. 99 D5
Mocun China 77 G4
Modan Indon. 69 I7
Modane France 56 H4
Modder *r.* S. Africa 101 G5
Modena Italy 58 D2
Modena U.S.A. 129 G3
Modesto U.S.A. 128 C3
Modesto Lake U.S.A. 128 C3
Modimolle S. Africa 101 I3
Modjadjiskloof S. Africa 101 J2
Modung China 76 C2
Moe Australia 112 C7
Moel Sych *hill* U.K. 49 D6
Moelv Norway 45 G6
Moen Norway 44 K2
Moenkopi U.S.A. 129 H3
Moenkopi Wash *r.* U.S.A. 129 H4
Moeraki Point N.Z. 113 C7
Moero, Lake Dem. Rep. Congo/Zambia *see* Mweru, Lake
Moers Germany 52 G3
Moffat U.K. 50 F5
Moga India 82 C3

▶Mogadishu Somalia 98 E3
Capital of Somalia.

Mogador Morocco *see* Essaouira
Mogadore Reservoir U.S.A. 134 E3
Moganyaka S. Africa 101 I3
Mogaung Myanmar 70 B1
Mogdy Russia 74 D2
Mögelin Germany 53 M2
Mogi das Cruzes Brazil 145 B3
Mogilev Belarus *see* Mahilyow
Mogilev Podol'skiy Ukr. *see* Mohyliv-Podil's'kyy
Mogi Mirim Brazil 145 B3
Mogiquiçaba Brazil 145 D2
Mogocha Russia 73 L2
Mogod *mts* Tunisia 58 C6
Mogoditshane Botswana 101 G3
Mogollon Mountains U.S.A. 129 I5
Mogollon Plateau U.S.A. 129 H4
Mogontiacum Germany *see* Mainz
Mogroum Chad 97 E3
Moguqi China 74 A3
Mogwadi S. Africa 101 I2
Mogwadi *r.* S. Africa 101 I2
Mogwase S. Africa 101 H3
Mogzon Russia 73 K2
Mohács Hungary 58 H2
Mohaka *r.* N.Z. 113 F4
Mohala India 84 D1
Mohale Dam Lesotho 101 I5
Mohale's Hoek Lesotho 101 H6
Mohali India 82 D3
Mohall U.S.A. 130 C1
Moḥammad Iran 88 E3
Moḥammadābād Iran 88 E4
Mohammadia Alg. 57 G6
Mohan *r.* India/Nepal 82 E3
Mohana India 82 D4
Mohave, Lake U.S.A. 129 F4
Mohawk *r.* U.S.A. 135 I2
Mohawk Mountains U.S.A. 129 G5
Mohenjo Daro *tourist site* Pak. 89 H5
Moher, Cliffs of Ireland 51 C5
Mohill Ireland 51 E4
Möhne *r.* Germany 53 H3
Möhnetalsperre *resr* Germany 53 I3
Mohon Peak U.S.A. 129 G4
Mohoro Tanz. 99 D4
Mohyliv-Podil's'kyy Ukr. 43 E6
Moi Norway 45 E7
Moijabana Botswana 101 H2
Moincêr China 82 E3
Moine Moz. 101 K3
Moinești Romania 59 L1
Mointy Kazakh. *see* Moyynty
Mo i Rana Norway 44 I3
Moirang India 76 B3
Mõisaküla Estonia 45 N7
Moisie Canada 123 I4
Moisie *r.* Canada 123 I4
Moissac France 56 E4
Mojave U.S.A. 128 D4
Mojave *r.* U.S.A. 128 E4
Mojave Desert U.S.A. 128 E4
Mojiang China 76 D4
Mojos, Llanos de *plain* Bol. 142 E6
Moju *r.* Brazil 143 I4
Mokala National Park S. Africa 100 G5
Mokama India 83 F4
Mokau N.Z. 113 E4
Mokau *r.* N.Z. 113 E4
Mokelumne *r.* U.S.A. 128 C2
Mokelumne Aqueduct *canal* U.S.A. 128 C2
Mokh, Gowd-e *l.* Iran 88 D4
Mokhoabong Pass Lesotho 101 I5
Mokhotlong Lesotho 101 I5
Mokhtārān Iran 88 E3
Moknine Tunisia 58 D7
Mokohinau Islands N.Z. 113 E2
Mokokchung India 83 H4
Mokolo Cameroon 97 E3
Mokolo *r.* S. Africa 101 H2
Mokopane S. Africa 101 I3
Mokpo S. Korea 75 B6
Mokrous Russia 43 J6
Moksha *r.* Russia 43 I5
Mokshan Russia 43 J5
Möksy Fin. 44 N5
Môktama Myanmar *see* Mottama
Môktama, Gulf of Myanmar *see* Mottama, Gulf of
Mokundurra India *see* Mukandwara
Mokwa Nigeria 96 D4
Molatón *mt.* Spain 57 F4
Moldavia *country* Europe *see* Moldova

Movas Mex. 127 F7
Mowbullan, Mount Australia 112 E1
Moxey Town Bahamas 133 E7
Moy r. Ireland 51 C3
Moyale Eth. 98 D3
Moyen Atlas mts Morocco 54 C5
Moyen-Congo country Africa see Congo
Moyeni Lesotho 101 H6
Moynalyk Russia 80 I1
Moynaq Uzbek. see Mo'ynoq
Mo'ynoq Uzbek. 80 A3
Moyo i. Indon. 108 B2
Moyobamba Peru 142 C5
Moyock U.S.A. 135 G5
Moyola r. U.K. 51 F3
Moyu China 82 D1
Moyynkum Kazakh. 80 D3
Moyynkum, Peski des. Kazakh. 80 C3
Moyynty Kazakh. 80 D2
Mozambique country Africa 99 D6
Mozambique Channel Africa 99 E6
Mozambique Ridge sea feature Indian Ocean 149 K7
Mozdok Russia 91 G2
Mozhaysk Russia 43 H5
Mozhga Russia 42 L4
Mozo Myanmar 76 B4
Mozyr' Belarus see Mazyr
Mpaathutlwa Pan salt pan Botswana 100 E3
Mpanda Tanz. 99 D4
Mpen India 83 I4
Mpika Zambia 99 D5
Mpolweni S. Africa 101 J5
Mporokoso Zambia 99 D4
Mpulungu Zambia 99 D4
Mpumalanga prov. S. Africa 101 I4
Mpunde mt. Tanz. 99 D4
Mpwapwa Tanz. 99 D4
Mqanduli S. Africa 101 I6
Mqinvartsveri mt. Georgia/Russia see Kazbek
Mrauk-U Myanmar 70 A2
Mrewa Zimbabwe see Murehwa
Mrkonjić-Grad Bos. & Herz. 58 G2
M'Saken Tunisia 58 D7
Mshinskaya Russia 45 P7
M'Sila Alg. 57 I6
Msta r. Russia 42 F4
Mstislavl' Belarus see Mstsislaw
Mstsislaw Belarus 43 F5
Mtelo Kenya 98 D3
Mthatha S. Africa 101 I6
Mtoko Zimbabwe see Mutoko
Mtorwi Tanz. 99 D4
Mtsensk Russia 43 H5
Mts'ire Kavkasioni Asia see Lesser Caucasus
Mtubatuba S. Africa 101 K5
Mtunzini S. Africa 101 J5
Mtwara Tanz. 99 E5
Mu r. Myanmar 70 A2
Mu'āb, Jibāl reg. Jordan see Moab
Muanda Dem. Rep. Congo 99 B4
Muang Ham Laos 70 D2
Muang Hiam Laos 70 C2
Muang Hinboun Laos 70 D3
Muang Hôngsa Laos 70 C3
Muang Khi Laos 70 C3
Muang Không Laos 71 D4
Muang Khoua Laos 70 C2
Muang Lamam Laos see Xékong
Muang Mok Laos 70 D3
Muang Ngoy Laos 70 C2
Muang Ou Nua Laos 70 C2
Muang Pakbeng Laos 70 C3
Muang Paktha Laos 70 C2
Muang Pakxan Laos see Pakxan
Muang Phalan Laos 68 D3
Muang Phin Laos 70 D3
Muang Sam Sip Thai. 70 D4
Muang Sing Laos 70 C2
Muang Soum Laos 70 C3
Muang Souy Laos 70 C3
Muang Thadua Laos 70 C3
Muang Thai country Asia see Thailand
Muang Va Laos 70 C2
Muang Vangviang Laos 70 C3
Muang Xon Laos 70 C2
Muar Malaysia 71 C7
Muarabungo Indon. 68 C7
Muarateweh Indon. 68 E7
Mubari, Ras pt Pak. 89 G5
Mu'ayqil, Khashm al hill Saudi Arabia 88 C5
Mubarek Uzbek. see Muborak
Mubarraz well Saudi Arabia 91 F5
Mubende Uganda 98 D3
Mubi Nigeria 96 E3
Muborak Uzbek. 89 G2
Mubur i. Indon. 71 D7
Mucajaí, Serra do mts Brazil 142 F3
Mucalic r. Canada 123 I2
Muccan Australia 108 C5
Much Germany 53 H4
Muchinga Escarpment Zambia 99 D5
Muchuan China 76 D2
Muck i. U.K. 50 C4
Mucojo Moz. 99 E5
Muconda Angola 99 C5
Mucubela Moz. 99 D5
Mucugê Brazil 145 C1
Mucur Turkey 90 D3
Mucuri Brazil 145 D2
Mucuri r. Brazil 145 D2
Mūd Iran 88 E3
Mudabidri India 84 B3
Mudan China see Heze
Mudanjiang China 74 C3
Mudan Jiang r. China 74 C3
Mudan Ling mts China 74 B4
Mudanya Turkey 59 M4
Mudaybī Oman 88 E6
Mudaysīsāt, Jabal al hill Jordan 85 C4
Muddus nationalpark nat. park Sweden 44 K3
Muddy r. U.S.A. 129 F3
Muddy Gap U.S.A. 126 G4
Muddy Peak U.S.A. 129 F3
Mudersbach Germany 53 H4
Mudgal India 84 C3
Mudgee Australia 112 D4
Mudhol India 84 B2
Mudigere India 84 B3
Mudjatik r. Canada 121 J3
Mud Lake U.S.A. 128 E3
Mudraya country Africa see Egypt
Mudurnu Turkey 59 N4
Mud'yuga Russia 42 H3
Mueda Moz. 99 D5
Mueller Range hills Australia 108 D4
Muertos Cays is Bahamas 133 D7
Muftyuga Russia 42 J2
Mufulira Zambia 99 C5
Mufumbwe Zambia 99 C5
Mufu Shan mts China 77 G2
Muğan Düzü lowland Azer. 91 H3
Mugarripug China 83 F2
Mughalbhin Pak. see Jati
Mughal Kot Pak. 89 H4
Mughal Sarai India 83 E4
Mūghār Iran 88 D3
Mughayrā' Saudi Arabia 85 C5
Mughayrā' well Saudi Arabia 88 B5
Muğla Turkey 59 M6
Mugodzhary, Gory mts Kazakh. 80 A2
Mugxung China 76 B1
Muḩ, Sabkhat al imp. l. Syria 85 D2
Muhammad Ashraf Pak. 89 H5
Muhammad Qol Sudan 86 E5
Muhammarah Iran see Khorramshahr
Muhashsham, Wādī al watercourse Egypt 85 B4
Muḩaysh, Wādī al watercourse Jordan 85 C5
Muḩaysinīyah Syria 85 D1
Mühlanger Germany 53 M3
Mühlberg/Elbe Germany 53 N3
Mühlhausen/Thüringen Germany 53 K3
Mühlig-Hofmann Mountains Antarctica 152 C2
Muhos Fin. 44 N4
Muḩradah Syria 85 C2
Mui Bai Bung c. Vietnam see Ca Mau, Mui
Muié Angola 99 C5
Muineachán Ireland see Monaghan
Muir U.S.A. 134 C2
Muirkirk U.K. 50 E5
Muir of Ord U.K. 50 E3
Muite Moz. 99 D5
Mūjān, Chāh-e well Iran 88 D3
Muji China 82 D1
Muju S. Korea 75 B5
Mukacheve Ukr. 43 D6
Mukachevo Ukr. see Mukacheve
Mukah Sarawak Malaysia 68 E6
Mukalla Yemen 86 G7
Mukandwara India 82 D4
Mukdahan Thai. 70 D3
Mukden China see Shenyang
Muketei r. Canada 122 D3
Mukhen Russia 74 E2
Mukhino Russia 74 B1
Mukhtuya Russia see Lensk
Mūkīk, Chashmeh-ye spring Iran 88 E3
Mukinbudin Australia 109 B7
Mu Ko Chang Marine National Park Thai. 71 C5
Mukojima-rettō is Japan 75 F8
Mukry Turkm. 89 G2
Muktsar India 82 C3
Mukutawa r. Canada 121 L4
Mukwonago U.S.A. 134 A2
Mula r. India 84 B2
Mulainagiri mt. India 84 B3
Mulakatholhu Maldives 81 D11
Mulaku Atoll atoll Maldives see Mulakatholhu
Mulan China 74 C3
Mulanje, Mount Malawi 99 D5
Mulapula, Lake salt flat Australia 111 B6
Mulatos Mex. 127 F7
Mulayḩ Saudi Arabia 88 B5
Mulayḩah, Jabal hill U.A.E. 88 D5
Mulayz, Wādī al watercourse Egypt 85 A4
Mulchatna r. U.S.A. 118 C3
Mulde r. Germany 53 M3
Mule Creek NM U.S.A. 129 I5
Mule Creek WY U.S.A. 126 G4
Mulegé Mex. 127 E8
Mules i. Indon. 108 C2
Muleshoe U.S.A. 131 C5
Mulga Park Australia 109 E6
Mulgathing Australia 109 F7
Mulhacén mt. Spain 57 E5
Mülhausen France see Mulhouse
Mülheim an der Ruhr Germany 52 G3
Mulhouse France 56 H3
Muli China 76 D3
Muli Russia see Vysokogorniy
Mulia Indon. 69 J7
Muling Heilong. China 74 C3
Muling Heilong. China 74 C3
Muling He r. China 74 D3
Mull i. U.K. 50 D4
Mull, Sound of sea chan. U.K. 50 C4
Mullaghcleevaun hill Ireland 51 F4
Mullaittivu Sri Lanka 84 D4
Mullaley Australia 112 D3
Mullengudgery Australia 112 C3
Mullens U.S.A. 134 E5
Muller watercourse Australia 108 F5
Muller, Pegunungan mts Indon. 68 E6
Mullett Lake U.S.A. 134 C1
Mullewa Australia 109 A7
Mullica r. U.S.A. 135 H4
Mullingar Ireland 51 E4
Mullion Creek Australia 112 D4
Mull of Galloway c. U.K. 50 E6
Mull of Kintyre hd U.K. 50 D5
Mull of Oa hd U.K. 50 C5
Mullumbimby Australia 112 F2
Mulobezi Zambia 99 C5
Mulshi Lake India 84 B2
Multai India 82 D5
Multan Pak. 89 H4
Multia Fin. 44 N5
Multien reg. France 52 C6
Mulug India 84 C2

▶Mumbai India 84 B2
4th most populous city in Asia and 6th in the world.

Mumbil Australia 112 D4
Mumbwa Zambia 99 C5
Muminabad Tajik. see Leningrad
Mŭ'minobod Tajik. see Leningrad
Mun, Mae Nam r. Thai. 70 D4
Muna i. Indon. 69 G8
Muna Mex. 136 G4
Muna r. Russia 65 N3
Munabao Pak. 89 H5
Munaðarnes Iceland 44 [inset 1]
Münchberg Germany 53 L4
München Germany see Munich
München-Gladbach Germany see Mönchengladbach
Münchhausen Germany 53 I4
Muncho Lake Canada 120 E3
Muncie U.S.A. 134 C3
Muncoonie West, Lake salt flat Australia 110 B5
Muncy U.S.A. 135 G3
Munda Pak. 89 H4
Mundel Lake Sri Lanka 84 C5
Mundesley U.K. 49 I6
Mundford U.K. 49 H6
Mundiwindi (abandoned) Australia 109 C5
Mundra India 82 B5
Mundrabilla Australia 106 C5
Munds Park U.S.A. 129 H4
Mundubbera Australia 111 E5
Mundwa India 82 C4
Munfordville U.S.A. 134 C5
Mungallala Australia 111 D5
Mungana Australia 110 D3
Mungap-do i. S. Korea 75 B5
Mungári Moz. 99 D5
Mungbere Dem. Rep. Congo 98 C3
Mungeli India 83 E5
Munger India 83 F4
Mu Nggava i. Solomon Is see Rennell
Mungindi Australia 112 D2
Mungla Bangl. see Mongla
Mungo Angola 99 B5
Mungo, Lake Australia 112 A4
Mungo National Park Australia 112 A4
Munich Germany 47 M6
Munising U.S.A. 132 C2
Munjpur India 82 B5
Munkács Ukr. see Mukacheve
Munkebakken Norway 44 P2
Munkedal Sweden 45 G7
Munkfors Sweden 45 H7
Munkhafaḑ al Qaţţārah depr. Egypt see Qattara Depression
Munku-Sardyk, Gora mt. Mongolia/Russia 72 I2
Münnerstadt Germany 53 K4
Munnik S. Africa 101 I2
Munroe Lake Canada 121 L3
Munsan S. Korea 75 B5
Münster Hessen Germany 53 I5
Münster Germany 53 K2
Münster Nordrhein-Westfalen Germany 53 H3
Munster reg. Ireland 51 D5
Münsterland reg. Germany 53 H3
Muntadgin Australia 109 B7
Muntervary hd Ireland 51 C6
Munyal-Par sea feature India see Bassas de Pedro Padua Bank
Munzur Vadisi Milli Parkı nat. park Turkey 55 L4
Muojärvi l. Fin. 44 P4
Mương Nhe Vietnam 70 C2
Muong Sai Laos see Oudômxai
Muonio Fin. 44 M3
Muonioälven r. Fin./Sweden 44 M3
Muonionjoki r. Fin./Sweden see Muonioälven
Mupa, Parque Nacional da nat. park Angola 99 B5
Muping China see Baoxing
Muqaynimah well Saudi Arabia 88 C6
Muqdisho Somalia see Mogadishu
Muqêr Afgh. 89 G3
Muquém Brazil 145 A1
Muqui Brazil 145 C3
Muqur Afgh. 89 F3
Mur r. Austria 47 P7
also known as Mura (Croatia/Slovenia)
Mura r. Croatia/Slovenia see Mur
Murai, Tanjong pt Sing. 71 [inset]
Murai Reservoir Sing. 71 [inset]
Murakami Japan 75 E5
Murallón, Cerro mt. Chile 144 B7
Muramvya Burundi 98 C4
Murashi Russia 42 K4
Murat r. Turkey 91 E3
Muratlı Turkey 59 L4
Muraysah, Ra's al pt Libya 90 B5
Murchison watercourse Australia 109 A6
Murchison, Mount Antarctica 152 H2
Murchison, Mount hill Australia 109 B6
Murchison Falls National Park Uganda 98 D3
Murcia Spain 57 F5
Murcia aut. comm. Spain 57 F5
Murdo U.S.A. 130 C3
Murehwa Zimbabwe 99 D5
Mureşul r. Romania 59 I1
Muret France 56 E5
Murewa Zimbabwe see Murehwa
Murfreesboro AR U.S.A. 131 E5
Murfreesboro TN U.S.A. 132 C5
Murg r. Germany 53 I6
Murgab Tajik. see Murghob
Murgab Turkm. see Murgap
Murgab r. Turkm. see Murgap
Murgap Turkm. 89 F2
Murgap r. Turkm. 87 J2
Murgh, Kōtal-e Afgh. 89 H3
Murghāb reg. Afgh. 89 F3
Murgha Kibzai Pak. 89 H4
Murghob Tajik. 89 I2
Murgon Australia 111 E5
Murgoo Australia 109 B6
Muri India 83 F5
Muriaé Brazil 145 C3
Murid Pak. 89 G4
Muriege Angola 99 C4
Müritz l. Germany 53 M1
Müritz, Nationalpark nat. park Germany 53 N1
Murmansk Russia 44 R2
Murmanskaya Oblast' admin. div. Russia 44 S2
Murmanskiy Bereg coastal area Russia 42 G1
Murmansk Oblast admin. div. Russia see Murmanskaya Oblast'
Muro, Capo di c. Corsica France 56 I6
Murom Russia 42 I5
Muroran Japan 74 F4
Muros Spain 57 B2
Muroto Japan 75 D6
Muroto-zaki pt Japan 75 D6
Murphy ID U.S.A. 126 D4
Murphy NC U.S.A. 133 D5
Murphysboro U.S.A. 130 F4
Murrah reg. Saudi Arabia 88 C6
Murrah al Kubrá, Al Buḩayrah al l. Egypt see Great Bitter Lake
Murrah aş Şughrá, Al Buḩayrah al l. Egypt see Little Bitter Lake
Murramarang National Park nat. park Australia 112 I5
Murra Murra Australia 112 C2
Murrat el Kubra, Buheirat l. Egypt see Great Bitter Lake
Murrat el Sughra, Buheirat l. Egypt see Little Bitter Lake

▶Murray r. S.A. Australia 111 B7
3rd longest river in Oceania, and a major part of the longest (Murray-Darling).

Murray r. W.A. Australia 109 A8
Murray KY U.S.A. 131 F4
Murray UT U.S.A. 129 H1
Murray, Lake P.N.G. 69 K8
Murray, Lake U.S.A. 133 D5
Murray, Mount Canada 120 D2
Murray Bridge Australia 111 B7

▶Murray-Darling r. Australia 106 E5
Longest river in Oceania.

Murray Downs Australia 108 F5
Murray Range hills Australia 109 E6
Murraysburg S. Africa 100 F6
Murray Sunset National Park Australia 111 C7
Murrhardt Germany 53 J6
Murrieta U.S.A. 128 E5
Murringo Australia 112 D5
Murrisk reg. Ireland 51 C4
Murroogh Ireland 51 C4

▶Murrumbidgee r. Australia 112 A5
4th longest river in Oceania.

Murrumburrah Australia 112 D5
Murrurundi Australia 112 E3
Mursan India 82 D4
Murshidabad India 83 G4
Murska Sobota Slovenia 58 G1
Mürt Iran 89 F5
Murtoa Australia 111 C8
Murua i. P.N.G. see Woodlark Island
Murud India 84 B2
Murud, Gunung mt. Indon. 68 F6
Murujuga National Park Australia 108 B5
Murunkan Sri Lanka 84 D4
Murupara N.Z. 113 F4
Mururoa atoll Fr. Polynesia 151 K7
Murviedro Spain see Sagunto
Murwara India see Katni
Murwillumbah Australia 112 F2
Murzechirla Turkm. 89 F2
Murzūq Libya 97 E2
Murzuq, Ḩamādat plat. Libya 98 B1
Murzuq, Idhān des. Libya 96 E2
Mürzzuschlag Austria 47 O7
Muş Turkey 91 F3
Mūsā, Khowr-e b. Iran 88 C4
Mūsá, Ţal'at mt. Lebanon/Syria 85 C2
Musakhel Pak. 89 H4
Musala mt. Bulg. 59 J3
Musala i. Indon. 71 B7
Musan N. Korea 74 C4
Musandam Peninsula Oman/U.A.E. 88 E5
Musay'īd Qatar see Umm Sa'id

▶Muscat Oman 88 E6
Capital of Oman.

Muscat reg. Oman 88 E5
Muscat and Oman country Asia see Oman
Muscatine U.S.A. 130 F3
Musgrave Australia 110 C2
Musgrave Harbour Canada 123 L4
Musgrave Ranges mts Australia 109 E6
Mushayyish, Wādī al watercourse Jordan 85 C4
Mushie Dem. Rep. Congo 98 B4
Mushkaf Pak. 89 G4
Music Mountain U.S.A. 129 G4
Musina S. Africa 101 J2
Musinia Peak U.S.A. 129 H2
Muskeg r. Canada 120 F2
Muskeget Channel U.S.A. 135 J3
Muskegon U.S.A. 134 B2
Muskegon r. U.S.A. 134 B2
Muskegon Heights U.S.A. 134 B2
Muskeg River Canada 120 G4
Muskogee U.S.A. 131 E5
Muskoka, Lake Canada 134 F1
Muskrat Dam Lake Canada 121 N4
Musmar Sudan 86 E6
Musoma Tanz. 98 D4
Musquanousse, Lac l. Canada 123 J4
Musquaro, Lac l. Canada 123 J4
Mussau Island P.N.G. 69 L7
Musselburgh U.K. 50 F5
Musselkanaal Neth. 52 H2
Musselshell r. U.S.A. 126 G3
Mussende Angola 99 B5
Mustafakemalpaşa Turkey 59 M4
Mustjala Estonia 45 M7
Mustvee Estonia 45 O7
Musu-dan pt N. Korea 74 C4
Muswellbrook Australia 112 E4
Mūţ Egypt 86 C4
Mut Turkey 85 A1
Mutá, Ponta do pt Brazil 145 D1
Mutare Zimbabwe 99 D5
Mutayr reg. Saudi Arabia 88 B5
Mutina Italy see Modena
Muting Indon. 69 K8
Mutis Col. 142 C2
Mutnyy Materik Russia 42 L2
Mutoko Zimbabwe 99 D5
Mutsamudu Comoros 99 E5
Mutsu Japan 74 F4
Muttaburra Australia 110 D4
Mutton Island Ireland 51 C5
Muttukuru India 84 D3
Muttupet India 84 C4
Mutum Brazil 145 C2
Mutunópolis Brazil 145 A1
Mutur Sri Lanka 84 D4
Mutusjärvi r. Fin. 44 O2
Muurola Fin. 44 N3
Mu Us Shadi des. China 73 J5
Muxaluando Angola 99 B4
Muxi China see Muchuan
Muxima Angola 99 B4
Muyezerskiy Russia 44 R5
Muyinga Burundi 98 D4
Mŭynoq Uzbek. see Mo'ynoq
Muyu China 77 F2
Muyumba Dem. Rep. Congo 99 C4
Muyunkum, Peski des. Kazakh. see Moyynkum, Peski
Muzaffarabad Pak. 89 I3
Muzaffargarh Pak. 89 H4
Muzaffarnagar India 82 D3
Muzaffarpur India 83 F4
Muzamane Moz. 101 K2
Muzbel', Uval hills Kazakh. 91 I2
Muzhi Russia 41 S2
Mūzīn Iran 89 F5
Muzon, Cape U.S.A. 120 C4
Múzquiz Mex. 131 C7
Muz Shan mt. China 82 E2
Muz Tag mt. China 83 F1
Muztagata mt. China 89 I2
Muztor Kyrg. see Toktogul
Mvadi Gabon 98 B3
Mvolo South Sudan 97 F4
Mvuma Zimbabwe 99 D5
Mwanza Malawi 99 D5
Mwanza Tanz. 98 D4
Mweelrea hill Ireland 51 C4
Mweka Dem. Rep. Congo 99 C4
Mwene-Ditu Dem. Rep. Congo 99 C4
Mwenezi Zimbabwe 99 D6
Mwenga Dem. Rep. Congo 98 C4
Mweru, Lake Dem. Rep. Congo/Zambia 99 C4
Mweru Wantipa National Park Zambia 99 C4
Mwimba Dem. Rep. Congo 99 C4
Mwinilunga Zambia 99 C5
Myadaung Myanmar 70 B2
Myadzyel Belarus 45 O9
Myajlar India 82 B4
Myall Lakes National Park Australia 112 F4
Myanaung Myanmar 70 A3
Myanmar country Asia 70 A2
Myauk-Oo Myanmar see Mrauk-U
Myaungmya Myanmar 70 A3
Myawadi Thai. 70 B3
Mybster U.K. 50 F2
Myebon Myanmar 70 A2
Myede Myanmar see Aunglan
Myeik Myanmar 71 B4
Myingyan Myanmar 70 A2
Myinkyado Myanmar 70 B2
Myinmoletkat mt. Myanmar 71 B4
Myitkyina Myanmar 70 B1
Myitson Myanmar 70 B2
Myitta Myanmar 71 B4
Myittha Myanmar 70 B2
Mykolayiv Ukr. 59 O1
Mykonos i. Greece 59 K6
Myla Russia 42 K2
Myla r. Russia 42 K2
Mylae Sicily Italy see Milazzo
Mylasa Turkey see Milas
Mymensing Bangl. see Mymensingh
Mymensingh Bangl. 83 G4
Mynämäki Fin. 45 M6
Myŏnggan N. Korea 74 C4
Myory Belarus 45 O9
My Phước Vietnam 71 D5
Mýrdalsjökull ice cap Iceland 44 [inset 1]
Myre Norway 44 I2
Myrheden Sweden 44 L4
Myrhorod Ukr. 43 G6
Myrnam Canada 121 I4
Myronivka Ukr. 43 F6
Myrtle Beach U.S.A. 133 E5
Myrtleford Australia 112 C6
Myrtle Point U.S.A. 126 B4
Myrtoo Pelagos sea Greece 59 J6
Mys Chelyuskin Russia 153 E1
Mysia hist. area Turkey 59 L5
Mys Lazareva Russia see Lazarev
Myślibórz Poland 47 O4
My Sơn Sanctuary tourist site Vietnam 70 E4
Mysore India see Mysuru
Mysore state India see Karnataka
Mys Shmidta Russia 65 T3
Mysuru India 84 C3
Mysy Russia 42 L3
My Tho Vietnam 71 D5
Mytikas mt. Greece see Olympus, Mount
Mytilene i. Greece see Lesbos
Mytilini Greece 59 L5
Mytilini Strait Greece/Turkey 59 L5
Mytishchi Russia 42 H5
Myton U.S.A. 129 H1
Myyeldino Russia 42 L3
Mzamomhle S. Africa 101 H6
Mže r. Czechia 53 M5
Mzimba Malawi 99 D5
Mzuzu Malawi 99 D5

N

Naab r. Germany 53 M5
Nā'ālehu U.S.A. 127 [inset]
Naantali Fin. 45 M6
Naas Ireland 51 F4
Náátsʼihchʼoh National Park Reserve nat. park Canada 120 D2
Naba Myanmar 70 B1
Nababeep S. Africa 100 C5
Nababganj Bangl. see Nawabganj
Nabadwip India see Navadwip
Nabarangapur India 84 D2
Nabarangpur India see Nabarangapur
Nabari Japan 75 E6
Nabatîyé et Tahta Lebanon 85 B3
Nabatiyet et Tahta Lebanon see Nabatîyé et Tahta
Nabberu, Lake salt flat Australia 109 C6
Nabburg Germany 53 M5
Naberera Tanz. 99 D4
Naberezhnyye Chelny Russia 41 Q4
Nabesna U.S.A. 120 A2
Nabeul Tunisia 58 D6
Nabha India 82 D3
Nabil'skiy Zaliv lag. Russia 74 F2
Nabire Indon. 69 J7
Nabi Younés, Ras en pt Lebanon 85 B3
Nāblus West Bank 85 B3
Nabq Protected Area nature res. Egypt 90 D5
Nābulus West Bank see Nāblus
Nacala Moz. 99 E5
Nachalovo Russia 43 K7
Nachicapau, Lac l. Canada 123 I2
Nachingwea Tanz. 99 D5
Nachna India 82 B4
Nachuge India 71 A5
Nacimiento Reservoir U.S.A. 128 C4
Naco U.S.A. 127 F7
Nacogdoches U.S.A. 131 E6
Nada China see Danzhou
Nadaleen r. Canada 120 C2
Nådendal Fin. see Naantali
Nadezhdinskoye Russia 74 D2
Nadiad India 82 C5
Nadol India 82 C4
Nador Morocco 57 E6
Nadqān, Qalamat well Saudi Arabia 88 C6
Nadūshan Iran 88 D3
Nadvirna Ukr. 43 E6
Nadvoitsy Russia 42 G3
Nadvornaya Ukr. see Nadvirna
Nadym Russia 64 I3
Næstved Denmark 45 G9
Nafarroa aut. comm. Spain see Navarra
Nafas, Ra's an mt. Egypt 85 B5
Nafḩa, Har hill Israel 85 B4
Nafpaktos Greece 59 I5
Nafplio Greece 59 J6
Naftalan Azer. 91 G2
Naft-e Safīd Iran 88 C4
Naft-e Shāh Iran see Naft Shahr
Naft Shahr Iran 88 B3
Nafūsah, Jabal hills Libya 96 E1
Nafy Saudi Arabia 86 F4
Nag, Co l. China 83 G2
Naga Phil. 69 G4
Nagagami r. Canada 122 D4
Nagagami Lake Canada 122 D4
Nagahama Japan 75 D6
Naga Hills India 83 H4
Naga Hills state India see Nagaland
Nagaland state India 83 H4
Nagamangala India 84 C3
Nagambie Australia 112 B6
Nagano Japan 75 E5
Nagaoka Japan 75 E5
Nagaon India 83 H4
Nagapatam India see Nagappattinam
Nagappattinam India 84 C4
Nagar Hima. Prad. India 87 M3
Nagar Karnataka India 84 B3
Nagaram India 84 D2
Nagari Hills India 84 C3
Nagarjuna Sagar Reservoir India 84 C2
Nagar Parkar Pak. 89 H5
Nagar Untari India 83 E4
Nagasaki Japan 75 C6
Nagato Japan 75 C6
Nagaur India 82 C4
Nagbhir India 84 C1
Nagda India 82 C5
Nageezi U.S.A. 129 J3
Nagercoil India 84 C4
Nagha Kalat Pak. 89 G5
Nag' Hammâdî Egypt see Naj' Ḩammādī
Nagina India 82 D3
Nagold r. Germany 53 I6
Nagong Chu r. China see Parlung Zangbo
Nagorno-Karabakh disp. terr. Azer. 91 G3
Nagornyy Karabakh disp. terr. Azer. see Nagorno-Karabakh
Nagorsk Russia 42 K4
Nagoya Japan 75 E6
Nagpur India 82 D5
Nagqu China 76 B2
Nag Qu r. China 76 B2
Nagurskoye Russia 64 F1
Nagyatád Hungary 58 G1
Nagybecskerek Serbia see Zrenjanin
Nagyenyed Romania see Aiud
Nagykanizsa Hungary 58 G1
Nagyvárad Romania see Oradea
Naha Japan 73 N7
Nahan India 82 D3
Nahanni Butte Canada 120 F2
Nahanni National Park Reserve Canada 120 E2
Nahanni Range mts Canada 120 F2
Naharāyim Jordan 85 B3
Nahariyya Israel 85 B3
Nahāvand Iran 88 C3
Nahr Dijlah r. Asia see Tigris

Nahrīn Afgh. 89 H2
Nahrīn reg. Afgh. 89 H2
Nahuel Huapí, Parque Nacional nat. park Arg. 144 B6
Nahunta U.S.A. 133 D6
Naica Mex. 131 B7
Nai Ga Myanmar 76 C3
Naij Tal China 83 H2
Naikliu Indon. 108 C2
Nain Canada 123 J2
Nā'īn Iran 88 D3
Nainital India 82 D3
Naini Tal India see Nainital
Nairn U.K. 50 F3
Nairn r. U.K. 50 F3

▶Nairobi Kenya 98 D4
Capital of Kenya.

Naissus Serbia see Niš
Naivasha Kenya 98 D4
Najafābād Iran 88 C3
Na'jān Saudi Arabia 88 B5
Najd reg. Saudi Arabia 86 F4
Nájera Spain 57 E2
Naj' Ḥammādī Egypt 86 D4
Naji China 74 A2
Najibabad India 82 D3
Najin N. Korea 74 C4
Najitun China see Naji
Najrān Saudi Arabia 86 F6
Nakadōri-shima i. Japan 75 C6
Na Kae Thai. 70 D3
Nakambé r. Burkina Faso/Ghana see White Volta
Nakanbe r. Burkina Faso/Ghana see White Volta
Nakanno Russia 65 L3
Nakano-shima i. Japan 75 D5
Nakasongola Uganda 97 G4
Nakatsu Japan 75 C6
Nakatsugawa Japan 75 E6
Nakdong-gang r. S. Korea 75 C6
Nakfa Eritrea 86 E6
Nakhichevan' Azer. see Naxçıvan
Nakhl Egypt 85 A5
Nakhodka Russia 74 D4
Nakhola India 83 H4
Nakhon Nayok Thai. 71 C4
Nakhon Pathom Thai. 71 C4
Nakhon Phanom Thai. 70 D3
Nakhon Ratchasima Thai. 70 C4
Nakhon Sawan Thai. 70 C4
Nakhon Si Thammarat Thai. 71 B5
Nakhtarana India 82 B5
Nakina Canada 122 D4
Nakina r. Canada 120 C3
Naknek U.S.A. 118 C4
Nakonde Zambia 99 D4
Nakskov Denmark 45 G9
Nakuru Kenya 98 D4
Nakusp Canada 120 G5
Nal Pak. 89 G5
Nal r. Pak. 89 G5
Na-lang Myanmar 70 B2
Nalázi Moz. 101 K3
Nalbari India 83 G4
Nal'chik Russia 91 F2
Naldurg India 84 C2
Nalgonda India 84 C2
Naliya India 82 B5
Nallamala Hills India 84 C3
Nallıhan Turkey 59 N4
Nālūt Libya 96 E1
Namaacha Moz. 101 K3
Namacurra Moz. 99 D5
Namadgi National Park Australia 112 D5
Namahadi S. Africa 101 I4
Namak, Daryācheh-ye salt flat Iran 88 C3
Namak, Kavīr-e salt flat Iran 88 E3
Namakkal India 84 C4
Namakwaland reg. Namibia see Great Namaqualand
Namakzar-e Shadad salt flat Iran 88 E4
Namaland reg. Namibia see Great Namaqualand
Namangan Uzbek. 80 D3
Namaqualand reg. Namibia see Great Namaqualand
Namaqualand reg. S. Africa 100 C5
Namaqua National Park S. Africa 100 C6
Namas Indon. 69 K8
Namatanai P.N.G. 106 F2
Nambour Australia 112 F1
Nambucca Heads Australia 112 F3
Nambung National Park Australia 109 A7
Năm Căn Vietnam 71 D5
Namcha Barwa mt. China see Namjagbarwa Feng
Namche Bazar Nepal 83 F4
Nam Co salt l. China 83 G3
Namdalen valley Norway 44 H4
Namdalseid Norway 44 G4
Nam Định Vietnam 70 D2
Nam Du, Quần Đao i. Vietnam 71 D5
Namen Belgium see Namur
Nam-gang r. N. Korea 75 B5
Namhae-do i. S. Korea 75 B6
Namhsan Myanmar 70 B2
Namib Desert Namibia 100 B3
Namibe Angola 99 B5
Namibia country Africa 99 B6
Namibia Abyssal Plain sea feature N. Atlantic Ocean 148 I8
Namib-Naukluft Park nature res. Namibia 100 B3
Namie (abandoned) Japan 75 F5
Namin Iran 91 H3
Namjagbarwa Feng mt. China 76 B2
Namlan Myanmar 70 B2
Nam Loi r. China see Nanlei He
Nam Nao National Park Thai. 70 C3
Namoi r. Australia 112 D3
Namonuito atoll Micronesia 69 L5
Nampa mt. Nepal 82 E3
Nampa U.S.A. 126 D4
Nampala Mali 96 C3
Nam Phong Thai. 70 C3
Namp'o N. Korea 75 B5
Nampula Moz. 99 D5
Namsai Myanmar 70 B1
Namsang Myanmar 70 B2
Namsen r. Norway 44 G4
Namsos Norway 44 G4
Nam Theun 2 resr Laos 70 D3
Namti Myanmar 70 B1
Namtok Myanmar 70 B3
Nam Tok Chattakan National Park Thai. 70 C3
Namton Myanmar 70 B2
Namtsy Russia 65 N3
Namtu Myanmar 70 B2
Namu Canada 120 E5
Namuli, Monte mt. Moz. 99 D5
Namuno Moz. 99 D5
Namur Belgium 52 E4
Namutoni Namibia 99 B5
Namwon S. Korea 75 B6
Namya Ra Myanmar 70 B1
Namyit Island S. China Sea 68 E4
Nan Thai. 70 C3
Nana Bakassa Cent. Afr. Rep. 98 B3
Nanaimo Canada 120 F5
Nanam N. Korea 74 C4
Nan'an China 77 H3
Nanango Australia 112 F1
Nananib Plateau Namibia 100 C3
Nanao Japan 75 E5
Nanatsu-shima i. Japan 75 E5
Nanbai China see Zunyi
Nanbin China see Shizhu
Nanbu China 76 E2
Nancha China 74 C3
Nanchang Jiangxi China 77 G2
Nanchang Jiangxi China 77 G2
Nanchong China 76 E2
Nanchuan China 76 E2
Nancowry i. India 71 A6
Nancun China 77 G1
Nancy France 52 G6
Nancy (Essey) airport France 52 G6
Nanda Devi mt. India 82 E3
Nanda Kot mt. India 82 E3
Nandan China 76 E3
Nandapur India 84 D2
Nanded India 84 C2
Nander India see Nanded
Nandewar Range mts Australia 112 E3
Nandod India 84 B1
Nandurbar India 82 C5
Nandyal India 84 C3
Nanfeng Guangdong China 77 F4
Nanfeng Jiangxi China 77 H3
Nang China 76 B2
Nanga Eboko Cameroon 96 E4

▶Nanga Parbat mt. Pak. 82 C2
9th highest mountain in Asia and the world.

Nangar National Park Australia 112 D4
Nangatayap Indon. 68 E7
Nangin Myanmar 71 B5
Nangnim-sanmaek mts N. Korea 75 B4
Nangqên China 76 C1
Nangulangwa Tanz. 99 D4
Nanguneri India 84 C4
Nanhua China 76 D3
Nanhui China 77 I2
Nanjian China 76 D3
Nanjiang China 76 E1
Nanjing China 77 H1
Nanji Shan i. China 77 I3
Nanka Jiang r. China 76 C4
Nankang China 77 G3
Nanking China see Nanjing
Nankova Angola 99 B5
Nanlei He r. China 76 C4
also known as Nam Loi (Myanmar)
Nanling China 77 H2
Nan Ling mts China 77 F3
Nanliu Jiang r. China 77 F4
Nanlong China see Nanbu
Nannilam India 84 C4
Nannine (abandoned) Australia 109 B6
Nanning China 77 F4
Nannup Australia 109 A8
Na Noi Thai. 70 C3
Nanortalik Greenland 119 N3
Nanouki atoll Kiribati see Nonouti
Nanouti atoll Kiribati see Nonouti
Nanpan Jiang r. China 76 E3
Nanping China 77 H3
Nanpu China see Pucheng
Nanri Dao i. China 77 H3
Nansei-shotō is Japan see Ryukyu Islands
Nansei-shotō Trench sea feature N. Pacific Ocean see Ryukyu Trench
Nansen Basin sea feature Arctic Ocean 153 H1
Nansen Sound sea chan. Canada 119 I1
Nan-sha Ch'ün-tao is S. China Sea see Spratly Islands
Nanshan China 77 [inset]
Nanshan Island S. China Sea 68 F4
Nansha Qundao is S. China Sea see Spratly Islands
Nansio Tanz. 98 D4
Nantes France 56 D3
Nantes à Brest, Canal de France 56 C3
Nanteuil-le-Haudouin France 52 C5
Nanthi Kadal Lagoon lag. Sri Lanka 84 D4
Nanticoke Canada 134 E2
Nanticoke U.S.A. 135 H4
Nantong China 77 I2
Nantou Taiwan 77 I4
Nantucket U.S.A. 135 J3
Nantucket Island U.S.A. 135 K3
Nantucket Sound g. U.S.A. 135 J3
Nantwich U.K. 49 E5
Nanumaga i. Tuvalu see Nanumanga
Nanumanga i. Tuvalu 107 H2
Nanumea atoll Tuvalu 107 H2
Nanuque Brazil 145 C2
Nanusa, Kepulauan is Indon. 69 H6
Nanxi China 76 E2
Nanxian China 77 G2
Nanxiong China 77 G3
Nanyang China 77 G1
Nanyuki Kenya 98 D4
Nanzhang China 77 F2
Nanzhao China see Zhao'an
Nanzhou China see Nanxian
Nao, Cabo de la c. Spain 57 G4
Naococane, Lac l. Canada 123 H3
Naoero country S. Pacific Ocean see Nauru
Naogaon Bangl. 83 G4
Naoli He r. China 74 D3
Nāomīd, Dasht-e des. Afgh./Iran 89 F3
Naoshera India 82 C2
Napa U.S.A. 128 B2
Napaktulik Lake Canada 121 H1
Napanee Canada 135 G1
Napasoq Greenland 119 M3
Naperville U.S.A. 134 A3
Napier N.Z. 113 F4
Napier Range hills Australia 108 D4
Napierville Canada 135 I1
Naples Italy 58 F4
Naples FL U.S.A. 133 D7
Naples ME U.S.A. 135 J2
Naples TX U.S.A. 131 E5
Naples UT U.S.A. 129 I1
Napo China 76 E4
Napoleon IN U.S.A. 134 C4
Napoleon ND U.S.A. 130 D2
Napoleon OH U.S.A. 134 C3
Napoli Italy see Naples
Naqadeh Iran 88 B2
Nara India 82 B5
Nara Japan 75 D6
Nara Mali 96 C3
Narach Belarus 45 O9
Naracoorte Australia 111 C8
Naradhan Australia 112 C4
Naralua India 83 F4
Naranjal Ecuador 142 C4
Naranjo Mex. 127 F8
Narasapur India 84 D2
Narasaraopet India 84 D2
Narasinghapur India 84 E1
Narathiwat Thai. 71 C6
Nara Visa U.S.A. 131 C5
Narayanganj Bangl. 83 G5
Narayanganj India 82 E5
Narayangarh India 82 C4
Narayanpur India 84 D2
Narbada r. India see Narmada
Narberth U.K. 49 C7
Narbo France see Narbonne
Narbonne France 56 F5
Narcea r. Spain 57 C2
Narcondam Island India 71 A4
Nardò Italy 58 H4
Narechi r. Pak. 89 H4
Narembeen Australia 109 B8
Nares Abyssal Plain sea feature S. Atlantic Ocean 148 D4
Nares Deep sea feature N. Atlantic Ocean 148 D4
Nares Strait Canada/Greenland 119 K2
Naretha Australia 109 D7
Narew r. Poland 47 R4
Narib Namibia 100 C3
Narikel Jinjira i. Bangl. see St Martin's Island
Narimanov Russia 43 J7
Narimskiy Khrebet mts Kazakh. see Naryn, Khrebet
Narince Turkey 90 E3
Narin Gol watercourse China 83 H1
Narizon, Punta pt Mex. 127 F8
Narkher India 82 D5
Narmada r. India 82 C5
Narman Turkey 91 F2
Narnaul India 82 D3
Narni Italy 58 E3
Narnia Italy see Narni
Narodnaya, Gora mt. Russia 41 S3
Naro-Fominsk Russia 43 H5
Narok Kenya 98 D4
Narooma Australia 112 E6
Narovchat Russia 43 I5
Narowlya Belarus 43 F6
Närpes Fin. 44 L5
Narrabri Australia 112 D3
Narragansett Bay U.S.A. 135 J3
Narran r. Australia 112 C2
Narrandera Australia 112 C5
Narran Lake Australia 112 C2
Narrogin Australia 109 B8
Narromine Australia 112 D4
Narrows U.S.A. 134 E5
Narrowsburg U.S.A. 135 H3
Narsapur India 84 C2
Narsaq Greenland 119 N3
Narshingdi Bangl. see Narsingdi
Narsimhapur India 82 D5
Narsingdi Bangl. 83 G5
Narsinghpur India see Narsimhapur
Narsipatnam India 84 D2
Nartkala Russia 91 F2
Naruto Japan 75 D6
Narva Estonia 45 P7
Narva Bay Estonia/Russia 45 O7
Narva laht b. Estonia/Russia see Narva Bay
Narva Reservoir resr Estonia/Russia 45 P7
Narva veehoidla resr Estonia/Russia see Narva Reservoir
Narvik Norway 44 J2
Narvskiy Zaliv b. Estonia/Russia see Narva Bay
Narvskoye Vodokhranilishche resr Estonia/Russia see Narva Reservoir
Narwana India 82 D3
Nar'yan-Mar Russia 42 L2
Naryn Kyrg. 80 E3
Naryn, Khrebet mts Kazakh. 80 F2
Näsåker Sweden 44 J5
Nashik India 84 B1
Nashua U.S.A. 135 J2
Nashville AR U.S.A. 131 E5
Nashville GA U.S.A. 133 D6
Nashville IN U.S.A. 134 B4
Nashville NC U.S.A. 132 E5
Nashville OH U.S.A. 134 D3

▶Nashville TN U.S.A. 132 C4
Capital of Tennessee.

Naşīb Syria 85 C3
Näsijärvi l. Fin. 45 M6
Nasik India see Nashik
Nasinu Fiji 107 H3
Nasir Pak. 89 H4
Nasir South Sudan 86 D8
Nāşir, Buḩayrat resr Egypt see Nasser, Lake
Nasirabad Bangl. see Mymensingh
Nasirabad India 82 C4
Naskaupi r. Canada 123 J3
Naşr Egypt 90 C5
Naşrānī, Jabal an mts Syria 85 C3
Naşrīān Iran 88 B3
Nass r. Canada 120 D4
Nassau r. Australia 110 C2

▶Nassau Bahamas 133 E7
Capital of the Bahamas.

Nassau i. Cook Is 107 J3
Nassau U.S.A. 135 I2
Nassawadox U.S.A. 135 H5
Nasser, Lake resr Egypt 86 D5
Nässjö Sweden 45 I8
Nassuttooq inlet Greenland 119 M3
Nastapoca r. Canada 122 F2
Nastapoka Islands Canada 122 F2
Nasugbu Phil. 69 G4
Nasushiobara Japan 75 F5
Nasva Russia 42 F4
Nata Botswana 99 C6
Natal Brazil 143 K5
Natal Indon. 68 B6
Natal prov. S. Africa see KwaZulu-Natal
Natal Basin sea feature Indian Ocean 149 K8
Naţanz Iran 88 C3
Natashquan Canada 123 J4
Natashquan r. Canada 123 J4
Natchez U.S.A. 131 F6
Natchitoches U.S.A. 131 E6
Nathalia Australia 112 B6
Nathia Gali Pak. 89 I3
Nati, Punta pt Spain 57 H3
Natillas Mex. 131 C7
National City U.S.A. 128 E5
Natitingou Benin 96 D3
Natividad, Isla i. Mex. 127 E8
Natividade Brazil 143 I6
Natkyizin Myanmar 70 B4
Natla r. Canada 120 D2
Natmauk Myanmar 70 A2
Nator Bangl. see Natore
Nátora Mex. 127 F7
Natore Bangl. 83 G4
Natori Japan 75 F5
Natron, Lake salt l. Tanz. 98 D4
Nattai National Park Australia 112 E5
Nattalin Myanmar 70 A3
Nattaung mt. Myanmar 70 B3
Na'tū Iran 89 F3
Natuashish Canada 123 J3
Natuna, Kepulauan is Indon. 71 D6
Natuna Besar i. Indon. 71 E6
Natural Bridges National Monument nat. park U.S.A. 129 H3
Naturaliste, Cape Australia 109 A8
Naturaliste Plateau sea feature Indian Ocean 149 P8
Naturita U.S.A. 129 I2
Nauchas Namibia 100 C2
Nau Co l. China 83 E2
Nauen Germany 53 M2
Naufragados, Ponta dos pt Brazil 145 A4
Naujoji Akmenė Lith. 45 M8
Naukh India 82 C4
Naukot Pak. 89 H5
Naumburg (Hessen) Germany 53 J3
Naumburg (Saale) Germany 53 L3
Naungion Myanmar 70 B3
Naungpale Myanmar 70 B3
Naupada India 84 E2
Na'ūr Jordan 85 B4
Nauroz Kalat Pak. 89 G4
Naurskaya Russia 91 G2
Nauru i. Nauru 107 G2
Nauru country S. Pacific Ocean 107 G2
Naustdal Norway 45 D6
Nauta Peru 142 D4
Nautaca Uzbek. see Qarshi
Naute Dam Namibia 100 C4
Nava Mex. 131 C6
Navadwip India 83 G5
Navahrudak Belarus 45 N10
Navajo Lake U.S.A. 129 J3
Navajo Mountain U.S.A. 129 H3
Navalmoral de la Mata Spain 57 D4
Navalvillar de Pela Spain 57 D4
Navan Ireland 51 F4
Navangar India see Jamnagar
Navapolatsk Belarus 45 P9
Navarin, Mys c. Russia 65 S3
Navarra aut. comm. Spain 57 F2
Navarra, Comunidad Foral de aut. comm. Spain see Navarra
Navarre Australia 112 A6
Navarre aut. comm. Spain see Navarra
Navarro r. U.S.A. 128 B2
Navashino Russia 42 I5
Navasota U.S.A. 131 D6

▶Navassa Island terr. West Indies 137 I5
United States Unincorporated Territory.

Naver r. U.K. 50 E2
Näverede Sweden 44 I5
Navi Mumbai India 84 B2
Navlakhi India 82 B5
Navlya Russia 43 G5
Năvodari Romania 59 M2
Navoi Uzbek. see Navoiy
Navoiy Uzbek. 89 G1
Navojoa Mex. 127 F8
Navolato Mex. 136 C4
Návpaktos Greece see Nafpaktos
Návplion Greece see Nafplio
Navşar Turkey see Şemdinli
Navsari India 84 B1
Nawá Syria 85 C3
Nawabganj Bangl. 83 G4
Nawabshah Pak. 89 H5
Nawada India 83 F4
Nāwah Afgh. 89 G3
Nāwah-ye Gurz Afgh. 89 G3
Nawalgarh India 82 C4
Nawanshahr India 82 D3
Nawan Shehar India see Nawanshahr
Nawar, Dasht-i- depr. Afgh. see Nāwêr, Dasht-e
Nawarangpur India see Nabarangapur
Nāwêr, Dasht-e depr. Afgh. 89 G3
Nawngcho Myanmar see Nawnghkio
Nawnghkio Myanmar 70 B2
Nawng Hpa Myanmar 70 B2
Nawngleng Myanmar 70 B2
Nawoiy Uzbek. see Navoiy
Naxçıvan Azer. 91 G3
Naxos i. Greece 59 K6
Nayagarh India 84 E1
Nayak Afgh. 89 G3
Nayar Mex. 136 D4
Nāy Band, Kūh-e mt. Iran 88 E3
Nayong China 76 E3
Nayoro Japan 74 F3

▶Nay Pyi Taw Myanmar 70 B3
Capital of Myanmar.

Nazaré Brazil 145 D1
Nazareno Mex. 131 C7
Nazareth Israel see Naẕerat
Nazário Brazil 145 A2
Nazas Mex. 131 B7
Nazas r. Mex. 131 B7
Nazca Peru 142 D6
Nazca Ridge sea feature S. Pacific Ocean 151 O7
Naẕerat Israel 85 B3
Nāzīl Iran 89 F4
Nazilli Turkey 59 M6
Nazimabad Pak. 89 G5
Nazımiye Turkey 91 E3
Nazir Hat Bangl. 83 G5
Nazko Canada 120 F4
Nazran' Russia 91 G2
Nazrēt Eth. 98 D3
Nazwá Oman 88 E6
Ncojane Botswana 100 E2
N'dalatando Angola 99 B4
Ndélé Cent. Afr. Rep. 98 C3
Ndendé Gabon 98 B4
Ndende i. Solomon Is see Nendo
N'Djamena Chad see Ndjamena

▶Ndjamena Chad 97 E3
Capital of Chad.

Ndjouani i. Comoros see Nzwani
Ndoi i. Fiji see Doi
Ndola Zambia 99 C5
Nduke i. Solomon Is see Kolombangara
Ndwedwe S. Africa 101 J5
Ndzuani i. Comoros 99 E5
Ne, Hon i. Vietnam 70 D3
Neabul Creek r. Australia 112 C1
Neagh, Lough l. U.K. 51 F3
Neah Bay U.S.A. 126 B2
Neale, Lake salt flat Australia 109 E6
Nea Liosia Greece 59 J5
Neapoli Greece 59 J6
Neapolis Italy see Naples
Nea Roda Greece 59 J4
Neath U.K. 49 D7
Neath r. U.K. 49 D7
Nebbi Uganda 98 D3
Nebine Creek r. Australia 112 C2
Neblina, Pico da mt. Brazil 142 E3
Nebo Australia 110 E4
Nebo, Mount U.S.A. 129 H2
Nebolchi Russia 42 G4
Nebraska state U.S.A. 130 C3
Nebraska City U.S.A. 130 E3
Nebrodi, Monti mts Sicily Italy 58 F6
Neches r. U.S.A. 131 E6
Nechisar National Park Eth. 98 D3
Nechranice, Vodní nádrž resr Czechia 53 N4
Neckar r. Germany 53 I5
Neckarsulm Germany 53 J5
Necker Island U.S.A. 150 J4
Necochea Arg. 144 E5
Nederland country Europe see Netherlands
Neder Rijn r. Neth. 52 F3
Nedlouc, Lac l. Canada 123 G2
Nedluk Lake Canada see Nedlouc, Lac
Nêdong China 83 G3
Nedre Soppero Sweden 44 L2
Nédroma Alg. 57 F6
Needle Mountain U.S.A. 126 F3
Needles U.S.A. 129 F4
Neemach India see Neemuch
Neemuch India 82 C4
Neenah U.S.A. 134 A1
Neepawa Canada 121 L5
Neergaard Lake Canada 119 J2
Neerijnen Neth. 52 F3
Neerpelt Belgium 52 F3
Neftçala Azer. 91 H3
Neftechala Azer. see Häsänabad
Neftechala Azer. see Neftçala
Neftegorsk Russia 43 K5
Neftegorsk (abandoned) Russia 74 F1
Neftekamsk Russia 41 Q4
Neftekumsk Russia 91 G1
Nefteyugansk Russia 64 I3
Neftezavodsk Turkm. see Seýdi
Neftezawodsk Turkm. see Seýdi
Nefyn U.K. 49 C6
Nefza Tunisia 58 C6
Negage Angola 99 B4
Negār Iran 88 E4
Negara Indon. 108 A2
Negēlē Eth. 98 D3
Negev des. Israel 85 B4
Negomane Moz. 99 D5
Negombo Sri Lanka 84 C5
Negotino Macedonia 59 J4
Negra, Cordillera mts Peru 142 C5
Negra, Punta pt Peru 142 B5
Negra, Serra mts Brazil 145 C2
Negrais, Cape Myanmar 70 A4
Nègrine Alg. 58 B7
Negro r. Arg. 144 D6
Negro r. Mato Grosso do Sul Brazil 143 G7
Negro r. Paraná/Santa Catarina Brazil 145 A4
Negro r. S. America 142 G4
Negro, Cabo c. Morocco 57 D6
Negroponte i. Greece see Evvoia
Negros i. Phil. 69 G5
Negru Vodă, Podişul plat. Romania 59 M3
Nehbandān Iran 89 F4
Nehe China 74 B2
Neijiang China 76 E2
Neilburg Canada 121 I4
Neimenggu aut. reg. China see Nei Mongol Zizhiqu
Nei Mongol Zizhiqu aut. reg. China 74 A2
Neinstedt Germany 53 L3
Neiva Col. 142 C3
Neixiang China 77 F1
Nejanilini Lake Canada 121 L3
Nejd reg. Saudi Arabia see Najd
Nekā Iran 88 D2
Nek'emtē Eth. 98 D3
Nekrasovskoye Russia 42 I4
Nelang India 82 D3
Nelia Australia 110 C4
Nelidovo Russia 42 G4
Neligh U.S.A. 130 D3
Nel'kan Russia 65 P3
Nelligere India 84 C3
Nellore India 84 C3
Nelluz watercourse Turkey 85 D1
Nel'ma Russia 74 E3
Nelson Canada 120 G5
Nelson r. Canada 121 M3
Nelson N.Z. 113 D5
Nelson U.K. 48 E5
Nelson U.S.A. 129 G4
Nelson, Cape Australia 111 C8
Nelson, Cape P.N.G. 69 L8
Nelson, Estrecho strait Chile 144 A8
Nelson Bay Australia 112 F4
Nelson Forks Canada 120 F3
Nelsonia U.S.A. 135 H5
Nelson Lakes National Park N.Z. 113 D6
Nelson Reservoir U.S.A. 126 G2
Nelspruit S. Africa see Mbombela
Néma Mauritania 96 C3
Nema Russia 42 K4
Neman r. Belarus/Lith. see Nyoman
Neman Russia 45 M9
Nemausus France see Nîmes
Nemawar India 82 D5
Nemed Russia 42 L3
Nementcha, Monts des mts Alg. 58 B7
Nemetocenna France see Arras
Nemetskiy, Mys c. Russia 44 Q2
Nemirov Ukr. see Nemyriv
Nemiscau r. Canada 122 F4
Nemiscau, Lac l. Canada 122 F4
Nemor He r. China 74 B2
Nemours Alg. see Ghazaouet
Nemours France 56 F2
Nemrut Dağı mt. Turkey 91 F3
Nemunas r. Belarus/Lith. see Nyoman
Nemuro Japan 74 G4
Nemuro-kaikyō sea chan. Japan/Russia 74 G4
Nemyriv Ukr. 43 F6
Nenagh Ireland 51 D5
Nenana U.S.A. 118 D3
Nendo i. Solomon Is 107 G3
Nene r. U.K. 49 H6
Nenjiang China 74 B2
Nen Jiang r. China 74 B3
Neosho U.S.A. 131 E4
Nepal country Asia 83 E3
Nepalganj Nepal 83 E3
Nepean Canada 135 H1
Nepean, Point Australia 112 B7
Nephi U.S.A. 129 H2
Nephin hill Ireland 51 C3
Nephin Beg Range hills Ireland 51 C3
Nepisiguit r. Canada 123 I5
Nepoko r. Dem. Rep. Congo 98 C3
Nérac France 56 E4
Nerang Australia 112 F1
Nera Tso l. China 83 H3
Nerchinsk Russia 73 L2
Nerekhta Russia 42 I4
Néret, Lac l. Canada 123 H3
Neretva r. Bos. & Herz./Croatia 58 G3
Nêri Pünco l. China 83 G3
Neriquinha Angola 99 C5
Neris r. Lith. 45 M9
also known as Viliya (Belarus/Lithuania)
Nerl' r. Russia 42 H4
Nerópolis Brazil 145 A2
Neryungri Russia 65 N4
Nes Neth. 52 F1
Nes Norway 45 F6
Nes' Russia 42 J2
Nesbyen Norway 45 F6
Neskaupstaður Iceland 44 [inset 1]
Nesle France 52 C5
Nesna Norway 44 H3
Nesri India 84 B2
Ness r. U.K. 50 E3
Ness, Loch l. U.K. 50 E3
Ness City U.S.A. 130 D4
Nesse r. Germany 53 K4
Nesselrode, Mount Canada/U.S.A. 120 C3
Nestor Falls Canada 121 M5
Nestos r. Greece 59 K4
also known as Mesta
Nesvizh Belarus see Nyasvizh
Netanya Israel 85 B3
Netherlands country Europe 52 F2

▶Netherlands Antilles West Indies 137 K6
The Netherlands Antilles was dissolved into 5 contsituent dependencies of the Netherlands in Oct 2010.

Netphen Germany 53 I4
Netrakona Bangl. 83 G4
Netrokona Bangl. see Netrakona
Nettilling Lake Canada 119 K3
Neubrandenburg Germany 53 N1
Neuburg an der Donau Germany 53 L6
Neuchâtel Switz. 56 H3
Neuchâtel, Lac de l. Switz. 56 H3
Neuendettelsau Germany 53 K5
Neuenhaus Germany 52 G2

Neuenkirchen Germany 53 J1
Neuenkirchen (Oldenburg) Germany 53 I2
Neufchâteau Belgium 52 F5
Neufchâteau France 56 G2
Neufchâtel-en-Bray France 52 B5
Neufchâtel-Hardelot France 52 B4
Neuharlingersiel Germany 53 H1
Neuhausen Russia see Gur'yevsk
Neuhof Germany 53 J4
Neu Kaliß Germany 53 L1
Neukirchen Germany 53 J4
Neukirchen/Erzgebirge Germany 53 M4
Neukuhren Russia see Pionerskiy
Neum Bos. & Herz. 58 G3
Neumarkt in der Oberpfalz Germany 53 L5
Neumayer III research station Antarctica 152 B2
Neumünster Germany 47 L3
Neunburg vorm Wald Germany 53 M5
Neunkirchen Austria 47 P7
Neunkirchen Germany 53 H5
Neuquén Arg. 144 C5
Neuruppin Germany 53 M2
Neu Sandez Poland see Nowy Sącz
Neuse r. U.S.A. 133 E5
Neusiedler See l. Austria/Hungary 47 P7
Neusiedler See Seewinkel, Nationalpark nat. park Austria 47 P7
Neuss Germany 52 G3
Neustadt (Wied) Germany 53 H4
Neustadt am Rübenberge Germany 53 J2
Neustadt an der Aisch Germany 53 K5
Neustadt an der Hardt Germany see Neustadt an der Weinstraße
Neustadt an der Waldnaab Germany 53 M5
Neustadt an der Weinstraße Germany 53 I5
Neustadt bei Coburg Germany 53 L4
Neustadt-Glewe Germany 53 L1
Neustrelitz Germany 53 N1
Neutraubling Germany 53 M6
Neuville-lès-Dieppe France 52 B5
Neuwied Germany 53 H4
Neu Wulmstorf Germany 53 J1
Nevada IA U.S.A. 130 E3
Nevada MO U.S.A. 130 E4
Nevada state U.S.A. 126 D5
Nevada, Sierra mts Spain 57 E5
Nevada, Sierra mts U.S.A. 128 C1
Nevada City U.S.A. 128 C2
Nevado, Cerro mt. Arg. 144 C5
Nevado, Sierra del mts Arg. 144 C5
Nevasa India 84 B2
Nevatim Israel 85 B4
Nevdubstroy Russia see Kirovsk
Nevel' Russia 42 F4
Nevel'sk Russia 74 F3
Never Russia 74 B1
Nevers France 56 F3
Nevertire Australia 112 C3
Nevesinje Bos. & Herz. 58 H3
Nevinnomyssk Russia 91 F1
Nevşehir Turkey 90 D3
Nevskoye Russia 74 D3
New r. CA U.S.A. 129 F5
New r. WV U.S.A. 134 E5
Newala Tanz. 99 D5
New Albany IN U.S.A. 134 C4
New Albany MS U.S.A. 131 F5
New Amsterdam Guyana 143 G2
New Amsterdam U.S.A. see New York
Newark DE U.S.A. 135 H4
Newark NJ U.S.A. 135 H3
Newark NY U.S.A. 135 G2
Newark OH U.S.A. 134 D3
Newark Lake U.S.A. 129 F2
Newark Liberty airport U.S.A. 132 F3
Newark-on-Trent U.K. 49 G5
New Bedford U.S.A. 135 J3
Newberg U.S.A. 126 C3
New Berlin U.S.A. 135 H2
New Bern U.S.A. 133 E5
Newberry IN U.S.A. 134 B4
Newberry MI U.S.A. 132 C2
Newberry SC U.S.A. 133 D5
Newberry National Volcanic Monument nat. park U.S.A. 126 C4
Newberry Springs U.S.A. 128 E4
New Bethlehem U.S.A. 134 F3
Newbiggin-by-the-Sea U.K. 48 F3
New Bight Bahamas 133 F7
New Bloomfield U.S.A. 135 G3
Newboro Canada 135 G1
New Boston OH U.S.A. 134 D4
New Boston TX U.S.A. 131 E5
New Braunfels U.S.A. 131 D6
Newbridge Ireland 51 F4
New Britain i. P.N.G. 69 L8
New Britain U.S.A. 135 I3
New Britain Trench sea feature S. Pacific Ocean 150 G6
New Brunswick prov. Canada 123 I5
New Brunswick U.S.A. 135 H3
New Buffalo U.S.A. 134 B3
Newburgh Canada 135 G1
Newburgh U.K. 50 G3
Newburgh U.S.A. 135 H3
Newbury U.K. 49 F7
Newburyport U.S.A. 135 J2
Newby Bridge U.K. 48 E4

▶New Caledonia terr. S. Pacific Ocean 107 G4
French Overseas Collectivity.

New Caledonia Trough sea feature Tasman Sea 150 G7
New Carlisle Canada 123 I4
Newcastle Australia 112 E4
Newcastle Canada 135 F2
Newcastle Ireland 51 F4
Newcastle S. Africa 101 I4
Newcastle U.K. 51 G3
New Castle CO U.S.A. 129 J2
New Castle IN U.S.A. 134 C4
New Castle KY U.S.A. 134 C4
New Castle PA U.S.A. 134 E3
Newcastle UT U.S.A. 129 G3
New Castle VA U.S.A. 134 E5
Newcastle WY U.S.A. 126 G4
Newcastle Emlyn U.K. 49 C6
Newcastle-under-Lyme U.K. 49 E5
Newcastle upon Tyne U.K. 48 F4
Newcastle Waters Australia 108 F4
Newcastle West Ireland 51 C5
Newchwang China see Yingkou
New City U.S.A. 135 I3
Newcomb U.S.A. 129 I3
New Concord U.S.A. 134 E4
New Cumberland U.S.A. 134 E3
New Cumnock U.K. 50 E5
New Deer U.K. 50 G3

▶New Delhi India 82 D3
Capital of India.

New Don Pedro Reservoir U.S.A. 128 C3
Newell U.S.A. 130 C2
Newell, Lake salt flat Australia 109 D6
Newell, Lake Canada 121 I5
New England National Park Australia 112 F3
New England Range mts Australia 112 E3
New England Seamounts sea feature N. Atlantic Ocean 148 E3
Newenham, Cape U.S.A. 118 B4
Newent U.K. 49 E7
New Era U.S.A. 134 B2
Newfane NY U.S.A. 135 F2
Newfane VT U.S.A. 135 I2
New Forest National Park nat. park U.K. 49 F8
Newfoundland i. Canada 123 K4
Newfoundland prov. Canada see Newfoundland and Labrador
Newfoundland and Labrador prov. Canada 123 K3
Newfoundland Evaporation Basin salt l. U.S.A. 129 G1
New Galloway U.K. 50 E5
New Georgia i. Solomon Is 107 F2
New Georgia Islands Solomon Is 107 F2
New Georgia Sound sea chan. Solomon Is 107 F2
New Glasgow Canada 123 J5

▶New Guinea i. Indon./P.N.G. 69 K8
Largest island in Oceania and 2nd in the world.

New Halfa Sudan 86 E6
New Hampshire state U.S.A. 135 J1
New Hampton U.S.A. 130 E3
New Hanover i. P.N.G. 106 F2
Newhaven U.K. 49 H8
New Haven CT U.S.A. 135 I3
New Haven IN U.S.A. 134 C3
New Haven WV U.S.A. 134 E4
New Hebrides country S. Pacific Ocean see Vanuatu
New Hebrides Trench sea feature S. Pacific Ocean 150 H7
New Holland country Oceania see Australia
New Holstein U.S.A. 134 A2
New Iberia U.S.A. 131 F6
Newinn Ireland 51 E5
New Ireland i. P.N.G. 106 F2
New Jersey state U.S.A. 135 H4
New Kensington U.S.A. 134 F3
New Kent U.S.A. 135 G5
Newkirk U.S.A. 131 D4
New Lanark U.K. 50 F5
Newland Range hills Australia 109 C7
New Lexington U.S.A. 134 D4
New Liskeard Canada 122 F5
New London CT U.S.A. 135 I3
New London MO U.S.A. 130 F4
New Madrid U.S.A. 131 F4
Newman Australia 109 B5
Newman U.S.A. 128 C3
Newmarket Canada 134 F1
Newmarket Ireland 51 C5
Newmarket U.K. 49 H6
New Market U.S.A. 135 F4
Newmarket-on-Fergus Ireland 51 D5
New Martinsville U.S.A. 134 E4
New Meadows U.S.A. 126 D3
New Mexico state U.S.A. 127 G6
New Miami U.S.A. 134 C4
New Milford U.S.A. 135 H3
Newnan U.S.A. 133 C5
New Orleans U.S.A. 131 F6
New Paris IN U.S.A. 134 C3
New Paris OH U.S.A. 134 C4
New Philadelphia U.S.A. 134 E3
New Pitsligo U.K. 50 G3
New Plymouth N.Z. 113 E4
Newport Mayo Ireland 51 C4
Newport Tipperary Ireland 51 D5
Newport England U.K. 49 E6
Newport England U.K. 49 F8
Newport Wales U.K. 49 D7
Newport AR U.S.A. 131 F5
Newport IN U.S.A. 134 B4
Newport KY U.S.A. 134 C4
Newport MI U.S.A. 134 D3
Newport NH U.S.A. 135 I2
Newport NJ U.S.A. 135 H4
Newport OR U.S.A. 126 B3
Newport RI U.S.A. 135 J3
Newport VT U.S.A. 135 I1
Newport WA U.S.A. 126 D2
Newport Beach U.S.A. 128 E5
Newport News U.S.A. 135 G5
Newport Pagnell U.K. 49 G6
New Port Richey U.S.A. 133 D6
New Providence i. Bahamas 133 E7
Newquay U.K. 49 B8
New Roads U.S.A. 131 F6
New Rochelle U.S.A. 135 I3
New Rockford U.S.A. 130 D2
New Romney U.K. 49 H8
New Ross Ireland 51 F5
Newry Australia 108 E4
Newry U.K. 51 F3
New Siberia Islands Russia 65 P2
New Smyrna Beach U.S.A. 133 D6
New South Wales state Australia 112 C4
New Stanton U.S.A. 134 F3
Newton U.K. 48 E5
Newton GA U.S.A. 133 C6
Newton IA U.S.A. 130 E3
Newton IL U.S.A. 130 F4
Newton KS U.S.A. 130 D4
Newton MA U.S.A. 135 J2
Newton MS U.S.A. 131 F5
Newton NC U.S.A. 132 D5
Newton NJ U.S.A. 135 H3
Newton TX U.S.A. 131 E6
Newton Abbot U.K. 49 D8
Newton Mearns U.K. 50 E5
Newton Stewart U.K. 50 E6
Newtown Ireland 51 D5
Newtown England U.K. 49 E6
Newtown Wales U.K. 49 D6
Newtown U.S.A. 134 C4
New Town U.S.A. 130 C1
Newtownabbey U.K. 51 G3
Newtownards U.K. 51 G3
Newtownbarry Ireland see Bunclody
Newtownbutler U.K. 51 E3
Newtown Mount Kennedy Ireland 51 F4
Newtown St Boswells U.K. 50 G5
Newtownstewart U.K. 51 E3
New Ulm U.S.A. 130 E2
Newville U.S.A. 135 G3
New World Island Canada 123 L4

▶New York U.S.A. 135 I3
2nd most populous city in North America and 5th in the world.

New York state U.S.A. 135 H2

▶New Zealand country Oceania 113 D5
3rd largest and 3rd most populated country in Oceania.

Nexø Denmark 45 I9
Neya Russia 42 I4
Ney Bīd Iran 88 E4
Neyrīz Iran 88 D4
Neyshābūr Iran 88 E2
Nezhin Ukr. see Nizhyn
Nezperce U.S.A. 126 D3
Ngabé Congo 98 B4
Nga Chong, Khao mt. Myanmar/Thai. 70 B4
Ngagahtawng Myanmar 76 C3
Ngagau mt. Tanz. 99 D4
Ngalu Indon. 108 C2
Ngamring China 83 F3
Ngangla Ringco salt l. China 83 E3
Nganglong Kangri mt. China 82 E2
Nganglong Kangri mts China 82 E2
Ngangzê Co salt l. China 83 F3
Ngangzê Shan mts China 83 F3
Ngân Sơn Vietnam 70 D2
Ngaoundal Cameroon 96 E4
Ngaoundéré Cameroon 97 E4
Ngape Myanmar 70 A2
Ngaputaw Myanmar 70 A3
Ngarrab China see Gyaca
Ngathainggyaung Myanmar 70 A3
Ngau i. Fiji see Gau
Ngawa China see Aba
Ngazidja i. Comoros 99 E5
Ngcobo S. Africa 101 H6
Ngeaur i. Palau see Angaur
Ngeruangel i. Palau 69 I5
Ngega Pulu mt. Indon. see Jaya, Puncak
Ngiap r. Laos 70 C3
Ngilmina Indon. 108 D2
Ngiva Angola see Ondjiva
Ngo Congo 98 B4
Ngoako Ramalepe S. Africa see Modjadjiskloof
Ngoin, Co salt l. China 83 G3
Ngoko r. Cameroon/Congo 97 E4
Ngola Shankou pass China 76 C1
Ngom Qu r. China see Ji Qu
Ngoqumaima China 83 F2
Ngoring China 76 C1
Ngoring Hu l. China 76 C1
Ngourti Niger 96 E3
Ngqamakhwe S. Africa 101 H7
Nguigmi Niger 96 E3
Nguiu Australia 108 E2
Ngükang China 76 B2
Ngukurr Australia 108 F3
Ngulu atoll Micronesia 69 J5
Ngum, Ang Kep Nam Laos 70 C3
Ngunza Angola see Sumbe
Ngunza-Kabolu Angola see Sumbe
Nguru Nigeria 96 E3
Ngwaketse admin. dist. Botswana see Southern
Ngwane country Africa see Swaziland
Ngwathe S. Africa 101 H4
Ngwavuma r. S. Africa/Swaziland 101 K4
Ngwelezana S. Africa 101 J5
Nhachengue Moz. 101 L2
Nhamalabué Moz. 99 D5
Nha Trang Vietnam 71 E4
Nhecolândia Brazil 143 G7
Nhill Australia 111 C8
Nhlangano Swaziland 101 J4
Nho Quan Vietnam 70 D2
Nhow i. Fiji see Gau
Nhulunbuy Australia 110 B2
Niacam Canada 121 J4
Niafounké Mali 96 C3
Niagara U.S.A. 132 C2
Niagara Falls Canada 134 F2
Niagara Falls U.S.A. 134 F2
Niagara-on-the-Lake Canada 134 F2
Niagzu China 82 D2
Niah Sarawak Malaysia 68 E6
Niakaramandougou Côte d'Ivoire 96 C4

▶Niamey Niger 96 D3
Capital of Niger.

Nīām Kand Iran 88 E5
Niampak Indon. 69 H6
Niangara Dem. Rep. Congo 98 C3
Niangay, Lac l. Mali 96 C3
Nianzishan China 74 A3
Nias i. Indon. 71 B7
Niassa, Lago l. Africa see Nyasa, Lake
Niaur i. Palau see Angaur
Nīāzābād Iran 89 F3
Nibil Well Australia 108 D5
Nīca Latvia 45 L8

▶Nicaragua country Central America 137 G6
4th largest country in North America.

Nicaragua, Lake l. Nicaragua 137 G6
Nicastro Italy 58 G5
Nice France 56 H5
Nice U.S.A. 128 B2
Nicephorium Syria see Ar Raqqah
Niceville U.S.A. 133 C6
Nichicun, Lac l. Canada 123 H3
Nicholas Channel Bahamas/Cuba 133 D8
Nicholasville U.S.A. 134 C5
Nichols U.S.A. 134 A1
Nicholson r. Australia 110 B3
Nicholson Lake Canada 121 K2
Nicholson Range hills Australia 109 B6
Nicholville U.S.A. 135 H1
Nicobar Islands India 71 A5
Nicolaus U.S.A. 128 C2
Nicomedia Turkey see İzmit

▶Nicosia Cyprus 85 A2
Capital of Cyprus.

Nicoya, Península de pen. Costa Rica 137 G7
Nida Lith. 45 L9
Nidagunda India 84 C2
Nidd r. U.K. 48 F4
Nidda Germany 53 J4
Nidder r. Germany 53 I4
Nidzica Poland 47 R4
Niebüll Germany 47 L3
Nied r. France 52 G5
Niederanven Lux. 52 G5
Niederaula Germany 53 J4
Niedere Tauern mts Austria 47 N7
Niedersachsen land Germany 53 I2
Niedersächsisches Wattenmeer, Nationalpark nat. park Germany 52 G1
Niefang Equat. Guinea 96 E4
Niellé Côte d'Ivoire 96 C3
Nienburg (Weser) Germany 53 J2
Niers r. Germany 52 F3
Nierstein Germany 53 I5
Nieuwe Niedorp Neth. 52 E2
Nieuwerkerk aan den IJssel Neth. 52 E3
Nieuw Nickerie Suriname 143 G2
Nieuwolda Neth. 52 G1
Nieuwoudtville S. Africa 100 D6
Nieuwpoort Belgium 52 C3
Nieuw-Vossemeer Neth. 52 E3
Niğde Turkey 90 D3
Niger country Africa 96 D3

▶Niger r. Africa 96 D4
3rd longest river in Africa.

Niger, Mouths of the Nigeria 96 D4
Niger Cone sea feature S. Atlantic Ocean 148 I5

▶Nigeria country Africa 96 D4
Most populous country in Africa and 7th in the world.

Nighthawk Lake Canada 122 E4
Nigrita Greece 59 J4
Nihing Pak. 89 G4
Nihon country Asia see Japan
Niigata Japan 75 E5
Niihama Japan 75 D6
Ni'ihau i. U.S.A. 127 [inset]
Nii-jima i. Japan 75 E6
Niimi Japan 75 D6
Niitsu Japan 75 E5
Nijil, Wādī watercourse Jordan 85 B4
Nijkerk Neth. 52 F2
Nijmegen Neth. 52 F3
Nijverdal Neth. 52 G2
Nikel' Russia 44 Q2
Nikki Benin 96 D4
Nikkō Japan 75 E5
Nikkō Kokuritsu-kōen nat. park Japan 75 E5
Nikolayev Ukr. see Mykolayiv
Nikolayevka Russia 43 J5
Nikolayevsk Russia 43 J6
Nikolayevskiy Russia see Nikolayevsk
Nikolayevsk-na-Amure Russia 74 F1
Nikol'sk Russia 42 J4
Nikol'skiy Kazakh. see Satpayev
Nikol'skoye Kamchatskiy Kray Russia 65 R4
Nikol'skoye Vologod. Obl. Russia see Sheksna
Nikopol' Ukr. 43 G7
Niksar Turkey 90 E2
Nīkshahr Iran 89 F5
Nikšić Montenegro 58 H3
Nīkū Jahān Iran 89 F5
Nikumaroro atoll Kiribati 107 I2
Nikunau i. Kiribati 107 H2
Nīl, Bahr el r. Africa see Nile
Nilagiri India 83 F5
Niland U.S.A. 129 F5
Nilande Atoll Maldives see Nilandhe Atholhu
Nilandhe Atholhu Maldives 81 D11
Nilandhe Atoll Maldives see Nilandhe Atholhu
Nilang India see Nelang
Nilanga India 84 C2
Nilaveli Sri Lanka 84 D4

▶Nile r. Africa 90 C5
Longest river in Africa and the world.

Niles MI U.S.A. 134 B3
Niles OH U.S.A. 134 E3
Nilgiri Hills India 84 C4
Nīlī Afgh. 89 G3
Nīl Kōtal Afgh. 89 G3
Nilphamari Bangl. 83 G4
Nilsiä Fin. 44 P5
Nimach India see Neemuch
Niman r. Russia 74 D2
Nimba, Mont mts Africa see Richard-Molard, Mont
Nimbal India 84 B2
Nimberra Well Australia 109 C5
Nimelen r. Russia 74 E1
Nîmes France 56 G5
Nimmitabel Australia 111 E8
Nimrod Glacier Antarctica 152 H1
Nimu India 82 D2
Nimule South Sudan 97 G4
Nimwegen Neth. see Nijmegen
Nindigully Australia 112 D2
Nine Degree Channel India 84 B4
Nine Islands P.N.G. see Kilinailau Islands
Ninepin Group is H.K. China 77 [inset]
Ninetyeast Ridge sea feature Indian Ocean 149 N8
Ninety Mile Beach Australia 112 C7
Ninety Mile Beach N.Z. 113 D2
Nineveh U.S.A. 135 H2
Ningaloo Coast tourist site Australia 109 A5
Ning'an China 74 C3
Ningbo China 77 I2
Ningde China 77 H3
Ning'er China 76 D4
Ningguo China 77 H2
Ninghai China 77 I2
Ninghsia Hui Autonomous Region aut. reg. China see Ningxia Huizu Zizhiqu
Ninghua China 77 H3
Ningjiang China see Songyuan
Ningjing Shan mts China 76 C2
Ninglang China 76 D3
Ningming China 76 E4
Ningnan China 76 D3
Ningqiang China 76 E1
Ningwu China 73 K5
Ningxia aut. reg. China see Ningxia Huizu Zizhiqu
Ningxia Huizu Zizhiqu aut. reg. China 76 E1
Ningxian China 73 J5
Ningxiang China 77 G2
Ningzhou China see Huaning
Ninh Binh Vietnam 70 D2
Ninh Hoa Vietnam 71 E4
Ninigo Group atolls P.N.G. 69 K7
Ninnis Glacier Antarctica 152 G2
Ninnis Glacier Tongue Antarctica 152 H2
Ninohe Japan 75 F4
Niobrara r. U.S.A. 130 D3
Niokolo Koba, Parc National du nat. park Senegal 96 B3
Niono Mali 96 C3
Nioro Mali 96 C3
Niort France 56 D3
Nipani India 84 B2
Nipawin Canada 121 J4
Niphad India 84 B1
Nipigon Canada 119 J5
Nipigon, Lake Canada 119 J5
Nipishish Lake Canada 123 J3
Nipissing, Lake Canada 122 F5
Nippon country Asia see Japan
Nippon Hai sea N. Pacific Ocean see Japan, Sea of
Nipton U.S.A. 129 F4
Niquelândia Brazil 145 A1
Nīr Iran 88 B2
Nir Iran 88 D4
Nira r. India 84 B2
Nirji China 74 B2
Nirmal India 84 C2
Nirmali India 83 F4
Nirmal Range hills India 84 C2
Niš Serbia 59 I3
Nisa Port. 57 C4
Nisarpur India 84 B1
Niscemi Sicily Italy 58 F6
Nīshāpūr Iran see Neyshābūr
Nishino-shima vol. Japan 75 F8
Nishi-Sonogi-hantō pen. Japan 75 C6
Nisibis Turkey see Nusaybin
Nísiros i. Greece see Nisyros
Niskibi r. Canada 121 N3
Nisling r. Canada 120 B2
Nispen Neth. 52 E3
Nissan r. Sweden 45 H8
Nistru r. Ukr. see Dniester
Nisutlin r. Canada 120 C2
Nisyros i. Greece 59 L6
Niṭā Saudi Arabia 88 C5
Nitchequon (abandoned) Canada 123 H3
Nitendi i. Solomon Is see Nendo
Niterói Brazil 145 C3
Nith r. U.K. 50 F5
Nitibe East Timor 108 D2
Niti Pass China/India 82 D3
Niti Shankou pass China/India see Niti Pass
Nitmiluk National Park Australia 108 F3
Nitra Slovakia 47 Q6
Nitro U.S.A. 134 E4
Niuafo'ou i. Tonga 107 I3
Niuatoputopu i. Tonga 107 I3

▶Niue terr. S. Pacific Ocean 107 J3
Self-governing New Zealand Overseas Territory.

Niujing China see Binchuan
Niulakita i. Tuvalu 107 H3
Niutao i. Tuvalu 107 H2
Niutoushan China 77 H2
Nivala Fin. 44 N5
Nive watercourse Australia 110 D5
Nivelles Belgium 52 E4
Niwai India 82 C4
Niwas India 82 E5
Nixia China see Sêrxü
Nixon U.S.A. 128 D2
Niya China see Minfeng
Niya He r. China 83 E1
Nizamabad India 84 C2
Nizam Sagar l. India 84 C2
Nizhnedevitsk Russia 43 H6
Nizhnekamsk Russia 42 K5
Nizhnekamskoye Vodokhranilishche resr Russia 41 Q4
Nizhnekolymsk Russia 65 R3
Nizhnetambovskoye Russia 74 E2
Nizhneudinsk Russia 72 H2
Nizhnevartovsk Russia 64 I3
Nizhnevolzhsk Russia see Narimanov
Nizhneyansk Russia 65 O2
Nizhniy Baskunchak Russia 43 J6
Nizhniye Kresty Russia see Cherskiy
Nizhniy Lomov Russia 43 I5
Nizhniy Novgorod Russia 42 I4
Nizhniy Odes Russia 42 L3
Nizhniy Pyandzh Tajik. see Panji Poyon
Nizhniy Tagil Russia 41 R4
Nizhnyaya Mola Russia 42 J2
Nizhnyaya Omra Russia 42 L3
Nizhnyaya Pirenga, Ozero l. Russia 44 R3
Nizhnyaya Tunguska r. Russia 64 J3
Nizhnyaya Tura Russia 41 R4
Nizhyn Ukr. 43 F6
Nizina r. U.S.A. 120 A2
Nizip Turkey 85 C1
Nízke Tatry, Národný park nat. park Slovakia 47 Q6
Nizwā Oman see Nazwá
Nizza France see Nice
Njallavarri mt. Norway 44 L2
Njavve Sweden 44 K3
Njombe Tanz. 99 D4
Njurundabommen Sweden 44 J5
Nkambe Cameroon 96 E4
Nkandla S. Africa 101 J5
Nkawkaw Ghana 96 C4
Nkhata Bay Malawi 99 D5
Nkhotakota Malawi 99 D5
Nkondwe Tanz. 99 D4
Nkongsamba Cameroon 96 D4
N'Kouilal, Tizi pass Alg. 57 I5
Nkululeko S. Africa 101 H6
Nkurenkuru Namibia 99 B5
Nkwenkwezi S. Africa 101 H7
Noakhali Bangl. 83 G5
Noatak r. U.S.A. 118 B3
Nobber Ireland 51 F4
Nobeoka Japan 75 C6
Noblesville U.S.A. 134 B3
Noboribetsu Japan 74 F4
Noccundra Australia 111 C5
Nockatunga Australia 111 C5
Nocona U.S.A. 131 D5
Noel Kempff Mercado, Parque Nacional nat. park Bol. 142 F6
Noelville Canada 122 E5
Nogales Mex. 127 F7
Nogales U.S.A. 127 F7
Nōgata Japan 75 C6
Nogent-le-Rotrou France 56 E2
Nogent-sur-Oise France 52 C5
Noginsk Russia 42 H5
Nogliki Russia 74 F2
Nogoa r. Australia 110 E4
Nohar India 82 C3
Noheji Japan 74 F4
Nohfelden Germany 52 H5
Noida India 82 D3
Noirmoutier, Île de i. France 56 C3
Noirmoutier-en-l'Île France 56 C3
Noisseville France 52 G5
Nokhowch, Kūh-e mt. Iran 89 F5
Nökis Uzbek. see Nukus
Nok Kundi Pak. 89 F4
Nokomis Canada 121 J5
Nokomis Lake Canada 121 K3
Nokou Chad 97 E3
Nokrek Peak India 83 G4
Nola Cent. Afr. Rep. 98 B3
Nolin River Lake U.S.A. 134 B5
Nolinsk Russia 42 K4
No Mans Land i. U.S.A. 135 J3
Nome U.S.A. 118 B3
Nomgon Mongolia 72 J4
Nomhon China 80 I4
Nomoi Islands Micronesia see Mortlock Islands
Nomonde S. Africa 101 H6
Nomzha Russia 42 I4
Nonacho Lake Canada 121 I2
Nondweni S. Africa 101 J5
Nong'an China 74 B3
Nonghui China see Guang'an
Nong Khai Thai. 70 C3
Nongoma S. Africa 101 J4
Nongstoin India 83 G4
Nonidas Namibia 100 B2
Nonni r. China see Nen Jiang
Nonning Australia 111 B7
Nonnweiler Germany 52 G5
Nonoava Mex. 127 G8
Nonouti atoll Kiribati 107 H2
Nonthaburi Thai. 71 C4
Nonzwakazi S. Africa 100 G6
Noolyeanna Lake salt flat Australia 111 B5
Noondie, Lake salt flat Australia 109 B7
Noonkanbah Australia 108 D4
Noonthorangee Range hills Australia 111 C6
Noorama Creek watercourse Australia 112 B1
Noordbeveland i. Neth. 52 D3
Noorderhaaks i. Neth. 52 E2
Noordoost Polder Neth. 52 F2
Noordwijk Neth. 52 E2
Nootka Island Canada 120 E5
Nora r. Russia 74 C2
Norak Tajik. 89 H2
Norak, Obanbori resr Tajik. 89 H2
Norala Phil. 69 G5
Noranda Canada 122 F4
Nor-Bayazet Armenia see Gavarr
Norberg Sweden 45 I6
Nord Greenland see Station Nord
Nord, Canal du France 52 D4
Nordaustlandet i. Svalbard 64 D2
Nordegg Canada 120 G4
Norden Germany 53 H1
Nordenshel'da, Arkhipelag is Russia 64 K2
Nordenskjold Archipelago is Russia see Nordenshel'da, Arkhipelag
Norderney Germany 53 H1
Norderstedt Germany 53 K1
Nordfjordeid Norway 44 D6
Nordfold Norway 44 I3

Oakwood *OH* U.S.A. 134 C3
Oakwood *TN* U.S.A. 134 B5
Oamaru N.Z. 113 C7
Oaro N.Z. 113 D6
Oasis *CA* U.S.A. 128 E3
Oasis *NV* U.S.A. 126 E4
Oates Coast *reg.* Antarctica *see* Oates Land
Oates Land *reg.* Antarctica 152 H2
Oaxaca Mex. 136 E5
Oaxaca de Juárez Mex. *see* Oaxaca

▶Ob' *r.* Russia 72 E2
Part of the Ob'-Irtysh, the 2nd longest river in Asia.

Ob, Gulf of *sea chan.* Russia *see* Obskaya Guba
Oba Canada 122 D4
Oba *i.* Vanuatu *see* Aoba
Obala Cameroon 96 E4
Obama Japan 75 D6
Oban U.K. 50 D4
O Barco Spain 57 C2
Obbia Somalia *see* Hobyo
Obdorsk Russia *see* Salekhard
Óbecse Serbia *see* Bečej
Obed Canada 120 G4
Ōbēh Afgh. 89 F3
Oberaula Germany 53 J4
Oberdorla Germany 53 K3
Oberhausen Germany 52 G3
Oberlin *KS* U.S.A. 130 C4
Oberlin *LA* U.S.A. 131 E6
Oberlin *OH* U.S.A. 134 D3
Obermoschel Germany 53 H5
Oberon Australia 112 D4
Oberpfälzer Wald *mts* Germany 53 M5
Obersinn Germany 53 J4
Oberthulba Germany 53 J4
Obertshausen Germany 53 I4
Oberwälder Land *reg.* Germany 53 J3
Obi *i.* Indon. 69 H7
Óbidos Brazil 143 G4
Obihiro Japan 74 F4
Obil'noye Russia 43 J7

▶Ob'-Irtysh *r.* Russia 64 H3
2nd longest river in Asia and 5th in the world.

Obluch'ye Russia 74 C2
Obninsk Russia 43 H5
Obo Cent. Afr. Rep. 98 C3
Obock Djibouti 86 F7
Ōbŏk N. Korea 74 C4
Obokote Dem. Rep. Congo 98 C4
Obo Liang China 80 H4
Obouya Congo 98 B4
Oboyan' Russia 43 H6
Obozerskiy Russia 42 I3
Obregón, Presa *resr* Mex. 127 F8
Obrenovac Serbia 59 I2
Obruk Turkey 90 D3
Observatory Hill *hill* Australia 109 F7
Obshchiy Syrt *hills* Russia 41 Q5
Obskaya Guba *sea chan.* Russia 64 I3
Obuasi Ghana 96 C4
Ob''yachevo Russia 42 K3
Ocala U.S.A. 133 D6
Ocampo Mex. 131 C7
Ocaña Col. 142 D2
Ocaña Spain 57 E4
Occidental, Cordillera *mts* Chile 142 E7
Occidental, Cordillera *mts* Col. 142 C3
Occidental, Cordillera *mts* Peru 142 D7
Oceana U.S.A. 134 E5
Ocean Cay *i.* Bahamas 133 E7
Ocean City *MD* U.S.A. 135 H4
Ocean City *NJ* U.S.A. 135 H4
Ocean Falls Canada 120 E4
Ocean Island Kiribati *see* Banaba
Ocean Island *atoll* U.S.A. *see* Kure Atoll
Oceanside U.S.A. 128 E5
Ocean Springs U.S.A. 131 F6
Ochakiv Ukr. 59 N1
Och'amchire Georgia 91 F2
Ocher Russia 41 Q4
Ochiishi-misaki *pt* Japan 74 G4
Ochil Hills U.K. 50 F4
Ochito *r.* Pak. 89 G5
Ochrida, Lake Albania/Macedonia *see* Ohrid, Lake
Ochsenfurt Germany 53 K5
Ochtrup Germany 53 H2
Ocilla U.S.A. 133 D6
Ockelbo Sweden 45 J6
Ocolaşul Mare, Vârful *mt.* Romania 59 K1
Oconomowoc U.S.A. 134 A2
Oconto U.S.A. 134 B1
Octeville-sur-Mer France 49 H9
October Revolution Island Russia *see* Oktyabr'skoy Revolyutsii, Ostrov
Ocussi *enclave* East Timor 108 D2
Ocussi-Ambeno *enclave* East Timor *see* Ocussi
Oda, Jebel *mt.* Sudan 86 E5
Ódáðahraun *lava field* Iceland 44 [inset 1]
Ŏdaejin N. Korea 74 C4
Odae-san National Park S. Korea 75 C5
Ōdate Japan 75 F4
Odawara Japan 75 E6
Odda Norway 45 E6
Odei *r.* Canada 121 L3
Odell U.S.A. 134 B3
Odem U.S.A. 131 D7
Odemira Port. 57 B5
Ödemiş Turkey 59 L5
Ödenburg Hungary *see* Sopron
Odense Denmark 45 G9
Odenwald *reg.* Germany 53 I5
Oder *r.* Germany 53 J3
also known as Odra (Poland)
Oderbucht *b.* Germany 47 O3
Oder-Havel-Kanal *canal* Germany 53 N2
Ödeshög Sweden 45 I7
Odessa Ukr. 59 N1
Odessa *TX* U.S.A. 131 C6
Odessa *WA* U.S.A. 126 D3
Odessus Bulg. *see* Varna
Odiel *r.* Spain 57 C5
Odienné Côte d'Ivoire 96 C4
Odintsovo Russia 42 H5
Odisha *state* India 84 E1
Ŏdŏngk Cambodia 71 D5
Odra *r.* Germany/Poland 47 Q6
also known as Oder (Germany)
Odzala-Kokoua, Parc National d' *nat. park* Congo 98 B3
Oea Libya *see* Tripoli
Oé-Cusse *enclave* East Timor *see* Ocussi
Oecussi *enclave* East Timor *see* Ocussi
Oeiras Brazil 143 J5
Oekussi *enclave* East Timor *see* Ocussi
Oelsnitz/Vogtland Germany 53 M4
Oenkerk Neth. 52 F1
Oenpelli Australia 108 F3
Oesel *i.* Estonia *see* Hiiumaa
Oeufs, Lac des *l.* Canada 123 G3
Of Turkey 91 F2
O'Fallon *r.* U.S.A. 126 G3
Ofanto *r.* Italy 58 G4
Ofaqim Israel 85 B4
Offa Nigeria 96 D4
Offenbach am Main Germany 53 I4
Offenburg Germany 47 K6
Oga Japan 75 E5
Ogadēn *reg.* Eth. 98 E3
Oga-hantō *pen.* Japan 75 E5
Ōgaki Japan 75 E6
Ogallala U.S.A. 130 C3
Ogasawara-shotō *is* Japan *see* Bonin Islands
Ogbomosho Nigeria *see* Ogbomoso
Ogbomoso Nigeria 96 D4
Ogden *IA* U.S.A. 130 E3
Ogden *UT* U.S.A. 126 F4
Ogden, Mount Canada 120 C3
Ogdensburg U.S.A. 135 H1
Ogidaki Canada 122 D5
Ogilvie *r.* Canada 118 E3
Ogilvie Mountains Canada 118 D3
Oglethorpe, Mount U.S.A. 133 C5
Oglio *r.* Italy 58 D2
Oglongi Russia 74 E1
Ogmore Australia 110 E4
Ogoamas, Gunung *mt.* Indon. 69 G6
Ogodzha Russia 74 D1
Ogoja Nigeria 96 D4
Ogoki *r.* Canada 122 D4
Ogoki Lake Canada 130 G1
Ogoki Reservoir Canada 122 C4
Ogoron Russia 74 C1
Ogosta *r.* Bulg. 59 J3
Ogre Latvia 45 N8
Ogulin Croatia 58 F2
Ogurchinskiy, Ostrov *i.* Turkm. *see* Ogurjaly Adasy
Ogurjaly Adasy *i.* Turkm. 88 D2
Oğuzeli Turkey 85 C1
Ohai N.Z. 113 A7
Ohakune N.Z. 113 E4
Ohanet Alg. 96 D2
Ōhata Japan 74 F4
Ohcejohka Fin. *see* Utsjoki
O'Higgins, Lago *l.* Chile 144 B7
Ohio *r.* U.S.A. 134 A5
Ohio *state* U.S.A. 134 D3
Ohm *r.* Germany 53 I4
Ohrdruf Germany 53 K4
Ohře *r.* Czechia 53 N4
Ohre *r.* Germany 53 L2
Ohrid Macedonia 59 I4
Ohrid, Lake Albania/Macedonia 59 I4
Ohridsko Ezero *l.* Albania/Macedonia *see* Ohrid, Lake
Ohrigstad S. Africa 101 J3
Öhringen Germany 53 J5
Ohrit, Liqeni i *l.* Albania/Macedonia *see* Ohrid, Lake
Ohura N.Z. 113 E4
Oich *r.* U.K. 50 E3
Oiga China 76 B2
Oignies France 52 C4
Oil City U.S.A. 134 F3
Oise *r.* France 52 C6
Oise à l'Aisne, Canal de l' France 52 D5
Ōita Japan 75 C6
Oiti *mt.* Greece 59 J5
Ojai U.S.A. 128 D4
Ojalava *i.* Samoa *see* 'Upolu
Ojinaga Mex. 131 B6
Ojiya Japan 75 E5
Ojo Caliente U.S.A. 127 G5
Ojo de Laguna Mex. 127 G7

▶Ojos del Salado, Nevado *mt.* Arg./Chile 144 C3
2nd highest mountain in South America.

Oka *r.* Russia 43 I4
Oka *r.* Russia 72 I1
Okahandja Namibia 100 C1
Okahukura N.Z. 113 E4
Okakarara Namibia 99 B6
Okak Islands Canada 123 J2
Okanagan Lake Canada 120 G5
Okanda Sri Lanka 84 D5
Okano *r.* Gabon 98 B4
Okanogan U.S.A. 126 D2
Okanogan *r.* U.S.A. 126 D2
Okapi, Parc National de la *nat. park* Dem. Rep. Congo 98 C3
Okara Pak. 89 I4
Okarem Turkm. *see* Ekerem
Okataina *vol.* N.Z. *see* Tarawera, Mount
Okaukuejo Namibia 99 B5
Okavango *r.* Africa 99 C5

▶Okavango Delta *swamp* Botswana 99 C5
Largest oasis in the world.

Okavango Swamps Botswana *see* Okavango Delta
Okaya Japan 75 E5
Okayama Japan 75 D6
Okazaki Japan 75 E6
Okeechobee U.S.A. 133 D7
Okeechobee, Lake U.S.A. 133 D7
Okeene U.S.A. 131 D4
Okefenokee Swamp U.S.A. 133 D6
Okehampton U.K. 49 C8
Okemah U.S.A. 131 D5
Oker *r.* Germany 53 K2
Okha India 82 B5
Okha Russia 74 F1
Okha Rann *marsh* India 82 B5
Okhotsk Russia 65 P4
Okhotsk, Sea of Japan/Russia 74 G3
Okhotskoye More *sea* Japan/Russia *see* Okhotsk, Sea of
Okhtyrka Ukr. 43 G6
Okinawa *i.* Japan 75 B8
Okinawa-guntō *is* Japan *see* Okinawa-shotō
Okinawa-shotō *is* Japan 75 B8
Okino-Daitō-jima *i.* Japan 73 O8
Okino-Tori-shima *i.* Japan 73 P8
Oki-shotō *is* Japan 75 D5
Okkan Myanmar 70 A3
Oklahoma *state* U.S.A. 131 D5

▶Oklahoma City U.S.A. 131 D5
Capital of Oklahoma.

Okmulgee U.S.A. 131 D5
Okolona *KY* U.S.A. 134 C4
Okolona *MS* U.S.A. 131 F5
Okondja Gabon 98 B4
Okovskiy Les *for.* Russia 42 G5
Okoyo Congo 98 B4
Okpan, Gora *hill* Kazakh. 91 H1
Øksfjord Norway 44 M1
Oktemberyan Armenia *see* Armavir
Oktwin Myanmar 70 B3
Oktyabr' Kazakh. *see* Kandyagash
Oktyabr'sk Kazakh. *see* Kandyagash
Oktyabr'skiy Belarus *see* Aktsyabrski
Oktyabr'skiy *Amurskaya Oblast'* Russia 74 C1
Oktyabr'skiy *Arkhangel'skaya Oblast'* Russia 42 I3
Oktyabr'skiy *Kamchatskiy Kray* Russia 65 Q4
Oktyabr'skiy *Respublika Bashkortostan* Russia 41 Q5
Oktyabr'skiy *Volgogradskaya Oblast'* Russia 43 I7
Oktyabr'skoye Russia 41 T3
Oktyabr'skoy Revolyutsii, Ostrov *i.* Russia 65 K2
Okulovka Russia 42 G4
Okushiri-tō *i.* Japan 74 E4
Okusi *enclave* East Timor *see* Ocussi
Okuta Nigeria 96 D4
Okwa *watercourse* Botswana 100 G1
Ólafsvík Iceland 44 [inset 1]
Olakkur India 84 C3
Olancha U.S.A. 128 D3
Olancha Peak U.S.A. 128 D3
Öland *i.* Sweden 45 J8
Olary Australia 111 C7
Olathe *CO* U.S.A. 129 J2
Olathe *KS* U.S.A. 130 E4
Olavarría Arg. 144 D5
Oława Poland 47 P5
Olbernhau Germany 53 N4
Olbia *Sardinia* Italy 58 C4
Old Bahama Channel Bahamas/Cuba 133 E8
Old Bastar India 84 D2
Oldcastle Ireland 51 E4
Old Cork Australia 110 C4
Old Crow Canada 118 E3
Oldeboorn Neth. *see* Aldeboarn
Oldenburg Germany 53 I1
Oldenburg in Holstein Germany 47 M3
Oldenzaal Neth. 52 G2
Olderdalen Norway 44 L2
Old Forge U.S.A. 135 H2
Old Gidgee Australia 109 B6
Oldham U.K. 48 E5
Old Harbor U.S.A. 118 C4
Old Head of Kinsale *hd* Ireland 51 D6
Oldman *r.* Canada 120 I5
Oldmeldrum U.K. 50 G3
Old Perlican Canada 123 L5
Old River U.S.A. 128 D4
Olds Canada 120 H5
Old Speck Mountain U.S.A. 135 J1
Old Station U.S.A. 128 C1
Old Wives Lake Canada 121 J5
Olean U.S.A. 135 F2
Olecko Poland 47 S3
Olekma *r.* Russia 65 N3
Olekminsk Russia 65 N3
Olekminskiy Stanovik *mts* Russia 73 M2
Oleksandrivs'k Ukr. *see* Zaporizhzhya
Oleksandriya Ukr. 43 G6
Ølen Norway 45 D7
Olenegorsk Russia 44 R2
Olenek Russia 65 M3
Olenek *r.* Russia 65 M2
Olenek Bay Russia *see* Olenekskiy Zaliv
Olenekskiy Zaliv *b.* Russia 65 N2
Olenino Russia 42 G4
Olenitsa Russia 42 G2
Olenivs'ki Kar"yery Ukr. *see* Dokuchayevs'k
Olenya Russia *see* Olenegorsk
Oleshky Ukr. *see* Tsyurupyns'k
Olevs'k Ukr. 43 E6
Ol'ga Russia 74 D4
Olga, Lac *l.* Canada 122 F4
Olga, Mount Australia 109 E6
Ol'ginsk Russia 74 D1
Olginskoye Russia *see* Kochubeyevskoye
Ölgiy Mongolia 80 G2
Olhão Port. 57 C5
Olia Chain *mts* Australia 109 E6
Olifants *r.* Moz./S. Africa 101 J3
also known as Elefantes
Olifants *watercourse* Namibia 100 D3
Olifants S. Africa 101 J2
Olifants *r.* *W. Cape* S. Africa 100 D6
Olifants *r.* *W. Cape* S. Africa 100 E7
Olifantshoek S. Africa 100 F4
Olifantsrivierberge *mts* S. Africa 100 D7
Olimarao *atoll* Micronesia 69 L5
Olimbos *hill* Cyprus *see* Olympos
Olimbos *mt.* Greece *see* Olympus, Mount
Olimpos Beydağları Milli Parkı *nat. park* Turkey 59 N6
Olinda Brazil 143 L5
Olinga Moz. 99 D5
Olio Australia 110 C4
Oliphants Drift S. Africa 101 H3
Olisipo Port. *see* Lisbon
Oliva Spain 57 F4
Oliva, Cordillera de *mts* Arg./Chile 144 C3
Olivares, Cerro de *mt.* Arg./Chile 144 C4
Olive Hill U.S.A. 134 D4
Olivehurst U.S.A. 128 C2
Oliveira dos Brejinhos Brazil 145 C1
Olivença Moz. *see* Lupilichi
Olivenza Spain 57 C4
Oliver Lake Canada 121 K3
Olivet *MI* U.S.A. 134 C2
Olivet *SD* U.S.A. 130 D3
Olivia U.S.A. 130 E2
Olji China 72 I4
Ol'khovka Russia 43 J6
Ollagüe Chile 144 C2
Ollombo Congo 98 B4
Olmaliq Uzbek. 80 C3
Olmos Peru 142 C5
Olmütz Czechia *see* Olomouc
Olney U.K. 49 G6
Olney *IL* U.S.A. 130 F4
Olney *MD* U.S.A. 135 G4
Olney *TX* U.S.A. 131 D5
Olofström Sweden 45 I8
Olomane *r.* Canada 123 J4
Olomouc Czechia 47 P6
Olonets Russia 42 G3
Olongapo Phil. 69 G4
Oloron-Ste-Marie France 56 D5
Olosenga *atoll* American Samoa *see* Swains Island
Olot Spain 57 H2
Olot Uzbek. 89 F2
Olovyannaya Russia 73 L2
Oloy *r.* Russia 65 Q3
Oloy, Qatorkŭhi *mts* Asia *see* Alai Range
Olpe Germany 53 H3
Olsztyn Poland 47 R4
Olt *r.* Romania 59 K3
Olten Switz. 56 H3
Olteniţa Romania 59 L2
Oltu Turkey 91 F2
Oluan Bi *c.* Taiwan 77 I4
Ol'viopol' Ukr. *see* Pervomays'k
Olymbos *hill* Cyprus *see* Olympos

▶Olympia U.S.A. 126 C3
Capital of Washington state.

Olympic National Park U.S.A. 126 C3
Olympos *hill* Cyprus 85 A2
Olympos Greece *see* Olympus, Mount
Olympos *nat. park* Greece *see* Olympou, Ethnikos Drymos
Olympou, Ethnikos Drymos *nat. park* Greece 59 J4
Olympus, Mount Cyprus 85 A2
Olympus, Mount Greece 59 J4
Olympus, Mount U.S.A. 126 C3
Olyutorskiy, Mys *c.* Russia 65 S4
Olyutorskiy Zaliv *b.* Russia 65 R4
Olzheras Russia *see* Mezhdurechensk
Oma China 83 E2
Oma *r.* Russia 42 J2
Omagh U.K. 51 E3
Omaha U.S.A. 130 E3
Omaheke *admin. reg.* Namibia 100 D2
Omal'skiy Khrebet *mts* Russia 74 E1
Oman *country* Asia 87 I6
Oman, Gulf of Asia 88 E5
Omaruru Namibia 99 B6
Omate Peru 142 D7
Omaweneno Botswana 100 F3
Omba *i.* Vanuatu *see* Aoba
Ombai, Selat *sea chan.* Indon. 108 D2
Ombalantu Namibia *see* Outapi
Omboué Gabon 98 A4
Ombu China 83 F3
Omdraaisvlei S. Africa 100 F6
Omdurman Sudan 86 D6
Omeo Australia 112 C6
Omer U.S.A. 134 D1
Ometepec Mex. 136 E5
Omgoy Wildlife Reserve *nature res.* Thai. 70 B3
Om Hajēr Eritrea 86 E7
Omīdīyeh Iran 88 C4
Omineca Mountains Canada 120 E3
Omirzak Kazakh. 91 H2
Omitara Namibia 100 C2
Ōmiya Japan 75 E6
Ommaney, Cape U.S.A. 120 C3
Ommen Neth. 52 G2
Omolon Russia 65 R3
Omo National Park Eth. 98 D3
Omsk Russia 64 I4
Omsukchan Russia 65 Q3
Ōmu Japan 74 F3
O-mu Myanmar 70 B2
Omu, Vârful *mt.* Romania 59 K2
Ōmura Japan 75 C6
Omutninsk Russia 42 L4
Onaman Lake Canada 122 D4
Onamia U.S.A. 130 E2
Onancock U.S.A. 135 H5
Onangué, Lac *l.* Gabon 98 B4
Onaping Lake Canada 122 E5
Onatchiway, Lac *l.* Canada 123 H4
Onavas Mex. 127 F7
Onawa U.S.A. 130 D3
Onaway U.S.A. 134 C1
Ōnay, Kōtal-e Afgh. 89 H3
Onbingwin Myanmar 71 B4
Oncativo Arg. 144 D4
Onchan Isle of Man 48 C4
Oncócua Angola 99 B5
Öncül Turkey 85 D1
Ondal India *see* Andal
Ondangwa Namibia 99 B5
Onderstedorings S. Africa 100 E6
Ondjiva Angola 99 B5
Ondo Nigeria 96 D4
Öndörhaan Mongolia 73 K3
Öndörshil Mongolia 73 J3
Ondozero Russia 42 G3
One Botswana 100 E2
One and a Half Degree Channel Maldives 81 D11
Onega Russia 42 H3
Onega *r.* Russia 42 H3

▶Onega, Lake Russia 42 G3
3rd largest lake in Europe.

Onega Bay *g.* Russia *see* Onezhskaya Guba
One Hundred and Fifty Mile House Canada *see* 150 Mile House
One Hundred Mile House Canada *see* 100 Mile House
Oneida *NY* U.S.A. 135 H2
Oneida *TN* U.S.A. 134 C5
Oneida Lake U.S.A. 135 H2
O'Neill U.S.A. 130 D3
Onekama U.S.A. 134 B1
Onekotan, Ostrov *i.* Russia 65 Q5
Oneonta *AL* U.S.A. 133 C5
Oneonta *NY* U.S.A. 135 H2
Oneşti Romania 59 L1
Onezhskaya Guba *g.* Russia 42 G2
Onezhskoye Ozero *l.* Russia *see* Onega, Lake
Ong *r.* India 84 D1
Onga Gabon 98 B4
Ongers *watercourse* S. Africa 100 F5
Ongiyn Gol *r.* Mongolia 80 J3
Ongjin N. Korea 75 B5
Ongole India 84 D3
Onida U.S.A. 130 C2
Onilahy *r.* Madag. 99 E6
Onistagane, Lac *l.* Canada 123 H4
Onitsha Nigeria 96 D4
Onjati Mountain Namibia 100 C2
Onjiva Angola *see* Ondjiva
Ono-i-Lau *i.* Fiji 107 I4
Onomichi Japan 75 D6
Onon *atoll* Micronesia *see* Namonuito
Onor, Gora *mt.* Russia 74 F2
Onotoa *atoll* Kiribati 107 H2
Onseepkans S. Africa 100 D5
Onslow Australia 108 A5
Onslow Bay U.S.A. 133 E5
Onstwedde Neth. 52 H1
Ontake-san *vol.* Japan 75 E6
Ontario *prov.* Canada 134 E1
Ontario U.S.A. 128 E4
Ontario, Lake Canada/U.S.A. 135 G2
Ontong Java Atoll Solomon Is 107 F2
Onutu *atoll* Kiribati *see* Onotoa
Onverwacht Suriname 143 G2
Onyx U.S.A. 128 D4
Oodnadatta Australia 111 A5
Oodweyne Somalia 98 E3
Oolambeyan National Park Australia 111 D7
Ooldea Australia 109 E7
Ooldea Range *hills* Australia 109 E7
Oologah Lake *resr* U.S.A. 131 E4
Ooratippra *r.* Australia 110 B4
Oos-Londen S. Africa *see* East London
Oostburg Neth. 52 D3
Oostende Belgium *see* Ostend
Oostendorp Neth. 52 F2
Oosterhout Neth. 52 E3
Oosterschelde *est.* Neth. 52 D3
Oosterwolde Neth. 52 G2
Oostvleteren Belgium 52 C4
Oost-Vlieland Neth. 52 F1
Ootacamund India *see* Udagamandalam
Ootsa Lake Canada 120 E4
Ootsa Lake *l.* Canada 120 E4
Opal Mex. 131 C7
Opala Dem. Rep. Congo 98 C4
Oparino Russia 42 K4
Oparo *i.* Fr. Polynesia *see* Rapa
Opasatika *r.* Canada 122 E4
Opasatika Lake Canada 122 E4
Opasquia Canada 121 M4
Opataca, Lac *l.* Canada 122 G4
Opava Czechia 47 P6
Opel *hill* Germany 53 H5
Opelika U.S.A. 133 C5
Opelousas U.S.A. 131 E6
Opeongo Lake Canada 122 F5
Opheim U.S.A. 126 G2
Opienge Dem. Rep. Congo 98 C3
Opinaca *r.* Canada 122 F3
Opinaca, Réservoir *resr* Canada 122 F3
Opinnagau *r.* Canada 122 E3
Opiscotéo, Lac *l.* Canada 123 H3
Op Luang National Park Thai. 70 B3
Opmeer Neth. 52 E2
Opochka Russia 45 P8
Opocopa, Lac *l.* Canada 123 I3
Opodepe Mex. 136 B3
Opole Poland 47 P5
Oporto Port. 57 B3
Opotiki N.Z. 113 F4
Opp U.S.A. 133 C6
Oppdal Norway 44 F5
Oppeid Norway 44 I2
Oppeln Poland *see* Opole
Opportunity U.S.A. 126 D3
Opunake N.Z. 113 D4
Opuwo Namibia 99 B5
Oqsu *r.* Tajik. 89 I2
Oracle U.S.A. 129 H5
Oradea Romania 59 I1
Orahovac Kosovo *see* Rahovec
Orai India 82 D4
Oraibi U.S.A. 129 H4
Oraibi Wash *watercourse* U.S.A. 129 H4
Oral Kazakh. *see* Ural'sk
Oran Alg. 57 F6
Orán Arg. 144 D2
Orang India 83 H4
Ŏrang N. Korea 74 C4
Orange Australia 112 D4
Orange France 56 G4
Orange *r.* Namibia/S. Africa 100 C5
Orange *CA* U.S.A. 128 E5
Orange *MA* U.S.A. 135 I2
Orange *TX* U.S.A. 131 E6
Orange *VA* U.S.A. 135 F4
Orange, Cabo *c.* Brazil 143 H3
Orangeburg U.S.A. 133 D5
Orange City U.S.A. 130 D3
Orange Cone *sea feature* S. Atlantic Ocean 148 I8
Orange Free State *prov.* S. Africa *see* Free State
Orangeville Canada 134 E2
Orange Walk Belize 136 G5
Oranienburg Germany 53 N2
Oranje *r.* Namibia/S. Africa *see* Orange
Oranje Gebergte *hills* Suriname 143 G3
Oranjemund Namibia 100 C5

▶Oranjestad Aruba 137 J6
Capital of Aruba.

Oranmore Ireland 51 D4
Orapa Botswana 99 C6
Orăştie Romania 59 J2
Oraşul Stalin Romania *see* Braşov
Oravais Fin. 44 M5
Orba Co *l.* China 82 E2
Orbetello Italy 58 D3
Orbost Australia 112 D6
Orcadas *research station* S. Atlantic Ocean 152 A2
Orchard City U.S.A. 129 J2
Orchha India 82 D4
Orchila, Isla *i.* Venez. 142 E1
Orchy *r.* U.K. 50 D4
Orcutt U.S.A. 128 C4
Ord *r.* Australia 108 E3
Ord U.S.A. 130 D3
Ord, Mount *hill* Australia 108 D4
Órdenes Spain *see* Ordes
Orderville U.S.A. 129 G3
Ordes Spain 57 B2
Ordesa y Monte Perdido, Parque Nacional de *nat. park* Spain 57 G2
Ord Mountain U.S.A. 128 E4
Ordos China *see* Dongsheng
Ord River Dam Australia 108 E4
Ordu *Hatay* Turkey *see* Yayladağı
Ordu *Ordu* Turkey 90 E2
Ordubad Azer. 91 G3
Ordway U.S.A. 130 C4
Ordzhonikidze Russia *see* Vladikavkaz
Ore Nigeria 96 D4
Oreana U.S.A. 128 D1
O Reăng Cambodia 71 D4
Örebro Sweden 45 I7
Oregon *IL* U.S.A. 130 F3
Oregon *OH* U.S.A. 134 D3
Oregon *state* U.S.A. 126 C4
Oregon City U.S.A. 126 C3
Orekhov Ukr. *see* Orikhiv
Orekhovo-Zuyevo Russia 42 H5
Orel' Kazakh. 80 G2
Orel Russia 43 H5
Orel, Gora *mt.* Russia 74 E1
Orel', Ozero *l.* Russia 74 E1
Orem U.S.A. 129 H1
Ore Mountains Czechia/Germany *see* Erzgebirge
Orenburg Russia 64 G4
Orense Spain *see* Ourense
Oreor Palau *see* Koror
Orepuki N.Z. 113 A8
Öresund *strait* Denmark/Sweden 45 H9
Oretana, Cordillera *mts* Spain *see* Toledo, Montes de
Orewa N.Z. 113 E3
Oreye Belgium 52 F4
Orfanou, Kolpos *b.* Greece 59 J4
Orford Australia 111 [inset]
Orford U.K. 49 I6
Orford Ness *hd* U.K. 49 I6
Organabo Fr. Guiana 143 H2
Organ Pipe Cactus National Monument *nat. park* U.S.A. 129 G5
Orge *r.* France 52 C6
Orhaneli Turkey 59 M5
Orhangazi Turkey 59 M4
Orhon Gol *r.* Mongolia 80 J2
Orichi Russia 42 K4
Oriental, Cordillera *mts* Bol. 142 E7
Oriental, Cordillera *mts* Col. 142 D2
Oriental, Cordillera *mts* Peru 142 E6
Orihuela Spain 57 F4
Orikhiv Ukr. 43 G7
Orillia Canada 134 F1
Orimattila Fin. 45 N6
Orin U.S.A. 126 G4
Orinoco *r.* Col./Venez. 142 F2
Orinoco, Delta del Venez. 142 F2
Orissa *state* India *see* Odisha
Orissaare Estonia 45 M7
Oristano *Sardinia* Italy 58 C5
Orivesi Fin. 45 N6
Orivesi *l.* Fin. 44 P5
Oriximiná Brazil 143 G4
Orizaba Mex. 136 E5

▶Orizaba, Pico de *vol.* Mex. 136 E5
Highest active volcano and 3rd highest mountain in North America.

Orizona Brazil 145 A2
Orkanger Norway 44 F5
Örkelljunga Sweden 45 H8
Orkla *r.* Norway 44 F5
Orkney S. Africa 101 H4
Orkney Islands *is* U.K. 50 F1
Orla U.S.A. 131 C6
Orland U.S.A. 128 B2
Orlândia Brazil 145 B3
Orlando U.S.A. 133 D6
Orland Park U.S.A. 134 B3
Orleans Brazil 145 A5
Orléans France 56 E3
Orleans *IN* U.S.A. 134 B4
Orleans *VT* U.S.A. 135 I1
Orléans, Île d' *i.* Canada 123 H5
Orléansville Alg. *see* Chlef
Orlik Russia 72 H2
Orlov Russia 42 K4
Orlov Gay Russia 43 K6
Orlovskiy Russia 43 I7
Ormara Pak. 89 G5
Ormara, Ras *hd* Pak. 89 G5
Ormiston Canada 121 J5
Ormoc Phil. 69 G4
Ormskirk U.K. 48 E5

Pentadaktylos Range mts Cyprus 85 A2
Pentakota India 84 D2
Pentecost Island Vanuatu 107 G3
Pentecôte, Île i. Vanuatu see Pentecost Island
Penticton Canada 120 G5
Pentire Point U.K. 49 B8
Pentland Australia 110 D4
Pentland Firth sea chan. U.K. 50 F2
Pentland Hills U.K. 50 F5
Pentwater U.S.A. 134 B2
Penwegon Myanmar 70 B3
Pen-y-bont ar Ogwr U.K. see Bridgend
Penygadair hill U.K. 49 D6
Penylan Lake Canada 121 J2
Penza Russia 43 J5
Penzance U.K. 49 B8
Penzhinskaya Guba b. Russia 65 R3
Peoria AZ U.S.A. 129 G5
Peoria IL U.S.A. 130 F3
Peotone U.S.A. 134 B3
Pequeña, Punta pt Mex. 127 E8
Pequop Mountains U.S.A. 129 F1
Peradeniya Sri Lanka 84 D5
Pera Head hd Australia 110 C2
Perak i. Malaysia 71 B6
Perales del Alfambra Spain 57 F3
Perambalur India 84 C4
Perämeren kansallispuisto nat. park Fin. 44 N4
Peräseinäjoki Fin. 44 M5
Percé Canada 123 I4
Percival Lakes salt flat Australia 108 D5
Percy U.S.A. 135 J1
Percy Isles Australia 110 E4
Percy Reach l. Canada 135 G1
Perdizes Brazil 145 B2
Perdu, Lac l. Canada 123 H4
Peregrebnoye Russia 41 T3
Pereira Col. 142 C3
Pereira Barreto Brazil 145 A3
Pereira de Eça Angola see Ondjiva
Pere Marquette r. U.S.A. 134 B2
Peremul Par reef India 84 B4
Peremyshlyany Ukr. 43 E6
Perenjori Australia 109 B7
Pereslavl'-Zalesskiy Russia 42 H4
Pereslavskiy Natsional'nyy Park nat. park Russia 42 H4
Pereyaslavka Russia 74 D3
Pereyaslav-Khmel'nitskiy Ukr. see Pereyaslav-Khmel'nyts'kyy
Pereyaslav-Khmel'nyts'kyy Ukr. 43 F6
Perforated Island Thai. see Bon, Ko
Pergamino Arg. 144 D4
Perhentian Besar, Pulau i. Malaysia 71 C6
Perho Fin. 44 N5
Péribonka, Lac l. Canada 123 H4
Perico Arg. 144 C2
Pericos Mex. 127 G8
Peridot U.S.A. 129 H5
Périgueux France 56 E4
Perijá, Parque Nacional nat. park Venez. 142 D2
Perijá, Sierra de mts Venez. 142 D2
Periyar India see Erode
Perkasie U.S.A. 135 H3
Perlas, Punta de pt Nicaragua 137 H6
Perleberg Germany 53 L1
Perm' Russia 41 R4
Permas Russia 42 J4
Pernambuco Brazil see Recife
Pernambuco Plain sea feature S. Atlantic Ocean 148 G6
Pernatty Lagoon salt flat Australia 111 B6
Pernem India 84 B3
Pernik Bulg. 59 J3
Pernov Estonia see Pärnu
Perojpur Bangl. see Pirojpur
Peron Islands Australia 108 E3
Péronne France 52 C5
Perpignan France 56 F5
Perranporth U.K. 49 B8
Perrégaux Alg. see Mohammadia
Perris U.S.A. 128 E5
Perros-Guirec France 56 C2
Perrot, Île i. Canada 135 I1
Perry FL U.S.A. 133 D6
Perry GA U.S.A. 133 D5
Perry MI U.S.A. 134 C2
Perry OK U.S.A. 131 D4
Perry Lake U.S.A. 130 E4
Perryton U.S.A. 131 C4
Perryville AK U.S.A. 118 C4
Perryville MO U.S.A. 130 F4
Perseverancia Bol. 142 F6
Pershore U.K. 49 E6
Persia country Asia see Iran
Persian Gulf Asia see The Gulf
Pertek Turkey 91 E3
▶Perth Australia 109 A7
Capital of Western Australia. 4th most populous city in Oceania.
Perth Canada 135 G1
Perth U.K. 50 F4
Perth Amboy U.S.A. 135 H3
Perth-Andover Canada 123 I5
Perth Basin sea feature Indian Ocean 149 P7
Pertominsk Russia 42 H2
Pertunmaa Fin. 45 O6
Pertusato, Capo c. Corsica France 56 I6
Peru atoll Kiribati see Beru
▶Peru country S. America 142 D6
3rd largest and 4th most populous country in South America.
Peru IL U.S.A. 130 F3
Peru IN U.S.A. 134 B3
Peru NY U.S.A. 135 I1
Peru-Chile Trench sea feature S. Pacific Ocean 151 O6
Perugia Italy 58 E3
Peruru India 84 C3
Perusia Italy see Perugia
Péruwelz Belgium 52 D4
Pervomaysk Russia 43 I5
Pervomays'k Ukr. 43 F6
Pervomayskiy Kazakh. 80 F1
Pervomayskiy Arkhangel'skaya Oblast' Russia see Novodvinsk
Pervomayskiy Tambovskaya Oblast' Russia 43 I5
Pervomays'kyy Ukr. 43 H6
Pervorechenskiy (abandoned) Russia 65 R3
Pervyy Brat, Gora hill Russia 74 F1
Pesaro Italy 58 E3
Pescadores is Taiwan see Penghu Qundao
Pescara Italy 58 F3
Pescara r. Italy 58 F3
Peschanokopskoye Russia 43 I7
Peschanoye Russia see Yashkul'
Peschanyy, Mys pt Kazakh. 91 H2
Pesha r. Russia 42 J2
Peshawar Pak. 89 H3
Peshkopi Albania 59 I4
Peshtera Bulg. 59 K3
Peski Turkm. 89 F2
Peskovka Russia 42 L4
Pesnica Slovenia 58 F1
Pessac France 56 D4
Pessin Germany 53 M2
Pestovo Russia 42 G4
Pestravka Russia 43 K5
Petah Tiqwa Israel 85 B3
Petäjävesi Fin. 44 N5
Petaling Jaya Malaysia 71 C7
Petalion, Kolpos sea chan. Greece 59 K5
Petaluma U.S.A. 128 B2
Pétange Lux. 52 F5
Petatlán Mex. 136 D5
Petauke Zambia 99 D5
Petenwell Lake U.S.A. 130 F2
Peterbell Canada 122 E4
Peterborough Australia 111 B7
Peterborough Canada 135 F1
Peterborough U.K. 49 G6
Peterborough U.S.A. 135 J2
Peterculter U.K. 50 G3
Peterhead U.K. 50 H3
Peter I Island Antarctica 152 K2
Peter I Øy i. Antarctica see Peter I Island
Peter Lake Canada 121 M2
Peterlee U.K. 48 F4
Petermann Bjerg nunatak Greenland 119 P2
Petermann Ranges mts Australia 109 E6
Peter Pond Lake Canada 121 I4
Peters, Lac l. Canada 123 H2
Petersberg Germany 53 J4
Petersburg AK U.S.A. 120 C3
Petersburg IL U.S.A. 130 F4
Petersburg IN U.S.A. 134 B4
Petersburg NY U.S.A. 135 I2
Petersburg VA U.S.A. 135 G5
Petersburg WV U.S.A. 134 F4
Petersfield U.K. 49 G7
Petershagen Germany 53 I2
Petersville U.S.A. 118 C3
Peter the Great Bay Russia see Petra Velikogo, Zaliv
Peth India 84 B2
Petilia Policastro Italy 58 G5
Petit Atlas mts Morocco see Anti-Atlas
Petitcodiac Canada 123 I5
Petitjean Morocco see Sidi Kacem
Petit Mécatina r. Canada 123 K4
Petit Mécatina, Île du i. Canada 123 K4
Petit Morin r. France 52 D6
Petitot r. Canada 120 F2
Petit St-Bernard, Col du pass France 56 H4
Petit Saut, Barrage du resr Fr. Guiana 143 H3
Peto Mex. 136 G4
Petoskey U.S.A. 132 C2
Petra tourist site Jordan 85 B4
Petra Velikogo, Zaliv b. Russia 74 C4
Petre, Point Canada 135 G2
Petrich Bulg. 59 J4
Petrified Forest National Park U.S.A. 129 I4
Petrikau Poland see Piotrków Trybunalski
Petrikov Belarus see Pyetrykaw
Petrinja Croatia 58 G2
Petroaleksandrovsk Uzbek. see To'rtko'l
Petroglyphic Complexes of the Mongolian Altai tourist site Mongolia 72 F3
Petrograd Russia see St Petersburg
Petrohanski Prohod pass Bulg. 59 J3
Petrokov Poland see Piotrków Trybunalski
Petrolia Canada 134 D2
Petrolia U.S.A. 128 A1
Petrolina Brazil 143 J5
Petrolina de Goiás Brazil 145 A2
Petropavl Kazakh. see Petropavlovskoye
Petropavlovsk Russia see Petropavlovsk-Kamchatskiy
Petropavlovsk-Kamchatskiy Russia 65 Q4
Petropavlovskoye Kazakh. 79 F1
Petrópolis Brazil 145 C3
Petroșani Romania 59 J2
Petrovsk Russia 43 J5
Petrovskoye Russia see Svetlograd
Petrovsk-Zabaykal'skiy Russia 73 J2
Petrozavodsk Russia 42 G3
Petrus Steyn S. Africa 101 I4
Petrusville S. Africa 100 G6
Petsamo Russia see Pechenga
Pettau Slovenia see Ptuj
Petten Neth. 52 E2
Pettigo U.K. 51 E3
Petukhovo Russia 64 H4
Petushki Russia 42 H5
Petzeck mt. Austria 47 N7
Peuetsagu, Gunung vol. Indon. 71 B6
Peureula Indon. 71 B6
Pevek Russia 65 S3
Pêxung China 76 B1
Pey Ostān Iran 88 E3
Peza r. Russia 42 J2
Pezinok Slovakia 47 P6
Pezu Pak. 89 H3
Pfälzer Wald hills Germany 53 H5
Pforzheim Germany 53 I6
Pfungstadt Germany 53 I5
Phac Mo, Phu mt. Vietnam 70 C2
Phagameng S. Africa 101 I3
Phagwara India 82 C3
Phahameng S. Africa 101 H5
Phalaborwa S. Africa 101 J2
Phalodi India 82 C4
Phalsund India 82 B4
Phalta India 83 G5
Phaluai, Ko i. Thai. 71 B5
Phalut Peak India/Nepal 83 G4
Phan Thai. 70 B3
Phanat Nikhom Thai. 71 C4
Phangan, Ko i. Thai. 71 C5
Phang Hoei, San Khao mts Thai. 70 C3
Phangnga Thai. 71 B5
Phăng Xi Păng mt. Vietnam 70 C2
Phanom Dong Rak, Thiu Khao mts Cambodia/Thai. 71 D4
Phan Rang-Thap Cham Vietnam 71 E5
Phan Thiêt Vietnam 71 E5
Phapon Myanmar see Pyapon
Phat Diêm Vietnam 70 D2
Phatthalung Thai. 71 C6
Phawngpui India 83 H5
Phayam, Ko i. Thai. 71 B5
Phayao Thai. 70 B3
Phayuhakhiri Thai. 70 C4
Phek India 83 H4
Phelps Lake Canada 121 K3
Phen Thai. 70 C3
Phenix U.S.A. 135 F5
Phenix City U.S.A. 133 C5
Phet Buri Thai. 71 B4
Phetchabun Thai. 70 C3
Phiafai Laos 70 D4
Phichai Thai. 70 C3
Phichit Thai. 70 C3
Philadelphia Jordan see 'Ammān
Philadelphia Turkey see Alaşehir
Philadelphia MS U.S.A. 131 F5
Philadelphia NY U.S.A. 135 H1
Philadelphia PA U.S.A. 135 H4
Philip U.S.A. 130 C2
Philip Atoll Micronesia see Sorol
Philippeville Alg. see Skikda
Philippeville Belgium 52 E4
Philippi U.S.A. 134 E4
Philippi, Lake salt flat Australia 110 B5
Philippine Neth. 52 D3
Philippine Basin sea feature N. Pacific Ocean 150 E4
Philippines country Asia 69 G4
Philippine Sea N. Pacific Ocean 69 G3
▶Philippine Trench sea feature N. Pacific Ocean 150 E4
3rd deepest trench in the world.
Philippolis S. Africa 101 G6
Philippopolis Bulg. see Plovdiv
Philippsburg Germany 53 I5
Philipsburg MT U.S.A. 126 E3
Philipsburg PA U.S.A. 135 F3
Philip Smith Mountains U.S.A. 118 D3
Philipstown S. Africa 100 G6
Phillip Island Australia 112 B7
Phillips ME U.S.A. 135 J1
Phillips WI U.S.A. 130 F2
Phillipsburg U.S.A. 130 D4
Phillips Range hills Australia 108 D4
Philmont U.S.A. 135 I2
Philomelium Turkey see Akşehir
Phiritona S. Africa 101 H4
Phitsanulok Thai. 70 C3
▶Phnom Penh Cambodia 71 D5
Capital of Cambodia.
Phnum Pénh Cambodia see Phnom Penh
Pho, Laem pt Thai. 71 C6
Phoenicia U.S.A. 135 H2
▶Phoenix U.S.A. 127 E6
Capital of Arizona.
Phoenix Island Kiribati see Rawaki
Phoenix Islands Kiribati 107 I2
Phô Lu Vietnam 70 D2
Phon Thai. 70 C4
Phong Nha Vietnam 70 D3
Phôngsali Laos 70 C2
Phong Saly Laos see Phôngsali
Phong Thô Vietnam 70 C2
Phon Phisai Thai. 70 C3
Phônsavan Laos 70 C3
Phônsavan mt. Laos 70 C3
Phon Thong Thai. 70 C3
Phosphate Hill Australia 110 C4
Phrae Thai. 70 C3
Phra Nakhon Si Ayutthaya Thai. see Ayutthaya
Phrao Thai. 70 B3
Phra Saeng Thai. 71 B5
Phrom Phiram Thai. 70 C3
Phsar Réam Cambodia 71 C5
Phu Bai Vietnam 70 D3
Phuchong-Nayoi National Park Thai. 71 D4
Phu Cương Vietnam see Thu Dâu Môt
Phuket Thai. 71 B6
Phuket, Ko i. Thai. 71 B6
Phu Khieo Wildlife Reserve nature res. Thai. 70 C3
Phulabani India see Phulbani
Phulbani India 84 E1
Phulchhari Ghat Bangl. see Fulchhari
Phulji Pak. 89 G5
Phu Lôc Soc Trăng Vietnam 71 D5
Phu Lôc Thưa Thiên-Huê Vietnam 70 D3
Phu Luang National Park Thai. 70 C3
Phu Ly Vietnam 70 D2
Phumiphon, Khuan Thai. 70 B3
Phu My Vietnam 71 E4
Phung Hiêp Vietnam 71 D5
Phước Bưu Vietnam 71 D5
Phước Hai Vietnam 71 D5
Phu Phan National Park Thai. 70 C3
Phu Quôc, Đao i. Vietnam 71 C5
Phu Quôc, Quân i. Vietnam see Phu Quôc, Đao
Phu Quy, Đao i. Vietnam 71 E5
Phu Tho Vietnam 70 D2
Phu Vinh Vietnam see Tra Vinh
Phyu Myanmar 70 B3
Piaca Brazil 143 I5
Piacenza Italy 58 C2
Piacouadie, Lac l. Canada 123 H4
Piagochioui r. Canada 122 F3
Piai, Tanjung pt Malaysia 71 C7
Pian r. Australia 112 D3
Pianosa, Isola i. Italy 58 D3
Piatra Neamț Romania 59 L1
Piave r. Italy 58 E2
Pibor Post South Sudan 97 G4
Pic r. Canada 122 D4
Picacho U.S.A. 129 H5
Picachos, Cerro dos mt. Mex. 127 E7
Picardie admin. reg. France 52 C5
Picardie reg. France see Picardy
Picardy admin. reg. France see Picardie
Picardy reg. France 52 B5
Picauville France 49 F9
Picayune U.S.A. 131 F6
Piceance Creek r. U.S.A. 129 I1
Pichanal Arg. 144 D2
Pichhor India 82 D4
Pichilemu Chile 144 B4
Pichilingue Mex. 136 B4
Pickens U.S.A. 134 E4
Pickering Canada 134 F2
Pickering U.K. 48 G4
Pickering, Vale of valley U.K. 48 G4
Pickle Lake Canada 119 I4
Pico da Neblina, Parque Nacional do nat. park Brazil 142 E3
Picos Brazil 143 J5
Picos de Europa, Parque Nacional de los nat. park Spain 57 D2
Pico Truncado Arg. 144 C7
Picton Australia 112 E5
Picton Canada 135 G2
Picton N.Z. 113 E5
Pictou Canada 123 J5
Picture Butte Canada 121 H5
Pidarak Pak. 89 F5
Pidurutalagala mt. Sri Lanka 84 D5
Piedade Brazil 145 B3
Piedra de Águila Arg. 144 B6
Piedras, Punta pt Arg. 144 E5
Piedras, Río de las r. Peru 142 E6
Piedras Blancas Point U.S.A. 128 C4
Piedras Negras Mex. 131 C6
Pie Island Canada 122 C4
Pieksämäki Fin. 44 O5
Pielavesi Fin. 44 O5
Pielinen l. Fin. 44 P5
Pieljekaise nationalpark nat. park Sweden 44 J3
Pienaarsrivier S. Africa 101 I3
Pieniński Park Narodowy nat. park Poland 47 R6
Pieninský národný park nat. park Slovakia 47 R6
Pierce U.S.A. 130 D3
Pierce Lake Canada 121 M4
Pierceland Canada 121 I4
Pierceton U.S.A. 134 C3
Pieria mts Greece 59 J4
Pierowall U.K. 50 G1
Pierpont U.S.A. 134 E3
▶Pierre U.S.A. 130 C2
Capital of South Dakota.
Pierrelatte France 56 G4
Pietermaritzburg S. Africa 101 J5
Pietersaari Fin. see Jakobstad
Pietersburg S. Africa see Polokwane
Pie Town U.S.A. 129 I4
Pietra Spada, Passo di pass Italy 58 G5
Piet Retief S. Africa see eMkhondo
Pietrosa mt. Romania 59 K1
Pigeon U.S.A. 134 D2
Pigeon Bay Canada 134 D3
Pigeon Lake Canada 120 H4
Piggott U.S.A. 131 F4
Pigg's Peak Swaziland 101 J3
Pigs, Bay of Cuba 133 D8
Pihij India 82 C5
Pihkva järv l. Estonia/Russia see Pskov, Lake
Pihlajavesi l. Fin. 44 P6
Pihlava Fin. 45 L6
Pihtipudas Fin. 44 N5
Piippola Fin. 44 N4
Piispajärvi Fin. 44 P4
Pikalevo Russia 42 G4
Pike U.S.A. 134 E4
Pike Bay Canada 134 E1
Pikelot i. Micronesia 69 L5
Pikes Peak U.S.A. 126 G5
Piketon U.S.A. 134 D4
Pikeville KY U.S.A. 134 D5
Pikeville TN U.S.A. 132 C5
Pikinni atoll Marshall Is see Bikini
Piła Poland 47 P4
Pila, Kyun i. Myanmar 71 B5
Pilanesberg National Park S. Africa 101 H3
Pilão Arcado Brazil 143 J5
Pilar Arg. 144 E4
Pilar Para. 144 E3
Pilar de Goiás Brazil 145 A1
Pilaya r. Bol. 142 F8
Pilbara reg. Australia 108 B5
Pilcomayo r. Bol./Para. 142 F8
Piler India 84 C3
Pili, Cerro mt. Chile 144 C2
Pilibangan India 82 C3
Pilibhit India 82 D3
Pilipinas country Asia see Philippines
Pillau Russia see Baltiysk
Pillcopata Peru 142 D6
Pilliga Australia 112 D3
Pillsbury, Lake U.S.A. 128 B2
Pil'na Russia 42 J5
Pil'nya, Ozero l. Russia 42 M1
Pilões, Serra dos mts Brazil 145 B2
Pilos Greece see Pylos
Pilot Knob mt. U.S.A. 126 E3
Pilot Peak U.S.A. 128 E2
Pilot Station U.S.A. 118 B3
Pilsen Czechia see Plzeň
Piltene Latvia 45 L8
Pil'tun, Zaliv lag. Russia 74 F1
Pilu Pak. 89 H5
Pima U.S.A. 129 I5
Pimenta Bueno Brazil 142 F6
Pimento U.S.A. 134 B4
Pimpalner India 84 B1
Pin r. India 82 D2
Pin r. Myanmar 70 A2
Pinahat India 82 D4
Pinaleno Mountains U.S.A. 129 H5
Pinamar Arg. 144 E5
Pinang Malaysia see George Town
Pinang i. Malaysia 71 C6
Pınarbaşı Turkey 90 E3
Pinar del Río Cuba 137 H4
Pinarhisar Turkey 59 L4
Piñas Ecuador 142 C4
Pincher Creek Canada 120 H5
Pinckneyville U.S.A. 130 F4
Pinconning U.S.A. 134 D2
Pińczów Poland 47 R5
Pindaí Brazil 145 C1
Pindamonhangaba Brazil 145 B3
Pindar Australia 109 A7
Pindaré r. Brazil 143 J4
Pindhos Óros mts Greece see Pindus Mountains
Pindos mts Greece see Pindus Mountains
Pindrei India 82 E5
Pindus Mountains Greece 59 I5
Pine watercourse Australia 111 C7
Pine r. MI U.S.A. 134 C1
Pine r. MI U.S.A. 134 C2
Pine Bluff U.S.A. 131 E5
Pine Bluffs U.S.A. 126 G4
Pine Creek Australia 108 E3
Pine Creek r. U.S.A. 135 G3
Pinecrest U.S.A. 128 C2
Pinedale NM U.S.A. 129 I4
Pinedale WY U.S.A. 126 F4
Pine Dock Canada 121 L5
Pine Falls Canada 121 L5
Pine Flat Lake U.S.A. 128 D3
Pinega Russia 42 I2
Pinega r. Russia 42 I2
Pinegrove Australia 109 A6
Pine Grove U.S.A. 135 G3
Pine Hills U.S.A. 133 D6
Pinehouse Lake Canada 121 J4
Pinehouse Lake l. Canada 121 J4
Pineimuta r. Canada 121 N4
Pineios r. Greece 59 J5
Pine Island Bay Antarctica 151 N10
Pine Island Glacier Antarctica 152 K1
Pine Islands FL U.S.A. 133 D7
Pine Islands FL U.S.A. 133 D7
Pine Knot U.S.A. 134 C5
Pineland U.S.A. 131 E6
Pine Mountain U.S.A. 128 C4
Pine Peak U.S.A. 129 G4
Pine Point pt Canada 120 H2
Pine Point (abandoned) Canada 120 H2
Pineridge U.S.A. 128 D3
Pine Ridge U.S.A. 130 C3
Pinerolo Italy 58 B2
Pines, Akrotirio pt Greece 59 K4
Pines, Isle of i. Cuba see Juventud, Isla de la
Pines, Isle of i. New Caledonia see Pins, Île des
Pinetop U.S.A. 129 I4
Pinetown S. Africa 101 J5
Pine Valley U.S.A. 135 G2
Pineville KY U.S.A. 134 D5
Pineville MO U.S.A. 131 E4
Pineville WV U.S.A. 134 E5
Ping, Mae Nam r. Thai. 70 C4
Ping'an China 72 I5
Ping'anyi China see Ping'an
Pingba China 76 E3
Pingbian China 76 D4
Ping Dao i. China 77 H1
Pingdingbu China see Guyuan
Pingdingshan China 77 G1
Pingdong Taiwan see Pingtung
Pingdu Jiangxi China see Anfu
Pingdu Shandong China 73 L5
Pinggang China 74 B4
Pinghe China 77 H3
Pinghu China see Pingtang
Pingjiang China 77 G2
Pingjin China 76 E2
Pingle China 77 F3
Pingli China 77 F1
Pingliang China 76 E1
Pinglu China 77 F1
Pingma China see Tiandong
Pingnan China 77 H3
Pingqiao China 77 G1
Pingshan Sichuan China 76 E2
Pingshan Yunnan China see Luquan
Pingshi China 77 G3
Pingtan China 77 H3
Pingtan Dao i. China see Haitan Dao
Pingtang China 76 E3
Pingtung Taiwan 77 I4
Pingxi China see Yuping
Pingxiang Guangxi China 76 E4
Pingxiang Jiangxi China 77 G3
Pingyang Heilong. China 74 B2
Pingyang Zhejiang China 77 I3
Pingyi China 77 H1
Pingyu China 77 G1
Pingyuan China 76 D4
Pingzhai China see Liuzhi
Pinheiro Brazil 143 I4
Pinhoe U.K. 49 D8
Pini i. Indon. 68 B6
Piniós r. Greece see Pineios
Pinjin Australia 109 C7
Pink Mountain Canada 120 F3
Pinlaung Myanmar 70 B2
Pinlebu Myanmar 70 A1
Pinnacle hill U.S.A. 135 F4
Pinnacles National Park nat. park U.S.A. 128 C3
Pinnau r. Germany 53 J1
Pinneberg Germany 53 J1
Pinnes, Akra pt Greece see Pines, Akrotirio
Pinon Hills U.S.A. 128 E4
Pinos, Isla de i. Cuba see Juventud, Isla de la
Pinos, Mount U.S.A. 128 D4
Pinotepa Nacional Mex. 136 E5
Pins, Île des i. New Caledonia 107 G4
Pins, Pointe aux pt Canada 134 E2
Pinsk Belarus 45 O10
Pinta, Sierra hill U.S.A. 129 G5
Pintada Creek watercourse U.S.A. 127 G6
Pintados Chile 144 C2
Pintura U.S.A. 129 G3
Pioche U.S.A. 129 F3
Piodi Dem. Rep. Congo 99 C4
Pioneer Mountains U.S.A. 126 E3
Pioner, Ostrov i. Russia 64 K2
Pionerskiy Kaliningradskaya Oblast' Russia 45 L9
Pionerskiy Khanty-Mansiyskiy Autonomnyy Okrug-Yugra Russia 41 S3
Pionki Poland 47 R5
Piopio N.Z. 113 E4
Piopiotahi inlet N.Z. see Milford Sound
Piorini, Lago l. Brazil 142 F4
Piotrków Trybunalski Poland 47 Q5
Pipa Dingzi mt. China 74 C4
Pipar India 82 C4
Pipar Road India 82 C4
Piperi i. Greece 59 K5
Piper Peak U.S.A. 128 E3
Pipestone Canada 121 K5
Pipestone r. Canada 121 N4
Pipestone U.S.A. 130 D3
Pipli India 82 C3
Pipmuacan, Réservoir resr Canada 123 H4
Piqua U.S.A. 134 C3
Piquiri r. Brazil 145 A4
Pira Benin 96 D4
Piracanjuba Brazil 145 A2
Piracicaba Brazil 145 B3
Piracicaba r. Brazil 145 C2
Piracuruca Brazil 143 J4
Piraeus Greece 59 J6
Piraí do Sul Brazil 145 A4
Piráievs Greece see Piraeus
Piraju Brazil 145 A3
Pirajuí Brazil 145 A3
Pirallahı Adası Azer. 91 H2
Piranhas Bahia Brazil 145 C1
Piranhas Goiás Brazil 143 H7
Piranhas r. Goiás Brazil 145 A2
Piranhas r. Rio Grande do Norte Brazil 143 K5
Pirapora Brazil 145 B2
Pirassununga Brazil 145 B3
Piraube, Lac l. Canada 123 H4
Pirawa India 82 D4
Pirenópolis Brazil 145 A1
Pires do Rio Brazil 145 A2
Pírgos Greece see Pyrgos
Pirin, Natsionalen Park nat. park Bulg. 59 J4
Pirineos mts Europe see Pyrenees
Piripiri Brazil 143 J4
Pirlerkondu Turkey see Taşkent
Pirmasens Germany 53 H5
Pirojpur Bangl. 83 G5
Pir Panjal Pass India 82 C2
Pir Panjal Range mts India/Pak. 89 I3
Pīr Shūrān, Selseleh-ye mts Iran 89 F4
Piryatin Ukr. see Pyryatyn
Pīr Zādah Afgh. 89 G4
Pisa Italy 58 D3
Pisae Italy see Pisa
Pisagua Chile 142 D7
Pisang, Kepulauan is Indon. 69 I7
Pisaurum Italy see Pesaro
Pisco Peru 142 C6
Písek Czechia 47 O6
Pisha China see Ningnan
Pishan China 82 D1
Pīshīn Iran 80 B6
Pishin Pak. 89 G4
Pīshīn Jān Afgh. 89 F3
Pishin Lora r. Pak. 89 G4
Pishpek Kyrg. see Bishkek
Pisidia hist. area Turkey 90 C3
▶Pissis, Cerro Arg. 144 C3
4th highest mountain in South America.
Pisté Mex. 136 G4
Pisticci Italy 58 G4
Pistoia Italy 58 D3
Pistoriae Italy see Pistoia
Pisuerga r. Spain 57 D3
Pita Guinea 96 B3
Pitaga Canada 123 I3
Pitanga Brazil 145 A4
Pitangui Brazil 145 B2
Pitar India 82 B5
Pitarpunga Lake imp. l. Australia 112 A5
Pitcairn, Henderson, Ducie and Oeno Islands terr. S. Pacific Ocean see Pitcairn Islands
Pitcairn Island Pitcairn Is 151 L7
▶Pitcairn Islands terr. S. Pacific Ocean 151 L7
United Kingdom Overseas Territory.
Piteå Sweden 44 L4
Piteälven r. Sweden 44 L4
Pitelino Russia 43 I5
Piterka Russia 43 J6
Pitești Romania 59 K2
Pithoragarh India 82 E3
Pitihra India 82 D5
Pitiquito Mex. 127 E7
Pitkyaranta Russia 42 F3
Pitlochry U.K. 50 F4
Pitong China see Pixian
Pitsane Siding Botswana 101 G3
Pitti i. India 84 B4
Pitt Island Canada 120 D4
Pitt Island N.Z. 107 I6
Pitt Islands Solomon Is see Vanikoro Islands
Pittsboro U.S.A. 131 F5
Pittsburg KS U.S.A. 131 E4
Pittsburg TX U.S.A. 131 E5
Pittsburgh U.S.A. 134 F3
Pittsfield MA U.S.A. 135 I2
Pittsfield ME U.S.A. 135 K1

Pittsfield VT U.S.A. 135 I2
Pittston U.S.A. 135 H3
Pittsworth Australia 112 E1
Pitz Lake Canada 121 L2
Piumhi Brazil 145 B3
Piura Peru 142 B5
Piute Mountains U.S.A. 129 F4
Piute Peak U.S.A. 128 D4
Piute Reservoir U.S.A. 129 G2
Piuthan Nepal 83 E3
Pivabiska r. Canada 122 E4
Pivka Slovenia 58 F2
Pixariá mt. Greece see Pyxaria
Pixian China 76 D2
Pixley U.S.A. 128 D4
Pizhanka Russia 42 K4
Pizhi Nigeria 96 D4
Pizhma Russia 42 J4
Pizhma r. Russia 42 K4
Pizhma r. Russia 42 L2
Pizhou China 77 H1
Placentia Canada 123 L5
Placentia Italy see Piacenza
Placentia Bay Canada 123 L5
Placerville CA U.S.A. 128 C2
Placerville CO U.S.A. 129 I2
Placetas Cuba 133 E8
Plácido de Castro Brazil 142 E6
Plain Dealing U.S.A. 131 E5
Plainfield CT U.S.A. 135 J3
Plainfield IN U.S.A. 134 B4
Plainfield VT U.S.A. 135 I1
Plains KS U.S.A. 131 C4
Plains TX U.S.A. 131 C5
Plainview U.S.A. 131 C5
Plainville IN U.S.A. 134 B4
Plainville KS U.S.A. 130 D4
Plainwell U.S.A. 134 C2
Plaka, Akra pt Greece see Plaka, Akrotirio
Plaka, Akrotirio pt Greece 59 L7
Plakoti, Cape Cyprus 85 B2
Plamondon Canada 121 H4
Planá Czechia 53 M5
Plana Cays is Bahamas 133 F8
Planada U.S.A. 128 C3
Planaltina Brazil 145 B1
Plane r. Germany 53 M2
Plankinton U.S.A. 130 D3
Plano U.S.A. 131 D5
Planura Brazil 145 A3
Plaquemine U.S.A. 131 F6
Plasencia Spain 57 C3
Plaster City U.S.A. 129 F5
Plaster Rock Canada 123 I5
Plastun Russia 74 E3
Platani r. Sicily Italy 58 E6
Platberg mt. S. Africa 101 I5
Plateau Antarctica
Platina U.S.A. 128 B1
Platinum U.S.A. 153 B3
Plato Col. 142 D2
Platte r. U.S.A. 130 E3
Platte City U.S.A. 130 E4
Plattling Germany 53 M6
Plattsburgh U.S.A. 135 I1
Plattsmouth U.S.A. 130 E3
Plau am See Germany 53 M1
Plauen Germany 53 M4
Plauer See l. Germany 53 M1
Plavsk Russia 43 H5
Playa Noriega, Lago l. Mex. 127 F7
Playas Ecuador 142 B4
Playas Lake U.S.A. 129 I6
Plây Ku Vietnam 71 E4
Pleasant, Lake U.S.A. 129 G5
Pleasant Bay U.S.A. 135 K3
Pleasant Grove U.S.A. 129 H1
Pleasant Hill Lake U.S.A. 134 D3
Pleasanton U.S.A. 131 D6
Pleasant Point N.Z. 113 C7
Pleasantville U.S.A. 135 H4
Pleasure Ridge Park U.S.A. 134 C4
Pleaux France 56 F4
Pledger Lake Canada 122 E4
Plei Doch Vietnam 71 D4
Plei Kân Vietnam 70 D4
Pleinfeld Germany 53 K5
Pleiße r. Germany 53 M3
Plenty watercourse Australia 110 B5
Plenty, Bay of g. N.Z. 113 F3
Plentywood U.S.A. 126 G2
Plesetsk Russia 42 I3
Pleshchentsy Belarus see Plyeshchanitsy
Plétipi, Lac l. Canada 123 H4
Plettenberg Germany 53 H3
Plettenberg Bay S. Africa 100 F8
Pleven Bulg. 59 K3
Plevna Bulg. see Pleven
Pljevlja Montenegro 59 H3
Płock Poland 47 Q4
Pločno mt. Bos. & Herz. 58 G3
Plodovoye Russia 42 F3
Ploemeur France 56 C3
Ploeşti Romania see Ploieşti
Ploieşti Romania 59 L2
Plomb du Cantal mt. France 56 F4
Ploskoye Russia see Stanovoye
Płoty Poland 47 O4
Ploudalmézeau France 56 B2
Plouzané France 56 B2
Plovdiv Bulg. 59 K3
Plover Cove Reservoir H.K. China 77 [inset]
Plozk Poland see Płock
Plum U.S.A. 134 F3
Plumridge Lakes salt flat Australia 109 D7
Plungė Lith. 45 L9
Plutarco Elías Calles, Presa resr Mex. 127 F7
Pluto, Lac l. Canada 123 H3
Plyeshchanitsy Belarus 45 O9
Ply Huey Wati, Khao mt. Myanmar/Thai. 70 B3
Plymouth U.K. 49 C8
Plymouth CA U.S.A. 128 C2
Plymouth IN U.S.A. 134 B3
Plymouth MA U.S.A. 135 J3
Plymouth NC U.S.A. 132 E5
Plymouth NH U.S.A. 135 J2
Plymouth WI U.S.A. 134 B2
▶Plymouth (abandoned) Montserrat 137 L5
Capital of Montserrat, abandoned in 1997 owing to volcanic activity. Temporary capital established at Brades.
Plymouth Bay U.S.A. 135 J3
Plynlimon hill U.K. 49 D6
Plyussa Russia 45 P7
Plzeň Czechia 47 N6
Pô Burkina Faso 96 C3
Po r. Italy 58 E2
Pobeda Peak China/Kyrg. 80 F3
Pobedy, Pik mt. China/Kyrg. see Pobeda Peak
Pocahontas U.S.A. 131 F4
Pocatello U.S.A. 126 E4
Pochayiv Ukr. 43 E6
Pochep Russia 43 G5
Pochinki Russia 43 J5
Pochinok Russia 43 G5
Pochutla Mex. 136 E5
Pocking Germany 47 N6
Pocklington U.K. 48 G5
Poções Brazil 145 C1
Pocomoke City U.S.A. 135 H4
Pocomoke Sound b. U.S.A. 135 H5
Poconé Brazil 143 G7
Pocono Mountains hills U.S.A. 135 H3
Pocono Summit U.S.A. 135 H3
Poços de Caldas Brazil 145 B3
Podanur India 84 C4
Poddor'ye Russia 42 F4
Podgorenskiy Russia 43 H6
▶Podgorica Montenegro 59 H3
Capital of Montenegro.
Podgornoye Russia 64 J4
Podile India 84 C3
Podişul Transilvaniei plat. Romania see Transylvanian Basin
Podkamennaya Tunguska r. Russia 65 K3
Podocarpus, Parque Nacional nat. park Ecuador 142 C4
Podol'sk Russia 43 H5
Podporozh'ye Russia 42 G3
Podujevë Kosovo 59 I3
Podujevo Kosovo see Podujevë
Podz' Russia 42 K3
Poelela, Lagoa l. Moz. 101 L3
Poeppel Corner salt flat Australia 111 B5
Poetovio Slovenia see Ptuj
Pofadder S. Africa 100 D5
Pogar Russia 43 G5
Poggibonsi Italy 58 D3
Pogradec Albania 59 I4
Pogranichnyy Russia 74 C3
Po Hai g. China see Bo Hai
Pohang S. Korea 75 C5
Pohnpei atoll Micronesia 150 G5
Pohri India 82 D4
Poi India 83 H4
Poiana Mare Romania 59 J3
Poindo China 83 G3
Poinsett, Cape Antarctica 152 F2
Point Arena U.S.A. 128 B2
Point au Fer Island U.S.A. 131 F6
Pointe à la Hache U.S.A. 131 F6
Pointe-à-Pitre Guadeloupe 137 L5
Pointe-Noire Congo 99 B4
Point Hope U.S.A. 118 B3
Point Lake Canada 120 H1
Point of Rocks U.S.A. 126 F4
Point Pelee National Park Canada 134 D3
Point Pleasant NJ U.S.A. 135 H3
Point Pleasant WV U.S.A. 134 D4
Poitiers France 56 E3
Poitou reg. France 56 E3
Poix-de-Picardie France 52 B5
Pojuca r. Brazil 145 D1
Pokaran India 82 B4
Pokataroo Australia 112 D2
Pokcha Russia 41 R3
Pokhara Nepal 83 E3
Pokhran Landi Pak. 89 G5
Pokhvistnevo Russia 41 Q5
Poko Dem. Rep. Congo 98 C3
Pokosnoye Russia 72 I1
P'ok'r Kovkas mts Asia see Lesser Caucasus
Pokrovka Primorskiy Kray Russia 74 C4
Pokrovka Zabaykal'skiy Kray Russia 74 A1
Pokrovsk Respublika Sakha (Yakutiya) Russia 65 N3
Pokrovsk Saratovskaya Oblast' Russia see Engel's
Pokrovskoye Russia 43 H7
Pokshen'ga r. Russia 42 J3
Pol India 82 C5
Pola Croatia see Pula
Polacca Wash watercourse U.S.A. 129 H4
Pola de Siero Spain see La Pola Siero
Poland country Europe 40 J5
Poland NY U.S.A. 135 H2
Poland OH U.S.A. 134 E3
Polar Plateau Antarctica 152 A1
Polatlı Turkey 90 D3
Polatsk Belarus 45 P9
Polavaram India 84 D2
Polcirkeln Sweden 44 L3
Pol-e Fasā Iran 88 D4
Pol-e Khātūn Iran 89 F2
Pol-e Sefīd Iran 88 D2
Polessk Russia 45 L9
Poles'ye marsh Belarus/Ukr. see Pripet Marshes
Polgahawela Sri Lanka 84 D5
Poli Cyprus see Polis
Políaigos i. Greece see Polyaigos
Police Poland 47 O4
Policoro Italy 58 G4
Poligny France 56 G3
Políkastron Greece see Polykastro
Polillo Islands Phil. 69 G3
Poliny Osipenko, imeni Russia 74 E1
Polis Cyprus 85 A2
Polis'ke (abandoned) Ukr. 43 F6
Polis'kyy Zapovidnyk nature res. Ukr. 43 F6
Politovo Russia 42 K2
Políyiros Greece see Polygyros
Polkowice Poland 47 P5
Pollachi India 84 C4
Pollard Islands U.S.A. see Gardner Pinnacles
Polle Germany 53 J3
Pollino, Monte mt. Italy 58 G5
Pollino, Parco Nazionale del nat. park Italy 58 G5
Pollock Pines U.S.A. 128 C2
Pollock Reef Australia 109 C8
Polmak Norway 44 O1
Polnovat Russia 41 T3
Polo Fin. 44 P4
Poloat atoll Micronesia see Puluwat
Pologi Ukr. see Polohy
Polohy Ukr. 43 H7
Polokwane S. Africa 101 I2
Polokwane r. S. Africa 101 J2
Polonne Ukr. 43 E6
Polonnoye Ukr. see Polonne
Polotsk Belarus see Polatsk
Polperro U.K. 49 C8
Polska country Europe see Poland
Polson U.S.A. 126 E3
Polta r. Russia 42 I2
Poltava Ukr. 43 G6
Poltoratsk Turkm. see Aşgabat
Põltsamaa Estonia 45 N7
Polunochnoye Russia 41 S3
Põlva Estonia 45 O7
Polvadera U.S.A. 127 G6
Polvijärvi Fin. 44 P5
Polyaigos i. Greece 59 K6
Polyanovgrad Bulg. see Karnobat
Polyarnyy Russia 44 R2
Polyarnyy (abandoned) Russia 65 S3
Polyarnyye Zori Russia 44 R3
Polyarnyy Ural mts Russia 41 S2
Polygyros Greece 59 J4
Polykastro Greece 59 J4
Polynesia is Pacific Ocean 150 I6
Polynésie Française terr. S. Pacific Ocean see French Polynesia
Pom Indon. 69 J7
Pomarkku Fin. 45 M6
Pombal Pará Brazil 143 H4
Pombal Paraíba Brazil 143 K5
Pombal Port. 57 B4
Pomene Moz. 101 L2
Pomeranian Bay Poland 47 O3
Pomeroy S. Africa 101 J5
Pomeroy U.K. 51 F3
Pomeroy OH U.S.A. 134 D4
Pomeroy WA U.S.A. 126 D3
Pomezia Italy 58 E4
Pomfret S. Africa 100 F3
Pomona Namibia 100 B4
Pomona U.S.A. 128 E4
Pomorie Bulg. 59 L3
Pomorskie, Pojezierze reg. Poland 47 O4
Pomorskiy Bereg coastal area Russia 42 G2
Pomorskiy Proliv sea chan. Russia 42 K1
Pomos Point Cyprus 85 A2
Pomo Tso l. China see Puma Yumco
Pomou, Akra pt Cyprus see Pomos Point
Pomozdino Russia 42 L3
Pompain China 76 B2
Pompano Beach U.S.A. 133 D7
Pompei Italy 58 F4
Pompéia Brazil 145 A3
Pompey France 52 G6
Pompeyevka Russia 74 C2
Ponape atoll Micronesia see Pohnpei
Ponask Lake Canada 121 M4
Ponazyrevo Russia 42 J4
Ponca City U.S.A. 131 D4
Ponce Puerto Rico 137 K5
Ponce de Leon Bay U.S.A. 133 D7
Poncheville, Lac l. Canada 122 F4
Pondichéry India see Puducherry
Pond Inlet Canada 153 K2
Ponds Bay Canada see Pond Inlet
Ponente, Riviera di coastal area Italy 58 B3
Poneto U.S.A. 134 C3
Ponferrada Spain 57 C2
Pongara, Pointe pt Gabon 98 A3
Pongaroa N.Z. 113 F5
Pongo watercourse South Sudan 97 F4
Pongola r. S. Africa 101 K4
Pongolapoort Dam l. S. Africa 101 J4
Ponnagyun Myanmar 70 A2
Ponnaiyar r. India 84 C4
Ponnampet India 84 B3
Ponnani India 84 B4
Ponnyadaung Range mts Myanmar 70 A2
Pono Indon. 69 I8
Ponoka Canada 120 H4
Ponoy r. Russia 42 I2
Pons r. Canada 123 H2
▶Ponta Delgada Arquipélago dos Açores 148 G3
Capital of the Azores.
Ponta Grossa Brazil 145 A4
Pontal Brazil 145 A3
Pontalina Brazil 145 A2
Pont-à-Mousson France 52 G6
Ponta Porã Brazil 144 E2
Pontarfynach U.K. see Devil's Bridge
Pont-Audemer France 49 H9
Pontault-Combault France 52 C6
Pontax r. Canada 122 F4
Pontchartrain, Lake U.S.A. 131 F6
Pontcysyllte Aqueduct tourist site U.K. 49 D6
Pont d'Arc tourist site France 56 G4
Pont-de-Loup Belgium 52 E4
Ponte Alta do Tocantins Brazil 143 I6
Ponte de Sor Port. 57 B4
Ponte Firme Brazil 145 B2
Pontefract U.K. 48 F5
Ponteix Canada 121 J5
Ponteland U.K. 48 F3
Ponte Nova Brazil 145 C3
Pontes e Lacerda Brazil 143 G7
Pontevedra Spain 57 B2
Ponthierville Dem. Rep. Congo see Ubundu
Pontiac IL U.S.A. 130 F3
Pontiac MI U.S.A. 134 D2
Pontiae is Italy see Ponziane, Isole
Pontianak Indon. 68 D7
Pontine Islands is Italy see Ponziane, Isole
Pont-l'Abbé France 56 B3
Ponto de Santa Cruz Brazil 145 C1
Pontoise France 52 C5
Ponton watercourse Australia 109 C7
Ponton Canada 121 L4
Pontotoc U.S.A. 131 F5
Pont-Ste-Maxence France 52 C5
Pontypool U.K. 49 D7
Pontypridd U.K. 49 D7
Ponza, Isola di i. Italy 58 E4
Ponziane, Isole is Italy 58 E4
Poochera Australia 109 F8
Poole U.K. 49 F8
Poole U.S.A. 134 B5
Poolowanna Lake salt flat Australia 111 B5
Poona India see Pune
Pooncarie Australia 111 C7
Poonch India see Punch
Poopelloe Lake salt l. Australia 112 B3
Poopó, Lago de l. Bol. 142 E7
Poor Knights Islands N.Z. 113 E2
Popayán Col. 142 C3
Poperinge Belgium 52 C4
Popigay r. Russia 65 L2
Popiltah Australia 111 C7
Popilta Lake imp. l. Australia 111 C7
Poplar r. Canada 121 L4
Poplar U.S.A. 126 G2
Poplar Bluff U.S.A. 131 F4
Poplar Camp U.S.A. 134 E5
Poplarville U.S.A. 131 F6
▶Popocatépetl, Volcán vol. Mex. 136 E5
5th highest mountain in North America.
Popokabaka Dem. Rep. Congo 99 B4
Popondetta P.N.G. 69 L8
Popovichskaya Russia see Kalininskaya
Popovo Bulg. 59 L3
Popovo Polje plain Bos. & Herz. 58 G3
Poppberg hill Germany 53 L5
Poppenberg hill Germany 53 K3
Poprad Slovakia 47 R6
Poquoson U.S.A. 135 G5
Porali r. Pak. 89 G5
Porangahau N.Z. 113 F5
Porangatu Brazil 145 A1
Porbandar India 82 B5
Porcher Island Canada 120 D4
Porcos r. Brazil 145 B1
Porcupine, Cape Canada 123 K3
Porcupine Abyssal Plain sea feature N. Atlantic Ocean 148 G2
Porcupine Gorge National Park Australia 110 D4
Porcupine Hills Canada 121 K4
Porcupine Mountains U.S.A. 130 F2
Poreč Croatia 58 E2
Porecatu Brazil 145 A3
Poretskoye Russia 43 J5
Pori Fin. 45 L6
Porirua N.Z. 113 E5
Porkhov Russia 45 P8
Porlamar Venez. 142 F1
Pormpuraaw Australia 110 C2
Pornic France 56 C3
Poronaysk Russia 74 F2
Porong China 83 G3
Poros Greece 59 J6
Porosozero Russia 42 G3
Porpoise Bay Antarctica 152 G2
Porsangerfjorden sea chan. Norway 44 N1
Porsangerhalvøya pen. Norway 44 N1
Porsgrunn Norway 45 F7
Porsuk r. Turkey 59 N5
Portadown U.K. 51 F3
Portaferry U.K. 51 G3
Portage MI U.S.A. 134 C2
Portage PA U.S.A. 135 F3
Portage WI U.S.A. 130 F3
Portage Lakes U.S.A. 134 E3
Portage la Prairie Canada 121 L5
Portal U.S.A. 130 C1
Port Alberni Canada 120 E5
Port Albert Australia 112 C7
Portalegre Port. 57 C4
Portales U.S.A. 131 C5
Port-Alfred Canada see La Baie
Port Alfred S. Africa 101 H7
Port Alice Canada 120 E5
Port Allegany U.S.A. 135 F3
Port Allen U.S.A. 131 F6
Port Alma Australia 110 E4
Port Angeles U.S.A. 126 C2
Port Antonio Jamaica 137 I5
Portarlington Ireland 51 E4
Port Arthur Australia 111 [inset]
Port Arthur U.S.A. 131 E6
Port Askaig U.K. 50 C5
Port Augusta Australia 111 B7
▶Port-au-Prince Haiti 137 J5
Capital of Haiti.
Port Austin U.S.A. 134 D1
Port aux Choix Canada 123 K4
Portavogie U.K. 51 G3
Port Beaufort S. Africa 100 E8
Port Blair India 71 A5
Port Bolster Canada 134 F1
Portbou Spain 57 H2
Port Burwell Canada 134 E2
Port Campbell Australia 112 A7
Port Campbell National Park Australia 112 A7
Port Carling Canada 134 F1
Port-Cartier Canada 123 I4
Port Chalmers N.Z. 113 C7
Port Charlotte U.S.A. 133 D7
Port Clements Canada 120 C4
Port Clinton U.S.A. 134 D3
Port Credit Canada 134 F2
Port-de-Paix Haiti 137 J5
Port Dickson Malaysia 71 C7
Port Douglas Australia 110 D3
Port Edward Canada 120 D4
Port Edward S. Africa 101 J6
Porteira Brazil 143 G4
Porteirinha Brazil 145 C1
Portel Brazil 143 H4
Port Elgin Canada 134 E1
Port Elizabeth S. Africa 101 G7
Port Ellen U.K. 50 C5
Port Erin Isle of Man 48 C4
Porter Lake N.W.T. Canada 121 J2
Porter Lake Sask. Canada 121 J3
Porter Landing Canada 120 D3
Porterville S. Africa 100 D7
Porterville U.S.A. 128 D3
Port Étienne Mauritania see Nouâdhibou
Port Everglades U.S.A. see Fort Lauderdale
Port Fitzroy N.Z. 113 E3
Port Francqui Dem. Rep. Congo see Ilebo
Port-Gentil Gabon 98 A4
Port Glasgow U.K. 50 E5
Port Harcourt Nigeria 96 D4
Port Harrison Canada see Inukjuak
Porthcawl U.K. 49 D7
Port Hedland Australia 108 B5
Port Henry U.S.A. 135 I1
Port Herald Malawi see Nsanje
Porthleven U.K. 49 B8
Porthmadog U.K. 49 C6
Port Hope Canada 135 F2
Port Hope Simpson Canada 123 L3
Port Hueneme U.S.A. 128 D4
Port Huron U.S.A. 134 D2
Portimão Port. 57 B5
Port Jackson Australia see Sydney
Port Jackson inlet Australia 112 E4
Port Keats Australia see Wadeye
Port Klang Malaysia see Pelabuhan Klang
Port Láirge Ireland see Waterford
Portland N.S.W. Australia 112 D4
Portland Vic. Australia 111 C8
Portland IN U.S.A. 134 C3
Portland ME U.S.A. 135 J2
Portland MI U.S.A. 134 C2
Portland OR U.S.A. 126 C3
Portland TN U.S.A. 134 B5
Portland, Isle of pen. U.K. 49 E8
Portland Bill hd U.K. see Bill of Portland
Portland Creek Pond l. Canada 123 K4
Portland Roads Australia 110 C2
Port-la-Nouvelle France 56 F5
Portlaoise Ireland 51 E4
Port Lavaca U.S.A. 131 D6
Portlaw Ireland 51 E5
Portlethen U.K. 50 G3
Port Lincoln Australia 111 A7
Port Loko Sierra Leone 96 B4
▶Port Louis Mauritius 149 L7
Capital of Mauritius.
Port-Lyautrey Morocco see Kenitra
Port Macquarie Australia 112 F3
Portmadoc U.K. see Porthmadog
Port McNeill Canada 120 E5
Port-Menier Canada 123 I4
▶Port Moresby P.N.G. 69 L8
Capital of Papua New Guinea.
Portnaguran U.K. 50 C2
Portnahaven U.K. 50 C5
Port nan Giúran U.K. see Portnaguran
Port Neill Australia 111 B7
Portneuf r. Canada 123 H4
Port Nis U.K. see Port of Ness
Port Noarlunga Australia 111 B7
Port Nolloth S. Africa 100 C5
Port Norris U.S.A. 135 H4
Port-Nouveau-Québec Canada see Kangiqsualujjuaq
Porto Port. see Oporto
Porto Acre Brazil 142 E5
Porto Alegre Brazil 145 A5
Porto Alexandre Angola see Tombua
Porto Amboim Angola 99 B5
Porto Amélia Moz. see Pemba
Porto Artur Brazil 143 G6
Porto Belo Brazil 145 A4
Porto de Moz Brazil 143 H4
Porto dos Gaúchos Óbidos Brazil 143 G6
Porto Esperança Brazil 143 G7
Porto Esperidião Brazil 143 G7
Portoferraio Italy 58 D3
Port of Ness U.K. 50 C2
Porto Franco Brazil 143 I5
▶Port of Spain Trin. and Tob. 137 L6
Capital of Trinidad and Tobago.
Porto Grande Brazil 143 H3
Portogruaro Italy 58 E2
Porto Jofre Brazil 143 G7
Portola U.S.A. 128 C2
Portomaggiore Italy 58 D2
Porto Mendes Brazil 144 F2
Porto Murtinho Brazil 144 E2
Porto Nacional Brazil 143 I6
▶Porto-Novo Benin 96 D4
Capital of Benin.
Porto Novo Cape Verde 96 [inset]
Porto Primavera, Represa resr Brazil 144 F2
Port Orchard U.S.A. 126 C3
Port Orford U.S.A. 126 B4
Porto Rico Angola 99 B4
Porto Santo, Ilha de i. Madeira 96 B1
Porto Seguro Brazil 145 D2
Porto Tolle Italy 58 E2
Porto Torres Sardinia Italy 58 C4
Porto União Brazil 145 A4
Porto-Vecchio Corsica France 56 I6
Porto Velho Brazil 142 F5
Portoviejo Ecuador 142 B4
Porto Walter Brazil 142 D5
Portpatrick U.K. 50 D6
Port Perry Canada 135 F1
Port Phillip Bay Australia 112 B7
Port Pirie Australia 111 B7
Port Radium Canada see Echo Bay
Portreath U.K. 49 B8
Portree U.K. 50 C3
Port Rexton Canada 123 L4
Port Royal U.S.A. 135 G4
Port Royal Sound inlet U.S.A. 133 D5
Portrush U.K. 51 F2
Port Safaga Egypt see Būr Safājah
Port Said Egypt 85 A4
Port St Joe U.S.A. 133 C6
Port St Mary Isle of Man 48 C4
Portsalon Ireland 51 E2
Port Sanilac U.S.A. 134 D2
Port Severn Canada 134 F1
Port Shepstone S. Africa 101 J6
Port Simpson Canada see Lax Kw'alaams
Portsmouth U.K. 49 F8
Portsmouth NH U.S.A. 135 J2
Portsmouth OH U.S.A. 134 D4
Portsmouth VA U.S.A. 135 G5
Portsoy U.K. 50 G3
Port Stanley Falkland Is see Stanley
Port Stephens b. Australia 112 F4
Portstewart U.K. 51 F2
Port St Lucie U.S.A. 133 D7
Port Sudan Sudan 86 E6
Port Swettenham Malaysia see Pelabuhan Klang
Port Talbot U.K. 49 D7
Porttipahdan tekojärvi l. Fin. 44 O2
Port Townsend U.S.A. 126 C2
Portugal country Europe 57 C4
Portugália Angola see Chitato
Portuguese East Africa country Africa see Mozambique
Portuguese Guinea country Africa see Guinea-Bissau
Portuguese Timor country Asia see East Timor
Portuguese West Africa country Africa see Angola
Portumna Ireland 51 D4
Portus Herculis Monoeci country Europe see Monaco
Port-Vendres France 56 F5
▶Port Vila Vanuatu 107 G3
Capital of Vanuatu.
Portville U.S.A. 135 F2
Port-Vladimir Russia 44 R2
Port Waikato N.Z. 113 E3
Port Washington U.S.A. 134 B2
Port William U.K. 50 E6
Porvenir Bol. 142 E6
Porvenir Chile 144 B8
Porvoo Fin. 45 N6
Posada Spain 57 D2
Posada de Llanera Spain see Posada
Posadas Arg. 144 E3
Posen Poland see Poznań
Posen U.S.A. 134 D1
Poseyville U.S.A. 134 B4
Poshekhon'ye Russia 42 H4
Poshekon'ye-Volodarsk Russia see Poshekhon'ye
Poshteh-ye Chaqvīr hill Iran 88 E4
Posht-e Kūh mts Iran 88 B3
Posht-e Rud va Zamīndāvar reg. Afgh. see Zamīndāwar
Posht Kūh hill Iran 88 C2
Posio Fin. 44 P3
Poso Indon. 69 G7
Posof Turkey 91 F2
Possession Island Namibia 100 B4
Pößneck Germany 53 L4
Post U.S.A. 131 C5
Postavy Belarus see Pastavy
Poste-de-la-Baleine Canada see Kuujjuarapik
Poste Weygand Alg. 96 D2
Postmasburg S. Africa 100 F5
Poston U.S.A. 129 F4
Postville Canada 123 K3
Postville U.S.A. 122 C6
Postysheve Ukr. see Krasnoarmiys'k
Pota Indon. 108 C2
Pótam Mex. 127 F8
Poté Brazil 145 C2
Poteau U.S.A. 131 E5
Potegaon India 84 D2
Potentia Italy see Potenza
Potenza Italy 58 F4
Poth U.S.A. 131 D6
Poti Georgia 91 F2
Potikal India 84 D2
Potiraguá Brazil 145 D1
Potiskum Nigeria 96 E3
Potlatch U.S.A. 126 D3
Pot Mountain U.S.A. 126 E3
Po Toi i. H.K. China 77 [inset]
Potomac r. U.S.A. 135 G4
Potosí Bol. 142 E7
Potosi U.S.A. 130 F4
Potosi Mountain U.S.A. 129 F4
Potrerillos Chile 144 C3
Potrero del Llano Mex. 131 B6
Potsdam Germany 53 N2
Potsdam U.S.A. 135 H1
Potter U.S.A. 130 C3
Potterne U.K. 49 E7
Potters Bar U.K. 49 G7
Potter Valley U.S.A. 128 B2
Pottstown U.S.A. 135 H3
Pottsville U.S.A. 135 G3
Pottuvil Sri Lanka 84 D5
Potwar reg. Pak. 89 I3
Pouch Cove Canada 123 L5
Poughkeepsie U.S.A. 135 I3
Poulin de Courval, Lac l. Canada 123 H4
Poulton-le-Fylde U.K. 48 E5
Pouso Alegre Brazil 145 B3
Poŭthĭsăt Cambodia 71 C4
Poŭthĭsăt, Stœng r. Cambodia 71 D4
Považská Bystrica Slovakia 47 Q6
Povenets Russia 42 G3
Poverty Bay N.Z. 113 F4
Poverty Point tourist site U.S.A. 131 F5
Povlen mt. Serbia 59 H2
Póvoa de Varzim Port. 57 B3
Povorino Russia 43 I6
Povorotnyy, Mys hd Russia 74 D4
Poway U.S.A. 128 E5
Powder r. U.S.A. 126 G3
Powder, South Fork r. U.S.A. 126 G4

Qazaqstan country Asia see Kazakhstan
Qazax Azer. 86 G1
Qazi Ahmad Pak. 89 H5
Qāzī Deh Afgh. 89 H2
Qazvīn Iran 88 C2
Qeisûm, Gezâ'ir is Egypt see Qaysūm, Juzur
Qeisum Islands Egypt see Qaysūm, Juzur
Qeładize Iraq 91 G3
Qena Egypt see Qinā
Qeqertarsuaq Greenland 119 M3
Qeqertarsuaq i. Greenland 119 M3
Qeqertarsuatsiaat Greenland 119 M3
Qeqertarsuup Tunua b. Greenland 119 M3
Qeshm Iran 88 E5
Qeydār Iran 88 C2
Qeydū Iran 88 C3
Qeyşar, Chāh-e well Iran 88 D4
Qeyşār, Kūh-e mt. Afgh. 89 G3
Qezel Owzan, Rūdkhāneh-ye r. Iran 88 C2
Qeẓi'ot Israel 85 B4
Qian'an China 74 B3
Qiandao Hu resr China 77 H2
Qian Gorlos China 74 B3
Qianjiang Chongqing China 77 F2
Qianjiang Hubei China 77 G2
Qianjin Heilong. China 74 D3
Qianjin Jilin China 74 C3
Qianqihao China 74 A3
Qian Shan mts China 74 A4
Qianshangjie China 73 L5
Qianxi China 76 E3
Qiaocheng China see Bozhou
Qiaojia China 76 D3
Qiaoshan China see Huangling
Qiaowa China see Muli
Qiaowan China 80 I3
Qiaozhuang China see Qingchuan
Qibā' Saudi Arabia 91 G6
Qibing S. Africa 101 H5
Qichun China 77 G2
Qidong China 77 G3
Qidukou China 76 B1
Qiemo China 80 G4
Qijiang China 76 E2
Qijiaojing China 80 H3
Qikiqtarjuaq Canada 119 L3
Qila Ladgasht Pak. 89 F5
Qila Saifullah Pak. 89 H4
Qilian China 80 J4
Qilian Shan mts China 80 I4
Qillak i. Greenland 119 O3
Qiman Tag mts China 83 G1
Qimusseriarsuaq b. Greenland 119 L2
Qinā Egypt 86 D4
Qin'an China 76 E1
Qincheng China see Nanfeng
Qing'an China 74 B3
Qingchuan China 76 E1
Qingdao China 73 M5
Qinggang China 74 B3
Qinggil China see Qinghe
Qinghai prov. China 76 B1
Qinghai Hu salt l. China 80 J4
Qinghai Nanshan mts China 80 I4
Qinghe Heilong. China 74 C3
Qinghe Xinjiang China 80 H2
Qinghecheng China 74 B4
Qinghua China see Bo'ai
Qingjiang Jiangsu China see Huai'an
Qingjiang Jiangxi China see Zhangshu
Qing Jiang r. China 77 F2
Qingkou China see Ganyu
Qinglan China 77 F5
Qingliu China 77 H3
Qinglung China 83 G3
Qingpu China 77 I2
Qingquan China see Xishui
Qingshan China see Wudalianchi
Qingshui China 76 E1
Qingshuihe Nei Mongol China 73 K5
Qingshuihe Qinghai China 76 C1
Qingtian China 77 I2
Qingyang Anhui China 77 H2
Qingyang Gansu China 76 E1
Qingyang Jiangsu China see Sihong
Qingyuan Gansu China see Weiyuan
Qingyuan Guangdong China 77 G4
Qingyuan Guangxi China see Yizhou
Qingyuan Liaoning China 74 B4
Qingyuan Zhejiang China 77 H3
Qingzang Gaoyuan plat. China see Tibet, Plateau of
Qingzhen China 76 E3
Qinhuangdao China 73 L5
Qinjiang China see Shicheng
Qin Ling mts China 76 E1
Qinshui China 77 G1
Qinting China see Lianhua
Qinzhou China 77 F4
Qionghai China 77 F5
Qiongjiexue China see Qonggyai
Qionglai China 76 D2
Qionglai Shan mts China 76 D2
Qiongxi China see Hongyuan
Qiongzhong China 77 F5
Qiongzhou Haixia strait China see Hainan Strait
Qiqian China 74 A1
Qiqihar China 74 A3
Qīr Iran 88 D4
Qira China 82 E1
Qîraîya, Wâdi watercourse Egypt see Qurayyah, Wādī
Qiryat Shemona Israel 85 B3
Qishan China 76 E1
Qishon, Naḥal r. Israel 85 B3
Qitab ash Shāmah vol. crater Saudi Arabia 85 C4
Qitaihe China 74 C3
Qiubei China 76 E3
Qiujin China 77 G2
Qixing He r. China 74 D3
Qiyang China 77 F3
Qizhou Liedao i. China 77 F5
Qızılağac Körfəzi b. Azer. 88 C2
Qizil-Art, Aghbai pass Kyrg./Tajik. see Kyzylart Pass
Qizil Qal'ah Afgh. 89 H2
Qizilqum des. Kazakh./Uzbek. see Kyzylkum Desert
Qizilrabot Tajik. 89 I2
Qobād, Chāh-e well Iran 88 D3
Qobustan Azer. 91 H2
Qogir Feng mt. China/Pak. see K2
Qog Qi China see Sain Us
Qom Iran 88 C3
Qomdo China see Qumdo
Qomīsheh Iran see Shahreẓā
Qomolangma Feng mt. China/Nepal see Everest, Mount
Qomsheh Iran see Shahreẓā
Qonāq, Kūh-e hill Iran 88 C3
Qondūz Afgh. see Kunduz
Qonggyai China 83 G3
Qo'ng'irot Uzbek. 80 A3
Qong Muztag mt. China 83 E2
Qongrat Uzbek. see Qo'ng'irot
Qoornoq Greenland 119 M3
Qoqek China see Tacheng
Qo'qon Uzbek. 80 D3
Qorako'l Uzbek. 89 F2
Qorghalzhyn Kazakh. see Korgalzhyn
Qornet es Saouda mt. Lebanon 85 C2
Qorovulbozor Uzbek. 89 G2
Qorowulbozor Uzbek. see Qorovulbozor
Qorveh Iran 88 B3
Qo'shrabot Uzbek. 89 G1
Qostanay Kazakh. see Kostanay
Qoubaiyat Lebanon 85 C2
Qowowuyag mt. China/Nepal see Cho Oyu
Qozide Tajik. 89 H2
Quabbin Reservoir U.S.A. 135 I2
Quadra Island Canada 120 E5
Quadros, Lago dos l. Brazil 145 A5
Quail Mountains U.S.A. 128 E4
Quairading Australia 109 B8
Quakenbrück Germany 53 H2
Quakertown U.S.A. 135 H3
Quambatook Australia 112 A5
Quambone Australia 112 C3
Quamby Australia 110 C4
Quanah U.S.A. 131 D5
Quanbao Shan mt. China 77 F1
Quan Dao Hoang Sa is S. China Sea see Paracel Islands
Quan Dao Truong Sa is S. China Sea see Spratly Islands
Quang Ha Vietnam 70 D2
Quang Ngai Vietnam 70 E4
Quang Tri Vietnam 70 D3
Quan Hoa Vietnam 70 D2
Quan Long Vietnam see Ca Mau
Quannan China 77 G3
Quantock Hills U.K. 49 D7
Quanzhou Fujian China 77 H3
Quanzhou Guangxi China 77 F3
Qu'Appelle r. Canada 121 K5
Quaqtaq Canada 119 L3
Quarry Bay H.K. China 77 [inset]
Quartu Sant'Elena Sardinia Italy 58 C5
Quartzite Mountain U.S.A. 128 E3
Quartzsite U.S.A. 129 F5
Quba Azer. 91 H2
Qūchān Iran 88 E2
Qudaym Syria 85 D2
Queanbeyan Australia 112 D5
▶Québec Canada 123 H5
Capital of Québec.
Québec prov. Canada 135 I1
Quebra Anzol r. Brazil 145 B2
Quedlinburg Germany 53 L3
Queen Adelaide Islands Chile see La Reina Adelaida, Archipiélago de
Queen Anne U.S.A. 135 H4
Queen Bess, Mount Canada 126 B2
Queen Charlotte Canada 120 C4
Queen Charlotte Islands Canada see Haida Gwaii
Queen Charlotte Sound sea chan. Canada 120 D5
Queen Charlotte Strait Canada 120 E5
Queen Creek U.S.A. 129 H5
Queen Elizabeth Islands Canada 119 H2
Queen Elizabeth Land reg. Antarctica 152 L1
Queen Elizabeth National Park Uganda 98 C4
Queen Mary Land reg. Antarctica 152 F2
Queen Maud Gulf Canada 119 H3
Queen Maud Land reg. Antarctica 152 C2
Queen Maud Mountains Antarctica 152 J1
Queenscliff Australia 112 B7
Queensland state Australia 112 B1
Queenstown Australia 111 [inset]
Queenstown Ireland see Cobh
Queenstown N.Z. 113 B7
Queenstown S. Africa 101 H6
Queenstown Sing. 71 [inset]
Que'er Shan mts China 76 C1
Queets U.S.A. 126 B3
Queimada, Ilha i. Brazil 143 H4
Quelimane Moz. 99 D5
Quellón Chile 144 B6
Quelpart Island S. Korea see Cheju-do
Quemado U.S.A. 129 I4
Quemoy i. Taiwan see Jinmen Dao
Que Que Zimbabwe see Kwekwe
Querétaro Mex. 136 D4
Querétaro de Arteaga Mex. see Querétaro
Querfurt Germany 53 L3
Querobabi Mex. 127 F7
Quesnel Canada 120 F4
Quesnel Lake Canada 120 F4
Quetta Pak. 89 G4
Quetzaltenango Guat. 136 F6
Queuco Chile 144 B5
Quezaltenango Guat. see Quetzaltenango
▶Quezon City Phil. 69 G4
Former capital of the Philippines.
Qufu China 77 H1
Quibala Angola 99 B5
Quibaxe Angola 99 B4
Quibdó Col. 142 C2
Quiberon France 56 C3
Quiçama, Parque Nacional do nat. park Angola 99 B4
Quiet Lake Canada 120 C2
Quilengues Angola 99 B5
Quillabamba Peru 142 D6
Quillacollo Bol. 142 E7
Quillan France 56 F5
Quill Lakes Canada 121 J5
Quilmes Arg. 144 E4
Quilon India see Kollam
Quilpie Australia 112 B1
Quilpué Chile 144 B4
Quimbele Angola 99 B4
Quimilí Arg. 144 D3
Quimper France 56 B3
Quimperlé France 56 C3
Quinag hill U.K. 50 D2
Quincy CA U.S.A. 128 C2
Quincy FL U.S.A. 133 C6
Quincy IL U.S.A. 130 F4
Quincy IN U.S.A. 134 B4
Quincy MA U.S.A. 135 J2
Quincy MI U.S.A. 134 C3
Quincy OH U.S.A. 134 D3
Quines Arg. 144 C4
Quinga Moz. 99 E5
Quinn Canyon Range mts U.S.A. 129 F3
Quinto Spain 57 F3
Quionga Moz. 99 E5
Quipungo Angola 99 B5
Quirima Angola 99 B5
Quirimbas, Parque Nacional das nat. park Moz. 99 E5
Quirindi Australia 112 E3
Quirinópolis Brazil 145 A2
Quissanga Moz. 99 E5
Quitapa Angola 99 B5
Quitilipi Arg. 144 D3
Quitman GA U.S.A. 133 D6
Quitman MS U.S.A. 131 F5
▶Quito Ecuador 142 C4
Capital of Ecuador.
Quitovac Mex. 127 E7
Quixadá Brazil 143 K4
Quixeramobim Brazil 143 K5
Qujiang Guangdong China 77 G3
Qujiang Sichuan China see Quxian
Qujie China 77 F4
Qujing China 76 D3
Qulandy Kazakh. see Kulandy
Qulansiyah Yemen 87 H7
Qulbān Layyah well Iraq 88 B4
Qulsary Kazakh. see Kul'sary
Qulyndy Zhazyghy plain Kazakh./Russia see Kulundinskaya Ravnina
Qulzum, Baḥr al Egypt see Suez Bay
Qumar He r. China 72 G6
Qumarheyan China 80 H4
Qumarlêb China see Sêrwolungwa
Qumarrabdün China 76 B1
Qumbu S. Africa 101 I6
Qumdo China 76 B2
Qumqo'rgo'n Uzbek. 89 G2
Qumqūrghon Uzbek. see Qumqo'rgo'n
Qumrha S. Africa 101 H7
Qumulangma mt. China/Nepal see Everest, Mount
Qunayfidhah, Nafūd des. Saudi Arabia 88 B5
Qunayy well Saudi Arabia 88 B6
Qundūz Afgh. see Kunduz
Qŭnghirot Uzbek. see Qo'ng'irot
Quntamari China 83 G2
Qu'nyido China 76 C2
Quoich r. Canada 121 M1
Quoich, Loch l. U.K. 50 D3
Quoile r. U.K. 51 G3
Quoin Point S. Africa 100 D8
Quoxo r. Botswana 100 G2
Qŭqon Uzbek. see Qo'qon
Qurama, Qatorkŭhi mts Asia see Kurama Range
Qurama tizmasi mts Asia see Kurama Range
Qurayyah, Wādī watercourse Egypt 85 B4
Qŭrghonteppa Tajik. 89 H2
Qusainka China 76 C2
Qusar Azer. 91 H2
Qushan China 76 E2
Qŭshrabot Uzbek. see Qo'shrabot
Qushtepe Iraq 91 F3
Qusmuryn Kazakh. see Kusmuryn
Qusum China 82 D2
Quthing Lesotho see Moyeni
Quttinirpaaq National Park Canada 119 K1
Quwayq, Nahr r. Syria/Turkey 85 C2
Quxar China see Lhazê
Quxian Sichuan China 76 E2
Quxian Zhejiang China see Quzhou
Quyang China see Jingzhou
Quy Châu Vietnam 70 D3
Quyghan Kazakh. see Kuygan
Quy Nhơn Vietnam 71 E4
Quyon Canada 135 G1
Qūyūn Eshek i. Iran 88 B2
Quzhou China 77 H2
Qypshaq Kōli salt l. Kazakh. see Azhibeksor, Ozero
Qyrghyz Zhotasy mts Kazakh./Kyrg. see Kirghiz Range
Qyteti Stalin Albania see Kuçovë
Qyzylorda Kazakh. see Kyzylorda
Qyzylqum des. Kazakh./Uzbek. see Kyzylkum Desert
Qyzyltū Kazakh. see Kishkenekol'
Qyzylzhar Kazakh. see Kyzylzhar

R

Raa Atoll Maldives see Maalhosmadulu Uthuruburi
Raab r. Austria 47 P7
Raab Hungary see Győr
Raahe Fin. 44 N4
Rääkkylä Fin. 44 P5
Raalte Neth. 52 G2
Raanujärvi Fin. 44 N3
Raasay i. U.K. 50 C3
Raasay, Sound of sea chan. U.K. 50 C3
Raba Indon. 108 B2
Rabang China 82 E2
Rabat Gozo Malta see Victoria
Rabat Malta 58 F7
▶Rabat Morocco 54 C5
Capital of Morocco.
Rabāṭak Afgh. 89 H2
Rabāṭ-e Jaldak Afgh. 89 G4
Rabaul P.N.G. 106 F2
Rabbath Ammon Jordan see 'Ammān
Rabbit r. Canada 120 E3
Rabbit Flat Australia 108 E5
Rabbitskin r. Canada 120 F2
Rābigh Saudi Arabia 86 E5
Rabnabad Islands Bangl. 83 G5
Râbniţa Moldova see Rîbniţa
Rabocheostrovsk Russia 42 G2
Racaka China 76 C2
Raccoon Cay i. Bahamas 133 F8
Race, Cape Canada 123 L5
Race Point U.S.A. 135 J2
Rachaïya Lebanon 85 B3
Rachal U.S.A. 131 D7
Rachaya Lebanon see Rachaïya
Rachel U.S.A. 129 F3
Rach Gia Vietnam 71 D5
Rach Gia, Vinh b. Vietnam 71 D5
Racibórz Poland 47 Q5
Racine WI U.S.A. 134 B2
Racine WV U.S.A. 134 E4
Rădăuţi Romania 43 E7
Radcliff U.S.A. 134 C5
Radde Russia 74 C2
Radford U.S.A. 134 E5
Radisson Que. Canada 122 F3
Radisson Sask. Canada 121 J4
Radlinski, Mount Antarctica 152 K1
Radnevo Bulg. 59 K3
Radom Poland 47 R5
Radom Sudan 97 F4
Radomir Bulg. 59 J3
Radom National Park Sudan 97 F4
Radomsko Poland 47 Q5
Radoviš Macedonia 90 A2
Radstock U.K. 49 E7
Radstock, Cape Australia 109 F8
Radun' Belarus 45 N9
Radviliškis Lith. 45 M9
Radyvyliv Ukr. 43 E6
Rae Bareli India 82 E4
Rae-Edzo Canada see Behchokò
Raeside, Lake salt flat Australia 109 C7
Raetihi N.Z. 113 E4
Rāf hill Saudi Arabia 91 E5
Rafaela Arg. 144 D4
Rafaḥ Gaza 85 B4
Rafaï Cent. Afr. Rep. 98 C3
Rafḥā' Saudi Arabia 91 F5
Rafiah Gaza see Rafaḥ
Rafsanjān Iran 88 D4
Raft r. U.S.A. 126 E4
Raga South Sudan 97 F4
Rägelin Germany 53 M1
Ragged, Mount hill Australia 109 C8
Ragged Island Bahamas 133 F8
Rāgh Afgh. 89 H2
Rago Nasjonalpark nat. park Norway 44 J3
Ragösen Germany 53 M2
Ragueneau Canada 123 H4
Raguhn Germany 53 M3
Ragusa Croatia see Dubrovnik
Ragusa Sicily Italy 58 F6
Ra'gya China 76 D1
Raha Indon. 69 G7
Rahachow Belarus 43 F5
Rahad r. Sudan 86 D7
Rahaeng Thai. see Tak
Raḥbah, Manqa' imp. l. Syria 85 C3
Rahden Germany 53 I2
Rahimyar Khan Pak. 89 H4
Raḥmān, Chāh-e well Iran 89 E4
Rahovec Kosovo 59 I3
Rahuri India 84 B2
Rai, Hon i. Vietnam 71 D5
Raiatea i. Fr. Polynesia 151 J7
Raibu i. Indon. see Air
Raichur India 84 C2
Raiganj India 83 G4
Raigarh Chhattisgarh India 83 E5
Raigarh Odisha India 84 D2
Raijua i. Indon. 108 C2
Railroad Pass U.S.A. 128 E2
Railroad Valley U.S.A. 129 F2
Raimangal r. Bangl. 83 G5
Raimbault, Lac l. Canada 123 H3
Rainbow Lake Canada 120 G3
Raine Island Australia 110 D1
Rainelle U.S.A. 134 E5
Raini r. Pak. 89 H4
Rainier, Mount vol. U.S.A. 126 C3
Rainy r. Canada/U.S.A. 121 M5
Rainy Lake Canada/U.S.A. 125 I2
Rainy River Canada 121 M5
Raipur Chhattisgarh India 83 E5
Raipur W. Bengal India 83 F5
Raisen India 82 D5
Raisio Fin. 45 M6
Raismes France 52 D4
Raitalai India 82 D5
Raivavae i. Fr. Polynesia 151 K7
Raiwind Pak. 89 I4
Raja, Ujung pt Indon. 71 B7
Rajaampat, Kepulauan is Indon. 69 H7
Rajahmundry India 84 D2
Raja-Jooseppi Fin. 44 P2
Rajanpur Pak. 89 H4
Rajapalayam India 84 C4
Rajapur India 84 B2
Rajasthan state India 82 C4
Rajasthan Canal India 82 C3
Rajauri India see Rajouri
Rajbiraj Nepal 83 F4
Rajevadi India 84 B2
Rajgarh India 82 D4
Rājijovsset Fin. see Raja-Jooseppi
Rajkot India 82 B5
Raj Mahal India 82 C4
Rajmahal Hills India 83 F4
Rajnandgaon India 82 E5
Rajouri India 82 C2
Rajpipla India 82 C5
Rajpur India 82 C5
Rajpura India 82 D3
Rajputana Agency state India see Rajasthan
Rajsamand India 82 C4
Rajshahi Bangl. 83 G4
Rājū Syria 85 C1
Rajula India 84 A1
Rajur India 84 C1
Rajura India 84 C2
Raka China 83 F3
Rakan, Ra's pt Qatar 88 C5
Rakaposhi mt. Pak. 82 C1
Raka Zangbo r. China see Dogxung Zangbo
Rakhiv Ukr. 43 E6
Rakhni Pak. 89 H4
Rakhni r. Pak. 89 H4
Rakhshan r. Pak. 89 F5
Rakitnoye Belgorodskaya Oblast' Russia 43 G6
Rakitnoye Primorskiy Kray Russia 74 D3
Rakiura i. N.Z. see Stewart Island
Rakiura National Park nat. park N.Z. 113 A8
Rakke Estonia 45 O7
Rakkestad Norway 45 G7
Rakovski Bulg. 59 K3
Rakushechnyy, Mys pt Kazakh. 91 H2
Rakvere Estonia 45 O7
▶Raleigh U.S.A. 132 E5
Capital of North Carolina.
Ralston U.S.A. 135 G3
Ram r. Canada 120 F2
Ramagiri India 84 E2
Ramah U.S.A. 129 I4
Ramalho, Serra do hills Brazil 145 B1
Rāmallāh West Bank 85 B4
Ramanagaram India 84 C3
Ramanathapuram India 84 C4
Ramapo Deep sea feature N. Pacific Ocean 150 F3
Ramapur India 84 D1
Ramas, Cape India 84 B3
Ramatlabama S. Africa 101 G3
Rambhapur India 82 C5
Rambouillet France 52 B6
Rambutyo Island P.N.G. 69 L7
Ramciel South Sudan 97 G4
Rame Head hd Australia 112 D6
Rame Head hd U.K. 49 C8
Rameshki Russia 42 H4
Ramezān Kalak Iran 89 F5
Ramgarh Jharkhand India 83 F5
Ramgarh Rajasthan India 82 B4
Ramgarh Rajasthan India 82 C3
Ramgul reg. Afgh. 89 H3
Rāmhormoz Iran 88 C4
Ramingining Australia 108 F3
Ramitan Uzbek. see Romiton
Ramla Israel 85 B4
Ramlat Rabyānah des. Libya see Rebiana Sand Sea
Ramm, Jabal mts Jordan 85 B5
Ramnad India see Ramanathapuram
Râmnicu Sărat Romania 59 L2
Râmnicu Vâlcea Romania 59 K2
Ramon' Russia 43 H6
Ramona U.S.A. 128 E5
Ramos r. Mex. 131 B7
Ramotswa Botswana 101 G3
Rampur India 82 D3
Rampur Boalia Bangl. see Rajshahi
Ramree Myanmar 70 A3
Ramree Island Myanmar 70 A3
Rāmsar Iran 88 C2
Ramsele Sweden 44 J5
Ramsey Isle of Man 48 C4
Ramsey U.K. 49 G6
Ramsey U.S.A. 135 H3
Ramsey Bay Isle of Man 48 C4
Ramsey Island U.K. 49 B7
Ramsey Lake Canada 122 E5
Ramsgate U.K. 49 I7
Rāmshīr Iran 88 C4
Ramu Bangl. 83 H5
Ramusio, Lac l. Canada 123 J3
Ramygala Lith. 45 N9
Ranaghat India 83 G5
Rana Pratap Sagar resr India 82 C4
Ranapur India 82 C5
Ranasar India 82 B4
Rancagua Chile 144 B4
Rancharia Brazil 145 A3
Rancheria Canada 120 D2
Rancheria r. Canada 120 D2
Ranchi India 83 F5
Ranco, Lago l. Chile 144 B6
Rand Australia 112 C5
Randalstown U.K. 51 F3
Randers Denmark 45 G8
Randijaure l. Sweden 44 K3
Randolph ME U.S.A. 135 K1
Randolph UT U.S.A. 126 F4
Randolph VT U.S.A. 135 I2
Randsjö Sweden 44 H5
Råneå Sweden 44 M4
Ranérou Senegal 96 B3
Ranfurly N.Z. 113 C7
Rangae Thai. 71 C6
Rangamati Bangl. 83 H5
Rangapara India 83 H4
Rangeley Lake U.S.A. 135 J1
Rangely U.S.A. 129 I1
Ranger Lake Canada 122 E5
Rangiora N.Z. 113 D6
Rangitata r. N.Z. 113 C7
Rangitikei r. N.Z. 113 E5
Rangke China see Zamtang
Rangkŭl Tajik. 89 I2
Rangôn Myanmar see Rangoon
▶Rangoon Myanmar 70 B3
Former capital of Myanmar.
Rangoon r. Myanmar 70 B3
Rangpur Bangl. 83 G4
Rangsang i. Indon. 71 C7
Rangse Myanmar 70 A1
Ranibennur India 84 B3
Raniganj India 83 F5
Ranipur Pak. 89 H5
Raniwara India 82 C4
Rānīyah/Ranye Iraq 91 G3
Rankin U.S.A. 131 C6
Rankin Inlet Canada 121 M2
Rankins Springs Australia 112 C4
Ranna Estonia 45 O7
Rannes Australia 110 E5
Rannoch, Loch U.K. 50 E4
Ranong Thai. 71 B5
Ranot Thai. 71 C6
Ranpur India 82 B5
Rānsa Iran 88 C3
Ransby Sweden 45 H6
Rantasalmi Fin. 44 P5
Rantau i. Indon. 71 C7
Rantauprapat Indon. 71 B7
Rantoul U.S.A. 134 A3
Rantsila Fin. 44 N4
Ranua Fin. 44 O4
Ranyah, Wādī watercourse Saudi Arabia 86 F5
Rao Go mt. Laos/Vietnam 70 D3
Raohe China 74 D3
Raoui, Erg er des. Alg. 54 D6
Raoul Island Kermadec Is 107 I4
Rapa i. Fr. Polynesia 151 K7
Rapa-iti i. Fr. Polynesia see Rapa
Rapallo Italy 58 C2
Rapar India 82 B5
Raphoe Ireland 51 E3
Rapidan r. U.S.A. 135 G4
Rapid City U.S.A. 130 C2
Rapid River U.S.A. 132 C2
Rapla Estonia 45 N7
Rapur Andhra Prad. India 84 C3
Rapur Gujarat India 82 B5
Raqqa Syria see Ar Raqqah
Raquette Lake U.S.A. 135 H2
Rara National Park Nepal 83 E3
Raritan Bay U.S.A. 135 H3
Rarkan Pak. 89 H4
Raroia atoll Fr. Polynesia 151 K7
Rarotonga i. Cook Is 151 J7
Ras India 82 C4
Rasa, Punta pt Arg. 144 D6
Ra's al Ḥikmah Egypt 90 B5
Ras al Khaimah U.A.E. see Ra's al Khaymah
Ra's al Khaymah U.A.E. 88 D5
Ra's an Naqb Jordan 85 B4
Ras Dashen mt. Eth. see Ras Dejen
▶Ras Dejen mt. Eth. 98 D2
5th highest mountain in Africa.
Raseiniai Lith. 45 M9
Râs el Hikma Egypt see Ra's al Ḥikmah
Ra's Ghārib Egypt 90 D5
Rashad Sudan 86 D7
Rashîd Egypt see Rashīd
Rashīd Egypt 90 C5
Rasht Iran 88 C2
Ras Koh mt. Pak. 89 G4
Raskoh mts Pak. 89 G4
Raso, Cabo c. Arg. 144 C6
Rason Lake salt flat Australia 109 D7
Rasony Belarus 45 P9
Rasra India 83 E4
Rasshua, Ostrov i. Russia 73 S3
Rass Jebel Tunisia 58 D6
Rasskazovo Russia 43 I5
Rastatt Germany 53 I6
Rastede Germany 53 I1
Rastow Germany 53 L1
Rasūl watercourse Iran 88 D5
Rasul Pak. 89 I3
Ratae U.K. see Leicester
Rätan Sweden 44 I5
Ratanda S. Africa 101 I4
Ratangarh India 82 C3
Rätansbyn Sweden 44 I5
Rat Buri Thai. 71 B4
Rathangan Ireland 51 F4
Rathbun Lake U.S.A. 130 E3
Rathdowney Ireland 51 E5
Rathdrum Ireland 51 F5
Rathedaung Myanmar 70 A2
Rathenow Germany 53 M2
Rathfriland U.K. 51 F3
Rathkeale Ireland 51 D5
Rathlin Island U.K. 51 F2
Ratibor Poland see Racibórz
Ratingen Germany 52 G3
Ratisbon Germany see Regensburg
Ratiya India 82 C3
Rat Lake Canada 121 L3
Ratlam India 82 C5
Ratnagiri India 84 B2
Ratnapura Sri Lanka 84 D5
Ratne Ukr. 43 E6
Ratno Ukr. see Ratne
Raton U.S.A. 127 G5
Rattray Head hd U.K. 50 H3
Rättvik Sweden 45 I6
Ratz, Mount Canada 120 C3
Ratzeburg Germany 53 K1
Raub Malaysia 71 C7
Rauðamýri Iceland 44 [inset 1]
Raudhatain Kuwait 88 B4
Rauenstein Germany 53 L4
Raufarhöfn Iceland 44 [inset 1]
Raukumara Range mts N.Z. 113 F4
Raul Soares Brazil 145 C3
Rauma Fin. 45 L6
Raurkela India 83 F5
Rauschen Russia see Svetlogorsk
Rausu Japan 74 G3
Rautavaara Fin. 44 P5
Ravānsar Iran 88 B3
Rāvar Iran 88 E4
Ravat Kyrg. 89 H2
Ravels Belgium 52 E3
Ravena U.S.A. 135 I2
Ravenglass U.K. 48 D4
Ravenna Italy 58 E2
Ravenna NE U.S.A. 130 D3
Ravenna OH U.S.A. 134 E3

Ravensburg Germany 47 L7
Ravenshoe Australia 110 D3
Ravenswood Australia 110 D4
Ravi r. Pak. 89 H4
Ravnina Turkm. see Rawnina
Rāwah Iraq 91 F4
Rawaki i. Kiribati 107 I2
Rawalpindi Pak. 89 I3
Rawalpindi Lake Canada 120 H1
Rawāndūz/Rewanduz Iraq 91 G3
Rawi, Ko i. Thai. 71 B6
Rawicz Poland 47 P5
Rawlinna Australia 109 D7
Rawlins U.S.A. 126 G4
Rawlinson Range hills Australia 109 E6
Rawnina Mary Turkm. 89 F2
Rawnina Mary Turkm. 89 F2
Rawson Arg. 144 C6
Rawu China 76 C2
Raxón, Cerro mt. Guat. 136 G5
Ray, Cape Canada 123 K5
Raya, Bukit mt. Indon. 68 E7
Rayachoti India 84 C3
Rayadurg India 84 C3
Rayagada India 84 D2
Rayagarha India see Rayagada
Rayak Lebanon 85 C3
Raychikhinsk Russia 74 C2
Raydah Yemen 86 F6
Rayes Peak U.S.A. 128 D4
Rayevskiy Russia 41 Q5
Rayleigh U.K. 49 H7
Raymond U.S.A. 135 J2
Raymond Terrace Australia 112 E4
Raymondville U.S.A. 131 D7
Raymore Canada 121 J5
Rayner Glacier Antarctica 152 D2
Rayong Thai. 71 C4
Raystown Lake U.S.A. 135 F3
Raz, Pointe du pt France 56 B2
Razan Iran 88 C3
Rāzān Iran 88 C3
Razani Pak. 89 H3
Razāzah, Buḥayrat ar l. Iraq 91 F4
Razdan Armenia see Hrazdan
Razdel'naya Ukr. see Rozdil'na
Razdol'noye Russia 74 C4
Razeh Iran 88 C3
Razgrad Bulg. 59 L3
Razim, Lacul lag. Romania 59 M2
Razisi China 76 D1
Razlog Bulg. 59 J4
Razmak Pak. 89 H3
Ré, Île de i. France 56 D3
Reading U.K. 49 G7
Reading MI U.S.A. 134 C3
Reading OH U.S.A. 134 C4
Reading PA U.S.A. 135 H3
Reagile S. Africa 101 H3
Realicó Arg. 144 D5
Réalmont France 56 F5
Reăng Kései Cambodia 71 C4
Reasi India 82 C2
Reate Italy see Rieti
Rebais France 52 D6
Rebecca, Lake salt flat Australia 109 C7
Rebiana Sand Sea des. Libya 97 F2
Reboly Russia 44 Q5
Rebrikha Russia 72 E2
Rebun-tō i. Japan 74 F3
Recherche, Archipelago of the is Australia 109 C8
Rechitsa Belarus see Rechytsa
Rechna Doab lowland Pak. 89 I4
Rechytsa Belarus 43 F5
Recife Brazil 143 L5
Recife, Cape S. Africa 101 G8
Recklinghausen Germany 53 H3
Reconquista Arg. 144 E3
Recreo Arg. 144 C3
Rectorville U.S.A. 134 D4
Red r. Australia 110 C3
Red r. Canada 120 E3
Red r. Canada/U.S.A. 130 D1
Red r. LA U.S.A. 131 F6
Red r. TN U.S.A. 134 B5
Red r. Vietnam 70 D2
Redang i. Malaysia 71 C6
Red Bank NJ U.S.A. 135 H3
Red Bank TN U.S.A. 133 C5
Red Basin China see Sichuan Pendi
Red Bay Canada 123 K4
Red Bay Basque Whaling Station tourist site Canada 123 K4
Redberry Lake Canada 121 J4
Red Bluff U.S.A. 128 B1
Red Bluff Lake U.S.A. 131 C6
Red Butte mt. U.S.A. 129 G4
Redcar U.K. 48 F4
Redcliff Canada 126 F2
Redcliffe, Mount hill Australia 109 C7
Red Cliffs Australia 111 C7
Red Cloud U.S.A. 130 D3
Red Deer Canada 120 H4
Red Deer r. Alba/Sask. Canada 121 I5
Red Deer r. Man./Sask. Canada 121 K4
Red Deer Lake Canada 121 K4
Reddersburg S. Africa 101 H5
Redding U.S.A. 128 B1
Redditch U.K. 49 F6
Rede r. U.K. 48 E3
Redenção Brazil 143 H5
Redeyef Tunisia 58 C7
Redfield U.S.A. 130 D2
Red Granite Mountain Canada 120 B2
Red Hills U.S.A. 131 D4
Red Hook U.S.A. 135 I3
Red Indian Lake Canada 123 K4
Redkey U.S.A. 134 C3
Redkino Russia 42 H4
Redknife r. Canada 120 G2
Red Lake Canada 121 M5
Red Lake U.S.A. 129 G4
Red Lake r. U.S.A. 130 D2
Red Lake Falls U.S.A. 121 L6
Red Lakes U.S.A. 130 E1
Redlands U.S.A. 128 E4
Red Lion U.S.A. 135 G4
Red Lodge U.S.A. 126 F3
Redmesa U.S.A. 129 I3
Redmond OR U.S.A. 126 C3
Redmond UT U.S.A. 129 H2
Red Oak U.S.A. 130 E3
Redonda Island Canada 120 E5
Redondo Port. 57 C4
Redondo Beach U.S.A. 128 D5
Red Peak U.S.A. 126 E3
Red River, Mouths of the Vietnam 70 D2
Red Rock Canada 122 C4
Red Rock AZ U.S.A. 129 H5
Redrock U.S.A. 129 I5
Red Rock PA U.S.A. 135 G3
Redrock Lake Canada 120 H1
Red Sea Africa/Asia 86 D4
Redstone r. Canada 120 E1
Red Sucker Lake Canada 121 M4
Reduzum Neth. 52 F1
Redwater Canada 120 H4
Redway U.S.A. 128 B1
Red Wing U.S.A. 130 E2
Redwood City U.S.A. 128 B3
Redwood Falls U.S.A. 130 E2
Redwood National Park U.S.A. 126 B4
Redwood Valley U.S.A. 128 B2
Ree, Lough l. Ireland 51 E4
Reed U.S.A. 134 B5
Reed City U.S.A. 134 C2
Reedley U.S.A. 128 D3
Reedsport U.S.A. 126 B4
Reedsville U.S.A. 134 E4
Reedville U.S.A. 135 G5
Reedy U.S.A. 134 E4
Reedy Glacier Antarctica 152 J1
Reefton N.Z. 113 C6
Rees Germany 52 G3
Reese U.S.A. 134 D2
Reese r. U.S.A. 128 E1
Refahiye Turkey 90 E3
Refugio U.S.A. 131 D6
Rēgay Afgh. 89 G3
Regen Germany 53 N6
Regen r. Germany 53 M5
Regência Brazil 145 D2
Regensburg Germany 53 M5
Regenstauf Germany 53 M5
Reggane Alg. 96 D2
Reggio Calabria Italy see Reggio di Calabria
Reggio Emilia-Romagna Italy see Reggio nell'Emilia
Reggio di Calabria Italy 58 F5
Reggio Emilia Italy see Reggio nell'Emilia
Reggio nell'Emilia Italy 58 D2
Reghin Romania 59 K1
▶Regina Canada 121 J5
Capital of Saskatchewan.
Régina Fr. Guiana 143 H3
Rēgistān reg. Afgh. 89 G4
Registro Brazil 144 G2
Registro do Araguaia Brazil 145 A1
Regium Lepidum Italy see Reggio nell'Emilia
Regozero Russia 44 Q4
Rehau Germany 53 M4
Rehburg (Rehburg-Loccum) Germany 53 J2
Rehli India 82 D5
Rehoboth Namibia 100 C2
Rehoboth Bay U.S.A. 135 H4
Rehovot Israel 85 B4
Reïbell Alg. see Ksar Chellala
Reibitz Germany 53 M3
Reichenbach im Vogtland Germany 53 M4
Reichshoffen France 53 H6
Reid Australia 109 E7
Reidh, Rubha pt U.K. 50 D3
Reidsville U.S.A. 132 E4
Reigate U.K. 49 G7
Reiley Peak U.S.A. 129 H5
Reims France 52 E5
Reinbek Germany 53 K1
Reindeer r. Canada 121 K4
Reindeer Island Canada 121 L4
Reindeer Lake Canada 121 K3
Reine Norway 44 H3
Reinosa Spain 57 D2
Reinsfeld Germany 52 G5
Reiphólsfjöll hill Iceland 44 [inset 1]
Reisaelva r. Norway 44 L2
Reisa Nasjonalpark nat. park Norway 44 M2
Reisjärvi Fin. 44 N5
Reitz S. Africa 101 I4
Rekapalle India 84 D2
Reken Germany 52 H3
Reliance Canada 121 I2
Relizane Alg. 57 G6
Rellano Mex. 131 B7
Rellingen Germany 53 J1
Remagen Germany 53 H4
Remarkable, Mount hill Australia 111 B7
Remedios Cuba 133 E8
Remeshk Iran 88 E5
Remhoogte Pass Namibia 100 C2
Remi France see Reims
Remmel Mountain U.S.A. 126 C2
Remscheid Germany 53 H3
Rena Norway 45 G6
Renaix Belgium see Ronse
Renam Myanmar 76 C3
Renapur India 84 C2
Rendsburg Germany 47 L3
René-Levasseur, Île i. Canada 123 H4
Renews Canada 123 L5
Renfrew Canada 135 G1
Renfrew U.K. 50 E5
Rengali Reservoir India 83 F5
Rengat Indon. 68 C7
Rengo Chile 144 B4
Renhe China 77 G2
Ren He r. China 77 F1
Renhua China 77 G3
Reni Ukr. 59 M2
Renland reg. Greenland see Tuttut Nunaat
Rennell i. Solomon Is 107 G3
Rennerod Germany 53 I4
Rennes France 56 D2
Rennick Glacier Antarctica 152 H2
Rennie Canada 121 M5
Reno r. Italy 58 E2
Reno U.S.A. 128 D2
Renovo U.S.A. 135 G3
Rensselaer U.S.A. 134 B3
Renswoude Neth. 52 F2
Renton U.S.A. 126 C3
Réo Burkina Faso 96 C3
Reo Indon. 108 C2
Repalle India 84 D2
Repetek Turkm. 89 F2
Repetek Döwlet Gorugy nature res. Turkm. 89 F2
Repolka Russia 45 P7
Repou, Tônle r. Laos 71 D4
Republic U.S.A. 126 D2
Republican r. U.S.A. 130 D4
Repulse Bay b. Australia 110 E4
Repulse Bay Canada 119 J3
Requena Peru 142 D5
Requena Spain 57 F4
Reşadiye Turkey 90 E2
Reserva Brazil 145 A4
Reserve U.S.A. 129 I5
Reshi China 77 F2
Reshm Iran 88 D3
Reshteh-ye Alborz mts Iran see Elburz Mountains
Resistencia Arg. 144 E3
Reşiţa Romania 59 I2
Resolute Canada 119 I2
Resolute Bay Canada see Resolute
Resolution Island Canada 119 L3
Resolution Island N.Z. 113 A7
Resplendor Brazil 145 C2
Restigouche r. Canada 123 I5
Resülayn Turkey see Ceylanpınar
Retalhuleu Guat. 136 F6
Retezat, Parcul Naţional nat. park Romania 59 J2
Retford U.K. 48 G5
Rethel France 52 E5
Rethem (Aller) Germany 53 J2
Réthimnon Greece see Rethymno
Rethymno Greece 59 K7
Retreat Australia 110 C5
Reuden Germany 53 M2
▶Réunion terr. Indian Ocean 149 L7
French Overseas Department.
Reus Spain 57 G3
Reusam, Pulau i. Indon. 71 B7
Reutlingen Germany 47 L6
Reval Estonia see Tallinn
Revda Russia 44 S3
Revel Estonia see Tallinn
Revel France 56 F5
Revelstoke Canada 120 G5
Revigny-sur-Ornain France 52 E6
Revillagigedo, Islas is Mex. 136 B5
Revillagigedo Island U.S.A. 120 D4
Revin France 52 E5
Revivim Israel 85 B4
Revolyutsii, Pik mt. Tajik. see Revolyutsiya, Qullai
Revolyutsiya, Qullai mt. Tajik. 89 I2
Rewa India 82 E4
Rewanduz Iraq see Rawāndūz/Rewanduz
Rewari India 82 D3
Rexburg U.S.A. 126 F4
Rexton Canada 123 I5
Rey Iran 88 C3
Reyābād Iran 88 D2
Reyes, Point U.S.A. 128 B2
Reyhanlı Turkey 85 C1
Reykir Iceland 44 [inset 1]
Reykjanes Ridge sea feature N. Atlantic Ocean 148 F2
Reykjanestá pt Iceland 44 [inset 1]
▶Reykjavík Iceland 44 [inset 1]
Capital of Iceland.
Reyneke, Ostrov i. Russia 74 E1
Reynoldsburg U.S.A. 134 D4
Reynolds Range mts Australia 108 F5
Reynosa Mex. 131 D7
Reẓā Iran 88 D3
Reẓā'iyeh Iran see Urmia
Reẓā'iyeh, Daryācheh-ye salt l. Iran see Urmia, Lake
Rēzekne Latvia 45 O8
Reẓvān Iran 89 F4
Reẓvāndeh Iran see Reẓvānshahr
Reẓvānshahr Iran 88 C2
Rhaeadr Gwy U.K. see Rhayader
Rhayader U.K. 49 D6
Rheda-Wiedenbrück Germany 53 I3
Rhede Germany 52 G3
Rhegium Italy see Reggio di Calabria
Rheims France see Reims
Rhein r. Germany see Rhine
Rheine Germany 53 H2
Rheinland-Pfalz land Germany 53 H5
Rheinsberg Germany 53 M1
Rheinstetten Germany 53 I6
Rhemilès well Alg. 96 C2
Rhin r. France see Rhine
Rhine r. Germany 53 G3
also spelt Rhein (Germany) or Rhin (France)
Rhinebeck U.S.A. 135 I3
Rhinelander U.S.A. 130 F2
Rhineland-Palatinate land Germany see Rheinland-Pfalz
Rhinkanal canal Germany 53 M2
Rhinow Germany 53 M2
Rhiwabon U.K. see Ruabon
Rho Italy 58 C2
Rhode Island state U.S.A. 135 J3
Rhodes Greece 59 M6
Rhodes i. Greece 59 M6
Rhodesia country Africa see Zimbabwe
Rhodes Peak U.S.A. 126 E3
Rhodope Mountains Bulg./Greece 59 J4
Rhodus i. Greece see Rhodes
Rhône r. France/Switz. 56 G5
Rhum i. U.K. see Rum
Rhuthun U.K. see Ruthin
Rhydaman U.K. see Ammanford
Rhyl U.K. 48 D5
Riachão Brazil 143 I5
Riacho Brazil 145 C2
Riacho de Santana Brazil 145 C1
Riacho dos Machados Brazil 145 C1
Rialma Brazil 145 A1
Rialto U.S.A. 128 E4
Riau, Kepulauan is Indon. 68 C6
Ribadeo Spain 57 C2
Ribadesella/Ribeseya Spain 57 D2
Ribas do Rio Pardo Brazil 144 F2
Ribat-i-Shur waterhole Iran 88 E3
Ribáuè Moz. 99 D5
Ribble r. U.K. 48 E5
Ribblesdale valley U.K. 48 E4
Ribe Denmark 45 F9
Ribécourt-Dreslincourt France 52 C5
Ribeira r. Brazil 145 B4
Ribeirão Preto Brazil 145 B3
Ribemont France 52 D5
Ribérac France 56 E4
Riberalta Bol. 142 E6
Rîbniţa Moldova 43 F7
Ribnitz-Damgarten Germany 47 N3
Říčany Czechia 47 O6
Rice U.S.A. 135 F5
Rice Lake Canada 135 F1
Richard-Molard, Mont Africa 96 C4
Richards Bay S. Africa 101 K5
Richards Inlet Antarctica 152 H1
Richards Island Canada 118 E3
Richardson r. Canada 121 I3
Richardson U.S.A. 131 D5
Richardson Island Canada 120 G1
Richardson Lakes U.S.A. 135 J1
Richardson Mountains Canada 118 E3
Richardson Mountains N.Z. 113 B7
Richfield U.S.A. 129 G2
Richfield Springs U.S.A. 135 H2
Richford NY U.S.A. 135 G2
Richford VT U.S.A. 135 I1
Richgrove U.S.A. 128 D4
Richland U.S.A. 126 D3
Richland Center U.S.A. 130 F3
Richmond N.S.W. Australia 112 E4
Richmond Qld Australia 110 C4
Richmond Canada 135 H1
Richmond N.Z. 113 D5
Richmond KwaZulu-Natal S. Africa 101 J5
Richmond N. Cape S. Africa 100 F6
Richmond U.K. 48 F4
Richmond CA U.S.A. 128 B3
Richmond IN U.S.A. 134 C4
Richmond KY U.S.A. 134 C5
Richmond MI U.S.A. 134 D2
Richmond MO U.S.A. 130 E4
Richmond TX U.S.A. 131 E6
▶Richmond VA U.S.A. 135 G5
Capital of Virginia.
Richmond Dale U.S.A. 134 D4
Richmond Hill U.S.A. 133 D6
Richmond Range hills Australia 112 F2
Richvale U.S.A. 128 C2
Richwood U.S.A. 134 E4
Rico U.S.A. 129 I3
Ricomagus France see Riom
Riddell Nunataks Antarctica 152 E2
Rideau Lakes Canada 135 G1
Ridge r. Canada 122 D4
Ridgecrest U.S.A. 128 E4
Ridge Farm U.S.A. 134 B4
Ridgeland MS U.S.A. 131 F5
Ridgeland SC U.S.A. 133 D5
Ridgetop U.S.A. 134 B5
Ridgetown Canada 134 E2
Ridgeway OH U.S.A. 134 D3
Ridgeway VA U.S.A. 134 F5
Ridgway CO U.S.A. 129 J2
Ridgway PA U.S.A. 135 F3
Riding Mountain National Park Canada 121 K5
Riecito Venez. 142 E1
Riemst Belgium 52 F4
Riesa Germany 53 N3
Riesco, Isla i. Chile 144 B8
Riet watercourse S. Africa 100 E6
Rietavas Lith. 45 L9
Rietfontein S. Africa 100 E4
Rieti Italy 58 E3
Rifā'ī, Tall mt. Jordan/Syria 85 C3
Rifeng China see Lichuan
Rifle U.S.A. 129 J2
Rifstangi pt Iceland 44 [inset 1]
Rift Valley Lakes National Park Eth. see Abijatta-Shalla National Park
▶Rīga Latvia 45 N8
Capital of Latvia.
Riga, Gulf of Estonia/Latvia 45 M8
Rigain Pünco l. China 83 F2
Rīgas jūras līcis b. Estonia/Latvia see Riga, Gulf of
Rigby U.S.A. 126 F4
Rīgestān reg. Afgh. see Rēgistān
Rigolet Canada 123 K3
Rigside U.K. 50 F5
Riia laht b. Estonia/Latvia see Riga, Gulf of
Riihimäki Fin. 45 N6
Riiser-Larsen Ice Shelf Antarctica 152 B2
Riito Mex. 129 F5
Rijau Nigeria 96 D3
Rijeka Croatia 58 F2
Rikā, Wādī ar watercourse Saudi Arabia 88 B6
Rikitgaib Indon. 71 B6
Rikor India 76 B2
Rikuchū-kaigan Kokuritsu-kōen nat. park Japan 75 F5
Rikuzen-takata Japan 75 F5
Rila mts Bulg. 59 J3
Rila China 83 F3
Riley U.S.A. 126 D4
Rileyville U.S.A. 135 F4
Rillieux-la-Pape France 56 G4
Rillito U.S.A. 129 H5
Rimah, Wādī ar watercourse Saudi Arabia 86 F4
Rimavská Sobota Slovakia 47 R6
Rimbey Canada 120 H4
Rimini Italy 58 E2
Rîmnicu Sărat Romania see Râmnicu Sărat
Rîmnicu Vîlcea Romania see Râmnicu Vâlcea
Rimouski Canada 123 H4
Rimpar Germany 53 J5
Rimsdale, Loch l. U.K. 50 E2
Rinbung China 83 G3
Rincão Brazil 145 A3
Rindal Norway 44 F5
Ringarooma Bay Australia 111 [inset]
Ringas India 82 C4
Ringe Germany 52 G2
Ringebu Norway 45 G6
Ringhkung Myanmar 70 B1
Ringkøbing Denmark 45 F8
Ringsend U.K. 51 F2
Ringsted Denmark 45 G9
Ringtor China 83 E3
Ringvassøya i. Norway 44 K2
Ringwood Australia 112 B6
Ringwood U.K. 49 F8
Rinjani, Gunung vol. Indon. 68 F8
Rinns Point U.K. 50 C5
Rinqênzê China 83 G3
Rinqin Xubco salt l. China 83 E3
Rinteln Germany 53 J2
Rinyirru (Lakefield) National Park Australia 110 D2
Río Abiseo, Parque Nacional nat. park Peru 142 C5
Rio Azul Brazil 145 A4
Riobamba Ecuador 142 C4
Rio Blanco U.S.A. 129 J2
Rio Bonito Brazil 145 C3
Rio Branco Brazil 142 E6
Rio Branco, Parque Nacional do nat. park Brazil 142 F3
Río Bravo, Parque Internacional del nat. park Mex. 131 C6
Rio Brilhante Brazil 144 F2
Rio Casca Brazil 145 C3
Rio Claro Brazil 145 B3
Río Colorado Arg. 144 D5
Río Cuarto Arg. 144 D4
Rio das Ostras Brazil 145 C3
Rio das Pedras Moz. 101 L2
Rio de Contas Brazil 145 C1
▶Rio de Janeiro Brazil 145 C3
Former capital of Brazil. 3rd most populous city in South America.
Rio de Janeiro state Brazil 145 C3
▶Río de la Plata-Paraná r. S. America 144 E4
2nd longest river in South America and 9th in the world.
Rio Dell U.S.A. 128 A1
Rio do Sul Brazil 145 A4
Río Gallegos Arg. 144 C8
Río Grande Arg. 144 C8
Rio Grande Brazil 144 F4
Río Grande Mex. 131 C8
Rio Grande r. Mex./U.S.A. 127 G5
also known as Río Bravo del Norte
Rio Grande City U.S.A. 131 D7
Rio Grande del Norte National Monument nat. park U.S.A. 127 G6
Rio Grande do Sul state Brazil 145 A5
Rio Grande Rise sea feature S. Atlantic Ocean 148 F8
Riohacha Col. 142 D1
Río Hondo, Embalse resr Arg. 144 C3
Rioja Peru 142 C5
Río Lagartos Mex. 133 B8
Rio Largo Brazil 143 K5
Riom France 56 F4
Rio Manso, Represa do resr Brazil 143 G6
Río Mulatos Bol. 142 E7
Río Muni reg. Equat. Guinea 96 E4
Río Negro, Embalse del resr Uruguay 144 E4
Rioni r. Georgia 91 F2
Rio Novo Brazil 145 C3
Rio Pardo de Minas Brazil 145 C1
Rio Preto Brazil 145 C3
Rio Preto, Serra do hills Brazil 145 B2
Rio Rancho U.S.A. 127 G6
Río Tigre Ecuador 142 C4
Riou Lake Canada 121 J3
Rio Verde Brazil 145 A2
Rio Verde de Mato Grosso Brazil 143 H7
Rio Vista U.S.A. 128 C2
Ripky Ukr. 43 F6
Ripley England U.K. 48 F4
Ripley England U.K. 49 F5
Ripley NY U.S.A. 134 F2
Ripley OH U.S.A. 134 D4
Ripley WV U.S.A. 134 E4
Ripoll Spain 57 H2
Ripon U.K. 48 F4
Ripon U.S.A. 128 C3
Ripu India 83 G4
Risca U.K. 49 D7
Rishiri-tō i. Japan 74 F3
Rishon LeZiyyon Israel 85 B4
Rīsh Pīsh Bālā Iran 89 F5
Rising Sun IN U.S.A. 134 C4
Rising Sun MD U.S.A. 135 G4
Risle r. France 49 H9
Risør Norway 45 F7
Rissa Norway 44 F5
Ristiina Fin. 45 O6
Ristijärvi Fin. 44 P4
Ristikent Russia 44 Q2
Risum China 82 D2
Ritchie S. Africa 100 G5
Ritchie's Archipelago is India 71 A4
Ritscher Upland mts Antarctica 152 B2
Ritsem Sweden 44 J3
Ritter, Mount U.S.A. 128 D3
Ritterhude Germany 53 I1
Ritzville U.S.A. 126 D3
Riu, Laem pt Thai. 71 B5
Riva del Garda Italy 58 D2
Rivas Nicaragua 137 G6
Rivera Arg. 144 D5
Rivera Uruguay 144 E4
Riverhead U.S.A. 135 I3
Riverhurst Canada 121 J5
Riverina Australia 109 C7
Riverina reg. Australia 112 B5
Riversdale S. Africa 100 E8
Riverside S. Africa 101 I6
Riverside U.S.A. 128 E5
Rivers Inlet Canada 120 E5
Riversleigh Australia 110 B3
Riverton N.Z. 113 B8
Riverton VA U.S.A. 135 F4
Riverton WY U.S.A. 126 F4
Riverview Canada 123 I5
Rivesaltes France 56 F5
Riviera Beach U.S.A. 133 D7
Rivière-du-Loup Canada 123 H5
Rivière-Pentecôte Canada 123 I4
Rivière-Pigou Canada 123 I4
Rivne Ukr. 43 E6
Rivungo Angola 99 C5
Riwaka N.Z. 113 D5
Riwoqê China see Racaka
▶Riyadh Saudi Arabia 86 G5
Capital of Saudi Arabia.
Riyan India 89 I5
Riza well Iran 88 D3
Rize Turkey 91 F2
Rizhao Shandong China see Donggang
Rizhao Shandong China 77 H1
Rizokarpaso Cyprus see Rizokarpason
Rizokarpason Cyprus 85 B2
Rīzū well Iran 88 E3
Rīzū'īyeh Iran 88 E4
Rjukan Norway 45 F7
Rjuvbrokkene mt. Norway 45 E7
Rkîz Mauritania 96 B3
Roa Norway 45 G6
Roachdale U.S.A. 134 B4
Roach Lake U.S.A. 129 F4
Roade U.K. 49 G6
Roads U.S.A. 134 D4
▶Road Town Virgin Is (U.K.) 137 L5
Capital of the British Virgin Islands.
Roan Norway 44 G4
Roan Fell hill U.K. 50 G5
Roan High Knob mt. U.S.A. 132 D4
Roanne France 56 G3
Roanoke IN U.S.A. 134 C3
Roanoke VA U.S.A. 134 F5
Roanoke r. U.S.A. 132 E4
Roanoke Rapids U.S.A. 132 E4
Roan Plateau U.S.A. 129 I2
Roaring Spring U.S.A. 135 F3
Roaringwater Bay Ireland 51 C6
Roatán Hond. 137 G5
Röbäck Sweden 44 L5
Robāţ-e Posht-e Bādām Iran 88 D3
Robāţ Karīm Iran 88 C3
Robāţ Sang Iran 88 E3
Robāţ Tork Iran 88 C3
Robb Canada 120 G4
Robbins Island Australia 111 [inset]
Robbinsville U.S.A. 133 D5
Robe Australia 111 B8
Robe r. Australia 108 A5
Robe r. Ireland 51 C4
Röbel/Müritz Germany 53 M1
Robe Noire, Lac de la l. Canada 123 J4
Robert-Bourassa, Réservoir resr Canada 122 F3
Robert Glacier Antarctica 152 D2
Robert Lee U.S.A. 131 C6
Roberts U.S.A. 126 E4
Roberts, Mount Australia 112 F2
Robertsburg U.S.A. 134 E4
Roberts Butte mt. Antarctica 152 H2
Roberts Creek Mountain U.S.A. 128 E2
Robertsfors Sweden 44 L4
Robertsganj India 83 E4
Robertson S. Africa 100 D7
Robertson, Lac l. Canada 123 K4
Robertson Bay Antarctica 152 H2
Robertson Island Antarctica 152 A2
Robertson Range hills Australia 109 C5
Robertsport Liberia 96 B4
Roberval Canada 123 G4
Robhanais, Rubha hd U.K. see Butt of Lewis
Robin Hood's Bay U.K. 48 G4
Robin's Nest hill H.K. China 77 [inset]
Robinson Canada 120 C2
Robinson U.S.A. 134 B4
Robinson Ranges hills Australia 109 B6
Robinson River Australia 110 B3
Robles Pass U.S.A. 129 H5
Roblin Canada 121 K5
Robsart Canada 121 I5
Robson, Mount Canada 120 G4
Robstown U.S.A. 131 D7
Roby U.S.A. 131 C5
Roçadas Angola see Xangongo
Rocha Uruguay 144 F4
Rochdale U.K. 48 E5
Rochechouart France 56 E4
Rochefort Belgium 52 F4
Rochefort France 56 D4
Rochefort, Lac l. Canada 123 G2
Rochegda Russia 42 I3
Rochester Australia 112 B6
Rochester U.K. 49 H7
Rochester IN U.S.A. 134 B3
Rochester MN U.S.A. 130 E2
Rochester NH U.S.A. 135 J2
Rochester NY U.S.A. 135 G2
Rochford U.K. 49 H7
Rochlitz Germany 53 M3
Roc'h Trévezel hill France 56 C2
Rock r. Canada 120 E2
Rockall i. N. Atlantic Ocean 40 D4
Rockall Bank sea feature N. Atlantic Ocean 148 G2
Rock Creek Canada 120 B1
Rock Creek U.S.A. 134 E3
Rock Creek r. U.S.A. 126 G2
Rockdale U.S.A. 131 D6

Rockefeller Plateau Antarctica 152 J1
Rockford AL U.S.A. 133 C5
Rockford IL U.S.A. 130 F3
Rockford MI U.S.A. 134 C2
Rockglen Canada 121 J5
Rockhampton Australia 110 E4
Rockhampton Downs Australia 108 F4
Rock Hill U.S.A. 133 D5
Rockingham Australia 109 A8
Rockingham U.S.A. 133 E5
Rockingham Bay Australia 110 D3
Rockinghorse Lake Canada 121 H1
Rock Island Canada 135 I1
Rock Island U.S.A. 130 F3
Rock Lake U.S.A. 130 D1
Rockland MA U.S.A. 135 J2
Rockland ME U.S.A. 132 G2
Rocknest Lake Canada 120 H1
Rockport IN U.S.A. 134 B5
Rockport TX U.S.A. 131 D7
Rock Rapids U.S.A. 130 D3
Rock River U.S.A. 126 G4
Rock Sound Bahamas 133 E7
Rock Springs MT U.S.A. 126 G3
Rocksprings U.S.A. 131 C6
Rock Springs WY U.S.A. 126 F4
Rockstone Guyana 143 G2
Rockville CT U.S.A. 135 I3
Rockville IN U.S.A. 134 B4
Rockville MD U.S.A. 135 G4
Rockwell City U.S.A. 130 E3
Rockwood MI U.S.A. 134 D2
Rockwood PA U.S.A. 134 F4
Rockyford Canada 120 H5
Rocky Harbour Canada 123 K4
Rocky Hill U.S.A. 134 D4
Rocky Island Lake Canada 122 E5
Rocky Lane Canada 120 G3
Rocky Mount U.S.A. 134 F5
Rocky Mountain House Canada 120 H4
Rocky Mountain National Park U.S.A. 126 G4
Rocky Mountains Canada/U.S.A. 124 F3
Rocourt-St-Martin France 52 D5
Rocroi France 52 E5
Rødberg Norway 45 F6
Rødbyhavn Denmark 45 G9
Roddickton Canada 123 L4
Rodeio Brazil 145 A4
Rodel U.K. 50 C3
Roden Neth. 52 G1
Rödental Germany 53 L4
Rodeo Arg. 144 C4
Rodeo Mex. 131 B7
Rodeo U.S.A. 127 F7
Rodez France 56 F4
Ródhos i. Greece see Rhodes
Rodi i. Greece see Rhodes
Roding Germany 53 M5
Rodney, Cape U.S.A. 118 B3
Rodniki Russia 42 I4
Rodolfo Sánchez Toboada Mex. 127 D7
Rodopi Planina mts Bulg./Greece see Rhodope Mountains
Rodos Greece see Rhodes
Rodos i. Greece see Rhodes
Rodosto Turkey see Tekirdağ
Rodrigues Island Mauritius 149 M7
Roe r. U.K. 51 F2
Roebourne Australia 108 B5
Roebuck Bay Australia 108 C4
Roedtan S. Africa 101 I3
Roe Plains Australia 109 D7
Roermond Neth. 52 F3
Roeselare Belgium 52 D4
Roes Welcome Sound sea chan. Canada 119 J3
Rogachev Belarus see Rahachow
Rogätz Germany 53 L2
Rogers U.S.A. 131 E4
Rogers, Mount U.S.A. 134 E5
Rogers City U.S.A. 134 D1
Rogers Lake U.S.A. 128 E4
Rogerson U.S.A. 126 E4
Rogersville U.S.A. 134 D5
Roggan r. Australia 110 A2
Roggan, Lac l. Canada 122 F3
Roggeveen Basin sea feature S. Pacific Ocean 151 O8
Roggeveld plat. S. Africa 100 E7
Roggeveldberge esc. S. Africa 100 E7
Roghadal U.K. see Rodel
Rognan Norway 44 G4
Rögnitz r. Germany 53 K1
Rogue r. U.S.A. 126 B4
Roha India 84 B2
Rohnert Park U.S.A. 128 B2
Rohrbach in Oberösterreich Austria 47 N6
Rohrbach-lès-Bitche France 53 H5
Rohri Sangar Pak. 89 H5
Rohtak India 82 D3
Roi Et Thai. 70 C3
Roi Georges, Îles du is Fr. Polynesia 151 K6
Rois-Bheinn hill U.K. 50 D4
Roisel France 52 D5
Roja Latvia 45 M8
Rojas Arg. 144 D4
Rokeby Australia 110 C2
Rokeby National Park Australia 110 C2
Rokiškis Lith. 45 N9
Roknäs Sweden 44 L4
Rokytne Ukr. 43 E6
Rolagang China 83 G2
Rola Kangri mt. China 83 G2
Rolândia Brazil 145 A3
Rolim de Moura Brazil 142 F6
Roll AZ U.S.A. 129 G5
Roll IN U.S.A. 134 C3
Rolla MO U.S.A. 130 F4
Rolla ND U.S.A. 130 D1
Rollag Norway 45 F6
Rolleston Australia 110 E5
Rolleville Bahamas 133 F8
Rolling Fork U.S.A. 131 F5
Rollins U.S.A. 126 E3
Roma Australia 111 E5
Roma Italy see Rome
Roma Lesotho 101 H5
Roma Sweden 45 K8
Romain, Cape U.S.A. 133 E5
Romaine r. Canada 123 J4
Roman Romania 59 L1
Română, Câmpia plain Romania 59 J2
Romanche Gap sea feature S. Atlantic Ocean 148 G6
Romanet, Lac l. Canada 123 I2
Romang, Pulau i. Indon. 108 D1
Romania country Europe 59 K2
Roman-Kosh mt. Crimea 90 D1
Romano, Cape U.S.A. 133 D7
Romanovka Russia 73 K2
Romans-sur-Isère France 56 G4
Romanzof, Cape U.S.A. 118 B3
Rombas France 52 G5
Romblon Phil. 69 G4

▶Rome Italy 58 E4
Capital of Italy.

Rome GA U.S.A. 133 C5
Rome ME U.S.A. 135 K1
Rome NY U.S.A. 135 H2
Rome TN U.S.A. 134 B5
Rome City U.S.A. 134 C3
Romeo U.S.A. 134 D2
Romford U.K. 49 H7
Romilly-sur-Seine France 56 F2
Romiton Uzbek. 89 G2
Romney U.S.A. 135 F4
Romney Marsh reg. U.K. 49 H7
Romny Ukr. 43 G6
Rømø i. Denmark 45 F9
Romodanovo Russia 43 J5
Romorantin-Lanthenay France 56 E3
Rompin r. Malaysia 71 C7
Romsey U.K. 49 F8
Romulus U.S.A. 134 D2
Ron India 84 B3
Ron, Mui hd Vietnam 70 D3
Rona i. U.K. 50 D1
Ronas Hill hill U.K. 50 [inset]
Roncador, Serra do hills Brazil 143 H6
Roncador Reef Solomon Is 107 F2
Ronda Spain 57 D5
Ronda, Serranía de mts Spain 57 D5
Rondane Nasjonalpark nat. park Norway 45 F6
Rondon Brazil 144 F2
Rondonópolis Brazil 143 H7
Rondout Reservoir U.S.A. 135 H3
Rongcheng Anhui China see Qingyang
Rongcheng Guangxi China see Rongxian
Rongcheng Hubei China see Jianli
Rong Chu r. China 83 G3
Rongelap atoll Marshall Is 150 H5
Rongjiang Guizhou China 77 F3
Rongjiang Jiangxi China see Nankang
Rongjiawan China see Yueyang
Rongklang Range mts Myanmar 70 A2
Rongmei China see Hefeng
Rongshui China 77 F3
Rongwo China see Tongren
Rongxian China 77 F4
Rongyul China 76 C2
Rongzhag China see Danba
Rönlap atoll Marshall Is see Rongelap
Rønne Denmark 45 I9
Ronneby Sweden 45 I8
Ronne Entrance strait Antarctica 152 L2
Ronne Ice Shelf Antarctica 152 L1
Ronnenberg Germany 53 J2
Ronse Belgium 52 D4
Roodeschool Neth. 52 G1
Rooke Island P.N.G. see Umboi
Roordahuizum Neth. see Reduzum
Roorkee India 82 D3
Roosendaal Neth. 52 E3
Roosevelt AZ U.S.A. 129 H5
Roosevelt UT U.S.A. 129 I1
Roosevelt, Mount Canada 120 E3
Roosevelt Sub-glacial Island Antarctica 152 I1
Root r. Canada 120 F2
Root r. U.S.A. 130 F3
Ropar India see Rupnagar
Roper r. Australia 110 A2
Roper Bar Australia 108 F3
Roquefort France 56 D4
Roraima, Mount Guyana 142 F2
Rori India 82 C3
Rori Indon. 69 J7
Røros Norway 44 G5
Rørvik Norway 44 G4
Rosa, Punta pt Mex. 127 F8
Rosalia U.S.A. 126 D3
Rosamond U.S.A. 128 D4
Rosamond Lake U.S.A. 128 D4
Rosario Arg. 144 D4
Rosário Brazil 143 J4
Rosario Baja California Mex. 127 E7
Rosario Coahuila Mex. 131 C7
Rosario Sinaloa Mex. 136 C4
Rosario Sonora Mex. 124 F6
Rosario Zacatecas Mex. 131 C7
Rosario Venez. 142 D1
Rosário do Sul Brazil 144 F4
Rosário Oeste Brazil 143 G6
Rosarito Baja California Mex. 127 E7
Rosarito Baja California Mex. 128 E5
Rosarito Baja California Sur Mex. 127 F8
Rosarno Italy 58 F5
Roscoff France 56 C2
Roscommon Ireland 51 D4
Roscommon U.S.A. 134 C1
Roscrea Ireland 51 E5
Rose r. Australia 110 A2
Rose, Mount U.S.A. 128 D2
Rose Atoll American Samoa see Rose Island

▶Roseau Dominica 137 L5
Capital of Dominica.

Roseau U.S.A. 130 E1
Roseau r. U.S.A. 130 D1
Roseberth Australia 111 B5
Rose Blanche Canada 123 K5
Rosebud r. Canada 120 H5
Rosebud U.S.A. 126 G3
Roseburg U.S.A. 126 C4
Rose City U.S.A. 134 C1
Rosedale U.S.A. 131 F5
Rosedale Abbey U.K. 48 G4
Roseires Reservoir Sudan 86 D7
Rose Island atoll American Samoa 107 J3
Rosenberg U.S.A. 131 E6
Rosendal Norway 45 E7
Rosendal S. Africa 101 H5
Rosenheim Germany 47 N7
Rose Peak U.S.A. 129 I5
Rose Point pt Canada 120 D4
Roseto degli Abruzzi Italy 58 F3
Rosetown Canada 121 J5
Rosetta Egypt see Rashīd
Rose Valley Canada 121 K4
Roseville CA U.S.A. 128 C2
Roseville MI U.S.A. 134 D2
Roseville OH U.S.A. 134 D4
Rosewood Australia 112 F1
Roshchino Russia 45 P6
Rosh Pinah Namibia 100 C4
Roshtkala Tajik. see Roshtqal'a
Roshtqal'a Tajik. 89 H2
Rosignano Marittimo Italy 58 D3
Roşiori de Vede Romania 59 K2
Roskilde Denmark 45 H9
Roskruge Mountains U.S.A. 129 H5
Roslavl' Russia 43 G5
Roslyakovo Russia 44 R2
Roslyatino Russia 42 J4
Ross N.Z. 113 C6
Ross, Mount hill N.Z. 113 E5
Rossano Italy 58 G5
Rossan Point Ireland 51 D3
Ross Barnett Reservoir U.S.A. 131 F5
Ross Bay Junction Canada 123 I3
Rosscarbery Ireland 51 C6
Ross Dependency reg. Antarctica 152 I2
Rosseau, Lake Canada 134 F1
Rossel Island P.N.G. 110 F1
Ross Ice Shelf Antarctica 152 I1
Rossignol, Lac l. Canada 122 G3
Rössing Namibia 100 B2
Ross Island Antarctica 152 H1
Rossiyskaya Sovetskaya Federativnaya Sotsialisticheskaya Respublika country Asia/Europe see Russia
Rossland Canada 120 G5
Rosslare Ireland 51 F5
Rosslare Harbour Ireland 51 F5
Roßlau Germany 53 M3
Rosso Mauritania 96 B3
Ross-on-Wye U.K. 49 E7
Rossony Belarus see Rasony
Rossosh' Russia 43 H6
Ross River Canada 120 C2
Ross Sea Antarctica 152 H1
Roßtal Germany 53 K5
Røssvatnet l. Norway 44 I4
Rossville U.S.A. 134 B3
Roßwein Germany 53 N3
Rosswood Canada 120 D4
Rostāq Iran 88 D5
Rosthern Canada 121 J4
Rostock Germany 47 N3
Rostov Russia 42 H4
Rostov-na-Donu Russia 43 H7
Rostov-on-Don Russia see Rostov-na-Donu
Rosvik Sweden 44 L4
Roswell U.S.A. 127 G6
Rota i. N. Mariana Is 69 L4
Rot am See Germany 53 K5
Rotch Island Kiribati see Tamana
Rote i. Indon. 108 C2
Rotenburg (Wümme) Germany 53 J1
Roth Germany 53 L5
Rothaargebirge hills Germany 53 I4
Rothbury U.K. 48 F3
Rothenburg ob der Tauber Germany 53 K5
Rother r. U.K. 49 G8
Rothera research station Antarctica 152 L2
Rotherham U.K. 48 F5
Rothes U.K. 50 F3
Rothesay U.K. 50 D5
Rothwell U.K. 49 G6
Roti Indon. 108 C2
Roti i. Indon. see Rote
Roto Australia 112 B4
Rotomagus France see Rouen
Rotomanu N.Z. 113 C6
Rotondo, Monte mt. Corsica France 56 I5
Rotorua N.Z. 113 F4
Rotorua, Lake N.Z. 113 F4
Röttenbach Germany 53 L5
Rottendorf Germany 53 K5
Rottenmann Austria 47 O7
Rotterdam Neth. 52 E3
Rottleberode Germany 53 K3
Rottnest Island Australia 109 A8
Rottumeroog i. Neth. 52 G1
Rottweil Germany 47 L6
Rotuma i. Fiji 107 H3
Rotung India 76 B2
Rötviken Sweden 44 I5
Rötz Germany 53 M5
Roubaix France 52 D4
Rouen France 52 B5
Rough River Lake U.S.A. 134 B5
Roulers Belgium see Roeselare
Roumania country Europe see Romania
Roundeyed Lake Canada 123 H3
Round Hill hill U.K. 48 F4
Round Mountain Australia 112 F3
Round Rock AZ U.S.A. 129 I3
Round Rock TX U.S.A. 131 D6
Roundup U.S.A. 126 F3
Rousay i. U.K. 50 F1
Rouses Point U.S.A. 135 I1
Rouxville S. Africa 101 H6
Rouyn-Noranda Canada 122 F4
Rovaniemi Fin. 44 N3
Roven'ki Russia 43 H6
Rovereto Italy 58 D2
Rôviĕng Cambodia 71 D4
Rovigo Italy 58 D2
Rovinj Croatia 58 E2
Rovno Ukr. see Rivne
Rovnoye Russia 43 J6
Rovuma r. Moz./Tanz. see Ruvuma
Rowena Australia 112 D2
Rowley Island Canada 119 K3
Rowley Shoals sea feature Australia 108 B4
Równe Ukr. see Rivne
Roxas Mindoro Phil. 69 G4
Roxas Palawan Phil. 68 F4
Roxas Panay Phil. 69 G4
Roxboro U.S.A. 132 E4
Roxburgh N.Z. 113 B7
Roxburgh Island Cook Is see Rarotonga
Roxby Downs Australia 111 B6
Roxo, Cabo c. Senegal 96 B3
Roy MT U.S.A. 126 F3
Roy NM U.S.A. 127 G5
Royal Canal Ireland 51 E4
Royal Chitwan National Park Nepal 83 F4
Royale, Île i. Canada see Cape Breton Island
Royale, Isle i. U.S.A. 130 F1
Royal Leamington Spa U.K. 49 F6
Royal Natal National Park S. Africa 101 I5
Royal National Park Australia 112 E5
Royal Oak U.S.A. 134 D2
Royal Sukla Phanta Wildlife Reserve Nepal 82 E3
Royal Tunbridge Wells U.K. 49 H7
Royal Wootton Bassett U.K. 49 F7
Royan France 56 D4
Roye France 52 C5
Roy Hill Australia 108 B5
Royston U.K. 49 G6
Rozdil'na Ukr. 59 N1
Rozivka Ukr. 43 H7
Rtishchevo Russia 43 I5
Ruabon U.K. 49 D6
Ruaha National Park Tanz. 99 D4
Ruahine Range mts N.Z. 113 F5
Ruanda country Africa see Rwanda

▶Ruapehu, Mount vol. N.Z. 113 E4
Highest active volcano in Oceania.

Ruapuke Island N.Z. 113 B8
Ruatoria N.Z. 113 G3
Ruba Belarus 43 F5

▶Rub' al Khālī des. Saudi Arabia 86 G6
Largest uninterrupted stretch of sand in the world.

Rubāṭ Māndêh r. Afgh. 89 F4
Rubaydā reg. Saudi Arabia 88 C5
Rubtsovsk Russia 80 F1
Ruby U.S.A. 118 C3
Ruby Dome mt. U.S.A. 129 F1
Ruby Mountains U.S.A. 129 F1
Rubys Inn U.S.A. 129 G3
Ruby Valley U.S.A. 129 F1
Rucheng China 77 G3
Ruckersville U.S.A. 135 F4
Rudall River National Park Australia 108 C5
Rudarpur India 83 E4
Ruda Śląska Poland 47 Q5
Rudauli India 83 E4
Rūdbār Iran 88 C2
Rudkøbing Denmark 45 G9
Rudnaya Pristan' Russia 74 D3
Rudnichnyy Russia 42 L4
Rudnik Ingichka Uzbek. see Ingichka
Rudnya Smolenskaya Oblast' Russia 43 F5
Rudnya Volgogradskaya Oblast' Russia 43 J6
Rudnyy Kazakh. 78 F1
Rudolf, Lake salt l. Eth./Kenya see Turkana, Lake

▶Rudol'fa, Ostrov i. Russia 64 G1
Most northerly point of Europe.

Rudolph Island Russia see Rudol'fa, Ostrov
Rudolstadt Germany 53 L4
Rudong China 77 I1
Rūdsar Iran 88 C2
Rue France 52 B4
Rufiji r. Tanz. 99 D4
Rufino Arg. 144 D4
Rufisque Senegal 96 B3
Rufrufua Indon. 69 I7
Rufunsa Zambia 99 C5
Rugao China 77 I1
Rugby U.K. 49 F6
Rugby U.S.A. 130 C1
Rugeley U.K. 49 F6
Rügen i. Germany 47 N3
Rugged Mountain Canada 120 E5
Rügland Germany 53 K5
Ruḥayyat al Ḥamr'ā' waterhole Saudi Arabia 88 B5
Ruhengeri Rwanda 98 C4
Ruhnu i. Estonia 45 M8
Ruhr r. Germany 53 G3
Ruhuna National Park Sri Lanka see Yala National Park
Rui'an China 77 I3
Ruicheng China 77 F1
Ruijin China 77 G3
Ruili China 76 C3
Ruin Point Canada 121 P2
Ruipa Tanz. 99 D4
Ruiz Mex. 136 C4
Ruiz, Nevado del vol. Col. 142 C3
Rujaylah, Ḥarrat ar lava field Jordan 85 C3
Rūjiena Latvia 45 N8
Ruk is Micronesia see Chuuk
Rukanpur Pak. 89 I4
Rukumkot Nepal 83 E3
Rukwa, Lake Tanz. 99 D4
Rulin China see Chengbu
Rulong China see Xinlong
Rum i. U.K. 50 C4
Rum, Jebel mts Jordan see Ramm, Jabal
Ruma Serbia 59 H2
Rumāh Saudi Arabia 86 G4
Rumania country Europe see Romania
Rumbek South Sudan 97 F4
Rumberpon i. Indon. 69 I7
Rum Cay i. Bahamas 133 F8
Rum Jungle (abandoned) Australia 108 E3
Rummānā hill Syria 85 D3
Rumphi Malawi 99 D5
Runan China 77 G1
Runaway, Cape N.Z. 113 F3
Runcorn U.K. 48 E5
Rundu Namibia 99 B5
Rundvik Sweden 44 K5
Rŭng, Kaôh i. Cambodia 71 C5
Rungwa Tanz. 99 D4
Rungwa r. Tanz. 99 D4
Runhe China 77 H1
Runing China see Runan
Runton Range hills Australia 109 C5
Ruokolahti Fin. 45 P6
Ruoqiang China 80 G4
Rupa India 83 H4
Rupat i. Indon. 71 C7
Rupert r. Canada 122 F4
Rupert ID U.S.A. 126 E4
Rupert WV U.S.A. 134 E5
Rupert Bay Canada 122 F4
Rupert Coast Antarctica 152 J1
Rupert House Canada see Waskaganish
Rupnagar India 82 D3
Rupshu reg. India 82 D2
Ruqqād, Wādī ar watercourse Israel 85 B3
Rural Retreat U.S.A. 134 E5
Rusaddir N. Africa see Melilla
Rusape Zimbabwe 99 D5
Ruschuk Bulg. see Ruse
Ruse Bulg. 59 K3
Rusera India 83 F4
Rush U.S.A. 134 D4
Rush Creek r. U.S.A. 130 C4
Rushden U.K. 49 G6
Rushinga Zimbabwe 99 D5
Rushville IL U.S.A. 130 F3
Rushville IN U.S.A. 134 C4
Rushville NE U.S.A. 130 C3
Rushworth Australia 112 B6
Rusk U.S.A. 131 E6
Russell Man. Canada 121 K5
Russell Ont. Canada 135 H1
Russell N.Z. 113 E2
Russell KS U.S.A. 130 D4
Russell PA U.S.A. 134 F3
Russell Bay Antarctica 152 J2
Russell Lake Man. Canada 121 K3
Russell Lake N.W.T. Canada 120 H2
Russell Lake Sask. Canada 121 J3
Russell Range hills Australia 109 C8
Russell Springs U.S.A. 134 C5
Russellville AL U.S.A. 131 G5
Russellville AR U.S.A. 131 E5
Russellville KY U.S.A. 134 B5
Rüsselsheim Germany 53 I4

▶Russia country Asia/Europe 64 I3
Largest country in Europe and Asia and the world. Most populous country in Europe and 9th in the world.

Russian r. U.S.A. 128 B2
Russian Federation country Asia/Europe see Russia
Russian Soviet Federal Socialist Republic country Asia/Europe see Russia
Russkiy, Ostrov i. Russia 74 C4
Russkiy Kameshkir Russia 43 J5
Rustāq Afgh. 89 H2
Rustavi Georgia 91 G2
Rustburg U.S.A. 134 F5
Rustenburg S. Africa 101 H3
Ruston U.S.A. 131 E5
Rutanzige, Lake Dem. Rep. Congo/Uganda see Edward, Lake
Ruteng Indon. 108 C2
Ruth U.S.A. 129 F2
Rüthen Germany 53 I3
Rutherglen Australia 112 C6
Ruther Glen U.S.A. 135 G5
Ruthin U.K. 49 D5
Ruthiyai India 82 D4
Ruth Reservoir U.S.A. 128 B1
Rutka r. Russia 42 J4
Rutland U.S.A. 135 I2
Rutland Water resr U.K. 49 G6
Rutledge Lake Canada 121 I2
Rutog Xizang China 76 B2
Rutög China see Dêrub
Rutog Xizang China 83 F3
Rutul Russia 91 G2
Ruukki Fin. 44 N4
Ruvuma r. Moz./Tanz. 99 E5
also known as Rovuma
Ruwayshid, Wādī watercourse Jordan 85 C3
Ruwayṭah, Wādī watercourse Jordan 85 C5
Ruweis U.A.E. 88 D5
Ruwenzori National Park Uganda see Queen Elizabeth National Park
Ruy Barbosa Brazil 145 C1
Rūy Dūāb Wuluswālī Afgh. 89 G3
Ruza Russia 42 H5
Ruzayevka Kazakh. 78 F1
Ruzayevka Russia 43 J5
Ruzhou China 77 G1
Ružomberok Slovakia 47 Q6
Rwanda country Africa 98 C4
Ryan, Loch b. U.K. 50 D5
Ryazan' Russia 43 H5
Ryazhsk Russia 43 I5
Rybachiy, Poluostrov pen. Russia 44 R2
Rybach'ye Kyrg. see Balykchy
Rybinsk Russia 42 H4

▶Rybinskoye Vodokhranilishche resr Russia 42 H4
5th largest lake in Europe.

Rybnik Poland 47 Q5
Rybnitsa Moldova see Rîbniţa
Rybnoye Russia 43 H5
Rybreka Russia 42 G3
Ryd Sweden 45 I8
Rydberg Peninsula Antarctica 152 L2
Ryde U.K. 49 F8
Rye U.K. 49 H8
Rye r. U.K. 48 G4
Rye Bay U.K. 49 H8
Ryegate U.S.A. 126 F3
Rye Patch Reservoir U.S.A. 128 D1
Rykovo Ukr. see Yenakiyeve
Ryl'sk Russia 43 G6
Rylstone Australia 112 D4
Ryn-Peski des. Kazakh. 41 P6
Ryukyu Islands Japan 75 B8
Ryūkyū-rettō is Japan see Ryukyu Islands
Ryukyu Trench sea feature N. Pacific Ocean 150 E4
Rzeszów Poland 43 D6
Rzhaksa Russia 43 I5
Rzhev Russia 42 G4

S

Sa'ādah al Barṣā' pass Saudi Arabia 85 C5
Saal an der Donau Germany 53 L6
Saale r. Germany 53 L3
Saalfeld/Saale Germany 53 L4
Saanich Canada 120 F5
Saar land Germany see Saarland
Saar r. Germany 52 G5
Saarbrücken Germany 52 G5
Saaremaa i. Estonia 45 M7
Saarenkylä Fin. 44 N3
Saargau reg. Germany 52 G5
Saarijärvi Fin. 44 N5
Saari-Kämä Fin. 44 O3
Saarikoski Fin. 44 L2
Saaristomeren kansallispuisto nat. park Fin. see Skärgårdshavets nationalpark
Saarland land Germany 52 G5
Saarlouis Germany 52 G5
Saatlı Azer. 91 H3
Saatly Azer. see Saatlı
Sab'a Egypt see Saba'ah
Saba'ah Egypt 85 A4
Sab' Ābār Syria 85 C3
Šabac Serbia 59 H2
Sabadell Spain 57 H3
Sabae Japan 75 E6
Sabak Malaysia 71 C7
Sabalana i. Indon. 68 F8
Sabalana, Kepulauan is Indon. 68 F8
Sabana, Archipiélago de is Cuba 137 H4
Sabang Indon. 71 A6
Şabanözü Turkey 90 D2
Sabará Brazil 145 C2
Sabasṭīyah West Bank 85 B3
Sab'atayn, Ramlat as des. Yemen 86 G6
Sabaudia Italy 58 E4
Sabaya Bol. 142 E7
Sabelo S. Africa 100 F6
Ṣabḥā Jordan 85 C3
Sabhā Libya 97 E2
Ṣabḥā' Saudi Arabia 88 B6
Sabhrai India 82 B5
Sabi r. India 82 D3
Sabi r. Moz./Zimbabwe see Save
Sabie Moz. 101 K3
Sabie r. Moz./S. Africa 101 K3
Sabie S. Africa 101 J3
Sabina U.S.A. 134 D4
Sabinal Mex. 127 G7
Sabinal, Cayo i. Cuba 133 E8
Sabinas Mex. 131 C7
Sabinas r. Mex. 131 C7
Sabinas Hidalgo Mex. 131 C7
Sabine r. U.S.A. 131 E6
Sabine Lake U.S.A. 131 E6
Sabine Pass U.S.A. 131 E6
Sabini, Monti mts Italy 58 E3
Sabirabad Azer. 91 H2
Sabkhat al Bardawīl Reserve nature res. Egypt see Lake Bardawil Reserve
Sable, Cape Canada 123 I6
Sable, Cape U.S.A. 133 D7
Sable, Lac du l. Canada 123 I3
Sable Island Canada 123 K6
Sable Island National Park Reserve nat. park Canada 123 K6
Sabon Kafi Niger 96 D3
Şabran Azer. 91 H2
Sabrina Coast Antarctica 152 F2
Sabugal Port. 57 C3
Şabyā Saudi Arabia 86 F6
Sabzak, Kōtal-e Afgh. 89 F3
Sabzawar Afgh. see Shīndand
Sabzevār Iran 88 E2
Sabzvārān Iran see Jīroft
Sacalinul Mare, Insula i. Romania 59 M2
Sacaton U.S.A. 129 H5
Sac City U.S.A. 130 E3
Săcele Romania 59 K2
Sacheon S. Korea 75 C6
Sachigo r. Canada 121 N4
Sachigo Lake Canada 121 M4
Sachin India 82 C5
Sach Pass India 82 D2
Sachsen land Germany 53 N3
Sachsen-Anhalt land Germany 53 L2
Sachsenheim Germany 53 J6
Sachs Harbour Canada 118 F2
Sacirsuyu r. Syria/Turkey see Sājūr, Nahr
Sackpfeife hill Germany 53 I4
Sackville Canada 123 I5
Saco ME U.S.A. 135 J2
Saco MT U.S.A. 126 G2
Sacramento Brazil 145 B2

▶Sacramento U.S.A. 128 C2
Capital of California.

Sacramento r. U.S.A. 128 C2
Sacramento Mountains U.S.A. 127 G6
Sacramento Valley U.S.A. 128 B1
Sada S. Africa 101 H7
Sádaba Spain 57 F2
Sá da Bandeira Angola see Lubango
Ṣadad Syria 85 C2
Ṣa'dah Yemen 86 F6
Sadakphu mt. India/Nepal 83 G4
Sadao Thai. 71 C6
Saddat al Hindīyah Iraq 91 G4
Saddleback Mesa mt. U.S.A. 131 C5
Saddle Hill hill Australia 110 D2
Saddle Peak hill India 71 A4
Sadê China 76 D2
Sa Đec Vietnam 71 D5
Sadêng China 76 B2
Sadieville U.S.A. 134 C4
Sadīj watercourse Iran 88 E5
Sadiola Mali 96 B3

Sadiqabad Pak. 89 H4
Sad Ishtrāgh mt. Afgh./Pak. 89 I2
Sa'dīyah, Hawr as imp. l. Iraq 91 G4
Sa'dīyyat i. U.A.E. 88 D5
Sado r. Port. 57 B4
Sadoga-shima i. Japan 75 E5
Sadot Egypt see Sadūt (abandoned)
Sadovoye Russia 43 J7
Sa Dragonera i. Spain 57 H4
Sadras India 84 D3
Sadūt Egypt see Sadūt (abandoned)
Sadūt (abandoned) Egypt 85 B4
Sæby Denmark 45 G8
Saena Julia Italy see Siena
Safad Israel see Ẕefat
Şafāshahr Iran 88 D4
Safayal Maqūf well Iraq 91 G5
Safēd Khir, Kōh-e mts Afgh. 89 H2
Safēd Kōh mts Afgh./Pak. 89 H3
Safēd Kōh, Silsilah-ye mts Afgh. 89 F3
Saffānīyah, Ra's as pt Saudi Arabia 88 C4
Säffle Sweden 45 H7
Safford U.S.A. 129 I5
Saffron Walden U.K. 49 H6
Safi Morocco 54 C5
Safīd, Chashmeh-ye spring Iran 88 E3
Safidār, Kūh-e mt. Iran 88 D4
Safiras, Serra das mts Brazil 145 C2
Şāfītā Syria 85 C2
Safonovo Arkhangel'skaya Oblast' Russia 42 K2
Safonovo Smolenskaya Oblast' Russia 43 G5
Safranbolu Turkey 90 D2
Saga China 83 F3
Saga Japan 75 C6
Saga Kazakh. 80 B1
Sagaing Myanmar 70 A2
Sagami-nada g. Japan 75 E6
Sagamore U.S.A. 134 F3
Saganthit Kyun i. Myanmar 71 B4
Sagar Karnataka India 84 B3
Sagar Karnataka India 84 C2
Sagar Madh. Prad. India 82 D5
Sagaredzho Georgia see Sagarejo
Sagarejo Georgia 91 G2
Sagar Island India 83 G5
Sagarmatha National Park Nepal 83 F4
Sagastyr Russia 65 N2
Sagavanirktok r. U.S.A. 118 D2
Sage U.S.A. 126 F4
Saggi, Har mt. Israel 85 B4
Sāghand Iran 88 D3
Saginaw U.S.A. 134 D2
Saginaw Bay U.S.A. 134 D2
Saglek Bay Canada 123 J2
Saglouc Canada see Salluit
Sagone, Golfe de b. Corsica France 56 I5
Sagres Port. 57 B5
Sagthale India 82 C5
Saguache U.S.A. 127 G5
Sagua la Grande Cuba 137 H4
Saguaro Lake U.S.A. 129 H5
Saguaro National Park U.S.A. 129 H5
Saguenay r. Canada 123 H4
Sagunt Spain see Sagunto
Sagunto Spain 57 F4
Saguntum Spain see Sagunto
Sagzī Iran 88 D3
Sahagún Spain 57 D2
Sahand, Kūh-e mt. Iran 88 B2

▶Sahara des. Africa 96 D3
Largest desert in the world.

Saharan Atlas mts Alg. see Atlas Saharien
Saharanpur India 82 D3
Sahara Well Australia 108 C5
Saharsa India 83 F4
Sahaswan India 82 D3
Sahat, Kūh-e hill Iran 88 D3
Sahatwar India 83 F4
Şahbuz Azer. 91 G3
Sahdol India see Shahdol
Sahebganj India see Sahibganj
Sahebgunj India see Sahibganj
Saheira, Wâdi el watercourse Egypt see Suhaymī, Wādī as
Sahel reg. Africa 96 C3
Sahibganj India 83 F4
Sahiwal Pak. 89 I4
Sahlābād Iran 89 E3
Şaḥm Oman 88 E5
Şaḥneh Iran 88 B3
Şaḥrā al Ḥijārah reg. Iraq 91 G5
Sahuaripa Mex. 127 F7
Sahuayo Mex. 136 D4
Sahuteng China see Zadoi
Sa Huynh Vietnam 71 E4
Sahyadri mts India see Western Ghats
Sahyadriparvat Range hills India 84 B1
Sai r. India 83 E4
Sai Buri Thai. 71 C6
Saïda Alg. 57 G6
Saïda Lebanon see Sidon
Sa'īdābād Iran 88 E5
Sai Dao Tai, Khao mt. Thai. 71 C4
Saïdia Morocco 57 E6
Sa'īdīyeh Iran see Solṭānīyeh
Saidpur Bangl. 83 G4
Saiha India 83 H5
Saihan Tal China 73 K4
Saijō Japan 75 D6
Saikai Kokuritsu-kōen nat. park Japan 75 C6
Saiki Japan 75 C6
Sai Kung H.K. China 77 [inset]
Sailana India 82 C5
Saimaa l. Fin. 45 P6
Saimbeyli Turkey 90 E3
Saindak Pak. 89 F4
St Abb's Head hd U.K. 50 G5
St Agnes U.K. 49 B8
St Agnes i. U.K. 49 A9
St Alban's Canada 123 L5
St Albans U.K. 49 G7
St Albans VT U.S.A. 135 I1
St Albans WV U.S.A. 134 E4
St Alban's Head hd U.K. see St Aldhelm's Head
St Albert Canada 120 H4
St Aldhelm's Head hd U.K. 49 E8
St-Amand-les-Eaux France 52 D4
St-Amand-Montrond France 56 F3
St-Amour France 56 G3
St-André, Cap pt Madag. see Vilanandro, Tanjona
St Andrews U.K. 50 G4
St Andrew Sound inlet U.S.A. 133 D6
St Anne U.S.A. 134 B3
St Ann's Bay Jamaica 137 I5
St Anthony Canada 123 L4
St Anthony U.S.A. 126 F4
St-Arnaud Alg. see El Eulma
St Arnaud Australia 112 A6
St Arnaud Range mts N.Z. 113 D6
St-Arnoult-en-Yvelines France 52 B6
St-Augustin Canada 123 K4
St Augustin r. Canada 123 K4
St Augustine U.S.A. 133 D6
St Austell U.K. 49 C8
St-Avertin France 56 E3
St-Avold France 52 G5
St Barbe Canada 123 K4

▶St-Barthélemy i. West Indies 137 L5
French Overseas Collectivity.

St Bees U.K. 48 D4
St Bees Head hd U.K. 48 D4
St Bride's Bay U.K. 49 B7
St-Brieuc France 56 C2
St Catharines Canada 134 F2
St Catherines Island U.S.A. 133 D6
St Catherine's Point U.K. 49 F8
St-Céré France 56 E4
St-Chamond France 56 G4
St Charles ID U.S.A. 126 F4
St Charles MD U.S.A. 135 G4
St Charles MI U.S.A. 134 C2
St Charles MO U.S.A. 130 F4
St-Chély-d'Apcher France 56 F4
St Christopher and Nevis country West Indies see St Kitts and Nevis
St Clair r. Canada/U.S.A. 134 D2
St Clair, Lake Canada/U.S.A. 134 D2
St-Claude France 56 G3
St Clears U.K. 49 C7
St Cloud U.S.A. 130 E2
St Croix r. U.S.A. 122 B5
St Croix Falls U.S.A. 130 E2
St David U.S.A. 129 H6
St David's Head hd U.K. 49 B7
St-Denis France 52 C6

▶St-Denis Réunion 149 L7
Capital of Réunion.

St-Denis-du-Sig Alg. see Sig
St-Dié-des-Vosges France 56 H2
St-Dizier France 52 E6
St-Domingue country West Indies see Haiti
Sainte Anne Canada 121 L5
Ste-Anne, Lac l. Canada 123 I4
St Elias, Cape U.S.A. 118 D4

▶St Elias, Mount U.S.A. 120 A2
4th highest mountain in North America.

St Elias Mountains Canada 120 A2
Ste-Marguerite r. Canada 123 I4
Ste-Marie, Cap c. Madag. see Vohimena, Tanjona
Sainte-Marie, Île i. Madag. see Boraha, Nosy
Ste-Maxime France 56 H5
Sainte Rose du Lac Canada 121 L5
Saintes France 56 D4
Sainte Thérèse, Lac l. Canada 120 F1
St-Étienne France 56 G4
St-Étienne-du-Rouvray France 52 B5
St-Fabien Canada 123 H4
St-Félicien Canada 123 G4
Saintfield U.K. 51 G3
St-Florent Corsica France 56 I5
St-Florent-sur-Cher France 56 F3
St-Flour France 56 F4
St Francis U.S.A. 130 C4
St Francis r. U.S.A. 131 F5
St Francis Isles Australia 109 F8
St Francisville U.S.A. 131 F6
St-François r. Canada 123 G5
St-François, Lac l. Canada 123 H5
St-Gaudens France 56 E5
St George Australia 112 D2
St George r. Australia 110 D3
St George AK U.S.A. 118 B4
St George SC U.S.A. 133 D5
St George UT U.S.A. 129 G3
St George, Point U.S.A. 126 B4
St George Island U.S.A. 118 B4
St George Range hills Australia 108 D4
St-Georges Canada 123 H5

▶St George's Grenada 137 L6
Capital of Grenada.

St George's Bay Nfld. and Lab. Canada 123 K4
St George's Bay N.S. Canada 123 J5
St George's Channel Ireland/U.K. 51 F6
St George's Channel P.N.G. 106 F2
St George's Head hd Australia 112 E5
St Gotthard Hungary see Szentgotthárd
St Gotthard Pass Switz. 56 I3
St Govan's Head hd U.K. 49 C7
St Helen U.S.A. 134 C1
St Helena i. S. Atlantic Ocean 148 H7
St Helena U.S.A. 128 B2

▶St Helena, Ascension and Tristan da Cunha terr. S. Atlantic Ocean 148 H7
United Kingdom Overseas Territory.

St Helena Bay S. Africa 100 D7
St Helens Australia 111 [inset]
St Helens U.K. 48 E5
St Helens U.S.A. 126 C3
St Helens, Mount vol. U.S.A. 126 C3
St Helens Point Australia 111 [inset]

▶St Helier Channel Is 49 E9
Capital of Jersey.

Sainthiya India 83 F5
St-Hubert Belgium 52 F4
St-Hyacinthe Canada 123 G5
St Ignace U.S.A. 132 C2
St Ignace Island Canada 122 D4
St Ishmael U.K. 49 C7
St Ives England U.K. 49 B8
St Ives England U.K. 49 G6
St-Jacques, Cap Vietnam see Vung Tau
St-Jacques-de-Dupuy Canada 122 F4
St James MN U.S.A. 130 E3
St James MO U.S.A. 130 F4
St James, Cape Canada 120 D5
St-Jean r. Canada 123 I4
St-Jean, Lac l. Canada 123 G4
St-Jean-d'Acre Israel see 'Akko
St-Jean-d'Angély France 56 D4
St-Jean-de-Monts France 56 C3
St-Jean-sur-Richelieu Canada 135 I1
St-Jérôme Canada 122 G5
St Joe r. U.S.A. 126 D3
Saint John Canada 123 I5
St John U.S.A. 130 D4
St John r. U.S.A. 132 H2
St John, Cape Canada 123 L4
St John Bay Canada 123 K4
St John Island Canada 123 K4

▶St John's Antigua and Barbuda 137 L5
Capital of Antigua and Barbuda.

▶St John's Canada 123 L5
Capital of Newfoundland and Labrador.

St Johns AZ U.S.A. 129 I4
St Johns MI U.S.A. 134 C2
St Johns OH U.S.A. 134 C3
St Johns r. U.S.A. 133 D6
St Johnsbury U.S.A. 135 I1
St John's Chapel U.K. 48 E4
St Joseph IL U.S.A. 134 A3
St Joseph LA U.S.A. 131 F6
St Joseph MI U.S.A. 134 B2
St Joseph MO U.S.A. 130 E4
St Joseph r. U.S.A. 134 C3
St Joseph, Lake Canada 121 N5
St-Joseph-d'Alma Canada see Alma
St Joseph Island Canada 122 E5
St-Junien France 56 E4
St Just U.K. 49 B8
St-Just-en-Chaussée France 52 C5
St Keverne U.K. 49 B8
St Kilda i. U.K. 40 E4
St Kilda is U.K. 46 C2
St Kitts and Nevis country West Indies 137 L5
St-Laurent inlet Canada see St Lawrence
St-Laurent, Golfe du g. Canada see St Lawrence, Gulf of
St-Laurent-du-Maroni Fr. Guiana 143 H2
St Lawrence Canada 123 L5
St Lawrence inlet Canada 123 H4
St Lawrence, Cape Canada 123 J5
St Lawrence, Gulf of Canada 123 J4
St Lawrence Island U.S.A. 118 B3
St Lawrence Islands National Park Canada 135 H1
St Lawrence Seaway sea chan. Canada/U.S.A. 135 H1
St-Léonard Canada 123 G5
St Leonard U.S.A. 135 G4
St Lewis r. Canada 123 K3
St-Lô France 56 D2
St-Louis Senegal 96 B3
St Louis MI U.S.A. 134 C2
St Louis MO U.S.A. 130 F4
St Louis r. U.S.A. 122 B5
St Lucia country West Indies 137 L6
St Lucia, Lake S. Africa 101 K5
St Lucia Estuary S. Africa 101 K5
St Luke's Island Myanmar see Zadetkale Kyun
St Magnus Bay U.K. 50 [inset]
St-Maixent-l'École France 56 D3
St-Malo France 56 C2
St-Malo, Golfe de g. France 56 C2
St-Marc Haiti 137 J5
St Maries U.S.A. 126 D3
St Marks S. Africa 101 H7
St Mark's S. Africa see Cofimvaba

▶St-Martin i. West Indies 137 L5
French Overseas Collectivity. The southern part of the island is the Dutch territory of Sint Maarten.

▶St Maarten terr. West Indies 137 L5
Self-governing Netherlands Territory. The northern part of the island is the French Overseas Collectivity of St-Martin.

St Martin, Cape S. Africa 100 C7
St Martin, Lake Canada 121 L5
St Martin's i. U.K. 49 A9
St Martin's Island Bangl. 70 A2
St Mary Peak Australia 111 B6
St Mary Reservoir Canada 120 H5
St Mary's Canada 134 E2
St Mary's U.K. 50 G2
St Mary's i. U.K. 49 A9
St Marys PA U.S.A. 135 F3
St Marys WV U.S.A. 134 E4
St Marys r. U.S.A. 134 C3
St Mary's, Cape Canada 123 L5
St Mary's Bay Canada 123 L5
St Marys City U.S.A. 135 G4
St Matthew Island U.S.A. 118 A3
St Matthews U.S.A. 134 C4
St Matthew's Island Myanmar see Zadetkyi Kyun
St Matthias Group is P.N.G. 69 L7
St-Maurice r. Canada 123 G5
St Mawes U.K. 49 B8
St-Médard-en-Jalles France 56 D4
St Meinrad U.S.A. 134 B4
St Michaels U.S.A. 135 G4
St Michael's Bay Canada 123 L3
St-Mihiel France 52 F6
St-Nazaire France 56 C3
St Neots U.K. 49 G6
St-Nicolas Belgium see Sint-Niklaas
St-Nicolas, Mont hill Lux. 52 G5
St-Nicolas-de-Port France 56 H2
St-Omer France 52 C4
Saintonge reg. France 56 D4
St-Pacôme Canada 123 H5
St-Palais France 56 D5
St Paris U.S.A. 134 D3
St-Pascal Canada 123 H5
St Paul r. Canada 123 K4
St-Paul atoll Fr. Polynesia see Hereheretue
St Paul AK U.S.A. 118 A4

▶St Paul MN U.S.A. 130 E2
Capital of Minnesota.

St Paul NE U.S.A. 130 D3
St-Paul, Île i. Indian Ocean 149 N8
St Paul Island U.S.A. 118 A4
St Peter and St Paul Rocks is N. Atlantic Ocean see São Pedro e São Paulo

▶St Peter Port Channel Is 49 E9
Capital of Guernsey.

St Peter's Canada 123 J5
St Peters Canada 123 J5
St Petersburg Russia 45 Q7
St Petersburg U.S.A. 133 D7
St-Pierre mt. France 56 G5

▶St-Pierre St Pierre and Miquelon 123 L5
Capital of St Pierre and Miquelon.

▶St Pierre and Miquelon terr. N. America 123 K5
French Territorial Collectivity.

St-Pierre-d'Oléron France 56 D4
St-Pierre-le-Moûtier France 56 F3
St-Pol-sur-Ternoise France 52 C4
St-Pourçain-sur-Sioule France 56 F3
St-Quentin France 52 D5
St Regis U.S.A. 126 E3
St Regis Falls U.S.A. 135 H1
St-Rémi Canada 135 I1
St-Saëns France 52 B5
St Sebastian Bay S. Africa 100 E8
St-Siméon Canada 123 H5
St Simons Island U.S.A. 133 D6
St Theresa Point Canada 121 M4
St Thomas Canada 134 E2
St-Trond Belgium see Sint-Truiden
St-Tropez France 56 H5
St-Tropez, Cap de c. France 56 H5
St-Vaast-la-Hougue France 49 F9
St-Valery-en-Caux France 49 H9
St-Véran France 56 H4
St Vincent U.S.A. 130 D1
St Vincent country West Indies see St Vincent and the Grenadines
St Vincent, Cape Australia 111 [inset]
St Vincent, Cape Port. see São Vicente, Cabo de
St Vincent, Gulf Australia 111 B7
St Vincent and the Grenadines country West Indies 137 L6
St Vincent Passage St Lucia/St Vincent 137 L6
St-Vith Belgium 52 G4
St Walburg Canada 121 I4
St Williams Canada 134 E2
St-Yrieix-la-Perche France 56 E4
Sain Us China 72 J4
Saioa mt. Spain 57 F2
Saipal mt. Nepal 82 E3
Saipan i. N. Mariana Is 69 L3
Saiteli Turkey see Kadınhanı
Saittanulkki hill Fin. 44 N3
Sai Yok National Park Thai. 71 B4
Sajam Indon. 69 I7
Sajama, Nevado mt. Bol. 142 E7
Sājir Saudi Arabia 88 B5
Sājūr, Nahr r. Syria/Turkey 85 D1
Sak watercourse S. Africa 100 E5
Sakaide Japan 75 D6
Sakākā Saudi Arabia 91 F5
Sakakawea, Lake U.S.A. 130 C2
Sakami Canada 122 G3
Sakami r. Canada 122 F3
Sakami Lake Canada 122 F3
Sakar mts Bulg. 59 L4
Sakaraha Madag. 99 E6
Sak'art'velo country Asia see Georgia
Sakarya Turkey see Adapazarı
Sakarya r. Turkey 59 N4
Sakassou Côte d'Ivoire 96 C4
Sakata Japan 75 E5
Sakchu N. Korea 75 B4
Sakesar Pak. 89 I3
Sakhalin i. Russia 74 F2
Sakhalin Oblast admin. div. Russia see Sakhalinskaya Oblast'
Sakhalinskaya Oblast' admin. div. Russia 74 F2
Sakhalinskiy Zaliv b. Russia 74 F1
Sakhi India 82 C3
Sakhile S. Africa 101 I4
Şäki Azer. 91 G2
Saki Crimea see Saky
Saki Nigeria 96 D4
Šakiai Lith. 45 M9
Sakir mt. Pak. 89 G4
Sakishima-shotō is Japan 73 M8
Sakoli India 82 D5
Sakon Nakhon Thai. 70 D3
Sakrivier S. Africa 100 E6
Sakura Japan 75 F6
Saky Crimea 90 D1
Säkylä Fin. 45 M6
Säkzā'ī Afgh. 89 F3
Sal i. Cape Verde 96 [inset]
Sal r. Russia 43 I7
Sala Sweden 45 J7
Salaberry-de-Valleyfield Canada 135 H1
Salacgrīva Latvia 45 N8
Sala Consilina Italy 58 F4
Salada, Laguna salt l. Mex. 129 F5
Saladas Arg. 144 E3
Salado r. Buenos Aires Arg. 144 E5
Salado r. Santa Fe Arg. 144 D4
Salado r. Arg. 144 C5
Salado r. Mex. 131 D7
Salaga Ghana 96 C4
Salairskiy Kryazh ridge Russia 72 E2
Salajwe Botswana 100 G2
Şalālah Oman 87 H6
Salamanca Mex. 136 D4
Salamanca Spain 57 D3
Salamanca U.S.A. 135 F2
Salamanga Moz. 101 K4
Salamantica Spain see Salamanca
Salamat, Bahr r. Chad 97 E4
Salāmī Iran 89 E3
Salamina i. Greece 59 J6
Salamis tourist site Cyprus 85 A2
Salamís i. Greece see Salamina
Salamīyah Syria 85 C2
Salamonie r. U.S.A. 134 C3
Salamonie Lake U.S.A. 134 C3
Salang, Tōnal-e Afgh. 89 H3
Salantai Lith. 45 L8
Salar de Pocitos Arg. 144 C2
Salari Pak. 89 G5
Salas Spain 57 C2
Salaspils Latvia 45 N8
Salavan Laos 70 D4
Salawati i. Indon. 69 I7
Salawin, Mae Nam r. China/Myanmar see Salween
Salaya India 82 B5
Sala y Gómez, Isla i. S. Pacific Ocean 151 M7
Salazar Angola see N'dalatando
Salbris France 56 F3
Šalčininkai Lith. 45 N9
Salcombe U.K. 49 D8
Saldae Alg. see Bejaïa
Saldaña Spain 57 D2
Saldanha S. Africa 100 C7
Saldanha Bay S. Africa 100 C7
Saldus Latvia 45 M8
Sale Australia 112 C7
Saleh, Teluk b. Indon. 68 F8
Şāleḥābād Iran 88 C3
Salekhard Russia 64 H3
Salem India 84 C4
Salem AR U.S.A. 131 F4
Salem IL U.S.A. 130 F4
Salem IN U.S.A. 134 B4
Salem MA U.S.A. 135 J2
Salem MO U.S.A. 130 F4
Salem NJ U.S.A. 135 H4
Salem NY U.S.A. 135 I2
Salem OH U.S.A. 134 E3

▶Salem OR U.S.A. 126 C3
Capital of Oregon.

Salem SD U.S.A. 130 D3
Salem VA U.S.A. 134 E5
Salen Scotland U.K. 50 D4
Salen Scotland U.K. 50 D4
Salerno Italy 58 F4
Salerno, Golfo di g. Italy 58 F4
Salernum Italy see Salerno
Salford U.K. 48 E5
Salgótarján Hungary 47 Q6
Salgueiro Brazil 143 K5
Salibabu i. Indon. 69 H6
Salida U.S.A. 127 G5
Salies-de-Béarn France 56 D5
Şāliḥān Afgh. 89 F4
Salihli Turkey 59 M5
Salihorsk Belarus 45 O10
Salima Malawi 99 D5
Salina KS U.S.A. 130 D4
Salina UT U.S.A. 129 H2
Salina, Isola i. Italy 58 F5
Salina Cruz Mex. 136 E5
Salinas Brazil 145 C2
Salinas Ecuador 142 B4
Salinas Mex. 136 D4
Salinas r. Mex. 131 D7
Salinas U.S.A. 128 C3
Salinas r. U.S.A. 128 C3
Salinas, Cabo de c. Spain see Salines, Cap de ses
Salinas, Ponta das pt Angola 99 B5
Salinas Peak U.S.A. 127 G6
Saline U.S.A. 134 D2
Saline r. U.S.A. 130 D4
Salines, Cap de ses c. Spain 57 H4
Saline Valley depr. U.S.A. 128 E3
Salinópolis Brazil 143 I4
Salinosó Lachay, Punta pt Peru 142 C6
Salisbury U.K. 49 F7
Salisbury MD U.S.A. 135 H4
Salisbury NC U.S.A. 132 D5
Salisbury Zimbabwe see Harare
Salisbury Plain U.K. 49 E7
Şalkhad Syria 85 C3
Salla Fin. 44 P3
Sallisaw U.S.A. 131 E5
Salluit Canada 153 K2
Sallum, Khalīj as b. Egypt 90 B5
Sallyana Nepal 83 E3
Salmās Iran 88 B2
Salmi Russia 42 F3
Salmo Canada 120 G5
Salmon U.S.A. 126 E3
Salmon r. U.S.A. 126 D3
Salmon Arm Canada 120 G5
Salmon Falls Creek r. U.S.A. 126 E4
Salmon Gums Australia 109 C8
Salmon Reservoir U.S.A. 135 H2
Salmon River Mountains U.S.A. 126 E3
Salmtal Germany 52 G5
Salo Fin. 45 M6
Salome U.S.A. 129 G5
Salon India 82 E4
Salon-de-Provence France 56 G5
Salonga Nord, Parc National de la nat. park Dem. Rep. Congo 98 C4
Salonica Greece see Thessaloniki
Salonika Greece see Thessaloniki
Saloum Delta tourist site Senegal 96 B3
Salpausselkä reg. Fin. 45 N6
Salqīn Syria 85 C1
Salses, Étang de l. France see Leucate, Étang de
Sal'sk Russia 43 I7
Salsomaggiore Terme Italy 58 C2
Salt Jordan see As Salṭ
Salt watercourse S. Africa 100 F7
Salt r. U.S.A. 129 G5
Salta Arg. 144 C2
Saltaire U.K. 48 F5
Saltash U.K. 49 C8
Saltcoats U.K. 50 E5
Saltee Islands Ireland 51 F5
Saltfjellet-Svartisen Nasjonalpark nat. park Norway 44 I3
Saltfjorden sea chan. Norway 44 H3
Salt Fork Arkansas r. U.S.A. 131 D4
Salt Fork Lake U.S.A. 134 E3
Saltillo Mex. 131 C7
Salt Lake India 89 I5

▶Salt Lake City U.S.A. 129 H1
Capital of Utah.

Salt Lick U.S.A. 134 D4
Salto Brazil 145 B3
Salto Uruguay 144 E4
Salto da Divisa Brazil 145 D2
Salto Grande Brazil 145 A3
Salton Sea salt l. U.S.A. 129 F5
Salto Santiago, Represa de resr Brazil 144 F3
Salt Range hills Pak. 89 I3
Salt River Canada 121 H2
Saluda U.S.A. 135 G5
Salūk, Kūh-e mt. Iran 88 E2
Salûm Egypt see As Sallūm
Salûm, Khalîg el b. Egypt see Sallum, Khalīj as
Salur India 84 D2
Saluzzo Italy 58 B2
Salvador Brazil 145 D1
Salvador country Central America see El Salvador
Salvador, Lake U.S.A. 131 F6
Salvaleón de Higüey Dom. Rep. see Higüey
Salvation Creek r. U.S.A. 129 H2
Salwah Saudi Arabia 98 F1
Salwah, Dawḥat b. Qatar/Saudi Arabia 88 C5
Salween r. China/Myanmar 76 C5
also known as Mae Nam Khong or Mae Nam Salawin or Nu Jiang (China) or Thanlwin (Myanmar)
Salyan Azer. 91 H3
Salyan Nepal see Sallyana
Sal'yany Azer. see Salyan
Salyersville U.S.A. 134 D5
Salzbrunn Namibia 100 C3
Salzburg Austria 47 N7
Salzgitter Germany 53 K2
Salzhausen Germany 53 K1
Salzkotten Germany 53 I3
Salzmünde Germany 53 L3
Salzwedel Germany 53 L2
Sam India 82 B4
Samae San, Ko i. Thai. 71 C4
Samagaltay Russia 80 H1
Samāh well Saudi Arabia 88 B4
Samaida Iran see Someydeh
Samaixung China 83 E2
Samakhixai Laos see Attapu
Samalanga Indon. 71 B6
Samalayuca Mex. 127 G7
Samalkot India 84 D2
Samālūṭ Egypt 90 C5
Samâlût Egypt see Samālūṭ
Samana Cay i. Bahamas 133 F8
Samanala mt. Sri Lanka see Adam's Peak
Samandağı Turkey 85 B1
Samangān Afgh. see Aībak
Samangān Iran 89 F3
Samani Japan 74 F4
Samanlı Dağları mts Turkey 59 M4
Samar Kazakh. see Samarskoye
Samar i. Phil. 69 H4
Samara Russia 43 K5
Samara r. Russia 41 Q5
Samarga Russia 74 E3
Samarinda Indon. 68 F7
Samarka Russia 74 D3
Samarkand Uzbek. see Samarqand
Samarkand, Pik mt. Tajik. see Samarqand, Qullai
Samarobriva France see Amiens
Samarqand Uzbek. 89 G2
Samarqand, Qullai mt. Tajik. 89 H2
Sāmarrā' Iraq 91 F4
Samarskoye Kazakh. 80 F2
Samasata Pak. 89 H4
Samastipur India 83 F4
Şamaxı Azer. 91 H2
Samba India 82 C2
Sambaliung mts Indon. 68 F6
Sambalpur India 83 E5
Sambar, Tanjung pt Indon. 68 E7
Sambas Indon. 71 E7
Sambat Ukr. see Kiev
Sambava Madag. 99 F5
Sambha India 83 G4
Sambhajinagar India see Aurangabad
Sambhal India 82 D3
Sambhar Lake India 82 C4
Sambir Ukr. 43 D6
Sambito r. Brazil 143 J5
Sâmbor Cambodia 71 D4
Sambor Ukr. see Sambir
Samborombón, Bahía b. Arg. 144 E5
Sambre r. Belgium/France 52 E4
Sambre à l'Oise, Canal de la France 52 D5
Samcheok S. Korea 75 C5
Samch'ŏnp'o S. Korea see Sacheon
Same Tanz. 98 D4
Samer France 52 B4
Sami India 82 B5
Samīrah Saudi Arabia 86 F4
Samīrum Iran see Īzad Khvāst

Samjiyŏn N. Korea 74 C4
Şämkir Azer. 91 G2
Sam Neua Laos see Xam Nua
Samoa country S. Pacific Ocean 107 I3
Samoa Basin sea feature S. Pacific Ocean 150 I7
Samoa i Sisifo country S. Pacific Ocean see Samoa
Samobor Croatia 58 F2
Samoded Russia 42 I3
Samokov Bulg. 59 J3
Šamorín Slovakia 47 P6
Samos i. Greece 59 L6
Samosir i. Indon. 71 B7
Samothrace i. Greece see Samothraki
Samothraki i. Greece 59 K4
Samoylovka Russia 43 I6
Sampit Indon. 68 E7
Sampit, Teluk b. Indon. 68 E7
Sâmraông Cambodia 71 C4
Sam Rayburn Reservoir U.S.A. 131 E6
Samrong Cambodia see Sâmraông
Samsang China 83 E3
Sam Sao, Phou mts Laos/Vietnam 70 C2
Samson U.S.A. 133 C6
Sâm Sơn Vietnam 70 D3
Samsun Turkey 90 E2
Samtī Afgh. 89 H2
Samuel, Represa de resr Brazil 142 F5
Samui, Ko i. Thai. 71 C5
Samut Prakan Thai. 71 C4
Samut Sakhon Thai. 71 C4
Samut Songkhram Thai. 71 C4
Samyai China 83 G3
San Mali 96 C3
San, Phou mt. Laos 70 C3
San, Tônlé r. Cambodia 71 D4

▶Şan'ā' Yemen 86 F6
Capital of Yemen.

Sanaa Yemen see Şan'ā'
SANAE IV research station Antarctica 152 B2
San Agostín U.S.A. see St Augustine
San Agustin, Cape Phil. 69 H5
San Agustin, Plains of U.S.A. 129 I5
San Agustín de Valle Fértil Arg. 144 C4
Sanak Island U.S.A. 118 B4
Sanandaj Iran 88 B3
San Andreas U.S.A. 128 C2
San Andrés, Isla de i. Caribbean Sea 137 H6
San Andres Mountains U.S.A. 127 G6
San Angelo U.S.A. 131 C6
San Antonio Chile 144 B4
San Antonio NM U.S.A. 127 G6
San Antonio TX U.S.A. 131 D6
San Antonio r. U.S.A. 131 D6
San Antonio, Cabo c. Cuba 137 H4
San Antonio del Mar Mex. 127 D7
San Antonio Oeste Arg. 144 D6
San Antonio Reservoir U.S.A. 128 C4
San Augustine U.S.A. 131 E6
San Benedetto del Tronto Italy 58 E3
San Benedicto, Isla i. Mex. 136 B5
San Benito U.S.A. 131 D7
San Benito r. U.S.A. 128 C3
San Benito Mountain U.S.A. 128 C3
San Bernardino U.S.A. 128 E4
San Bernardino Mountains U.S.A. 128 E4
San Bernardo Chile 144 B4
San Blas Mex. 127 F8
San Blas, Cape U.S.A. 133 C6
San Borja Bol. 142 E6
Sanbornville U.S.A. 135 J2
Sanbu China see Kaiping
San Buenaventura Mex. 131 C7
San Carlos Chile 144 B5
San Carlos Equat. Guinea see Luba
San Carlos Coahuila Mex. 131 C6
San Carlos Tamaulipas Mex. 131 D7
San Carlos U.S.A. 129 H5
San Carlos Venez. 142 E2
San Carlos de Bariloche Arg. 144 B6
San Carlos de Bolívar Arg. 144 D5
San Carlos Lake U.S.A. 129 H5
Sancha China 76 E1
Sanchahe China see Fuyu
Sancha He r. China 76 E3
Sanchakou China 80 I4
Sanchi India 82 D5
San Chien Pau mt. Laos 70 C2
Sanchor India 82 B4
San Clemente U.S.A. 128 E5
San Clemente Island U.S.A. 128 D5
Sanclêr U.K. see St Clears
San Cristóbal Arg. 144 D4
San Cristóbal i. Solomon Is see Makira
San Cristóbal Venez. 142 D2
San Cristóbal, Isla i. Galápagos Ecuador 142 [inset]
San Cristóbal de las Casas Mex. 136 F5
Sancti Spíritus Cuba 137 I4
Sandagou Russia 74 D4
Sanda Island U.K. 50 D5
Sandakan Sabah Malaysia 68 F5
Sândăn Cambodia 71 D4
Sandane Norway 44 E6
Sandanski Bulg. 59 J4
Sandaré Mali 96 B3
Sandau (Elbe) Germany 53 M2
Sanday i. U.K. 50 G1
Sandbach U.K. 49 E5
Sandborn U.S.A. 134 B4
Sand Cay reef India 84 B4
Sandefjord Norway 45 G7
Sandercock Nunataks Antarctica 152 D2
Sanders U.S.A. 129 I4
Sandersleben Germany 53 L3
Sanderson U.S.A. 131 C6
Sandfire Australia 108 C4
Sand Fork U.S.A. 134 E4
Sandgate Australia 112 F1
Sandhead U.K. 50 E6
Sand Hill r. U.S.A. 130 D2
Sand Hills U.S.A. 130 C3
Sandia Peru 142 E6
San Diego Mex. 131 B6
San Diego CA U.S.A. 128 E5
San Diego TX U.S.A. 131 D7
San Diego, Sierra mts Mex. 127 F7
Sandıklı Turkey 59 N5
Sandila India 82 E4
Sand Lake Canada 122 D5
Sand Lake l. Canada 121 M5
Sandnes Norway 45 D7
Sandnessjøen Norway 44 H3
Sandoa Dem. Rep. Congo 99 C4
Sandomierz Poland 43 D6
San Donà di Piave Italy 58 E2
Sandover watercourse Australia 110 B4
Sandovo Russia 42 H4
Sandoway Myanmar see Thandwe
Sandown U.K. 49 F8
Sandoy i. Faroe Is 44 [inset 2]
Sand Point U.S.A. 118 B4
Sandpoint U.S.A. 126 D2
Sandray i. U.K. 50 B4
Sandringham Australia 110 B5
Şandrul Mare, Vârful mt. Romania 59 L1
Sandsjö Sweden 45 I6
Sandspit Canada 120 D4
Sand Springs U.S.A. 131 D4
Sand Springs Salt Flat U.S.A. 128 D2
Sandstone Australia 109 B6
Sandstone U.S.A. 130 E2
Sandu Guizhou China 76 E3
Sandu Hunan China 77 G3
Sandur Faroe Is 44 [inset 2]
Sandusky MI U.S.A. 134 D2
Sandusky OH U.S.A. 134 D3
Sandveld mts S. Africa 100 D6
Sandverhaar Namibia 100 C4
Sandvika Akershus Norway 45 G7
Sandvika Nord-Trøndelag Norway 44 H5
Sandviken Sweden 45 J6
Sandwich Bay Canada 123 K3
Sandwich Island Vanuatu see Éfaté
Sandwich Islands is N. Pacific Ocean see Hawai'ian Islands
Sandwick U.K. 50 [inset]
Sandwip Bangl. 83 G5
Sandy U.S.A. 129 H1
Sandy r. U.S.A. 135 K1
Sandy Bay Canada 121 K4
Sandy Cape Qld Australia 110 F5
Sandy Cape Tas. Australia 111 [inset]
Sandy Hook U.S.A. 134 D4
Sandy Hook pt U.S.A. 135 H3
Sandy Island Australia 108 C3
Sandykgachy Turkm. see Sandykgaçy
Sandykgaçy Turkm. 89 F2
Sandykly Gumy des. Turkm. 89 F2
Sandy Lake Alta Canada 120 H4
Sandy Lake Ont. Canada 121 M4
Sandy Lake l. Canada 121 M4
Sandy Springs U.S.A. 133 C5
San Estanislao Para. 144 E2
San Esteban, Isla i. Mex. 127 E7
San Felipe Chile 144 B4
San Felipe Baja California Mex. 127 E7
San Felipe Chihuahua Mex. 127 G8
San Felipe Venez. 142 E1
San Felipe, Cayos de is Cuba 133 D8
San Felipe de Puerto Plata Dom. Rep. see Puerto Plata
San Fernando Chile 144 B4
San Fernando Mex. 131 D7
San Fernando watercourse Mex. 127 E7
San Fernando Phil. 69 G3
San Fernando Spain 57 C5
San Fernando Trin. and Tob. 137 L6
San Fernando U.S.A. 128 D4
San Fernando de Apure Venez. 142 E2
San Fernando de Atabapo Venez. 142 E3
San Fernando de Monte Cristi Dom. Rep. see Monte Cristi
Sanford FL U.S.A. 133 D6
Sanford ME U.S.A. 135 J2
Sanford MI U.S.A. 134 C2
Sanford NC U.S.A. 132 E5
Sanford, Mount U.S.A. 118 D3
Sanford Lake U.S.A. 134 C2
San Francisco Arg. 144 D4
San Francisco U.S.A. 128 B3
San Francisco, Cabo de c. Ecuador 142 B3
San Francisco, Passo de pass Arg./Chile 144 C3
San Francisco Bay inlet U.S.A. 128 B3
San Francisco del Oro Mex. 131 B7
San Francisco de Paula, Cabo c. Arg. 144 C7
Sang, Loi mt. Myanmar 70 B2
San Gabriel, Punta pt Mex. 127 E7
San Gabriel Mountains U.S.A. 128 D4
Sangachaly Azer. see Sanqaçal
Sangameshwar India 84 B2
Sangamon r. U.S.A. 130 F3
Sangān, Kōh-e mt. Afgh. 89 G3
Sangan, Koh-i- mt. Afgh. see Sangān, Kōh-e
Sangar Russia 65 N3
Sangareddi India see Sangareddy
Sangareddy India 84 C2
San Gavino Monreale Sardinia Italy 58 C5
Sangay, Parque Nacional nat. park Ecuador 142 C4
Sang Bar Afgh. 89 F3
Sangdankangsang Feng mt. China 83 G3
Sangeang i. Indon. 108 B2
Sanger U.S.A. 128 D3
Sangerfield U.S.A. 135 H2
Sangerhausen Germany 53 L3
Sang-e Surakh Iran 88 E2
Sanggarmai China 76 D1
Sanggau Indon. 68 E6
San Giovanni in Fiore Italy 58 G5
Sangir India 82 C5
Sangir i. Indon. 69 H6
Sangir, Kepulauan is Indon. 69 G6
Sangkapura Indon. 68 E8
Sangkulirang Indon. 68 F6
Sangli India 84 B2
Sangmai China see Dêrong
Sangmélima Cameroon 96 E4
Sangngagqoiling China 76 B2
Sango Zimbabwe 99 D6
Sangole India 84 B2
San Gorgonio Mountain U.S.A. 128 E4
Sangre de Cristo Range mts U.S.A. 127 G5
Sangrur India 82 C3
Sangu r. Bangl. 83 G5
Sanguem India 84 B3
Sangutane r. Moz. 101 K3
Sangzhi China 77 F2
Sanhe China see Sandu
San Hipólito, Punta pt Mex. 127 E8
Sanhūr Egypt 90 C5
Sanhûr Egypt see Sanhūr
San Ignacio Beni Bol. 142 E6
San Ignacio Santa Cruz Bol. 142 F7
San Ignacio Santa Cruz Bol. 142 F7
San Ignacio Baja California Mex. 127 E7
San Ignacio Durango Mex. 131 C7
San Ignacio Sonora Mex. 127 F7
San Ignacio Para. 144 E3
San Ignacio, Laguna l. Mex. 127 E8
Sanikiluaq Canada 122 F2
Sanin-kaigan Kokuritsu-kōen nat. park Japan 75 D6
San Jacinto U.S.A. 128 E5
San Jacinto Peak U.S.A. 128 E5
San Javier Bol. 142 F7
Sanjiang Guangdong China see Liannan
Sanjiang Guangxi China 77 F3
Sanjiang Guizhou China see Jinping
Sanjiangkou China 74 A4
Sanjiaocheng China see Haiyan
Sanjiaoping China 77 F2
Sanjō Japan 75 E5
San Joaquin r. U.S.A. 128 C2
San Joaquin Valley U.S.A. 128 C3
Sanjoli India 82 C5
San Jon U.S.A. 131 C5
San Jorge, Golfo de g. Arg. 144 C7
San Jorge, Golfo de g. Spain see Sant Jordi, Golf de

▶San José Costa Rica 137 H7
Capital of Costa Rica.

San Jose Phil. 69 G3
San Jose CA U.S.A. 128 C3
San Jose NM U.S.A. 127 G6
San Jose watercourse U.S.A. 129 J4
San José, Isla i. Mex. 136 B4
San José de Amacuro Venez. 142 F2
San José de Bavicora Mex. 127 G7
San Jose de Buenavista Phil. 69 G4
San José de Chiquitos Bol. 142 F7
San José de Comondú Mex. 127 F8
San José de Gracia Mex. 127 E8
San José de la Brecha Mex. 127 F8
San José de las Lajas Cuba 133 D8
San José del Cabo Mex. 136 C4
San José del Guaviare Col. 142 D3
San José de Mayo Uruguay 144 E4
San José de Raíces Mex. 131 C7
San Juan Arg. 144 C4
San Juan r. Costa Rica/Nicaragua 137 H6
San Juan mt. Cuba 133 D8
San Juan Mex. 127 G8
San Juan r. Mex. 131 D7

▶San Juan Puerto Rico 137 K5
Capital of Puerto Rico.

San Juan U.S.A. 129 J5
San Juan r. U.S.A. 129 H3
San Juan, Cabo c. Arg. 144 D8
San Juan, Cabo c. Equat. Guinea 96 D4
San Juan Bautista Para. 144 E3
San Juan Bautista de las Misiones Para. see San Juan Bautista
San Juan de Guadalupe Mex. 131 C7
San Juan de los Morros Venez. 142 E2
San Juan Mountains U.S.A. 129 J3
San Juan y Martínez Cuba 133 D8
San Justo Arg. 144 D4
Sankari Drug India 84 C4
Sankh r. India 81 F7
Sankhu India 82 C3
Sankra Chhattisgarh India 84 D1
Sankra Rajasthan India 82 B4
Sankt Augustin Germany 53 H4
Sankt Gallen Switz. 56 I3
Sankt-Peterburg Russia see St Petersburg
Sankt Pölten Austria 47 O6
Sankt Veit an der Glan Austria 47 O7
Sankt Vith Belgium see St-Vith
Sankt Wendel Germany 53 H5
Sanku India 82 D2
Şanlıurfa Turkey 90 E3
Şanlıurfa prov. Turkey 85 D1
San Lorenzo Arg. 144 D4
San Lorenzo Beni Bol. 142 E7
San Lorenzo Tarija Bol. 142 F8
San Lorenzo Ecuador 142 C3
San Lorenzo mt. Spain 57 E2
San Lorenzo, Isla i. Mex. 127 E7
San Lorenzo, Monte mt. Arg./Chile 144 B7
Sanlúcar de Barrameda Spain 57 C5
San Lucas Mex. 127 E8
San Lucas, Serranía de mts Col. 142 D2
San Luis Arg. 144 C4
San Luis AZ U.S.A. 129 F5
San Luis AZ U.S.A. 129 H5
San Luis CO U.S.A. 131 B4
San Luis, Isla i. Mex. 127 E7
San Luisito Mex. 127 E7
San Luis Obispo U.S.A. 128 C4
San Luis Obispo Bay U.S.A. 128 C4
San Luis Potosí Mex. 136 D4
San Luis Reservoir U.S.A. 128 C3
San Luis Río Colorado Mex. 129 F5
San Manuel U.S.A. 129 H5
San Marcial, Punta pt Mex. 127 F8
San Marcos U.S.A. 131 D6
San Marcos, Isla i. Mex. 127 E8
San Marino country Europe 58 E3

▶San Marino San Marino 58 E3
Capital of San Marino.

San Martín research station Antarctica 152 L2
San Martín Catamarca Arg. 144 C3
San Martín Mendoza Arg. 144 C4
San Martín, Lago l. Arg./Chile 144 B7
San Martín de los Andes Arg. 144 B6
San Mateo U.S.A. 128 B3
San Mateo Mountains U.S.A. 129 J4
San Matías Bol. 143 G7
San Matías, Golfo g. Arg. 144 D6
Sanmen China 77 I2
Sanmen Wan b. China 77 I2
Sanmenxia China 77 F1
San Miguel El Salvador 136 G6
San Miguel U.S.A. 128 C4
San Miguel r. U.S.A. 129 I2
San Miguel de Huachi Bol. 142 E7
San Miguel de Tucumán Arg. 144 C3
San Miguel Island U.S.A. 128 C4
Sanming China 77 H3
Sanndraigh i. U.K. see Sandray
Sannicandro Garganico Italy 58 F4
San Nicolás Durango Mex. 131 B7
San Nicolás Tamaulipas Mex. 131 D7
San Nicolas Island U.S.A. 128 D5
Sannieshof S. Africa 101 G4
Sanniquellie Liberia 96 C4
Sanok Poland 43 D6
San Pablo Bol. 142 E8
San Pablo Phil. 69 G4
San Pablo de Manta Ecuador see Manta
San Pedro Arg. 144 D2
San Pedro Bol. 142 F7
San Pedro Chile 144 C2
San-Pédro Côte d'Ivoire 96 C4
San Pedro Baja California Sur Mex. 124 E7
San Pedro Chihuahua Mex. 127 G7
San Pedro Para. see San Pedro de Ycuamandyyú
San Pedro watercourse U.S.A. 129 H5
San Pedro, Sierra de mts Spain 57 C4
San Pedro Channel U.S.A. 128 D5
San Pedro de Arimena Col. 142 D3
San Pedro de Atacama Chile 144 C2
San Pedro de las Colonias Mex. 131 C7
San Pedro de Macorís Dom. Rep. 137 K5
San Pedro de Ycuamandyyú Para. 144 E2
San Pedro Martir, Parque Nacional nat. park Mex. 127 E7
San Pedro Sula Hond. 136 G5
San Pierre U.S.A. 134 B3
San Pietro, Isola di i. Sardinia Italy 58 C5
San Pitch r. U.S.A. 129 H2
Sanqaçal Azer. 91 H2
Sanquhar U.K. 50 F5
Sanquianga, Parque Nacional nat. park Col. 142 C3
San Quintín, Cabo c. Mex. 127 D7
San Rafael Arg. 144 C4
San Rafael CA U.S.A. 128 B3
San Rafael NM U.S.A. 129 J4
San Rafael r. U.S.A. 129 H2
San Rafael Knob mt. U.S.A. 129 H2
San Rafael Mountains U.S.A. 128 C4
San Ramón Bol. 142 F6
Sanrao China 77 H3
Sanremo Italy 58 B3
San Roque Spain 57 B2
San Roque, Punta pt Mex. 127 E8
San Saba U.S.A. 131 D6
San Salvador i. Bahamas 133 F7

▶San Salvador El Salvador 136 G6
Capital of El Salvador.

San Salvador de Jujuy Arg. 144 C2
Sansanné-Mango Togo 96 D3
San Sebastián Arg. 144 C8
San Sebastián Spain 57 F2
San Sebastián de los Reyes Spain 57 E3
Sansepolcro Italy 58 E3
San Severo Italy 58 F4
San Simon U.S.A. 129 I5
Sanski Most Bos. & Herz. 58 G2
Sansoral Islands Palau see Sonsorol Islands
Sansui China 77 F3
Santa r. Peru 142 C5
Santa Ana Bol. 142 E7
Santa Ana El Salvador 136 G6
Santa Ana Mex. 127 F7
Santa Ana i. Solomon Is 107 G3
Santa Ana U.S.A. 128 E5
Santa Ana de Yacuma Bol. 142 E6
Santa Anna U.S.A. 131 D6
Santa Bárbara Brazil 145 C2
Santa Bárbara Cuba see La Demajagua
Santa Bárbara Mex. 131 B7
Santa Barbara U.S.A. 128 D4
Santa Bárbara, Ilha i. Brazil 145 D2
Santa Barbara Channel U.S.A. 128 C4
Santa Bárbara d'Oeste Brazil 145 B3
Santa Barbara Island U.S.A. 128 D5
Santa Catalina, Gulf of U.S.A. 128 E5
Santa Catalina, Isla i. Mex. 127 F8
Santa Catalina de Armada Spain 57 B2
Santa Catalina Island U.S.A. 128 D5
Santa Catarina state Brazil 145 A4
Santa Catarina Baja California Mex. 127 E7
Santa Catarina Nuevo León Mex. 131 C7
Santa Catarina, Ilha de i. Brazil 145 A4
Santa Clara Col. 142 E4
Santa Clara Cuba 137 I4
Santa Clara Mex. 131 B6
Santa Clara CA U.S.A. 128 C3
Santa Clara NM U.S.A. 129 I5
Santa Clara UT U.S.A. 129 G3
Santa Clarita U.S.A. 128 D4
Santa Clotilde Peru 142 D4
Santa Comba Angola see Waku-Kungo
Santa Croce, Capo c. Sicily Italy 58 F6
Santa Cruz Bol. 142 F7
Santa Cruz Brazil 143 K5
Santa Cruz Costa Rica 142 A1
Santa Cruz U.S.A. 128 B3
Santa Cruz watercourse U.S.A. 129 G5
Santa Cruz, Isla i. Galápagos Ecuador 142 [inset]
Santa Cruz, Isla i. Mex. 127 F8
Santa Cruz Cabrália Brazil 145 D2
Santa Cruz de Goiás Brazil 145 A2
Santa Cruz de la Palma Canary Is 96 B2
Santa Cruz del Sur Cuba 137 I4
Santa Cruz de Moya Spain 57 F4

▶Santa Cruz de Tenerife Canary Is 96 B2
Joint capital of the Canary Islands.

Santa Cruz do Sul Brazil 144 F3
Santa Cruz Island U.S.A. 128 D4
Santa Cruz Islands Solomon Is 107 G3
Santa Elena, Bahía de b. Ecuador 142 B4
Santa Elena, Cabo c. Costa Rica 137 G6
Santa Elena, Punta pt Ecuador 142 B4
Santa Eudóxia Brazil 145 B3
Santa Eufemia, Golfo di g. Italy 58 G5
Santa Fe Arg. 144 D4
Santa Fe Cuba 133 D8

▶Santa Fe U.S.A. 127 G6
Capital of New Mexico.

Santa Fé de Bogotá Col. see Bogotá
Santa Fé de Minas Brazil 145 B2
Santa Fé do Sul Brazil 145 A3
Santa Helena Brazil 143 I4
Santa Helena de Goiás Brazil 145 A2
Santai Sichuan China 76 E2
Santai Yunnan China 76 D3
Santa Inês Brazil 143 I4
Santa Inés, Isla i. Chile 152 L3
Santa Isabel Arg. 144 C5
Santa Isabel Equat. Guinea see Malabo
Santa Isabel i. Solomon Is 107 F2
Santa Juliana Brazil 145 B2
Santalpur India 82 B5
Santa Lucia Range mts U.S.A. 128 C3
Santa Margarita U.S.A. 128 C4
Santa Margarita, Isla i. Mex. 136 B4
Santa María Arg. 144 C3
Santa Maria Amazonas Brazil 143 G4
Santa Maria Distrito Federal Brazil 145 A1
Santa Maria Rio Grande do Sul Brazil 144 F3
Santa Maria Cape Verde 96 [inset]
Santa María r. Mex. 127 G7
Santa María Peru 142 D4
Santa Maria U.S.A. 128 C4
Santa Maria r. U.S.A. 129 G4
Santa Maria, Cabo de c. Moz. 101 K4
Santa Maria, Cabo de c. Port. 57 C5
Santa Maria, Chapadão de hills Brazil 145 B1
Santa Maria, Serra de hills Brazil 145 B1
Santa Maria da Vitória Brazil 145 B1
Santa María de Cuevas Mex. 131 B7
Santa Maria do Suaçuí Brazil 145 C2
Santa Maria Island Vanuatu 107 G3
Santa Maria Madalena Brazil 145 C3
Santa Maria Mountains U.S.A. 129 G4
Santa Marta Col. 142 D1
Santa Marta, Cabo de c. Angola 99 B5
Santa Marta Grande, Cabo de c. Brazil 145 A5
Santa Maura i. Greece see Lefkada
Santa Monica U.S.A. 128 D4
Santa Monica, Pico mt. Mex. 127 E8
Santa Monica Bay U.S.A. 128 D5
Santan Indon. 68 F7
Santana Brazil 145 C1
Santana r. Brazil 145 A2
Santana do Araguaia Brazil 143 H5
Santander Spain 57 E2
Santa Nella U.S.A. 128 C3
Santanilla, Islas is Caribbean Sea see Cisne, Islas del
Santan Mountain hill U.S.A. 129 H5
Sant'Antioco Sardinia Italy 58 C5
Sant'Antioco, Isola di i. Sardinia Italy 58 C5
Sant Antoni de Portmany Spain 57 G4
Santapilly India 84 D2
Santaquin U.S.A. 129 H2
Santa Quitéria Brazil 143 J4
Santarém Brazil 143 H4
Santarém Port. 57 B4
Santa Rita Mex. 131 C7
Santa Rosa Arg. 144 D5
Santa Rosa Brazil 144 F3
Santa Rosa Mex. 131 C7
Santa Rosa CA U.S.A. 128 B2
Santa Rosa NM U.S.A. 127 G6
Santa Rosa de Copán Hond. 136 G6
Santa Rosa de la Roca Bol. 142 F7
Santa Rosa do Purus Brazil 142 D5
Santa Rosa Island U.S.A. 128 C5
Santa Rosalía Mex. 127 E8
Santa Rosa Range mts U.S.A. 126 D4
Santa Rosa Wash watercourse U.S.A. 129 G5
Santa Sylvina Arg. 144 D3
Santa Tecla El Salvador 136 G6
Santa Teresa Australia 109 F6
Santa Teresa r. Brazil 145 A1
Santa Teresa Mex. 131 D7
Santa Vitória Brazil 145 A2
Santa Ynez r. U.S.A. 128 C4
Santa Ysabel i. Solomon Is see Santa Isabel
Santee U.S.A. 128 E5
Santee r. U.S.A. 133 E5
Sant Francesc de Formentera Spain 57 G4
Santiago Brazil 144 F3
Santiago i. Cape Verde 96 [inset]

▶Santiago Chile 144 B4
Capital of Chile.

Santiago Dom. Rep. 137 J5
Santiago Panama 137 H7
Santiago Phil. 69 G3
Santiago, Isla i. Galápagos Ecuador 142 [inset]
Santiago de Compostela Spain 57 B2
Santiago de Cuba Cuba 137 I4
Santiago del Estero Arg. 144 D3
Santiago de los Caballeros Dom. Rep. see Santiago
Santiago de Veraguas Panama see Santiago
Santiaguillo, Laguna de l. Mex. 131 B7
Santianna Point Canada 121 P2
Santipur India see Shantipur
Sant Jordi, Golf de g. Spain 57 G3
Santo Amaro Brazil 145 D1
Santo Amaro de Campos Brazil 145 C3
Santo Anastácio Brazil 145 A3
Santo André Brazil 145 B3
Santo Ângelo Brazil 144 F3

▶Santo Antão i. Cape Verde 96 [inset]
Most westerly point of Africa.

Santo Antônio Brazil 142 F4
Santo Antônio r. Brazil 145 C2
Santo António São Tomé and Príncipe 96 D4
Santo Antônio, Cabo c. Brazil 145 D1
Santo Antônio da Platina Brazil 145 A3
Santo Antônio de Jesus Brazil 145 D1
Santo Antônio do Içá Brazil 142 E4
Santo Corazón Bol. 143 G7
Santo Domingo Cuba 133 D8

▶Santo Domingo Dom. Rep. 137 K5
Capital of the Dominican Republic.

Santo Domingo Baja California Mex. 127 E7
Santo Domingo Baja California Sur Mex. 127 F8
Santo Domingo country West Indies see Dominican Republic
Santo Domingo de Guzmán Dom. Rep. see Santo Domingo
Santo Hipólito Brazil 145 B2
Santorini i. Greece 59 K6
Santos Brazil 145 B3
Santos Dumont Brazil 145 C3
Santos Luzardo, Parque Nacional nat. park Venez. 142 E2
Santos Plateau sea feature S. Atlantic Ocean 148 E7
Santo Tomás Mex. 127 E7
Santo Tomás Peru 142 D6
Santo Tomé Arg. 144 E3
Sanup Plateau U.S.A. 129 G3
San Valentín, Cerro mt. Chile 144 B7
San Vicente El Salvador 136 G6
San Vicente Mex. 127 D7
San Vicente de Baracaldo Spain see Barakaldo
San Vicente de Cañete Peru 142 C6
San Vincenzo Italy 58 D3
San Vito, Capo c. Sicily Italy 58 E5
Sanwer India 82 C5
Sanya China 77 F5
Sanyuan China 77 F1
S. A. Nyýazow Adyndaky Turkm. 89 F2
Sanza Pombo Angola 99 B4
Sao, Phou mt. Laos 70 C3
São Bernardo do Campo Brazil 145 B3
São Borja Brazil 144 E3
São Carlos Brazil 145 B3
São Cristóvão Brazil 143 K6
São Domingos Brazil 145 B1
São Felipe, Serra de hills Brazil 145 B1
São Félix Brazil 145 D1
São Félix do Araguaia Brazil 143 H6
São Félix do Xingu Brazil 143 H5
São Fidélis Brazil 145 C3
São Francisco Brazil 145 B1

▶São Francisco r. Brazil 145 C1
5th longest river in South America.

São Francisco, Ilha de i. Brazil 145 A4
São Francisco de Paula Brazil 145 A5
São Francisco de Sales Brazil 145 A2
São Francisco do Sul Brazil 145 A4
São Gabriel Brazil 144 F4
São Gonçalo Brazil 145 C3
São Gonçalo do Abaeté Brazil 145 B2
São Gonçalo do Sapucaí Brazil 145 B3
São Gotardo Brazil 145 B2
São João, Ilhas de is Brazil 143 J4
São João da Barra Brazil 145 C3
São João da Boa Vista Brazil 145 B3
São João da Madeira Port. 57 B3
São João da Ponte Brazil 145 B1
São João del Rei Brazil 145 B3
São João do Paraíso Brazil 145 C1
São Joaquim Brazil 145 A5
São Joaquim da Barra Brazil 145 B3
São José Amazonas Brazil 142 E4
São José Santa Catarina Brazil 145 A4
São José do Rio Preto Brazil 145 A3
São José dos Campos Brazil 145 B3
São José dos Pinhais Brazil 145 A4
São Leopoldo Brazil 145 A5
São Lourenço Brazil 145 B3
São Lourenço r. Brazil 143 G7
São Luís Maranhão Brazil 143 J4
São Luís Pará Brazil 143 G4
São Luís de Montes Belos Brazil 145 A2
São Manuel Brazil 145 A3
São Marcos r. Brazil 145 B2
São Mateus Brazil 145 D2
São Mateus do Sul Brazil 145 A4
São Miguel i. Arquipélago dos Açores 148 G3
São Miguel r. Brazil 145 B2
São Miguel do Araguaia Brazil 145 A1
São Miguel do Tapuio Brazil 143 J5
Saône r. France 56 G4
Saoner India 82 D5
São Nicolau i. Cape Verde 96 [inset]

▶São Paulo Brazil 145 B3
Most populous city in South America and 7th in the world.

São Paulo state Brazil 145 A3
São Paulo de Olivença Brazil 142 E4
São Pedro da Aldeia Brazil 145 C3
São Pedro e São Paulo is N. Atlantic Ocean 148 G5
São Pires r. Brazil see Teles Pires
São Raimundo Nonato Brazil 143 J5
São Romão Amazonas Brazil 142 E5
São Romão Minas Gerais Brazil 145 B2
São Roque Brazil 145 B3
São Roque, Cabo de c. Brazil 143 K5
São Salvador Angola see M'banza Congo
São Salvador do Congo Angola see M'banza Congo
São Sebastião Brazil 145 B3
São Sebastião, Ilha do i. Brazil 145 B3
São Sebastião do Paraíso Brazil 145 B3
São Sebastião dos Poções Brazil 145 B1
São Simão Goiás Brazil 143 H7
São Simão São Paulo Brazil 145 B3
São Simão, Barragem de resr Brazil 145 A2

Sengirli, Mys *pt* Kazakh. *see* Syngyrli, Mys
Senhor do Bonfim Brazil 143 J6
Senigallia Italy 58 E3
Senj Croatia 58 F2
Senja *i.* Norway 44 J2
Sen'kina Russia 42 K2
Şenköy Turkey 85 C1
Senlac S. Africa 100 F3
Senlin Shan *mt.* China 74 C4
Senlis France 52 C5
Senmonorom Cambodia 71 D4
Sennar Sudan 86 D7
Sennen U.K. 49 B8
Senneterre Canada 122 F4
Senqu *r.* Lesotho 101 H6
Sens France 56 F2
Sensuntepeque El Salvador 136 G6
Senta Serbia 59 I2
Senthal India 82 D3
Sentinel U.S.A. 129 G5
Sentinel Peak Canada 120 F4
Sentosa *i.* Sing. 71 [inset]
Sento Sé Brazil 143 J5
Senwabarwana S. Africa 101 I2
Şenyurt Turkey 91 F3
Seocheon S. Korea 75 B5
Seo de Urgell Spain *see* La Seu d'Urgell
Seonath *r.* India 84 D1
Seongnam S. Korea 75 B5
Seoni India 82 D5
Seorak-san *mt.* S. Korea 75 C5
Seorak-san National Park S. Korea 75 C5
Seorinarayan India 83 E5
Seosan S. Korea 75 B5

▶**Seoul** S. Korea 75 B5
Capital of South Korea.

Separation Well Australia 108 C5
Sepik *r.* P.N.G. 69 K7
Sep'o N. Korea 75 B5
Sepon India 83 H4
Seppa India 83 H4
Sept-Îles Canada 123 I4
Sequoia National Park U.S.A. 128 D3
Serafimovich Russia 43 I6
Sêraitang China *see* Baima
Seram *i.* Indon. 69 H7
Seram, Laut *sea* Indon. 69 I7
Serang Indon. 68 D8
Serangoon Harbour *b.* Sing. 71 [inset]
Serapi, Gunung *hill* Indon. 71 E7
Serapong, Mount *hill* Sing. 71 [inset]
Serasan *i.* Indon. 71 E7
Serasan, Selat *sea chan.* Indon. 71 E7
Seraya *i.* Indon. 71 E7
Serbâl, Gebel *mt.* Egypt *see* Sirbāl, Jabal

▶**Serbia** *country* Europe 59 I3
Formerly known as Yugoslavia and as Serbia and Montenegro. Up to 1993 included Bosnia-Herzegovina, Croatia, Macedonia, Montenegro and Slovenia. Became independent from Montenegro in June 2006. Kosovo declared independence in February 2008.

Sêrbug Co *l.* China 83 G2
Sêrca China 76 B2
Serchhip India 83 H5
Serdar Turkm. 88 E2
Serdica Bulg. *see* Sofia
Serdo Eth. 98 E2
Serdoba *r.* Russia 43 J5
Serdobsk Russia 43 J5
Serebryansk Kazakh. 80 F2
Seredka Russia 45 P7
Şereflikoçhisar Turkey 90 D3
Serekunda Gambia 96 B3
Seremban Malaysia 71 C7
Serengeti National Park Tanz. 98 D4
Serenje Zambia 99 D5
Serezha *r.* Russia 42 I5
Sergach Russia 42 J5
Sergeyevka Russia 74 B2
Sergiyev Posad Russia 42 H4
Sergo Ukr. *see* Stakhanov
Serh China 80 I4
Serhetabat Turkm. 89 F3
Serifos *i.* Greece 59 K6
Sérigny *r.* Canada 123 H3
Sérigny, Lac *l.* Canada 123 H3
Serik Turkey 90 C3
Seringapatam Reef Australia 108 C3
Sêrkang China *see* Nyainrong
Sermata *i.* Indon. 69 H8
Sermata, Kepulauan *is* Indon. 108 E2
Sermersuaq *glacier* Greenland 119 M2
Sermilik *inlet* Greenland 119 O3
Sernovodsk Russia 43 K5
Sernur Russia 42 K4
Sernyy Zavod Turkm. *see* Kükürtli
Seronga Botswana 99 C5
Serov Russia 41 S4
Serowe Botswana 101 H2
Serpa Port. 57 C5
Serpa Pinto Angola *see* Menongue
Serpentine Lakes *salt flat* Australia 109 E7
Serpukhov Russia 43 H5
Serra Brazil 145 C3
Serra Alta Brazil 145 A4
Serrachis *r.* Cyprus 85 A2
Serra da Bocaina, Parque Nacional da *nat. park* Brazil 145 B3
Serra da Canastra, Parque Nacional da *nat. park* Brazil 145 B3
Serra da Mesa, Represa *resr* Brazil 145 A1
Serra das Araras Brazil 145 B1
Serra do Divisor, Parque Nacional da *nat. park* Brazil 142 D5
Sérrai Greece *see* Serres
Serranía de la Neblina, Parque Nacional *nat. park* Venez. 142 E3
Serraria, Ilha *i.* Brazil *see* Queimada, Ilha
Serra Talhada Brazil 143 K5
Serre *r.* France 52 D5
Serres Greece 59 J4
Serrinha Brazil 143 K6
Serro Brazil 145 C2
Sers Tunisia 58 C6
Sertanópolis Brazil 145 A3
Sertãozinho Brazil 145 B3
Sêrtar China 76 D1
Sertavul Geçidi *pass* Turkey 85 A1
Sertolovo Russia 45 Q6
Seruai Indon. 71 B6
Serui Indon. 69 J7
Serule Botswana 99 C6
Seruna India 82 C3
Sêrwolungwa China 76 B1
Sêrxü China 76 C1
Seryshevo Russia 74 C2
Seseganaga Lake Canada 122 C4
Sese Islands Uganda 98 D4
Sesel *country* Indian Ocean *see* Seychelles
Sesfontein Namibia 99 B5
Seshachalam Hills India 84 C3
Sesheke Zambia 99 C5
Sesostris Bank *sea feature* India 84 A3
Sestri Levante Italy 58 C2
Sestroretsk Russia 45 P6
Set, Phou *mt.* Laos 70 D4
Sète France 56 F5
Sete Lagoas Brazil 145 B2
Setermoen Norway 44 K2
Setesdal *valley* Norway 45 E7
Seti *r.* Nepal 82 E3
Sétif Alg. 54 F4
Seto Japan 75 E6
Seto-naikai *sea* Japan 73 O6
Seto-naikai Kokuritsu-kōen *nat. park* Japan 75 D6
Setsan Myanmar 70 A3
Settat Morocco 54 C5
Settepani, Monte *mt.* Italy 58 C2
Settle U.K. 48 E4
Setúbal Port. 57 B4
Setúbal, Baía de *b.* Port. 57 B4
Seul, Lac *l.* Canada 121 M5
Sevan Armenia 91 G2
Sevan, Lake Armenia 91 G2
Sevan, Ozero *l.* Armenia *see* Sevan, Lake
Sevana Lich *l.* Armenia *see* Sevan, Lake
Sevastopol' Crimea 90 D1
Seven Islands Canada *see* Sept-Îles
Seven Islands Bay Canada 123 J2
Sevenoaks U.K. 49 H7
Seventy Mile House Canada *see* 70 Mile House
Sévérac-le-Château France 56 F4
Severn *r.* Australia 112 E2
Severn *r.* Canada 122 D3
Severn S. Africa 100 F4
Severn *r.* U.K. 49 E7
also known as Hafren
Severnaya Dvina *r.* Russia 42 I2
Severnaya Sos'va *r.* Russia 41 T3
Severnaya Zemlya *is* Russia 65 L1
Severn Lake Canada 121 N4
Severnoye Russia 41 Q5
Severnyy *Nenetskiy Avtonomnyy Okrug* Russia 42 K1
Severnyy *Respublika Komi* Russia 64 H3

▶**Severnyy, Ostrov** *i.* Russia 64 G2
4th largest island in Europe.

Severobaykal'sk Russia 73 J1
Severo-Baykal'skoye Nagor'ye *mts* Russia 65 M4
Severodonetsk Ukr. *see* Syeverodonets'k
Severodvinsk Russia 42 H2
Severo-Kuril'sk Russia 65 Q4
Severomorsk Russia 44 R2
Severoonezhsk Russia 42 H3
Severo-Sibirskaya Nizmennost' *lowland* Russia *see* North Siberian Lowland
Severoural'sk Russia 41 R3
Severo-Yeniseyskiy Russia 64 K3
Severskaya Russia 90 E1
Severskiy Donets *r.* Russia/Ukr. *see* Northern Donets
Sevier U.S.A. 129 G2
Sevier *r.* U.S.A. 129 G2
Sevier Desert U.S.A. 129 G2
Sevier Lake U.S.A. 129 G2
Sevierville U.S.A. 132 D5
Sevilla Col. 142 C3
Sevilla Spain *see* Seville
Seville Spain 57 D5
Sevlyush Ukr. *see* Vynohradiv
Sewani India 82 C3
Seward *AK* U.S.A. 118 D3
Seward *NE* U.S.A. 130 D3
Seward Mountains Antarctica 152 L2
Seward Peninsula U.S.A. 118 B3
Sexi Spain *see* Almuñécar
Sexsmith Canada 120 G4
Sextín Mex. 131 B7
Seyakha Russia 153 F2
Seychelles *country* Indian Ocean 149 L6
Seydi Turkm. 89 F2
Seydişehir Turkey 90 C3
Seyðisfjörður Iceland 44 [inset 1]
Seyhan Turkey *see* Adana
Seyhan *r.* Turkey 85 B1
Seyitgazi Turkey 59 N5
Seym *r.* Russia/Ukr. 43 G6
Seymchan Russia 65 Q3
Seymour Australia 112 B6
Seymour S. Africa 101 H7
Seymour *IN* U.S.A. 134 C4
Seymour *TX* U.S.A. 131 D5
Seymour Inlet Canada 120 E5
Seymour Range *mts* Australia 109 F6
Seypan *i.* N. Mariana Is *see* Saipan
Sézanne France 52 D6
Sfakia Greece *see* Chora Sfakion
Sfântu Gheorghe Romania 59 K2
Sfax Tunisia 58 D7
Sfikia, Limni *resr* Greece *see* Sfikias, Limni
Sfikias, Limni *resr* Greece 59 J4
Sfintu Gheorghe Romania *see* Sfântu Gheorghe
Sgiersch Poland *see* Zgierz
's-Graveland Neth. 52 F2
's-Gravenhage Neth. *see* The Hague
Sgurr Alasdair *hill* U.K. 50 C3
Sgurr Dhomhnuill *hill* U.K. 50 D4
Sgurr Mòr *mt.* U.K. 50 D3
Sgurr na Ciche *mt.* U.K. 50 D3
Shaanxi *prov.* China 76 F1
Shaartuz Tajik. *see* Shahritus
Shaban Pak. 89 G4
Shabani Zimbabwe *see* Zvishavane
Shabestar Iran 88 B2
Shabībī, Jabal ash *mt.* Jordan 85 B5
Shabla, Nos *pt* Bulg. 59 M3
Shabogamo Lake Canada 123 I3
Shabunda Dem. Rep. Congo 98 C4
Shache China 80 E4
Shackleton Coast Antarctica 152 H1
Shackleton Glacier Antarctica 152 I1
Shackleton Ice Shelf Antarctica 152 F2
Shackleton Range *mts* Antarctica 152 A1
Shadaogou China 77 F2
Shadaw Myanmar 70 B3
Shādegān Iran 88 C4
Shadihar Pak. 89 G4
Shady Cove U.S.A. 126 C4
Shady Spring U.S.A. 134 E5
Shadzud Tajik. 89 I2
Shafer, Lake U.S.A. 134 B3
Shafer Peak Antarctica 152 H2
Shafter U.S.A. 128 D4
Shaftesbury U.K. 49 E7
Shagamu *r.* Canada 122 D3
Shagedu China 73 K5
Shageluk U.S.A. 118 C3
Shaghyray Üstirti *plat.* Kazakh. *see* Shagyray, Plato
Shagonar Russia 80 H1
Shag Point N.Z. 113 C7
Shag Rocks *is* S. Georgia 144 H8
Shagyray, Plato *plat.* Kazakh. 80 A2
Shahabad *Karnataka* India 84 C2
Shahabad *Rajasthan* India 82 D4
Shahabad *Uttar Prad.* India 82 E4
Shāhābād Iran *see* Eslāmābād-e Gharb
Shah Alam Malaysia 71 C7
Shah Bandar Pak. 89 G5
Shahdād Iran 88 E4
Shahdol India 82 E5
Shahe China 77 F2
Shahejie China *see* Jiujiang
Shahezhen China *see* Jiujiang
Shāh Fōlād *mt.* Afgh. 89 G3
Shahid, Ras *pt* Pak. 89 F5
Shāhīn Dezh Iran 88 B2
Shāh Ismā'īl Afgh. 89 G4
Shāh Jahān, Kūh-e *mts* Iran 88 E2
Shahjahanpur India 82 D4
Shāh Kūh *mt.* Iran 88 E4
Shāhpūr Iran *see* Salmās
Shahrak Afgh. 89 G3
Shāhrakht Iran 89 F3
Shahr-e Bābak Iran 88 D4
Shahr-e Ghulghulah *tourist site* Afgh. 89 F4
Shahr-e Kord Iran 88 C3
Shahr-e Şafā Afgh. 89 G4
Shahrezā Iran 88 C3
Shahrig Pak. 89 G4
Shahrisabz Uzbek. 89 G2
Shahr-i Sokhta *tourist site* Iran 89 F4
Shahriston Tajik. 89 H2
Shahritus Tajik. 89 H2
Shahr Sultan Pak. 89 H4
Shāhrūd Iran 88 D2
Shāhrūd, Rūdkhāneh-ye *r.* Iran 88 C2
Shāhrūd Bustām *reg.* Iran 88 D3
Shāh Savārān, Kūh-e *mts* Iran 88 E4
Shāh Taqī Iran *see* Emām Taqī
Shaighalu Pak. 89 H4
Shaikh Husain *mt.* Pak. 89 G4
Shaikhpura India *see* Sheikhpura
Sha'īr, Jabal *mts* Syria 85 C2
Sha'īra, Gebel *mt.* Egypt *see* Sha'īrah, Jabal
Sha'īrah, Jabal *mt.* Egypt 85 B5
Shaj'ah, Jabal *hill* Saudi Arabia 88 C5
Shajapur India 82 D5
Shajianzi China 74 B4
Shakaville S. Africa 101 J5
Shakh Tajik. *see* Shoh
Shakhbuz Azer. *see* Şahbuz
Shākhen Iran 89 E3
Shakhovskaya Russia 42 G4
Shakhrisabz Uzbek. *see* Shahrisabz
Shakhristan Tajik. *see* Shahriston
Shakhtinsk Kazakh. 80 D2
Shakhty *Respublika Buryatiya* Russia *see* Gusinoozersk
Shakhty *Rostovskaya Oblast'* Russia 43 I7
Shakhun'ya Russia 42 J4
Shaki Nigeria *see* Saki
Shakotan-hantō *pen.* Japan 74 F4
Shalakusha Russia 42 I3
Shalang China 77 F4
Shali Russia 91 G2
Shaliuhe China *see* Gangca
Shalkar India 82 D3
Shalkar Kazakh. 80 A2
Shalkarteniz, Solonchak *salt marsh* Kazakh. 80 B2
Shalqar Kazakh. *see* Shalkar
Shaluli Shan *mts* China 76 C2
Shaluni *mt.* India 83 I3
Shama *r.* Tanz. 99 D4
Shamâl Sînâ' *governorate* Egypt *see* Shamāl Sīnā'
Shamāl Sīnā' *governorate* Egypt 85 A4
Shāmat al Akbād *des.* Saudi Arabia 91 F5
Shamattawa Canada 121 N4
Shamattawa *r.* Canada 122 D3
Shambār Iran 88 C3
Shamgong Bhutan *see* Zhemgang
Shamīl Iran 88 E5
Shāmīyah *des.* Iraq/Syria 85 D2
Shamkhor Azer. *see* Şämkir
Shamrock U.S.A. 131 C5
Shancheng *Fujian* China *see* Taining
Shancheng *Henan* China 73 K5
Shancheng *Shandong* China *see* Shanxian
Shand Afgh. 89 F4
Shandan China 80 J4
Shandong *prov.* China 77 H1
Shandong Bandao *pen.* China 73 M5
Shandur Pass Pak. 89 I2
Shangchao China 77 F3
Shangcheng China 77 G2
Shangchuan Dao *i.* China 77 G4
Shangdu China 73 K4
Shangganling China 74 C3

▶**Shanghai** China 77 I2
3rd most populous city in Asia and the world.

Shanghai *mun.* China 77 I2
Shangji China *see* Xichuan
Shangjie China *see* Yangbi
Shangjin China 77 F1
Shangluo China 77 F1
Shangmei China *see* Xinhua
Shangnan China 77 F1
Shangpa China *see* Fugong
Shangpai China *see* Feixi
Shangpaihe China *see* Feixi
Shangqiu *Henan* China *see* Suiyang
Shangqiu *Henan* China 77 G1
Shangrao China 77 H2
Shangshui China 77 G1
Shangyou China 77 G3
Shangyou Shuiku *resr* China 80 F3
Shangyu China 77 I2
Shangzhi China 74 B3
Shangzhou China *see* Shangluo
Shanhe *Gansu* China *see* Zhengning
Shanhe *Heilong.* China 74 B3
Shankou China 77 F4
Shanlaragh Ireland 51 C6
Shannon *airport* Ireland 51 D5
Shannon *est.* Ireland 51 D5
Shannon *r.* Ireland 51 D5
Shannon, Mouth of the Ireland 51 C5
Shannon National Park Australia 109 B8
Shannon Ø *i.* Greenland 153 I1
Shan Plateau Myanmar 70 B2
Shansi *prov.* China *see* Shanxi
Shantipur India 83 G5
Shantou China 77 H4
Shantung *prov.* China *see* Shandong
Shanwei China 77 G4
Shanxi *prov.* China 77 F1
Shanxian China 77 H1
Shanyang China 77 F1
Shaodong China 77 F3
Shaoguan China 77 G3
Shaowu China 77 H3
Shaoxing China 77 I2
Shaoyang China 77 F3
Shap U.K. 48 E4
Shapa China 77 F4
Shaping China *see* Ebian
Shapinsay *i.* U.K. 50 G1
Shapkina *r.* Russia 42 L2
Shapshal'skiy Khrebet *mts* Russia 80 G1
Shaqrā' Saudi Arabia 86 G4
Shār, Jabal *mt.* Saudi Arabia 90 D6
Sharaf *well* Iraq 91 F5
Sharan Jogizai Pak. 89 H4
Shardara Kazakh. 80 C3
Shardara, Step' *plain* Kazakh. 80 C3
Shari *r.* Cameroon/Chad *see* Chari
Shārī, Buḩayrat *imp. l.* Iraq 91 G4
Shari-dake *vol.* Japan 74 G4
Shārīmā Iran 88 E4
Sharjah U.A.E. 88 D5
Sharka-leb La *pass* China 83 G3
Sharkawshchyna Belarus 45 O9
Shark Bay Australia 109 A6
Shark Reef Australia 110 D2
Sharlyk Russia 41 Q5
Sharm ash Shaykh Egypt 90 D6
Sharm el Sheikh Egypt *see* Sharm ash Shaykh
Sharon U.S.A. 134 E3
Sharon Springs U.S.A. 130 C4
Sharpe Lake Canada 121 M4
Sharp Peak *hill* H.K. China 77 [inset]
Sharqat Iraq *see* Ash Sharqāṭ
Sharqī, Jabal ash *mts* Lebanon/Syria 85 B3
Sharqiy Ustyurt Chink *esc.* Uzbek. 80 A3
Sharur Azer. *see* Şärur
Shar'ya Russia 42 J4
Shashe *r.* Botswana/Zimbabwe 99 C6
Shashemenē Eth. 98 D3
Shashi China *see* Jingzhou
Shasta U.S.A. 128 B1
Shasta, Mount *vol.* U.S.A. 126 C4
Shasta Lake U.S.A. 128 B1
Shatilki Belarus *see* Svyetlahorsk
Sha Tin H.K. China 77 [inset]
Shatki Russia 43 J5
Shaţnat as Salmās, Wādī *watercourse* Syria 85 D2
Shatoy Russia 91 G2
Shatsk Russia 43 I5
Shatsky Rise *sea feature* Pacific Ocean 150 G3
Shatt al Arab *r.* Iran/Iraq 91 H5
Shatura Russia 43 H5
Shaubak Jordan *see* Ash Shawbak
Shaunavon Canada 121 I5
Shaver Lake U.S.A. 128 D3
Shaw *r.* Australia 108 B5
Shawangunk Mountains *hills* U.S.A. 135 H3
Shawano U.S.A. 134 A1
Shawano Lake U.S.A. 134 A1
Shawinigan Canada 123 G5
Shawnee *OK* U.S.A. 131 D5
Shawnee *WY* U.S.A. 126 G4
Shawneetown U.S.A. 130 F4
Shaxian China 77 H3
Shay Gap (abandoned) Australia 108 C5
Shaykh, Jabal ash *mt.* Lebanon/Syria *see* Hermon, Mount
Shaykh Miskīn Syria 85 C3
Shāzand Iran 88 C3
Shchekino Russia 43 H5
Shchel'yayur Russia 42 L2
Shcherbakov Russia *see* Rybinsk
Shchigry Russia 43 H6
Shchors Ukr. 43 F6
Shchuchin Belarus *see* Shchuchyn
Shchuchyn Belarus 45 N10
Shebalino Russia 80 G1
Shebekino Russia 43 H6
Shebelē Wenz, Wabē *r.* Eth. 98 E3

▶**Shebelē Wenz, Wabē** *r.* Somalia 98 E3
5th longest river in Africa.

Sheboygan U.S.A. 134 B2
Shebshi Mountains Nigeria 96 E4
Shebunino Russia 74 F3
Shediac Canada 123 I5
Shedin Peak Canada 120 E4
Shedok Russia 91 F1
Sheelin, Lough *l.* Ireland 51 E4
Sheep Haven *b.* Ireland 51 E2
Sheepmoor S. Africa 101 J4
Sheep Mountain U.S.A. 129 J2
Sheep Peak U.S.A. 129 F3
Sheep's Head *hd* Ireland *see* Muntervary
Sheerness U.K. 49 H7
Sheet Harbour Canada 123 J5
Shefar'am Israel 85 B3
Sheffield N.Z. 113 D6
Sheffield U.K. 48 F5
Sheffield *AL* U.S.A. 133 C5
Sheffield *PA* U.S.A. 134 F3
Sheffield *TX* U.S.A. 131 C6
Sheffield Lake Canada 123 K4
Shêgê 'Alāqahdārī Afgh. 89 G4
Sheghnān Afgh. 89 H2
Shegmas Russia 42 K2
Shehong China 76 E2
Sheikh, Jebel esh *mt.* Lebanon/Syria *see* Hermon, Mount
Sheikhpura India 83 F4
Sheikhupura Pak. 89 I4
Shējā' ul Mulk Kêlay Afgh. 89 H4
Shekak *r.* Canada 122 D4
Shekār Āb Iran 88 D3
Shekhawati *reg.* India 89 I5
Shekhem West Bank *see* Nāblus
Shekhpura India *see* Sheikhpura
Sheki Azer. *see* Şäki
Shek Kwu Chau *i.* H.K. China 77 [inset]
Shekou China 77 [inset]
Sheksna Russia 42 H4
Sheksninskoye Vodokhranilishche *resr* Russia 42 H4
Shek Uk Shan *mt.* H.K. China 77 [inset]
Shela China 76 B2
Shelagskiy, Mys *pt* Russia 65 S2
Shelbina U.S.A. 130 E4
Shelburn U.S.A. 134 B4
Shelburne *N.S.* Canada 123 I6
Shelburne *Ont.* Canada 134 E1
Shelburne Bay Australia 110 C1
Shelby *MI* U.S.A. 134 B2
Shelby *MS* U.S.A. 131 F5
Shelby *MT* U.S.A. 126 F2
Shelby *NC* U.S.A. 133 D5
Shelbyville *IL* U.S.A. 130 F4
Shelbyville *IN* U.S.A. 134 C4
Shelbyville *KY* U.S.A. 134 C4
Shelbyville *TN* U.S.A. 132 C5
Sheldon *IA* U.S.A. 130 E3
Sheldon *IL* U.S.A. 134 B3
Sheldrake Canada 123 I4
Shelek Kazakh. *see* Shilik
Shelikhova, Zaliv *g.* Russia 65 Q3
Shelikof Strait U.S.A. 118 C4
Shell U.S.A. 130 B2
Shellbrook Canada 121 J4
Shelley U.S.A. 126 E4
Shellharbour Australia 112 E5
Shell Lake Canada 121 J4
Shell Lake U.S.A. 130 F2
Shell Mountain U.S.A. 128 B1
Shelter Bay Canada *see* Port-Cartier
Shelter Island U.S.A. 135 I3
Shelter Point N.Z. 113 B8
Shelton U.S.A. 126 C3
Shemakha Azer. *see* Şamaxı
Shemordan Russia 42 K4
Shenandoah *IA* U.S.A. 130 E3
Shenandoah *PA* U.S.A. 135 G3
Shenandoah Mountains U.S.A. 134 F4
Shenandoah National Park U.S.A. 135 F4
Shendam Nigeria 96 D4
Shending Shan *hill* China 74 D3
Shengena *mt.* Tanz. 99 D4
Shengli China 77 G2
Shengli Feng *mt.* China/Kyrg. *see* Pobeda Peak
Shengping China 74 B3
Shengrenjian China *see* Pinglu
Sheng Shan *i.* China 77 I2
Shengsi China 77 I2
Shengsi Liedao *is* China 77 I2
Shenjiamen China *see* Putuo
Shenkursk Russia 42 I3
Shenmu China 73 K5
Shennong Ding *mt.* China 77 F2
Shennongjia China 77 F2
Shenqiu China 77 G1
Shenshu China 74 C3
Shensi *prov.* China *see* Shaanxi
Shentala Russia 43 K5
Shenton, Mount *hill* Australia 109 C7
Shenyang China 74 A4
Shenzhen China 77 G4
Sheopur India 82 D4
Shepetivka Ukr. 43 E6
Shepetovka Ukr. *see* Shepetivka
Shepherd Islands Vanuatu 107 G3
Shepherdsville U.S.A. 134 C5
Shepparton Australia 112 B6
Sheppey, Isle of *i.* U.K. 49 H7
Sheqi China 77 G1
Sherabad Uzbek. *see* Sherobod
Sherborne U.K. 49 E8
Sherbro Island Sierra Leone 96 B4
Sherbrooke Canada 123 H5
Sherburne U.S.A. 135 H2
Shercock Ireland 51 F4
Shereiq Sudan 86 D6
Shergaon India 83 H4
Shergarh India 82 C4
Sheridan *AR* U.S.A. 131 E5
Sheridan *WY* U.S.A. 126 G3
Sheringham U.K. 49 I6
Sherman U.S.A. 131 D5
Sherman Mountain U.S.A. 129 F1
Sherobod Uzbek. 89 G2
Sherpur *Dhaka* Bangl. 83 G4
Sherpur *Rajshahi* Bangl. 83 G4
Sherridon Canada 121 K4
's-Hertogenbosch Neth. 52 F3
Sherwood Forest *reg.* U.K. 49 F5
Sherwood Lake Canada 121 K2
Sheslay Canada 120 D3
Sheslay *r.* Canada 120 C3
Shethanei Lake Canada 121 L3
Shetland Islands *is* U.K. 50 [inset]
Shetpe Kazakh. 78 E2
Sheung Shui H.K. China 77 [inset]
Sheung Sze Mun *sea chan.* H.K. China 77 [inset]
Shevchenko Kazakh. *see* Aktau
Shevli *r.* Russia 74 D1
Shexian China 77 H2
Sheyang China 77 I1
Sheyenne *r.* U.S.A. 130 D2
Shey Phoksundo National Park Nepal 83 E3
Sheyṭūr Iran 88 D4
Shezhin II Kazakh. 43 K6
Shiant Islands U.K. 50 C3
Shiashkotan, Ostrov *i.* Russia 65 Q5
Shibām Yemen 86 G6
Shibar, Kōtal-e Afgh. 89 H3
Shibata Japan 75 E5
Shibazhan China 74 B1
Shibh Jazīrat Sīnā' *pen.* Egypt *see* Sinai
Shibīn al Kawm Egypt 90 C5
Shibîn el Kôm Egypt *see* Shibīn al Kawm
Shibirghān Afgh. 89 G2
Shibogama Lake Canada 122 C3
Shibotsu-jima *i.* Russia *see* Zelenyy, Ostrov
Shicheng *Fujian* China *see* Zhouning
Shicheng *Jiangxi* China 77 H3
Shidād al Mismā' *hill* Saudi Arabia 85 D4
Shidao China 73 M5
Shidian China 76 C3
Shiel, Loch *l.* U.K. 50 D4
Shield, Cape Australia 110 B2
Shīeli Kazakh. *see* Shiyeli
Shīf Iran 88 C4
Shifa, Jabal ash *mts* Saudi Arabia 90 D5
Shifang China 76 E2
Shigatse China *see* Xigazê
Shiḩān *mt.* Jordan 85 B4
Shihezi China 80 G3
Shihkiachwang China *see* Shijiazhuang
Shijiao China *see* Fogang
Shijiazhuang China 73 K5
Shijiu Hu *l.* China 77 H2
Shijiusuo China *see* Rizhao
Shikag Lake Canada 122 C4
Shikar *r.* Pak. 89 F4
Shikarpur Pak. 89 H5
Shikengkong *mt.* China 77 G3
Shikhany Russia 43 J5
Shikohabad India 82 D4
Shikoku *i.* Japan 75 D6
Shikoku-sanchi *mts* Japan 75 D6
Shikotan, Ostrov *i.* Russia 74 G4
Shikotan-tō *i.* Russia *see* Shikotan, Ostrov
Shikotsu-Tōya Kokuritsu-kōen *nat. park* Japan 74 F4
Shildon U.K. 48 F4
Shilega Russia 42 J2
Shiliguri India 83 G4
Shilik Kazakh. 80 E3
Shilin China 76 D3
Shilipu China 77 G2
Shiliu China *see* Changjiang
Shilla *mt.* India 82 D2
Shillelagh Ireland 51 F5
Shillo, Naḩal *r.* Israel 85 B3
Shillong India 83 G4
Shillong Peak *mt.* India 83 G4
Shilovo Russia 43 I5
Shimada Japan 75 E6
Shimanovsk Russia 74 B1
Shimbiris *mt.* Somalia 98 E2
Shimen *Gansu* China 76 D1
Shimen *Hunan* China 77 F2
Shimen *Yunnan* China *see* Yunlong
Shimla India 82 D3
Shimoga India *see* Shivamogga
Shimokita-hantō *pen.* Japan 74 F4
Shimoni Kenya 99 D4
Shimonoseki Japan 75 C6
Shimsk Russia 42 F4
Shin, Loch *l.* U.K. 50 E2
Shināfīyah Iraq *see* Ash Shanāfīyah
Shinan China *see* Xingye
Shīndand Afgh. 89 F3
Shingbwiyang Myanmar 70 B1
Shing-gai Myanmar 70 B1
Shinghshal Pass Pak. 89 I2
Shingletown U.S.A. 128 C1
Shingū Japan 75 E6
Shingwedzi S. Africa 101 J2
Shingwedzi *r.* S. Africa 101 J2
Shīnkai Afgh. 89 G4
Shīnkay Ghar Afgh. 89 H3
Shinnston U.S.A. 134 E4
Shinshār Syria 85 C2
Shinyanga Tanz. 98 D4
Shiocton U.S.A. 134 A1
Shiogama Japan 75 F5
Shiono-misaki *c.* Japan 75 D6
Shipai China 77 H2
Shiping China 76 D4
Shipki La China/India 82 D3
Shipman U.S.A. 135 F5
Shippegan Island Canada 123 I5
Shippensburg U.S.A. 135 G3
Shiprock U.S.A. 129 I3
Shiprock Peak U.S.A. 129 I3
Shipu China 77 I2
Shipunovo Russia 72 E2
Shiqi China *see* Zhongshan
Shiqian China 77 F3
Shiqiao China *see* Panyu
Shiquan China 77 F1
Shiquanhe *Xizang* China *see* Ali
Shiquanhe *Xizang* China *see* Gar
Shiquan He *r.* China *see* Indus
Shiquan Shuiku *resr* China 77 F1
Shira Russia 72 F2
Shīrābād Iran 88 C2
Shirakawa-go and Gokayama *tourist site* Japan 75 E5
Shirane-san *vol.* Japan 75 E5
Shirase Coast Antarctica 152 J1
Shirase Glacier Antarctica 152 D2
Shīrāz Iran 88 D4

Shire r. Malawi 99 D5
Shireza Pak. 89 G5
Shiriya-zaki c. Japan 74 F4
Shirkala reg. Kazakh. 80 A2
Shiroro Reservoir Nigeria 96 D3
Shirpur India 82 C5
Shirten Holoy Gobi des. China 80 I3
Shīrvān Iran 88 E2
Shisanzhan China 74 B2
Shishaldin Volcano U.S.A. 118 B4
Shisha Pangma mt. China see Xixabangma Feng
Shishou China 77 G2
Shitan China 77 G3
Shitang China 77 I2
Shithāthah Iraq 91 F4
Shīū' Iran 88 D5
Shiv India 82 B4
Shivamogga India 84 B3
Shiveegovĭ Mongolia 73 J3
Shiveluch, Vulkan vol. Russia 65 R4
Shivpuri India 82 D4
Shivwits U.S.A. 129 G3
Shivwits Plateau U.S.A. 129 G3
Shiwan Dashan mts China 76 E4
Shiwa N'gandu Zambia 99 D5
Shixing China 77 G3
Shiyan China 77 F1
Shiyeli Kazakh. 80 C3
Shizhong China 77 H1
Shizhu China 77 F2
Shizi China 77 H2
Shizilu China see Junan
Shizong China 76 D3
Shizuishan China 72 J5
Shizuoka Japan 75 E6

▶Shkhara mt. Georgia/Russia 91 F2
3rd highest mountain in Europe.

Shklov Belarus see Shklow
Shklow Belarus 43 F5
Shkodër Albania 59 H3
Shkodra Albania see Shkodër
Shkodrës, Liqeni i l. Albania/Montenegro see Scutari, Lake
Shmidta, Ostrov i. Russia 64 K1
Shmidta, Poluostrov pen. Russia 74 F1
Shoal Lake Canada 121 K5
Shoals U.S.A. 134 B4
Shōbara Japan 75 D6
Shoh Tajik. 89 H2
Shohi Pass Pak. see Tal Pass
Shokanbetsu-dake mt. Japan 74 F4
Sholakkorgan Kazakh. 80 C3
Sholapur India see Solapur
Sholaqqorghan Kazakh. see Sholakkorgan
Shomba r. Russia 44 R4
Shomvukovo Russia 42 K3
Shona Ridge sea feature S. Atlantic Ocean 148 I9
Shonzhy Kazakh. 80 E3
Shor India 82 D2
Shōrābak reg. Afgh. 89 G4
Shorap Pak. 89 G5
Shorapur India 84 C2
Sho'rchi Uzbek. 89 G2
Shorewood IL U.S.A. 134 A3
Shorewood WI U.S.A. 134 B2
Shorkot Pak. 89 I4
Shorkozakhly, Solonchak salt flat Turkm. 91 J2
Shoshone CA U.S.A. 128 E4
Shoshone ID U.S.A. 126 E4
Shoshone r. U.S.A. 126 F3
Shoshone Mountains U.S.A. 128 E2
Shoshone Peak U.S.A. 128 E3
Shoshong Botswana 101 H2
Shoshoni U.S.A. 126 F4
Shostka Ukr. 43 G6
Shotoran, Chashmeh-ye well Iran 88 D3
Shotor Khūn Afgh. 89 G3
Shouyang Shan mt. China 77 F1
Showak Sudan 86 E7
Show Low U.S.A. 129 H4
Shoyna Russia 42 J2
Shpola Ukr. 43 F6
Shqipëria country Europe see Albania
Shreve U.S.A. 134 D3
Shreveport U.S.A. 131 E5
Shrewsbury U.K. 49 E6
Shri Lanka country Asia see Sri Lanka
Shri Mohangarh India 82 B4
Shrirampur India 83 G5
Shu Kazakh. 80 D3
Shu r. Kazakh./Kyrg. 80 C3
Shū r. Kazakh./Kyrg. see Shu
Shu'ab, Ra's pt Yemen 87 H7
Shuajingsi China 76 D1
Shuangbai China 76 D3
Shuangcheng Fujian China see Zherong
Shuangcheng Heilong. China 74 B3
Shuanghe Hubei China 77 G2
Shuanghe Sichuan China 76 E2
Shuanghedagang China 74 C2
Shuangjiang Guizhou China see Jiangkou
Shuangjiang Hunan China see Tongdao
Shuangjiang Yunnan China see Eshan
Shuangliao China 74 A4
Shuangliu China 76 D2
Shuangpai China 77 F3
Shuangshipu China see Fengxian
Shuangxi China see Shunchang
Shuangyang China 74 B4
Shuangyashan China 74 C3
Shubarkudyk Kazakh. 80 A2
Shubayḩ well Saudi Arabia 85 D4
Shugozero Russia 42 G4
Shuidong China see Dianbai
Shuijing China 76 E1
Shuikou Guangxi China 76 E4
Shuikou Hunan China 77 F3
Shu-Ile, Gory mts Kazakh. 80 D3
Shuiluocheng China see Zhuanglang
Shuizhai China see Wuhua
Shulan China 74 B3
Shumagin Islands U.S.A. 118 B4
Shumba Zimbabwe 99 C5
Shumen Bulg. 59 L3
Shumerlya Russia 42 J5
Shumilina Belarus 43 F5
Shumyachi Russia 43 G5
Shūnan Japan 75 C6
Shunchang China 77 H3
Shuncheng China 74 A4
Shunde China 77 G4
Shuoxian China see Shuozhou
Shuozhou China 73 K5
Shuqrah Yemen 86 G7
Shūr r. Iran 88 D4
Shūr r. Iran 89 F3
Shūr watercourse Iran 88 D5
Shur watercourse Iran 88 E3
Shūr, Chāh-e well Iran 88 D3
Shūr, Rūd-e watercourse Iran 88 E4
Shūr Āb watercourse Iran 88 D4
Shūrjestān Iran 88 D4
Shūrū Iran 89 F4
Shuryshkarskiy Sor, Ozero l. Russia 41 T2
Shūsh Iran 88 C3
Shusha Azer. see Şuşa
Shūshtar Iran 88 C3
Shutfah, Qalamat well Saudi Arabia 88 D6
Shuwayḩān Syria 85 D2
Shuwaysh, Tall ash hill Jordan 85 C4
Shuya Ivanovskaya Oblast' Russia 42 I4
Shuya Respublika Kareliya Russia 42 G3
Shuyskoye Russia 42 I4
Shuzāz, Jabal mt. Saudi Arabia 91 F6
Shwebo Myanmar 70 A2
Shwedwin Myanmar 70 A1
Shwegun Myanmar 70 B3
Shwegyin Myanmar 70 B3
Shweudaung mt. Myanmar 70 B2
Shyganak Kazakh. 80 D2
Shyghanaq Kazakh. see Shyganak
Shymkent Kazakh. 80 C3
Shyngystau, Khrebet mts Kazakh. 80 E2
Shyok India 82 D2
Shypuvate Ukr. 43 H6
Shyroke Ukr. 43 G7
Sia Indon. 69 I8
Siabu Indon. 71 B7
Siahan Range mts Pak. 89 F5
Sīāh Cheshmeh Iran 88 B2
Sialkot Pak. 89 I3
Siam country Asia see Thailand
Sian China see Xi'an
Sian Russia 74 B1
Siang r. India see Brahmaputra
Siantan i. Indon. 71 D7
Siargao i. Phil. 69 H5
Siatlai Myanmar 70 A2
Siau i. Indon. 69 H6
Šiauliai Lith. 45 M9
Siazan' Azer. see Siyäzän
Si Bai, Lam r. Thai. 70 D4
Sibasa S. Africa 101 J2
Sibayi, Lake S. Africa 101 K4
Sibda China 76 C2
Šibenik Croatia 58 F3
Siberia reg. Russia 65 M3
Siberut i. Indon. 68 B7
Siberut, Selat sea chan. Indon. 68 B7
Sibi Pak. 89 G4
Sibidiri P.N.G. 69 K8
Sibigo Indon. 71 A7
Sibiloi National Park Kenya 98 D3
Sibir' reg. Russia see Siberia
Sibiti Congo 98 B4
Sibiu Romania 59 K2
Sibley U.S.A. 130 E3
Siboa Indon. 69 G6
Sibolga Indon. 71 B7
Siborongborong Indon. 71 B7
Sibu Sarawak Malaysia 68 E6
Sibut Cent. Afr. Rep. 98 B3
Sibuyan i. Phil. 69 G4
Sibuyan Sea Phil. 69 G4
Sicamous Canada 120 G5
Sicca Veneria Tunisia see Le Kef
Siccus watercourse Australia 111 B6
Sicheng Anhui China see Sixian
Sicheng Guangxi China see Lingyun
Sichon Thai. 71 B5
Sichuan prov. China 76 D2
Sichuan Pendi basin China 76 E2
Sicié, Cap c. France 56 G5
Sicilia i. Italy see Sicily
Sicilian Channel Italy/Tunisia 58 E6
Sicily i. Italy 58 F5
Sicuani Peru 142 D6
Siddhapur India see Sidhpur
Siddipet India 84 C2
Sideros, Akra pt Greece see Sideros, Akrotirio
Sideros, Akrotirio pt Greece 59 L7
Sidesaviwa S. Africa 100 F7
Sidhauli India 82 E4
Sidhi India 83 E4
Sidhpur India 82 C5
Sidi Aïssa Alg. 57 H6
Sidi Ali Alg. 57 G5
Sīdī Barrānī Egypt 90 B5
Sidi Bel Abbès Alg. 57 F6
Sidi Bennour Morocco 54 C5
Sidi Bou Sa'id Tunisia see Sidi Bouzid
Sidi Bouzid Tunisia 58 C7
Sidi el Barráni Egypt see Sīdī Barrānī
Sidi El Hani, Sebkhet de salt pan Tunisia 58 D7
Sidi Ifni Morocco 96 B2
Sidi Kacem Morocco 54 C5
Sidikalang Indon. 71 B7
Sidi Khaled Alg. 54 E5
Sid Lake Canada 121 J2
Sidlaw Hills U.K. 50 F4
Sidley, Mount Antarctica 152 J1
Sidli India 83 G4
Sidmouth U.K. 49 D8
Sidney IA U.S.A. 130 E3
Sidney MT U.S.A. 126 G3
Sidney NE U.S.A. 130 C3
Sidney OH U.S.A. 134 C3
Sidney Lanier, Lake U.S.A. 133 D5
Sidoktaya Myanmar 70 A2
Sidon Lebanon 85 B3
Sidr Egypt see Sudr
Siedlce Poland 43 D5
Sieg r. Germany 53 H4
Siegen Germany 53 I4
Siĕm Réab Cambodia 71 C4
Siem Reap Cambodia see Siĕm Réab
Si'en China see Huanjiang
Siena Italy 58 D3
Sieradz Poland 47 Q5
Si'erdingka China 76 B2
Sierra Blanca U.S.A. 127 G7
Sierra Colorada Arg. 144 C6
Sierra Grande Arg. 144 C6
Sierra Leone country Africa 96 B4
Sierra Leone Basin sea feature N. Atlantic Ocean 148 G5
Sierra Leone Rise sea feature N. Atlantic Ocean 148 G5
Sierra Madre Mountains U.S.A. 128 C4
Sierra Mojada Mex. 131 C7
Sierra Nevada, Parque Nacional nat. park Venez. 142 D2
Sierra Nevada de Santa Marta, Parque Nacional nat. park Col. 142 D1
Sierraville U.S.A. 128 C2
Sierra Vista U.S.A. 127 F7
Sierre Switz. 56 H3
Sievi Fin. 44 N5
Sifang Ling mts China 76 E4
Sifangtai China 74 B3
Sīfenī Eth. 98 E2
Sifnos i. Greece 59 K6
Sig Alg. 57 F6
Sigguup Nunaa pen. Greenland 119 M2
Sighetu Marmaţiei Romania 43 D7
Sighişoara Romania 59 K1
Siglap Sing. 71 [inset]
Sigli Indon. 71 A6
Siglufjörður Iceland 44 [inset 1]
Signal de Botrange hill Belgium 52 G4
Signal de la Ste-Baume mt. France 56 G5
Signal Peak U.S.A. 129 F5
Signy research station Antarctica 152 A2
Signy-l'Abbaye France 52 E5
Sigourney U.S.A. 130 E3
Sigri, Akra pt Greece see Saratsina, Akrotirio
Sigsbee Deep sea feature G. of Mexico 151 N4
Sigüenza Spain 57 E3
Siguiri Guinea 96 C3
Sigulda Latvia 45 N8
Sigurd U.S.A. 129 H2
Sihanoukville Cambodia 71 C5
Sihaung Myauk Myanmar 70 A2
Sihawa India 84 D1
Sihong China 77 H1
Sihora India 82 E5
Sihui China 77 G4
Siikajoki Fin. 44 N4
Siilinjärvi Fin. 44 O5
Siirt Turkey 91 F3
Sijawal Pak. 82 B4
Sikaka Saudi Arabia see Sakākā
Sikandra Rao India 82 D4
Sikanni Chief Canada 120 F3
Sikanni Chief r. Canada 120 F3
Sikar India 82 C4
Sikaram mt. Afgh. 89 H3
Sikasso Mali 96 C3
Sikaw Myanmar 70 B2
Sikeston U.S.A. 131 F4
Sikhote-Alin' mts Russia 74 D4
Sikhote-Alinskiy Zapovednik nature res. Russia 74 E3
Sikinos i. Greece 59 K6
Sikka India 82 B5
Sikkim state India 83 G4
Siksjö Sweden 44 J4
Sil r. Spain 57 C2
Şila' i. Saudi Arabia 90 D6
Šilalė Lith. 45 M9
Si Lanna National Park Thai. 70 B3
Silas U.S.A. 131 F6
Silavatturai Sri Lanka 84 C4
Silawaih Agam vol. Indon. 71 A6
Silberberg hill Germany 53 J1
Silchar India 83 H4
Şile Turkey 59 M4
Sileru r. India 84 D2
Silesia reg. Czechia/Poland 47 P5
Silety r. Kazakh. 72 C2
Siletyteniz, Ozero salt l. Kazakh. 79 G1
Silghat India 83 H4
Siliana Tunisia 58 C6
Silifke Turkey 85 A1
Siliguri India see Shiliguri
Siling Co salt l. China 83 G3
Silipur India 82 D4
Silistra Bulg. 59 L2
Silistria Bulg. see Silistra
Silivri Turkey 59 M4
Siljan l. Sweden 45 I6
Silkeborg Denmark 45 F8
Sillajhuay mt. Chile 142 E7
Sillamäe Estonia 45 O7
Sille Turkey 90 D3
Silli India 83 F5
Sillod India 84 B1
Silobela S. Africa 101 J4
Silsby Lake Canada 121 M4
Silt U.S.A. 129 J2
Siltaharju Fin. 44 O3
Sīlūp r. Iran 89 F5
Šilutė Lith. 45 L9
Silvan Turkey 91 F3
Silvânia Brazil 145 A2
Silvassa India 84 B1
Silver Bank Passage Turks and Caicos Is 137 J4
Silver Bay U.S.A. 130 F2
Silver City NM U.S.A. 129 I5
Silver City NV U.S.A. 128 D2
Silver City (abandoned) Canada 120 B2
Silver Creek r. U.S.A. 129 H4
Silver Lake U.S.A. 126 C4
Silver Lake l. U.S.A. 128 E4
Silvermine Mountains hills Ireland 51 D5
Silver Peak Range mts U.S.A. 128 E3
Silver Spring U.S.A. 135 G4
Silver Springs U.S.A. 128 D2
Silverthrone Mountain Canada 120 E5
Silvertip Mountain Canada 120 F5
Silverton U.K. 49 D8
Silverton CO U.S.A. 129 J3
Silverton TX U.S.A. 131 C5
Sima China 83 G3
Simanggang Sarawak Malaysia see Sri Aman
Simao China 76 D4
Simard, Lac l. Canada 122 F5
Simaria India 83 F4
Simav Turkey 59 M5
Simav Dağları mts Turkey 59 M5
Simba Dem. Rep. Congo 98 C3
Simbirsk Russia see Ul'yanovsk
Simcoe Canada 134 E2
Simcoe, Lake Canada 134 F1
Simdega India 84 E1
Simēn mts Eth. 98 D2
Simēn Mountains Eth. see Simēn
Simeulue i. Indon. 71 B7

▶Simferopol' Crimea 90 D1
Capital of Crimea.

Sími i. Greece see Symi
Simikot Nepal 83 E3
Similan, Ko i. Thai. 71 B5
Simi Valley U.S.A. 128 D4
Simla India see Shimla
Simla U.S.A. 126 G5
Şimleu Silvaniei Romania 59 J1
Simlipal National Park India 83 F5
Simmerath Germany 52 G4
Simmern/Hunsrück Germany 53 H5
Simmesport U.S.A. 131 F6
Simms U.S.A. 126 F3
Simojärvi l. Fin. 44 O3
Simon Mex. 131 C7
Simonette r. Canada 120 G4
Simon Wash watercourse U.S.A. 129 I5
Simoom Sound Canada 120 E5
Simoon Sound Canada see Simoom Sound
Simpang Indon. 68 C7
Simpang Mangayau, Tanjung pt Malaysia 68 F5
Simpele Fin. 45 P6
Simplício Mendes Brazil 143 J5
Simplon Pass Switz. 56 I3
Simpson Canada 121 J5
Simpson U.S.A. 126 F2
Simpson Desert Australia 110 B5
Simpson Desert National Park Australia 110 B5
Simpson Desert Regional Reserve nature res. Australia 111 B5
Simpson Islands Canada 121 H2
Simpson Park Mountains U.S.A. 128 E2
Simpson Peninsula Canada 119 J3
Simrishamn Sweden 45 I9
Simushir, Ostrov i. Russia 73 S3
Sina r. India 84 B2
Sinabang Indon. 71 B7
Sinabung vol. Indon. 71 B7
Sinai pen. Egypt 85 A5
Sinai, Mont hill France 52 E5
Sinai al Janûbîya governorate Egypt see Janūb Sīnā'
Sinai ash Shamâlîya governorate Egypt see Shamāl Sīnā'
Si Nakarin, Ang Kep Nam Thai. 70 B4
Sinaloa state Mex. 127 F8
Sinalunga Italy 58 D3
Sinan China 77 F3
Sinancha Russia see Cheremshany
Sinbo Myanmar 70 B1
Sinbyubyin Myanmar 71 B4
Sinbyugyun Myanmar 70 A2
Sincan Turkey 90 E3
Sincelejo Col. 142 C2
Sinchu Taiwan see Taoyuan
Sinclair Mills Canada 120 F4
Sincora, Serra do hills Brazil 145 C1
Sind r. India 82 D4
Sind Pak. see Thul
Sind prov. Pak. see Sindh
Sinda Russia 74 E2
Sindari India 82 B4
Sindelfingen Germany 53 I6
Sindh prov. Pak. 89 H5
Sindhulimadi Nepal see Kamalamai
Sındırgı Turkey 59 M5
Sindor Russia 42 K3
Sindou Burkina Faso 96 C3
Sindri India 83 F5
Sind Sagar Doab lowland Pak. 89 H4
Sinel'nikovo Ukr. see Synel'nykove
Sines Port. 57 B5
Sines, Cabo de c. Port. 57 B5
Sinettä Fin. 44 N3
Sinfra Côte d'Ivoire 96 C4
Sing Myanmar 70 B2
Singa Sudan 86 D7
Singanallur India 84 C4
Singapore country Asia 71 [inset]

▶Singapore Sing. 71 [inset]
Capital of Singapore.

Singapore r. Sing. 71 [inset]
Singapore, Strait of Indon./Sing. 71 [inset]
Singapura country Asia see Singapore
Singapura Sing. see Singapore
Singapuru India 84 D2
Singaraja Indon. 108 A2
Sing Buri Thai. 70 C4
Singhampton Canada 134 E1
Singhana India 82 C3
Singida Tanz. 99 D4
Singidunum Serbia see Belgrade
Singkaling Hkamti Myanmar 70 A1
Singkawang Indon. 68 D6
Singkep i. Indon. 68 C7
Singkil Indon. 71 B7
Singkuang Indon. 71 B7
Singleton Australia 112 E4
Singleton, Mount hill N.T. Australia 108 E5
Singleton, Mount hill W.A. Australia 109 B7
Singora Thai. see Songkhla
Sin'gosan N. Korea see Kosan
Singra India 83 G4
Singri India 83 H4
Singu Myanmar 76 B4
Singwara India 84 D1
Sin'gye N. Korea 75 B5
Sinhala country Asia see Sri Lanka
Sinhkung Myanmar 70 B1
Sining China see Xining
Siniscola Sardinia Italy 58 C4
Sinj Croatia 58 G3
Sinjai Indon. 69 G8
Sinjār, Jabal mt. Iraq 91 F3
Sinkat Sudan 86 E6
Sinkiang aut. reg. China see Xinjiang Uygur Zizhiqu
Sinkiang Uighur Autonomous Region aut. reg. China see Xinjiang Uygur Zizhiqu
Sinmi-do i. N. Korea 75 B5
Sinn Germany 53 I4
Sinnamary Fr. Guiana 143 H2
Sinn Bishr, Gebel hill Egypt see Sinn Bishr, Jabal
Sinn Bishr, Jabal hill Egypt 85 A5
Sinneh Iran see Sanandaj
Sinoia Zimbabwe see Chinhoyi
Sinop Brazil 143 G6
Sinop Turkey 90 D2
Sinope Turkey see Sinop
Sinp'a N. Korea see Kimjŏngsuk
Sinp'o N. Korea 75 C4
Sinsang N. Korea 75 B5
Sinsheim Germany 53 I5
Sintang Indon. 68 E6
Sint Eustatius mun. West Indies 137 L5
Sint-Laureins Belgium 52 D3
Sint Maarten terr. West Indies see St Maarten
Sint-Niklaas Belgium 52 E3
Sinton U.S.A. 131 D6
Sintra Port. 57 B4
Sint-Truiden Belgium 52 F4
Sinŭiju N. Korea 75 B4
Sinzig Germany 53 H4
Siófok Hungary 58 H1
Sioma Ngwezi National Park Zambia 99 C5
Sion Switz. 56 H3
Sion Mills U.K. 51 E3
Siorapaluk Greenland 119 K2
Sioux Center U.S.A. 125 H3
Sioux City U.S.A. 130 D3
Sioux Falls U.S.A. 130 D3
Sioux Lookout Canada 121 N5
Siphaqeni S. Africa see Flagstaff
Siping China 74 B4
Sipiwesk Canada 121 L4
Sipiwesk Lake Canada 121 L4
Siple, Mount Antarctica 152 J2
Siple Coast Antarctica 152 I1
Siple Dome ice feature Antarctica 152 J1
Siple Island Antarctica 152 J2
Siponj Tajik. see Bartang
Sipsey r. U.S.A. 131 F5
Sipura i. Indon. 68 B7
Sīq, Wādī as watercourse Egypt 85 A5
Sir r. Pak. 89 H6
Sir, Dar"yoi r. Asia see Syrdar'ya
Sira India 84 C3
Sira r. Norway 45 E7
Şīr Abū Nu'āyr i. U.A.E. 88 D5
Siracusa Sicily Italy see Syracuse
Siraha Nepal see Sirha
Sirajganj Bangl. 83 G4
Sir Alexander, Mount Canada 120 F4
Şiran Turkey 91 E2
Sirbāl, Jabal mt. Egypt 90 D5
Şīr Banī Yās i. U.A.E. 88 D5
Sircilla India see Sirsilla
Sirdaryo r. Asia see Syrdar'ya
Sirdaryo Uzbek. 80 C3
Sirdingka China see Si'erdingka
Sir Edward Pellew Group is Australia 110 B2
Sirha Nepal 83 F4
Sirḩān, Wādī as watercourse Jordan/Saudi Arabia 85 C4
Sirik, Tanjung pt Malaysia 68 E6
Siri Kit, Khuan Thai. 70 C3
Sirina i. Greece see Syrna
Sīrjā Iran 89 F5
Sir James MacBrien, Mount Canada 120 E2
Sīrjān Iran 88 D4
Sīrjān salt flat Iran 88 D4
Sirkazhi India 84 C4
Sirmilik National Park Canada 119 K2
Şırnak Turkey 91 F3
Sirohi India 82 C4
Sirombu Indon. 71 B7
Sironj India 82 D4
Síros i. Greece see Syros
Sirpur India 84 C2
Sirr, Nafūd as des. Saudi Arabia 88 B5
Sirretta Peak U.S.A. 128 D4
Sīrrī, Jazīreh-ye i. Iran 88 D5
Sirsa India 82 C3
Sir Sandford, Mount Canada 120 G5
Sirsi Karnataka India 84 B3
Sirsi Madh. Prad. India 82 D4
Sirsi Uttar Prad. India 82 D3
Sirsilla India 84 C2
Sirte Libya 97 E1
Sirte, Gulf of Libya 97 E1
Sir Thomas, Mount hill Australia 109 E6
Siruguppa India 84 C3
Sirur India 84 B2
Şirvan Azer. 91 H3
Şirvan Turkey 91 F3
Sirvel India 84 C3
Širvintai Lith. see Širvintos
Širvintos Lith. 45 N9
Sīrwān r. Iraq 91 G4
Sir Wilfrid Laurier, Mount Canada 120 G4
Sis Turkey see Kozan
Sisak Croatia 58 G2
Sisaket Thai. 70 D4
Siscia Croatia see Sisak
Sishen S. Africa 100 F4
Sishilipu China 76 E1
Sishuang Liedao is China 77 I3
Sisian Armenia 91 G3
Sisimiut Greenland 119 M3
Sisipuk Lake Canada 121 K4
Sisŏphŏn Cambodia 71 C4
Sissano P.N.G. 69 K7
Sisseton U.S.A. 130 D2
Sīstān reg. Iran 89 F4
Sisteron France 56 G4
Sisters is India 71 A5
Sīt Iran 88 E5
Sitamarhi India 83 F4
Sitang China see Sinan
Sitapur India 82 E4
Siteia Greece 59 L7
Siteki Swaziland 101 J4
Sithonia pen. Greece see Sithonias, Chersonisos
Sithonias, Chersonisos pen. Greece 59 J4
Sitía Greece see Siteia
Sitidgi Lake Canada 118 E3
Sitila Moz. 101 L2
Siting China 76 E3
Sítio do Mato Brazil 145 C1
Sitka U.S.A. 120 C3
Sitka National Historical Park nat. park U.S.A. 120 C3
Sitra oasis Egypt see Sitrah
Sitrah oasis Egypt 90 B5
Sittang r. Myanmar see Sittaung
Sittard Neth. 52 F4
Sittaung Myanmar 70 A1
Sittaung r. Myanmar 70 B3
Sittensen Germany 53 J1
Sittingbourne U.K. 49 H7
Sittoung r. Myanmar see Sittaung
Sittwe Myanmar see Akyab
Situbondo Indon. 68 E8
Siumpu i. Indon. 69 G8
Siuri India 83 F5
Sivaganga India 84 C4
Sivakasi India 84 C4
Sivaki Russia 74 B1
Sivan India see Siwan
Sivas Turkey 90 E3
Sivasagar India 83 H4
Sivaslı Turkey 59 M5
Siverek Turkey 91 E3
Siverskiy Russia 45 Q7
Sivers'kyy Donets' r. Russia/Ukr. see Northern Donets
Sivomaskinskiy Russia 41 S2
Sivrice Turkey 91 E3
Sivrihisar Turkey 59 N5
Sivukile S. Africa 101 I4
Sīwa Egypt see Sīwah
Sīwah Egypt 90 B5
Sīwah, Wāḩāt oasis Egypt 90 B5
Siwalik Range mts India/Nepal 82 D3
Siwan India 83 F4
Siwana India 82 C4
Siwa Oasis oasis Egypt see Sīwah, Wāḩāt
Sixian China 77 H1
Sixmilecross U.K. 51 E3
Siyabuswa S. Africa 101 I3
Siyāh Band, Kōh-e mts Afgh. 89 F3
Siyāh Gird Afgh. 89 G2
Siyāh Kōh mts Afgh. 89 G3
Siyäzän Azer. 91 H2
Sīyunī Iran 88 D3
Siziwang Qi China see Ulan Hua
Sjælland i. Denmark see Zealand
Sjenica Serbia 59 I3
Sjöbo Sweden 45 H9
Sjøvegan Norway 44 J2
Skadarsko Jezero, Nacionalni Park nat. park Montenegro 59 H3
Skadovs'k Ukr. 59 O1
Skaftárós r. mouth Iceland 44 [inset 1]
Skagafjörður inlet Iceland 44 [inset 1]
Skagen Denmark 45 G8
Skagerrak strait Denmark/Norway 45 F8
Skagit r. U.S.A. 126 C2
Skagway U.S.A. 153 A3
Skaidi Norway 44 N1
Skaland Norway 44 J2
Skalmodal Sweden 44 I4
Skanderborg Denmark 45 F8
Skaneateles Lake U.S.A. 135 G2
Skara Sweden 45 H7
Skardarsko Jezero l. Albania/Montenegro see Scutari, Lake
Skardu Pak. 82 C2
Skärgårdshavets nationalpark nat. park Fin. 45 L7
Skarnes Norway 45 G6
Skarżysko-Kamienna Poland 47 R5
Skaulo Sweden 44 L3
Skawina Poland 47 Q6
Skeena r. Canada 120 D4
Skeena Mountains Canada 120 D3
Skegness U.K. 48 H5
Skellefteå Sweden 44 L4
Skellefteälven r. Sweden 44 L4
Skelleftehamn Sweden 44 L4
Skelmersdale U.K. 48 E5
Skerries Ireland 51 F4
Ski Norway 45 G7
Skiathos i. Greece 59 J5
Skibbereen Ireland 51 C6
Skibotn Norway 44 L2
Skiddaw hill U.K. 48 D4
Skien Norway 45 F7
Skiermûntseach Neth. see Schiermonnikoog
Skiermûntseach i. Neth. see Schiermonnikoog
Skierniewice Poland 47 R5
Skikda Alg. 58 B6
Skipsea U.K. 48 G5
Skipton Australia 112 A6
Skipton U.K. 48 E5
Skirlaugh U.K. 48 G5
Skíros i. Greece see Skyros
Skive Denmark 45 F8
Skjern Denmark 45 F9
Skjolden Norway 45 E6
Skobelev Uzbek. see Farg'ona
Skobeleva, Pik mt. Kyrg. 89 I2
Skodje Norway 44 E5
Skoganvarri Norway 44 N2
Skokie U.S.A. 134 B2
Skomer Island U.K. 49 B7

Skopelos *i.* Greece 59 J5
Skopin Russia 43 H5

▶Skopje Macedonia 59 I4
Capital of Macedonia.

Skoplje Macedonia *see* Skopje
Skövde Sweden 45 H7
Skovorodino Russia 74 A1
Skowhegan U.S.A. 135 K1
Skrunda Latvia 45 M8
Skukum, Mount Canada 120 C2
Skukuza S. Africa 101 J3
Skull Valley U.S.A. 129 G4
Skuodas Lith. 45 L8
Skurup Sweden 45 H9
Skutskär Sweden 45 J6
Skvyra Ukr. 43 F6
Skye *i.* U.K. 50 C3
Skylge *i.* Neth. *see* Terschelling
Skyring, Seno *b.* Chile 144 B8
Skyros Greece 59 K5
Skyros *i.* Greece 59 K5
Skytrain Ice Rise Antarctica 152 L1
Slættaratindur *hill* Faroe Is 44 [inset 2]
Slagelse Denmark 45 G9
Slagnäs Sweden 44 K4
Slane Ireland 51 F4
Slaney *r.* Ireland 51 F5
Slantsy Russia 45 P7
Slashers Reefs Australia 110 D3
Slatina Croatia 58 G2
Slatina Romania 59 K2
Slaty Fork U.S.A. 134 E4
Slava Russia 74 C1
Slave *r.* Canada 121 H2
Slave Coast Africa 96 D4
Slave Lake Canada 120 H4
Slave Point Canada 120 H2
Slavgorod Belarus *see* Slawharad
Slavgorod Russia 72 D2
Slavkovichi Russia 45 P8
Slavonska Požega Croatia *see* Požega
Slavonski Brod Croatia 58 H2
Slavuta Ukr. 43 E6
Slavutych Ukr. 43 F6
Slavyanka Russia 74 C4
Slavyansk Ukr. *see* Slov"yans'k
Slavyanskaya Russia *see* Slavyansk-na-Kubani
Slavyansk-na-Kubani Russia 90 E1
Slawharad Belarus 43 F5
Sławno Poland 47 P3
Slayton U.S.A. 130 E3
Sleaford U.K. 49 G5
Slea Head *hd* Ireland 51 B5
Sleat Neth. *see* Sloten
Sleat, Sound of *sea chan.* U.K. 50 D3
Sled Lake Canada 121 J4
Sleeper Islands Canada 122 F2
Sleeping Bear Dunes Wilderness *nature res.* U.S.A. 134 B1
Slessor Glacier Antarctica 152 B1
Slick Rock U.S.A. 129 I2
Slide Mountain U.S.A. 135 H3
Slieve Bloom Mountains *hills* Ireland 51 E5
Slieve Car *hill* Ireland 51 C3
Slieve Donard *hill* U.K. 51 G3
Slieve Mish Mountains *hills* Ireland 51 B5
Slieve Snaght *hill* Ireland 51 E2
Sligachan U.K. 50 C3
Sligeach Ireland *see* Sligo
Sligo Ireland 51 D3
Sligo U.S.A. 134 F3
Sligo Bay Ireland 51 D3
Slinger U.S.A. 134 A2
Slippery Rock U.S.A. 134 E3
Slite Sweden 45 K8
Sliven Bulg. 59 L3
Sloan U.S.A. 129 F4
Sloat U.S.A. 128 C2
Sloboda Russia *see* Ezhva
Slobodchikovo Russia 42 K3
Slobodskoy Russia 42 K4
Slobozia Romania 59 L2
Slochteren Neth. 52 G1
Slonim Belarus 45 N10
Slootdorp Neth. 52 E2
Sloten Neth. 52 F2
Slough U.K. 49 G7
Slovakia *country* Europe 40 J6
Slovenia *country* Europe 58 F2
Slovenija *country* Europe *see* Slovenia
Slovenj Gradec Slovenia 58 F1
Slovensko *country* Europe *see* Slovakia
Slovenský raj, Národný park *nat. park* Slovakia 47 R6
Slov"yans'k Ukr. 43 H6
Słowiński Park Narodowy *nat. park* Poland 47 P3
Sluch *r.* Ukr. 43 E6
S'Lung, B'Nom *mt.* Vietnam 71 D5
Słupsk Poland 47 P3
Slussfors Sweden 44 J4
Slutsk Belarus 45 O10
Slyne Head *hd* Ireland 51 B4
Slyudyanka Russia 72 I2
Smăch, Kaôh *i.* Cambodia 71 C5
Small Point U.S.A. 135 K2
Smallwood Reservoir Canada 123 I3
Smalyavichy Belarus 45 P9
Smalyenskaya Wzwyshsha *hills* Belarus/Russia *see* Smolensko-Moskovskaya Vozvyshennost'
Smarhon' Belarus 45 O9
Smeaton Canada 121 J4
Smederevo Serbia 59 I2
Smederevska Palanka Serbia 59 I2
Smela Ukr. *see* Smila
Smethport U.S.A. 135 F3
Smidovich Russia 74 D2
Smila Ukr. 43 F6
Smilde Neth. 52 G2
Smiltene Latvia 45 N8
Smirnykh Russia 74 F2
Smith Canada 120 H4
Smith Center U.S.A. 130 D4
Smithers Canada 120 E4
Smithfield S. Africa 101 H6
Smithfield *NC* U.S.A. 132 E5
Smithfield *UT* U.S.A. 126 F4
Smith Glacier Antarctica 152 K1
Smith Island India 71 A4
Smith Island *MD* U.S.A. 135 G4
Smith Island *VA* U.S.A. 135 H5
Smith Mountain Lake U.S.A. 134 F5
Smith River Canada 120 E3
Smiths Falls Canada 135 G1
Smithton Australia 111 [inset]
Smithtown Australia 112 F3
Smithville *OK* U.S.A. 131 E5
Smithville *WV* U.S.A. 134 E4
Smoke Creek Desert U.S.A. 128 D1
Smoky Bay Australia 109 F8
Smoky Cape Australia 112 F3
Smoky Falls Canada 122 E4
Smoky Hill *r.* U.S.A. 130 C4
Smoky Hills *KS* U.S.A. 124 H4
Smoky Hills *KS* U.S.A. 130 D4
Smoky Lake Canada 121 H4
Smoky Mountains U.S.A. 126 E4
Smøla *i.* Norway 44 E5
Smolenka Russia 43 K6
Smolensk Russia 43 G5
Smolensk-Moscow Upland *hills* Belarus/Russia 43 G5
Smolensko-Moskovskaya Vozvyshennost' *hills* Belarus/Russia *see* Smolensk-Moscow Upland
Smolevichi Belarus *see* Smalyavichy
Smolyan Bulg. 59 K4
Smooth Rock Falls Canada 122 E4
Smoothrock Lake Canada 122 C4
Smoothstone Lake Canada 121 J4
Smørfjord Norway 44 N1
Smorgon' Belarus *see* Smarhon'
Smyley Island Antarctica 152 L2
Smyrna Turkey *see* İzmir
Smyrna U.S.A. 135 H4
Smyth Island *atoll* Marshall Is *see* Taongi
Snæfell *mt.* Iceland 44 [inset 1]
Snaefell *hill* Isle of Man 48 C4
Snag (abandoned) Canada 120 A2
Snake *r.* Canada 120 C1
Snake *r.* U.S.A. 126 D3
Snake Island Australia 112 C7
Snake Range *mts* U.S.A. 129 F2
Snake River Canada 120 F3
Snake River Plain U.S.A. 126 E4
Snare *r.* Canada 120 G2
Snare Lake Canada 121 J3
Snare Lakes Canada *see* Wekweètì
Snares Islands N.Z. 107 G6
Snåsa Norway 44 H4
Sneedville U.S.A. 134 D5
Sneek Neth. 52 F1
Sneem Ireland 51 C6
Sneeuberge *mts* S. Africa 100 G6
Snegamook Lake Canada 123 J3
Snegurovka Ukr. *see* Tetiyiv
Snelling U.S.A. 128 C3
Snettisham U.K. 49 H6
Snezhnogorsk Russia 64 J3
Snežnik *mt.* Slovenia 58 F2
Sniečkus Lith. *see* Visaginas
Snihurivka Ukr. 43 G7
Snits Neth. *see* Sneek
Snizort, Loch *b.* U.K. 50 C3
Snoqualmie Pass U.S.A. 126 C3
Snøtinden *mt.* Norway 44 H3
Snoul Cambodia *see* Snuŏl
Snover U.S.A. 134 D2
Snovsk Ukr. *see* Shchors
Snowbird Lake Canada 121 K2
Snowcrest Mountain Canada 120 G5
Snowdon *mt.* U.K. 49 C5
Snowdonia National Park U.K. 49 D6
Snowdrift Canada *see* Łutselk'e
Snowdrift *r.* Canada 121 I2
Snowflake U.S.A. 129 H4
Snow Hill U.S.A. 135 H4
Snow Lake Canada 121 K4
Snowville U.S.A. 126 E4
Snow Water Lake U.S.A. 129 F1
Snowy *r.* Australia 112 D6
Snowy Mountain U.S.A. 135 H2
Snowy Mountains Australia 112 C6
Snowy River National Park Australia 112 D6
Snug Corner Bahamas 133 F8
Snug Harbour *Nfld. and Lab.* Canada 123 L3
Snug Harbour *Ont.* Canada 134 E1
Snuŏl Cambodia 71 D4
Snyder U.S.A. 131 C5
Soalala Madag. 99 E5
Soalara Madag. 99 E6
Soan *r.* Pak. 89 H3
Soan-gundo *is* S. Korea 75 B6
Soanierana-Ivongo Madag. 99 E5
Soavinandriana Madag. 99 E5
Sobat *r.* South Sudan 86 D8
Sobger *r.* Indon. 69 K7
Sobinka Russia 42 I5
Sobradinho, Barragem de *resr* Brazil 143 J6
Sobral Brazil 143 J4
Sochi Russia 91 E2
Society Islands Fr. Polynesia 151 J7
Socorro Brazil 145 B3
Socorro Col. 142 D2
Socorro U.S.A. 127 G6
Socorro, Isla *i.* Mex. 136 B5
Socotra *i.* Yemen 87 H7
Soc Trăng Vietnam 71 D5
Socuéllamos Spain 57 E4
Soda Lake *CA* U.S.A. 128 D4
Soda Lake *CA* U.S.A. 128 E4
Sodankylä Fin. 44 O3
Soda Plains China 82 D2
Soda Springs U.S.A. 126 F4
Söderhamn Sweden 45 J6
Söderköping Sweden 45 J7
Södertälje Sweden 45 J7
Sodiri Sudan 86 C7
Sodo Eth. 98 D3
Södra Kvarken *strait* Fin./Sweden 45 K6
Sodus U.S.A. 135 G2
Soë Indon. 69 G8
Soekarno, Puntjak *mt.* Indon. *see* Jaya, Puncak
Soerabaia Indon. *see* Surabaya
Soerendonk Neth. 52 F3
Soest Germany 53 I3
Soest Neth. 52 F2
Sofala Australia 112 D4

▶Sofia Bulg. 59 J3
Capital of Bulgaria.

Sofiya Bulg. *see* Sofia
Sofiyevka Ukr. *see* Vil'nyans'k
Sofiysk *Khabarovskiy Kray* Russia 74 D1
Sofiysk *Khabarovskiy Kray* Russia 74 E2
Sofporog Russia 44 Q4
Sofrana *i.* Greece 59 L6
Sofra Kalesi *tourist site* Turkey 85 A1
Sōfu-gan *i.* Japan 75 F7
Sog China 76 B2
Soğanlı Dağları *mts* Turkey 91 E2
Sogda Russia 74 D2
Sögel Germany 53 H2
Sogma China 82 E2
Søgne Norway 45 E7
Sognefjorden *inlet* Norway 45 D6
Soguma China 76 D1
Söğüt Turkey 59 N4
Söğüt Dağı *mts* Turkey 59 M6
Soh Iran 88 C3
Sohâg Egypt *see* Sūhāj
Sohagpur India 82 D5
Soham U.K. 49 H6
Sohano P.N.G. 106 F2
Sohar Oman *see* Şuḩār
Sohawal India 82 E4
Sohela India 83 E5
Soheuksan-do *i.* S. Korea 75 B6
Sohng Gwe, Khao *hill* Myanmar/Thai. 71 B4
Sŏho-ri N. Korea 75 C4
Soignies Belgium 52 E4
Soila China 76 C2
Soini Fin. 44 N5
Soissons France 52 D5
Sojat India 82 C4
Sojat Road India 82 C4
Sok *r.* Russia 43 K5
Sokal' Ukr. 43 E6
Sokcho S. Korea 75 C5
Söke Turkey 59 L6
Sokhor, Gora *mt.* Russia 72 J2

▶Sokhumi Georgia 91 F2
Capital of Abkhazia.

Sokiryany Ukr. *see* Sokyryany
Sokodé Togo 96 D4
Soko Islands *H.K.* China 77 [inset]
Sokol Russia 42 I4
Sokolo Mali 96 C3
Sokolov Czechia 53 M4
Sokoto Nigeria 96 D3
Sokoto *r.* Nigeria 96 D3
Sokyryany Ukr. 43 E6
Sola Cuba 133 E8
Sola *i.* Tonga *see* Ata
Solan India 82 D3
Solana Beach U.S.A. 128 E5
Solander Island N.Z. 113 A8
Solapur India 84 B2
Soldotna U.S.A. 118 C3
Soledad U.S.A. 128 C3
Soledade Brazil 144 F3
Solenoye Russia 43 I7
Solfjellsjøen Norway 44 H3
Solginskiy Russia 42 I3
Solhan Turkey 91 F3
Soligalich Russia 42 I4
Soligorsk Belarus *see* Salihorsk
Solihull U.K. 49 F6
Solikamsk Russia 41 R4
Sol'-Iletsk Russia 64 G4
Solimões *r.* S. America *see* Amazon
Solingen Germany 52 H3
Solitaire Namibia 100 B2
Sol-Karmala Russia *see* Severnoye
Şollar Azer. 91 H2
Sollefteå Sweden 44 J5
Söllichau Germany 53 M3
Solling *hills* Germany 53 J3
Sollstedt Germany 53 K3
Sollum, Gulf of Egypt *see* Sallum, Khalīj as
Solms Germany 53 I4
Solnechnogorsk Russia 42 H4
Solnechnyy *Amurskaya Oblast'* Russia 74 A1
Solnechnyy *Khabarovskiy Kray* Russia 74 E2
Solok Indon. 68 C7
Solomon U.S.A. 129 I5
Solomon, North Fork *r.* U.S.A. 130 D4

▶Solomon Islands *country* S. Pacific Ocean 107 G2
4th largest and 5th most populous country in Oceania.

Solomon Sea S. Pacific Ocean 106 F2
Solon U.S.A. 135 K1
Solon Springs U.S.A. 130 F2
Solor *i.* Indon. 108 C2
Solor, Kepulauan *is* Indon. 108 C2
Solothurn Switz. 56 H3
Solovetskiye Ostrova *is* Russia 42 G2
Solov'yevsk Russia 74 B1
Šolta *i.* Croatia 58 G3
Solţānābād *Kermān* Iran 88 E4
Solţānābād *Khorāsān-e Razavī* Iran 89 E3
Solţānābād *Tehrān* Iran 88 C3
Solţānīyeh Iran 88 C2
Soltau Germany 53 J2
Sol'tsy Russia 42 F4
Solvay U.S.A. 135 G2
Sölvesborg Sweden 45 I8
Solway Firth *est.* U.K. 50 F6
Solwezi Zambia 99 C5
Soma Turkey 59 L5
Somain France 52 D4
Somalia *country* Africa 98 E3
Somali Basin *sea feature* Indian Ocean 149 L6
Somaliland *disp. terr.* Somalia 98 E3
Somali Republic *country* Africa *see* Somalia
Sombo Angola 99 C4
Sombor Serbia 59 H2
Sombrero Channel India 71 A6
Sombrio, Lago do *l.* Brazil 145 A5
Somero Fin. 45 M6
Somerset *KY* U.S.A. 134 C5
Somerset *MI* U.S.A. 134 C2
Somerset *OH* U.S.A. 134 D4
Somerset *PA* U.S.A. 134 F4
Somerset, Lake Australia 112 F1
Somerset East S. Africa 101 G7
Somerset Island Canada 119 I2
Somerset Reservoir U.S.A. 135 I2
Somerset West S. Africa 100 D8
Somersworth U.S.A. 135 J2
Somerton U.S.A. 129 F5
Somerville *NJ* U.S.A. 135 H3
Somerville *TN* U.S.A. 131 F5
Someydeh Iran 88 B3
Somme *r.* France 52 B4
Somme, Canal de la France 52 C5
Sommen *l.* Sweden 45 I7
Sömmerda Germany 53 L3
Sommet, Lac du *l.* Canada 123 H3
Somnath India 82 B5
Somoniyon Tajik. 89 H2
Somutu Myanmar 70 B1
Son *r.* India 83 F4
Sonag China *see* Zêkog
Sonapur India *see* Subarnapur
Sonar *r.* India 82 D4
Sŏnbong N. Korea 74 C4
Sŏnch'ŏn N. Korea 75 B5
Sønderborg Denmark 45 F9
Sondershausen Germany 53 K3
Søndre Strømfjord Greenland *see* Kangerlussuaq
Søndre Strømfjord *inlet* Greenland *see* Kangerlussuaq
Sondrio Italy 58 C1
Sonepat India *see* Sonipat
Sonepur India *see* Subarnapur
Song, Loi *mt.* Myanmar 70 B2
Songbai *Hubei* China *see* Shennongjia
Songbai *Hunan* China 77 G3
Songbu China 77 G2
Sông Câu Vietnam 71 E4
Songcheng China *see* Xiapu
Sông Đa, Hô *resr* Vietnam 70 D2
Songea Tanz. 99 D5
Songhua Hu *resr* China 74 B4
Songhua Jiang *r. Heilongjiang/Jilin* China 74 D3
Songhua Jiang *r. Jilin* China 74 B3
Songjiang China 77 I2
Songjianghe China 74 B4
Sŏngjin N. Korea *see* Kimch'aek
Songkan China 76 E2
Songkhla Thai. 71 C6
Songling China *see* Tarqi
Songlong Myanmar 70 B2
Songnim N. Korea 75 B5
Songo Angola 99 B4
Songo Moz. 99 D5
Songpan China 76 D1
Songshan China *see* Ziyun
Song Shan *mt.* China 77 G1
Songtao China 77 F2
Songxi China 77 H3
Songxian China 77 G1
Songyuan *Fujian* China *see* Songxi
Songyuan *Jilin* China 74 B3
Songzi China 77 F2
Sơn Hai Vietnam 71 E5
Sonid Youqi China *see* Saihan Tal
Sonid Zuoqi China *see* Mandalt
Sonipat India 82 D3
Sonkajärvi Fin. 44 O5
Sonkovo Russia 42 H4
Sơn La Vietnam 70 C2
Sonmiani Pak. 89 G5
Sonmiani Bay Pak. 89 G5
Sonneberg Germany 53 L4
Sono *r. Minas Gerais* Brazil 145 B2
Sono *r. Tocantins* Brazil 143 I5
Sonoma U.S.A. 128 B2
Sonoma Peak U.S.A. 128 E1
Sonora *r.* Mex. 127 F7
Sonora *state* Mex. 127 F7
Sonora *CA* U.S.A. 128 C3
Sonora *KY* U.S.A. 134 C5
Sonora *TX* U.S.A. 131 C6
Sonoran Desert U.S.A. 129 G5
Sonoran Desert National Monument *nat. park* U.S.A. 127 E6
Sonqor Iran 88 B3
Sonsogad *mt.* India 84 B3
Sonsonate El Salvador 136 G6
Sonsorol Islands Palau 69 I5
Sơn Tây Vietnam 70 D2
Sonwabile S. Africa 101 I6
Soochow China *see* Suzhou
Soomaaliya *country* Africa *see* Somalia
Sopi, Tanjung *pt* Indon. 69 H6
Sopo *watercourse* South Sudan 97 F4
Sopot Bulg. 59 K3
Sopot Poland 47 Q3
Sop Prap Thai. 70 B3
Sopron Hungary 58 G1
Sopur India 82 C2
Sora Italy 58 E4
Sorab India 84 B3
Sorada India 84 E2
Söråker Sweden 44 J5
Sorel Canada 123 G5
Soreq, Naḥal *r.* Israel 85 B4
Sorgun Turkey 90 D3
Sorgun *r.* Turkey 85 B1
Soria Spain 57 E3
Sorkh, Daqq-e *salt flat* Iran 88 D3
Sorkh, Kūh-e *mts* Iran 88 D3
Sorkhān Iran 88 E4
Sorkh Doz Afgh. 89 G4
Sorkheh Iran 88 D3
Sørli Norway 44 H4
Soro India 83 F5
Soroca Moldova 43 F6
Sorocaba Brazil 145 B3
Soroki Moldova *see* Soroca
Sorol *atoll* Micronesia 69 K5
Sorong Indon. 69 I7
Soroti Uganda 98 D3
Sørøya *i.* Norway 44 M1
Sorraia *r.* Port. 57 B4
Sørreisa Norway 44 K2
Sorrento Italy 58 F4
Sorsele Sweden 44 J4
Sorsogon Phil. 69 G4
Sortavala Russia 44 Q6
Sortland Norway 44 I2
Sortopolovskaya Russia 42 K3
Sorvizhi Russia 42 K4
Sosenskiy Russia 43 G5
Soshanguve S. Africa 101 I3
Sosna *r.* Russia 43 H5
Sosneado *mt.* Arg. 144 C4
Sosnogorsk Russia 42 L3
Sosnovka *Arkhangel'skaya Oblast'* Russia 42 J3
Sosnovka *Kaliningradskaya Oblast'* Russia 41 K5
Sosnovka *Murmanskaya Oblast'* Russia 42 I2
Sosnovka *Tambovskaya Oblast'* Russia 43 I5
Sosnovo Russia 45 Q6
Sosnovo-Ozerskoye Russia 73 K2
Sosnovyy Russia 44 R4
Sosnovyy Bor Russia 45 P7
Sosnowiec Poland 47 Q5
Sosnowitz Poland *see* Sosnowiec
Sos'va *Khanty-Mansiyskiy Avtonomnyy Okrug-Yugra* Russia 41 S3
Sos'va *Sverdlovskaya Oblast'* Russia 41 S4
Sotang China 76 B2
Sotara, Volcán *vol.* Col. 142 C3
Sotkamo Fin. 44 P4
Sotteville-lès-Rouen France 52 B5
Souanké Congo 98 B3
Soubré Côte d'Ivoire 96 C4
Souderton U.S.A. 135 H3
Soufflenheim France 53 H6
Soufli Greece 59 L4
Soufrière St Lucia 137 L6
Soufrière *vol.* St Vincent 137 L6
Sougueur Alg. 57 G6
Souillac France 56 E4
Souilly France 52 F5
Souk Ahras Alg. 58 B6
Souk el Arbaâ du Rharb Morocco 54 C5
Sŏul S. Korea *see* Seoul
Soulac-sur-Mer France 56 D4
Soulom France 56 D5
Sounding Creek *r.* Canada 121 I4
Souni Cyprus 85 A2
Soûr Lebanon *see* Tyre
Soure Brazil 143 I4
Sour el Ghozlane Alg. 57 H5
Souris Canada 121 K5
Souris *r.* Canada 121 L5
Souriya *country* Asia *see* Syria
Sousa Brazil 143 K5
Sousa Lara Angola *see* Bocoio
Sousse Tunisia 58 D7
Soustons France 56 D5

▶South Africa *country* Africa 100 F5
5th most populous country in Africa.

Southampton Canada 134 E1
Southampton U.K. 49 F8
Southampton U.S.A. 135 I3
Southampton, Cape Canada 119 J3
Southampton Island Canada 119 J3
South Andaman *i.* India 71 A5
South Anna *r.* U.S.A. 135 G5
South Anston U.K. 48 F5
South Aulatsivik Island Canada 123 J2
South Australia *state* Australia 106 D5
South Australian Basin *sea feature* Indian Ocean 149 P8
Southaven U.S.A. 131 F5
South Baldy *mt.* U.S.A. 127 G6
South Bank U.K. 48 F4
South Bass Island U.S.A. 134 D3
South Bend *IN* U.S.A. 134 B3
South Bend *WA* U.S.A. 126 C3
South Bluff *pt* Bahamas 133 F8
South Boston U.S.A. 135 F5
South Brook Canada 123 K4
South Carolina *state* U.S.A. 133 D5
South Charleston *OH* U.S.A. 134 D4
South Charleston *WV* U.S.A. 134 E4
South China Sea N. Pacific Ocean 68 F4
South Coast Town Australia *see* Gold Coast
South Dakota *state* U.S.A. 130 C2
South Downs *hills* U.K. 49 G8
South Downs National Park *nat. park* U.K. 49 G8
South East *admin. dist.* Botswana 101 G3
South East Cape Australia 111 [inset]
Southeast Cape U.S.A. 118 B3
Southeast Indian Ridge *sea feature* Indian Ocean 149 N8
South East Isles Australia 109 C8
Southeast Pacific Basin *sea feature* S. Pacific Ocean 151 M10
South East Point Australia 112 C7
Southend Canada 121 K3
Southend U.K. 50 D5
Southend-on-Sea U.K. 49 H7
Southern *admin. dist.* Botswana 100 G3
Southern Alps *mts* N.Z. 113 C6
Southern Cross Australia 109 B7
Southern Indian Lake Canada 121 L3
Southern Lau Group *is* Fiji 107 I3
Southern National Park South Sudan 97 F4
Southern Ocean 152 C2
Southern Pines U.S.A. 133 E5
Southern Rhodesia *country* Africa *see* Zimbabwe
Southern Uplands *hills* U.K. 50 E5
South Esk *r.* U.K. 50 F4
South Esk Tableland *reg.* Australia 108 D4
Southey Canada 121 J5
Southfield U.S.A. 134 D2
South Fiji Basin *sea feature* S. Pacific Ocean 150 H7
South Fork U.S.A. 128 B1
South Geomagnetic Pole Antarctica 152 F1
South Georgia *i.* S. Atlantic Ocean 144 I8

▶South Georgia and South Sandwich Islands *terr.* S. Atlantic Ocean 144 I8
United Kingdom Overseas Territory

South Harris *pen.* U.K. 50 B3
South Haven U.S.A. 134 B2
South Henik Lake Canada 121 L2
South Hill U.S.A. 135 F5
South Honshu Ridge *sea feature* N. Pacific Ocean 150 F3
South Indian Lake Canada 121 L3

▶South Island N.Z. 113 D7
2nd largest island in Oceania.

South Junction Canada 121 M5
South Korea *country* Asia 75 B5
South Lake Tahoe U.S.A. 128 C2
South Luangwa National Park Zambia 99 D5
South Magnetic Pole Antarctica 152 G2
South Mills U.S.A. 135 G5
Southminster U.K. 49 H7
South Mountains *hills* U.S.A. 135 G4
South New Berlin U.S.A. 135 H2
South Orkney Islands S. Atlantic Ocean 148 F10
South Ossetia *disp. terr.* Georgia 91 G2
South Paris U.S.A. 135 J1
South Platte *r.* U.S.A. 130 C3
South Point Bahamas 133 F8
South Pole Antarctica 152 C1
Southport *Qld* Australia 112 F1
Southport *Tas.* Australia 111 [inset]
Southport U.K. 48 D5
Southport U.S.A. 135 G2
South Portland U.S.A. 135 J2
South Ronaldsay *i.* U.K. 50 G2
South Royalton U.S.A. 135 I2
South Salt Lake U.S.A. 129 H1
South Sand Bluff *pt* S. Africa 101 J6
South Sandwich Islands S. Atlantic Ocean 148 G9
South Sandwich Trench *sea feature* S. Atlantic Ocean 148 G9
South San Francisco U.S.A. 128 B3
South Saskatchewan *r.* Canada 121 J4
South Seal *r.* Canada 121 L3
South Shetland Islands Antarctica 152 A2
South Shetland Trough *sea feature* S. Atlantic Ocean 152 L2
South Shields U.K. 48 F3
South Sinai *governorate* Egypt *see* Janūb Sīnā'
South Solomon Trench *sea feature* S. Pacific Ocean 150 G6

▶South Sudan *country* Africa 97 G4
Gained independence from Sudan on 9 July 2011.

South Taranaki Bight *b.* N.Z. 113 E4
South Tasman Rise *sea feature* Southern Ocean 150 F9
South Tent *mt.* U.S.A. 129 H2
South Tons *r.* India 83 E4
South Twin Island Canada 122 F3
South Tyne *r.* U.K. 48 E4
South Uist *i.* U.K. 50 B3
South Wellesley Islands Australia 110 B3
South-West Africa *country* Africa *see* Namibia
South West Cape N.Z. 113 A8
South West Entrance *sea chan.* P.N.G. 110 E1
Southwest Indian Ridge *sea feature* Indian Ocean 149 K8
South West National Park Australia 111 [inset]
Southwest Pacific Basin *sea feature* S. Pacific Ocean 150 I8
South-West Peru Ridge *sea feature* S. Pacific Ocean *see* Nazca Ridge
South West Rocks Australia 112 F3
South Whitley U.S.A. 134 C3
South Wichita *r.* U.S.A. 131 D5
South Windham U.S.A. 135 J2
Southwold U.K. 49 I6
Southwood National Park Australia 112 E1
Soutpansberg *mts* S. Africa 101 I2
Souttouf, Adrar *mts* W. Sahara 96 B2
Soverato Italy 58 G5
Sovetsk *Kaliningradskaya Oblast'* Russia 45 L9
Sovetsk *Kirovskaya Oblast'* Russia 42 K4
Sovetskaya Gavan' Russia 74 F2
Sovetskiy *Khanty-Mansiyskiy Avtonomnyy Okrug-Yugra* Russia 41 S3
Sovetskiy *Leningradskaya Oblast'* Russia 45 P6
Sovetskiy *Respublika Mariy El* Russia 42 K4
Sovetskoye *Chechenskaya Respublika* Russia *see* Shatoy
Sovetskoye *Stavropol'skiy Kray* Russia *see* Zelenokumsk
Sovyets'kyy Crimea 90 D1
Sowa China 76 C2
Soweto S. Africa 101 H4
Şowma'eh Sarā Iran 88 C2
So'x Tajik. 89 H2
Sōya-kaikyō *strait* Japan/Russia *see* La Pérouse Strait
Sōya-misaki *c.* Japan 74 F3
Soyana *r.* Russia 42 I2
Soyma *r.* Russia 42 K2
Soyopa Mex. 127 F7
Sozh *r.* Europe 43 F6
Sozopol Bulg. 59 L3
Spa Belgium 52 F4

▶Spain *country* Europe 57 E3
4th largest country in Europe.

Spalato Croatia *see* Split
Spalatum Croatia *see* Split
Spalding U.K. 49 G6
Spanish Canada 122 E5
Spanish Fork U.S.A. 129 H1
Spanish Guinea *country* Africa *see* Equatorial Guinea
Spanish Netherlands *country* Europe *see* Belgium
Spanish Sahara *disp. terr.* Africa *see* Western Sahara

Spanish Town Jamaica 137 I5
Sparks U.S.A. 128 D2
Sparta Greece see Sparti
Sparta GA U.S.A. 133 D5
Sparta KY U.S.A. 134 C4
Sparta MI U.S.A. 134 C2
Sparta NC U.S.A. 134 E5
Sparta TN U.S.A. 132 C5
Spartanburg U.S.A. 133 D5
Sparti Greece 59 J6
Spartivento, Capo c. Italy 58 G6
Spas-Demensk Russia 43 G5
Spas-Klepiki Russia 43 I5
Spassk-Dal'niy Russia 74 D3
Spassk-Ryazanskiy Russia 43 I5
Spata (Eleftherios Venizelos) airport Greece 59 J6
Spatha, Akra pt Greece see Spatha, Akrotirio
Spatha, Akrotirio pt Greece 59 J7
Spearman U.S.A. 131 C4
Speedway U.S.A. 134 B4
Spence Bay Canada see Taloyoak
Spencer IA U.S.A. 130 E3
Spencer ID U.S.A. 126 E3
Spencer IN U.S.A. 134 B4
Spencer NE U.S.A. 130 D3
Spencer WV U.S.A. 134 E4
Spencer, Cape U.S.A. 120 B3
Spencer Bay Namibia 100 B3
Spencer Gulf est. Australia 111 B7
Spencer Range hills Australia 108 E3
Spennymoor U.K. 48 F4
Sperrgebiet National Park nat. park Namibia 100 B4
Sperrin Mountains hills U.K. 51 E3
Sperryville U.S.A. 135 F4
Spessart reg. Germany 53 J5
Spétsai i. Greece see Spetses
Spetses i. Greece 59 J6
Spey r. U.K. 50 F3
Speyer Germany 53 I5
Spezand Pak. 89 G4
Spice Islands Indon. see Moluccas
Spijk Neth. 52 G1
Spijkenisse Neth. 52 E3
Spilimbergo Italy 58 E1
Spilsby U.K. 48 H5
Spīn Bōldak Afgh. 89 G4
Spintangi Pak. 89 H4
Spirit Lake U.S.A. 130 E3
Spirit River Canada 120 G4
Spirovo Russia 42 G4
Spišská Nová Ves Slovakia 43 D6
Spiti r. India 82 D3

▶Spitsbergen i. Svalbard 64 C2
5th largest island in Europe.

Spittal an der Drau Austria 47 N7
Spitzbergen i. Svalbard see Spitsbergen
Split Croatia 58 G3
Split Lake Canada 121 L3
Split Lake l. Canada 121 L3
Spokane U.S.A. 126 D3
Spoletium Italy see Spoleto
Spoleto Italy 58 E3
Spóng Cambodia 71 D4
Spoon r. U.S.A. 130 F3
Spooner U.S.A. 130 F2
Spornitz Germany 53 L1
Spotsylvania U.S.A. 135 G4
Spotted Horse U.S.A. 126 G3
Spranger, Mount Canada 120 F4
Spratly Islands S. China Sea 68 E4
Spray U.S.A. 126 D3
Spree r. Germany 47 N4
Sprimont Belgium 52 F4
Springbok S. Africa 100 C5
Springdale Canada 123 L4
Springdale U.S.A. 134 C4
Springe Germany 53 J2
Springer U.S.A. 127 G5
Springerville U.S.A. 129 I4
Springfield CO U.S.A. 130 C4

▶Springfield IL U.S.A. 130 F4
Capital of Illinois.

Springfield KY U.S.A. 134 C5
Springfield MA U.S.A. 135 I2
Springfield MO U.S.A. 131 E4
Springfield OH U.S.A. 134 D4
Springfield OR U.S.A. 126 C3
Springfield TN U.S.A. 134 B5
Springfield VT U.S.A. 135 I2
Springfield WV U.S.A. 135 F4
Springfontein S. Africa 101 G6
Spring Glen U.S.A. 129 H2
Spring Grove U.S.A. 134 A2
Springhill Canada 123 I5
Spring Hill U.S.A. 133 D6
Springhouse Canada 120 F5
Spring Mountains U.S.A. 129 F3
Springs Junction N.Z. 113 D6
Springsure Australia 110 E5
Spring Valley MN U.S.A. 130 E3
Spring Valley NY U.S.A. 135 H3
Springview U.S.A. 130 D3
Springville CA U.S.A. 128 D3
Springville NY U.S.A. 135 F2
Springville PA U.S.A. 135 H3
Springville UT U.S.A. 129 H1
Sprowston U.K. 49 I6
Spruce Grove Canada 120 H4
Spruce Knob mt. U.S.A. 132 E4
Spruce Mountain CO U.S.A. 129 I2
Spruce Mountain NV U.S.A. 129 F1
Spurn Head hd U.K. 48 H5
Spuzzum Canada 120 F5
Squam Lake U.S.A. 135 J2
Square Lake U.S.A. 123 H5
Squillace, Golfo di g. Italy 58 G5
Squires, Mount hill Australia 109 D6
Srbija country Europe see Serbia
Srbinje Bos. & Herz. see Foča
Srê Âmběl Cambodia 71 C5
Srebrenica Bos. & Herz. 59 H2
Sredets Burgas Bulg. 59 L3
Sredets Sofia-Grad Bulg. see Sofia
Sredinnyy Khrebet mts Russia 65 Q4
Sredna Gora mts Bulg. 59 J3
Srednekolymsk Russia 65 Q3
Sredne-Russkaya Vozvyshennost' hills Russia see Central Russian Upland
Sredne-Sibirskoye Ploskogor'ye plat. Russia see Central Siberian Plateau
Sredneye Kuyto, Ozero l. Russia 44 Q4
Sredniy Ural mts Russia 41 R4
Srednyaya Akhtuba Russia 43 J6
Sreepur Bangl. see Sripur
Srê Khtum Cambodia 71 D4
Srê Noy Cambodia 71 D4
Sretensk Russia 73 L2
Sri Aman Sarawak Malaysia 68 E6
Sriharikota Island India 84 D3

▶Sri Jayewardenepura Kotte Sri Lanka 84 C5
Capital of Sri Lanka.

Srikakulam India 84 E2
Sri Kalahasti India 84 C3
Sri Lanka country Asia 84 D5
Srinagar India 82 C2
Sri Pada mt. Sri Lanka see Adam's Peak
Sripur Bangl. 83 G4
Srirangam India 84 C4
Sri Thep tourist site Thai. 70 C3
Srivardhan India 84 B2
Staaten r. Australia 110 C3
Staaten River National Park Australia 110 C3
Stabroek Guyana see Georgetown
Stade Germany 53 J1
Staden Belgium 52 D4
Stadskanaal Neth. 52 G2
Stadtallendorf Germany 53 J4
Stadthagen Germany 53 J2
Stadtilm Germany 53 L4
Stadtlohn Germany 52 G3
Stadtoldendorf Germany 53 J3
Stadtroda Germany 53 L4
Staffa i. U.K. 50 C4
Staffelberg hill Germany 53 L4
Stafford U.K. 49 E6
Stafford U.S.A. 135 G4
Stafford Creek Bahamas 133 E7
Stafford Springs U.S.A. 135 I3
Stagg Lake Canada 120 H2
Staicele Latvia 45 N8
Staines-upon-Thames U.K. 49 G7
Stakhanov Ukr. 43 H6
Stakhanovo Russia see Zhukovskiy
Stalbridge U.K. 49 E8
Stalham U.K. 49 I6
Stalin Bulg. see Varna
Stalinabad Tajik. see Dushanbe
Stalingrad Russia see Volgograd
Staliniri Georgia see Tskhinvali
Stalino Ukr. see Donets'k
Stalinogorsk Russia see Novomoskovsk
Stalinogród Poland see Katowice
Stalinsk Russia see Novokuznetsk
Stalowa Wola Poland 43 D6
Stamboliyski Bulg. 59 K3
Stamford Australia 110 C4
Stamford U.K. 49 G6
Stamford CT U.S.A. 135 I3
Stamford NY U.S.A. 135 H2
Stampalia i. Greece see Astypalaia
Stampriet Namibia 100 D3
Stamsund Norway 44 H2
Stanardsville U.S.A. 135 F4
Stanberry U.S.A. 130 E3
Stancomb-Wills Glacier Antarctica 152 B1
Standard Canada 120 H5
Standdaarbuiten Neth. 52 E3
Standerton S. Africa 101 I4
Standish U.S.A. 134 D2
Stanfield U.S.A. 129 H5
Stanford KY U.S.A. 134 C5
Stanford MT U.S.A. 126 F3
Stanger S. Africa see KwaDukuza
Stanislaus r. U.S.A. 128 C3
Stanislav Ukr. see Ivano-Frankivs'k
Stanke Dimitrov Bulg. see Dupnitsa
Staňkov Czechia 53 N5
Stanley Australia 111 [inset]
Stanley H.K. China 77 [inset]

▶Stanley Falkland Is 144 E8
Capital of the Falkland Islands (Islas Malvinas).

Stanley U.K. 48 F4
Stanley ID U.S.A. 126 E3
Stanley KY U.S.A. 134 B5
Stanley ND U.S.A. 130 C1
Stanley VA U.S.A. 135 F4
Stanley, Mount hill N.T. Australia 108 E5
Stanley, Mount hill Tas. Australia 111 [inset]
Stanley, Mount Dem. Rep. Congo/Uganda see Margherita Peak
Stanleyville Dem. Rep. Congo see Kisangani
Stann Creek Belize see Dangriga
Stannington U.K. 48 F3
Stanovoye Russia 43 H5
Stanovoye Nagor'ye mts Russia 73 L1
Stanovoy Khrebet mts Russia 65 N4
Stansmore Range hills Australia 108 E5
Stanthorpe Australia 112 E2
Stanton U.K. 49 H6
Stanton KY U.S.A. 134 D5
Stanton MI U.S.A. 134 C2
Stanton ND U.S.A. 130 C2
Stanton TX U.S.A. 131 C5
Stapleton U.S.A. 130 C3
Starachowice Poland 47 R5
Stara Planina mts Bulg./Serbia see Balkan Mountains
Staraya Russa Russia 42 F4
Stara Zagora Bulg. 59 K3
Starbuck Island Kiribati 151 J6
Star City U.S.A. 134 B3
Starcke National Park Australia 110 D2
Stargard in Pommern Poland see Stargard Szczeciński
Stargard Szczeciński Poland 47 O4
Staritsa Russia 42 G4
Starke U.S.A. 133 D6
Starkville U.S.A. 131 F5
Star Lake U.S.A. 135 H1
Starnberger See l. Germany 47 M7
Starobel'sk Ukr. see Starobil's'k
Starobil's'k Ukr. 43 H6
Starogard Gdański Poland 47 Q4
Starokonstantinov Ukr. see Starokostyantyniv
Starokostyantyniv Ukr. 43 E6
Starominskaya Russia 43 H7
Staroshcherbinovskaya Russia 43 H7
Star Peak U.S.A. 128 D1
Start Point U.K. 49 D8
Starve Island Kiribati see Starbuck Island
Staryya Darohi Belarus 43 F5
Staryye Dorogi Belarus see Staryya Darohi
Staryy Kayak Russia 65 L2
Staryy Oskol Russia 43 H6
Staßfurt Germany 53 L3
State College U.S.A. 135 G3
State Line U.S.A. 131 F6
Staten Island Arg. see Estados, Isla de los
Statenville U.S.A. 133 D6
Statesboro U.S.A. 133 D5
Statesville U.S.A. 132 D5
Statia mun. West Indies see Sint Eustatius
Station U.S.A. 134 C4

▶Station Nord Greenland 153 I1
Most northerly point of North America.

Stauchitz Germany 53 N3
Staufenberg Germany 53 I4
Staunton U.S.A. 134 F4
Stavanger Norway 45 D7
Staveley U.K. 48 F5
Stavropol' Russia 91 F1
Stavropol Kray admin. div. Russia see Stavropol'skiy Kray
Stavropol'-na-Volge Russia see Tol'yatti
Stavropol'skaya Vozvyshennost' hills Russia 91 F1
Stavropol'skiy Kray admin. div. Russia 91 F1
Stayner Canada 134 E1
Stayton U.S.A. 126 C3
Steadville S. Africa 101 I5
Steamboat Springs U.S.A. 126 G4
Stearns U.S.A. 134 C5
Stebbins U.S.A. 118 B3
Steele Island Antarctica 152 L2
Steelville U.S.A. 130 F4
Steen r. Canada 120 G3
Steenderen Neth. 52 G2
Steenkampsberge mts S. Africa 101 J3
Steen River Canada 120 G3
Steens Mountain U.S.A. 126 D4
Steenstrup Gletscher glacier Greenland see Sermersuaq
Steenvoorde France 52 C4
Steenwijk Neth. 52 G2
Stefansson Island Canada 119 H2
Stegi Swaziland see Siteki
Steigerwald mts Germany 53 K5
Stein Germany 53 L5
Steinach Germany 53 L4
Steinaker Reservoir U.S.A. 129 I1
Steinbach Canada 121 L5
Steinfeld (Oldenburg) Germany 53 I2
Steinfurt Germany 53 H2
Steinhausen Namibia 99 B6
Steinheim Germany 53 J3
Steinkjer Norway 44 G4
Steinkopf S. Africa 100 C5
Steinsdalen Norway 44 G4
Stella S. Africa 100 G4
Stella Maris Bahamas 133 F8
Stellenbosch S. Africa 100 D7
Stello, Monte mt. Corsica France 56 I5
Stelvio, Parco Nazionale dello nat. park Italy 58 D1
Stenay France 52 F5
Stendal Germany 53 L2
Stenhousemuir U.K. 50 F4
Stenungsund Sweden 45 G7
Steornabhagh U.K. see Stornoway
Stepanakert Azer. see Xankändi
Stephens, Cape N.Z. 113 D5
Stephens City U.S.A. 135 F4
Stephens Lake Canada 121 M3
Stephenville U.S.A. 131 D5
Stepnoy Russia see Elista
Stepnoye Russia 43 J6
Sterkfontein Dam resr S. Africa 101 I5
Sterkstroom S. Africa 101 H6
Sterlet Lake Canada 121 I1
Sterlibashevo Russia 41 R5
Sterling S. Africa 100 E6
Sterling CO U.S.A. 130 C3
Sterling IL U.S.A. 130 F3
Sterling MI U.S.A. 134 C1
Sterling UT U.S.A. 129 H2
Sterling City U.S.A. 131 C6
Sterling Heights U.S.A. 134 D2
Sterlitamak Russia 64 G4
Stettin Poland see Szczecin
Stettler Canada 121 H4
Steubenville KY U.S.A. 134 C5
Steubenville OH U.S.A. 134 E3
Stevenage U.K. 49 G7
Stevenson U.S.A. 126 C3
Stevenson Lake Canada 121 L4
Stevens Point U.S.A. 130 F2
Stevens Village U.S.A. 118 D3
Stevensville MI U.S.A. 134 B2
Stevensville PA U.S.A. 135 G3
Stevns Klint cliff Denmark 45 H9
Stewart Canada 120 D4
Stewart r. Canada 120 B2
Stewart, Isla i. Chile 144 B8
Stewart Crossing Canada 120 B2
Stewart Island N.Z. 113 A8
Stewart Islands Solomon Is 107 G2
Stewart Lake Canada 119 J3
Stewarton U.K. 50 E5
Stewarts Point U.S.A. 128 B2
Stewiacke Canada 123 J5
Steynsburg S. Africa 101 G6
Steyr Austria 47 O6
Steytlerville S. Africa 100 G7
Stiens Neth. 52 F1
Stif Alg. see Sétif
Stigler U.S.A. 131 E5
Stikine r. Canada 120 C3
Stikine Plateau Canada 120 D3
Stikine Strait U.S.A. 120 C3
Stilbaai S. Africa 100 E8
Stiles U.S.A. 134 A1
Stillwater MN U.S.A. 130 E2
Stillwater OK U.S.A. 131 D4
Stillwater Range mts U.S.A. 128 D2
Stillwell U.S.A. 134 B3
Stilton U.K. 49 G6
Stilwell U.S.A. 131 E5
Stinnett U.S.A. 131 C5
Štip Macedonia 59 J4
Stirling Australia 108 F5
Stirling Canada 135 G1
Stirling U.K. 50 F4
Stirling Creek r. Australia 108 E4
Stirling Range National Park Australia 109 B8
Stittsville Canada 135 H1
Stjørdalshalsen Norway 44 G5
Stockbridge U.S.A. 134 C2
Stockerau Austria 47 P6
Stockheim Germany 53 L4

▶Stockholm Sweden 45 K7
Capital of Sweden.

Stockinbingal Australia 112 C5
Stockport U.K. 48 E5
Stockton CA U.S.A. 128 C3
Stockton KS U.S.A. 130 D4
Stockton MO U.S.A. 130 E4
Stockton UT U.S.A. 129 G1
Stockton Lake U.S.A. 130 E4
Stockton-on-Tees U.K. 48 F4
Stockville U.S.A. 130 C3
Stod Czechia 53 N5
Stœng Trêng Cambodia 71 D4
Stoer, Point of U.K. 50 D2
Stoke-on-Trent U.K. 49 E5
Stokesley U.K. 48 F4
Stokes Point Australia 111 [inset]
Stokes Range hills Australia 108 E4
Stokkseyri Iceland 44 [inset 1]
Stokkvågen Norway 44 H3
Stokmarknes Norway 44 I2
Stolac Bos. & Herz. 58 G3
Stolberg (Rheinland) Germany 52 G4
Stolbovoy Russia 153 G2
Stolbtsy Belarus see Stowbtsy
Stolin Belarus 45 O11
Stollberg Germany 53 M4
Stolp Poland see Słupsk
Stolzenau Germany 53 J2
Stone U.K. 49 E6
Stoneboro U.S.A. 134 E3
Stonecliffe Canada 122 F5
Stonecutters' Island pen. H.K. China 77 [inset]
Stonehaven U.K. 50 G4
Stonehenge Australia 110 C5
Stonehenge tourist site U.K. 49 F7
Stoner U.S.A. 129 I3
Stone Spheres of the Diquís tourist site Costa Rica 137 H7
Stonewall Canada 121 L5
Stonewall Jackson Lake U.S.A. 134 E4
Stony Creek U.S.A. 135 G5
Stony Lake Canada 121 L3
Stony Point U.S.A. 135 G2
Stony Rapids Canada 121 J3
Stony River U.S.A. 118 C3
Stooping r. Canada 122 E3
Stora Lulevatten l. Sweden 44 K3
Stora Sjöfallets nationalpark nat. park Sweden 44 J3
Storavan l. Sweden 44 K4
Store Bælt sea chan. Denmark see Great Belt
Støren Norway 44 G5
Storfjordbotn Norway 44 O1
Storforshei Norway 44 I3
Storjord Norway 44 I3
Storkerson Peninsula Canada 119 H2
Storm Bay Australia 111 [inset]
Stormberg S. Africa 101 H6
Storm Lake U.S.A. 130 E3
Stornosa mt. Norway 44 E6
Stornoway U.K. 50 C2
Storozhevsk Russia 42 L3
Storozhynets' Ukr. 43 E6
Storrs U.S.A. 135 I3
Storseleby Sweden 44 J4
Storsjön l. Sweden 44 I5
Storskrymten mt. Norway 44 F5
Storslett Norway 44 L2
Stortemelk sea chan. Neth. 52 F1
Storuman Sweden 44 J4
Storuman l. Sweden 44 J4
Storvik Sweden 45 J6
Storvorde Denmark 45 G8
Storvreta Sweden 45 J7
Story U.S.A. 126 G3
Stotfold U.K. 49 G6
Stoughton Canada 121 K5
Stour r. England U.K. 49 F6
Stour r. England U.K. 49 F8
Stour r. England U.K. 49 I7
Stour r. England U.K. 49 I7
Stourbridge U.K. 49 E6
Stourport-on-Severn U.K. 49 E6
Stout Lake Canada 121 M4
Stowbtsy Belarus 45 O10
Stowe U.S.A. 135 I1
Stowmarket U.K. 49 H6
Stoyba Russia 74 C1
Strabane U.K. 51 E3
Stradbally Ireland 51 E4
Stradbroke U.K. 49 I6
Stradella Italy 58 C2
Strakonice Czechia 47 N6
Stralsund Germany 47 N3
Strand S. Africa 100 D8
Stranda Norway 44 E5
Strangford U.K. 51 G3
Strangford Lough inlet U.K. 51 G3
Strangways r. Australia 108 F3
Stranraer U.K. 50 D6
Strasbourg France 56 H2
Strasburg U.S.A. 135 F4
Strasburg (Uckermark) Germany 53 N1
Strassburg France see Strasbourg
Stratford Australia 112 C6
Stratford Canada 134 E2
Stratford CA U.S.A. 128 D3
Stratford TX U.S.A. 131 C4
Stratford-upon-Avon U.K. 49 F6
Strathaven U.K. 50 E5
Strathmore Canada 120 H5
Strathmore r. U.K. 50 E2
Strathnaver Canada 120 F4
Strathroy Canada 134 E2
Strathspey valley U.K. 50 F3
Strathy U.K. 50 F2
Stratton U.K. 49 C8
Stratton U.S.A. 135 J1
Stratton Mountain U.S.A. 135 I2
Straubing Germany 53 M6
Straumnes pt Iceland 44 [inset 1]
Strawberry U.S.A. 129 H4
Strawberry Mountain U.S.A. 126 D3
Strawberry Reservoir U.S.A. 129 H1
Streaky Bay Australia 109 F8
Streaky Bay b. Australia 109 F8
Streator U.S.A. 130 F3
Street U.K. 49 E7
Streetsboro U.S.A. 134 E3
Strehaia Romania 59 J2
Strehla Germany 53 N3
Streich Mound hill Australia 109 C7
Strelka Russia 65 Q3
Strel'na r. Russia 42 H2
Strenči Latvia 45 N8
Streymoy i. Faroe Is 44 [inset 2]
Stříbro Czechia 53 M5
Strichen U.K. 50 G3
Strimonas r. Greece see Strymonas
Stroeder Arg. 144 D6
Strokestown Ireland 51 D4
Stroma, Island of U.K. 50 F2
Stromboli, Isola i. Italy 58 F5
Stromness S. Georgia 144 I8
Stromness U.K. 50 F2
Strömstad Sweden 45 G7
Strömsund Sweden 44 I5
Strongsville U.S.A. 134 E3
Stronsay i. U.K. 50 G1
Stroud Australia 112 E4
Stroud U.K. 49 E7
Stroud Road Australia 112 E4
Stroudsburg U.S.A. 135 H3
Struer Denmark 45 F8
Struga Macedonia 59 I4
Strugi-Krasnyye Russia 45 P7
Struis Bay S. Africa 100 E8
Strullendorf Germany 53 K5
Struma r. Bulg. 59 J4
also known as Strymonas (Greece)
Strumble Head hd U.K. 49 B6
Strumica Macedonia 59 J4
Struthers U.S.A. 134 E3
Stryama r. Bulg. 59 K3
Strydenburg S. Africa 100 F5
Strymonas r. Greece 59 J4
also known as Struma (Bulgaria)
Stryn Norway 44 E6
Stryy Ukr. 43 D6
Strzelecki, Mount hill Australia 108 F5
Strzelecki Regional Reserve nature res. Australia 111 B6
Stuart FL U.S.A. 133 D7
Stuart NE U.S.A. 130 D3
Stuart VA U.S.A. 134 E5
Stuart Lake Canada 120 E4
Stuart Range hills Australia 111 A6
Stuarts Draft U.S.A. 134 F4
Stuart Town Australia 112 D4
Stuchka Latvia see Aizkraukle
Stučka Latvia see Aizkraukle
Studholme Junction N.Z. 113 C7
Studsviken Sweden 44 K5
Stukely, Lac l. Canada 135 I1
Stung Treng Cambodia see Stœng Trêng
Stupart r. Canada 121 M4
Stupino Russia 43 H5
Sturge Island Antarctica 152 H2
Sturgeon r. Ont. Canada 122 F5
Sturgeon r. Sask. Canada 121 J4
Sturgeon Bay b. Canada 121 L4
Sturgeon Bay U.S.A. 134 B1
Sturgeon Bay Canal lake channel U.S.A. 134 B1
Sturgeon Falls Canada 122 F5
Sturgeon Lake Ont. Canada 121 N5
Sturgeon Lake Ont. Canada 135 F1
Sturgis MI U.S.A. 134 C3
Sturgis SD U.S.A. 130 C2
Sturt, Mount hill Australia 111 C6
Sturt Creek watercourse Australia 108 D4
Sturt National Park Australia 111 C6
Sturt Stony Desert Australia 111 C6
Stutterheim S. Africa 101 H7
Stuttgart Germany 53 J6
Stuttgart U.S.A. 131 F5
Stykkishólmur Iceland 44 [inset 1]
Styr r. Belarus/Ukr. 43 E5
Suaçuí Grande r. Brazil 145 C2
Suai East Timor 108 D2
Suakin Sudan 86 E6
Su'ao Taiwan 77 I3
Suaqui Grande Mex. 127 F7
Suau P.N.G. 110 E1
Subačius Lith. 45 N9
Subankhata India 83 G4
Subarnapur India 84 D1
Sūbāshī Iran 88 C3
Subay reg. Saudi Arabia 88 B5
Şubayḩah Saudi Arabia 85 D4
Subei China 80 H4
Subi Besar i. Indon. 71 E7
Subi Kecil i. Indon. 71 E7
Sublette U.S.A. 131 C4
Subotica Serbia 59 H1
Success, Lake U.S.A. 128 D3
Succiso, Alpe di mts Italy 58 D2
Suceava Romania 43 E7
Suchan Russia see Partizansk
Suck r. Ireland 51 D4
Suckling, Mount P.N.G. 110 E1
Suckow Germany 53 L1

▶Sucre Bol. 142 E7
Joint capital (with La Paz) of Bolivia.

Suczawa Romania see Suceava
Sud, Grand Récif du reef New Caledonia 107 G4
Suda Russia 42 H4
Sudak Crimea 90 D1

▶Sudan country Africa 97 F3
3rd largest country in Africa.

Suday Russia 42 I4
Sudayr reg. Saudi Arabia 88 B5
Sudbury Canada 122 E5
Sudbury U.K. 49 H6
Sudd swamp South Sudan 86 C8
Sude r. Germany 53 K1
Sudest Island P.N.G. see Tagula Island
Sudetenland mts Czechia/Poland see Sudety
Sudety mts Czechia/Poland 47 O5
Sudislavl' Russia 42 I4
Sudlersville U.S.A. 135 H4
Süd-Nord-Kanal canal Germany 52 H2
Sudogda Russia 42 I5
Sudr Egypt 85 A5
Suðuroy i. Faroe Is 44 [inset 2]
Sue watercourse South Sudan 97 F4
Sueca Spain 57 F4
Suez Egypt 85 A5
Suez, Gulf of Egypt 85 A5
Suez Bay Egypt 85 A5
Suez Canal Egypt 85 A4
Suffolk U.S.A. 135 G5
Sugarbush Hill hill U.S.A. 130 F2
Sugarloaf Mountain U.S.A. 135 J1
Sugarloaf Point Australia 112 F4
Sugun China 80 E4
Sūhāj Egypt 86 D4
Şuḩār Oman 88 E5
Suhaymī, Wādī as watercourse Egypt 85 A4
Sühbaatar Mongolia 72 J2
Suheli Par i. India 84 B4
Suhl Germany 53 K4
Suhlendorf Germany 53 K2
Suhul reg. Saudi Arabia 88 B6
Suhūl al Kidan plain Saudi Arabia 88 D6
Şuhut Turkey 59 N5
Sui Pak. 89 H4
Sui, Laem pt Thai. 71 B5
Suibin China 74 C3
Suid-Afrika country Africa see South Africa
Suide China 73 K5
Sui Dehar Pak. 89 H4
Suidzhikurmsy Turkm. see Madaw
Suifenhe China 74 C3
Suihua China 74 B3
Suileng China 74 B3
Suining Hunan China 77 F3
Suining Jiangsu China 77 H1
Suining Sichuan China 76 E2
Suippes France 52 E5
Suir r. Ireland 51 E5
Suisse country Europe see Switzerland
Suixi China 77 H1
Suixian Henan China 77 G1
Suixian Hubei China see Suizhou
Suiyang Guizhou China 76 E3
Suiyang Henan China 77 G1
Suiza country Europe see Switzerland
Suizhong China 73 M4
Suizhou China 77 G2
Sujangarh India 82 C4
Sujawal Pak. 89 H5
Suk atoll Micronesia see Pulusuk
Sukabumi Indon. 68 D8
Sukagawa Japan 75 F5
Sukarnapura Indon. see Jayapura
Sukarno, Puncak mt. Indon. see Jaya, Puncak
Sukchŏn N. Korea 75 B5
Sukhinichi Russia 43 G5
Sukhona r. Russia 42 J3
Sukhothai Thai. 70 B3
Sukhumi Georgia see Sokhumi
Sukhum-Kale Georgia see Sokhumi
Sukkertoppen Greenland see Maniitsoq
Sukkozero Russia 42 G3
Sukkur Pak. 89 H5
Sukma India 84 D2
Sukpay Russia 74 E3
Sukpay r. Russia 74 E3
Sukri r. Rajasthan India 82 C4
Sukri r. Rajasthan India 82 C4
Suktel r. India 84 D1
Sukun i. Indon. 108 C2
Sula i. Norway 45 D6
Sula r. Russia 42 K2
Sula, Kepulauan is Indon. 69 H7
Sulaiman Range mts Pak. 89 H4
Sulak Russia 91 G2
Sülär Iran 88 C4
Sula Sgeir i. U.K. 50 C1
Sulawesi i. Indon. see Celebes
Sulaymān Beg Iraq 91 G4
Sulayyimah Saudi Arabia 88 B6
Sulci Sardinia Italy see Sant'Antioco
Sulcis Sardinia Italy see Sant'Antioco
Sule Skerry i. U.K. 50 E1
Sule Stack i. U.K. 50 E1
Sulingen Germany 53 I2
Sulitjelma Norway 44 J3
Sulkava Fin. 44 P6
Sullana Peru 142 B4
Sullivan IL U.S.A. 130 F4
Sullivan IN U.S.A. 134 B4
Sullivan Bay Canada 120 E5
Sullivan Island Myanmar see Lanbi Kyun
Sullivan Lake Canada 121 I5
Sulmo Italy see Sulmona
Sulmona Italy 58 E3
Sulphur LA U.S.A. 131 E6
Sulphur OK U.S.A. 131 D5
Sulphur r. U.S.A. 131 E5
Sulphur Springs U.S.A. 131 E5
Sultan Canada 122 E5

Tall al Aḥmar Syria 85 D1
Tall Baydar Syria 91 F3
Tall-e Ḥalāl Iran 88 D4
Tallimarjon Uzbek. 89 G2

▶Tallinn Estonia 45 N7
Capital of Estonia.

Tall Kalakh Syria 85 C2
Tall Kayf Iraq 91 F3
Tallow Ireland 51 D5
Tallulah U.S.A. 131 F5
Tall 'Uwaynāt Iraq 91 F3
Tallymerjen Uzbek. *see* Tallimarjon
Talmont-St-Hilaire France 56 D3
Tal'ne Ukr. 43 F6
Tal'noye Ukr. *see* Tal'ne
Taloda India 82 C5
Talodi Sudan 86 D7
Taloga U.S.A. 131 D4
Talon, Lac *l.* Canada 123 I3
Ta-long Myanmar 70 B2
Talos Dome *ice feature* Antarctica 152 H2
Ta Loung San *mt.* Laos 70 C2
Talovaya Russia 43 I6
Taloyoak Canada 119 I3
Tal Pass Pak. 89 I3
Talsi Latvia 45 M8
Tal Sīyāh Iran 89 F4
Taltal Chile 144 B3
Taltson *r.* Canada 121 H2
Talu China 76 B2
Tāluqān Afgh. 89 H2
Talvik Norway 44 M1
Talwood Australia 112 D2
Talyshskiye Gory *mts* Azer./Iran *see* Talış Dağları
Talyy Russia 42 L2
Tamala Australia 109 A6
Tamala Russia 43 I5
Tamale Ghana 96 C4
Tamana *i.* Kiribati 107 H2
Taman Negara National Park Malaysia 71 C6
Tamano Japan 75 D6
Tamanrasset Alg. 96 D2
Tamanthi Myanmar 70 A1
Tamaqua U.S.A. 135 H3
Tamar India 83 F5
Tamar Syria *see* Tadmur
Tamar *r.* U.K. 49 C8
Tamar Qareh Qūzī Iran 88 D2
Tamarugal, Pampa de *plain* Chile 142 E7
Tamasane Botswana 101 H2
Tamatave Madag. *see* Toamasina
Tamaulipas *state* Mex. 131 D7
Tambacounda Senegal 96 B3
Tambaqui Brazil 142 F5
Tambar Springs Australia 112 D3
Tambelan, Kepulauan *is* Indon. 71 D7
Tambelan Besar *i.* Indon. 71 D7
Tambo *r.* Australia 112 C6
Tambohorano Madag. 99 E5

▶Tambora, Gunung *vol.* Indon. 108 B2
Deadliest recorded volcanic eruption (1815).

Tamboritha *mt.* Australia 112 C6
Tambov Russia 43 I5
Tambovka Russia 74 C2
Tambura South Sudan 97 F4
Tamburi Brazil 145 C1
Tâmchekket Mauritania 96 B3
Tamdybulak Uzbek. *see* Tomdibuloq
Tâmega *r.* Port. 57 B3
Tamenghest Alg. *see* Tamanrasset
Tamenglong India 83 H4
Tamerza Tunisia 58 B7
Tamgak, Adrar *mt.* Niger 96 D3
Tamgué, Massif du *mt.* Guinea 96 B3
Tamiahua, Laguna de *lag.* Mex. 136 E4
Tamiang, Ujung *pt* Indon. 71 B6
Tamil Nadu *state* India 84 C4
Tamitsa Russia 42 H2
Ṭâmîya Egypt *see* Ṭāmīyah
Ṭāmīyah Egypt 90 C5
Tamkuhi India 83 F4
Tam Ky Vietnam 70 E4
Tammarvi *r.* Canada 121 K1
Tammerfors Fin. *see* Tampere
Tammisaari Fin. *see* Ekenäs
Tampa U.S.A. 133 D7
Tampa Bay U.S.A. 133 D7
Tampere Fin. 45 M6
Tampico Mex. 136 E4
Tampin Malaysia 71 C7
Tampines Sing. 71 [inset]
Tamsagbulag Mongolia 73 L3
Tamsweg Austria 47 N7
Tamu Myanmar 70 A1
Tamworth Australia 112 E3
Tamworth U.K. 49 F6
Tana *r.* Fin./Norway *see* Tenojoki
Tana *r.* Kenya 98 E4
Tana Madag. *see* Antananarivo
Tana *i.* Vanuatu *see* Tanna
Tana, Lake Eth. 98 D2
Tanabe Japan 75 D6
Tanabi Brazil 145 A3
Tana Bru Norway 44 P1
Tanada Lake U.S.A. 120 A2
Tanafjorden *inlet* Norway 44 P1
Tanah, Tanjung *pt* Indon. 68 D8
T'ana Hāyk' *l.* Eth. *see* Tana, Lake
Tanahgrogot Indon. 68 F7
Tanah Merah Malaysia 71 C6
Tanahputih Indon. 71 C7
Tanakeke *i.* Indon. 68 E8
Tanami Australia 108 E4
Tanami Desert Australia 108 E4
Tân An Vietnam 71 D5
Tanana *r.* U.S.A. 120 A2
Tananarive Madag. *see* Antananarivo
Tanandava Madag. 99 E6
Tancheng China *see* Pingtan
Tanch'ŏn N. Korea 75 C4
Tanda Côte d'Ivoire 96 C4
Tanda *Uttar Prad.* India 82 D3
Tanda *Uttar Prad.* India 83 E4
Tandag Phil. 69 H5
Ţăndărei Romania 59 L2
Tandaué Angola 99 B5
Tandi India 82 D2
Tandil Arg. 144 E5
Tando Adam Pak. 89 H5
Tando Allahyar Pak. 89 H5
Tando Bago Pak. 89 H5
Tandou Lake *imp. l.* Australia 111 C7
Tandragee U.K. 51 F3
Tandur India 84 C2
Tanduri Pak. 89 G4
Tanega-shima *i.* Japan 75 C7
Tanen Taunggyi *mts* Thai. 70 B3
Tanezrouft *reg.* Alg./Mali 96 C2
Ţanf, Jabal aţ *hill* Syria 85 D3
Tang, Kaôh *i.* Cambodia 71 C5
Tang, Ra's-e *pt* Iran 89 E5
Tanga Tanz. 99 D4
Tangail Bangl. 83 G4
Tanga Islands P.N.G. 106 F2
Tanganyika *country* Africa *see* Tanzania

▶Tanganyika, Lake Africa 99 C4
Deepest and 2nd largest lake in Africa, and 6th largest in the world.

Tangará Brazil 145 A4
Tangasseri India 84 C4
Tangdan China 76 D3
Tangeli Iran 88 D2
Tanger Morocco *see* Tangier
Tangerhütte Germany 53 L2
Tangermünde Germany 53 L2
Tang-e Sarkheh Iran 89 E5
Tanggor China 76 D1
Tanggulashan China 76 B1
Tanggula Shan *mt.* China 83 G2
Tanggula Shan *mts* China 83 G2
Tanggula Shankou *pass* China 83 G2
Tangguo China 83 F3
Tanghe China 77 G1
Tangier Morocco 57 D6
Tangiers Morocco *see* Tangier
Tang La *pass* China 83 G4
Tangla India 83 G4
Tanglag China 76 C1
Tanglin Sing. 71 [inset]
Tangmai China 76 B2
Tangnag China 76 D1
Tangorin Australia 110 D4
Tangra Yumco *salt l.* China 83 F3
Tangse Indon. 71 A6
Tangshan *Guizhou* China *see* Shiqian
Tangshan *Hebei* China 73 L5
Tangte *mt.* Myanmar 70 B2
Tangtse India *see* Tanktse
Tangwan China 77 F3
Tangwanghe China 74 C2
Tangyuan China 74 C3
Tangyung Tso *salt l.* China 83 F3
Tanhaçu Brazil 145 C1
Tanhua Fin. 44 O3
Tani Cambodia 71 D5
Taniantaweng Shan *mts* China 76 B2
Tanimbar, Kepulauan *is* Indon. 108 E1
Tanintharyi Myanmar *see* Tenasserim
Tanintharyi Myanmar *see* Tenasserim
Taninthayi Myanmar *see* Tenasserim
Tanjah Morocco *see* Tangier
Tanjay Phil. 69 G5
Tanjore India *see* Thanjavur
Tanjung Indon. 68 F7
Tanjungbalai Indon. 71 B7
Tanjungkarang-Telukbetung Indon. *see* Bandar Lampung
Tanjungpandan Indon. 68 D7
Tanjungpinang Indon. 71 D7
Tanjungpura Indon. 71 B7
Tanjung Puting, Taman Nasional *nat. park* Indon. 68 E7
Tanjungredeb Indon. 68 F6
Tanjungselor Indon. 68 F6
Tankse India *see* Tanktse
Tanktse India 82 D2
Tankwa-Karoo National Park S. Africa 100 D7
Tanna *i.* Vanuatu 107 G3
Tannadice U.K. 50 G4
Tännäs Sweden 44 H5
Tanner, Mount Canada 120 G5
Tannu-Ola, Khrebet *mts* Russia 80 H1
Tanot India 82 B4
Tanout Niger 96 D3
Tansen Nepal 83 E4
Tanshui Taiwan *see* Danshui
Ţanţa Egypt *see* Ţanţā
Ţanţā Egypt 90 C5
Tan-Tan Morocco 96 B2
Tantu China 74 A3
Tanuku India 84 D2
Tanumbirini Australia 108 F4
Tanumshede Sweden 45 G7
Tanzania *country* Africa 99 D4
Tanzilla *r.* Canada 120 D3
Tao, Ko *i.* Thai. 71 B5
Tao'an China *see* Taonan
Taobh Tuath U.K. *see* Northton
Taocheng China *see* Daxin
Tao He *r.* China 76 D1
Taohong China *see* Longhui
Taohuajiang China *see* Taojiang
Taohuaping China *see* Longhui
Taojiang China 77 G2
Taolanaro Madag. *see* Tôlañaro
Taonan China 74 A3
Taongi *atoll* Marshall Is 150 H5
Taos U.S.A. 127 G5
Taounate Morocco 54 D5
Taourirt Morocco 54 D5
Taoxi China 77 H3
Taoyang China *see* Lintao
Taoyuan China 77 F2
Taoyuan Taiwan 77 I3
Tapa Estonia 45 N7
Tapachula Mex. 136 F6
Tapah Malaysia 71 C6
Tapajós *r.* Brazil 143 H4
Tapaktuan Indon. 71 B7
Tapauá Brazil 142 F5
Tapauá *r.* Brazil 142 F5
Taperoá Brazil 145 D1
Tapiau Russia *see* Gvardeysk
Tapis, Gunung *mt.* Malaysia 71 C6
Tapisuelas Mex. 127 F8
Taplejung Nepal 83 F4
Tap Mun Chau *i. H.K.* China 77 [inset]
Ta-pom Myanmar 70 B2
Tappahannock U.S.A. 135 G5
Tappeh, Kūh-e *hill* Iran 88 C3
Taprobane *country* Asia *see* Sri Lanka
Tapti *r.* India 82 C5
Tapuae-o-Uenuku *mt.* N.Z. 113 D5
Tapulonanjing *mt.* Indon. 71 B7
Tapurucuara Brazil 142 E4
Taputeouea *atoll* Kiribati *see* Tabiteuea
Taquara Brazil 145 A5
Taquari Brazil 145 A5
Taquarí *r.* Brazil 143 G7
Taquaritinga Brazil 145 A3
Tar *r.* Ireland 51 E5
Tara Australia 112 E1
Ţarābulus Lebanon *see* Tripoli
Ţarābulus Libya *see* Tripoli
Tarahuwan India 82 E4
Tarai *reg.* India 83 G4
Tarakan Indon. 68 F6
Tarakan *i.* Indon. 68 F6
Tārakī *reg.* Afgh. 89 G3
Taraklı Turkey 59 N4
Taran, Mys *pt* Russia 45 K9
Tarana Australia 112 D4
Taranagar India 82 C3
Taranaki, Mount *vol.* N.Z. 113 E4
Tarancón Spain 57 E3
Tarangambadi India 84 C4
Tarangire National Park Tanz. 98 D4
Taranto Italy 58 G4
Taranto, Golfo di *g.* Italy 58 G4
Taranto, Gulf of Italy *see* Taranto, Golfo di
Tarapoto Peru 142 C5
Tarapur India 84 B2
Tararua Range *mts* N.Z. 113 E5
Tarascon-sur-Ariège France 56 E5
Tarasovskiy Russia 43 I6
Tarauacá Brazil 142 D5
Tarauacá *r.* Brazil 142 E5
Tarawera N.Z. 113 F4
Tarawera, Mount *vol.* N.Z. 113 F4
Taraz Kazakh. 80 D3
Tarazona Spain 57 F3
Tarazona de la Mancha Spain 57 F4
Tarbagatay, Khrebet *mts* Kazakh. 80 F2
Tarbat Ness *pt* U.K. 50 F3
Tarbert Ireland 51 C5
Tarbert *Scotland* U.K. 50 C3
Tarbert *Scotland* U.K. 50 D5
Tarbes France 56 E5
Tarboro U.S.A. 132 E5
Tarcoola Australia 109 F7
Tarcoon Australia 112 C3
Tarcoonyinna *watercourse* Australia 109 F6
Tarcutta Australia 112 C5
Tardoki-Yangi, Gora *mt.* Russia 74 E2
Taree Australia 112 F3
Tarella Australia 111 C6
Tarentum Italy *see* Taranto
Ţarfā', Baţn aţ *depr.* Saudi Arabia 88 C6
Tarfaya Morocco 96 B2
Targa *well* Niger 96 D3
Targan China *see* Talin Hiag
Targhee Pass U.S.A. 126 F3
Targovishte Bulg. 59 L3
Târgovişte Romania 59 K2
Targuist Morocco 57 D6
Târgu Jiu Romania 59 J2
Târgu Mureş Romania 59 K1
Târgu Neamţ Romania 59 L1
Târgu Secuiesc Romania 59 L1
Targyailing China 83 F3
Tari P.N.G. 69 K8
Tariat Mongolia 80 I2
Tarif U.A.E. 88 D5
Tarifa Spain 57 D5
Tarifa, Punta de *pt* Spain 57 D5
Tarija Bol. 142 F8
Tarikere India 84 B3
Tariku *r.* Indon. 69 J7
Tarīm Yemen 86 G6
Tarim Basin China 80 F4
Tarime Tanz. 98 D4
Tarim He *r.* China 80 G3
Tarim Pendi *basin* China *see* Tarim Basin
Tarīn Kōṭ Afgh. 89 G3
Taritatu *r.* Indon. 69 J7
Tarka *r.* S. Africa 101 G7
Tarkastad S. Africa 101 H7
Tarkio U.S.A. 130 E3
Tarko-Sale Russia 64 I3
Tarkwa Ghana 96 C4
Tarlac Phil. 69 G3
Tarlag China 76 C1
Tarlo River National Park Australia 112 D5
Tarma Peru 142 C6
Tarmstedt Germany 53 J1
Tarn *r.* France 56 E4
Tärnaby Sweden 44 I4
Tarnak Rōd *r.* Afgh. 89 G4
Târnăveni Romania 59 K1
Tarnobrzeg Poland 43 D6
Tarnogskiy Gorodok Russia 42 I3
Tarnopol Ukr. *see* Ternopil'
Tarnów Poland 43 D6
Tarnowitz Poland *see* Tarnowskie Góry
Tarnowskie Góry Poland 47 Q5
Taro Co *salt l.* China 83 F3
Ţārom Iran 88 D4
Taroom Australia 111 E5
Taroudannt Morocco 54 C5
Tarpaulin Swamp Australia 110 B3
Ţarq Iran 88 C3
Tarqi China 73 M3
Tarquinia Italy 58 D3
Tarquinii Italy *see* Tarquinia
Tarrabool Lake *salt flat* Australia 110 A3
Tarraco Spain *see* Tarragona
Tarrafal Cape Verde 96 [inset]
Tarragona Spain 57 G3
Tårrajaur Sweden 44 K3
Tarran Hills *hill* Australia 112 C4
Tarrant Point Australia 110 B3
Tàrrega Spain 57 G3
Tarrong China *see* Nyêmo
Tarsus Turkey 85 B1
Tart China 83 H1
Tärtär Azer. 91 G2
Tartu Estonia 45 O7
Ţarţūs Syria 85 B2
Tarumovka Russia 91 G1
Tarung Hka *r.* Myanmar 70 B1
Tarutao, Ko *i.* Thai. 71 B6
Tarutao National Park Thai. 71 B6
Tarutung Indon. 71 B7
Tarvisium Italy *see* Treviso
Ţarz Iran 88 E4
Tasai, Ko *i.* Thai. 71 B5
Taschereau Canada 122 F4
Taseko Mountain Canada 120 F5
Tashauz Turkm. *see* Daşoguz
Tashi Chho Bhutan *see* Thimphu
Tashigang Bhutan *see* Trashigang
Tashikuzuke Shan *mts* China 82 C1
Tashino Russia *see* Pervomaysk
Tashir Armenia 91 G2
Tashk, Daryācheh-ye *l.* Iran 88 D4
Tashkent Uzbek. *see* Toshkent
Tāshqurghān Afgh. *see* Khulm
Tashtagol Russia 72 F2
Tashtyp Russia 72 F2
Tasialujjuaq, Lac *l.* Canada 123 G2
Tasiat, Lac *l.* Canada 122 G2
Tasiilap Karra *c.* Greenland 119 O3
Tasiilaq Greenland 153 J2
Tasīl Syria 85 B3
Tasiujaq Canada 123 H2
Tasiusaq Greenland 119 M2
Taskala Kazakh. 41 Q5
Taşkent Turkey 85 A1
Tasker Niger 96 E3
Taskesken Kazakh. 80 F2
Taşköprü Turkey 90 D2
Tasman Abyssal Plain *sea feature* Tasman Sea 150 G8
Tasman Basin *sea feature* Tasman Sea 150 G8
Tasman Bay N.Z. 113 D5

▶Tasmania *state* Australia 111 [inset]
4th largest island in Oceania.

Tasman Islands P.N.G. *see* Nukumanu Islands
Tasman Mountains N.Z. 113 D5
Tasman Peninsula Australia 111 [inset]
Tasman Sea S. Pacific Ocean 106 H6
Taşova Turkey 90 E2
Tassara Niger 96 D3
Tassialouc, Lac *l.* Canada 122 G2
Tassili n'Ajjer, Parc National de *nat. park* Alg. 96 D2
Tasty Kazakh. 80 C3
Taşucu Turkey 85 A1
Tas-Yuryakh Russia 65 M3
Tata Morocco 54 C6
Tatabánya Hungary 58 H1
Tatamailau, Foho *mt.* East Timor 108 D2
Tataouine Tunisia 54 G5
Tatarbunary Ukr. 59 M2
Tatarsk Russia 64 I4
Tatarskiy Proliv *strait* Russia 74 F2
Tatar Strait Russia *see* Tatarskiy Proliv
Tate *r.* Australia 110 C3
Tateyama Japan 75 E6
Tathlina Lake Canada 120 G2
Tathlīth Saudi Arabia 86 F6
Tathlīth, Wādī *watercourse* Saudi Arabia 86 F5
Tathra Australia 112 D6
Tatinnai Lake Canada 121 L2
Tatishchevo Russia 43 J6
Tatkon Myanmar 70 B2
Tatla Lake Canada 120 E5
Tatla Lake *l.* Canada 120 E5
Tatlayoko Lake Canada 120 E5
Tatnam, Cape Canada 121 N3
Tatra Mountains Poland/Slovakia 47 Q6
Tatry *mts* Poland/Slovakia *see* Tatra Mountains
Tatrzański Park Narodowy *nat. park* Poland 47 Q6
Tatshenshini-Alsek Provincial Wilderness Park Canada 120 B3
Tatsinskaya Russia 43 I6
Tatuí Brazil 145 B3
Tatuk Mountain Canada 120 E4
Tatum U.S.A. 131 C5
Tatvan Turkey 91 F3
Tau Norway 45 D7
Tauá Brazil 143 J5
Tauapeçaçu Brazil 142 F4
Taubaté Brazil 145 B3
Tauber *r.* Germany 53 J5
Tauberbischofsheim Germany 53 J5
Taucha Germany 53 M3
Taufstein *hill* Germany 53 J4
Taukum, Peski *des.* Kazakh. 80 D3
Taumarunui N.Z. 113 E4
Taumaturgo Brazil 142 D5
Taung S. Africa 100 G4
Taungdwingyi Myanmar 70 A2
Taunggyi Myanmar 70 B2
Taung-ngu Myanmar 70 B3
Taungnyo Range *mts* Myanmar 70 B3
Taungtha Myanmar 70 A2
Taungup Myanmar 76 B5
Taunton U.K. 49 D7
Taunton U.S.A. 135 J3
Taunus *hills* Germany 53 H4
Taupo N.Z. 113 F4
Taupo, Lake N.Z. 113 E4
Tauragė Lith. 45 M9
Tauranga N.Z. 113 F3
Taurasia Italy *see* Turin
Taureau, Réservoir *resr* Canada 122 G5
Taurianova Italy 58 G5
Tauroa Point N.Z. 113 D2
Taurus Mountains Turkey 85 A1
Taute *r.* France 49 F9
Tauz Azer. *see* Tovuz
Tavas Turkey 59 M6
Tavastehus Fin. *see* Hämeenlinna
Taverham U.K. 49 I6
Taveuni *i.* Fiji 107 I3
Tavildara Tajik. 89 H2
Tavira Port. 57 C5
Tavistock Canada 134 E2
Tavistock U.K. 49 C8
Tavoy Myanmar *see* Dawei
Tavoy *r. mouth* Myanmar 71 B4
Tavoy Island Myanmar *see* Mali Kyun
Tavoy Point Myanmar 71 B4
Tavşanlı Turkey 59 M5
Taw *r.* U.K. 49 C7
Tawakkul China 82 E1
Tawang India 83 G4
Tawas City U.S.A. 134 D1
Tawau *Sabah* Malaysia 68 F6
Tawè Myanmar *see* Dawei
Tawe *r.* U.K. 49 D7
Ţawī Ḥafir *well* U.A.E. 88 D5
Ţawī Murra *well* U.A.E. 88 D5
Tawmaw Myanmar 70 B1
Tawu Taiwan *see* Dawu
Taxkorgan China 80 E4
Tay *r.* Canada 120 C2
Tay *r.* U.K. 50 F4
Tay, Firth of *est.* U.K. 50 F4
Tay, Lake *salt flat* Australia 109 C8
Tay, Loch *l.* U.K. 50 E4
Tayandu, Kepulauan *is* Indon. 69 I8
Tāybād Iran 89 F3
Taybola Russia 44 R2
Taycheedah U.S.A. 134 A2
Tayinloan U.K. 50 D5
Taylor Canada 120 F3
Taylor *AK* U.S.A. 118 B3
Taylor *MI* U.S.A. 134 D2
Taylor *NE* U.S.A. 130 D3
Taylor *TX* U.S.A. 131 D6
Taylor, Mount U.S.A. 129 J4
Taylorsville U.S.A. 134 C4
Taylorville U.S.A. 130 F4
Taymā' Saudi Arabia 90 E6
Taymanī *reg.* Afgh. 89 F3
Taymura *r.* Russia 65 K3
Taymyr, Ozero *l.* Russia 65 L2
Taymyr, Poluostrov *pen.* Russia *see* Taymyr Peninsula
Taymyr Peninsula Russia 64 J2
Tây Ninh Vietnam 71 D5
Taypak Kazakh. 41 Q6
Taypaq Kazakh. *see* Taypak
Tayshet Russia 72 H1
Taytay Phil. 68 F4
Tayuan China 74 B2
Taz *r.* Russia 64 I3
Taza Morocco 54 D5
Tāza Khurmātū Iraq 91 G4
Taze Myanmar 70 A2
Tazewell *TN* U.S.A. 134 D5
Tazewell *VA* U.S.A. 134 E5
Tazin *r.* Canada 121 I2
Tazin Lake Canada 121 I3
Tāzirbū Libya 97 F2
Tazmalt Alg. 57 I5
Tazovskaya Guba *sea chan.* Russia 64 I3
Tbessa Alg. *see* Tébessa

▶Tbilisi Georgia 91 G2
Capital of Georgia.

Tbilisskaya Russia 43 I7
Tchad *country* Africa *see* Chad
Tchamba Togo 96 D4
Tchibanga Gabon 98 B4
Tchigaï, Plateau du Niger 97 E2
Tchin-Tabaradene Niger 96 D3
Tcholliré Cameroon 97 E4
Tchula U.S.A. 131 F5
Tczew Poland 47 Q3
Té, Prêk *r.* Cambodia 71 D4
Teague, Lake *salt flat* Australia 109 C6
Te Anau N.Z. 113 A7
Te Anau, Lake N.Z. 113 A7
Teapa Mex. 136 F5
Te Araroa N.Z. 113 G3
Teate Italy *see* Chieti
Te Awamutu N.Z. 113 E4
Teba Indon. 69 J7
Tébarat Niger 96 D3
Tebas Indon. 71 E7
Tebay U.K. 48 E4
Tebesjuak Lake Canada 121 L2
Tébessa Alg. 58 C7
Tébessa, Monts de *mts* Alg. 58 C7
Tebingtinggi Indon. 71 B7
Tébourba Tunisia 58 C6
Téboursouk Tunisia 58 C6
T'ebulos Mta Georgia/Russia 91 G2
Tecate Mex. 128 E5
Tece Turkey 85 B1
Techiman Ghana 96 C4
Tecka Arg. 144 B6
Tecklenburger Land *reg.* Germany 53 H2
Tecoripa Mex. 127 F7
Técpan Mex. 136 D5
Tecuala Mex. 136 C4
Tecuci Romania 59 L2
Tecumseh *MI* U.S.A. 134 D3
Tecumseh *NE* U.S.A. 130 D3
Tedzhen Turkm. *see* Tejen
Teec Nos Pos U.S.A. 129 I3
Tees *r.* U.K. 48 F4
Teeswater Canada 134 E1
Tefé *r.* Brazil 142 F4
Tefenni Turkey 59 M6
Tegal Indon. 68 D8
Tegel *airport* Germany 53 N2
Tegid, Llyn *l.* U.K. *see* Bala Lake

▶Tegucigalpa Hond. 137 G6
Capital of Honduras.

Teguidda-n-Tessoumt Niger 96 D3
Tehachapi U.S.A. 128 D4
Tehachapi Mountains U.S.A. 128 D4
Tehachapi Pass U.S.A. 128 D4
Tehek Lake Canada 121 M1
Teheran Iran *see* Tehrān
Tehery Lake Canada 121 M1
Téhini Côte d'Ivoire 96 C4

▶Tehrān Iran 88 C3
Capital of Iran.

Tehri India *see* Tikamgarh
Tehuacán Mex. 136 E5
Tehuantepec, Gulf of *g.* Mex. 136 F5
Tehuantepec, Istmo de *isthmus* Mex. 136 F5
Teide, Pico del *vol.* Canary Is 96 B2
Teifi *r.* U.K. 49 C6
Teignmouth U.K. 49 D8
Teixeira de Freitas Brazil 145 D2
Teixeira de Sousa Angola *see* Luau
Teixeiras Brazil 145 C3
Teixeira Soares Brazil 145 A4
Tejakula Indon. 108 A2
Tejen Turkm. 89 F2
Tejo *r.* Port. *see* Tagus
Tejon Pass U.S.A. 128 D4
Tekapo, Lake N.Z. 113 C6
Tekax Mex. 136 G4
Tekeli Kazakh. 80 E3
Tekes China 80 F3
Tekeze *resr* Eth. 98 D2
Tekiliktag *mt.* China 82 E1
Tekin Russia 74 D2
Tekirdağ Turkey 59 L4
Tekka India 84 D2
Tekkali India 84 E2
Teknaf Bangl. 83 H5
Tekong Kechil, Pulau *i.* Sing. 71 [inset]
Te Kuiti N.Z. 113 E4
Tel *r.* India 84 D1
Télagh Alg. 57 F6
Telanaipura Indon. *see* Jambi
Telangana *state* India 84 C3
Tel Ashqelon *tourist site* Israel 85 B4
Télataï Mali 96 D3
Tel Aviv-Yafo Israel 85 B3
Telč Czechia 47 O6
Telchac Puerto Mex. 136 G4
Telekhany Belarus *see* Tsyelyakhany
Telêmaco Borba Brazil 145 A4
Teleorman *r.* Romania 59 K3
Telertheba, Djebel *mt.* Alg. 96 D2
Telescope Peak U.S.A. 128 E3
Teles Pires *r.* Brazil 143 G5
Telford U.K. 49 E6
Telgte Germany 53 H3
Télimélé Guinea 96 B3
Teljo, Jebel *mt.* Sudan 86 C7
Telkwa Canada 120 E4
Tell Atlas *mts* Alg. *see* Atlas Tellien
Tell City U.S.A. 134 B5
Teller U.S.A. 118 B3
Tell es Sultan West Bank *see* Jericho
Tellicherry India *see* Thalassery
Tellin Belgium 52 F4
Telloh Iraq 91 G5
Telluride U.S.A. 129 J3
Tel'mana, imeni Russia 74 D2
Tel'novskiy Russia 74 F2
Telok Anson Malaysia *see* Teluk Intan
Telo Martius France *see* Toulon
Telpoziz, Gora *mt.* Russia 41 R3
Telsen Arg. 144 C6
Telšiai Lith. 45 M9
Teltow Germany 53 N2
Teluk Anson Malaysia *see* Teluk Intan
Telukbetung Indon. *see* Bandar Lampung
Teluk Cenderawasih, Taman Nasional *nat. park* Indon. 69 I7
Teluk Intan Malaysia 71 C6
Temagami Lake Canada 122 F5
Temanggung Indon. 68 E8
Têmarxung China 83 G2
Temba S. Africa 101 I3
Tembagapura Indon. 69 J7
Tembenchi *r.* Russia 65 K3
Tembilahan Indon. 68 C7
Tembisa S. Africa 101 I4
Tembo Aluma Angola 99 B4
Teme *r.* U.K. 49 E6
Temecula U.S.A. 128 E5
Temerloh Malaysia *see* Temerluh
Temerluh Malaysia 71 C7
Teminabuan Indon. 69 I7
Temirtau Kazakh. 80 D1
Témiscamie *r.* Canada 123 G4
Témiscamie, Lac *l.* Canada 123 G4
Témiscaming Canada 122 F5
Témiscamingue, Lac *l.* Canada 122 F5
Témiscouata, Lac *l.* Canada 123 H5
Temmes Fin. 44 N4
Temnikov Russia 43 I5
Temora Australia 112 C5
Temósachic Mex. 127 G7
Tempe U.S.A. 129 H5
Tempe Downs Australia 109 F6
Temple *MI* U.S.A. 134 C1
Temple *TX* U.S.A. 131 D6
Temple Bar U.K. 49 C6
Temple Dera Pak. 89 H4
Templemore Ireland 51 E5
Temple Sowerby U.K. 48 E4
Templeton *watercourse* Australia 110 B4
Templin Germany 53 N1
Tempué Angola 99 B5
Temryuk Russia 90 E1
Temryukskiy Zaliv *b.* Russia 43 H7
Temuco Chile 144 B5
Temuka N.Z. 113 C7
Temuli China *see* Butuo
Tena Ecuador 142 C4
Tenabo Mex. 136 F4
Tenabo, Mount U.S.A. 128 E1
Tenali India 84 D2
Tenasserim Myanmar 71 B4
Tenasserim *r.* Myanmar 71 B4
Tenbury Wells U.K. 49 E6
Tenby U.K. 49 C7
Tendaho Eth. 98 E2
Tende, Col de *pass* France/Italy 56 H4
Ten Degree Channel India 71 A5
Tendō Japan 75 F5
Tenedos *i.* Turkey *see* Bozcaada
Ténenkou Mali 96 C3
Ténéré *reg.* Niger 96 D2
Ténéré du Tafassâsset *des.* Niger 96 E2
Tenerife *i.* Canary Is 96 B2
Ténès Alg. 57 G5
Teng, Nam *r.* Myanmar 70 B3
Tengah, Kepulauan *is* Indon. 68 F8

Tisza r. Serbia see Tisa
Titalya Bangl. see Tetulia
Titan Dome ice feature Antarctica 152 H1
Titao Burkina Faso 96 C3
Tit-Ary Russia 65 N2
Titawin Morocco see Tétouan
Titicaca, Lago Bol./Peru see Titicaca, Lake

▶Titicaca, Lake Bol./Peru 142 E7
Largest lake in South America.

Titi Islands N.Z. 113 A8
Titiea mt. N.Z. see Aspiring, Mount
Titlagarh India 84 D1
Titograd Montenegro see Podgorica
Titova Mitrovica Kosovo see Mitrovicë
Titovo Užice Serbia see Užice
Titovo Velenje Slovenia see Velenje
Titov Veles Macedonia see Veles
Titov Vrbas Serbia see Vrbas
Ti Tree Australia 108 F5
Titu Romania 59 K2
Titusville FL U.S.A. 133 D6
Titusville PA U.S.A. 134 F3
Tiu Chung Chau i. H.K. China 77 [inset]
Tiumpain, Rubha an hd U.K. see Tiumpan Head
Tiumpan Head hd U.K. 50 C2
Tiva watercourse Kenya 98 D4
Tivari India 82 C4
Tiverton Canada 134 E1
Tiverton U.K. 49 D8
Tivoli Italy 58 E4
Ţīwī Oman 88 E6
Ti-ywa Myanmar 71 B4
Tizimín Mex. 136 G4
Tizi Ouzou Alg. 57 I5
Tiznap He r. China 82 D1
Tiznit Morocco 96 C2
Tiztoutine Morocco 57 E6
Tjaneni Swaziland 101 J3
Tjappsåive Sweden 44 K4
Tjeukemeer l. Neth. 52 F2
Tjirebon Indon. see Cirebon
Tjolotjo Zimbabwe see Tsholotsho
Tjorhom Norway 45 E7
Tkibuli Georgia see T'q'ibuli
Tlahualilo Mex. 131 C7
Tlaxcala Mex. 136 E5
Tl'ell Canada 120 D4
Tlemcen Alg. 57 F6
Tlhakalatlou S. Africa 100 F5
Tlholong S. Africa 101 I5
Tlokweng Botswana 101 G3
Tlyarata Russia 91 G2
To r. Myanmar 70 B3
Toad r. Canada 120 E3
Toad River Canada 120 E3
Toamasina Madag. 99 E5
Toana mts U.S.A. 129 F1
Toano U.S.A. 135 G5
Toa Payoh Sing. 71 [inset]
Toba China 76 C2
Toba, Danau l. Indon. 71 B7
Toba, Lake Indon. see Toba, Danau
Toba and Kakar Ranges mts Pak. 89 G4
Toba Gargaji Pak. 89 I4
Tobago i. Trin. and Tob. 137 L6
Tobelo Indon. 69 H6
Tobercurry Ireland 51 D3
Tobermorey Australia 110 B4
Tobermory Australia 112 A1
Tobermory Canada 134 E1
Tobermory U.K. 50 C4
Tobi i. Palau 69 I6
Tobin, Lake salt flat Australia 108 D5
Tobin, Mount U.S.A. 128 E1
Tobin Lake Canada 121 K4
Tobin Lake l. Canada 121 K4
Tobi-shima i. Japan 75 E5
Tobli Liberia 96 C4
Tobol r. Kazakh./Russia see Tobyl
Tobol'sk Russia 64 H4
Tobruk Libya see Tubruq
Tobseda Russia 42 L1
Tobyl r. Kazakh./Russia 78 F1
Tobysh r. Russia 42 K2
Tocache Nuevo Peru 142 C5
Tocantinópolis Brazil 143 I5
Tocantins r. Brazil 145 A1
Tocantins state Brazil 145 A1
Tocantinzinha r. Brazil 145 A1
Toccoa U.S.A. 133 D5
Tochi r. Pak. 89 H3
Töcksfors Sweden 45 G7
Tocopilla Chile 144 B2
Tocumwal Australia 112 B5
Tod, Mount Canada 120 G5
Todd watercourse Australia 110 A5
Todi Italy 58 E3
Todoga-saki pt Japan 75 F5
Todos Santos Mex. 136 B4
Toe Head hd U.K. 50 B3
Tofino Canada 120 E5
Toft U.K. 50 [inset]
Tofua i. Tonga 107 I3
Togatax China 82 E2
Togian i. Indon. 69 G7
Togian, Kepulauan is Indon. 69 G7
Togliatti Russia see Tol'yatti
Togo country Africa 96 D4
Togtoh China 73 K4
Togton He r. China 83 H2
Togton Heyan China see Tanggulashan
Tohatchi U.S.A. 129 I4
Toholampi Fin. 44 N5
Toiba China 83 G3
Toibalewe India 71 A5
Toijala Fin. 45 M6
Toili Indon. 69 G7
Toi-misaki pt Japan 75 C7
Toivakka Fin. 44 O5
Toiyabe Range mts U.S.A. 128 E2
Tojikiston country Asia see Tajikistan
Tok U.S.A. 120 A2
Tokar Sudan 86 E6
Tokara-rettō is Japan 75 C7
Tokarevka Russia 43 I6
Tokat Turkey 90 E2
Tok-do i. N. Pacific Ocean see Liancourt Rocks

▶Tokelau terr. S. Pacific Ocean 107 I2
New Zealand Overseas Territory.

Tokmak Kyrg. see Tokmok
Tokmak Ukr. 43 G7
Tokmok Kyrg. 80 E3
Tokomaru Bay N.Z. 113 G4
Tokoroa N.Z. 113 E4
Tokoza S. Africa 101 I4
Toksun China 80 G3
Tok-to i. N. Pacific Ocean see Liancourt Rocks
Toktogul Kyrg. 80 D3
Tokur Russia 74 D1
Tokushima Japan 75 D6

▶Tōkyō Japan 75 E6
Capital of Japan. Most populous city in Asia and the world.

Tolaga Bay N.Z. 113 G4
Tôlañaro Madag. 99 E6
Tolbo Mongolia 80 H2
Tolbukhin Bulg. see Dobrich
Tolbuzino Russia 74 B1
Toledo Brazil 144 F2
Toledo Spain 57 D4
Toledo IA U.S.A. 130 E3
Toledo OH U.S.A. 134 D3
Toledo OR U.S.A. 126 C3
Toledo, Montes de mts Spain 57 D4
Toledo Bend Reservoir U.S.A. 131 E6
Toletum Spain see Toledo
Toliara Madag. 99 E6
Tolitoli Indon. 69 G6
Tol'ka Russia 64 J3
Tolleson U.S.A. 129 G5
Tolmachevo Russia 45 P7
Tolo Dem. Rep. Congo 98 B4
Tolo Channel H.K. China 77 [inset]
Tolochin Belarus see Talachyn
Tolo Harbour b. H.K. China 77 [inset]
Tolosa France see Toulouse
Tolosa Spain 57 E2
Toluca Mex. 136 E5
Toluca de Lerdo Mex. see Toluca
To-lun China see Duolun
Tol'yatti Russia 43 K5
Tom' r. Russia 74 B2
Tomah U.S.A. 130 F3
Tomakomai Japan 74 F4
Tomales U.S.A. 128 B2
Tomali Indon. 69 G7
Tomamae Japan 74 F3
Tomanivi mt. Fiji 107 H3
Tomar Brazil 142 F4
Tomar Port. 57 B4
Tomari Russia 74 F3
Tomarza Turkey 90 D3
Tomaszów Lubelski Poland 43 D6
Tomaszów Mazowiecki Poland 47 R5
Tomatin U.K. 50 F3
Tomatlán Mex. 136 C5
Tomazina Brazil 145 A3
Tombador, Serra do hills Brazil 143 G6
Tombigbee r. U.S.A. 133 C6
Tomboco Angola 99 B4
Tombouctou Mali see Timbuktu
Tombstone U.S.A. 127 F7
Tombua Angola 99 B5
Tom Burke S. Africa 101 H2
Tomdibuloq Uzbek. 80 B3
Tome Moz. 101 L2
Tomelilla Sweden 45 H9
Tomelloso Spain 57 E4
Tomi Romania see Constanța
Tomingley Australia 112 D4
Tomini, Teluk g. Indon. 69 G7
Tominian Mali 96 C3
Tomintoul U.K. 50 F3
Tomislavgrad Bos. & Herz. 58 G3
Tomkinson Ranges mts Australia 109 E6
Tømmerneset Norway 44 I3
Tommot Russia 65 N4
Tomo r. Col. 142 E2
Tomóchic Mex. 127 G7
Tomortei China 73 K4
Tompkinsville U.S.A. 134 C5
Tom Price Australia 108 B5
Tomra China 83 F3
Tomsk Russia 64 J4
Toms River U.S.A. 135 H4
Tomtabacken hill Sweden 45 I8
Tomtor Russia 65 P3
Tomur Feng mt. China/Kyrg. see Pobeda Peak
Tomuzlovka r. Russia 43 J7
Tom White, Mount U.S.A. 118 D3
Tonalá Mex. 136 F5
Tonantins Brazil 142 E4
Tonb-e Bozorg, Jazīreh-ye i. The Gulf 88 D5
Tonb-e Kūchek, Jazīreh-ye i. The Gulf 88 D5
Tonbridge U.K. 49 H7
Tondano Indon. 69 G6
Tønder Denmark 45 F9
Tondi India 84 C4
Tone r. U.K. 49 E7
Tonekābon Iran 88 C2
Toney Mountain Antarctica 152 K1
Tonga country S. Pacific Ocean 107 I4
Tongariro National Park N.Z. 113 E4
Tongatapu Group is Tonga 107 I4

▶Tonga Trench sea feature S. Pacific Ocean 150 I7
2nd deepest trench in the world.

Tongbai Shan mts China 77 G1
Tongcheng China 77 H2
T'ongch'ŏn N. Korea 75 B5
Tongchuan Shaanxi China 77 F1
Tongchuan Sichuan China see Santai
Tongdao China 77 F3
Tongde China 76 D1
Tongeren Belgium 52 F4
Tonggu China 77 G2
Tonggu Zui pt China 77 F5
Tonghai China 76 D3
Tonghe China 74 C3
Tonghua Jilin China 74 B4
Tonghua Jilin China 74 B4
Tongi Bangl. see Tungi
Tongjiang Heilong. China 74 D3
Tongjiang Sichuan China 76 E2
Tongking, Gulf of China/Vietnam 70 E2
Tonglau Myanmar 70 B2
Tongle China see Leye
Tongliang China 76 E2
Tongliao China 73 M4
Tongling China 77 H2
Tonglu China 77 H2
Tongo Australia 112 A3
Tongo Lake salt flat Australia 112 A3
Tongren Guizhou China 77 F3
Tongren Qinghai China 76 D1
Tongres Belgium see Tongeren
Tongsa Bhutan see Trongsa
Tongshan China see Xuzhou
Tongta Myanmar 70 B2
Tongtian He r. Qinghai China see Yangtze
Tongue U.K. 50 E2
Tongue r. U.S.A. 126 G3
Tongue of the Ocean sea chan. Bahamas 133 E7
Tongxin China 72 J5
Tongyeong S. Korea 75 C6
Tongzi China 76 E2
Tónichi Mex. 127 F7
Tonk India 82 C4
Tonkin reg. Vietnam 70 D2
Tônlé Sab l. Cambodia see Tonle Sap

▶Tonle Sap l. Cambodia 71 C4
Largest lake in south-east Asia.

Tonopah AZ U.S.A. 129 G5
Tonopah NV U.S.A. 128 E2
Tønsberg Norway 45 G7
Tonstad Norway 45 E7
Tonto Creek watercourse U.S.A. 129 H5
Tonūrjeh Iran 88 E3
Tonzang Myanmar 70 A2
Tonzi Myanmar 70 A1
Toobeah Australia 112 D2
Tooele U.S.A. 129 G1
Toogoolawah Australia 112 F1
Tooma r. Australia 112 D6
Toompine Australia 112 B1
Toora Australia 112 C7
Tooraweenah Australia 112 D3
Toorberg mt. S. Africa 100 G7
Toowoomba Australia 112 E1
Tooxin Somalia 98 F2
Tōp Afgh. 89 H3
Top Boğazı Geçidi pass Turkey 85 C1

▶Topeka U.S.A. 130 E4
Capital of Kansas.

Topia Mex. 127 G8
Töplitz Germany 53 M2
Topoľčany Slovakia 47 Q6
Topolobampo Mex. 127 F8
Topolovgrad Bulg. 59 L3
Topozero, Ozero l. Russia 44 R4
Topsfield U.S.A. 132 H2
Torbalı Turkey 59 L5
Torbat-e Ḩeydarīyeh Iran 88 E3
Torbat-e Jām Iran 89 F3
Torbay Bay Australia 109 B8
Torbert, Mount U.S.A. 118 C3
Torbeyevo Russia 43 I5
Torch r. Canada 121 K4
Tordesillas Spain 57 D3
Tordesilos Spain 57 F3
Töre Sweden 44 M4
Torelló Spain 57 H2
Torenberg hill Neth. 52 F2
Toretam Kazakh. see Baykonyr
Torgau Germany 53 M3
Torgay Kazakh. 80 B2
Torghay Kazakh. see Torgay
Torgun r. Russia 43 J6
Torhout Belgium 52 D3
Tori Eth. 97 G4
Torino Italy see Turin
Tori-shima i. Japan 75 F7
Torit South Sudan 97 G4
Torkamānchāy Iran 88 B2
Tōr Kham Afgh. 89 H3
Torkovichi Russia 42 F4
Tornado Mountain Canada 120 H5
Torneå Fin. see Tornio
Torneälven r. Sweden 44 N4
Torneträsk l. Sweden 44 K2
Torngat, Monts mts Canada see Torngat Mountains
Torngat Mountains Canada 123 I2
Tornio Fin. 44 N4
Toro Spain 57 D3
Toro, Pico del mt. Mex. 131 C7
Torom Russia 74 D1

▶Toronto Canada 134 F2
Capital of Ontario.

Toro Peak U.S.A. 128 E5
Toropets Russia 42 F4
Tororo Uganda 98 D3
Toros Dağları mts Turkey see Taurus Mountains
Torphins U.K. 50 G3
Torquay Australia 112 B7
Torquay U.K. 49 D8
Torrance U.S.A. 128 D5
Torrão Port. 57 B4
Torre mt. Port. 57 C3
Torreblanca Spain 57 G3
Torre Blanco, Cerro mt. Mex. 127 E6
Torrecerredo mt. Spain 57 D2
Torre del Greco Italy 58 F4
Torre de Moncorvo Port. 57 C3
Torrelavega Spain 57 D2
Torremolinos Spain 57 D5

▶Torrens, Lake imp. l. Australia 111 B6
2nd largest lake in Oceania.

Torrens Creek Australia 110 D4
Torrent Spain 57 F4
Torrente Spain see Torrent
Torreón Mex. 131 C7
Torres Brazil 145 A5
Torres Mex. 127 F7
Torres del Paine, Parque Nacional nat. park Chile 144 B8
Torres Islands Vanuatu 107 G3
Torres Novas Port. 57 B4
Torres Strait Australia 106 E2
Torres Vedras Port. 57 B4
Torrevieja Spain 57 F5
Torrey U.S.A. 129 H2
Torridge r. U.K. 49 C8
Torridon, Loch b. U.K. 50 D3
Torrijos Spain 57 D4
Torrington Australia 112 E2
Torrington CT U.S.A. 132 F3
Torrington WY U.S.A. 126 G4
Torsby Sweden 45 H6

▶Tórshavn Faroe Is 44 [inset 2]
Capital of the Faroe Islands.

Tortilla Flat U.S.A. 129 H5
To'rtko'l Uzbek. 80 B3
Törtköl Uzbek. see To'rtko'l
Tortolì Sardinia Italy 58 C5
Tortona Italy 58 C2
Tortosa Spain 57 G3
Tortum Turkey 91 F2
Ţorūd Iran 88 D3
Torugart, Pereval pass China/Kyrg. see Turugart Pass
Torul Turkey 91 E2
Toruń Poland 47 Q4
Tory Island Ireland 51 D2
Tory Sound sea chan. Ireland 51 D2
Torzhok Russia 42 G4
Tōrzī Afgh. 89 G4
Tosa Japan 75 D6
Tosbotn Norway 44 H4
Tosca S. Africa 100 F3
Toscano, Arcipelago is Italy 58 C3
Tosham India 82 C3
Tōshima-yama mt. Japan 75 F4

▶Toshkent Uzbek. 80 C3
Capital of Uzbekistan.

Tosno Russia 42 F4
Toson Hu l. China 83 I1
Tostado Arg. 144 D3
Tostedt Germany 53 J1
Tosya Turkey 90 D2
Totapola mt. Sri Lanka 84 D5
Tôtes France 52 B5
Tot'ma Russia 42 I4
Totness Suriname 143 G2
Totten Glacier Antarctica 152 F2
Tottenham Australia 112 C4
Totton U.K. 49 F8
Tottori Japan 75 D6
Touba Côte d'Ivoire 96 C4
Touba Senegal 96 B3
Toubkal, Jebel mt. Morocco 54 C5
Toubkal, Parc National du nat. park Morocco 54 C5
Touboro Cameroon 97 E4
Tougan Burkina Faso 96 C3
Touggourt Alg. 54 F5
Tougué Guinea 96 B3
Touil Mauritania 96 B3
Toul France 52 F6
Touliu Taiwan see Douliu
Toulon France 56 G5
Toulon U.S.A. 130 F3
Toulouse France 56 E5
Toumodi Côte d'Ivoire 96 C4
Toupai China 77 F3
Tourane Vietnam see Đa Năng
Tourcoing France 52 D4
Tourgis Lake Canada 121 J1
Tourlaville France 49 F9
Tournai Belgium 52 D4
Tournon-sur-Rhône France 56 G4
Tournus France 58 A1
Touros Brazil 143 K5
Tours France 56 E3
Tousside, Pic mt. Chad 97 E2
Toussoro, Mont mt. Cent. Afr. Rep. 98 C3
Toutai China 74 B3
Touwsrivier S. Africa 100 E7
Toužim Czechia 53 M4
Tovarkovo Russia 43 G5
Tovil'-Dora Tajik. see Tavildara
Tovuz Azer. 91 G2
Towada Japan 74 F4
Towak Mountain hill U.S.A. 118 B3
Towanda U.S.A. 135 G3
Towaoc U.S.A. 129 I3
Towcester U.K. 49 G6
Tower Ireland 51 D6
Towner U.S.A. 130 C1
Townes Pass U.S.A. 128 E3
Townsend U.S.A. 126 F3
Townsend, Mount Australia 112 D6
Townshend Island Australia 110 E4
Townsville Australia 110 D3
Towot South Sudan 97 G4
Towson U.S.A. 135 G4
Towyn U.K. see Tywyn
Toy U.S.A. 128 D1
Toyah U.S.A. 131 C6
Toyama Japan 75 E5
Toyama-wan b. Japan 75 E5
Toyohashi Japan 75 E6
Toyokawa Japan 75 E6
Toyonaka Japan 75 D6
Toyooka Japan 75 D6
Toyota Japan 75 E6
Tozanlı Turkey see Almus
Tozê Kangri mt. China 83 E2
Tozeur Tunisia 54 F5
Tozi, Mount U.S.A. 118 C3
T'q'ibuli Georgia 91 F2
Traben Germany 52 H5
Trâblous Lebanon see Tripoli
Trabotivište Macedonia 59 J4
Trabzon Turkey 91 E2
Tracy CA U.S.A. 128 C3
Tracy MN U.S.A. 130 E2
Trading r. Canada 122 C4
Traer U.S.A. 130 E3
Trafalgar U.S.A. 134 B4
Trafalgar, Cabo c. Spain 57 C5
Traffic Mountain Canada 120 D2
Trail Canada 120 G5
Tràille, Rubha na pt U.K. 50 D5
Traill Island Greenland see Traill Ø
Traill Ø i. Greenland 119 P2
Trainor Lake Canada 120 F2
Trajectum Neth. see Utrecht
Trakai Lith. 45 N9
Tra Khuc, Sông r. Vietnam 70 E4
Trakiya reg. Europe see Thrace
Trakt Russia 42 K3
Trakya reg. Europe see Thrace
Tralee Ireland 51 C5
Tralee Bay Ireland 51 C5
Trá Li Ireland see Tralee
Tramandaí Brazil 145 A5
Tramán Tepuí mt. Venez. 142 F2
Trá Mhór Ireland see Tramore
Trâm Kák Cambodia 71 D5
Tramore Ireland 51 E5
Tranås Sweden 45 I7
Trancas Arg. 144 C3
Trancoso Brazil 145 D2
Tranemo Sweden 45 H8
Tranent U.K. 50 G5
Trang Thai. 71 B6
Trangan i. Indon. 108 F1
Trang An tourist site Vietnam 70 D2
Trangie Australia 112 C4
Trân Ninh, Cao Nguyên Laos 70 C3
Transantarctic Mountains Antarctica 152 H2
Trans Canada Highway Canada 121 H5
Transnistria disp. terr. Moldova 43 F7
Transylvanian Alps mts Romania 59 J2
Transylvanian Basin plat. Romania 59 K1
Trapani Sicily Italy 58 E5
Trapezus Turkey see Trabzon
Trapper Peak U.S.A. 126 E3
Trappes France 52 C6
Traralgon Australia 112 C7
Trashigang Bhutan 83 G4
Trasimeno, Lago l. Italy 58 E3
Trasvase, Canal de Spain 57 E4
Trat Thai. 71 C4
Tratani r. Pak. 89 H4
Traunsee l. Austria 47 N7
Traunstein Germany 47 N7
Travellers Lake imp. l. Australia 111 C7
Travers, Mount N.Z. 113 D6
Traverse City U.S.A. 134 C1
Tra Vinh Vietnam 71 D5
Travnik Bos. & Herz. 58 G2
Trbovlje Slovenia 58 F1
Tre, Hon i. Vietnam 71 E4
Treasury Islands Solomon Is 106 F2
Trebbin Germany 53 N2
Trebević, Nacionalni Park nat. park Bos. & Herz. 58 H3
Třebíč Czechia 47 O6
Trebinje Bos. & Herz. 58 H3
Trebišov Slovakia 43 D6
Trebizond Turkey see Trabzon
Trebnje Slovenia 58 F2
Trebur Germany 53 I5
Tree Island India 84 B4
Trefaldwyn U.K. see Montgomery
Treffurt Germany 53 K3
Treffynnon U.K. see Holywell
Tref-y-clawdd U.K. see Knighton
Trefynwy U.K. see Monmouth
Tregosse Islets and Reefs Australia 110 E3
Treinta y Tres Uruguay 144 F4
Trelew Arg. 144 C6
Trelleborg Sweden 45 H9
Trélon France 52 E4
Tremblant, Mont hill Canada 122 G5
Trembleur Lake Canada 120 E4
Tremiti, Isole is Italy 58 F3
Tremont U.S.A. 135 G3
Tremonton U.S.A. 126 E4
Tremp Spain 57 G2
Trenance U.K. 49 B8
Trenary U.S.A. 132 C2
Trenche r. Canada 123 G5
Trenčín Slovakia 47 Q6
Trendelburg Germany 53 J3
Trêng Cambodia 71 C4
Trenque Lauquén Arg. 144 D5
Trent r. Italy see Trento
Trent r. U.K. 49 G5
Trento Italy 58 D1
Trenton Canada 135 G1
Trenton FL U.S.A. 133 D6
Trenton GA U.S.A. 133 C5
Trenton KY U.S.A. 134 B5
Trenton MO U.S.A. 130 E3
Trenton NC U.S.A. 133 E5
Trenton NE U.S.A. 130 C3

▶Trenton NJ U.S.A. 135 H3
Capital of New Jersey.

Treorchy U.K. 49 D7
Trepassey Canada 123 L5
Tres Arroyos Arg. 144 D5
Tresco i. U.K. 49 A9
Três Corações Brazil 145 B3
Tres Esquinas Col. 142 C3
Tres Forcas, Cabo c. Morocco see Trois Fourches, Cap des
Três Lagoas Brazil 145 A3
Três Marias, Represa resr Brazil 145 B2
Tres Picachos, Sierra mts Mex. 127 G7
Tres Picos, Cerro mt. Arg. 144 D5
Três Pontas Brazil 145 B3
Tres Puntas, Cabo c. Arg. 144 C7
Três Rios Brazil 145 C3
Tretiy Severnyy Russia 41 S3
Tretten Norway 45 G6
Treuchtlingen Germany 53 K6
Treuenbrietzen Germany 53 M2
Treungen Norway 45 F7
Treves Germany see Trier
Treviglio Italy 58 C2
Treviso Italy 58 E2
Trevose Head hd U.K. 49 B8
Tri An, Hồ resr Vietnam 71 D5
Triánda Greece see Trianta
Triangle U.S.A. 135 G4
Trianta Greece 59 M6
Tribal Areas admin. div. Pak. 89 H3
Tribune U.S.A. 130 C4
Tricase Italy 58 H5
Trichinopoly India see Tiruchchirappalli
Trichur India see Thrissur
Tricot France 52 C5
Trida Australia 112 B4
Tridentum Italy see Trento
Trier Germany 52 G5
Trieste Italy 58 E2
Trieste, Golfo di g. Europe see Trieste, Gulf of
Trieste, Gulf of Europe 58 E2
Triglav mt. Slovenia 58 E1
Triglavski narodni park nat. park Slovenia 58 E1
Trikala Greece 59 I5
Tríkkala Greece see Trikala

▶Trikora, Puncak mt. Indon. 69 J7
2nd highest mountain in Oceania.

Trim Ireland 51 F4
Trincomalee Sri Lanka 84 D4
Trindade Brazil 145 A2
Trindade, Ilha da i. S. Atlantic Ocean 148 G7
Trinidad Bol. 142 F6
Trinidad Cuba 137 I4
Trinidad i. Trin. and Tob. 137 L6
Trinidad Uruguay 144 E4
Trinidad U.S.A. 127 G5
Trinidad country West Indies see Trinidad and Tobago
Trinidad and Tobago country West Indies 137 L6
Trinity U.S.A. 131 E6
Trinity r. CA U.S.A. 128 B1
Trinity r. TX U.S.A. 131 E6
Trinity Bay Canada 123 L5
Trinity Islands U.S.A. 118 C4
Trinity Range mts U.S.A. 128 D1
Trinkat Island India 71 A5
Trionto, Capo c. Italy 58 G5
Tripa r. Indon. 71 B7
Tripkau Germany 53 L1
Tripoli Greece 59 J6
Tripoli Lebanon 85 B2

▶Tripoli Libya 97 E1
Capital of Libya.

Trípolis Greece see Tripoli
Tripolis Lebanon see Tripoli
Tripolitania hist. area Libya 96 E1
Tripunittura India 84 C4
Tripura state India 83 G5

▶Tristan da Cunha i. S. Atlantic Ocean 148 H8
Part of St Helena, Ascension and Tristan da Cunha.

Trisul mt. India 82 D3
Triton Canada 123 L4
Triton Island atoll Paracel Is 68 E3
Trittau Germany 53 K1
Trittenheim Germany 52 G5
Trivandrum India see Thiruvananthapuram
Trivento Italy 58 F4
Trnava Slovakia 47 P6
Trobriand Islands P.N.G. 106 F2
Trochu Canada 120 H5
Trofors Norway 44 H4
Trogir Croatia 58 G3
Troia Italy 58 F4
Troisdorf Germany 53 H4
Trois Fourches, Cap des c. Morocco 57 E6
Trois-Ponts Belgium 52 F4
Trois-Rivières Canada 123 G5
Troitsko-Pechorsk Russia 41 R3
Troitskoye Altayskiy Kray Russia 72 E2
Troitskoye Khabarovskiy Kray Russia 74 E2
Troitskoye Respublika Kalmykiya-Khalm'g-Tangch Russia 43 J7
Troll research station Antarctica 152 C2
Trollhättan Sweden 45 H7
Trombetas r. Brazil 143 G4
Tromelin, Île i. Indian Ocean 149 L7
Tromelin Island Micronesia see Fais
Tromen, Volcán vol. Arg. 144 B5
Tromie r. U.K. 50 E3
Trompsburg S. Africa 101 G6
Tromsø Norway 44 K2
Trona U.S.A. 128 E4
Tronador, Monte mt. Arg. 144 B6
Trondheim Norway 44 G5
Trondheimsfjorden sea chan. Norway 44 F5
Trongsa Bhutan 83 G4
Troödos Mountains Cyprus 85 A2
Troon U.K. 50 E5
Tropeiros, Serra dos hills Brazil 145 B1
Tropic U.S.A. 129 G3
Tropic of Cancer 131 B8
Tropic of Capricorn 110 G4
Trosh Russia 42 L2
Trostan hill U.K. 51 F2
Trout r. B.C. Canada 120 E3
Trout r. N.W.T. Canada 120 G2
Trout Lake Alta Canada 120 H3
Trout Lake N.W.T. Canada 120 F2
Trout Lake l. N.W.T. Canada 120 F2
Trout Lake l. Ont. Canada 121 M5
Trout Peak U.S.A. 126 F3
Trout Run U.S.A. 135 G3
Trouville-sur-Mer France 49 H9
Trowbridge U.K. 49 E7
Troy tourist site Turkey 59 L5
Troy AL U.S.A. 133 C6
Troy KS U.S.A. 130 E4
Troy MI U.S.A. 134 D2

Troy MT U.S.A. 130 F4
Troy MT U.S.A. 126 E2
Troy NH U.S.A. 135 I2
Troy NY U.S.A. 135 I2
Troy OH U.S.A. 134 C3
Troy PA U.S.A. 135 G3
Troyan Bulg. 59 K3
Troyes France 56 G2
Troy Lake U.S.A. 128 E4
Troy Peak U.S.A. 129 F2
Trstenik Serbia 59 I3
Truc Giang Vietnam see Bên Tre
Trucial States country Asia see United Arab Emirates
Trud Russia 42 G4
Trufanova Russia 42 J2
Trujillo Hond. 137 G5
Trujillo Peru 142 C5
Trujillo Spain 57 D4
Trujillo Venez. 142 D2
Trujillo, Monte mt. Dom. Rep. see Duarte, Pico
Truk is Micronesia see Chuuk
Trulben Germany 53 H5
Trumbull, Mount U.S.A. 129 G3
Trumon Indon. 71 B7
Trundle Australia 112 C4
Trưng Hiệp Vietnam 70 D4
Trưng Khanh Vietnam 70 D2
Truong Sa is S. China Sea see Spratly Islands
Truro Canada 123 J5
Truro U.K. 49 B8
Truskmore hill Ireland 51 D3
Trutch Canada 120 F3
Truth or Consequences U.S.A. 127 G6
Trutnov Czechia 47 O5
Truuli Peak U.S.A. 118 C4
Truva tourist site Turkey see Troy
Trypiti, Akra pt Greece see Trypiti, Akrotirio
Trypiti, Akrotirio pt Greece 59 K7
Trysil Norway 45 H6
Trzebiatów Poland 47 O3
Tsagaannuur Mongolia 80 G2
Tsagaan-Uul Mongolia 80 I2
Tsagan Aman Russia 43 J7
Tsagan Nur Russia 43 J7
Tsaidam Basin China see Qaidam Pendi
Tsaka La pass China/India 82 D2
Ts'alenjikha Georgia 91 F2
Tsaratanana, Massif du mts Madag. 99 E5
Tsarevo Bulg. 59 L3
Tsaris Mountains Namibia 100 C3
Tsaritsyn Russia see Volgograd
Tsaukaib Namibia 100 B4
Tsavo East National Park Kenya 98 D4
Tsavo West National Park Africa 98 D3
Tsefat Israel see Ẕefat
Tselinograd Kazakh. see Astana
Tsenhermandal Mongolia 73 J3
Tsenogora Russia 42 J2
Tses Namibia 100 D3
Tsetseg Mongolia 80 H2
Tsetseng Botswana 100 F2
Tsetserleg Arhangay Mongolia 80 J2
Tsetserleg Hövsgöl Mongolia 80 I2
Tshabong Botswana 100 F4
Tshad country Africa see Chad
Tshane Botswana 100 E3
Tshela Dem. Rep. Congo 99 B4
Tshibala Dem. Rep. Congo 99 C4
Tshikapa Dem. Rep. Congo 99 C4
Tshing S. Africa 101 H4
Tshipise S. Africa 101 J2
Tshitanzu Dem. Rep. Congo 99 C4
Tshofa Dem. Rep. Congo 99 C4
Tshokwane S. Africa 101 J3
Tsholotsho Zimbabwe 99 C5
Tshootsha Botswana 100 E2
Tshuapa r. Dem. Rep. Congo 97 F5
Tshwane S. Africa see Pretoria
Tsil'ma r. Russia 42 K2
Tsimlyansk Russia 43 I7
Tsimlyanskoye Vodokhranilishche resr Russia 43 I7
Tsimmermanovka Russia 74 E2
Tsinan China see Jinan
Tsineng S. Africa 100 F4
Tsinghai prov. China see Qinghai
Tsingtao China see Qingdao
Tsing Yi i. H.K. China 77 [inset]
Tsining China see Ulan Qab
Tsiombe Madag. 99 E6
Tsiroanomandidy Madag. 99 E5
Tsitsihar China see Qiqihar
Tsitsutl Peak Canada 120 E4
Tsivil'sk Russia 42 J5
Tskhaltubo Georgia see Ts'q'alt'ubo

▶Tskhinvali Georgia 91 F2
Capital of South Ossetia.

Tsna r. Russia 43 I5
Ts'nori Georgia 91 G2
Tsokar Chumo l. India 82 D2
Tsolo S. Africa 101 I6
Tsomo S. Africa 101 H7
Tsona China see Cona
Ts'q'alt'ubo Georgia 91 F2
Tsu Japan 75 E6
Tsuchiura Japan 75 F5
Tsuen Wan H.K. China 77 [inset]
Tsugarū-kaikyō strait Japan 74 F4
Tsugaru Strait Japan see Tsugarū-kaikyō
Tsumeb Namibia 99 B5
Tsumis Park Namibia 100 C2
Tsumkwe Namibia 99 C5
Tsuruga Japan 75 E6
Tsurugi-san mt. Japan 75 D6
Tsurukhaytuy Russia see Priargunsk
Tsuruoka Japan 75 E5
Tsushima Japan 75 C6
Tsushima is Japan 75 C6
Tsushima-kaikyō strait Japan/S. Korea see Korea Strait
Tsuyama Japan 75 D6
Tswaane Botswana 100 E2
Tswaraganang S. Africa 101 G5
Tswelelang S. Africa 101 G4
Tsyelyakhany Belarus 45 N10
Tsypnavolok Russia 44 R2
Tsyurupyns'k Ukr. 59 O1
Tthenaagoo Canada see Nahanni Butte
Tu, Nam r. Myanmar 70 B2
Tua Dem. Rep. Congo 98 B4
Tual Indon. 69 I8
Tuam Ireland 51 D4
Tuamotu Archipelago is Fr. Polynesia see Tuamotu Islands
Tuamotu Islands Fr. Polynesia 151 K6
Tuân Giao Vietnam 70 C2
Tuangku i. Indon. 71 B7
Tuapse Russia 90 E1
Tuas Sing. 71 [inset]
Tuath, Loch a' b. U.K. 50 C2
Tuba City U.S.A. 129 H3
Tubarão Brazil 145 A5
Tubarjal Saudi Arabia 85 D4
Tübingen Germany 47 L6
Tubmanburg Liberia 96 B4
Tubruq Libya 90 A4
Tubuai i. Fr. Polynesia 151 K7
Tubuai Islands Fr. Polynesia 151 J7
Tucano Brazil 143 K6
Tucavaca Bol. 143 G7
Tüchen Germany 53 M1
Tuchheim Germany 53 M2
Tuchitua Canada 120 D2
Tuchodi r. Canada 120 F3
Tuckerton U.S.A. 135 H4
Tucopia i. Solomon Is see Tikopia
Tucson U.S.A. 129 H5
Tucson Mountains U.S.A. 129 H5
Tuctuc r. Canada 123 I2
Tucumán Arg. see San Miguel de Tucumán
Tucumcari U.S.A. 131 C5
Tucupita Venez. 142 F2
Tucuruí Brazil 143 I4
Tucuruí, Represa de resr Brazil 143 I4
Tudela Spain 57 F2
Tuder Italy see Todi
Tüdevtey Mongolia 80 I2
Tudun Wada Nigeria 96 D3
Tuela r. Port. 57 C3
Tuen Mun H.K. China 77 [inset]
Tuensang India 83 H4
Tufts Abyssal Plain sea feature N. Pacific Ocean 151 K2
Tuglung China 76 B2
Tuguegarao Phil. 69 G3
Tugur Russia 74 E1
Tuhemberua Indon. 71 B7
Tujiabu China see Yongxiu
Tukangbesi, Kepulauan is Indon. 69 G8
Tukarak Island Canada 122 F2
Ţukhmān, Banī reg. Saudi Arabia 88 C6
Tukituki r. N.Z. 113 F4
Tuktoyaktuk Canada 118 E3
Tuktut Nogait National Park Canada 118 F3
Tukums Latvia 45 M8
Tukuringra, Khrebet mts Russia 74 B1
Tukuyu Tanz. 99 D4
Tukzār Afgh. 89 G3
Tula Russia 43 H5
Tulach Mhór Ireland see Tullamore
Tulagt Ar Gol r. China 83 H1
Tūlak Afgh. 89 F3
Tulameen Canada 120 F5
Tula Mountains Antarctica 152 D2
Tulancingo Mex. 136 E4
Tulare U.S.A. 128 D3
Tulare Lake Bed U.S.A. 128 D4
Tularosa Mountains U.S.A. 129 I5
Tulasi mt. India 84 D2
Tulbagh S. Africa 100 D7
Tulcán Ecuador 142 C3
Tulcea Romania 59 M2
Tule r. U.S.A. 131 C5
Tuléar Madag. see Toliara
Tulemalu Lake Canada 121 L2
Tule Springs Fossil Beds National Monument nat. park U.S.A. 129 F3
Tulia U.S.A. 131 C5
Tulihe China 74 A2
Tulita Canada 120 E1
Tulkarem West Bank see Ţūlkarm
Ţūlkarm West Bank 85 B3
Tulla Ireland 51 D5
Tullahoma U.S.A. 132 C5
Tullamore Australia 112 C4
Tullamore Ireland 51 E4
Tulle France 56 E4
Tulleråsen Sweden 44 I5
Tullibigeal Australia 112 C4
Tullow Ireland 51 F5
Tully Australia 110 D3
Tully r. Australia 110 D3
Tully U.K. 51 E3
Tulos Russia 44 Q5
Tulqarem West Bank see Ţūlkarm
Tulsa U.S.A. 131 E4
Tulsipur Nepal 83 E3
Tuluá Col. 142 C3
Tuluksak U.S.A. 153 B2
Tulūl al Ashāqif hills Jordan 85 C3
Tulun Russia 72 I2
Tulu-Tuloi, Serra hills Brazil 142 F3
Tulu Welel mt. Eth. 98 D3
Tuma Russia 43 I5
Tumaco Col. 142 C3
Tumahole S. Africa 101 H4
Tumain China 83 G2
Tumakuru India 84 C3
Tumannyy Russia 44 S2
Tumasik Sing. see Singapore
Tumba Dem. Rep. Congo 98 C4
Tumba Sweden 45 J7
Tumba, Lac l. Dem. Rep. Congo 98 B4
Tumbarumba Australia 112 D5
Tumbes Peru 142 B4
Tumbler Ridge Canada 120 F4
Tumby Bay Australia 111 B7
Tumen Jilin China 74 C4
Tumen Shaanxi China 77 F1
Tumereng Guyana 142 F2
Tumindao i. Phil. 68 F6
Tumiritinga Brazil 145 C2
Tumkur India see Tumakuru
Tummel r. U.K. 50 F4
Tummel, Loch l. U.K. 50 F4
Tumnin r. Russia 74 F2
Tump Pak. 89 F5
Tumpat Malaysia 71 C6
Tumpôr, Phnum mt. Cambodia 71 C4
Tumshuk Uzbek. 89 G2
Tumu Ghana 96 C3
Tumucumaque, Serra hills Brazil 143 G3
Tumudibandh India 84 D2
Tumut Australia 112 D5
Tuna India 82 B5
Ţunb al Kubrá i. The Gulf see Tonb-e Bozorg, Jazīreh-ye
Ţunb aş Şughrá i. The Gulf see Tonb-e Küchek, Jazīreh-ye
Tunceli Turkey 91 E3
Tunchang China 77 F5
Tuncurry Australia 112 F4
Tundi imp. l. Afgh. 89 F3
Tunduru Tanz. 99 D5
Tunes Tunisia see Tunis
Tunga Nigeria 96 D4
Tungabhadra Reservoir India 84 C3
Tungi Bangl. 83 G5
Tung Lung Island i. H.K. China 77 [inset]
Tungnaá r. Iceland 44 [inset 1]
Tungor Russia 74 F1
T'ung-shan China see Xuzhou
Tungsten (abandoned) Canada 120 D2
Tung Wan b. H.K. China 77 [inset]
Tuni India 84 D2
Tūnī, Chāh-e well Iran 88 E3
Tunica U.S.A. 131 F5
Tūnis country Africa see Tunisia

▶Tunis Tunisia 58 D6
Capital of Tunisia.

Tunis, Golfe de g. Tunisia 58 D6
Tunisia country Africa 54 F5
Tunja Col. 142 D2
Tunkhannock U.S.A. 135 H3
Tunnsjøen l. Norway 44 H4
Tunstall U.K. 49 I6
Tuntsa Fin. 44 P3
Tuntsajoki r. Fin./Russia see Tuntsayoki
Tuntsayoki r. Fin./Russia 44 Q3
also known as Tuntsajoki
Tunulic r. Canada 123 I2
Tununak U.S.A. 118 B3
Tunungayualok Island Canada 123 J2
Tunxi China see Huangshan
Tuodian China see Shuangbai
Tuojiang China see Fenghuang
Tuŏl Khpós Cambodia 71 D5
Tuoniang Jiang r. China 76 E3
Tuotuo He r. China see Togton He
Tuotuoheyan China see Tanggulashan
Tüp Kyrg. 80 E3
Tupã Brazil 145 A3
Tupelo U.S.A. 131 F5
Tupik Russia 73 L2
Tupinambarama, Ilha i. Brazil 143 G4
Tupiraçaba Brazil 145 A1
Tupiza Bol. 142 E8
Tupper Canada 120 F4
Tupper Lake U.S.A. 135 H1
Tupper Lake l. U.S.A. 135 H1

▶Tupungato, Cerro mt. Arg./Chile 144 C4
5th highest mountain in South America.

Tuqayyid well Iraq 88 B4
Tuquan China 73 M3
Tuqu Wan b. China see Lingshui Wan
Tura China 83 F1
Tura India 83 G4
Tura Russia 65 L3
Turabah Saudi Arabia 86 F5
Turakina N.Z. 113 E5
Turan Russia 72 G2
Turana, Khrebet mts Russia 74 C2
Turan Lowland Asia 80 A4
Turan Oypaty lowland Asia see Turan Lowland
Turan Pesligi lowland Asia see Turan Lowland
Turanskaya Nizmennost' lowland Asia see Turan Lowland
Ţurāq al 'Ilab hills Syria 85 D3
Turar Ryskulov Kazakh. 80 D3
Tura-Ryskulova Kazakh. see Turar Ryskulov
Ţurayf Saudi Arabia 85 D4
Ţurayf, Kutayfat vol. Saudi Arabia 85 D4
Turba Estonia 45 N7
Turbat Pak. 89 F5
Turbo Col. 142 C2
Turda Romania 59 J1
Türeh Iran 88 C3
Turfan China see Turpan
Turfan Basin depr. China see Turpan Pendi
Turfan Depression China see Turpan Pendi
Turgayskaya Dolina valley Kazakh. 80 B2
Turgutlu Turkey 59 L5
Turhal Turkey 90 E2
Türi Estonia 45 N7
Turia r. Spain 57 F4
Turin Canada 121 H5
Turin Italy 58 B2
Turiy Rog Russia 74 C3

▶Turkana, Lake salt l. Eth./Kenya 98 D3
5th largest lake in Africa.

Turkestan Range mts Asia 89 G2
Turkey country Asia/Europe 90 D3
Turkey U.S.A. 134 D5
Turkey r. U.S.A. 130 F3
Turki Russia 43 I6
Turkish Republic of Northern Cyprus disp. terr. Asia see Northern Cyprus
Turkistan Kazakh. 80 C3
Türkistan Kazakh. see Turkistan
Turkistān, Silsilah-ye Band-e mts Afgh. 89 F3
Türkiye country Asia/Europe see Turkey
Türkmenabat Turkm. 89 F2
Türkmen Adasy i. Turkm. see Ogurjaly Adasy
Türkmen Aýlagy b. Turkm. see Türkmen Aýlagy
Türkmen Aýlagy b. Turkm. 88 D2
Türkmenbaşy Turkm. 88 D1
Türkmenbaşy Turkm. see Türkmenbaşy
Türkmenbaşy Aýlagy b. Turkm. see Türkmenbaşy Aýlagy
Türkmenbaşy Aýlagy b. Turkm. 88 D2
Türkmenbaşy Döwlet Gorugy nature res. Turkm. 88 D2
Türkmen Dağı mt. Turkey 59 N5
Turkmenistan country Asia 87 I2
Turkmeniya country Asia see Turkmenistan
Türkmenostan country Asia see Turkmenistan
Turkmenskaya S.S.R. country Asia see Turkmenistan
Türkoğlu Turkey 90 E3

▶Turks and Caicos Islands terr. West Indies 137 J4
United Kingdom Overseas Territory.

Turks Island Passage Turks and Caicos Is 133 G8
Turks Islands Turks and Caicos Is 137 J4
Turku Fin. 45 M6
Turkwel watercourse Kenya 98 D3
Turlock U.S.A. 128 C3
Turlock Lake U.S.A. 128 C3
Turmalina Brazil 145 C2
Turnagain r. Canada 120 E3
Turnagain, Cape N.Z. 113 F5
Turnberry U.K. 50 E5
Turnbull, Mount U.S.A. 129 H5
Turneffe Islands atoll Belize 136 G5
Turner U.S.A. 134 D1
Turner Valley Canada 120 H5
Turnhout Belgium 52 E3
Turnor Lake Canada 121 I3
Tŭrnovo Bulg. see Veliko Tarnovo
Turnu Măgurele Romania 59 K3
Turnu Severin Romania see Drobeta-Turnu Severin
Turon r. Australia 112 D4
Turones France see Tours
Turon pasttekisligi lowland Asia see Turan Lowland
Turovets Russia 42 I4
Turpan China 80 G3

▶Turpan Pendi depr. China 80 G3
Lowest point in northern Asia.

Turquino, Pico mt. Cuba 137 I4
Turriff U.K. 50 G3
Turris Libisonis Sardinia Italy see Porto Torres
Tursāq Iraq 91 G4
Turtle Island Fiji see Vatoa
Turtle Lake Canada 121 I4
Turugart Pass China/Kyrg. 80 E3
Turugart Shankou pass China/Kyrg. see Turugart Pass
Turuvanur India 84 C3
Turvo r. Goiás Brazil 145 A2
Turvo r. São Paulo Brazil 145 A2
Tusayan U.S.A. 129 G4
Tuscaloosa U.S.A. 133 C5
Tuscarawas r. U.S.A. 134 E3
Tuscarora Mountains hills U.S.A. 135 G3
Tuscola IL U.S.A. 130 F4
Tuscola TX U.S.A. 131 D5
Tuscumbia U.S.A. 133 C5
Tuskegee U.S.A. 133 C5
Tussey Mountains hills U.S.A. 135 F3
Tustin U.S.A. 134 C1
Tutak Turkey 91 F3
Tutayev Russia 42 H4
Tutera Spain see Tudela
Tuticorin India 84 C4
Tutong Brunei 68 E6
Tuttle Creek Reservoir U.S.A. 130 D4
Tuttlingen Germany 47 L7
Tuttut Nunaat reg. Greenland 119 P2
Tutuala East Timor 108 D2
Tutubu P.N.G. 110 E1
Tutubu Tanz. 99 D4
Tutuila i. American Samoa 107 I3
Tutume Botswana 99 C6
Tutwiler U.S.A. 131 F5
Tuun-bong mt. N. Korea 74 B4
Tuupovaara Fin. 44 Q5
Tuusniemi Fin. 44 P5
Tuvalu country S. Pacific Ocean 107 H2
Tuwayq, Jabal hills Saudi Arabia 86 G4
Tuwayq, Jabal mts Saudi Arabia 86 G5
Ţuwayyil ash Shihāq mt. Jordan 85 C4
Tuwwal Saudi Arabia 86 E5
Tuxpan Mex. 136 E4
Tuxtla Gutiérrez Mex. 136 F5
Tuya Lake Canada 120 D3
Tuyên Quang Vietnam 70 D2
Tuy Hoa Vietnam 71 E4
Tuz, Lake salt l. Turkey 90 D3
Tuz Gölü salt l. Turkey see Tuz, Lake
Tuzha Russia 42 J4
Tuz Khurmātū Iraq 91 G4
Tuzla Bos. & Herz. 58 H2
Tuzla Turkey 85 B1
Tuzla Gölü lag. Turkey 59 L4
Tuzlov r. Russia 43 I7
Tuzu r. Myanmar 70 A1
Tvedestrand Norway 45 F7
Tver' Russia 42 G4
Twain Harte U.S.A. 128 C2
Tweed Canada 135 G1
Tweed r. U.K. 50 G5
Tweed Heads Australia 112 F2
Tweedie Canada 121 I4
Tweefontein S. Africa 100 D7
Twee Rivier Namibia 100 D3
Twentekanaal canal Neth. 52 G2
Twentynine Palms U.S.A. 128 E4
Twin Bridges CA U.S.A. 128 C2
Twin Bridges MT U.S.A. 126 E3
Twin Buttes Reservoir U.S.A. 131 C6
Twin Falls Canada 123 I3
Twin Falls U.S.A. 126 E4
Twin Heads hill Australia 108 D5
Twin Peak U.S.A. 128 C2
Twistringen Germany 53 I2
Twitchen Reservoir U.S.A. 128 C4
Twitya r. Canada 120 D1
Twizel N.Z. 113 C7
Twofold Bay Australia 112 D6
Two Harbors U.S.A. 130 F2
Two Hills Canada 121 I4
Two Rivers U.S.A. 134 B1
Tyan' Shan' mts China/Kyrg. see Tien Shan
Tyao r. India/Myanmar 76 B4
Tyatya, Vulkan vol. Russia 74 G3
Tydal Norway 44 G5
Tygart Valley U.S.A. 134 F4
Tygda Russia 74 B1
Tygda r. Russia 74 B1
Tyler U.S.A. 131 E5
Tylertown U.S.A. 131 F6
Tym' r. Russia 74 F2
Tymovskoye Russia 74 F2
Tynda Russia 73 M1
Tyndall U.S.A. 130 D3
Tyndinskiy Russia see Tynda
Tyne r. U.K. 50 G4
Tynemouth U.K. 48 F3
Tynset Norway 44 G5
Tyoploozyorsk Russia see Teploozersk
Tyoploye Ozero Russia see Teploozersk
Tyr Lebanon see Tyre
Tyras Ukr. see Bilhorod-Dnistrovs'kyy
Tyre Lebanon 85 B3
Tyree, Mount Antarctica 152 L1
Tyrma Russia 74 D2
Tyrma r. Russia 74 C2
Tyrnävä Fin. 44 N4
Tyrnavos Greece 59 J5
Tyrnyauz Russia 91 F2
Tyrone U.S.A. 135 F3
Tyrrell r. Australia 112 A5
Tyrrell, Lake dry lake Australia 111 C7
Tyrrell Lake Canada 121 J2
Tyrrhenian Sea France/Italy 58 D4
Tyrus Lebanon see Tyre
Tysa r. Serbia see Tisa
Tyukalinsk Russia 64 I4
Tyulen'i, Ostrova is Kazakh. 91 H1
Tyumen' Russia 64 H4
Tyup Kyrg. see Tüp
Tyuratam Kazakh. see Baykonyr
Tywi r. U.K. 49 C7
Tywyn U.K. 49 C6
Tzaneen S. Africa 101 J2
Tzia i. Greece 59 K6

U

Uaco Congo Angola see Waku-Kungo
Ualan atoll Micronesia see Kosrae
Uamanda Angola 99 C5
Uarc, Ras c. Morocco see Trois Fourches, Cap des
Uaroo Australia 109 A5
Uatumã r. Brazil 143 G4
Uauá Brazil 143 K5
Uaupés r. Brazil 142 E3
U'aylī, Wādī al watercourse Saudi Arabia 85 D4
U'aywij well Saudi Arabia 88 B4
U'aywij, Wādī al watercourse Saudi Arabia 91 F5
Ubá Brazil 145 C3
Ubaí Brazil 145 B2
Ubaitaba Brazil 145 D1
Ubangi r. Cent. Afr. Rep./Dem. Rep. Congo 98 B4
Ubangi-Shari country Africa see Central African Republic
Ubauro Pak. 89 H4
Ubayyiḍ, Wādī al watercourse Iraq/Saudi Arabia 91 F4
Ube Japan 75 C6
Úbeda Spain 57 E4
Uberaba Brazil 145 B2
Uberlândia Brazil 145 A2
Ubin, Pulau i. Sing. 71 [inset]
Ubiña, Peña mt. Spain 57 D2
Ubly U.S.A. 134 D2
Ubolratna, Ang Kep Nam Thai. 70 C3
Ubombo S. Africa 101 K4
Ubon Ratchathani Thai. 70 D4
Ubstadt-Weiher Germany 53 I5
Ubundu Dem. Rep. Congo 97 F5
Üçajy Turkm. 89 F2
Ucar Azer. 91 G2
Uçarı Turkey 85 A1
Ucayali r. Peru 142 D4
Uch Pak. 89 H4
Üchajy Turkm. see Üçajy
Üchān Iran 88 C2
Uchiura-wan b. Japan 74 F4
Uchkeken Russia 91 F2
Uchkuduk Uzbek. see Uchquduq
Uchquduq Uzbek. 80 B3
Uchte Germany 53 I2
Uchte r. Germany 53 L2
Uchur r. Russia 65 O4
Uckermark reg. Germany 53 N1
Uckfield U.K. 49 H8
Ucluelet Canada 120 E5
Ucross U.S.A. 126 G3
Uda r. Russia 73 J2
Uda r. Russia 74 D1
Udachnoye Russia 43 J7
Udachnyy Russia 153 E2
Udagamandalam India 84 C4
Udaipur Rajasthan India 82 C4
Udaipur Tripura India 83 G5
Udanti r. India/Myanmar 83 E5
Uday r. Ukr. 43 G6
'Udaynān well Saudi Arabia 88 C6
Uddevalla Sweden 45 G7
Uddingston U.K. 50 E5
Uddjaure l. Sweden 44 J4
'Udeid, Khōr al inlet Qatar 88 C5
Uden Neth. 52 F3
Udgir India 84 C2
Udhagamandalam India see Udagamandalam
Udhampur India 82 C2
Udia-Milai atoll Marshall Is see Bikini
Udimskiy Russia 42 J3
Udine Italy 58 E1
Udit India 89 I5
Udjuktok Bay Canada 123 J3
Udmalaippettai India see Udumalaippettai
Udomlya Russia 42 G4
Udon Thani Thai. 70 C3
Udskaya Guba b. Russia 65 O4
Udskoye Russia 74 D1
Udumalaippettai India 84 C4
Udupi India 84 B3
Udyl', Ozero l. Russia 74 E1
Udzhary Azer. see Ucar
Udzungwa Mountains National Park Tanz. 99 D4
Uéa atoll New Caledonia see Ouvéa
Ueckermünde Germany 47 O4
Ueda Japan 75 E5
Uele r. Dem. Rep. Congo 98 C3
Uelen Russia 65 U3
Uelzen Germany 53 K2
Uetersen Germany 53 J1
Uettingen Germany 53 J5
Uetze Germany 53 K2
Ufa Russia 41 R5
Ufa r. Russia 41 R5
Uffenheim Germany 53 K5
Uftyuga r. Russia 42 J3
Ugab watercourse Namibia 99 B6
Ugalla r. Tanz. 99 D4
Uganda country Africa 98 D3
Ugie S. Africa 101 I6
Ūgīnak Iran 89 F5
Uglegorsk Russia 74 F2
Uglich Russia 42 H4
Ugljan i. Croatia 58 F2
Uglovoye Russia 74 C2
Ugol'noye Russia 65 P3
Ugolnyy Russia see Beringovskiy
Ugol'nyye Kopi Russia 65 S3
Ugra Russia 43 G5
Uherské Hradiště Czechia 47 P6
Úhlava r. Czechia 53 N5
Uhrichsville U.S.A. 134 E3
Uibhist a' Deas i. U.K. see South Uist
Uibhist a' Tuath i. U.K. see North Uist
Uig U.K. 50 C3
Uíge Angola 99 B4
Uijeongbu S. Korea 75 B5
Ŭiju N. Korea 75 B4
Uimaharju Fin. 44 Q5
Uinta Mountains U.S.A. 129 H1
Uis Mine Namibia 99 B6
Uitenhage S. Africa 101 G7
Uithoorn Neth. 52 E2
Uithuizen Neth. 52 G1
Uivak, Cape Canada 123 J2
Ujhani India 82 D4
Uji Japan 75 D6
Uji-guntō is Japan 75 C7
Ujiyamada Japan see Ise
Ujjain India 82 C5
Ujung Pandang Indon. see Makassar
Újvidék Serbia see Novi Sad
Ukal Sagar l. India 82 C5
Ukata Nigeria 96 D3
'Ukayrishah well Saudi Arabia 88 B5
uKhahlamba-Drakensberg Park nat. park S. Africa 101 I5
Ukholovo Russia 43 I5
Ukhrul India 83 H4
Ukhta Respublika Kareliya Russia see Kalevala
Ukhta Respublika Komi Russia 42 L3
Ukiah CA U.S.A. 128 B2
Ukiah OR U.S.A. 126 D3
Ukkusiksalik National Park nat. park Canada 119 J3
Ukkusissat Greenland 119 M2
Ukmergė Lith. 45 N9

▶Ukraine country Europe 43 F6
2nd largest country in Europe.

Ukrainskaya S.S.R. country Europe see Ukraine
Ukrayina country Europe see Ukraine
Uku-jima i. Japan 75 C6
Ukwi Botswana 100 E2
Ukwi Pan salt pan Botswana 100 E2
Ulaanbaatar Mongolia see Ulan Bator
Ulaangom Mongolia 80 H2
Ulan Australia 112 D4

▶Ulan Bator Mongolia 72 J3
Capital of Mongolia.

Ulanbel' Kazakh. 80 D3
Ulan Erge Russia 43 J7
Ulanhad China see Chifeng
Ulanhot China 74 A3
Ulan Hua China 73 K4
Ulan-Khol Russia 43 J7
Ulan Qab China 73 K4
Ulan-Ude Russia 73 J2
Ulan Ul Hu l. China 83 G2
Ulaş Turkey 90 E3
Ulawa Island Solomon Is 107 G2
Ulayyah reg. Saudi Arabia 88 B6
Ul'banskiy Zaliv b. Russia 74 E1
Uldz Gol r. Mongolia 73 L3
Uleåborg Fin. see Oulu
Ulefoss Norway 45 F7
Ülenurme Estonia 45 O7
Ulety Russia 73 K2
Ulhasnagar India 84 B2
Uliastai China 73 L3
Uliastay Mongolia 80 I2
Uliatea i. Fr. Polynesia see Raiatea
Ulicoten Neth. 52 E3
Ulie atoll Micronesia see Woleai
Ulita r. Russia 44 R2
Ulithi atoll Micronesia 69 J4
Uljin S. Korea 75 C5
Ul'ken Naryn Kazakh. 80 F2
Ulladulla Australia 112 E5
Ullapool U.K. 50 D3
Ulla Ulla, Parque Nacional nat. park Bol. 142 E6
Ullava Fin. 44 M5
Ullersuaq c. Greenland 119 K2
Ulleung-do i. S. Korea 75 C5
Ullswater l. U.K. 48 E4

Ulm Germany 47 L6
Ulmarra Australia 112 F2
Ulmen Germany 52 G4
Uloowaranie, Lake *salt flat* Australia 111 B5
Ulricehamn Sweden 45 H8
Ulrum Neth. 52 G1
Ulsan S. Korea 75 C6
Ulsberg Norway 44 F5
Ulster *reg.* Ireland/U.K. 51 E3
Ulster U.S.A. 135 G3
Ulster Canal Ireland/U.K. 51 E3
Ultima Australia 112 A5
Ulubat Gölü *l.* Turkey 59 M4
Ulubey Turkey 59 M5
Uluborlu Turkey 59 N5
Uludağ *mt.* Turkey 59 M4
Uludağ Milli Parkı *nat. park* Turkey 59 M4
Ulugqat China 80 D4
Ulu Kali, Gunung *mt.* Malaysia 71 C7
Ulukhaktok Canada 118 G2
Ulukışla Turkey 90 D3
Ulundi S. Africa 101 J5
Ulungur Hu *l.* China 80 G2
Uluqsaqtuuq Canada *see* Ulukhaktok
Uluṟu *hill* Australia 109 E6
Uluṟu-Kata Tjuṯa National Park Australia 109 E6
Uluru National Park Australia *see* Uluṟu-Kata Tjuṯa National Park
Ulutau Kazakh. *see* Ulytau
Ulutau, Gory *mts* Kazakh. *see* Ulytau, Gory
Uluyatır Turkey 85 C1
Ulva *i.* U.K. 50 C4
Ulvenhout Neth. 52 E3
Ulverston U.K. 48 D4
Ulvsjön Sweden 45 I6
Ül'yanov Kazakh. *see* Botakara
Ul'yanovsk Russia 43 K5
Ul'yanovskoye Kazakh. *see* Botakara
Ulysses *KS* U.S.A. 130 C4
Ulysses *KY* U.S.A. 134 D5
Ulytau Kazakh. 80 C2
Ulytau, Gory *mts* Kazakh. 80 C2
Ulyunkhan Russia 73 K2
Uma Russia 74 A1
Umal'ta (abandoned) Russia 74 D2
'Umān *country* Asia *see* Oman
Uman' Ukr. 43 F6
Umarao Pak. 89 G4
'Umarī, Qā' al *salt pan* Jordan 85 C4
Umaria India 82 E5
Umarkhed India 84 C2
Umarkot India 84 D2
Umarkot *Punjab* Pak. 89 H4
Umarkot *Sindh* Pak. 89 H5
Umaroona, Lake *salt flat* Australia 111 B5
Umarpada India 82 C5
Umatilla U.S.A. 126 D3
Umba Russia 42 G2
Umbagog Lake U.S.A. 135 J1
Umbeara Australia 109 F6
Umboi *i.* P.N.G. 69 L8
Umeå Sweden 44 L5
Umeälven *r.* Sweden 44 L5
Umfreville Lake Canada 121 M5
uMhlanga S. Africa 101 J5
Umiiviip Kangertiva *inlet* Greenland 119 N3
Umingmaktok Canada 153 L2
Umiujaq Canada 122 F2
Umkomaas S. Africa 101 J6
Umlaiteng India 83 H4
Umlazi S. Africa 101 J5
Umm ad Daraj, Jabal *mt.* Jordan 85 B3
Umm al 'Amad Syria 85 C2
Umm al Jamājim *well* Saudi Arabia 88 B5
Umm al Qaiwain U.A.E. *see* Umm al Qaywayn
Umm al Qaywayn U.A.E. 88 D5
Umm al Qulbān Saudi Arabia 91 F6
Umm ar Raqabah, Khabrat *imp. l.* Saudi Arabia 85 C5
Umm az Zumūl *well* Oman 88 D6
Umm Bāb Qatar 88 C5
Umm Bel Sudan 86 C7
Umm Keddada Sudan 86 C7
Umm Lajj Saudi Arabia 86 E4
Umm Nukhaylah *hill* Saudi Arabia 85 D5
Umm Qaṣr Iraq 91 G5
Umm Quṣūr *i.* Saudi Arabia 90 D6
Umm Ruwaba Sudan 86 D7
Umm Sa'ad Libya 90 B5
Umm Sa'id Qatar 88 C5
Umm Ṣalāl Muḥammad Qatar 88 C5
Umm Shugeira Sudan 86 C7
Umm Wa'āl *hill* Saudi Arabia 85 D4
Umm Wazīr *well* Saudi Arabia 88 B6
Umnak Island U.S.A. 118 B4
Um Phang Wildlife Reserve *nature res.* Thai. 70 B4
Umpqua *r.* U.S.A. 126 B4
Umpulo Angola 99 B5
Umraniye Turkey 59 N5
Umred India 84 C1
Umri India 82 D4
Umtali Zimbabwe *see* Mutare
Umtata S. Africa *see* Mthatha
Umtentweni S. Africa 101 J6
Umuahia Nigeria 96 D4
Umuarama Brazil 144 F2
Umvuma Zimbabwe *see* Mvuma
Umzimkulu S. Africa 101 I6
Una *r.* Bos. & Herz./Croatia 58 G2
Una Brazil 145 D1
Una India 82 D3
'Unāb, Jabal al *hill* Jordan 85 C5
'Unāb, Wādī al *watercourse* Jordan 85 C4
Unaí Brazil 145 B2
Unalaska Island U.S.A. 118 B4
Unapool U.K. 50 D2
'Unayzah Saudi Arabia 86 F4
'Unayzah, Jabal *hill* Iraq 91 E4
Uncia Bol. 142 E7
Uncompahgre Peak U.S.A. 129 J2
Uncompahgre Plateau U.S.A. 129 I2
Undara National Park Australia 110 D3
Underberg S. Africa 101 I5
Underbool Australia 111 C7
Underwood U.S.A. 134 C4
Undur Indon. 69 I7
Unecha Russia 43 G5
Ungama Bay Kenya *see* Ungwana Bay
Ungarie Australia 112 C4
Ungava, Baie d' *b.* Canada *see* Ungava Bay
Ungava, Péninsule d' *pen.* Canada 122 G1
Ungava Bay Canada 123 I2
Ungava Peninsula Canada *see* Ungava, Péninsule d'
Ungeny Moldova *see* Ungheni
Ungheni Moldova 59 L1
Unguana Moz. 101 L2
Unguja *i.* Tanz. *see* Zanzibar Island
Unguz, Solonchakovyye Vpadiny *salt flat* Turkm. 88 E2
Üngüz Angyrsyndaky Garagum *des.* Turkm. 88 E1
Ungvár Ukr. *see* Uzhhorod
Ungwana Bay Kenya 98 E4
Uni Russia 42 K4
União Brazil 143 J4
União da Vitória Brazil 145 A4
União dos Palmares Brazil 143 K5
Unimak Island U.S.A. 118 B4
Unini *r.* Brazil 142 F4
Union *MO* U.S.A. 130 F4
Union *WV* U.S.A. 134 E5
Union, Mount U.S.A. 129 G4
Union City *OH* U.S.A. 134 C3
Union City *PA* U.S.A. 134 F3
Union City *TN* U.S.A. 131 F4
Uniondale S. Africa 100 F7
Unión de Reyes Cuba 133 D8

▶Union of Soviet Socialist Republics
Divided in 1991 into 15 independent nations: Armenia, Azerbaijan, Belarus, Estonia, Georgia, Latvia, Kazakhstan, Kyrgyzstan, Lithuania, Moldova, Russia, Tajikistan, Turkmenistan, Ukraine and Uzbekistan.

Union Springs U.S.A. 133 C5
Uniontown U.S.A. 134 F4
Unionville U.S.A. 135 G3
United Arab Emirates *country* Asia 88 D6
United Arab Republic *country* Africa *see* Egypt

▶United Kingdom *country* Europe 46 G3
3rd most populous country in Europe.

United Provinces *state* India *see* Uttar Pradesh

▶United States of America *country* N. America 124 F3
Most populous country in North America and 3rd most populous in the world. Also 2nd largest country in North America and 3rd in the world.

United States Range *mts* Canada 119 L1
Unity Canada 121 I4
Unjha India 82 C5
Unna Germany 53 H3
Unnao India 82 E4
Ŭnp'a N. Korea 75 B5
Unsan N. Korea 75 B4
Ŭnsan N. Korea 75 B5
Unst *i.* U.K. 50 [inset]
Unstrut *r.* Germany 53 L3
Untor, Ozero *l.* Russia 41 T3
Unuk *r.* Canada/U.S.A. 120 D3
Unuli Horog China 83 G2
Unzen-dake *vol.* Japan 75 C6
Unzha Russia 42 J4
Upalco U.S.A. 129 H1
Upar Ghat *reg.* India 83 F5
Upemba, Lac *l.* Dem. Rep. Congo 99 C4
Upemba, Parc National de l' *nat. park* Dem. Rep. Congo 99 C4
Uperbada India 83 F5
Upernavik Greenland 119 M2
Upington S. Africa 100 E5
Upland U.S.A. 128 E4
Upleta India 82 B5
Upoloksha Russia 44 Q3
'Upolu *i.* Samoa 107 I3
Upper Arlington U.S.A. 134 D3
Upper Arrow Lake Canada 120 G5
Upper Chindwin Myanmar *see* Mawlaik
Upper Fraser Canada 120 F4
Upper Garry Lake Canada 121 K1
Upper Hutt N.Z. 113 E5
Upper Klamath Lake U.S.A. 126 C4
Upper Lough Erne *l.* U.K. 51 E3
Upper Marlboro U.S.A. 135 G4
Upper Mazinaw Lake Canada 135 G1
Upper Missouri Breaks National Monument *nat. park* U.S.A. 130 A2
Upper Peirce Reservoir Sing. 71 [inset]
Upper Red Lake U.S.A. 130 E1
Upper Sandusky U.S.A. 134 D3
Upper Saranac Lake U.S.A. 135 H1
Upper Seal Lake Canada *see* Iberville, Lac d'
Upper Tunguska *r.* Russia *see* Angara
Upper Volta *country* Africa *see* Burkina Faso
Upper Yarra Reservoir Australia 112 B6
Uppinangadi India 84 B3
Uppsala Sweden 45 J7
Upsala Canada 122 C4
Upshi India 82 D2
Upton U.S.A. 135 J2
'Uqayqah, Wādī *watercourse* Jordan 85 B4
'Uqayribāt Syria 85 C2
'Uqlat al 'Udhaybah *well* Iraq 91 G5
Uqturpan China *see* Wushi
Uracas *vol.* N. Mariana Is *see* Farallon de Pajaros
Urad Houqi China *see* Sain Us
Ūrāf Iran 88 E4
Urakawa Japan 74 F4
Ural *hill* Australia 112 C4
Ural *r.* Kazakh./Russia 78 E2
Uralla Australia 112 E3
Ural Mountains Russia 41 S2
Ural'sk Kazakh. 78 E1
Ural'skaya Oblast' *admin. div.* Kazakh. *see* Zapadnyy Kazakhstan
Ural'skiye Gory *mts* Russia *see* Ural Mountains
Ural'skiy Khrebet *mts* Russia *see* Ural Mountains
Urambo Tanz. 99 D4
Uran India 84 B2
Urana Australia 112 C5
Urana, Lake Australia 112 C5
Urandangi Australia 110 B4
Urandi Brazil 145 C1
Uranium City Canada 121 I3
Uranquinty Australia 112 C5
Uraricoera *r.* Brazil 142 F3
Urartu *country* Asia *see* Armenia
Ura-Tyube Tajik. *see* Istaravshan
Uravakonda India 84 C3
Uravan (abandoned) U.S.A. 129 I2
Urawa Japan 75 E6
'Urayf an Nāqah, Jabal *hill* Egypt 85 B4
Uray'irah Saudi Arabia 88 C5
'Urayq ad Duḥūl *des.* Saudi Arabia 88 B5
'Urayq Sāqān *des.* Saudi Arabia 88 B5
Urbana *IL* U.S.A. 130 F3
Urbana *OH* U.S.A. 134 D3
Urbino Italy 58 E3
Urbinum Italy *see* Urbino
Urbs Vetus Italy *see* Orvieto
Urdoma Russia 42 K3
Urdyuzhskoye, Ozero *l.* Russia 42 K2
Ure *r.* U.K. 48 F4
Urek'i Georgia 91 F2
Uren' Russia 42 J4
Urengoy Russia 64 I3
Uréparapara *i.* Vanuatu 107 G3
Urfa Turkey *see* Şanlıurfa
Urfa *prov.* Turkey *see* Şanlıurfa
Urga Mongolia *see* Ulan Bator
Urgal *r.* Russia 74 D2
Urganch Uzbek. 80 B3
Urgench Uzbek. *see* Urganch
Ürgün-e Kalān Afgh. 89 H3
Ürgüp Turkey 90 D3
Urgut Uzbek. 89 G2
Urho China 80 G2
Urho Kekkosen kansallispuisto *nat. park* Fin. 44 O2
Urie *r.* U.K. 50 G3
Uril Russia 74 C2
Urisino Australia 112 A2
Urjala Fin. 45 M6
Urk Neth. 52 F2
Urkan Russia 74 B1
Urkan *r.* Russia 74 B1
Urla Turkey 59 L5
Urlingford Ireland 51 E5
Urluk Russia 73 J2
Ūrmā aş Şughrá Syria 85 C1
Urmai China 83 F3
Urmia Iran 88 B2
Urmia, Lake *salt l.* Iran 88 B2
Urmston Road *sea chan.* H.K. China 77 [inset]
Uromi Nigeria 96 D4
Uroševac Kosovo *see* Ferizaj
Urosozero Russia 42 G3
Urru Co *salt l.* China 83 F3
Urt Moron China 80 H4
Uruáchic Mex. 124 F6
Uruaçu Brazil 145 A1
Uruana Brazil 145 A1
Uruapan *Baja California* Mex. 127 D7
Uruapan *Michoacán* Mex. 136 D5
Urubamba *r.* Peru 142 D6
Urucará Brazil 143 G4
Urucu *r.* Brazil 142 F4
Uruçuca Brazil 145 D1
Uruçuí Brazil 143 J5
Uruçuí, Serra do *hills* Brazil 143 I5
Urucuia Brazil 145 B2
Urucurituba Brazil 143 G4
Uruguai *r.* Arg./Uruguay *see* Uruguay
Uruguaiana Brazil 144 E3
Uruguay *r.* Arg./Uruguay 144 E4 *also known as Uruguai*
Uruguay *country* S. America 144 E4
Uruhe China 74 B2
Urumchi China *see* Ürümqi
Ürümqi China 80 G3
Urundi *country* Africa *see* Burundi
Urup, Ostrov *i.* Russia 73 S3
Urusha Russia 74 A1
Urutaí Brazil 145 A2
Uruzgān Afgh. 89 G3
Uryupino Russia 73 M2
Uryupinsk Russia 43 I6
Ürzhar Kazakh. *see* Urzhar
Urzhar Kazakh. 80 F2
Urzhum Russia 42 K4
Urziceni Romania 59 L2
Usa Japan 75 C6
Usa *r.* Russia 42 M2
Uşak Turkey 59 M5
Usakos Namibia 100 B1
Usarp Mountains Antarctica 152 H2
Usborne, Mount *hill* Falkland Is 144 E8
Ushakova, Ostrov *i.* Russia 64 I1
Ushant *i.* France *see* Ouessant, Île d'
Üsharal Kazakh. *see* Usharal
Usharal Kazakh. 80 F2
Ush-Bel'dir Russia 72 H2
Ushtobe Kazakh. 80 E2
Ush-Tyube Kazakh. *see* Ushtobe
Ushuaia Arg. 144 C8
Ushumun Russia 74 B1
Usingen Germany 53 I4
Usinsk Russia 41 R2
Usk U.K. 49 E7
Usk *r.* U.K. 49 E7
Uskhodni Belarus 45 O10
Uskoplje Bos. & Herz. *see* Gornji Vakuf
Üsküdar Turkey 59 M4
Uslar Germany 53 J3
Usman' Russia 43 H5
Usmanabad India *see* Osmanabad
Usmas ezers *l.* Latvia 45 M8
Usogorsk Russia 42 K3
Usol'ye-Sibirskoye Russia 72 I2
Ussel France 56 F4
Ussuri *r.* China/Russia 74 D2
Ussuriysk Russia 74 C4
Ust'-Abakanskoye Russia *see* Abakan
Usta Muhammad Pak. 89 H4
Ust'-Balyk Russia *see* Nefteyugansk
Ust'-Donetskiy Russia 43 I7
Ust'-Dzheguta Russia 91 F1
Ust'-Dzhegutinskaya Russia *see* Ust'-Dzheguta
Ustica, Isola di *i. Sicily* Italy 58 E5
Ust'-Ilimsk Russia 65 L4
Ust'-Ilimskoye Vodokhranilishche *resr* Russia 65 L4
Ust'-Ilych Russia 41 R3
Ústí nad Labem Czechia 47 O5
Ustinov Russia *see* Izhevsk
Üstirt *plat.* Kazakh./Uzbek. *see* Ustyurt Plateau
Ustka Poland 47 P3
Ust'-Kamchatsk Russia 65 R4
Ust'-Kamenogorsk Kazakh. 80 F2
Ust'-Kan Russia 80 F1
Ust'-Koksa Russia 80 G1
Ust'-Kulom Russia 42 L3
Ust'-Kut Russia 65 L4
Ust'-Kuyga Russia 65 O2
Ust'-Labinsk Russia 91 E1
Ust'-Labinskaya Russia *see* Ust'-Labinsk
Ust'-Lyzha Russia 42 M2
Ust'-Maya Russia 65 O3
Ust'-Nera Russia 65 P3
Ust'-Ocheya Russia 42 K3
Ust'-Olenek Russia 65 M2
Ust'-Omchug Russia 65 P3
Ust'-Ordynskiy Russia 72 I2
Ust'-Port Russia 64 J3
Ustrem Russia 41 T3
Ust'-Tsil'ma Russia 42 L2
Ust'-Uda Russia 72 I2
Ust'-Umalta (abandoned) Russia 74 D2
Ust'-Undurga Russia 73 L2
Ust'-Ura Russia 42 J3
Ust'-Urgal Russia 74 D2
Ust'-Usa Russia 42 M2
Ust'-Vayen'ga Russia 42 I3
Ust'-Voya Russia 41 R3
Ust'-Vyyskaya Russia 42 J3
Ust'ya *r.* Russia 42 I3
Ust'ye Russia 42 H4
Ustyurt, Plato *plat.* Kazakh./Uzbek. *see* Ustyurt Plateau
Ustyurt Plateau Kazakh./Uzbek. 78 E2
Ustyurt Platosi *plat.* Kazakh./Uzbek. *see* Ustyurt Plateau
Ustyuzhna Russia 42 H4
Usulután El Salvador 136 G6
Usumbura Burundi *see* Bujumbura
Usvyaty Russia 42 F5
Utah *state* U.S.A. 126 F5
Utah Lake U.S.A. 129 H1
Utajärvi Fin. 44 O4
Utashinai Russia *see* Yuzhno-Kuril'sk
'Utaybah, Buḥayrat al *imp. l.* Syria 85 C3
Utena Lith. 45 N9
Uterlai India 82 B4
Uthai Thani Thai. 70 C4
Uthal Pak. 89 G5
'Uthmānīyah Syria 85 C2
uThukela *r.* S. Africa 101 J5
Utiariti Brazil 143 G6
Utica *NY* U.S.A. 135 H2
Utica *OH* U.S.A. 134 D3
Utiel Spain 57 F4
Utikuma Lake Canada 120 H4
Utlwanang S. Africa 101 G4
Utrecht Neth. 52 F2
Utrecht S. Africa 101 J4
Utrera Spain 57 D5
Utsjoki Fin. 44 O2
Utsunomiya Japan 75 E5
Utta Russia 43 J7
Uttaradit Thai. 70 C3
Uttarakhand *state* India 82 D3
Uttaranchal *state* India *see* Uttarakhand
Uttarkashi India 82 D3
Uttar Kashi India *see* Uttarkashi
Uttar Pradesh *state* India 82 D4
Uttoxeter U.K. 49 F6
Uttranchal *state* India *see* Uttarakhand
Utubulak China 80 G2
Utupua *i.* Solomon Is 107 G3
Uturuncu, Cerro *mt.* Bol. 142 E8
Uummannaq Fjord *inlet* Greenland 153 J2
Uummannarsuaq *c.* Greenland *see* Farewell, Cape
Uurainen Fin. 44 N5
Uusikaarlepyy Fin. *see* Nykarleby
Uusikaupunki Fin. 45 L6
Uva Russia 42 L4
Uvalde U.S.A. 131 D6
Uvarovo Russia 43 I6
Uvéa *atoll* New Caledonia *see* Ouvéa
Uvinza Tanz. 99 D4
Uvs Nuur *salt l.* Mongolia 80 H1
Uwajima Japan 75 D6
'Uwayriḍ, Ḥarrat al *lava field* Saudi Arabia 86 E4
Uwaysiṭ *well* Saudi Arabia 85 D4
Uweinat, Jebel *mt.* Sudan 86 C5
Uwi *i.* Indon. 71 D7
Uxbridge Canada 134 F1
Uxbridge U.K. 49 G7
Uxin Qi China *see* Dabqig
Uyaly Kazakh. 80 B3
Uyar Russia 72 G1
Uyo Nigeria 96 D4
Uyu Chaung *r.* Myanmar 70 A1
Uyuni Bol. 142 E8
Uyuni, Salar de *salt flat* Bol. 142 E8
Uza *r.* Russia 43 J5
Uzbekistan *country* Asia 80 B3
Ŭzbekiston *country* Asia *see* Uzbekistan
Uzbekskaya S.S.R. *country* Asia *see* Uzbekistan
Uzbek S.S.R. *country* Asia *see* Uzbekistan
Uzboý Turkm. 88 D2
Uzen' Kazakh. *see* Kyzylsay
Uzhgorod Ukr. *see* Uzhhorod
Uzhhorod Ukr. 43 D6
Užhorod Ukr. *see* Uzhhorod
Užice Serbia 59 H3
Uzlovaya Russia 43 H5
Üzümlü Turkey 59 M6
Uzun Uzbek. 89 H2
Uzunköprü Turkey 59 L4
Uzynkair Kazakh. 80 B3

V

Vaajakoski Fin. 44 N5
Vaal *r.* S. Africa 101 F5
Vaala Fin. 44 O4
Vaalbos National Park S. Africa 100 G5
Vaal Dam S. Africa 101 I4
Vaalwater S. Africa 101 I3
Vaasa Fin. 44 L5
Vaavu Atoll Maldives *see* Felidhe Atholhu
Vác Hungary 47 Q7
Vacaria Brazil 145 A5
Vacaria, Campo da *plain* Brazil 145 A5
Vacaville U.S.A. 128 C2
Vachon *r.* Canada 123 H1
Vad Russia 42 J5
Vad *r.* Russia 43 I5
Vada India 84 B2
Vadakara India 84 B4
Vadla Norway 45 E7
Vadodara India 82 C5
Vadsø Norway 44 P1

▶Vaduz Liechtenstein 56 I3
Capital of Liechtenstein.

Værøy *i.* Norway 44 H3
Vaga *r.* Russia 42 I3
Vågåmo Norway 45 F6
Vaganski Vrh *mt.* Croatia 58 F2
Vágar *i.* Faroe Is 44 [inset 2]
Vagharshapat Armenia 91 G2
Vägsele Sweden 44 K4
Vágur Faroe Is 44 [inset 2]
Váh *r.* Slovakia 47 Q7
Vähäkyrö Fin. 44 M5

▶Vaiaku Tuvalu 107 H2
Capital of Tuvalu, on Funafuti atoll.

Vaida Estonia 45 N7
Vaiden U.S.A. 131 F5
Vail U.S.A. 124 F4
Vailly-sur-Aisne France 52 D5
Vaitupu *i.* Tuvalu 107 H2
Vajrakarur India *see* Kanur
Vakhsh Tajik. 89 H2
Vakhsh *r.* Tajik. 89 H2
Vakhstroy Tajik. *see* Vakhsh
Vakīlābād Iran 88 E4
Valbo Sweden 45 J6
Valcheta Arg. 144 C6
Valdai Hills Russia *see* Valdayskaya Vozvyshennost'
Valday Russia 42 G4
Valdayskaya Vozvyshennost' *hills* Russia 42 G4
Valdecañas, Embalse de *resr* Spain 57 D4
Valdemārpils Latvia 45 M8
Valdemarsvik Sweden 45 J7
Valdepeñas Spain 57 E4
Val-de-Reuil France 52 B5
Valdés, Península *pen.* Arg. 144 D6
Valdez U.S.A. 118 D3
Valdivia Chile 144 B5
Val-d'Or Canada 122 F4
Valdosta U.S.A. 133 D6
Valdres *valley* Norway 45 F6
Vale Georgia 91 F2
Vale U.S.A. 126 D3
Valemount Canada 120 G4
Valença *Bahia* Brazil 145 D1
Valença *Rio de Janeiro* Brazil 145 C3
Valence France 56 G4
Valencia Spain 57 F4
València Spain *see* Valencia
Valencia *reg.* Spain 57 F4
Valencia Venez. 142 E1
Valencia, Golfo de *g.* Spain 57 G4
Valencia de Don Juan Spain 57 D2
Valencia Island Ireland 51 B6
Valenciennes France 52 D4
Valensole, Plateau de France 56 H5
Valentia Spain *see* Valencia
Valentin Russia 74 D4
Valentine U.S.A. 130 C3
Våler Norway 45 G6
Valera Venez. 142 D2
Vale Verde Brazil 145 D2
Val Grande, Parco Nazionale della *nat. park* Italy 58 C1
Valiyakara, Suheli India 84 B4
Valjevo Serbia 59 H2
Valka Latvia 45 O8
Valkeakoski Fin. 45 N6
Valkenswaard Neth. 52 F3
Valky Ukr. 43 G6
Valkyrie Dome *ice feature* Antarctica 152 D1
Valladolid Mex. 136 G4
Valladolid Spain 57 D3
Vallard, Lac *l.* Canada 123 H3
Valle Norway 45 E7
Vallecillos Mex. 131 D7
Vallecito Reservoir U.S.A. 129 J3
Valle de la Pascua Venez. 142 E2
Valledupar Col. 142 D1
Vallée-Jonction Canada 123 H5
Valle Fértil, Sierra de *mts* Arg. 144 C4
Valle Grande Bol. 142 F7
Valle Hermoso Mex. 131 D7
Vallejo U.S.A. 128 B2
Vallenar Chile 144 B3
Valles Caldera National Preserve *nat. park* U.S.A. 127 G6

▶Valletta Malta 58 F7
Capital of Malta.

Valley *r.* Canada 121 L5
Valley U.K. 48 C5
Valley City U.S.A. 130 D2
Valleyview Canada 120 G4
Valls Spain 57 G3
Val Marie Canada 121 J5
Valmiera Latvia 45 N8
Valmy U.S.A. 128 E1
Valnera *mt.* Spain 57 E2
Valognes France 49 F9
Valona Albania *see* Vlorë
Valozhyn Belarus 45 O9
Val-Paradis Canada 122 F4
Valparai India 84 C4
Valparaíso Chile 144 B4
Valparaiso U.S.A. 134 B3
Valpoi India 84 B3
Valréas France 56 G4
Vals, Tanjung *c.* Indon. 69 J8
Valsad India 84 B1
Valspan S. Africa 100 G4
Valtimo Fin. 44 P5
Valuyevka Russia 43 I7
Valuyki Russia 43 H6
Vammala Fin. 45 M6
Van Turkey 91 F3
Van, Lake *salt l.* Turkey 91 F3
Vanadzor Armenia 91 G2
Van Buren *AR* U.S.A. 131 E5
Van Buren *MO* U.S.A. 131 F4
Van Buren *OH* U.S.A. *see* Kettering
Vanceburg U.S.A. 134 D4
Vanch Tajik. *see* Vanj
Vancleve U.S.A. 134 D5
Vancouver Canada 120 F5
Vancouver U.S.A. 126 C3
Vancouver, Mount Canada/U.S.A. 120 B2
Vancouver Island Canada 120 E5
Vanda Fin. *see* Vantaa
Vandalia *IL* U.S.A. 130 F4
Vandalia *OH* U.S.A. 134 C4
Vandekerckhove Lake Canada 121 K3
Vanderbijlpark S. Africa 101 H4
Vanderbilt U.S.A. 134 C1
Vandergrift U.S.A. 134 F3
Vanderhoof Canada 120 E4
Vanderkloof Dam *resr* S. Africa 100 G6
Vanderlin Island Australia 110 B2
Vanderwagen U.S.A. 129 I4
Van Diemen, Cape *N.T.* Australia 108 E2
Van Diemen, Cape *Qld* Australia 110 B3
Van Diemen Gulf Australia 108 F2
Vändra Estonia 45 N7
Väner, Lake Sweden *see* Vänern

▶Vänern *l.* Sweden 45 H7
4th largest lake in Europe.

Vänersborg Sweden 45 H7
Vangaindrano Madag. 99 E6
Van Gia Vietnam 71 E4
Van Gölü *salt l.* Turkey *see* Van, Lake
Van Horn U.S.A. 127 G7
Vanikoro Islands Solomon Is 107 G3
Vanimo P.N.G. 69 K7
Vanino Russia 74 F2
Vanivilasa Sagara *resr* India 84 C3
Vaniyambadi India 84 C3
Vanj Tajik. 89 H2
Vännäs Sweden 44 K5
Vannes France 56 C3
Vannes, Lac *l.* Canada 123 I3
Vannovka Kazakh. *see* Turar Ryskulov
Vannøya *i.* Norway 44 K1
Vanoise, Massif de la *mts* France 56 H4
Vanoise, Parc National de la *nat. park* France 56 H4
Van Rees, Pegunungan *mts* Indon. 69 J7
Vanrhynsdorp S. Africa 100 D6
Vansant U.S.A. 134 D5
Vansbro Sweden 45 I6
Vansittart Island Canada 119 J3
Van Starkenborgh Kanaal *canal* Neth. 52 G1
Vantaa Fin. 45 N6
Van Truer Tableland *reg.* Australia 109 C6
Vanua Lava *i.* Vanuatu 107 G3
Vanua Levu *i.* Fiji 107 H3
Vanuatu *country* S. Pacific Ocean 107 G3
Van Wert U.S.A. 134 C3
Van Wyksvlei S. Africa 100 E6
Van Wyksvlei Dam *l.* S. Africa 100 E6
Văn Yên Vietnam 70 D2
Van Zylsrus S. Africa 100 F4
Varadero Cuba 133 D8
Varahi India 82 B5
Varakļāni Latvia 45 O8
Varalé Côte d'Ivoire 96 C4
Varāmīn Iran 88 C3
Varanasi India 83 E4
Varandey Russia 42 M1
Varangerfjorden *sea chan.* Norway 44 P1
Varangerhalvøya *pen.* Norway 44 P1
Varaždin Croatia 58 G1
Varberg Sweden 45 H8
Vardar *r.* Macedonia 59 J4
Varde Denmark 45 F9
Vardenis Armenia 91 G2
Vardø Norway 44 Q1
Varel Germany 53 I1
Varėna Lith. 45 N9
Varese Italy 58 C2
Varfolomeyevka Russia 74 D3
Vårgårda Sweden 45 H7
Varginha Brazil 145 B3
Varik Neth. 52 F3
Varillas Chile 144 B2
Varkaus Fin. 44 O5
Varna Bulg. 59 L3
Värnamo Sweden 45 I8
Värnäs Sweden 45 H6
Varnavino Russia 42 J4
Várnjárg *pen.* Norway *see* Varangerhalvøya
Varpaisjärvi Fin. 44 O5
Várpalota Hungary 58 H1
Varsh, Ozero *l.* Russia 42 J2
Varto Turkey 91 F3
Várzea da Palma Brazil 145 B2
Várzea Grande Brazil 143 G7
Vasa Fin. *see* Vaasa
Vasai India 84 B2
Vashka *r.* Russia 42 J2
Vasht Iran *see* Khāsh
Vasilkov Ukr. *see* Vasyl'kiv
Vasknarva Estonia 45 O7
Vaslui Romania 59 L1
Vassar U.S.A. 134 D2
Vas-Soproni-síkság *hills* Hungary 58 G1
Vastan Turkey *see* Geveş
Västerås Sweden 45 J7

234

Volos Greece 59 J5
Volosovo Russia 45 P7
Volot Russia 42 F4
Volovo Russia 43 H5
Volozhin Belarus *see* **Valozhyn**
Volsinii Italy *see* **Orvieto**
Vol'sk Russia 43 J5

▶**Volta, Lake** *resr* Ghana 96 D4
4th largest lake in Africa.

Volta Blanche *r.* Burkina Faso/Ghana *see* **White Volta**
Voltaire, Cape Australia 108 D3
Volta Redonda Brazil 145 B3
Vol'tevo Russia 42 J2
Volturno *r.* Italy 58 E4
Volubilis *tourist site* Morocco 54 C5
Volvi, Limni *l.* Greece 59 J4
Volzhsk Russia 42 K5
Volzhskiy *Samarskaya Oblast'* Russia 43 K5
Volzhskiy *Volgogradskaya Oblast'* Russia 43 J6
Vondanka Russia 42 J4
Vontimitta India 84 C3
Vopnafjörður Iceland 44 [inset 1]
Vopnafjörður *b.* Iceland 44 [inset 1]
Vörå Fin. 44 M5
Voranava Belarus 45 N9
Voreies Sporades *is* Greece 59 J5
Voríai Sporádhes *is* Greece *see* **Voreies Sporades**
Voring Plateau *sea feature* N. Atlantic Ocean 148 I1
Vorjing *mt.* India 83 H3
Vorkuta Russia 64 H3
Vormsi *i.* Estonia 45 M7
Vorona *r.* Russia 43 I6
Voronezh Russia 43 H6
Voronezh *r.* Russia 43 H6
Voronov, Mys *pt* Russia 42 I2
Vorontsovo-Aleksandrovskoye Russia *see* **Zelenokumsk**
Voroshilov Russia *see* **Ussuriysk**
Voroshilovgrad Ukr. *see* **Luhans'k**
Voroshilovsk Russia *see* **Stavropol'**
Voroshilovsk Ukr. *see* **Alchevs'k**
Vorotynets Russia 42 J4
Vorozhba Ukr. 43 G6
Vorpommersche Boddenlandschaft, Nationalpark *nat. park* Germany 47 N3
Vorskla *r.* Russia 43 G6
Võrtsjärv *l.* Estonia 45 N7
Võru Estonia 45 O8
Vorukh Tajik. 89 H2
Vosburg S. Africa 100 F6
Vose' Tajik. 89 H2
Vosges *mts* France 56 H3
Voskresensk Russia 43 H5
Voskresenskoye Russia 42 H4
Voss Norway 45 E6
Vostochno-Sakhalinskiye Gory *mts* Russia 74 F2
Vostochno-Sibirskoye More *sea* Russia *see* **East Siberian Sea**
Vostochnyy *Kirovskaya Oblast'* Russia 42 L4
Vostochnyy *Sakhalinskaya Oblast'* Russia 74 F2
Vostochnyy Sayan *mts* Russia 72 G2

▶**Vostok** *research station* Antarctica 152 F1
Lowest recorded screen temperature in the world.

Vostok *Primorskiy Kray* Russia 74 D3
Vostok *Sakhalinskaya Oblast'* Russia *see* **Neftegorsk (abandoned)**
Vostok Island Kiribati 151 J6
Vostroye Russia 42 J3
Votkinsk Russia 41 Q4
Votkinskoye Vodokhranilishche *resr* Russia 41 R4
Votuporanga Brazil 145 A3
Vouziers France 52 E5
Voves France 56 E2
Voyageurs National Park U.S.A. 130 E1
Voynitsa Russia 44 Q4
Vöyri Fin. *see* **Vörå**
Voyvozh Russia 42 L3
Vozhayel' Russia 42 K3
Vozhe, Ozero *l.* Russia 42 H3
Vozhega Russia 42 I3
Vozhgaly Russia 42 K4
Voznesens'k Ukr. 43 F7
Vozonin Trough *sea feature* Arctic Ocean 153 F1
Vozrozhdenya Island *i.* Uzbek. 80 A3
Vozzhayevka Russia 74 C2
Vrangel' Russia 74 D4
Vrangelya, Mys *pt* Russia 74 E1
Vranje Serbia 59 I3
Vratnik *pass* Bulg. 59 L3
Vratsa Bulg. 59 J3
Vrbas Serbia 59 H2
Vrede S. Africa 101 I4
Vredefort S. Africa 101 H4
Vredenburg S. Africa 100 C7
Vredendal S. Africa 100 D6
Vresse-sur-Semois Belgium 52 E5
Vriddhachalam India 84 C4
Vries Neth. 52 G1
Vrigstad Sweden 45 I8
Vršac Serbia 59 I2
Vryburg S. Africa 100 G4
Vryheid S. Africa 101 J4
Vsevidof, Mount *vol.* U.S.A. 118 B4
Vsevolozhsk Russia 42 F3
Vu Ban Vietnam 70 D2
Vučitrn Kosovo *see* **Vushtrri**
Vukovar Croatia 59 H2
Vuktyl Russia 41 R3
Vukuzakhe S. Africa 101 I4
Vulcan Canada 120 H5
Vulcan Island P.N.G. *see* **Manam Island**
Vulcano, Isola *i.* Italy 58 F5
Vu Liêt Vietnam 70 D3
Vulkathunha-Gammon Ranges National Park Australia 111 B6
Vulture Mountains U.S.A. 129 G5
Vung Tau Vietnam 71 D5
Vuohijärvi Fin. 45 O6
Vuolijoki Fin. 44 O4
Vuollerim Sweden 44 L3
Vuostimo Fin. 44 O3
Vurnary Russia 42 J5
Vushtrri Kosovo 59 I3
Vvedenovka Russia 74 C2
Vyara India 82 C5
Vyarkhowye Belarus *see* **Ruba**
Vyatka Russia *see* **Kirov**
Vyatka *r.* Russia 42 K5
Vyatskiye Polyany Russia 42 K4
Vyazemskiy Russia 74 D3
Vyaz'ma Russia 43 G5
Vyazniki Russia 42 I4
Vyazovka Russia 43 J5
Vyborg Russia 45 P6
Vychegda *r.* Russia 42 J3
Vychegodskiy Russia 42 J3
Vyerkhnyadzvinsk Belarus 45 O9
Vyetryna Belarus 45 P9
Vygozero, Ozero *l.* Russia 42 G3
Vyksa Russia 43 I5
Vylkove Ukr. 59 M2
Vym' *r.* Russia 42 K3
Vynohradiv Ukr. 43 D6
Vypin Island India 84 C4
Vypolzovo Russia 42 G4
Vyritsa Russia 45 Q7
Vyrnwy, Lake U.K. 49 D6
Vyselki Russia 43 H7
Vysha Russia 43 I5
Vyshhorod Ukr. 43 F6
Vyshnevolotskaya Gryada *ridge* Russia 42 G4
Vyshniy-Volochek Russia 42 G4
Vyškov Czechia 47 P6
Vysokaya Gora Russia 42 K5
Vysokogorniy Russia 74 E2
Vystupovychi Ukr. 43 F6
Vytegra Russia 42 H3
Vyya *r.* Russia 42 J3
Vyžuona *r.* Lith. 45 N9

W

Wa Ghana 96 C3
Waal *r.* Neth. 52 E3
Waalwijk Neth. 52 F3
Waat South Sudan 86 D8
Wabag P.N.G. 69 K8
Wabakimi Lake Canada 122 C4
Wabasca *r.* Canada 120 H3
Wabasca-Desmarais Canada 120 H4
Wabash U.S.A. 134 C3
Wabash *r.* U.S.A. 134 A5
Wabasha U.S.A. 130 E2
Wabassi *r.* Canada 122 D4
Wabatongushi Lake Canada 122 D4
Wabigoon Lake Canada 121 M5
Wabowden Canada 121 L4
Wabrah *well* Saudi Arabia 88 B5
Wabu China 77 H1
Wabuk Point Canada 122 D3
Wabush Canada 123 I3
Waccasassa Bay U.S.A. 133 D6
Wächtersbach Germany 53 J4
Waco Canada 123 I4
Waco U.S.A. 131 D6
Waconda Lake U.S.A. 130 D4
Wadbilliga National Park Australia 112 D6
Waddān Libya 55 H6
Waddell Dam U.S.A. 129 G5
Waddeneilanden Neth. *see* **West Frisian Islands**
Waddenzee *sea chan.* Neth. 52 E2
Waddington, Mount Canada 120 E5
Waddinxveen Neth. 52 E2
Wadebridge U.K. 49 C8
Wadena Canada 121 K5
Wadena U.S.A. 130 E2
Wadern Germany 52 G5
Wadesville U.S.A. 134 B4
Wadeye Australia 108 E3
Wadgassen Germany 52 G5
Wadh Pak. 89 G5
Wadhwan India *see* **Surendranagar**
Wadi India 84 C2
Wādī as Sīr Jordan 85 B4
Wadi Halfa Sudan 86 D5
Wadi Howar National Park *nat. park* Sudan 98 C2
Wadi Rum Protected Area *tourist site* Jordan 85 B5
Wad Madani Sudan 86 D7
Wad Rawa Sudan 86 D6
Wadsworth U.S.A. 128 D2
Wafangdian China 73 M5
Wafra Kuwait *see* **Al Wafrah**
Wagenfeld Germany 53 I2
Wagenhoff Germany 53 K2
Wagga Wagga Australia 112 C5
Wagner U.S.A. 130 D3
Wagoner U.S.A. 131 E4
Wagon Mound U.S.A. 127 G5
Wah Pak. 89 I3
Wahai Indon. 69 H7
Wāḩāt Jālū Libya 97 F2
Wahemen, Lac *l.* Canada 123 H3
Wahiawā U.S.A. 127 [inset]
Wahlhausen Germany 53 J3
Wahpeton U.S.A. 130 D2
Wahran Alg. *see* **Oran**
Wah Wah Mountains U.S.A. 129 G2
Wai India 84 B2
Waialua U.S.A. 127 [inset]
Waiau N.Z. *see* **Franz Josef Glacier**
Waiau *r.* N.Z. 113 D6
Waiblingen Germany 53 J6
Waidhofen an der Ybbs Austria 47 O7
Waigeo *i.* Indon. 69 I7
Waiheke Island N.Z. 113 E3
Waikabubak Indon. 108 B2
Waikaia *r.* N.Z. 113 B7
Waikari N.Z. 113 D6
Waikerie Australia 111 B7
Waikouaiti N.Z. 113 C7
Wailuku U.S.A. 127 [inset]
Waimangaroa N.Z. 113 C5
Waimarama N.Z. 113 F4
Waimate N.Z. 113 C7
Waimea U.S.A. 127 [inset]
Wainganga *r.* India 84 C2
Waingapu Indon. 108 C2
Wainhouse Corner U.K. 49 C8
Waini Point Guyana 143 G2
Wainwright Canada 121 I4
Wainwright U.S.A. 118 C2
Waiouru N.Z. 113 E4
Waipahi N.Z. 113 B8
Waipaoa *r.* N.Z. 113 F4
Waipara N.Z. 113 D6
Waipawa N.Z. 113 F4
Waipukurau N.Z. 113 F4
Wairarapa, Lake N.Z. 113 E5
Wairau *r.* N.Z. 113 E5
Wairoa N.Z. 113 F4
Wairoa *r.* N.Z. 113 F4
Waitahanui N.Z. 113 F4
Waitahuna N.Z. 113 B7
Waitakaruru N.Z. 113 E3
Waitaki *r.* N.Z. 113 C7
Waitangi N.Z. 107 I6
Waite River Australia 108 F5
Waiuku N.Z. 113 E3
Waiwera South N.Z. 113 B8
Waiyang China 77 H3
Wajima Japan 75 E5
Wajir Kenya 98 E3
Waka Indon. 108 C2
Wakasa-wan *b.* Japan 75 D6
Wakatipu, Lake N.Z. 113 B7
Wakaw Canada 121 J4
Wakayama Japan 75 D6
Wake Atoll *terr.* N. Pacific Ocean *see* **Wake Island**
WaKeeney U.S.A. 130 D4
Wakefield N.Z. 113 D5
Wakefield U.K. 48 F5
Wakefield *MI* U.S.A. 130 F2
Wakefield *RI* U.S.A. 135 J3
Wakefield *VA* U.S.A. 135 G5

▶**Wake Island** *terr.* N. Pacific Ocean 150 H4
United States Unincorporated Territory.

Wakema Myanmar 70 A3
Wākhān *reg.* Afgh. 89 I2
Wakkanai Japan 74 F3
Wakkerstroom S. Africa 101 J4
Wakool Australia 112 B5
Wakool *r.* Australia 112 A5
Wakuach, Lac *l.* Canada 123 I3
Waku-Kungo Angola 99 B5
Wałbrzych Poland 47 P5
Walcha Australia 112 E3
Walcott U.S.A. 126 G4
Walcourt Belgium 52 E4
Wałcz Poland 47 P4
Waldburg Range *mts* Australia 109 B6
Walden U.S.A. 135 H3
Waldenbuch Germany 53 J6
Waldenburg Poland *see* **Wałbrzych**
Waldkraiburg Germany 47 N6
Waldo U.S.A. 134 D3
Waldoboro U.S.A. 135 K1
Waldorf U.S.A. 135 G4
Waldport U.S.A. 126 B3
Waldron U.S.A. 131 E5
Waldron, Cape Antarctica 152 F2
Walebing Australia 109 B7
Walêg China 76 D2
Wales *admin. div.* U.K. 49 D6
Walgaon India 82 D5
Walgett Australia 112 D3
Walgreen Coast Antarctica 152 K1
Walhalla *MI* U.S.A. 134 B2
Walhalla *ND* U.S.A. 130 D1
Walikale Dem. Rep. Congo 97 F5
Walingai P.N.G. 69 L8
Walker *r.* Australia 110 A2
Walker *watercourse* Australia 109 F6
Walker *MI* U.S.A. 134 C2
Walker *MN* U.S.A. 130 E2
Walker *r.* U.S.A. 128 D2
Walker Bay S. Africa 100 D8
Walker Creek *r.* Australia 110 C3
Walker Lake Canada 121 L4
Walker Lake U.S.A. 128 D2
Walker Pass U.S.A. 128 D4
Walkersville U.S.A. 135 G4
Walkerton Canada 134 E1
Walkerton U.S.A. 134 B3
Wall, Mount *hill* Australia 108 B5
Wallaby Island Australia 110 C2
Wallace *ID* U.S.A. 126 D3
Wallace *NC* U.S.A. 133 E5
Wallace *VA* U.S.A. 134 D5
Wallaceburg Canada 134 D2
Wallal Downs Australia 108 C4
Wallangarra Australia 112 E2
Wallaroo Australia 111 B7
Wallasey U.K. 48 D5
Walla Walla Australia 112 C5
Walla Walla U.S.A. 126 D3
Walldürn Germany 53 J5
Wallekraal S. Africa 100 C6
Wallendbeen Australia 112 D5
Wallingford U.K. 49 F7
Wallis, Îles *is* Wallis and Futuna 107 I3

▶**Wallis and Futuna** *terr.* S. Pacific Ocean 107 I3
French Overseas Collectivity.

Wallis et Futuna, Îles *terr.* S. Pacific Ocean *see* **Wallis and Futuna**
Wallis Islands Wallis and Futuna *see* **Wallis, Îles**
Wallis Lake *inlet* Australia 112 F4
Wall of Genghis Khan *tourist site* Asia 73 K3
Wallonia, Major Mining Sites of *tourist site* Belgium 52 E4
Wallops Island U.S.A. 135 H5
Wallowa Mountains U.S.A. 126 D3
Walls U.K. 50 [inset]
Walls of Jerusalem National Park Australia 111 [inset]
Wallumbilla Australia 111 E5
Walmsley Lake Canada 121 I2
Walney, Isle of *i.* U.K. 48 D4
Walnut Creek U.S.A. 128 B3
Walnut Grove U.S.A. 128 C2
Walnut Ridge U.S.A. 131 F4
Walong India 83 I3
Walpole U.S.A. 135 I2
Walsall U.K. 49 F6
Walsenburg U.S.A. 127 G5
Walsh U.S.A. 131 C4
Walsrode Germany 53 J2
Waltair India 84 D2
Walterboro U.S.A. 133 D5
Walters U.S.A. 131 D5
Walter's Range *hills* Australia 112 B2
Walthall U.S.A. 131 F5
Waltham U.S.A. 135 J2
Walton *IN* U.S.A. 134 B3
Walton *KY* U.S.A. 134 C4
Walton *NY* U.S.A. 135 H2
Walton *WV* U.S.A. 134 E4
Walvisbaai Namibia *see* **Walvis Bay**
Walvisbaai *b.* Namibia *see* **Walvis Bay**
Walvis Bay Namibia 100 B2
Walvis Bay *b.* Namibia 100 B2
Walvis Ridge *sea feature* S. Atlantic Ocean 148 H8
Wāmā Afgh. 89 H3
Wamba *Équateur* Dem. Rep. Congo 97 F5
Wamba *Orientale* Dem. Rep. Congo 98 C3
Wamba Nigeria 96 D4
Wampum U.S.A. 134 E3
Wampusirpi Hond. 137 H5
Wamsutter U.S.A. 126 G4
Wana Pak. 89 H3
Wanaaring Australia 112 B2
Wanaka N.Z. 113 B7
Wanaka, Lake N.Z. 113 B7
Wan'an China 77 G3
Wanapitei Lake Canada 122 E5
Wanbi Australia 111 C7
Wanbrow, Cape N.Z. 113 C7
Wanda Shan *mts* China 74 D3
Wandering River Canada 121 H4
Wandersleben Germany 53 K4
Wandlitz Germany 53 N2
Wando S. Korea 75 B6
Wandoan Australia 111 E5
Wanganui N.Z. 113 E4
Wanganui *r.* N.Z. 113 E4
Wangaratta Australia 112 C6
Wangcang China 76 E1
Wangda China *see* **Zogang**
Wangdain China 83 G3
Wangdue Phodrang Bhutan 83 G4
Wanggamet, Gunung *mt.* Indon. 108 C2
Wanggao China 77 F3
Wang Gaxun China 83 I1
Wangguan China 76 E1
Wangiwangi *i.* Indon. 69 G8
Wangkui China 74 B3
Wangmo China 76 E3
Wangqing China 74 C4
Wangwu Shan *mts* China 77 F1
Wangying China *see* **Huaiyin**
Wanham Canada 120 G4
Wan Hsa-la Myanmar 70 B2
Wanie-Rukula Dem. Rep. Congo 98 C3
Wankaner India 82 B5
Wankie Zimbabwe *see* **Hwange**
Wanlaweyn Somalia 98 E3
Wanna Germany 53 I1
Wanna Lakes *salt flat* Australia 109 E7
Wannian China 77 H2
Wanning China 77 F5
Wanroij Neth. 52 F3
Wanshan China 77 F3
Wanshan Qundao *is* China 77 G4
Wansheng China 76 E2
Wanshengchang China *see* **Wansheng**
Wantage U.K. 49 F7
Wanxian China *see* **Wanzhou**
Wanyuan China 77 F1
Wanzai China 77 G2
Wanze Belgium 52 F4
Wanzhou China 77 F2
Wapakoneta U.S.A. 134 C3
Wapawekka Lake Canada 121 J4
Wapello U.S.A. 130 F3
Wapikaimaski Lake Canada 122 C4
Wapikopa Lake Canada 122 C3
Wapiti *r.* Canada 120 G4
Wapusk National Park Canada 121 M3
Waqên China 76 D1
Waqf aş Şawwān, Jibāl *hills* Jordan 85 C4
War U.S.A. 134 E5
Warangal India 84 C2
Waranga Reservoir Australia 112 B6
Waratah Bay Australia 112 B7
Warbreccan Australia 110 C5
Warburg Germany 53 J3
Warburton Australia 109 D6
Warburton *watercourse* Australia 111 B5
Warburton Bay Canada 121 I2
Warche *r.* Belgium 52 F4
Ward, Mount N.Z. 113 B6
Warden S. Africa 101 I4
Wardenburg Germany 53 I1
Warder Eth. 98 E3
Wardha India 84 C1
Wardha *r.* India 84 C2
Ward Hill *hill* U.K. 50 F2
Ward Hunt, Cape P.N.G. 69 L8
Ware Canada 120 E3
Ware U.S.A. 135 I2
Wareham U.K. 49 E8
Waremme Belgium 52 F4
Waren (Müritz) Germany 53 M1
Warendorf Germany 53 H3
Warginburra Peninsula Australia 110 E4
Wargla Alg. *see* **Ouargla**
Warialda Australia 112 E2
Warin Chamrap Thai. 70 D4
Warkum Neth. *see* **Workum**
Warkworth U.K. 48 F3
Warli China *see* **Walêg**
Warloy-Baillon France 52 C4
Warman Canada 121 J4
Warmbad Namibia 100 D5
Warmbad S. Africa *see* **Bela-Bela**
Warmbaths S. Africa *see* **Bela-Bela**
Warminster U.K. 49 E7
Warminster U.S.A. 135 H3
Warmond Neth. 52 E2
Warm Springs *NV* U.S.A. 128 E2
Warm Springs *VA* U.S.A. 134 F4
Warmwaterberg *mts* S. Africa 100 E7
Warner Canada 121 H5
Warner Lakes U.S.A. 126 D4
Warner Mountains U.S.A. 126 C4
Warnes Bol. 142 F7
Warning, Mount Australia 112 F2
Waronda India 84 C2
Warora India 84 C1
Warra Australia 112 E1
Warragamba Reservoir Australia 112 E5
Warragul Australia 112 B7
Warrambool *r.* Australia 112 C3
Warrandirinna, Lake *salt flat* Australia 111 B5
Warrandyte Australia 112 B6
Warrap South Sudan 86 C8
Warrawagine Australia 108 C5
Warrego *r.* Australia 112 B3
Warrego Range *hills* Australia 110 D5
Warren Australia 112 C3
Warren *AR* U.S.A. 131 E5
Warren *MI* U.S.A. 134 D2
Warren *MN* U.S.A. 130 D1
Warren *OH* U.S.A. 134 E3
Warren *PA* U.S.A. 134 F3
Warren Hastings Island Palau *see* **Merir**
Warren Island U.S.A. 120 C4
Warrenpoint U.K. 51 F3
Warrensburg *MO* U.S.A. 130 E4
Warrensburg *NY* U.S.A. 135 I2
Warrenton S. Africa 100 G5
Warrenton *GA* U.S.A. 133 D5
Warrenton *MO* U.S.A. 130 F4
Warrenton *VA* U.S.A. 135 G4
Warri Nigeria 96 D4
Warriners Creek *watercourse* Australia 111 B6
Warrington N.Z. 113 C7
Warrington U.K. 48 E5
Warrington U.S.A. 133 C6
Warrnambool Australia 111 C8
Warroad U.S.A. 130 E1
Warrumbungle National Park Australia 112 D3
Warsaj 'Alāqahdārī Afgh. 89 H2

▶**Warsaw** Poland 47 R4
Capital of Poland.

Warsaw *IN* U.S.A. 134 C3
Warsaw *KY* U.S.A. 134 C4
Warsaw *MO* U.S.A. 130 E4
Warsaw *NY* U.S.A. 135 F2
Warsaw *VA* U.S.A. 135 G5
Warshiikh Somalia 98 E3
Warstein Germany 53 I3
Warszawa Poland *see* **Warsaw**
Warta *r.* Poland 47 O4
Wartburg, Schloss *tourist site* Germany 53 K3
Warwick Australia 112 F2
Warwick U.K. 49 F6
Warwick U.S.A. 135 J3
Warzhong China 76 D2
Wasaga Beach Canada 134 E1
Wasatch Range *mts* U.S.A. 126 F5
Wasbank S. Africa 101 J5
Wasco U.S.A. 128 D4
Washburn *ND* U.S.A. 130 C2
Washburn *WI* U.S.A. 130 F2
Wāshēr Afgh. 89 F3
Washim India 84 C1

▶**Washington** *DC* U.S.A. 135 G4
Capital of the United States of America.

Washington *GA* U.S.A. 133 D5
Washington *IA* U.S.A. 130 F3
Washington *IN* U.S.A. 134 B4
Washington *MO* U.S.A. 130 F4
Washington *NC* U.S.A. 132 E5
Washington *NJ* U.S.A. 135 H3
Washington *PA* U.S.A. 134 E3
Washington *UT* U.S.A. 129 G3
Washington *state* U.S.A. 126 C3
Washington, Cape Antarctica 152 H2
Washington, Mount U.S.A. 135 J1
Washington Court House U.S.A. 134 D4
Washington Island U.S.A. 132 C2
Washington Land *reg.* Greenland 119 L2
Washita *r.* U.S.A. 131 D5
Washpool National Park Australia 112 F2
Washtucna U.S.A. 126 D3
Washuk Pak. 89 G5
Wasi India 84 B2
Wasi' Saudi Arabia 88 B5
Wasi' *well* Saudi Arabia 88 C6
Waskaganish Canada 122 F4
Waskaghegamish Canada *see* **Waskaganish**
Waskaiowaka Lake Canada 121 L3
Waskey, Mount U.S.A. 118 C4
Wassenaar Neth. 52 E2
Wasser Namibia 100 D4
Wasserkuppe *hill* Germany 53 J4
Wassertrüdingen Germany 53 K5
Wassuk Range *mts* U.S.A. 128 D2
Wasua P.N.G. 69 K8
Wasum P.N.G. 69 L8
Waswanipi *r.* Canada 122 F4
Waswanipi, Lac *l.* Canada 122 F4
Watam P.N.G. 69 K7
Watampone Indon. 69 G7
Watapi Lake Canada 121 I4
Watarrka National Park Australia 109 E6
Watenstadt-Salzgitter Germany *see* **Salzgitter**
Waterbury *CT* U.S.A. 135 I3
Waterbury *VT* U.S.A. 135 I1
Waterbury Lake Canada 121 J3
Water Cays *i.* Bahamas 133 E8
Waterdown Canada 134 F2
Wateree *r.* U.S.A. 133 D5
Waterfall U.S.A. 120 C4
Waterford Ireland 51 E5
Waterford *PA* U.S.A. 134 F3
Waterford *WI* U.S.A. 134 A2
Waterford Harbour Ireland 51 F5
Watergrasshill Ireland 51 D5
Waterhen Lake Canada 121 L4
Waterloo Australia 108 E4
Waterloo Belgium 52 E4
Waterloo *Ont.* Canada 134 E2
Waterloo *Que.* Canada 135 I1
Waterloo *IA* U.S.A. 130 E3
Waterloo *IL* U.S.A. 130 F4
Waterloo *NY* U.S.A. 135 G2
Waterlooville U.K. 49 F8
Waterton Lakes National Park Canada 120 H5
Watertown *NY* U.S.A. 135 H2
Watertown *SD* U.S.A. 130 D2
Watertown *WI* U.S.A. 130 F3
Water Valley U.S.A. 131 F5
Waterville *ME* U.S.A. 135 K1
Waterville *WA* U.S.A. 126 C3
Watford Canada 134 E2
Watford U.K. 49 G7
Watford City U.S.A. 130 C2
Wathaman *r.* Canada 121 K3
Wathaman Lake Canada 121 K3
Watheroo National Park Australia 109 A7
Wathlingen Germany 53 K2
Watino Canada 120 G4
Watīr, Wādī *watercourse* Egypt 85 B5
Watkins Glen U.S.A. 135 G2
Watling Island Bahamas *see* **San Salvador**
Watmuri Indon. 108 E1
Watonga U.S.A. 131 D5
Watrous Canada 121 J5
Watrous U.S.A. 127 G6
Watseka U.S.A. 134 B3
Watsi Kengo Dem. Rep. Congo 97 F5
Watson *r.* Australia 110 C2
Watson Canada 121 J4
Watson Lake Canada 120 D2
Watsontown U.S.A. 135 G3
Watsonville U.S.A. 128 C3
Watten U.K. 50 F2
Watterson Lake Canada 121 L2
Watton U.K. 49 H6
Watts Bar Lake *resr* U.S.A. 132 C5
Wattsburg U.S.A. 134 F2
Watubela, Kepulauan *is* Indon. 69 I7
Wau P.N.G. 69 L8
Wau South Sudan 86 C8
Waubay Lake U.S.A. 130 D2
Wauchope *N.S.W.* Australia 112 F3
Wauchope *N.T.* Australia 108 F5
Waukaringa (abandoned) Australia 111 B7
Waukarlycarly, Lake *salt flat* Australia 108 C5
Waukegan U.S.A. 134 B2
Waukesha U.S.A. 134 A2
Waupaca U.S.A. 130 F2
Waupun U.S.A. 130 F3
Waurika U.S.A. 131 D5
Wausau U.S.A. 130 F2
Wausaukee U.S.A. 132 C2
Wauseon U.S.A. 134 C3
Wautoma U.S.A. 130 F2
Wave Hill Australia 108 E4
Waveney *r.* U.K. 49 I6
Waverly *IA* U.S.A. 130 E3
Waverly *NY* U.S.A. 135 G2
Waverly *OH* U.S.A. 134 D4
Waverly *TN* U.S.A. 132 C4
Waverly *VA* U.S.A. 135 G5
Wavre Belgium 52 E4
Waw Myanmar 70 B3
Wawa Canada 122 D5
Wawalalindu Indon. 69 G7
Wāw al Kabīr Libya 97 E2
Wawasee, Lake U.S.A. 134 C3
Wawo Indon. 69 G7
Waxahachie U.S.A. 131 D5
Waxü China 76 D1
Waxxari China 80 G4
Way, Lake *salt flat* Australia 109 C6
Waycross U.S.A. 133 D6
Wayland *KY* U.S.A. 134 D5
Wayland *MI* U.S.A. 134 C2
Wayne *NE* U.S.A. 130 D3
Wayne *WV* U.S.A. 134 D4
Waynesboro *GA* U.S.A. 133 D5
Waynesboro *MS* U.S.A. 131 F6
Waynesboro *TN* U.S.A. 132 C5
Waynesboro *VA* U.S.A. 135 F4
Waynesburg U.S.A. 134 E4
Waynesville *MO* U.S.A. 130 E4
Waynesville *NC* U.S.A. 132 D5
Waynoka U.S.A. 131 D4
Waza, Parc National de *nat. park* Cameroon 97 E3
Wāzah Khwāh Afgh. *see* **Mashōrêy**
Wazirabad Pak. 89 I3
W du Niger, Parc National du *nat. park* Niger 96 D3
We, Pulau *i.* Indon. 71 A6
Weagamow Lake Canada 121 N4
Weam P.N.G. 69 K8
Wear *r.* U.K. 48 F4
Weare U.S.A. 135 J2
Weatherford U.S.A. 131 D5
Weaver Lake Canada 121 L4
Weaverville U.S.A. 126 C4
Webb, Mount *hill* Australia 108 E5
Webequie Canada 122 D3
Weber, Mount Canada 120 D4
Weber Basin *sea feature* Laut Banda 150 E6
Webster *IN* U.S.A. 134 C4
Webster *MA* U.S.A. 135 J2
Webster *SD* U.S.A. 130 D2
Webster City U.S.A. 130 E3
Webster Springs U.S.A. 134 E4
Wecho Lake Canada 120 H2
Wedau P.N.G. 110 E1
Weddell Abyssal Plain *sea feature* Southern Ocean 152 A2
Weddell Island Falkland Is 144 D8
Weddell Sea Antarctica 152 A2
Wedderburn Australia 112 A6

Weddin Mountains National Park Australia 112 D4
Wedel Germany 53 J1
Wedge Mountain Canada 120 F5
Wedowee U.S.A. 133 C5
Weedville U.S.A. 135 F3
Weenen S. Africa 101 J5
Weener Germany 53 H1
Weert Neth. 52 F3
Weethalle Australia 112 C4
Wee Waa Australia 112 D3
Wegberg Germany 52 G3
Węgorzewo Poland 47 R3
Weichang China 73 L4
Weida Germany 53 M4
Weidenberg Germany 53 L5
Weiden in der Oberpfalz Germany 53 M5
Weifang China 73 L5
Weihai China 73 M5
Wei He r. Henan China 77 G1
Wei He r. Shaanxi China 76 F1
Weilburg Germany 53 I4
Weilmoringle Australia 112 C2
Weimar Germany 53 L4
Weinan China 77 F1
Weinheim Germany 53 I5
Weining China 76 E3
Weinsberg Germany 53 J5
Weipa Australia 110 C2
Weiqu China see Chang'an
Weir r. Australia 112 D2
Weir River Canada 121 M3
Weirton U.S.A. 134 E3
Weiser U.S.A. 126 D3
Weishan China 76 D3
Weishan Hu l. China 77 H1
Weishi China 77 G1
Weiße Elster r. Germany 53 L3
Weißenburg in Bayern Germany 53 K5
Weißenfels Germany 53 L3
Weißkugel mt. Austria/Italy 47 M7
Weissrand Mountains Namibia 100 D3
Weiterstadt Germany 53 I5
Weitzel Lake Canada 121 J3
Weixi China 76 C3
Weixin China 76 E3
Weiya China 80 H3
Weiyuan Gansu China 76 E1
Weiyuan Sichuan China 76 E2
Weiyuan Yunnan China see Jinggu
Weiyuan Jiang r. China 76 D4
Weiz Austria 47 O7
Weizhou China see Wenchuan
Weizhou Dao i. China 77 F4
Wejherowo Poland 47 Q3
Wekilbazar Turkm. 89 F2
Wekusko Canada 121 L4
Wekusko Lake Canada 121 L4
Wekweètì Canada 120 H1
Welatam Myanmar 70 B1
Welbourn Hill Australia 109 F6
Welch U.S.A. 134 E5
Weld U.S.A. 135 J1
Weldiya Eth. 98 D2
Welford National Park Australia 110 C5
Welk'īt'ē Eth. 98 D3
Welkom S. Africa 101 H4
Welland Canada 134 F2
Welland r. U.K. 49 G6
Welland Canal Canada 134 F2
Wellesley Canada 134 E2
Wellesley Islands Australia 110 B3
Wellesley Lake Canada 120 B2
Wellfleet U.S.A. 135 J3
Wellin Belgium 52 F4
Wellingborough U.K. 49 G6
Wellington Australia 112 D4
Wellington Canada 135 G2

▶Wellington N.Z. 113 E5
Capital of New Zealand.

Wellington S. Africa 100 D7
Wellington England U.K. 49 D8
Wellington England U.K. 49 E6
Wellington CO U.S.A. 126 G4
Wellington IL U.S.A. 134 B3
Wellington KS U.S.A. 131 D4
Wellington NV U.S.A. 128 D2
Wellington OH U.S.A. 134 D3
Wellington TX U.S.A. 131 C5
Wellington UT U.S.A. 129 H2
Wellington, Isla i. Chile 144 B7
Wellington Range hills N.T. Australia 108 F3
Wellington Range hills W.A. Australia 109 C6
Wells Canada 120 F4
Wells U.K. 49 E7
Wells U.S.A. 126 E4
Wells, Lake salt flat Australia 109 C6
Wellsboro U.S.A. 135 G3
Wellsburg U.S.A. 134 E3
Wellsford N.Z. 113 E3
Wells-next-the-Sea U.K. 49 H6
Wellston U.S.A. 134 C1
Wellsville U.S.A. 135 G2
Wellton U.S.A. 129 F5
Wels Austria 47 O6
Welshpool U.K. 49 D6
Welsickendorf Germany 53 N3
Welwitschia Namibia see Khorixas
Welwyn Garden City U.K. 49 G7
Welzheim Germany 53 J6
Wem U.K. 49 E6
Wembesi S. Africa 101 I5
Wembley Canada 120 G4
Wemindji Canada 122 F3
Wenatchee U.S.A. 126 C3
Wenatchee Mountains U.S.A. 126 C3
Wenbu China see Cozhê
Wenceslau Braz Brazil 145 A3
Wenchang China see Zitong
Wencheng China 77 F5
Wenchow China see Wenzhou
Wenchuan China 76 D2
Wendelstein Germany 53 L5
Wenden Germany 53 H4
Wenden Latvia see Cēsis
Wenden U.S.A. 129 G5
Wendover U.S.A. 129 F1
Weng'an China 76 E3
Wengda China 76 D2
Wengshui China 76 C2
Wengyuan China 77 G3
Wenhua China see Weishan
Wenlan China see Mengzi
Wenling China 77 I2
Wenlock r. Australia 110 C2
Wenping China see Ludian
Wenquan Guizhou China 76 E2
Wenquan Henan China see Wenxian
Wenquan Hubei China see Yingshan

▶Wenquan Qinghai China 83 G2
Highest settlement in the world.

Wenquan Xinjiang China 80 F3
Wenshan China 76 E4
Wenshui China 76 E2
Wensum r. U.K. 49 I6
Wentorf bei Hamburg Germany 53 K1
Wentworth Australia 111 C7
Wenxi China 77 F1
Wenxian Gansu China 76 E1
Wenxian Henan China 77 G1
Wenxing China see Xiangyin
Wenzhou China 77 I3
Wenzlow Germany 53 M2
Wepener S. Africa 101 H5
Wer India 82 D4
Werben (Elbe) Germany 53 L2
Werda Botswana 100 F3
Werdau Germany 53 M4
Werder (Havel) Germany 53 M2
Werdohl Germany 53 H3
Werl Germany 53 H3
Wernberg-Köblitz Germany 53 M5
Werne Germany 53 H3
Wernecke Mountains Canada 120 B1
Wernigerode Germany 53 K3
Werra r. Germany 53 J3
Werris Creek Australia 112 E3
Wertheim Germany 53 J5
Wervik Belgium 52 D4
Wesel Germany 52 G3
Wesel-Datteln-Kanal canal Germany 52 G3
Wesenberg Germany 53 M1
Wesendorf Germany 53 K2
Weser r. Germany 53 I1
Weser sea chan. Germany 53 I1
Wesergebirge hills Germany 53 I2
Weslaco U.S.A. 131 D7
Weslemkoon Lake Canada 135 G1
Wesleyville Canada 123 L4
Wessel, Cape Australia 110 B1
Wessel Islands Australia 110 B1
Wesselsbron S. Africa 101 H4
Wesselton S. Africa 101 I4
Wessington Springs U.S.A. 130 D2
Westall, Point Australia 109 F8
West Allis U.S.A. 134 A2
West Antarctica reg. Antarctica 152 J1
West Australian Basin sea feature Indian Ocean 149 O7
West Bank disp. terr. Asia 85 B3
West Bay Canada 123 K3
West Bay inlet U.S.A. 133 C6
West Bend U.S.A. 134 A2
West Bengal state India 83 F5
West Branch U.S.A. 134 C1
West Bromwich U.K. 49 F6
Westbrook U.S.A. 135 J2
West Burke U.S.A. 135 J1
Westbury U.K. 49 E7
West Caicos i. Turks and Caicos Is 133 F8
West Cape Howe Australia 109 B8
West Caroline Basin sea feature N. Pacific Ocean 150 F5
West Chester U.S.A. 135 H4
Westcliffe U.S.A. 127 G5
West Coast National Park S. Africa 100 D7
West End Bahamas 133 E7
Westerburg Germany 53 H4
Westerholt Germany 53 H1
Westerland Germany 47 L3
Westerlo Belgium 52 E3
Westerly U.S.A. 135 J3
Western r. Canada 121 J1
Western Australia state Australia 109 C6
Western Cape prov. S. Africa 100 E7
Western Desert Egypt 90 C6
Western Dvina r. Europe see Zapadnaya Dvina
Western Ghats mts India 84 B3
Western Port b. Australia 112 B7
Western Sahara disp. terr. Africa 96 B2
Western Samoa country S. Pacific Ocean see Samoa
Western Sayan Mountains reg. Russia see Zapadnyy Sayan
Westerschelde est. Neth. 52 D3
Westerstede Germany 53 H1
Westerville U.S.A. 134 D3
Westerwald hills Germany 53 H4
West Falkland i. Falkland Is 144 D8
West Fargo U.S.A. 130 D2
West Fayu atoll Micronesia 69 L5
Westfield IN U.S.A. 134 B3
Westfield MA U.S.A. 135 I2
Westfield NY U.S.A. 134 F2
Westfield PA U.S.A. 135 G3
West Frisian Islands Neth. 52 E1
Westgat sea chan. Neth. 52 G1
Westgate Australia 112 C1
West Glacier U.S.A. 126 E2
West Grand Lake U.S.A. 132 H2
West Hartford U.S.A. 135 I3
Westhausen Germany 53 K6
West Haven U.S.A. 135 I3
Westhill U.K. 50 G3
Westhope U.S.A. 130 C1
West Ice Shelf Antarctica 152 E2
West Indies is Caribbean Sea 137 J4
West Island India 71 A4
Westkapelle Neth. 52 D3
West Kazakhstan Oblast admin. div. Kazakh. see Zapadnyy Kazakhstan
West Kelowna Canada 120 F5
West Kingston U.S.A. 135 J3
West Lafayette U.S.A. 134 B3
West Lamma Channel H.K. China 77 [inset]
Westland Australia 110 C4
Westland Tai Poutini National Park N.Z. 113 C6
Westleigh S. Africa 101 H4
Westleton U.K. 49 I6
West Liberty U.S.A. 134 D5
West Linton U.K. 50 F5
West Loch Roag b. U.K. 50 C2
Westlock Canada 120 H4
West Lorne Canada 134 E2
West Lunga National Park Zambia 99 C5
West MacDonnell National Park Australia 109 F5
West Malaysia pen. Malaysia see Peninsular Malaysia
Westmalle Belgium 52 E3
Westman Islands Iceland see Vestmannaeyjar
Westmar Australia 112 D1
West Mariana Basin sea feature N. Pacific Ocean 150 F4
West Memphis U.S.A. 131 F5
Westminster U.S.A. 135 G4
Westmoreland Australia 110 B3
Westmoreland U.S.A. 134 B5
Westmorland U.S.A. 129 F5
Weston OH U.S.A. 134 D3
Weston WV U.S.A. 134 E4
Weston-super-Mare U.K. 49 E7
West Palm Beach U.S.A. 133 D7
West Plains U.S.A. 131 F4
West Point pt Australia 111 [inset]
West Point CA U.S.A. 128 C2
West Point KY U.S.A. 134 C5
West Point MS U.S.A. 131 F5
West Point NE U.S.A. 130 D3
West Point VA U.S.A. 135 G5
West Point Lake resr U.S.A. 133 C5
Westport Canada 135 G1
Westport Ireland 51 C4
Westport N.Z. 113 C5
Westport CA U.S.A. 128 B2
Westport KY U.S.A. 134 C4
Westport NY U.S.A. 135 I1
Westray Canada 121 K4
Westray i. U.K. 50 F1
Westray Firth sea chan. U.K. 50 F1
Westree Canada 122 E5
West Rutland U.S.A. 135 I2
West Salem U.S.A. 134 D3
West Siberian Plain Russia 64 J3
West-Skylge Neth. see West-Terschelling
West Stewartstown U.S.A. 135 J1
West-Terschelling Neth. 52 F1
West Topsham U.S.A. 135 I1
West Union IA U.S.A. 130 F3
West Union IL U.S.A. 134 B4
West Union OH U.S.A. 134 D4
West Union WV U.S.A. 134 E4
West Valley City U.S.A. 129 H1
Westville U.S.A. 134 B3
West Virginia state U.S.A. 134 E4
Westwood U.S.A. 128 C1
West Wyalong Australia 112 C4
West York U.S.A. 135 G4
Westzaan Neth. 52 E2
Wetar i. Indon. 108 D1
Wetar, Selat sea chan. Indon. 108 D2
Wetaskiwin Canada 120 H4
Wete Tanz. 99 D4
Wetter r. Germany 53 I4
Wettin Germany 53 L3
Wetumpka U.S.A. 133 C5
Wetwun Myanmar 70 B2
Wetzlar Germany 53 I4
Wewahitchka U.S.A. 133 C6
Wewak P.N.G. 69 K7
Wewoka U.S.A. 131 D5
Wexford Ireland 51 F5
Wexford Harbour b. Ireland 51 F5
Weyakwin Canada 121 J4
Weybridge U.K. 49 G7
Weyburn Canada 121 K5
Weyhe Germany 53 I2
Weymouth U.K. 49 E8
Weymouth U.S.A. 135 J2
Wezep Neth. 52 G2
Whakaari i. N.Z. 113 F3
Whakatane N.Z. 113 F3
Whalan Creek r. Australia 112 D2
Whale r. Canada see Baleine, Rivière à la
Whalsay i. U.K. 50 [inset]
Whampoa China see Huangpu
Whangamata N.Z. 113 E3
Whanganui National Park N.Z. 113 E4
Whangarei N.Z. 113 E2
Whapmagoostui Canada 122 F3
Wharfe r. U.K. 48 F5
Wharfedale valley U.K. 48 F4
Wharton U.S.A. 131 D6
Wharton Lake Canada 121 L1
Whatî Canada 120 G2
Wheatland IN U.S.A. 134 B4
Wheatland WY U.S.A. 126 G4
Wheaton IL U.S.A. 134 A3
Wheaton MD U.S.A. 135 G4
Wheaton MN U.S.A. 130 D2
Wheeler U.S.A. 131 C5
Wheeler Lake Canada 120 H2
Wheeler Lake resr U.S.A. 133 C5
Wheeler Peak NM U.S.A. 127 G5
Wheeler Peak NV U.S.A. 129 F2
Wheelersburg U.S.A. 134 D4
Wheeling U.S.A. 134 E3
Whernside hill U.K. 48 E4
Whinham, Mount Australia 109 E6
Whiskey Jack Lake Canada 121 K3
Whitburn U.K. 50 F5
Whitby Canada 135 F2
Whitby U.K. 48 G4
Whitchurch U.K. 49 E6
Whitchurch-Stouffville Canada 134 F2
White r. Canada 122 D4
White r. Canada/U.S.A. 120 B2
White r. AR U.S.A. 131 F5
White r. CO U.S.A. 129 I1
White r. IN U.S.A. 134 B4
White r. MI U.S.A. 134 B2
White r. NV U.S.A. 129 F3
White r. SD U.S.A. 130 D3
White r. VT U.S.A. 135 I2
White watercourse U.S.A. 129 H5
White, Lake salt flat Australia 108 E5
White Bay Canada 123 K4
White Butte mt. U.S.A. 130 C2
White Canyon U.S.A. 129 H3
White Cloud U.S.A. 134 C2
Whitecourt Canada 120 H4
Whiteface Mountain U.S.A. 135 I1
Whitefield U.S.A. 135 J1
Whitefish r. Canada 120 E1
Whitefish U.S.A. 126 E2
Whitefish Bay U.S.A. 134 B1
Whitefish Lake Canada 121 J2
Whitefish Point U.S.A. 132 C2
Whitehall U.K. 50 G1
Whitehall NY U.S.A. 135 I2
Whitehall WI U.S.A. 130 F2
Whitehaven U.K. 48 D4
Whitehead U.K. 51 G3
White Hill hill Canada 123 J5
Whitehill U.K. 49 G7

▶Whitehorse Canada 120 C2
Capital of Yukon.

Whitehorse U.S.A. 129 J4
White Horse, Vale of valley U.K. 49 F7
White Horse Pass U.S.A. 129 F1
White House U.S.A. 134 B5
White Island Antarctica 152 D2
White Island N.Z. see Whakaari
White Lake Ont. Canada 122 D4
White Lake Ont. Canada 135 G1
White Lake LA U.S.A. 131 E6
White Lake MI U.S.A. 134 B2
Whitemark Australia 111 [inset]
White Mountain Peak U.S.A. 128 D3
White Mountains U.S.A. 135 J1
White Mountains National Park Australia 110 D4
Whitemouth Lake Canada 121 M5
Whitemud r. Canada 120 G3
White Nile r. Africa 86 D6
also known as Bahr el Abiad or Bahr el Jebel
White Nossob watercourse Namibia 100 D2
White Oak U.S.A. 134 D5
White Otter Lake Canada 121 N5
White Pass Canada/U.S.A. 120 C3
White Pine Range mts U.S.A. 129 F2
White Plains U.S.A. 135 I3
White River Canada 122 D4
Whiteriver U.S.A. 129 I5
White River U.S.A. 130 C3
White River Valley U.S.A. 129 F2
White Rock Peak U.S.A. 129 F2
White Russia country Europe see Belarus
Whitesail Lake Canada 120 E4
White Salmon U.S.A. 126 C3
Whitesand r. Canada 120 H2
White Sands National Monument nat. park U.S.A. 127 G6
Whitesburg U.S.A. 134 D5
White Sea Russia 42 H2
White Stone U.S.A. 135 G5
White Sulphur Springs MT U.S.A. 126 F3
White Sulphur Springs WV U.S.A. 134 E5
Whitesville U.S.A. 134 E5
Whiteville U.S.A. 133 E5
White Volta r. Burkina Faso/Ghana 96 C4
also known as Nakambé or Nakanbe or Volta Blanche
Whitewater U.S.A. 129 I2
Whitewater Baldy mt. U.S.A. 129 I5
Whitewater Lake Canada 122 C4
Whitewood Australia 110 C4
Whitewood Canada 121 K5
Whitfield U.K. 49 I7
Whithorn U.K. 50 E6
Whitianga N.Z. 113 E3
Whitland U.K. 49 C7
Whitley Bay U.K. 48 F3
Whitmore Mountains Antarctica 152 K1
Whitney Canada 135 F1
Whitney, Mount U.S.A. 128 D3
Whitney Point U.S.A. 135 H2
Whitstable U.K. 49 I7
Whitsunday Group is Australia 110 E4
Whitsunday Island National Park Australia 110 E4
Whitsun Island Vanuatu see Pentecost Island
Whittemore U.S.A. 134 D1
Whittlesea Australia 112 B6
Whittlesey U.K. 49 G6
Whitton Australia 112 C5
Wholdaia Lake Canada 121 J2
Why U.S.A. 129 G5
Whyalla Australia 111 B7
Wiang Sa Thai. 70 C3
Wiarton Canada 134 E1
Wibaux U.S.A. 126 G3
Wichelen Belgium 52 D3
Wichita U.S.A. 130 D4
Wichita r. U.S.A. 131 D5
Wichita Falls U.S.A. 131 D5
Wichita Mountains U.S.A. 131 D5
Wick U.K. 50 F2
Wick r. U.K. 50 F2
Wickenburg U.S.A. 129 G5
Wickes U.S.A. 131 E5
Wickford U.K. 49 H7
Wickham r. Australia 108 E4
Wickham, Cape Australia 111 [inset]
Wickham, Mount hill Australia 108 E4
Wickliffe U.S.A. 131 F4
Wicklow Ireland 51 F5
Wicklow Head hd Ireland 51 G5
Wicklow Mountains Ireland 51 F5
Wicklow Mountains National Park Ireland 51 F4
Widerøe, Mount Antarctica 152 C2
Widerøefjellet mt. Antarctica see Widerøe, Mount
Widgeegoara watercourse Australia 112 B1
Widgiemooltha (abandoned) Australia 109 C7
Widnes U.K. 48 E5
Wi-do i. S. Korea 75 B6
Wied r. Germany 53 H4
Wiehengebirge hills Germany 53 I2
Wiehl Germany 53 H4
Wielkopolskie, Pojezierze reg. Poland 47 O4
Wielkopolski Park Narodowy nat. park Poland 47 P4
Wieluń Poland 47 Q5
Wien Austria see Vienna
Wiener Neustadt Austria 47 P7
Wierden Neth. 52 G2
Wieren Germany 53 K2
Wieringerwerf Neth. 52 F2
Wiesbaden Germany 53 I4
Wiesenfelden Germany 53 M5
Wiesentheid Germany 53 K5
Wiesloch Germany 53 I5
Wiesmoor Germany 53 H1
Wietze Germany 53 J2
Wietzendorf Germany 53 J2
Wieżyca hill Poland 47 Q3
Wigan U.K. 48 E5
Wiggins U.S.A. 131 F6
Wight, Isle of i. U.K. 49 F8
Wigierski Park Narodowy nat. park Poland 45 M9
Wignes Lake Canada 121 J2
Wigston U.K. 49 F6
Wigton U.K. 48 D4
Wigtown U.K. 50 E6
Wigtown Bay U.K. 50 E6
Wijchen Neth. 52 F3
Wijhe Neth. 52 G2
Wilberforce, Cape Australia 110 B1
Wilbur U.S.A. 126 D3
Wilburton U.S.A. 131 E5
Wilcannia Australia 112 A3
Wilcox U.S.A. 135 F3
Wilczek Land i. Russia see Vil'cheka, Zemlya
Wildberg Germany 53 M2
Wildcat Peak U.S.A. 128 E2
Wild Coast S. Africa 101 I6
Wildeshausen Germany 53 I2
Wild Horse Hill mt. U.S.A. 130 C3
Wildspitze mt. Austria 47 M7
Wildwood FL U.S.A. 133 D6
Wildwood NJ U.S.A. 135 H4
Wilge r. Free State S. Africa 101 I4
Wilge r. Gauteng/Mpumalanga S. Africa 101 I3
Wilgena Australia 109 F7

▶Wilhelm, Mount P.N.G. 69 L8
5th highest mountain in Oceania.

Wilhelm II Land reg. Antarctica see Kaiser Wilhelm II Land
Wilhelmina Gebergte mts Suriname 143 G3
Wilhelmina Kanaal canal Neth. 52 F3
Wilhelmshaven Germany 53 I1
Wilhelmshöhe, Bergpark tourist site Germany 53 J3
Wilhelmstal Namibia 100 C1
Wilkes-Barre U.S.A. 135 H3
Wilkesboro U.S.A. 132 D4
Wilkes Coast Antarctica 152 G2
Wilkes Land reg. Antarctica 152 G2
Wilkie Canada 121 I4
Wilkins Coast Antarctica 152 L2
Wilkins Ice Shelf Antarctica 152 L2
Wilkinson Lakes salt flat Australia 109 F7
Will, Mount Canada 120 D3
Willand U.K. 49 D8
Willandra Billabong watercourse Australia 112 B4
Willandra National Park Australia 112 B4
Willapa Bay U.S.A. 126 B3
Willard Mex. 127 F7
Willard NM U.S.A. 127 G6
Willard OH U.S.A. 134 D3
Willcox U.S.A. 129 I5
Willcox Playa salt flat U.S.A. 129 I5
Willebadessen Germany 53 J3
Willebroek Belgium 52 E3
Willemstad Curaçao 137 K6
Willeroo Australia 108 E3
Willette U.S.A. 134 C5
William, Mount Australia 111 C8
William Creek Australia 111 B6
William Lake Canada 121 L4
Williams AZ U.S.A. 129 G4
Williams CA U.S.A. 128 B2
Williamsburg KY U.S.A. 134 C5
Williamsburg OH U.S.A. 134 C4
Williamsburg VA U.S.A. 135 G5
Williams Lake Canada 120 F4
William Smith, Cap c. Canada 123 I1
Williamson NY U.S.A. 135 G2
Williamson WV U.S.A. 134 D5
Williamsport IN U.S.A. 134 B3
Williamsport PA U.S.A. 135 G3
Williamston U.S.A. 132 E5
Williamstown KY U.S.A. 134 C4
Williamstown NJ U.S.A. 135 H4
Willimantic U.S.A. 135 I3
Willis Group atolls Australia 110 E3
Williston S. Africa 100 E6
Williston ND U.S.A. 130 C1
Williston SC U.S.A. 133 D5
Williston Lake Canada 120 F4
Williton U.K. 49 D7
Willits U.S.A. 128 B2
Willmar U.S.A. 130 E2
Willoughby, Lake U.S.A. 135 I1
Willow Beach U.S.A. 129 F4
Willow Bunch Canada 121 J5
Willow Hill U.S.A. 135 G3
Willow Lake Canada 120 G2
Willowlake r. Canada 120 F2
Willowmore S. Africa 100 F7
Willowra Australia 108 F5
Willows U.S.A. 128 B2
Willow Springs U.S.A. 131 F4
Willowvale S. Africa 101 I7
Wills, Lake salt flat Australia 108 E5
Wilma U.S.A. 133 C6
Wilmington DE U.S.A. 135 H4
Wilmington NC U.S.A. 133 E5
Wilmington OH U.S.A. 134 D4
Wilmore U.S.A. 134 C5
Wilmslow U.K. 48 E5
Wilno Lith. see Vilnius
Wilnsdorf Germany 53 I4
Wilpattu National Park Sri Lanka 84 D4
Wilseder Berg hill Germany 53 J1
Wilson watercourse Australia 111 C5
Wilson atoll Micronesia see Ifalik
Wilson KS U.S.A. 130 D4
Wilson NC U.S.A. 132 E5
Wilson NY U.S.A. 135 F2
Wilson, Mount CO U.S.A. 129 J3
Wilson, Mount NV U.S.A. 129 F2
Wilson, Mount OR U.S.A. 126 C3
Wilsonia U.S.A. 128 D3
Wilson's Promontory pen. Australia 112 C7
Wilson's Promontory National Park Australia 112 C7
Wilsum Germany 52 G2
Wilton r. Australia 108 F3
Wilton U.S.A. 135 J1
Wiltz Lux. 52 F5
Wiluna Australia 109 C6
Wimereux France 52 B4
Wina r. Cameroon see Vina
Winamac U.S.A. 134 B3
Winbin watercourse Australia 111 D5
Winburg S. Africa 101 H5
Wincanton U.K. 49 E7
Winchester Canada 135 H1
Winchester U.K. 49 F7
Winchester IN U.S.A. 134 C3
Winchester KY U.S.A. 134 C5
Winchester NH U.S.A. 135 I2
Winchester TN U.S.A. 133 C5
Winchester VA U.S.A. 135 F4
Wind r. Canada 120 C1
Wind r. U.S.A. 126 F4
Windau Latvia see Ventspils
Windber U.S.A. 135 F3
Wind Cave National Park U.S.A. 130 C3
Windermere U.K. 48 E4
Windermere l. U.K. 48 E4
Windham U.S.A. 120 C3

▶Windhoek Namibia 100 C2
Capital of Namibia.

Windigo Lake Canada 121 N4
Windlestraw Law hill U.K. 50 G5
Wind Mountain U.S.A. 127 G6
Windom U.S.A. 130 E3
Windom Peak U.S.A. 129 J3
Windorah Australia 110 C5
Window Rock U.S.A. 129 I4
Wind Point U.S.A. 134 B2
Wind River Range mts U.S.A. 126 F4
Windrush r. U.K. 49 F7
Windsbach Germany 53 K5
Windsor Australia 112 E4
Windsor N.S. Canada 123 I5
Windsor Ont. Canada 134 D2
Windsor U.K. 49 G7
Windsor NC U.S.A. 132 E4
Windsor NY U.S.A. 135 H2
Windsor VA U.S.A. 135 G5
Windsor VT U.S.A. 135 I2
Windsor Locks U.S.A. 135 I3
Windward Islands Caribbean Sea 137 L5
Windward Passage Cuba/Haiti 137 J5
Windy U.S.A. 118 D3
Winefred Lake Canada 121 I4
Winfield KS U.S.A. 131 D4
Winfield WV U.S.A. 134 E4
Wingate U.K. 48 F4
Wingen Australia 112 E3
Wingene Belgium 52 D3
Wingen-sur-Moder France 53 H6
Wingham Australia 112 F3
Wingham Canada 134 E2
Winisk r. Canada 122 D3
Winisk (abandoned) Canada 122 D3
Winisk Lake Canada 122 D3
Winkana Myanmar 70 B4
Winkelman U.S.A. 129 H5
Winkler Canada 121 L5
Winlock U.S.A. 126 C3
Winneba Ghana 96 C4
Winnebago, Lake U.S.A. 134 A1
Winnecke Creek watercourse Australia 108 E4
Winnemucca U.S.A. 128 E1
Winnemucca Lake U.S.A. 128 D1
Winner U.S.A. 130 C3
Winnett U.S.A. 126 F3
Winnfield U.S.A. 131 E6
Winnibigoshish, Lake U.S.A. 130 E2
Winnie U.S.A. 131 E6
Winning Australia 109 A5

▶Winnipeg Canada 121 L5
Capital of Manitoba.

Winnipeg r. Canada 121 L5
Winnipeg, Lake Canada 121 L5
Winnipegosis Canada 121 L5
Winnipegosis, Lake Canada 121 K4
Winnipesaukee, Lake U.S.A. 135 J2
Winona AZ U.S.A. 129 H4
Winona MN U.S.A. 130 F2
Winona MO U.S.A. 131 F4
Winona MS U.S.A. 131 F5
Winschoten Neth. 52 H1
Winsen (Aller) Germany 53 J2
Winsen (Luhe) Germany 53 K1
Winsford U.K. 48 E5
Winslow AZ U.S.A. 129 H4
Winslow ME U.S.A. 135 K1
Winsop, Tanjung pt Indon. 69 I7
Winsted U.S.A. 135 I3
Winston-Salem U.S.A. 132 D4
Winterberg Germany 53 I3
Winter Haven U.S.A. 133 D6
Winters CA U.S.A. 128 C2
Winters TX U.S.A. 131 D6
Wintersville U.S.A. 134 E3
Winterswijk Neth. 52 G3
Winterthur Switz. 56 I3
Winterton S. Africa 101 I5
Winthrop U.S.A. 135 K1
Winton Australia 110 C4
Winton N.Z. 113 B8
Winton U.S.A. 132 E4

Winwick U.K. 49 G6
Wirral pen. U.K. 48 D5
Wirrulla Australia 111 A7
Wisbech U.K. 49 H6
Wiscasset U.S.A. 135 K1
Wisconsin r. U.S.A. 130 F3
Wisconsin state U.S.A. 134 A1
Wisconsin Rapids U.S.A. 130 F2
Wise U.S.A. 134 D5
Wiseman U.S.A. 118 C3
Wishaw U.K. 50 F5
Wishek U.S.A. 130 D2
Wisil Dabarow Somalia 98 E3
Wisła r. Poland see Vistula
Wismar Germany 47 M4
Wistaria Canada 120 E4
Witbank S. Africa see eMalahleni
Witbooisvlei Namibia 100 D3
Witham U.K. 49 H7
Witham r. U.K. 49 H6
Witherbee U.S.A. 135 I1
Withernsea U.K. 48 H5
Witjira National Park Australia 111 A5
Witmarsum Neth. 52 F1
Witney U.K. 49 F7
Witrivier S. Africa 101 J3
Witry-lès-Reims France 52 E5
Witteberg mts S. Africa 101 H6
Wittenberg Germany see Wittenberg, Lutherstadt
Wittenberg, Lutherstadt Germany 53 M3
Wittenberge Germany 53 L2
Wittenburg Germany 53 L1
Wittingen Germany 53 K2
Wittlich Germany 52 G5
Wittmund Germany 53 H1
Wittstock/Dosse Germany 53 M1
Witu Islands P.N.G. 69 L7
Witvlei Namibia 100 D2
Witzenhausen Germany 53 J3
Wivenhoe, Lake Australia 112 F1
Władysławowo Poland 47 Q3
Włocławek Poland 47 Q4
Wobkent Uzbek. see Vobkent
Wodonga Australia 112 C6
Wœrth France 53 H6
Woëvre, Plaine de la plain France 52 F5
Wohlthat Mountains Antarctica 152 C2
Woippy France 52 G5
Wōjjā atoll Marshall Is see Wotje
Wokam i. Indon. 69 I8
Woken He r. China 74 C3
Wokha India 83 H4
Woking U.K. 49 G7
Wokingham watercourse Australia 110 C4
Wokingham U.K. 49 G7
Woko National Park Australia 112 E3
Wolcott IN U.S.A. 134 B3
Wolcott NY U.S.A. 135 G2
Woldegk Germany 53 N1
Wolea atoll Micronesia see Woleai
Woleai atoll Micronesia 69 K5
Wolf r. Canada 120 C2
Wolf r. TN U.S.A. 131 F5
Wolf r. WI U.S.A. 130 F2
Wolf Creek MT U.S.A. 126 E3
Wolf Creek OR U.S.A. 126 C4
Wolf Creek Pass U.S.A. 127 G5
Wolfen Germany 53 M3
Wolfenbüttel Germany 53 K2
Wolfhagen Germany 53 J3
Wolf Lake Canada 120 D2
Wolf Point U.S.A. 126 G2
Wolfsberg Austria 47 O7
Wolfsburg Germany 53 K2
Wolfstein Germany 53 H5
Wolfville Canada 123 I5
Wolgast Germany 47 N3
Wolin Poland 47 O4
Wollaston Lake Canada 121 K3
Wollaston Lake l. Canada 121 K3
Wollaston Peninsula Canada 118 G3
Wollemi National Park Australia 112 E4
Wollongong Australia 112 E5
Wolmaransstad S. Africa 101 G4
Wolmirstedt Germany 53 L2
Wolong Natural Reserve nature res. China 76 D2
Wolseley Australia 111 C8
Wolseley S. Africa 100 D7
Wolsey U.S.A. 130 D2
Wolsingham U.K. 48 F4
Wolvega Neth. 52 G2
Wolvegea Neth. see Wolvega
Wolverhampton U.K. 49 E6
Wolverine U.S.A. 134 C1
Wommelgem Belgium 52 E3
Womrather Höhe hill Germany 53 H5
Wonarah Australia 110 B3
Wondai Australia 111 E5
Wongalarroo Lake salt l. Australia 112 B3
Wongarbon Australia 112 D4
Wong Chuk Hang H.K. China 77 [inset]
Wong Leng hill H.K. China 77 [inset]
Wonju S. Korea 75 B5
Wonowon Canada 120 F3
Wŏnsan N. Korea 75 B5
Wonthaggi Australia 112 B7
Wonyulgunna, Mount hill Australia 109 B6
Woocalla Australia 111 B6
Wood, Mount Canada 120 A2
Woodbine GA U.S.A. 133 D6
Woodbine NJ U.S.A. 135 H4
Woodbridge U.K. 49 I6
Woodbridge U.S.A. 135 G4
Wood Buffalo National Park Canada 120 H3
Woodburn U.S.A. 126 C3
Woodbury NJ U.S.A. 135 H4
Woodbury TN U.S.A. 131 G5
Wooded Bluff hd Australia 112 F2
Wood Lake Canada 121 K4
Woodlake U.S.A. 128 D3
Woodland CA U.S.A. 128 C2
Woodland PA U.S.A. 135 F3
Woodland WA U.S.A. 126 C3
Woodlands Sing. 71 [inset]
Woodlark Island P.N.G. 106 F2
Woodridge Canada 121 L5
Woodroffe watercourse Australia 110 B4
Woodroffe, Mount Australia 109 E6
Woodruff UT U.S.A. 126 F4
Woodruff WI U.S.A. 130 F2
Woods, Lake salt flat Australia 108 F4
Woods, Lake of the Canada/U.S.A. 125 I2
Woodsfield U.S.A. 134 E4
Woodside Australia 112 C7
Woodstock N.B. Canada 123 I5
Woodstock Ont. Canada 134 E2
Woodstock IL U.S.A. 130 F3
Woodstock VA U.S.A. 135 F4
Woodstock VT U.S.A. 135 I2
Woodsville U.S.A. 135 I1
Woodville Canada 135 F1
Woodville MS U.S.A. 131 F6
Woodville OH U.S.A. 134 D3
Woodville TX U.S.A. 131 E6
Woodward U.S.A. 131 D4
Woody U.S.A. 128 D4
Wooler U.K. 48 E3
Woolgoolga Australia 112 F3
Wooli Australia 112 F2
Woollard, Mount Antarctica 152 K1
Woollett, Lac l. Canada 122 G4
Woolyeenyer Hill hill Australia 109 C8
Woomera Australia 111 B6
Woomera Prohibited Area Australia 109 F7
Woonsocket RI U.S.A. 135 J2
Woonsocket SD U.S.A. 130 D2
Woorabinda Australia 110 E5
Wooramel r. Australia 109 A6
Wooster U.S.A. 134 E3
Wootton Bassett U.K. see Royal Wootton Bassett
Worbis Germany 53 K3
Worbody Point Australia 110 C2
Worcester S. Africa 100 D7
Worcester U.K. 49 E6
Worcester MA U.S.A. 135 J2
Worcester NY U.S.A. 135 H2
Wörgl Austria 47 N7
Workai i. Indon. 69 I8
Workington U.K. 48 D4
Worksop U.K. 48 F5
Workum Neth. 52 F2
Worland U.S.A. 126 G3
Wörlitz Germany 53 M3
Wormerveer Neth. 52 E2
Worms Germany 53 I5
Worms Head hd U.K. 49 C7
Wortel Namibia 100 C2
Wörth am Rhein Germany 53 I5
Worthing U.K. 49 G8
Worthington IN U.S.A. 134 B4
Worthington MN U.S.A. 130 E3
Wotje atoll Marshall Is 150 H5
Wotu Indon. 69 G7
Woudrichem Neth. 52 E3
Woustviller France 52 H5
Wowoni i. Indon. 69 G7
Wozrojdeniye oroli i. Uzbek. see Vozrozhdenya Island
Wrangel Island Russia 65 T2
Wrangell Island U.S.A. 120 C3
Wrangell Mountains U.S.A. 153 B3
Wrangell-St Elias National Park and Preserve U.S.A. 120 A2
Wrath, Cape U.K. 50 D2
Wray U.S.A. 130 C3
Wreake r. U.K. 49 F6
Wreck Point S. Africa 100 C5
Wreck Reef Australia 110 F4
Wrecsam U.K. see Wrexham
Wrestedt Germany 53 K2
Wrexham U.K. 49 E5
Wrightmyo India 71 A5
Wrightson, Mount U.S.A. 127 F7
Wrightwood U.S.A. 128 E4
Wrigley Canada 120 F2
Wrigley U.S.A. 134 D4
Wrigley Gulf Antarctica 152 J2
Wrocław Poland 47 P5
Września Poland 47 P4
Wu'an China see Changtai
Wubin Australia 109 B7
Wuchang Heilong. China 74 B3
Wuchang Hubei China see Jiangxia
Wuchow China see Wuzhou
Wuchuan Guangdong China 77 F4
Wuchuan Guizhou China 76 E2
Wudalianchi China 74 B2
Wudām 'Alwā Oman 88 E6
Wudang Shan mt. China 77 F1
Wudaoliang China 76 B1
Wuding China 76 D3
Wudinna Australia 109 F8
Wufeng Hubei China 77 F2
Wufeng Yunnan China see Zhenxiong
Wugang China 77 F3
Wuhai China 72 J5
Wuhan China 77 G2
Wuhe China 77 H1
Wuhu China 77 H2
Wuhua China 77 G4
Wuhubei China 77 H2
Wūjang China 82 D2
Wu Jiang r. China 76 E2
Wujin Jiangsu China see Changzhou
Wujin Sichuan China see Xinjin
Wukari Nigeria 96 D4
Wulang China 76 B2
Wulêswālī Bihsūd Afgh. 89 G3
Wuli China 76 B1
Wulian Feng mts China 76 D2
Wuliang Shan mts China 76 D3
Wuliaru i. Indon. 108 E1
Wuli Jiang r. China 77 F4
Wuling Shan mts China 77 F2
Wulong China 76 E2
Wulongji China see Huaibin
Wulur Indon. 108 E1
Wumeng Shan mts China 76 D3
Wuming China 77 F4
Wümme r. Germany 53 I1
Wundwin Myanmar 70 B2
Wuning China 77 G2
Wünnenberg Germany 53 I3
Wunnummin Lake Canada 119 J4
Wunsiedel Germany 53 M4
Wunstorf Germany 53 J2
Wupatki National Monument nat. park U.S.A. 129 H4
Wuping China 77 H3
Wuppertal Germany 53 H3
Wuppertal S. Africa 100 D7
Wuqi China 73 J5
Wuquan China see Wuyang
Wuranga Australia 109 B7
Wurno Nigeria 96 D3
Würzburg Germany 53 J5
Wurzen Germany 53 M3
Wushan Chongqing China 77 F2
Wushan Gansu China 76 E1
Wu Shan mts China 77 F2
Wushi Guangdong China 77 F4
Wushi Xinjiang China 80 E3
Wüstegarten hill Germany 53 J3
Wusuli Jiang r. China/Russia see Ussuri
Wuvulu Island P.N.G. 69 K7
Wuwei China 72 I5
Wuxi Chongqing China 77 F2
Wuxi Hunan China 77 F2
Wuxi Hunan China see Qiyang
Wuxi Jiangsu China 77 I2
Wuxia China see Wushan
Wuxian China see Suzhou
Wuxing China see Huzhou
Wuxu China 77 F4
Wuxuan China 77 F4
Wuxue China 77 G2
Wuyang Guizhou China see Zhenyuan
Wuyang Henan China 77 G1
Wuyang Zhejiang China see Wuyi
Wuyi China 77 H2
Wuyiling China 74 C2
Wuyi Shan mts China 77 H3
Wuyuan Jiangxi China 77 H2
Wuyuan Nei Mongol China 73 J4
Wuyuan Zhejiang China see Haiyan
Wuyun China see Jinyun
Wuzhishan China 77 F5
Wuzhi Shan mts China 77 F5
Wuzhong China 72 J5
Wuzhou China 77 F4
Wyalkatchem Australia 109 B7
Wyalong Australia 112 C4
Wyandra Australia 112 B1
Wyangala Reservoir Australia 112 D4
Wyara, Lake salt flat Australia 112 B2
Wycheproof Australia 112 A6
Wylliesburg U.S.A. 135 F5
Wyloo Australia 108 B5
Wylye r. U.K. 49 F7
Wymondham U.K. 49 I6
Wymore U.S.A. 130 D3
Wynbring Australia 109 F7
Wyndham Australia 108 E3
Wyndham-Werribee Australia 112 B6
Wynne U.S.A. 131 F5
Wynyard Canada 121 J5
Wyola Lake salt flat Australia 109 E7
Wyoming U.S.A. 134 C2
Wyoming state U.S.A. 126 G4
Wyoming Peak U.S.A. 126 F4
Wyoming Range mts U.S.A. 126 F4
Wyong Australia 112 E4
Wyperfeld National Park Australia 111 C7
Wysox U.S.A. 135 G3
Wyszków Poland 47 R4
Wythall U.K. 49 F6
Wytheville U.S.A. 134 E5
Wytmarsum Neth. see Witmarsum

X

Xaafuun Somalia 98 F2
▶Xaafuun, Raas pt Somalia 86 H7
Most easterly point of Africa.
Xabyaisamba China 76 C2
Xaçmaz Azer. 91 H2
Xago China 83 G3
Xagquka China 76 B2
Xaidulla China 82 D1
Xaignabouli Laos 70 C3
Xaignabouri Laos see Xaignabouli
Xainza China 83 G3
Xai-Xai Moz. 101 K3
Xalapa Mex. 136 E5
Xaltan Aşırımı Azer. 91 H2
Xambioá Brazil 143 I5
Xamgyi'nyilha China 76 C3
Xam Nua Laos 70 D2
Xá-Muteba Angola 99 B4
Xan r. Laos 70 C3
Xanagas Botswana 100 E2
Xangda China see Nangqên
Xangdin Hural China 73 K4
Xangdoring China see Xungba
Xangongo Angola 99 B5
Xanh, Cu Lao i. Vietnam 71 E4
▶Xankändi Azer. 91 G3
Capital of Nagorno-Karabakh.
Xanthi Greece 59 K4
Xarag China 83 I1
Xarardheere Somalia 98 E3
Xàtiva Spain 57 F4
Xavantes, Serra dos hills Brazil 143 I6
Xaxa China 83 E2
Xayar China 80 F3
Xékong Laos 70 D4
Xela Guat. see Quetzaltenango
Xelva Spain see Chelva
Xenia U.S.A. 134 D4
Xero Potamos r. Cyprus see Xeros
Xeros r. Cyprus 85 A2
Xhora S. Africa see Elliotdale
Xiabole Shan mt. China 74 B2
Xiachuan Dao i. China 77 G4
Xiaguan China see Dali
Xiahe China 76 D1
Xiamen China 77 H3
Xi'an China 77 F1
Xianfeng China 77 F2
Xiangcheng Sichuan China 76 C2
Xiangcheng Yunnan China see Xiangyun
Xiangfan China see Xiangyang
Xiangfeng China see Laifeng
Xianggang H.K. China see Hong Kong
Xianggang Tebie Xingzhengqu aut. reg. China see Hong Kong
Xiangkou China see Wulong
Xiangning China 73 K5
Xiangquan He r. China see Langqên Zangbo
Xiangride China 83 I2
Xiangshan China see Menghai
Xiangshui China 77 H1
Xiangshuiba China 77 F3
Xiangtan China 77 G3
Xiangxiang China 77 G3
Xiangyang China 77 G1
Xiangyang Hu l. China 83 G2
Xiangyin China 77 G2
Xiangyun China 76 D3
Xianju China 77 I2
Xianning China 77 G2
Xiannümiao China see Jiangdu
Xianshui He r. China 76 D2
Xiantao China 77 G2
Xianxia Ling mts China 77 H3
Xianyang China 77 F1
Xiaocaohu China 80 G3
Xiaodong China 77 F4
Xiaodongliang China 76 C1
Xiao'ergou China 74 A2
Xiaogan China 77 G2
Xiaogang China see Dongxiang
Xiao Hinggan Ling mts China 74 B2
Xiaojin China 76 D2
Xiaonanchuan China 83 H2
Xiaosanjiang China 77 G3
Xiaoshan China 77 I2
Xiao Shan mts China 77 F1
Xiaoshi China see Benxi
Xiao Surmang China 76 C1
Xiaotao China 77 H3
Xiaoxi China see Pinghe
Xiaoxian China 77 H1
Xiaoxiang Ling mts China 76 D2
Xiaoxita China see Yiling
Xiapu China 77 I3
Xiaqiong China see Batang
Xiashan China see Zhanjiang
Xiayang China see Yanling
Xiayingpan China see Liuzhi
Xiayukou China 77 F1
Xiazhuang China see Linshu
Xibdê China 76 C2
Xibing China 77 H3
Xibu China see Dongshan
Xichang China 76 D3
Xichou China 76 E4
Xichuan China 77 F1
Xide China 76 D2
Xidu China see Hengyang
Xiema China 77 F2
Xiêng Lam Vietnam 70 D3
Xieyang Dao i. China 77 F4
Xifeng Guizhou China 76 E3
Xifeng Liaoning China 74 B4
Xifengzhen China see Qingyang
Xigazê China 83 G3
Xihan Shui r. China 76 E1
Xi He r. China 76 E2
Xi Jiang r. China 77 G4
Xijir China 83 G2
Xijir Ulan Hu salt l. China 83 G2
Xiliao He r. China 74 A4
Xilin China 76 E3
Xilinhot China 73 L4
Ximiao China 80 J3
Xin'an Anhui China see Lai'an
Xin'an Guizhou China see Anlong
Xin'an Henan China 77 G1
Xinavane Moz. 101 K3
Xin Barag Zuoqi China see Amgalang
Xincai China 77 G1
Xinchang Jiangxi China see Yifeng
Xinchang Zhejiang China 77 I2
Xincheng Fujian China see Gutian
Xincheng Guangdong China see Xinxing
Xincheng Guangxi China 77 F3
Xincheng Sichuan China see Zhaojue
Xincun China see Dongchuan
Xindi Guangxi China 77 F4
Xindi Hubei China see Honghu
Xindian China 74 B3
Xindu Guangxi China 77 F4
Xindu Sichuan China see Luhuo
Xindu Sichuan China 76 E2
Xinduqiao China 76 D2
Xinfeng Guangdong China 77 G3
Xinfeng Jiangxi China 77 G3
Xinfengjiang Shuiku resr China 77 G4
Xing'an Guangxi China 77 F3
Xingan China 77 G3
Xing'an Shaanxi China see Ankang
Xingba China see Lhünzê
Xingguo Gansu China see Qin'an
Xingguo Hubei China see Yangxin
Xingguo Jiangxi China 77 G3
Xinghai China 80 I4
Xinghua China 77 H1
Xinghua Wan b. China 77 H3
Xingkai China 74 D3
Xingkai Hu l. China/Russia see Khanka, Lake
Xinglong Heilong. China 74 B2
Xinglong Heilong. China 74 B3
Xinglongzhen China 76 E1
Xingning Guangdong China 77 G3
Xingning Hunan China 77 G3
Xingou China 77 G2
Xingping China 77 F1
Xingqêngoin China 76 D2
Xingren China 76 E3
Xingsagoinba China 76 D1
Xingshan Guizhou China see Majiang
Xingshan Hubei China 77 F2
Xingtai China 73 K5
Xingu r. Brazil 143 H4
Xingu, Parque Indígena do res. Brazil 143 H6
Xinguara Brazil 143 H5
Xingye China 77 F4
Xingyi China 76 E3
Xinhua Guangdong China see Huadu
Xinhua Hunan China 77 F3
Xinhua Yunnan China see Qiaojia
Xinhua Yunnan China see Funing
Xinhuang China 77 F3
Xinhui China 77 G4
Xining China 72 I5
Xinjian China 77 G2
Xinjiang China 77 F1
Xinjiang aut. reg. China see Xinjiang Uygur Zizhiqu
Xinjiangkou China see Songzi
Xinjiang Uygur Zizhiqu aut. reg. China 82 E1
Xinjie Qinghai China 76 D1
Xinjie Yunnan China 76 C3
Xinjie Yunnan China 76 D4
Xinjin China 76 D2
Xinjing China see Jingxi
Xinkai He r. China 74 A4
Xinkou China 73 K5
Xinling China see Badong
Xinlitun China 74 B2
Xinlong China 76 D2
Xinmi China 77 G1
Xinmin China 74 B2
Xinning Gansu China see Ningxian
Xinning Hunan China 77 F3
Xinning Jiangxi China see Wuning
Xinning Sichuan China see Kaijiang
Xinping China 76 D3
Xinqiao China 77 G1
Xinqing China 74 C2
Xinquan China 77 H3
Xinshan China see Anyuan
Xinshiba China see Ganluo
Xinsi China 76 E1
Xintai China 73 L5
Xintanpu China 77 G2
Xintian China 77 G3
Xinxiang China 77 G1
Xinxing China 77 G4
Xinyang Henan China see Pingqiao
Xinyang Henan China 77 G1
Xinye China 77 G1
Xinyi Guangdong China 77 F4
Xinyi Jiangsu China 77 H1
Xinying China 77 F5
Xinying Taiwan 77 I4
Xinyu China 77 G3
Xinyuan Qinghai China see Tianjun
Xinyuan Xinjiang China 80 F3
Xinzhangfang China 74 A2
Xinzhou Guangxi China see Longlin
Xinzhou Hubei China 77 G2
Xinzhu Taiwan see Hsinchu
Xinzo de Limia Spain 57 C2
Xiongshan China see Zhenghe
Xiongshi China see Guixi
Xiongzhou China see Nanxiong
Xiping Henan China 77 F1
Xiping Henan China 77 G1
Xiqing Shan mts China 76 D1
Xique-Xique Brazil 143 J6
Xisa China see Xichou
Xisha Qundao is S. China Sea see Paracel Islands
Xishuangbanna reg. China 76 D4
Xishui Guizhou China 76 E2
Xishui Hubei China 77 G2
Xitianmu Shan mt. China 77 H2
Xiugu China see Jinxi
Xi Ujimqin Qi China see Bayan Ul
Xiuning China 77 H2
Xiushan Chongqing China 77 F2
Xiushan Yunnan China see Tonghai
Xiushui China 77 G2
Xiuwen China 76 E3
Xiuwu China 77 G1
Xiuying China 77 F4
Xiwol China 82 E1
Xiwu China 76 C1
Xixabangma Feng mt. China 83 F3
Xixia China 77 F1
Xixiang China 76 E1
Xixiu China see Anshun
Xixón Spain see Gijón/Xixón
Xiyang Dao i. China 77 I3
Xiyang Jiang r. China 76 E3
Xiyuping Yu i. Taiwan 77 H4
Xizang aut. reg. China see Xizang Zizhiqu
Xizang Gaoyuan plat. China see Tibet, Plateau of
Xizang Zizhiqu aut. reg. China 83 G3
Xo'japiryox tog'i mt. Uzbek. 89 G2
Xo'jayli Uzbek. 80 A3
Xorkol China 80 H4
Xuancheng China 77 H2
Xuande Qundao is Paracel Is see Amphitrite Group
Xuan'en China 77 F2
Xuanhua China 73 L4
Xuân Lôc Vietnam 71 D5
Xuanwei China 76 E3
Xuanzhou China see Xuancheng
Xuchang China 77 G1
Xucheng China see Xuwen
Xuddur Somalia 98 E3
Xuefeng China see Mingxi
Xuefeng Shan mts China 77 F3
Xue Shan mts China 76 C3
Xue Shan mt. Taiwan 77 I3
Xugui China 80 I4
Xuguit Qi China see Yakeshi
Xujiang China see Guangchang
Xümatang China 76 C1
Xungba China 83 E2
Xungmai China 83 G3
Xunhe China 74 B2
Xun He r. China 74 C2
Xun Jiang r. China 77 F4
Xunwu China 77 G3
Xunyi China 77 F1
Xúquer, Riu r. Spain 57 F4
Xuru Co salt l. China 83 F3
Xuwen China 68 E2
Xuyi China 77 H1
Xuyong China 76 E2
Xuzhou China 77 H1

Y

Ya'an China 76 D2
Yabanabat Turkey see Kızılcahamam
Yabēlo Eth. 98 D3
Yablonovyy Khrebet mts Russia 73 J2
Yabrīn reg. Saudi Arabia 88 C6
Yabuli China 74 C3
Yacha China see Baisha
Yacheng China 77 F5
Yachi He r. China 76 E3
Yacuma r. Bol. 142 E6
Yadgir India 84 C2
Yadrin Russia 42 J5
Yaeyama-rettō is Japan 73 M8
Yafa Israel see Tel Aviv-Yafo
Yagaba Ghana 96 C3
Yagan China 72 I4
Yağda Turkey see Erdemli
Yaghan Basin sea feature S. Atlantic Ocean 148 D9
Yagman Turkm. 88 D2
Yagmo China 83 F3
Yagodnoye Russia 65 P3
Yagodnyy Russia 74 E2
Yagoua Cameroon 97 E3
Yagra China 83 E3
Yagradagzê Feng mt. China 76 B1
Yaguajay Cuba 133 E8
Yagul and Mitla, Prehistoric Caves of tourist site Mex. 136 E5
Yaha Thai. 71 C6
Yahk Canada 120 G5
Yahualica Mex. 136 D4
Yahyalı Turkey 55 L4
Yai Myanmar see Ye
Yai, Khao mt. Thai. 71 B4
Yaizu Japan 75 E6
Yajiang China 76 D2
Yakacık Turkey 85 C1
Yakeshi China 73 M3
Yakhab waterhole Iran 88 E3
Yakhchāl Afgh. 89 G4
Yakima U.S.A. 126 C3
Yakima r. U.S.A. 126 D3
Yakmach Pak. 89 F4
Yako Burkina Faso 96 C3
Yakovlevka Russia 74 D3
Yaku-shima i. Japan 75 C7
Yakutat U.S.A. 120 B3
Yakutat Bay U.S.A. 120 A3
Yakutsk Russia 65 N3
Yakymivka Ukr. 43 G7
Yala Thai. 71 C6
Yala National Park Sri Lanka 84 D5
Yalan Dünya Mağarası tourist site Turkey 85 A1
Yale Canada 120 F5
Yale U.S.A. 134 D2
Yalgoo Australia 109 B7
Yalleroi Australia 110 D5
Yaloké Cent. Afr. Rep. 98 B3
Yalova Turkey 59 M4
Yalta Crimea 90 D1
Yalu Jiang r. China/N. Korea 74 B4
Yalujiang Kou r. mouth China/N. Korea 75 B5
Yalvaç Turkey 59 N5
Yamagata Japan 75 F5
Yamaguchi Japan 75 C6
Yamal, Poluostrov pen. Russia see Yamal Peninsula
Yam-Alin', Khrebet mts Russia 74 D1
Yamal Peninsula Russia 64 H2
Yamanie Falls National Park Australia 110 D3
Yamba Australia 112 F2
Yamba Lake Canada 121 I1
Yambarran Range hills Australia 108 E3
Yambi, Mesa de hills Col. 142 D3
Yambio South Sudan 97 F4
Yambol Bulg. 59 L3
Yamdena i. Indon. 108 E1
Yamethin Myanmar 70 B2
▶Yamin, Puncak mt. Indon. 69 J7
4th highest mountain in Oceania.
Yamkanmardi India 84 B2
Yamkhad Syria see Aleppo
Yamm Russia 45 P7
Yamma Yamma, Lake salt flat Australia 111 C5
▶Yamoussoukro Côte d'Ivoire 96 C4
Capital of Côte d'Ivoire (Ivory Coast).
Yampa r. U.S.A. 129 I1
Yampil' Ukr. 43 F6
Yampol' Ukr. see Yampil'
Yamuna r. India 82 E4
Yamunanagar India 82 D3
Yamzho Yumco l. China 83 G3
Yana r. Russia 65 O2
Yanam India 84 D2
Yan'an China 73 J5
Yanaoca Peru 142 D6
Yanaon India see Yanam
Yanaul Russia 41 Q4
Yanbu' al Baḩr Saudi Arabia 86 E5
Yanceyville U.S.A. 132 E4
Yancheng Henan China 77 G1
Yancheng Jiangsu China 77 I1
Yanchep Australia 109 A7
Yanco Australia 112 C5
Yanco Creek r. Australia 112 B5
Yanco Glen Australia 111 C6
Yanda watercourse Australia 112 B3
Yandama Creek watercourse Australia 111 C6
Yandao China see Yingjing
Yandoon Myanmar 70 A3
Yandun China 80 H3
Yanfolila Mali 96 C3
Ya'ngamdo China 76 B2
Yangbi China 76 C3
Yangchang China 76 E3
Yangcheng Guangdong China see Yangshan

Z

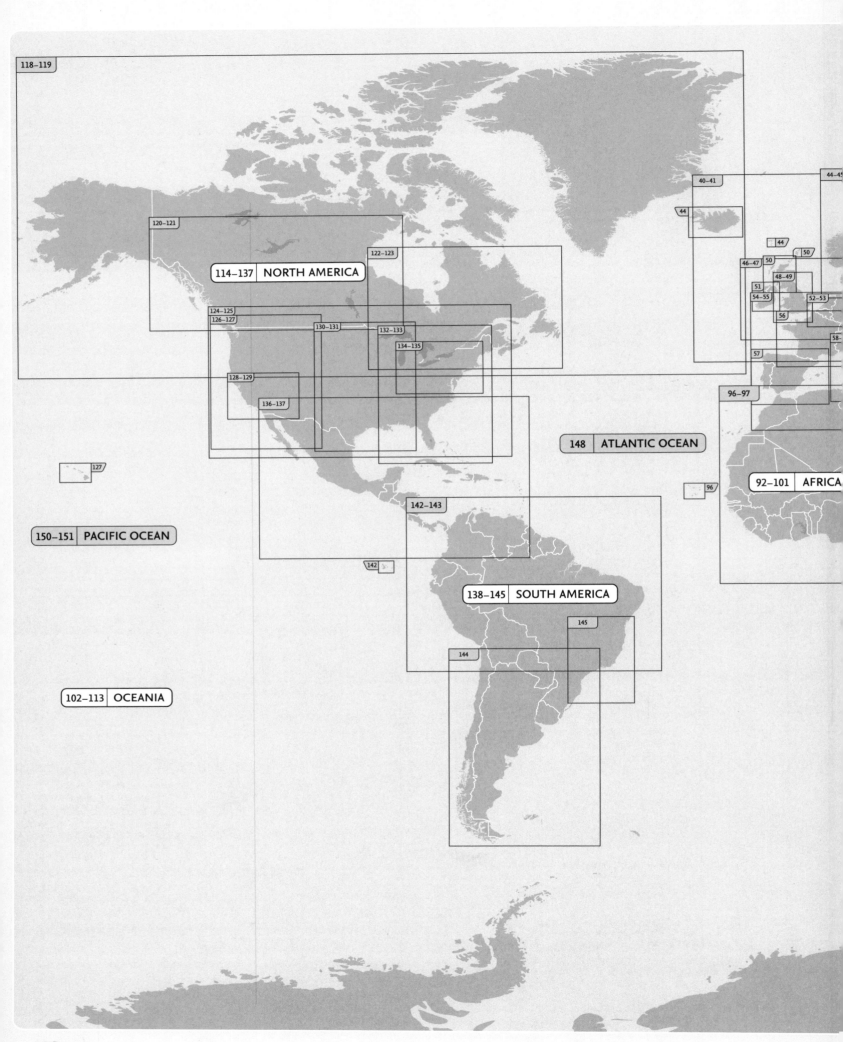

118–119

120–121

122–123 | 114–137 NORTH AMERICA

124–125
126–127

130–131 | 132–133

134–135

128–129

136–137

127

148 | ATLANTIC OCEAN

150–151 | PACIFIC OCEAN

142–143

142

138–145 | SOUTH AMERICA

145

144

102–113 | OCEANIA

40–41

44–4

44

44

50

46–47 | 50

48–49

51
54–55
56

52–53

58–

57

96–97

92–101 | AFRICA

96

Find your map